Introduction to Poetry:
British, American, Canadian

General Editors: Jack David/Robert Lecker

Co-ordinating Editor: David A. Kent

Editors: 400 - 1500   David Lyle Jeffrey/University of Ottawa
          1500 - 1660   Michael F.N. Dixon/New College, University of Toronto
          1660 - 1800   R.G. Moyles/University of Alberta
          1800 - 1832   Herbert J. Rosengarten/University of British Columbia
          1832 - 1900   D.M.R. Bentley/University of Western Ontario
          1900 - 1945   Paul Denham/University of Saskatchewan
          1945 - 1980   George Bowering/Simon Fraser University

Canadian Cataloguing in Publication Data
　　Main entry under title:
　　Introduction to poetry

　　ISBN 0-03-920279-8

　　1. English poetry.　2. American poetry.　3. Canadian
　　poetry (English).*　I. David, Jack, 1946–
　　II. Lecker, Robert, 1951–

　　PN6101.I58　　821'.008　　C81–094002-7

Acquisitions Editor: Joe McKeon
Copy Editor: Robert Billings
Production Editor: Marilyn S. Brooks
Cover Design: René Demers
Interior Design: Peggy Heath
Typesetting and Assembly: Trigraph

Special thanks to Russell Brown, Louis K. MacKendrick, and Julie Mari.

Printed in Canada

1　　2　　3　　4　　5　　85　　84　　83　　82　　81

Introduction to Poetry: British, American, Canadian

Preface

This anthology brings together the best poetry of Britain, the United States, and Canada. The selection is designed primarily for introductory courses in literature or poetry and, whenever possible, aims at depth of representation rather than at breadth or variety. *Introduction to Poetry: British, American, Canadian* is therefore an anthology of major poets. What distinguishes this collection is its inclusion of significant Canadian poets (more than twenty are represented) alongside their British and American counterparts in the overall tradition of English-language poetry. It should also be noted that the Medieval period, so often treated in a cursory manner, here is represented by an unusually large and varied group of poems.

The ordering principle governing the arrangement of poets and poems is generally chronological (whenever chronology can be accurately established). Because cultural movements may occur historically at later dates in different countries, the usual periodization tags (such as "Romantic" or "Victorian") have been avoided in section headings. Each of the anthology's seven sections has been edited by a Canadian scholar who was responsible for selecting poems from authoritative texts, for annotating them with an audience of undergraduate students in mind, and for writing a general introduction to the period to provide an overview of the poetry's characteristic features. The only exception to these general guidelines is, again, the Medieval section, in which a marginal gloss is often used to aid comprehension and where the editor has sometimes provided his own translations and edited texts. As a rule, annotations have been made for names, concepts, obsolete words, and unusual usages whenever it was thought that these would be alien to a student reading widely in English-language poetry for the first time. Such annotations do not, however, obviate the student's need to refer to a good dictionary.

Teachers will find that the selections from major poets are normally generous enough to allow some concentrated study of a particular poet's work. Nevertheless, the anthology is also capacious enough to permit a more eclectic approach, i.e., movement from period to period or poetic form to poetic form when that is deemed the best strategy for introducing poetry to the student.

J. D.
R. L.
D. A. K.

Contents

1200–1500

Introduction: 1500–1660

Introduction: 1660 – 1800

Introduction: 1800-32   276

Introduction: 1832–1900

Introduction: 1900–45

Introduction: 1945–80

Introduction: 400–1500

The heritage of English poetry which is left to us from the Middle Ages is rich, varied, and much more entertaining than we are likely to imagine until we begin to read it. One of the great difficulties facing an anthologist who tries to represent this richness fairly is, in fact, the achievement of an adequate selection. Although we have undoubtedly only a small proportion of the poetry of the Middle Ages still preserved in surviving manuscripts, the time embraced by the "medieval period," as we call it loosely, is more than 1100 years—from the time of Boethius and Augustine in the fourth century until about A.D. 1500. There survives an astonishing amount of good poetry from this epoch, of which the present selection is only a slight representation.

Our British ancestors' traditional poetry was oral, and only a portion of it was transcribed, beginning in the sixth century. This happened in Ireland as well as England, as educated persons began to consider not only the Latin (and Greek) with which they were educated, but also their own vernacular languages fit for preservation in a written form. We must acknowledge that it is of the essence of our English poetic heritage that the first transcriptions always took place in a multi-lingual context; though the point is often overlooked, multi-linguality is one of the most important single factors to consider in tracing the roots of English poetic tradition throughout the Middle Ages.

The people of the British Isles were made up of many vital linguistic groups. In the fourth and fifth centuries, while the Angles, Saxons, and Jutes were moving in from Germany, Denmark, and Friesland, the Romans were about to rescind occupation of a largely Celtic country, whose inhabitants were speaking antecedents of modern Irish, Welsh, or Scots Gaelic. The Romans' introduction of Latin and of Christianity, extended especially in Scotland and the north of England by Irish monks, was further strengthened by missionary visits in the south and a general conversion of England to Christianity by the late sixth and seventh centuries. During this time Latin became the "language of letters," hence of much of the earliest poetry which was written down. But in England and Ireland especially the strength of the vernacular languages, Old Irish and Old English (Anglo-Saxon), was so strong that vernacular poems began to be transcribed with increasing regularity—at first in flyleaves, then as the substance of manuscript books.

Most of this early transcription took place in monastic centres of learning, both in Ireland and in England. The Venerable Bede's account of the first Christian poet to compose in English is a helpful index to many features of the old poetry. Bede, writing in Latin, tells us that a humble stockman and shepherd named Caedmon was living near the Benedictine monastery of Whitby in the late seventh century. According to Bede he had lived a secular life until an advanced age and ". . . had never learned any poetry. Therefore, sometimes at a banquet, when for the sake of merrymaking it was agreed that all should sing in turn, and he saw the harp coming towards him, he would get up from the table, go out quietly and return home." One night when Caedmon had done this, he returned to the stables to care for the animals, and fell asleep. In a vision he was challenged to receive a special gift for the composition of poetry in praise of God. He promptly composed a Creation hymn, and when in the morning this became known he was asked by the brothers to versify a passage of Scripture. He soon produced such accomplished poetry that he was invited to take holy orders. Thereafter, Bede says, Caedmon composed much fine religious verse; indeed, one of the selections in this volume is attributed to his "school," or tradition. Yet it is significant that we can ascribe to Caedmon with certainty nothing more than the hymn Bede records; early English poetry, like most of later medieval poetry, is persistently anonymous.

We are reminded by Bede's story that our Anglo-Saxon ancestors were fond of reciting poetry orally, in public, as entertainment following a meal, and to the music of the harp, upon which most were expected to be able to chord themselves an accompaniment. A propos of Caedmon, it is noteworthy that the first of five references in *Beowulf* to the harp is an account of its use in Hrothgar's hall to accompany a poet's recitation of the biblical story of Creation. Yet there is more which is typical in the story of Caedmon. For example, one of the most significant features of all medieval poetry is its public and communal character, even if, in the modern sense, it was in its own day unpublished. (Modern poetry, by contrast, is widely published, but almost always notably "personal" in character.) Also, the early medieval association of poetry with music and oral tradition continues strongly into the later medieval lyric, and even Chaucer's poetry, often free translations of Latin, Italian, or French tales, was similarly "public" in its vision rather than private, and was recited orally to courtly audiences. *Sir Orfeo*, written late in the fourteenth century (perhaps first in Anglo-French), explicitly calls up old and familiar shared stories, requires a harp in accompaniment, and indeed has as its protagonist a poet-harpist.

These features, then, are characteristic of much of our early poetry: a multi-lingual background, frequent musical accompaniment, oral performance in a public setting, anonymity of authorship, and communal rather than private orientation. To these may be added a typical medieval love of layered language, a semantic richness in which the entire world of things seen has poetic potential because of a perceived relationship binding the "seen" physical elements of creation to "the unseen things of God," the spiritual element of human experience. No very sharp discontinuity between sacred and secular, or physical and spiritual realms was held to exist; in all that was in the modern sense "substantial" (i.e., physical) medieval poets saw traces or signs of all that was in *their* sense "substantial" (i.e., spiritual). Accordingly their language had about it a rich multivalence and a poetic power that even now can be exhilarating for the modern person who reads it carefully.

The period between 1066 and about 1200 saw a swift rise to dominance in England of yet another language, the French of the Norman conquerors, and some of the selections in this volume are from the peculiar "Anglo-French" which came to be used in England down to the fourteenth century. But the medieval poetry in our collection is divided at 1200 because after this point there is a tremendous burgeoning of manuscripts containing vernacular lyric poetry, in both English and Anglo-French. The preservation of much of this lyric verse was strongly influenced by the popularized mendicant preaching and entertainments of the new orders of friars which came to England from France and Italy about 1225. In this third major wave of Christian spiritual and cultural awakening in Britain, the authors of the poetry remain largely anonymous. Their audience, however, is evidently more diversified, and a clearer distinction between popular verse (e.g., many of the lyrics) and courtly poetry, as represented by Geffrey Chaucer or Charles d'Orleans, is becoming evident. Also, preservation of poems in written form is increasingly common, and some humorous and bawdy songs get added to the manuscript collections. From this point we can date a tremendous rise in the preservation of popular songs, although in the manuscripts many have their "pub-lyrics" transformed into religious verse, as the friars and others engaged in the practice of making "old songs new." But also in this period, especially during the fourteenth century, comes some of the greatest of English verse in highly literate style, here represented especially by the "Orfeo" poet and Chaucer.

In the fifteenth century a trend towards more "secular" poetry grew rapidly, embracing the work of the Scots Chaucerians, including Dunbar and Henryson, as well as English poets like John Skelton. Yet many readers find the fifteenth century less than a match for the great poetic achievement of the fourteenth century.

Finally, it will be evident that despite their many strong particular characteristics, Old Irish, Old English, Anglo-Norman, Middle English, and Middle Scots poetry all share one further element: most of their authors were profoundly affected by the impact of the Christian message and biblical story upon their culture, and a majority of their poems—even many light-hearted love songs—are markedly influenced by renewed expressions of this central medieval cultural phenomenon. It may surprise us that so much of our poetic heritage, from each of the British languages and medieval sub-periods, is so thoroughly permeated with an essentially biblical understanding of humanity and nature, as well as a religious, even liturgical, sense of the function of poetry. But a strong sacramental sense of the power of language, especially poetic language, remains a dominant characteristic of medieval cultural consciousness from the philosophical metres of Boethius through to the beautiful and enigmatic "*Corpus Christi* Carol" written more than 1100 years later. Thus, though the "Middle Ages" comprises a very long and complex period in the history of our poetry, in the central aspects of its poetry this generous millenium is perhaps as aesthetically unified as any single century which follows.

David Lyle Jeffrey

400 – 1200

BOETHIUS (480 – 524)[1]

Of Partial Truths

This discord in the pact of things,
This endless war twixt truth and truth,
That singly hold, yet give the lie
To him who seeks to yoke them both –[2]   20
5 Do the gods know the reason why?

Or is truth one without a flaw,
And all things to each other turn,
But the soul, sunken in desire,
No longer can the links discern,   25
10 In glimmering of her smothered fire?

Then why with travail does she yearn
To find the hidden mysteries?
Knows she the thing for which she burns?
Yet who will seek what he hath got?
15 Yet who will seek he knows not what?   30

How shall he follow the unknown?
How shall he find it, and when found
How shall he know it? Did the soul
Once see the universal mind,[3]
And know the part, and know the whole?

Now sunken in the mirk of sense,
Not wholly doth the soul forget,
Still grasps the whole, lets go the part:
And therefore whoso seeks the truth
Shall find in no wise peace of heart.

For neither doth he wholly know,
And neither doth he all forget:
But that high thing which once he saw,
And still remembers, that he holds,
And seeks to bring the truth forgot
Again to that which he hath yet.

COLUMBANUS (543 – 615)

En Silvis Caesa

En, silvis caesa fluctu meat acta carina
Bicornis Rheni et pelagus perlabitur uncta.
  Heia viri! nostrum reboans echo sonet
                                    heia!

Extollunt venti flatus, nocet horridus imber,
5 Sed vis apta virum superat sternitque
                                    procellam.
  Heia viri! nostrum reboans echo sonet   5
                                    heia!

Nam cedunt nimbi studio, ceditque procella,
cuncta domat nisus, labor improbus omnia
                                    vincit.
  Heia viri! nostrum reboans echo sonet
                                    heia!

10 Durate et vosmet rebus servate secundis,
O passi graviora, dabit deus his quoque   10
                                    finem.

Columbanus to His Monks[1]

See, cut in woods, through flood of
                          twin-horned Rhine
passes the keel, and greased slips over seas—
  Heave, men! And let resounding echo
                    sound our 'heave.'[2]

The winds raise blasts, wild rain-storms
                          wreak their spite
but ready strength of men subdues it all—
  Heave, men! And let resounding echo
                    sound our 'heave.'

Clouds melt away and the harsh tempest
                                    stills,
effort tames all, great toil is conqueror—
  Heave, men! And let resounding echo
                    sound our 'heave.'

Endure and keep yourselves for happy
                                    things;

---

1. Boethius was a fourth-century Roman philosopher and senator, contemporary with St. Augustine (and buried in the same church). Executed under the Emperor Theodoric on false charges, he became known as St. Severinus. He wrote *The Consolation of Philosophy*, a book of enormous influence in the Middle Ages and translated in England by King Alfred the Great, Chaucer, King James I of Scotland, and Queen Elizabeth I among others. Through Chaucer especially he has become an important part of English poetic tradition. This poem is from Book V of his *Consolation*.
2. This poem discusses the partiality of limited individual perspectives on truth, as this might be experienced by one who is frustrated in the search for a unified view.
3. There are important Platonic elements in Boethius' thought.

1. The poem refers to a monastic voyage (ca. 610). The use of a sea voyage as an image for the Christian life is common in early Christian literature, and has a particular immediacy for a northern European culture in the Middle Ages. Columbanus was a notable Irish monk and abbott.
2. A rowing song refrain.

Heia viri! nostrum reboans echo sonet
heia!

Sic inimicus agit invisus corda fatigans,
Ac male temptando quatit intima corda
furore.
15   *Vestra, viri, Christum memorans mens*
personet heia!

State animo fixi, hostisque spernite strofas,
Virtutum vosmet armis defendite rite.
Vestra, viri, Christum memorans mens
personet heia!

Firma fides cuncta superat studiumque
beatum,
20   Hostis et antiquus cedens sua spicula frangit.
Vestra, viri, Christum memorans mens
personet heia!

Rex quoque virtutum, rerum fons, summa
potestas,
Certanti spondet, vincenti praemia donat.
Vestra, viri, Christum memorans mens
personet heia!

you suffered worse, and these too God shall
end—
Heave, men! And let resounding echo
sound our 'heave.'

Thus acts the foul fiend: wearing out the
heart
and with temptation shaking inmost parts—
15   *You men, remember Christ with mind still*
sounding 'heave.'

Stand firm in soul and spurn the foul fiend's
tricks
and seek defence in virtue's armoury—[3]
You men, remember Christ with mind still
sounding 'heave.'

Firm faith will conquer all and blessed zeal
20   and the old fiend yielding breaks at last his
darts—
You men, remember Christ with mind still
sounding 'heave.'

Supreme, of virtues King, and fount of
things,
He promises in strife, gives prize in
victory—[4]
You men, remember Christ with mind still
sounding 'heave.'

ANONYMOUS

Quis Est Deus?

Quis est Deus
et ubi est Deus
et cuius est Deus
et ubi habitaculum eius?

5   Si habet filios et filias,
aurum et argentum, Deus vester?

Si vivus semper,
si pulcher,
si filium eius
10   nutrierunt multi?

Si filiae eius
carae et pulchrae sunt
hominibus mundi?

Si in caelo
15   an in terra est?
In aequore,
in fluminibus,
in montanis,
in convallibus?

Questions[1]

Who is God
and where is God,
of whom is God,
and where His dwelling?

5   Has He sons and daughters,
gold and silver, this God of yours?

Is He ever-living,
is He beautiful,
was His son
10   fostered by many?

Are His daughters
dear and beautiful
to the men of the world?

Is He in heaven
15   or on the earth?
In the sea,
in the rivers,
in the mountains,
in the valleys?

3. Here and in the stanza following the reference is to the preparation of a spiritual warrior. Cf. Eph. vi.6–17.
4. An allusion to *comitatus*, the bond between a warrior king and his men such as is modelled in *Beowulf*.

1. This riddle is probably catechetical. By its form it invokes in reply various psalms and other passages from the Psalter, e.g., Ps. xviii (xix), Isa. lv.6, etc.

20 Dic nobis
notitiam eius:
Quomodo videbitur,
quomodo diligitur,
quomodo invenitur?

20 Speak to us
tidings of Him:
How will He be seen,
how is He loved,
how is He found?

25 Si in iuventute,
si in senectute
invenitur?

25 Is it in youth
or is it in old age
He is found?

Dom-Farcai Fidbaidæ Fál

Dom-farcai fidbaidæ fál,
    fom-chain loíd luin –lúad nad cél;
húas mo lebrán, ind línech,
    fom-chain trírech inna n-én.

Fomm-chain coí menn –medair mass –
    hi mbrot glass de dindgnaib doss.
Débrad! nom-choimmdiu coíma,
    caín-scríbaimm fo foída ross.

Writing in the Woods

A wall of forest looms above
    and sweetly the blackbird[1] sings;
all the birds make melody
    over me and my books and things.

There sings to me the cuckoo[2]
    from bush-citadels in grey hood.
God's doom! May the Lord protect me
    writing well, under the great wood.

A Scholar of Malmesbury
Carmen Aldhelmo Datum

Ecce, nocturno tempore,
orto brumali turbine
quatiens terram tempestas
turbabat atque vastitas,
5 cum fracto venti federe
bacharentur in aethere
et rupto retinaculo
desevirent in saeculo. . . .
ac totidem torrentibus
10 septem latet lampadibus
Pliadis pulchra copula
ab Athlantis prosapia: . . .
Zodiacus cum cetera
cyclus fuscatur caterva,
15 quem Mazaroth reperimus
nuncupari antiquitus,
bis senis cum sideribus
per Olimpum lucentibus;
nec radiabat rutilus,
20 sicut solebat, Sirius,
quia nubis nigerrima
abscondunt polos pallia.
attamen flagrant fulmina
late per caeli culmina,
25 quando pallentem pendula
flammam vomunt fastigia,
quorum natura nubibus
procedit conlidentibus,
nec non marina cerula

Storm
To Aldhelm[1]

Storm and destruction shattering
    Strike fear upon the world,
The winds are out, and through high heaven
    Their Bacchanals are hurled.
5 Their league is broken, burst the girth,
And launched their fury on the earth.

Torrent on torrent falls the rain,
    Dark are the lovely Pleiades,
Their seven lamps are out, and dark
10   The Houses where abide the stars.
And Sirius shines no more at all,
And heaven is hung with blackest pall.

Yet through the summits of the sky
    Flashes afar the livid levin,
15 And cataracts of pallid fire
    Pour from the toppling crests of heaven.
Struggling with clouds the mountains stand,
The dark sea masses on the strand,
Following wave on wave behind
20 The rush and ruin of the wind.

Along the pathways of the sea
    The salt waves rise in foam.
The deep is boiling like a pot,
    Dark water seething furiously,
25 And Ocean with his might of war
And thunder of his waves afar,

---

1. The blackbird was associated with penitence and a religious life.
2. The cuckoo was associated with pleasures of the flesh and carnal infidelity.

1. This poem (eighth century) is addressed to Aldhelm, the abbot of Malmesbury (675–705) whose memory was so much revered by King Alfred. The poem recalls a miraculous escape from a raging storm which destroyed the entire monastery, except for the abbey church in which the brothers, singing matins, were saved.

30 glomerantur in glarea,
qua inruit inruptio
ventorum ac correptio.
per pelagi itinera
salsa spumabant equora,
35 cum bulliret brumalibus
undosus vortex fluctibus;
Oceanus cum motibus
atque diris dodrantibus
pulsabat promontoria
40 suffragante victoria.

Storming the headlands, shock on shock,
And shouting victory.

Fuitt Co Bráth

Fuitt co bráth!
 Is mó in doinenn ar cách;
is ob cach etriche án,
 ocus is loch lán cach áth.

Is méit muir mór cech loch lonn,
 is drong cech cuire gúr gann,
méit taul scéith banna dond linn,
 méit moltchrocann finn cech slamm.

Méit cuithe cach lathrach léig,
 coirthe cach réid, caill cach móin,
inna helta, nís tá dín,
 snechtae finn fír do-roich tóin.

Ro-íad réod rótu gribb
 iar ngléo glicc im choirthi Cuilt,
con-gab doinenn dar cach leth
 coná apair nech acht 'Fuitt.'

Forever Cold

Forever cold!
Weather grim and grimmer still,
glittering brook a river
and ford a brimming lake.

The lake a great sea
(each meagre band a company)
rain-drop like shield-boss
and snow-flake like wether-skin.

The dirty puddle is a great pit,
level land is risen, the moor a wood,
no shelter for the flocks of birds
and white snow reaches up to haunch.

Sudden frost has closed the roads
encircling with cunning the standing-stone at
                                          Colt;
grim weather lies entrenched on every side
and no one utters anything but: 'Cold.'

Scél Lemm Dúib

Scél lemm dúib:
dordaid dam,
snigid gaim,
ro-fáith sam;

gáeth ard úar,
ísel grían,
gair a rith,
ruirthech rían;

rorúad rath,
ro-cleth cruth,
ro-gab gnáth
giugrann guth;

ro-gab úacht
etti én,
aigre ré:
é mo scél.

Winter[1]

News I bring:
bells[2] the stag,
winter snow,
summer past;

wind high and cold,
low the sun,
short its course,
seas run strong;

russet bracken,
shape awry,
wild goose raises
wonted cry;

cold lays hold
on wings of bird,
icy time:
this I heard.

---

1. A song or chant in an unusual, compressed metre and syntax.

2. "Bellows" or "bugles" – the call of the stag in mating season.

Is Acher in Gáith In-Nocht

Is acher in gáith in-nocht,
fu-fúasna fairggæ findfolt:
ní ágor réimm mora minn
dond láechraid lainn úa Lothlind.

The Vikings[1]

Bitter and wild is the wind to-night
tossing the tresses of the sea to white.
On such a night as this I feel at ease:
fierce Northmen only course the quiet seas.

Deor[1]

Wayland[2] knew the wanderer's fate:
that single-willed earl suffered agonies,
sorrow and longing the sole companions
of his ice-cold exile. Anxieties bit
5   when Nithhad put a knife to his hamstrings,
laid clever bonds on the better man.

    That changed; this may too.[3]

Beadohild mourned her murdered brothers:[4]
but her own plight pained her more
10 - her womb grew great with child.
When she knew that, she could never hold
steady before her wit what was to happen.

    That has gone; this may too.

All have heard of Hild's ravishing:
15 the Geat's lust was ungovernable,
their bitter love banished sleep.

    That passed over; this may too.

Thirty winters Theodric ruled[5]
the Maering city: and many knew it.

20   That went by; this may too.

We all know that Eormanric[6]
had a wolf's wit. Wide Gothland
lay in the grasp of that grim king,
and through it many sat, by sorrows environed,
25 foreseeing only sorrow; sighed for the downfall
and thorough overthrow of the thrall-maker.

    That blew by; this may too.

When each gladness has gone, gathering sorrow
may cloud the brain; and in his breast a man
30 can not then see how his sorrows shall end.

---

1. The Irish monasteries were regular recipients of savage visitations from Viking raiding parties.

1. This poem (early eighth century) is the lament of a poet who has lost his place in the court of the Heodenings to a new poet (*makar*, or *scop*), Heorrenda. Now he is exiled and destitute. The poem is unique among Anglo-Saxon poems in having a strophic form and a regular refrain.
2. Wayland was captured and mutilated by his enemies.

3. *Thaes oferode, thisses swa maeg* is a strong, recurrent lyric refrain which expresses a kind of "stoic" resignation and resolve.
4. Beadohild was raped by Wayland.
5. Theordoric the Ostrogoth, the emperor who had Boethius executed.
6. A tyrant who oppressed his own people. Each story exemplifies a misfortune outlived.

But he may think how throughout this world
it is the way of God, who is wise, to deal
to the most part of men much favour
and a flourishing fame; to a few the sorrow-share.

35   Of myself in this regard I shall say this only:
that in the hall of the Heodenings I held long the makarship,
lived dear to my prince, Deor my name;
many winters I held this happy place
and my lord was kind. Then came Heorrenda,
40   whose lays were skilful; the lord of fighting-men
settled on him the estate bestowed once on me.

That has gone; this may too.

From Beowulf[1]

The Fight with Grendel's Dam

The Geat, son of Ecgtheow,[2] spoke:
'Great son of Healfdene,[3] gracious ruler,
gold-friend of men, remember now—
for I am now ready to go—
1480   what we agreed if I, fighting on your behalf,
should fail to return: that you would always
be like a father to me after I had gone.
Guard my followers, my dear friends,
if I die in battle; and, beloved Hrothgar,
1485   send to Hygelac[4] the treasures you gave me.
When the lord of the Geats, Hrethel's son,
sees those gifts of gold, he will know
that I found a noble giver of rings
and enjoyed his favour for as long as I lived.
1490   And, O Hrothgar, let renowned Unferth[5]
have the ancient treasure, the razor sharp
ornamented sword; and I will make my name
with Hrunting,[6] or death will destroy me.'
After these words the leader of the Geats
1495   dived bravely from the bank, did not even
wait for an answer; the seething water
received the warrior. A full day elapsed
before he could perceive the bottom of the lake.
She who had guarded the lake's length and breadth
1500   for fifty years, vindictive, fiercely ravenous for blood,
soon realized that one of the race of men
was looking down into the monsters' lair.
Then she grasped him, clutched the Geat
in her ghastly claws; and yet she did not
1505   so much as scratch his skin; his coat of mail

1. The greatest of Old English poems, epic in form (ca. 720). The three selections in this anthology represent only about five percent of the poem's 3182 lines. The story is about an heroic warrior who is called upon to rid a neighbouring people of two hominid monsters, Grendel and his even more awesome mother. These sasquatch-like creatures, who maim and devour people, attacking them while they sleep, are finally overcome by Beowulf in titanic battle. This first selection deals with Beowulf's pursuit and destruction of Grendel's mother in her underwater lair. The second is the tribute by the chieftain of the liberated people, Hrothgar, with some words of advice to the young hero. The third selection describes the breathless report of one who escapes from a great dragon which, near the end of the story, will destroy Beowulf even as it is being vanquished by the now aged warrior.
2. Beowulf himself.
3. Hrothgar was son of Half-Dane.
4. Hygelac was Beowulf's own present ruler.
5. A warrior in Hrothgar's retinue.
6. A famous gift-sword.

protected him; she could not penetrate
the linked metal rings with her loathsome fingers.
Then the sea-wolf dived to the bottom-most depths,
swept the prince to the place where she lived,
1510 so that he, for all his courage, could not
wield a weapon; too many wondrous creatures
harassed him as he swam; many sea-serpents
with savage tusks tried to bore through his corslet,
the monsters molested him. Then the hero saw
1515 that he had entered some loathsome hall
in which there was no water to impede him,
a vaulted chamber where the floodrush
could not touch him. A light caught his eye,
a lurid flame flickering brightly.
1520   Then the brave man saw the sea-monster,
fearsome, infernal; he whirled his blade,
swung his arm with all his strength,
and the ring-hilted sword sang a greedy war-song
on the monster's head. Then that guest realized
1525 that his gleaming blade could not bite into her flesh,
break open her bone-chamber; its edge failed Beowulf
when he needed it; yet it had endured
many a combat, sheared often through the helmet,
split the corslet of a fated man; for the first time
1530 that precious sword failed to live up to its name.
     Then, resolute, Hygelac's kinsman took his courage
in both hands, trusted in his own strength.
Angrily the warrior hurled Hrunting away,
the damascened sword with serpent patterns on its hilt;
1535 tempered and steel-edged, it lay useless on the earth.
Beowulf trusted in his own strength,
the might of his hand. So must any man
who hopes to gain long-lasting fame
in battle; he must risk his life, regardless.
1540 Then the prince of the Geats seized the shoulder
of Grendel's mother—he did not mourn their feud;
when they grappled, that brave man in his fury
flung his mortal foe to the ground.
Quickly she came back at him, locked him
1545 in clinches and clutched at him fearsomely.
Then the greatest of warriors stumbled and fell.
She dropped on her hall-guest, drew her dagger,
broad and gleaming; she wanted to avenge her son,
her only offspring. The woven corslet
1550 that covered his shoulders saved Beowulf's life,
denied access to both point and edge.
Then Ecgtheow's son, leader of the Geats,
would have died far under the wide earth
had not his corslet, his mighty chain-mail,
1555 guarded him, and had not holy God
granted him victory; the wise Lord,
Ruler of the Heavens, settled the issue
easily after the hero had scrambled to his feet.[7]

---

7. The message here, as elsewhere in Old English poetry,
seems to be that "God helps those who help themselves."

Hrothgar's Advice

Hrōðgār maðelode—   hylt scēawode,
ealde lāfe,   on ðǣm wæs ōr writen
fyrngewinnes,   syðþan flōd ofslōh,
1690 gifen gēotende   gīganta cyn,
frēcne gefērdon;   þæt wæs fremde þēod
ēcea–htne;   him þæs endelēan
þurh wæteres wylm   Waldend sealde.
Swā wæs on ðǣm scennum   scīran goldes
1695 þurh rūnstafas   rihte gemearcod,
geseted ond gesǣd,   hwām þæt sweord
                              geworht,
īrena cyst   ǣrest wǣre,
wreoþenhilt ond wyrmfāh.   Ðā se wīsa sprǣc
sunu Healfdenes   —swīgedon ealle—:
1700 ' þæt, lā, mæg secgan   sē þe sōð ond riht
fremeð on folce,   feor eal gemon,
eald ēþelweard,   þæt ðes eorl wǣre
geboren betera!   Blǣd is ārǣred
geond wīdwegas,   wine mīn Bēowulf,
1705 ðīn ofer þēoda gehwylce.   Eal þū hit
                              geþyldum healdest,
mægen mid mōdes snyttrum.   Ic þē sceal mīne
                              gelǣstan
frēode, swā wit furðum sprǣcon.   Ðū scealt tō
                              frōfre weorþan
eal langtwīdig   lēodum þīnum,
hæleðum tō helpe.
                              Ne wearð Heremōd swā
1710 eaforum Ecgwelan,   Ār-Scyldingum;
ne gewēox hē him tō willan,   ac tō wælfealle
ond tō dēaðcwalum   Deniga lēodum;
brēat bolgenmōd   bēodgenēatas,
eaxlgesteallan,   oþ þæt hē āna hwearf,
1715 mǣre þēoden   mondrēamum from,
ðēah þe hine mihtig God   mægenes wynnum,
eafeþum stēpte,   ofer ealle men
forð gefremede.   Hwæþere him on ferhþe
                              grēow
brēosthord blōdrēow;   nallas bēagas geaf
1720 Denum æfter dōme;   drēamlēas gebād,
þæt hē þæs gewinnes   weorc þrōwade,
lēodbealo longsum.   Ðū þē lǣr be þon,
gumcyste ongit!   Ic þis gid be þē
āwrǣc wintrum frōd.
                              Wundor is tō secganne,
1725 hū mihtig God   manna cynne
þurh sīdne sefan   snyttru bryttað,
eard ond eorlscipe;   hē āh ealra geweald.
Hwīlum hē on lufan   lǣteð hworfan
monnes mōdgeþonc   mǣran cynnes,
1730 seleð him on ēþle   eorþan wynne
tō healdanne   hlēoburh wera,
gedēð him swā gewealdene   worolde dǣlas,
sīde rīce,   þæt hē his selfa ne mæg
his unsnyttrum   ende geþencean.
1735 Wunað hē on wiste;   nō hine wiht dweleð
ādl nē yldo,   nē him inwitsorh
on sefa(n) sweorceð,   nē gesacu ōhwǣr
ecghete ēoweð,   ac him eal worold

Hrothgar spoke, first examining the hilt,
the ancient heirloom. On it was engraved
the origins of strife in time immemorial,
when the tide of rising water drowned
1690 the race of giants; their end was horrible;
they were opposed to the Eternal Lord,
and their reward was the downpour and the
                              flood.[1]
Also, on the sword-guards of pure gold,
it was recorded in runic letters, as is the
                              custom,
1695 for whom that sword, finest of blades,
with twisted hilt and serpentine patterning
had first been made.
                              Then Healfdene's wise
                              son
lifted his voice—everyone listened:
1700 'This land's grizzled guardian, who promotes
                              truth
and justice amongst his people, and forgets
                              nothing
though the years pass, can say for certain
                              that this man
is much favoured by fate! Beowulf my friend,
your name is echoed in every country
1705 to earth's end. You wear your enormous
                              might
with wisdom and with dignity. I shall keep
my promise made when last we spoke. You
                              will
beyond doubt be the shield of the Geats
for days without number, and a source
1710 of strength to warriors.
                              Heremod[2] was hardly
                              that
to Ecgwala's sons, the glorious Scyldings;
he grew to spread slaughter and destruction
rather than happiness amongst the Danish
                              people.
In mad rage he murdered his
                              table-companions,
1715 his most loyal followers; it came about
that the great prince cut himself off
from all earthly pleasures, though God had
                              endowed him
with strength and power above all other
                              men,
and had sustained him. For all that, his heart
1720 was filled with savage blood-lust. He never
                              gave
gifts to the Danes, to gain glory. He lived
                              joyless,
agony racked him; he was long an affliction
to his people. Be warned, Beowulf,
learn the nature of nobility. I who tell you
1725 this story am many winters old.
                              It is a miracle
how the mighty Lord in his generosity
gives wisdom and land and high estate

---

1. The reference is to the Flood of Noah, Gen. vi.8, esp.
vi.4 ff.

2. Heremod was a notorious betrayer and tyrant.

wendeð on willan;   hē þæt wyrse ne con—,
1740 oð þæt him on innan   oferhygda dǣl
weaxeð ond wrīdað;   þonne se weard swefeð,
sāwele hyrde;   bið se slǣp tō fæst,
bisgum gebunden,   bona swīðe nēah,
sē þe of flānbogan   fyrenum scēoteð.
1745 þonne bið on hreþre   under helm drepen
biteran strǣle   —him bebeorgan ne con—,
wōm wundorbebodum   wergan gāstes;
þinceð him tō lȳtel,   þæt hē lange hēold,
gȳtsað gromhȳdig,   nallas on gylp seleð
1750 fǣtte bēagas,   ond hē þā forðgesceaft
forgyteð ond forgȳmeð,   þæs þe him ǣr God
sealde,
wuldres Waldend,   weorðmynda dǣl.
Hit on endestæf   eft gelimpeð,
þæt se līchoma   lǣne gedrēoseð,
1755 fǣge gefealleð;   fēhð ōþer tō,
sē þe unmurnlīce   māðmas dǣleþ,
eorles ǣrgestrēon,   egesan ne gȳmeð.
Bebeorh þē ðone bealonīð,   Bēowulf lēofa,
secg betsta,   ond þē þæt sēlre gecēos.
1760 ēce rǣdas;   oferhȳda ne gȳm,
mǣre cempa!   Nū is þīnes mægnes blǣd
āne hwīle;   eft sōna bið,
þæt þec ādl oððe ecg   eafoþes getwǣfeð,
oððe fȳres feng,   oððe flōdes wylm,
1765 oððe gripe mēces,   oððe gāres fliht,
oððe atol yldo;   oððe ēagena bearhtm
forsiteð ond forsworceð;   semninga bið,
þæt ðec, dryhtguma,   dēað oferswȳðeð.
      Swā ic Hring-Dena   hund missēra
1770 wēold under wolcnum   ond hig wigge belēac
manigum mǣgþa   geond þysne middangeard,
æscum ond ecgum,   þæt ic mē ǣnigne
under swegles begong   gesacan ne tealde.
Hwæt, mē þæs on ēþle   edwenden cwōm,
1775 gyrn æfter gomene,   seoþðan Grendel wearð,
ealdgewinna,   ingenga mīn;
ic þǣre sōcne   singāles wæg
mōdceare micle.   þæs sig Metode þanc,
ēcean Dryhtne,   þæs ðe ic on aldre gebād,
1780 þæt ic on þone hafelan   heorodrēorigne
ofer eald gewin   ēagum starige!
Gā nū tō setle,   symbelwynne drēoh
wīggeweorþad;   unc sceal worn fela
māþma gemǣnra,   siþðan morgen bið.'

to people on earth; all things are in His
power.
At times he allows a noble man's mind to
experience
1730 happiness, grants he should rule over a
pleasant,
prosperous country, a stronghold of men,
makes subject to him regions of earth,
a wide kingdom, until in his stupidity
there is no end to his ambition.
1735 His life is unruffled—neither old age
nor illness afflict him, no unhappiness
gnaws at his heart, in his land no hatred
flares up in mortal feuds, but all the world
bends to his will. He suffers no setbacks
1740 until the seed of arrogance is sown and grows
within him, while still the watchman
slumbers;
how deeply the soul's guardian[3] sleeps
when a man is enmeshed in matters of this
world;
the evil archer stands close with his drawn
bow,
1745 his bristling quiver. Then the poisoned shaft
pierces his mind under his helmet
and he does not know how to resist
the devil's insidious, secret temptations.
What had long contented him now seems
insufficient;
1750 he becomes embittered, begins to hoard
his treasures, never parts with gold rings
in ceremonial splendour; he soon forgets
his destiny and disregards the honours
given him of God, the Ruler of Glory.
1755 In time his transient body wizens and
withers,
and dies as fate decrees; then another man
succeeds to his throne who gives treasures
and heirlooms
with great generosity; *he* is not obsessed
with suspicions.
Arm yourself, dear Beowulf, best of men,
1760 against such diseased thinking; always
swallow pride;
remember, renowned warrior, what is more
worthwhile—
gain everlasting. Today and tomorrow
you will be in your prime; but soon you will
die,
in battle or in bed; either fire or water,
1765 the fearsome elements, will embrace you,
or you will succumb to the sword's flashing
edge,
or to the arrow's flight, or to extreme old
age;
then your eyes, once bright, will be clouded
over;
all too soon, O warrior, death will destroy
you.
1770 I have ruled the Ring-Danes under the
skies
for fifty years, shielded them in war
from many tribes of men in this world,

---

3. Conscience, prudence.

from swords and from ash-spears, and the
                                            time had come
when I thought I had no enemies left on
                                                    earth.

1775 All was changed utterly, gladness
      became grief, after Grendel,
      my deadly adversary, invaded Heorot.
      His visitations caused me continual pain.
      Thus I thank the Creator, the Eternal Lord,

1780 that after our afflictions I have lived to see,
      to see with my own eyes this blood-stained
                                                    head.

Now, Beowulf, brave in battle,
go to your seat and enjoy the feast;
tomorrow we shall share many treasures.'

The Lay of the Last Survivor

There were heaps of hoard-things in this hall
                                    underground[1]
which once in gone days gleamed and rang;
the thesaurus of a race rusts derelict.

In another age an unknown man,
2235 brows bent, brought and hid here
      the beloved hoard. The whole race
      death-rapt, and of the ring of earls
      one left alive; living on in that place
      heavy with friend-loss, the hoard-guard
2240 waited the same wierd.[2] His wit acknowledged
      that the treasures gathered and guarded over the years
      were his for the briefest while.
                            Barrow stood ready
      on flat ground where breakers beat at the headland,
      new, near at hand, made narrow of access.
2245 The keeper of rings carried into it
      the earls' holdings, the hoard-worthy part
      fraught with gold, few words spoke:

      'Hold, ground, the gold of the earls!
      Men could not. Cowards they were not
2250 who took it from thee once, but war-death took them,
      that stops life, struck them, spared not one
      man of my people, passed on now.
      They have had their hall-joys. I have not with me
      a man able to unsheathe this. . . .

2255 Who shall polish this plated vessel?
      This cup was dear. The company is elsewhere.[3]

      This hardened helmet healed with gold
      shall lose its shell. They sleep now
      whose work was to burnish the battle-mask;
2260 so the cuirass that in the crash took
      bite of iron amid breaking shields:
      it moulders with the man. This mailshirt travelled far,
      hung from a shoulder shouldered warriors;
      it shall not jingle again.
                            There's no joy from harp-play,
2265 gleewood's gladness, no good hawk
      swings through hall now, no swift horse
      tramps at threshold. The threat came:
      falling, has felled a flowering kingdom.'

---

1. The survivor describes a hoard of treasure guarded
over by the dragon.
2. *Wierd* is an Old English word meaning "fate" or
"destiny."

3. Old English literature reiterates the theme that *lif is
laene*, life is transitory and mortal happiness
fleeting—peoples and families, tribes and nations are all
temporary in their existence. The hoards are relics,
antiques of people now dead.

A Dream of the Cross
(Dream of the Rood)[1]

Lo! I will tell   the dearest of dreams
That I dreamed in the midnight   when mortal men
Were sunk in slumber.   Me-seemed I saw
A wondrous Tree[2]   towering in air,
5   Most shining of crosses   compassed with light.
Brightly that beacon   was gilded with gold;
Jewels adorned it   fair at the foot,
Five on the shoulder-beam,   blazing in splendour.
Through all creation   the angels of God
10   Beheld it shining—   no cross of shame!
Holy spirits   gazed on its gleaming,
Men upon earth   and all this great creation.
        Wondrous that Tree,   that Token of triumph,
And I a transgressor   soiled with my sins!
15   I gazed on the Rood   arrayed in glory,
Shining in beauty   and gilded with gold,
The Cross of the Saviour   beset with gems.
But through the gold-work   outgleamed a token
Of the ancient evil   of sinful men
20   Where the Rood on its right side   once sweat blood.
Saddened and rueful,   smitten with terror
At the wondrous Vision,   I saw the Cross
Swiftly varying   vesture and hue,
Now wet and stained   with the Blood outwelling,
25   Now fairly jewelled   with gold and gems.
        Then, as I lay there,   long I gazed
In rue and sadness   on my Saviour's Tree,
Till I heard in dream   how the Cross addressed me,
Of all woods worthiest,   speaking these words:[3]
30   "Long years ago   (well yet I remember)
They hewed me down   on the edge of the holt.
Severed my trunk;   strong foemen took me,
For a spectacle wrought me,   a gallows for rogues.
High on their shoulders   they bore me to hilltop,
35   Fastened me firmly,   an army of foes!
        "Then I saw the King   of all mankind
In brave mood hasting   to mount upon me.
Refuse I dared not,   nor bow nor break,
Though I felt earth's confines   shudder in fear;
40   All foes I might fell,   yet still I stood fast.
        "Then the young Warrior,   God, the All-Wielder,
Put off His raiment,   steadfast and strong;
With lordly mood   in the sight of many
He mounted the Cross   to redeem mankind.
45   When the Hero clasped me   I trembled in terror,
But I dared not bow me   nor bend to earth;
I must needs stand fast.   Upraised as the Rood
I held the High King,   the Lord of heaven.
I dared not bow!   With black nails driven
50   Those sinners pierced me;   the prints are clear,
The open wounds.   I dared injure none.
They mocked us both.   I was wet with blood
From the Hero's side   when He sent forth His spirit.
        "Many a bale   I bore on that hill-side

---

1. This early poem (ca. 750) has a portion of its lines
inscribed in runic characters on an eighteen-foot-high
stone cross, now preserved in the church at Ruthwell,
Dumfriesshire, Scotland, indicating that it was a poem of
some reputation and esteem. "Rood" was an early name
for "cross," spelt *rod* in OE, *rode* in Middle English.

2. A continuous association in Christian tradition, in
which the cross is associated with other symbolic biblical
trees, such as the trees in the Garden of Eden (see "The
Fall of Lucifer" below), particularly the "tree of life."
3. An early English example of personification.

55 Seeing the Lord   in agony outstretched.
Black darkness covered   with clouds God's body,
That radiant splendour.   Shadow went forth
Wan under heaven;   all creation wept
Bewailing the King's death.   Christ was on the Cross.
60   "Then many came quickly,   faring from far,
Hurrying to the Prince.   I beheld it all.
Sorely smitten with sorrow   in meekness I bowed
To the hands of men.   From His heavy and bitter pain
They lifted Almighty God.   Those warriors left me
65 Standing bespattered with blood;   I was wounded with spears.
Limb-weary they laid Him down;   they stood at His head,
Looked on the Lord of heaven   as He lay there at rest
From His bitter ordeal all forspent.   In sight of His slayers
They made Him a sepulchre   carved from the shining stone;
70 Therein laid the Lord of triumph.   At evening tide
Sadly they sang their dirges   and wearily turned away
From their lordly Prince;   there He lay all still and alone.
   "There at our station   a long time we stood
Sorrowfully weeping   after the wailing of men
75 Had died away.   The corpse grew cold,
The fair life-dwelling.   Down to earth
Men hacked and felled us,   a grievous fate!
They dug a pit   and buried us deep.
But there God's friends   and followers found me
80 And graced me with treasure   of silver and gold.
   "Now may you learn,   O man beloved,
The bitter sorrows   that I have borne,
The work of caitiffs.[4]   But the time is come
That men upon earth   and through all creation
85 Show me honour   and bow to this sign.
On me a while   God's Son once suffered;
Now I tower under heaven   in glory attired
With healing for all   that hold me in awe.
Of old I was once   the most woeful of tortures,
90 Most hateful to all men,   till I opened for them
The true Way of life.   Lo! the Lord of glory,
The Warden of heaven,   above all wood
Has glorified me   as Almighty God
Has honoured His Mother,   even Mary herself,
95 Over all womankind   in the eyes of men.
   "Now I give you bidding,   O man beloved,
Reveal this Vision   to the sons of men,
And clearly tell   of the Tree of glory
Whereon God suffered   for man's many sins
100 And the evil that Adam   once wrought of old.
   "Death He suffered,   but our Saviour rose
By virtue of His great might   as a help to men.
He ascended to heaven.   But hither again
He shall come unto earth   to seek mankind,
105 The Lord Himself   on the Day of Doom,
Almighty God   with His angel hosts.
And then will He judge,   Who has power of judgment,
To each man according   as here on earth
In this fleeting life   he shall win reward.
110   "Nor there may any   be free from fear
Hearing the words   which the Wielder shall utter.
He shall ask before many: Where is the man
Who would taste bitter death   as He did on the Tree?
And all shall be fearful   and few shall know
115 What to say unto Christ.   But none at His Coming

4. Scavenging dogs.

Shall need to fear   if he bears in his breast
This best of symbols;   and every soul
From the ways of earth   through the Cross shall come
To heavenly glory,   who would dwell with God."
120   Then with ardent spirit   and earnest zeal,[5]
Companionless, lonely,   I prayed to the Cross.
My soul was fain of death.   I had endured
Many an hour of longing.   It is my life's hope
That I may turn   to this Token of triumph,
125   I above all men,   and revere it well.
          That is my heart's desire,   and all my hope
Waits on the Cross.   In this world now
I have few powerful friends;   they have fared hence
Away from these earthly gauds   seeking the King of glory,
130   Dwelling now with the High Father   in heaven above,
Abiding in rapture.   Each day I dream
Of the hour when the Cross of my Lord,   whereof here on earth
I once had vision,   from this fleeting life may fetch me
And bring me where is great gladness   and heavenly bliss,
135   Where the people of God   are planted and stablished for ever
In joy everlasting.   There may it lodge me
Where I may abide in glory   knowing bliss with the saints.
          May the Lord befriend me   who on earth of old
Once suffered on the Cross   for the sins of men.
140   He redeemed us, endowed us with life   and a heavenly home.
Therein was hope renewed   with blessing and bliss
For those who endured the burning.   In that great deed
God's Son was triumphant,   possessing power and strength!
Almighty, Sole-Ruling   He came to the kingdom of God
145   Bringing a host of souls   to angelic bliss,
To join the saints   who abode in the splendour of glory,
When the Lord, Almighty God,   came again to His throne.

ALCUIN[1]

Lost Nightingale
Written for his lost nightingale

De Luscinia

Quae te dextra mihi rapuit, luscinia, ruscis,
     illa meae fuerat invida laetitiae.
tu mea dulcisonis implesti pectora musis,
     atque animum moestum carmine mellifluo.
qua propter veniant volucrum simul undique
                                   coetus
     carmine te mecum plangere Pierio.
spreta colore tamen fueras non spreta
                                   canendo.
     lata sub angusto gutture vox sonuit,
dulce melos iterans vario modulamine Musae,
     atque creatorem semper in ore canens.
noctibus in furvis nusquam cessavit ab odis,
     vox veneranda sacris, o decus atque decor.
quid mirum, cherubim, seraphim si voce

Whoever stole you from that bush of broom,[2]
     I think he envied me my happiness,
O little nightingale, for many a time
     You lightened my sad heart from its
                                   distress,
     And flooded my whole soul with melody.
And I would have the other birds all come,
     And sing along with me thy threnody.[3]

So brown and dim that little body was,
     But none could scorn thy singing. In that
                                   throat
That tiny throat, what depth of harmony,
     And all night long ringing thy changing
                                   note.

5. At this point it is the poet (persona) who speaks,
identifying himself, in the figural Christian sense, with
the Cross.

1. Alcuin (735–804) was a famous early English scholar,

instrumental in the revival of learning in the court of
Charlemagne.
2. A hardy shrub, common in the British Isles.
3. A lamentation, a dirge.

tonantem
perpetua laudent, dum tua sic potuit?

What marvel if the cherubim[4] in heaven
Continually do praise Him, when to thee,
O small and happy, such a grace was
given?

SEDULIUS SCOTTUS[1]

On the Slaying of a Ram

Wherein his guilt—so simple, straight and true?
Bacchus[2] he shunned, sherbet avoided too;
not him did liquor from narrow path entice,
not meal with king, or lesser lord, his vice;
his solemn feast was grazing on the grass,
his sweetest drink from brink of limpid Maas,
nor did he plead that he be vested in
purple or red—felt happy with a skin;
and never did he ride astride a horse
but steady on his legs he plied a course,
lied not, nor idle word did ever say,
but utterance of depth—just 'baa' and 'beh.'
Adieu good chief of gleaming herd—alas!
  I see you not a-feeding on my grass.
Ah! Were you there a hot bath I had planned
(only to please the guest you understand!)
and self would minister with devoted breast
to head and horn and hoof and all the rest.
You have I loved, and love your widow too,
mother I love, and brothers all—Adieu.

Nunc Viridant Segetes

Nunc viridant segetes, nunc florent germine
campi,
Nunc turgent vites, est nunc pulcherrimus
annus,
Nunc pictae volucres permulcent aethera
cantu,
Nunc mare, nunc tellus, nunc caeli sidera
rident.

Ast nos tristificis perturbat potio sucis,
Cum medus atque Ceres, cum Bachi munera
desint;
Heu—quam multiplicis defit substantia
carnis,
Quam mitis tellus generat, quam roscidus
aether.

Scriptor sum (fateor), sum Musicus alter et
Orpheus,
Sum bos triturans, prospera quaeque volo,
Sum vester miles sophiae praeditus armis:
Pro nobis nostrum, Musa, rogato patrem.

Complaint of His Larder

The crops are green and fields are all in
flower,
budding the vine—the year now has its hour;
gay-painted songbirds fill the air with glee,
there's smile on land and sky and laughs the
sea.

Of mirth-provoking sap I too have need,
some beer, or Bacchus' gift,[1] or perhaps some
mead;[2]
and then there's meat, produce of earth and
sky,
and I have none, but ask the reason why.

Now, Muse, I write and sing, am Orpheus[3]
reborn,
but too have needs, the ox that treads the
corn;
your champion I, with wisdom's arms I fight:
Off to the bishop, and tell him of my plight.

4. An order of angels.

1. Sedulius Scottus (ninth century) was an Irish monk
who founded an important centre of Irish culture in Liège
in A.D. 848. He knew Greek literature well, and wrote
Greek. This poem was written ca. 850.

2. The Greek god of the vine.

1. Wine.
2. Liquor made with honey.
3. Orpheus, the archetypal poet whose music was so
immortal as to return him from the dead (see *Sir Orfeo* below).

Aut Lego Vel Scribo

Aut lego vel scribo, doceo scrutorve sophiam:
  Obsecro celsithronum nocte dieque meum.
Vescor, poto libens, rithmizans invoco
                                    Musas,
  Dormisco stertens: oro deum vigilans.
Conscia mens scelerum deflet peccamina
                                    vitae:
  Parcite vos misero, Christe Maria, viro.

Confession

I read and write and teach, philosophy
                                    peruse.
I eat and freely drink, with rhymes invoke
                                    the muse,
I call on heaven's throne both night and day,
snoring I sleep, or stay awake and pray.
And sin and fault inform each act I plan:
Ah! Christ and Mary, pity this miserable
                                    man.

ANONYMOUS

Atá Uarboth Dam I Caill

Atá úarboth dam i caill,
  nís-fitir acht mo Fhíada:
uinnius di-síu, coll an-all,
  bile rátha nosn-íada.

5 Dí ersainn fraích fri fulong
  ocus fordorus féithe;
feraid in chaill imma cress
  a mess for mucca méithe.

Mét mo boithe: beccnat becc,
10 baile sétae sognath;
canaid sian mbinn día beinn
  ben a lleinn co londath.

            *   *   *

Monga lebra ibair éoglais,
  nósta cél!
15 Caín in magan márglas darach
  darsin sén.

Aball ubull (már a ratha)
  mbruidnech mbras;
barr dess dornach, collán cnobecc
20 cróebach nglas.

Glére thibrat, essa uisci,
  úais do dig;
bruinnit ilair, cáera ibair,
  fidait fir.

25 Foilgit impe mucca cenntai,
  cadlaid, uirc,
mucca alltai, oiss aird, eillti,
  bruicnech, bruic.

Buidnech, sídech, slúag tromm tírech,
30 dál dom thig;
ina erchaill tecat cremthainn,
  álainn sin.

            *   *   *

Líne ugae, mil, mess, melle,
  Dia dod-roíd;

The Hermit

I have a bothy[1] in the wood—
none knows it but the Lord, my God;
one wall an ash, the other hazel,
and a great fern makes the door.

5 The doorsteps are of heather,
the lintel of honeysuckle;
and wild forest all around
drops mast for well-fed swine.

This size my hut: the smallest thing,
10 homestead amid well-trod paths;
a woman—blackbird clothed and coloured—
is singing sweetly from its gable.

            *   *   *

Smooth the tresses of yew-green yew-trees,
  glorious portent;
15 place delicious with great green oakwoods
  increasing blessing.

Tree of apples huge and magic,
  great its graces;
crop in fistfulls from clustered hazel,
20 green and branching.

Sparkling wells and water-torrents,
  best for drinking;
green privet there and bird-cherry
  and yew-berries.

25 Resting there are herded swine,
  goats and piglings;
wild swine too, deer and doe,
  speckled badgers.

Great woodland bands troop like fairies
30 to my bothy;
and great delight when timid foxes
  show their faces.

            *   *   *

Eggs in clutches and God gives mast,
  honey, heath-pease;

1. A hut or cottage such as might be used by a farm
labourer or game-keeper.

35 ubla milsi, mónainn derca,
     derena froích.

          *   *   *

Cúach meda colláin chunnla
     co ndáil daith;
durcháin donna, dristin monga
40   mérthain maith.

Mad fri samrad suaire snobrat
     somlas mlas,
curair, orcáin, foltáin glaise,
     glaine glas.

45 Céola ferán mbruinne forglan
     foram ndil,
dordán smálcha caíne gnáthcha
     úas mo thig.

Tellinn, cíarainn, cerdán cruinne,
50   crónán séim;
gigrainn, cadain, gair ré Samain
     seinm ngairb chéir.

          *   *   *

Tecat caínfinn, corra, faílinn,
     fos-cain cúan;
55 ní céol ndogra cerca odra
     a fráech rúad.

          *   *   *

Fogur gaíthe fri fid flescach
     forglas néol,
essa aba, esnad eala,
60   álainn céol.

Caíne ailmi ardom peitet,
     ní íarna creic,
do Chríst cech than ní messa dam
     oldás deit.

65 Cid maith lat-su a ndo-mil-siu,
     mó cach maín,
buidech lem-sa do-berr dam-sa
     óm Chríst chaín.

Cen úair n-augrai, cen deilm ndebtha
70   immut foich,
buidech dond Fhlaith do-beir cach maith
     dom im boith.

---

35 sweet the apples and the berries
     of bog and heather.

          *   *   *

A cup of mead from noble hazel,
     swift the service;
acorns brown, bramble tresses
40   and their berries.

Then in summer pleasant mantle
     of tasty savour;
marjoram, earth-nuts, and the tresses
     of the streamlet.

45 Pigeons cooing, breasts are gleaming.
     beloved flutter;
on my house-top constant music,
     song of thrushes.

Bees and chafers, gentle humming
50   and soft crooning;
wild geese come with rough dark music
     before All Hallows.

          *   *   *

Then come dear white ones, herons, sea-gulls
     sea-chant hearing;
55 no harsh music when grouse is calling
     from russet heather.

          *   *   *

The sound of wind in branching trees,
     day grey and cloudy;
stream in torrent, swans are singing,
60   sweet the music.

I hear the soughing of the pine-trees
     and pay no money;
I am richer far through Christ, my Lord,
     than ever you were.

65 Though you enjoy all you consume
     and wealth exceeding,
I am grateful for the riches
     my dear Christ brings me.

No hour of trouble like you endure,
70   no din of combat:
I thank the Prince who so endows me
     in my bothy.

Teicht Do Róim

Teicht do Róim,
     mór saído, becc torbai!
In rí chon-daigi hi foss,
manim-bera latt, ní fogbai.

Pilgrimage to Rome

Pilgrim, take care your journey's not in vain,
a hazard without profit, without gain;
the King you seek you'll find in Rome, it's
                                        true,
but only if he travels on the way with you.

COLMAN[1]

Since Your Heart Is Set
Written by Colman the Irishman to Colman returning to his own land

So, since your heart is set on those sweet fields
    And you must leave me here,
Swift be your going, heed not any prayers,
    Although the voice be dear.

5 Vanquished art thou by love of thine own land,[2]
    And who shall hinder love?
Why should I blame thee for thy weariness,
    And try thy heart to move?

Since, if but Christ would give me back the past,
10   And that first strength of days,
And this white head of mine were dark again,
    I too might go your ways.

Do but indulge an idle fond old man
    Whose years deny his heart.
15 The years take all away, the blood runs slow,
    No leaping pulses start.

All those far seas and shores that must be crossed,
    They terrify me: yet
Go thou, my son, swift be thy cleaving prow,
20   And do not quite forget.

Hear me, my son; little have I to say.
    Let the world's pomp go by.
Swift is it as a wind, an idle dream,
    Smoke in an empty sky.

25 Go to the land whose love gives thee no rest,
    And may Almighty God,
Hope of our life, lord of the sounding sea,
    Of winds and waters lord,

Give thee safe passage on the wrinkled sea,
30   Himself thy pilot stand,
Bring thee through mist and foam to thy desire,
    Again to Irish land.

Live, and be famed and happy: all the praise
    Of honoured life to thee.
35 Yea, all this world can give thee of delight,
    And then eternity.

1. Nothing more is known about the author (ninth century). The name Colman means "little dove," and was one of the most popular Irish names of that period, probably because of the fame of St. Columba (521–527).

2. The poem is written in a monastery in Scotland or England, and sent as a verse letter from an older monk to a younger monk of the same Irish name.

ANONYMOUS

Aithbe Dam Cen Bés Mora

Aithbe dam cen bés mora—
  sentu fom-dera croan;
toirse oca cía dono?—
  sona do-táet a loan.

5 Is mé caillech Bérri Buí,
no-meilinn léini mbithnuí;
indíu táthum do séimi
ná melainn cid aithléini.

It moíni
10 cartar lib, nídat doíni;
sinni, indbaid marsaimme
batar doíni carsaimme.

Batar inmaini doíni
  ata maige mad-ríadam;
15 ba maith no-meilmis leo,
  ba becc no-mmoítis íaram.

Indíu trá cáin timgarat
  ocus ní mór nond-oídet;
cíasu becc do-n-indnagat
20 is mór a mét no-mmoídet.

Carpait lúaith
ocus eich no beirtis búaid,
ro boí, denus, tuile díb;
bennacht ar ríg do-da-úaid.

25 Tocair mo chorp co n-aichri
  dochum adba dían aithgni;
tan bas mithig la mac nDé
  do-té do brith a aithni.

Ó do-éctar mo láma,
30 ot é cnámacha cáela,
nítat fíu turcbáil, taccu,
  súas tar na maccu cáema.

Ot é cnámacha cáela
  ó do-éctar mo láma,
35 ba inmainiu tan gnítis
  bítis im ríga rána.

It fáilti na ingena
  ó thic dóib co Beltaine;
is deithbiriu dam-sa brón,
40 sech am tróg, am sentainne.

Ní feraim cobrai milis,
  ní marbtar muilt dom banais;
is becc, is líath mo thrilis,
  ní líach droch-caille tarais.

Ebb Tide

The ebbing that has come on me
is not the ebbing of the sea.
What knows the sea of grief or pain?—
Happy tide will flood again.

5 I am Bui, the hag of Beare—[1]
the richest cloth I used to wear.
Now with meanness and with thrift
I even lack a change of shift.

It is wealth
10 and not men that you love.
In the time that we lived
it was men that we loved.

Those whom we loved, the plains
we ride today bear their names;
15 gaily they feasted with laughter
nor boasted thereafter.

To-day they gather in the tax
but, come to handing out, are lax;
the very little they bestow
20 be sure that everyone will know.

Chariots there were, and we
had horses bred for victory.
Such things came in a great wave;
pray for the dead kings who gave.

25 Bitterly does my body race
seeking its destined place;
now let God's Son come and take
that which he gave of his grace.

These arms, these scrawny things you see,
30   scarce merit now their little joy
when lifted up in blessing
    over sweet student boy.

These arms you see,
    these bony scrawny things,
35 had once more loving craft
    embracing kings.

When Maytime comes
    the girls out there are glad,
and I, old hag, old bones,
40   alone am sad.

No wedding wether killed for me,
an end to all coquetry;
a pitiful veil I wear
on thin and faded hair.

---

1. The old woman of Bérri (Beare) was an immortal mythological figure reminiscent of Sheela-Na-Gig, the Celtic goddess of Motherhood, ancestress of races and a builder of cairns. The author of this poem regards her as a very old woman, facing encroaching decrepitude and senility.

45 Ní olc lium
ce beith caille finn form chiunn;
boí móirmeither cech datha
form chiunn oc ól dag-latha.

Ním-gaib format fri nach sen
50 inge nammá fri Feimen:
meisse, rom-melt forbaid sin,
buide beus barr Feimin.

Lia na Ríg hi Femun,
Caithir Rónáin hi mBregun,
55 cían ó ro-s-siachtat sína,
a lleicne nít sen-chrína.

Is labar tonn moro máir,
ros-gab in gaim cumgabáil;
fer maith, mac mogo in-díu
60 ní freiscim do chéilidiu.

Is éol dam a ndo-gniat,
rait ocus do-raat;
curchasa Átha Alma,
is úar ind adba hi faat.

65 Is mó láu
nád muir n-oíted imma-ráu;
testa már mblíadnae dom chruth,
dáig fo-rroimled mo chétluth.

Is mó dé
70 dam-sa in-díu, cibé de;
gaibthium étach cid fri gréin,
do-fil áes dam, at-gén féin.

Sam oíted i rrabamar
do-miult cona fagamur;
75 gaim aís báides cech nduine,
domm-ánaic a fochmuine.

Ro-miult m'oítid ar thuus
is buide lem ron-gleus;
cid becc mo léim dar duae
80 níbu nuae in bratt beus.

Is álainn in bratt úaine
ro-scar mo Rí tar dromman;
is sáer in Fer no-d-lúaidi:
do-rat loí fair íar lommad.

85 Aminecán morúar dam
— cech n-érchaín is erchraide—
íar feis fri caindlib sorchaib
bith i ndorchuib derthaige!

Rom-boí denus la ríga
90 oc ól meda ocus fína;
indíu ibim medcuisce
eter sentainni crína.

45 Well do I wear
plain veil on faded hair;
many colours I wore
and we feasting before.

Were it not for Feven's plain[2]
50 I'd envy nothing old;
I have a shroud of aged skin,
Feven's crop[3] is gold.

Ronan's city there in Bregon
and in Feven the royal standing stone,
55 why are their cheeks not weathered,
only mine alone?

Winter comes and the sea will rise
crying out with welcoming wave;
but no welcome for me from nobleman's son
60 or from son of a slave.

What they do now, I know, I know:
to and fro they row and race;
but they who once sailed Alma's ford
rest in a cold place.

65 It's more than a day
since I sailed youth's sea,
beauty's years not devoured
and sap flowing free.

It's more than a day, God's truth,
70 that I'm lacking in youth;
I wrap myself up in the sun—
I know Old Age, I see him come.

There was a summer of youth
nor was autumn the worst of the year,
75 but winter is doom
and its first days are here.

God be thanked, I had joy of my youth.
I swear that it's true,
if I hadn't leapt the wall
80 this old cloak still were not new.

The Lord on the world's broad back
threw a lovely cloak of green;
first fleecy, then it's bare,
and again the fleece is seen.

85 All beauty is doomed.
God! Can it be right
to kneel in a dark prayer-house
after feasting by candlelight?

I sat with kings drinking wine and mead
90 for many a day,
and now, a crew of shrivelled hags,
we toast in whey.

---

2. A plain in County Tipperary.

3. OI *barr* means both "crop" and "hair."

Rop ed mo choirm: cóid in mide,
   ropo toil Dé cecham-theirp
95 oc do guidi-siu, a Dé bí,
   do-rat a chró clí fri feirg.

Ad-cíu form brott brodrad n-aís,
ro-gab mo chíall mo thogaís;
líath a finn ásas trim thoinn,
100 is samlaid crotball senchruinn.

Rucad úaim-se mo súil des
día reic ar thír mbithdíles;
ocus rucad int súil chlé
do formach a foirdílse.

105 Tonn tuili
   ocus ind í aithbi áin,
a ndo-beir tonn tuili dait
   beirid tonn aithbi as do láim.

Tonn tuili
110 ocus ind aile aithbi,
dom-áncatar-sa uili
   conda éola a n-aithgni.

Tonn tuili
ní cos tar socht mo chuili;
115 cid mór mo dám fo deimi
fo-cress lám forru uili.

Mad ro-feissed mac Maire
   co mbeith fo chlí mo chuile:
cení dernus gart cenae
120 ní érburt 'nac' fri duine.

Tróg n-uile!—
   doíriu dúilib don duiniu
nád ndecha asind aithbiu-se
   feib do-ndecha asin tuiliu.

125 Mo thuile,
   is maith con-roíter m'aithne;
ra-sócr fsu mac Maire
   conda toirsech co aithbe.

Céin mair ailén mora máir,
130 dosn-ic tuile íarna tráig;
os mé, ní frescu dom-í
tuile tar éisi n-aithbi.

Be this my feast, these cups of whey;
   and let me always count as good
95 the vexing things that come of Christ
   who stayed God's ire with flesh and blood.

The mind is not so clear,
   there's mottling of age on my cloak,
grey hairs sprouting through skin,
100 I am like a stricken oak.

For deposit on heaven
   of right eye bereft,
I concluded the purchase
   with loss of the left.

105 Great wave of flood
   and wave of ebb and lack!
What flooding tide brings in
   the ebbing tide takes back.

Great wave of flood
110 and wave of ebbing sea,
and two of them I know
   for both have washed on me.

Great wave of flood
   brings no step to silent cellar floor;
115 a hand fell on all the company
   that feasted there before.

The Son of Mary knew right well
   he'd walk that floor one day;
grasping I was, but never sent
120 man hungry on his way.

Pity Man!—
   If only like the elements he could
come out of ebbing in the very way
   that he comes out of flood.

125 Christ left with me on loan
   flood tide of youth, and now it seems
there's ebb and misery, for Mary's Son
   too soon redeems.

Blessed the island in the great sea
130 with happy ebb and happy flood.
For me, for me alone, no hope:
   the ebbing is for good.

From Junius MS.[1]

Rebellion and Fall of Lucifer
Genesis B

    Then spoke the proud prince,   once fairest of angels,
Most shining in heaven,   beloved of his lord,
Dear to his leader,   till error misled him
And Almighty God   was roused to wrath.
5   He cast him down   to the depths of torment,
The couch of corpses,   and named him anew;
Said his name thenceforth   should be known as Satan;
He bade him reign over   Hell's black abyss
And never again   contend with God!
10   Then spoke Satan   in sorrow of spirit,
Who must henceforth rule   o'er the depths of hell.
Once he was white,   God's angel in heaven,
Till his heart betrayed him,   his haughty pride,
And he would not obey   or honour the word
15   Of the Lord of hosts.   Hell's heat was around him,
His heart surged within him;   he spoke these words:
    "Unlike indeed   is this narrow land
To that other home   that of old we held
In heaven's high realm,   though we could not keep
20   What our Lord had granted,   or govern our kingdom
Against God's will.   He has wrought us wrong,
In hurling us down   to the fiery depths of hell,
Deprived of heaven.   He has marked those heights
For man to settle.   'Tis my greatest sorrow
25   That Adam, fashioned   and formed of earth,
Should hold my high seat   and abide in bliss
While we suffer this torture,   this torment in hell.
    "Woe! Alas!   Could I lift my hands
And feel their strength,   be free for an hour,
30   One winter hour,   with this host I would—
But bands of iron   bind me about,
Sorely the rings   of my bondage ride me!
I am stripped of my kingdom.   Firmly hell's fetters
Are fastened upon me;   the fires burn
35   Above and below.   A loathlier landscape
I never have seen,   flame unassuaged
Surging through hell.   These clasping shackles,
These cruel-hard chains,   hinder my going.
Hell's doors are bolted,   the ways are barred,
40   My hands are fastened,   my feet are bound,
I can no way get free   of these fettering chains.
Gratings huge   of heavy iron,
Hammered hot,   press hard upon me,
Wherewith God has fastened me   firm by the neck.
45   I know full well   that He knew my purpose
Of evil for Adam   and all his hopes
Of the heavenly realm,   had I power of my hands.
    "But now we endure   the darkness of hell,
Its bottomless fires   blazing and grim.
50   God has banished us   into the black mists!
Though He may not charge us   with any evil
Or any wrong   that we wrought in that realm,
He has cut us off from light   and cast us down

---

1. This poem is a free poetic adaptation of the biblical book of Genesis with other interpolations traditionally ascribed to the poet Caedmon, whose story is preserved in Bede's *History of the Church in England*. The Junius manuscript (tenth-eleventh centuries) may have been seen by Milton, and it has been argued that portions of *Genesis B* were an influence on his *Paradise Lost*. The story of Lucifer and his angels is a part of Christian tradition, but does not actually occur in the biblical Genesis.

To the worst of all woes.   Nor may we requite it,
55   Or repay Him with harm   Who deprived us of light.
       "He has marked out the margins   of middle-earth
And created man   in His own image
By whom to re-people   the plains of heaven
With pure souls.   We must earnestly ponder
60   How we on Adam   and on his offspring,
If ever we can,   may avenge this wrong
And pervert His will   by any device.
       "No longer have I any   hope of that light
That He thinks long to enjoy   in bliss with His angels,
65   Nor may we in any way   soften the mood
Of Almighty God.   Since we may not regain it
Let us wrest heaven's realm   from the sons of men,
Make them forfeit His favour,   break His command.
Then His rage will be kindled.   He will cast them from grace;
70   They shall be banished   to hell's grim abyss.
We shall have them to serve us,   the sons of men,
As slaves fast-bound   in these fettering bonds.
       "Begin now to plan   and plot this assault!
If to any thane ever   in days of old
75   When we dwelt in that good kingdom   and happily held our thrones
I dealt out princely treasure,   at no dearer time
Could he give me requital,   repayment for gifts,
If some thane would be my helper   and outward hence
Break through these bolted gates,   with strength to wing
80   On feathered pinions   circling in the sky
To where new-shaped on earth   Adam and Eve
Abide in bliss   surrounded with abundance,
While we are cast out hither   to this deep hell.
       "They now indeed   are dearer unto God
85   And have the wealth   that we should have in heaven,
Our rightful realm.   The advantage lies with man!
My soul is sorrowful,   my heart is sore
That they should hold   the heavenly realms for ever.
If one of you can win them   in any way
90   To forsake God's law,   they will lose His love;
If they break His commandment   His mood will be roused
And all their wealth   will be changed for the worse,
Their punishment made ready,   some penalty grim.
Take thought how you may ensnare them.   More softly then
95   Shall I lie in these chains   if they lose the heavenly kingdom.
Whoever shall bring that to pass   shall have portion for ever
In all we may win of advantage   in these wide flames.
I will let him sit next myself   who returns to tell,
In this hot hell,   that the will of the King of heaven
100   Unworthily they forswore   by their words and works. . . ."[2]
       Then God's enemy   began to arm,
To put on his war-gear.   He had a wily heart.
He placed on his head   the helmet of darkness,
Fastened the buckles   and bound it firm.
105   He had craft of speech   and cunning of word.
He circled upward   and darted out
Through the portals of hell.   (He had a pitiless heart.)
Fell of purpose   he soared in flight
Cleaving the fire   with fiendish craft.
110   He wished to ensnare   God's servants in sin,
Seduce and beguile them   until they had gained God's hate.
       With fiendish cunning   he found his way
To where on earth   he came upon Adam,
God's own handiwork   wisely fashioned
115   And Eve beside him,   fairest of women,

2. At this point a leaf or two is missing from the text. It appears as though the text would have dealt with Satan's appeal to *comitatus* loyalty from his followers.

Serving God well   in all good works
For the Maker of man   had made them His stewards.
  By them two trees stood   filled with fruit
And clothed with increase.   Heaven's High King,
120   The Almighty, had set them   that the sons of men
Might choose of good or evil,   weal or woe.
  Unlike was their fruit.   One tree was fair,[3]
Lovely and shining,   pleasant and sweet.
That was the tree of life!   He might live for ever,
125   Who ate of that fruit.   Nor would age thereafter
Or woeful sickness   work him a hurt;
But long might he live   in happiness for ever,
Have here on earth   the favour of heaven's King
And the glory ordained on high   when he went hence.
130   The other tree was in shadow,   sunless and dark;
That was the tree of death!   Deadly its fruit!
Disgraced in this world,   knowing good and evil,
He needs must suffer   in sorrow and sweat
Who ate of the fruit   that formed on that tree.
135   Old age would despoil him   of deeds of strength,
Of bliss and lordship,   with death for his lot.
A little time only   he might joy in this life,
Then seek in the flames   the most loathsome of lands,
Be subject to fiends   where most fearful horrors
140   Afflict men for ever.   That the fiend knew well,
The devil's dark steward   who strove against God.

From ms of St. Augustine at Canterbury

Zephyrus[1]

Levis exsurgit Zephyrus,	Softly the west wind blows;
et sol procedit tepidus;	Gaily the warm sun goes;
iam terra sinus aperit,	The earth her bosom sheweth,
dulcore suo diffluit.	And with all sweetness floweth.

5 Ver purpuratum exiit,   5 Goes forth the scarlet spring,
ornatus suos induit: Clad with all blossoming,
aspergit terram floribus,   Sprinkles the fields with flowers,
ligna silvarum frondibus.   Leaves on the forest

Struunt lustra quadrupedes,   Dens for four-footed things,
10 et dulces nidos volucres;   10 Sweet nests for all with wings.
inter ligna florentia   On every blossomed bough
sua decantant gaudia.   Joy ringeth now.

Quod oculis dum video   I see it with my eyes,
et auribus dum audio,   I hear it with my ears,
15 heu, pro tantis gaudiis   15 But in my heart are sighs,
tantis inflor suspiriis.   And I am full of tears.

Cum mihi sola sedeo   Alone with thought I sit,
et hec revolvens palleo,   And blench, remembering it;
si forte caput sublevo,   Sometimes I lift my head,
20 nec audio nec video.   20 I neither hear nor see.

Tu saltim, Veris gratia,   Do thou, O Spring most fair,
exaudi et considera   Squander thy care
frondes, flores et gramina;   On flower and leaf and grain.
nam mea languet anima.   —Leave me alone with pain!

---

3. See Gen. ii.9.

1. Deity of the west wind. The Latin verb "exsurgit" means "rises up"—the time is early morning.

From The Exeter Book

The Wanderer[1]

Who liveth alone longeth for mercy,
Maker's mercy. Though he must traverse
tracts of sea, sick at heart,
—trouble with oars ice-cold waters,
5   the ways of exile,[2]—Wierd[3] is set fast.

     Thus spoke such a 'grasshopper,'[4] old griefs in his mind,
cold slaughters, the death of dear kinsmen:

'Alone am I driven each day before daybreak
to give my cares utterance.
10   None are there now among the living
to whom I dare declare me thoroughly,
tell my heart's thought. Too truly I know
it is in a man no mean virtue
that he keep close his heart's chest,
15   hold his thought-hoard, think as he may.

No weary mind may stand against Wierd
nor may a wrecked will work new hope;
wherefore, most often, those eager for fame
bind the dark mood fast in their breasts.

20   So must I also curb my mind,
cut off from country, from kind far distant,
by cares overworn, bind it in fetters;
this since, long ago, the ground's shroud
enwrapped my gold-friend.[5] Wretched I went thence,
25   winter-wearied, over the waves' bound;
dreary I sought hall of a gold-giver,
where far or near I might find
him who in meadhall might take heed of me,
furnish comfort to a man friendless,
30   win me with cheer.
             He knows who makes trial
how harsh and bitter is care for companion
to him who hath few friends to shield him.
Track ever taketh him, never the torqued gold,
not earthly glory, but cold heart's cave.
35   He minds him of hall-men, of treasure-giving,
how in his youth his gold-friend
gave him to feast. Fallen all this joy.

He knows this who is forced to forgo his lord's,
his friend's counsels, to lack them for long:
40   oft sorrow and sleep, banded together,
come to bind the lone outcast;
he thinks in his heart then that he his lord
claspeth and kisseth, and on knee layeth
hand and head, as he had at otherwhiles
45   in days now gone, when he enjoyed the gift-stool.

Awakeneth after this friendless man,
seeth before him fallow waves,

---

1. This poem is from The Exeter Book (eleventh century).
2. Many protagonists of OE lyric poetry are presented as exiles, pilgrims, wanderers, or strangers—people outcast from their *cynn* (kin, family, or tribe) and isolate, in search of another group or society in which they might live.

3. Fate or destiny.
4. *Eardstapa*—lit. "earth-stepper."
5. Patron, chief.

seabirds bathing, broading out feathers,
snow and hail swirl, hoar-frost falling.
50 Then all the heavier his heart's wounds,
sore for his loved lord. Sorrow freshens.

Remembered kinsmen press through his mind;
he singeth out gladly, scanneth eagerly
men from the same hearth. They swim away.
55 Sailors' ghosts bring not many
known songs there. Care grows fresh
in him who shall send forth too often
over locked waves his weary spirit.

Therefore I may not think, throughout this world,
60 why cloud cometh not on my mind
when I think over all the life of earls,
how at a stroke they have given up hall,
mood-proud thanes. So this middle earth
each of all days ageth and falleth.'

65 Wherefore no man grows wise without he have
his share of winters. A wise man holds out;
he is not too hot-hearted, nor too hasty in speech,
nor too weak a warrior, not wanting in fore-thought,
nor too greedy of goods, nor too glad, nor too mild,
70 nor ever too eager to boast, ere he knows all.

A man should forbear boastmaking
until his fierce mind fully knows
which way his spleen shall expend itself.

A wise man may grasp how ghastly it shall be
75 when all this world's wealth standeth waste,
even as now, in many places, over the earth
walls stand, wind-beaten,
hung with hoar-frost; ruined habitations.
The wine-halls crumble; their wielders lie
80 bereft of bliss, the band all fallen
proud by the wall. War took off some,
carried them on their course hence; one a bird bore
over the high sea; one the hoar wolf
dealt to death; one his drear-cheeked
85 earl stretched in an earthen trench.

The Maker of men hath so marred this dwelling
that human laughter is not heard about it
and idle stand these old giant-works.

A man who on these walls wisely looked
90 who sounded deeply this dark life
would think back to the blood spilt here,
weigh it in his wit. His word would be this:
'Where is that horse now? Where are those men? Where is the hoard-sharer?
Where is the house of the feast? Where is the hall's uproar?[6]

95   Alas, bright cup! Alas, burnished fighter!
    Alas, proud prince! How that time has passed,
    dark under night's helm, as though it never had been!

There stands in the stead of staunch thanes
a towering wall wrought with worm-shapes;

6. The *lif is laene* transitoriness of life theme, familiar
also in Latin poetry in the refrain *ubi sunt*? ("where are
they now").

100 the earls are off-taken by the ash-spear's point,
   —that thirsty weapon. Their Wierd is glorious.

   Storms break on the stone hillside,
   the ground bound by driving sleet,
   winter's wrath. Then wanness cometh,
105 night's shade spreadeth, sendeth from north
   the rough hail to harry mankind.

   In the earth-realm all is crossed;
   Wierd's will changeth the world.
   Wealth is lent us, friends are lent us,
110 man is lent, kin is lent;
   all this earth's frame shall stand empty.'

   So spoke the sage in his heart; he sat apart in thought.
   Good is he who keeps faith: nor should care too fast
   be out of a man's breast before he first know the cure:
115 a warrior fights on bravely. Well is it for him who seeks forgiveness,
   the Heavenly Father's solace, in whom all our fastness stands.

The Seafarer[1]

   The tale I frame shall be found to tally:
   the history is of myself.
        Sitting day-long
   at an oar's end clenched against clinging sorrow,
   breast-drought I have borne, and bitternesses too.
5 I have coursed my keel through care-halls without end
   over furled foam, I forward in the bows
   through the narrowing night, numb, watching
   for the cliffs we beat along.
        Cold then
   nailed my feet, frost shrank on
10 its chill clamps, cares sighed
   hot about heart, hunger fed
   on a mere-wearied mind.
        No man blessed
   with a happy land-life is like to guess
   how I, aching-hearted, on ice-cold seas
15 have wasted whole winters; the wanderer's beat,
   cut off from kind. . . .
   hung with hoar-frost.
        Hail flew in showers,
   there was no sound there but the slam of waves
   along an icy sea. The swan's blare
20 my seldom amusement; for men's laughter
   there was curlew-call, there were the cries of gannets,
   for mead-drinking the music of the gull.
   To the storm striking the stone cliffs
   gull would answer, eagle scream
25 from throats frost-feathered. No friend or brother
   by to speak with the despairing mind.

   This he little believes whose life has run
   sweet in the burgs, no banished man,
   but well-seen at wine-round, my weariness of mind
30 on the ways stretching over the salt plains.

---

1. Here the wandering protagonist is engaged in a
pilgrimage over the sea. The structure of the monologue is
somewhat less clear than is the case for *The Wanderer*,
but the general tenor and affirmations of the poem are
evident enough.

Night thickened, and from the north snowflakes;
hail fell on the frost-bound earth,
coldest of grains.

Now come thoughts
knocking my heart, of the high waves,
35   clashing salt-crests, I am to cross again.
Mind-lust maddens, moves as I breathe
soul to set out, seek out the way
to a far folk-land flood-beyond.

For no man above mould is so mood-proud,
40   so thoroughly equipped, so quick to do,
so strong in his youth, or with so staunch a lord
that before seafaring he does not fear a little
whither the Lord shall lead him in the end.
His heart is not in harping nor in the having of rings,
45   has no delight in women nor the world's gladnesses
nor can think of any thing outside the thrash of waves,
sea-struck, is distracted, stillness lost.

The thriving of the treeland, the town's briskness,
a lightness over the leas, life gathering,
50   everything urges the eagerly mooded
man to venture on the voyage he thinks of,
the faring over flood, the far bourn.
And the cuckoo calls him in his care-laden voice,
scout of summer, sings of new griefs
55   that shall make breast-hoard bitter.   Blithe heart cannot know,
through its happiness, what hardships they suffer
who drive the foam-furrow furthest from land.
Spirit breaks from the body's chest
to the sea's acres; over earth's breadth
60   and whale's range roams the mind now,
homes to the breast hungry and thirsty.

Lone-flier's song drags out my heart,[2]
whets will to the whale's beat
across wastes of water: far warmer to me
65   are the Lord's kindnesses than this life of death
lent us on land.   I do not believe
earthly estate is everlasting:
three things that all ways threaten a man's peace
and one before the end shall overthrow his mind;
70   either illness or age or the edge of vengeance
shall draw out the breath from the doom-shadowed.
Wherefore, for earl whosoever, it is afterword,
the praise of livers-on, that, lasting, is best:
won in the world before wayfaring,
75   forged, framed here, in the face of enmity,
in the Devil's spite: deeds, achievements.
That after-speakers should respect the name
and after them angels have honour toward it
for always and ever. From those everlasting joys
the daring shall not die.
80   Days are soon over,
on earth imperium with the earl's hand fails;
kings are not now, kaisers are not,
there are no gold-givers like the gone masters

---

2. *Gielleth anfloga*: the anfloga (lone-flier) is a sea bird,
sometimes taken as a symbol of the soul.

who between them framed the first deeds in the world,
85   in their lives lordly, in the lays renowned.
That chivalry is changed, cheer is gone away,
it is a weaker kind who wields earth now,
sweats for its bread. Brave men are fewer,
all excellence on earth grows old and sere
90   as now does every man over the world;
age fares against him, his face bleaches
and his thatch thins: had a throng of friends
of noble houses, knows now they all
are given to the ground. That grieves his white head.
95   Once life is going, this gristle slackens;
nothing can pain or please flesh then,
he cannot stir a finger, fix his thinking.

A man may bury his brother with the dead
and strew his grave with the golden things
100 he would have him take, treasures of all kinds,
but gold hoarded when he here lived
cannot allay the anger of God
towards a soul sin-freighted.

The Wife's Complaint[1]

I have wrought these words together out of a wryed existence,
the heart's tally, telling off
the griefs I have undergone from girlhood upwards,
old and new, and now more than ever;
5   for I have never not had some new sorrow,
some fresh affliction to fight against.

The first was my lord's leaving his people here:
crossed crests. To what country I knew not,
wondered where, awoke unhappy.
10   I left, fared any road, friendless, an outcast,
sought any service to staunch the lack of him.

Then his kinsmen ganged, began to think
thoughts they did not speak, of splitting the wedlock;
so—estranged, alienated—we lived each
15   alone, a long way apart; how I longed for him!

In his harshness he had me brought here;
and in these parts there were few friendly-minded,
worth trusting.
            Trouble in the heart now:
I saw the bitterness, the bound mind
20   of my matched man, mourning-browed,
mirk in his mood, murder in his thoughts.

Our lips had smiled to swear hourly
that nothing should split us—save dying—
nothing else. All that has changed:
25   it is now as if it never had been,
our friendship. I feel in the wind
that the man dearest to me detests me.
I was banished to this knoll knotted by woods
to live in a den dug beneath an oak.
30   Old is this earthen room; it eats at my heart.

1. This poem is the lament of a woman whose husband is misled by his kinsmen and banishes her to live in exile in an underground hovel far from her home. She recalls her former joys, curses the courtier whose advice caused the estrangement, and imagines her husband, also now rejected, stranded far on a distant shore.

I see the thorns thrive up there in thick coverts
on the banks that baulk these black hollows:
not a gay dwelling. Here the grief bred
by lordlack preys on me. Some lovers in this world
35 live dear to each other, lie warm together
at day's beginning; I go by myself
about these earth caves under the oak tree.
Here I must sit the summer day through,
here weep out the woes of exile,
40 the hardships heaped upon me. My heart shall never
suddenly sail into slack water,
all the longings of a lifetime answered.

May grief and bitterness blast the mind
of that young man! May his mind ache
45 behind his smiling face! May a flock of sorrows
choke his chest! He would change his tune
if he lived alone in a land of exile
far from his folk.
                    Where my friend is stranded
frost crusts the cracked cliff-face
50 grey waves grind the shingle.
The mind cannot bear in such a bleak place
very much grief.
                    He remembers too often
less grim surroundings. Sorrow follows
this too long wait for one who is estranged.

From The Exeter Book [*continued*]

Advent Lyrics

O Rex gentium et desideratus earum,
lapisque angularis qui facis utraque unum:
veni, et salva hominem quem de limo
formasti.

> . . . . cyninge.
> Ðu eart se weallstan   þe ða wyrhtan iu
> wiðwurpon to weorce.   Wel þe geriseð
> þæt þu heafod sie   healle mærre
> ond gesomnige   side weallas
> fæste gefoge,   flint unbræcne,
> þæt geond eorðbyrg eall   eagna gesihþe
> wundrien to worlde   wuldres ealdor.
> Gesweotula nu þurh searocræft   þin sylfes
>   weorc,
> soðfæst, sigorbeorht,   ond sona forlæt
> weall wið wealle.   Nu is þam weorce þearf
> þæt se cræftga cume   ond se cyning sylfa,
> ond þonne gebete—   nu gebrosnad is—
> hus under hrofe.   He þæt hra gescop,
> leomo læmena.   Nu sceal liffrea
> þone wergan heap   wraþum ahreddan,
> earme from egsan,   swa he oft dyde.

I. To the King

> . . . . to the King.
> You are the wall-stone[1] which the workmen
>   of old
> rejected from the work. Indeed it is fitting
> that you be the head of the great hall,
> and draw together the vast walls,
> the unbroken flint, with a firm joining,
> in order that throughout earth's cities all
>   things with the gift of sight
> may wonder eternally, O Lord of Glory.
> Reveal now by your mysterious skill your
>   own work,
> O true and victorious One, and then leave
>   standing
> wall against wall. Now for your works there
>   is need
> that the Maker come, the King himself,
> and thereupon repair—it is now decayed—
> the house under its roof. He created the
>   body,
> the limbs of clay. Now must the Lord
> save this weary multitude from wrath,
> the wretched ones from terror, as He has
>   often done.

1. The Bible has "corner-stone" (Cf. Ps. cxviii.22 and
Eph. ii.20). The lyric is a poem of praise which acts like an
expanding commentary on the biblical passages.

O Hierusalem, civitas Dei summi: leva in circuitu oculos tuos, et vide Dominum tuum, quia jam veniet solvere te a vinculis.

Eala sibbe gesihð,   sancta hierusalem,
cynestola cyst,   cristes burglond,
engla eþelstol,   ond þa ane in þe
saule soðfæstra   simle gerestað,
5 wuldrum hremgē.   Næfre wommes tacn
in þam eardgearde   eawed weorþeð,
ac þe firena gehwylc   feor abugeð,
wærgðo ond gewinnes.   Bist to wuldre full
halgan hyhtes,   swa þu gehaten eart.
10 Sioh nu sylfa,   þe geond þas sidan gesceaft,
swylce rodores hrof   rume geondwlite
ymb healfa gehwone,   hu þec heofones
                    cyning
siðe geseceð,   ond sylf cymeð.
Nimeð eard in þe,   swa hit ær gefyrn
15 witgan wisfæste   wordum sægdon;
cyðdon cristes gebyrd,   cwædon þe to frofre,
burga betlicast.   Nu is þæt bearn cymen,
awæcned to wyrpe   weorcum ebrea,
bringeð blisse þe,   benda onlyseð,
20 niþum genedde.   Nearoþearfe conn,
hu se earma sceal   are gebidan.

O Emmanuel, Rex et Legifer noster, exspectatio gentium et salvator earum: veni ad salvandum nos, Dominus Deus noster.

Eala gæsta god,   hu þu gleawlice
mid noman ryhte   nemned wære
emmanuhel,   swa hit engel gecwæð
ærest on ebresc!   þæt is eft gereht,
5 rume bi gerynum: "Nu is rodera weard,
god sylfa mid us."   Swa þæt gomele gefyrn
ealra cyninga cyning   ond þone clænan eac
sacerd soðlice   sægdon toweard;
swa se mæra iu,   melchisedech,
10 gleaw in gæste   godþrym onwrah
eces alwaldan.   Se wæs æ bringend,
lara lædend,   þam longe his
hyhtan hidercyme,   swa him gehaten wæs,
þætte sunu meotudes   sylfa wolde
15 gefælsian   foldan mægðe,
swylce grundas eac   gæstes mægne
siþe gesecan.   Nu hie softe þæs
bidon in bendum   hwonne bearn godes
cwome to cearigum.   Forþon cwædon swa,
20 suslum geslæhte: "Nu þu sylfa cum,

III. O Vision of Peace

O vision of peace, holy Jerusalem,[1]
best of royal thrones, homeland of Christ,
native seat of angels, where those alone,
the souls of the steadfast, always dwell
exultant in glory. Never a touch of vileness
in that region is ever seen,
rather every crime is exiled far from you,
every evil and struggle. You are gloriously
                  full
of holy joy, as your name promises.
Look yourself now, that through the wide
                  creation
you may broadly survey, the roof of heaven
                  also
on every side, how Heaven's King
seeks you widely and Himself comes.
He makes his home in you, as long ago
wise prophets predicted;
they proclaimed Christ's birth, they spoke
                comfort to you,
brightest of cities. Now has that man come,
been born to mitigate the pain of the
                  Hebrews;
He brings joy to you, He loosens the chains
imposed by sin. He knows the dire need,
that the wretched must await grace.

VI. Emmanuel

O God of Spirits, how wisely you
were justly called by the name
Emmanuel, as the angel spoke it
first in Hebrew.[1] That is interpreted
broadly by the meaning: "Now is the
              Guardian of the Heavens,
God Himself, with us." As prophets of old
said truly the King of all kings and also
the spotless priest was to come,
so of old the great Melchisedech,[2]
wise in spirit, revealed the divine power
of the eternal Ruler. He was the Bringer of
              Law,
the Guide of Wisdom to those to those who
              long
had wished for his coming, as was promised
              to them,
that the son of God Himself would
cleanse the people of earth,
and also with a journey by the might of his
              spirit

---

1. The reference is to "that Jerusalem which is above" (Gal. iv.27), the heavenly Jerusalem described in the prophets and Apocalypse of St. John, not the earthly city.

1. The Old English culture found the Hebrew Scriptures, with its saga of the trials and tribulations of the exiled Jewish peoples and their heroic leaders, almost more congenial than the New Testament. This reference to the

name of The Messiah comes from Isa. vii.14, and is repeated in Matt. i.23 by the angel.
2. In one of the Messianic Psalms (cix [cx].4) it is foretold that the Messiah should be a priest after the order of Melchizedek—that is, combining characteristics of prophet, priest, and king. The passage is quoted in Heb. vi.20 to identify the Melchizedek of Gen. xiv.18-20 as a type of Christ.

```
        heofones heahcyning.        Bring us hælo lif,
        werigum witeþeowum,        wope forcymenum,
        bitrum brynetearum.        Is seo bot gelong
        eal æt þe anum        ::::::::oferþearfum.
25    Hæftas hygegeomre        hider ::::::es,
        ne læt þe behindan,        þonne þu heonan cyrre,
        mænigo þus micle,        ac þu miltse on us
        gecyð cynelice,        crist nergende,
        wuldres æþeling,        ne læt awyrgde ofer us
30    onwald agan.        Læf us ecne gefean
        wuldres þines,        þæt þec weorðien,
        weoroda wuldorcyning,        þa þu geworhtes ær
        hondum þinum.        þu in heannissum
        wunast wideferh        mid waldend fæder."
```

visit the depths. For that they patiently
awaited in chains the time when the Son of
                                        God
should come to the wretched. They then
                                    spoke thus,
20   weakened by torment: "Now come yourself,
High King of Heaven. Bring the life of
                                    salvation to us,
to the weary prisoners overcome with
                                        crying,
with bitter salt tears. The remedy is
                                    completely
yours alone ....
25   heart-saddened captives hither....
Nor leave behind you when you turn hence
this great crowd, but your mercy upon us
make known royally, Savior Christ,
Prince of Heaven, nor let the cursed one over
                                        us
30   wield power. Leave us the eternal joy
of your glory that we may praise you,
Glory-King of people whom you long ago
                                    made
with your hands. In the highest
you live eternally with the Ruling Father."

X. Lord of Heaven

```
        Eala þu halga        heofona dryhten,
        þu mid fæder þinne        gefyrn wære
        efenwesende        in þam æþelan ham.
        Næs ænig þa giet        engel geworden,
5      ne þæs miclan        mægenþrymmes nan
        ðe in roderum up        rice biwitigað,
        þeodnes þryðgesteald        ond his þegnunga,
        þa þu ærest wære        mid þone ecan frean
        sylf settende        þas sidan gesceaft,
10    brade brytengrundas.        Bæm inc is gemæne
        heahgæst hleofæst.        We þe, hælend crist,
        þurh eaðmedu        ealle biddað
        þæt þu gehyre        hæfta stefne,
        þinra *nied*þiowa,        nergende god,
15    hu we sind geswencte        þurh ure sylfra gewill.
        Habbað wræcmæcgas,        wergan gæstas,
        hetl*a*n helsceaþa*n*,        hearde genyrw*a*d,
        gebunden bealorapum.        Is seo bot gelong
        eal æt þe anum,        ece dryhten.
20    Hreowcearigum help,        þæt þin hidercyme
        afrefre feasceafte,        þeah we fæhþo wið þec
        þurh firena lust        gefremed hæbben.
        Ara nu onbehtum        ond usse yrmþa geþenc,
        Hu *we* tealtrigað        tydran mode,
25    hwearfiað heanlice.        Cym nu, hæleþa cyning,
        ne lata to lange.        Us is lissa þearf,
        þæt þu us ahredde        ond us hælogiefe
        soðfæst sylle,        þæt we siþþan forð
```

O holy Lord of Heaven
you of old were with your Father
coexisting in that excellent home.
Not any angel was yet created,
5   nor any of that great mighty host
which up in the heavens watches over the
                                    kingdom,
God's magnificent dwelling and His service,
when you first were with the eternal Lord
yourself establishing this wide creation,
10   the broad earth-space. Common to you both
                                        is
the protecting Holy Spirit. We all, Savior
                                        Christ,
in humility pray you
that you hear the voice of captives,
of your servants, God the Savior,
15   how we are afflicted through our own willing.
Exiled wretches,[1] evil spirits,
hateful hell-fiends have narrowly pressed us,
bound with dire ropes. The relief belongs
completely to you alone, eternal Lord.
20   Help the care-burdened, so that your advent
may comfort the miserable, although we
                                        against you
through our appetite for sin have carried on a
                                        feud.
Have mercy now on your servants and
                                consider our misery,

1. The "exiled wretches" (cf. the *wraecca* of *The Wan-*
derer and *The Seafarer*) are the singers of the lyric; the
"evil spirits" and "hateful hell-fiends" are those spirits
which oppress them in their struggle to serve their Lord
in adverse times.

þa sellan þing   symle moten
30 geþeon on þeode,   þinne willan.

25 how we totter with sickly spirits,
we wander abjectly. Come now, King of men,
do not delay too long. For us there is a need
of grace,
that you save us and to us your salvation,
True One, give in order that we afterward
may always perform among men
30 the better thing, your will.

From The Exeter Book [*continued*]

Physiologus

The Panther[1]

Many are the creatures,   the manifold kinds,
Throughout the earth   whose natures we may not
Fully interpret,   or tell their numbers,
So wide-spread are they   over the world:
5 These teeming legions   of birds and beasts
That range the world   as far as the waters,
The roaring ocean   and salt sea-streams,
Brightly encircle   the bosom of earth.
Lo! we have learned   of a wondrous beast
10 Living in far lands,   famed among men,
In mountain caverns   making his home.
His name is Panther,   as men who know
In their writings tell   of the lonely rover.
He is full of kindness,   friendly to all
15 Save the Dragon[2] only   with whom for ever
He wages eternal,   unceasing war
By every means   of hurt he can muster.
He's a winsome creature   most wondrous fair,
Of varied hues.   As holy men tell
20 How Joseph's coat   was coloured with dyes
Of every shading,   each shining more fair,[3]
More excellent than the others   to the eyes of men,
So the coat of this beast   is wondrous bright,
Glowing in beauty   and gleaming with hues
25 Each than the others   more rich and more rare.
He is mild and loving,   unique of nature,
Meek and gentle   and kindly of mood.
None will he assail   save the venomous Serpent,
His Ancient Foe   whom I spoke of before.
30 When, fain of his fill,   he tastes of food,
After each meal   in the mountain caverns
He seeks his rest   in a secret spot.
There the Great Warrior   a three days' while
Heavy with sleep   sinks into slumber;
35 And on the third day   endowed with glory
The Mighty One wakens   straightway from sleep.
Out of the beast's mouth   melody cometh,
Loveliest music;   and after that strain
A fragrance[4] rises   from the fields of earth,
40 A breath more winsome,   sweeter and stronger
Than any savour,   than flowering spice
Or fruits of the forest;   more excellent far

---

1. The curious choice of the Panther to represent Christ
may derive from the Septuagint Greek translation of Hos.
v.14, in which the Hebrew word for "young lion" is so
rendered.

2. Symbolically associated with Satan.
3. Gen. xxxvii.3.
4. The odour of sanctity.

Than all earthly treasures.   Then out from the towns,
From kingly dwellings   and castle halls,
45   Men in multitudes   throng the roads
Hurrying onward   in crowding hosts,
Warriors in battle-gear;   even the beasts
After that sweet strain   fare towards the fragrance.
       So is the Lord God,   Giver of joys,
50   Kindly to every   creature of earth
With all loving gifts,   save alone to the Dragon,
The Author of venom,   the Ancient Foe
Whom once He bound   in the bottomless pit,
Fettered him there,   by force constrained him
55   In the grip of the flames.   Then He rose from the grave,
The God of angels,   the Giver of triumph,
On the third day   after He died for men.
That was sweet fragrance   winsome and fair
Over all the world;   and unto that odour
60   Righteous men gathered   from every region
Through all the limits   and lands of earth.
       Thus spake of old   St Paul the wise.[5]
"Manifold and abounding   are the blessings of earth
God gives unto men   for salvation and grace,
65   The Almighty Father   and only Hope
Of every being   in the heavens above,
And the world below."   That is lovely fragrance!

The Whale

       Now I will fashion   the tale of a fish,
With wise wit singing   in measured strains
The song of the Great Whale.   Often unwittingly
Ocean-mariners   meet with this monster,
5   Fastitocalon,[1]   fierce and menacing,
The Great Sea-Swimmer   of the ocean-streams.
       Like a rough rock   is the Whale's appearance,
Or as if there were swaying   by the shore of the sea
A great mass of sedge   in the midst of the sand dunes;
10   So it seems to sailors   they see an island,
And they firmly fasten   their high-prowed ships
With anchor-ropes   to the land that is no land,
Hobble their sea-steeds   at ocean's end,
Land bold on the island   and leave their barks
15   Moored at the water's edge   in the wave's embrace.
       There they encamp,   the sea-weary sailors,
Fearing no danger.   They kindle a fire;
High on the island   the hot flames blaze
And joy returns   to travel-worn hearts
20   Eager for rest.   Then, crafty in evil,
When the Whale feels the sailors   are fully set
And firmly lodged,   enjoying fair weather,
Suddenly with his prey   Ocean's Guest plunges
Down in the salt wave   seeking the depths,
25   In the hall of death   drowning sailors and ships.
       Such is the manner of demons,   the devils' way,[2]
Luring from virtue,   inciting to lust,
By secret power   deceiving men's souls
That they may seek help   at the hands of their foes

5. The reference to the epistles of St. Paul is unclear.

1. A corruption of the Greek name for shield-turtle, the beast associated with the false-island story in the Greek *Physiologus*.

2. The whale is associated with Leviathan, the satanic monster of chaos who struggles against divine order and provision.

30 And, fixed in sin,   find abode with the Fiend.
Sly and deceitful,   when the Devil perceives
Out of hell-torment   that each of mankind,
Of the race of men,   is bound with his ring,
Then with cunning craft   the Dark Destroyer
35 Takes proud and humble   who here on earth
Through sin did his will.   Seizing them suddenly
Shrouded in darkness,   estranged from good,
He seeks out hell,   the bottomless abyss
In the misty gloom;   even as the Great Whale
40 Who drowns the mariners,   sea-steeds and men.
    A second trait has he,   the proud Sea-Thrasher,
Even more marvellous: when hunger torments
And the fierce Water-Monster   is fain of food,
Then the Ocean-Warden   opens his mouth,
45 Unlocks his wide jaws,   and a winsome odour
Comes from his belly;   other kinds of fish
Are deceived thereby,   all eagerly swimming
To where the sweet fragrance[3]   comes flowing forth.
In unwary schools   they enter within
50 Till the wide mouth is filled.   Then swiftly the Whale
Over his sea-prey   snaps his grim jaws.
    So is it with him   in this transient time
Who takes heed to his life   too late and too little,
Letting vain delights   through their luring fragrance
55 Ensnare his soul   till he slips away,
Soiled with sin,   from the King of glory.
Before them the Devil   after death's journey
Throws open hell   for all who in folly
Fulfilled the lying   lusts of the flesh
60 Against the law.   But when the Wily One,
Expert in evil,   has brought into bonds
In the burning heat   those cleaving to him
Laden with sins,   who during their life-days
Did his bidding,   on them after death
65 His savage jaws   he snaps together,
The gates of hell.   Who gather there
Know no retreat,   no return out thence,
Any more than the fishes   swimming the sea
Can escape from the grip   of the Great Whale.
70   Therefore by every means   (should every man
Serve the Lord God)   and strive against devils
By words and works,   that we may behold
The King of glory.   In this transient time
Let us seek for peace   and healing at His hands,
75 That we in grace may dwell   with Him so dear
And have His bliss   and blessedness for ever!

ANONYMOUS

Love's Gift Is Life[1]

Ipsa vivere   mihi reddidit!
cessit prospere,   spe plus accidit
menti misere:
que dum temere   totam tradidit

Herself hath given back my life to me,
Herself hath yielded far
More than had ever hoped my misery.
And when she recklessly

3. Like other characteristics of the "Deceiver," a false fragrance.

1. This poem comes from one of the great collections of medieval lyrics and was written in England during the time of Thomas à Beckett. It expresses the style and tone of the "twelfth century Renaissance" of classical learning, which tended to express itself poetically in revived Latin verse in England.

5   se sub Venere,
      Venus ethere   risus edidit
      leto sidere.

      Desiderio   nimis officit,
      dum vix gaudio   pectus sufficit,
10   quod concipio
      dum Venerio   Flora reficit
      me colloquio,
      dum, quem haurio,   favus allicit
      dato basio.

15   Sepe refero   cursum liberum
      sinu tenero: sic me superum
      addens numero.
      cunctis impero,   felix iterum
      si tetigero
20   quem desidero,   sinum tenerum
      tactu libero.

5   Gave herself wholly unto Love and me,
      Beauty in heaven afar
      Laughed from her joyous star.

      Too great desire hath overwhelmed me,
      My heart's not great enough
10 For this huge joy that overmastered me,
      What time my love
      Made in her arms another man of me,
      And all the gathered honey of her lips
      Drained in one yielded kiss.

15 Again, again, I dream the freedom given
      Of her soft breast,
      And so am come, another god, to heaven
      Among the rest.
      Yea, and serene would govern gods and men,
20 If I might find again
      My hand upon her breast.

Monk Song

Myrie songen the monkes binne° Ely[1]   *within*
Whan Cnut Kyng[2] rewe° ther-by: *rowed*
Roweth, knightes, neer the lond
And here we thise monkes song.

1200–1500

ANONYMOUS

Mirie It Is[1]

Mirie it is while sumer ilast°   *lasts*
with fugheles° song,   *birds*
oc nu necheth windes blast[2]
and weder° strong.   *weather*
Ej! ej! what this nicht is long,
and ich wid wel michel wrong[3]
soregh° and murne and fast.   *sorrow*

Sumer Is I-Cumen In[1]

Sumer° is i-cumen in,   *summer*
Loude° syng cuckow!   *loudly*
Groweth seed and bloweth° meed   *burst into bloom*
And spryngeth the wode now.
Syng cuckow!
Ewe bleteth after lamb,
Loweth after calve cow;
Bullock sterteth,° bukke° farteth,—   *leap / stag*
Myrie syng cuckow!

1. Ely, near Cambridge.
2. King Canute.

1. The text appears with music in the original ms (ca. 1225).

2. "But now draws nigh the blast of wind."
3. "And I with very much wrong" (i.e., "too much on my conscience").

1. This text appears with music in the original ms (ca. 1225).

Cuckow! Cuckow!
Wel syngest thou cuckow:
Ne swik° thou nevere now.   *stop*
  Syng cuckow, now, syng cuckow!
  Syng cuckow, syng cuckow, now!

Sonne under Wode[1]

Now goth sonne under wode,°—   *wood; dark anger*
Me reweth, Marie, thy faire rode.°   *cross; countenance*
Now goth sonne under tree,—
Me reweth,° Marie, thy sone and thee.   *pity; consider*

Love's Madness[1]

  Amor est quedam mentis insania
Que vagum hominem ducit per devia;
Sitit delicias et bibit tristia,
Crebris doloribus commiscens gaudia.

  Amur est une pensee enragee
Ke le udif humme meyne par veie deveye,
Ke a seyf de delices e ne beyt ke tristesces,
E od sovens dolurs medle sa tristesce.[2]

  Love is a selkud° wodenesse   *silly madness*
That the idel mon ledeth by wildernesse,
That thurstes of wilfuscipe and drinket sorwenesse,
And with lomful° sorwes menget° his blithnesse.   *frequent / disturb*

Wight in the Broom

Sey me, wight in the broom,°   *brush, shrub*
Teche me how I shal don
That myn housebonde
Me loven wolde.

"Hold thy tonge stille
And have al thy wylle."

Whan the Turf Is Thy Tour[1]

Whan the turf is thy tour
And thy put° is thy bour,   *grave*
Thy fel° and thy white throte   *skin*
Shullen wormes to note.°   *have to use*
What helpeth thee than
Al the worlde wenne?°   *world's joys; to win the world*

1. This poem (ca. 1240) appears in either Latin, French, or English in thirty-six different manuscripts. The poem depends on the double meanings of *wode*, *rode*, and *reweth*.

1. One of many early Middle English lyrics (ca. 1240) which are simply translations from the Latin. Here the original is preserved in the text, the Latin in four lines, with the Anglo-French inscribed alongside in a stanza, and the English written underneath across the folio.
2. "Love is a madness in the mind that leads astray an idle man, so that, thirsty for pleasure, he drinks only the cup of bitterness, and finds sorrow often mingled with his joy...."

1. This poem (ca. 1250) is translated directly from Latin verses and is one example of a large medieval genre called *memento mori*—"death reminders." One associates them with the *danse macabre*, paintings of skeletons dancing away with living people come to their final hour. Death, we recognize, was a much more immediate concern for our medieval ancestors than it is for most of us.

Angelus ad Virginem[1]

Gabriel, fram evene-king
  sent to the maide swete,
broute hire blisful tiding
   And faire he gan hire greten:
5   'heil be thu ful of grace a-rith!
      for godes sone, this euene lith,°   *heavenly light*
        for mannes louen
        wile man bicomen,
        and taken
10   fles of the maiden brith,°   *bright*
        manken fre for to maken
      of senne and deules mith.'°   *might*

Mildeliche im gan andsweren
  the milde maiden thanne:
15 'Wichewise sold ichs beren°   *bear*
  child with-huten manne?'[2]
     the angle seide, 'ne dred te nout;
     thurw holigast° sal ben iwrout   *The Holy Spirit*
     this ilche° thing,   *very*
20   war-of tiding
     ichs bringe,
     al manken wrth ibout[3]
     thur thi swete chiltinge,
     and hut of pine ibrout.'[4]

25 Wan the maiden understud
  and angles wordes herde,
mildeliche with milde mud°   *mood*
  to the angle hie° andswerde: *she*
     'hur lordes theumaiden iwis[5]
30   ics am, that her a-bouen is.
     anenttis° me,   *in respect of*
     fulfurthed° be   *fulfilled*
     thi sawe;°   *word*
     that ics, sithen° his wil is,   *since*
35   maiden, withhuten lawe
     of moder, haue the blis.

The angle wente a-wei mid than,
  al hut of hire sithte;°   *sight*
hire wombe arise gan
40   thurw holigastes mithe.°   *might*
     in hire was crist biloken° anon,   *enclosed*
     Sutli° god, soth man ine fleas and bon,   *truly*
     and of hir fleas°   *flesh*
     iboren was
45   at time.
     War thurw us kam god won,
     that he bout us hut of pine
     and let im for us slon.[6]

1. This famous Annunciation lyric (ca. 1260) was part of the repertoire of "hende Nicholas," the randy clerk of Chaucer's *Miller's Tale*. It is a direct translation of the Latin sequence *"Angelus ad virginem"* and in the Arundel MS. (f. 154ª) the text of the Latin original, accompanied with music, precedes the English text.
2. "How should I bear a child without intercourse with a man?"
3. "All mankind worthily redeemed."
4. "Through thy sweet child, and brought out of pain [of childbirth]."
5. "Her Lord's handmaiden, certainly, I am. . . ."
6. "Wherefore through us [humankind] came good hope; he bought [redeemed] us out of pain, and allowed himself to be slain for us."

Maiden, moder makeles,°   *mateless, matchless*
50   of milche ful ibunden,[7]
bid for hus im that the ches
    at wam thu grace funde,
        that he forgiue hus senne° and wrake,°   *sin and wickedness*
        and clene of euri gelt us make,
55   and eune° blis,   *heavenly*
        wan hure time is
        to steruen,°   *die*
        hus giue, for thine sake
        him so her for to seruen
60   that he us to him take.

Wanne Mine Eyhnen Misten[1]

Wanne mine eyhnen misten,
and mine heren sissen,°   *hearing ceases*
and mi nose koldet,°   *grows cold*
and mi tunge ffoldet,
5   and mi rude° slaket,   *face*
And mine lippes blaken,
and mi muth grennet,°   *grimaces*
and mi spotel rennet,°   *spittle runs*
and min her riset,°   *hair rises*
10   and min herte griset,°   *trembles*
and mine honden biuien,°   *shake*
and mine ffet stiuien,°   *stiffen*
al to late, al to late,
wanne the bere ys ate gate.[2]

15   Thanne y schel fflutte°   *go*
ffrom bedde te fflore,
ffrom fflore to here,°   *shroud*
ffrom here to bere,
ffrom bere to putte,°   *pit, grave*
20   and te putt ffor-dut.
Thanne lyd min hus vppe min nose,
off al this world ne gyffe ihic a pese.°   *a pea*

Ubi Sunt[1]

Wher beth they biforn us weren,
Houndes ladden and haukes° beren   *hawks*
And hadden feeld and wode?
The riche ladies in her bour
5   That werede gold in her tresour,°   *head-dress*
Wyth her brighte rode?°   *countenance*

They eten and dronken and maden hem glad—
Her lyf was al wyth gamen i-lad;
Men kneleden hem biforn;
10   They beren hem wel swithe heighe,°   *great pomp*
And, in a twynkelyng of an eye,
Her soules weren forlorn.°   *lost*

---

7. "Of abundant mercy."

1. This song (thirteenth century) is of the genre now
represented by the children's street song, "When your
eyes fall in, your teeth fall out, you won't know what it's
all about. . . ."

2. "When the bier is at the gate"—the hearse is there to
pick up the corpse.

1. *"Ubi sunt qui ante nos ferunt"* (where are they who
were before us) signifies another major medieval theme,
related to the *memento mori* poems above.

Wher is that laughyng and that song,
That trailyng° and that proude yong,°   *trailing gowns / walk*
15 Tho haukes and tho houndes?
Al that joye is went awey—
That wele is comen to weylawey,
To many harde stoundes.°   *hard hours*

Her paradys they nomen° heer,   *took*
20 And now they liggen in helle y-fere;°   *lie in hell together*
The fyr it brenneth evere.
Long is ay and long is o,
Long is wei and long is wo—
Thennes ne comen they nevere.

25 Drey° heer, man, than if thou wylt   *Endure*
A litel pyne that me thee bit;°   *I ask you*
Wythdraw thyne eses° ofte.   *comforts*
Thogh thy pyne be unrede,°   *severe*
And thou thenke on thy mede
30 It shal thee thynken softe.²

If that feend, that foule thyng,
Thurgh wikked roun,° thurgh fals eggyng,   *advice*
Nethere° thee hath i-cast,   *downward*
Up and be good champioun!
35 Stond, ne fal namore adoun
For a litel blast!

Thou tak the rode to thy staf,
And thenk on him that ther-on yaf
His lyf that was so leef.
40 He it yaf for thee, thou yeld it him:³
Ayeins his fo that staf thou nim°   *sieze*
And wrek° him of that theef.   *avenge*

Of right bileve, thou nim that sheeld
The whiles that thou best in that feeld,
45 Thyn hond to strengthen fond!°   *try*
And keep thy fo wyth staves ord,⁴
And do that traytour seyn that word:°   *... of surrender*
Biget that myrie lond!⁵

Ther-inne is day wythouten nyght,
50 Wythouten ende strengthe and myght,
And wreche° of every fo;   *vengeance*
Wyth God him-selve eche° lyf,   *everlasting*
And pees and reste wythouten strif—
Wele wythouten wo.

55 Mayden moder, hevenes quene,
Thou myghte and canst and owest to ben
Oure sheeld ayeins the feend.
Help us synnes for-to fleen,
That we mote thy sone seen
60 In joye wythouten ende. Amen.

2. "If you think about your [eternal] reward it [the severe pain] shall seem soft to you."
3. "He gave it [his life] for you, you yield it [yours] to him."
4. "Keep off your foe with stiff opposition."
5. "Win [your place in] that merry land."

Stond Wel, Moder[1]

"Stond wel, Moder, under rode,°   *the cross*
Bihold thy child wyth gladde mood;
Blithe, Moder, myghtestow be."
"Sone, how may I blithe stonde?
5   I see thy feet, I see thyne honde°   *hands*
Nayled to the harde tree."

"Moder, do wey thy wepyng,
I thole° this deeth for mannes thyng;[2]   *suffer*
For my gilt ne thole I non."
10   "Sone, I fele the dethes stounde;°   *time, hour*
That swerd is at myn hertes ground
That me bihete° Simeon."   *promised*

"Moder, rewe upon thy bern;°   *son*
Thou wassh awey the blody teren:°   *tears*
15   It doth me worse thanne my deeth.'
"Sone, how myghte I teres werne?°   *restrain*
I see thy blody woundes erne°   *flow*
From thyn herte to my feet."

"Moder, now I may thee seye,
20   Bettre is that ich oone deye
Thanne al mankynde to helle go."
"Sone, I see thy body i-swongen—
Thy brest, thyne honde, thy feet thurgh-stongen:
No sely° is thogh me be wo."   *wonder*

25   "Moder, if I thee durste telle,
If I ne deye thou gost to helle;
I thole this deeth for mannes sake."
"Sone, thou best so meke and mynde,°   *thoughtful*
Ne wyte° me noght—it is my kynde[3]   *blame*
30   That I for thee this sorwe make."

"Moder, mercy! lat me deye
And Adam out of helle beye,°   *redeem*
And al mankynde that is forlorn."
"Sone, what shal me to rede?
35   Thy pyne pyneth me to dede:°   *death*
Lat me deye thee biforn."

"Moder, now thou myghte wel lernen
What pyne tholen that children beren,
What sorwe han that child forgon."°   *relinquish*
40   "Sone, I wot I may thee telle
But it be the pyne of helle;
Of more pyn ne wot I non."

"Moder, rewe° of modres care   *regret*
Now thou wost of modres fare,°   *fate*
45   Thogh thou be clene mayden-man."°   *virgin*
"Sone, thou helpest at the nede

---

1. A popular spiritual song (ca. 1270) deriving from Latin prose versions of Anselm and Bernard of Clairvaux, with Latin and Italian poetic versions by the Franciscan Jacopone da Todi. One version includes music and one is found in extracts from a Latin sermon written about 1300, in which it is evident that the preacher intended it to be a sung dialogue with voices inpersonating both Christ and His Mother.

2. *Thyng* in ME can have precisely the same force as in the contemporary expression "to do one's own thing"—i.e., "deeds" or "actions." (Chaucer makes frequent use of this sense of the word.)

3. "Don't blame me, it's only natural [my nature]."

Alle tho that to thee grede,° *pray*
Mayden, wyfe, and fole° womman." *foolish*

50 "Moder, I may no lenger dwelle—
The tyme is comen I shal to helle:
The thridde day I rise upon."
"Sone, I wyl wyth thee founden,° *go away*
I deye y-wis of thyne wounden;° *wounds*
So reweful deeth was nevere non."

55 Whan he ros than fil hir sorwe;
The blisse sprong the thridde morwe.
Blithe moder were thou tho!
Lady, for that ilke blisse,
Biseech thy Sone oure synnes lisse;° *sin's remission*
60 Thou be oure sheeld ayeins oure fo.

Blessed be thou, quene of hevene!
Bryng us out of helle levene° *hell fire*
Thurgh thy dere sones myght.
Moder, for that heighe blood
65 That He shedde upon the rode,
Leed us into hevenes light.

Foweles in the Frith[1]

Foweles in the frith,° *woodland*
The fisshes in the flood,
And I mon° waxe wood:° *must / distressed*
Muche sorwe I walke wyth
For best° of bon and blood. *the lust person*

The End of Peace

Pes est acravente e amur refreidie,
La terre est desconforté e de plur enmoistie,
Amur et amisté tut est ane[e]ntie,
N'i ad nul ki ne quert confort et aye.

Peace is destroyed and love grown cold,
The land lies desolate, damp with tears,
All love and friendship seems to have
       vanished
Everyone seeks shelter, from comfort
       banished.

Ave Maria[1]

Dieu vous sauve, Marie,
De grace replenie:
  Li sires est en vous;
De tut femmes qe sunt
Parmy ceste mound,
  Beneit seez vus;
E beneit seit le frut
K'en vostre ventre crust:
  Jhesu li tresduz.
Amen.

Hail Mary

God save you, Mary full of grace: the Lord is
      within you;
May you be blessed above all other women on
      earth;
And blessed be the fruit that grew in your
      womb: gentle Jesus.
Amen.

1. The text appears with music in the original ms (ca. 1270).

1. Written in tailed couplets.

Veni Creator Spiritus[1]

Seint esperiz, a nus venez
E nos penseies visitez,
De vostre grace paremplez
Les quers ke crié avez.

Vous ki estes confortur
E graunt doun del haut seignur,
Sosteine vive veroie amur,
L'oignement de bon odur.

Nos sens del seint fu embracez,
De bon amur nos quers emplez. . . .

Come to us, Holy Ghost, visit us in our
sadness, fill with your Grace the hearts
that you have created.

You who are the comforter and the
great gift of the Lord on High, preserve
that love which is true, that sweet-
smelling balm.

Kindle our minds with the Holy Fire,
and fill our hearts with goodness and
love. . . .

The Trumpet

Wel, who shal thise hornes blowe
　　Holy Rode thy day?[1]
Now is he deed and lieth lowe
　　Was wont to blowe hem ay.

Lady Fortune and Her Wheel

The leuedi° fortune[1] is bothe frend and fo,　　*lady*
　　Of pore che makit riche, of riche pore also,
Che turnes wo al into wele, and wele al into wo,
No triste no man to this wele, the whel it turnet so.

Three Troublesome Thoughts

Whan I thenke thynges three
Ne may I nevere blithe be:
That oon is that I shal awey;
That other is I ne wot which day;
The thridde is my moste care—
I ne wot whider I shal fare.

Whan I See on Rode I-Don[1]

Whan I see on rode i-don°　　*done-in*
Jhesus my lemman,°　　*love*
And by him stonden
Marie and Iohan,[2]
His herte depe i-stongen,
His body wyth scourge i-swongen°　　*beaten*
For the synne of man:
Ethe° I may wepe　　*readily*
And salte teres lete
If I of love can.

---

1. A translation of the liturgical prayer, written out as prose with the balance lost from the end of the ms (ca. 1290).

1. Holy Cross Day (September 14). A late thirteenth-century poem.

1. Lady Fortune is a figure from Boethian tradition. Reminiscent of Blind Justice, she is often pictured turning a wheel upon which ride the hopeful and the ambitious on the way up, who then must suffer the downward turn since it is Fortune's property to be always turning her wheel. A fourteenth-century poem.

1. This poem (ca. 1310) evokes a typical theme of Franciscan spirituality—an identification with Christ in his humanity on the cross. The reference to him as "lemman" (*leofman*—beloved) alludes to the language of the Song of Songs.
2. Mary and John at each side of the cross.

Loket to Me

Man and wyman, loket° to me,   *look*
u michel pine ich tholede for the;[1]
loke up-one mi rig,° u sore ich was i-biten;   *back*
loke to mi side, wat Blode ich haue i-leten.
mine uet an mine honden nailed beth to the rode;
of the thornes prikung min hiued urnth° a blode.   *runs*
fram side to side, fro hiued to the fot,
turn mi bodi abuten, oueral thu findest blod.
man, thin hurte, thin hurre° thu turne to me,   *favour*
for the vif wndes the ich tholede for the.[2]

Al Nist by the Rose

Al nist by the rose, rose—
al nist bi the rose i lay;
darf ich noust the rose stele,[1]
ant yet ich bar the flour away.

Mayden in the Moor

Mayden in the moor lay—
In the moor lay—
   Seven-nyght fulle,
    Seven-nyght fulle.
5 Mayden in the moor lay—
In the moor lay—
   Seven-nyghtes fulle and a day.

Wel° was hir mete.   *good*
What was hir mete?
10   The prymerole° and the—   *primrose*
    The prymerole and the—
Wel was hir mete.
What was hir mete?
   The prymerole and the vyolete.

15 Wel was hir drynke.
What was hir drynke?
   The colde water of the—
    The colde water of the—
Wel was hir drynke.
20 What was hir drynke?
   The colde water of the welle-spryng.

Wel was hir bour.
What was hir bour?
   The rede rose and the—
25   The rede rose and the—
Wel was hir bour.
What was hir bour?
   The rede rose and the lilye-flour.

1. "How much pain I suffered for thee."
2. There was a traditional exposition of the five wounds of
Christ which paralleled The Five Joys of the Virgin, The

Seven Last Words, etc.

1. "I did not dare to steal the rose."

From MS. Harley 2253[1]

Cest rym fust fet al bois, desouz un lorer,
La chaunte merle, russinole e eyre
                    l'esperver;
Escrit estoit en perchemyn pur mout
                   remenbrer
E gitté en haut chemyn qe um le dust trover.

Secret Poem

This ryme was made in the wood, beneath a
                   laurel tree,
There sing black bird and nightingale, and
                 sparrow-hawk hovers;
it was written on a parchment the better to
                 remember
and thrown on the highroad for someone to
                 discover.

Lenten Is Comen wyth Love

Lenten[1] is comen wyth love to toun—
Wyth blosmes and wyth briddes roun°—   *song*
   That al this blisse bryngeth;
Dayesyes in thise dales,
5   Notes swete of nyghtengales—
   Ech fowel song syngeth.
The thrustelcok him threteth° oo;   *chides*
Awey is here wynter wo
   Whan woderove° spryngeth.   *woodruff*
10   Thise foweles syngen ferly fele°   *wondrously many*
And wlyten° on her wynne wele°   *warbles | wealth of joy*
   That al the wode ryngeth.

The rose raileth hire rode,[2]
The leves on the lighte wode
15   Waxen al wyth wylle;
The mone mandeth hire blee,[3]
The lilye is lufsom to see,
   The fenel and the fille.

Wowen thise wilde drakes;
20   Miles myrien here makes,[4]
   As streem that striketh stille.°   *flows softly*
Mody meneth, so doth mo;[5]
I wot I am oon of tho,
   For love that liketh ille.

25   The mone mandeth hire light,
So doth the seemly sonne bright,
   Whan briddes syngen breme;°   *clearly*
Dewes donken° thise dounes,   *moisten*
Deres wyth her derne rounes
30   Domes for-to deme.[6]
Wormes wowen under cloude,°   *clod, earth*
Wommen waxen wonder proude,
   So wel it wol hem seme.°   *befit*
If me shal wante wylle of oon
35   This wynne° wele I wol forgon   *joy*
   And wyght° in wode be fleme.°   *quickly | flee*

1. Ca. 1320.

1. The season of Lent—spring.
2. "Puts on her rosy countenance."
3. "Sends forth her radiance."

4. "Male animals gladden their mates."
5. "The moody [spirited] man laments; so do more
[others]."
6. "Deer with their secret cries make their own judgements."

Blow, Northren Wynd

Blow, Northren Wynd,
Send thou me my swetying!°   sweetheart
Blow, Northren Wynd,
Blow, blow, blow![1]

I wot a burde in boure bright[2]
That fully seemly is on sight,
Menskful° mayden of myght,   honourable
Faire and free to fonde;°   examine
5   In al this worthly won°   goodly country
A burde of blood and of bon
Nevere yet I niste non°   ... knew I one
Lufsomer° in londe.   more lovely

Wyth lokkes leefly° and longe,   lovely
10   Wyth frount° and face faire to fonde,   forehead
Wyth myrthes many moot she monge,°   mingle
That brid so brem° in boure;   bright
Wyth lufsom eye greet and good
Wyth browes blisful under hood—
15   He that reste him on the rode,°   cross
That leefly lyf honoure!

Hir lere lumeth° lighte   complexion gleams
As a lanterne a-nyghte,
Hir blee bliketh° so brighte   face shines
20   So faire she is and fyne;
A swetely swire° she hath to holde,   neck
Wyth armes, shuldres as man wolde,
Any fyngres faire for to folde—
God wolde she were myn!

25   Myddel she hath menskful smal,°   gracefully slender
Hir lovely chere as cristal,
Thighes, legges, feet, and al
I-wroght was of the best;
A lufsom lady lasteles°   faultless
30   That swetyng is and evere was—
A bettre burde nevere nas
I-heried° wyth the best.   praised

She is dereworthe° in day,   dearworthy, beloved
Gracious, stout, and gay,
35   Gentil, joly so the jay,
Worthly whan she waketh;
Mayden muriest of mouth,
By est, by west, by north and south
Ther nis fiele° ne crouth°   stringed musical instruments
40   That swiche myrthes maketh.

She is coral of goodnesse,
She is ruby of rightfulnesse,
She is cristal of clennesse,
And baner of bealtee;°   beauty
45   She is lilye of largesse,°   generosity
She is pervynke° of prowesse,   periwinkle
She is solsecle° of sweetnesse,   marigold
And lady of lealtee.°   faithfulness

1. A refrain, to be sung after each stanza.
2. "I know a bird in a bright bower"—"bird" was then, as now in some English-speaking countries, a slang term for an attractive woman.

To Love, that lovely is in londe,
50 I tolde him as I understonde
How this hende hath hent in hond[3]
An herte that myn was;
And hir knightes me han so soght—
Sikyng, Sorwyng, and Thoght—
55 Tho three me han in bale broght
Ayeins the power of Pees.

To Love I putte pleyntes mo,
How Sikyng me hath sewed so,
And eke Thoght me thrat to slo°   *threatened to slay*
60 Wyth maistrye if he myghte;
And Sorwe, sore in baleful bend°   *bondage*
That he wolde, for this hende,
Me lede to my lyves ende
Unlawefully in lighte.°   *openly*

65 Love me listned ech a word,
And bowed him to me over bord,
And bad me hente that hord[4]
Of myn herte hele;
"And biseech that swete and swoot,°   *sweet person*
70 Er-than thou falle as fen° offe foot,   *mud*
That she wyth thee wol of boot°   *remedy*
Dereworthly dele."°   *perform*

For hir love I carke and care,°   *sorrow and grieve*
For hir love I droupe and dare,°   *droop and tremble*
75 For hir love my blisse is bare,
And al I waxe wan;°   *pale*
For hir love in sleep I slake,°   *diminish*
For hir love all nyght I wake,
For hir love murnyng I make,
80 More thanne any man.

Love-Sickness

Whan the nyghtengale syngeth the wodes waxen grene,
Leef and gras and blosme spryngeth in Aperil, I wene;
And love is to myne herte gon wyth oon spere so kene,
Nyght and day my blood it drynketh, myn herte doth me tene.°   *suffering*

I have loved al this year, that I may love namore;
I have siked many sik, lemman, for thyn ore.[1]
Me nis love nevere the neer,[2] and that me reweth sore:
Swete lemman, thenk on me,—I have loved thee yore.

Swete lemman, I preye thee of love oon speche;
While I lyve in world so wide other nyl I seche.
Wyth thy love, my swete leef, my blisse thou myghte eche;°   *increase*
A swete cosse of thyn mouth myghte be my leche.°   *physician*

Swete lemman, I preye thee of a love-bene;[3]
If thou me lovest, as men seyn—lemman, as I wene—
And if it thy wylle be, thou loke that it be sene.
So muche I thenke upon thee, that al I waxe grene.

3. "How this gracious [lady] had seized in her hand" (his metaphor appears to involve more wishful thinking).
4. The "God of Love" bids him "seize the treasure" of his heart's healing—in other words urges him to stint his song and speak to the lady directly. The last stanza suggests that the persona has not taken the advice.

1. "I have sighed many a sigh, lover, for thy favour."
2. "For all that the satisfaction of love is no nearer to me."
3. Not a vegetable, but a lover's gift.

Bitwene Lyncoln and Lindeseye, Northamptoun and Lounde,°   *London*
Ne wot I non so faire a may, as I go forbounde.°   *enslaved (by love)*
Swete lemman, I preye thee thou love me a stounde;°   *hour*
I wol mone° my song on whom that it is on ylong.[4]   *mention*

Alysoun

Bitwene March and Aperil,
Whan spray bigynneth to sprynge,[1]
The litel fowel hath hir wyl
On hir lede° to synge.   *language*
5 I lyve in love-longynge
For semlokest° of alle thyng;   *seemliest, most fair*
She may me blisse brynge:
I am in hir baundoun.°   *control*
    An hende hap I have i-hent,[2]
10   I wot from hevene it is me sent;—
    From alle wommen my love is lent°   *taken away*
    And light on Alysoun.

On hewe hir heer is faire ynough,
Hir browes broune, hir eyen blake,
15 Wyth lufsom chere she on me lough,°   *smiled*
Wyth myddel smal and wel i-mak.

But she me wol to hire take
For-to ben hir owene make,
Longe to lyve I wyl forsake
20 And feye° falle adoun.   *doomed*
    An hende hap I have i-hent,
    I wol from hevene it is me sent;—
    From alle wommen my love is lent
    And light on Alysoun.

25 Nyghtes whan I wende° and wake—   *toss*
For-thy myne wonges waxen wan;[3]
Lady, al for thy sake
Longyng is i-lent° me on.   *come-up*
In world nis non so witter° man   *wise*
30 That al hir bountee° telle can: *excellence*
Hir swire° is whiter thanne the swan,   *neck*
And fairest may in toun.
    An hende hap I have i-hent,
    I wot from hevene it is me sent;—
35   From alle wommen my love is lent
    And light on Alysoun.

I am for wowyng al forwake,[4]
Wery as water in wore;°   *troubled pool*
Lest any reve° me my make   *bereave, rob*
40 I have i-yerned yore.[5]
Bettre is tholen while sore
Thanne murnen evermore.
Geynest under gore,[6]
Herkne to my roun:°   *speech*

---

4. A thinly veiled threat. He will mention in his song the woman who is the cause of his love-sickness, unless, presumably, she grants him the "stounde" he is asking for.

1. "When the branch begins to blossom."

2. "A happy fortune has come to me."
3. "For you my cheeks wax pale."
4. "I am all worn out from lying awake."
5. "I have been yearning for a long time."
6. "Most gracious under gown."

45 An hende hap I have i-hent,
    I wot from hevene it is me sent;—
    From alle wommen my love is lent
    And light on Alysoun.

Winter Thoughts

Wynter wakeneth al my care;
Now thise leves waxen bare.
Ofte I sike and murne sare[1]
   Whan it cometh in my thoght
   Of this worldes joye, how it goth all to noght.

Now it is and now it nis,
Also it ner nere,° y-wis.   *never was*
That many man seyth, sooth it is—
   Al goth but Goddes wille;
   Alle we shullen deye, thogh us like ille.[2]

Al that greyn me graveth grene,[3]
Now it faleweth° al bidene.°   *withers / already*
Jhesu, help that it be sene,
   And shilde us from helle;
   For I not° whider I shal, ne how longe heer dwelle.   *know not*

As I Me Rod This Endre Day

As I me rod this endre day
By grene wode to seche pley,°   *pleasure*
Wyth herte I thoghte al on a may,
   Swettest of alle thyng.
5 Lith° and I you telle may   *listen*
   Al of that swete thyng.

This mayden is swete and free of blood,
Bright and faire, of mylde mood;
Al she may don us good
10   Thurgh hir bisechyng:
Of hire He took flessh and blood,
   Jhesus, hevenes kyng.

Wyth al my lyf I love that may;
She is my solas nyght and day,
15 My joye and eke my beste pley,
   And eke my love-longynge.
Al the bettre me is that day
   That I of hire synge.

Of alle thyng I love hire meste,°   *most*
20 My dayes blisse, my nyghtes reste;
She counseileth and helpeth best
   Bothe olde and yinge.°   *young*
Now I may if that you leste
   The five joyes mynge.[1]

1. "Often I sigh and mourn sorrowfully."
2. "Though we like it ill" (i.e., not very much).
3. "All that grain [seed] I bury [plant] green [unripe—too green to be good seed]." The allusion is to John xii.24, 25.

1. *mynge*: "mention." "The Five Joys of the Virgin Mary"—a standard typology and chatechetical device which appears quite frequently in religious lyrics and litanies of the period. Here the device appears as a surprise; one expects from the beginning of the poem that bodily and not spiritual love will be the poet's subject.

25 The firste joye of that womman:—
Whan Gabriel from hevene cam
And seyde God sholde bicomen man
    And of hire be born,
And bryngen up of helle-pyne
30   Mankynde that was forlorn.

That othere joye of that may
Was on Cristemasse day
Whan God was born on thorugh lay[2]
    And broghte us lightnesse;
35 The sterre was seen bifore day—
    This hierdes° beren witnesse.   *shepherds*

The thridde joye of that lady,
That men clepe the epiphany:—
Whan the kynges comen wery
40   To presente hir sone
Wyth myrre, gold and encense,
    That was man bicome.

The ferthe joye we telle mowen:
On Ester-morwe whan it gan dawen
45 Hir sone that was slawen
    Aros in flessh and bon;
More joye ne may me haven,
    Wyf ne mayden non.

The fifte joye of that womman:—
50 Whan hir body to hevene cam
Hir soule to the body nam°   *went*
    As it was wont to ben.
Crist leve° us alle wyth that womman   *grant*
That joye al for-to sen.

55 Preye we alle to oure lady,
And to the seintes that wone hire by,
That they of us han mercy,
    And that we ne mysse°   *miss, fail*
In this world to ben holy
60   And wynne hevenes blisse. Amen.

Erthe Took of Erthe[1]

Erthe took of erthe, erthe wyth wogh;°   *wrong; harm*
Erthe other erthe to the erthe drough;°   *drew down; added*
Erthe leyde erthe in erthen through:°   *graves; furrow*
Than hadde erthe of erthe erthe ynough.

2. To fulfill the story.

1. A popular riddle-song (ca. 1320) with many variant versions and expansions. That it is designed to be inter- preted playfully on a number of levels of intention has been suggested by Prof. Russell A. Peck in his excellent introduction to the sensibility of medieval vernacular poetry; cf. *PMLA*, 90 (1975), 461–69.

Lord, Thou Clepedest Me[1]

Lord, thou clepedest me
And I noght ne answerde thee.
But wordes slowe and slepy:
"Thole° yet! Thole a litel!"   *be patient*
But "yet" and "yet" was endeles,
And "thole a litel" a long weye is.

NICOLE DE BOHUN[1]

Seignours, Ore Escotez Haute Chivalerye

Coment le fiz Deu fu armé en la croyz

Seignours, ore escotez haute chivalerye,
De un noble chivaler qe pur l'amour s'amye
Tant se myst avaunt qe il dona sa vye
Pur reyndre sa espouse q'ele fu forbanye.

5 C'est l'ame de homme qe jadis fu trayhé,
Mes son tredouz amy ne se hasta mye
Pur fere rescouz qe ele veist sa folye
E coment de haut en bas out chaungé sa vie.

Il suffry bien longtemps qe ele fu grevee,
10 Qe par taunt puyt veer come ele out
                              meschaungé;
Mes qant ele cria mercy, il en out pytee,
E par taunt le plus q'ele fu engignee.

Soul se myst as champ pur reyndre sa amye,
Si venquist la batayle e conquist seygnurie,
15 Partye par poer e partie par mestrie,
E suffrist dures playes par douce jolouzie.

Mout est beaus li chivaler par taunt esprové
Quant pur l'amour s'amye si forment fu
                              playé,
E bien deveroyt s'amye en chaumbre
                              courtynee
20 Son escu depeyndre qe si est devisé:

Il porte l'escu d'argent e tencelé de goules;
En chef, la couroune de verges espynouses,
Blef la bordure, a quatre signes coustouses,
E en my, la fontayne des veynes
                              plentyvouses.

High Chivalry

The Arming on the Cross of the Son of God:

Listen now, my lords, to a tale of the highest chivalry, of a noble knight who so strove for the love of his lady that he gave his life in winning back his exiled bride.

5   This lady's name was Soul: she had earlier been led falsely astray, and her gentle lover delayed coming to her rescue until she realised her folly and the way in which she had quite debased her life.

10   He allowed her to suffer long torment, so that she might see the extent of her decline; but as soon as she cried out for help he took pity on her, the more so because she had been ensnared.

15   Alone he took the field to rescue his love; partly through force of arms and partly through strategy, he won the victory and triumphed over all—but his jealousy in love caused him to be sorely wounded.

20   How fair and handsome he was in this trial, this knight who suffered such wounds for the love of his mistress! His lady had the clear duty to paint his shield in her tapestried chamber. These were the bearings on the shield he bore: argent, stencilled with gules; in chief a crown of sharp thorns; a fair white-coloured border on which were four signs of great cost and worth; and in the middle of the field a rich fountain of blood.

30   Tall and strong was the steed he mounted that day; its coat all over was of four kinds of fur:[2] cypress for the body, cedar for the hooves, olive for the back, and palms for the great mane.

---

1. This poem (early fourteenth century) recalls the story of Samuel, called by God in the night to wake up and listen to what were the divine expectations for his life, but is in the form of a direct translation of certain lines from *The Confessions* of St. Augustine (VIII, 5), which text immediately precedes the poem in the manuscript.

1. Nicole de Bohun, a Franciscan friar from the vicinity of

Hereford, composed many narrative poems, fables, and lyrics of high quality, of which this poem (ca. 1340) is an example. Bohun's constituency would have consisted of both Anglo-French and Saxon families, but he wrote almost all of his poetry in Anglo-French.
2. The pun on "fur" and "fir" here is successful in Anglo-French as well as English.

25 Son cheval fu haut e fort q'il mounta la
                jornee;
  De quatre manere de pyel ly fust envyrouné:
  Cypres fu le cors, de cedre fu lé pyé,
  L'eschine fu de olyve, de palme le haut cryné.

  Hyaume out a la teste de chevelure
                ensanglantee;
30 Sa qwyree fu qwir, en plusurs lyws percee,
  Son hauberk fu de sofraunce qe ren fu
                entamee,
  L'espeye q'yl tynt en poyn fu sa deité.

  Dunt yl venqy celi qe do touz nous ad vencu;
  Pur ceo il se degwisa qe yl ne fust coneu,
35 Qar si ly enemy l'eut ben aparceu,
  Ja de ly assaut pur nule rien n'out eu.

  Mes coyntement le fist nostre chivaler,
  Qar il prist les armes de un son bacheler
  Qe Adam fu nomé, sy les fist rouler
40 E de une damoysele de eus se fist armer.

  Il entra la chaumbre cele damoysele
  Qe de totes autres estoit la plus bele;
  Il entra si qucyntcment, saunz noyse u
                favele,
  Qe nul home nel sout for qe soule cele.

45 La damoysele l'arma de estraunge armeyure:
  Pur aketoun ly bayle blaunche char e pure,
  Pur cadaz e cotoun de saunk fu le encusture,
  Pur quyssers e mustelers ly dona fourchure.

  Pur les chauces de fer de ners fist la
                ceynture;
50 Les plates furent des os qe estoyent a
                mesure,
  Le gambeson de seye la pel par deusure,
  De tutes pars sunt assiz les veynes pur
                urlure.

  Quant estoyt armé, hors de la chaumbre issy
  Pur combatre pur nous fraunchement se
                profry;
55 De tutes se geyta le deceyvaunt enemy,
  Mes il ne sout de veyr qy esteyt cely.

  Il regarda les armes, si out graunt dedeyng,
  E Jhesu le suffryst de travailer en vayn;
  Ben entendist le houre de lever sa meyn
60 Quant jugé fu a la mort, lors nous tuz fist
                seyn.

  Il lessa ses armes au fust atachee,
  Si entra la batayle com champion prové;
  Trova la s'amye dur emprysonee,
  Si la mena ove ly e myst en salveté.

35 On his head the knight wore a helm of bloody locks; his over-jerkin was of skin, pierced through and through, and his coat of the mail of suffering was all split and riven; 40 but the sword he held in his hand was the sword of divinity.

And thus it was that he conquered the conqueror of us all; but to this end he had disguised his identity, for had his adversary recognised him he would on no account have 45 ridden against him.

Our champion acted very wisely: he borrowed the arms of one of his knights bachelor, Adam by name, had them refurbished, and had a damsel arm him with 50 them.

He entered this damsel's chamber—she was the fairest of all—so quietly, without word or sound, that no one knew he was there save she alone.

55 And then she armed him with his borrowed armour: pure white flesh was the aketon she gave him, padded out not with silken cloth or cotton, but with blood; for cuisses and greaves she gave him groin and thighs, and 60 sinews around his legs for hose of mail. His shin-plates were bones, well-fitting; and on top of all skin formed his silken gambeson, trimmed all about with veins.

Once armed, the knight left the chamber, 65 nobly offering to do battle for us; his deceitful enemy flung himself from the ranks, not knowing his true identity.

He took one look at the armour, and sneered in great disdain; but Jesus let him 70 carry on his vain assault, awaiting the right time to raise his hand: the moment when he was himself doomed to death, for it was then that he made us all whole. . . .

Then he left his armour hanging on the 75 tree, and took the field as proven champion; he found his mistress in her vile prison, and led her away with him to salvation.

ANONYMOUS

Hond by Hond[1]

Hond by hond we shullen us take,
And joye and blisse shullen we make,
For the devel of helle man hath forsake,
And Goddes Sone is maked oure make.

A child is born amonges man,
And in that child was no wam;°   *blemish*
That child is God, that child is man
And in that child oure lyf bigan.

Synful man, be blithe and glad,
For youre mariage thy pees is grad°   *peace is proclaimed*
   Whan Crist was born!
Com to Crist—thy pees is grad;
For thee was his blood i-shad,
   That were forlorn.

Synful man, be blithe and bold,
For hevene is bothe boght and sold
   Everich a foot!
Com to Crist—thy pees is told;
For thee he yaf a hundredfold
   His lyf to boot.°   *as compensation*

Against Hasty Marriage

Man, bewar of thin wowyng,
for weddying is the longe wo.

Loke er° thin herte be set;   *before*
   lok thou wowe° er thou be knet;°   *woo / knit, knotted*
& if thou se thou mow do bet,°   *better*
   knet vp the heltre and let her goo.[1]

Wyuys be bothe stowte and bolde,
   her husbondes ayens hem durn not holde;
& if he do, his herte is colde,[2]
   howsoeuere the game go.

---

1. This poem (ca. 1350) is in the genuine *carol*, or round dance form, and may have been sung and danced to at the same time.

1. "Knot up the halter and let her go."
2. I.e., if the husband tries to resist his wife, he's sure to die for it.

JOHN GRIMESTONE

Gold and Al This Werdis Wyn

Gold and al this werdis wyn[1]
Is nouth but cristis rode;°   *Christ's cross*
I wolde ben clad in cristes skyn,[2]
that ran so longe on blode,
& gon t'is herte and taken myn in—
ther is a fulsum fode.
than yef i litel of kith or kyn,[3]
For ther is alle gode.[4]
                    Amen.

GEFFREY CHAUCER (ca. 1343–1400)

To Rosemounde

Madame, ye ben of alle beaute shryne
As fer as cercled is the mapamounde,°   *map of the world*
For as the cristall glorious ye shyne,
And lyke ruby ben your chekes rounde.
5   Therwyth ye ben so mery and so jocounde
That at a revell whan that I se you daunce,
It is an oynement unto my wounde,
Thogh ye to me ne do no daliaunce.[1]

For thogh I wepe of teres ful a tyne,°   *tub*
10   Yet may that wo myn herte nat confounde.
Your semy voys, that ye so small out twyne,[2]
Maketh my thoght in joy and blys habounde.
So curtaysly I go, with love bounde,
That to myself I sey, in my penaunce,
15   "Suffyseth me to love you, Rosemounde,
Thogh ye to me ne do no daliaunce."

Nas never pyk walwed in galauntyne°   *galantine sauce*
As I in love am walwed and iwounde,
For whych ful ofte I of myself devyne
20   That I am trewe Tristam the secounde.[3]
My love may not refreyde° nor affounde;°   *grow cold / founder*
I brenne ay in an amorouse plesaunce.
Do what you lyst; I wyl your thral be founde,
Thogh ye to me ne do no daliaunce.

Tregentil. Chaucer.

1. *Werdis* can mean both "of words" and "of the world"; *wyn* can mean both "wine" and "joy." Here all combinations of meaning and nuance are apropos of the balance of the poem. John Grimestone was a Franciscan friar who collected a large number of lyrics in a commonplace book of 1372. Therefore, it may be that the poem is not his.
2. This "metaphysical" image is a striking anticipation of seventeenth-century lyricism, but is consistent with the style and content of Franciscan spirituality as it influences the medieval lyric.
3. The allusion is to Matt. x.37.

4. *Gode* can signify both "good" and "God"; *alle* can mean both "all" and "wholly," or "very."

1. "Though you engage in no love-play with me."
2. "Your tiny [not 'seamy'] voice that you turn out so softly."
3. Tristam was one of the most famous of unfortunate lovers in medieval legend. He fell in love with his own uncle's wife, Isolde, and their affair caused much tragedy. Therefore, the reference may not be without irony.

The Former Age

Chawcer upon the fyfte metrum of the second book.[1]

A blysful lyf, a paysyble and a swete,
Ledden the poeples in the former age.
They helde hem paied of the fruttes that they ete,
Whiche that the feldes yave hem by usage.

5   They ne were nat forpampred with owtrage.°   *outrageously pampered*
Unknowen was the quyerne and ek the melle;°   *handmill or windmill*
They eten mast,° hawes, and swych pownage,°   *acorns / roughage*
And dronken water of the colde welle.

Yit nas the grownd nat wownded with the plowh,
10   But corn up-sprong, unsowe of mannes hond,
The which they gnodded,° and eete nat half inowh.   *husked*
No man yit knew the forwes° of his lond;   *borders*
No man the fyr owt of the flynt yit fond;
Unkorven° and ungrobbed° lay the vyne;   *unpruned / uncultivated*
15   No man yit in the morter spices grond
To clarre, ne to sawse of galentyne.[2]

No mader, welde, or wod no litestere[3]
Ne knew; the fles was of his former hewe.[4]
No flessh ne wyste offence of egge° or spere;   *sword edge*
20   No coyn ne knew man which was fals or trewe;
No ship yit karf the wawes grene and blewe;
No marchaunt yit ne fette owtlandissh ware;[5]
No batails trompes for the werres folk ne knewe,
No towres heye, and walles rownde or square.

25   What sholde it han avayled to werreye?°   *make war*
Ther lay no profyt, ther was no rychesse.
But corsed was the tyme, I dar wel seye,
That men fyrst dede her swety bysynesse
To grobbe up metal, lurkinge in derknesse,
30   And in the ryveres fyrst gemmes sowhte.
Allas, than sprong up al the cursednesse
Of covetyse, that fyrst owr sorwe browhte!

Thyse tyrauntz putte hem gladly nat in pres°   *to trouble*
No places wyldnesse ne no busshes for to wynne
35   Ther poverte is, as seithe Diogenes,
Ther as vitalye is ek so skars and thinne
That noght but mast° or apples is therinne.   *acorns*
But ther as bagges ben, and fat vitaile,
Ther wol they gon and spare for no synne
40   With al hir ost the cyte for t'assayle.

Yit were no paleis chaumbres, ne non halle
In kaves and wodes softe and swete
Slepten this blyssed folk withowte walles,
On gras or leves in parfyt joye and quiete.
45   No down of fetheres ne no bleched° shete   *bleached white*
Was kyd° to hem, but in surte° they slepte.   *known / security*
Hir hertes were al oon withowte galles;°   *twinge of envy*
Everych of hem his feith to oother kepte.

---

1. This is a free translation of Book II, poem 5, of
Boethius' *Consolation of Philosophy*, the whole of which,
with commentaries, was translated by Chaucer.
2. "For claret [spiced wine] or [galantine] spiced sauce."

3. Plants whose roots give red, yellow, and blue dye.
Dyer of cloths.
4. The fleece (wool) was its natural colour.
5. "Fetched foreign wares."

Unforged was the hawberk° and the plate;°   *armour*
50   The lambyssh poeple, voyd of alle vyce,
Hadden no fantasye to debate,
But eche of hem wolde oother wel cheryce.
No pryde, non envye, non avaryce,
No lord, no taylage by no tyranye:
55   Umblesse° and pes; good feith the emperice.°   *humility | empress*

Yit was nat Juppiter the lykerous,°   *lecherous*
That fyrst was fader of delicacie,
Come in this world; ne Nembrot,[6] desyrous
To regne, had nat maad his towres hye.
60   Allas, allas, now may men wepe and crye!
For in owr dayes nis but covetyse,
Dowblenesse, and tresoun, and envye,
Poysoun, and manslawhtre, and mordre in sondry wyse.

Finit etas prima. Chaucers.

Balade de Bon Conseil
Truth.

Fle fro the prees° and dwell with sothfastnesse,°   *crowd | truthfulness*
Suffise unto thy good, though it be smal,[1]
For hord hath hate, and clymbyng tykelnesse,°   *insecurity*
Prees hath envye, and wele blent overal.°   *prosperity blinds*
5   Savour no more than the byhove° shal.   *profit*
Reule wel thiself, that other folk canst rede;
And trouthe the shal delivere, it is no drede.°/[2]   *fear not*

Tempest the noght al croked to redresse,
In trust of hir that turneth as a bal.[3]
10   Gret reste stant in lytel bisynesse.
Bewar also to sporne ayeyns an al.[4]
Styrve noght as doth the crokke with the wal.
Daunte° thiself, that dauntest otheres dede;   *govern*
And trouthe the shal delivere, it is no drede.

15   That the is sent, receyve in boxomnesse.°   *generous, humble spirit*
The wrastling for this world axeth a fal.
Here nis non home, here nis but wyldernesse:
Forth, pilgrym, forth! Forth, beste, out of thi stal!
Know thi contree, lok up, thank God of al;
20   Hold the hye wey, and lat thi gost° the lede;   *spirit*
And trouthe the shal delivere, it is no drede.

Envoy

Therfore, thou Vache,[5] leve thine old wrechedenesse;
Unto the world leve° now to be thral.   *stop*
Crie Hym mercy, that of His hie godnesse
25   Made the of noght, and in especial
Draw unto Him, and pray in general
For the, and eke for other hevenlyche mede;
And trouthe the shal delivere, it is no drede.

6. Nimrod, according to medieval tradition, was builder of the tower of Babel—cf. Gen. x.10.

1. "Let your goods be sufficient for you, even if small."
2. The allusion is to John viii.32: "And you shall know the truth, and the truth shall make you free."

3. Lady Fortune, who turns her wheel.
4. "To kick against an awl," or, "to kick against the pricks." The allusion is to Acts ix.5.
5. At first taken to be the French word for cow. Subsequently it has been suggested that the reference is to Sir Philip de la Vache, who, like Chaucer, lost his government job in 1386 with the demise of the "peace party."

Lack of Steadfastnesse
Envoy to King Richard.[1]

Somtyme the world was so stedfast and stable
That mannes word was obligacioun,
And now it is so fals and deceivable
That word and dede, as in conclusioun,
5 Ben nothing lyk, for turned up so doun°   *upside down, perverted*
Is al this world for mede and wilfulnesse,
That all is lost for lak of stedfastnesse.

What maketh this world to be so veriable
But lust that folk have in discencioun?
10 For among us now a man is holde unable,
But if he can by som collusioun
Do his neyghburgh wrong or oppressioun.
What causeth this but wilfull wrecchednesse,
That all is lost for lak of stedfastnesse?

15 Trouthe is putte doun, resoun is holden fable,
Vertu hath now no domynacioun;
Pite exiled, no man is merciable;
Through covetise is blent° discrecioun.   *blinded*
The world hath mad a permutacioun
20 Fro right to wrong, fro trouthe to fikelnesse,
That all is lost for lak of stedfastnesse.

Lenvoy to King Richard

O prince, desire to be honourable;
Cherice thi folk and hate extorcioun.
Suffre nothing that may be reprevable
25 To thyn estaat don in thi regioun.
Shew forth thy swerd of castigacioun.
Dred God, do law, love trouthe and worthynesse,
And wed thy folk ageyn to stedfastnesse.

Friar's Tale[1]
The Prologe of the Freres Tale.

1265 This worthy lymytour, this noble Frere,[2]
He made alwey a maner louryng chiere°   *lowering (sullen) expression (manner)*
Upon the Somonour, but for honestee°   *propriety*
No vileyns° word as yet to hym spak he.   *rude*
But atte laste he seyde unto the wyf,
1270 "Dame," quod he, "God yeve yow right good lyf.
Ye han heer touched, also moot I thee,°   *prosper*
In scole-matere greet difficultee.°   *on difficult scholastic matters*
Ye han seyd muche thyng right wel, I seye.
But dame, heere as we ryde by the weye
1275 Us nedeth nat to speken but of game,°   *entertainment*
And lete° auctoritees, on Goddes name,   *leave*

1. The latter years of the fourteenth century were not altogether unlike the present age. Chaucer urges the King to represent a standard of moral and political leadership which can help to restore confidence in better values.

1. *The Friar's Tale* is one of twenty-four tales told by twenty-three of thirty pilgrims en route from an inn in south London to the Cathedral at Canterbury. The tales are told in a contest to see who will win a free supper for the best performance. The friars come in for particularly harsh treatment from Chaucer (in fact, he was once fined for beating a friar in Fleet Street), as do the summoners, both of whom represent to him hypocrisy and an extreme falling away from the religious ideals they once pledged themselves to espouse. Between this friar and summoner, moreover, there is a typical and intense rivalry; they contested with each other in trying to extract money from people who could ill afford to part with it.

2. A begging friar with an assigned limit or territory. "Friar" is an anglicization of the French for brother—frère.

To prechyng and to scole of clergye.
But if it lyke to this compaignye,
I wol yow of a somonour telle a game.
1280 Pardee, ye may wel knowe by the name
That of a somonour may no good be sayd;
I praye that noon of you be yvele apayd.°   *be displeased*
A somonour is a rennere up and doun
With mandementz³ for fornicacioun,
1285 And is ybet° at every townes ende.”   *beaten*
     Oure Hoost⁴ tho spak, “A, sire, ye sholde be hende°   *gracious*
And curteys, as a man of youre estaat;
In compaignye we wol have no debaat.°   *quarrel*
Telleth youre tale and lat the Somonour be.”
1290   “Nay,” quod the Somonour, “lat hym seye to me
Whatso hym list. Whan it comth to my lot,
By God, I shal hym quiten° every grot.°   *repay / groat (silver fourpence)*
I shal hym tellen which a greet honour
It is to be a flaterynge lymytour,
1295 And of many another manere cryme
Which nedeth nat rehercen for this tyme.
And his office I shal hym telle, ywis.”
     Oure Hoost answerde, “Pees, namoore of this!”
And after this he seyde unto the Frere,
1300 “Tel forth youre tale, my leeve maister deere.”

Heere bigynneth the Freres Tale.

     Whilom ther was dwellynge in my contree
An erchedekene,⁵ a man of heigh degree,
That boldely dide execucioun
In punysshynge of fornicacioun,
1305 Of wicchecraft, and eek of bawderye,
Of diffamacioun,° and avowtrye,°   *slander / adultery*
Of chirche reves,⁶ and of testamentz,
Of contractes, and of lakke of sacramentz,⁷
Of usure, and of symonye⁸ also.
1310 But certes, lecchours dide he grettest wo⁹—
They sholde syngen° if that they were hent°—   *wail / caught*
And smale tytheres weren foule yshent°   *treated harshly*
If any persone wolde upon hem pleyne.
Ther myghte asterte hym no pecunyal peyne.¹⁰
1315 For smale tithes and for smal offrynge
He made the peple pitously to synge,¹¹
For er the bisshop caughte hem with his hook,
They were in the erchedeknes book.
And thanne hadde he, thurgh his jurisdiccioun,
1320 Power to doon on hem correccioun.
He hadde a somonour redy to his hond—
A slyer boye nas noon in Engelond,
For subtilly he hadde his espiaille°   *network of spies*
That taughte hym wher that hym myghte availle.°   *profit*
1325 He koude spare of lecchours oon or two

3. Summonses. Literally to come before the ecclesiastical court, but with the suggestion of invitation to fornication itself.
4. The Host, Harry Bailey, was master at the inn from which the pilgrims first set out, and judge of the stories told.
5. Archdeacon. The disciplinary officer of a diocese who administered its ecclesiastical court and was charged with overseeing the moral health of the community.
6. Church wardens (i.e., their behaviour), or possibly church robberies.
7. Failure to observe any of the seven sacraments: bap-

tism, confirmation, communion, marriage, ordination, penance, and extreme unction.
8. The buying and selling of church offices.
9. He was hardest on lechery—an unusual order of priorities, since it ought to have been the mortal sins (pride, envy, wrath, sloth, covetousness) which most concerned him. Lechery, like gluttony, was considered to be a venial sin, hence not as serious.
10. The tithe cheater could in no way escape financial punishment (a fine).
11. He was really an extortioner, abusing his power to run something not very different from a modern criminal “insurance” racket.

To techen° hym to foure and twenty mo.   *lead*
For thogh this somonour wood° was as an hare,   *crazy*
To telle his harlotrye I wol nat spare,[12]
For we° been out of his correccioun.   *i.e., friars*
1330   They han of us no jurisdiccioun,
Ne nevere shullen, terme of alle hir lyves.
    "Peter, so been wommen of the styves,"°   *brothels*
Quod the Somonour, "yput out of my cure!"°   *responsibility*
    "Pees, with myschance and with mysaventure,"
Thus seyde oure Hoost, "and lat hym telle his tale.
1335   Now telleth forth, thogh that the Somonour gale,°   *make a commotion*
Ne spareth nat, myn owene maister deere."
    This false theef, this somonour, quod the Frere,
Hadde alwey bawdes° redy to his hond,   *procurers*
1340   As any hauk to lure in Engelond,
That tolde hym al the secree that they knewe,
For hire acqueyntance was nat come of newe.[13]
They weren his approwours° prively.   *profit makers*
He took hymself a greet profit therby;
1345   His maister knew nat alwey what he wan.
Withouten mandement° a lewed° man   *official document / ignorant*
He koude somne, on peyne of Cristes curs,[14]
And they were glade for to fille his purs
And make hym grete feestes atte nale.°   *at the ale house*
1350   And right as Judas hadde purses smale,
And was a theef, right swich a theef was he;
His maister hadde but half his duetee.[15]
He was, if I shal yeven hym his laude,°   *praise*
A theef and eek a somnour and a baude.
1355   He hadde eek wenches at his retenue
That wheither that Sir Robert or Sir Huwe,
Or Jakke, or Rauf, or whoso that it were
That lay by hem, they tolde it in his ere.
Thus was the wenche and he of oon assent;
1360   And he wolde fecche a feyned mandement
And somne hem to chapitre° bothe two,   *chapter (ecclesiastical) court*
And pile° the man and lete the wenche go.   *pluck, despoil*
    Thanne wolde he seye, "Freend, I shal for thy sake
Do striken hire° out of oure lettres blake.   *erase her name*
1365   Thee thar namoore, as in this cas, travaille;°   *trouble (yourself)*
I am thy freend ther I thee may availle."
Certeyn he knew of briberyes mo
Than is possible to telle in yeres two.
For in this world nys dogge for the bowe[16]
1370   That kan an hurt deer from an hool knowe
Bet than this somnour knew a sly lecchour
Or an avowtier° or a paramour.   *adulterer*
And for that was the fruyt° of al his rente,°   *best part / income*
Therfore on it he sette al his entente.
1375   And so bifel that ones on a day
This somnour evere waityng on his pray
Rood for to somne an old wydwe, a ribibe,[17]
Feynynge a cause, for he wolde brybe.
And happed that he saugh bifore hym ryde
1380   A gay yeman under a forest syde.
A bowe he bar and arwes brighte and kene;

12. The summoner himself was apparently an extreme
case—presumably the wicked archdeacon's serpentine
wisdom suggested to him that "it takes one to catch one."
13. The summoner used a system of informers.
14. The threat of excommunication had a seriousness
comparable to the threat of exile in Anglo-Saxon times—it

meant a complete cutting off from society.
15. As Judas was reputed to have done, he filched money
from the purse.
16. Dog trained to hunt with a bowman.
17. Fiddle. Slang term for old woman.

He hadde upon a courtepy° of grene;[18]   *short coat*
An hat upon his heed with frenges blake.
    "Sire," quode this somnour, "hayl, and wel atake."
1385   "Welcome," quod he, "and every good felawe.
Wher rydestow, under this grenewode shawe?"°   *grove*
Seyde this yeman, "Wiltow fer to day?"
    This somnour hym answerde and seyde, "Nay.
Heere faste by," quod he, "is myn entente
1390 To ryden for to reysen° up a rente[19]   *collect*
That longeth to my lordes duetee."
    "Artow thanne a bailly?"° "Ye," quod he.   *bailiff*
He dorste nat, for verray filthe and shame
Seye that he was a somonour, for the name.
1395   "Depardieux,"° quod this yeman, "deere broother,   *in God's name*
Thou art a bailly, and I am another.
I am unknowen as in this contree;
Of thyn aqueyntance I wolde praye thee
And eek of bretherhede,[20] if that yow leste.°   *are agreeable*
1400 I have gold and silver in my cheste;
If that thee happe to comen in oure shire,
Al shal be thyn, right as thou wolt desire."
    "Grantmercy," quod this somonour, "by my feith!"
Everych in ootheres hand his trouthe° leith,   *troth*
1405 For to be sworne bretheren til they deye.
In daliance° they ryden forth hir weye.   *merriment*
    This somonour, that was as ful of jangles°   *idle chatter*
As ful of venym been thise waryangles[21]
And evere enqueryng upon everythyng,
1410 "Brother," quod he, "where is now youre dwellyng
Another day if that I sholde yow seche?"
This yeman hym answerde in softe speche,
    "Brother," quod he, "fer in the north contree,[22]
Where as I hope som tyme I shal thee see.
1415 Er we departe I shal thee so wel wisse°   *inform*
That of myn hous ne shaltow nevere mysse."
    "Now, brother," quod this somonour, "I yow preye,
Teche me whil that we ryden by the weye[23]—
Syn that ye been a baillif as am I—
1420 Som subtiltee,° and tel me feithfully   *trick*
In myn office how that I may moost wynne;
And spareth nat for conscience ne synne,
But as my brother tel me how do ye."
    "Now by my trouthe, brother deere," seyde he,
1425 "As I shal tellen thee a feithful tale:
My wages been ful streite and ful smale.
My lord is hard to me and daungerous,°   *demanding*
And myn office is ful laborous,
And therfore by extorcions I lyve.
1430 For sothe, I take al that men wol me yeve.
Algate,° by sleyghte or by violence   *always*
Fro yeer to yeer I wynne° al my dispence.°   *earn / expenditure*
I kan no bettre telle, feithfully."
    "Now certes," quod this somonour, "so fare I.
1435 I spare nat to taken, God it woot,
But if it be to hevy or to hoot.
What I may gete in conseil prively,

18. Green is sometimes the colour of the devil in medieval story.
19. "Rente" has the significance of "love service" in this period—it had not yet taken on its modern monetary connotations. It was thus service one performed for his lord in the feudal system.

20. Guild, or confraternity.
21. Shrikes or butcher-birds who impaled their prey on thorns which were thereafter considered poisonous.
22. Often the abode of devils in English medieval story.
23. This phrase suggests, as elsewhere in Chaucer, "off the track."

No maner conscience of that have I.

Nere° myn extoricioun, I myghte nat lyven,   *were it not*

1440   Nor of swiche japes° wol I nat be shryven.°   *tricks / absolved*

Stomak ne conscience ne knowe I noon;

I shrewe° thise shrifte-fadres° everychoon.   *curse / confessors*

Wel be we met, by God and by Seint Jame!

But, leeve° brother, tel me thanne thy name,"   *dear*

1445   Quod this somonour. In this meene while

This yeman gan a litel for to smyle,

    "Brother," quod he, "wiltow that I thee telle?

I am a feend; my dwellyng is in helle.

And heere I ryde about my purchasyng°   *acquiring*

1450   To wite where° men wold me yeven anythyng.   *know whether*

My purchas is th'effect of al my rente.[24]

Looke how thou rydest for the same entente—

To wynne good, thou rekkest° nevere how.   *care*

Right so fare I, for ryde I wold right now

1455   Unto the worldes ende for a preye."

    "A," quod this somonour, "benedicite, what sey ye?

I wende° ye were a yemen trewely.   *thought*

Ye han a mannes shap as wel as I.

Han ye a figure thanne determinat[25]

1460   In helle, ther ye been in youre estat?"

    "Nay, certeinly," quod he, "ther have we noon;

But whan us liketh we kan take us oon,

Or elles make yow seme° we been shape.   *make it seem to you*

Somtyme lyk a man, or lyk an ape,

1465   Or lyk an angel kan I ryde or go.

It is no wonder thyng thogh it be so;

A lowsy jogelour kan deceyve thee,

And pardee, yet kan° I moore craft than he."   *know*

    "Why," quod this somonour, "ryde ye thanne or goon

1470   In sondry shap and nat alwey in oon?"

    "For we," quod he, "wol us swiche formes make

As moost able is oure preyes for to take."

    "What maketh yow to han al this labour?"

    "Ful many a cause, leeve sire somonour,"

1475   Seyde this feend, "but alle thyng hath tyme.

The day is short and it is passed pryme,°   *9:00 a.m.*

And yet ne wan I nothyng in this day.

I wol entende to wynnen,° if I may,   *attend to business (capturing souls)*

And nat entende oure wittes to declare.°   *intellect to display*

1480   For, brother myn, thy wit is al to bare

To understonde althogh I tolde hem thee.

But, for thou axest why labouren we,

For somtyme we been Goddes instrumentz

And meenes to doon his comandementz,

1485   Whan that hym list,° upon his creatures,   *it pleases him*

In divers art and in diverse figures.

Withouten hym we have no myght, certayn,

If that hym list to stonden ther-agayn.°   *it pleases him to oppose*

And somtyme, at oure prayere,° han we leve   *entreaty*

1490   Oonly the body and nat the soule greve:°   *to punish*

Witnesse on Job, whom that we diden wo.

And somtyme han we myght of° bothe two,   *power over*

This is to seyn, of soule and body eke.

And somtyme be we suffred for to seke

1495   Upon a man and doon his soule unreste,

And nat his body, and al is for the beste.

24. "What I seize for myself is the net effect of my service
to my lord."

25. Since it was known that devils could assume any
shape, it was a question for theological debate as to what
their natural form was in hell.

Whan he withstandeth oure temptacioun,
It is a cause of his savacioun,
Al be it that it was nat oure entente
1500 He sholde be sauf but that we wolde hym hente.°   *get*
And somtyme be we servant unto man,
As to the erchebisshop Seint Dunstan,
And to the apostles servant eek was I."[26]
    "Yet tel me," quod the somonour, "feithfully,
1505 Make ye yow newe bodies thus alway
Of elementz?"[27] The feend answerde, "Nay.
Somtyme we feyne,° and somtyme we aryse   *pretend*
With dede bodyes in ful sondry wyse,
And speke as renably° and faire and wel   *reasonably*
1510 As to the Phitonissa dide Samuel[28]—
And yet wol som men seye it was nat he;
I do no fors° of youre dyvynytee.°   *regard / study of theology*
But o thyng warne I thee, I wol nat jape:°   *joke*
Thou wolt algates wite how we been shape;
1515 Thou shalt herafterwardes, my brother deere,
Come there thee nedeth nat of me to leere,°   *learn*
For thou shalt by thyn owene experience
Konne in a chayer rede[29] of this sentence
Bet than Virgile while he was on lyve,
1520 Or Dant also. Now lat us ryde blyve,°   *briskly*
For I wole holde compaignye with thee
Til it be so that thou forsake me."
    "Nay," quod this somonour, "that shal nat bityde.°   *happen*
I am a yeman knowen is ful wyde;
1525 My trouthe° wol I holde, as in this cas.   *troth (promise)*
For though thou were the devel Sathanas,
My trouthe wol I holde to thee my brother,
As I am sworn—and ech of us til oother—
For to be trewe brother in this cas.
1530 And bothe we goon abouten oure purchas.
Taak thou thy part, what that men wol thee yeve,
And I shal myn; thus may we bothe lyve.
And if that any of us have moore than oother,
Lat hym be trewe and parte° it with his brother."   *share*
1535 "I graunte," quod the devel, "by my fey."
And with that word they ryden forth hir wey.
And right at the entryng of the townes ende,
To which this somonour shoop hym for to wende,°   *go*
They saugh a cart that charged° was with hey,   *full*
1540 Which that a cartere droof forth in his wey.
Deep° was the wey, for which the carte stood.°   *Deep with mud / stuck*
The cartere smoot and cryde as he were wood,
"Hayt, Brok! Hayt, Scot! What, spare ye for the stones?
The feend," quod he, "yow fecche, body and bones,
1545 As ferforthly as evere were ye foled,°   *sure as you were born*
So muche wo as I have with yow tholed!°   *suffered*
The devel have al, bothe hors and cart and hey."
    This somonour seyde, "Heere shal we have a pley."°   *some fun*
And neer the feend he drough, as noght ne were,°   *i.e., casually*
1550 Ful prively, and rowned° in his ere,   *whispered*
"Herkne, my brother, herkne, by thy feith!
Herestow nat how that the cartere seith?
Hent° it anon,° for he hath yeve it thee,   *take / at once*

---

26. St. Dunstan, Archbishop of Canterbury (961–88), was
reputed to have subjected demons. The apostles, in some
saints' legends, subject demons to their service.
27. "Are your temporal shapes created of substance (or
are they merely illusions)?"

28. In the Vulgate, the Witch of Endor is called
"pythonissam." The spirit called up in 1 Sam. xxviii.11 ff.
was reputed to be not Samuel but a fiend.
29. Will know how to deliver lectures on the subject.

Bothe hey and cart, and eek his caples° thre."   *cart horses*

1555   "Nay," quod the devel, "God woot,° never a deel.°   *knows / not at all*
It is nat his entente, trust thou me weel.³⁰
Axe hym thyself, if thou nat trowest° me;   *believe*
Or elles stynt° a while, and thou shalt see."   *stop*
    This cartere thakketh° his hors upon the croupe,°   *pats / rump*
1560   And they bigonne drawen and to stoupe.
"Heyt now," quod he, "ther Jhesu Crist yow blesse,
And al his handwerk,° bothe moore and lesse!   *creations*
That was wel twight,° myn owene lyard° boy.   *pulled / gray*
I pray God save thee, and Seinte Loy!³¹
1565   Now is my cart out of the slow,° pardee."   *mud (slough)*
    "Lo, brother," quod the feend, "what tolde I thee?
Heere may ye se, myn owene deere brother,
The carl spak oon, but he thoghte another.
Lat us go forth abouten oure viage;
1570   Heere wynne I nothyng upon cariage."³²
    Whan that they coomen somwhat out of towne,
This somonour to his brother gan to rowne:
"Brother," quod he, "heere woneth° an old rebekke°   *lives / fiddle*
That hadde almoost as lief to lese hire nekke
1575   As for to yeve a peny of hir good.
I wole han twelf pens, though that she be wood,°   *mad*
Or I wol sompne° hire unto oure office;   *summon*
And yet, God woot, of hire knowe I no vice.
But for thou kanst nat, as in this contree,
1580   Wynne° thy cost,° taak heer ensample of me."   *earn / expenses*
    This somonour clappeth at the wydwes gate.
"Com out," quod he, "thou olde virytrate!°   *hag*
I trowe thou hast som frere or preest with thee."
    "Who clappeth?" seyde this wyf, "Benedicitee,
1585   God save you, sire; what is youre sweete wille?"³³
    "I have," quod he, "of somonce here a bille.°   *document*
Upon peyne of cursyng,° looke that thou be   *excommunication*
Tomorn bifore the erchedeknes knee
T'answere to the court of certeyn thynges."
1590   "Now, Lord," quod she, "Crist Jhesus, kyng of kynges,
So wisly helpe me, as I ne may.
I have been syk, and that ful many a day.
I may nat go so fer," quod she, "ne ryde,
But I be deed, so priketh it in my syde.
1595   May I nat axe a libel,³⁴ sire somonour,
And answere there by my procuratour°   *proxy*
To swich thyng as men wole opposen° me?"   *bring against*
    "Yis," quod this somonour, "pay anon—lat se—
Twelf pens to me, and I wol thee acquite.
1600   I shal no profit han therby but lite;
My maister hath the profit and nat I.
Com of, and lat me ryden hastily;
Yif me twelf pens; I may no lenger tarye."
    "Twelf pens!" quod she, "Now, lady Seinte Marie
1605   So wisly help me out of care and synne,
This wyde world thogh that I sholde wynne,

---

30. Here the Devil teaches good medieval theology. The
teamster's cursing is simply a venting of anger and
frustration; he doesn't *mean*, premeditatively, what he
says. The play on *entente* (intention, will) is Augustinian
and biblical, suggesting that it is what the heart commits
itself to which determines judgement. The summoner,
being literal-minded and evidencing no theology at all,
doesn't get the point.

31. Patron saint of carters.
32. Technical term for a feudal lord's claim on the use of
his tenant's horses and carts, which could be commuted by
money payment called *cariage*. I.e., the devil will make no
profit on this cart and horses.
33. I.e., "What is your good intention?"
34. Written copy of the accusation.

Ne have I nat tweft pens withinne myn hoold.°   *possession*
Ye knowen wel that I am poure and oold;
Kithe° youre almesse° on me, poure wrecche."   *show / charity*
1610   "Nay thanne," quod he, "the foule feend me fecche
If I th'excuse, though thou shul be spilt!"°   *ruined*
    "Allas!" quod she, "God woot, I have no gilt."
    "Pay me," quod he, "or by the sweete Seinte Anne,
As I wol bere awey thy newe panne
1615   For dette which that thou owest me of old.
Whan that thou madest thyn housbonde cokewold,
I payde at hoom for thy correccioun."°   *fine*
    "Thou lixt,"° quod she, "by my savacioun,   *lie*
Ne was I nevere er now, wydwe ne wyf,
1620   Somoned unto youre court in al my lyf;
Ne nevere I nas but of my body trewe.
Unto the devel, blak and rough of hewe,
Yeve I thy body and my panne also!"
    And whan the devel herde hire cursen so
1625   Upon hir knees, he seyde in this manere,
"Now Mabely, myn owene moder deere,
Is this youre wyl in ernest that ye seye?"
    "The devel," quod she, "so fecche hym er he deye,
And panne and al, but he wol hym repente!"
1630   "Nay, olde stot,° that is nat myn entente,"   *cow*
Quod this somonour, "for to repente me
For any thyng that I have had of thee.
I wolde I hadde thy smok° and every clooth."°   *underclothes / rag*
    "Now brother," quod the devel, "be nat wrooth;
1635   Thy body and this panne been myne by right.
Thou shalt with me to helle yet tonyght,
Where thou shalt knowen of ouro privetcc
Moore than a maister of dyvyntee."
    And with that word this foule feend hym hente;°   *grabbed*
1640   Body and soule he with the devel wente
Where as that somonours han hir heritage.
And God, that maked after his ymage
Mankynde, save and gyde us alle and some,
And leve° thise somonours goode men bicome!   *let*

1645   Lordynges, I koude han toold yow, quod this Frere,
Hadde I had leyser for° this Somnour heere,   *permission of*
After the text of Crist, Poul, and John,
And of oure othere doctours many oon,
Swiche peynes that youre heretes myghte agryse,°   *terrify*
1650   Al be it so° no tonge may it devyse,   *nevertheless*
Thogh that I myghte a thousand wynter telle,
The peynes of thilke cursed hous of helle.
But for to kepe us fro that cursed place,
Waketh and preyeth Jhesu for his grace
1655   So kepe us fro the temptour Sathanas.
Herketh this word, beth war as in this cas:
The leoun sit in his awayt° alway   *lies in wait*
To sle the innocent, if that he may.
Disposeth ay youre hertes to withstonde
The feend that yow wolde make thral° and bonde.   *slave*
1660   He may nat tempte yow over youre myght,
For Crist wol be youre champion and knyght.
And prayeth that thise somonours hem repente
Of hir mysdedes er that the feend hem hente!

Heere endeth the Freres Tale.

ANONYMOUS

Sir Orfeo[1]

We often read and written find,
as learned men do us remind,
that lays that now the harpers sing
are wrought of many a marvellous thing.[2]
5   Some are of weal, and some of woe,
and some do joy and gladness know;
in some are guile and treachery told,
in some the deeds that chanced of old;
some are of jests and ribaldry,
10 and some are tales of Faërie.[3]
Of all the things that men may heed
'tis most of love they sing indeed.
   In Britain all these lays are writ,
there issued first in rhyming fit,
15 concerning adventures in those days
whereof the Britons made their lays;[4]
for when they heard men anywhere
tell of adventures that there were,
they took their harps in their delight
20 and made a lay and named it right.
   Of adventures that did once befall
some can I tell you, but not all.
Listen now, lordings good and true,
and 'Orfeo' I will sing to you.
25   Sir Orfeo was a king of old,
in England lordship high did hold;
valour he had and hardihood,
a courteous king whose gifts were good.
His father from King Pluto came,
30 his mother from Juno, king of fame,
who once of old as gods were named
for mighty deeds they did and claimed.
Sir Orfeo, too, all things beyond
of harping's sweet delight was fond,
35 and sure were all good harpers there
of him to earn them honour fair;
himself he loved to touch the harp
and pluck the strings with fingers sharp.
He played so well, beneath the sun
40 a better harper was there none;
no man hath in this world been born
who would not, hearing him, have sworn
that as before him Orfeo played
to joy of Paradise he had strayed
45 and sound of harpers heavenly,
such joy was there and melody.
This king abode in Tracience,
a city proud of stout defence;
for Winchester, 'tis certain, then
50 as Tracience was known to men.

There dwelt his queen in fairest bliss,
whom men called Lady Heurodis,[5]
of ladies then the one most fair
who ever flesh and blood did wear;
55 in her did grace and goodness dwell,
but none her loveliness can tell.

   It so did chance in early May,
when glad and warm doth shine the day,
and gone are bitter winter showers,
60 and every field is filled with flowers,
on every branch the blossom blows,
in glory and in gladness grows,
the lady Heurodis, the queen,
two maidens fair to garden green
65 with her she took at drowsy tide
of noon to stroll by orchard-side,
to see the flowers there spread and spring
and hear the birds on branches sing.
   There down in shade they sat all three
70 beneath a fair young grafted tree;[6]
and soon it chanced the gentle queen
fell there asleep upon the green.
Her maidens durst her not awake,
but let her lie, her rest to take;
75 and so she slept, till midday soon
was passed, and come was afternoon.
Then suddenly they heard her wake,
and cry, and grievous clamour make;
she writhed with limb, her hands she wrung,
80 she tore her face till blood there sprung,
her raiment rich in pieces rent;
thus sudden out of mind she went.
   Her maidens two then by her side
no longer durst with her abide,
85 but to the palace swiftly ran
and told there knight and squire and man
their queen, it seemed, was sudden mad;
'Go and restrain her,' they them bade.
Both knights and ladies thither sped,
90 and more than sixty damsels fled;
to the orchard to the queen they went,
with arms to lift her down they bent,
and brought her to her bed at last,
and raving there they held her fast;
95 but ceaselessly she still would cry,
and ever strove to rise and fly.
   When Orfeo heard these tidings sad,
more grief than ever in life he had;
and swiftly with ten knights he sped

---

1. One of the most beautiful of medieval romances (ca.
1390–1400), and one of the briefest, this poem offers a
distinctive treatment of the Orpheus story by departing
from the usual ending—the second death of Eurydice—to
offer a strikingly different conclusion.
2. The subject matter of romance is that which is "marvel-
ous" or "wonderful," not that which is, in the modern

sense, "realistic."
3. The supernatural world.
4. The form of the original is a Breton *lai*, a sung variant
of the romance accompanied by a harp.
5. Eurydice.
6. The tree is called *ympe* (or *ente*) in the original text,
and grafted, is an orchard tree.

100 to bower, and stood before her bed,
and looking on her ruefully,
'Dear life,' he said, 'what troubles thee,
who ever quiet hast been and sweet,
why dost thou now so shrilly greet?
105 Thy body that peerless white was born
is now by cruel nails all torn.
Alas! thy cheeks that were so red
are now as wan as thou wert dead;
thy fingers too, so small and slim,
110 are strained with blood, their hue is dim.
Alas! thy lovely eyes in woe
now stare on me as on a foe.
A! lady, mercy I implore.
These piteous cries, come, cry no more,
115 but tell me what thee grieves, and how,
and say what may thee comfort now.'
    Then, lo! at last she lay there still,
and many bitter tears did spill,
and thus unto the king she spake:
120 'Alas! my lord, my heart will break.
Since first together came our life,
between us ne'er was wrath nor strife,
but I have ever so loved thee
as very life, and so thou me.
125 Yet now we must be torn in twain,
and go I must, for thy pain.'
    'Alas!' said he, 'then dark my doom.
Where wilt thou go, and go to whom?
But where thou goest, I come with thee,
130 and where I go, thou shalt with me.'
    'Nay, nay, sir, words avail thee naught.
I will tell thee how this woe was wrought:
as I lay in the quiet noontide
and slept beneath our orchard-side,
135 there came two noble knights to me
arrayed in armour gallantly.
"We come," they said, "thee swift to bring
to meeting with our lord and king."
Then answered I both bold and true
140 that dared I not, and would not do.
They spurred then back on swiftest steed;
then came their king himself with speed;
a hundred knights with him and more,
and damsels, too, were many a score,
145 all riding there on snow-white steeds,
and white as milk were all their weeds;[7]
I saw not ever anywhere
a folk so peerless and so fair.
The king was crowned with crown of light,
150 not of red gold nor silver white,
but of one single gem 'twas hewn
that shone as bright as sun at noon.
And coming, straightway he me sought,
and would I or no, he up me caught,
155 and made me by him swiftly ride
upon a palfrey at his side;
and to his palace thus me brought,
a dwelling fair and wondrous wrought.
He castles showed me there and towers,
160 Water and wild, and woods, and flowers,

and pastures rich upon the plain;
and then he brought me home again,
and to our orchard he me led,
and then at parting this he said:
165 "See, lady, tomorrow thou must be
right here beneath this grafted tree,
and then beside us thou shalt ride,
and with us evermore abide.
If let or hindrance thou dost make,
170 where'er thou be, we shall thee take,
and all thy limbs shall rend and tear—
no aid of man shall help thee there;
and even so, all rent and torn,
thou shalt away with us be borne."'
175   When all those tidings Orfeo heard,
then spake he many a bitter word:
'Alas! I had liever lose my life
than lose thee thus, my queen and wife!'
He counsel sought of every man,
180 but none could find him help or plan.
    On the morrow, when the noon drew near,
in arms did Orfeo appear,
and full ten hundred knights with him,
all stoutly armed, all stern and grim;
185 and with their queen now went that band
beneath the grafted tree to stand.
A serried rank on every side
they made, and vowed there to abide,
and die there sooner for her sake
190 than let men thence their lady take.
And yet from midst of that array
the queen was sudden snatched away;
by magic was she from them caught,
and none knew whither she was brought.
195   Then was there wailing, tears, and woe;
the king did to his chamber go,
and oft he swooned on floor of stone,
and such lament he made and moan
that nigh his life then came to end;
200 and nothing could his grief amend.
His barons he summoned to his board,
each mighty earl and famous lord,
and when they all together came,
'My lords,' he said, 'I here do name
205 my steward high before you all
to keep my realm, whate'er befall,
to hold my place instead of me
and keep my lands where'er they be.
For now that I have lost my queen,
210 the fairest lady men have seen,
I wish not woman more to see.
Into the wilderness I will flee,
and there will live for evermore
with the wild beasts in forests hoar.
215 But when ye learn my days are spent,
then summon ye a parliament,
and choose ye there a king anew.
With all I have now deal ye true.'
    Then weeping was there in the hall,
220 and great lament there made they all,

7. Clothes, garments.

and hardly there might old or young
for weeping utter word with tongue.
They knelt them down in company,
and prayed, if so his will might be,
225   that never should he from them go.
'Have done!' said he. 'It must be so.'

Now all his kingdom he forsook.
Only a beggar's cloak he took;
he had no kirtle and no hood,
230   no shirt, nor other raiment good.
His harp yet bore he even so,
and barefoot from the gate did go;
no man might keep him on the way.
A me! the weeping woe that day,
235   when he that had been king with crown
went thus beggarly out of town!
Through wood and over moorland bleak
he now the wilderness doth seek,
and nothing finds to make him glad,
240   but ever liveth lone and sad.
He once had ermine worn and vair,
on bed had purple linen fair,
now on the heather hard doth lie,
in leaves is wrapped and grasses dry.
245   He once had castles owned and towers,
water and wild, and woods, and flowers,
now though it turn to frost or snow,
this king with moss his bed must strow.
He once had many a noble knight
250   before him kneeling, ladies bright,
now nought to please him doth he keep;
only wild serpents by him creep.
He that once had in plenty sweet
all dainties for his drink and meat,
255   now he must grub and dig all day,
with roots his hunger to allay.
In summer on wildwood fruit he feeds,
or berries poor to serve his needs;
in winter nothing can he find
260   save roots and herbs and bitter rind.
All his body was wasted thin
by hardship, and all cracked his skin.
A Lord! who can recount the woe
for ten long years that king did know?
265   His hair and beard all black and rank
down to his waist hung long and lank.
His harp wherein was his delight
in hollow tree he hid from sight;
when weather clear was in the land
270   his harp he took then in his hand
and harped thereon at his sweet will.
Through all the wood the sound did thrill,
and all the wild beasts that there are
in joy approached him from afar;
275   and all the birds that might be found
there perched on bough and bramble round
to hear his harping to the end,
such melodies he there did blend;
and when he laid his harp aside,
280   no bird or beast would near him bide.

There often by him would he see,
when noon was hot on leaf and tree,
the king of Faërie with his rout
came hunting in the woods about
285   with blowing far and crying dim,
and barking hounds that were with him;
yet never a beast they took nor slew,
and where they went he never knew.
At other times he would descry
290   a mighty host, it seemed, go by,
ten hundred knights all fair arrayed
with many a banner proud displayed.
Each face and mien was fierce and bold,
each knight a drawn sword there did hold,
295   and all were armed in harness fair
and marching on he knew not where.
Or a sight more strange would meet his eye:
knights and ladies came dancing by
in rich array and raiment meet,
300   softly stepping with skilful feet;
tabour and trumpet went along,
and marvellous minstrelsy and song.

And one fair day he at his side
saw sixty ladies on horses ride,
305   each fair and free as bird on spray,
and never a man with them that day.
There each on hand a falcon bore,
riding a-hawking by river-shore.
Those haunts with game in plenty teem,
310   cormorant, heron, and duck in stream;
there off the water fowl arise,
and every falcon them descries;
each falcon stooping slew his prey,
and Orfeo laughing loud did say:
315   'Behold, in faith, this sport is fair!
Fore Heaven, I will betake me there!
I once was wont to see such play.'
He rose and thither made his way,
and to a lady came with speed,
320   and looked at her, and took good heed,
and saw as sure as once in life
'twas Heurodis, his queen and wife.
Intent he gazed, and so did she,
but no word spake; no word said he.
325   For hardship that she saw him bear,
who had been royal, and high, and fair,
then from her eyes the tears there fell.
The other ladies marked it well,
and away they made her swiftly ride;
330   no longer might she near him bide.
'Alas!' said he, 'unhappy day!
Why will not now my death me slay?
Alas! unhappy man, ah why
may I not, seeing her, now die?
335   Alas! too long hath lasted life,
when I dare not with mine own wife
to speak a word, nor she with me.
Alas! my heart should break,' said he.
'And yet, fore Heaven, tide what betide,
340   and whithersoever these ladies ride,

that road I will follow they now fare;
for life or death no more I care.'
  His beggar's cloak he on him flung,
his harp upon his back he hung;
345 with right good will his feet he sped,
for stock nor stone he stayed his tread.
Right into a rock the ladies rode,
and in behind he fearless strode.
He went into that rocky hill
350 a good three miles or more, until
he came into a country fair
as bright as sun in summer air.
Level and smooth it was and green,
and hill nor valley there was seen.
355 A castle he saw amid the land
princely and proud and lofty stand;
the outer wall around it laid
of shining crystal clear was made.
A hundred towers were raised about
360 with cunning wrought, embattled stout;
and from the moat each buttress bold
in arches sprang of rich red gold.
The vault was carven and adorned
with beasts and birds and figures horned;
365 within were halls and chambers wide
all made of jewels and gems of pride;
the poorest pillar to behold
was builded all of burnished gold.
And all that land was ever light,
370 for when it came to dusk of night
from precious stones there issued soon
a light as bright as sun at noon.
No man may tell nor think in thought
how rich the works that there were wrought;
375 indeed it seemed he gazed with eyes
on the proud court of Paradise.
  The ladies to that castle passed.
Behind them Orfeo followed fast.
There knocked he loud upon the gate;
380 the porter came, and did not wait,
but asked him what might be his will.
'In faith, I have a minstrel's skill
with mirth and music, if he please,
thy lord to cheer, and him to ease.'
385 The porter swift did then unpin
the castle gates, and let him in.
  Then he began to gaze about,
and saw within the walls a rout
of folk that were thither drawn below,
390 and mourned as dead, but were not so.
For some there stood who had no head,
and some no arms, nor feet; some bled
and through their bodies wounds were set,
and some were strangled as they ate,
395 and some lay raving, chained and bound,
and some in water had been drowned;
and some were withered in the fire,
and some on horse, in war's attire;
and wives there lay in their childbed,
400 and mad were some, and some were dead;
and passing many there lay beside

as though they slept at quiet noon-tide.
Thus in the world was each one caught
and thither by fairy magic brought.
405 There too he saw his own sweet wife,
Queen Heurodis, his joy and life,
asleep beneath a grafted tree:
by her attire he knew 'twas she.
  When he had marked these marvels all,
410 he went before the king in hall,
and there a joyous sight did see,
a shining throne and canopy.
Their king and lord there held his seat
beside their lady fair and sweet.
415 Their crowns and clothes so brightly shone
that scarce his eyes might look thereon.
  When he had marked this wondrous thing,
he knelt him down before the king:
'O lord,' said he, 'if it be thy will,
420 now shalt thou hear my minstrel's skill.'
The king replied: 'What man art thou
that hither darest venture now?
Not I nor any here with me
have ever sent to summon thee,
425 and since here first my reign began
I have never found so rash a man
that he to us would dare to wend,
unless I first for him should send.'
'My lord,' said he, 'I thee assure,
430 I am but a wandering minstrel poor;
and, sir, this custom use we all
at the house of many a lord to call,
and little though our welcome be,
to offer there our minstrelsy.'
435 Before the king upon the ground
he sat, and touched his harp to sound;
his harp he tuned as well he could,
glad notes began and music good,
and all who were in palace found
440 came unto him to hear the sound,
and lay before his very feet,
they thought his melody so sweet.
He played, and silent sat the king
for great delight in listening;
445 great joy this minstrelsy he deemed,
and joy to his noble queen it seemed.
  At last when he his harping stayed,
this speech the king to him then made:
'Minstrel, thy music pleaseth me.
450 Come, ask of me whate'er it be,
and rich reward I will thee pay.
Come, speak, and prove now what I say!"
'Good sir,' he said, 'I beg of thee
that this thing thou wouldst give to me,
455 that very lady fair to see
who sleeps beneath the grafted tree.'
'Nay,' said the king, 'that would not do!
A sorry pair ye'd make, ye two;
for thou art black, and rough, and lean,
460 and she is faultless, fair and clean.
A monstrous thing then would it be
to see her in thy company.'

'O sir,' he said, 'O gracious king,
but it would be a fouler thing
465 from mouth of thine to hear a lie.
Thy vow, sir, thou canst not deny,
Whate'er I asked, that should I gain,
and thou must needs thy word maintain.'
The king then said: 'Since that is so,
470 now take her hand in thine, and go;
I wish thee joy of her, my friend!"

He thanked him well, on knees did bend;
his wife he took then by the hand,
and departed swiftly from that land,
475 and from that country went in haste;
the way he came he now retraced.

Long was the road. The journey passed;
to Winchester he came at last,[8]
his own beloved city free;
480 but no man knew that it was he.
Beyond the town's end yet to fare,
lest men them knew, he did not dare;
but in a beggar's narrow cot
a lowly lodging there he got
485 both for himself and for his wife,
as a minstrel poor of wandering life.
He asked for tidings in the land,
and who that kingdom held in hand;
the beggar poor him answered well
490 and told all things that there befell:
how fairies stole their queen away
ten years before, in time of May;
and how in exile went their king
in unknown countries wandering,
495 while still the steward rule did hold;
and many things beside he told.

Next day, when hour of noon was near,
he bade his wife await him here;
the beggar's rags he on him flung,
500 his harp upon his back he hung,
and went into the city's ways
for men to look and on him gaze.
Him earl and lord and baron bold,
lady and burgess, did behold.
505 'O look! O what a man!' they said,
'How long the hair hangs from his head!
His beard is dangling to his knee!
He is gnarled and knotted like a tree!'
Then he walked along the street
510 He chanced his steward there to meet,
and after him aloud cried he:
'Mercy, sir steward, have on me!
A harper I am from Heathenesse;
to thee I turn in my distress.'
515 The steward said: 'Come with me, come!
Of what I have thou shalt have some.
All harpers good I welcome make
For my dear lord Sir Orfeo's sake.'
The steward in castle sat at meat,
520 and many a lord there had his seat;

trumpeters, tabourers there played
harpers and fiddlers music made.
Many a melody made they all,
but Orfeo silent sat in hall
525 and listened. And when they all were still
he took his harp and tuned it shrill.
Then notes he harped more glad and clear
than ever a man hath heard with ear;
his music delighted all those men.
530 The steward looked and looked again;
the harp in hand at once he knew.
'Minstrel,' he said, 'come, tell me true,
whence came this harp to thee, and how?
I pray thee, tell me plainly now.'
535 'My lord,' said he, 'in lands unknown
I walked a wilderness alone,
and there I found in dale forlorn
a man by lions to pieces torn,
by wolves devoured with teeth so sharp;
540 by him I found this very harp,
and that is full ten years ago.'
'Ah!' said the steward, 'news of woe!
'Twas Orfeo, my master true.
Alas! poor wretch, what shall I do,
545 who must so dear a master mourn?
A! woe is me that I was born,
for him so hard a fate designed,
a death so vile that he should find!'
Then on the ground he fell in swoon;
550 his barons stooping raised him soon
and bade him think how all must end—
for death of man no man can mend.

King Orfeo now had proved and knew
his steward was both loyal and true,
555 and loved him as he duly should.
'Lo!' then he cried, and up he stood,
'Steward, now to my words give ear!
If thy king, Orfeo, were here,[9]
and had in wilderness full long
560 suffered great hardship sore and strong,
had won his queen by his own hand
out of the deeps of fairy land,
and led at last his lady dear
right hither to the town's[10] end near,
565 and lodged her in a beggar's cot;
if I were he, whom ye knew not,
thus come among you, poor and ill,
in secret to prove thy faith and will,
if then I thee had found so true,
570 thy loyalty never shouldst thou rue:
nay, certainly, tide what betide,
thou shouldst be king when Orfeo died.
Hadst thou rejoiced to hear my fate,
I would have thrust thee from the gate.'
575 Then clearly knew they in the hall
that Orfeo stood before them all.
The steward understood at last;
in his haste the table down he cast

8. In all other versions the audience would know, as with modern versions such as those of Anouilh or Cocteau, Orpheus looks back at Eurydice on the way out, against the command of the King of the underworld, and she is therefore condemned to remain in the realm of the dead.

9. The speech of revelation is cast in the form of an hypothesis.
10. The Middle English text has "tounes ende," a pun for "town's ende" or "tune's ende," or end of the song.

and flung himself before his feet,
580   and each lord likewise left his seat,
and this one cry they all let ring:
'Ye are our lord, sir, and our king!'
To know he lived so glad they were.
To his chamber soon they brought him there;
585   they bathed him and they shaved his beard,
and robed him, till royal he appeared;
and brought them in procession long
the queen to town with merry song,
with many a sound of minstrelsy.
590   A Lord! how great the melody!
For joy the tears were falling fast
of those who saw them safe at last.
    Now was King Orfeo crowned anew,
and Heurodis his lady too;
595   and long they lived, till they were dead,
and king was the steward in their stead.
    Harpers in Britain in aftertime
these marvels heard, and in their rhyme
a lay they made of fair delight,
600   and after the king it named aright,
'Orfeo' called it, as was meet:
good is the lay, the music sweet.
    Thus came Sir Orfeo out of care.
God grant that well we all may fare!

Complaint to the Lord of Love

O Lord of loue, here my complaynt,
    And do me Ryght I the requere!
Why suffers thou me to be ataynt?°   *condemned*
    loue in the lore,° the I Requyre.   *learning*
5   Syth thou haste set me on the fyere,
        My hert to bren thou wyll not spare;
    thou get me here that I desyre—
        that fygure fresch that ys so fayre.

So fayre she ys and also fresch,
10   that all me loue ys on here set;
She is the fayreste of face and flesch,
    And here to loue y kan not let.°   *give up*
    So myld a mayde neuer yet I met,
        here commely countenance caste me in care,
15   To that dyrlyng yt ys me deute°—   *debt*
        that fygure fraysch that ys so fayre.

Of schynyng schappes° I here comand—   *shapes*
    here stedfast stature standes full bryght;
here cors° can not all kynde° amende,   *body / nature*
20   So ys she wroght,[1] that worthe wyght.°   *person*
    when I of here may haue a syght,
        there may no payne me hert emperre;°   *impair*
    I am all here, as yt ys Ryght—
        that fygure fresche that ys so fayre.[2]

1. The sense is "All of nature could not improve on her body, she is so wonderfully made. . . ."
2. The sense: "She has my full attention, as is appropriate, that figure fresh. . . ." The play on "Right" is to imply a consequent or reciprocal "attention" on the part of the lady, with the entire poem couched in legal terms.

25   Here feete, here hondys that byth full smale,
     And all that to here body longe,
of kynde the comlyste° I here calle,   *comliest*
     full fayn wollde I, y myght here fonde.³
     But she me loue, she dose me wronge,
30   And of my blyse I may be bare;
     fore here y laye in paynes stronge—
      that fygure fresch that ys so fayre.

And when that ferly° fallys in my thoght,   *wonder, miracle*
     full sore I sygh and say allas;
35 In butyr balles thus am I broght,
     And in paynes that wyll not fro me passe.
     In so grete wo neuer yet I was,
      And but she cewre me of me care,
     Intoloreable ys here trespasse—
40   [that fygure fresch that ys so fayre.]

Gentle Cock

I haue a gentil cook,
     crowyt me day;
he doth me rysyn erly,
     my matyins° for to say.   *morning prayers*

I haue a gentil cook,
     comyn he is of gret;°   *great lineage*
his comb is of reed corel,
     his tayl is of get.°   *jet (black)*

I haue a gentyl cook,
     comyn he is of kynde;°   *gentlefolk (nature)*
his comb is of red corel,
     his tayl is of Inde.

his legges ben of asor,°   *azure blue*
     so geintil & so smale;
his spores arn of syluer qwyt,
     in-to the worte-wale.¹

his eynyn° arn of cristal,   *eyes*
     lokyn al in aumbyr;
& euery nyȝt he perchit hym
     in myn ladyis chaumbyr.

---

3. *Fonde*—lit. "try her out" or "have knowledge of her."   1. *Worte-wal:* the root of a cock's spur.

A Boar's Head Carol
Hey, hey, hey, hey!
the borrys hede is armyd gay.

The boris hede in hond I bryng,
Witt garlond gay in porttoryng;°   *carrying*
I pray yow all witt me to synge,
      Witt hay![1]

5   Lordys, knyghttis, and skyers,°   *squires*
Persons, prystis, and wycars°—   *vicars*
The boris hede ys the furst mes,
      Witt hay!

The boris hede, as I yow say,
10 He takis his leyfe, & gothe his way
Son after the tweylffyt Day,[2]
      Witt hay!

Then commys in the secund kowrs witt mykyll° pryid:°   *much pride*
the crannis & the heyrrons, the bytteris by ther syde,
15 the pertrychys & the plowers, the wodcokis & the snyt,
      Witt hay!

Larkys in hoot schow,[3] ladys for to pyk,
Good drynk therto, lycyvs° and fyn—   *luscious*
Blwet of allmayn,° romnay° and wyin,   *almond soup / sweet wine*
20   Witt hay!

Gud bred, alle, & wyin, dare I well say,
the boris hede witt musterd armyd soo gay.

furmante to potdtage,° witt wennissun° fyn,[4]   *soup / venison*
& the hombuls of the dow,° & all that euer commis in.   *entrails of the dove*

25 Cappons ibake, witt the pesys of the roow,°   *roe deer*
Reysons of corrans,° witt odyr spysis moo.   *raisins and currants*

CHARLES d'ORLEANS (1391–1465)

Ofte in My Thought[1]

Ofte in my thought fulle besily haue y sought
Ayens the bigynnyng of this fresshe newe yere
What praty° thyng that y best yeven ought   *pleasing*
To hir that was myn hertis lady dere
5   But alle that thought bitane° is fro me clere   *taken away*
Sith deth allas hath closid hir vndir cley
And hath this world fornakid with hir here
God haue hir sowle y kan no bettir say

1. "With a hey, hey" etc. introduces the refrain. This song (ca. 1425) is sung at the entrance of the boar's head, on a platter, into the banqueting hall—a custom still observed at Queen's College, Oxford.
2. The twelfth day of Christmas.
3. "Larks in hot sauce."
4. Wheat boiled in milk with fine venison.

1. Charles d'Orleans was born in France and taken prisoner at the battle of Agincourt in 1415. As a distinguished French nobleman he had various forms of court arrest in England, during which time he grew to a great facility in English and composed many poems in English as well as French. This poem (ca. 1425) is from a ballad sequence, commencing probably as an amorous correspondence, and was written at the New Year.

But forto kepe in custome lo my thought
10   And of my sely° seruice the manere   *innocent*
In shewyng allys° that y forget hir nought   *all; Alice*
Vnto eche wight y shall*e* to my powere
This dede hir serue w*ith* massis and prayere
For a to fowle a shame were me mafay°   *my faith*
15   Hir to forgete this tyme that neigheth nere[2]
God haue hir sowle y kan no bettir say

To hir profit now nys ther to ben bought
Noon othir thyng all*e* wol y bay hit dere
Wherfore thou lord that lordist all*e* aloft
20   Mi deedis take suche as goodnes stere°   *star*
And crowne hir lord w*ith*in thyn hevenly spere°   *sphere*
As for most trewist lady may y say
Most good most fayre and most benygne of chere
God haue hir sowle y kan no bettir say

25   When y hir prayse/or praysyng of hir here
All*e* though it whilom° were to me plesere   *betimes*
Hit fill*e* y-nough hit doth myn hert to-day
And doth me wisshe y clothid had my bere[3]
God haue hir sowle y kan no bettir say

ANONYMOUS

Money

Synge we alle and seye we thus:
Gramercy,° myn owene purs.   *great thanks*

Whan I have in my purs ynough,
I may have bothe hors and plough
And also frendes ynough—
   Thurgh the vertu of my purs.

Whan my purs gynneth to slake,
And ther is noght in my pak,
They wol seyn, "Go! Farewel, Jakke,
   Thou shalt namore drynke wyth us."

Thus is al my good i-lorn,
And my purs is al to-torn;°   *torn to pieces*
I may pleye wyth an horn
   In the stede al of my purs.

Farewel, hors, and farewel, cow,
Farewel, carte, and farewel, plough;
As I pleyde me wyth a bowe
   I seyde, "God, what is al this?"

2. "For ever to be a fool's shame were my fidelity if I
forgot her at this time. . . ."

3. "And makes me wish I were already wrapped in my
coffin."

A Walk in the Woods

I moot go walke the wode so wilde,
   And wandren heer and ther
   In drede and deedly fere;
For wher I trusted I am bigiled,
   And al for oon.[1]

Thus am I banysshed from my blisse
   By craft and fals pretence,
   Fautles wythoute offence;
As of retourn no certeyn° is,   *certainty*
   And al for fere of oon.

My bed shal be under the grene-wode tree,
   A toft of brakes° under myn hed,   *tuft of bracken*
   As oon from joye were fled;
Thus from my lyf day by day I flee,
   And al for oon.

The rennyng stremes shullen be my drynke,
   Accornes shullen be my fode;
   No-thyng may do me good
But whan of thy beautee I do thenke—
   And al for love of oon.

Go, Litel Ryng

Go, litel ryng, to that ilke swete
   That hath myn herte in hir demeyne,°   *possession*
And loke thou knele doun at hir feet
   Bisechyng hire she wolde not desdeyne
   On hir smale fyngres thee to streyne;°   *encircle*
     Than I wyl thee seye boldely:
     "My maister wolde that he were I."

I Have a Yong Suster[1]

I have a yong suster
   Fer biyonde the see;
Many ben the drueries°   *presents*
   That she sente me.

5   She sente me the chery
   Wythouten any ston,
And so she dide the dowve
   Wythouten any bon.

She sente me the brere°   *wild rose*
10   Wythouten any rynde,°   *bark*
She bad me love my lemman
   Wythouten longynge.

How sholde any chery
   Ben wythouten ston?
15   And how sholde any dowve
   Ben wythouten bon?

---

1. "All on account of one [person]." The persona appears
to be a would-be lover who has overplayed his hand and is
now banished.

1. Traditional English paradox song (ca. 1430), which has
modern versions.

How sholde any brere
   Ben wythouten rynde?
How sholde I love my lemman
20   Wythouten longynge?

Whan the chery was a flour,
   Than hadde it non ston;
Whan the dowve was an ey,°   *egg*
   Than hadde it non bon.

25 Whan the brere was unbred,°   *unborn (a seed)*
   Than hadde it non rynde;
Whan the mayden hath that she loveth,
   She is wythouten longynge.

I Synge of a Mayden

I synge of a mayden
That is makeles:[1]
Kyng of alle kynges
To hir sone she ches.°   *chose*

He cam also stille°   *as silently*
Ther° his moder was   *where*
As dewe in Aprill
That falleth on the gras.

He cam also stille
To his modres bour
As dewe in Aprill
That falleth on the flour.

He cam also stille
Ther his moder lay
As dewe in Aprill
That falleth on the spray.°   *branch of buds*

Moder and mayden
Was nevere non but she:
Wel may swich a lady
Goddes moder be.

Verbum Caro Factum Est

I passed thurgh a gardyn grene,
I fond an herber made ful newe;
A seemlier sight I have not seen—
On ilke tree song a turtel trewe.
5 Ther-inne a mayden bright of hewe,
And evere she song and nevere she cessed;
Thise were the notes that she gan shewe:
"*Verbum caro factum est.*"[1]

---

1. One of the most beautiful nativity lyrics, this poem (ca. 1430) makes striking use of *double entendres.* In this one we understand the maiden to be *matchless* and also *mate-less*, i.e., without carnal knowledge of a man.

1. "The Word is Made Flesh," John i.14—the incarnation.

10   I axed that mayden what she mente,
     She bad me bide and I sholde here;
     What she seyde I took good tente°—   *attention*
     In hir song hadde she vois ful clere.
     She seyde, "A prince wythouten pere
15   Is born and leyd bitwene two beste;[2]
     Ther-fore I synge as thou mayst here,
     'Verbum caro factum est.'"

     And thurghout that frith° as I gan wende,   *woodland*
     A blisful song yet herde I mo;
     And that was of three shepherdes hende:
20   *"Gloria in excelsis deo."*[3]
     I wolde not they hadde faren me fro,
     And after hem ful faste I prest;
     Than tolde they me that they songen so,
     For *verbum caro factum est.*

25   They seyde that song was this to seye:
     "To God above be joye and blisse,
     For pees in erthe also we preye
     To alle men that in goodnesse is.
     The may that is wythouten mys°   *fault*
30   Hath born a child bitwene two beste;
     She is the cause ther-of, y-wis,
     That *verbum caro factum est.*

     I fared me furthe° in that frith,   *onward*
     I mette three comly kynges wyth croune;[4]
35   I spedde me forth to speke hem wyth,
     And on my knees I knelede doun.
     The royalest of hem to me gan roune°   *address*
     And seyde, "We fared wel at the feste;
     From Bethleem now are we boun,°   *bound*
40   For *verbum caro factum est.*

     "For we sawen God bicomen in mannes flessh,
     That boot has boght of al oure bale,[5]
     Awey oure synnes for-to wasshe;
     A may him herberd° in hir halle,   *harboured*
45   She socoured him soothly in hir sall°   *chamber*
     And held that hende in hir arest;[6]
     Ful trewely may she telle that tale
     That *verbum caro factum est.*"

     Unto that princesse wol we preye,
50   As she is bothe moder and mayde;
     She be oure help as she wel may
     To him that in hir lappe was leyd;
     To serve him we ben prest and payed,°   *ready and content*
     And ther-to make we oure biheste;°   *request*
55   For I herde when she song and seyde,
     "Verbum caro factum est."

2. Two beasts—the ox and the ass. Cf. Isa .i.3.
3. "Glory to God in the highest." Cf. Luke ii.14.
4. Traditional representation of the Magi (wise men) after the fourteenth century—previously there could be as many as eight.
5. "That remedy has redeemed us from our misfortune."
6. "And kept that lad in her own room."

Adam Lay I-Bounde

Adam lay i-bounde,
   Bounden in a bond;
Foure thousand wynter[1]
   Thoghte he not to longe.
And al was for an appel,[2]
   An appel that he took,
As clerkes fynden writen
   In here book.

Ne hadde the appel take ben,
   The appel take ben,
Ne hadde nevere oure lady
   A ben hevenes quene.
Blessed be the tyme
   That appel take was,—
Ther-fore we mowen synge
   "Deo gracias."[3]

In the Vale of Resteles Mynde

In the vale of resteles mynde
I soghte in mountayne and in meed
Trustyng a trewe-love for-to fynde.
Upon an hil than took I hede;
5   A vois I herde (and neer I yede°)   *went*
In greet dolour compleynyng tho:
"See, dere soule, my sides blede,
   Quia amore langueo."[1]

Upon this mount I fond a tree;
10 Under this tree a man sittyng.
From hed to foot wounded was he,
His herte blood I saw bledyng;
A seemly man to ben a kyng,
A gracious face to loke unto.
15 I axed him how he hadde peynyng:
He seyde, "*Quia amore langueo.*

"I am trewe-love that fals was nevere;
My suster, mannes soule, I lovede hire thus:
Bicause I wolde on no wyse dissevere°   *separate*
20 I lefte my kyngdom glorious;
I purveiede° hire a place ful precious.   *provided*
She flitte, I folwed, I lovede hire so
That I suffred thise peynes piteous,
   Quia amore langueo.

25 "My faire love and my spouse brighte
I savede hire from betyng and she hath me bette;
I clothede hire in grace and hevenly light:
This blody sherte° she hath on me set.   *shirt*
For longyng love I wol not lete.°   *cease*
30 Swete strokes ben thise, lo!
I have loved evere as I hette,°   *promised*
   Quia amore langueo.

"I crounede hire wyth blisse and she me wyth thorn;
I ledde hire to chambre and she me to deye;
35 I broghte hire to worshipe and she me to scorn:
I dide hire reverence and she me vilanye.

1. It was thought that Christ's "Harrowing of Hell," when during the three days of his death he delivered the captive souls of godly men and women of the past, took place approximately 4,000 years after the Fall of Man from Eden.
2. The Bible does not specify the fruit the serpent offered, but because of the similarity between the Latin word for evil (*malus*) and the Latin word for apple (*malum*) the association was imaginatively irresistable.

3. This is the notion of the *felix culpa*, or "fortunate fault"; if man had not first sinned, there would not have been the joy of his redemption.

1. "Because I languish with love." The Latin is a quotation from the Bible, *Song* (of Songs) v.8, and was taken in the Middle Ages to refer to the pains of the unrequited love God (or Christ) feels for the world, his desired "bride." This poem (ca. 1430) is in the form of a liturgical sequence, and has often been set to music.

To love that° loveth is no maistrye;   *that one who*
Hir hate made nevere my love hir fro.
Axe than no more questiouns why,
40   But *quia amore langueo*.

"Loke unto myne hondes, man!
Thise gloves were yeven me whan I hire soghte.
They ben not white, but rede and wan;°   *pale*
45   Enbrouded wyth blood my spouse hem boghte.
They wol not offe; I leve hem noght;
I wowe hire wyth hem wher-evere she go.
Thise hondes ful freendly for hire foghte,
    Quia amore langueo.

"Merveil not, man, thogh I sitte stille,—
50   My love hath shod me wonder streyte:°   *very closely*
She bokeled my feet, as was hir wylle,
Wyth sharpe nayles—wel thou mayst waite.°   *attend, observe*
In my love was nevere disceite,
For alle my membres I have opened hire to;
55   My body I made hir hertes baite,°   *enticement*
    Quia amore langueo.

"In my side I have made hir neste.
Loke in, how wide a wounde is heer:
This is hir chambre, heer shal she reste,
60   That she and I mowen slepe in fere.°   *together*
Heer may she wasshe if any filthe were;
Heer is socour for al hir wo.
Come if she wyl, she shal have chere,
    Quia amore langueo.

65   "I wol abide til she be redy;
I wol to hire sende er she seye nay;
If she be reccheles° I wol be redy,   *negligent*
If she be daungerous° I wol hire preye;   *disdainful*
If she do wepe than bidde I nay:
70   Myne armes ben sprad to clyppe° hire to.   *clasp*
Cry ones° 'I come,' now, soule, assay,   *once*
    Quia amore langueo.

"I sitte on an hil for to see fer;
I loke to the vale my spouse to see.
75   Now renneth she aweyward, now cometh she nere,
Yet from myn eye-sight she may not be.
Som wayte her pray to make hire flee,
I renne to-fore to fleme° hir fo.   *to drive to flight*
Retourn, my soule, ageyn to me,
80   *Quia amore langueo*.

"My swete spouse, lat us go pleye—
Apples ben ripe in my gardyn;
I shal thee clothe in newe array,
Thy mete shal be milk, hony, and wyne.
85   Now, dere soule, lete us go dyne—
Thy sustenaunce is in my scrippe,° lo!   *wallet, bag*
Tary not now, faire spouse myn,
    Quia amore langueo.

"If thou be foule I shal make thee clene;
90   If thou be sik I shal thee hele;
If thou aught murne I shal thee mene.°   *pity*
Spouse, why wyltow not wyth me dele?

Thou founde nevere love so lele.°   *loyal*
What wyltow, soule, that I shal do?
95   I may of unkyndenesse thee appele,°   *accuse*
    Quia amore langueo.

"What shal I do now wyth my spouse?
Abide I wol hir gentilnesse.
Wolde she loke ones out of hir hous
100   Of flesshly affecciouns and unclennesse,
Hir bed is made, hir bolster is in blisse,
Hir chambre is chosen, swiche are no mo.
Loke out at the wyndowes of kyndenesse,
    Quia amore langueo.

105   "My spouse is in chambre—hold thy pees!
Make no noise, but lat hire slepe.
My babe shal suffre no disese;
I may not here my dere child wepe;
For wyth my pappe I shal hire kepe.
110   No wonder thogh I tende hire to,
This hole in my side hadde nevere ben so depe,
    But *quia amore langueo.*

"Longe and love thou nevere so heighe,
Yet is my love more thanne thyn may be;
115   Thou gladdest, thou wepest, I sitte thee by;
Yet myghte thou, spouse, loke ones at me.
Spouse, sholde I alwey fede thee
Wyth childes mete? Nay, love, not so!
I wol preve° thy love wyth adversitee,   *prove*
120   *Quia amore langueo.*

"Wax not wery, myn owene dere wyf!
What mede is ay to lyve in confort?
For in tribulacioun I regne more rife
Ofter tymes thanne in desport;°   *amusement*
125   In welthe, in wo, evere I supporte.
Than, dere soule, go nevere me fro—
Thy mede is marked, whan thou art mort°   *dead*
    In blisse; *quia amore langueo.*"

In Praise of Women[1]

I am as lyght as any roe
To preyse wemen wher that I goo.

To onpreyse wemen yt were a shame,
For a woman was thy dame;
Our blessyd lady beryth the name
    of all women wher that they goo.

A woman ys a worthy thyng—
they do the washe and do the wrynge;
'lullay, lullay,' she dothe the synge,
    And yet she hath but care and woo.

A woman ys a worthy wyght,
she seruyth a man both daye and nyght,
therto she puttyth all her myght,
    And yet she hathe bot care and woo.

1. Feminists might regard this as an adequate description, but not much praise. Actually, the poet intends a serious plea to respect medieval women for their thankless tasks and difficult life.

The Fox and the Goose

'Pax uobis,' quod the ffox,[1]
'for I am comyn to toowne.'

It fell ageyns the next nyght
the fox yede° to with all his myghte, *went to work*
with-outen cole or candlelight,
 whan that he cam vnto the toowne.

5 Whan he cam all in the yarde,
soore te geys° wer ill a-ferde; *geese*
"I shall macke some of youre berde,[2]
 or that I goo from the toowne!'

whan he cam all in the croofte,
10 there he stalkyd wundirfull soofte;
'for here haue I be frayed° full ofte *frightened*
 whan that i haue come to toowne.'

he hente a goose all be the heye,° *eye*
faste the goos began to creye!
15 oowte yede men as they myght heye,
 and seyde, 'fals fox, ley it doowne!'

'Nay,' he saide, 'soo mot I the—
sche shall goo vnto the wode with me;
sche and I wnther a tre,
20 e-mange° the beryis browne. *among*

I haue a wyf, and sche lyeth seke;
many smale whelppis sche haue to eke—
many bonys they muste pike
 will they ley a-downe.'

Allas, Allas!

Allas, allas the while!
Thoghte I on no gile,
 So have I good chaunce.
Allas, allas the while —
 That evere I coude daunce!

Ledde I the daunce a mydsomer day;
I made smal trippes,° soth for-to seye. *steps in a dance*
Jak, oure holy water clerk, cam by the weye,
And he loked me upon, he thoghte that I was gay.
5 Thoghte I on no gile.

Jak, oure holy water clerk, the yonge strippelyng,° *youth*
For the chesoun of me° he cam to the ryng; *because of me*
And he tripped on my too° and made a twynkelyng°— *toe / wink*
Evere he cam neer, he spared for no thyng.
10 Thoghte I on no gile.

Jak, I wot, pryed° in my faire face; *searched*
He thoghte me worly,° so have I good grace. *attractive*
As we turnden oure daunce in a narwe place,
Jak bad me the mouth—a kissing ther was.
15 Thoghte I on no gile.

---

1. "Peace be with you." The fox often has clerical attributes and figures largely in anti-clerical, especially anti-fraternal, satire (Cf. Chaucer's *The Nun's Priest's Tale*).

2. "I shall beard some of you." I.e., "I'll get the best of some of you."

Jak tho bigan to roune° in myn ere,°   *whisper / ear*
"Loke that thou be privee and graunte that thou bere;
A paire white gloves I have to thy were."°   *wearing*
"Gramercy, Jak," that was myn answere.
20   Thoghte I on no gile.

Soon after evensong Jak me mette:
"Com hom after thy gloves that I thee bihete."°   *promise*
Whan I to his chambre cam, doun he me sette;
From him myghte I not go whan we were mette.
25   Thoghte I on no gile.

Shetes and chalones,° I wot, were i-spred;   *blankets*
For sothe tho Jak and I wenten to bed.
He priked and he praunced—nolde° he nevere lynne:°   *nor would / cease*
It was the muriest nyght that evere I cam inne.
30   Thoghte I on no gile.

Whan Jak hadde don tho he rong the belle;
Al nyght ther he made me to dwelle.
Oft, I trewe,° we hadden i-served the ragged devil of helle;   *suppose*
Of other smal bourdes° kepe I not to tell.   *frivolities*
35   Thoghte I on no gile.

The other day at pryme° I cam hom, as I wene,   *dawn*
Mete I my dame copped and kene:°   *peevish and sharp*
"Sey, thou stronge strompet, wher hastow ben?
Thy trippyng and thy daunsyng, wel it wol be sene!"
40   Thoghte I on no gile.

Evere by oon and by oon° my dame raughte me clout.[1]   *again and again*
Evere I bar it privee whil that I moghte,°   *might*
Til my girdel aros, my womb wex out:
"Yvele i-spun yerne° evere it wol out."   *ill-spun yarn*
45   Thoghte I on no gile.

Suddenly Terrified

Sodeynly affrayed, half wakyng, half slepyng,
And greetly dismayde, a womman sat wepyng.[1]

Wyth favour in hir face fer passyng my resoun,
And of hir sore wepyng this was the enchesoun:°   *occasion*
Hir sone in hir lappe lay, she seyde, slayn by tresoun.
If wepyng myghte ripe ben, it semed than in sesoun.
5   "Jhesu!" so she sobbed,
        So hir sone was bobbed°   *beaten*
        And of his lyf robbed;
Seying thise wordes, as I seye thee:
"Who can not wepe, come lerne at me."

10 I seyde I coude not wepe, I was so hard-herted.
She answerde me wyth wordes shortely that smerted:
"Lo, nature shal meve° thee, thou most be converted.   *move*
Thyn owene fader this nyght is deed," lo, thus she thwarted,°   *retorted*
        "So my sone is bobbed
15   And of his lyf robbed."
        For sothe than I sobbed,

1. "Every once in a while my mistress caught me a clout."

1. This poem (fifteenth-century) recounts a dream or   vision in which the persona sees the (Virgin) Mother of
                                                            Christ suddenly bereft.

Verifying the wordes she seyde to me:
Who can not wepe may lerne at thee.

20 "Now breek, herte, I thee preye! This cors lieth so rewely,°   *ruefully*
So beten, so wounded, entreted so Jewely,[2]
What wight may me biholde and wepe not? Non, trewely,
To see my dede dere sone lie bledyng, lo, this newely."
    Ay stille she sobbed
    So hir sone was bobbed
25   And of his lyf robbed,
Newyng the wordes, as I seye thee:
"Who can not wepe, come lerne at me."

On me she caste hir eye, seyde, "See, man, thy brother!"
She kiste him and seyde, "Swete, am I not thy moder?"
30 In swownyng° she fil ther, it wolde be non other.   *swooning*
I not° which more deedly, that oon or that other.   *know not*
    Yet she revived and sobbed
    So hir sone was bobbed
    And of his lyf robbed.
35 "Who can not wepe"—this was the laye°—   *refrain, song*
And wyth that word she vanisht awey.

Timor Mortis Conturbat Me

In what estat° so evere I be,   *circumstance*
Timor mortis conturbat me.[1]

As I went in a myrie morwenynge
I herde a brid° bothe wepe and synge;   *bird*
This was the tenour° of hir talkynge—   *substance*
Timor mortis conturbat me.

5 I axed that brid what she mente.
"I am a musket[2] bothe faire and gent;
For drede of deeth I am al shent:°   *undone, helpless*
Timor mortis conturbat me.

"Whan I shal deye I knowe no day,
10 What contree or place I can not seye;
Wher-fore this song synge I may—
Timor mortis conturbat me.

"Jhesu Crist, whan he sholde deye,
To his Fader he gan seye,
15 'Fader,' he seyde, 'in trinitee,
Timor mortis conturbat me.'

"Alle cristen peple biholde and see
This world is but a vanytee,
And repleet wyth necessitee.
20 *Timor mortis conturbat me.*

"Wake I or slepe, ete or drynke,
Whan I on my laste ende do thenke,
For greet fere° my soule doth shrynke: *fear*
Timor mortis conturbat me."

2. "Treated like a Jew"—the phrase is ironic as well as compassionate.

1. "The fear of death distresses." This Latin refrain occurs in a member of vernacular poems meant to cause people to consider the fragility of life.
2. *Musket* was a name for the male sparrowhawk.

25 God graunte us grace Him for-to serve,
  And be at oure ende when we sterve,°   *die*
  And from the feend° He us preserve!   *fiend, Satan*
  Timor mortis conturbat me.

Bryng Us in Good Ale![1]

Bryng us in good ale, and bryng us in good ale!
For oure blessed Ladies[2] sake, bryng us in good ale!

Bryng us in no broun breed, for that is made of bren,
Nor bryng us in no white breed, for ther-inne is no game—
  But bryng us in good ale.

Bryng us in no beef, for there is many bones,
5 But bryng us in good ale, for that goth doun at ones—
  And bryng us in good ale.

Bryng us in no bacoun, for that is passyng fat,
But bryng us in good ale, and yif us ynough of that—
  And bryng us in good ale.

10 Bryng us in no moton, for that is ofte lene,
Nor bryng us in no trypes, for they ben selden clene—
  But bryng us in good ale.

Bryng us in no eyren,° for ther are many shelles, *eggs*
But bryng us in good ale, and yif us no thyng elles—
15 And bryng us in good ale.

Bryng us in no butter, for ther-inne are many heres,
Nor bryng us in no pigges flessh, for that wyl make us bores—
  But bryng us in good ale.

Bryng us in no podynges, for ther-inne is al gotes blood,
20 Nor bryng us in no venysoun, for that is not for oure good—
  But bryng us in good ale.

Bryng us in no capons flessh, for that is often dere,° *expensive*
Nor byrng us in no dokes flessh, for they slobere in the mere,
  But bryng us in good ale.

ROBERT HENRYSON (1420–90)

The Complaint of Orpheus[1]

'O dulfull harp with mony dolly° stryng,   *jolly*
135 Turne all thi mirth and musik in murnyng,
  And ces of all thi subtell sangis sweit;
  Now wepe with me, thi lord and carefull° kyng, *full of care*
  Quhilk losit has in erd all his lyking;[2]
  And all thi game thow change in gule and greit,° *weeping and lamentation*
140 Thy goldin pynnis with thi teris weit,
  And all my pane for to report thow press,

---

1. A famous fifteenth-century student's drinking song (ca. 1470).
2. Deliberate ambiguity.

1. Adapted (ca. 1480) from the story of Orpheus, known to medieval audiences through the Latin versions of Boethius, Virgil, and Ovid, as well as other adaptations. Henryson was one of a group of poets known as the "Scottish Chaucerians."
2. "Who has lost everything on earth which pleased him."

Cryand with me in every steid° and streit: *place*
"Quhar art thou gane, my luf Erudices?"'

Him to rejos yit playit he a spryng,
145 Quhill all the foulis of the wod can syng,
And treis dansit with thair leves grene,
Him to devoid of his gret womenting:°   *lamenting*
Bot all in vane—thai comfort him nothing,
His hart was sa apon his lusty° quene;   *youthful*
150 The bludy teres sprang out of his eyne,
Thar was na solace mycht his sobbing ces,
Bot cryit ay with caris cald and kene:
'Quhar art thow gane, my luf Erudices?

'Fairweill my place, fairweile plesance and play,
155 And welcome woddis wyld and wilsome way,°   *bewildering paths*
My wikit werd° in wildernes to wair;³   *stewardship, rule*
My rob ryall and all my riche array
Changit sall be in rude russat of gray,
My diademe intill ane hat of hair;
160 My bed sall be with bever, broke and bair
In buskis bene with mony bustuous bes,⁴
Withoutin sang, saying with siching° sair: *sighing*
"Quhar art thow gane, my luf Erudices?"

'I the beseike, my fair fader Phebus,⁵
165 Have pete of thi awne sone Orpheus;
Wait thow nocht wele I am thi barne and childe?
Now heir my plant, panefull and petuous;
Direct me fra this deid sa dolorus,
Quhilk gois thus withoutin gilt begild;⁶
170 Lat nocht thi [face] with clowdis be [oursyld];
Len me thi licht, and lat me nocht ga les
To fynd the fair in fame that never was fyld,°   *fulfilled*
My lady, quene and luf Eurdices.

'O Jupiter, thow god celestial
175 And grantschir° to myself, on the I call   *grandfather*
To mend my murnyng and my drery mone;
Thow gif me fors that I nocht fant nor fall
Quhill I hir fynd; for seik hir suth I sall,
And nother stynt nor stand for stok nor stone.
180 Throw thi godhed gyde me quhar scho° is gone,   *she*
Gar° hir appeir and put myne hert in pes.'   *cause*
Thus King Orpheus with his harpe allone
Sore wepit for his wyf Erudices.

JOHN SKELTON (1460–1529)

To Mistress Anne

Mistress Anne,
I am your man,
As you may well espy.
If you will be
5 Content with me,
I am your man.

But if you will
Keep company still
With every knave that comes by,
10 Then you will be
Forsaken of me,
That am your man.

3. "My evil stewardship [weard] in the wilderness to spend."
4. "In protective bushes with many wild beasts."
5. Phoebus was the Roman sun-god.
6. "Who goes thus as one without guilt yet treated as guilty [beguiled]."

But if you fain,
I tell you plain,
15 If I presently shall die,
I will not such
As loves too much,
That am your man.

For if you can
20 Love every man
That can flatter and lie,
Then are ye
No match for me,
That am your man.

25 For I will not take
No such kind of make
(May all full well it try!),
But off will ye cast
At any blast,
30 That am your man.

Mannerly Margery Milk and Ale[1]

Ay, beshrew you! by my fay,°   *faith*
These wanton clerks be nice alway!
Avaunt, avaunt° my popinjay!   *boast*
What, will ye do nothing but play?
5   Tilly vally, straw, let be I say!
Gup, Christian Clout, gup, Jack of the Vale!
With Mannerly Margery Milk and Ale.

By God, ye be a pretty pode,°   *pudding*
And I love you an whole cart-load.
10 Straw, James Foder, ye play the fode,
I am no hackney for your rod:
Go watch a bull, your back is broad!
Gup, Christian Clout, gup, Jack of the Vale!
With Mannerly Margery Milk and Ale.

15 Ywis ye deal uncourteously;
What, would ye frumple° me? now fy!   *mock*
What, and ye shall be my pigesney?[2]
By Christ, ye shall not, no hardely:
I will not be japéd° bodily!   *tricked*
20 Gup, Christian Clout, gup, Jack of the Vale!
With Mannerly Margery Milk and Ale.

Walk forth your way, ye cost me nought;
Now have I found that I have sought:
The best cheap flesh that ever I bought.
25 Yet, for His love that all hath wrought,
Wed me, or else I die for thought.
Gup, Christian Clout, your breath is stale!
Go, Mannerly Margery Milk and Ale!
Gup, Christian Clout, gup, Jack of the Vale!
30 With Mannerly Margery Milk and Ale.

My Darling Dear, My Daisy Flower

With lullay, lullay, like a child,
Thou sleepest too long, thou art beguiled.

My darling dear, my daisy flower,
    Let me, quod he, lie in your lap.
Lie still, quod she, my paramour.
Lie still hardely, and take a nap.
5   His head was heavy, such was his hap,
All drowsy dreaming, drowned in sleep,
That of his love he took no keep.
    With hey lullay, lullay, like a child,
    Thou sleepest too long, thou art beguiled.

10 With ba, ba, ba! and bas, bas, bas!
    She cherished him both cheek and chin,
That he wist never where he was:
    He had forgotten all deadly sin.
    He wanted wit her love to win:
15 He trusted her payment and lost all his pay;
She left him sleeping and stole away.
    With hey lullay, lullay, like a child,
    Thou sleepest too long, thou art beguiled.

1. A nonsense song written during the period Skelton was made poet laureate in a ceremony at Oxford in the summer of 1488 attended by Henry VIII. This is a hearty song, set to music by William Cornish about 1492.
2. "Pig's-eye": a folk term of endearment; possibly also a flower, the trillium.

The rivers rough, the waters wan,
20   She spouréd not to wet her feet;
She waded over, she found a man
      That halséd° her heartily and kissed her sweet: *embraced*
      Thus after her cold she caught a heat.
My love, she said, routeth in his bed;
25 Ywis he hath an heavy head.
      With hey lullay, lullay, like a child,
      Thou sleepest too long, thou art beguiled.

What dreamest thou, drunkard, drowsy pate?
      Thy lust and liking is from thee gone;
30 Thou blinkard blowbowl, thou wakest too late,
      Behold thou liest, luggard, alone!
      Well may thou sigh, well may thou groan,
To deal with her so cowardly:
Ywis, pole hatchet, she bleared thine eye.[1]

JAMES RYMAN[1]

Revert, Revert

Revert, revert, revert, revert!
O synful man, yif me thyn herte.

Have mynde how I mankynde° have take   *human form*
Of a pure mayde, man, for thy sake,
That were most bounde most free to make.
      O synful man, yif me thyn herte.

5 Have mynde, thou synful creature,
I took baptesme in thy nature
From filthe of synne to make thee pure.
      O synful man, yif me thyn herte.

Have mynde, man, how I took the feeld,
10 Upon my bak beryng my sheeld;
For peyne ne deeth I wolde not yelde.
      O synful man, yif me thyn herte.

Have mynde, I was put on the rode
And for thy sake shedde myn herte blood;
15 Bihold my peyne—bihold my mood!
      O synful man, yif me thyn herte.

Bihold me, hed, hond, foot, and side!
Bihold my woundes five so wide!
Bihold the peyne that I abide!
20   O synful man, yif me thyn herte.

Have mynde, man, how faste I was bounde
For thy sake to a piler rounde,
Scourged til my blood fil to grounde.
      O synful man, yif me thyn herte.

1. "She did you in the eye."

1. James Ryman is one of the few authors of medieval lyrics about whom we know very much. He was a Franciscan, and Archbishop of Canterbury in the later part of the fifteenth century.

25   Have mynde how I in forme of breed
     Have left my flessh and blood to wedde°   *as a covenant*
     To make thee quik whan thou art deed.
        O synful man, yif me thyn herte.

     Have mynde, man, how I have thee wroght,
30   How wyth my blood I have thee boght,
     And how to blisse I have thee broght.
        O synful man, yif me thyn herte.

     O synful man, bihold and see
     What I have don and do for thee,
35   If thou wylt be in blisse wyth me.
        O synful man, yif me thyn herte.

     Bothe for my deeth and peynes smerte
     That I suffred for thy desserte[2]
     I axe namore, man, but thyn herte.
40   Revert, revert, revert, revert.

ANONYMOUS

Pennillion[1]

Bachgen wyf o bridd a lludw,	### Beer and the Inner Man

Beer and the Inner Man

Bachgen wyf o bridd a lludw,   I am made of ash and clay,
Yfodd llawer iawn o gwrw.   I've put a lot of beer away.
Rhyfedd yw, wrth yfed llawer,   Strange that all that liquids never
Nid ai'r pridd a'r ewrw'n forter.   Made in me a little mortar.

Gathering Bouquets

Mynd i'r ardd i dorri pwysi   I went out to pick a posy
Pasio'r lafant, pasio'r lili,   Passed the lavender, the lily,
Pasio'r pines a'r rhosys cochion,   Passed the pink and the red rose
Torri pwysi o ddanadl poethion.   Instead a bunch of nettles chose.

---

2. "On your account."   1. Fifteenth-century Welsh verse form.

WILLIAM DUNBAR[1]

Meditation in Winter

In to thir dirk and drublie° dayis,   *wet*
Quhone sabill° all the hevin arrayis   *sable*
   With mystie vapouris, cluddis, and skyis,
   Nature all curage me denyis
5 Off sangis, ballattis, and of playis.

Quhone that the nycht dois lenthin houris,
With wind, with haill, and havy schouris,
   My dule spreit dois lurk for schoir,°   *threatening*
   My hairt for languor dois foloir°   *perish*
10 For laik of symmer° with his flouris.   *summer*

I walk, I turne, sleip may I nocht,
I vexit am with havie thocht;
   This warld all ouir I cast about,
   And ay the mair I am in dout,
15 The mair that I remeid have socht.

I am assayit on everie syde:
Dispair sayis ay, "In tyme provyde
   And get sum thing quhairon to leif,[2]
   Or with grit trouble and mischeif
20 Thow sall in to this court abyd."

Than Patience sayis, "Be not agast:
Hald Hoip and Treuthe within the fast,
   And lat Fortoun wirk furthe hir rage,
   Quhome that no rasoun may assuage,
25 Quhill that hir glas be run and past."

And Prudence in my eir sayis ay,
"Quhy wald thow hald that will away?[3]
   Or craif° that thow may have no space,   *crave*
   Thow tending to ane uther place,
30 A journay going everie day?"

And than sayis Age, "My freind, cum neir,
And be not strange, I the requeir:
   Cum, brodir, by the hand me tak,
   Remember thow hes compt to mak
35 Off all thi tyme thow spendit heir."

Syne Deid castis upe his yettis° wyd,   *gates*
Saying, "Thir oppin° sall the abyd;   *thereupon*
   Albeid that thow wer never sa stout,
   Undir this lyntall° sall thow lowt:°   *lintel / bow down*
40 Thair is nane uther way besyde."

---

1. Like Henryson, Dunbar was a "Scottish Chaucerian" about whom little of a biographical nature is not conjectural. He is best known for his occasional and longer narrative poems, such as *The Goldyn Targe*. At one time he may have been a novitiate with the Franciscans.

2. "And get something in which to believe."

3. "Why do you try to hang on to that which, by Nature, will pass away?"

For feir of this all day I drowp;
No gold in kist,° nor wyne in cowp,   *chest*
　　No ladeis bewtie,° nor luiffis blys,[4]   *beauty*
　　May lat me to remember this,
45   How glaid that ever I dyne or sowp.

Yit, quhone the nycht begynnis to schort,
It dois my spreit sum pairt confort,
　　Off thocht oppressit with the schowris.
　　Cum, lustie symmer! with thi flowris,
50   That I may leif in sum disport.

ANONYMOUS

Corpus Christi Carol[1]

Lully, lullay, lully, lullay,[2]
The faucon° hath born my make° awey.   *falcon | mate*

He bar him up, he bar him down,
He bar him into an orchard broun.

In that orchard ther was an halle
That was hanged wyth purpre[3] and palle.[4]

And in that halle ther was a bed,
It was hanged wyth gold so red.[5]

And in that bed ther lieth a knight,
His woundes bledying day and nyght.

By that beddes side ther kneleth a may,
And she wepeth bothe nyght and day.

And by that beddes side ther stondeth a ston,
Corpus Cristi writen ther-on.[6]

---

4. "No ladies' beauty or hues of love."

1. This late fifteenth- or early sixteenth-century carol would have been sung with the initial *burden* or refrain following each stanza, to a four-line melody. It has, because of the falcon image, sometimes been attributed to events surrounding Henry VIII's banishment of Anne Boleyn, whose heraldic symbol was a white falcon. More likely, perhaps, is that the poem should be read according to more general allegorical values in which the ever-dying knight and his ever-weeping lady create a mysterious reciprocity of flowing tears and flowing blood, an image whose reference is clarified by the stone and its inscription in the last stanza.

2. This is a lullaby refrain.
3. Purple is a royal as well as penitential colour.
4. Rich cloth, canopy. Also, altar cloth or linen cloth with which the chalice is covered.
5. Gold is also royal and the colour of wisdom. When red-gold, it is often the colour of sacrifice.
6. (Latin) "The Body of Christ"—usually referring to the Sacrament in Holy Communion and to the Community of the Church, though initially to the Crucifixion.

Introduction: 1500–1660

"The Middle Ages produced nothing quite so medieval as the Renaissance." English poetry, of course, constitutes only one of the seething phenomena encompassed by the rubrics "Renaissance" and "Middle Ages," but it exemplifies both the validity and the limitations of this witty truism. Even a casual comparison of the selective sample from each of these periods in this collection reveals immediate, obvious differences of poetic form, the result of major developments in prosody during the sixteenth and seventeenth centuries. The influence of Middle English verse on this process was attenuated and largely submerged by a competing stream of models for mimetic adaptation flowing from classical sources through the methodological and conceptual filter of the Italian and French Humanists.

Sir Thomas Wyatt stands at the point where these currents cross. His songs, such as "Blame Not My Lute" and "My Lute, Awake!" in their simple stanzaic regularity and metre based on stressed syllables exemplify the remnant of Middle English prosody surviving into the sixteenth century, while his adaptations of Petrarch's sonnets inaugurate a new era of experimentation and discovery. Wyatt confronted major problems of transposition. Italian is inflected; English is not. Italian permits a poetic line of regular rhythm based on syllabic stress; English patterns of stress are irregular and largely independent of syllabic sequence. Petrarch's eleven-syllable line, therefore, was unsuitable for English sonnets, and Wyatt's compromise of intermingled rhythms based upon both stressed syllables and the accentuations of spoken English, while uneven and often awkward, effectively rediscovers Chaucer's iambic pentameter line, which had been lost through failure to recognize that the final "e" was pronounced in Middle English, and which became the normative metre in English poetry.

A succeeding generation of poets, led by Sidney and Spenser, faced similar problems as they struggled to make English an instrument equal to Italian and French in absorbing and developing the admired achievements of classical writers. Scores of verse forms and metres were invented, discarded, modified, elaborated, as one by one the classical modes of pastoral, satire, elegy, ode, and epic joined the erotic lyric in the harvest of genres realized from the potential of English. By the end of the sixteenth century, the resources of Elizabethan prosody included a range of stanzaic and metrical flexibility equal to the generic range demonstrated most graphically, perhaps, by comparing the simplicity of songs by Wyatt and Shakespeare with the complexity of Spenser's masterful schemes devised for *The Faerie Queene* and, especially, *Epithalamion*. Even the sonnet, that most prevalent and regular of Elizabethan forms, showed considerable schematic flexibility. Sidney adapted the Italian model divided into an octave, rhyming abba abba, and a sestet, rhyming cddc ee (with some variation); Shakespeare preferred the "English" sonnet of three quatrains and a couplet rhyming abab cdcd efef gg; Spenser developed a more demanding version with enlarged capacity for rhyme: abab bcbc cdcd ee. While the sonnet fell from favour in the seventeenth century, other types of lyric and other genres showed a similar capacity for structural diversity. The sustained melody and controlled, metrical precision of Jonson's verse contrasts markedly with Donne's irregular, dense, reverberative lines, which disrupt the smooth harmonies of iambic pentameter and exploit tensions between metric regularity and the abrupt, unpredictable rhythms of colloquial discourse. Herrick is one of those who followed Jonson's lead; Marvell and Herbert responded to Donne. Milton transcends classification with any group, but his heroic couplets and blank verse (unrhymed iambic pentameter) inform a dynamic marriage of English phrasing with Latinate structure which represents the crowning culmination to the long process of adaptive innovation begun by Wyatt.

Despite large differences in prosodic form created by this process, a common substratum founded on Latin culture and Christian tradition supports poets of both the Renaissance and the Middle Ages, and generates fundamental questions of common concern: "Who am I?" as an individual in a social complex; "Where am I?" in history and the natural order; "Why am I?" the ultimate puzzle of human purpose and destiny. Historical flux inevitably changes the context in which these issues are perceived, rendering the perspective of one epoch inappropriate for the next without negating either the validity of the questions or the imperative to seek answers. In English poetry, if the Middle Ages depicted its prototypical "seeker" as a "pilgrim," the Renaissance equivalent might be capsulized as a "courtier."

Humanism was the dominant intellectual movement of the Renaissance. It conceived of "courtship" as a ritualistic striving to overcome three essential types of perceived estrangement: between the sexes, between social classes, and between orders of Being. Each of these separations generates its own response, but the social hierarchy, with the sovereign at its apex as the ultimate object of courtship, was the model for erotic and mystical courtship, with the loved one and God as the respective hierarchical ultimates. As sources of poetic structure and image, the three hierarchies are equivalent in function, therefore interchangeable. The resulting flexibility produced a high degree of allegorical density in Renaissance art, especially literature, and allowed the simultaneous representation of Man as a sociopolitical, erotic, and religious questor, driven by the complex interactions of reason, will, and passion (the corresponding hierarchy of the individual psyche) to court an elusive and sometimes perversely conceived ideal. Spenser's Redcrosse in Book I of *The Faerie Queene* is perhaps the clearest example of such a multi-faceted questor, and Milton's Satan in *Paradise Lost* epitomizes the perverse antithesis.

Even in works less explicitly allegorical, however, readers can discern the same intermingling of erotic, social, and mystical motives. Sidney's Astrophil, for example, courts Stella through his verse ostensibly as an erotic ideal; but an accumulation of imagery gives her attributes of reason, sovereignty, the muse of artistic inspiration, the locus of "honour" or communal values, and an icon of Divinity. Thus Sidney, like Spenser and Shakespeare, uses the lyric form of the sonnet to explore "love" as the impetus to "courtship," and thereby to reveal its corresponding range of implications from sexual passion to civil and spiritual communion. Donne's sonnets, addressed to God, and his songs, addressed to a lady, both use the strategies of seductive courtship, and both inform, through paradoxical tension, Man's conflicting desires for, and tendency to confuse, the sacred and the profane. In varying degrees, explicitly or implicitly, this paradox also gives both ethical and emotional resonance to the work of Herbert, Marvell, Jonson, and Herrick.

Indeed, Renaissance poets generally are themselves "courtiers" in the Humanist image, seeking to emulate the formal accomplishments of their exemplars from the past and, through a rich texture of allusion to contemporary, classical, and biblical sources, to court a defining model of human possibilities within a large cultural vision. At the core of this vision, however, stands a figure of ambiguous potential, poised in the moral creation between angel and animal, good and evil, capable of moving in either direction by his free volition and acts of rational choice. The many ramifications of that ambiguity are the subject and the substance of major Renaissance poetry.

Michael F. N. Dixon

SIR THOMAS WYATT (1503–42)

My Galley Chargèd with Forgetfulness

My galley[1] chargèd with forgetfulness
   Through sharp seas, in winter night doth pass
   Tween rock and rock; and eke[2] mine enemy, alas,
   That is my lord steereth with cruelness.
And every oar a thought in readiness,
   As though that death were light in such a case.[3]
   An endless wind doth tear the sail apace
   Of forcèd sighs and trusty fearfulness.
A rain of tears, a cloud of dark disdain,
   Hath done the wearied cords[4] great hinderance,
   Wreathed with error and eke with ignorance.
The stars be hid that led me to this pain
   Drownèd is reason that should me consort,
   And I remain despairing of the port.

Whoso List to Hunt

Whoso list[1] to hunt, I know where is an hind,
   But as for me alas, I may no more—
   The vain travail hath wearied me so sore,
   I am of them that farthest cometh behind.
Yet may I, by no means, my wearied mind
   Draw from the deer, but as she fleeth afore,
   Fainting I follow. I leave off therefore,
   Since in a net I seek to hold the wind.
Who list her hunt, I put him out of doubt,
   As well as I, may spend his time in vain.
   And graven with diamonds in letters plain
There is written her fair neck round about:
   '*Noli me tangere*,[2] for Caesar's[3] I am,
   And wild for to hold, though I seem tame.'

My Lute, Awake!

My lute, awake! Perform the last
Labour that thou and I shall waste,
And end that I have now begun:
For when this song is sung and past,
5 My lute, be still, for I have done.

As to be heard where ear is none,
As lead to grave in marble stone,
My song may pierce her heart as soon.[1]
Should we then sigh or sing or moan?
10 No, no, my lute, for I have done.

The rocks do not so cruelly
Repulse the waves continually
As she my suit and affectiòn,
So that I am past remedy,
15 Whereby my lute and I have done.

Proud of the spoil that thou hast got
Of simple hearts, thorough love's shot,
By whom, unkind,[2] thou hast them won—
Think not he hath his bow forgot,
20 Although my lute and I have done.

1. The extended metaphor of the individual as a ship navigating the treacherous seas of life, needing reason at the helm for safe passage, was derived by Wyatt from Petrarch and became a commonplace in Renaissance literature.
2. Also.
3. I.e., as if death were inconsequential.
4. Rigging.

1. Wishes.
2. Touch me not.
3. This poem reputedly concerns Anne Boleyn, who became mistress to Henry VIII ("Caesar") in 1526.

1. I.e., her heart will be touched when sound is heard with no ears to listen and soft lead carves ("graves") hard marble.
2. Unnatural.

Vengeance shall fall on thy disdain
That makest but game on earnest pain.
Think not alone under the sun,
Unquit,[3] to cause thy lovers plain,[4]
25   Although my lute and I have done.

Perchance thee lie withered and old
The winter nights that are so cold,
Plaining in vain unto the moon.
Thy wishes then dare not be told.
30   Care then who list,[5] for I have done.

And then may chance thee to repent
The time that thou hast lost and spent
To cause thy lovers sigh and swoon.
Then shalt thou know beauty but lent,
35   And wish and want as I have done.

Now cease, my lute. This is the last
Labour that thou and I shall waste,
And ended is that we begun.
Now is this song both sung and past;
40   My lute, be still, for I have done.

Blame Not My Lute

Blame not my lute, for he must sound
Of this or that as liketh me,
For lack of wit the lute is bound
To give such tunes as pleaseth me.
5   Though my songs be somewhat strange
And speaks such words as touch thy change,
Blame not my lute.

My lute, alas, doth not offend,
Though that perforce he must agree
10   To sound such tunes as I intend,
To sing to them that heareth me.
Then, though my songs be somewhat plain,
And toucheth some that use to feign,[1]
Blame not my lute.

15   My lute and strings may not deny
But as I strike they must obey:
Break not them then so wrongfully,
But wreak[2] thyself some wiser way.
And though the songs which I indite[3]
20   Do quit[4] thy change with rightful spite,
Blame not my lute.

Spite asketh spite and changing change,
And falsèd faith must needs be known.
The fault so great, the case so strange,
25   Of right it must abroad be blown.[5]
Then since that by thine own desért[6]
My songs do tell how true thou art,
Blame not my lute.

Blame but thyself that hast misdone
30   And well deservèd to have blame.
Change thou thy way so evil begun
And then my lute shall sound that same.
But if till then my fingers play,
By thy desért, their wonted way,
35   Blame not my lute.

Farewell, unknown, for though thou brake
My strings in spite, with great disdain,
Yet have I found out for thy sake
Strings for to string my lute again.
40   And if perchance this foolish rhyme
Do make thee blush at any time,
Blame not my lute.

SIR PHILIP SIDNEY (1554–86)

From Astrophil and Stella

1[1]

Loving in truth, and fain[2] in verse my love to show,   A
   That[3] she (dear She) might take some pleasure of my pain: B
   Pleasure might cause her read, reading might make her know,   A
   Knowledge might pity win, and pity grace obtain;   B

3. Unrevenged.
4. To lament.
5. Likes.

1. Habitually are deceitful.
2. Avenge.
3. Compose.
4. Requite.

5. Broadcast.
6. Deserving.

1. With this sonnet, Sidney introduces the hexameter line
to English poetry. He experiments with it in five other
sonnets and his *Arcadia*.
2. Desiring.
3. I.e., "so that."

I sought fit words to paint the blackest face of woe, *A*
    Studying inventions fine, her wits to entertain: *B*
    Oft turning others' leaves, to see if thence would flow *A*
    Some fresh and fruitful showers upon my sun-burn'd brain. *B*

But words came halting forth, wanting Invention's stay,[4] *C*
    Invention, Nature's child, fled step-dame Study's blows, *D*
    And others' feet still seem'd but strangers in my way. *C*

Thus, great with child to speak, and helpless in my throes, *D*
    Biting my truant pen, beating myself for spite— *E*
    "Fool," said my Muse to me, "look in thy heart[5] and write." *E*

5

It is most true, that eyes are form'd to serve *A*
    The inward light; and that the heavenly part[1] *B*
    Ought to be king, from whose rules who do swerve,[2] *A*
    Rebels to Nature, strive for their own smart.[3] *B*

It is most true, what we call Cupid's dart, *B*
    An image is, which for ourselves we carve; *C*
    And, fools, adore in temple of our heart, *B*
    Till that good god make Church and churchman starve. *C*

True, that true beauty virtue is indeed, *D*
    Whereof this beauty can be but a shade, *E*
    Which elements with mortal mixture breed:[4] *D*

True, that on earth we are but pilgrims made, *E*
    And should in soul up to our country move: *F*
    True, and yet true that I must Stella love. *F*

14

Alas have I not pain enough, my friend,[1] *A*
    Upon whose breast a fiercer gripe doth tire,[2] *B*
    Than did on him who first stale down the fire,[3] *B*
    While Love on me doth all his quiver spend, *A*

But with your rhubarb[4] words you must contend, *A*
    To grieve me worse, in saying that desire *B*
    Doth plunge my well-form'd soul even in the mire *B*
    Of sinful thoughts, which do in ruin end? *A*

4. "Crutch," support.
5. Locus of the passions. What Astrophil finds in his "heart," of course, is not Stella, but an image fashioned by his desire and frustration.

1. Intellect, the rational faculty.
2. I.e., "those who swerve."
3. Pain, punishment.
4. In Platonism, all material things composed of "elements" (earth, air, fire, water) are subject to change and decay. Consequently, they represent imperfect imitations, or shadows ("but a shade"), of an immutable, perfect Idea or "Form." Beauty, Virtue, and Truth are examples of such "Forms": indeed, the first thirteen lines constitute a series of concessions to major tenets in the doctrine of rational love central to neo-Platonism, a Christianized adaptation of Plato's thought.

1. One of a series of sonnets in which Astrophil addresses a "friend" who apparently speaks for the neo-Platonic view of love outlined in Sonnet 5.
2. I.e., "fiercer grasp does tear."
3. Prometheus stole fire from the gods to save mankind from destruction. In punishment, he was chained to a rocky, mountainous summit by Zeus, who sent a vulture to devour his liver, which regenerated itself each day and was devoured again daily.
4. Bitter, used as a purgative.

If that be sin which doth the manners[5] frame,
  Well stayed with truth in word and faith of deed,
  Ready of wit and fearing nought but shame:

If that be sin which in fix'd hearts doth breed
  A loathing of all loose unchastity,
  Then love is sin, and let me sinful be.

31

With how sad steps, oh Moon, thou climb'st the skies,
  How silently, and with how wan a face.
  What, may it be, that even in heav'nly place
  That busy archer[1] his sharp arrows tries?

Sure, if that long with Love acquainted eyes
  Can judge of Love, thou feel'st a lover's case;
  I read it in thy looks; thy languish'd grace
  To me that feel the like, thy state descries.

Then ev'n of fellowship, oh Moon, tell me
  Is constant love deem'd there but want of wit?
  Are beauties there as proud as here they be?

Do they above love to be lov'd, and yet
  Those lovers scorn whom that Love doth possess?
  Do they call virtue there ungratefulness?

64

No more, my dear, no more these counsels try,
  Oh give my passions leave to run their race:
  Let Fortune lay on me her worst disgrace,
  Let folk o'ercharg'd with brain against me cry,

Let clouds bedim my face, break in mine eye,
  Let me no steps but of lost labor trace,
  Let all the earth with scorn recount my case,
  But do not will me from my love to fly.

I do not envy Aristotle's wit,
  Nor do aspire to Caesar's bleeding fame;
  Nor aught do care, though some above me sit;

Nor hope, nor wish another course to frame,
  But that which once may win thy cruel heart:
  Thou art my wit, and thou my virtue art.

71

Who will in fairest book of Nature know
  How Virtue may best lodg'd in beauty be;
  Let him but learn of Love to read in thee,
  Stella, those fair lines which true goodness show.

---

5. Code of virtuous social behaviour.   1. Cupid.

There shall he find all vices' overthrow,
  Not by rude force, but sweetest sovereignty
  Of reason, from whose light those night birds[1] flee;
  That inward sun in thine eyes shineth so.

And not content to be Perfection's heir
  Thyself, dost strive all minds that way to move,
  Who mark in thee what is in thee most fair.

So while thy beauty draws the heart to love,
  As fast thy virtue bends that love to good:
  "But ah," Desire still cries, "give me some food."

Eighth Song[1]

In a grove most rich of shade,
Where birds wanton music made,
May, then young, his pied weeds[2] showing,   35
New perfumed with flowers growing,

5 Astrophil with Stella sweet
Did for mutual comfort meet,
Both within themselves oppressed,
But each in the other blessed.   40

Him great harms had taught much care,
10 Her fair neck a foul yoke bare;
But her sight his cares did banish,
In his sight her yoke did vanish.

Wept they had, alas the while,   45
But now tears themselves did smile,
15 While their eyes by love directed,
Interchangeably reflected.

Sigh they did, but now betwixt
Sighs of woe were glad sighs mix'd,   50
With arms cross'd, yet testifying
20 Restless rest, and living dying.

Their ears hungry of each word,
Which the dear tongue would afford,
But their tongues restrained from walking   55
Till their hearts had ended talking,

25 But when their tongues could not speak,
Love itself did silence break;
Love did set his lips asunder,
Thus to speak in love and wonder: 60

"Stella, sovereign of my joy,
30 Fair triumpher of annoy,[3]
Stella star of heavenly fire,
Stella loadstone of desire;

"Stella, in whose shining eyes
Are the lights of Cupid's skies,
Whose beams where they once are darted,
Love therewith is straight imparted;

"Stella, whose voice when it speaks,
Senses all asunder breaks;
Stella, whose voice when it singeth,
Angels to acquaintance bringeth;

"Stella, in whose body is
Writ each character of bliss,
Whose face all, all beauty passeth,
Save thy mind, which yet surpasseth:

"Grant, oh grant—but speech alas,
Fails me, fearing on to pass—
Grant, oh me, what am I saying?
But no fault there is in praying.

"Grant, oh dear, on knees I pray,"
(Knees on ground he then did stay)
"That not I, but since I love you,
Time and place for me may move you.

"Never season was more fit,
Never room more apt for it;
Smiling air allows my reason,
These birds sing, 'Now use the season.'

"This small wind which so sweet is,
See how it the leaves doth kiss;
Each tree in his best attiring,
Sense of love to love inspiring.

"Love makes earth the water drink,
Love to earth makes water sink;
And if dumb things be so witty,
Shall a heavenly grace want pity?"

1. E.g., owls and ravens, emblems of vice.

1. One of a series of "songs" appearing between Sonnets 85 and 86 in the Folio edition of *Astrophil and Stella* (1598). Here Sidney provides our only view of the lovers from a perspective other than that of Astrophil. Its trochaic metrical form is derived from Chaucer's comically inept "Tale of Sir Topas" in the *Canterbury Tales*.
2. Multi-coloured garments.
3. I.e., victor over grief.

65   There his hands in their speech, fain
      Would have made tongue's language plain;
      But her hands his hands repelling,
      Gave repulse all grace excelling.

      Then she spake; her speech was such
70   As not ear but heart did touch:
      While such wise she love denied,
      As yet love she signified.

      "Astrophil," said she, "my love,
      Cease in these effects to prove:
75   Now be still, yet still believe me,
      Thy grief more than death would grieve me.

      "If that any thought in me
      Can taste comfort but of thee,
      Let me, fed with hellish anguish,
80   Joyless, hopeless, endless languish.

      "If those eyes you praised, be
      Half so dear as you to me,
      Let me home return, stark blinded
      Of those eyes, and blinder minded.[4]

85   "If to secret of my heart
      I do any wish impart
      Where thou art not foremost placed,
      Be both wish and I defaced.

      "If more may be said, I say,
90   All my bliss in thee I lay;
      If thou love, my love content thee,
      For all love, all faith is meant thee.

      "Trust me, while I thee deny,
      In myself the smart I try;
95   Tyrant Honour doth thus use thee
      Stella's self might not refuse thee.

      "Therefore, dear, this no more move,
      Lest, though I leave not thy love,
      Which too deep in me is framed,
100   I should blush when thou art named."

      Therewithal away she went,
      Leaving him so passion-rent
      With what she had done and spoken,
      That therewith my song is broken.

107

Stella, since thou so right[1] a princess art
    Of all the powers which life bestows on me,
    That ere by them aught undertaken be
    They first resort unto that sovereign part;[2]

Sweet, for a while give respite to my hart,
    Which pants as though it still should leap to thee,
    And on my thoughts give thy lieutenancy[3]
    To this great cause, which needs both use and art.[4]

And as a queen, who from her presence sends
    Whom she employs, dismiss from thee my wit,
    Till it have wrought what thy own will attends.

On servant's shame oft master's blame doth sit;
    Oh let not fools in me thy works reprove,
    And scorning say, "See what it is to love."

108[1]

When sorrow (using mine own fire's might)
    Melts down his lead into my boiling breast;
    Through that dark furnace to my heart oppress'd
    There shines a joy from thee, my only light;

4. I.e., mind more blinded.

1. True.
2. Stella identified with "that sovereign part," i.e., reason
(cf. Sonnet 5, ll. 2–3).

3. I.e., place my thoughts under your command. Deputize
my mind.
4. I.e., both experience and knowledge.

1. Final sonnet in the cycle.

But soon as thought of thee breeds my delight,
    And my young soul flutters to thee his nest,
    Most rude despair, my daily unbidden guest,
    Clips straight my wings, straight wraps me in his night,

And makes me then bow down my head and say,
    "Ah, what doth Phoebus'[2] gold that wretch avail
    Whom iron doors do keep from use of day?"

So strangely (alas) thy works in me prevail,
    That in my woes for thee thou art my joy
    And in my joys for thee my only annoy.

EDMUND SPENSER (1552–99)

From The Faerie Queene

Book I, Canto i

The Patron of true Holinesse,
Foule Errour doth defeate:
Hypocrisie him to entrape,
Doth to his home entreate.

A gentle Knight was pricking[1] on the plaine,
    Ycladd in mightie armes and siluer shielde,
    Wherein old dints of deepe wounds did remaine,
    The cruell markes of many' a bloudy fielde;
    Yet armes till that time did he neuer wield:[2]
    His angry steede did chide his foming bitt,
    As much disdayning to the curbe to yield:
    Full iolly knight he seemd, and faire did sitt,
As one for knightly giusts[3] and fierce encounters fitt.

2

But on his brest a bloudie Crosse he bore,
    The deare remembrance of his dying Lord,
    For whose sweet sake that glorious badge he wore,
    And dead as liuing euer him ador'd:
    Vpon his shield the like was also scor'd,
    For soueraine hope, which in his helpe he had:
    Right faithfull true he was in deede and word,
    But of his cheere[4] did seeme too solemne sad;[5]
Yet nothing did he dread, but euer was ydrad.[6]

3

Vpon a great aduenture he was bond,[7]
    That greatest *Gloriana* to him gaue,
    That greatest Glorious Queene of *Faerie* lond,
    To winne him worship,[8] and her grace to haue,
    Which of all earthly things he most did craue;
    And euer as he rode, his hart did earne[9]

2. An epithet for Apollo, particularly in his role as sun-god.

1. Cantering.
2. Redcrosse is an untested knight wearing borrowed armour. In a letter to Sir Walter Raleigh, Spenser identifies the significance of the armour in an allusion to Eph. vi. 10–22: "put on the whole armour of God, that ye may be able to stand against the wiles of the devil."
3. Jousts.
4. Facial expression.
5. Serious.
6. Feared.
7. Bound.
8. Honour.
9. Yearn.

To proue his puissance in battell braue
Vpon his foe, and his new force to learne;
Vpon his foe, a Dragon horrible and stearne.

4

A louely Ladie rode him faire beside,
Vpon a lowly Asse more white then snow,
Yet she much whiter, but the same did hide
Vnder a vele,[10] that wimpled[11] was full low,
And ouer all a blacke stole she did throw,
As one that inly mourned: so was she sad,
And heauie sat vpon her palfrey slow;
Seemed in heart som hidden care she had,
And by her in a line a milke white lambe she lad.[12]

5

So pure an innocent, as that same lambe,
She was in life and euery vertuous lore,
And by descent from Royall lynage came
Of ancient Kings and Queenes, that had of yore
Their scepters stretcht from East to Westerne shore,
And all the world in their subiection held;
Till that infernall feend[13] with foule vprore
Forwasted all their land, and them expeld:
Whom to auenge, she had this Knight from far compeld.[14]

6

Behind her farre away a Dwarfe did lag,
That lasie[15] seemd in being euer last,
Or wearied with bearing of her bag
Of needments at his backe. Thus as they past,
The day with cloudes was suddeine ouercast,
And angry *Ioue* an hideous storme of raine
Did poure into his Lemans[16] lap so fast,
That euery wight[17] to shrowd[18] it did constrain,
And this faire couple eke[19] to shroud themselues were fain.

7

Enforst to seeke some couert nigh at hand,
A shadie groue not far away they spide,
That promist ayde the tempest to withstand:
Whose loftie trees yclad with sommers pride,
Did spred so broad, that heauens light did hide,
Not perceable with power of any starre:
And all within were pathes and alleies wide,
With footing worne, and leading inward farre:
Faire harbour that them seemes;[20] so in they entred arre.

8

And foorth they passe, with pleasure forward led,
Ioying to heare the birds sweete harmony,
Which therein shrouded from the tempest dred,
Seemd in their song to scorne the cruel sky.

10. Veil.
11. Folded.
12. Lead.
13. I.e., the Dragon, an allegorization of evil.
14. In his letter to Raleigh, Spenser explains that Una had come to the court of Gloriana seeking help for her parents, beseiged in their castle by the Dragon. Redcrosse, a country boy untrained in the arts of knighthood, begged to be given the task. Because it was the time of an annual twelve-day festival, the Queen was bound by tradition to grant his request.
15. Lazy.
16. Paramour, i.e., the Earth.
17. Creature.
18. Cover.
19. Also.
20. It seems to them.

Much can[21] they prayse the trees so straight and hy,[22]
    The sayling Pine, the Cedar proud and tall,
    The vine-prop Elme, the Poplar neuer dry,
    The builder Oake, sole king of forrests all,
The Aspine good for staues, the Cypresse funerall.

9

The Laurell, meed[23] of mightie Conquerours
    And Poets sage, the Firre that weepeth still,
    The Willow worne of forlorne Paramours,
    The Eugh[24] obedient to the benders will,
    The Birch for shaftes,[25] the Sallow for the mill,
    The Mirrhe sweete bleeding in the bitter wound,
    The warlike Beech, the Ash for nothing ill,
    The fruitfull Oliue, and the Platane[26] round,
The caruer Holme,[27] the Maple seeldom inward sound.

10

Led with delight, they thus beguile the way,
    Vntill the blustring storme is ouerblowne;
    When weening[28] to returne, whence they did stray,
    They cannot finde that path, which first was showne,
    But wander too and fro in wayes vnknowne,
    Furthest from end then, when they neerest weene,
    That makes them doubt, their wits be not their owne:
    So many pathes, so many turnings seene,
That which of them to take, in diuerse doubt they been.

11

At last resoluing forward still to fare,
    Till that some end they finde or[29] in or out,
    That path they take, that beaten seemd most bare,
    And like to lead the labyrinth about;[30]
    Which when by tract[31] they hunted had throughout,
    At length it brought them to a hollow caue,
    Amid the thickest woods. The Champion stout
    Eftsoones dismounted from his courser braue,
And to the Dwarfe a while his needlesse spere he gaue.

12

Be well aware, quoth then that Ladie milde,
    Least suddaine mischiefe ye too rash prouoke:
    The danger hid, the place vnknowne and wilde,
    Breedes dreadfull doubts: Oft fire is without smoke,
    And perill without show: therefore your stroke
    Sir knight with-hold, till further triall made.
    Ah Ladie (said he) shame were to reuoke
    The forward footing for[32] an hidden shade:[33]
Vertue giues her selfe light, through darknesse for to wade.

13

Yea but (quoth she) the perill of this place
    I better wot then you, though now too late
    To wish you backe returne with foule disgrace,

21. Did, began.
22. The catalogue of trees, or "topos of the mixed grove,"
is a conventional device in Classical and Medieval, as well
as Renaissance, poetry. It appears as early as Ovid's
Metamorphoses. Spenser's immediate inspiration may
have been Chaucer's *Parlement of Foules*, 176–82.
23. Reward.
24. Yew.
25. Arrows.

26. Plane-tree.
27. Holly, or holm-oak.
28. Supposing.
29. Either.
30. Through, out of.
31. I.e., by following the track.
32. Because of.
33. Shadow.

Yet wisedome warnes, whilest foot is in the gate,
To stay the steppe, ere forced to retrate.
This is the wandring wood, this *Errours den*,
A monster vile, whom God and man does hate:
Therefore I read[34] beware. Fly fly (quoth then
The fearefull Dwarfe:) this is no place for liuing men.

14

But full of fire and greedy hardiment,[35]
The youthfull knight could not for ought be staide,
But forth vnto the darksome hole he went,
And looked in: his glistring armor made
A litle glooming light, much like a shade,
By which he saw the vgly monster plaine,
Halfe like a serpent horribly displaide,
But th'other halfe did womans shape retaine,[36]
Most lothsom, filthie, foule, and full of vile disdaine.

15

And as she lay vpon the durtie ground,
Her huge long taile her den all ouerspred,
Yet was in knots and many boughtes[37] vpwound,
Pointed with mortall sting. Of her there bred
A thousand yong ones, which she dayly fed,
Sucking vpon her poisonous dugs, eachone
Of sundry shapes, yet all ill fauored:
Soone as that vncouth light vpon them shone,
Into her mouth they crept, and suddain all were gone.

16

Their dam vpstart, out of her den effraide,[38]
And rushed forth, hurling her hideous taile
About her cursed head, whose folds displaid
Were stretcht now forth at length without entraile.[39]
She lookt about, and seeing one in mayle
Armed to point,[40] sought backe to turne againe;
For light she hated as the deadly bale,[41]
Ay wont in desert darknesse to remaine,
Where plaine none might her see, nor she see any plaine.

17

Which when the valiant Elfe[42] perceiu'd, he lept
As Lyon fierce vpon the flying pray,
And with his trenchand blade her boldly kept
From turning backe, and forced her to stay:
Therewith enrag'd she loudly gan to bray,
And turning fierce, her speckled taile aduaunst,
Threatning her angry sting, him to dismay:
Who nought aghast, his mightie hand enhaunst:[43]
The stroke down from her head vnto her shoulder glaunst.

18

Much daunted with that dint,[44] her sence was dazd,
Yet kindling rage, her selfe she gathered round,
And all attonce her beastly body raizd

34. Advise.
35. Boldness.
36. Such monsters, compounded of human and animal, are common in both medieval romance and classical epic. *Errour*, combining the generative qualities of woman and the demonic power to deceive of Biblical serpents (cf. Gen. iii.1–6; Rev. ix.7–10), represents false doctrine.
37. Coils.
38. Affrighted.
39. Winding, twisting.
40. Head to foot.
41. Evil.
42. A knight of Faerie Land.
43. Raised.
44. Blow, stroke.

With doubled forces high aboue the ground:
Tho[45] wrapping vp her wrethed sterne[46] arownd,
Lept fierce vpon his shield, and her huge traine
All suddenly about his body wound,
That hand or foot to stirre he stroue in vaine:
God helpe the man so wrapt in *Errours* endlesse traine.

19

His Lady sad to see his sore constraint,
    Cride out, Now now Sir knight, shew what ye bee,
    Add faith vnto your force and be not faint:
    Strangle her, else she sure will strangle thee.
    That when he heard in great perplexitie,
    His gall did grate for griefe and high disdaine,
    And knitting all his force got one hand free,
    Wherewith he grypt her gorge[47] with so great paine,
That soone to loose her wicked bands did her constraine.

20

Therewith she spewd out of her filthy maw
    A floud of poyson horrible and blacke,
    Full of great lumpes of flesh and gobbets raw,
    Which stunck so vildly, that it forst him slacke
    His grasping hold, and from her turne him backe:
    Her vomit full of bookes and papers[48] was,
    With loathly frogs and toades, which eyes did lacke,[49]
    And creeping sought way in the weedy gras:
Her filthy parbreake[50] all the place defiled has.

21

As when old father *Nilus* gins to swell
    With timely[51] pride aboue the *Aegyptian* vale,
    His fattie[52] waues do fertile slime outwell,
    And ouerflow each plaine and lowly dale:
    But when his later spring gins to auale,[53]
    Huge heapes of mudd he leaues, wherein there breed
    Ten thousand kindes of creatures, partly male
    And partly female of his fruitfull seed;
Such vgly monstrous shapes elswhere may no man reed.[54]

22

The same so sore annoyed has the knight,
    That welnigh choked with the deadly stinke,
    His forces faile, ne can no longer fight.
    Whose corage when the feend perceiu'd to shrinke,
    She poured forth out of her hellish sinke
    Her fruitfull cursed spawne of serpents small,
    Deformed monsters, fowle, and blacke as inke,
    Which swarming all about his legs did crall,
And him encombred sore, but could not hurt at all.

---

45. Then.
46. Coiled tail.
47. Throat.
48. A topical reference to the flood of violent politico-religious controversy and propaganda issued in pamphlets during the 1580s and 1590s. Modern readers, however, subjected to electronic as well as printed bombardment, may readily emphathize with the predicament of Redcrosse.
49. Cf. Rev. xvi.13: "And I saw three unclean spirits like frogs come out of the mouth of the dragon, and out of the mouth of the beast, and out of the mouth of the false prophet."
50. Vomit.
51. Seasonal.
52. Fecund.
53. Subside.
54. See.

23

As gentle Shepheard in sweete euen-tide,
  When ruddy *Phœbus* gins to welke[55] in west,
  High on an hill, his flocke to vewen wide,
  Markes which do byte their hasty supper best;
  A cloud of combrous gnattes do him molest,
  All striuing to infixe their feeble stings,
  That from their noyance he no where can rest,
  But with his clownish[56] hands their tender wings
He brusheth oft, and oft doth mar their murmurings.

24

Thus ill bestedd,[57] and fearefull more of shame,
  Then of the certaine perill he stood in,
  Halfe furious vnto his foe he came,
  Resolv'd in minde all suddenly to win,
  Or soone to lose, before he once would lin;[58]
  And strooke at her with more then manly force,
  That from her body full of filthie sin
  He raft[59] her hatefull head without remorse;
A streame of cole black bloud forth gushed from her corse.

25

Her scattred brood, soone as their Parent deare
  They saw so rudely falling to the ground,
  Groning full deadly, all with troublous feare,
  Gathred themselues about her body round,
  Weening their wonted entrance to haue found
  At her wide mouth: but being there withstood
  They flocked all about her bleeding wound,
  And sucked vp their dying mothers blood,
Making her death their life, and eke[60] her hurt their good.

26

That detestable sight him much amazde
  To see th'vnkindly Impes of heauen accurst,
  Deuoure their dam; on whom while so he gazd,
  Hauing all satisfide their bloudy thurst,
  Their bellies swolne he saw with fulnesse burst,
  And bowels gushing forth: well worthy end
  Of such as drunke her life, the which them nurst;
  Now needeth him no lenger labour spend,
His foes haue slaine themselues, with whom he should contend.

27

His Ladie seeing all, that chaunst, from farre
  Approcht in hast to greet his victorie,
  And said, Faire knight, borne vnder happy starre
  Who see your vanquisht foes before you lye:
  Well worthy be you of that Armorie,[61]
  Wherein ye haue great glory wonne this day,
  And proou'd your strength on a strong enimie,
  Your first aduenture: many such I pray,
And henceforth euer wish, that like succeed it may.

28

Then mounted he vpon his Steede againe,
  And with the Lady backward sought to wend;
  That path he kept, which beaten was most plaine,

---

55. Sink, set.
56. Rustic.
57. Positioned.
58. Rest, stop.

59. Cut off.
60. Also.
61. I.e., the Christian armour.

Ne euer would to any by-way bend,
But still did follow one vnto the end,
The which at least out of the wood them brought.
So forward on his way (with God to[62] frend)
He passed forth, and new aduenture sought;
Long way he trauelled, before he heard of ought.

29

At length they chaunst to meet vpon the way
An aged Sire, in long blacke weedes yclad,[63]
His feete all bare, his beard all hoarie gray,
And by his belt his booke he hanging had;
Sober he seemde, and very sagely sad,
And to the ground his eyes were lowly bent,
Simple in shew, and voyde of malice bad,
And all the way he prayed, as he went,
And often knockt his brest, as one that did repent.

30

He faire the knight saluted, louting[64] low,
Who faire him quited,[65] as that courteous was:
And after asked him, if he did know
Of straunge aduentures, which abroad did pas.
Ah my deare Sonne (quoth he) how should, alas,
Silly[66] old man, that liues in hidden cell,
Bidding his beades all day for his trespas,
Tydings of warre and worldly trouble tell?
With holy father sits not with such things to mell.[67]

31

But if of daunger which hereby doth dwell,
And homebred euill ye desire to heare,
Of a straunge man I can you tidings tell,
That wasteth all this countrey farre and neare.
Of such (said he) I chiefly do inquere,
And shall you well reward to shew the place,
In which that wicked wight his dayes doth weare:[68]
For to all knighthood it is foule disgrace,
That such a cursed creature liues so long a space.

32

Far hence (quoth he) in wastfull wildernesse
His dwelling is, by which no liuing wight
May euer passe, but thorough great distresse.
Now (sayd the Lady) draweth toward night,
And well I wote, that of your later[69] fight
Ye all forwearied be: for what so strong,
But wanting rest will also want of might?
The Sunne that measures heauen all day long,
At night doth baite[70] his steedes the *Ocean* wau emong.

33

Then with the Sunne take Sir, your timely rest,
And with new day new worke at once begin:
Vntroubled night they say giues counsell best.
Right well Sir knight ye haue aduised bin,
(Quoth then that aged man;) the way to win
Is wisely to aduise: now day is spent;

---

62. As.
63. Clothed in long, black garments.
64. Bowing.
65. Answered, requited.
66. Simple, innocent.

67. Meddle.
68. Spend.
69. Recent.
70. Refresh.

Therefore with me ye may take vp your In[71]
For this same night. The knight was well content:
So with that godly father to his home they went.

34

A little lowly Hermitage it was,
    Down in a dale, hard by a forests side,
    Far from resort of people, that did pas
    In trauell to and froe: a little wyde[72]
    There was an holy Chappell edifyde,[73]
    Wherein the Hermite dewly wont[74] to say
    His holy things each morne and euentyde:
    Thereby a Christall streame did gently play,
Which from a sacred fountaine welled forth alway.

35

Arriued there, the little house they fill,
    Ne looke for entertainement, where none was:
    Rest is their feast, and all things at their will;
    The noblest mind the best contentment has.
    With faire discourse the euening so they pas:
    For that old man of pleasing wordes had store,
    And well could file his tongue as smooth as glas;
    He told of Saintes and Popes, and euermore
He strowd an *Aue-Mary* after and before.

36

The drouping Night thus creepeth on them fast,
    And the sad humour[75] loading their eye liddes,
    As messenger of *Morpheus*[76] on them cast
    Sweet slombring deaw, the which to sleepe them biddes.
    Vnto their lodgings then his guestes he riddes:[77]
    Where when all drownd in deadly sleepe[78] he findes,
    He to his study goes, and there amiddes
    His Magick bookes and artes of sundry kindes,
He seekes out mighty charmes, to trouble sleepy mindes.

37

Then choosing out few wordes most horrible,
    (Let none them read) thereof did verses frame,
    With which and other spelles like terrible,
    He bad awake blacke *Plutoes* griesly Dame,[79]
    And cursed heauen, and spake reprochfull shame
    Of highest God, the Lord of life and light;
    A bold bad man, that dar'd to call by name
    Great *Gorgon*, Prince of darknesse and dead night,
At which *Cocytus* quakes, and *Styx*[80] is put to flight.

38

And forth he cald out of deepe darknesse dred
    Legions of Sprights, the which like little flyes
    Fluttring about his euer damned hed,
    A-waite whereto their seruice he applyes,
    To aide his friends, or fray[81] his enimies:
    Of those he chose out two, the falsest twoo,
    And fittest for to forge true-seeming lyes;
    The one of them he gaue a message too,
The other by him selfe staide other worke to doo.

71. Lodging.
72. Apart.
73. Built.
74. Was wont.
75. Heavy dew.
76. God of sleep.

77. Leads.
78. Death-like sleep. Sleep and Death were mythical twins, sons of Night.
79. I.e., Proserpine.
80. Cocytus and Styx are rivers in Hades.
81. Frighten and attack.

39

He making speedy way through spersed[82] ayre,
   And through the world of waters wide and deepe,
   To *Morpheus* house doth hastily repaire.
   Amid the bowels of the earth full steepe,
   And low, where dawning day doth neuer peepe,
   His dwelling is; there *Tethys*[83] his wet bed
   Doth euer wash, and *Cynthia*[84] still doth steepe
   In siluer deaw his euerdrouping hed,
Whiles sad Night ouer him her mantle black doth spred.

40

Whose double gates he findeth locked fast,
   The one faire fram'd of burnisht Yuory,
   The other all with siluer ouercast;[85]
   And wakefull dogges before them farre do lye,
   Watching to banish Care their enimy,
   Who oft is wont to trouble gentle Sleepe.
   By them the Sprite doth passe in quietly,
   And vnto *Morpheus* comes, whom drowned deepe
In drowsie fit he findes: of nothing he takes keepe.[86]

41

And more, to lulle him in his slumber soft,
   A trickling streame from high rocke tumbling downe
   And euer-drizling raine vpon the loft,
   Mixt with a murmuring winde, much like the sowne
   Of swarming Bees, did cast him in a swowne:
   No other noyse, nor peoples troublous cryes,
   As still are wont t'annoy the walled towne,
   Might there be heard: but carelesse Quiet lyes,
Wrapt in eternall silence farre from enemyes.

42

The messenger approaching to him spake,
   But his wast[87] wordes returnd to him in vaine:
   So sound he slept, that nought mought him awake.
   Then rudely he him thrust, and pusht with paine,
   Whereat he gan to stretch: but he againe
   Shooke him so hard, that forced him to speake.
   As one then in a dreame, whose dryer braine[88]
   Is tost with troubled sights[89] and fancies weake,
He mumbled soft, but would not all his silence breake.

43

The Sprite then gan more boldly him to wake,
   And threatned vnto him the dreaded name
   Of *Hecate:*[90] whereat he gan to quake,
   And lifting vp his lumpish head, with blame
   Halfe angry asked him, for what he came.
   Hither (quoth he) me *Archimago*[91] sent,
   He that the stubborne Sprites can wisely tame,
   He bids thee to him send for his intent
A fit false dreame, that can delude the sleepers sent.[92]

---

82. Dispersed.
83. Wife of Oceanus.
84. I.e., Diana, goddess of the moon.
85. In Homer's *Odyssey*, XIX.562–67, a gate of horn releases true visions and a gate of ivory releases false visions. Cf. Virgil, *Aeneid*, VI.893–96.
86. Notice.
87. Wasted.

88. In antique physiology, people who slept lightly were thought to lack normal moisture in the brain.
89. Visions.
90. Fearsome Queen of Hades, i.e., Proserpine.
91. Lit. "original magician," primal creator of false illusions. Spenser calls him "Hypocrisie" in the Argument to Canto i (l. 3).
92. Senses.

44

The God obayde, and calling forth straight way
   A diuerse dreame out of his prison darke,
   Deliuered it to him, and downe did lay
   His heauie head, deuoide of carefull carke,[93]
   Whose sences all were straight benumbd and starke.
   He backe returning by the Yuorie dore,
   Remounted vp as light as chearefull Larke,
   And on his litle winges the dreame he bore
In hast vnto his Lord, where he him left afore.

45

Who all this while with charmes and hidden artes,
   Had made a Lady of that other Spright,
   And fram'd of liquid ayre her tender partes
   So liuely,[94] and so like in all mens sight,
   That weaker[95] sence it could haue rauisht quight:
   The maker selfe[96] for all his wondrous witt,
   Was nigh beguiled with so goodly sight:
   Her all in white he clad, and ouer it
Cast a blacke stole, most like to seeme for *Vna*[97] fit.

46

Now when that ydle dreame was to him brought,
   Vnto that Elfin knight he bad him fly,
   Where he slept soundly void of euill thought,
   And with false shewes abuse his fantasy,[98]
   In sort as[99] he him schooled priuily:
   And that new creature borne without her dew,[100]
   Full of the makers guile, with vsage sly
   He taught to imitate that Lady trew,
Whose semblance she did carrie vnder feigned hew.

47

Thus well instructed, to their worke they hast,
   And comming where the knight in slomber lay,
   The one vpon his hardy head him plast,
   And made him dreame of loues and lustfull play,
   That nigh his manly hart did melt away,
   Bathed in wanton blis and wicked ioy:
   Then seemed him his Lady by him lay,
   And to him playnd,[101] how that false winged boy,[102]
Her chast hart had subdewd, to learne Dame pleasures toy.

48

And she her selfe of beautie soueraigne Queene,
   Faire *Venus* seemde vnto his bed to bring
   Her, whom he waking euermore did weene,
   To be the chastest flowre, that ay[103] did spring
   On earthly braunch, the daughter of a king,
   Now a loose Leman[104] to vile seruice bound:
   And eke the *Graces* seemed all to sing,
   Hymen iō Hymen,[105] dauncing all around,
Whilst freshest *Flora*[106] her with Yuie[107] girlond crownd.

---

93. Anxiety.
94. Life-like.
95. Too weak.
96. Himself, i.e., Archimago.
97. "One," or "Unity," echoing Latin *Una Vera Fides*, "one true faith." She is called "Truth" in the Argument to Canto ii.
98. Imagination.
99. In the way that.
100. Born unnaturally.

101. Complained.
102. I.e., Cupid.
103. Ever.
104. Paramour.
105. A call to physical consummation of marriage. Hymen was god of marriage.
106. Goddess of flowers.
107. Ivy was sacred to Bacchus, and emblematic of wantonness.

49

In this great passion of vnwonted lust,
  Or wonted feare of doing ought amis,
  He started vp, as seeming to mistrust
  Some secret ill, or hidden foe of his:
  Lo there before his face his Lady is,
  Vnder blake stole hyding her bayted hooke,
  And as halfe blushing offred him to kis,
  With gentle blandishment and louely looke,
Most like that virgin true, which for her knight him took.

50

All cleane[108] dismayd to see so vncouth sight,
  And halfe enraged at her shamelesse guise,
  He thought haue slaine her in his fierce despight:[109]
  But hasty heat tempring with sufferance wise,
  He stayde his hand, and gan himselfe aduise
  To proue[110] his sense, and tempt her faigned truth.
  Wringing her hands in wemens pitteous wise,
  Tho can[111] she weepe, to stirre vp gentle ruth,[112]
Both for her noble bloud, and for her tender youth.

51

And said, Ah Sir, my liege Lord and my loue,
  Shall I accuse the hidden cruell fate,
  And mightie causes wrought in heauen aboue,
  Or the blind God, that doth me thus amate,[113]
  For hoped loue to winne me certaine hate?
  Yet thus perforce he bids me do, or die.
  Die is my dew: yet rew[114] my wretched state
  You, whom my hard auenging destinie
Hath made iudge of my life or death indifferently.

52

Your owne deare sake forst me at first to leaue
  My Fathers kingdome, There she stopt with teares;
  Her swollen hart her speach seemd to bereaue,
  And then againe begun, My weaker yeares
  Captiu'd to fortune and frayle worldly feares,
  Fly to your faith for succour and sure ayde:
  Let me not dye in languor and long teares.
  Why Dame (quoth he) what hath ye thus dismayd?
What frayes ye, that were wont to comfort me affrayd?

53

Loue of your selfe, she said, and deare constraint
  Lets me not sleepe, but wast the wearie night
  In secret anguish and vnpittied plaint,
  Whiles you in carelesse sleepe are drowned quight.
  Her doubtfull words made that redoubted knight
  Suspect her truth: yet since no'vntruth he knew,
  Her fawning loue with foule disdainefull spight
  He would not shend,[115] but said, Deare dame I rew,
That for my sake vnknowne such griefe vnto you grew.

108. Completely.
109. Indignation.
110. Test.
111. Began.

112. Compassion.
113. Dismay.
114. Pity.
115. Reject.

54

Assure your selfe, it fell not all to ground;
　　For all so deare as life is to my hart,
　　I deeme your loue, and hold me to you bound;
　　Ne let vaine feares procure your needlesse smart,[116]
　　Where cause is none, but to your rest depart.
　　Not all content, yet seemd she to appease[117]
　　Her mournefull plaintes, beguiled of her art,
　　And fed with words, that could not chuse but please,
So slyding softly forth, she turnd as to her ease.

55

Long after lay he musing at her mood,
　　Much grieu'd to thinke that gentle Dame so light,
　　For whose defence he was to shed his blood.
　　At last dull wearinesse of former fight
　　Hauing yrockt a sleepe his irkesome spright,[118]
　　That troublous dreame gan freshly tosse his braine,
　　With bowres, and beds, and Ladies deare delight:
　　But when he[119] saw his labour all was vaine,
With that misformed spright he backe returnd againe.

From Book I, Canto ix

21

So as they[1] traueild, lo they gan espy
　　An armed knight towards them gallop fast,
　　That seemed from some feared foe to fly,
　　Or other griesly thing, that him agast.[2]
　　Still as he fled, his eye was backward cast,
　　As if his feare still followed him behind;
　　Als flew his steed, as he his bands had brast,[3]
　　And with his winged heeles did tread the wind,
As he had been a fole of *Pegasus* his kind.[4]

22

Nigh as he drew, they might perceiue his head
　　To be vnarmd, and curld vncombed heares
　　Vpstaring[5] stiffe, dismayd with vncouth dread;
　　Nor drop of bloud in all his face appeares
　　Nor life in limbe: and to increase his feares,
　　In fowle reproch[6] of knighthoods faire degree,[7]
　　About his neck an hempen rope he weares,[8]
　　That with his glistring armes does ill agree;
But he of rope or armes has now no memoree.

23

The *Redcrosse* knight toward him crossed fast,
　　To weet, what mister[9] wight was so dismayd:
　　There him he finds all sencelesse and aghast,
　　That of him selfe he seemd to be afrayd;
　　Whom hardly he from flying forward stayd,

---

116. Pain.
117. Cease.
118. Spirit.
119. I.e., Archimago.

1. I.e., Redcrosse and Una.
2. Horrified.

3. Burst.
4. I.e., like Pegasus, the winged horse of Greek mythology.
5. Standing on end.
6. Disgrace.
7. Status.
8. The rope suggests attempted suicide.
9. Sort of.

Till he these wordes to him deliuer might;
 Sir knight, aread who hath ye thus arayd,
 And eke from whom make ye this hasty flight:
For neuer knight I saw in such misseeming[10] plight.

24

He answered nought at all, but adding new
 Feare to his first amazment, staring wide
 With stony eyes, and hartlesse hollow hew,
 Astonisht stood, as one that had aspide
 Infernall furies, with their chaines vntide.
 Him yet againe, and yet againe bespake
 The gentle knight; who nought to him replide,
 But trembling euery ioynt did inly quake,
And foltring tongue at last these words seemd forth to shake.

25

For Gods deare loue, Sir knight, do me not stay;
 For loe he comes, he comes fast after mee.
 Eft[11] looking backe would faine haue runne away;
 But he him forst to stay, and tellen free
 The secret cause of his perplexitie:
 Yet nathemore[12] by his bold hartie speach,
 Could his bloud-frosen hart emboldned bee,
 But through his boldnesse rather feare did reach,
Yet forst, at last he made through silence suddein breach.

26

And am I now in safetie sure (quoth he)
 From him, that would haue forced me to dye?
 And is the point of death now turnd fro mee,
 That I may tell this haplesse history?
 Feare nought: (quoth he) no daunger now is nye.
 Then shall I you recount a ruefull cace,
 (Said he) the which with this vnlucky eye
 I late beheld, and had not greater grace
Me reft from it, had bene partaker of the place.[13]

27

I lately chaunst (Would I had neuer chaunst)
 With a faire knight to keepen companee,
 Sir *Terwin* hight,[14] that well himselfe aduaunst
 In all affaires, and was both bold and free,
 But not so happie as mote happie bee:
 He lou'd, as was his lot, a Ladie gent,[15]
 That him againe lou'd in the least degree:[16]
 For she was proud, and of too high intent,
And ioyd[17] to see her louer languish and lament.

28

From whom returning sad and comfortlesse,
 As on the way together we did fare,
 We met that villen (God from him me blesse[18])
 That cursed wight, from whom I scapt whyleare,[19]

10. Unseemly.
11. Again.
12. Not at all.
13. I.e., shared the same fate.
14. Named.

15. Noble.
16. Loved not at all.
17. Enjoyed.
18. Protect.
19. Recently.

A man of hell, that cals himselfe *Despaire*:[20]
Who first vs greets, and after faire areedes[21]
Of tydings strange, and of aduentures rare:
So creeping close, as Snake in hidden weedes,
Inquireth of our states, and of our knightly deedes.

29

Which when he knew, and felt our feeble harts
Embost with bale,[22] and bitter byting griefe,
Which loue had launched with his deadly darts,
With wounding words and terms of foule repriefe,
He pluckt from vs all hope of due reliefe,
That earst vs held in loue of lingring life;
Then hopelesse hartlesse gan the cunning thiefe
Perswade vs die, to stint[23] all further strife:
To me he lent this rope, to him a rustie knife.

30

With which sad instrument of hastie death,
That wofull louer, loathing lenger light,
A wide way made to let forth liuing breath.
But I more fearefull, or more luckie wight,
Dismayd with that deformed dismall sight,
Fled fast away, halfe dead with dying feare:[24]
Ne yet assur'd of life by you, Sir knight,
Whose like infirmitie like chaunce may beare:
But God you neuer let his charmed speeches heare.

31

How may a man (said he)[25] with idle speach
Be wonne, to spoyle the Castle of his health?
I wote (quoth he) whom triall late did teach,
That like would not[26] for all this worldes wealth:
His[27] subtill tongue, like dropping honny, mealt'h[28]
Into the hart, and searcheth euery vaine,
That ere one be aware, by secret stealth
His powre is reft, and weakenesse doth remaine.
O neuer Sir desire to try his guilefull traine.

32

Certes (said he) hence shall I neuer rest,
Till I that treachours art haue heard and tride;
And you Sir knight, whose name mote[29] I request,
Of grace do me vnto his cabin guide.
I that hight *Treuisan* (quoth he) will ride
Against my liking backe, to doe you grace:
But nor for gold nor glee will I abide
By you, when ye arriue in that same place;
For leuer[30] had I die, then see his deadly face.

33

Ere long they come, where that same wicked wight
His dwelling has, low in an hollow caue,
Farre vnderneath a craggie clift ypight,[31]
Darke, dolefull, drearie, like a greedie graue,

20. Despair is, theologically, the only unforgiveable
Christian sin because, by its very nature, despair negates
hope. Those who cannot believe in the possibility of
redemption cannot be redeemed. *Despaire* is the last
figure of evil encountered by Redcrosse prior to his battle
with the Dragon, a structural placement appropriate to
his status as the ultimate Christian sin.
21. Tells.
22. Weakened with sorrow.

23. End.
24. Fear of death.
25. I.e., Redcrosse.
26. I.e., would not do the like again.
27. I.e., Despaire's.
28. Melts.
29. Might.
30. Rather.
31. Placed.

That still for carrion carcases doth craue:
On top whereof aye dwelt the ghastly Owle,
Shrieking his balefull note, which euer draue
Farre from that haunt all other chearefull fowle;
And all about it wandring ghostes did waile and howle.

34

And all about old stockes and stubs of trees,
Whereon nor fruit, nor leafe was euer seene,
Did hang vpon the ragged rocky knees;[32]
On which had many wretches hanged beene,
Whose carcases were scattered on the greene,
And throwne about the cliffs. Arriued there,
That bare-head knight for dread and dolefull teene,[33]
Would faine haue fled, ne durst approchen neare,
But th'other forst him stay, and comforted in feare.

35

That darkesome caue they enter, where they find
That cursed man, low sitting on the ground,
Musing full sadly in his sullein mind;
His griesie lockes, long growen, and vnbound,
Disordred hong about his shoulders round,
And hid his face; through which his hollow eyne
Lookt deadly dull, and stared as astound;
His raw-bone cheekes through penurie and pine,[34]
Were shronke into his iawes, as he did neuer dine.

36

His garment nought but many ragged clouts,[35]
With thornes together pind and patched was,
The which his naked sides he wrapt abouts;
And him beside there lay vpon the gras
A drearie corse, whose life away did pas,
All wallowd in his owne yet luke-warme blood,
That from his wound yet welled fresh alas;
In which a rustie knife fast fixed stood,
And made an open passage for the gushing flood.

37

Which piteous spectacle, approuing trew[36]
The wofull tale that *Treuisan* had told,
When as the gentle *Redcrosse* knight did vew,
With firie zeale he burnt in courage bold,
Him to auenge, before his bloud were cold,
And to the villein said, Thou damned wight,
The author of this fact, we here behold,
What iustice can but iudge against thee right,
With thine owne bloud to price[37] his bloud, here shed in sight.

38

What franticke fit (quoth he) hath thus distraught
Thee, foolish man, so rash a doome[38] to giue?
What iustice euer other iudgement taught,
But he should die, who merites not to liue?

32. Crags.
33. Grief.
34. Famine.
35. Strips of cloth.

36. Confirming.
37. Pay for.
38. Judgement.

None else to death this man despayring driue,[39]
But his owne guiltie mind deseruing death.
Is then vniust to each his due to giue?
Or let him die, that loatheth liuing breath?
Or let him die at ease, that liueth here vneath?[40]

39

Who trauels by the wearie wandring way,
　To come vnto his wished home in haste,
　And meetes a flood, that doth his passage stay,
　Is not great grace to helpe him ouer past,
　Or free his feet, that in the myre sticke fast?
　Most enuious man, that grieues at neighbours good,
　And fond,[41] that ioyest in the woe thou hast,
　Why wilt not let him passe, that long hath stood
Vpon the banke, yet wilt thy selfe not passe the flood?

40

He there does now enioy eternall rest
　And happie ease, which thou doest want and craue,
　And further from it daily wanderest:
　What if some litle paine the passage haue,
　That makes fraile flesh to feare the bitter waue?
　Is not short paine well borne, that brings long ease,
　And layes the soule to sleepe in quiet graue?
　Sleepe after toyle, port after stormie seas,
Ease after warre, death after life does greatly please.

41

The knight much wondred at his suddeine wit,
　And said, The terme of life is limited,
　Ne may a man prolong, nor shorten it;
　The souldier may not moue from watchfull sted,[42]
　Nor leaue his stand, vntill his Captaine bed.[43]
　Who life did limit by almightie doome,
　(Quoth he)[44] knowes best the terms established;
　And he, that points the Centonell his roome,[45]
Doth license him depart at sound of morning droome.[46]

42

Is not his deed, what euer thing is donne,
　In heauen and earth? did not he all create
　To die againe? all ends that was begonne.
　Their times in his eternall booke of fate
　Are written sure, and haue their certaine date.
　Who then can striue with strong necessitie,
　That holds the world in his[47] still chaunging state,
　Or shunne the death ordaynd by destinie?
When houre of death is come, let none aske whence, nor why.

43

The lenger life, I wote the greater sin,
　The greater sin, the greater punishment:
　All those great battels, which thou boasts to win,
　Through strife, and bloud-shed, and auengement,
　Now praysd, hereafter deare thou shalt repent:

39. Drove.
40. Uneasily.
41. Foolish.
42. Post.
43. Bids, commands.

44. I.e., Despaire.
45. Station.
46. Drum.
47. Its.

For life must life, and bloud must bloud repay.
Is not enough thy euill life forespent?
For he, that once hath missed the right way,
The further he doth goe, the further he doth stray.

44

Then do no further goe, no further stray,
  But here lie downe, and to thy rest betake,
  Th'ill to preuent, that life ensewen may.[48]
  For what hath life, that may it loued make,
  And guies not rather cause it to forsake?
  Feare, sicknesse, age, losse, labour, sorrow, strife,
  Paine, hunger cold that makes the hart to quake;
  And euer fickle fortune rageth rife,
All which, and thousands mo[49] do make a loathsome life.

45

Thou wretched man, of death hast greatest need,
  If in true ballance thou wilt weigh thy state:
  For neuer knight, that dared warlike deede,
  More lucklesse disauentures did amate:[50]
  Witnesse the dongeon deepe,[51] wherein of late
  Thy life shut vp, for death so oft did call;
  And though good lucke[52] prolonged hath thy date,[53]
  Yet death then, would the like mishaps forestall,
Into the which hereafter thou maiest happen fall.

46

Why then doest thou, O man of sin, desire
  To draw thy dayes forth to their last degree?
  Is not the measure of thy sinfull hire[54]
  High heaped vp with huge iniquitie,
  Against the day of wrath,[55] to burden thee?
  Is not enough, that to this Ladie milde
  Thou falsed hast thy faith with periurie,
  And sold thy selfe to serue *Duessa*[56] vilde,[57]
With whom in all abuse thou hast thy selfe defilde?

47

Is not he iust, that all this doth behold
  From highest heauen, and beares an equall[58] eye?
  Shall he thy sins vp in his knowledge fold,
  And guiltie be of thine impietie?
  Is not his law, Let euery sinner die:
  Die shall all flesh? what then must needs be donne,
  Is it not better to doe willinglie,
  Then linger, till the glasse be all out ronne?
Death is the end of woes: die soone, O faeries sonne.

48. I.e., to prevent the evil that will come in later life.
49. More.
50. Amass.
51. Redcrosse is overcome in battle by the giant, Orgoglio, an allegorization of spiritual pride, and imprisoned in the giant's dungeon (Canto vii–viii).
52. What Despaire attributes to chance ("good lucke") was, in fact, an act of Providential purpose. Redcrosse was released from Orgoglio's dungeon by Prince Arthur, represented as Divine Grace, and by Una, the personification of revealed Truth (Canto viii).
53. Term of life.
54. Service.
55. Day of Judgement.
56. Trusting the evidence of his deluded senses, Redcrosse accepts the false vision of Una as a harlot created by Archimago and deserts her. He then comes under the influence of her antithesis, Duessa, whose physical beauty disguises moral ugliness. She seduces Redcrosse successively into worldly pride, concupiscence, and spiritual pride.
57. Vile.
58. Impartial.

48

The knight was much enmoued with his speach,
   That as a swords point through his hart did perse,
   And in his conscience made a secret breach,
   Well knowing true all, that he did reherse,[59]
   And to his fresh remembrance did reuerse[60]
   The vgly vew of his deformed crimes,
   That all his manly powres it did disperse,
   As[61] he were charmed with inchaunted rimes,
That oftentimes he quakt, and fainted oftentimes.

49

In which amazement, when the Miscreant
   Perceiued him to wauer weake and fraile,
   Whiles trembling horror did his conscience dant,[62]
   And hellish anguish did his soule assaile,
   To driue him to despaire, and quite to quaile,
   He shew'd him painted in a table[63] plaine,
   The damned ghosts, that doe in torments waile,
   And thousand feends that doe them endlesse paine
With fire and brimstone, which for euer shall remaine.

50

The sight whereof so thoroughly him dismaid,
   That nought but death before his eyes he saw,
   And euer burning wrath before him laid,
   By righteous sentence of th'Almighties law:
   Then gan the villein him to ouercraw,[64]
   And brought vnto him swords, ropes, poison, fire,
   And all that might him to perdition draw;
   And bad him choose, what death he would desire:
For death was due to him, that had prouokt Gods ire.

51

But when as none of them he saw him take,
   He to him raught[65] a dagger sharpe and keene,
   And gaue it him in hand: his hand did quake,
   And tremble like a leafe of Aspin greene,
   And troubled bloud through his pale face was seene
   To come, and goe with tydings from the hart,
   As it a running messenger had beene.
   At last resolu'd to worke his finall smart,
He lifted vp his hand, that backe againe did start.

52

Which when as *Vna* saw, through euery vaine
   The crudled[66] cold ran to her well of life,[67]
   As in a swowne: but soone reliu'd[68] againe,
   Out of his hand she snatcht the cursed knife,
   And threw it to the ground, enraged rife,[69]
   And to him said, Fie, fie, faint harted knight,
   What meanest thou by this reprochfull strife?
   Is this the battell, which thou vauntst to fight
With that fire-mouthed Dragon, horrible and bright?

59. Recount.
60. Bring back.
61. As if.
62. Daunt.
63. Picture.
64. Exult over, crow over.

65. Reached.
66. Congealing.
67. Heart.
68. Revived.
69. Deeply.

53

Come, come away, fraile, feeble, fleshly wight,
    Ne let vaine words bewitch thy manly hart,
    Ne diuelish thoughts dismay thy constant[70] spright.
    In heauenly mercies hast thou not a part?
    Why shouldst thou then despeire, that chosen art?
    Where iustice growes, there grows eke greater grace,
    The which doth quench the brond[71] of hellish smart,
    And that accurst hand-writing doth deface.[72]
Arise, Sir knight arise, and leaue this cursed place.[73]

54

So vp he rose, and thence amounted streight.
    Which when the carle[74] beheld, and saw his guest
    Would safe depart, for all his subtill sleight,[75]
    He chose an halter from among the rest,
    And with it hung himselfe, vnbid[76] vnblest.
    But death he could not worke himselfe thereby;
    For thousand times he so himselfe had drest,[77]
    Yet nathelesse it could not doe him die,[78]
Till he should die his last, that is eternally.

From Amoretti

Sonnet 8

More then[1] most faire, full of the living fire,
Kindled above unto the maker neere:
No eyes but joyes, in which al powers conspire,
That to the world naught else be counted deare.
Thrugh your bright beames doth not the blinded guest,[2]
Shoot out his darts to base affections wound:
But Angels come to lead fraile mindes to rest
In chast desires on heavenly beauty bound.[3]
You frame my thoughts and fashion me within,
You stop my toung, and teach my hart to speake,
You calme the storme that passion did begin,
Strong thrugh[4] your cause, but by your vertue[5] weak.
Dark is the world, where your light shined never;
Well is he borne,[6] that may behold you ever.

---

70. Eternal.
71. Brand.
72. Blot out.
73. Despaire's fundamental rhetorical strategy has been to suppress Mercy as an element of Divine Judgement and to stress Justice alone. Una need only supply the concealed term to undermine the whole elaborate edifice of Despaire's propaganda.
74. Churl, villain.
75. Deceptive adroitness.
76. Unprayed for.

77. Attempted.
78. I.e., could not kill him.

1. Than.
2. I.e., Cupid.
3. Seeking. In neo-Platonic thought, the mind seeks to transcend temporal, earthly beauties and to comprehend ideal or absolute Beauty.
4. Through, because of.
5. Physical powers.
6. Both "born" and "supported."

Sonnet 34

Lyke as a ship that through the ocean wyde,
By conduct of some star doth make her way,
Whenas a storme hath dimd her trusty guyde,
Out of her course doth wander far astray.
So I whose star, that wont with her bright ray,
Me to direct, with cloudes is overcast,
Doe wander now in darknesse and dismay,
Through hidden perils round about me plast.[1]
Yet hope I well, that when this storme is past
My Helice[2] the lodestar[3] of my lyfe
Will shine again, and looke on me at last,
With lovely light to cleare my cloudy grief.
Till then I wander carefull[4] comfortlesse,
In secret sorow and sad pensivenesse.

Sonnet 54

Of this worlds theatre in which we stay,
My love like the spectator ydly sits
Beholding me that all the pageants play,
Disguysing diversly my troubled wits.
Sometimes I joy when glad occasion fits,
And mask in myrth lyke to a comedy:
Soone after when my joy to sorrow flits,
I waile and make my woes a tragedy.
Yet she, beholding me with constant eye,
Delights not in my merth nor rues my smart:[1]
But when I laugh she mocks, and when I cry
She laughs and hardens evermore her heart.
What then can move her? if nor[2] merth nor mone,[3]
She is no woman, but a sencelesse stone.

[Handwritten annotation: He is on the stage but she is simply watching dully. She won't respond to him. Has to disguise his troubled wits.]

[Handwritten annotation: If he cannot move her]

Sonnet 75

One day I wrote her name upon the strand,   *A*
But came the waves and washéd it away: *B*
Agayne I wrote it with a second hand,   *A*
But came the tyde, and made my paynes his pray.   *B*
"Vayne man," sayd she, "that doest in vaine assay,[1]   *B*
A mortall thing so to immortalize,   *C*
For I my selve shall lyke to this decay,   *B*
And eek[2] my name bee wypéd out lykewize."   *C*
"Not so," quod[3] I, "let baser things devize[4]   *C*
To dy in dust, but you shall live by fame: *D*
My verse your vertues rare shall eternize,   *C*
And in the heavens wryte your glorious name.   *D*
Where whenas death shall all the world subdew,   *E*
Our love shall live, and later life renew."   *E*

[Handwritten annotation: contrast between what poet is trying to do and to what she is saying]

[Handwritten annotation: contrast here]

1. Placed.
2. Constellation of the Great Bear.
3. Guiding star, i.e., the North Star.
4. Full of care.

1. Pities my suffering.
2. Neither.

3. Moan.

1. Attempt.
2. Also.
3. Quoth.
4. Plan.

Epithalamion[1]

Ye learned sisters[2] which haue oftentimes
Beene to me ayding, others to adorne:
Whom ye thought worthy of your gracefull rymes,
That euen the greatest did not greatly scorne
5   To heare theyr names sung in your simple layes,
But ioyed in theyr prayse.
And when ye list your owne mishaps to mourne,
Which death, or loue, or fortunes wreck did rayse,
Your string could soone to sadder tenor[3] turne,
10 And teach the woods and waters to lament
Your dolefull dreriment.
Now lay those sorrowfull complaints aside,
And hauing all your heads with girland crownd,
Helpe me mine owne loues prayses to resound,
15 Ne let the same of any be enuide:
So Orpheus[4] did for his owne bride,
So I vnto my selfe alone will sing.
The woods shall to me answer and my Eccho ring.

Early before the worlds light giuing lampe,
20 His golden beame vpon the hils doth spred,
Hauing disperst the nights vnchearefull dampe,
Doe ye awake and with fresh lusty hed,
Go to the bowre[5] of my beloued loue,
My truest turtle doue,
25 Bid her awake; for Hymen[6] is awake,
And long since ready forth his maske[7] to moue,
With his bright Tead[8] that flames with many a flake,[9]
And many a bachelor to waite on him,
In theyr fresh garments trim.
30 Bid her awake therefore and soone her dight,[10]
For lo the wished day is come at last,
That shall for al the paynes and sorrowes past,
Pay to her vsury[11] of long delight:
And whylest she doth her dight,
35 Doe ye to her of ioy and solace[12] sing,
That all the woods may answer and your eccho ring.

Bring with you all the Nymphes that you can heare[13]
Both of the riuers and the forrests greene:
And of the sea that neighbours to her neare,
40 Al with gay girlands goodly wel beseene.
And let them also with them bring in hand
Another gay girland
For my fayre loue of lillyes and of roses,
Bound trueloue wize with a blew silke riband.
45 And let them make great store of bridale poses,[14]
And let them eeke bring store of other flowers
To deck the bridale bowers.
And let the ground whereas her foot shall tread,
For feare the stones her tender foot should wrong
50 Be strewed with fragrant flowers all along,

1. Greek word for wedding song. Spenser draws on a long tradition; examples of the epithalamion occur in Greek, Latin, Italian, and French literature.
2. I.e., the Muses.
3. Strain.
4. Mythical musician whose art could move inanimate objects and calm storms. He descended into Hades, braving its terrors to search for his beloved wife, Eurydice.
5. Bedchamber.
6. God of marriage, represented as a young man bearing a

torch to lead the wedding procession.
7. Pageant, procession.
8. Ceremonial torch associated with weddings since classical antiquity.
9. Spark.
10. Dress.
11. Large interest.
12. Pleasure.
13. I.e., that can hear you.
14. Bouquets.

And diapred[15] lyke the discolored mead.[16]
Which done, doe at her chamber dore awayt,
For she will waken strayt,[17]
The whiles doe ye this song vnto her sing,
55   The woods shall to you answer and your Eccho ring.

Ye Nymphes of Mulla[18] which with carefull heed,
The siluer scaly trouts doe tend full well,
And greedy pikes which vse therein to feed,
(Those trouts and pikes all others doo excell)
60   And ye likewise which keepe the rushy lake,
Where none doo fishes take,
Bynd vp the locks the which hang scatterd light,
And in his waters which your mirror make,
Behold your faces as the christall bright,
65   That when you come whereas my loue doth lie,
No blemish she may spie.
And eke ye lightfoot mayds which keepe the deere,[19]
That on the hoary mountayne vse to towre,[20]
And the wylde wolues which seeke them to deuoure,
70   With your steele darts doo chace from comming neer,
Be also present heere,
To helpe to decke her and to help to sing,
That all the woods may answer and your eccho ring.

Wake, now my loue, awake; for it is time,
75   The Rosy Morne long since left Tithones[21] bed,
All ready to her siluer coche to clyme,
And Phœbus gins to shew his glorious hed.
Hark how the cheerefull birds do chaunt theyr laies
And carroll of loues praise.
80   The merry Larke hir mattins[22] sings aloft,
The thrush replyes, the Mauis[23] descant[24] playes,
The Ouzell[25] shrills, the Ruddock[26] warbles soft,
So goodly all agree with sweet consent,[27]
To this dayes merriment.
85   Ah my deere loue why doe ye sleepe thus long,
When meeter were that ye should now awake,
T'awayt the comming of your ioyous make,[28]
And hearken to the birds louelearned song,
The deawy leaues among.
90   For they of ioy and pleasance to you sing,
That all the woods them answer and theyr eccho ring.

My loue is now awake out of her dreames,
And her fayre eyes like stars that dimmed were
With darksome cloud, now shew theyr goodly beames
95   More bright than Hesperus[29] his head doth rere.
Come now ye damzels, daughters of delight,
Helpe quickly her to dight,
But first come ye fayre houres which were begot
In Ioues sweet paradice, of Day and Night,
100   Which doe the seasons of the yeare allot,
And al that euer in this world is fayre
Doe make and still repayre.

---

15. Ornamented.
16. Multi-coloured meadow.
17. Directly, immediately.
18. The Vale of Mulla, near Spenser's home in Ireland.
19. A general term for wild animals.
20. A term from falconry meaning "to occupy the heights."
21. Husband of the goddess Aurora, mythological personification of the dawn.

22. Morning prayers.
23. Thrush.
24. Melodic soprano counterpoint.
25. Blackbird.
26. Robin.
27. Harmony.
28. Mate.
29. Evening star.

And ye three handmayds of the Cyprian Queene,[30]
The which doe still adorne her beauties pride,
105   Helpe to addorne my beautifullest bride:
And as ye her array, still throw betweene
Some graces to be seene,
And as ye vse to Venus, to her sing,
The whiles the woods shal answer and your eccho ring.

110   Now is my loue all ready forth to come,
Let all the virgins therefore well awayt,
And ye fresh boyes that tend vpon her groome
Prepare your selues; for he is comming strayt.
Set all your things in seemely good aray
115   Fit for so ioyfull day,
The ioyfulst day that euer sunne did see.
Faire Sun, shew forth thy fauourable ray,
And let thy lifull[31] heat not feruent be
For feare of burning her sunshyny face,
120   Her beauty to disgrace.
O fayrest Phœbus, father of the Muse,
If euer I did honour thee aright,
Or sing the thing, that mote[32] thy mind delight,
Doe not thy seruants simple boone[33] refuse,
125   But let this day let this one day be myne,
Let all the rest be thine.
Then I thy souerayne prayses loud wil sing,
That all the woods shal answer and theyr eccho ring.

Harke how the Minstrels gin to shrill aloud
130   Their merry Musick that resounds from far,
The pipe, the tabor,[34] and the trembling Croud,[35]
That well agree withouten breach or iar.[36]
But most of all the Damzels doe delite,
When they their tymbrels[37] smyte,
135   And thereunto doe daunce and carrol sweet,
That all the sences they doe rauish quite,
The whyles the boyes run vp and downe the street,
Crying aloud with strong confused noyce,
As if it were one voyce.
140   Hymen io[38] Hymen, Hymen they do shout,
That euen to the heauens theyr shouting shrill
Doth reach, and all the firmament doth fill,
To which the people standing all about,
As in approuance doe thereto applaud
145   And loud aduance her laud,
And euermore they Hymen Hymen sing,
That al the woods them answer and theyr eccho ring.

Loe where she comes along with portly pace,
Lyke Phœbe[39] from her chamber of the East,
150   Arysing forth to run her mighty race,
Clad all in white, that seemes[40] a virgin best.
So well it her beseemes that ye would weene
Some angell she had beene.
Her long loose yellow locks lyke golden wyre,

30. Venus, whose handmaids are the Graces Aglaia, "the
brilliant one," Thalia, "she who brings flowers," and
Euphrosyne, "she who gladdens the heart."
31. Life-giving.
32. Might.
33. Request.
34. Small drum.

35. Primitive fiddle.
36. Discord.
37. Tambourines.
38. Greek for a cry of joy or exultation.
39. The moon.
40. Befits.

155   Sprinckled with perle, and perling[41] flowres a tweene,
Doe lyke a golden mantle her attyre,
And being crowned with a girland greene,
Seeme lyke some mayden Queene.
Her modest eyes abashed to behold
160   So many gazers, as on her do stare,
Vpon the lowly ground affixed are.
Ne dare lift vp her countenance too bold,
But blush to heare her prayses sung so loud,
So farre from being proud.
165   Nathlesse[42] doe ye still loud her prayses sing,
That all the woods may answer and your eccho ring.

Tell me ye merchants daughters did ye see
So fayre a creature in your towne before?
So sweet, so louely, and so mild as she,
170   Adornd with beautyes grace and vertues store,[43]
Her goodly eyes lyke Saphyres shining bright,
Her forehead yuory white,
Her cheekes lyke apples which the sun hath rudded,
Her lipes lyke cherryes charming men to byte,
175   Her brest like to a bowle of creame vncrudded,[44]
Her paps lyke lyllies budded,
Her snowie necke lyke to a marble towre,
And all her body like a pallace fayre,
Ascending vppe with many a stately stayre,
180   To honors seat and chastities sweet bowre.
Why stand ye still ye virgins in amaze,
Vpon her so to gaze,
Whiles ye forget your former lay to sing,
To which the woods did answer and your eccho ring?

185   But if ye saw that which no eyes can see,
The inward beauty of her liuely spright,
Garnisht with heauenly guifts of high degree,
Much more then would ye wonder at that sight,
And stand astonisht lyke to those which red
190   Medusaes mazeful hed.[45]
There dwels sweet loue and constant chastity,
Vnspotted fayth and comely womanhed,
Regard of honour and mild modesty,
There Vertue raynes as Queene in royal throne,
195   And giueth lawes alone.
The which the base affections[46] doe obay,
And yeeld theyr seruices vnto her will,
Ne thought of thing vncomely euer may
Thereto approch to tempt her mind to ill.
200   Had ye once seene these her celestial threasures,
And vnreuealed pleasures,
Then would ye wonder and her prayses sing,
That al the woods should answer and your echo ring.

Open the temple gates vnto my loue,
205   Open them wide that she may enter in,
And all the postes adorne as doth behoue,[47]
And all the pillours deck with girlands trim,
For to recyue this Saynt with honour dew,
That commeth in to you.

---

41. Dewy.
42. Nevertheless.
43. Wealth.
44. Uncurdled.

45. Medusa's head was covered with serpents in place of hair. Anyone who beheld her was turned to stone.
46. Lower passions.
47. I.e., as is fitting.

210 With trembling steps and humble reuerence,
     She commeth in, before th'almighties vew:
     Of her ye virgins learne obedience,
     When so ye come into those holy places,
     To humble your proud faces;
215 Bring her vp to th'high altar that she may,
     The sacred ceremonies there partake,
     The which do endlesse matrimony make,
     And let the roring Organs loudly play
     The praises of the Lord in liuely notes,
220 The whiles with hollow throates
     The Choristers the ioyous Antheme sing,
     That al the woods may answere and their eccho ring.

     Behold whiles she before the altar stands
     Hearing the holy priest that to her speakes
225 And blesseth her with his two happy hands,
     How the red roses flush vp in her cheekes,
     And the pure snow with goodly vermill stayne,
     Like crimsin dyde in grayne,[48]
     That euen th'Angels which continually,
230 About the sacred Altare doe remaine,
     Forget their seruice and about her fly,
     Ofte peeping in her face that seemes more fayre,
     The more they on it stare.
     But her sad[49] eyes still fastened on the ground,
235 Are gouerned with goodly modesty,
     That suffers not one looke to glaunce awry,
     Which may let in a little thought vnsownd.
     Why blush ye loue to giue to me your hand,
     The pledge of all our band?[50]
240 Sing ye sweet Angels, Alleluya sing,
     That all the woods may answere and your eccho ring.

     Now al is done; bring home the bride againe,
     Bring home the triumph of our victory,
     Bring home with you the glory of her gaine,[51]
245 With ioyance bring her and with iollity.
     Neuer had man more ioyfull day then this,
     Whom heauen would heape with blis.
     Make feast therefore now all this liue long day,
     This day for euer to me holy is,
250 Poure out the wine without restraint or stay,
     Poure not by cups, but by the belly full,
     Poure out to all that wull,[52]
     And sprinkle all the postes and wals with wine,
     That they may sweat, and drunken be withall.
255 Crowne ye God Bacchus with a coronall,[53]
     And Hymen also crowne with wreathes of vine,
     And let the Graces daunce vnto the rest;
     For they can doo it best:
     The whiles the maydens doe theyr carroll sing,
260 To which the woods shal answer and theyr eccho ring.

     Ring ye the bels, ye yong men of the towne,
     And leaue your wonted[54] labors for this day:
     This day is holy; doe ye write it downe,
     That ye for euer it remember may.

48. I.e., dyed permanently.
49. Steady, modest.
50. Bond.
51. I.e., the glory of gaining her.

52. Wish it.
53. Garland.
54. Usual.

265 This day the sunne is in his chiefest hight,
With Barnaby the bright,[55]
From whence declining daily by degrees,
He somewhat loseth of his heat and light,
When once the Crab[56] behind his back he sees.
270 But for this time it ill ordained was,
To chose the longest day in all the yeare,
And shortest night, when longest fitter weare:
Yet neuer day so long, but late[57] would passe.
Ring ye the bels, to make it weare away,
275 And bonefiers make all day,
And daunce about them, and about them sing:
That all the woods may answer, and your eccho ring.

Ah when will this long weary day haue end,
And lende me leaue to come vnto my loue?
280 How slowly do the houres theyr numbers spend?
How slowly does sad Time his feathers moue?
Hast thee O fayrest Planet to thy home[58]
Within the Westerne fome:
Thy tyred steedes long since haue need of rest.
285 Long though it be, at last I see it gloome,
And the bright euening star with golden creast
Appeare out of the East.
Fayre childe of beauty, glorious lampe of loue
That all the host of heauen in rankes doost lead,
290 And guydest louers through the nights dread,
How chearefully thou lookest from aboue,
And seemst to laugh atweene thy twinkling light
As ioying in the sight
Of these glad many which for ioy doe sing,
295 That all the woods them answer and their echo ring.

Now ceasse ye damsels your delights forepast;
Enough is it, that all the day was youres:
Now day is doen, and night is nighing fast:
Now bring the Bryde into the brydall boures.
300 Now night is come, now soone her disaray,
And in her bed her lay;
Lay her in lillies and in violets,
And silken courteins ouer her display,[59]
And odourd sheetes, and Arras[60] couerlets.
305 Behold how goodly my faire loue does ly
In proud humility;
Like vnto Maia,[61] when as Ioue her tooke,
In Tempe, lying on the flowry gras,
Twixt sleepe and wake, after she weary was,
310 With bathing in the Acidalian brooke.
Now it is night, ye damsels may be gon,
And leaue my loue alone,
And leaue likewise your former lay to sing:
The woods no more shal answere, nor your echo ring.

315 Now welcome night, thou night so long expected,
That long daies labour doest at last defray,[62]
And all my cares, which cruell loue collected,

---

55. St. Barnabas Day, the summer solstice. By the calendar then in use, 11 June 1594, not 21 June.
56. Fourth constellation in the zodiac, the sign of Cancer.
The sun completes its passage ("sees behind its back")
through the Crab late in July.
57. At last.
58. In Ptolemaic astronomy, still used as a source of

imagery in Renaissance art, the sun was regarded as a
planet in orbit around the earth.
59. Cover.
60. Tapestry.
61. Most beautiful of the Pleiades.
62. Cancel the debt.

Hast sumd in one, and cancelled for aye:
Spread thy broad wing ouer my loue and me,
320   That no man may vs see,
And in thy sable mantle vs enwrap,
From feare of perrill and foule horror free.
Let no false treason seeke vs to entrap,
Nor any dread disquiet once annoy
325   The safety of our ioy:
But let the night be calme and quietsome,
Without tempestuous storms or sad afray:
Lyke as when Ioue with fayre Alcmena[63] lay,
When he begot the great Tirynthian groome:
330   Or lyke as when he with thy selfe[64] did lie,
And begot Maiesty.
And let the mayds and yongmen cease to sing:
Ne let the woods them answer, nor theyr eccho ring.

Let no lamenting cryes, nor dolefull teares,
335   Be heard all night within nor yet without:
Ne let false whispers breeding hidden feares,
Breake gentle sleepe with misconceiued dout.
Let no deluding dreames, nor dreadful sights
Make sudden sad affrights;
340   Ne let housefyres, nor lightnings helpelesse harmes,
Ne let the Pouke,[65] nor other euill sprights,
Ne let mischiuous witches with theyr charmes,
Ne let hob Goblins, names whose sence we see not,
Fray[66] vs with things that be not.
345   Let not the shriech Oule, nor the Storke be heard:
Nor the night Rauen that still deadly yels,[67]
Nor damned ghosts cald vp with mighty spels,
Nor griesly vultures make vs once affeard:
Ne let th'unpleasant Quyre of Frogs still croking
350   Make vs to wish theyr choking.
Let none of these theyr drery accents sing;
Ne let the woods them answer, nor theyr eccho ring.

Bvt let stil Silence trew night watches keepe,
That sacred peace may in assurance rayne,
355   And tymely sleep, when it is tyme to sleepe,
May poure his limbs forth on your pleasant playne,
The whiles an hundred little winged loues,[68]
Like diuers fethered doues,
Shall fly and flutter round about your bed,
360   And in the secret darke, that none reproues,
Their prety stealthes shal worke, and snares shal spread
To filch away sweet snatches of delight,
Conceald through couert night.
Ye sonnes of Venus, play your sports at will,
365   For greedy pleasure, carelesse of your toyes,[69]
Thinks more vpon her paradise of ioyes,
Then what ye do, albe it good or ill.
All night therefore attend your merry play,
For it will soone be day:
370   Now none doth hinder you, that say or sing,
Ne will the woods now answer, nor your Eccho ring.

---

63. Mother of Hercules, who performed twelve great labours as a servant (groom) to the King of Tiryns.
64. I.e., Night.
65. Puck. Shakespeare's Puck, or Robin Goodfellow, in *A Midsummer Night's Dream* depicts the goblin as mischievous fairy, not the traditional figure of sinister power alluded to by Spenser.
66. Frighten.
67. Owls and ravens were traditional birds of ill omen. In Chaucer's *Parlement of Foules*, the stork is called an avenger of adultery.
68. Cupids.
69. Amorous games.

Who is the same, which at my window peepes?
Or whose is that faire face, that shines so bright?
Is it not Cinthia,[70] she that neuer sleepes,
375   But walkes about high heauen al the night?
O fayrest goddesse, do thou not enuy
My loue with me to spy:
For thou likewise didst loue, though now vnthought[71]
And for a fleece of woll,[72] which priuily,
380   The Latmian shephard[73] once vnto thee brought,
His pleasures with thee wrought.
Therefore to vs be fauorable now;
And sith of wemens labours[74] thou hast charge,[75]
And generation goodly dost enlarge,
385   Encline thy will t'effect our wishfull vow,
And the chast wombe informe[76] with timely seed,
That may our comfort breed:
Till which we cease our hopefull hap to sing,
Ne let the woods vs answere, nor our Eccho ring.

390   And thou great Iuno, which with awful[77] might
The lawes of wedlock still dost patronize,
And the religion[78] of the faith first plight
With sacred rites hast taught to solemnize:
And eeke for comfort often called art
395   Of women in their smart,[79]
Eternally bind thou this louely band,
And all thy blessings vnto vs impart.
And thou glad Genius,[80] in whose gentle hand,
The bridale bowre and geniall bed remaine,
400   Without blemish or staine,
And the sweet pleasures of theyr loues delight
With secret ayde doest succour and supply,
Till they bring forth the fruitfull progeny,
Send vs the timely fruit of this same night.
405   And thou fayre Hebe,[81] and thou Hymen free,
Grant that it may so be.
Til which we cease your further prayse to sing,
Ne any woods shal answer, nor your Echo ring.

And ye high heauens, the temple of the gods,
410   In which a thousand torches flaming bright
Doe burne, that to vs wretched earthly clods,
In dreadful darknesse lend desired light;
And all ye powers which in the same remayne,
More then we men can fayne,[82]
415   Poure out your blessing on vs plentiously,
And happy influence vpon vs raine,
That we may raise a large posterity,
Which from the earth, which they may long possesse,
With lasting happinesse,
420   Vp to your haughty pallaces may mount,
And for the guerdon[83] of theyr glorious merit
May heauenly tabernacles there inherit,
Of blessed Saints for to increase the count.

70. Like Phoebe (l. 149), another name for Diana, goddess of the moon.
71. Unsuspected, forgotten.
72. Wool.
73. Endymion, beloved of Diana, who visited him in his sleep. Spenser has apparently conflated this myth with that of Pan, who sought to entice Diana disguised in the fleece of a white ram ("fleece of wool").
74. I.e., of childbirth.
75. Diana in one of her many mythological aspects was patroness of births.
76. Animate, give life to.
77. Awesome.
78. Sanctity.
79. Pains of childbirth.
80. Universal principle of generation.
81. Daughter of Juno, and goddess of youth.
82. Imagine.
83. Reward.

So let vs rest, sweet loue, in hope of this,
425 And cease till then our tymely ioyes to sing,
The woods no more vs answer, nor our eccho ring.

Song made in lieu of many ornaments,[84]
With which my loue should duly haue bene dect,[85]
Which cutting off through hasty accidents,
430 Ye would not stay your dew time to expect,[86]
But promist both to recompens,
Be vnto her a goodly ornament,
And for short time an endlesse moniment.[87]

WILLIAM SHAKESPEARE (1564–1616)

From Sonnets

15

When I consider everything that grows
Holds in perfection[1] but a little moment,
That this huge stage[2] presenteth nought but shows
Whereon the stars in secret[3] influence comment;
When I perceive that men as plants increase,
Cheerèd and checked even by the selfsame sky,
Vaunt in their youthful sap,[4] at height decrease,
And wear their brave[5] state out of memory:[6]
Then the conceit[7] of this inconstant stay
Sets you most rich in youth before my sight,
Where wasteful Time debateth with Decay
To change your day of youth to sullied night;
   And, all in war with Time for love of you,
   As he takes from you, I ingraft[8] you new.

18

Shall I compare thee to a summer's day?
Thou art more lovely and more temperate.
Rough winds do shake the darling buds of May,
And summer's lease hath all too short a date.
Sometime too hot the eye of heaven shines,
And often is his gold complexion dimmed;
And every fair from fair sometime declines,
By chance, or nature's changing course, untrimmed:[1]
But thy eternal summer shall not fade
Nor lose possession of that fair thou ow'st,[2]
Nor shall Death brag thou wand'rest in his shade
When in eternal lines[3] to time thou grow'st.
   So long as men can breathe or eyes can see,
   So long lives this, and this gives life to thee.

84. The poem is offered apologetically in lieu of wedding presents (ornaments).
85. Adorned.
86. Await.
87. I.e., the poem as a timeless monument to the single day it celebrates.

1. Remains perfect.
2. The world.
3. Occult.

4. I.e., vigour.
5. Splendid.
6. I.e., until forgotten.
7. Concept, idea.
8. Graft, renew (with poetry).

1. Divested of its beauty.
2. Ownest.
3. Poetry.

29

When, in disgrace with Fortune and men's eyes,
I all alone beweep my outcast state,
And trouble deaf heaven with my bootlesss[1] cries,
And look upon myself and curse my fate,
Wishing me like to one more rich in hope,
Featured like him, like him with friends possessed,
Desiring this man's art, and that man's scope,
With what I most enjoy contented least;
Yet in these thoughts myself almost despising,
Haply[2] I think on thee, and then my state,
Like to the lark at break of day arising
From sullen earth, sings hymns at heaven's gate;
    For thy sweet love rememb'red such wealth brings
    That then I scorn to change my state with kings.

30

When to the sessions[1] of sweet silent thought
I summon up remembrance of things past,
I sigh the lack of many a thing I sought,
And with old woes new wail my dear time's waste:
Then can I drown an eye, unused to flow,
For precious friends hid in death's dateless[2] night,
And weep afresh love's long since cancelled woe,
And moan th' expense of many a vanished sight.
Then can I grieve at grievances foregone,
And heavily from woe to woe tell o'er[3]
The sad account of fore-bemoanèd moan,
Which I new pay as if not paid before.
    But if the while I think on thee, dear friend,
    All losses are restored and sorrows end.

33

Full many a glorious morning have I seen
Flatter the mountain tops with sovereign eye,
Kissing with golden face the meadows green,
Gilding pale streams with heavenly alchemy;
Anon permit the basest clouds to ride
With ugly rack[1] on his celestial face,
And from the forlorn world his visage hide,
Stealing unseen to west with this disgrace:
Even so my sun one early morn did shine
With all-triumphant splendour on my brow;
But, out alack,[2] he was but one hour mine,
The region cloud[3] hath masked him from me now.
    Yet him for this my love no whit disdaineth;
    Suns of the world may stain[4] when heaven's sun staineth.

1. Futile.
2. By chance.

1. Sittings of a court.
2. Eternal.
3. Count.

1. Streamers of cloud driven by wind.
2. Alas.
3. Local clouds.
4. I.e., be stained.

55

Not marble nor the gilded monuments
Of princes shall outlive this pow'rful rime,
But you shall shine more bright in these contents[1]
Than unswept stone, besmeared with sluttish[2] time.
When wasteful war shall statues overturn,
And broils[3] root out the work of masonry,
Nor Mars his sword[4] nor war's quick fire shall burn
The living record of your memory.
'Gainst death and all oblivious enmity
Shall you pace forth; your praise shall still find room
Even in the eyes of all posterity
That wear this world out to the ending doom.[5]
   So, till the judgment that yourself arise,
    You live in this, and dwell in lovers' eyes.

60

Like as the waves make towards the pebbled shore,
So do our minutes hasten to their end;
Each changing place with that which goes before,
In sequent[1] toil all forwards[2] do contend.
Nativity,[3] once in the main of light,
Crawls to maturity, wherewith being crowned,
Crooked[4] eclipses 'gainst his glory fight,
And Time that gave doth now his gift confound.
Time doth transfix the flourish set on youth
And delves[5] the parallels in beauty's brow,
Feeds on the rarities of nature's truth,
And nothing stands but for his scythe to mow:
   And yet to times in hope[6] my verse shall stand,[7]
    Praising thy worth, despite his cruel hand.

71

No longer mourn for me when I am dead
Than you shall hear the surly sullen bell
Give warning to the world that I am fled
From this vile world, with vilest worms to dwell.
Nay, if you read this line, remember not
The hand that writ it, for I love you so
That I in your sweet thoughts would be forgot
If thinking on me then should make you woe.[1]
O, if, I say, you look upon this verse
When I, perhaps, compounded am with clay,
Do not so much as my poor name rehearse,
But let your love even with my life decay,
   Lest the wise world should look into your moan
    And mock you with me[2] after I am gone.

1. What is contained here, i.e., these poems.
2. Untidy, slovenly.
3. Battles.
4. I.e., the sword of Mars.
5. The Day of Judgement, Doomsday.

1. Successive.
2. Forward.

3. I.e., the new-born child.
4. Adverse, malignant.
5. Digs.
6. Hoped-for times, i.e., the future.
7. Endure.

1. Cause you woe.
2. Because of me.

73

That time of year thou mayst in me behold   A
When yellow leaves, or none, or few, do hang   B
Upon those boughs which shake against the cold,   A
Bare ruined choirs where late[1] the sweet birds sang.   B
In me thou seest the twilight of such day   C
As after sunset fadeth in the west,   D
Which by and by black night doth take away,   C
Death's second self that seals up[2] all in rest.   D
In me thou seest the glowing of such fire   E
That[3] on the ashes of his youth doth lie,   F
As the deathbed whereon it must expire,   E
Consumed with that which it was nourished by.   F
  This thou perceiv'st, which makes thy love more strong,   G
  To love that well which thou must leave ere long.   G

(Handwritten annotations: "fall ending of the year"; "dark and sinister"; "I am asleep"; "ending couplet"; "concerned with his youth." At right: "Address to a lover. 3 avatars — progression of seasons, day & earth. zeros in on smallest point. seasons and day will return. fire will not, unlike nature man is finite." "you see my physical aging")

97

How like a winter hath my absence been
From thee, the pleasure[1] of the fleeting year!
What freezings have I felt, what dark days seen!
What old December's bareness everywhere!
And yet this time removed[2] was summer's time,
The teeming autumn, big with rich increase,
Bearing the wanton burden of the prime,[3]
Like widowed wombs after their lords' decease:
Yet this abundant issue seemed to me
But hope of orphans and unfathered fruit;
For summer and his pleasures wait on thee,
And, thou away, the very birds are mute;
  Or, if they sing, 'tis with so dull a cheer
  That leaves look pale, dreading the winter's near.

106

When in the chronicle of wasted time[1]
I see descriptions of the fairest wights,[2]
And beauty making beautiful old rime
In praise of ladies dead and lovely knights;
Then, in the blazon[3] of sweet beauty's best,
Of hand, of foot, of lip, of eye, of brow,
I see their antique pen would have expressed
Even such a beauty as you master[4] now.
So all their praises are but prophecies
Of this our time, all you prefiguring;[5]
And, for[6] they looked but with divining[7] eyes,
They had not skill enough your worth to sing:
  For we,[8] which now behold these present days,
  Have eyes to wonder, but lack tongues to praise.

1. Lately.
2. Closes.
3. As.

1. I.e., pleasant part.
2. Time of separation.
3. Spring.

1. Used-up time, bygone days.
2. Persons.
3. Catalogue.
4. Possess, command.
5. Picturing you in advance.
6. Because.
7. Predicting without actually seeing.
8. I.e., even we.

116

Let me not to the marriage of true minds
Admit impediments;[1] love is not love
Which alters when it alteration finds
Or bends[2] with the remover to remove.
O, no, it is an ever-fixèd mark
That looks on tempests and is never shaken;
It is the star to every wand'ring bark,
Whose worth's unknown, although his height be taken.[3]
Love's not Time's fool, though rosy lips and cheeks
Within his bending sickle's compass come;
Love alters not with his[4] brief hours and weeks,
But bears it out even to the edge of doom.[5]
   If this be error, and upon me proved,
   I never writ, nor no man ever loved.

129

Th' expense[1] of spirit[2] in a waste of shame[3]
Is lust in action; and, till action, lust
Is perjured, murd'rous, bloody, full of blame,
Savage, extreme, rude, cruel, not to trust;[4]
Enjoyed no sooner but despisèd straight;
Past reason hunted, and no sooner had,
Past reason hated as a swallowed bait
On purpose laid to make the taker mad:
Mad in pursuit, and in possession so;
Had, having, and in quest to have, extreme;
A bliss in proof,[5] and proved, a very woe;
Before, a joy proposed; behind, a dream.
   All this the world well knows; yet none knows well
   To shun the heaven that leads men to this hell.

130

My mistress' eyes are nothing like the sun;   *A*
Coral is far more red than her lips' red;   *B*
If snow be white, why then her breasts are dun;   *A*
If hairs be wires, black wires grow on her head.   *B*
I have seen roses damasked,[1] red and white,   *c*
But no such roses see I in her cheeks;   *d*
And in some perfumes is there more delight   *c*
Than in the breath that from my mistress reeks.[2]   *d*
I love to hear her speak; yet well I know   *e f*
That music hath a far more pleasing sound: *f*
I grant I never saw a goddess go;[3]   *e*
My mistress, when she walks, treads on the ground.   *f*
   And yet, by heaven, I think my love as rare   *e*
   As any she belied with false compare.[4]   *e*

His women is not perfect but he loves her for what she is.

Shakespaore says there is no way to describe Kathys hair

his actual love belys the false comparisons his love superior to any love to base on nackneyed conceptions

1. An echo of the marriage service: "If any of you know cause or just impediment why these persons should not be joined together...."
2. Collaborates.
3. I.e., although elevation (height above the horizon) may be measured.
4. Time's.
5. Brink of Doomsday.

1. Expenditure.
2. Vital power.
3. Shameful waste.
4. Not to be trusted.
5. While being experienced.

1. Variegated in colour.
2. Is exhaled.
3. Walk.
4. Comparison.

144

Two loves I have, of comfort and despair,
Which like two spirits do suggest[1] me still:[2]
The better angel is a man right fair,
The worser spirit a woman coloured ill.[3]
To win me soon to hell, my female evil
Tempteth my better angel from my side,
And would corrupt my saint to be a devil,
Wooing his purity with her foul pride.
And whether that my angel be turned fiend
Suspect I may, yet not directly tell;
But being both from me, both to each friend,[4]
I guess one angel in another's hell.
    Yet this shall I ne'er know, but live in doubt,
    Till my bad angel fire[5] my good one out.

Songs from the Plays

Under the Greenwood Tree[1]

Under the greenwood tree
  Who loves to lie with me,
And turn his merry note
  Unto the sweet bird's throat,
Come hither, come hither, come hither:
  Here shall he see
  No enemy
But winter and rough weather.

Who doth ambition shun
  And loves to live i' the sun,
Seeking the food he eats,
  And pleased with what he gets,
Come hither, come hither, come hither:
  Here shall he see
  No enemy
But winter and rough weather.

Blow, Blow, Thou Winter Wind[1]

Blow, blow, thou winter wind,
  Thou art not so unkind
    As man's ingratitude;
  Thy tooth is not so keen,
  Because thou art not seen,
    Although thy breath be rude.
Heigh-ho! sing, heigh-ho! unto the green holly:[2]
Most friendship is feigning, most loving mere folly:
  Then, heigh-ho, the holly!
    This life is most jolly.

Freeze, freeze, thou bitter sky,
  That dost not bite so nigh
    As benefits forgot:
  Though thou the waters warp,[3]
  Thy sting is not so sharp
    As friend remembered not.
Heigh-ho! sing, etc.

1. Urge.
2. Constantly.
3. I.e., dark, swarthy.
4. I.e., each the other's friend.
5. Drive out. Also, colloquially, "infect with venereal disease."

1. From *As You Like It*.

1. From *As You Like It*.
2. Emblem of mirth and fellowship.
3. Freeze, or distort by freezing.

When That I Was and a Little Tiny Boy[1]

When that I was and a little tiny boy,
    With hey, ho, the wind and the rain,
A foolish thing was but a toy,
    For the rain it raineth every day.

But when I came to man's estate,
    With hey, ho, . . .
'Gainst knaves and thieves men shut their gate,
    For the rain, . . .

But when I came, alas! to wive,
    With hey, ho, . . .
By swaggering could I never thrive,
    For the rain, . . .

But when I came unto my beds,[2]
    With hey, ho, . . .
With toss-pots[3] still had drunken heads,
    For the rain, . . .

A great while ago the world begun,
    With hey, ho, . . .
But that's all one, our play is done,
    And we'll strive to please you every day.

Come Away, Come Away, Death[1]

Come away, come away, death,
    And in sad cypress[2] let me be laid.
Fly away, fly away, breath;
    I am slain by a fair cruel maid.
My shroud of white, stuck all with yew,
        O, prepare it!
My part of death, no one so true
        Did share it.[3]

Not a flower, not a flower sweet,
    On my black coffin let there be strown.
Not a friend, not a friend greet
    My poor corpse, where my bones shall be thrown.
A thousand thousand sighs to save,
        Lay me, O, where
Sad true lover never find my grave,
        To weep there!

Oh Mistress Mine[1]

Oh mistress mine! where are you roaming?
Oh! stay and hear; your true love's coming,
    That can sing both high and low.
Trip no further, pretty sweeting;
Journeys end in lovers meeting,
    Every wise man's son doth know.

What is love? 'tis not hereafter;
Present mirth hath present laughter;
    What's to come is still[2] unsure:
In delay there lies no plenty;
Then come kiss me, sweet and twenty,[3]
    Youth's a stuff will not endure.

---

1. Sung by the clown, Feste, at the end of *Twelfth Night*.
2. To old age (?).
3. Drunkards.

1. From *Twelfth Night*.
2. Cyprus, like yew (l. 5), was often planted in graveyards and became emblematic of death.

3. I.e., I had to act my role ("part") of dying alone, with no one of equal constancy to share it.

1. From *Twelfth Night*.
2. Always, forever.
3. "Twenty" is used here as an intensive, i.e., "sweet and twenty-times sweet."

Full Fathom Five[1]

Full fathom five thy father lies;
   Of his bones are coral made;
Those are pearls that were his eyes:
   Nothing of him that doth fade,
But doth suffer a sea change
Into something rich and strange.
Sea nymphs hourly ring his knell:
   Ding-dong.
Hark! now I hear them— Ding-dong, bell.

Where the Bee Sucks, There Suck I[1]

Where the bee sucks, there suck I:
In a cowslip's bell I lie;
There I couch when owls do cry.
On the bat's back I do fly
After summer merrily.
Merrily, merrily shall I live now
Under the blossom that hangs on the bough.

JOHN DONNE

From Songs and Sonnets

The Good-Morrow

I wonder, by my troth, what thou and I
Did, till we loved? were we not weaned till then?
But sucked on country pleasures, childishly?
Or snorted we in the Seven Sleepers' den?[1]
5   'Twas so; but this,[2] all pleasures fancies be.
If ever any beauty I did see,
Which I desired, and got, 'twas but a dream of thee.

And now good-morrow to our waking souls,
Which watch not one another out of fear;
10 For love, all love of other sights controls,
And makes one little room an everywhere.
Let sea-discoverers to new worlds have gone,
Let maps to others, worlds on worlds have shown,[3]
Let us possess one world, each hath one, and is one.

15 My face in thine eye, thine in mine appears,
And true plain hearts do in the faces rest;
Where can we find two better hemispheres,
Without sharp north, without declining west?
Whatever dies was not mixed equally;[4]
20 If our two loves be one, or thou and I
Love so alike that none do slacken, none can die.

---

1. From *The Tempest*.

1. From *The Tempest*.

1. A reference to the legend of seven Christian youths from Ephesus, who fled Roman persecution to hide in a cave where they slept for 187 years.
2. Except for this.
3. I.e., let maps reveal new worlds to others.
4. The mutability of material things was attributed, in scholastic thought, to an imperfect blending of contrary elements.

Song

Go and catch a falling star,
   Get with child a mandrake root,[1]
Tell me where all past years are,
   Or who cleft the Devil's foot,
5 Teach me to hear mermaids singing,
   Or to keep off envy's stinging,
      And find
      What wind
Serves to advance an honest mind.

10 If thou be'st born to strange sights,
   Things invisible to see,
Ride ten thousand days and nights,
   Till age snow white hairs on thee,
Thou, when thou return'st, wilt tell me
15 All strange wonders that befell thee,
      And swear
      Nowhere
Lives a woman true, and fair.

If thou findst one, let me know,
20 Such a pilgrimage were sweet.
Yet do not; I would not go,
   Though at next door we might meet;
Though she were true, when you met her,
   And last till you write your letter,
25   Yet she
      Will be
False, ere I come, to two, or three.

The Indifferent

I can love both fair and brown,[1]
Her whom abundance melts, and her whom want betrays,
Her who loves loneness best, and her who masks and plays,
Her whom the country formed, and whom the town,
5 Her who believes, and her who tries,
Her who still weeps with spongy eyes,
And her who is dry cork, and never cries;
I can love her, and her, and you, and you,
I can love any, so she be not true.

10 Will no other vice content you?
Will it not serve your turn to do as did your mothers?
Or have you all old vices spent, and now would find out others?
Or doth a fear, that men are true, torment you?
Oh we are not, be not you so;
15 Let me, and do you, twenty know.
Rob me, but bind me not, and let me go.
Must I, who came to travail[2] thorough[3] you,
Grow your fixed subject, because you are true?

---

1. The forked shape of the mandragora plant (mandrake) resembles the lower part of the human body. It was considered an aphrodisiac, a soporific, and an aid to fertility in women.

1. I.e., both blond and brunette.
2. Suffering, striving, with a suggestion of "journey" or "travel."
3. Through.

Venus heard me sigh this song,
20   And by love's sweetest part, variety, she swore
She heard not this till now; and that it should be so no more.
She went, examined, and returned ere long,
And said, "Alas, some two or three
Poor heretics in love there be,
25   Which think to 'stablish[4] dangerous constancy.
But I have told them, 'Since you will be true,
You shall be true to them who are false to you.' "

The Canonization

For God's sake, hold your tongue, and let me love,
   Or chide my palsy, or my gout,
My five gray hairs, or ruined fortune flout,
   With wealth your state, your mind with arts improve,
5   Take you a course, get you a place,[1]
         Observe his honour, or his grace,
Or the King's real, or his stamped[2] face
      Contemplate; what you will, approve,[3]
      So you will let me love.

10   Alas, alas, who's injured by my love?
      What merchant's ships have my sighs drowned?
Who says my tears have overflowed his ground?
      When did my colds a forward spring remove?
         When did the heats which my veins fill
15   Add one more to the plaguy bill?[4]
Soldiers find wars, and lawyers find out still[5]
      Litigious men, which quarrels move,
      Though she and I do love.

Call us what you will, we are made such by love;
20   Call her one, me another fly,[6]
We're tapers too, and at our own cost die,[7]
      And we in us find the eagle and the dove.[8]
         The phoenix[9] riddle hath more wit
         By us; we two being one, are it.
25   So, to one neutral thing both sexes fit.
      We die and rise the same, and prove
      Mysterious by this love.

We can die by it, if not live by love,
   And if unfit for tombs and hearse
30   Our legend be, it will be fit for verse;
   And if no piece of chronicle we prove,
      We'll build in sonnets pretty rooms;[10]
      As well a well-wrought urn becomes
The greatest ashes, as half-acre tombs,
35   And by these hymns, all shall approve
      Us *canonized* for Love.

---

4. Establish.

1. I.e., settle on a way of life, get a position at court.
2. I.e., on coins.
3. Test by experience.
4. List of plague victims.
5. Always.
6. Flies, or moths, symbolize ephemeral pleasures consumed by the stimulus that attracts them.

7. "To die" was a slang euphemism for sexual consummation, implying each sexual act reduced the span of life.
8. Symbols of war and peace, power and meekness, the worldly and the spiritual.
9. A mythical bird, only one of which exists at a time, that consumes itself in its own funeral pyre, sings its funeral song, then rises reincarnated from its own ashes.
10. *Stanza* in Italian means "room."

And thus invoke us: "You, whom reverend love
   Made one another's hermitage;
40 You, to whom love was peace, that now is rage;
   Who did the whole world's soul extract, and drove
     Into the glasses of your eyes
     (So made such mirrors, and such spies,
That they did all to you epitomize)
45   Countries, towns, courts: beg from above
   A pattern of your love!"

The Flea

Mark but this flea, and mark in this
How little that which thou deny'st me is;
It sucked me first, and now sucks thee,
And in this flea our two bloods mingled be;
5 Thou know'st that this cannot be said
A sin, nor shame, nor loss of maidenhead,
   Yet this enjoys before it woo,
   And pampered swells with one blood made of two,
   And this, alas, is more than we would do.

10 Oh stay, three lives in one flea spare,
Where we almost, yea more than married are.
This flea is you and I, and this
Our marriage bed, and marriage temple is;
Though parents grudge, and you, we're met
15 And cloistered in these living walls of jet.
   Though use[1] make you apt to kill me,
   Let not to that, self-murder added be,
   And sacrilege, three sins in killing three.

Cruel and sudden, hast thou since
20 Purpled thy nail in blood of innocence?
Wherein could this flea guilty be,
Except in that drop which it sucked from thee?
Yet thou triumph'st, and say'st that thou
Find'st not thyself, nor me, the weaker now;
25   'Tis true; then learn how false fears be;
   Just so much honour, when thou yield'st to me,
   Will waste, as this flea's death took life from thee.

The Bait[1]

Come live with me, and be my love,
And we will some new pleasures prove[2]
Of golden sands, and crystal brooks:
With silken lines, and silver hooks.

5 There will the river whispering run
Warmed by thine eyes more than the sun.
And there the enamored fish will stay,
Begging themselves they may betray.

10 When thou wilt swim in that live bath,
Each fish, which every channel hath,
Will amorously to thee swim,
Gladder to catch thee, than thou him.

If thou to be so seen be'st loath
By sun, or moon, thou dark'nest both,
15 And if myself have leave to see,
I need not their light, having thee.

1. Custom, habit.

1. A response to Christopher Marlowe's poem "The Passionate Shepherd to His Love."
2. Test.

Let others freeze with angling reeds,
And cut their legs with shells and weeds,
Or treacherously poor fish beset,
20   With strangling snare or windowy net:

Let coarse bold hands, from slimy nest
The bedded fish in banks out-wrest;
Or curious traitors, sleave-silk[3] flies,
Bewitch poor fishes' wand'ring eyes.

25   For thee, thou need'st no such deceit,
For thou thyself art thine own bait;
That fish that is not catched thereby,
Alas, is wiser far than I.

A Valediction: Forbidding Mourning

As virtuous men pass mildly away,
    And whisper to their souls to go,
Whilst some of their sad friends do say,
    "The breath goes now," and some say, "No,"

5   So let us melt, and make no noise,
    No tear-floods, nor sigh-tempests move;
'Twere profanation of our joys
    To tell the laity our love.

Moving of the earth[1] brings harms and fears,
10   Men reckon what it did and meant;
But trepidation of the spheres,[2]
    Though greater far, is innocent.[3]

Dull sublunary[4] lovers' love
    (Whose soul[5] is sense) cannot admit
15   Absence, because it doth remove
    Those things which elemented[6] it.

But we, by a love so much refined
    That our selves know not what it is,
Inter-assured of the mind,
20   Care less, eyes, lips, and hands to miss.

Our two souls therefore, which are one,
    Though I must go, endure not yet
A breach, but an expansion,
    Like gold to airy thinness beat.

25   If they be two, they are two so
    As stiff twin compasses are two:
Thy soul, the fixed foot, makes no show
    To move, but doth, if the other do;

And though it in the center sit,
30   Yet when the other far doth roam,
It leans, and hearkens after it,
    And grows erect, as that comes home.

Such wilt thou be to me, who must,
    Like the other foot, obliquely run;
35   Thy firmness makes my circle just,[7]
    And makes me end where I begun.

The Ecstasy[1]

Where, like a pillow on a bed,
    A pregnant bank swelled up, to rest
The violet's reclining head,
    Sat we two, one another's best.

5   Our hands were firmly cemented
    With a fast balm, which thence did spring;
Our eye-beams twisted,[2] and did thread
    Our eyes, upon one double string;

10   So to intergraft our hands, as yet
    Was all the means to make us one,
And pictures in our eyes to get[3]
    Was all our propagation.

As, 'twixt two equal armies, Fate
    Suspends uncertain victory,
15   Our souls (which to advance their state
    Were gone out) hung 'twixt her and me.

---

3. Untangled silk.

1. Earthquakes.
2. Ptolemaic astronomers postulated oscillatory disturbances in the celestial spheres to account for observed variations in stellar movement that did not accord with theory.
3. I.e., disturbances in the stellar spheres are far greater in magnitude than earthquakes, but they are "innocent," cause no "harms and fears," because they are so remote from earth.
4. Beneath or inside the moon's orbit, therefore earthly.

The sublunar world is, like the moon, subject to constant change.
5. Essence.
6. Composed.
7. Perfect, precise.

1. In literal derivation, the term means "outside the place," and Donne alludes in his title to its use by religious mystics to describe a transcendent state of heightened insight when the soul seems to move outside the body.
2. Eyes were thought to emit beams which made objects visible.
3. Beget.

And whilst our souls negotiate there,
   We like sepulchral statues lay;   50
All day, the same our postures were,
20   And we said nothing, all the day.

If any, so by love refined
   That he souls' language understood,
And by good love were grown all mind,   55
   Within convenient distance stood,

25   He (though he knew not which soul spake,
   Because both meant, both spake the same)
Might thence a new concoction⁴ take,
   And part far purer than he came.   60

This Ecstasy doth unperplex,
30   We said, and tell us what we love;
We see by this it was not sex;
   We see we saw not what did move:⁵

But as all several⁶ souls contain   65
   Mixture of things, they know not what,
35   Love these mixed souls doth mix again,
   And makes both one, each this and that.

A single violet transplant,
   The strength, the color, and the size,   70
(All which before was poor, and scant)
40   Redoubles still, and multiplies.

When love, with one another so
   Interinanimates two souls,
That abler soul, which thence doth flow,⁷
   Defects of loneliness controls.   75

45   We then, who are this new soul, know
   Of what we are composed, and made,
For the atomies⁸ of which we grow
   Are souls, whom no change can invade.

But oh, alas, so long, so far
   Our bodies why do we forbear?
They're ours, though they're not we, we are
   The intelligences, they the sphere.⁹

We owe them thanks because they thus
   Did us to us at first convey,
Yielded their forces, sense, to us,
   Nor are dross to us, but allay.¹⁰

On man heaven's influence works not so,
   But that it first imprints the air;¹¹
So soul into the soul may flow,
   Though it to body first repair.

As our blood labours to beget
   Spirits as like souls as it can,¹²
Because such fingers need to knit
   That subtle knot which makes us man:

So must pure lovers' souls descend
   To affections, and to faculties,
Which sense may reach and apprehend,
   Else a great Prince in prison lies.

To our bodies turn we then, that so
   Weak men on love revealed may look;
Love's mysteries in souls do grow,
   But yet the body is his book.¹³

And if some lover, such as we,
   Have heard this dialogue of one,
Let him still mark us, he shall see
   Small change, when we're to bodies gone.

From Holy Sonnets

Death be not proud, though some have called thee
Mighty and dreadful, for thou art not so;
For those whom thou think'st thou dost overthrow
Die not, poor death, nor yet canst thou kill me.
From rest and sleep, which but thy pictures be,
Much pleasure; then from thee much more must flow,
And soonest our best men with thee do go,
Rest of their bones, and soul's delivery.¹

---

4. Alchemical term for a mixture highly refined by heat.
5. I.e., what motivated us.
6. Individual.
7. I.e., flows from the union of two "less able" souls.
8. Atoms.
9. Each of the nine celestial spheres was thought to have, like the body, its "soul," or angelic intelligence.
10. Alloy.
11. Stellar influence on men required the medium of air;

angels assumed bodies of air when manifesting themselves to men.
12. The "animal spirits," refined from the blood, act as a medium between body and soul.
13. I.e., Love's Bible, the physical manifestation of spiritual mystery.

1. Escape, deliverance.

Thou art slave to fate, chance, kings, and desperate men,
And dost with poison, war, and sickness dwell;
And poppy[2] or charms can make us sleep as well,
And better than thy stroke; why swell'st[3] thou then?
One short sleep past, we wake eternally,
And death shall be no more; death, thou shalt die.

Batter my heart, three-personed God; for You
As yet but knock, breathe, shine, and seek to mend;
That I may rise and stand, o'erthrow me, and bend
Your force, to break, blow, burn, and make me new.
I, like an usurped town, to another due,[1]
Labor to admit You, but Oh, to no end!
Reason, Your viceroy in me, me should defend,
But is captived, and proves weak or untrue.
Yet dearly I love You, and would be loved fain,
But am betrothed unto Your enemy:
Divorce me, untie or break that knot again,
Take me to You, imprison me, for I,
Except You enthrall me, never shall be free,
Nor ever chaste, except You ravish me.

I am a little world made cunningly
Of elements and an angelic sprite,
But black sin hath betrayed to endless night
My world's both parts, and, oh, both parts must die.
You[1] which beyond that heaven which was most high
Have found new spheres, and of new lands can write,
Pour new seas in mine eyes, that so I might
Drown my world with my weeping earnestly,
Or wash it if it must be drowned no more.[2]
But oh it must be burnt![3] Alas, the fire
Of lust and envy have burnt it heretofore,
And made it fouler; let their flames retire,
And burn me, O Lord, with a fiery zeal
Of Thee and Thy house, which doth in eating heal.[4]

Show me, dear Christ, Thy spouse,[1] so bright and clear.
What, is it she which on the other shore
Goes richly painted?[2] or which robbed and tore
Laments and mourns in Germany and here?[3]
Sleeps she a thousand, then peeps up one year?
Is she self-truth and errs? now new, now outwore?
Doth she, and did she, and shall she evermore
On one,[4] on seven,[5] or on no hill appear?[6]
Dwells she with us, or like adventuring knights
First travail[7] we to seek, and then make love?
Betray, kind husband, Thy spouse to our sights,
And let mine amorous soul court Thy mild Dove,
Who is most true and pleasing to Thee then
When she is embraced and open to most men.

---

2. Opium.
3. Puff up (with pride).

1. Owing allegiance.

1 Addressed to post Copernican astronomers and global explorers such as Magellan and Columbus whose discoveries revolutionized people's conception of the world.
2. God made a covenant with Noah to guarantee forever seed-time and harvest; "neither shall there any more be a flood to destroy the earth" (Gen. ix.11).
3. I.e., in the apocalyptic fire at the end of the world.

4. An echo of Ps. lxix.9: "For the zeal of thine house hath eaten me up."

1. I.e., the true Church, the "bride of Christ."
2. I.e., the Roman Church.
3. I.e., the Protestant Church.
4. Perhaps the Mount of Olives, scene of Christ's Ascension, Mount Sinai, or Mount Moriah, site of Solomon's temple.
5. The seven hills of Rome.
6. Perhaps Geneva (centre of Calvinism) or Canterbury (centre of Anglicanism).
7. Both "strive" and "journey" seem to be implied.

BEN JONSON (1572–1637)

To John Donne

Donne, the delight of Phoebus[1] and each Muse,
Who, to thy one, all other brains refuse;[2]
Whose every work, of thy most early wit,
Came forth example and remains so yet;
Longer a-knowing than most wits do live,
And which no affection praise enough can give.
To it[3] thy language, letters, arts, best life,
Which might with half mankind maintain a strife.
All which I meant to praise, and yet I would,
But leave, because I cannot as I should.

On My First Daughter

Here lies, to each her parents' ruth,[1]
Mary, the daughter of their youth:
Yet, all heavens' gifts, being heavens' due,
It makes the father less to rue.
At six months' end, she parted hence
With safety of her innocence;
Whose soul heaven's Queen, (whose name she bears)
In comfort of her mother's tears,
Hath placed amongst her virgin-train;
Where, while that severed doth remain,
This grave partakes the fleshly birth—
Which cover lightly, gentle earth.

To Penshurst[1]

Thou art not, Penshurst, built to envious show,
Of touch[2] or marble; nor canst boast a row
Of polished pillars, or a roof of gold;
Thou hast no lantern,[3] whereof tales are told,
5 Or stair, or courts; but stand'st an ancient pile,
And, these grudged at,[4] art reverenced the while.
Thou joy'st in better marks, of soil, of air,
Of wood, of water; therein thou art fair.
Thou hast thy walks for health, as well as sport;
10 Thy mount, to which the dryads[5] do resort,
Where Pan and Bacchus their high feasts have made,
Beneath the broad beech and the chestnut shade;
That taller tree, which of a nut was set
At his great birth where all the Muses met.[6]
15 There in the writhéd bark are cut the names
Of many a sylvan,[7] taken with his flames;[8]
And thence the ruddy satyrs oft provoke
The lighter fauns to reach thy Lady's Oak.

1. Apollo, god of poetry.
2. Re-ignite, gain new fire.
3. "To add" is understood.

1. Sorrow.

1. Country home in Kent of the Sidney family.
2. Touchstone, an expensive variety of basalt.

3. Small, glassed-in copula.
4. I.e., lacking these.
5. Wood nymphs.
6. An oak was planted at Penshurst on the day Sir Philip Sidney was born.
7. Woodsman.
8. I.e., Sidney's love-poetry.

Thy copse too, named of Gamage,[9] thou hast there,

20   That never fails to serve thee seasoned deer
When thou wouldst feast or exercise thy friends.
The lower land, that to the river bends,
Thy sheep, thy bullocks, kine, and calves do feed;
The middle grounds thy mares and horses breed.

25   Each bank doth yield thee conies;[10] and the tops,
Fertile of wood, Ashore and Sidney's copse,
To crown thy open table, doth provide
The purpled pheasant with the speckled side;
The painted partridge lies in every field,

30   And for thy mess is willing to be killed.
And if the high-swollen Medway[11] fail thy dish,
Thou hast thy ponds, that pay thee tribute fish,
Fat aged carps that run into thy net,
And pikes, now weary their own kind to eat,

35   As loath the second draught or cast to stay,[12]
Officiously[13] at first themselves betray;
Bright eels that emulate them, and leap on land
Before the fisher, or into his hand.
Then hath thy orchard fruit, thy garden flowers,

40   Fresh as the air, and new as are the hours.
The early cherry, with the later plum,
Fig, grape, and quince, each in his time doth come;
The blushing apricot and woolly peach
Hang on thy walls, that every child may reach.

45   And though thy walls be of the country stone,
They are reared with no man's ruin, no man's groan;
There's none that dwell about them wish them down;
But all come in, the farmer and the clown,[14]
And no one empty-handed, to salute

50   Thy lord and lady, though they have no suit.
Some bring a capon, some a rural cake,
Some nuts, some apples; some that think they make
The better cheeses bring them, or else send
By their ripe daughters, whom they would commend

55   This way to husbands, and whose baskets bear
An emblem of themselves in plum or pear.
But what can this (more than express their love)
Add to thy free provisions, far above
The need of such? whose liberal board doth flow

60   With all that hospitality doth know;
Where comes no guest but is allowed to eat,
Without his fear, and of thy lord's own meat;
Where the same beer and bread, and selfsame wine,
That is his lordship's shall be also mine,

65   And I not fain to sit (as some this day
At great men's tables), and yet dine away.[15]
Here no man tells[16] my cups; nor, standing by,
A waiter doth my gluttony envy,
But gives me what I call, and lets me eat;

70   He knows below he shall find plenty of meat.
Thy tables hoard not up for the next day;
Nor, when I take my lodging, need I pray
For fire, or lights, or livery;[17] all is there,
As if thou then wert mine, or I reigned here:

---

9. Barbara Gamage, wife of Philip Sidney's younger
brother Robert. Sir Robert is the present owner of
Penshurst addressed in the poem.
10. Rabbits.
11. The local river.
12. Wait for.

13. Dutifully.
14. Rustic.
15. I.e., go away still hungry.
16. Counts.
17. Provision.

75   There's nothing I can wish, for which I stay.[18]
     That found King James when, hunting late this way
     With his brave son, the prince, they saw thy fires
     Shine bright on every hearth, as the desires
     Of thy Penates[19] had been set on flame
80   To entertain them; or the country came
     With all their zeal to warm their welcome here.
     What (great I will not say, but) sudden cheer
     Didst thou then make 'em! and what praise was heaped
     On thy good lady then, who therein reaped
85   The just reward of her high housewifery;
     To have her linen, plate, and all things nigh,
     When she was far; and not a room but dressed
     As if it had expected such a guest!
     These, Penshurst, are thy praise, and yet not all.
90   Thy lady's noble, fruitful, chaste withal.
     His children thy great lord may call his own,
     A fortune in this age but rarely known.
     They are, and have been, taught religion; thence
     Their gentler spirits have sucked innocence.
95   Each morn and even they are taught to pray,
     With the whole household, and may, every day,
     Read in their virtuous parents' noble parts
     The mysteries of manners, arms, and arts.
     Now, Penshurst, they that will proportion[20] thee
100 With other edifices, when they see
     Those proud, ambitious heaps, and nothing else,
     May say their lords have built, but thy lord dwells.

Song: To Celia

Drink to me only with thine eyes,
   And I will pledge with mine;
Or leave a kiss but in the cup,
   And I'll not look for wine.
The thirst that from the soul doth rise
   Doth ask a drink divine;
But might I of Jove's nectar sup,
   I would not change for thine.

I sent thee late a rosy wreath,
   Not so much honoring thee,
As giving it a hope that there
   It could not withered be.
But thou thereon didst only breathe,
   And sent'st it back to me—
Since when it grows and smells, I swear,
   Not of itself, but thee.

Song: To Celia[1]

Come, my Celia, let us prove,[2]
While we may, the sports of love.
Time will not be ours forever;
He, at length, our good will sever.
Spend not then his gifts in vain;
Suns that set may rise again,
But if once we lose this light,
'Tis with us perpetual night.
Why should we defer our joys?

Fame and rumour are but toys.
Cannot we delude the eyes
Of a few poor household spies?
Or his[3] easier ears beguile,
So removèd by our wile?
'Tis no sin love's fruit to steal,
But the sweet theft to reveal:
To be taken, to be seen,
These have crimes accounted been.

18. Wait.
19. Roman household gods.
20. Compare.

1. From *Volpone*. The amorous Volpone attempts to seduce the virtuous Celia.
2. Experience.
3. Celia's husband, Corvino.

Still to Be Neat[1]

Still to be neat, still to be dressed
As you were going to a feast;
Still to be powdered, still perfumed:
Lady, it is to be presumed,
Though art's hid causes are not found,
All is not sweet, all is not sound.

Give me a look, give me a face
That makes simplicity a grace;
Robes loosely flowing, hair as free:
Such sweet neglect more taketh me
Than all the adulteries of art;
They strike mine eyes, but not my heart.

To the Memory of My Beloved William Shakespeare and What He Hath Left Us[1]

To draw no envy, Shakespeare, on thy name,
Am I thus ample to thy book and fame,
While I confess thy writings to be such
As neither man nor muse can praise too much.
5 'Tis true, and all men's suffrage.[2] But these ways
Were not the paths I meant unto thy praise;
For silliest ignorance on these may light,
Which, when it sounds at best, but echoes right;
Or blind affection, which doth ne'er advance
10 The truth, but gropes, and urgeth all by chance;
Or crafty malice might pretend this praise,
And think to ruin, where it seemed to raise.
These are, as some infamous bawd or whore
Should praise a matron; what could hurt her more?
15 But thou art proof against them, and indeed
Above the ill fortune of them, or the need.
I, therefore will begin. Soul of the Age!
The applause, delight, the wonder of our stage!
My Shakespeare, rise; I will not lodge thee by
20 Chaucer or Spenser, or bid Beaumont lie[3]
A little further, to make thee a room:
Thou art a monument without a tomb,
And art alive still, while thy book doth live,
And we have wits to read, and praise to give.
25 That I not mix thee so, my brain excuses;
I mean with great but disproportioned[4] Muses.
For, if I thought my judgment were of years,
I should commit thee surely with thy peers,
And tell how far thou didst our Lyly out-shine,
30 Or sporting Kyd, or Marlowe's[5] mighty line.
And though thou hadst small Latin and less Greek,
From thence to honor thee, I would not seek
For names; but call forth thundering Aeschylus,
Euripides, and Sophocles to us,
35 Pacuvius, Accius, him of Cordoba dead,[6]
To life again, to hear thy buskin[7] tread,
And shake a stage; or when thy socks were on,
Leave thee alone, for the comparison
Of all, that insolent Greece or haughty Rome
40 Sent forth, or since did from their ashes come.

---

1. From *The Silent Woman*.

1. Prefixed to the first Folio edition of Shakespeare's
plays, published in 1623.
2. Consent.
3. Chaucer, Spenser, and Beaumont are all buried in
Westminster Abbey. Shakespeare is buried in Stratford-
Upon-Avon.

4. Lesser, not comparable.
5. John Lyly, Thomas Kyd, and Christopher Marlowe are
Elizabethan dramatists.
6. Pacurius, Accius, and Seneca ("him of Cordoba") are
Roman tragedians.
7. High boots, worn by actors in classical tragedy. They
contrast with the "socks" (l. 37) or light slippers worn by
comic actors.

Triumph, my Britain, thou hast one to show,
To whom all scenes of Europe homage owe.
He was not of an age, but for all time!
And all the Muses still were in their prime,
45 When like Apollo he came forth to warm
Our ears, or like a Mercury to charm!
Nature herself was proud of his designs,
And joyed to wear the dressing of his lines!
Which were so richly spun, and woven so fit,
50 As, since, she will vouchsafe no other wit.
The merry Greek, tart Aristophanes,
Neat Terence, witty Plautus,[8] now not please,
But antiquated and deserted lie
As they were not of Nature's family.
55 Yet must I not give Nature all: thy art,
My gentle Shakespeare, must enjoy a part.
For though the Poet's matter nature be,
His art doth give the fashion.[9] And, that he
Who casts to write a living line, must sweat,
60 (Such as thine are) and strike the second heat
Upon the Muses' anvil, turn the same,
And himself with it, that he thinks to frame—
Or for the laurel, he may gain a scorn;
For a good poet's made, as well as born.
65 And such wert thou. Look how the father's face
Lives in his issue; even so the race
Of Shakespeare's mind and manners brightly shines
In his well turnëd, and true-filëd lines,
In each of which he seems to shake a lance,
70 As brandished at the eyes of Ignorance.
Sweet swan of Avon! what a sight it were
To see thee in our waters yet appear,
And make those flights upon the banks of Thames
That so did take Eliza and our James![10]
75 But stay, I see thee in the hemisphere
Advanced, and made a constellation there!
Shine forth, thou star of poets, and with rage,
Or influence,[11] chide, or cheer the drooping stage,
Which, since thy flight from hence, hath mourned like night,
80 And despairs day, but for thy volume's light.

ROBERT HERRICK (1591 – 1674)

Delight in Disorder

A Sweet disorder in the dresse
Kindles in cloathes a wantonnesse:
A Lawne[1] about the shoulders thrown
Into a fine distraction:
An erring[2] Lace, which here and there
Enthralls the Crimson Stomacher:[3]
A Cuffe neglectfull, and thereby
Ribbands to flow confusedly:
A winning wave (deserving Note)
In the tempestuous petticote:
A carelesse shooe-string, in whose tye
I see a wilde civility:
Doe more bewitch me, then when Art
Is too precise in every part.

8. Terence and Plautus are Roman comic dramatists of
the third and second centuries B.C.
9. Form.
10. Queen Elizabeth and King James.
11. In astrology, the planets are thought to affect human

affairs. "Rage" also implies poetic inspiration.

1. Fine linen scarf.
2. Wandering.
3. An ornamental, frilled accent worn under the bodice.

Corinna's Going A-Maying

Get up, get up for shame, the Blooming Morne
Upon her wings presents the god unshorne.[1]
     See how *Aurora*[2] throwes her faire
     Fresh-quilted colours through the aire:
5   Get up, sweet-Slug-a-bed, and see
     The Dew-bespangling Herbe and Tree.
Each Flower has wept, and bow'd toward the East,
Above an houre since; yet you not drest,
     Nay! not so much as out of bed?
10   When all the Birds have Mattens[3] seyd,
     And sung their thankfull Hymnes: 'tis sin,
     Nay, profanation to keep in,
Whenas a thousand Virgins on this day,
Spring, sooner then the Lark, to fetch in May.[4]

15 Rise; and put on your Foliage, and be seene
To come forth, like the Spring-time, fresh and greene;
     And sweet as *Flora*.[5] Take no care
     For Jewels for your Gowne, or Haire:
     Feare not; the leaves will strew
20   Gemms in abundance upon you:
Besides, the childhood of the Day has kept,
Against[6] you come, some *Orient*[7] *Pearls* unwept:
     Come, and receive them while the light
     Hangs on the Dew-locks of the night:
25   And *Titan*[8] on the Eastern hill
     Retires himselfe, or else stands still
Till you come forth. Wash, dresse, be briefe in praying:
Few Beads[9] are best, when once we goe a Maying.

  Come, my *Corinna*, come; and comming, marke
30 How each field turns a street; each street a Parke
     Made green, and trimm'd with trees: see how
     Devotion gives each House a Bough,
     Or Branch: Each Porch, each doore, ere this,
     An Arke a Tabernacle is
35 Made up of white-thorn neatly enterwove;
As if here were those cooler shades of love.
     Can such delights be in the street,
     And open fields, and we not see't?
     Come, we'll abroad; and let's obay
40   The Proclamation made for May:
And sin no more, as we have done, by staying;
But my *Corinna*, come, let's goe a Maying.

  There's not a budding Boy, or Girle, this day,
But is got up, and gone to bring in May.
45   A deale of Youth, ere this, is come
     Back, and with *White-thorn* laden home.
     Some have dispatcht their Cakes and Creame,
     Before that we have left to dreame:
And some have wept, and woo'd, and plighted Troth,
50 And chose their Priest, ere we can cast off sloth:
     Many a green-gown[10] has been given;
     Many a kisse, both odde and even:

1. Apollo, god of the sun. His "unshorne" hair represents
the sun's rays.
2. Goddess of the dawn.
3. Morning prayers.
4. Boughs of white hawthorne, emblematic of marriage,
gathered traditionally on Mayday morning.

5. Goddess of flowers and vegetation.
6. Until.
7. Eastern, glowing with the rising sun.
8. The sun.
9. I.e., prayers, devotions.
10. Grass-stained from rolling amorously on the ground.

Many a glance too has been sent
From out the eye, Loves Firmament:
55 Many a jest told of the Keyes betraying
This night, and Locks pickt, yet we're not a Maying.

Come, let us goe, while we are in our prime;
And take the harmlesse follie of the time.
      We shall grow old apace, and die
60   Before we know our liberty.
      Our life is short; and our dayes run
      As fast away as do's the Sunne:
And as a vapour, or a drop of raine
Once lost, can ne'r be found againe:
65   So when or you or I are made
      A fable, song, or fleeting shade;
      All love, all liking, all delight
      Lies drown'd with us in endlesse night.
Then while time serves, and we are but decaying;
70 Come, my *Corinna*, come, let's goe a Maying.

To the Virgins, to Make Much of Time

Gather ye Rose-buds while ye may,
   Old Time is still a flying:
And this same flower that smiles today,
   To morrow will be dying,

The glorious Lamp of Heaven, the Sun,
   The higher he's a getting;
The sooner will his Race be run,
   And neerer he's to Setting.

That Age is best, which is the first,
   When Youth and Blood are warmer;
But being spent, the worse, and worst
   Times, still succeed the former.

Then be not coy, but use your time;
   And while ye may, goe marry:
For having lost but once your prime,
   You may for ever tarry.

Upon *Julia's* Clothes

Whenas in silks my *Julia* goes,
Then, then (me thinks) how sweetly flowes
That liquefaction of her clothes.

Next, when I cast mine eyes and see
That brave[1] Vibration each way free;
O how that glittering taketh me!

To His Conscience

Can I not sin, but thou wilt be
My private *Protonotarie?*[1]
Can I not wooe thee to passe by
A short and sweet iniquity?
I'le cast a mist and cloud, upon
My delicate transgression,
So utter dark, as that no eye
Shall see the hug'd impietie:
Gifts blind the wise,[2] and bribes do please,

And winde[3] all other witnesses:
And wilt not thou, with gold, be ti'd
To lay thy pen and ink aside?
That in the mirk[4] and tonguelesse night,
Wanton I may, and thou not write?
It will not be: And, therefore, now,
For times to come, I'le make this Vow,
From aberrations to live free;
So I'le not feare the Judge, or thee.

1. Boldly splendid.

1. The clerk who records testimony in a law court.
2. Allusion to Deut. xvi.19: "a gift doth blind the eyes of

the wise, and pervert the words of the righteous."
3. Silence, corrupt.
4. Dark, murky.

GEORGE HERBERT (1593–1633)

The Altar

A broken ALTAR, Lord, thy servant rears,
Made of a heart, and cemented with tears:
   Whose parts are as thy hand did frame;
   No workman's tool hath touched the same.[1]
        A HEART alone
        Is such a stone,
        As nothing but
        Thy pow'r doth cut.
        Wherefore each part
        Of my hard heart
        Meets in this frame,
        To praise thy name.
That, if I chance to hold my peace,
These stones to praise thee may not cease.
O let thy blessed SACRIFICE be mine,
And sanctify this ALTAR to be thine.

Easter-Wings

Lord, who createdst man in wealth and store,[1]
   Though foolishly he lost the same,
      Decaying more and more,
         Till he became
           Most poor:
           With thee
         O let me rise
      As larks, harmoniously,
   And sing this day thy victories:
Then shall the fall[2] further the flight in me.

My tender age in sorrow did begin:
   And still with sicknesses and shame
      Thou didst so punish sin,
         That I became
           Most thin.
           With thee
         Let me combine,
      And feel this day thy victory:
For, if I imp[3] my wing on thine,
Affliction shall advance the flight in me.

---

1. An allusion to Exod. xx.25, where Moses is commanded by God to build an altar of uncut stone without using tools.

1. Abundance.

2. An allusion to the paradox of the "fortunate Fall" (*felix culpa*), "fortunate" or "happy" because man's loss of grace resulted in the coming of Christ as redeemer.

3. Graft feathers on a damaged wing (from falconry).

Virtue

Sweet day, so cool, so calm, so bright,
The bridal of the earth and sky:
The dew shall weep thy fall to night;
        For thou must die.

Sweet rose, whose hue angry[1] and brave[2]
Bids the rash gazer wipe his eye:
Thy root is ever in its grave,
        And thou must die.

Sweet spring, full of sweet days and roses,
A box where sweets[3] compacted lie:
My music shows ye have your closes,[4]
        And all must die.

Only a sweet and virtuous soul,
Like seasoned timber, never gives;
But though the whole world turn to coal,[5]
        Then chiefly lives.

Man

      My God, I heard this day,
That none doth build a stately habitation,
      But he that means to dwell therein.
5   What house more stately hath there been,
Or can be, than is Man? to[1] whose creation
      All things are in decay.

      For Man is ev'ry thing,
And more: he is a tree, yet bears more fruit;
      A beast, yet is, or should be more:
10   Reason and speech we only bring.
Parrots may thank us, if they are not mute.
      They go upon the score.[2]

      Man is all symmetry,
Full of proportions, one limb to another,
15   And all to all the world besides:
      Each part may call the farthest, brother:
For head with foot hath private amity,
      And both with moons and tides.[3]

      Nothing hath got so far,
20   But Man hath caught and kept it, as his prey.
      His eyes dismount the highest star:
      He is in little all the sphere.
Herbs gladly cure our flesh; because that they
      Find their acquaintance there.

25   For us the winds do blow,
The earth doth rest, heav'n move, and fountains flow.
      Nothing we see, but means our good,
      As our *delight*, or as our *treasure:*
The whole is, either our cupboard of *food*,
30   Or cabinet of *pleasure*.

---

1. Red.
2. Splendid.
3. Perfumes.
4. Musical cadences.
5. I.e., be reduced to cinders in the apocalyptic conflagration at the Last Judgement.

1. Compared to.
2. I.e., parrots can say only what they have been taught to speak by men.
3. The proportions of the human body were thought to correspond to the symmetric proportions of the created cosmos, and human rhythms to respond to those of the moon and tides.

The stars have us to bed;
Night draws the curtain, which the sun withdraws;
Music and light attend our head.
All things unto our *flesh* are kind[4]
35   In their *descent* and *being;* to our *mind*
In their *ascent* and *cause.*

Each thing is full of duty:
Waters united are our navigation;
Distinguished, our habitation;
40   Below, our drink; above, our meat;
Both are our cleanliness. Hath one such beauty?
Then how are all things neat![5]

More servants wait on Man,
Than he'll take notice of: in ev'ry path
45   He treads down that which doth befriend him,
When sickness makes him pale and wan.
Oh mighty love! Man is one world, and hath
Another to attend him.

Since then, my God, thou hast
50   So brave a Palace built; O dwell in it,
That it may dwell with thee at last!
Till then, afford us so much wit,
That, as the world serves us, we may serve thee,
And both thy servants be.

The Pulley

When God at first made man,
Having a glass of blessings standing by;
Let us (said he) pour on him all we can:
Let the world's riches, which dispersed lie,
Contract into a span.[1]

So strength first made a way;
Then beauty flowed, then wisdom, honour, pleasure:
When almost all was out, God made a stay,
Perceiving that alone of all his treasure
Rest in the bottom lay.

For if I should (said he)
Bestow this jewel also on my creature,
He would adore my gifts instead of me,
And rest in Nature, not the God of Nature:
So both should losers be.

Yet let him keep the rest,
But keep them with repining restlessness:
Let him be rich and weary, that at least,
If goodness lead him not, yet weariness
May toss him to my breast.

4. Kindred.
5. I.e., if one element serves us so well, how wonderful
are the blessings of all elements (earth, air, and fire as

well as water).

1. Width of a hand.

The Flower

How fresh, O Lord, how sweet and clean
Are thy returns! ev'n as the flowers in spring;
        To which, besides their own demean,[1]
The late-past frosts tributes of pleasure bring.
5   Grief melts away
                Like snow in May,
        As if there were no such cold thing.

        Who would have thought my shriveled heart
Could have recovered greenness? It was gone
10   Quite under ground; as flowers depart
To see their mother-root, when they have blown;[2]
                Where they together
                All the hard weather,
        Dead to the world, keep house unknown.

15   These are thy wonders, *Lord of power*,
Killing and quick'ning,[3] bringing down to hell
        And up to heaven in an hour;
Making a chiming of a passing-bell.[4]
                We say amiss,
20   This or that is:
        Thy word is all, if we could spell.

        O that I once past changing were,
Fast in thy Paradise, where no flower can wither!
        Many a spring I shoot up fair,
25 Off'ring at[5] heav'n, growing and groaning thither:
                Nor doth my flower
                Want a spring-shower,
        My sins and I joining together.

        But while I grow in a straight line,
30 Still upwards bent, as if heav'n were mine own,
        Thy anger comes, and I decline:
What frost to that? what pole is not the zone
                Where all things burn,
                When thou dost turn
35   And the least frown of thine is shown?

        And now in age I bud again,
After so many deaths I live and write,
         I once more smell the dew and rain,
And relish versing: O my only light,
40   It cannot be
                That I am he
        On whom thy tempests fell all night.

        These are thy wonders, *Lord of love*,
To make us see we are but flowers that glide:[6]
45   Which when we once can find and prove,[7]
Thou hast a garden for us, where to bide.
                Who would be more,
                Swelling through store,
        Forfeit their Paradise by their pride.

1. Demeanor, appearance.
2. Bloomed.
3. Giving life.
4. The bell that tolls to mark a death.

5. Striving for.
6. Slip away.
7. Understand (the "wonders").

Discipline

Throw away thy rod,
Throw away thy wrath:
        O my God,
Take the gentle path.

5   For my heart's desire
Unto thine is bent:
        I aspire
To a full consent.

Not a word or look
10   I affect to own,
        But by book,
And thy book alone.

Though I fail, I weep:
Though I halt in pace,
15   Yet I creep
To the throne of grace.

20   Then let wrath remove;
Love will do the deed;
        For with love
Stony hearts will bleed.

Love is swift of foot;
Love's a man of war,
        And can shoot,
And can hit from far.

25   Who can scape his bow?
That which wrought on thee,
        Brought thee low,
Needs must work on me.

Throw away thy rod;
30   Though man frailties hath,
        Thou art God:
Throw away thy wrath.

The Elixir

Teach me, my God and King,
In all things thee to see,
And what I do in any thing,
    To do it as for thee:

5   Not rudely as a beast,
To run into an action;
But still to make thee prepossest,
    And give it his[1] perfection.

A man that looks on glass,
10 On it may stay his eye;
Or if he pleaseth, through it pass,
    And then the heav'n espy.

15 All may of thee partake:
Nothing can be so mean,
Which with his tincture[2] (for thy sake)
    Will not grow bright and clean.

A servant with this clause
Makes drudgery divine:
20 Who sweeps a room, as for thy laws,
    Makes that and th'action fine.

This is the famous stone[3]
That turneth all to gold:
For that which God doth touch[4] and own
    Cannot for less be told.

Love (III)

Love bade me welcome. Yet my soul drew back
        Guilty of dust and sin.
But quick-eyed Love, observing me grow slack[1]
        From my first entrance in,
Drew nearer to me, sweetly questioning,
        If I lacked any thing.

A guest, I answered, worthy to be here:
        Love said, You shall be he.
I the unkind, ungrateful? Ah my dear,
        I cannot look on thee.
Love took my hand, and smiling did reply,
        Who made the eyes but I?

1. Its.
2. In alchemy, "tincture" is an immaterial substance capable of infusing and altering in character material substances.
3. The "philosopher's stone" or "elixir," sought by

alchemists as the instrument for transmuting base metals into gold.
4. I.e., "touchstone," used to test the purity of gold.

1. Hesitant, reluctant.

Truth Lord, but I have marred them: let my shame
                    Go where it doth deserve.
And know you not, says Love, who bore the blame?
                    My dear, then I will serve.
You must sit down, says Love, and taste my meat:
                    So I did sit and eat.

JOHN MILTON (1608–74)

On Shakespeare

What needs my Shakespeare for his honoured bones
The labor of an age in piléd stones,
Or that his hallowed relics should be hid
Under a star-ypointing[1] pyramid?
Dear son of memory,[2] great heir of fame,
What need'st thou such weak witness of thy name?
Thou in our wonder and astonishment
Hast built thyself a livelong monument.
For whilst to th' shame of slow-endeavoring art,
Thy easy numbers flow, and that each heart
Hath from the leaves of thy unvalued book[3]
Those delphic[4] lines with deep impression took,
Then thou, our fancy of itself bereaving,
Dost make us marble with too much conceiving;
And so sepulchered in such pomp dost lie,
That kings for such a tomb would wish to die.

L'Allegro[1]

Hence loathéd Melancholy
   Of Cerberus[2] and blackest midnight born,
In Stygian[3] cave forlorn
'Mongst horrid shapes, and shrieks, and sights unholy,
5 Find out some uncouth cell,
   Where brooding Darkness spreads his jealous wings,
And the night-raven sings;
   There under ebon shades, and low-browed rocks,
As ragged as thy locks,
10   In dark Cimmerian[4] desert ever dwell.
But come thou goddess fair and free,
In Heaven yclept[5] Euphrosyne,[6]
And by men, heart-easing Mirth,
Whom lovely Venus at a birth
15 With two sister Graces more
To ivy-crownéd Bacchus[7] bore;
Or whether (as some sager sing)[8]

1. I.e., "pointing." The y-prefix represents an archaic form of the past participle.
2. Memory (Mneymosyne) is mother to the Muses.
3. I.e., book beyond value.
4. Apollo, god of poetry, had an oracle in his temple at Delphi.

1. Milton apparently did not translate the title because English lacks an entirely satisfactory equivalent. "Cheerful, sociable man" is, perhaps, a fair approximation. The companion poem, *Il Penseroso*, explores the complementary type of spirit: contemplative, solitary, melancholy.

2. Three-headed watchdog of Hell.
3. From "Styx," one of the rivers of Hell.
4. The Cimmerians appear in classical myth as a mysterious people living beyond the seas, at the edge of the world, in perpetual twilight.
5. Called.
6. One of the three Graces. Aglaia and Thalia are her "sister Graces" (l. 15).
7. God of wine.
8. Milton apparently invented this myth of Euphrosyne's birth, i.e., he is the "sager' singer.

The frolic wind that breathes the spring,
Zephyr[9] with Aurora[10] playing,
20   As he met her once a-Maying,
There on beds of violets blue,
And fresh-blown roses washed in dew,
Filled her with thee a daughter fair,
So buxom, blithe, and debonair.
25   Haste thee nymph, and bring with thee
Jest and youthful Jollity,
Quips and Cranks,[11] and wanton Wiles,
Nods, and Becks,[12] and wreathéd Smiles,
Such as hang on Hebe's[13] cheek,
30   And love to live in dimple sleek;
Sport that wrinkled Care derides,
And Laughter, holding both his sides.
Come, and trip it as ye go
On the light fantastic toe,
35   And in thy right hand lead with thee,
The mountain nymph, sweet Liberty;
And if I give thee honor due,
Mirth, admit me of thy crew
To live with her and live with thee,
40   In unreprovéd pleasures free;
To hear the lark begin his flight,
And, singing, startle the dull night,
From his watch-tower in the skies,
Till the dappled dawn doth rise;
45   Then to come in spite of sorrow,
And at my window bid good morrow,
Through the sweetbriar, or the vine,
Or the twisted eglantine.
While the cock with lively din,
50   Scatters the rear of darkness thin,
And to the stack, or the barn door,
Stoutly struts his dames before;
Oft listening how the hounds and horn
Cheerly rouse the slumbering morn,
55   From the side of some hoar hill,
Through the high wood echoing shrill.
Sometime walking not unseen
By hedgerow elms, on hillocks green,
Right against the eastern gate,
60   Where the great sun begins his state,[14]
Robed in flames, and amber light,
The clouds in thousand liveries dight;[15]
While the plowman near at hand,
Whistles o'er the furrowed land,
65   And the milkmaid singeth blithe,
And the mower whets his scythe,
And every shepherd tells his tale,
Under the hawthorn in the dale.
Straight mine eye hath caught new pleasures

70   Whilst the landscape round it measures,
Russet lawns and fallows gray,
Where the nibbling flocks do stray,
Mountains on whose barren breast
The laboring clouds do often rest;
75   Meadows trim with daisies pied,[16]
Shallow brooks, and rivers wide.
Towers and battlements it sees
Bosomed high in tufted trees,
Where perhaps some beauty lies,
80   The cynosure[17] of neighboring eyes.
Hard by, a cottage chimney smokes,
From betwixt two aged oaks,
Where Corydon and Thyrsis[18] met,
Are at their savory dinner set
85   Of herbs, and other country messes,
Which the neat-handed Phyllis dresses;
And then in haste her bower she leaves,
With Thestylis to bind the sheaves;
Or if the earlier season lead
90   To the tanned haycock in the mead.
Sometimes with secure[19] delight
The upland hamlets will invite,
When the merry bells ring round
And the jocund rebecks[20] sound
95   To many a youth and many a maid,
Dancing in the checkered shade;
And young and old come forth to play
On a sunshine holiday,
Till the livelong daylight fail;
100   Then to the spicy nut-brown ale,
With stories told of many a feat,
How fairy Mab[21] the junkets eat;
She was pinched and pulled, she said,
And he, by Friar's lantern led,
105   Tells how the drudging goblin[22] sweat
To earn his cream-bowl, duly set,
When in one night, ere glimpse of morn,
His shadowy flail hath threshed the corn
That ten day-laborers could not end;
110   Then lies him down the lubber fiend,[23]
And, stretched out all the chimney's length,
Basks at the fire his hairy strength;
And crop-full out of doors he flings
Ere the first cock his matin rings.
115   Thus done the tales, to bed they creep,
By whispering winds soon lulled asleep.
Towered cities please us then,
And the busy hum of men,
Where throngs of knights and barons bold,
120   In weeds[24] of peace high triumphs hold,
With store of ladies, whose bright eyes

---

9. West wind.
10. Dawn.
11. Jokes.
12. Curtseys.
13. Cupbearer to Zeus, and goddess of youth.
14. Stately progress, procession.
15. Dressed.
16. Variously coloured.
17. Polestar.
18. Corydon, Thyrsis, Phyllis (l. 86), and Thestylis (l. 88)

are traditional names for shepherds and country girls in
pastoral poetry.
19. Carefree.
20. Primitive three-stringed fiddle.
21. Wife of Oberon, king of the fairies. The domestic
calamities recounted here are traditional fairie-lore.
22. Puck, or Robin Goodfellow. "Friar's lantern" is will-
o'-the-wisp.
23. Loutish spirit.
24. Garments.

Rain influence,[25] and judge the prize
Of wit, or arms, while both contend
To win her grace, whom all commend.
125 There let Hymen[26] oft appear
In saffron robe, with taper clear,
And pomp, and feast, and revelry,
With masque, and antique pageantry;
Such sights as youthful poets dream
130 On summer eves by haunted stream.
Then to the well-trod stage anon,
If Jonson's learned sock[27] be on,
Or sweetest Shakespeare, fancy's child,
Warble his native wood-notes wild.
135 And ever against eating cares
Lap me in soft Lydian airs,[28]
Married to immortal verse

Such as the meeting soul may pierce
In notes, with many a winding bout[29]
140 Of linkéd sweetness long drawn out,
With wanton heed, and giddy cunning,
The melting voice through mazes running;
Untwisting all the chains that tie
The hidden soul of harmony;
145 That Orpheus' self[30] may heave his head
From golden slumber on a bed
Of heaped Elysian flowers, and hear
Such strains as would have won the ear
Of Pluto, to have quite set free
150 His half-regained Eurydice.
These delights if thou canst give,
Mirth, with thee I mean to live.

Il Penseroso

Hence vain deluding Joys,
   The brood of Folly without father bred.
How little you bestead,[1]
   Or fill the fixéd mind with all your toys;
5 Dwell in some idle brain,
   And fancies fond[2] with gaudy shapes possess,
As thick and numberless
   As the gay motes that people the sunbeams,
Or likest hovering dreams,
10   The fickle pensioners of Morpheus'[3] train.
But hail thou Goddess, sage and holy,
Hail, divinest Melancholy,
Whose saintly visage is too bright
To hit[4] the sense of human sight;
15 And therefore to our weaker view,
O'erlaid with black, staid Wisdom's hue.
Black, but such as in esteem,
Prince Memnon's[5] sister might beseem,
Or that starred Ethiope queen[6] that strove
20 To set her beauty's praise above
The sea nymphs, and their powers offended.
Yet thou art higher far descended;
Thee bright-haired Vesta long of yore
To solitary Saturn bore;[7]

25. Astrologers believed that stars exert powerful influence on men through the medium of an ethereal fluid.
26. God of marriage.
27. The slipper worn by comic actors in classical comedy.
28. The Lydian mode of music was considered sensual and languid.
29. Passage.
30. The primal musician of Greek mythology, whose wife, Eurydice, died on their wedding day. Seeking to regain her, Orpheus journeys to the underworld and charms the powers of death with his music. They grant her release on condition he not look back during the return journey to life. Orpheus violates the condition and so loses Eurydice forever.

1. Avail, profit.
2. Foolish.
3. God of sleep.
4. Affect.
5. Ethiopian prince who fought for Troy (*Odyssey* XI), noted for his handsomeness. His sister's name, Hemera, means "day."
6. Cassiopeia was made a constellation ("starred") for boasting that her beauty exceeded that of the Nereids ("sea nymphs").
7. Milton invented this account of Melancholy's origins. Saturn was associated with the "saturnine" complexion and disposition thought to be symptomatic of melancholia. Vesta was goddess of purity.

25 His daughter she (in Saturn's reign
    Such mixture was not held a stain).
    Oft in glimmering bowers and glades
    He met her, and in secret shades
    Of woody Ida's[8] inmost grove,
30 While yet there was no fear of Jove.
    Come pensive nun, devout and pure,
    Sober, steadfast, and demure,
    All in a robe of darkest grain,[9]
    Flowing with majestic train,
35 And sable stole of cypress lawn[10]
    Over thy decent shoulders drawn.
    Come, but keep thy wonted state,
    With even step and musing gait,
    And looks commercing with the skies,
40 Thy rapt soul sitting in thine eyes:
    There held in holy passion still,
    Forget thyself to marble, till
    With a sad leaden downward cast,
    Thou fix them on the earth as fast.
45 And join with thee calm Peace and Quiet,
    Spare Fast, that oft with gods doth diet,
    And hears the Muses in a ring
    Aye round about Jove's altar sing.
    And add to these retired Leisure,
50 That in trim gardens takes his pleasure;
    But first, and chiefest, with thee bring,
    Him that yon soars on golden wing,
    Guiding thy fiery-wheeléd throne,
    The cherub Contemplation;[11]
55 And the mute Silence hist[12] along
    'Less Philomel[13] will deign a song,
    In her sweetest, saddest plight,
    Smoothing the rugged brow of night,
    While Cynthia[14] checks her dragon yoke
60 Gently o'er th' accustomed oak;
    Sweet bird that shunn'st the noise of folly,
    Most musical, most melancholy!
    Thee chantress oft the woods among,
    I woo to hear thy evensong;
65 And missing thee, I walk unseen
    On the dry smooth-shaven green,
    To behold the wandering moon,

        Riding near her highest noon,
        Like one that had been led astray
70   Through the Heaven's wide pathless way;
        And oft as if her head she bowed,
        Stooping through a fleecy cloud.
        Oft on a plat[15] of rising ground,
        I hear the far-off curfew sound,
75   Over some wide-watered shore,
        Swinging slow with sullen roar;
        Or if the air will not permit,
        Some still removéd place will fit,
        Where glowing embers through the room
80   Teach light to counterfeit a gloom
        Far from all resort of mirth,
        Save the cricket on the hearth,
        Or the bellman's[16] drowsy charm,
        To bless the doors from nightly harm;
85   Or let my lamp at midnight hour
        Be seen in some high lonely tower,
        Where I may oft outwatch the Bear,[17]
        With thrice great Hermes,[18] or unsphere[19]
        The spirit of Plato to unfold
90   What worlds, or what vast regions hold
        The immortal mind that hath forsook
        Her mansion in this fleshly nook:
        And of those demons[20] that are round
        In fire, air, flood, or underground,
95   Whose power hath a true consent[21]
        With planet, or with element.
        Some time let gorgeous Tragedy
        In sceptered pall[22] come sweeping by,
        Presenting Thebes', or Pelops' line,
100   Or the tale of Troy divine.[23]
        Or what (though rare) of later age
        Ennobled hath the buskined[24] stage.
        But, O sad virgin, that thy power
        Might raise Musaeus[25] from his bower,
105   Or bid the soul of Orpheus[26] sing
        Such notes as, warbled to the string,
        Drew iron tears down Pluto's cheek,
        And made Hell grant what Love did seek.
        Or call up him[27] that left half told
110   The story of Cambuscan bold,

8. Mount Ida in Crete, where Saturn ruled before his son,
Jove, overthrew him.
9. Colour.
10. A delicate cloth, often dyed black for mourning.
11. Milton associates Contemplation with the four
cherubim pictured in Ezek. i and x.
12. Summon.
13. The nightingale.
14. Diana, goddess of the moon, sometimes represented
as driving two sleepless dragons.
15. Plain.
16. Night watchman.
17. The constellation of the Great Bear never sets in the
northern hemisphere, so can never be "outwatched."
18. The Egyptian god Thoth, identified with Hermes
Trismegistus, who was thought to be the author of various
books, of the third and fourth centuries A.D., on magic and
alchemy.
19. I.e., to call back Plato from the sphere he presently
inhabits.

20. In Plato's metaphysic, intermediate beings between
men and gods. Neo-Platonists associated them with the
four primary material elements (fire, air, water, earth)
and their corresponding planets.
21. Mystical correspondence.
22. Royal robe.
23. Greek tragedy was largely based on stories about the
royal house of Thebes (e.g., Sophocles' Oedipus cycle), the
sons of Pelops (e.g., Aeschylus' *Oresteia*), and the Trojan
war (e.g., Euripides' *Trojan Women*).
24. High boots worn by tragic actors. Cf. "sock,"
L'Allegro, l. 132 and note.
25. Legendary poet-priest, thought to be either the son or
pupil of Orpheus.
26. See note to l. 145 of *L'Allegro*.
27. Chaucer, who left the tale of Cambuscan unfinished in
his *Squire's Tale*.

Of Camball, and of Algarsife,
And who had Canacee to wife
That owned the virtuous[28] ring and glass,
And of the wondrous horse of brass,
115 On which the Tartar king did ride;
And if aught else great bards beside
In sage and solemn tunes have sung,
Of tourneys and of trophies hung,
Of forests and enchantments drear,
120 Where more is meant than meets the ear.
Thus, Night, oft see me in thy pale career,
Till civil-suited morn appear,[29]
Not tricked and frounced[30] as she was wont,
With the Attic boy to hunt,
125 But kerchiefed in a comely cloud,
While rocking winds are piping loud,
Or ushered with a shower still,
When the gust hath blown his fill,
Ending on the rustling leaves,
130 With minute-drops from off the eaves.
And when the sun begins to fling
His flaring beams, me, Goddess, bring
To archéd walks of twilight groves,
And shadows brown that Sylvan[31] loves
135 Of pine or monumental oak,
Where the rude ax with heavéd stroke,
Was never heard the nymphs to daunt,
Or fright them from their hallowed haunt.
There in close covert by some brook,
140 Where no profaner eye may look,
Hide me from day's garish eye,
While the bee with honeyed thigh,
That at her flowery work doth sing,

And the waters murmuring
145 With such consort[32] as they keep,
Entice the dewy-feathered sleep;
And let some strange mysterious dream,
Wave at his wings in airy stream,
Of lively portraiture displayed,
150 Softly on my eyelids laid.
And as I wake, sweet music breathe
Above, about, or underneath,
Sent by some spirit to mortals good,
Or th' unseen genius[33] of the wood.
155 But let my due feet never fail
To walk the studious cloister's pale,[34]
And love the high embowéd roof,
With antic[35] pillars massy proof,[36]
And storied windows[37] richly dight,[38]
160 Casting a dim religious light.
There let the pealing organ blow,
To the full-voiced choir below,
In service high, and anthems clear,
As may with sweetness, through mine ear,
165 Dissolve me into ecstasies,
And bring all heaven before mine eyes.
And may at last my weary age
Find out the peaceful hermitage,
The hairy gown and mossy cell,
170 Where I may sit and rightly spell[39]
Of every star that Heaven doth show,
And every herb that sips the dew
Till old experience do attain
To something like prophetic strain.
175 These pleasures, Melancholy, give,
And I with thee will choose to live.

How Soon Hath Time

How soon hath Time, the subtle thief of youth,
    Stoln on his wing my three and twentieth year!
    My hasting days fly on with full career,
    But my late spring no bud or blossom show'th.
Perhaps my semblance might deceive the truth,
    That I to manhood am arrived so near,
    And inward ripeness doth much less appear,
    That some more timely-happy spirits endu'th.[1]
Yet be it less or more, or soon or slow,
    It shall be still in strictest measure even[2]
    To that same lot, however mean or high,
Toward which Time leads me, and the will of Heaven;
    All is, if I have grace to use it so,
    As ever in my great Taskmaster's eye.

28. Possessing mysterious power.
29. Aurora, goddess of the dawn, who once loved Cephalus, "the Attic boy," and hunted with him.
30. Adorned and curled.
31. Sylvanus, Roman god of woodlands.
32. Harmony.
33. Guardian spirit.
34. Enclosure.
35. Elaborately, or grotesquely carved.

36. Massive in strength.
37. I.e., windows depicting biblical stories in stained glass.
38. Dressed.
39. Speculate.

1. Endoweth.
2. Adequate.

Lycidas

**In this monody[1] the author bewails a learned friend,
unfortunately drowned in his passage from Chester
on the Irish Seas, 1637. And by occasion foretells
the ruin of our corrupted clergy,
then in their height.**

Yet once more, O ye laurels,[2] and once more
Ye myrtles brown, with ivy never sere,[3]
I come to pluck your berries harsh and crude,[4]
And with forced fingers rude,
5   Shatter your leaves before the mellowing year.
Bitter constraint, and sad occasion dear,[5]
Compels me to disturb your season due;
For Lycidas is dead, dead ere his prime,
Young Lycidas, and hath not left his peer.
10   Who would not sing for Lycidas? He knew
Himself to sing, and build the lofty rhyme.
He must not float upon his watery bier
Unwept, and welter to the parching wind,
Without the meed[6] of some melodious tear.
15   Begin then, sisters of the sacred well[7]
That from beneath the seat of Jove doth spring,
Begin, and somewhat loudly sweep the string.
Hence with denial vain, and coy excuse;
So may some gentle Muse[8]
20   With lucky words favor my destined urn,
And as he passes turn,
And bid fair peace be to my sable shroud.
For we were nursed upon the selfsame hill,
Fed the same flock, by fountain, shade, and rill.
25   Together both, ere the high lawns[9] appeared
Under the opening eyelids of the morn,
We drove afield, and both together heard
What time the grayfly winds her sultry horn.
Battening[10] our flocks with the fresh dews of night,
30   Oft till the star that rose at evening bright
Toward Heaven's descent had sloped his westering wheel.
Meanwhile the rural ditties were not mute,
Tempered to th' oaten flute,[11]
Rough satyrs danced, and fauns with cloven heel
35   From the glad sound would not be absent long,
And old Damoetas[12] loved to hear our song.
But O the heavy change, now thou art gone,
Now thou art gone, and never must return!
Thee, shepherd, thee the woods and desert caves,
40   With wild thyme and the gadding[13] vine o'ergrown,

---

1. A song in Greek drama, sung by a solo voice. The
"learned friend" is Edward King, Milton's fellow-student
at Cambridge, who was drowned when his ship capsized in
the Irish Sea.
2. Laurel, myrtle, and ivy are all evergreens associated
with poetic inspiration and achievement.
3. Withered.
4. Unripe.
5. Both "profoundly affecting" and "dire."
6. Reward, tribute.

7. The nine Muses, whose "sacred well" was Aganippe, at
the foot of Mt. Helicon.
8. Poet.
9. Pastures.
10. Fattening.
11. Traditional shepherd's Panpipes.
12. A typical name from pastoral poetry, perhaps referring to a tutor at Cambridge.
13. Struggling.

And all their echoes mourn.
The willows and the hazel copses green
Shall now no more be seen,
Fanning their joyous leaves to thy soft lays.
45 As killing as the canker to the rose,
Or taint-worm to the weanling herds that graze,
Or frost to flowers that their gay wardrobe wear,
When first the white thorn blows;[14]
Such, Lycidas, thy loss to shepherd's ear.
50   Where were ye, nymphs, when the remorseless deep
Closed o'er the head of your loved Lycidas?
For neither were ye playing on the steep,
Where your old Bards, the famous Druids lie,
Nor on the shaggy top of Mona high,[15]
55 Nor yet where Deva spreads her wizard stream:
Ay me! I fondly dream—
Had ye been there—for what could that have done?
What could the Muse[16] herself that Orpheus bore,
The Muse herself, for her inchanting son
60 Whom universal Nature did lament,
When by the rout[17] that made the hideous roar,
His gory visage down the stream was sent,
Down the swift Hebrus to the Lesbian shore?
      Alas! What boots[18] it with incessant care
65 To tend the homely slighted shepherd's trade,
And strictly meditate the thankless Muse?
Were it not better done as others use,
To sport with Amaryllis in the shade,
Or with the tangles of Neaera's hair?[19]
70 Fame is the spur that the clear spirit doth raise
(That last infirmity of noble mind)
To scorn delights, and live laborious days;
But the fair guerdon[20] when we hope to find,
And think to burst out into sudden blaze,
75 Comes the blind Fury with th' abhorréd shears,[21]
And slits the thin spun life. "But not the praise,"
Phoebus[22] replied, and touched my trembling ears;
"Fame is no plant that grows on mortal soil,
Not in the glistering foil[23]
80 Set off to th' world, nor in broad rumor lies,
But lives and spreads aloft by those pure eyes,
And perfect witness of all-judging Jove;
As he pronounces lastly on each deed,
Of so much fame in Heaven expect thy meed."
85   O fountain Arethuse,[24] and thou honored flood,
Smooth-sliding Mincius, crowned with vocal reeds,
That strain I heard was of a higher mood.

14. Blooms.
15. The "steep" is probably Kerig-y-Druidion, a mountain in northern Wales with a Druid burial ground at its foot. Mona is the island of Anglesey, Deva the River Dee, designated "wizard" because changes in its course were believed to foreshadow the country's fortunes. These sites are directly south of the Irish Sea.
16. Calliope, Muse of epic poetry.
17. Orpheus was dismembered by a mob ("rout") of crazed Thracian Maenads who threw his head into the river Hebrus. It floated across the Aegean to the island of Lesbos.
18. Profits.
19. Amaryllis and Neaera are conventional names for nymphs in pastoral poetry.
20. Reward.
21. Atropos, third of the Three Fates, who cuts the thread of life after her sisters have spun and measured it.
22. Apollo, god of poetic inspiration.
23. An ornate setting to enhance the appearance of fake or poor-quality gems.
24. A fountain in Sicily, representing the pastoral poetry of Theocritus. Mincius is a river in Lombardy representing Virgil's pastoral poetry.

But now my oat[25] proceeds,
And listens to the herald of the sea[26]
90   That came in Neptune's plea.
He asked the waves, and asked the felon winds,
"What hard mishap hath doomed this gentle swain?"
And questioned every gust of rugged wings
That blows from off each beakéd promontory;
95   They knew not of his story,
And sage Hippotades[27] their answer brings,
That not a blast was from his dungeon strayed,
The air was calm, and on the level brine,
Sleek Panope[28] with all her sisters played.
100   It was that fatal and perfidious bark
Built in th' eclipse, and rigged with curses dark,
That sunk so low that sacred head of thine.
    Next Camus,[29] reverend sire, went footing slow,
His mantle hairy, and his bonnet sedge,
105   Inwrought with figures dim, and on the edge
Like to that sanguine flower inscribed with woe.[30]
"Ah! who hath reft," quoth he, "my dearest pledge?"
Last came and last did go
The pilot of the Galilean lake,[31]
110   Two massy keys he bore of metals twain
(The golden opes, the iron shuts amain).
He shook his mitered locks,[32] and stern bespake:[33]
"How well could I have spared for thee, young swain,
Enow[34] of such as for their bellies' sake,
115   Creep and intrude, and climb into the fold!
Of other care they little reckoning make,
Than how to scramble at the shearer's feast,
And shove away the worthy bidden guest.
Blind mouths! That scarce themselves know how to hold
120   A sheep-hook, or have learned aught else the least
That to the faithful herdsman's art belongs!
What recks it them?[35] What need they? They are sped;[36]
And when they list,[37] their lean and flashy songs
Grate on their scrannel[38] pipes of wretched straw.
125   The hungry sheep look up, and are not fed,
But swoln with wind, and the rank mist they draw,
Rot inwardly, and foul contagion spread,
Besides what the grim wolf with privy paw[39]
Daily devours apace, and nothing said.
130   But that two-handed engine at the door[40]
Stands ready to smite once, and smite no more."
    Return, Alpheus,[41] the dread voice is past,
That shrunk thy streams; return, Sicilian muse,

---

25. I.e., oaten pipe, hence "song."
26. Triton, a merman, who appears as advocate for his master Neptune, god of the sea.
27. Aeolus, son of Hippotus, and god of the winds.
28. A Nereid, or daughter of Nerius, the Old Man of the Sea.
29. God of the River Cam, representing Cambridge University.
30. The hyacinth was reputedly marked by Apollo with the Greek letters AI AI ("alas, alas") from the blood of the youth Hyacinthus, who died accidentally when hit by Apollo's discus.
31. St. Peter, the fisherman of Galilee, to whom Christ pledged custody of the keys to the Kingdom of Heaven (Matt. xvi.19).
32. St. Peter wears the mitre to signify his role as first bishop of Christ's Church.
33. Spoke.

34. Enough.
35. I.e., what does it matter to them?
36. Prosperous.
37. Choose.
38. Harsh, meager.
39. Protestant writers conventionally referred to Roman Catholicism as a Papal wolf operating secretly ("privy") in sheep's clothing.
40. If Milton alluded to a specific instrument of retribution in these lines, it is now difficult to identify. Speculative suggestions include: the shears of Atropos (l. 75), St. Peter's keys (l. 110), the two Houses of the English Parliament, the two-handed sword of the archangel Michael, and Christ's second coming and the day of Judgement.
41. A river-deity who loved and pursued the nymph Arethusa. She was metamorphosed into a fountain (see l. 35), and their waters flowed together.

And call the vales, and bid them hither cast
135   Their bells and flowerets of a thousand hues.
Ye valleys low where the mild whispers use,[42]
Of shades and wanton winds, and gushing brooks,
On whose fresh lap the swart star[43] sparely looks,
Throw hither all your quaint enameled eyes,
140   That on the green turf suck the honeyed showers,
And purple all the ground with vernal flowers.
Bring the rathe[44] primrose that forsaken dies.
The tufted crow-toe, and pale jessamine,
The white pink, and the pansy freaked[45] with jet,
145   The glowing violet,
The musk-rose, and the well attired woodbine.
With cowslips wan that hang the pensive head,
And every flower that sad embroidery wears:
Bid amaranthus[46] all his beauty shed,
150   And daffadillies fill their cups with tears,
To strew the laureate hearse[47] where Lycid lies.
For so to interpose a little ease,
Let our frail thoughts dally with false surmise.
Ay me! Whilst thee the shores and sounding seas
155   Wash far away, where'er thy bones are hurled,
Whether beyond the stormy Hebrides,
Where thou perhaps under the whelming tide
Visit'st the bottom of the monstrous world;
Or whether thou, to our moist vows denied,
160   Sleep'st by the fable of Bellerus old,[48]
Where the great vision of the guarded mount
Looks toward Namancos and Bayona's hold;[49]
Look homeward angel now, and melt with ruth:[50]
And, O ye dolphins,[51] waft the hapless youth.
165   Weep no more, woeful shepherds, weep no more,
For Lycidas your sorrow is not dead,
Sunk though he be beneath the watery floor,
So sinks the day-star[52] in the ocean bed,
And yet anon repairs his drooping head,
170   And tricks[53] his beams, and with new-spangled ore,
Flames in the forehead of the morning sky:
So Lycidas sunk low, but mounted high,
Through the dear might of him that walked the waves,
Where other groves, and other streams along,
175   With nectar pure his oozy locks he laves,
And hears the unexpressive nuptial song,[54]
In the blest kingdoms meek of joy and love.
There entertain him all the saints above,
In solemn troops and sweet societies

---

42. Frequent.
43. Sirius, the Dog Star, associated with the withering heat of late summer.
44. Early.
45. Flecked, spotted.
46. Legendary flower that never fades.
47. Bier.
48. A giant of legend, buried at Land's End on the Cornish coast.
49. On St. Michael's Mount at the tip of Land's End, the archangel Michael keeps protective watch (hence "guarded mount") on the threatening strongholds of Catholicism, Namancos and Bayona, in northern Spain.
50. Pity.
51. The Greek poet Arion was saved from drowning by a dolphin and carried safely to shore.
52. Sun.
53. Dresses.
54. An allusion to the transcendent music, beyond human perception ("unexpressive") at "the marriage supper of the Lamb" (Rev. xix.9).

180   That sing, and singing in their glory move,
And wipe the tears forever from his eyes.
Now, Lycidas, the shepherds weep no more:
Henceforth thou art the genius[55] of the shore,
In thy large recompense, and shalt be good
185   To all that wander in that perilous flood.
        Thus sang the uncouth[56] swain to th' oaks and rills,
While the still morn went out with sandals gray;
He touched the tender stops of various quills,[57]
With eager thought warbling his Doric[58] lay.
190   And now the sun had stretched out all the hills,
And now was dropped into the western bay;
At last he rose, and twitched his mantle blue:
Tomorrow to fresh woods, and pastures new.

On the Late Massacre in Piedmont[1]

Avenge, O Lord, thy slaughtered saints, whose bones
    Lie scattered on the Alpine mountains cold,
    Even them who kept thy truth so pure of old
    When all our fathers worshiped stocks and stones,[2]
Forget not: in thy book record their groans
    Who were thy sheep and in their ancient fold
    Slain by the bloody Piemontese that rolled
    Mother with infant down the rocks. Their moans
The vales redoubled to the hills, and they
    To Heaven. Their martyred blood and ashes sow
    O'er all th' Italian fields where still doth sway
The triple tyrant:[3] that from these may grow
    A hundredfold, who having learnt thy way
    Early may fly the Babylonian woe.[4]

When I Consider How My Light Is Spent[1]

When I consider how my light is spent
    Ere half my days, in this dark world and wide,
    And that one talent which is death to hide,
    Lodged with me useless, though my soul more bent
To serve therewith my Maker, and present
    My true account, lest he returning chide;
    "Doth God exact day-labor, light denied?"
    I fondly[2] ask; but Patience to prevent
That murmur, soon replies, "God doth not need
    Either man's work or his own gifts; who best
    Bear his mild yoke, they serve him best. His state
Is kingly. Thousands at his bidding speed
    And post o'er land and ocean without rest:
    They also serve who only stand and wait."

---

55. Protective spirit.
56. Unlettered.
57. Reeds in a set of Panpipes.
58. I.e., pastoral. Doric was the Greek dialect used by the earliest pastoral poets.

1. A district in north-west Italy where 1,700 members of the Waldenses, a Protestant sect, were killed in an attack by forces of the Duke of Savoy in April 1655.
2. The Waldenses, like many Protestant sects, attacked as idolatry the worship of saints' relics and "graven images" practised in the Roman Church.
3. I.e., the Pope, who wears a three-crowned tiara.
4. Protestants during the Reformation conventionally identified the Roman Church with the "whore of Babylon" in Rev. xvii, xviii.

1. Milton, aged forty-two or forty-three, became totally blind in 1651.
2. Foolishly.

Methought I Saw My Late Espoused Saint

Methought I saw my late espoused saint[1]
    Brought to me like Alcestis[2] from the grave,
    Whom Jove's great son to her glad husband gave,
    Rescued from death by force though pale and faint.
Mine, as whom washed from spot of childbed taint,
    Purification in the old law did save,[3]
    And such, as yet once more I trust to have
    Full sight of her in Heaven[4] without restraint,
Came vested all in white, pure as her mind.
    Her face was veiled, yet to my fancied sight,
    Love, sweetness, goodness, in her person shined
So clear, as in no face with more delight.
    But O, as to embrace me she inclined,
    I waked, she fled, and day brought back my night.

From Paradise Lost

Book IX

The Argument

      Satan, having compassed the earth, with meditated guile returns as a mist by night into Paradise, enters into the serpent sleeping. Adam and Eve in the morning go forth to their labours, which Eve proposes to divide in several places, each labouring apart: Adam consents not, alleging the danger, lest that enemy, of whom they were forewarned, should attempt her found alone: Eve loath to be thought not circumspect or firm enough, urges her going apart, the rather desirous to make trial of her strength; Adam at last yields: the Serpent finds her alone, his subtle approach, first gazing, then speaking, with much flattery extolling Eve above all other creatures. Eve wondering to hear the Serpent speak, asks how he attained to human speech and such understanding not till now; the Serpent answers, that by tasting of a certain tree in the garden he attained both to speech and reason, till then void of both: Eve requires him to bring her to that tree, and finds it to be the Tree of Knowledge forbidden: the Serpent now grown bolder, with many wiles and arguments induces her at length to eat; she pleased with the taste deliberates a while whether to impart thereof to Adam or not, at last brings him of the fruit, relates what persuaded her to eat thereof: Adam at first amazed, but perceiving her lost, resolves through vehemence of love to perish with her; and extenuating the trespass, eats also of the fruit: the effects thereof in them both; they seek to cover their nakedness; then fall to variance and accusation of one another.

No more of talk where God or angel guest
With man, as with his friend, familiar used
To sit indulgent, and with him partake
Rural repast, permitting him the while
5   Venial[1] discourse unblamed:[2] I now must change
Those notes to tragic; foul distrust, and breach
Disloyal on the part of man, revolt,
And disobedience: on the part of heav'n
Now alienated, distance and distaste,
10   Anger and just rebuke, and judgment giv'n,

---

1. Milton's second wife, Katharine Woodcock, died in 1658 after less than two years of marriage.
2. In Euripides' *Alcestis*, Hercules ("Jove's great son") brings Alcestis back from death to her husband Admetus.
3. Hebraic law required ritual purification of women after childbirth (Lev. xii).
4. Milton became blind in 1651. It is likely that he never saw his second wife.

1. Allowable.
2. Adam has just completed a long conversation with the archangel Raphael, who instructed him in the history of Creation, Satan's rebellion, and the expulsion of the rebellious angels from heaven. Adam now possesses sufficient knowledge to withstand Satan's attempt to gain vengeance on God by corrupting His newest creatures.

That brought into this world a world of woe,
Sin and her shadow Death, and misery
Death's harbinger: sad task, yet argument
Not less but more heroic than the wrath
15 Of stern Achilles on his foe pursued
Thrice fugitive about Troy wall,[3] or rage
Of Turnus for Lavinia disespoused,[4]
Or Neptune's ire or Juno's, that so long
Perplexed the Greek and Cytherea's son;[5]
20 If answerable style I can obtain
Of my celestial patroness;[6] who deigns
Her nightly visitation unimplored,
And dictates to me slumb'ring, or inspires
Easy my unpremeditated verse:
25 Since first this subject for heroic song
Pleased me, long choosing, and beginning late;
Not sedulous by nature to indite[7]
Wars, hitherto the only argument
Heroic deemed, chief maistry to dissect
30 With long and tedious havoc fabled knights
In battles feigned; the better fortitude
Of patience and heroic martyrdom
Unsung; or to describe races and games,
Or tilting furniture,[8] emblazoned shields,
35 Impresses[9] quaint, caparisons and steeds;
Bases[10] and tinsel trappings; gorgeous knights
At joust and tournament; then marshaled feast
Served up in hall with sewers, and seneschals;[11]
The skill of artifice or office mean,
40 Not that which justly gives heroic name
To person or to poem. Me of these
Nor skilled nor studious, higher argument
Remains, sufficient of itself to raise
That name, unless an age too late, or cold
45 Climate, or years damp my intended wing
Depressed, and much they may, if all be mine,
Nor hers who brings it nightly to my ear.
   The sun was sunk, and after him the star
Of Hesperus, whose office is to bring
50 Twilight upon the earth, short arbiter
'Twixt day and night, and now from end to end
Night's hemisphere had veiled the horizon round:
When Satan who late fled before the threats
Of Gabriel out of Eden, now improved
55 In meditated fraud and malice, bent
On man's destruction, maugre[12] what might hap
Of heavier on himself, fearless returned.
By night he fled, and at midnight returned
From compassing the earth, cautious of day,
60 Since Uriel[13] regent of the sun descried
His entrance, and forewarned the Cherubim
That kept their watch; thence full of anguish driv'n,
The space of seven continued nights he rode

---

3. In Homer's *Iliad*, Achilles pursues Hector three times
around the walls of Troy before killing the Trojan champion.
4. In Virgil's *Aeneid*, Lavinia is betrothed to Turnus, but
given by her father in marriage to Aeneas.
5. In Homer's *Odyssey*, Neptune attempts to prevent the
safe return of Odysseus ("the Greek") to Ithaca from the
Trojan wars. In the *Aeneid*, Juno's jealous quarrel with
Venus ("Cytherea") has a similar effect on the quest of
Venus' son, Aeneas.
6. Urania, the Muse of astronomy.

7. Write about.
8. The equipment or "furnishings" conventional to
descriptions of "joust and tournament" in Romance-epic.
9. Heraldic emblems.
10. Decorative and protective skirts of chain-mail for
horses.
11. Senior household servants.
12. Despite.
13. An archangel in the celestial sphere of the sun keeping
watch over Paradise.

With darkness, thrice the equinoctial line[14]
65 He circled, four times crossed the car of Night
From pole to pole, traversing each colure;
On the eighth returned; and on the coast averse[15]
From entrance or Cherubic watch, by stealth
Found unsuspected way. There was a place,
70 Now not, though sin, not time, first wrought the change,
Where Tigris at the foot of Paradise
Into a gulf shot under ground, till part
Rose up a fountain by the Tree of Life;
In with the river sunk, and with it rose
75 Satan involved in rising mist, then sought
Where to lie hid; sea he had searched and land
From Eden over Pontus,[16] and the pool
Maeotis, up beyond the river Ob;
Downward as far antarctic; and in length
80 West from Orontes to the ocean barred
At Darien, thence to the land where flows
Ganges and Indus: thus the orb he roamed
With narrow search; and with inspection deep
Considered every creature, which of all
85 Most opportune might serve his wiles, and found
The serpent subtlest beast of all the field.
Him after long debate, irresolute
Of thoughts revolved, his final sentence chose
Fit vessel, fittest imp[17] of fraud, in whom
90 To enter, and his dark suggestions hide
From sharpest sight: for in the wily snake,
Whatever sleights none would suspicious mark,
As from his wit and native subtlety
Proceeding, which in other beasts observed
95 Doubt[18] might beget of diabolic pow'r
Active within beyond the sense of brute.
Thus he resolved, but first from inward grief
His bursting passion into plaints thus poured:
"O earth, how like to heav'n, if not preferred
100 More justly, seat worthier of gods, as built
With second thoughts, reforming what was old!
For what God after better worse would build?
Terrestial heav'n, danced round by other heav'ns
That shine, yet bear their bright officious[19] lamps,
105 Light above light, for thee alone, as seems,
In thee concentring all their precious beams
Of sacred influence: as God in heav'n
Is center, yet extends to all, so thou
Centring receiv'st from all those orbs; in thee,
110 Not in themselves, all their known virtue appears
Productive in herb, plant, and nobler birth
Of creatures animate with gradual[20] life
Of growth, sense, reason, all summed up in man.
With what delight could I have walked thee round,
115 If I could joy in aught, sweet interchange
Of hill and valley, rivers, woods and plains,

---

14. The equator. "Colures" (l. 66) are two vast circles intersecting at the celestial poles in Ptolemaic astronomy. Satan circles the globe from east to west for three days and over the poles for four days, remaining hidden in darkness by always keeping the earth between himself and the sun.
15. Opposite.
16. Ll. 77–81. *Pontus*: the Black Sea. *Maeotis*: Sea of Azoo in Russia. *Ob*: Siberian river flowing into the Arctic Ocean. *Orontes*: Syrian river. *Darien*: Isthmus of Panama.
17. Offshoot, graft.
18. Suspicion.
19. Dutiful.
20. I.e., graduated, from the vegetable kingdom possessing the power to grow, through the animal kingdom, possessing growth and sensation, to man, who has all the powers of the lower orders as well as reason.

Now land, now sea, and shores with forest crowned,
Rocks, dens, and caves; but I in none of these
Find place or refuge; and the more I see
120 Pleasures about me, so much more I feel
Torment within me, as from the hateful siege
Of contraries; all good to me becomes
Bane,[21] and in heav'n much worse would be my state.
But neither here seek I, no nor in heav'n
125 To dwell, unless by maistring heav'n's Supreme;
Nor hope to be myself less miserable
By what I seek, but others to make such
As I, though thereby worse to me redound:
For only in destroying I find ease
130 To my relentless thoughts; and him[22] destroyed,
Or won to what may work his utter loss,
For whom all this[23] was made, all this will soon
Follow, as to him linked in weal or woe:
In woe then; that destruction wide may range:
135 To me shall be the glory sole among
The infernal Powers, in one day to have marred
What he Almighty styled, six nights and days
Continued making, and who knows how long
Before had been contriving, though perhaps
140 Not longer than since I in one night freed[24]
From servitude inglorious well-nigh half
Th' angelic name, and thinner left the throng
Of his adorers: he to be avenged,
And to repair his numbers thus impaired,
145 Whether such virtue spent of old now failed
More angels to create, if they at least
Are his created, or to spite us more,
Determined to advance into our room
A creature formed of earth, and him endow,
150 Exalted from so base original,
With heav'nly spoils, our spoils: what he decreed
He effected; man he made, and for him built
Magnificent this world, and earth his seat,
Him lord pronounced, and, O indignity!
155 Subjected to his service angel wings,
And flaming ministers to watch and tend
Their earthy charge: of these the vigilance
I dread, and to elude, thus wrapped in mist
Of midnight vapor glide obscure, and pry
160 In every bush and brake, where hap may find
The serpent sleeping, in whose mazy folds
To hide me, and the dark intent I bring.
O foul descent! that I who erst contended
With gods to sit the highest, am now constrained
165 Into a beast, and mixed with bestial slime,
This essence to incarnate and imbrute,
That to the highth of deity aspired;
But what will not ambition and revenge
Descend to? Who aspires must down as low
170 As high he soared, obnoxious[25] first or last
To basest things. Revenge, at first though sweet,
Bitter ere long back on itself recoils;
Let it; I reck not, so it light well aimed,
Since higher I fall short, on him who next

---

21. Poison.
22. I.e., Man.
23. I.e., the Cosmos.

24. Satan refers to his revolt, which "freed" his followers
from "servitude" by causing them to be imprisoned in hell.
25. Subject.

175 Provokes my envy, this new favorite
Of Heav'n, this man of clay, son of despite,
Whom us the more to spite his Maker raised
From dust: spite them with spite is best repaid."
 So saying, through each thicket dank or dry,
180 Like a black mist low creeping, he held on
His midnight search, where soonest he might find
The serpent: him fast sleeping soon he found
In labyrinth of many a round self-rolled,
His head the midst, well stored with subtle wiles:
185 Not yet in horrid shade or dismal den,
Nor nocent[26] yet, but on the grassy herb
Fearless unfeared he slept: in at his mouth
The Devil entered, and his brutal sense,
In heart or head, possessing soon inspired
190 With act intelligential; but his sleep
Disturbed not, waiting close th' approach of morn.
Now whenas sacred light began to dawn
In Eden on the humid flow'rs, that breathed
Their morning incense, when all things that breathe,
195 From th' earth's great altar send up silent praise
To the Creator, and his nostrils fill
With grateful smell, forth came the human pair
And joined their vocal worship to the choir
Of creatures wanting voice; that done, partake
200 The season, prime for sweetest scents and airs:
Then cómmune how that day they best may ply
Their growing work; for much their work outgrew
The hands' dispatch of two gard'ning so wide.
And Eve first to her husband thus began.
205 "Adam, well may we labour still to dress
This garden, still to tend plant, herb and flow'r,
Our pleasant task enjoined, but till more hands
Aid us, the work under our labour grows,
Luxurious by restraint; what we by day
210 Lop overgrown, or prune, or prop, or bind,
One night or two with wanton growth derides,
Tending to wild. Thou therefore now advise
Or hear what to my mind first thoughts present,
Let us divide our labors, thou where choice
215 Leads thee, or where most needs, whether to wind
The woodbine round this arbor, or direct
The clasping ivy where to climb, while I
In yonder spring of roses intermixed
With myrtle, find what to redress till noon:
220 For while so near each other thus all day
Our task we choose, what wonder if so near
Looks intervene and smiles, or object new
Casual discourse draw on, which intermits
Our day's work brought to little, though begun
225 Early, and th' hour of supper comes unearned."
 To whom mild answer Adam thus returned.
"Sole Eve, associate sole, to me beyond
Compare above all living creatures dear!
Well hast thou motioned,[27] well thy thoughts employed
230 How we might best fulfill the work which here
God hath assigned us, nor of me shalt pass

---

26. Harmful, criminal.   27. Proposed.

Unpraised: for nothing lovelier can be found
In woman, than to study household good,
And good works in her husband to promote.
235 Yet not so strictly hath our Lord imposed
Labour, as to debar us when we need
Refreshment, whether food, or talk between,
Food of the mind, or this sweet intercourse
Of looks and smiles, for smiles from reason flow,
240 To brute denied, and are of love the food,
Love not the lowest end of human life.
For not to irksome toil, but to delight
He made us, and delight to reason joined.
These paths and bowers doubt not but our joint hands
245 Will keep from wilderness with ease, as wide
As we need walk, till younger hands ere long
Assist us: but if much convérse perhaps
Thee satiate, to short absence I could yield.
For solitude sometimes is best society,
250 And short retirement urges sweet return.
But other doubt possesses me, lest harm
Befall thee severed from me; for thou know'st
What hath been warned us, what malicious foe
Envying our happiness, and of his own
255 Despairing, seeks to work us woe and shame
By sly assault; and somewhere high at hand
Watches, no doubt, with greedy hope to find
His wish and best advantage, us asunder,
Hopeless to circumvent us joined, where each
260 To other speedy aid might lend at need;
Whether his first design be to withdraw
Our fealty from God, or to disturb
Conjugal love, than which perhaps no bliss
Enjoyed by us excites his envy more;
265 Or this, or worse, leave not the faithful side
That gave thee being, still shades thee and protects.
The wife, where danger or dishonour lurks,
Safest and seemliest by her husband stays,
Who guards her, or with her the worst endures."
270 To whom the virgin[28] majesty of Eve,
As one who loves, and some unkindness meets,
With sweet austere composure thus replied.
"Offspring of heav'n and earth, and all earth's lord,
That such an enemy we have, who seeks
275 Our ruin, both by thee informed I learn,
And from the parting angel overheard
As in a shady nook I stood behind,
Just then returned at shut of evening flow'rs.
But that thou shouldst my firmness therefore doubt
280 To God or thee, because we have a foe
May tempt it, I expected not to hear.
His violence thou fear'st not, being such,
As we, not capable of death or pain,
Can either not receive, or can repel.
285 His fraud is then thy fear, which plain infers
Thy equal fear that my firm faith and love
Can by his fraud be shaken or seduced;
Thoughts, which how found they harbour in thy breast,
Adam, misthought of her to thee so dear?"
290 To whom with healing words Adam replied.

28. Innocent.

"Daughter of God and man, immortal Eve,
For such thou art, from sin and blame entire:[29]
Not diffident[30] of thee do I dissuade
Thy absence from my sight, but to avoid
295   Th' attempt itself, intended by our foe.
For he who tempts, though in vain, at least asperses[31]
The tempted with dishonour foul, supposed
Not incorruptible of faith, not proof
Against temptation: thou thyself with scorn
300   And anger wouldst resent the offered wrong,
Though ineffectual found; misdeem not then,
If such affront I labour to avert
From thee alone, which on us both at once
The enemy, though bold, will hardly dare,
305   Or daring, first on me th' assault shall light.
Nor thou his malice and false guile contemn;[32]
Subtle he needs must be, who could seduce
Angels, nor think superfluous others' aid.
I from the influence of thy looks receive
310   Access[33] in every virtue, in thy sight
More wise, more watchful, stronger, if need were
Of outward strength; while shame, thou looking on,
Shame to be overcome or overreached
Would utmost vigour raise, and raised unite.
315   Why shouldst not thou like sense within thee feel
When I am present, and thy trial choose
With me, best witness of thy virtue tried."
    So spake domestic Adam in his care
And matrimonial love; but Eve, who thought
320   Less[34] attribúted to her faith sincere,
Thus her reply with accent sweet renewed.
    "If this be our condition, thus to dwell
In narrow circuit straitened by a foe,
Subtle or violent, we not endued[35]
325   Single with like defense, wherever met,
How are we happy, still in fear of harm?
But harm precedes not sin: only our foe
Tempting affronts us with his foul esteem
Of our integrity: his foul esteem
330   Sticks no dishonour on our front,[36] but turns
Foul on himself; then wherefore shunned or feared
By us? who rather double honour gain
From his surmise proved false, find peace within,
Favour from Heav'n, our witness from th' event.
335   And what is faith, love, virtue unassayed
Alone, without exterior help sustained?
Let us not then suspect our happy state
Left so imperfect by the Maker wise,
As not secure to single or combined.
340   Frail is our happiness, if this be so,
And Eden were no Eden thus exposed."
    To whom thus Adam fervently replied.
"O woman, best are all things as the will
Of God ordained them, his creating hand
345   Nothing imperfect or deficient left
Of all that he created, much less man,
Or aught that might his happy state secure,
Secure from outward force; within himself
The danger lies, yet lies within his power:

29. Free.
30. Distrustful.
31. Maligns.
32. Treat with contempt.

33. Increase.
34. Too little.
35. Endowed.
36. Forehead, countenance.

350   Against his will he can receive no harm.
       But God left free the will, for what obeys
       Reason is free, and reason he made right,
       But bid her well beware, and still erect,[37]
       Lest by some fair appearing good surprised
355   She dictate false, and misinform the will
       To do what God expressly hath forbid.
       Not then mistrust, but tender love enjoins,
       That I should mind[38] thee oft, and mind thou me.
       Firm we subsist, yet possible to swerve,
360   Since reason not impossibly may meet
       Some specious object by the foe suborned,
       And fall into deception unaware,
       Not keeping strictest watch, as she was warned.
       Seek not temptation then, which to avoid
365   Were better, and most likely if from me
       Thou sever not: trial will come unsought.
       Wouldst thou approve thy constancy, approve[39]
       First thy obedience; th' other who can know,
       Not seeing thee attempted, who attest?
370   But if thou think, trial unsought may find
       Us both securer than thus warned thou seem'st,
       Go; for thy stay, not free, absents thee more;
       Go in thy native innocence, rely
       On what thou hast of virtue, summon all,
375   For God towards thee hath done his part, do thine."
          So spake the patriarch of mankind, but Eve
       Persisted, yet submiss,[40] though last, replied.
          "With thy permission then, and thus forewarned
       Chiefly by what thy own last reasoning words
380   Touched only, that our trial, when least sought,
       May find us both perhaps far less prepared,
       The willinger I go, nor much expect
       A foe so proud will first the weaker seek;
       So bent, the more shall shame him his repulse."
385   Thus saying, from her husband's hand her hand
       Soft she withdrew, and like a wood-nymph light
       Oread or Dryad, or of Delia's train,[41]
       Betook her to the groves, but Delia's self
       In gait surpassed and goddess-like deport,
390   Though not as she with bow and quiver armed,
       But with such gardening tools as art yet rude,
       Guiltless of fire had formed, or angels brought.
       To Pales, or Pomona, thus adorned,
       Likest she seemed, Pomona when she fled
395   Vertumnus, or to Ceres in her prime,
       Yet virgin of Proserpina from Jove.[42]
       Her long with ardent look his eye pursued
       Delighted, but desiring more her stay.
       Oft he to her his charge of quick return
400   Repeated, she to him as oft engaged
       To be returned by noon amid the bow'r,
       And all things in best order to invite
       Noontide repast, or afternoon's repose.
       O much deceived, much failing, hapless Eve,
405   Of thy presumed return! event[43] perverse!

37. I.e., remain always alert.
38. Remind.
39. Prove.
40. Still submissive.
41. *Oread*: nymph of the mountain. *Dryad*: nymph of the
wood. *Delia* is Diana, chaste goddess of the chase, especially the hunt for large, dangerous animals.
42. Pales, Pomona, and Ceres are agricultural goddesses.
Pamona long resisted the courtship of Vertumnus, god of
the spring. Proserpina was the daughter of Ceres and
Jupiter.
43. Outcome.

Thou never from that hour in Paradise
Found'st either sweet repast, or sound repose;
Such ambush hid among sweet flow'rs and shades
Waited with hellish rancour imminent
410   To intercept thy way, or send thee back
Despoiled of innocence, of faith, of bliss.
For new, and since first break of dawn the Fiend,
Mere serpent in appearance, forth was come,
And on his quest, where likeliest he might find
415   The only two of mankind, but in them
The whole included race, his purposed[44] prey.
In bow'r and field he sought, where any tuft
Of grove or garden-plot more pleasant lay,
Their tendance[45] or plantation for delight,
420   By fountain or by shady rivulet
He sought them both, but wished his hap[46] might find
Eve separate, he wished, but not with hope
Of what so seldom chanced, when to his wish,
Beyond his hope, Eve separate he spies,
425   Veiled in a cloud of fragrance, where she stood,
Half spied, so thick the roses bushing round
About her glowed, oft stooping to support
Each flow'r of slender stalk, whose head though gay
Carnation, purple, azure, or specked with gold,
430   Hung drooping unsustained, them she upstays
Gently with myrtle band, mindless the while,
Herself, though fairest unsupported flow'r,
From her best prop so far, and storm so nigh.
Nearer he drew, and many a walk traversed
435   Of stateliest covert, cedar, pine, or palm,
The voluble[47] and bold, now hid, now seen
Among thick-woven arborets and flow'rs
Embordered on each bank, the hand of Eve:
Spot more delicious than those gardens feigned
440   Or of revived Adonis,[48] or renowned
Alcinous, host of old Laertes' son,[49]
Or that, not mystic,[50] where the sapient king[51]
Held dalliance with his fair Egyptian spouse.
Much he the place admired, the person more.
445   As one who long in populous city pent,
Where houses thick and sewers annoy the air,
Forth issuing on a summer's morn to breathe
Among the pleasant villages and farms
Adjoined, from each thing met conceives delight,
450   The smell of grain, or tedded grass,[52] or kine,[53]
Or dairy, each rural sight, each rural sound;
If chance with nymph-like step fair virgin pass,
What pleasing seemed, for her now pleases more,
She most, and in her look sums all delight.
455   Such pleasure took the Serpent to behold
This flow'ry plat,[54] the sweet recess of Eve
Thus early, thus alone; her heav'nly form
Angelic, but more soft, and feminine,
Her graceful innocence, her every air
460   Of gesture or least action overawed

---

44. Intended.
45. I.e., place they tended.
46. Luck.
47. Coiling, undulating.
48. Adonis, wounded by a boar, was nursed in a heavenly bower by Venus.
49. Odysseus ("Laertes' son") visited the garden of Alcin-

ous, where springtime and harvest occur constantly at the same time.
50. I.e., historical, not mythical or "feigned" (l. 439).
51. Solomon. Cf. Song Sol. vi.2.
52. Drying hay.
53. Cattle.
54. Plot.

His malice, and with rapine[55] sweet bereaved
His fierceness of the fierce intent it brought:
That space the Evil One abstracted stood
From his own evil, and for the time remained
465 Stupidly good, of enmity disarmed,
Of guile, of hate, of envy, of revenge;
But the hot hell that always in him burns,
Though in mid-heav'n, soon ended his delight,
And tortures him now more, the more he sees
470 Of pleasure not for him ordained: then soon
Fierce hate he recollects, and all his thoughts
Of mischief, gratulating,[56] thus excites.
    "Thoughts, whither have ye led me, with what sweet
Compulsion thus transported to forget
475 What hither brought us, hate, not love, nor hope
Of Paradise for hell, hope here to taste
Of pleasure, but all pleasure to destroy,
Save what is in destroying, other joy
To me is lost. Then let me not let pass
480 Occasion which now smiles, behold alone
The woman, opportune to all attempts,
Her husband, for I view far round, not nigh,
Whose higher intellectual[57] more I shun,
And strength, of courage haughty, and of limb
485 Heroic built, though of terrestrial mold,
Foe not informidable, exempt from wound,
I not; so much hath hell debased, and pain
Enfeebled me, to what I was in heav'n.
She fair, divinely fair, fit love for gods,
490 Not terrible, though terror be in love
And beauty, not[58] approached by stronger hate,
Hate stronger, under show of love well feigned,
The way which to her ruin now I tend."
    So spake the Enemy of mankind, enclosed
495 In serpent, inmate bad, and toward Eve
Addressed his way, not with indented wave,
Prone on the ground, as since, but on his rear,
Circular base of rising folds, that tow'red
Fold above fold a surging maze, his head
500 Crested aloft, and carbuncle[59] his eyes;
With burnished neck of verdant gold, erect
Amidst his circling spires, that on the grass
Floated redundant:[60] pleasing was his shape,
And lovely, never since of serpent kind
505 Lovelier, not those that in Illyria changed
Hermione and Cadmus,[61] or the god
In Epidaurus;[62] nor to which transformed
Ammonian Jove, or Capitoline was seen,
He with Olympias, this with her who bore
510 Scipio, the height of Rome.[63] With tract oblique
At first, as one who sought accéss, but feared
To interrupt, sidelong he works his way.
As when a ship by skilful steersman wrought
Nigh river's mouth or foreland, where the wind
515 Veers oft, as oft so steers, and shifts her sail;
So varied he, and of his tortuous train

55. Violent seizure ("rapine sweet" is an oxymoron).
56. Exulting.
57. Intellect.
58. Unless.
59. Ruby-red.
60. Undulating.
61. Cadmus and his wife Harmonia ("Hermione") were transformed into serpents when driven to despair by the suffering of their children.
62. Aesculaplus, god of healing, sometimes appeared in the form of a serpent at his temple in Epidaurus.
63. Jupiter, worshipped as Ammon in Syria ("Ammonian Jove"), is said to have fathered Alexander the Great after visiting his mother, Olympias, in the form of a serpent. "Capitoline Jove," the Roman Jupiter, reputedly sired Scipio Africanus by visting Sempronia in the same form.

Curled many a wanton wreath in sight of Eve,
To lure her eye; she busied heard the sound
Of rustling leaves, but minded not, as used
520 To such disport before her through the field,
From every beast, more duteous at her call,
Than at Circean call the herd disguised.[64]
He bolder now, uncalled before her stood;
But as in gaze admiring: oft he bowed
525 His turret crest, and sleek enameled neck,
Fawning, and licked the ground whereon she trod.
His gentle dumb expression turned at length
The eye of Eve to mark his play; he glad
Of her attention gained, with serpent tongue
530 Organic, or impulse of vocal air,
His fraudulent temptation thus began.
    "Wonder not, sovran mistress, if perhaps
Thou canst, who art sole wonder, much less arm
Thy looks, the heav'n of mildness, with disdain,
535 Displeased that I approach thee thus, and gaze
Insatiate, I thus single, nor have feared
Thy awful brow, more awful thus retired.
Fairest resemblance of thy Maker fair,
Thee all things living gaze on, all things thine
540 By gift, and thy celestial beauty adore
With ravishment beheld, there best beheld
Where universally admired; but here
In this enclosure wild, these beasts among,
Beholders rude, and shallow to discern
545 Half what in thee is fair, one man except,
Who sees thee? (and what is one?) who shouldst be seen
A goddess among gods, adored and served
By angels numberless, thy daily train."
    So glozed[65] the Tempter, and his proem tuned;
550 Into the heart of Eve his words made way,
Though at the voice much marveling; at length
Not unamazed she thus in answer spake.
"What may this mean? Language of man pronounced
By tongue of brute, and human sense expressed?
555 The first at least of these I thought denied
To beasts, whom God on their creation-day
Created mute to all articulate sound;
The latter I demur,[66] for in their looks
Much reason, and in their actions oft appears.
560 Thee, serpent, subtlest beast of all the field
I knew, but not with human voice endued;
Redouble then this miracle, and say,
How cam'st thou speakable of mute, and how
To me so friendly grown above the rest
565 Of brutal kind, that daily are in sight?
Say, for such wonder claims attention due."
    To whom the guileful Tempter thus replied.
"Empress of this fair world, resplendent Eve,
Easy to me it is to tell thee all
570 What thou command'st, and right thou shouldst be obeyed:
I was at first as other beasts that graze
The trodden herb, of abject thoughts and low,
As was my food, nor aught but food discerned
Or sex, and apprehended nothing high:
575 Till on a day roving the field, I chanced
A goodly tree far distant to behold

---

64. In the *Odyssey*, Circe the witch changed men into
obedient swine.

65. Flattered.
66. Doubt.

Loaden with fruit of fairest colors mixed,
Ruddy and gold: I nearer drew to gaze;
When from the boughs a savoury odour blown,
580   Grateful to appetite, more pleased my sense
Than smell of sweetest fennel, or the teats
Of ewe or goat dropping with milk at ev'n,
Unsucked of lamb or kid, that tend their play.
To satisfy the sharp desire I had
585   Of tasting those fair apples, I resolved
Not to defer; hunger and thirst at once,
Powerful persuaders, quickened at the scent
Of that alluring fruit, urged me so keen.
About the mossy trunk I wound me soon,
590   For high from ground the branches would require
Thy utmost reach or Adam's: round the tree
All other beasts that saw, with like desire
Longing and envying stood, but could not reach.
Amid the tree now got, where plenty hung
595   Tempting so nigh, to pluck and eat my fill
I spared not, for such pleasure till that hour
At feed or fountain never had I found.
Sated at length, ere long I might perceive
Strange alteration in me, to degree
600   Of reason in my inward powers, and speech
Wanted not long, though to this shape retained.[67]
Thenceforth to speculations high or deep
I turned my thoughts, and with capacious mind
Considered all things visible in heav'n,
605   Or earth, or middle, all things fair and good;
But all that fair and good in thy divine
Semblance, and in thy beauty's heav'nly ray
United I beheld; no fair to[68] thine
Equivalent or second, which compelled
610   Me thus, though importune perhaps, to come
And gaze, and worship thee of right declared
Sovran of creatures, universal dame."
    So talked the spirited[69] sly snake; and Eve
Yet more amazed unwary thus replied.
615   "Serpent, thy overpraising leaves in doubt
The virtue of that fruit, in thee first proved:
But say, where grows the tree, from hence how far?
For many are the trees of God that grow
In Paradise, and various, yet unknown
620   To us, in such abundance lies our choice,
As leaves a greater source of fruit untouched,
Still hanging incorruptible, till men
Grow up to their provision,[70] and more hands
Help to disburden nature of her bearth."[71]
625   To whom the wily adder, blithe and glad.
"Empress, the way is ready, and not long,
Beyond a row of myrtles, on a flat,
Fast by a fountain, one small thicket past
Of blowing myrrh and balm; if thou accept
630   My conduct, I can bring thee thither soon."
    "Lead then," said Eve. He leading swiftly rolled
In tangles, and made intricate seem straight,
To mischief swift. Hope elevates, and joy
Brightens his crest, as when a wand'ring fire,
635   Compact of unctuous[72] vapor, which the night
Condenses, and the cold environs round,

---

67. I.e., retained the form of a serpent.
68. Was comparable to.
69. I.e., possessed by a spirit.

70. I.e., increase to equal the supply.
71. I.e., what nature bears.
72. Oily. A reference to *ignis fatuus*, or will-o'-the-wisp.

Kindled through agitation to a flame,
Which oft, they say, some evil spirit attends,
Hovering and blazing with delusive light,
640 Misleads th' amazed night-wanderer from his way
To bogs and mires, and oft through pond or pool,
There swallowed up and lost, from succour far.
So glistered the dire snake, and into fraud
Led Eve our credulous mother, to the tree
645 Of prohibition, root of all our woe;
Which when she saw, thus to her guide she spake.
 "Serpent, we might have spared our coming hither,
Fruitless to me, though fruit be here to excess,
The credit of whose virtue rest with thee,[73]
650 Wondrous indeed, if cause of such effects.
But of this tree we may not taste nor touch;
God so commanded, and left that command
Sole daughter of his voice; the rest, we live
Law to ourselves, our reason is our law."
655 To whom the Tempter guilefully replied.
"Indeed? hath God then said that of the fruit
Of all these garden trees ye shall not eat,
Yet lords declared of all in earth or air?"
 To whom thus Eve yet sinless. "Of the fruit
660 Of each tree in the garden we may eat,
But of the fruit of this fair tree amidst
The garden, God hath said, 'Ye shall not eat
Thereof, nor shall ye touch it, lest ye die.' "
 She scarce had said, though brief, when now more bold
665 The Tempter, but with show of zeal and love
To man, and indignation at his wrong,
New part puts on, and as to passion moved,
Fluctuates disturbed, yet comely, and in act
Raised, as of some great matter to begin.
670 As when of old some orator renowned
In Athens or free Rome, where eloquence
Flourished, since mute, to some great cause addressed,
Stood in himself collected, while each part,
Motion, each act won audience ere the tongue,
675 Sometimes in height began, as no delay
Of preface brooking through his zeal of right.
So standing, moving, or to height upgrown
The Tempter all impassioned thus began.
 "O sacred, wise, and wisdom-giving plant,
680 Mother of science,[74] now I feel thy power
Within me clear, not only to discern
Things in their causes, but to trace the ways
Of highest agents, deemed however wise.
Queen of this universe, do not believe
685 Those rigid threats of death; ye shall not die:
How should ye? By the fruit? It gives you life
To[75] knowledge. By the Threat'ner? Look on me,
Me who have touched and tasted, yet both live,
And life more perfect have attained than fate
690 Meant me, by vent'ring higher than my lot.
Shall that be shut to man, which to the beast
Is open? Or will God incense his ire
For such a petty trespass, and not praise
Rather your dauntless virtue, whom the pain
695 Of death denounced, whatever thing death be,
Deterred not from achieving what might lead

---

73. I.e., the reputation of the fruit's powers must rest
solely on your testimony.

74. Knowledge.
75. In addition to.

To happier life, knowledge of good and evil;
Of good, how just? Of evil, if what is evil
Be real, why not known, since easier shunned?
700 God therefore cannot hurt ye, and be just;
Not just, not God; not feared then, nor obeyed:
Your fear itself of death removes the fear.
Why then was this forbid? Why but to awe,
Why but to keep ye low and ignorant,
705 His worshipers; he knows that in the day
Ye eat thereof, your eyes that seem so clear,
Yet are but dim, shall perfectly be then
Opened and cleared, and ye shall be as gods,
Knowing both good and evil as they know.
710 That ye should be as gods, since I as man,
Internal man,[76] is but proportion meet,
I of brute human, ye of human gods.
So ye shall die perhaps, by putting off
Human, to put on gods,[77] death to be wished,
715 Though threatened, which no worse than this can bring.
And what are gods that man may not become
As they, participating[78] godlike food?
The gods are first, and that advantage use
On our belief, that all from them proceeds;
720 I question it, for this fair earth I see,
Warmed by the sun, producing every kind,
Them nothing: if they all things,[79] who enclosed
Knowledge of good and evil in this tree,
That whoso eats thereof, forthwith attains
725 Wisdom without their leave? And wherein lies
Th' offense, that man should thus attain to know?
What can your knowledge hurt him, or this tree
Impart against his will if all be his?
Or is it envy, and can envy dwell
730 In heav'nly breasts? These, these and many more
Causes import your need of this fair fruit.
Goddess humane, reach then, and freely taste."
    He ended, and his words replete with guile
Into her heart too easy entrance won:
735 Fixed on the fruit she gazed, which to behold
Might tempt alone, and in her ears the sound
Yet rung of his persuasive words, impregned[80]
With reason, to her seeming, and with truth;
Meanwhile the hour of noon drew on, and waked
740 An eager appetite, raised by the smell
So savory of that fruit, which with desire,
Inclinable now grown to touch or taste,
Solicited her longing eye; yet first
Pausing a while, thus to herself she mused:
745 "Great are thy virtues, doubtless, best of fruits,
Though kept from man, and worthy to be admired,
Whose taste, too long forborne, at first assay
Gave elocution to the mute, and taught
The tongue not made for speech to speak thy praise:
750 Thy praise he also who forbids thy use,
Conceals not from us, naming thee the Tree
Of Knowledge, knowledge both of good and evil;
Forbids us then to taste, but his forbidding
Commends thee more, while it infers the good
755 By thee communicated, and our want:

---

76. I.e., intellectually a man.
77. Satan parodies St. Paul's doctrine of spiritual resur-
rection in 1 Cor. xv.51–54.

78. Sharing.
79. I.e., produced all things.
80. Impregnated.

For good unknown, sure is not had, or had
And yet unknown, is as not had at all.
In plain[81] then, what forbids he but to know,
Forbids us good, forbids us to be wise?
760 Such prohibitions bind not. But if death
Bind us with after-bands, what profits then
Our inward freedom? In the day we eat
Of this fair fruit, our doom is, we shall die.
How dies the serpent? He hath eat'n and lives,
765 And knows, and speaks, and reasons, and discerns,
Irrational till then. For us alone
Was death invented? Or to us denied
This intellectual food, for beasts reserved?
For beasts it seems: yet that one beast which first
770 Hath tasted, envies not, but brings with joy
The good befall'n him, author unsuspect,[82]
Friendly to man, far from deceit or guile.
What fear I then, rather what know to fear
Under this ignorance of good and evil,
775 Of God or death, of law or penalty?
Here grows the cure of all, this fruit divine,
Fair to the eye, inviting to the taste,
Of virtue[83] to make wise: what hinders then
To reach, and feed at once both body and mind?"
780 So saying, her rash hand in evil hour
Forth reaching to the fruit, she plucked, she eat:[84]
Earth felt the wound, and nature from her seat
Sighing through all her works gave signs of woe,
That all was lost. Back to the thicket slunk
785 The guilty serpent, and well might, for Eve
Intent now wholly on her taste, naught else
Regarded, such delight till then, as seemed,
In fruit she never tasted, whether true
Or fancied so, through expectation high
790 Of knowledge, nor was Godhead from her thought.
Greedily she engorged without restraint,
And knew not eating death: satiate at length,
And highthened as with wine, jocund and boon,[85]
Thus to herself she pleasingly began.
795 "O sovran, virtuous, precious of all trees
In Paradise, of operation blest
To sapience, hitherto obscured, infamed,[86]
And thy fair fruit let hang, as to no end
Created; but henceforth my early care,
800 Not without song, each morning, and due praise
Shall tend thee, and the fertile burden ease
Of thy full branches offered free to all;
Till dieted by thee I grow mature
In knowledge, as the gods who all things know;
805 Though others envy what they cannot give;
For had the gift been theirs, it had not here
Thus grown. Experience, next to thee I owe,
Best guide; not following thee, I had remained
In ignorance, thou open'st wisdom's way,
810 And giv'st accéss, though secret she retire.
And I perhaps am secret; Heav'n is high,
High and remote to see from thence distinct
Each thing on earth; and other care perhaps
May have diverted from continual watch

81. I.e., plainly speaking.
82. Authority beyond suspicion.
83. With power.
84. Ate.

85. Liberal.
86. Unknown, lacking fame—with a suggestion of "defamed."

815　Our great Forbidder, safe with all his spies
　　　About him. But to Adam in what sort
　　　Shall I appear? shall I to him make known
　　　As yet my change, and give him to partake
　　　Full happiness with me, or rather not,
820　But keep the odds of knowledge in my power
　　　Without copartner? so to add what wants
　　　In female sex, the more to draw his love,
　　　And render me more equal, and perhaps,
　　　A thing not undesirable, sometime
825　Superior; for inferior who is free?
　　　This may be well: but what if God have seen,
　　　And death ensue? Then I shall be no more,
　　　And Adam wedded to another Eve,
　　　Shall live with her enjoying, I extinct;
830　A death to think. Confirmed then I resolve,
　　　Adam shall share with me in bliss or woe:
　　　So dear I love him, that with him all deaths
　　　I could endure, without him live no life."
　　　　　So saying, from the tree her step she turned,
835　But first low reverence done, as to the power
　　　That dwelt within, whose presence had infused
　　　Into the plant sciential[87] sap, derived
　　　From nectar, drink of gods. Adam the while
　　　Waiting desirous her return, had wove
840　Of choicest flow'rs a garland to adorn
　　　Her tresses, and her rural labors crown,
　　　As reapers oft are wont their harvest queen.
　　　Great joy he promised to his thoughts, and new
　　　Solace in her return, so long delayed;
845　Yet oft his heart, divine of[88] something ill,
　　　Misgave him; he the falt'ring measure felt;
　　　And forth to meet her went, the way she took
　　　That morn when first they parted; by the Tree
　　　Of Knowledge he must pass; there he her met,
850　Scarce from the tree returning; in her hand
　　　A bough of fairest fruit that downy smiled,
　　　New gathered, and ambrosial smell diffused.
　　　To him she hasted, in her face excuse
　　　Came prologue, and apology to prompt,[89]
855　Which with bland words at will she thus addressed.
　　　　　"Hast thou not wondered, Adam, at my stay?
　　　Thee I have missed, and thought it long, deprived
　　　Thy presence, agony of love till now
　　　Not felt, nor shall be twice, for never more
860　Mean I to try, what rash untried I sought,
　　　The pain of absence from thy sight. But strange
　　　Hath been the cause, and wonderful to hear:
　　　This tree is not as we are told, a tree
　　　Of danger tasted,[90] nor to evil unknown
865　Op'ning the way, but of divine effect
　　　To open eyes, and make them gods who taste;
　　　And hath been tasted such: the serpent wise,
　　　Or not restrained as we, or not obeying,
　　　Hath eaten of the fruit, and is become,
870　Not dead, as we are threatened, but thenceforth
　　　Endued with human voice and human sense,
　　　Reasoning to admiration,[91] and with me
　　　Persuasively hath so prevailed, that I
　　　Have also tasted, and have also found

87. Knowledge-giving.
88. Foreboding.
89. I.e., her facial expression is an excuse acting as

prologue and prompter for the apology.
90. If tasted.
91. So as to create admiration.

875 Th' effects to correspond, opener mine eyes,
Dim erst, dilated spirits, ampler heart,
And growing up to godhead; which for thee
Chiefly I sought, without thee can despise.
For bliss, as thou hast part, to me is bliss,
880 Tedious, unshared with thee, and odious soon.
Thou therefore also taste, that equal lot
May join us, equal joy, as equal love;
Lest thou not tasting, different degree[92]
Disjoin us, and I then too late renounce
885 Deity for thee, when fate will not permit."
    Thus Eve with count'nance blithe her story told;
But in her cheek distemper[93] flushing glowed.
On th' other side, Adam, soon as he heard
The fatal trespass done by Eve, amazed,
890 Astonied[94] stood and blank, while horror chill
Ran through his veins, and all his joints relaxed;
From his slack hand the garland wreathed for Eve
Down dropped, and all the faded roses shed:
Speechless he stood and pale, till thus at length
895 First to himself he inward silence broke.
    "O fairest of creation, last and best
Of all God's works, creature in whom excelled
Whatever can to sight or thought be formed,
Holy, divine, good, amiable, or sweet!
900 How art thou lost, how on a sudden lost,
Defaced, deflow'red, and now to death devote?[95]
Rather how hast thou yielded to transgress
The strict forbiddance, how to violate
The sacred fruit forbidd'n! some cursèd fraud
905 Of enemy hath beguiled thee, yet unknown,
And me with thee hath ruined, for with thee
Certain my resolution is to die;
How can I live without thee, how forgo
Thy sweet converse and love so dearly joined,
910 To live again in these wild woods forlorn?
Should God create another Eve, and I
Another rib afford, yet loss of thee
Would never from my heart; no no, I feel
The link of nature draw me: flesh of flesh,
915 Bone of my bone thou art, and from thy state
Mine never shall be parted, bliss or woe."
    So having said, as one from sad dismay
Recomforted, and after thoughts disturbed
Submitting to what seemed remédiless,
920 Thus in calm mood his words to Eve he turned.
    "Bold deed thou hast presumed, advent'rous Eve,
And peril great provoked, who thus hast dared
Had it been only coveting to eye
That sacred fruit, sacred[96] to abstinence,
925 Much more to taste it under ban to touch.
But past who can recall, or done undo?
Not God omnipotent, nor fate; yet so
Perhaps thou shalt not die, perhaps the fact
Is not so heinous now, foretasted fruit,
930 Profaned first by the serpent, by him first
Made common and unhallowed ere our taste;
Nor yet on him found deadly, he yet lives,
Lives, as thou saidst, and gains to live as man
Higher degree of life, inducement strong

92. Status in the order of Creation.
93. Intemperance, physical disorder.
94. Stunned.

95. Doomed.
96. Consecrated.

935 To us, as likely tasting to attain
Proportional ascent, which cannot be
But to be gods, or angels demi-gods.
Nor can I think that God, Creator wise,
Though threat'ning, will in earnest so destroy
940 Us his prime creatures, dignified so high,
Set over all his works, which in our fall,
For us created, needs with us must fail,
Dependent made; so God shall uncreate,
Be frustrate, do, undo, and labour lose,
945 Not well conceived of God, who though his power
Creation could repeat, yet would be loath
Us to abolish, lest the Adversary
Triumph and say; 'Fickle their state whom God
Most favors, who can please him long? Me first
950 He ruined, now mankind; whom will he next?'
Matter of scorn, not to be given the Foe.
However I with thee have fixed my lot,
Certain[97] to undergo like doom; if death
Consort with thee, death is to me as life;
955 So forcible within my heart I feel
The bond of nature draw me to my own,
My own in thee, for what thou art is mine;
Our state cannot be severed, we are one,
One flesh; to lose thee were to lose myself."
960   So Adam, and thus Eve to him replied.
"O glorious trial of exceeding love,
Illustrious evidence, example high!
Engaging me to emulate, but short
Of thy perfection, how shall I attain,
965 Adam, from whose dear side I boast me sprung,
And gladly of our union hear thee speak,
One heart, one soul in both; whereof good proof
This day affords, declaring thee resolved,
Rather than death or aught than death more dread
970 Shall separate us, linked in love so dear,
To undergo with me one guilt, one crime,
If any be, of tasting this fair fruit,
Whose virtue, for of good still good proceeds,
Direct, or by occasion hath presented
975 This happy trial of thy love, which else
So eminently never had been known.
Were it I thought death menaced would ensue
This my attempt, I would sustain alone
The worst, and not persuade thee, rather die
980 Deserted, than oblige thee[98] with a fact[99]
Pernicious to thy peace, chiefly assured
Remarkably so late of thy so true,
So faithful love unequaled; but I feel
Far otherwise th' event,[100] not death, but life
985 Augmented, opened eyes, new hopes, new joys,
Taste so divine, that what of sweet before
Hath touched my sense, flat seems to this, and harsh.
Of my experience, Adam, freely taste,
And fear of death deliver to the winds."
990   So saying, she embraced him, and for joy
Tenderly wept, much won that he his love
Had so ennobled, as of choice to incur
Divine displeasure for her sake, or death.
In recompense (for such compliance bad

97. Determined, resolved.   99. Act, deed.
98. Make you liable to penalty.   100. Outcome.

995 Such recompense best merits) from the bough
     She gave him of that fair enticing fruit
     With liberal hand: he scrupled not to eat
     Against his better knowledge, not deceived,
     But fondly overcome with female charm.
1000 Earth trembled from her entrails, as again
     In pangs, and nature gave a second groan;
     Sky loured, and muttering thunder, some sad drops
     Wept at completing of the mortal sin
     Original; while Adam took no thought,
1005 Eating his fill, nor Eve to iterate[101]
     Her former trespass feared, the more to soothe
     Him with her loved society, that now
     As with new wine intoxicated both
     They swim in mirth, and fancy that they feel
1010 Divinity within them breeding wings
     Wherewith to scorn the earth: but that false fruit
     Far other operation first displayed,
     Carnal desire inflaming, he on Eve
     Began to cast lascivious eyes, she him
1015 As wantonly repaid; in lust they burn:
     Till Adam thus 'gan Eve to dalliance move.
        "Eve, now I see thou art exact[102] of taste,
     And elegant, of sapience no small part,
     Since to each meaning savour we apply,
1020 And palate call judicious; I the praise
     Yield thee, so well this day thou hast purveyed.
     Much pleasure we have lost, while we abstained
     From this delightful fruit, nor known till now
     True relish, tasting; if such pleasure be
1025 In things to us forbidden, it might be wished,
     For this one tree had been forbidden ten.
     But come, so well refreshed, now let us play,
     As meet is, after such delicious fare;
     For never did thy beauty since the day
1030 I saw thee first and wedded thee, adorned
     With all perfections, so inflame my sense
     With ardour to enjoy thee, fairer now
     Than ever, bounty of this virtuous tree."
        So said he, and forebore not glance or toy[103]
1035 Of amorous intent, well understood
     Of Eve, whose eye darted contagious fire.
     Her hand he seized, and to a shady bank,
     Thick overhead with verdant roof embow'red
     He led her nothing loath; flow'rs were the couch,
1040 Pansies, and violets, and asphodel,
     And hyacinth, earth's freshest softest lap.
     There they their fill of love and love's disport
     Took largely, of their mutual guilt the seal,
     The solace of their sin, till dewy sleep
1045 Oppressed them, wearied with their amorous play.
     Soon as the force of that fallacious fruit,
     That with exhilarating vapour bland
     About their spirits had played, and inmost powers
     Made err, was now exhaled, and grosser sleep
1050 Bred of unkindly[104] fumes, with conscious dreams
     Encumbered, now had left them, up they rose
     As from unrest, and each the other viewing,
     Soon found their eyes how opened, and their minds
     How darkened; innocence, that as a veil

101. Repeat.
102. Discriminating.

103. Caress.
104. Unnatural.

1055   Had shadowed them from knowing ill, was gone,
        Just confidence, and native righteousness,
        And honour from about them, naked left
        To guilty Shame: he covered, but his robe
        Uncovered more.[105] So rose the Danite strong
1060   Hercúlean Samson from the harlot-lap
        Of Philistéan Dálilah, and waked
        Shorn of his strength,[106] they destitute and bare
        Of all their virtue: silent, and in face
        Confounded long they sat, as strucken mute,
1065   Till Adam, though not less than Eve abashed,
        At length gave utterance to these words constrained.
            "O Eve, in evil hour thou didst give ear
        To that false worm,[107] of whomsoever taught
        To counterfeit man's voice, true in our fall,
1070   False in our promised rising; since our eyes
        Opened we find indeed, and find we know
        Both good and evil, good lost and evil got,
        Bad fruit of knowledge, if this be to know,
        Which leaves us naked thus, of honour void,
1075   Of innocence, of faith, of purity,
        Our wonted ornaments now soiled and stained,
        And in our faces evident the signs
        Of foul concupiscence; whence evil store;
        Even shame, the last of evils; of the first
1080   Be sure then. How shall I behold the face
        Henceforth of God or angel, erst with joy
        And rapture so oft beheld? Those heav'nly shapes
        Will dazzle now this earthly, with their blaze
        Insufferably bright. O might I here
1085   In solitude live savage, in some glade
        Obscured, where highest woods impenetrable
        To star or sunlight, spread their umbrage broad,
        And brown[108] as evening: cover me ye pines,
        Ye cedars, with innumerable boughs
1090   Hide me, where I may never see them more.
        But let us now, as in bad plight, devise
        What best may for the present serve to hide
        The parts of each from other, that seem most
        To shame obnoxious,[109] and unseemliest seen,
1095   Some tree whose broad smooth leaves together sewed,
        And girded on our loins, may cover round
        Those middle parts, that this newcomer, Shame,
        There sit not, and reproach us as unclean."
            So counseled he, and both together went
1100   Into the thickest wood, there soon they chose
        The figtree, not that kind for fruit renowned,
        But such as at this day to Indians known
        In Malabar or Deccan spreads her arms
        Branching so broad and long, that in the ground
1105   The bended twigs take root, and daughters grow
        About the mother tree, a pillared shade
        High overarched, and echoing walks between;
        There oft the Indian herdsman shunning heat
        Shelters in cool, and tends his pasturing herds
1110   At loopholes cut through thickest shade: those leaves
        They gathered, broad as Amazonian targe,[110]
        And with what skill they had, together sewed,

105. I.e., the covering of Shame (here personified) makes
them more conscious of their nakedness, physical and
spiritual.
106. The story of Samson and Delilah is told in Judg.
xvi.4–20.

107. Serpent.
108. Dark.
109. Liable, subject.
110. Shield.

To gird their waist, vain covering if to hide
Their guilt and dreaded shame; O how unlike
1115 To that first naked glory. Such of late
Columbus found th' American so girt
With feathered cincture,[111] naked else and wild,
Among the trees on isles and woody shores.
Thus fenced, and as they thought, their shame in part
1120 Covered, but not at rest or ease of mind,
They sat them down to weep, nor only tears
Rained at their eyes, but high winds worse within
Began to rise, high passions, anger, hate,
Mistrust, suspicion, discord, and shook sore
1125 Their inward state of mind, calm region once
And full of peace, now tossed and turbulent:
For understanding ruled not, and the will
Heard not her lore, both in subjection now
To sensual appetite, who from beneath
1130 Usurping over sovran reason claimed
Superior sway: from thus distempered breast,
Adam, estranged in look and altered style,
Speech intermitted thus to Eve renewed.
  "Would thou hadst hearkened to my words, and stayed
1135 With me, as I besought thee, when that strange
Desire of wand'ring this unhappy morn,
I know not whence possessed thee; we had then
Remained still happy, not as now, despoiled
Of all our good, shamed, naked, miserable.
1140 Let none henceforth seek needless cause to approve[112]
The faith they owe;[113] when earnestly they seek
Such proof, conclude, they then begin to fail."
  To whom soon moved with touch of blame thus Eve.
"What words have passed thy lips, Adam severe,
1145 Imput'st thou that to my default, or will
Of wand'ring, as thou call'st it, which who knows
But might as ill have happened thou being by,
Or to thyself perhaps: hadst thou been there,
Or here th' attempt, thou couldst not have discerned
1150 Fraud in the serpent, speaking as he spake;
No ground of enmity between us known,
Why he should mean me ill, or seek to harm.
Was I to have never parted from thy side?
As good have grown there still a lifeless rib.
1155 Being as I am, why didst not thou the head[114]
Command me absolutely not to go,
Going into such danger as thou saidst?
Too facile then thou didst not much gainsay,
Nay didst permit, approve, and fair dismiss.
1160 Hadst thou been firm and fixed in thy dissent,
Neither had I transgressed, nor thou with me."
  To whom then first incensed Adam replied.
"Is this the love, is this the recompense
Of mine to thee, ingrateful Eve, expressed[115]
1165 Immutable when thou wert lost, not I,
Who might have lived and joyed immortal bliss,
Yet willingly chose rather death with thee:
And am I now upbraided, as the cause
Of thy transgressing? not enough severe,
1170 It seems, in thy restraint: what could I more?

111. Belt.
112. Test, prove.
113. Own.

114. Cf. "the head of the woman is the man" 1 Cor. xi.3.
115. Demonstrated to be.

I warned thee, I admonished thee, foretold
The danger, and the lurking Enemy
That lay in wait; beyond this had been force,
And force upon free will hath here no place.
1175   But confidence then bore thee on, secure
Either to meet no danger, or to find
Matter of glorious trial; and perhaps
I also erred in overmuch admiring
What seemed in thee so perfect, that I thought
1180   No evil durst attempt thee, but I rue
That error now, which is become my crime,
And thou th' accuser. Thus it shall befall
Him who to worth in women overtrusting
Lets her will rule; restraint she will not brook,
1185   And left to herself, if evil thence ensue,
She first his weak indulgence will accuse."
   Thus they in mutual accusation spent
The fruitless hours, but neither self-condemning,
And of their vain contést appeared no end.

ANDREW MARVELL (1621–78)

To His Coy Mistress

Had we but world enough, and time,
This coyness, lady, were no crime.
We would sit down, and think which way
To walk, and pass our long love's day.
5   Thou by the Indian Ganges' side
Shouldst rubies find; I by the tide
Of Humber[1] would complain.[2] I would
Love you ten years before the flood,
And you should, if you please, refuse
10   Till the conversion of the Jews.[3]
My vegetable love should grow
Vaster than empires and more slow;
An hundred years should go to praise
Thine eyes, and on thy forehead gaze;
15   Two hundred to adore each breast,
But thirty thousand to the rest;
An age at least to every part,
And the last age should show your heart.
For, lady, you deserve this state,[4]
20   Nor would I love at lower rate.
   But at my back I always hear
Time's wingéd chariot hurrying near;
And yonder all before us lie

Deserts of vast eternity.
25   Thy beauty shall no more be found.
Nor, in thy marble vault, shall sound
My echoing song; then worms shall try
That long-preserved virginity,
And your quaint[5] honour turn to dust,
30   And into ashes all my lust:
The grave's a fine and private place,
But none, I think, do there embrace.
   Now therefore, while the youthful hue
Sits on thy skin like morning dew,
35   And while thy willing soul transpires[6]
At every pore with instant fires,
Now let us sport us while we may,
And now, like amorous birds of prey,
Rather at once our time devour
40   Than languish in his slow-chapped power.[7]
Let us roll all our strength and all
Our sweetness up into one ball,
And tear our pleasures with rough strife
Thorough the iron gates of life:
45   Thus, though we cannot make our sun
Stand still,[8] yet we will make him run.

1. A river running through Marvell's home town of Hull.
The Ganges and Humber contrast the exotic and the
ordinary.
2. A reference to conventional poems lamenting unrequited love.
3. An event not anticipated in popular superstition until
the end of the world.
4. Dignity.

5. Fastidious. Also a slang term for female sexual organs.
6. Breathes out.
7. I.e., power of Time's relentlessly devouring jaws.
8. Zeus stopped the sun so he could enjoy a week-long
night of pleasure with the mortal Alcmena. Joshua caused
the same phenomenon "until the people had avenged
themselves upon their enemies" in Josh. x.12–13.

The Garden

How vainly men themselves amaze[1]
To win the palm, the oak, or bays,[2]
And their incessant labours see
Crowned from some single herb, or tree,
5   Whose short and narrow-vergéd shade
Does prudently their toils upbraid;
While all flowers and all trees do close[3]
To weave the garlands of repose!

Fair Quiet, have I found thee here,
10   And Innocence, thy sister dear?
Mistaken long, I sought you then
In busy companies of men.
Your sacred plants, if here below,
Only among the plants will grow;
15   Society is all but rude[4]
To this delicious solitude.

No white nor red[5] was ever seen
So amorous as this lovely green.[6]
Fond lovers, cruel as their flame,
20   Cut in these trees their mistress' name:
Little, alas, they know or heed
How far these beauties hers exceed!
Fair trees, wheresoe'er your barks I wound,
No name shall but your own[7] be found.

25   When we have run our passion's heat,
Love hither makes his best retreat.
The gods, that mortal beauty chase,
Still in a tree did end their race:
Apollo hunted Daphne so,
30   Only that she might laurel grow;
And Pan did after Syrinx speed,
Not as a nymph, but for a reed.[8]

What wondrous life is this I lead!
Ripe apples drop about my head;
35   The luscious clusters of the vine
Upon my mouth do crush their wine;
The nectarine and curious peach
Into my hands themselves do reach;
Stumbling on melons, as I pass,
40   Insnared with flowers, I fall on grass.

Meanwhile the mind, from pleasure less,[9]
Withdraws into its happiness;
The mind, that ocean where each kind
Does straight its own resemblance find;[10]
45   Yet it creates, transcending these,
Far other worlds and other seas,
Annihilating all that's made
To a green thought in a green shade.[11]

Here at the fountain's sliding foot,
50   Or at some fruit tree's mossy root,
Casting the body's vest[12] aside,
My soul into the boughs does glide:
There, like a bird, it sings and sings,
Then whets[13] and combs its silver wings,
55   And, till prepared for longer flight,
Waves in its plumes the various light.[14]

Such was that happy garden-state,
While man there walked without a mate:
After a place so pure and sweet,
60   What other help could yet be meet!
But 'twas beyond a mortal's share
To wander solitary there:
Two paradises 'twere in one
To live in paradise alone.[15]

65   How well the skillful gardener drew
Of flowers and herbs this dial[16] new,
Where, from above, the milder sun
Does through a fragrant zodiac run;
And as it works, th' industrious bee
70   Computes its time as well as we!
How could such sweet and wholesome hours
Be reckoned but with herbs and flowers?

---

1. Bewilder, lose themselves in a maze.
2. Emblems, respectively, of athletic, civic, and poetic achievement.
3. Join.
4. Barbarous.
5. Conventional colours representing a woman's complexion.
6. Contrasted with "white and red," "green" becomes representative of love without sexual passion.
7. I.e., Marvell's speaker would carve the names of the trees in their own bark.
8. In Ovid's *Metamorphoses*, Daphne turns into a laurel to escape Apollo's pursuit, and Syrinx becomes a reed to escape Pan. Marvell's speaker has changed the gods' motives from amorous to horticultural.
9. I.e., lesser pleasures.
10. It was believed that everything on land had its counterpart in the ocean.
11. Cf. ll. 17–18. "Green" has taken on connotations of pure contemplative abstraction, completely removed from the world of sense and matter.
12. Vestment, garment.
13. Preens.
14. A neo-Platonic image of the pure, white light of Eternity fragmented into the multi-coloured light of a fallen, temporal world.
15. An assertion contrary to God's will as expressed in Gen. ii.18: "It is not good that the man should be alone; I will make him a help meet for him."
16. Sundial.

The Definition of Love

My Love is of a birth as rare
As 'tis, for object, strange and high;
It was begotten by Despair
Upon Impossibility.

5   Magnanimous Despair alone
Could show me so divine a thing,
Where feeble Hope could ne'er have flown
But vainly flapped its tinsel wing.

And yet I quickly might arrive
10 Where my extended[1] soul is fixed;
But Fate does iron wedges drive,
And always crowds itself betwixt.

For Fate with jealous eye does see
Two perfect loves, nor lets them close;[2]
15 Their union would her ruin be,
And her tyrannic power depose.

20 And therefore her decrees of steel
Us as the distant poles have placed
(Though Love's whole world on us doth wheel),[3]
Not by themselves to be embraced,

Unless the giddy heaven fall,
And earth some new convulsion tear,
And, us to join, the world should all
Be cramped into a planisphere.[4]

25 As lines, so loves oblique may well
Themselves in every angle greet;[5]
But ours, so truly parallel,
Though infinite, can never meet.

Therefore the love which us doth bind,
30 But Fate so enviously debars,
Is the conjunction of the mind,
And opposition of the stars.[6]

Bermudas

Where the remote Bermudas ride,
In th' ocean's bosom unespied,
From a small boat that rowed along,
The listening winds received this song:

5   "What should we do but sing His praise,
That led us through the watery maze
Unto an isle so long unknown,
And yet far kinder than our own?
Where He the huge sea monsters wracks,[1]
10 That lift the deep upon their backs;
He lands us on a grassy stage,
Safe from the storms, and prelate's rage.[2]
He gave us this eternal spring
Which here enamels everything,
15 And sends the fowls to us in care,
On daily visits through the air;
He hangs in shades the orange bright,
Like golden lamps in a green night,
And does in the pomegranates close[3]
20 Jewels more rich than Ormus[4] shows;

25 He makes the figs our mouths to meet,
And throws the melons at our feet;
But apples[5] plants of such a price,
No tree could ever bear them twice;
With cedars, chosen by His hand,
From Lebanon, He stores the land;
And makes the hollow seas, that roar,
Proclaim the ambergris[6] on shore;
He cast (of which we rather boast)
30 The Gospel's pearl upon our coast,
And in these rocks for us did frame
A temple, where to sound His name.
O! let our voice His praise exalt,
Till it arrive at heaven's vault,
35 Which, thence (perhaps) rebounding, may
Echo beyond the Mexique Bay."[7]

Thus sung they in the English boat,
An holy and a cheerful note;
And all the way, to guide their chime,
40 With falling oars they kept the time.

---

1. I.e., from himself to the object of his love.
2. Unite.
3. Turn on its axis.
4. A sphere projected onto a plane surface, as with a map of the world.
5. Where oblique lines meet, an angle is formed. Parallel lines meet at infinity.
6. In astronomy, "conjunction" occurs when two planets appear to occupy the same point in their orbits; "opposition" occurs when they are diametrically opposite each other.

1. Runs aground.
2. An allusion to the persecution of Puritan sects by bishops of the Established Church.
3. Hide.
4. Hormuz, on the Persian Gulf, was famous as a trading centre for jewels.
5. Pineapple.
6. A secretion of the sperm whale used in the making of perfumes.
7. Gulf of Mexico.

An Horatian Ode
Upon Cromwell's Return from Ireland[1]

The forward[2] youth that would appear,
Must now forsake his Muses dear,
    Nor in the shadows sing
    His numbers languishing:

5 'Tis time to leave the books in dust,
And oil the unuséd armor's rust;
    Removing from the wall
    The corselet[3] of the hall.

So restless Cromwell could not cease
10 In the inglorious arts of peace,[4]
    But through adventurous war
    Urgéd his active star;

And, like the three-forked lightning, first
Breaking the clouds where it was nursed,
15   Did thorough his own side
    His fiery way divide.[5]

For 'tis all one to courage high,
The emulous, or enemy;
    And with such, to enclose,[6]
20   Is more than to oppose;

Then burning through the air he went,
And palaces and temples rent;
    And Caesar's head at last
    Did through his laurels blast.[7]

25 'Tis madness to resist or blame
The face of angry Heaven's flame;
    And if we would speak true,
    Much to the man is due,

Who from his private gardens, where
30 He lived reservéd and austere,
    As if his highest plot
    To plant the bergamot;[8]

Could by industrious valour climb
To ruin the great work of Time,
35   And cast the kingdom old,
    Into another mold;

40 Though Justice against Fate complain,
And plead the ancient rights in vain;
    But those do hold or break,
    As men are strong or weak.

Nature that hateth emptiness,[9]
Allows of penetration[10] less,
    And therefore must make room
    Where greater spirits come.

45 What field of all the civil wars
Where his were not the deepest scars?
    And Hampton[11] shows what part
    He had of wiser art;

Where, twining subtle fears with hope,
50 He wove a net of such a scope
    That Charles himself might chase
    To Caresbrooke's narrow case,

That thence the royal actor borne,
The tragic scaffold might adorn;
55   While round the arméd bands
    Did clap their bloody hands.

He[12] nothing common did or mean
Upon that memorable scene,
    But with his keener eye
60   The ax's edge did try;

Nor called the gods with vulgar spite
To vindicate helpless right;
    But bowed his comely head
    Down, as upon a bed.

65 This was that memorable hour,
Which first assured the forcéd power;
    So when they did design
    The capitol's first line,

A bleeding head where they begun,
70 Did fright the architects to run;
    And yet in that the state
    Foresaw its happy fate.[13]

1. Oliver Cromwell returned from his Irish campaign in May 1650 and began making preparations for an invasion of Scotland in July.
2. Ambitious, presumptuous.
3. Suit of armour.
4. An allusion to Lucan's epic of the Roman Civil Wars, *Pharsalia*. Lucan represents Caesar as "restless" in peace. Lucan's hero, however, is neither Caesar nor his rival Pompey, but Liberty and the Stoic philosopher Cato who defends it.
5. Cromwell left the Presbyterian party to become leader of a more radical revolutionary faction.
6. Ambiguously "to make common cause" or "to neutralize by absorbing."
7. "Caesar" here is Charles I, beheaded some eighteen months previously. The laurel, symbol of civic leadership, was supposed to give its wearer immunity from Jove's tyrannical bolt of retributive lightning ("angry Heaven's flame").
8. An exotic species of pear, known as "pear of princes," suggesting Cromwell may have harboured royal ambitions even while in early "private" life.
9. Vacuum.
10. I.e., two objects occupying the same space.
11. Charles I escaped from confinement at Hampton Court to seek sanctuary at Carisbrooke, but Carisbrooke became another prison ("narrow case"). It was rumoured that Cromwell had arranged the escape to convince Parliament that Charles should be executed.
12. I.e., Charles.
13. Livy and Pliny report that workmen digging foundations for the temple of Jupiter in Rome uncovered a bloody head. This was taken as a sign of Rome's destiny to become "head" of an empire, and the temple hill was called Capitoline (from *caput*: head).

And now the Irish are ashamed
To see themselves in one year tamed;
75   So much one man can do,
    That does both act and know.

They can affirm his praises best,
And have, though overcome, confessed
    How good he is, how just,
80   And fit for highest trust.

Nor yet grown stiffer with command,
But still in the republic's hand—
    How fit he is to sway,
    That can so well obey.

85 He to the Commons' feet presents
A kingdom for his first year's rents;
    And, what he may, forbears
    His fame to make it theirs;

And has his sword and spoils ungirt,
90 To lay them at the public's skirt:
    So, when the falcon high
    Falls heavy from the sky,

She, having killed, no more does search,
But on the next green bough to perch;
95   Where, when he first does lure,
    The falconer has her sure.

What may not then our isle presume,
While victory his crest does plume!
    What may not others fear,
100   If thus he crown each year!

A Caesar he ere long to Gaul,
To Italy an Hannibal,
    And to all states not free,
    Shall climactéric[14] be.

105 The Pict no shelter now shall find
Within his party-colored mind,
    But from his valour sad,
    Shrink underneath the plaid;[15]

Happy if in the tufted brake
110 The English hunter him mistake,
    Nor lay his hounds in near
    The Caledonian[16] deer.

But thou, the war's and fortune's son,
March indefatigably on;
115   And for the last effect,
    Still keep thy sword erect;[17]

Besides the force it has to fright
The spirits of the shady night,
    The same arts that did gain
120   A power must it maintain.

14. I.e., instrument of crucial change, for better or worse.
15. The Romans called the Scots *picti* because their warriors painted themselves for battle. Marvell plays on the term to suggest factional divisions in Scotland—a nation divided by "party-coloured" minds, each "party" wearing its own colour of "plaid."
16. Scottish.
17. An erect sword makes the sign of the Cross.

Introduction: 1660 – 1800

If one should ask what common features of English poetry between 1660 and 1800 made it different from that which preceded it—different enough to warrant this section—and if one should demand a brief reply, the following might suffice: the date which begins the period (1660) marks a clear break in England's political history; Oliver Cromwell's attempt to establish a Puritan republic was clearly rejected and monarchial rule was restored. The age thus saw a return to courtly traditions and to more secular concerns and was, to a large extent, more rational, peaceful, and even-tempered than the preceding one. Reflecting that restoration, the poetry of the period was primarily concerned with social order. Poets emphasized the supremacy of reason as the key to achieving both personal and social stability, and lamented those many occasions when the passions brought chaos to the individual and society; their verse was therefore social rather than personal, public rather than introspective, secular rather than spiritual, and it belonged to the immediate and practical life of the time. The epic and lyric gave way to satire and epigrammatic verse; pure inspiration, in both content and style, was replaced by a seeming subservience to classical rules; correctness was preferred to extravagance, order to effusion, and common sense to exuberance.

Such superficial syntheses, however, though generally unavoidable in introductions to the period, are misleading in their simplicity. They make the age seem static and homogenous, when in fact, like all human history, it was part of a continuously evolving process. The poetry of the period represents an evolution of ideas; it is not completely free of preceding influences, it changes as it progresses, and, most significant, it partakes of the individuality of each author. What Dryden practised, Pope refined; what Pope refined, Gray discarded. The preponderance of satire in the first half of the period gave way to a preponderance of descriptive-reflective poetry in the latter. That is why some literary historians, in an attempt to disabuse us of the notion that all writers were of the same mind and to give an impression of change, divide the age into other categories: the "Neo-Classic Age" takes us to the death of Pope in 1774 and includes that poetry most influenced by classical tradition; the "Age of Sensibility," which follows, witnesses a reaction against those rules and the development of a more introspective, reflective, and personal kind of poetry, whose authors are often seen as the precursors of the so-called Romantics. But even these categories have the disadvantage of offering the age in neatly bundled packages, each with its identifying label.

What one must see—indeed, what makes the poetry of this period worth reading—is that the age was paradoxical, as most are, and that it produced paradoxical poets, whose individual tastes, stubborn egotism, and idiosyncratic ideas resulted in an amazing variety of original poems. These poems demand to be read not only as reflections of the intellectual and social concerns of the century, but also as poetry in its own right—as works of art, fascinating not only for *what* they say but also for *how* they say it. Although one might define the term "Neo-Classic" by showing just how Dryden, Pope, and others relied on classical models and precepts, one should not confuse adherence with servitude; one might also recognize that the common occurrence of the mock-heroic was as much an assertion of poets' independence as it was a testimony to their regard for the classical tradition. They gave to the elegy, the ode, the panegyric, and the heroic epistle a new energy and force. A poet like Pope could be extremely contradictory—savagely satiric ("An Epistle to Dr. Arbuthnot") or poignantly tragic ("Eloïsa to Abelard"), pessimistic or optimistic. And, though Pope believed in the supremacy of reason, he could be very cynical of man's so-called rational achievements and was often bewildered by the human dilemma.

It is therefore important to read the poetry as expressions of unique personalities, to discover as intuitively as possible the particular features of each expression, and to thereby become acquainted with the diversity of pleasures which the poetry of this period has to offer. For example:

(1) Pope's brilliant handling of the heroic couplet and his pointed wit:

> Eternal smiles his emptiness betray,
> As shallow streams run dimpling all the way.

> The hungry judges soon the sentence sign,
> And wretches hang that jurymen may dine.

(2) The richness of the mock-heroic form. How, in *The Rape of the Lock*, for example, the meaning resides as much in the form of the poem as in the words themselves.

(3) The variety of diction in eighteenth-century poetry, from the startling vividness of Swift:

> Sweepings from butchers' stalls, dung, guts, and blood,
> Drowned puppies, stinking sprats, all drenched in mud,
> Dead cats, and turnip-tops come tumbling down the flood.

to the abstract, yet equally apt, descriptions of Goldsmith:

> Sweet smiling village, loveliest of the lawn,
> Thy sports are fled, and all thy charms withdrawn;
> Amidst thy bowers the tyrant's hand is seen,
> And desolation saddens all thy green.

(4) The perfectly controlled tone of Gray's *Elegy Written in a Country Church-Yard*, in which "the effect is of a series of waves, each growing with almost imperceptible power, then sinking back to the original starting-point."[1]

These are a very few suggestions, to be sure, but are enough to tantalize and to indicate that the best of this poetry is as rewarding, in its imagery, diction, tone, and structure, as any other and that close analysis reveals it to be rich in texture, varied in form, complex and paradoxical, and highly original.

R. G. Moyles

1. Norman Callan, "Augustan Reflective Poetry," *The Pelican Guide to English Literature*, Vol. IV, ed. Boris Ford (Harmondsworth: Penguin, 1965), pp. 346–71.

JOHN DRYDEN (1631–1700)

Absalom and Achitophel[1]

In pious times, ere priestcraft did begin,
Before polygamy was made a sin;
When man on many multiplied his kind,
Ere one to one was cursedly confined;
5   When nature prompted, and no law denied
Promiscuous use of concubine and bride;
Then Israel's monarch after Heaven's own heart,
His vigorous warmth did variously impart
To wives and slaves; and, wide as his command,
10   Scattered his Maker's image thro' the land.
Michal,[2] of royal blood, the crown did wear;
A soil ungrateful to the tiller's care:
Not so the rest; for several mothers bore
To godlike David[3] several sons before.
15   But since like slaves his bed they did ascend,
No true succession could their seed attend.
Of all this numerous progeny was none
So beautiful, so brave, as Absalon:[4]
Whether, inspired by some diviner lust,
20   His father got him with a greater gust;
Or that his conscious destiny made way,
By manly beauty, to imperial sway.
Early in foreign fields he won renown,
With kings and states allied to Israel's crown:
25   In peace the thoughts of war he could remove,
And seemed as he were only born for love.
Whate'er he did, was done with so much ease,
In him alone 'twas natural to please:
His motions all accompanied with grace;
30   And paradise was opened in his face.
With secret joy indulgent David viewed
His youthful image in his son renewed:
To all his wishes nothing he denied;
And made the charming Annabel[5] his bride.
35   What faults he had, (for who from faults is free?)
His father could not, or he would not see.
Some warm excesses which the law forbore,
Were construed youth that purged by boiling o'er,
And Amnon's murther,[6] by a specious name,
40   Was called a just revenge for injured fame.
Thus praised and loved the noble youth remained,
While David, undisturbed, in Sion[7] reigned.

1. *Absalom and Achitophel* was published in 1681 at the height of a complicated political crisis involving a disagreement between Charles II and his parliament. Charles II, who ascended the English throne in 1660, failed (as had his father) to get along with his parliament; in addition he failed to produce a legitimate heir to the throne. The natural successor, therefore, was his brother James, the Duke of York, a Roman Catholic. The Whig party, under the Earl of Shaftesbury, opposed James and supported Charles's illegitimate son James, the Duke of Monmouth, who was (of course) a Protestant. Charges of Popish interference, indeed alleged attempts at assassination, threw the country into a state of turmoil. In 1680 Parliament passed an Exclusion Bill (excluding the Duke of York from the right to be king), but it was rejected by the House of Lords. In a counter-attack by the king's supporters, Shaftesbury was arrested on a charge of high treason;

on 17 November, a week before the trial, Dryden produced his *Absalom and Achitophel*, supporting the king's cause under the guise of a well-known biblical story of King David (2 Sam. xiii–xx). For a more detailed but succinct account of the political background, see *The Works of John Dryden* (Berkeley: Univ. of California Press, 1972), II, 209–36.

2. Catherine of Braganza, Charles's wife, who (like Michal) failed to bear her husband any children.

3. Charles II, like David, had a large number of children by his several mistresses.

4. James, the Duke of Monmouth, son to Charles by Lucy Walters.

5. Anne Scott, Monmouth's wife.

6. The account of Amnon's murder in 2 Sam. xiii has puzzled annotators; the specific reference is not known.

7. London.

But life can never be sincerely blest;
Heaven punishes the bad, and proves the best.
45 The Jews,[8] a headstrong, moody, murmuring race,
As ever tried the extent and stretch of grace;
God's pampered people, whom, debauched with ease,
No king could govern, nor no God could please;
(Gods they had tried of every shape and size,
50 That god-smiths could produce, or priests devise:)
These Adam-wits, too fortunately free,
Began to dream they wanted liberty;
And when no rule, no precedent was found,
Of men by laws less circumscribed and bound;
55 They led their wild desires to woods and caves,
And thought that all but savages were slaves.
They who, when Saul[9] was dead, without a blow,
Made foolish Ishbosheth the crown forego;
Who banished David did from Hebron[10] bring,
60 And with a general shout proclaimed him king:
Those very Jews, who, at their very best,
Their humor more than loyalty expressed,
Now wondered why so long they had obeyed
An idol monarch, which their hands had made;
65 Thought they might ruin him they could create,
Or melt him to that golden calf, a State.[11]
But these were random bolts; no formed design,
Nor interest made the factious crowd to join:
The sober part of Israel, free from stain,
70 Well knew the value of a peaceful reign;
And, looking backward with a wise affright,
Saw seams of wounds, dishonest to the sight:
In contemplation of whose ugly scars
They cursed the memory of civil wars.
75 The moderate sort of men, thus qualified,
Inclined the balance to the better side;
And David's mildness managed it so well,
The bad found no occasion to rebel.
But when to sin our biased nature leans,
80 The careful Devil is still at hand with means;
And providently pimps for ill desires.
The Good Old Cause revived, a plot requires:
Plots, true or false, are necessary things,
To raise up commonwealths, and ruin kings.
85   The inhabitants of old Jerusalem[12]
Where Jebusites; the town so called from them;
And theirs the native right—
But when the chosen people grew more strong,
The rightful cause at length became the wrong;
90 And every loss the men of Jebus bore,
They still were thought God's enemies the more.
Thus worn and weakened, well or ill content,
Submit they must to David's government:
Impoverished and deprived of all command,
95 Their taxes doubled as they lost their land;
And, what was harder yet to flesh and blood,
Their gods disgraced, and burnt like common wood.
This set the heathen priesthood in a flame;
For priests of all religions are the same:

---

8. The English.
9. Oliver Cromwell, the English Protector during the interregnum (1649–60). He died in 1658 and was succeeded for a very brief time by his son, Richard (here *Ishbosheth*).
10. David was crowned king of Judah in Hebron (2 Sam.

ii.4). Here Hebron may refer to Scotland where Charles had been crowned before his coronation in London.
11. Commonwealth or republic.
12. London. The "Jebusites" are the Roman Catholics and "the chosen people" are the Protestants.

100 Of whatsoe'er descent their godhead be,
     Stock, stone, or other homely pedigree,
     In his defense his servants are as bold,
     As if he had been born of beaten gold.
     The Jewish rabbins,[13] tho' their enemies,
105 In this conclude them honest men and wise:
     For 'twas their duty, all the learnèd think,
     T'espouse his cause, by whom they eat and drink.
     From hence began that Plot,[14] the nation's curse,
     Bad in itself, but represented worse;
110 Raised in extremes, and in extremes decried;
     With oaths affirmed, with dying vows denied;
     Not weighed or winnowed by the multitude;
     But swallowed in the mass, unchewed and crude.
     Some truth there was, but dashed and brewed with lies,
115 To please the fools, and puzzle all the wise.
     Succeeding times did equal folly call,
     Believing nothing, or believing all.
     The Egyptian[15] rites the Jebusites embraced;
     Where gods were recommended by their taste.
120 Such savory deities must needs be good,
     As served at once for worship and for food.
     By force they could not introduce these gods,
     For ten to one in former days was odds;
     So fraud was used (the sacrificer's trade):
125 Fools are more hard to conquer than persuade.
     Their busy teachers mingled with the Jews,
     And raked for converts even the court and stews:
     Which Hebrew priests the more unkindly took,
     Because the fleece accompanies the flock.
130 Some thought they God's anointed meant to slay
     By guns, invented since full many a day:
     Our author swears it not; but who can know
     How far the Devil and Jebusites may go?
     This Plot, which failed for want of common sense,
135 Had yet a deep and dangerous consequence:
     For, as when raging fevers boil the blood,
     The standing lake soon floats into a flood,
     And every hostile humor, which before
     Slept quiet in its channels, bubbles o'er;
140 So several factions from this first ferment
     Work up to foam, and threat the government.
     Some by their friends, more by themselves thought wise,
     Opposed the power to which they could not rise.
     Some had in courts been great, and thrown from thence,
145 Like fiends were hardened in impenitence.
     Some, by their monarch's fatal mercy, grown
     From pardoned rebels kinsmen to the throne,
     Were raised in power and public office high;
     Strong bands, if bands ungrateful men could tie.
150   Of these the false Achitophel[16] was first;
     A name to all succeeding ages curst:
     For close designs and crooked counsels fit;
     Sagacious, bold, and turbulent of wit;
     Restless, unfixed in principles and place;
155 In power unpleased, impatient of disgrace:
     A fiery soul, which, working out its way,

13. Church of England clergy.
14. The Popish Plot. See *The Works*, II, 213–19.
15. French.
16. Anthony Ashley Cooper, First Earl of Shaftesbury.

The biblical counterpart was David's counsellor, who later turned traitor and tried to persuade Absalom to rebel against his father.

Fretted the pigmy body to decay,
And o'er-informed the tenement of clay.
A daring pilot in extremity;
160 Pleased with the danger, when the waves went high,
He sought the storms; but, for a calm unfit,
Would steer too nigh the sands, to boast his wit.
Great wits are sure to madness near allied,
And thin partitions do their bounds divide;
165 Else why should he, with wealth and honor blest,
Refuse his age the needful hours of rest?
Punish a body which he could not please;
Bankrupt of life, yet prodigal of ease?
And all to leave what with his toil he won,
170 To that unfeathered two-legged thing, a son;
Got, while his soul did huddled notions try;
And born a shapeless lump, like anarchy.
In friendship false, implacable in hate;
Resolved to ruin or to rule the State.
175 To compass this the triple bond[17] he broke;
The pillars of the public safety shook;
And fitted Israel for a foreign yoke:
Then seized with fear, yet still affecting fame,
Usurped a patriot's all-atoning name.
180 So easy still it proves in factious times,
With public zeal to cancel private crimes.
How safe is treason, and how sacred ill,
Where none can sin against the people's will!
Where crowds can wink, and no offense be known,
185 Since in another's guilt they find their own!
Yet fame deserved no enemy can grudge;
The statesman we abhor, but praise the judge.
In Israel's courts ne'er sat an Abbethdin[18]
With more discerning eyes, or hands more clean;
190 Unbribed, unsought, the wretched to redress;
Swift of dispatch, and easy of access.
O, had he been content to serve the crown,
With virtues only proper to the gown;
Or had the rankness of the soil been freed
195 From cockle, that oppressed the noble seed;
David for him his tuneful harp had strung,
And Heaven had wanted one immortal song.
But wild Ambition loves to slide, not stand,
And Fortune's ice prefers to Virtue's land.
200 Achitophel, grown weary to possess
A lawful fame, and lazy happiness,
Disdained the golden fruit to gather free,
And lent the crowd his arm to shake the tree.
Now, manifest of crimes contrived long since,
205 He stood at bold defiance with his prince;
Held up the buckler of the people's cause
Against the crown, and skulked behind the laws.
The wished occasion of the Plot he takes;
Some circumstances finds, but more he makes.
210 By buzzing emissaries fills the ears
Of listening crowds with jealousies and fears
Of arbitrary counsels brought to light,
And proves the king himself a Jebusite.
Weak arguments! which yet he knew full well
215 Were strong with people easy to rebel.

---

17. An alliance between England, Holland, and Sweden.   18. An officer of the Jewish high court.

For, governed by the moon, the giddy Jews
Tread the same track when she the prime renews;
And once in twenty years, their scribes record,
By natural instinct they change their lord.[19]
220 Achitophel still wants a chief, and none
Was found so fit as warlike Absalon:
Not that he wished his greatness to create,
(For politicans neither love nor hate,)
But, for he knew his title not allowed,
225 Would keep him still depending on the crowd:
That kingly power, thus ebbing out, might be
Drawn to the dregs of a democracy.
Him he attempts with studied arts to please,
And sheds his venom in such words as these:
230 "Auspicious prince, at whose nativity
Some royal planet ruled the southern sky;
Thy longing country's darling and desire;
Their cloudy pillar and their guardian fire:
Their second Moses, whose extended wand
235 Divides the seas, and shews the promised land;
Whose dawning day in every distant age
Has exercised the sacred prophets' rage:
The people's prayer, the glad diviners' theme,
The young men's vision, and the old men's dream!
240 Thee, Savior, thee, the nation's vows confess,
And, never satisifed with seeing, bless:
Swift unbespoken pomps thy steps proclaim,
And stammering babes are taught to lisp thy name.
How long wilt thou the general joy detain,
245 Starve and defraud the people of thy reign?
Content ingloriously to pass thy days
Like one of Virtue's fools that feeds on praise;
Till thy fresh glories, which now shine so bright,
Grow stale and tarnish with our daily sight.
250 Believe me, royal youth, thy fruit must be
Or gathered ripe, or rot upon the tree.
Heaven has to all allotted, soon or late,
Some lucky revolution of their fate;
Whose motions if we watch and guide with skill,
255 (For human good depends on human will,)
Our Fortune rolls as from a smooth descent,
And from the first impression takes the bent:
But, if unseized, she glides away like wind,
And leaves repenting Folly far behind.
260 Now, now she meets you with a glorious prize,
And spreads her locks before her as she flies.
Had thus old David, from whose loins you spring,
Not dared, when Fortune called him, to be king,
At Gath[20] an exile he might still remain,
265 And Heaven's anointing oil had been in vain.
Let his successful youth your hopes engage;
But shun the example of declining age:
Behold him setting in his western skies,
The shadows lengthening as the vapors rise.
270 He is not now, as when on Jordan's sand
The joyful people thronged to see him land,
Covering the beach, and blackening all the strand;
But, like the Prince of Angels, from his height
Comes tumbling downward with diminished light;

---

19. Charles II ascended the throne in 1660; it is now 1680.
20. See 1 Sam. xxvii.107; its parallel is perhaps Brussels, where Charles spent time in exile.

275 Betrayed by one poor plot to public scorn,
    (Our only blessing since his curst return;)
    Those heaps of people which one sheaf did bind,
    Blown off and scattered by a puff of wind.
    What strength can he to your designs oppose,
280 Naked of friends, and round beset with foes?
    If Pharaoh's doubtful succor he should use,
    A foreign aid would more incense the Jews:
    Proud Egypt would dissembled friendship bring;
    Foment the war, but not support the king:
285 Nor would the royal party e'er unite
    With Pharaoh's arms[21] to assist the Jebusite;
    Or if they should, their interest soon would break,
    And with such odious aid make David weak.
    All sorts of men by my successful arts,
290 Abhorring kings, estrange their altered hearts
    From David's rule: and 'tis the general cry,
    'Religion, commonwealth, and liberty.'
    If you, as champion of the public good,
    Add to their arms a chief of royal blood,
295 What may not Israel hope, and what applause
    Might such a general gain by such a cause?
    Not barren praise alone, that gaudy flower
    Fair only to the sight, but solid power;
    And nobler is a limited command,
300 Given by the love of all your native land,
    Than a successive title, long and dark,
    Drawn from the moldy rolls of Noah's ark."
        What cannot praise effect in mighty minds,
    When flattery soothes, and when ambition blinds!
305 Desire of power, on earth a vicious weed,
    Yet, sprung from high, is of celestial seed:
    In God 'tis glory; and when men aspire,
    'Tis but a spark too much of heavenly fire.
    The ambitious youth, too covetous of fame,
310 Too full of angels' metal in his frame,
    Unwarily was led from virtue's ways,
    Made drunk with honor, and debauched with praise.
    Half loth, and half consenting to the ill,
    (For loyal blood within him struggled still,)
315 He thus replied: "And what pretense have I
    To take up arms for public liberty?
    My father governs with unquestioned right;
    The faith's defender, and mankind's delight;
    Good, gracious, just, observant of the laws:
320 And Heaven by wonders has espoused his cause.
    Whom has he wronged in all his peaceful reign?
    Who sues for justice to his throne in vain?
    What millions has he pardoned of his foes,
    Whom just revenge did to his wrath expose?
325 Mild, easy, humble, studious of our good;
    Enclined to mercy, and averse from blood;
    If mildness ill with stubborn Israel suit,
    His crime is God's beloved attribute.
    What could he gain, his people to betray,
330 Or change his right for arbitrary sway?
    Let haughty Pharaoh curse with such a reign
    His fruitful Nile, and yoke a servile train.
    If David's rule Jerusalem displease,
    The Dog-star[22] heats their brains to this disease.

21. Louis XIV's help. Hence "Egypt" is France.

22. Sirius, which is most prominent during August, sometimes causing madness (hence "dog days").

335   Why then should I, encouraging the bad,
       Turn rebel and run popularly mad?
       Were he a tyrant, who, by lawless might
       Oppressed the Jews, and raised the Jebusite,
       Well might I mourn; but nature's holy bands
340   Would curb my spirits and restrain my hands:
       The people might assert their liberty;
       But what was right in them were crime in me.
       His favor leaves me nothing to require,
       Prevents my wishes, and outruns desire.
345   What more can I expect while David lives?
       All but his kingly diadem he gives:
       And that"— But there he paused; then sighing, said—
       "Is justly destined for a worthier head.
       For when my father from his toils shall rest,
350   And late augment the number of the blest,
       His lawful issue shall the throne ascend,
       Or the *collateral* line, where that shall end.
       His brother,[23] tho' oppressed with vulgar spite,
       Yet dauntless, and secure of native right,
355   Of every royal virtue stands possessed;
       Still dear to all the bravest and the best.
       His courage foes, his friends his truth proclaim;
       His loyalty the king, the world his fame.
       His mercy even the offending crowd will find;
360   For sure he comes of a forgiving kind.
       Why should I then repine at Heaven's decree,
       Which gives me no pretense to royalty?
       Yet O that fate, propitiously inclined,
       Had raised my birth, or had debased my mind;
365   To my large soul not all her treasure lent,
       And then betrayed it to a mean descent!
       I find, I find my mounting spirits bold,
       And David's part disdains my mother's mold.
       Why am I scanted by a niggard birth?
370   My soul disclaims the kindred of her earth;
       And, made for empire, whispers me within,
       'Desire of greatness is a godlike sin.' "
         Him staggering so when hell's dire agent found,
       While fainting Virtue scarce maintained her ground,
375   He pours fresh forces in, and thus replies:
         "The eternal God, supremely good and wise,
       Imparts not these prodigious gifts in vain:
       What wonders are reserved to bless your reign!
       Against your will, your arguments have shown,
380   Such virtue's only given to guide a throne.
       Not that your father's mildness I contemn;
       But manly force becomes the diadem.
       'Tis true he grants the people all they crave;
       And more, perhaps, than subjects ought to have:
385   For lavish grants suppose a monarch tame,
       And more his goodness than his wit proclaim.
       But when should people strive their bonds to break,
       If not when kings are negligent or weak?
       Let him give on till he can give no more,
390   The thrifty Sanhedrin[24] shall keep him poor;
       And every shekel which he can receive,
       Shall cost a limb of his prerogative.
       To ply him with new plots shall be my care;
       Or plunge him deep in some expensive war;

23. James, the Duke of York.

24. The highest Jewish court. The parallel is the English parliament.

395 Which when his treasure can no more supply,
     He must, with the remains of kingship, buy.
     His faithful friends, our jealousies and fears
     Call Jebusites, and Pharaoh's pensioners;
     Whom when our fury from his aid has torn,
400 He shall be naked left to public scorn.
     The next successor, whom I fear and hate,
     My arts have made obnoxious to the State;
     Turned all his virtues to his overthrow,
     And gained our elders to pronounce a foe.
405 His right, for sums of necessary gold,
     Shall first be pawned, and afterwards be sold;
     Till time shall ever-wanting David draw,
     To pass your doubtful title into law:
     If not, the people have a right supreme
410 To make their kings; for kings are made for them.
     All empire is no more than power in trust,
     Which, when resumed, can be no longer just.
     Succession, for the general good designed,
     In its own wrong a nation cannot bind;
415 If altering that the people can relieve,
     Better one suffer than a nation grieve.
     The Jews well know their power: ere Saul they chose,
     God was their king, and God they durst depose.
     Urge now your piety, your filial name,
420 A father's right, and fear of future fame;
     The public good, that universal call,
     To which even Heaven submitted, answers all.
     Nor let his love enchant your generous mind;
     'Tis Nature's trick to propagate her kind.
425 Our fond begetters, who would never die,
     Love but themselves in their posterity.
     Or let his kindness by the effects be tried,
     Or let him lay his vain pretense aside.
     God said he loved your father; could he bring
430 A better proof, than to anoint him king?
     It surely shewed he loved the shepherd well,
     Who gave so fair a flock as Israel.
     Would David have you thought his darling son?
     What means he then, to alienate the crown?
435 The name of godly he may blush to bear:
     'Tis after God's own heart to cheat his heir.
     He to his brother gives supreme command,
     To you a legacy of barren land:
     Perhaps the old harp, on which he thrums his lays,
440 Or some dull Hebrew ballad in your praise.
     Then the next heir, a prince severe and wise,
     Already looks on you with jealous eyes;
     Sees thro' the thin disguises of your arts,
     And marks your progress in the people's hearts.
445 Tho' now his mighty soul its grief contains,
     He meditates revenge who least complains;
     And, like a lion, slumbering in the way,
     Or sleep dissembling, while he waits his prey,
     His fearless foes within his distance draws,
450 Constrains his roaring, and contracts his paws;
     Till at the last, his time for fury found,
     He shoots with sudden vengeance from the ground;
     The prostrate vulgar passes o'er and spares,
     But with a lordly rage his hunters tears.
455 Your case no tame expedients will afford:
     Resolve on death, or conquest by the sword,
     Which for no less a stake than life you draw;

And self-defense is nature's eldest law.
Leave the warm people no considering time;
460 For then rebellion may be thought a crime.
Prevail yourself of what occasion gives,
But try your title while your father lives;
And that your arms may have a fair pretense,
Proclaim you take them in the king's defense;
465 Whose sacred life each minute would expose
To plots, from seeming friends, and secret foes.
And who can sound the depth of David's soul?
Perhaps his fear his kindness may control.
He fears his brother, tho' he loves his son,
470 For plighted vows too late to be undone.
If so, by force he wishes to be gained;
Like women's lechery, to seem constrained.
Doubt not: but, when he most affects the frown,
Commit a pleasing rape upon the crown.
475 Secure his person to secure your cause:
They who possess the prince, possess the laws."
    He said, and this advice above the rest,
With Absalom's mild nature suited best:
Unblamed of life, (ambition set aside,)
480 Not stained with cruelty, nor puffed with pride;
How happy had he been, if destiny
Had higher placed his birth, or not so high!
His kingly virtues might have claimed a throne,
And blest all other countries but his own.
485 But charming greatness since so few refuse,
'Tis juster to lament him than accuse.
Strong were his hopes a rival to remove,
With blandishments to gain the public love;
To head the faction while their zeal was hot,
490 And popularly prosecute the Plot.
To farther this, Achitophel unites
The malcontents of all the Israelites;
Whose differing parties he could wisely join,
For several ends, to serve the same design:
495 The best, (and of the princes some were such,)
Who thought the power of monarchy too much;
Mistaken men, and patriots in their hearts;
Not wicked, but seduced by impious arts.
By these the springs of property were bent,
500 And wound so high, they cracked the government.
The next for interest sought to embroil the State,
To sell their duty at a dearer rate;
And make their Jewish markets of the throne,
Pretending public good, to serve their own.
505 Others thought kings an useless heavy load,
Who cost too much, and did too little good.
These were for laying honest David by,
On principles of pure good husbandry.
With them joined all the haranguers of the throng,
510 That thought to get preferment by the tongue.
Who follow next, a double danger bring,
Not only hating David, but the king:
The Solymaean rout,[25] well-versed of old
In godly faction, and in treason bold;
515 Cowering and quaking at a conquerer's sword;
But lofty to a lawful prince restored;
Saw with disdain an Ethnic plot begun,
And scorned by Jebusites to be outdone.

25. Belonging to Jerusalem—here, the London mob.

Hot Levites[26] headed these; who, pulled before
520   From the ark, which in the Judges' days they bore,
Resumed their cant, and with a zealous cry
Pursued their old beloved Theocracy:
Where Sanhedrin and priest enslaved the nation,
And justified their spoils by inspiration:
525   For who so fit for reign as Aaron's race,[27]
If once dominion they could found in grace.
These led the pack; tho' not of surest scent,
Yet deepest mouthed against the government.
A numerous host of dreaming saints succeed,
530   Of the true old enthusiastic breed:
'Gainst form and order they their power imploy,
Nothing to build, and all things to destroy.
But far more numerous was the herd of such,
Who think too little, and who talk too much.
535   These, out of mere instinct, they knew not why,
Adored their fathers' God and property;
And, by the same blind benefit of fate,
The Devil and the Jebusite did hate:
Born to be saved, even in their own despite,
540   Because they could not help believing right.
Such were the tools; but a whole Hydra more
Remains, of sprouting heads too long to score.
Some of their chiefs were princes of the land:
In the first rank of these did Zimri[28] stand;
545   A man so various, that he seemed to be
Not one, but all mankind's epitome:
Stiff in opinions, always in the wrong;
Was everything by starts, and nothing long;
But, in the course of one revolving moon,
550   Was chymist, fiddler, statesman, and buffoon:
Then all for women, painting, rhyming, drinking,
Besides ten thousand freaks that died in thinking.
Blest madman, who could every hour employ,
With something new to wish, or to enjoy!
555   Railing and praising were his usual themes;
And both (to shew his judgment) in extremes:
So over-violent, or over-civil,
That every man, with him, was God or Devil.
In squandering wealth was his peculiar art:
560   Nothing went unrewarded but desert.
Beggared by fools, whom still he found too late,
He had his jest, and they had his estate.
He laughed himself from court; then sought relief
By forming parties, but could ne'er be chief;
565   For, spite of him, the weight of business fell
On Absalom and wise Achitophel:
Thus, wicked but in will, of means bereft,
He left not faction, but of that was left.
    Titles and names 'twere tedious to rehearse
570   Of lords, below the dignity of verse.
Wits, warriors, Commonwealth's-men, were the best;
Kind husbands, and mere nobles, all the rest.
And therefore, in the name of dulness, be
The well-hung Balaam[29] and cold Caleb, free;
575   And canting Nadab let oblivion damn,

---

26. Nonconformist clergymen who, in 1662, were deprived of their religious positions by the Act of Uniformity.
27. The clergy.
28. George Villiers, the Duke of Buckingham, who had been a close friend to the king, but who went over to the opposition in 1674 and later helped fan the flames of the Popish Plot.
29. Ll. 574–85. Balaam, Caleb, Nadab, Jonas, and Shimei: the parallels here are between well-known biblical characters and supporters of the Whig parliamentarians. For more detail see *The Works*, II, 260–62.

Who made new porridge for the paschal lamb.
Let friendship's holy band some names assure;
Some their own worth, and some let scorn secure.
Nor shall the rascal rabble here have place,
580 Whom kings no titles gave, and God no grace:
Not bull-faced Jonas, who could statutes draw
To mean rebellion, and make treason law.
But he, tho' bad, is followed by a worse,
The wretch who Heaven's anointed dared to curse:
585 Shimei, whose youth did early promise bring
Of zeal to God and hatred to his king,
Did wisely from expensive sins refrain,
And never broke the Sabbath, but for gain;
Nor ever was he known an oath to vent,
590 Or curse, unless against the government.
Thus heaping wealth, by the most ready way
Among the Jews, which was to cheat and pray,
The city, to reward his pious hate
Against his master, chose him magistrate.
595 His hand a vare[30] of justice did uphold;
His neck was loaded with a chain of gold.
During his office, treason was no crime;
The sons of Belial had a glorious time;
For Shimei, tho' not prodigal of pelf,[31]
600 Yet loved his wicked neighbor as himself.
When two or three were gathered to declaim
Against the monarch of Jerusalem,
Shimei was always in the midst of them;
And if they cursed the king when he was by,
605 Would rather curse than break good company.
If any durst his factious friends accuse,
He packed a jury of dissenting Jews;
Whose fellow-feeling in the godly cause
Would free the suffering saint from human laws.
610 For laws are only made to punish those
Who serve the king, and to protect his foes.
If any leisure time he had from power,
(Because 'tis sin to misimploy an hour,)
His business was, by writing, to persuade
615 That kings were useless, and a clog to trade;
And, that his noble style he might refine,
No Rechabite[32] more shunned the fumes of wine.
Chaste were his cellars, and his shrieval[33] board
The grossness of a city feast abhorred:
620 His cooks, with long disuse, their trade forgot;
Cool was his kitchen, tho' his brains were hot.
Such frugal virtue malice may accuse,
But sure 'twas necessary to the Jews;
For towns once burnt such magistrates require
625 As dare not tempt God's providence by fire.
With spiritual food he fed his servants well,
But free from flesh that made the Jews rebel;
And Moses' laws he held in more account,
For forty days of fasting in the mount.
630 To speak the rest, who better are forgot,
Would tire a well-breathed witness of the Plot.
Yet, Corah,[34] thou shalt from oblivion pass:

---

30. Wand.
31. A depreciatory term for "wealth."
32. Total abstainer (see Jer. xxxv).
33. Sheriff's.

34. Titus Oates, the chief perpetrator of the Popish Plot, who falsely accused many of treason. He was later found guilty of perjury.

Erect thyself, thou monumental brass,
High as the serpent[35] of thy metal made,
635 While nations stand secure beneath thy shade.
What tho' his birth were base, yet comets rise
From earthy vapors, ere they shine in skies.
Prodigious actions may as well be done
By weaver's issue, as by prince's son.
640 This arch-attestor for the public good
By that one deed ennobles all his blood.
Who ever asked the witnesses' high race,
Whose oath with martyrdom did Stephen grace?
Ours was a Levite, and as times went then,
645 His tribe were God Almighty's gentlemen.
Sunk were his eyes, his voice was harsh and loud,
Sure signs he neither choleric was nor proud:
His long chin proved his wit; his saintlike grace
A church vermilion, and a Moses' face.
650 His memory, miraculously great,
Could plots, exceeding man's belief, repeat;
Which therefore cannot be accounted lies,
For human wit could never such devise.
Some future truths are mingled in his book;
655 But where the witness failed, the prophet spoke:
Some things like visionary flights appear;
The spirit caught him up, the Lord knows where;
And gave him his rabbinical degree,
Unknown to foreign university.
660 His judgment yet his memory did excel;
Which pieced his wondrous evidence so well,
And suited to the temper of the times,
Then groaning under Jebusitic crimes.
Let Israel's foes suspect his heavenly call,
665 And rashly judge his writ apocryphal;
Our laws for such affronts have forfeits made:
He takes his life, who takes away his trade.
Were I myself in witness Corah's place,
The wretch who did me such a dire disgrace,
670 Should whet my memory, tho' once forgot,
To make him an appendix of my plot.
His zeal to Heaven made him his prince despise,
And load his person with indignities;
But zeal peculiar privilege affords,
675 Indulging latitude to deeds and words;
And Corah might for Agag's murther[36] call,
In terms as coarse as Samuel used to Saul.
What others in his evidence did join,
(The best that could be had for love or coin,)
680 In Corah's own predicament will fall;
For *witness* is a common name to all.
   Surrounded thus with friends of every sort,
Deluded Absalom forsakes the court;
Impatient of high hopes, urged with renown,
685 And fired with near possession of a crown.
The admiring crowd are dazzled with surprise,
And on his goodly person feed their eyes.
His joy concealed, he sets himself to show,
On each side bowing popularly low;
690 His looks, his gestures, and his words he frames,
And with familiar ease repeats their names.

---

35. See Num. xxi.6–9 for a description of Moses' brazen
serpent.

36. The reference is to 1 Sam. xv.11–33, but the parallel
is not positively known.

Thus formed by nature, furnished out with arts,
He glides unfelt into their secret hearts.
Then, with a kind compassionating look,
695   And sighs, bespeaking pity ere he spoke,
Few words he said; but easy those and fit,
More slow than Hybla-drops,[37] and far more sweet.
    "I mourn, my countrymen, your lost estate;
Tho' far unable to prevent your fate:
700   Behold a banished man, for your dear cause
Exposed a prey to arbitrary laws!
Yet O! that I alone could be undone,
Cut off from empire, and no more a son!
Now all your liberties a spoil are made;
705   Egypt and Tyrus intercept your trade,
And Jebusites your sacred rites invade.
My father, whom with reverence yet I name,
Charmed into ease, is careless of his fame;
And, bribed with petty sums of foreign gold,
710   Is grown in Bathsheba's[38] embraces old;
Exalts his enemies, his friends destroys;
And all his power against himself imploys.
He gives, and let him give, my right away;
But why should he his own and yours betray?
715   He, only he, can make the nation bleed,
And he alone from my revenge is freed.
Take then my tears, (with that he wiped his eyes,)
'Tis all the aid my present power supplies:
No court-informer can these arms accuse;
720   These arms may sons against their fathers use:
And 'tis my wish, the next successor's reign
May make no other Israelite complain."
    Youth, beauty, graceful action seldom fail;
But common interest always will prevail;
725   And pity never ceases to be shown
To him who makes the people's wrongs his own.
The crowd, that still believe their kings oppress,
With lifted hands their young Messiah bless:
Who now begins his progress to ordain
730   With chariots, horsemen, and a numerous train;
From east to west his glories he displays,
And, like the sun, the promised land surveys.
Fame runs before him as the morning star,
And shouts of joy salute him from afar:
735   Each house receives him as a guardian god,
And consecrates the place of his abode.
But hospitable treats did most commend
Wise Issachar,[39] his wealthy western friend.
This moving court, that caught the people's eyes,
740   And seemed but pomp, did other ends disguise:
Achitophel had formed it, with intent
To sound the depths, and fathom, where it went,
The people's hearts; distinguish friends from foes,
And try their strength, before they came to blows.
745   Yet all was colored with a smooth pretense
Of specious love, and duty to their prince.
Religion, and redress of grievances,
Two names that always cheat and always please,
Are often urged; and good King David's life
750   Endangered by a brother and a wife.[40]

37. Honey.
38. The Duchess of Portsmouth and mistress to the king.
39. Thomas Thynne, friend to Monmouth, who was anything but "wise." The biblical reference is to Gen. xlix.
40. The Duke of York and his wife, Catherine.

Thus in a pageant shew a plot is made,
And peace itself is war in masquerade.
O foolish Israel! never warned by ill!
Still the same bait, and circumvented still!
755   Did ever men forsake their present ease,
In midst of health imagine a disease;
Take pains contingent mischiefs to foresee,
Make heirs for monarchs, and for God decree?
What shall we think! Can people give away,
760   Both for themselves and sons, their native sway?
Then they are left defenseless to the sword
Of each unbounded, arbitrary lord:
And laws are vain, by which we right enjoy,
If kings unquestioned can those laws destroy.
765   Yet if the crowd be judge of fit and just,
And kings are only officers in trust,
Then this resuming covenant was declared
When kings were made, or is for ever barred.
If those who gave the scepter could not tie
770   By their own deed their own posterity,
How then could Adam bind his future race?
How could his forfeit on mankind take place?
Or how could heavenly justice damn us all,
Who ne'er consented to our father's fall?
775   Then kings are slaves to those whom they command,
And tenants to their people's pleasure stand.
Add, that the power for property allowed
Is mischievously seated in the crowd;
For who can be secure of private right,
780   If sovereign sway may be dissolved by might?
Nor is the people's judgment always true:
The most may err as grossly as the few.
And faultless kings run down, by common cry,
For vice, oppression, and for tyranny.
785   What standard is there in a fickle rout,
Which, flowing to the mark, runs faster out?
Nor only crowds, but Sanhedrins may be
Infected with this public lunacy,
And share the madness of rebellious times,
790   To murther monarchs for imagined crimes.
If they may give and take whene'er they please,
Not kings alone, (the Godhead's images,)
But government itself at length must fall
To nature's state, where all have right to all.
795   Yet, grant our lords the people kings can make,
What prudent men a settled throne would shake?
For whatsoe'er their sufferings were before,
That change they covet makes them suffer more.
All other errors but disturb a state,
800   But innovation is the blow of fate.
If ancient fabrics nod, and threat to fall,
To patch the flaws, and buttress up the wall,
Thus far 'tis duty: but here fix the mark;
For all beyond it is to touch our ark.[41]
805   To change foundations, cast the frame anew,
Is work for rebels, who base ends pursue,
At once divine and human laws control,
And mend the parts by ruin of the whole.
The tampering world is subject to this curse,
810   To physic their disease into a worse.

41. Commit sacrilege.

Now what relief can righteous David bring?
How fatal 'tis to be too good a king!
Friends he has few, so high the madness grows:
Who dare be such, must be the people's foes.
815　Yet some there were, even in the worst of days;
Some let me name, and naming is to praise.
　　In this short file Barzillai[42] first appears;
Barzillai, crowned with honor and with years.
Long since, the rising rebels he withstood
820　In regions waste, beyond the Jordan's flood:
Unfortunately brave to buoy the State;
But sinking underneath his master's fate:
In exile with his godlike prince he mourned;
For him he suffered, and with him returned.
825　The court he practiced, not the courtier's art:
Large was his wealth, but larger was his heart,
Which well the noblest objects knew to choose,
The fighting warrior, and recording Muse.
His bed could once a fruitful issue boast;
830　Now more than half a father's name is lost.
His eldest hope,[43] with every grace adorned,
By me (so Heaven will have it) always mourned,
And always honored, snatched in manhood's prime
By unequal fates, and Providence's crime;
835　Yet not before the goal of honor won,
All parts fulfilled of subject and of son:
Swift was the race, but short the time to run.
O narrow circle, but of power divine,
Scanted in space, but perfect in thy line!
840　By sea, by land, thy matchless worth was known,
Arms thy delight, and war was all thy own:
Thy force, infused, the fainting Tyrians[44] propped;
And haughty Pharaoh found his fortune stopped.
O ancient honor! O unconquered hand,
845　Whom foes unpunished never could withstand!
But Israel was unworthy of thy name;
Short is the date of all immoderate fame.
It looks as Heaven our ruin had designed,
And durst not trust thy fortune and thy mind.
850　Now, free from earth, thy disencumbered soul
Mounts up, and leaves behind the clouds and starry pole:
From thence thy kindred legions mayst thou bring,
To aid the guardian angel of thy king.
Here stop, my Muse, here cease thy painful flight;
855　No pinions can pursue immortal height:
Tell good Barzillai thou canst sing no more,
And tell thy soul she should have fled before.
Or fled she with his life, and left this verse
To hang on her departed patron's hearse?
860　Now take thy steepy flight from heaven, and see
If thou canst find on earth another *he*:
Another *he* would be too hard to find;
See then whom thou canst see not far behind.
Zadoc[45] the priest, whom, shunning power and place,
865　His lowly mind advanced to David's grace.
With him the Sagan of Jerusalem,[46]
Of hospitable soul, and noble stem;

42. A man loyal to King David during Absalom's rebellion. The parallel is James Butler, the Duke of Ormonde.
43. Butler's eldest son.
44. The Dutch. A reference to Butler's campaign against the French.
45. A priest in David's camp— here, William Sancroft, the Archbishop of Canterbury.
46. The Bishop of London.

Him of the western dome,[47] whose weighty sense
Flows in fit words and heavenly eloquence.
870　The prophets' sons, by such example led,
To learning and to loyalty were bred:
For colleges on bounteous kings depend,
And never rebel was to arts a friend.
To these succeed the pillars of the laws;
875　Who best could plead, and best can judge a cause.
Next them a train of loyal peers ascend;
Sharp-judging Adriel,[48] the Muses' friend;
Himself a Muse— in Sanhedrin's debate
True to his prince, but not a slave of state:
880　Whom David's love with honors did adorn,
That from his disobedient son were torn.
Jotham of piercing wit, and pregnant thought;
Endued by nature, and by learning taught
To move assemblies, who but only tried
885　The worse a while, then chose the better side:
Nor chose alone, but turned the balance too;
So much the weight of one brave man can do.
Hushai, the friend of David in distress;
In public storms, of manly steadfastness:
890　By foreign treaties he informed his youth,
And joined experience to his native truth.
His frugal care supplied the wanting throne;
Frugal for that, but bounteous of his own:
'Tis easy conduct when exchequers flow,
895　But hard the task to manage well the low;
For sovereign power is too depressed or high,
When kings are forced to sell, or crowds to buy.
Indulge one labor more, my weary Muse,
For Amiel: who can Amiel's praise refuse?
900　Of ancient race by birth, but nobler yet
In his own worth, and without title great:
The Sanhedrin long time as chief he ruled,
Their reason guided, and their passion cooled:
So dextrous was he in the crown's defense,
905　So formed to speak a loyal nation's sense,
That, as their band was Israel's tribes in small,
So fit was he to represent them all.
Now rasher charioteers the seat ascend,
Whose loose careers his steady skill commend:
910　They, like the unequal ruler of the day,
Misguide the seasons, and mistake the way;
While he withdrawn at their mad labor smiles,
And safe enjoys the sabbath of his toils.
　　These were the chief, a small but faithful band
915　Of worthies, in the breach who dared to stand,
And tempt the united fury of the land.
With grief they viewed such powerful engines bent,
To batter down the lawful government:
A numerous faction, with pretended frights,
920　In Sanhedrins to plume the regal rights;
The true successor from the court removed;
The Plot, by hireling witnesses, improved.
These ills they saw, and, as their duty bound,
They shewed the king the danger of the wound;
925　That no concessions from the throne would please,
But lenitives fomented the disease;
That Absalom, ambitious of the crown,

---

47. The Dean of Westminster.

48. Ll. 877–99: Adriel, Jotham, Hushai, and Amiel, all
identifiable supporters of Charles II.

Was made the lure to draw the people down;
That false Achitophel's pernicious hate
930 Had turned the Plot to ruin Church and State;
The council violent, the rabble worse;
That Shimei taught Jerusalem to curse.
    With all these loads of injuries oppressed,
And long revolving in his careful breast
935 The event of things, at last, his patience tired,
Thus from his royal throne, by Heaven inspired,
The godlike David spoke: with awful fear
His train their Maker in their master hear.
    "Thus long have I, by native mercy swayed,
940 My wrongs dissembled, my revenge delayed:
So willing to forgive the offending age;
So much the father did the king assuage.
But now so far my clemency they slight,
The offenders question my forgiving right.
945 That one was made for many, they contend;
But 'tis to rule; for that's a monarch's end.
They call my tenderness of blood, my fear;
Tho' manly tempers can the longest bear.
Yet, since they will divert my native course,
950 'Tis time to shew I am not good by force.
Those heaped affronts that haughty subjects bring,
Are burthens for a camel, not a king.
Kings are the public pillars of the State,
Born to sustain and prop the nation's weight;
955 If my young Samson will pretend a call
To shake the column, let him share the fall:
But O that yet he would repent and live!
How easy 'tis for parents to forgive!
With how few tears a pardon might be won
960 From nature, pleading for a darling son!
Poor pitied youth, by my paternal care
Raised up to all the height his frame could bear!
Had God ordained his fate for empire born,
He would have given his soul another turn:
965 Gulled with a patriot's name, whose modern sense
Is one that would by law supplant his prince;
The people's brave, the politician's tool;
Never was patriot yet, but was a fool.
Whence comes it that religion and the laws
970 Should more be Absalom's than David's cause?
His old instructor, ere he lost his place,
Was never thought indued with so much grace.
Good heavens, how faction can a patriot paint!
My rebel ever proves my people's saint.
975 Would *they* impose an heir upon the throne?
Let Sanhedrins be taught to give their own.
A king's at least a part of government,
And mine as requisite as their consent;
Without my leave a future king to choose,
980 Infers a right the present to depose.
True, they petition me to approve their choice;
But Esau's hands suit ill with Jacob's voice.
My pious subjects for my safety pray;
Which to secure, they take my power away.
985 From plots and treasons Heaven preserve my years,
But save me most from my petitioners!
Unsatiate as the barren womb or grave;
God cannot grant so much as they can crave.
What then is left, but with a jealous eye

990   To guard the small remains of royalty?
  The law shall still direct my peaceful sway,
  And the same law teach rebels to obey:
  Votes shall no more established power control—
  Such votes as make a part exceed the whole:
995   No groundless clamors shall my friends remove,
  Nor crowds have power to punish ere they prove;
  For gods and godlike kings their care express,
  Still to defend their servants in distress.
  O that my power to saving were confined!
1000   Why am I forced, like Heaven, against my mind,
  To make examples of another kind?
  Must I at length the sword of justice draw?
  O curst effects of necessary law!
  How ill my fear they by my mercy scan!
1005   Beware the fury of a patient man.
  Law they require, let Law then shew her face;[49]
  They could not be content to look on Grace,
  Her hinder parts, but with a daring eye
  To tempt the terror of her front and die.
1010   By their own arts, 'tis righteously decreed,
  Those dire artificers of death shall bleed.
  Against themselves their witnesses will swear,
  Till viper-like their mother Plot they tear;
  And suck for nutriment that bloody gore,
1015   Which was their principle of life before.
  Their Belial with their Belzebub will fight;[50]
  Thus on my foes, my foes shall do me right.
  Nor doubt the event; for factious crowds engage,
  In their first onset, all their brutal rage.
1020   Then let 'em take an unresisted course;
  Retire, and traverse, and delude their force;
  But, when they stand all breathless, urge the fight,
  And rise upon 'em with redoubled might;
  For lawful power is still superior found;
1025   When long driven back, at length it stands the ground."
   He said. The Almighty, nodding, gave consent;
  And peals of thunder shook the firmament.
  Henceforth a series of new time began,
  The mighty years in long procession ran:
1030   Once more the godlike David was restored,
  And willing nations knew their lawful lord.

To the Memory of Mr. Oldham[1]

  Farewell, too little, and too lately known,
  Whom I began to think and call my own:
  For sure our souls were near allied, and thine
  Cast in the same poetic mold with mine.
5 One common note on either lyre did strike,
  And knaves and fools we both abhorred alike.
  To the same goal did both our studies drive;
  The last set out the soonest did arrive.

49. Ll. 1006–09. See Exod. xxxiii.19–23.
50. Belial, Belzebub: princes among demons. They are evil personified.

1. "To the Memory of Mr. Oldham" commemorates the brief career and laments the loss of a promising poet, John Oldham, who died in 1683 at the age of thirty. That he was a friend of Dryden's seems obvious; how well they knew each other is unclear. The poem appeared in the *Remains of Mr. John Oldham* (1684).

Thus Nisus[2] fell upon the slippery place,
10   While his young friend performed and won the race.
O early ripe! to thy abundant store
What could advancing age have added more?
It might (what nature never gives the young)
Have taught the numbers of thy native tongue.
15   But satire needs not those, and wit will shine
Thro' the harsh cadence of a rugged line:
A noble error, and but seldom made,
When poets are by too much force betrayed.
Thy generous fruits, tho' gathered ere their prime,
20   Still shewed a quickness; and maturing time
But mellows what we write to the dull sweets of rhyme.
Once more, hail and farewell; farewell, thou young,
But ah too short, Marcellus of our tongue;
Thy brows with ivy, and with laurels bound;
25   But fate and gloomy night encompass thee around.

A Song for St. Cecilia's Day, 1687[1]

I

From harmony, from heavenly harmony
         This universal frame began:
         When Nature underneath a heap
             Of jarring atoms lay,
5   And could not heave her head,
The tuneful voice was heard from high:
             "Arise, ye more than dead."
Then cold, and hot, and moist, and dry,
In order to their stations leap,
10   And Music's power obey.
From harmony, from heavenly harmony
         This universal frame began:
         From harmony to harmony
Thro' all the compass of the notes it ran,
15   The diapason closing full in Man.

II

What passion cannot Music raise and quell!
             When Jubal[2] struck the corded shell,
             His listening brethren stood around,
             And, wondering, on their faces fell
20   To worship that celestial sound.
Less than a god they thought there could not dwell
             Within the hollow of that shell
             That spoke so sweetly and so well.
What passion cannot Music raise and quell!

III

25   The Trumpet's loud clangor
                 Excites us to arms,
             With shrill notes of anger,
                 And mortal alarms.

2. The references in the poem are to Virgil's *Aeneid*, which Dryden had translated; Nisus and Euryalus ("his young friend") ran together in a race, in which Nisus slipped and fell, allowing Euryalus to win. *Marcellus* (l. 23), who also died young, was also celebrated by Virgil.

1. St. Cecilia is the patron saint of music; the celebration of St. Cecilia's Day (22 November) was common well into the eighteenth century and was the occasion for new music and poetry. Dryden was one among many poets who sang the praises of St. Cecilia.

2. According to the Bible (Gen. iv.21), the inventor of the harp and organ.

        The double double double beat
30   Of the thundering Drum
Cries: "Hark! the foes come;
Charge, charge, 'tis too late to retreat."

IV

        The soft complaining Flute
        In dying notes discovers
35   The woes of hopeless lovers,
Whose dirge is whispered by the warbling Lute.

V

        Sharp Violins proclaim
Their jealous pangs, and desperation,
Fury, frantic indignation,
40   Depth of pains, and height of passion,
        For the fair, disdainful dame.

VI

        But O! what art can teach,
        What human voice can reach,
The sacred Organ's praise?
45   Notes inspiring holy love,
Notes that wing their heavenly ways
        To mend the choirs above.

VII

Orpheus could lead the savage race;
And trees unrooted left their place,
50   Sequacious of the lyre;
But bright Cecilia raised the wonder higher:
When to her Organ vocal breath was given,
An angel heard, and straight appeared,
        Mistaking earth for heaven.

Grand Chorus

55   *As from the power of sacred lays*
        The spheres began to move,
And sung the great Creator's praise
        To all the blest above;
So, when the last and dreadful hour
60   *This crumbling pageant shall devour,*
The Trumpet shall be heard on high,
The dead shall live, the living die,
And Music shall untune the sky.

JONATHAN SWIFT (1667–1745)

A Description of the Morning[1]

Now hardly here and there a hackney-coach
Appearing, showed the ruddy morn's approach.
Now Betty[2] from her master's bed had flown,
And softly stole to discompose her own;
The slip-shod 'prentice from his master's door
Had pared the dirt, and sprinkled round the floor.

---

1. "A Description of the Morning" and "A Description of a
City Shower" (which follows) were first published in *The
Tatler* in 1709 and 1710. The texts here are based on the
1735 authoritative edition of the *Works*.
2. Maid-servant.

Now Moll[3] had whirled her mop with dext'rous airs,
Prepared to scrub the entry and the stairs.
The youth with broomy stumps began to trace
The kennel-edge, where wheels had worn the place.[4]
The small-coal man was heard with cadence deep,
Till drowned in shriller notes of chimney-sweep:
Duns[5] at his lordship's gate began to meet;
And brickdust Moll had screamed through half the street.
The turnkey[6] now his flock returning sees,
Duly let out a-nights to steal for fees:
The watchful bailiffs take their silent stands,
And schoolboys lag with satchels in their hands.

A Description of a City Shower

Careful observers may foretell the hour
(By sure prognostics) when to dread a shower.
While rain depends,[1] the pensive cat gives o'er
Her frolics, and pursues her tail no more.
5   Returning home at night, you'll find the sink[2]
Strike your offended sense with double stink.
If you be wise, then go not far to dine:
You'll spend in coach-hire more than save in wine.
A coming shower your shooting corns presage,
10 Old aches throb, your hollow tooth will rage;
Sauntering in coffeehouse is Dulman seen;
He damns the climate, and complains of spleen.
   Meanwhile the South, rising with dabbled wings,
A sable cloud athwart the welkin[3] flings,
15 That swilled more liquor than it could contain,
And like a drunkard gives it up again.
Brisk Susan[4] whips her linen from the rope,
While the first drizzling shower is borne aslope;
Such is that sprinkling which some careless quean[5]
20 Flirts on you from her mop, but not so clean:
You fly, invoke the gods; then, turning, stop
To rail; she singing, still whirls on her mop.
Not yet the dust had shunned th' unequal strife,
But, aided by the wind, fought still for life,
25 And wafted with its foe by violent gust,
'Twas doubtful which was rain, and which was dust.
Ah! where must needy poet seek for aid,
When dust and rain at once his coat invade?
His only coat, where dust confused with rain,
30 Roughen the nap,[6] and leave a mingled stain.
   Now in contiguous drops the flood comes down,
Threatening with deluge this *devoted* town.
To shops in crowds the daggled[7] females fly,
Pretend to cheapen goods, but nothing buy.
35 The Templar spruce,[8] while every spout's abroach,
Stays till 'tis fair, yet seems to call a coach.
The tucked-up sempstress walks with hasty strides,
While streams run down her oiled umbrella's sides.
Here various kinds by various fortunes led,
40 Commence acquaintance underneath a shed.

3. A charwoman.
4. According to an early editor, the boys were trying to
find old nails.
5. Collectors of debts.
6. Jailer.

1. Impends.

2. Outdoor cesspool.
3. Sky.
4. Servant.
5. Hussy or bold woman.
6. Soft, fuzzy surface of his coat
7. Muddy.
8. Law student from the Inner or Middle Temple.

Triumphant Tories, and desponding Whigs,
Forget their feuds, and join to save their wigs.
Boxed in a chair the beau impatient sits,
While spouts run clattering o'er the roof by fits,
45   And ever and anon with frightful din
The leather sounds; he trembles from within.
So when Troy chairmen bore the wooden steed,
Pregnant with Greeks impatient to be freed,
(Those bully Greeks, who, as the moderns do,
50   Instead of paying chairmen, ran them through),
Laoccon struck the outside with his spear,
And each imprisoned hero quaked for fear.[9]
   Now from all parts the swelling kennels[10] flow,
And bear their trophies with them as they go:
55   Filth of all hues and odor seem to tell
What street they sailed from, by their sight and smell.
They, as each torrent drives with rapid force,
From Smithfield or St. Pulchre's shape their course,
And in huge confluent join at Snow Hill Ridge,
60   Fall from the conduit prone to Holborn bridge.
Sweepings from butchers' stalls, dung, guts, and blood,
Drowned puppies, stinking sprats, all drenched in mud,
Dead cats, and turnip-tops, come tumbling down the flood.[11]

A Beautiful Young Nymph Going to Bed[1]

Corinna, pride of Drury-Lane,
For whom no shepherd sighs in vain;
Never did Covent-Garden boast
So bright a battered, strolling toast;
5   No drunken rake to pick her up,
No cellar where on tick to sup;
Returning at the midnight hour,
Four stories climbing to her bower;
Then, seated on a three-legged chair,
10   Takes off her artificial hair;
Now picking out a crystal eye,
She wipes it clean, and lays it by.
Her eyebrows from a mouse's hide
Stuck on with art on either side,
15   Pulls off with care, and first displays 'em,
Then in a play-book smoothly lays 'em.
Now dext'rously her plumpers[2] draws,
That serve to fill her hollow jaws,
Untwists a wire, and from her gums
20   A set of teeth completely comes;
Pulls out the rags contrived to prop
Her flabby dugs, and down they drop.
Proceeding on, the lovely goddess
Unlaces next her steel-ribbed bodice,
25   Which, by the operator's skill,
Press down the lumps, the hollows fill.

Up goes her hand, and off she slips
The bolsters that supply her hips:
With gentlest touch she next explores
30   Her chancres,[3] issues, running sores;
Effects of many a sad disaster,
And then to each applies a plaster:
But must, before she goes to bed,
Rub off the daubs of white and red,
35   And smooth the furrows in her front
With greasy paper stuck upon't.
She takes a bolus[4] ere she sleeps;
And then between two blankets creeps.
With pains of love tormented lies;
40   Or, if she chance to close her eyes,
Of Bridewell and the Compter[5] dreams,
And feels the lash, and faintly screams;
Or by a faithless bully drawn,
At some hedge-tavern lies in pawn;
45   Or to Jamaica seems transported
Alone, and by no planter courted;
Or, near Fleet-ditch's oozy brinks,
Surrounded with a hundred stinks,
Belated, seems on watch to lie,
50   And snap some cully[6] passing by;
Or, struck with fear, her fancy runs
On watchmen, constables, and duns,

---

9. Ll. 47–52: The reference here is to the well-known
story of the Trojan horse.
10. Gutters.
11. Ll. 61–3: In a note appended to the 1735 edition Swift
wrote: "These last three lines were intended against that
licentious manner of modern poets, in making three
rhymes together, which they call *Triplets*; and the last of
the three was two or sometimes more syllables longer,
called an Alexandrian."

1. "A Beautiful Young Nymph," written (states Swift)
"for the honour of the fair sex," was first published in 1734
and again in the *Works* (1735).
2. Pads carried in the mouth to plump out shrivelled
cheeks.
3. Sores or ulcers (denoting venereal disease).
4. Large pill.
5. Prisons for vagrants and harlots.
6. Gullible fool.

From whom she meets with frequent rubs;
But never from religious clubs;
55 Whose favor she is sure to find,
Because she pays them all in kind.
   Corinna wakes. A dreadful sight!
Behold the ruins of the night!
A wicked rat her plaster stole,
60 Half eat, and dragged it to his hole.
The crystal eye, alas! was missed;
And puss had on her plumpers p-ssed.
A pigeon picked her issue-pease:

65 And Shock her tresses filled with fleas.
   The nymph, though in this mangled plight,
Must every morn her limbs unite.
But how shall I describe her arts
To re-collect the scattered parts?
Or show the anguish, toil, and pain,
70 Of gathering up herself again?
The bashful Muse will never bear
In such a scene to interfere.
Corinna in the morning dizened,[7]
Who sees, will spew; who smells, be poisoned.

ALEXANDER POPE (1688–1744)

The Rape of the Lock[1]

Canto I

What dire offence from amorous causes springs,
What mighty contests rise from trivial things,
I sing—This verse to CARYLL, Muse! is due:
This, even Belinda[2] may vouchsafe to view:
5 Slight is the subject, but not so the praise,
If She inspire, and He approve my lays.
   Say what strange motive, Goddess! could compel
A well-bred Lord t' assault a gentle Belle?
O say what stranger cause, yet unexplored,
10 Could make a gentle Belle reject a Lord?
In tasks so bold, can little men engage,
And in soft bosoms dwells such mighty Rage?
   Sol through white curtains shot a timorous ray,
And oped those eyes that must eclipse the day:
15 Now lap dogs give themselves the rousing shake,
And sleepless lovers, just at twelve, awake:
Thrice rung the bell, the slipper knocked the ground,
And the pressed watch[3] returned a silver sound.
Belinda still her downy pillow prest,
20 Her guardian SYLPH[4] prolonged the balmy rest:
'Twas He had summoned to her silent bed
The morning dream that hovered o'er her head;
A Youth more glittering than a Birth-night Beau,[5]
(That even in slumber caused her cheek to glow)
25 Seemed to her ear his winning lips to lay,
And thus in whispers said, or seemed to say.
   Fairest of mortals, thou distinguished care
Of thousand bright Inhabitants of Air!
If e'er one Vision touched thy infant thought,
30 Of all the Nurse and all the Priest have taught;

7. To be dressed or decked out in finery.

1. *The Rape of the Lock* was written in an attempt to reconcile two families of Pope's acquaintance who had become estranged after Lord Petre had surreptitiously cut off a lock of Arabella Fermor's hair. "The stealing of Miss Belle Fermor's hair," wrote Pope, "was taken too seriously. . . . A common acquaintance and well-wisher to both (John Caryll) desired me to write a poem to make a jest of it, and laugh them together again." Pope's effort succeeded; the rift was healed. The poem was first published in 1712 in two cantos; it was expanded to five cantos in 1714 and appeared again with minor revisions in 1717. For the most succinct commentary on the poem, see Geoffrey

Tillotson's "Introduction" to *The Rape of the Lock* in the *Poems of Alexander Pope* (London, 1940), II, 81–124. A most intriguing edition, designed to "draw attention to the visual element of the poem," is Clarence Tracy's *The Rape Observ'd* (Toronto: Univ. of Toronto Press, 1974).
2. Arabella Fermor.
3. When pressure was applied to a pin ("pressed"), this relatively new invention—a repeater watch—sounded the previous hour and a quarter hour.
4. A spirit of the air. Any mortal who remains chaste may enjoy the protection of a sylph. See l. 67.
5. A courtier at a royal birthday (or birth-night) party would have been splendidly dressed.

Of airy Elves by moonlight shadows seen,
The silver token, and the circled green,[6]
Or virgins visited by Angel powers,
With golden crowns and wreaths of heavenly flowers;
35   Hear and believe! thy own importance know,
Nor bound thy narrow views to things below.
Some secret truths, from learnèd pride concealed,
To Maids alone and Children are revealed:
What though no credit doubting Wits may give?
40   The Fair and Innocent shall still believe.
Know, then, unnumbered Spirits round thee fly,
The light Militia of the lower sky:
These, though unseen, are ever on the wing,
Hang o'er the Box, and hover round the Ring.[7]
45   Think what an equipage thou hast in Air,
And view with scorn two Pages and a Chair.[8]
As now your own, our beings were of old,
And once enclosed in Woman's beauteous mould;
Thence, by a soft transition, we repair
50   From earthly Vehicles to these of air.
Think not, when Woman's transient breath is fled,
That all her vanities at once are dead;
Succeeding vanities she still regards,
And though she plays no more, o'erlooks the cards.
55   Her joy in gilded Chariots, when alive,
And love of Ombre,[9] after death survive.
For when the Fair in all their pride expire,
To their first Elements[10] their Souls retire:
The Sprites of fiery Termagants in Flame[11]
60   Mount up, and take a Salamander's name.
Soft yielding minds to Water glide away,
And sip, with Nymphs, their elemental Tea.
The graver Prude sinks downward to a Gnome,
In search of mischief still on Earth to roam.
65   The light Coquettes in Sylphs aloft repair,
And sport and flutter in the fields of Air.
    Know further yet; whoever fair and chaste
Rejects mankind, is by some Sylph embraced:
For Spirits, freed from mortal laws, with ease
70   Assume what sexes and what shapes they please.
What guards the purity of melting Maids,
In courtly balls, and midnight masquerades,
Safe from the treacherous friend, the daring spark,
The glance by day, the whisper in the dark,
75   When kind occasion prompts their warm desires,
When music softens, and when dancing fires?
'Tis but their Sylph, the wise Celestials know,
Though Honour is the word with Men below.
    Some nymphs there are, too conscious of their face,
80   For life predestined to the Gnomes' embrace.
These swell their prospects and exalt their pride,
When offers are disdained, and love denied:
Then gay Ideas crowd the vacant brain,
While Peers, and Dukes, and all their sweeping train,
85   And Garters, Stars, and Coronets appear,
And in soft sounds, Your Grace salutes their ear.
'Tis these that early taint the female soul,

6. In folklore fairies are reported to leave coins for the food they take and bright green "rings" of grass appear where they have danced.
7. *Box*: theatre box. *Ring*: a fashionable circular drive in Hyde Park, London.
8. A sedan-chair, carried by two men.

9. See Canto II, ll. 25–100.
10. All matter was considered to have been composed of four essential elements: fire, air, water, and earth. The dominance of one or another of these determined a person's temperament.
11. Shrewish, scolding women.

Instruct the eyes of young Coquettes to roll,
Teach Infant cheeks a bidden blush to know,
90 And little hearts to flutter at a Beau.
    Oft, when the world imagine women stray,
The Sylphs through mystic mazes guide their way,
Through all the giddy circle they pursue,
And old impertinence[12] expel by new.
95 What tender maid but must a victim fall
To one man's treat, but for another's ball?
When Florio speaks what virgin could withstand,
If gentle Damon did not squeeze her hand?
With varying vanities, from every part,
100 They shift the moving toyshop of their heart;
Where wigs with wigs, with sword-knots[13] sword-knots strive,
Beaux banish beaux, and coaches coaches drive.
This erring mortals Levity may call;
Oh blind to truth! the Sylphs contrive it all.
105   Of these am I, who thy protection claim,
A watchful sprite, and Ariel[14] is my name.
Late, as I ranged the crystal wilds of air,
In the clear mirror of thy ruling Star
I saw, alas! some dread event impend,
110 Ere to the main this morning sun descend,
But heaven reveals not what, or how, or where:
Warned by the Sylph, oh pious maid, beware!
This to disclose is all thy guardian can:
Beware of all, but most beware of Man!
115   He said; when Shock,[15] who thought she slept too long,
Leaped up, and waked his mistress with his tongue.
'Twas then, Belinda, if report say true,
Thy eyes first opened on a Billet-doux;[16]
Wounds, Charm, and Ardors were no sooner read,
120 But all the Vision vanished from thy head.
    And now, unveiled, the Toilet stands displayed,
Each silver Vase in mystic order laid.
First, robed in white, the Nymph intent adores,
With head uncovered, the cosmetic powers.
125 A heavenly image in the glass appears,
To that she bends, to that her eyes she rears;
Th' inferior Priestess, at her altar's side,
Trembling, begins the sacred rites of Pride.
Unnumbered treasures ope at once, and here
130 The various offerings of the world appear;
From each she nicely culls with curious toil,
And decks the Goddess with the glittering spoil.
This casket India's glowing gems unlocks,
And all Arabia breathes from yonder box.
135 The Tortoise here and Elephant unite,
Transformed to combs, the speckled, and the white.
Here files of pins extend their shining rows,
Puffs, Powders, Patches, Bibles, Billet-doux.
Now awful Beauty puts on all its arms;
140 The fair each moment rises in her charms,
Repairs her smiles, awakens every grace,
And calls forth all the wonders of her face;
Sees by degrees a purer blush arise,
And keener lightnings quicken in her eyes.

12. Trifle.
13. Ribbons tied to the hilts of swords.
14. A spirit who, in many literary sources, has control over the elements.

15. Belinda's lap-dog. A "shock" is a long-haired poodle.
16. A love letter. If, however, l. 138 is correct, this could not have been the first time her eyes "opened on a billet-doux."

145   The busy Sylphs surround their darling care,
These set the head, and those divide the hair,
Some fold the sleeve, whilst others plait the gown;
And Betty's[17] praised for labours not her own.

Canto II

Not with more glories, in th' etherial plain,
The Sun first rises o'er the purpled main,
Than, issuing forth, the rival of his beams[18]
Launched on the bosom of the silver Thames.
5   Fair Nymphs, and well-dressed Youths around her shone,
But every eye was fixed on her alone.
On her white breast a sparkling Cross she wore,
Which Jews might kiss, and infidels adore.
Her lively looks a sprightly mind disclose,
10   Quick as her eyes, and as unfixed as those:
Favours to none, to all she smiles extends;
Oft she rejects, but never once offends.
Bright as the sun, her eyes the gazers strike,
And, like the sun, they shine on all alike.
15   Yet graceful ease, and sweetness void of pride,
Might hide her faults, if Belles had faults to hide:
If to her share some female errors fall,
Look on her face, and you'll forget 'em all.
    This Nymph, to the destruction of mankind,
20   Nourished two Locks, which graceful hung behind
In equal curls, and well conspired to deck
With shining ringlets the smooth ivory neck.
Love in these labyrinths his slaves detains,
And mighty hearts are held in slender chains.
25   With hairy springes[19] we the birds betray,
Slight lines of hair surprise the finny prey,
Fair tresses man's imperial race ensnare,
And beauty draws us with a single hair.
    Th' adventurous Baron[20] the bright locks admired;
30   He saw, he wished, and to the prize aspired.
Resolved to win, he meditates the way,
By force to ravish, or by fraud betray;
For when success a Lover's toil attends,
Few ask, if fraud or force attained his ends.
35   For this, ere Phœbus rose, he had implored
Propitious heaven, and every power adored,
But chiefly Love—to Love an altar built,
Of twelve vast French Romances, neatly gilt.
There lay three garters, half a pair of gloves;
40   And all the trophies of his former loves;
With tender Billets-doux he lights the pyre,
And breathes three amorous sighs to raise the fire.
Then prostrate falls, and begs with ardent eyes
Soon to obtain, and long possess the prize:
45   The powers gave ear, and granted half his prayer,
The rest, the winds dispersed in empty air.
    But now secure the painted vessel[21] glides,
The sunbeams trembling on the floating tides:
While melting music steals upon the sky,
50   And softened sounds along the waters die;
Smooth flow the waves, the Zephyrs gently play,
Belinda smiled, and all the world was gay.

---

17. A generic name for lady's maid.
18. Belinda's "fair nymphs and well-dressed youths" who rival the sun in brilliance.
19. Traps or snares.

20. Robert, Lord Petre.
21. It was quite usual to travel from London to Hampton Court by water (via the Thames).

All but the Sylph—with careful thoughts opprest,
Th' impending woe sat heavy on his breast.
55 He summons strait his Denizens of air;
The lucid squadrons round the sails repair:
Soft o'er the shrouds aërial whispers breathe,
That seemed but Zephyrs to the train beneath.
Some to the sun their insect wings unfold,
60 Waft on the breeze, or sink in clouds of gold;
Transparent forms, too fine for mortal sight,
Their fluid bodies half dissolved in light,
Loose to the wind they airy garments flew,
Thin glittering textures of the filmy dew,
65 Dipped in the richest tincture of the skies,
Where light disports in ever-mingling dyes,
While every beam new transient colours flings,
Colours that change whene'er they wave their wings.
Amid the circle, on the gilded mast,
70 Superior by the head, was Ariel placed;
His purple pinions opening to the sun,
He raised his azure wand, and thus begun.
      Ye Sylphs and Sylphids, to your chief give ear!
Fays, Fairies, Genii, Elves, and Dæmons, hear!
75 Ye know the spheres and various tasks assigned
By laws eternal to th' aërial kind.
Some in the fields of purest Æther play,
And bask and whiten in the blaze of day.
Some guide the course of wandering orbs on high,
80 Or roll the planets through the boundless sky.
Some less refined, beneath the moon's pale light
Pursue the stars that shoot athwart the night,
Or suck the mists in grosser air below,
Or dip their pinions in the painted bow,
85 Or brew fierce tempests on the wintry main,
Or o'er the glebe[22] distil the kindly rain.
Others on earth o'er human race preside,
Watch all their ways, and all their actions guide:
Of these the chief the care of Nations own,
90 And guard with Arms divine the British Throne.
      Our humbler province is to tend the Fair,
Not a less pleasing, though less glorious care;
To save the powder from too rude a gale,
Nor let th' imprisoned essences exhale;
95 To draw fresh colours from the vernal flowers;
To steal from rainbows e'er they drop in showers
A brighter wash; to curl their waving hairs,
Assist their blushes, and inspire their airs;
Nay oft, in dreams, invention we bestow,
100 To change a Flounce, or add a Furbelow.[23]
      This day, black Omens threat the brightest Fair
That e'er deserved a watchful spirit's care;
Some dire disaster, or by force, or slight;
But what, or where, the fates have wrapped in night.
105 Whether the nymph shall break Diana's[24] law,
Or some frail China jar receive a flaw;
Or stain her honour, or her new brocade;
Forget her prayers, or miss a masquerade;
Or lose her heart, or necklace, at a ball;
110 Or whether Heaven has doomed that Shock must fall.
Haste, then, ye spirits! to your charge repair:

22. "*glebe*": earth or field.
23. A "flounce" is a piece of cloth sewn on a gown by its edge and left hanging; a "furbelow" is a piece of puckered cloth placed on gowns for decoration. Pope seems to be suggesting that female "invention" is restricted to the trimmings on gowns. For a vivid illustration see Tracy, *The Rape Observ'd*, p. 26 and p. 29.
24. The goddess of chastity.

The fluttering fan be Zephyretta's care;
The drops[25] to thee, Brillante, we consign;
And, Momentilla, let the watch be thine;
115   Do thou, Crispissa, tend her favorite Lock;
Ariel himself shall be the guard of Shock.
    To fifty chosen Sylphs, of special note,
We trust th' important charge, the Petticoat:
Oft have we known that sevenfold fence to fail,
120   Though stiff with hoops, and armed with ribs of whale;
Form a strong line about the silver bound,
And guard the wide circumference around.
    Whatever spirit, careless of his charge,
His post neglects, or leaves the fair at large,
125   Shall feel sharp vengeance soon o'ertake his sins,
Be stopped in vials, or transfixed with pins;
Or plunged in lakes of bitter washes lie,
Or wedged whole ages in a bodkin's[26] eye:
Gums and Pomatums[27] shall his flight restrain,
130   While clogged he beats his silken wings in vain;
Or Alum styptics[28] with contracting power
Shrink his thin essence like a rivelled[29] flower:
Or, as Ixion[30] fixed, the wretch shall feel
The giddy motion of the whirling Mill,
135   In fumes of burning chocolate shall glow,
And tremble at the sea that froths below!
    He spoke; the spirits from the sails descend;
Some, orb in orb, around the nymph extend;
Some thrid the mazy ringlets of her hair;
140   Some hang upon the pendants of her ear;
With beating hearts the dire event they wait,
Anxious, and trembling for the birth of Fate.

Canto III

Close by those meads, for ever crowned with flowers,
Where Thames with pride surveys his rising towers,
There stands a structure of majestic frame,
Which from the neighboring Hampton takes its name.
5   Here Britain's statesmen oft the fall foredoom
Of foreign Tyrants, and of Nymphs at home;
Here thou, great ANNA![31] whom three realms obey,
Dost sometimes counsel take— and sometimes Tea.
    Hither the heroes and the nymphs resort,
10   To taste awhile the pleasures of a Court;
In various talk th' instructive hours they past,
Who gave the ball, or paid the visit last;
One speaks the glory of the British Queen,
And one describes a charming Indian screen;
15   A third interprets motions, looks, and eyes;
At every word a reputation dies.
Snuff, or the fan, supply each pause of chat,
With singing, laughing, ogling, *and all that*.
    Meanwhile, declining from the noon of day,
20   The sun obliquely shoots his burning ray;
The hungry Judges soon the sentence sign,
And wretches hang that jurymen may dine;

25. Earrings.
26. A blunt needle with a large eye. At IV.98 and V.95 Pope uses "bodkin" to mean a hair ornament and at V.55 and V.88 to mean a dagger.
27. Ointments.
28. Substances able to contract organic tissue and used to stop bleeding.
29. Shrivelled.
30. In Greek legend Ixion was punished by being bound to a turning wheel.
31. Queen Anne, who, according to Samuel Johnson, had no talent for governing.

The merchant from th' Exchange returns in peace,
And the long labours of the Toilet cease.
25   Belinda now, whom thirst of fame invites,
Burns to encounter two adventurous Knights,
At Ombre[32] singly to decide their doom;
And swells her breast with conquests yet to come.
Straight the three bands prepare in arms to join,
30   Each band the number of the sacred nine.
Soon as she spreads her hand, th' aërial guard
Descend, and sit on each important card:
First Ariel perched upon a Matadore,
Then each, according to the rank they bore;
35   For Sylphs, yet mindful of their ancient race,
Are, as when women, wondrous fond of place.
      Behold, four Kings in majesty revered,
With hoary whiskers and a forky beard;
And four fair Queens whose hands sustain a flower,
40   Th' expressive emblem of their softer power;
Four Knaves in garbs succinct, a trusty band,
Caps on their heads, and halberts in their hand;
And particoloured troops, a shining train,
Draw forth to combat on the velvet plain.
45   The skilful Nymph reviews her force with care:
Let Spades be trumps! she said, and trumps they were.
      Now move to war her sable Matadores,
In show like leaders of the swarthy Moors.
Spadillio first, unconquerable Lord!
50   Led off two captive trumps, and swept the board.
As many more Manillio forced to yield,
And marched a victor from the verdant field.
Him Basto followed, but his fate more hard
Gained but one trump and one Plebeian card.
55   With his broad sabre next, a chief in years,
The hoary Majesty of Spades appears,
Puts forth one manly leg, to sight revealed,
The rest, his many-coloured robe concealed.
The rebel Knave, who dares his prince engage,
60   Proves the just victim of his royal rage.
Even mighty Pam, that Kings and Queens o'erthrew
And mowed down armies in the fights of Lu,
Sad chance of war! now destitute of aid,
Falls undistinguished by the victor Spade!
65   Thus far both armies to Belinda yield;
Now to the Baron fate inclines the field.
His warlike Amazon her host invades,
Th' imperial consort of the crown of Spades.
The Club's black Tyrant first her victim died
70   Spite of his haughty mien, and barbarous pride:
What boots the regal circle on his head,
His giant limbs, in state unwieldy spread;
That long behind he trails his pompous robe,
And, of all monarchs, only grasps the globe?
75   The Baron now his Diamonds pours apace;
Th' embroidered King who shows but half his face,
And his refulgent Queen, with powers combined
Of broken troops an easy conquest find.

32. A card game much in fashion at the time, played with ordinary cards after removing the tens, nines, and eights. The cards are dealt to three players (nine to each and a "kitty" of thirteen). The high bidder is called the *ombre* (Spanish, *hombre*); he or she names trumps and then has to win more tricks than the opponents combined. Failure to do so is *codille*. "The ones of highest value, called Matadores, were the ace of spades ("Spadillio"), the most valuable, the ace of clubs ("Basto"), the third most valuable, and, when spades were trumps, as they are here, the two of spades ("Manillio"), which came between the other two." See "Appendix I: The Game of Ombre" in Tracy's *The Rape Observ'd.*

Clubs, Diamonds, Hearts, in wild disorder seen,
80 With throngs promiscuous strew the level green.
Thus when dispersed a routed army runs,
Of Asia's troops, and Afric's sable sons,
With like confusion different nations fly,
Of various habit, and of various dye,
85 The pierced battalions disunited fall,
In heaps on heaps; one fate o'erwhelms them all.
    The Knave of Diamonds tries his wily arts,
And wins (oh shameful chance!) the Queen of Hearts.
At this, the blood the virgin's cheek forsook,
90 A livid paleness spreads o'er all her look;
She sees, and trembles at th' approaching ill,
Just in the jaws of ruin, and Codille.
And now (as oft in some distempered State)
On one nice Trick depends the general fate.
95 An Ace of Hearts steps forth: The King unseen
Lurked in her hand, and mourned his captive Queen:
He springs to vengeance with an eager pace,
And falls like thunder on the prostrate Ace.
The nymph exulting fills with shouts the sky;
100 The walls, the woods, and long canals reply.
    Oh thoughtless mortals! ever blind to fate,
Too soon dejected, and too soon elate.
Sudden, these honours shall be snatched away,
And cursed for ever this victorious day.
105   For lo! the board with cups and spoons is crowned,
The berries crackle, and the mill turns round;
On shining Altars of Japan[33] they raise
The silver lamp; the fiery spirits blaze:
From silver spouts the grateful liquors glide,
110 While China's earth receives the smoking tide:
At once they gratify their scent and taste,
And frequent cups prolong the rich repast.
Straight hover round the Fair her airy band;
Some, as she sipped, the fuming liquor fanned,
115 Some o'er her lap their careful plumes displayed,
Trembling, and conscious of the rich brocade.
Coffee, (which makes the politician wise,
And see through all things with his half-shut eyes)
Sent up in vapours to the Baron's brain
120 New stratagems, the radiant Lock to gain.
Ah cease, rash youth! desist ere 'tis too late,
Fear the just Gods, and think of Scylla's Fate![34]
Changed to a bird, and sent to flit in air,
She dearly pays for Nisus' injured hair!
125   But when to mischief mortals bend their will,
How soon they find fit instruments of ill!
Just then, Clarissa[35] drew with tempting grace
A two-edged weapon from her shining case:
So Ladies in Romance assist their Knight,
130 Present the spear, and arm him for the fight.
He takes the gift with reverence, and extends
The little engine on his fingers' ends;
This just behind Belinda's neck he spread,
As o'er the fragrant steams she bends her head.
135 Swift to the Lock a thousand Sprites repair,
A thousand wings, by turns, blow back the hair;
And thrice they twitched the diamond in her ear;

33. Lacquered tables.
34. In Ovid's *Metamorphosis* Scylla was turned into a
bird for daring to steal a hair from her father's (Nisus')
head.
35. An unknown female accessory to the "rape" who
provided the scissors (the "forfex," l. 147).

Thrice she looked back, and thrice the foe drew near.
Just in that instant, anxious Ariel sought
140 The close recesses of the Virgin's thought;
As on the nosegay in her breast reclined,
He watched th' Ideas rising in her mind,
Sudden he viewed, in spite of all her art,
An earthly Lover lurking at her heart.
145 Amazed, confused, he found his power expired,
Resigned to fate, and with a sigh retired.
    The Peer now spreads the glittering Forfex wide,
T' enclose the Lock; now joins it, to divide.
Even then, before the fatal engine closed,
150 A wretched Sylph too fondly interposed;
Fate urged the shears, and cut the Sylph in twain,
(But airy substance soon unites again)
The meeting points the sacred hair dissever
From the fair head, for ever, and for ever!
155   Then flashed the living lightning from her eyes,
And screams of horror rend th' affrighted skies.
Not louder shrieks to pitying heaven are cast,
When husbands, or when lap dogs breathe their last;
Or when rich China vessels fallen from high,
160 In glittering dust, and painted fragments lie!
    Let wreaths of triumph now my temples twine,
(The Victor cried) the glorious Prize is mine!
While fish in streams, or birds delight in air,
Or in a coach and six the British Fair,
165 As long as Atalantis[36] shall be read,
Or the small pillow grace a Lady's bed,
While visits shall be paid on solemn days,
When numerous wax-lights in bright order blaze,
While nymphs take treats, or assignations give,
170 So long my honour, name, and praise shall live!
What Time would spare, from Steel receives its date,
And monuments, like men, submit to fate!
Steel could the labour of the Gods destroy,
And strike to dust th' imperial towers of Troy;
175 Steel could the works of mortal pride confound,
And hew triumphal arches to the ground.
What wonder then, fair nymph! thy hairs should feel,
The conquering force of unresisted steel?

Canto IV

But anxious cares the pensive nymph oppressed,
And secret passions laboured in her breast.
Not youthful kings in battle seized alive,
Not scornful virgins who their charms survive,
5 Not ardent lovers robbed of all their bliss,
Not ancient ladies when refused a kiss,
Not tyrants fierce that unrepenting die,
Not Cynthia when her manteau's[37] pinned awry,
E'er felt such rage, resentment, and despair,
10 As thou, sad Virgin! for thy ravished Hair.
    For, that sad moment, when the Sylphs withdrew,
And Ariel weeping from Belinda flew,
Umbriel, a dusky, melancholy sprite,
As ever sullied the fair face of light,
15 Down to the central earth, his proper scene,

---

36. A scandal-revealing novel by Mrs. Manley, published in 1709.

37. Loose robe.

Repaired to search the gloomy Cave of Spleen.[38]
    Swift on his sooty pinions flits the Gnome,
And in a vapour reached the dismal dome.
No cheerful breeze this sullen region knows,
20   The dreaded East is all the wind that blows.
Here in a grotto, sheltered close from air,
And screened in shades from day's detested glare,
She sighs for ever on her pensive bed,
Pain at her side, and Megrim[39] at her head.
25   Two handmaids wait the throne: alike in place,
But differing far in figure and in face.
Here stood Ill Nature like an ancient maid,
Her wrinkled form in black and white arrayed;
With store of prayers, for mornings, nights, and noons,
30   Her hand is filled; her bosom with lampoons.
    There Affectation, with a sickly mien,
Shows in her cheek the roses of eighteen,
Practised to lisp, and hang the head aside,
Faints into airs, and languishes with pride,
35   On the rich quilt sinks with becoming woe,
Wrapped in a gown, for sickness, and for show.
The fair ones feel such maladies as these,
When each new nightdress gives a new disease.
    A constant Vapour o'er the palace flies;
40   Strange phantoms rising as the mists arise;
Dreadful, as hermit's dreams in haunted shades,
Or bright, as visions of expiring maids.
Now glaring fiends, and snakes on rolling spires,
Pale spectres, gaping tombs, and purple fires:
45   Now lakes of liquid gold, Elysian scenes,[40]
And crystal domes, and Angels in machines.[41]
    Unnumbered throngs on every side are seen,
Of bodies changed to various forms by Spleen.
Here living Teapots stand, one arm held out,
50   One bent; the handle this, and that the spout:
A Pipkin there, like Homer's Tripod walks;[42]
Here sighs a Jar, and there a Goose Pie talks;
Men prove with child, as powerful fancy works,
And maids turned bottles, call aloud for corks.
55   Safe passed the Gnome through this fantastic band,
A branch of healing Spleenwort[43] in his hand.
Then thus addressed the power: "Hail, wayward Queen!
Who rule the sex to fifty from fifteen:
Parent of vapours and of female wit,
60   Who give th' hysteric, or poetic fit,
On various tempers act by various ways,
Make some take physic, others scribble plays;
Who cause the proud their visits to delay,
And send the godly in a pet to pray.
65   A nymph there is, that all thy power disdains,
And thousands more in equal mirth maintains.
But oh! if e'er thy Gnome could spoil a grace,
Or raise a pimple on a beauteous face,
Like Citron waters matrons cheeks inflame,
70   Or change complexions at a losing game;
If e'er with airy horns I planted heads,

---

38. A fashionable name for Ill-temper or fit of spite and a common excuse offered when rejecting a lover's invitations. Pope here is indulging in a common epic convention—the journey to the underworld.
39. A severe headache.
40. Blissful (from Elysium, the place of bliss).
41. Stage machinery then introduced in operas. In this and the preceding lines, Pope is satirizing the various stage effects of contemporary opera and pantomime.
42. "Pipkin": an earthen pot. "Homer's tripod": in the *Iliad* Vulcan provided the gods with self-propelling three-legged stools (tripods).
43. Herb, protection against splenetic diseases.

Or rumpled petticoats, or tumbled beds,
Or caused suspicion when no soul was rude,
Or discomposed the headdress of a Prude,
75 Or e'er to costive lap dog gave disease,
Which not the tears of brightest eyes could ease:
Hear me, and touch Belinda with chagrin,
That single act gives half the world the spleen."
    The Goddess with a discontented air
80 Seems to reject him, though she grants his prayer.
A wondrous Bag with both her hands she binds,
Like that where once Ulysses held the winds;
There she collects the force of female lungs,
Sighs, sobs, and passions, and the war of tongues.
85 A Vial next she fills with fainting fears,
Soft sorrows, melting griefs, and flowing tears.
The Gnome rejoicing bears her gifts away,
Spreads his black wings, and slowly mounts to day.
    Sunk in Thalestris'[44] arms the nymph he found,
90 Her eyes dejected and her hair unbound.
Full o'er their heads the swelling bag he rent,
And all the Furies issued at the vent.
Belinda burns with more than mortal ire,
And fierce Thalestris fans the rising fire.
95 "O wretched maid!" she spread her hands, and cried,
(While Hampton's echoes, "Wretched maid!" replied)
"Was it for this you took such constant care
The bodkin, comb, and essence to prepare?
For this your locks in paper durance bound,
100 For this with torturing irons wreathed around?
For this with fillets strained your tender head,
And bravely bore the double loads of lead?
Gods! shall the ravisher display your hair,
While the Fops envy, and the Ladies stare!
105 Honour forbid! at whose unrivalled shrine
Ease, pleasure, virtue, all our sex resign.
Methinks already I your tears survey,
Already hear the horrid things they say,
Already see you a degraded toast,
110 And all your honour in a whisper lost!
How shall I, then, your helpless fame defend?
'Twill then be infamy to seem your friend!
And shall this prize, th' inestimable prize,
Exposed through crystal to the gazing eyes,[45]
115 And heightened by the diamond's circling rays,
On that rapacious hand for ever blaze?
Sooner shall grass in Hyde Park Circus grow,
And wits take lodgings in the sound of Bow;[46]
Sooner let earth, air, sea, to Chaos fall,
120 Men, monkeys, lap dogs, parrots, perish all!"
    She said; then raging to Sir Plume[47] repairs,
And bids her Beau demand the precious hairs:
(Sir Plume of amber snuffbox justly vain,
And the nice conduct of a clouded cane)
125 With earnest eyes, and round unthinking face,
He first the snuffbox opened, then the case,
And thus broke out—"My Lord, why, what the devil?

44. Queen of the Amazons—in this case, one of the ladies present.
45. Tracy, in *The Rape Observ'd* (p. 57), has a picture of an eighteenth-century diamond ring with a lock of hair visible through the "crystal."
46. Persons born within hearing of the bells of St. Mary-le-Bow are considered "cockneys." No fashionable person, in Pope's day, would live in that district.
47. One of the males present, perhaps Sir George Browne, a cousin of Arabella's mother.

Z-ds! damn the lock! 'fore Gad, you must be civil!
Plague on't! 'tis past a jest—nay prithee, pox!
130   Give her the hair"—he spoke, and rapped his box.
    "It grieves me much" (replied the Peer again)
"Who speaks so well should ever speak in vain.
But by this Lock, this sacred Lock I swear,
(Which never more shall join its parted hair;
135   Which never more its honours shall renew,
Clipped from the lovely head where late it grew)
That while my nostrils draw the vital air,
This hand, which won it, shall for ever wear."
He spoke, and speaking, in proud triumph spread
140   The long-contended honours of her head.
    But Umbriel, hateful Gnome! forbears not so;
He breaks the Vial whence the sorrows flow.
Then see! the nymph in beauteous grief appears,
Her eyes half languishing, half drowned in tears;
145   On her heaved bosom hung her drooping head,
Which, with a sigh, she raised; and thus she said.
    "For ever cursed be this detested day,
Which snatched my best, my favorite curl away!
Happy! ah ten times happy had I been,
150   If Hampton Court these eyes had never seen!
Yet am not I the first mistaken maid,
By love of Courts to numerous ills betrayed.
Oh had I rather unadmired remained
In some lone isle, or distant Northern land;
155   Where the gilt Chariot never marks the way,
Where none learn Ombre, none e'er taste Bohea![48]
There kept my charms concealed from mortal eye,
Like roses, that in deserts bloom and die.
What moved my mind with youthful Lords to roam?
160   O had I stayed, and said my prayers at home!
'Twas this, the morning omens seemed to tell,
Thrice from my trembling hand the patch box[49] fell;
The tottering China shook without a wind,
Nay, Poll sat mute, and Shock was most unkind!
165   A Sylph too warned me of the threats of fate,
In mystic visions, now believed too late!
See the poor remnants of these slighted hairs!
My hands shall rend what even thy rapine spares:
These in two sable ringlets taught to break,
170   Once gave new beauties to the snowy neck;
The sister lock now sits uncouth, alone,
And in its fellow's fate foresees its own;
Uncurled it hangs, the fatal shears demands,
And tempts once more, thy sacrilegious hands.
175   Oh hadst thou, cruel! been content to seize
Hairs less in sight, or any hairs but these!"

Canto V

She said: the pitying audience melt in tears.
But Fate and Jove had stopped the Baron's ears.
In vain Thalestris with reproach assails,
For who can move when fair Belinda fails?
5   Not half so fixed the Trojan[50] could remain,
While Anna begged and Dido raged in vain.
The grave Clarissa graceful waved her fan;
Silence ensued, and thus the nymph began.

48. A fancy brand of tea.
49. Container for the beauty patches worn by both sexes.

50. Aeneas, who forsook Dido in spite of the pleadings of her sister, Anna.

    "Say why are Beauties praised and honoured most,
10   The wise man's passion, and the vain man's toast?
    Why decked with all that land and sea afford,
    Why Angels called, and Angel-like adored?
    Why round our coaches crowd the white-gloved Beaux,
    Why bows the side-box from its inmost rows;
15   How vain are all these glories, all our pains,
    Unless good sense preserve what beauty gains:
    That men may say, when we the front-box grace,
    'Behold the first in virtue as in face!'
    Oh! if to dance all night, and dress all day,
20   Charmed the smallpox, or chased old age away;
    Who would not scorn what housewife's cares produce,
    Or who would learn one earthly thing of use?
    To patch, nay ogle, might become a Saint,
    Nor could it sure be such a sin to paint.
25   But since, alas! frail beauty must decay,
    Curled or uncurled, since Locks will turn to grey;
    Since painted, or not painted, all shall fade,
    And she who scorns a man, must die a maid;
    What then remains but well our power to use,
30   And keep good humour still whate'er we lose?
    And trust me, dear! good humour can prevail,
    When airs, and flights, and screams, and scolding fail.
    Beauties in vain their pretty eyes may roll;
    Charms strike the sight, but merit wins the soul."
35   So spoke the Dame, but no applause ensued;
    Belinda frowned, Thalestris called her Prude.
    "To arms, to arms!" the fierce Virago cries,
    And swift as lightning to the combat flies.[51]
    All side in parties, and begin th' attack;
40   Fans clap, silks rustle, and tough whalebones crack;
    Heroes' and Heroines' shouts confusedly rise,
    And bass and treble voices strike the skies.
    No common weapons in their hands are found,
    Like Gods they fight, nor dread a mortal wound.
45   So when bold Homer makes the Gods engage,
    And heavenly breasts with human passions rage;
    'Gainst Pallas, Mars; Latona, Hermes arms;
    And all Olympus rings with loud alarms:
    Jove's thunder roars, heaven trembles all around,
50   Blue Neptune storms, the bellowing deeps resound:
    Earth shakes her nodding towers, the ground gives way,
    And the pale ghosts start at the flash of day!
      Triumphant Umbriel on a sconce's[52] height
    Clapped his glad wings, and sat to view the fight:
55   Propped on their bodkin spears, the Sprites survey
    The growing combat, or assist the fray.
      While through the press enraged Thalestris flies,
    And scatters death around from both her eyes,
    A Beau and Witling perished in the throng,
60   One died in metaphor, and one in song.
    "O cruel nymph! a living death I bear,"
    Cried Dapperwit, and sunk beside his chair.
    A mournful glance Sir Fopling upwards cast,
    "Those eyes are made so killing"— was his last.
65   Thus on Mæander's[53] flowery margin lies

---

51. "The following scene," states Tracy in *The Rape Observ'd* (p. 66), "is a parody of countless battle scenes in epics and romances. Pope's lines are full of innuendoes and ambiguities that may puzzle a modern reader, who must not imagine that any of Belinda's well-bred party stooped to physical violence, unless Belinda's making the Baron sneeze by means of a well-aimed pinch of snuff constitutes violence. . . . Instead the battle was fought with dirty looks, snide remarks, and improper gestures."

52. Bracket candlestick on a wall.

53. A winding river in Asia Minor from which we get the word "meander."

Th' expiring Swan, and as he sings he dies.
        When bold Sir Plume had drawn Clarissa down,
Chloe stepped in, and killed him with a frown;
She smiled to see the doughty hero slain,
70   But, at her smile, the Beau revived again.
        Now Jove suspends his golden scales in air,
Weighs the Men's wits against the Lady's hair;
The doubtful beam long nods from side to side;
At length the wits mount up, the hairs subside.
75   See, fierce Belinda on the Baron flies,
With more than usual lightning in her eyes:
Nor feared the Chief th' unequal fight to try,
Who sought no more than on his foe to die.
But this bold Lord with manly strength endued,
80   She with one finger and a thumb subdued:
Just where the breath of life his nostrils drew,
A charge of Snuff the wily virgin threw;
The Gnomes direct, to every atom just,
The pungent grains of titillating dust.
85   Sudden with starting tears each eye o'erflows,
And the high dome re-echoes to his nose.
        Now meet thy fate, incensed Belinda cried,
And drew a deadly bodkin from her side.
(The same, his ancient personage to deck,
90   Her great great grandsire wore about his neck,
In three seal rings; which after, melted down,
Formed a vast buckle for his widow's gown:
Her infant grandame's whistle next it grew,
The bells she jingled, and the whistle blew;
95   Then in a bodkin graced her mother's hairs,
Which long she wore, and now Belinda wears.)
        "Boast not my fall" (he cried) "insulting foe!
Thou by some other shalt be laid as low.
Nor think, to die dejects my lofty mind:
100   All that I dread is leaving you behind!
Rather than so, ah let me still survive,
And burn in Cupid's flames—but burn alive."
        "Restore the Lock!" she cries; and all around
"Restore the Lock!" the vaulted roofs rebound.
105   Not fierce Othello in so loud a strain
Roared for the handkerchief that caused his pain.
But see how oft ambitious aims are crossed,
And chiefs contend till all the prize is lost!
The Lock, obtained with guilt, and kept with pain,
110   In every place is sought, but sought in vain:
With such a prize no mortal must be blest,
So heaven decrees! with heaven who can contest?
        Some thought it mounted to the Lunar sphere,
Since all things lost on earth are treasured there.
115   There Heroes' wits are kept in ponderous vases,
And beaux' in snuffboxes and tweezer cases.
There broken vows and deathbed alms are found,
And lovers' hearts with ends of riband bound,
The courtier's promises, and the sick man's prayers,
120   The smiles of harlots, and the tears of heirs,
Cages for gnats, and chains to yoke a flea,
Dried butterflies, and tomes of casuistry.
        But trust the Muse—she saw it upward rise,
Though marked by none but quick, poetic eyes:
125   (So Rome's great founder to the heavens withdrew,
To Proculus alone confessed in view)[54]

54. Romulus, the founder of Rome, was snatched up into
heaven, a scene witnessed only by Proculus.

A sudden Star, it shot through liquid air,
And drew behind a radiant trail of hair.
Not Berenice's Locks[55] first rose so bright,
130   The heavens bespangling with dishevelled light.
The Sylphs behold it kindling as it flies,
And pleased pursue its progress through the skies.
    This the Beau monde shall from the Mall survey,
And hail with music its propitious ray.
135   This the blest Lover shall for Venus take,
And send up vows from Rosamonda's lake.[56]
This Partridge[57] soon shall view in cloudless skies,
When next he looks through Galileo's eyes;
And hence th' egregious wizard shall foredoom
140   The fate of Louis, and the fall of Rome.
    Then cease, bright Nymph! to mourn thy ravished hair,
Which adds new glory to the shining sphere!
Not all the tresses that fair head can boast,
Shall draw such envy as the Lock you lost.
145   For, after all the murders of your eye,
When, after millions slain, yourself shall die;
When those fair suns shall set, as set they must,
And all those tresses shall be laid in dust,
This Lock, the Muse shall consecrate to fame,
150   And midst the stars inscribe Belinda's name.

Eloïsa to Abelard[1]

In these deep solitudes and awful cells,
Where heavenly-pensive contemplation dwells,
And ever musing melancholy reigns;
What means this tumult in a Vestal's veins?[2]
5   Why rove my thoughts beyond this last retreat?
Why feels my heart its long-forgotten heat?
Yet, yet I love!—From Abelard it came,
And Eloïsa yet must kiss the name.
    Dear fatal name! rest ever unrevealed,
10   Nor pass these lips in holy silence sealed:
Hide it, my heart, within that close disguise,
Where mixed with God's, his loved Idea lies:
O write it not my hand—the name appears
Already written—wash it out, my tears!
15   In vain lost Eloïsa weeps and prays,
Her heart still dictates, and her hand obeys.
    Relentless walls! whose darksome round contains
Repentant sighs, and voluntary pains:
Ye rugged rocks! which holy knees have worn;
20   Ye grots and caverns shagged with horrid thorn![3]
Shrines! where their vigils pale-eyed virgins keep,

---

55. Berenice, wife of Egypt's Ptolemy III, dedicated a lock of her hair to the gods; it too was taken up into the heavens where it became a constellation.
56. A lake associated with unrequited love in St. James' Park, London, where one also finds the Mall, a fashionable resort for strollers and oglers.
57. John Partridge who, according to Pope's note, "was a ridiculous star-gazer, who in his Almanacks every year, never failed to predict the downfall of the Pope, and the King of France."

1. *Eloïsa to Abelard* (published in 1717) is based on a single aspect of a well-known love story: Peter Abelard (1079–1142), a brilliant theologian, fell in love with his pupil, Heloise, which so enraged her uncle that he contrived to have Abelard castrated. Forced apart, the lovers entered separate monasteries and devoted themselves to the Church; later in life they renewed their love through a series of letters, through which their story became known to the world (for a fuller account see Tillotson, *The Poems of Alexander Pope*, II, Appendix I, pp. 411–13). It is on Heloise's letters—"which," says Pope, "give so lively a picture of the struggles of grace and nature, virtue and passion"—that this "heroic epistle" is based, the particular source being the *Letters of Abelard and Heloise*, translated by John Hughes, published in 1713.
2. Virgin's. From Vesta, goddess of the hearth, whose virgin priestesses were known as vestal virgins.
3. See Milton's *Comus*, l. 429: "By grots, and caverns shag'd with horrid shades." There are in *Eloïsa to Abelard* many significant echoes of Milton, though they are too numerous to note here.

And pitying saints, whose statues learn to weep![4]
Though cold like you, unmoved and silent grown,
I have not yet forgot myself to stone.
25   All is not Heaven's while Abelard has part,
Still rebel nature holds out half my heart;
Nor prayers nor fasts its stubborn pulse restrain,
Nor tears for ages taught to flow in vain.
    Soon as thy letters trembling I unclose,
30   That well-known name awakens all my woes.
Oh name for ever sad! for ever dear!
Still breathed in sighs, still ushered with a tear.
I tremble too, where'er my own I find,
Some dire misfortune follows close behind.
35   Line after line my gushing eyes o'erflow,
Led through a sad variety of woe:
Now warm in love, now withering in thy bloom,
Lost in a convent's solitary gloom!
There stern Religion quenched th' unwilling flame,
40   There died the best of passions, Love and Fame.
    Yet write, oh write me all, that I may join
Griefs to thy griefs, and echo sighs to thine.
Nor foes nor fortune take this power away;
And is my Abelard less kind than they?
45   Tears still are mine, and those I need not spare,
Love but demands what else were shed in prayer;
No happier task these faded eyes pursue;
To read and weep is all they now can do.
    Then share thy pain, allow that sad relief;
50   Ah, more than share it, give me all thy grief.
Heaven first taught letters for some wretch's aid,
Some banished lover, or some captive maid;
They live, they speak, they breathe what love inspires,
Warm from the soul, and faithful to its fires,
55   The virgin's wish without her fears impart,
Excuse the blush, and pour out all the heart,
Speed the soft intercourse from soul to soul,
And waft a sigh from Indus to the Pole.
    Thou knowst how guiltless first I met thy flame,
60   When Love approached me under Friendship's name;
My fancy formed thee of angelic kind,
Some emanation of th' all-beauteous Mind.
Those smiling eyes, attempering[5] every ray,
Shone sweetly lambent with celestial day.
65   Guiltless I gazed; heaven listened while you sung;
And truths divine came mended from that tongue.[6]
From lips like those what precept failed to move?
Too soon they taught me 'twas no sin to love:
Back through the paths of pleasing sense I ran,
70   Nor wished an Angel whom I loved a Man.
Dim and remote the joys of saints I see;
Nor envy them that heaven I lose for thee.
    How oft, when pressed to marriage, have I said,
Curse on all laws but those which love has made?
75   Love, free as air, at sight of human ties,
Spreads his light wings, and in a moment flies.
Let wealth, let honour, wait the wedded dame,
August her deed, and sacred be her fame;
Before true passion all those views remove,
80   Fame, wealth, and honour! what are you to Love?

---

4. Literally, condensation.
5. Moderating.

6. Abelard was, states Pope, Eloisa's "preceptor in Philosophy and Divinity."

The jealous God, when we profane his fires,
Those restless passions in revenge inspires,
And bids them make mistaken mortals groan,
Who seek in love for aught but love alone.
85 Should at my feet the world's great master fall,
Himself, his throne, his world, I'd scorn 'em all:
Not Cæsar's empress would I deign to prove;
No, make me mistress to the man I love;
If there be yet another name more free,
90 More fond than mistress, make me that to thee!
Oh! happy state! when souls each other draw,
When love is liberty, and nature, law:
All then is full, possessing, and possessed,
No craving void left aching in the breast:
95 Even thought meets thought, ere from the lips it part,
And each warm wish springs mutual from the heart.
This sure is bliss (if bliss on earth there be)
And once the lot of Abelard and me.
　　Alas, how changed! what sudden horrors rise!
100 A naked Lover bound and bleeding lies!
Where, where was Eloïse? her voice, her hand,
Her poniard, had opposed the dire command.
Barbarian, stay! that bloody stroke restrain;
The crime was common, common be the pain.[7]
105 I can no more; by shame, by rage suppressed,
Let tears, and burning blushes speak the rest.
　　Canst thou forget that sad, that solemn day,
When victims at yon altar's foot we lay?
Canst thou forget what tears that moment fell,
110 When, warm in youth, I bade the world farewell?
As with cold lips I kissed the sacred veil,
The shrines all trembled, and the lamps grew pale:
Heaven scarce believed the Conquest it surveyed,
And Saints with wonder heard the vows I made.
115 Yet then, to those dread altars as I drew,
Not on the Cross my eyes were fixed, but you:
Not grace, or zeal, love only was my call,
And if I lose thy love, I lose my all.
Come! with thy looks, thy words, relieve my woe;
120 Those still at least are left thee to bestow.
Still on that breast enamoured let me lie,
Still drink delicious poison from thy eye,
Pant on thy lip, and to thy heart be pressed;
Give all thou canst—and let me dream the rest.
125 Ah no! instruct me other joys to prize,
With other beauties charm my partial eyes,
Full in my view set all the bright abode,
And make my soul quit Abelard for God.
　　Ah, think at least thy flock deserves thy care,
130 Plants of thy hand, and children of thy prayer.
From the false world in early youth they fled,
By thee to mountains, wilds, and deserts led.
You raised these hallowed walls;[8] the desert smiled,
And Paradise was opened in the Wild.[9]
135 No weeping orphan saw his father's stores
Our shrines irradiate, or emblaze the floors;
No silver saints, by dying misers given,
Here bribed the rage of ill-requited heaven:

7. "common": shared. "pain": punishment (although the literal meaning need not be ignored).
8. "He founded the monastery," states Pope.
9. "The sudden oasis—'beauty in the lap of horror'—had been strongly presented in *Paradise Lost*, IV, 131 ff. (cf. Isa. 1.3) and was to endear itself to all eighteenth-century aestheticians." John Butt, ed. *The Poems of Alexander Pope* (London: Oxford Univ. Press, 1963), p. 255.

But such plain roofs as Piety could raise,
140   And only vocal with the Maker's praise.
In these lone walls (their days eternal bound)
These moss-grown domes with spiry turrets crowned,
Where awful arches make a noonday night,
And the dim windows shed a solemn light;
145   Thy eyes diffused a reconciling ray,
And gleams of glory brightened all the day.
But now no face divine contentment wears,
'Tis all blank sadness, or continual tears.
See how the force of others' prayers I try,
150   (O pious fraud of amorous charity!)
But why should I on others' prayers depend?
Come thou, my father, brother, husband, friend!
Ah let thy handmaid, sister, daughter move,
And all those tender names in one, thy love!
155   The darksome pines that o'er yon rocks reclined
Wave high, and murmur to the hollow wind,
The wandering streams that shine between the hills,
The grots that echo to the tinkling rills,
The dying gales that pant upon the trees,
160   The lakes that quiver to the curling breeze;
No more these scenes my meditation aid,
Or lull to rest the visionary maid.
But o'er the twilight groves and dusky caves,
Long-sounding aisles, and intermingled graves,
165   Black Melancholy sits, and round her throws
A deathlike silence, and a dead repose:
Her gloomy presence saddens all the scene,
Shades every flower, and darkens every green,
Deepens the murmur of the falling floods,
170   And breathes a browner horror on the woods.
     Yet here for ever, ever must I stay;
Sad proof how well a lover can obey!
Death, only death, can break the lasting chain;
And here, even then, shall my cold dust remain,
175   Here all its frailties, all its flames resign,
And wait till 'tis no sin to mix with thine.
     Ah wretch! believed the spouse of God in vain,
Confessed within the slave of love and man.
Assist me, heaven! but whence arose that prayer?
180   Sprung it from piety, or from despair?
Even here, where frozen chastity retires,
Love finds an altar for forbidden fires.
I ought to grieve, but cannot what I ought;
I mourn the lover, not lament the fault;
185   I view my crime, but kindle at the view,
Repent old pleasures, and solicit new;
Now turned to heaven, I weep my past offence,
Now think of thee, and curse my innocence.
Of all affliction taught a lover yet,
190   'Tis sure the hardest science to forget!
How shall I lose the sin, yet keep the sense,[10]
And love th' offender, yet detest th' offence?
How the dear object from the crime remove,
Or how distinguish penitence from love?
195   Unequal task! a passion to resign,
For hearts so touched, so pierced, so lost as mine.
Ere such a soul regains its peaceful state,
How often must it love, how often hate!
How often hope, despair, resent, regret,
200   Conceal, disdain, — do all things but forget.

10. Both perception and sensation.

But let heaven seize it, all at once 'tis fired;
Not touched, but rapt; not wakened, but inspired!
Oh come! oh teach me nature to subdue,
Renounce my love, my life, myself—and you.
205 Fill my fond heart with God alone, for he
Alone can rival, can succeed to thee.
　　How happy is the blameless Vestal's lot!
The world forgetting, by the world forgot:
Eternal sunshine of the spotless mind!
210 Each prayer accepted, and each wish resigned;
Labour and rest, that equal periods keep;
"Obedient slumbers that can wake and weep;"[11]
Desires composed, affections ever even;
Tears that delight, and sighs that waft to heaven.
215 Grace shines around her with serenest beams,
And whispering Angels prompt her golden dreams.
For her th' unfading rose of Eden blooms,
And wings of Seraphs shed divine perfumes,
For her the Spouse prepares the bridal ring,
220 For her white virgins Hymeneals[12] sing,
To sounds of heavenly harps she dies away,
And melts in visions of eternal day.
　　Far other dreams my erring soul employ,
Far other raptures, of unholy joy:
225 When at the close of each sad, sorrowing day,
Fancy restores what vengeance snatched away,
The conscience sleeps, and leaving nature free,
All my loose soul unbounded springs to thee.
Oh cursed, dear horrors of all-conscious night!
230 How glowing guilt exalts the keen delight!
Provoking Dæmons all restraint remove,
And stir within me every source of love.
I hear thee, view thee, gaze o'er all thy charms,
And round thy phantom glue my clasping arms.
235 I wake:—no more I hear, no more I view,
The phantom flies me, as unkind as you.
I call aloud; it hears not what I say:
I stretch my empty arms; it glides away.
To dream once more I close my willing eyes;
240 Ye soft illusions, dear deceits, arise!
Alas, no more! methinks we wandering go
Through dreary wastes, and weep each other's woe,
Where round some mouldering tower pale ivy creeps,
And low-browed rocks hang nodding o'er the deeps.
245 Sudden you mount, you beckon from the skies;
Clouds interpose, waves roar, and winds arise.
I shriek, start up, the same sad prospect find,
And wake to all the griefs I left behind.
　　For thee the fates, severely kind, ordain
250 A cool suspense from pleasure and from pain;
Thy life a long dead calm of fixed repose;
No pulse that riots, and no blood that glows.
Still as the sea, ere winds were taught to blow,
Or moving spirit bade the waters flow;
255 Soft as the slumbers of a saint forgiven,
And mild as opening gleams of promised heaven.
　　Come, Abelard! for what hast thou to dread?
The torch of Venus burns not for the dead.
Nature stands checked; Religion disapproves;
260 Even thou art cold—yet Eloïsa loves.
Ah hopeless, lasting flames! like those that burn

11. A quotation from Richard Crashaw's poem "Description of a Religious House" (1648).

12. Wedding hymns. Nuns are the "brides of Christ."

To light the dead, and warm th' unfruitful urn.
　　What scenes appear where'er I turn my view?
The dear Ideas, where I fly, pursue,
265　Rise in the grove, before the altar rise,
Stain all my soul, and wanton in my eyes.
I waste the Matin lamp in sighs for thee,
Thy image steals between my God and me,
Thy voice I seem in every hymn to hear,
270　With every bead I drop too soft a tear.
When from the censer clouds of fragrance roll,
And swelling organs lift the rising soul,
One thought of thee puts all the pomp to flight,
Priests, tapers, temples, swim before my sight:
275　In seas of flame my plunging soul is drowned,
While Altars blaze, and Angels tremble round.
　　While prostrate here in humble grief I lie,
Kind, virtuous drops just gathering in my eye,
While praying, trembling, in the dust I roll,
280　And dawning grace is opening on my soul:
Come, if thou darst, all charming as thou art!
Oppose thyself to heaven; dispute my heart;
Come, with one glance of those deluding eyes
Blot out each bright Idea of the skies;
285　Take back that grace, those sorrows, and those tears;
Take back my fruitless penitence and prayers;
Snatch me, just mounting, from the blest abode;
Assist the fiends, and tear me from my God!
　　No, fly me, fly me, far as Pole from Pole;
290　Rise Alps between us! and whole oceans roll!
Ah, come not, write not, think not once of me,
Nor share one pang of all I felt for thee.
Thy oaths I quit, thy memory resign;
Forget, renounce me, hate whate'er was mine.
295　Fair eyes, and tempting looks (which yet I view!)
Long loved, adored ideas, all adieu!
Oh Grace serene! oh virtue heavenly fair!
Divine oblivion of low-thoughted care!
Fresh blooming Hope, gay daughter of the sky!
300　And Faith, our early immortality!
Enter, each mild, each amicable guest;
Receive, and wrap me in eternal rest!
　　See in her cell sad Eloïsa spread,
Propped on some tomb, a neighbour of the dead.
305　In each low wind methinks a Spirit calls,
And more than Echoes talk along the walls.
Here, as I watched the dying lamps around,
From yonder shrine I heard a hollow sound.
"Come, sister, come!" (it said, or seemed to say)
310　"Thy place is here, sad sister, come away!
Once like thyself, I trembled, wept, and prayed,
Love's victim then, though now a sainted maid:
But all is calm in this eternal sleep;
Here grief forgets to groan, and love to weep,
315　Even superstition loses every fear:
For God, not man, absolves our frailties here."
　　I come, I come! prepare your roseate bowers,
Celestial palms, and ever-blooming flowers.
Thither, where sinners may have rest, I go,
320　Where flames refined in breasts seraphic glow:
Thou, Abelard! the last sad office pay,
And smooth my passage to the realms of day;
See my lips tremble, and my eyeballs roll,
Suck my last breath, and catch my flying soul!

325   Ah no—in sacred vestments mayst thou stand,
       The hallowed taper trembling in thy hand,
       Present the Cross before my lifted eye,
       Teach me at once, and learn of me to die.
       Ah then, thy once-loved Eloïsa see!
330   It will be then no crime to gaze on me.
       See from my cheek the transient roses fly!
       See the last sparkle languish in my eye!
       Till every motion, pulse, and breath be o'er;
       And even my Abelard be loved no more.
335   O Death all-eloquent! you only prove
       What dust we dote on, when 'tis man we love.
          Then too, when fate shall thy fair frame destroy,
       (That cause of all my guilt, and all my joy)
       In trance ecstatic may thy pangs be drowned,
340   Bright clouds descend, and Angels watch thee round,
       From opening skies may streaming glories shine,
       And saints embrace thee with a love like mine.
          May one kind grave unite each hapless name,[13]
       And graft my love immortal on thy fame!
345   Then, ages hence, when all my woes are o'er,
       When this rebellious heart shall beat no more;
       If ever chance two wandering lovers brings
       To Paraclete's white walls and silver springs,
       O'er the pale marble shall they join their heads,
350   And drink the falling tears each other sheds;
       Then sadly say, with mutual pity moved,
       "Oh may we never love as these have loved!"
       From the full choir when loud Hosannas rise,
       And swell the pomp of dreadful sacrifice,[14]
355   Amid that scene if some relenting eye
       Glance on the stone where our cold relics lie,
       Devotion's self shall steal a thought from heaven,
       One human tear shall drop, and be forgiven.
       And sure, if fate some future bard[15] shall join
360   In sad similitude of griefs to mine,
       Condemned whole years in absence to deplore,
       And image charms he must behold no more;
       Such if there be, who loves so long, so well;
       Let him our sad, our tender story tell;
365   The well-sung woes will soothe my pensive ghost;
       He best can paint 'em who shall feel 'em most.

Elegy to the Memory of an Unfortunate Lady[1]

       What beckoning ghost, along the moonlight shade
       Invites my steps, and points to yonder glade?
       'Tis she!—but why that bleeding bosom gored,
       Why dimly gleams the visionary sword?[2]
5   Oh ever beauteous, ever friendly! tell,
       Is it, in heaven, a crime to love too well?
       To bear too tender, or too firm a heart,
       To act a Lover's or a Roman's part?[3]

13. "Abelard and Eloisa were," states Pope, "interred in the same grave, or in monuments adjoining in the monastery of Paraclete."
14. The celebration of the Eucharist.
15. Pope may here and in the last lines be referring to himself and to the absence of his friend, Lady Mary Montagu (see Tillotson, *The Poems of Alexander Pope*, II, 312).

1. Though many early commentators believed otherwise, this "elegy" was written not to lament any particular lady but as an elegiac exercise, having as its subject an idealized "unfortunate lady." It was published in 1717.
2. The lady's ghost carries the sword with which she committed suicide. "That the wound has been carried over unhealed unto the ghostly body suggests that heaven has failed to honour the virtue of the unfortunate lady" (Tillotson, *The Poems of Alexander Pope*, II, 362).
3. To commit suicide.

Is there no bright reversion in the sky,
10   For those who greatly think, or bravely die?
    Why bade ye else, ye Powers! her soul aspire
Above the vulgar flight of low desire?
Ambition first sprung from your blest abodes;
The glorious fault of Angels and of Gods:
15   Thence to their images on earth it flows,
And in the breasts of Kings and Heroes glows.
Most souls, 'tis true, but peep out once an age,
Dull sullen prisoners in the body's cage:
Dim lights of life, that burn a length of years
20   Useless, unseen, as lamps in sepulchres;
Like Eastern Kings a lazy state they keep,
And close confined to their own palace, sleep.
    From these perhaps (ere nature bade her die)
Fate snatched her early to the pitying sky.
25   As into air the purer spirits flow,
And separate from their kindred dregs below;
So flew the soul to its congenial place,
Nor left one virtue to redeem her Race.
    But thou, false guardian of a charge too good,
30   Thou, mean deserter of thy brother's blood!
See on these ruby lips the trembling breath,
These cheeks, now fading at the blast of death;
Cold is that breast which warmed the world before,
And those love-darting eyes must roll no more.
35   Thus, if Eternal justice rules the ball,[4]
Thus shall your wives, and thus your children fall:
On all the line a sudden vengeance waits,
And frequent hearses shall besiege your gates.
There passengers shall stand, and pointing say,
40   (While the long funerals blacken all the way)
Lo these were they, whose souls the Furies steeled,
And cursed with hearts unknowing how to yield.
Thus unlamented pass the proud away,
The gaze of fools, and pageant of a day!
45   So perish all, whose breast ne'er learned to glow
For others' good, or melt at others' woe.
    What can atone (oh ever-injured shade!)
Thy fate unpitied, and thy rites unpaid?
No friend's complaint, no kind domestic tear
50   Pleased thy pale ghost, or graced thy mournful bier.
By foreign hands[5] thy dying eyes were closed,
By foreign hands thy decent limbs composed,
By foreign hands thy humble grave adorned,
By strangers honoured, and by strangers mourned!
55   What though no friends in sable weeds appear,
Grieve for an hour, perhaps, then mourn a year,
And bear about the mockery of woe
To midnight dances, and the public show?
What though no weeping Loves thy ashes grace,
60   Nor polished marble emulate thy face?
What though no sacred earth allow thee room,
Nor hallowed dirge be muttered o'er thy tomb?
Yet shall thy grave with rising flowers be drest,
And the green turf lie lightly on thy breast:
65   There shall the morn her earliest tears bestow,
There the first roses of the year shall blow;
While Angels with their silver wings o'ershade
The ground, now sacred by thy reliques made.

---

4. The world, though the image Pope intends here is the orb placed in the hands of statues of Justice.

5. Because death by suicide would have caused both family and Church to spurn the deceased.

So peaceful rests, without a stone, a name,
70 What once had beauty, titles, wealth, and fame.
How loved, how honoured once, avails thee not,
To whom related, or by whom begot;
A heap of dust alone remains of thee,
'Tis all thou art, and all the proud shall be!
75   Poets themselves must fall, like those they sung,
Deaf the praised ear, and mute the tuneful tongue.
Even he, whose soul now melts in mournful lays,
Shall shortly want the generous tear he pays;
Then from his closing eyes thy form shall part,
80 And the last pang shall tear thee from his heart,
Life's idle business at one gasp be o'er,
The Muse forgot, and thou beloved no more!

An Epistle to Dr. Arbuthnot[1]

P. Shut, shut the door, good John![2] fatigued, I said,
Tie up the knocker say I'm sick, I'm dead.
The Dog Star[3] rages! nay 'tis past a doubt,
All Bedlam, or Parnassus,[4] is let out:
5 Fire in each eye, and papers in each hand,
They rave, recite, and madden round the land.
    What walls can guard me, or what shades can hide?
They pierce my thickets, through my Grot[5] they glide;
By land, by water, they renew the charge:
10 They stop the chariot, and they board the barge.
No place is sacred, not the Church is free;
Even Sunday shines no Sabbath day to me:
Then from the Mint[6] walks forth the Man of rhyme,
Happy! to catch me just at Dinner time.
15   Is there a Parson, much bemused in beer,
A maudlin Poetess, a rhyming Peer,
A Clerk, foredoomed his father's soul to cross,
Who pens a Stanza, when he should engross?[7]
Is there, who, locked from ink and paper, scrawls
20 With desperate charcoal round his darkened walls?
All fly to TWITNAM,[8] and in humble strain
Apply to me, to keep them mad or vain.
Arthur,[9] whose giddy son neglects the Laws,
Imputes to me and my damned works the cause:
25 Poor Cornus[10] sees his frantic wife elope,
And curses Wit, and Poetry, and Pope.
    Friend to my Life! (which did not you prolong,
The world had wanted many an idle song)
What Drop or Nostrum can this plague remove?
30 Or which must end me, a Fool's wrath or love?
A dire dilemma! either way I'm sped,
If foes, they write, if friends, they read me dead.

1. "An Epistle to Dr. Arbuthnot" is, as Pope described it, primarily "a sort of bill of complaint" against "some persons of rank and fortune" who had attacked not only his writing but also his "person, morals, and family." More than that, however, the poem is a defence of his kind of poetry and of poets who dared to attack evil in high places. The "Epistle" was completed in 1734 at the request of his lifelong friend, Dr. Arbuthnot, who (then on his deathbed) urged him to "continue that noble disdain and abhorrence of vice which you seem naturally endued with." It was published in 1735, a few weeks before Arbuthnot's death.
2. John Searl, Pope's servant.
3. Sirius, associated with the heat of August, sometimes causing madness. August was also the time for rehearsing poetry in ancient Rome.

4. "Bedlam": the hospital of St. Mary of Bethlehem in London, for the insane. "Parnassus": a mountain in Greece inhabited by the Muses and thus sacred to poets (and to poetasters as well).
5. Pope's grotto, a cave-like passage built by him to link his house and grounds.
6. A sanctuary for insolvent debtors in Southwark. They emerged on Sundays when they were free from arrest.
7. Write legal documents.
8. Twickenham, the district of London where Pope lived.
9. Arthur Moore, whose son had plagiarized a few of Pope's verses in one of his plays.
10. Another name for cuckold—a man whose wife has deceived him.

Seized and tied down to judge, how wretched I!
Who can't be silent, and who will not lie:
35   To laugh, were want of goodness and of grace,
And to be grave, exceeds all Power of face.
I sit with sad civility, I read
With honest anguish, and an aching head;
And drop at last, but in unwilling ears,
40   This saving counsel, "Keep your piece nine years."[11]
   "Nine years!" cries he, who high in Drury Lane,
Lulled by soft Zephyrs through the broken pane,
Rhymes ere he wakes, and prints before term[12] ends,
Obliged by hunger, and request of friends:
45   "The piece, you think, is incorrect? why, take it,
I'm all submission, what you'd have it, make it."
   Three things another's modest wishes bound,
My Friendship, and a Prologue, and ten pound.
   Pitholeon[13] sends to me: "You know his Grace,
50   I want a Patron; ask him for a Place."
Pitholeon libelled me—"but here's a letter
Informs you, Sir, 'twas when he knew no better.
Dare you refuse him? Curll invites to dine,
He'll write a Journal, or he'll turn Divine."
55   Bless me! a packet.—" 'Tis a stranger sues,
A Virgin Tragedy, an Orphan Muse."
If I dislike it, "Furies, death and rage!"
If I approve, "Commend it to the Stage."
There (thank my stars) my whole commission ends,
60   The Players and I are, luckily, no friends.
Fired that the house reject him, "'Sdeath I'll print it,
And shame the fools—— Your Interest, Sir, with Lintot."[14]
Lintot, dull rogue! will think your price too much:
"Not, Sir, if you revise it, and retouch."
65   All my demurs but double his attacks;
At last he whispers, "Do; and we go snacks."[15]
Glad of a quarrel, straight I clap the door,
"Sir, let me see your works and you no more."
   'Tis sung, when Midas' Ears began to spring,
70   (Midas, a sacred person and a King)
His very Minister who spied them first,
(Some say his Queen) was forced to speak, or burst.
And is not mine, my friend, a sorer case,
When every coxcomb perks them in my face?
75   A. Good friend, forbear! you deal in dangerous things.
I'd never name Queens, Ministers, or Kings;
Keep close to Ears, and those let asses prick;
'Tis nothing— P. Nothing? if they bite and kick?
Out with it, DUNCIAD! let the secret pass,
80   That secret to each fool, that he's an Ass:
The truth once told (and wherefore should we lie?)
The Queen of Midas slept, and so may I.
   You think this cruel? take it for a rule,
No creature smarts so little as a fool.
85   Let peals of laughter, Codrus![16] round thee break,
Thou unconcerned canst hear the mighty crack:
Pit, Box, and gallery in convulsions hurled,
Thou standst unshook amidst a bursting world.
Who shames a Scribbler? break one cobweb through,
90   He spins the slight, self-pleasing thread anew:

---

11. The advice given by Horace in his *Ars Poetica*.
12. The law-court session, which coincided with the publishing term.
13. Any bad poet who might get Edmund Curll, the unscrupulous publisher, to print his libellous verse.
14. Pope's former publisher.
15. Go shares.
16. A poet ridiculed by Virgil.

Destroy his fib or sophistry, in vain,
The creature's at his dirty work again,
Throned in the centre of his thin designs,
Proud of a vast extent of flimsy lines!
95 Whom have I hurt? has Poet yet, or Peer,
Lost the arched eyebrow, or Parnassian sneer?
And has not Colley[17] still his Lord, and whore?
His butchers Henley, his Freemasons Moore?
Does not one table Bavius still admit?
100 Still to one Bishop Philips seem a wit?
Still Sappho— A. Hold! for God's sake— you'll offend,
No Names— be calm— learn prudence of a friend:
I too could write, and I am twice as tall;[18]
But foes like these— P. One Flatterer's worse than all.
105 Of all mad creatures, if the learned are right,
It is the slaver kills, and not the bite.
A fool quite angry is quite innocent:
Alas! 'tis ten times worse when they repent.
   One dedicates in high heroic prose,
110 And ridicules beyond a hundred foes:
One from all Grubstreet[19] will my fame defend,
And, more abusive, calls himself my friend.
This prints my Letters, that expects a bribe,
And others roar aloud, "Subscribe, subscribe."
115   There are, who to my person pay their court:
I cough like Horace, and, though lean, am short,
Ammon's great son one shoulder had too high,
Such Ovid's nose, and "Sir! you have an Eye"—
Go on, obliging creatures, make me see
120 All that disgraced my Betters, met in me.
Say for my comfort, languishing in bed,
"Just so immortal Maro held his head:"
And when I die, be sure you let me know
Great Homer died three thousand years ago.
125   Why did I write? what sin to me unknown
Dipped me in ink, my parents', or my own?
As yet a child, nor yet a fool to fame,
I lisped in numbers, for the numbers came.
I left no calling for this idle trade,
130 No duty broke, no father disobeyed.
The Muse but served to ease some friend, not Wife,
To help me through this long disease, my Life,
To second, ARBUTHNOT! thy Art and Care,
And teach the Being you preserved, to bear.
135   But why then publish? Granville[20] the polite,
And knowing Walsh, would tell me I could write;
Well-natured Garth inflamed with early praise;
And Congreve loved, and Swift endured my lays;
The courtly Talbot, Somers, Sheffield read,
140 Even mitred Rochester would nod the head,
And St. John's self (great Dryden's friends before)
With open arms received one Poet more.
Happy my studies, when by these approved!
Happier their author, when by these beloved!
145 From these the world will judge of men and books,
Not from the Burnets, Oldmixons, and Cookes.

17. Ll. 97–101. "Colley": Colley Cibber, poet laureate.
"Henley": John Henley, a preacher in Hutcher Row.
"Bavius": minor Roman poetaster. "Philips": Ambrose
Philips, nicknamed "Namby-Pamby" because of the overt
adulation in his poetry. "Sappho": a seventh-century Lesbian poetess.
18. Pope was only four-feet-six-inches tall.

19. A section of London inhabited by hack writers.
20. Ll. 135–53. These are the names of writers and
statesmen who encouraged Pope, set against those who
denounced him (among the former, Jonathan Swift and
William Congreve; among the latter, Charles Gildon and
John Dennis).

Soft were my numbers; who could take offence
While pure Description held the place of Sense?
Like gentle Fanny's was my flowery theme,
150 A painted mistress, or a purling stream.
Yet then did Gildon draw his venal quill;
I wished the man a dinner, and sat still.
Yet then did Dennis rave in furious fret;
I never answered— I was not in debt.
155 If want provoked, or madness made them print,
I waged no war with Bedlam or the Mint.
Did some more sober Critic come abroad;
If wrong, I smiled; if right, I kissed the rod.
Pains, reading, study, are their just pretence,
160 And all they want is spirit, taste, and sense.
Commas and points they set exactly right,
And 'twere a sin to rob them of their mite.
Yet ne'er one sprig of laurel graced these ribalds,
From slashing Bentley down to pidling Tibalds:[21]
165 Each wight, who reads not, and but scans and spells,
Each Word-catcher, that lives on syllables,
Even such small Critics some regard may claim,
Preserved in Milton's or in Shakespeare's name.
Pretty! in amber to observe the forms
170 Of hairs, or straws, or dirt, or grubs, or worms!
The things, we know, are neither rich nor rare,
But wonder how the devil they got there.
Were others angry: I excused them too;
Well might they rage, I gave them but their due.
175 A man's true merit 'tis not hard to find;
But each man's secret standard in his mind,
That Casting weight pride adds to emptiness,
This, who can gratify? for who can guess?
The Bard whom pilfered Pastorals renown,
180 Who turns a Persian tale for half a Crown,
Just writes to make his barrenness appear,
And strains, from hard-bound brains, eight lines a year;
He, who still wanting, though he lives on theft,
Steals much, spends little, yet has nothing left:
185 And He, who now to sense, now nonsense leaning,
Means not, but blunders round about a meaning:
And He, whose fustian's so sublimely bad,
It is not Poetry, but prose run mad:
All these, my modest Satire bade translate,
190 And owned that nine such Poets made a Tate.[22]
How did they fume, and stamp, and roar, and chafe!
And swear, not ADDISON himself was safe.
Peace to all such! but were there One whose fires
True Genius kindles, and fair Fame inspires;
195 Blest with each talent and each art to please,
And born to write, converse, and live with ease:
Should such a man, too fond to rule alone,
Bear, like the Turk, no brother near the throne,
View him with scornful, yet with jealous eyes,
200 And hate for arts that caused himself to rise;
Damn with faint praise, assent with civil leer,
And without sneering, teach the rest to sneer;
Willing to wound, and yet afraid to strike,
Just hint a fault, and hesitate dislike;
205 Alike reserved to blame, or to commend,
A timorous foe, and a suspicious friend;

---

21. "Bentley," "Theobald": two pedants who had edited
Milton and Shakespeare.

22. Nahum Tate, minor versifier and translator.

Dreading even fools, by Flatterers besieged,
And so obliging, that he ne'er obliged;
Like Cato,²³ give his little Senate laws,
210 And sit attentive to his own applause;
While Wits and Templars²⁴ every sentence raise,
And wonder with a foolish face of praise—
Who but must laugh, if such a man there be?
Who would not weep, if ATTICUS²⁵ were he?
215   What though my Name stood rubric²⁶ on the walls,
Or plastered posts, with claps,²⁷ in capitals?
Or smoking forth, a hundred hawkers' load,
On wings of wind came flying all abroad?
I sought no homage from the Race that write;
220 I kept, like Asian Monarchs, from their sight:
Poems I heeded (now berhymed so long)
No more than thou, great GEORGE! a birthday song.²⁸
I ne'er with wits or witlings passed my days,
To spread about the itch of verse and praise;
225 Nor like a puppy, daggled through the town,
To fetch and carry singsong up and down;
Nor at Rehearsals sweat, and mouthed, and cried,
With handkerchief and orange at my side;
But sick of fops, and poetry, and prate,
230 To Bufo²⁹ left the whole Castalian state.
   Proud as Apollo on his forkèd hill,
Sat full-blown Bufo, puffed by every quill;
Fed with soft Dedication all day long,
Horace and he went hand in hand in song.
235 His Library (where busts of Poets dead
And a true Pindar stood without a head)
Received of wits an undistinguished race,
Who first his judgment asked, and then a place:
Much they extolled his pictures, much his seat,
240 And flattered every day, and some days eat:
Till grown more frugal in his riper days,
He paid some bards with port, and some with praise;
To some a dry rehearsal was assigned,
And others (harder still) he paid in kind.
245 Dryden alone (what wonder?) came not nigh,
Dryden alone escaped this judging eye:
But still the Great have kindness in reserve,
He helped to bury whom he helped to starve.
   May some choice patron bless each grey goose quill!
250 May every Bavius have his Bufo still!
So, when a Statesman wants a day's defence,
Or Envy holds a whole week's war with Sense,
Or simple pride for flattery makes demands,
May dunce by dunce be whistled off my hands!
255 Blest be the Great! for those they take away,
And those they left me; for they left me GAY;³⁰
Left me to see neglected Genius bloom,
Neglected die, and tell it on his tomb:
Of all thy blameless life the sole return
260 My Verse, and QUEENSBURY weeping o'er thy urn!
   Oh let me live my own, and die so too!

23. Roman senator, "the conscience of Rome." The reference here is to Addison's play about Cato.
24. Law students from the Inner and Middle Temples.
25. A respected Roman critic, meant to suggest that Addison had many respected qualities as well as faults, thus causing sadness rather than mirth.
26. In red letters.
27. Posters.

28. A reference to the execrable verses of Cibber written to celebrate the king, who had not the taste to know whether they were good or bad.
29. Ll. 230–48. "Bufo": a type of ostentatious patron of the arts.
30. John Gay, author of *The Beggar's Opera* and good friend to Pope. Gay lost all his money in the South Sea Bubble and had to rely on the kindness of the Duke of Queensbury.

(To live and die is all I have to do:)
Maintain a Poet's dignity and ease,
And see what friends, and read what books I please:
265   Above a Patron, though I condescend
Sometimes to call a Minister my friend.
I was not born for Courts or great affairs;
I pay my debts, believe, and say my prayers;
Can sleep without a Poem in my head,
270   Nor know, if Dennis be alive or dead.
     Why am I asked what next shall see the light?
Heavens! was I born for nothing but to write?
Has Life no joys for me? or, (to be grave)
Have I no friend to serve, no soul to save?
275   "I found him close with Swift"—'Indeed? no doubt,'
(Cries prating Balbus) 'something will come out.'
'Tis all in vain, deny it as I will.
'No, such a Genius never can lie still;'
And then for mine obligingly mistakes
280   The first Lampoon Sir Will. or Bubo makes.[31]
Poor guiltless I! and can I choose but smile,
When every Coxcomb knows me by my Style?
     Cursed be the verse, how well soe'er it flow,
That tends to make one worthy man my foe,
285   Give Virtue scandal, Innocence a fear,
Or from the soft-eyed Virgin steal a tear!
But he who hurts a harmless neighbour's peace,
Insults fallen worth, or Beauty in distress,
Who loves a Lie, lame slander helps about,
290   Who writes a Libel, or who copies out:
That Fop, whose pride affects a patron's name,
Yet absent, wounds an author's honest fame:
Who can your merit selfishly approve,
And show the sense of it without the love;
295   Who has the vanity to call you friend,
Yet wants the honour, injured, to defend;
Who tells whate'er you think, whate'er you say,
And, if he lie not, must at least betray:
Who to the Dean, and silver bell can swear,
300   And sees at Canons what was never there;
Who reads, but with a lust to misapply,
Make Satire a Lampoon, and Fiction, Lie.
A lash like mine no honest man shall dread,
But all such babbling blockheads in his stead.
305   Let Sporus[32] tremble— A. What? that thing of silk,
Sporus, that mere white curd of Ass's milk?
Satire or sense, alas! can Sporus feel?
Who breaks a butterfly upon a wheel?
P. Yet let me flap this bug with gilded wings,
310   This painted child of dirt, that stinks and stings;
Whose buzz the witty and the fair annoys,
Yet wit ne'er tastes, and beauty ne'er enjoys:
So well-bred spaniels civilly delight
In mumbling of the game they dare not bite.
315   Eternal smiles his emptiness betray,
As shallow streams run dimpling all the way.
Whether in florid impotence he speaks,
And, as the prompter breathes, the puppet squeaks;
Or at the ear of Eve, familiar Toad,
320   Half froth, half venom, spits himself abroad,

31. "Sir Will": Sir William Yonge, a politician. "Bubo":
George Bubb Dodington, perhaps the "Bufo" in ll. 230–48.
32. A homosexual in Nero's court—here referring to
Lord Hervey, a favourite at Queen Anne's court known
for his poetastery, effeminancy, and love of gossip. This is
Pope's most caustic character-satire; note the variety of
imagery.

In puns, or politics, or tales, or lies,
Or spite, or smut, or rhymes, or blasphemies.
His wit all seesaw, between that and this,
Now high, now low, now master up, now miss,
325 And he himself one vile Antithesis.
Amphibious thing! that acting either part,
The trifling head, or the corrupted heart,
Fop at the toilet, flatterer at the board,
Now trips a Lady, and now struts a Lord.
330 Eve's tempter thus the Rabbins have exprest,
A Cherub's face, a reptile all the rest;
Beauty that shocks you, parts that none will trust,
Wit that can creep, and pride that licks the dust.
     Not Fortune's worshipper, nor Fashion's fool,
335 Not Lucre's madman, nor Ambition's tool,
Not proud, nor servile; Be one Poet's praise,
That, if he pleased, he pleased by manly ways:
That Flattery, even to Kings, he held a shame,
And thought a Lie in verse or prose the same.
340 That not in Fancy's maze he wandered long,
But stooped to Truth and moralized his song:
That not for Fame, but Virtue's better end,
He stood the furious foe, the timid friend,
The damning critic, half approving wit,
345 The coxcomb hit, or fearing to be hit;
Laughed at the loss of friends he never had,
The dull, the proud, the wicked, and the mad;
The distant threats of vengeance on his head,
The blow unfelt, the tear he never shed;
350 The tale revived, the lie so oft o'erthrown,
Th' imputed trash, and dulness not his own;
The morals blackened when the writings 'scape,
The libeled person, and the pictured shape;
Abuse, on all he loved, or loved him, spread,
355 A friend in exile, or a father, dead;
The whisper, that to greatness still too near,
Perhaps, yet vibrates on his SOVEREIGN's ear—
Welcome for thee, fair Virtue! all the past:
For thee, fair Virtue! welcome even the last!
360   A. But why insult the poor, affront the great?
P. A knave's a knave, to me, in every state:
Alike my scorn, if he succeed or fail,
Sporus at court, of Japhet[33] in a jail,
A hireling scribbler, or a hireling peer,
365 Knight of the post corrupt, or of the shire;
If on a Pillory, or near a Throne,
He gain his Prince's ear, or lose his own.
     Yet soft by nature, more a dupe than wit,
Sappho can tell you how this man was bit:
370 This dreaded Satirist Dennis will confess
Foe to his pride, but friend to his distress:
So humble, he has knocked at Tibbald's door,
Has drunk with Cibber, nay, has rhymed for Moore.
Full ten years slandered, did he once reply?
375 Three thousand suns went down on Welsted's lie.[34]
To please a Mistress one aspersed his life;
He lashed him not, but let her be his wife:
Let Budgel[35] charge low Grubstreet on his quill,
And write whate'er he pleased, except his Will;

33. A criminal who, Pope intimates, committed lesser crimes than Sporus yet was sentenced to the pillory, had his ears cut off, his nose slit, his goods confiscated, and was imprisoned for life.
34. A minor poet, who slandered Pope.
35. Another slanderer who, says Pope, "got to himself almost the whole fortune of a man entirely unrelated to him" by forging a will.

380   Let the two Curlls of Town and Court, abuse
His father, mother, body, soul, and muse.
Yet why? that Father held it for a rule,
It was a sin to call our neighbour fool:
That harmless Mother thought no wife a whore:
385   Hear this, and spare his family, James Moore!
Unspotted names, and memorable long!
If there be force in Virtue, or in Song.
   Of gentle blood (part shed in Honour's cause,
While yet in Britain Honour had applause)
390   Each parent sprung— A. What fortune, pray?— P. Their own,
And better got, than Bestia's[36] from the throne.
Born to no Pride, inheriting no Strife,
Nor marrying Discord in a noble wife,
Stranger to civil and religious rage,
395   The good man walked innoxious through his age.
No Courts he saw, no suits would ever try,
Nor dared an Oath, nor hazarded a Lie.
Unlearned, he knew no schoolman's subtle art,
No language, but the language of the heart.
400   By Nature honest, by Experience wise,
Healthy by temperance, and by exercise;
His life, though long, to sickness past unknown,
His death was instant, and without a groan.
O grant me, thus to live, and thus to die!
405   Who sprung from Kings shall know less joy than I.
   O Friend! may each domestic bliss be thine!
Be no unpleasing Melancholy mine:
Me, let the tender office long engage,
To rock the cradle of reposing Age,
410   With lenient arts extend a Mother's breath,
Make Languor smile, and smooth the bed of Death,
Explore the thought, explain the asking eye,
And keep a while one parent from the sky!
On cares like these if length of days attend,
415   May Heaven, to bless those days, preserve my friend,
Preserve him social, cheerful and serene,
And just as rich as when he served a QUEEN.
A. Whether that blessing be denied or given,
Thus far was right, the rest belongs to Heaven.

JAMES THOMSON (1700–48)

From The Seasons

Spring[1]

Come, gentle Spring—ethereal Mildness, come,
And from the bosom of yon dropping cloud,
While music wakes around, veiled in a shower
Of shadowing roses, on our plains descend.
5   O Hertford,[2] fitted or to shine in courts
With unaffected grace, or walk the plain
With Innocence and Meditation joined

36. A Roman bribe-taker.

1. "Spring" is the first book of Thomson's famous poem of
natural description, which established its author as the
foremost nature poet of the century. Thomson's venture
began in 1726 when he published a descriptive poem called

"Winter." In 1727 he followed with "Summer"; "Spring"
appeared in 1728 and "Autumn" in the first collected
edition of *The Seasons* in 1730. The whole poem was
considerably revised in 1744 and finally revised in 1746.
2. Frances, Countess of Hertford, Thomson's patroness.

In soft assemblage, listen to my song,
Which thy own season paints— when nature all
10   Is blooming and benevolent, like thee.
        And see where surly Winter passes off
Far to the north, and calls his ruffian blasts:
His blasts obey, and quit the howling hill,
The shattered forest, and the ravaged vale;
15   While softer gales succeed, at whose kind touch,
Dissolving snows in livid torrents lost,
The mountains lift their green heads to the sky.
        As yet the trembling year is unconfirmed,
And Winter oft at eve resumes the breeze,
20   Chills the pale morn, and bids his driving sleets
Deform the day delightless; so that scarce
The bittern knows his time with bill engulfed
To shake the sounding marsh; or from the shore
The plovers when to scatter o'er the heath,
25   And sing their wild notes to the listening waste.
        At last from Aries rolls the bounteous sun,
And the bright Bull receives him. Then no more
The expansive atmosphere is cramped with cold;
But, full of life and vivifying soul,
30   Lifts the light clouds sublime, and spreads them thin,
Fleecy, and white o'er all-surrounding heaven.
        Forth fly the tepid airs; and unconfined,
Unbinding earth, the moving softness strays.
Joyous the impatient husbandman perceives
35   Relenting Nature, and his lusty steers
Drives from their stalls to where the well-used plow
Lies in the furrow loosened from the frost.
There, unrefusing, to the harnessed yoke
They lend their shoulder, and begin their toil,
40   Cheered by the simple song and soaring lark.
Meanwhile incumbent o'er the shining share
The master leans, removes the obstructing clay,
Winds the whole work, and sidelong lays the glebe.³
        White through the neighboring fields the sower stalks
45   With measured step, and liberal throws the grain
Into the faithful bosom of the ground:
The harrow follows harsh, and shuts the scene.
        Be gracious, Heaven, for now laborious man
Has done his part. Ye fostering breezes, blow;
50   Ye softening dews, ye tender showers, descend;
And temper all, thou world-reviving sun,
Into the perfect year. Nor, ye who live
In luxury and ease, in pomp and pride,
Think these lost themes unworthy of your ear:
55   Such themes as these the rural Maro⁴ sung
To wide-imperial Rome, in the full height
Of elegance and taste, by Greece refined.
In ancient times the sacred plow employed
The kings and awful fathers of mankind;
60   And some, with whom compared your insect-tribes
Are but the beings of a summer's day,
Have held the scale of empire, ruled the storm
Of mighty war; then, with victorious hand,
Disdaining little delicacies seized
65   The plow, and, greatly independent, scorned
All the vile stores Corruption can bestow.

3. Earth or field.

4. Virgil, the great Roman poet, who wrote extensively of rural life.

Ye generous Britons, venerate the plow;
And o'er your hills, and long withdrawing vales,
Let Autumn spread his treasures to the sun,
70   Luxuriant and unbounded: as the sea,
Far through his azure turbulent domain,
Your empire owns, and from a thousand shores
Wafts all the pomp of life into your ports;
So with superior boon may your rich soil,
75   Exuberant, Nature's better blessings pour
O'er every land, the naked nations clothe,
And be the exhaustless granary of a world!
   Nor only through the lenient air this change,
Delicious, breathes; the penetrative sun,
80   His force deep-darting to the dark retreat
Of vegetation, sets the steaming Power
At large, to wander o'er the vernant earth,
In various hues; but chiefly thee, gay green,
Thou smiling Nature's universal robe!
85   United light and shade! where the sight dwells
With growing strength and ever-new delight.
   From the moist meadow to the withered hill,
Led by the breeze, the vivid verdure runs,
And swells, and deepens, to the cherished eye.
90   The hawthorn whitens; and the juicy groves
Put forth their buds, unfolding by degrees,
Till the whole leafy forest stands displayed
In full luxuriance to the sighing gales—
Where the deer rustle through the twining brake,
95   And the birds sing concealed. At once arrayed
In all the colors of the flushing year
By Nature's swift and secret-working hand,
The garden glows, and fills the liberal air
With lavish fragrance; while the promised fruit
100 Lies yet a little embryo, unperceived,
Within its crimson folds. Now from the town,
Buried in smoke and sleep and noisome damps,
Oft let me wander o'er the dewy fields
Where freshness breathes, and dash the trembling drops
105 From the bent bush, as through the verdant maze
Of sweetbriar hedges I pursue my walk;
Or taste the smell of dairy; or ascend
Some eminence, Augusta,[5] in thy plains,
And see the country, far diffused around,
110 One boundless blush, one white-empurpled shower
Of mingled blossoms; where the raptured eye
Hurries from joy to joy, and, hid beneath
The fair profusion, yellow Autumn spies.
   If, brushed from Russian wilds, a cutting gale
115 Rise not, and scatter from his humid wings
The clammy mildew; or, dry-blowing, breathe
Untimely frost—before whose baleful blast
The full-blown Spring through all her foliage shrinks,
Joyless and dead, a wide-dejected waste.
120 For oft, engendered by the hazy north,
Myriads on myriads, insect armies waft
Keen in the poisoned breeze, and wasteful eat
Through buds and bark into the blackened core
Their eager way. A feeble race, yet oft
125 The sacred sons of vengeance, on whose course
Corrosive famine waits, and kills the year.
To check this plague, the skilful farmer chaff

5. London.

And blazing straw before his orchard burns;
Till, all involved in smoke, the latent foe
130 From every cranny suffocated falls;
Or scatters o'er the blooms the pungent dust
Of pepper, fatal to the frosty tribe;
Or, when the envenomed leaf begins to curl,
With sprinkled water drowns them in their nest:
135 Nor, while they pick them up with busy bill,
The little trooping birds unwisely scares.
 Be patient, swains; these cruel-seeming winds
Blow not in vain. Far hence they keep repressed
Those deepening clouds on clouds, surcharged with rain,
140 That o'er the vast Atlantic hither borne
In endless train would quench the Summer blaze,
And cheerless drown the crude unripened year.
 The North-east spends his rage, and now shut up
Within his iron caves, the effusive South
145 Warms the wide air, and o'er the void of heaven
Breathes the big clouds with vernal showers distent.
At first a dusky wreath they seem to rise,
Scarce staining ether; but by fast degrees,
In heaps on heaps the doubling vapor sails
150 Along the loaded sky, and mingling deep
Sits on the horizon round a settled gloom;
Not such as wintry storms on mortals shed,
Oppressing life; but lovely, gentle, kind,
And full of every hope and every joy,
155 The wish of Nature. Gradual sinks the breeze
Into a perfect calm; that not a breath
Is heard to quiver through the closing woods,
Or rustling turn the many-twinkling leaves
Of aspen tall. The uncurling floods, diffused
160 In glassy breadth, seem through delusive lapse
Forgetful of their course. 'Tis silence all,
And pleasing expectation. Herds and flocks
Drop the dry sprig, and mute-imploring eye
The falling verdure. Hushed in short suspense,
165 The plumy people streak their wings with oil
To throw the lucid moisture trickling off,
And wait the approaching sign to strike at once
Into the general choir. Even mountains, vales,
And forests seem, impatient, to demand
170 The promised sweetness. Man superior walks
Amid the glad creation, musing praise
And looking lively gratitude. At last
The clouds consign their treasures to the fields,
And, softly shaking on the dimpled pool
175 Prelusive drops, let all their moisture flow,
In large effusion o'er the freshened world.
The stealing shower is scarce to patter heard
By such as wander through the forest walks,
Beneath the umbrageous multitude of leaves.
180 But who can hold the shade while Heaven descends
In universal bounty, shedding herbs
And fruits and flowers on Nature's ample lap?
Swift fancy fired anticipates their growth;
And, while the milky nutriment distils,
185 Beholds the kindling country color round.
 Thus all day long the full-distended clouds
Indulge their genial stores, and well-showered earth
Is deep enriched with vegetable life;
Till, in the western sky, the downward sun
190 Looks out effulgent from amid the flush

Of broken clouds, gay-shifting to his beam.
The rapid radiance instantaneous strikes
The illumined mountain, through the forest streams,
Shakes on the floods, and in the yellow mist,
195   Far smoking o'er the interminable plain,
In twinkling myriads lights the dewy gems.
Moist, bright, and green, the landscape laughs around.
Full swell the woods; their every music wakes,
Mixed in wild concert, with the warbling brooks
200   Increased, the distant bleatings of the hills,
The hollow lows responsive from the vales,
Whence, blending all, the sweetened zephyr springs.
Meantime, refracted from yon eastern cloud,
Bestriding earth, the grand ethereal bow
205   Shoots up immense; and every hue unfolds
In fair proportion running from the red
To where the violet fades into the sky.
Here, awful Newton, the dissolving clouds
Form, fronting on the sun, thy showery prism;
210   And to the sage-instructed eye unfold
The various twine of light, by thee disclosed
From the white mingling maze. Not so the swain;
He wondering views the bright enchantment bend
Delightful o'er the radiant fields, and runs
215   To catch the falling glory; but amazed
Beholds the amusive[6] arch before him fly,
Then vanish quite away. Still night succeeds,
A softened shade, and saturated earth
Awaits the morning beam, to give to light,
220   Raised through ten thousand different plastic tubes,
The balmy treasures of the former day.
    Then spring the living herbs, profusely wild,
O'er all the deep-green earth, beyond the power
Of botanist to number up their tribes:
225   Whether he steals along the lonely dale
In silent search; or through the forest, rank
With what the dull incurious weeds account,
Bursts his blind way; or climbs the mountain rock,
Fired by the nodding verdure of its brow.
230   With such a liberal hand has Nature flung
Their seeds abroad, blown them about in winds,
Innumerous mixed them with the nursing mold,
The moistening current, and prolific rain.
                    *   *   *
    Now, when the first foul torrent of the brooks,
380   Swelled with the vernal rains, is ebbed away,
And whitening down their mossy-tinctured stream
Descends the billowy foam; now is the time,
While yet the dark-brown water aids the guile,
To tempt the trout. The well-dissembled fly,
385   The rod fine-tapering with elastic spring,
Snatched from the hoary steed the floating line,
And all thy slender watery stores prepare.
But let not on thy hook the tortured worm
Convulsive twist in agonizing folds;
390   Which, by rapacious hunger swallowed deep,
Gives, as you tear it from the bleeding breast
Of the weak helpless uncomplaining wretch,
Harsh pain and horror to the tender hand.
    When with his lively ray the potent sun
395   Has pierced the streams and roused the finny race,

6. Illusory.

Then, issuing cheerful, to thy sport repair;
Chief should the western breezes curling play,
And light o'er ether bear the shadowy clouds.
High to their fount, this day, amid the hills
400 And woodlands warbling round, trace up the brooks;
The next, pursue their rocky-channelled maze,
Down to the river, in whose ample wave
Their little naiads love to sport at large.
Just in the dubious point where with the pool
405 Is mixed the trembling stream, or where it boils
Around the stone, or from the hollowed bank
Reverted plays in undulating flow,
There throw, nice-judging, the delusive fly;
And, as you lead it round in artful curve,
410 With eye attentive mark the springing game.
Straight as above the surface of the flood
They wanton rise, or urged by hunger leap,
Then fix with gentle twitch the barbèd hook—
Some lightly tossing to the grassy bank,
415 And to the shelving shore slow-dragging some,
With various hand proportioned to their force.
If, yet too young and easily deceived,
A worthless prey scarce bends your pliant rod,
Him, piteous of his youth and the short space
420 He has enjoyed the vital light of heaven,
Soft disengage, and back into the stream
The speckled infant throw. But, should you lure
From his dark haunt beneath the tangled roots
Of pendent trees the monarch of the brook,
425 Behoves you then to ply your finest art.
Long time he, following cautious, scans the fly,
And oft attempts to seize it, but as oft
The dimpled water speaks his jealous fear.
At last, while haply o'er the shaded sun
430 Passes a cloud, he desperate takes the death
With sullen plunge. At once he darts along,
Deep-struck, and runs out all the lengthened line;
Then seeks the farthest ooze, the sheltering weed,
The caverned bank, his old secure abode;
435 And flies aloft, and flounces round the pool,
Indignant of the guile. With yielding hand,
That feels him still, yet to his furious course
Gives way, you, now retiring, following now
Across the stream, exhaust his idle rage;
440 Till floating broad upon his breathless side,
And to his fate abandoned, to the shore
You gaily drag your unresisting prize.
   Thus pass the temperate hours: but when the sun
Shakes from his noon-day throne the scattering clouds,
445 Even shooting listless languor through the deeps,
Then seek the bank where flowering elders crowd,
Where scattered wild the lily of the vale
Its balmy essence breathes, where cowslips hang
The dewy head, where purple violets lurk,
450 With all the lowly children of the shade;
Or lie reclined beneath yon spreading ash,
Hung o'er the steep, whence, borne on liquid wing,
The sounding culver[7] shoots, or where the hawk,
High in the beetling cliff, his eyry[8] builds.
455 There let the classic page thy fancy lead

---

7. Wood pigeon.   8. "Eyrie": an eagle's nest.

Through rural scenes, such as the Mantuan swain[9]
Paints in the matchless harmony of song;
Or catch thyself the landscape, gliding swift
Athwart imagination's vivid eye;
460   Or by the vocal woods and waters lulled,
And lost in lonely musing, in a dream,
Confused of careless solitude, where mix
Ten thousand wandering images of things,
Soothe every gust of passion into peace—
465   All but the swellings of the softened heart,
That waken, not disturb, the tranquil mind.
Behold yon breathing prospect bids the muse
Throw all her beauty forth. But who can paint
Like Nature? Can imagination boast,
470   Amid its gay creation, hues like hers?
Or can it mix them with that matchless skill,
And lose them in each other, as appears
In every bud that blows? If fancy then
Unequal fails beneath the pleasing task,
475   Ah, what shall language do? Ah, where find words
Tinged with so many colors and whose power,
To life approaching, may perfume my lays
With that fine oil, those aromatic gales,
That inexhaustive flow continual round?
480   Yet, though successless, will the toil delight.
Come then, ye virgins and ye youths, whose hearts
Have felt the raptures of refining love;
And thou, Amanda,[10] come, pride of my song!
Formed by the Graces, loveliness itself!
485   Come with those downcast eyes, sedate and sweet,
Those looks demure that deeply pierce the soul,
Where, with the light of thoughtful reason mixed,
Shines lively fancy and the feeling heart:
Oh come! and while the rosy-footed May
490   Steals blushing on, together let us tread
The morning dews, and gather in their prime
Fresh-blooming flowers to grace thy braided hair
And thy loved bosom, that improves their sweets....

SAMUEL JOHNSON (1709–84)

The Young Author[1]

When first the peasant, long inclined to roam,
Forsakes his rural seats and peaceful home,
Charmed with the scene the smiling ocean yields,
He scorns the flow'ry vales and verdant fields;
5   Jocund he dances o'er the wat'ry way,
While the breeze whispers and the streamers play.
Joys insincere! thick clouds invade the skies,
Loud roars the tempest, high the billows rise,
Sick'ning with fear he longs to view the shore,
10   And vows to trust the faithless deep no more.
So the young author panting for a name,
And fired with pleasing hope of endless fame,
Entrusts his happiness to humankind,

---

9. Virgil, who was born in Mantua.
10. Elizabeth Young, with whom Thomson was in love.

1. First published in *The Gentleman's Magazine* in 1743,

"The Young Author" was probably written as early as 1729 when Johnson prematurely left Oxford. The poem anticipates (and invites comparison with) the passage on the scholar's life in *The Vanity of Human Wishes*.

More false, more cruel than the seas and wind.
15 "Toil on, dull crowd," in ecstasy he cries,
"For wealth or title, perishable prize;
While I these transitory blessings scorn,
Secure of praise from nations yet unborn."
This thought once formed, all counsel comes too late,
20 He plies the press, and hurries on his fate;
Swiftly he sees the imagined laurels spread,
He feels th' unfading wreath surround his head;
Warned by another's fate, vain youth, be wise,
These dreams were Settle's once and Ogilby's.[2]
25 The pamphlet[3] spreads, incessant hisses rise,
To some retreat the baffled writer flies,
Where no sour critics damn, nor sneers molest,
Safe from the keen lampoon and stinging jest;
There begs of heav'n a less distinguished lot;
30 Glad to be hid, and proud to be forgot.

The Vanity of Human Wishes[1]

Let observation with extensive view,
Survey mankind, from China to Peru;
Remark each anxious toil, each eager strife,
And watch the busy scenes of crowded life;
5 Then say how hope and fear, desire and hate,
O'erspread with snares the clouded maze of fate,
Where wav'ring man, betrayed by vent'rous pride,
To tread the dreary paths without a guide,
As treach'rous phantoms in the mist delude,
10 Shuns fancied ills, or chases airy good;
How rarely reason guides the stubborn choice,
Rules the bold hand, or prompts the suppliant voice;
How nations sink, by darling schemes oppressed,
When vengeance listens to the fool's request.
15 Fate wings with every wish th'afflictive dart,
Each gift of nature, and each grace of art,
With fatal heat impetuous courage glows,
With fatal sweetness elocution flows,
Impeachment stops the speaker's pow'rful breath,
20 And restless fire precipitates on death.
But scarce observed, the knowing and the bold
Fall in the gen'ral massacre of gold;
Wide-wasting pest! that rages unconfined,
And crowds with crimes the records of mankind;
25 For gold his sword the hireling ruffian draws,
For gold the hireling judge distorts the laws;
Wealth heaped on wealth, nor truth nor safety buys,
The dangers gather as the treasures rise.
Let hist'ry tell where rival kings command,
30 And dubious title shakes the madded land,
When statutes glean the refuse of the sword,
How much more safe the vassal than the lord;
Low skulks the hind[2] beneath the rage of pow'r,
And leaves the wealthy traitor in the Tow'r,

2. "Settle": Elkanah Settle, a minor poet who enjoyed popularity in his youth but who died in poverty and obscurity. "Ogilby": a poet of similar talent and fame.
3. Critical response.

1. *The Vanity of Human Wishes* is an updated imitation of the tenth satire of the famous Roman writer Juvenal, whose work was well known to English readers. "The peculiarity of Juvenal," wrote Johnson in his *Life of*

Dryden, "is a mixture of gaiety and stateliness, of pointed sentences, and declamatory grandeur." These qualities Johnson has managed to re-capture, but there are so many original qualities that *The Vanity of Human Wishes* cannot be considered a mere copy of the tenth satire but a companion to it. Johnson's poem was first published in 1749 and revised in 1755.
2. Farm servant.

35   Untouched his cottage, and his slumbers sound,
       Though confiscation's vultures hover round.
          The needy traveler, serene and gay,
       Walks the wild heath, and sings his toil away.
       Does envy seize thee? crush th' upbraiding joy,
40   Increase his riches and his peace destroy;
       Now fears in dire vicissitude invade,
       The rustling brake[3] alarms, and quiv'ring shade,
       Nor light nor darkness bring his pain relief,
       One shows the plunder, and one hides the thief.
45   Yet still one gen'ral cry the skies assails,
       And gain and grandeur load the tainted gales;[4]
       Few know the toiling statesman's fear or care,
       Th' insidious rival and the gaping heir.
          Once more, Democritus,[5] arise on earth.
50   With cheerful wisdom and instructive mirth,
       See motley life in modern trappings dressed,
       And feed with varied fools th' eternal jest:
       Thou who couldst laugh where want enchained caprice,
       Toil crushed conceit, and man was of a piece;
55   Where wealth unloved without a mourner died,
       And scarce a sycophant was fed by pride;
       Where ne'er was known the form of mock debate,
       Or seen a new-made mayor's unwieldy state;
       Where change of fav'rites made no change of laws,
60   And senates heard before they judged a cause;
       How wouldst thou shake at Britain's modish tribe,
       Dart the quick taunt, and edge the piercing gibe?
       Attentive truth and nature to descry,
       And pierce each scene with philosophic eye.
65   To thee were solemn toys or empty show,
       The robes of pleasure and the veils of woe:
       All aid the farce, and all thy mirth maintain,
       Whose joys are causeless, or whose griefs are vain.
          Such was the scorn that filled the sage's mind,
70   Renewed at every glance on humankind;
       How just that scorn ere yet thy voice declare,
       Search every state, and canvass every pray'r.
          Unnumbered suppliants crowd Preferment's gate,
       Athirst for wealth, and burning to be great;
75   Delusive Fortune hears th' incessant call,
       They mount, they shine, evaporate, and fall.
       On every stage the foes of peace attend,
       Hate dogs their flight, and insult mocks their end.
       Love ends with hope, the sinking statesman's door
80   Pours in the morning worshiper no more;
       For growing names the weekly scribbler[6] lies,
       To growing wealth the dedicator flies,
       From every room descends the painted face,
       That hung the bright Palladium[7] of the place,
85   And smoked in kitchens, or in auctions sold,
       To better features yields the frame of gold;
       For now no more we trace in every line
       Heroic worth, benevolence divine:
       The form distorted justifies the fall,
90   And detestation rids th' indignant wall.
          But will not Britain hear the last appeal,
       Sign her foes' doom, or guard her fav'rites' zeal?
       Through Freedom's sons no more remonstrance rings,

---

3. Thicket or brushwood.
4. Even the air is tainted with greed.
5. Known as the "laughing philosopher," this fifth-

century Greek writer also ridiculed human folly.
6. Weekly political newspapers.
7. The statue of Pallas Athene which safeguarded Troy.

Degrading nobles and controlling kings;
95 Our supple tribes repress their patriot throats,
And ask no questions but the price of votes;
With weekly libels and septennial ale,[8]
Their wish is full to riot and to rail.
    In full-blown dignity, see Wolsey[9] stand,
100 Law in his voice, and fortune in his hand:
To him the church, the realm, their pow'rs consign,
Through him the rays of regal bounty shine,
Turned by his nod the stream of honor flows,
His smile alone security bestows:
105 Still to new heights his restless wishes tow'r,
Claim leads to claim, and pow'r advances pow'r;
Till conquest unresisted ceased to please,
And rights submitted, left him none to seize.
At length his sov'reign frowns—the train of state
110 Mark the keen glance, and watch the sign to hate.
Where'er he turns he meets a stranger's eye,
His suppliants scorn him, and his followers fly;
At once is lost the pride of aweful state,
The golden canopy, the glitt'ring plate,
115 The regal palace, the luxurious board,
The liv'ried army, and the menial lord.
With age, with cares, with maladies oppressed,
He seeks the refuge of monastic rest.
Grief aids disease, remembered folly stings,
120 And his last sighs reproach the faith of kings.
    Speak thou, whose thoughts at humble peace repine,
Shall Wolsey's wealth, with Wolsey's end be thine?
Or liv'st thou now, with safer pride content,
The wisest justice on the banks of Trent?
125 For why did Wolsey near the steeps of fate,
On weak foundations raise th' enormous weight?
Why but to sink beneath misfortune's blow,
With louder ruin to the gulfs below?
    What gave great Villiers[10] to th' assassin's knife,
130 And fixed disease on Harley's closing life?
What murdered Wentworth, and what exiled Hyde,
By kings protected, and to kings allied?
What but their wish indulged in courts to shine,
And pow'r too great to keep, or to resign?
135   When first the college rolls receive his name,
The young enthusiast quits his ease for fame;
Through all his veins the fever of renown
Burns from the strong contagion of the gown;
O'er Bodley's dome[11] his future labors spread,
140 And Bacon's mansion[12] trembles o'er his head.
Are these thy views? proceed, illustrious youth,
And virtue guard thee to the throne of Truth!
Yet should thy soul indulge the gen'rous heat,
Till captive Science yields her last retreat;
145 Should Reason guide thee with her brightest ray,
And pour on misty Doubt resistless day;
Should no false Kindness lure to loose delight,

8. Parliamentary elections were held every seven years;
voters were bribed with food and drink as well as with
money.
9. Cardinal Wolsey (1475–1530) who rose to great power
under Henry VIII but who, when his foreign policies
failed, fell quickly out of favour.
10. L1. 129–31. "Villiers": first Duke of Buckingham
(1592–1628), favourite of James I, was assassinated.
Robert Harley: favourite of Queen Anne, was imprisoned
under George I. Thomas Wentworth: a favourite of
Charles I, was executed under Cromwell. Edward Hyde:
Lord Chancellor under Charles II, was impeached and
fled to France for safety.
11. The Bodleian Library, Oxford.
12. Roger Bacon (1214–94?), Oxford philosopher and sci-
entist. Johnson noted: "There is a tradition, that the study
of Friar Bacon, built on an arch over the bridge (Folly
Bridge), will fall, when a man greater than Bacon shall
pass under it."

Nor Praise relax, nor Difficulty fright;
Should tempting Novelty thy cell refrain,
150 And Sloth effuse her opiate fumes in vain;
Should Beauty blunt on fops her fatal dart,
Nor claim the triumph of a lettered heart;
Should no Disease thy torpid veins invade,
Nor Melancholy's phantoms haunt thy shade;
155 Yet hope not life from grief or danger free,
Nor think the doom of man reversed for thee:
Deign on the passing world to turn thine eyes,
And pause awhile from letters, to be wise;
There mark what ills the scholar's life assail,
160 Toil, envy, want, the patron, and the jail.
See nations slowly wise, and meanly just,
To buried merit raise the tardy bust.
If dreams yet flatter, once again attend,
Hear Lydiat's life, and Galileo's[13] end.
165   Nor deem, when learning her last prize bestows,
The glitt'ring eminence exempt from foes;
See when the vulgar 'scape, despised or awed,
Rebellion's vengeful talons seize on Laud.[14]
From meaner minds, though smaller fines content,
170 The plundered palace or sequestered rent;
Marked out by dangerous parts he meets the shock,
And fatal Learning leads him to the block:
Around his tomb let Art and Genius weep,
But hear his death, ye blockheads, hear and sleep.
175   The festal blazes, the triumphal show,
The ravished standard, and the captive foe,
The senate's thanks, the gazette's pompous tale,
With force resistless o'er the brave prevail.
Such bribes the rapid Greek[15] o'er Asia whirled,
180 For such the steady Romans shook the world;
For such in distant lands the Britons shine,
And stain with blood the Danube or the Rhine;
This pow'r has praise, that virtue scarce can warm,
Till fame supplies the universal charm.
185 Yet Reason frowns on War's unequal game,
Where wasted nations raise a single name,
And mortgaged states their grandsires' wreaths regret,
From age to age in everlasting debt;
Wreaths which at last the dear-bought right convey
190 To rust on medals, or on stones decay.
  On what foundation stands the warrior's pride,
How just his hopes let Swedish Charles[16] decide;
A frame of adamant, a soul of fire,
No dangers fright him, and no labors tire;
195 O'er love, o'er fear, extends his wide domain,
Unconquered lord of pleasure and of pain;
No joys to him pacific scepters yield,
War sounds the trump, he rushes to the field;
Behold surrounding kings their pow'r combine,
200 And one capitulate, and one resign;
Peace courts his hand, but spreads her charms in vain;
"Think nothing gained," he cries, "till nought remain,
On Moscow's walls till Gothic standards fly,

13. "Lydiat": Thomas Lydiat (1572–1646), Oxford mathematician, died in poverty because he supported the Royalist cause. "Galileo" (1564–1642), one of the world's greatest astronomers, was a victim of the Inquisition and lived his last days in seclusion and blindness.
14. William Laud, Archbishop of Canterbury (1573–1645) under Charles I and champion of high-church policies, was executed under Cromwell.
15. Alexander the Great.
16. Charles XII of Sweden (1682–1718), known as the "Alexander of the North," forced Frederick IV of Denmark to "capitulate" and Augustus II of Poland to "resign" (l. 200).

And all be mine beneath the polar sky."
205   The march begins in military state,
And nations on his eye suspended wait;
Stern Famine guards the solitary coast,
And Winter barricades the realms of Frost;
He comes, not want and cold his course delay;—
210   Hide, blushing Glory, hide Pultowa's[17] day:
The vanquished hero leaves his broken bands,
And shows his miseries in distant lands;
Condemned a needy supplicant to wait,
While ladies interpose, and slaves debate.
215   But did not Chance at length her error mend?
Did no subverted empire mark his end?
Did rival monarchs give the fatal wound?
Or hostile millions press him to the ground?
His fall was destined to a barren strand,
220   A petty fortress, and a dubious hand;
He left the name, at which the world grew pale,
To point a moral, or adorn a tale.
    All times their scenes of pompous woes afford,
From Persia's tyrant to Bavaria's lord.[18]
225   In gay hostility, and barb'rous pride,
With half mankind embattled at his side,
Great Xerxes comes to seize the certain prey,
And starves exhausted regions in his way;
Attendant Flatt'ry counts his myriads o'er,
230   Till counted myriads soothe his pride no more;
Fresh praise is tried till madness fires his mind,
The waves he lashes, and enchains the wind;
New pow'rs are claimed, new pow'rs are still bestowed,
Till rude resistance lops the spreading god,
235   The daring Greeks deride the martial show,
And heap their valleys with the gaudy foe;
Th' insulted sea with humbler thoughts he gains,
A single skiff to speed his flight remains;
Th' encumbered oar scarce leaves the dreaded coast
240   Through purple billows and a floating host.
    The bold Bavarian, in a luckless hour,
Tries the dread summits of Cesarean pow'r,
With unexpected legions bursts away,
And sees defenceless realms receive his sway;
245   Short sway! fair Austria spreads her mournful charms,
The queen, the beauty, sets the world in arms;
From hill to hill the beacons' rousing blaze
Spreads wide the hope of plunder and of praise;
The fierce Croatian, and the wild Hussar,
250   And all the sons of ravage crowd the war;
The baffled prince in honor's flattering bloom
Of hasty greatness finds the fatal doom,
His foes' derision, and his subjects' blame,
And steals to death from anguish and from shame.
255   "Enlarge my life with multitude of days,"
In health, in sickness, thus the suppliant prays;
Hides from himself his state, and shuns to know,
That life protracted is protracted woe.
Time hovers o'er, impatient to destroy,
260   And shuts up all the passages of joy:
In vain their gifts the bounteous seasons pour,

17. "Pultowa": where Charles was finally defeated by Peter the Great of Russia in 1709. Charles took refuge in Turkey, but was later killed at the siege of Fredericksten in Norway.

18. "Persia's tyrant": Xerxes, who unsuccessfully invaded Greece in 480 B.C. "Bavaria's lord": Charles Albert of Bavaria caused the War of the Austrian Succession (1740–48).

The fruit autumnal, and the vernal flow'r,
With listless eyes the dotard views the store,
He views, and wonders that they please no more;
265   Now pall the tasteless meats, and joyless wines,
And Luxury with sighs her slave resigns.
Approach, ye minstrels, try the soothing strain,
Diffuse the tuneful lenitives[19] of pain:
No sounds alas would touch th' impervious ear,
270   Though dancing mountains witnessed Orpheus[20] near;
Nor lute nor lyre his feeble pow'rs attend,
Nor sweeter music of a virtuous friend,
But everlasting dictates crowd his tongue,
Perversely grave, or positively wrong.
275   The still returning tale, and ling'ring jest,
Perplex the fawning niece and pampered guest,
While growing hopes scarce awe the gath'ring sneer,
And scarce a legacy can bribe to hear;
The watchful guests still hint the last offence,
280   The daughter's petulance, the son's expense,
Improve his heady rage with treach'rous skill,
And mould his passions till they make his will.
    Unnumbered maladies his joints invade,
Lay siege to life, and press the dire blockade;
285   But unextinguished Avarice still remains,
And dreaded losses aggravate his pains;
He turns, with anxious heart and crippled hands,
His bonds of debt, and mortgages of lands;
Or views his coffers with suspicious eyes,
290   Unlocks his gold, and counts it till he dies.
    But grant, the virtues of a temp'rate prime
Bless with an age exempt from scorn or crime;
An age that melts with unperceived decay,
And glides in modest innocence away;
295   Whose peaceful day Benevolence endears,
Whose night congratulating Conscience cheers;
The gen'ral fav'rite as the gen'ral friend:
Such age there is, and who shall wish its end?
    Yet ev'n on this her load Misfortune flings,
300   To press the weary minutes' flagging wings:
New sorrow rises as the day returns,
A sister sickens, or a daughter mourns.
Now kindred Merit fills the sable bier,
Now lacerated Friendship claims a tear.
305   Year chases year, decay pursues decay,
Still drops some joy from with'ring life away;
New forms arise, and diff'rent views engage,
Superfluous lags the vet'ran on the stage,
Till pitying Nature sign the last release,
310   And bids afflicted worth retire to peace.
    But few there are whom hours like these await,
Who set unclouded in the gulfs of fate.
From Lydia's monarch[21] should the search descend,
By Solon cautioned to regard his end,
315   In life's last scene what prodigies surprise,
Fears of the brave, and follies of the wise?
From Marlb'rough's eyes the streams of dotage flow,
And Swift[22] expires a driv'ler and a show.

19. Pain-relieving medicines.
20. Mythological poet-musician whose music had the power to move mountains.
21. Croesus, wealthy king of Lydia, was warned by Solon not to consider himself happy until his life was over.
22. Ll. 317–18. "Marlb'rough": the illustrious Duke of Marlborough, one of England's most brilliant soldiers, suffered several strokes before he died. Jonathan Swift became senile in his last years.

The teeming mother, anxious for her race,
320   Begs for each birth the fortune of a face:
Yet Vane could tell what ills from beauty spring;
And Sedley[23] cursed the form that pleased a king.
Ye nymphs of rosy lips and radiant eyes,
Whom Pleasure keeps too busy to be wise,
325   Whom Joys with soft varieties invite,
By day the frolic, and the dance by night,
Who frown with vanity, who smile with art,
And ask the latest fashion of the heart,
What care, what rules your heedless charms shall save,
330   Each nymph your rival, and each youth your slave?
Against your fame with fondness hate combines,
The rival batters, and the lover mines.
With distant voice neglected Virtue calls,
Less heard and less, the faint remonstrance falls;
335   Tired with contempt, she quits the slipp'ry reign,
And Pride and Prudence take her seat in vain.
In crowd at once, where none the pass defend,
The harmless Freedom, and the private friend.
The guardians yield, by force superior plied;
340   By Int'rest, Prudence; and by Flatt'ry, Pride.
Now beauty falls betrayed, despised, distressed,
And hissing Infamy proclaims the rest.
        Where then shall Hope and Fear their objects find?
Must dull Suspense corrupt the stagnant mind?
345   Must helpless man, in ignorance sedate,
Roll darkling down the torrent of his fate?
Must no dislike alarm, no wishes rise,
No cries attempt the mercies of the skies?
Enquirer, cease, petitions yet remain,
350   Which heav'n may hear, nor deem religion vain.
Still raise for good the supplicating voice,
But leave to heav'n the measure and the choice,
Safe in His pow'r, whose eyes discern afar
The secret ambush of a specious pray'r.
355   Implore His aid, in His decisions rest,
Secure whate'er He gives, He gives the best.
Yet when the sense of sacred presence fires,
And strong devotion to the skies aspires,
Pour forth thy fervors for a healthful mind,
360   Obedient passions, and a will resigned;
For love, which scarce collective man can fill;
For patience sov'reign o'er transmuted ill;
For faith, that panting for a happier seat,
Counts death kind Nature's signal of retreat:
365   These goods for man the laws of heav'n ordain,
These goods He grants, who grants the pow'r to gain;
With these celestial wisdom calms the mind,
And makes the happiness she does not find.

---

23. Ll. 321–22. "Vane": Anne Vane (1705–36) was mistress to the Prince of Wales. "Sedley": Catherine Sedley
(1657–1717) was mistress to the Duke of York (later
James II).

THOMAS GRAY (1716–71)

Ode on the Death of a Favourite Cat, Drowned in a Tub of Gold Fishes[1]

'Twas on a lofty vase's side,
Where China's gayest art had dyed
   The azure flowers, that blow;[2]
Demurest of the tabby kind,
5 The pensive Selima reclined,
   Gazed on the lake below.

Her conscious tail her joy declared;
The fair round face, the snowy beard,
   The velvet of her paws,
10 Her coat, that with the tortoise vies,
Her ears of jet, and emerald eyes,
   She saw; and purred applause.

Still had she gazed; but 'midst the tide
Two angel forms were seen to glide,
15   The Genii of the stream:
Their scaly armour's Tyrian hue[3]
Thro' richest purple to the view
   Betrayed a golden gleam.

The hapless Nymph with wonder saw:
20 A whisker first and then a claw,
   With many an ardent wish,
She stretched in vain to reach the prize.
What female heart can gold despise?
   What Cat's averse to fish?

25 Presumptuous Maid! with looks intent
Again she stretched, again she bent,
   Nor knew the gulf between.
(Malignant Fate sat by, and smiled)
The slipp'ry verge her feet beguiled,
30   She tumbled headlong in.

Eight times emerging from the flood
She mewed to every watry God,
   Some speedy aid to send.
No Dolphin came, no Nereid[4] stirred:
35 Nor cruel *Tom*, nor *Susan*[5] heard.
   A Fav'rite has no friend!

From hence, ye Beauties, undeceived,
Know, one false step is ne'er retrieved,
   And be with caution bold.
40 Not all that tempts your wand'ring eyes
And heedless hearts, is lawful prize;
   Nor all, that glisters, gold.

Elegy Written in a Country Church-Yard[1]

The Curfew tolls the knell of parting day,
The lowing herd wind slowly o'er the lea,
The plowman homeward plods his weary way,
And leaves the world to darkness and to me.

5 Now fades the glimmering landscape on the sight,
And all the air a solemn stillness holds,
Save where the beetle wheels his droning flight,
And drowsy tinklings lull the distant folds;

Save that from yonder ivy-mantled tow'r
10 The moping owl does to the moon complain
Of such, as wand'ring near her secret bow'r,
Molest her ancient solitary reign.

---

1. This ode was written in 1747 at the request of Horace Walpole, whose cat (Selima) had drowned in a small water cistern. It was first published in 1748; this version is based on the authoritative *Poems* (1768).
2. Bloom.
3. Purple.
4. Sea nymphs. Beautiful maidens helpful to sailors.

5. "Tom," "Susan": servants.

1. The *Elegy* circulated among Gray's friends for a number of years in manuscript form before being published in 1751. More than thirty editions were printed in his lifetime, the version here being based on the 1768 *Poems*.

Beneath those rugged elms, that yew-tree's shade,
Where heaves the turf in many a mould'ring heap,
15 Each in his narrow cell for ever laid,
The rude[2] Forefathers of the hamlet sleep.

The breezy call of incense-breathing Morn,
The swallow twitt'ring from the straw-built shed,
The cock's shrill clarion, or the echoing horn,
20 No more shall rouse them from their lowly bed.

For them no more the blazing hearth shall burn,
Or busy housewife ply her evening care:
No children run to lisp their sire's return,
Or climb his knees the envied kiss to share.

25 Oft did the harvest to their sickle yield,
Their furrow oft the stubborn glebe[3] has broke;
How jocund did they drive their team afield!
How bow'd the woods beneath their sturdy stroke!

Let not Ambition mock their useful toil,
30 Their homely joys, and destiny obscure;
Nor Grandeur hear with a disdainful smile,
The short and simple annals of the poor.

The boast of heraldry, the pomp of pow'r,
And all that beauty, all that wealth e'er gave,
35 Awaits alike th' inevitable hour.
The paths of glory lead but to the grave.

Nor you, ye Proud, impute to these the fault,
If Memory o'er their Tomb no Trophies raise,
Where thro' the long-drawn isle and fretted[4] vault
40 The pealing anthem swells the note of praise.

Can storied urn or animated bust
Back to its mansion call the fleeting breath?
Can Honour's voice provoke the silent dust,
Or Flatt'ry sooth the dull cold ear of Death?

45 Perhaps in this neglected spot is laid
Some heart once pregnant with celestial fire;
Hands, that the rod of empire might have sway'd,
Or waked to ecstasy the living lyre.

But Knowledge to their eyes her ample page
50 Rich with the spoils of time did ne'er unroll;
Chill Penury repress'd their noble rage,
And froze the genial current of the soul.

Full many a gem of purest ray serene,
The dark unfathomed caves of ocean bear:
55 Full many a flower is born to blush unseen,
And waste its sweetness on the desert air.

Some village-Hampden,[5] that with dauntless breast
The little Tyrant of his fields withstood;
Some mute inglorious Milton here may rest,
60 Some Cromwell guiltless of his country's blood.

2. Uneducated or unsophisticated.
3. Earth or field.
4. Ornamental pattern of straight lines joined at right
angles.

5. John Hampden (1594–1643), a member of the English
parliament who defended both the rights of parliament
and the people against the policies of Charles I.

Th' applause of list'ning senates to command,
The threats of pain and ruin to despise,
To scatter plenty o'er a smiling land,
And read their history in a nation's eyes,

65 Their lot forbad: nor circumscrib'd alone
Their growing virtues, but their crimes confined;
Forbad to wade through slaughter to a throne,
And shut the gates of mercy on mankind,

The struggling pangs of conscious truth to hide,
70 To quench the blushes of ingenuous shame,
Or heap the shrine of Luxury and Pride
With incense kindled at the Muse's flame.

Far from the madding crowd's ignoble strife,
Their sober wishes never learned to stray;
75 Along the cool sequestered vale of life
They kept the noiseless tenor of their way.

Yet ev'n these bones from insult to protect
Some frail memorial still erected nigh,
With uncouth rhymes and shapeless sculpture decked,
80 Implores the passing tribute of a sigh.

Their name, their years, spelt by th' unletter'd muse,
The place of fame and elegy supply:
And many a holy text around she strews,
That teach the rustic moralist to die.

85 For who to dumb Forgetfulness a prey,
This pleasing anxious being e'er resigned,
Left the warm precincts of the cheerful day,
Nor cast one longing ling'ring look behind?

On some fond breast the parting soul relies,
90 Some pious drops the closing eye requires;
Ev'n from the tomb the voice of Nature cries,
Ev'n in our Ashes live their wonted Fires.

For thee, who mindful of th' unhonour'd Dead
Dost in these lines their artless tale relate;
95 If chance, by lonely contemplation led,
Some kindred Spirit shall inquire thy fate,

Haply some hoary-headed Swain may say,
'Oft have we seen him at the peep of dawn
'Brushing with hasty steps the dews away
100 'To meet the sun upon the upland lawn.

'There at the foot of yonder nodding beech
'That wreathes its old fantastic roots so high,
'His listless length at noontide would he stretch,
'And pore upon the brook that babbles by.

105 'Hard by yon wood, now smiling as in scorn,
'Mutt'ring his wayward fancies he would rove,
'Now drooping, woeful wan, like one forlorn,
'Or crazed with care, or crossed in hopeless love.

'One morn I missed him on the customed hill,
110 'Along the heath and near his fav'rite tree;
'Another came; nor yet beside the rill,
'Nor up the lawn, nor at the wood was he;

'The next with dirges due in sad array
'Slow thro' the church-way path we saw him born.
115 'Approach and read (for thou can'st read) the lay,
'Graved on the stone beneath yon aged thorn.'

The Epitaph

*HERE rests his head upon the lap of Earth
A Youth to Fortune and to Fame unknown.
Fair Science frown'd not on his humble birth,*
120 *And Melancholy mark'd him for her own.*

*Large was his bounty, and his soul sincere,
Heav'n did a recompence as largely send:
He gave to Mis'ry all he had, a tear,
He gained from Heav'n ('twas all he wished) a friend.*

125 *No farther seek his merits to disclose,
Or draw his frailties from their dread abode,
(There they alike in trembling hope repose,)
The bosom of his Father and his God.*

Sonnet on the Death of Mr. Richard West[1]

In vain to me the smiling Mornings shine,
And redd'ning Phœbus[2] lifts his golden fire:
The birds in vain their amorous descant join;
Or cheerful fields resume their green attire:
These ears, alas! for other notes repine,
A different object do these eyes require.
My lonely anguish melts no heart but mine,
And in my breast the imperfect joys expire.
Yet Morning smiles the busy race to cheer,
And new-born pleasure brings to happier men:
The fields to all their wonted tribute bear:
To warm their little loves the birds complain:
I fruitless mourn to him, that cannot hear,
And weep the more, because I weep in vain.

WILLIAM COLLINS (1721–59)

Ode on the Poetical Character[1]

Strophe

As once, if not with light regard
I read aright that gifted bard[2]
(Him whose school above the rest
His loveliest Elfin Queen has blest),
5 One, only one, unrivaled fair
Might hope the magic girdle wear,
At solemn tourney hung on high,
The wish of each love-darting eye;
Lo! to each other nymph in turn applied,

1. This sonnet, written in 1742, was published posthumously in Mason's edition of the *Poems* in 1775. Richard West, a promising scholar and close friend of Gray's, died in 1742 at the age of twenty-six.
2. Another name for Apollo, god of the sun, and used here for the sun itself.

1. In the "Ode on the Poetical Character" Collins is imitating the Pindaric form with its three-strophe (stanza) division, in which the *strophe* and *antistrophe* are metrically similar and the *epode* provides a formal contrast and a lull in the emotional pitch. It was published in 1746.
2. Edmund Spenser (1552–99), author of *The Faerie Queene*, in which Florimel owned a magic girdle (the cest of Venus) which only the chaste lover might wear without harm.

10   As if, in air unseen, some hov'ring hand,
Some chaste and angel friend to virgin fame,
With whispered spell had burst the starting band,
It left unblest her loathed, dishonored side;
Happier hopeless fair, if never
15   Her baffled hand with vain endeavor
Had touched that fatal zone to her denied!
Young Fancy thus, to me divinest name,[3]
To whom, prepared and bathed in heav'n,
The cest of amplest pow'r is giv'n,
20   To few the godlike gift assigns,
To gird their blest, prophetic loins,
And gaze[4] her visions wild, and feel unmixed her flame!

Epode

The band, as fairy legends say,
Was wove on that creating day
25   When He who called with thought to birth
Yon tented sky, this laughing earth,
And dressed with springs and forests tall,
And poured the main engirting all,
Long by the loved enthusiast[5] wooed,
30   Himself in some diviner mood,
Retiring, sat with her alone,
And placed her on his sapphire throne,
The whiles, the vaulted shrine around,
Seraphic wires were heard to sound,
35   Now sublimest triumph swelling,
Now on love and mercy dwelling;
And she, from out the veiling cloud,
Breathed her magic notes aloud:
And thou, thou rich-haired Youth of Morn,[6]
40   And all thy subject life, was born!
The dang'rous Passions kept aloof,
Far from the sainted growing woof:
But near it sat ecstatic Wonder,
List'ning the deep applauding thunder;
45   And Truth, in sunny vest arrayed,
By whose the tarsel's[7] eyes were made;
All the shad'wy tribes of mind
In braided dance their murmurs joined,
And all the bright uncounted Pow'rs
50   Who feed on heav'n's ambrosial flow'rs.
Where is the bard whose soul can now
Its high presuming hopes avow?
Where he who thinks, with rapture blind,
This hallowed work for him designed?

Antistrophe

55   High on some cliff, to heav'n up-piled,
Of rude access, of prospect wild,
Where, tangled round the jealous steep,
Strange shades o'er-brow the valleys deep,
And holy genii guard the rock,
60   Its glooms embrown, its springs unlock,
While on its rich ambitious head
An Eden, like his[8] own, lies spread,

---

3. Imagination (fancy) was, for Collins, the supreme
poetic faculty.
4. Gaze on.
5. Poetic inspiration or fancy.

6. Apollo, god of the sun and poetry.
7. "tarsel": male hawk.
8. Milton's. The scene described is reminiscent of that in
Paradise Lost IV, 130 ff.

I view that oak, the fancied glades[9] among,
By which as Milton lay, his ev'ning ear,
65   From many a cloud that dropped ethereal dew,
Nigh sphered in heav'n its native strains could hear,
On which that ancient trump he reached was hung:
     Thither oft, his glory greeting,
     From Waller's[10] myrtle shades retreating,
70   With many a vow from Hope's aspiring tongue,
My trembling feet his guiding steps pursue;
     In vain— such bliss to one alone[11]
     Of all the sons of soul was known,
     And Heav'n and Fancy, kindred pow'rs,
75   Have now o'erturned th' inspiring bow'rs,
Or curtained close such scene from ev'ry future view.

Ode Written in the Beginning of the Year 1746[1]

How sleep the brave who sink to rest
By all their country's wishes blessed!
When Spring, with dewy fingers cold,
Returns to deck their hallowed mold,
She there shall dress a sweeter sod
Than Fancy's feet have ever trod.

By fairy hands their knell is rung,
By forms unseen their dirge is sung;
There Honor comes, a pilgrim grey,
To bless the turf that wraps their clay;
And freedom shall awhile repair,
To dwell a weeping hermit there!

Ode to Evening

If ought of oaten stop,[1] or pastoral song,
May hope, chaste Eve, to soothe thy modest ear,
     Like thy own solemn springs,
     Thy springs and dying gales,

5   O nymph reserved, while now the bright-haired sun
Sits in yon western tent, whose cloudy skirts,
     With brede[2] ethereal wove,
     O'erhang his wavy bed:

Now air is hushed, save where the weak-eyed bat,
10   With short shrill shriek, flits by on leathern wing.
     Or where the beetle winds
     His small but sullen horn,

As oft he rises 'midst the twilight path,
Against the pilgrim borne in heedless hum:
15   Now teach me, maid composed,
     To breathe some softened strain,

Whose numbers, stealing through thy dark'ning vale,
May not unseemly with its stillness suit,
     As, musing slow, I hail
20   Thy genial loved return!

---

9. A reference to Milton's "Il Penseroso," ll. 60–64. See also *Paradise Lost* II, 26 ff.
10. "Waller": Edmund Waller (1606–87), whose secular love poetry (represented by the myrtle) is considered trifling compared to Milton's.
11. Milton alone wears the magic girdle and can have no successor.

1. This "Ode" was, according to its title, probably written after the Battle of Falkirk (17 January 1746) during the war between the English and the Scots Jacobites (under Bonnie Prince Charlie). The absence of specific references, however, implies that Collins wished the poem to be read not as a commemorative one but as a poem of grief "recollected in tranquillity."

1. Literally, the hole in the shepherd's pipe, but here referring to pastoral music.
2. Braid or embroidery.

For when thy folding-star[3] arising shows
His paly circlet, at his warning lamp
   The fragrant Hours, and elves
   Who slept in flow'rs the day,

25   And many a nymph who wreathes her brows with sedge,
And sheds the fresh'ning dew, and, lovelier still,
   The pensive Pleasures sweet,
   Prepare thy shadowy car.

Then lead, calm vot'ress, where some sheety lake
30   Cheers the lone heath, or some time-hallowed pile
   Or upland fallows grey
   Reflect its last cool gleam.

But when chill blust'ring winds, or driving rain,
Forbid my willing feet, be mine the hut
35   That from the mountain's side
   Views wilds, and swelling floods,

And hamlets brown, and dim-discovered spires,
And hears their simple bell, and marks o'er all
   Thy dewy fingers draw
40   The gradual dusky veil.

While Spring shall pour his show'rs, as oft he wont,
And bathe thy breathing[4] tresses, meekest Eve;
   While Summer loves to sport
   Beneath thy ling'ring light;

45   While sallow Autumn fills thy lap with leaves;
Or Winter, yelling through the troublous air,
   Affrights thy shrinking train
   And rudely rends thy robes;

So long, sure-found beneath the sylvan shed,
50   Shall Fancy, Friendship, Science, rose-lipped Health,
   Thy gentlest influence own,
   And hymn thy fav'rite name!

OLIVER GOLDSMITH (1728–74)

The Deserted Village[1]

Sweet AUBURN, loveliest village of the plain,[2]
   Where health and plenty cheered the labouring swain,
Where smiling spring its earliest visit paid,
And parting summer's lingering blooms delayed,
5   Dear lovely bowers of innocence and ease,

---

3. Evening star, which rises when the sheep return to the folds.
4. Giving off fragrance.

1. The publication of *The Deserted Village* was advertised in the *Public Advertiser* (London) on 16 November 1769; it appeared on 26 May 1770 as a quarto pamphlet and sold for two shillings. Five other editions of the poem were also published in 1770, the second and fourth of which were revised by the author. The text printed here is that of the fourth edition (1770), the last to be revised by Goldsmith; several of the major changes are noted.

2. The prototype of Goldsmith's village, if there was one, has been the subject of much speculation, most favouring the town of Lissoy, Ireland, where Goldsmith spent his youth. It is, however, entirely unnecessary for the reader to indulge in such speculation (this applies also to the identity of the people in the poem), for Goldsmith was concerned to show that Auburn was not one but many small villages, and his people not a few but representative of many who suffered at the hands of country noblemen who displaced them to create vast private parks or landscape gardens.

Seats of my youth, when every sport could please,
How often have I loitered o'er thy green,
Where humble happiness endeared each scene;
How often have I paused on every charm,
10   The sheltered cot, the cultivated farm,
The never failing brook, the busy mill,
The decent church that topt the neighbouring hill,
The hawthorn bush, with seats beneath the shade,
For talking age and whispering lovers made.
15   How often have I blest the coming day,
When toil remitting lent its turn to play,
And all the village train from labour free
Led up their sports beneath the spreading tree,
While many a pastime circled in the shade,
20   The young contending as the old surveyed;
And many a gambol frolicked o'er the ground,
And slights[3] of art and feats of strength went round.
And still as each repeated pleasure tired,
Succeeding sports the mirthful band inspired;
25   The dancing pair that simply sought renown
By holding out to tire each other down,
The swain mistrustless of his smutted face,
While secret laughter tittered round the place,
The bashful virgin's side-long looks of love,
30   The matron's glance that would those looks reprove.
These were thy charms, sweet village; sports like these,
With sweet succession, taught even toil to please;
These round thy bowers their cheerful influence shed,
These were thy charms—
But all these charms are fled.

35   Sweet smiling village, loveliest of the lawn,
Thy sports are fled, and all thy charms withdrawn;
Amidst thy bowers the tyrant's hand is seen,
And desolation saddens all thy green:
One only master[4] grasps the whole domain,
40   And half a tillage stints thy smiling plain;
No more thy glassy brook reflects the day,
But choaked with sedges, works its weedy way.
Along thy glades, a solitary guest,
The hollow sounding bittern guards its nest;
45   Amidst thy desert walks the lapwing flies,
And tires their echoes with unvaried cries.
Sunk are thy bowers in shapeless ruin all,
And the long grass o'ertops the mouldering wall,
And trembling, shrinking from the spoiler's hand,
50   Far, far away thy children leave the land.

Ill fares the land, to hastening ills a prey,
Where wealth accumulates, and men decay;
Princes and lords may flourish, or may fade;
A breath can make them, as a breath has made.
55   But a bold peasantry, their country's pride,
When once destroyed, can never be supplied.

---

3. As in sleight-of-hand, juggling, etc.
4. In an essay on "The Revolution in Low Life" (1762), Goldsmith had lamented the "depopulation of the country": "I was informed that a merchant of immense fortune in London, who had lately purchased the estate on which they lived, intended to lay the whole out in a seat of pleasure for himself. . . . I was grieved to see a generous, virtuous race of men, who should be considered as the strength and the ornament of their country, torn from their little habitations." See A. Friedman, ed., *Collected Works of Oliver Goldsmith* (Oxford: Oxford Univ. Press, 1966), III, 196.

A time there was, ere England's griefs began,
When every rood of ground maintained its man;
For him light labour spread her wholesome store,
60   Just gave what life required, but gave no more.
His best companions, innocence and health;
And his best riches, ignorance of wealth.

But times are altered; trade's unfeeling train
Usurp the land and dispossess the swain;
65   Along the lawn, where scattered hamlets rose,
Unwieldy wealth, and cumbrous pomp repose;
And every want to oppulence[5] allied,
And every pang that folly pays to pride.
These gentle hours that plenty bade to bloom,
70   Those calm desires that asked but little room,
Those healthful sports that graced the peaceful scene,
Lived in each look, and brightened all the green;
These far departing seek a kinder shore,
And rural mirth and manners are no more.

75   Sweet AUBURN! parent of the blissful hour,
Thy glades forlorn confess the tyrant's power.
Here as I take my solitary rounds,
Amidst thy tangling walks, and ruined grounds,
And, many a year elapsed, return to view
80   Where once the cottage stood, the hawthorn grew,[6]
Remembrance wakes with all her busy train,
Swells at my breast, and turns the past to pain.

In all my wanderings round this world of care,
In all my griefs— and GOD has given my share—
85   I still had hopes my latest hours to crown,
Amidst these humble bowers to lay me down;
To husband out life's taper at the close,[7]
And keep the flame from wasting by repose.
I still had hopes, for pride attends us still,
90   Amidst the swains to shew my book-learned skill,
Around my fire an evening group to draw,
And tell of all I felt, and all I saw;
And, as an hare whom hounds and horns pursue,
Pants to the place from whence at first she flew,
95   I still had hopes, my long vexations past,
Here to return— and die at home at last.

O blest retirement, friend to life's decline,
Retreats from care that never must be mine,
How happy he who crowns in shades like these,
100   A youth of labour with an age of ease;
Who quits a world where strong temptations try,
And, since 'tis hard to combat, learns to fly.
For him no wretches, born to work and weep,
Explore the mine, or tempt the dangerous deep;
105   No surly porter stands in guilty state
To spurn imploring famine from the gate,
But on he moves to meet his latter end,
Angels around befriending virtue's friend;
Bends to the grave with unperceived decay,
110   While resignation gently slopes the way;
And all his prospects brightening to the last,
His Heaven commences ere the world be past!

5. The first edition reads "luxury."
6. In editions 1–3, the following two lines came between 80 and 81: "Here, as with doubtful, pensive steps I range, / Trace every scene, and wonder at the change."
7. In editions 1–3 this line less artfully reads: "My anxious day to husband near the close."

Sweet was the sound when oft at evening's close,
Up yonder hill the village murmur rose;
115 There as I past with careless steps and slow,
The mingling notes came softened from below;
The swain responsive as the milk-maid sung,
The sober herd that lowed to meet their young;
The noisy geese that gabbled o'er the pool,
120 The playful children just let loose from school;
The watch-dog's voice that bayed the whispering wind,
And the loud laugh that spoke the vacant[8] mind,
These all in sweet confusion sought the shade,
And filled each pause the nightingale had made.
125 But now the sounds of population fail,
No cheerful murmurs fluctuate in the gale,
No busy steps the grass-grown foot-way tread,
For all the bloomy flush of life is fled.
All but yon widowed, solitary thing
130 That feebly bends beside the plashy[9] spring;
She, wretched matron, forced, in age, for bread,
To strip the brook with mantling cresses spread,
To pick her wintry faggot from the thorn,
To seek her nightly shed, and weep till morn;
135 She only left of all the harmless train,
The sad historian of the pensive plain.

Near yonder copse, where once the garden smil'd,
And still where many a garden flower grows wild;
There, where a few torn shrubs the place disclose,
140 The village preacher's modest mansion rose.
A man he was, to all the country dear,
And passing rich with forty pounds a year;
Remote from towns he ran his godly race,
Nor ere had changed, nor wish'd to change his place;
145 Unpractised he to fawn, or seek for power,
By doctrines fashioned to the varying hour;
Far other aims his heart had learned to prize,
More skilled to raise the wretched than to rise.
His house was known to all the vagrant train,
150 He chid their wanderings, but relieved their pain;
The long remembered beggar was his guest,
Whose beard descending swept his aged breast;
The ruined spendthrift, now no longer proud,
Claimed kindred there, and had his claims allowed;
155 The broken soldier, kindly bade to stay,
Sat by his fire, and talked the night away;
Wept o'er his wounds, or tales of sorrow done,
Shouldered his crutch, and shewed how fields were won.
Pleased with his guests, the good man learned to glow,
160 And quite forgot their vices in their woe;
Careless their merits, or their faults to scan,
His pity gave ere charity began.

Thus to relieve the wretched was his pride,
And even his failings leaned to Virtue's side;
165 But in his duty prompt at every call,
He watched and wept, he prayed and felt, for all.
And, as a bird each fond endearment tries,
To tempt its new fledged offspring to the skies;
He tried each art, reproved each dull delay,
170 Allured to brighter worlds, and led the way.

8. Carefree or not rationally occupied; see l. 257.   9. Splashing.

Beside the bed where parting life was layed,
And sorrow, guilt, and pain, by turns dismayed,
The reverend champion stood. At his control,
Despair and anguish fled the struggling soul;
175   Comfort came down the trembling wretch to raise,
And his last faultering accents whispered praise.

At church, with meek and unaffected grace,
His looks adorned the venerable place;
Truth from his lips prevailed with double sway,
180   And fools, who came to scoff, remained to pray.
The service past, around the pious man,
With steady zeal each honest rustic ran;
Even children followed with endearing wile,
And plucked his gown, to share the good man's smile.
185   His ready smile a parent's warmth exprest,
Their welfare pleased him, and their cares distrest;
To them his heart, his love, his griefs were given,
But all his serious thoughts had rest in Heaven.
As some tall cliff that lifts its awful form
190   Swells from the vale, and midway leaves the storm,
Tho' round its breast the rolling clouds are spread,
Eternal sunshine settles on its head.

Beside yon straggling fence that skirts the way,
With blossomed furze unprofitably gay,
195   There, in his noisy mansion, skill'd to rule,
The village master taught his little school;
A man severe he was, and stern to view,
I knew him well, and every truant knew;
Well had the boding tremblers learned to trace
200   The day's disasters in his morning face;
Full well they laugh'd with counterfeited glee,
At all his jokes, for many a joke had he;
Full well the busy whisper circling round,
Conveyed the dismal tidings when he frowned;
205   Yet he was kind, or if severe in aught,
The love he bore to learning was in fault;
The village all declared how much he knew;
'Twas certain he could write, and cypher too;
Lands he could measure, terms and tides presage,[10]
210   And even the story ran that he could gauge.[11]
In arguing too, the parson owned his skill,
For even tho' vanquished, he could argue still;
While words of learned length, and thundering sound,
Amazed the gazing rustics ranged around,
215   And still they gazed, and still the wonder grew,
That one small head could carry all he knew.

But past is all his fame. The very spot
Where many a time he triumphed, is forgot.
Near yonder thorn, that lifts its head on high,
220   Where once the sign-post caught the passing eye,
Low lies that house where nut-brown draughts inspired,
Where grey-beard mirth and smiling toil retired,
Where village statesmen talked with looks profound,
And news much older than their ale went round.
225   Imagination fondly stoops to trace
The parlour splendours of that festive place;
The white-washed wall, the nicely sanded floor,
The varnished clock that clicked behind the door;

10. Could keep the uneducated farmers informed of their
contract terms (rents and leases) and of the seasons of the
Church calendar such as Whitsuntide and Christmastide.
11. Measure the contents of barrels and casks.

The chest contrived a double debt to pay,
230   A bed by night, a chest of drawers by day;
The pictures placed for ornament and use,
The twelve good rules, the royal game of goose;[12]
The hearth, except when winter chill'd the day,
With aspen boughs, and flowers, and fennel gay,
235   While broken tea-cups, wisely kept for shew,
Ranged o'er the chimney, glistened in a row.

    Vain transitory splendours! Could not all
Reprieve the tottering mansion from its fall!
Obscure it sinks, nor shall it more impart
240   An hour's importance to the poor man's heart;
Thither no more the peasant shall repair
To sweet oblivion of his daily care;
No more the farmer's news, the barber's tale,
No more the wood-man's ballad shall prevail;
245   No more the smith his dusky brow shall clear,
Relax his ponderous strength, and lean to hear;
The host himself no longer shall be found
Careful to see the mantling[13] bliss go round;
Nor the coy maid, half willing to be prest,
250   Shall kiss the cup to pass it to the rest.

    Yes! let the rich deride, the proud disdain,
These simple blessings of the lowly train,
To me more dear, congenial to my heart,
One native charm, than all the gloss of art;
255   Spontaneous joys, where Nature has its play,[14]
The soul adopts, and owns their first born sway,
Lightly they frolic o'er the vacant mind,
Unenvied, unmolested, unconfined.
But the long pomp, the midnight masquerade,
260   With all the freaks of wanton wealth arrayed,
In these, ere trifflers half their wish obtain,
The toiling pleasure sickens into pain;
And, even while fashion's brightest arts decoy,
The heart distrusting asks, if this be joy.

265   Ye friends to truth, ye statesmen who survey
The rich man's joys encrease, the poor's decay,
'Tis yours to judge, how wide the limits stand
Between a splendid and an happy land.
Proud swells the tide with loads of freighted ore,
270   And shouting Folly hails them from her shore;
Hoards, even beyond the miser's wish abound,
And rich men flock from all the world around.
Yet count our gains. This wealth is but a name
That leaves our useful products still the same.
275   Not so the loss. The man of wealth and pride,
Takes up a space that many poor supplied;
Space for his lake, his park's extended bounds,
Space for his horses, equipage, and hounds;
The robe that wraps his limbs in silken sloth,
280   Has robbed the neighbouring fields of half their growth;
His seat, where solitary sports are seen,
Indignant spurns the cottage from the green;
Around the world each needful product flies,

---

12. "rules": rules of good conduct promulgated by Charles I, often hung on the walls of taverns; "goose": a board game played with dice and counters, similar to snakes-and-ladders.
13. Foamy ale.

14. In "A Lady of Fashion" (1760) Goldsmith wrote: "Happy they who pursue pleasure as far as Nature directs, and no farther; pleasure rightly understood, and prudently followed, is but another name for virtue" (Friedman, *Collected Works*, II, 149).

For all the luxuries the world supplies.
285 While thus the land adorned for pleasure all
In barren splendour feebly waits the fall.

As some fair female unadorned and plain,
Secure to please while youth confirms her reign,
Slights every borrowed charm that dress supplies,
290 Nor shares with art the triumph of her eyes.
But when those charms are past, for charms are frail,
When time advances, and when lovers fail,
She then shines forth sollicitous to bless,
In all the glaring impotence of dress.
295 Thus fares the land, by luxury betrayed,
In nature's simplest charms at first arrayed,
But verging to decline, its splendours rise,
Its vistas strike, its palaces surprize;
While scourged by famine from the smiling land,
300 The mournful peasant leads his humble band;
And while he sinks without one arm to save,
The country blooms—a garden, and a grave.

Where then, ah, where shall poverty reside,
To scape the pressure of contiguous pride;
305 If to some common's fenceless limits strayed,
He drives his flock to pick the scanty blade,
Those fenceless fields the sons of wealth divide,
And even the bare-worn common is denied.

If to the city sped—What waits him there?
310 To see profusion that he must not share;
To see ten thousand baneful arts combined
To pamper luxury, and thin mankind;
To see those joys the sons of pleasure know,
Extorted from his fellow-creature's woe.
315 Here, while the courtier glitters in brocade,
There the pale artist plies the sickly trade;
Here, while the proud their long drawn pomps display,
There the black gibbet glooms beside the way.[15]
The dome where pleasure holds her midnight reign,
320 Here richly deckt admits the gorgeous train,
Tumultuous grandeur crowds the blazing square,
The rattling chariots clash, the torches glare;
Sure scenes like these no troubles ere annoy!
Sure these denote one universal joy!
325 Are these thy serious thoughts—Ah, turn thine eyes
Where the poor houseless shivering female lies.
She once, perhaps, in village plenty blest,
Has wept at tales of innocence distrest;
Her modest looks the cottage might adorn,
330 Sweet as the primrose peeps beneath the thorn;
Now lost to all; her friends, her virtue fled,
Near her betrayer's door she lays her head,
And pinch'd with cold, and shrinking from the shower,
With heavy heart deplores that luckless hour,
335 When idly first, ambitious of the town,
She left her wheel and robes of country brown.

Do thine, sweet AUBURN, thine, the lovliest train,
Do thy fair tribes participate her pain?

15. In *The Vicar of Wakefield*, chap. 27, Goldsmith wrote: "...as if the more enormous our wealth, the more extensive our fears, all our possessions are piled up with new edicts every day, and hung round with gibbets to scare every invader" (Friedman, *Collected Works*, IV, 150).

Even now, perhaps, by cold and hunger led,
340 At proud men's doors they ask a little bread!

Ah, no. To distant climes, a dreary scene,
Where half the convex world intrudes between,
Through torrid tracts with fainting steps they go,
Where wild Altama[16] murmurs to their woe.
345 Far different there from all that charm'd before,
The various terrors of that horrid shore.
Those blazing suns that dart a downward ray,
And fiercely shed intolerable day;
Those matted woods where birds forget to sing,
350 But silent bats in drowsy clusters cling,
Those poisonous fields with rank luxuriance crowned
Where the dark scorpion gathers death around;
Where at each step the stranger fears to wake
The rattling terrors of the vengeful snake;
355 Where crouching tigers wait their hapless prey,
And savage men more murderous still than they;
While oft in whirls the mad tornado flies,
Mingling the ravaged landscape with the skies.
Far different these from every former scene,
360 The cooling brook, the grassy vested green,
The breezy covert of the warbling grove,
That only sheltered thefts of harmless love.

Good Heaven! what sorrows gloom'd that parting day,
That called them from their native walks away;
365 When the poor exiles, every pleasure past,
Hung round their bowers, and fondly looked their last,
And took a long farewell, and wished in vain
For seats like these beyond the western main;
And shuddering still to face the distant deep,
370 Returned and wept, and still returned to weep.
The good old sire, the first prepared to go
To new found worlds, and wept for others woe.
But for himself, in conscious virtue brave,
He only wished for worlds beyond the grave.
375 His lovely daughter, lovelier in her tears,
The fond companion of his helpless years,
Silent went next, neglectful of her charms,
And left a lover's for a father's arms.
With louder plaints the mother spoke her woes,
380 And blest the cot where every pleasure rose;
And kist her thoughtless babes with many a tear,
And claspt them close in sorrow doubly dear;
Whilst her fond husband strove to lend relief
In all the silent manliness of grief.

385 O luxury! Thou curst by heaven's decree,
How ill exchanged are things like these for thee!
How do thy potions with insidious joy,
Diffuse their pleasures only to destroy!
Kingdoms by thee, to sickly greatness grown,
390 Boast of a florid vigour not their own.
At every draught more large and large they grow,
A bloated mass of rank unwieldy woe;
Till sapped their strength, and every part unsound,
Down, down they sink, and spread a ruin round.

16. A river in Georgia, U.S.A. Here, and in the following
eighteen lines, Goldsmith is describing that part of North
America according to the popular tradition of his day.

395   Even now the devastation is begun,
  And half the business of destruction done;
  Even now, methinks, as pondering here I stand,
  I see the rural virtues leave the land.
  Down where yon anchoring vessel spreads the sail
400   That idly waiting flaps with every gale,
  Downward they move a melancholy band,
  Pass from the shore, and darken all the strand.
  Contented toil, and hospitable care,
  And kind connubial tenderness, are there;
405   And piety with wishes placed above,
  And steady loyalty, and faithful love.
  And thou, sweet Poetry, thou loveliest maid,
  Still first to fly where sensual joys invade;
  Unfit in these degenerate times of shame,
410   To catch the heart, or strike for honest fame;
  Dear charming nymph, neglected and decried,
  My shame in crowds, my solitary pride.
  Thou source of all my bliss, and all my woe,
  That found'st me poor at first, and keep'st me so;
415   Thou guide by which the nobler arts excell,
  Thou nurse of every virtue, fare thee well.
  Farewell, and O where'er thy voice be tried,
  On Torno's cliffs, or Pambamarca's side,[17]
  Whether where equinoctial fervours glow,
420   Or winter wraps the polar world in snow,
  Still let thy voice prevailing over time,
  Redress the rigours of the inclement clime;
  Aid slighted truth, with thy persuasive strain
  Teach erring man to spurn the rage of gain;
425   Teach him that states of native strength possest,
  Tho' very poor, may still be very blest;
  That trade's proud empire hastes to swift decay,
  As ocean sweeps the labour'd mole[18] away;
  While self dependent power can time defy,
430   As rocks resist the billows and the sky.

  Finis.

An Elegy on the Death of a Mad Dog[1]

Good people all, of every sort,
  Give ear unto my song;
And if you find it wond'rous short,
  It cannot hold you long.

5   In Isling town there was a man,
  Of whom the world might say,
That still a godly race he ran,
  Whene'er he went to pray.

A kind and gentle heart he had,
10   To comfort friends and foes;
The naked every day he clad,
  When he put on his clothes.

And in that town a dog was found,
  As many dogs there be,
15   Both mungrel, puppy, whelp, and hound,
  And curs of low degree.

This dog and man at first were friends;
  But when a pique began,
The dog, to gain some private ends,
20   Went mad and bit the man.

Around from all the neighbouring streets,
  The wondering neighbours ran,
And swore the dog had lost his wits,
  To bite so good a man.

---

17. "Torno": a river in Sweden. "Pambamarca": a mountain in Equador.
18. Breakwater.

1. This poem occurs in chap. 17 of *The Vicar of Wakefield* (1766) where it is facetiously described as an "elegy that may truly be called tragical." See Friedman, *Collected Works*, IV, 88–89.

<table>
<tr><td>25</td><td>The wound it seemed both sore and sad,
  To every christian eye;
And while they swore the dog was mad,
  They swore the man would die.</td><td>30</td><td>But soon a wonder came to light,
  That showed the rogues they lied,
The man recovered of the bite,
  The dog it was that died.</td></tr>
</table>

WILLIAM COWPER (1731–1800)

From The Task:[1] Book I

The Sofa

I sing the sofa. I, who lately sang
Truth, Hope, and Charity,[2] and touched with awe
The solemn chords, and with a trembling hand,
Escaped with pain from that advent'rous flight,
5 Now seek repose upon an humbler theme;
The theme though humble, yet august and proud
Th' occasion—for the Fair[3] commands the song.
  Time was, when clothing sumptuous or for use,
Save their own painted skins, our sires had none.
10 As yet black breeches were not; satin smooth,
Or velvet soft, or plush with shaggy pile;
The hardy chief upon the rugged rock
Washed by the sea, or on the gravelly bank
Thrown up by wintry torrents roaring loud,
15 Fearless of wrong, reposed his weary strength.
Those barb'rous ages past, succeeded next
The birth-day of invention; weak at first,
Dull in design, and clumsy to perform.
Joint-stools were then created; on three legs
20 Upborne they stood. Three legs upholding firm
A massy slab, in fashion square or round.
On such a stool immortal Alfred sat,
And swayed the sceptre of his infant realms:
And such in ancient halls and mansions drear
25 May still be seen; but perforated sore,
And drilled in holes, the solid oak is found,
By worms voracious eating through and through.
  At length a generation more refined
Improved the simple plan; made three legs four,
30 Gave them a twisted form vermicular,[4]
And o'er the seat, with plenteous wadding stuffed,
Induced a splendid cover, green and blue,
Yellow and red, of tap'stry richly wrought
And woven close, or needlework sublime.
35 There might you see the peony spread wide,
The full blown rose, the shepherd and his lass,
Lapdog and lambkin with black staring eyes,
And parrots with twin cherries in their beak.
  Now came the cane from India, smooth and bright
40 With Nature's varnish; severed into stripes,

1. *The Task* takes its title from the fact that it was also written at the request of Lady Austen who, being an admirer of Milton, solicited Cowper to try his hand at blank verse. "After repeated solicitations, he promised her, if she would furnish the subject, to comply with her request. 'Oh,' she replied, 'you can never be in want of a subject—you can write upon any—write upon this sofa!'" The poem indeed begins, in a mock-heroic vein, with a history of chairs, but it soon becomes a more serious affair—a series of vignettes depicting many aspects of life, having as its unifying theme the Christian man's duty or "task." The whole poem contains approximately five thousand lines in six books; for the remaining five, an excellent edition is Brian Spiller's *Cowper: Verse and Letters* (Cambridge, Mass.: Harvard Univ. Press, 1968).
2. "Truth," "Hope," and "Charity" were the titles of three poems published in 1782.
3. Lady Austen.
4. Worm-like.

That interlaced each other, these supplied
Of texture firm a lattice-work, that braced
The new machine, and it became a chair.
But restless was the chair; the back erect
45 Distressed the weary loins, that felt no ease;
The slipp'ry seat betrayed the sliding part
That pressed it, and the feet hung dangling down,
Anxious in vain to find the distant floor.
These for the rich: the rest, whom fate had placed
50 In modest mediocrity, content
With base materials, sat on well tanned hides,
Obdurate and unyielding, glassy smooth,
With here and there a tuft of crimson yarn,
Or scarlet crewel,[5] in the cushion fixed,
55 If cushion might be called, what harder seemed
Than the firm oak of which the frame was formed.
No want of timber then was felt or feared
In Albion's happy isle. The lumber stood
Pond'rous and fixed by its own massy weight.
60 But elbows still were wanting; these, some say
An alderman of Cripplegate contrived;
And some ascribe th' invention to a priest,
Burly and big, and studious of his ease.
But, rude at first, and not with easy slope
65 Receding wide, they pressed against the ribs,
And bruised the side; and, elevated high,
Taught the raised shoulders to invade the ears.
Long time elapsed or e'er our rugged sires
Complained, though incommodiously pent in,
70 And ill at ease behind. The ladies first
'Gan murmur, as became the softer sex.
Ingenious fancy, never better pleased,
Than when employed t' accommodate the fair,
Heard the sweet moan with pity, and devised
75 The soft settee; one elbow at each end,
And in the midst an elbow it received,
United yet divided, twain at once.
So sit two kings of Brentford[6] on one throne;
As so two citizens who take the air,
80 Close packed, and smiling, in a chaise and one.
But relaxation of the languid frame,
By soft recumbency of outstretched limbs,
Was bliss reserved for happier days. So slow
The growth of what is excellent; so hard
85 T' attain perfection in this nether world.
Thus first necessity invented stools,
Convenience next suggested elbow chairs,
And luxury th' accomplished sofa last.
    The nurse sleeps sweetly, hired to watch the sick,
90 Whom snoring she disturbs. As sweetly he,
Who quits the coach-box at the midnight hour
To sleep within the carriage more secure,
His legs depending at the open door.
Sweet sleep enjoys the curate in his desk,
95 The tedious rector drawling o'er his head;
And sweet the clerk below. But neither sleep
Of lazy nurse, who snores the sick man dead,
Nor his who quits the box at midnight hour
To slumber in the carriage more secure,
100 Nor sleep enjoyed by curate in his desk,

5. Thin worsted for embroidery.
6. Characters in *The Rehearsal*, a satiric play by George
Villiers (1628–87).

Nor yet the dozings of the clerk, are sweet,
Compared with the repose the sofa yields.
   Oh may I live exempted (while I live
Guiltless of pampered appetite obscene)
105 From pangs arthritic, that infest the toe
Of libertine excess. The sofa suits
The gouty limb, 'tis true; but gouty limb
Though on a sofa, may I never feel:
For I have loved the rural walk through lanes
110 Of grassy swarth, close cropped by nibbling sheep,
And skirted thick with intertexture firm
Of thorny boughs; have loved the rural walk
O'er hills, through valleys, and by rivers' brink,
E'er since a truant boy I passed my bounds
115 T' enjoy a ramble on the banks of Thames;
And still remember, nor without regret
Of hours that sorrow since has much endeared,
How oft, my slice of pocket store consumed,
Still hungering, pennyless, and far from home,
120 I fed on scarlet hips and stony haws,[7]
Or blushing crabs,[8] or berries, that emboss
The bramble, black as jet, or sloes[9] austere.
Hard fare! but such as boyish appetite
Disdains not; nor the palate, undepraved
125 By culinary arts, unsav'ry deems.
No sofa then awaited my return;
Nor sofa then I needed. Youth repairs
His wasted spirits quickly, by long toil
Incurring short fatigue; and, though our years
130 As life declines speed rapidly away,
And not a year but pilfers as he goes
Some youthful grace that age would gladly keep;
A tooth or auburn lock, and by degrees
Their length and color from the locks they spare;
135 Th' elastic spring of an unwearied foot,
That mounts the stile with ease, or leaps the fence;
That play of lungs, inhaling and again
Respiring freely the fresh air, that makes
Swift pace or steep ascent, no toil to me,
140 Mine have not pilfered yet; nor yet impaired
My relish of fair prospect; scenes that soothed
Or charmed me young, no longer young, I find
Still soothing, and of pow'r to charm me still.
              * * *
   Nor rural sights alone, but rural sounds,
Exhilarate the spirit, and restore
The tone of languid Nature. Mighty winds,
That sweep the skirt of some far-spreading wood
185 Of ancient growth, make music not unlike
The dash of ocean on his winding shore,
And lull the spirit while they fill the mind;
Unnumbered branches waving in the blast,
And all their leaves fast flutt'ring, all at once.
190 Nor less composure waits upon the roar
Of distant floods, or on the softer voice
Of neighb'ring fountain, or of rills that slip
Through the cleft rock, and, chiming as they fall
Upon loose pebbles, lose themselves at length
195 In matted grass, that with a livelier green
Betrays the secret of their silent course.

7. Hawthorn fruit.
8. Crab-apples.   9. Blackthorn fruit.

Nature inanimate employs sweet sounds,
But animated nature sweeter still,
To sooth and satisfy the human ear.
200 Ten thousand warblers cheer the day, and one
The livelong night: nor these alone, whose notes
Nice-fingered art must emulate in vain,
But cawing rooks, and kites that swim sublime
In still repeated circles, screaming loud,
205 The jay, the pie, and ev'n the boding owl
That hails the rising moon, have charms for me.
Sounds inharmonious in themselves and harsh,
Yet heard in scenes where peace for ever reigns,
And only there, please highly for their sake.

                    *   *   *

By ceaseless action all that is subsists.
Constant rotation of th' unwearied wheel
That Nature rides upon maintains her health,
370 Her beauty, her fertility. She dreads
An instant's pause, and lives but while she moves.
Its own revolvency upholds the world.
Winds from all quarters agitate the air,
And fit the limpid element for use,
375 Else noxious: oceans, rivers, lakes, and streams,
All feel the fresh'ning impulse, and are cleansed
By restless undulation: ev'n the oak
Thrives by the rude concussion of the storm:
He seems indeed indignant, and to feel
380 Th' impression of the blast with proud disdain,
Frowning as if in his unconscious arm
He held the thunder: but the monarch owes
His firm stability to what he scorns—
More fixed below, the more disturbed above.
385 The law, by which all creatures else are bound,
Binds man the lord of all. Himself derives
No mean advantage from a kindred cause,
From strenuous toil his hours of sweetest ease.
The sedentary stretch their lazy length
390 When custom bids, but no refreshment find,
For none they need: the languid eye, the cheek
Deserted of its bloom, the flaccid, shrunk,
And withered muscle, and the vapid soul,
Reproach their owner with that love of rest
395 To which he forfeits ev'n the rest he loves.
Not such th' alert and active. Measure life
By its true worth, the comforts it affords,
And theirs alone seems worthy of the name.
Good health, and, its associate in most,
400 Good temper; spirits prompt to undertake,
And not soon spent, though in an arduous task;
The pow'rs of fancy and strong thought are theirs;
Ev'n age itself seems privileged in them
With clear exemption from its own defects.
405 A sparkling eye beneath a wrinkled front
The vet'ran shows, and, gracing a gray beard
With youthful smiles, descends toward the grave
Sprightly, and old almost without decay.

The Castaway[1]

Obscurest night involved the sky,
  Th' Atlantic billows roared,
When such a destined wretch as I,
  Washed headlong from on board,
5 Of friends, of hope, of all bereft,
His floating home for ever left.

No braver chief could Albion boast
  Than he with whom he went,
Nor ever ship left Albion's coast,
10 With warmer wishes sent.
He loved them both, but both in vain,
Nor him beheld, nor her again.

Not long beneath the whelming brine,
  Expert to swim, he lay;
15 Nor soon he felt his strength decline,
  Or courage die away;
But waged with death a lasting strife,
Supported by despair of life.

He shouted: nor his friends had failed
20 To check the vessel's course,
But so the furious blast prevailed,
  That, pitiless perforce.
They left their outcast mate behind,
And scudded still before the wind.

25 Some succor yet they could afford;
  And, such as storms allow,
The cask, the coop, the floated cord,
  Delayed not to bestow.
But he (they knew) nor ship, nor shore,
30 Whate'er they gave, should visit more.

Nor, cruel as it seemed, could he
  Their haste himself condemn,
Aware that flight, in such a sea,
  Alone could rescue them;
35 Yet bitter felt it still to die
Deserted, and his friends so nigh.

He long survives, who lives an hour
  In ocean, self-upheld:
And so long he, with unspent pow'r,
40 His destiny repelled;
And ever as the minutes flew,
Entreated help, or cried—"Adieu!"

At length, his transient respite past,
  His comrades, who before
45 Had heard his voice in ev'ry blast,
  Could catch the sound no more.
For then, by toil subdued, he drank
The stifling wave, and then he sank.

No poet wept him: but the page
50 Of narrative sincere,
That tells his name, his worth, his age,
  Is wet with Anson's tear.
And tears by bards or heroes shed
Alike immortalize the dead.

55 I therefore purpose not, or dream,
  Descanting on his fate,
To give the melancholy theme
  A more enduring date:
But misery still delights to trace
60 Its 'semblance in another's case.

No voice divine the storm allayed
  No light propitious shone;
When, snatched from all effectual aid,
  We perished, each alone:
65 But I beneath a rougher sea,
And whelmed in deeper gulfs than he.

1. "The Castaway" was the last poem written by Cowper—written in 1799 and published posthumously in 1803. It was based on a passage in George Anson's *A Voyage Round the World* (1748) in which Anson vividly describes the fate of a seaman who was thrown overboard during a storm and lost.

Introduction: 1800-32

No term has been given more definitions and explanations, and no term has more success-fully eluded definition, than "Romanticism." In one context it may suggest a search for the infinite; in another, more narrowly, a search for self. It is at once the rejection of classicism and a love of the past. Romanticism is the elevation of feeling over thought, of emotion over reason. It reveals a numinous truth behind the stark forms of external reality, adding, in Walter Pater's words, "strangeness to beauty" (*Appreciations*, 1889). It is the voice of the rebel striving to realize transcendent ideals in defiance of the norms of a materialistic and hostile society. Such explanations are helpful in any attempt to identify the special qualities of Romanticism; but they can never be more than rough guides to the startling variety of forms and ideas which emerged from a movement encompassing Europe and North America over the span of a hundred years: a movement that could embrace thinkers as different as Rousseau and Carlyle, or link poets as unlike as Wordsworth and Byron.

The period of Romantic poetry in English is usually taken as having begun with the anonymous publication in 1798 of *Lyrical Ballads, with a Few Other Poems* by Wordsworth and Coleridge. In that collection, as Wordsworth's "Preface" to the edition of 1800 makes clear, the authors saw themselves as making a deliberate break with the literary conven-tions of their day. Wordsworth was critical of "the gaudiness and inane phraseology" of his contemporaries; poets had separated themselves from "the sympathies of men," indulging in "arbitrary and capricious habits of expression, in order to furnish food for fickle tastes, and fickle appetites, of their own creation." In place of such triviality, and in defiance of the rules of contemporary criticism which favoured a highly artificial poetic diction, Wordsworth proposed to keep his readers "in the company of flesh and blood," and to write in "a selection of language really used by men."

The publication of *Lyrical Ballads* undoubtedly marks an important stage in the growth of the Romantic movement; but Wordsworth and Coleridge were not the first writers to feel dissatisfied with the limiting prescriptions of neo-classical critical theory. The eighteenth century is sometimes thought of as the Age of Reason, with Pope and Johnson as its literary high priests; but it was also the age of Thomson and Cowper, of Macpherson's *Ossian* and Percy's *Reliques*, of the novel of sensibility and the Gothic romance. Many of the features we associate with Romantic poetry—for example, its preoccupation with the beauties of nature, its belief in the importance of individual emotion and intuition, its interest in the medieval period and in folk-traditions—were evident in much of the literature of the eighteenth century. Not that writers like Thomson or Gray or Burns thought of their work as "Romantic"; indeed, the word had pejorative overtones, being associated for the most part with excessive feeling, foolish impracticality, or the tendency to dwell on the improbable and fantastic. Not until the 1830s was "Romantic" to be used as a serious critical term in England. Nevertheless, it is important to remember that the work of the Lake poets and their great contemporaries was the culmination of influen-ces and tendencies that had been gathering force throughout western Europe in the eighteenth century. Of especial significance in this regard is the contribution made by French and German writers. From mid-century onwards, there was a growing reaction on the continent against classicism and the subordination of feeling to prescribed forms; the work of Jean-Jacques Rousseau, and of Goethe and the members of the "Sturm und Drang" (Storm and Stress) school, introduced a new note of passionate intensity that linked literature to the rising tide of political fervour in Europe.

The evolution of Romantic literature occurred at a time of immense social upheaval. The old aristocratic order was crumbling; first the rebellion of the British colonies in America, then the outbreak of revolution in France, signalled the decline of feudal power and aroused people to the possibility of a new freedom, spiritual as well as social. This seemed a time when dreams of a just and humane society might be realized; when, as Wordsworth noted in *The Prelude*, "the whole Earth / The beauty wore of promise." In England, however, the establishment viewed events abroad with fear and suspicion; the cause of reform was set back by repressive legislation, made harsher after 1793 by the bitter and debilitating war with France which brought economic depression in its wake. During the same period, advances in machine technology were turning England from a primarily agrarian society into an industrial one, with far-reaching consequences for the quality of life. The industrial revolution transformed the nature of production and led to an immense expansion of England's power and wealth; but it also brought harsh working conditions, crowded and unhealthy living quarters, mass unemployment, and a new sense of division in English society that was to lead the Victorian novelist and politician Disraeli to describe England as "The Two Nations."

To Wordsworth, writing in the Preface to *Lyrical Ballads*, the social and political events of his time seemed evidence of a general decline in moral and aesthetic sensibility, especially manifested by "the increasing accumulation of men in cities, where the uniformity of their occupations produces a craving for extraordinary incident, which the rapid communication of intelligence hourly gratifies." He viewed the poet's task as one of putting men back in touch with the deeper truths of their nature by examining the human mind in relation to "the great and permanent objects that act upon it." This he hoped to accomplish in part by focusing on humble, rustic life; here, he felt, one might see the passions of the human heart in their purest and most durable forms. In turning to the ordinary and the commonplace for poetic subjects, Wordsworth had been anticipated by other writers, notably Robert Burns, whose dialect poems and comic portrayals of Scottish life and manners had already won critical acclaim; but Wordsworth went further by making such materials the basis of a poetic theory and relating them to his vision of humanity's essential unity with all aspects of the natural world.

This unity is a recurring theme in the poetry of all the Romantics. They returned again and again to nature in all its rugged grandeur or its unsullied beauty, not as observers merely (though to the description of natural phenomena they brought a new accuracy of detail born of close observation) but as participants in a cosmic process whose workings were discernible through the interaction of natural forms. This consciousness of spiritual kinship with nature and, through nature, with the unseen forces operative in the universe is most fully developed by Wordsworth, in such poems as "Tintern Abbey" and *The Prelude*; but it is equally central to the works of his major contemporaries. Coleridge's Mariner is relieved of his burden only when he can find love in his heart for all living things; Byron, in *Childe Harold*, is disgusted by human society and finds consolation in the prospect of ultimate union with the "mountains, waves, and skies"; Shelley draws a revivifying power from a sense of affinity with the west wind; Keats (whose death is celebrated by Shelley in *Adonais* as a return to nature) can find release from earthly pain by an imaginative leap into the world of the nightingale. The nature that is described by these poets is conceived as an extension of their own being, a source of spiritual strength, and the manifestation of a transcendent reality not governed by human concepts of space and time: "The types and symbols of Eternity, / Of first, and last, and midst, and without end" (*The Prelude*, Book VI, 639–40).

The world of nature presented in Romantic poetry is one that is transformed by the poet's own needs, experiences, and feelings and by his conviction of the validity of individual perception. Like his Augustan predecessors, the poet is concerned with general truths; however, those truths are no longer sought by the application of judgement and reason alone to the objects of the external world, but by heeding the force of intuition and inner vision. For the poet and painter William Blake, the true artist possessed a visionary power that could pierce outward creation: "I question not my Corporeal or Vegetative Eye any more than I would Question a Window concerning a Sight. I look thro' it and not with it" ("A Vision of the Last Judgment," 1810). To Keats, nothing was certain but "the holiness of the Heart's affections and the truth of Imagination—What the imagination seizes as Beauty must be truth—whether it existed before or not" (letter to Bailey, 22 November 1817). Such assertions of the primacy of the poet's imagination sharply distinguish the Romantics from the neo-classical poets and critics of the eighteenth century. In *Rasselas* (1759), Samuel Johnson devoted a chapter to "The Dangerous Prevalence of the Imagination," which he equated with idle fictions, "dreams of rapture or of anguish" that might warp our sense of reality if they were left unchecked. To the Romantics, however, imagination was the channel by which the artist gained access to universal truth, and at the same time the creative principle which enabled him to give form and significance to his subjective perceptions. Coleridge drew a distinction between imagination and fancy (what the eighteenth-century critic would have called "wit"); whereas fancy concerns itself only with "fixities and definites," the primary imagination is "the living power and prime agent of all human perception, and . . . a repetition in the finite mind of the eternal act of creation in the infinite I AM" (*Biographia Literaria*, 1817).

A corollary of this emphasis on imagination is the importance attached by the Romantics to the role of feeling, which has implications for form as well as content. According to Wordsworth, "all good poetry is the spontaneous overflow of powerful feelings." Such a view inevitably conflicted with eighteenth-century theories of poetic "kinds" and poetic decorum, whereby a writer would be expected to match subject, form, and diction; the shape a poem took under the guidance of feeling was much less likely to be predetermined by such considerations. "If Poetry comes not as naturally as the Leaves to a tree," wrote Keats to his friend Taylor, "it had better not come at all" (27 February 1818). Liberated from the constraints of the heroic couplet which had dominated the verse of their predecessors, the Romantics experimented widely with a variety of forms, especially the lyric, which offered unlimited possibilities for the exploration of emotion. Feeling itself became a subject, as the poet examined his responses to the external world; nature thus became a medium for the delineation of emotional states, as in Canto III of *Childe Harold*, where the contemplation of a storm over Lake Leman arouses Byron's thoughts of the turmoil in his own spirit.

Romantic poetry was thus rooted in the writer's subjective response to experience; but it was a subjectivity that merged with an awareness of the poet's traditional role as guide and teacher. In its reflective or philosophic moods especially, Romantic poetry is characterized by a sense of moral purpose and conviction bordering on the oracular. Indeed, to a greater or lesser degree, all the great Romantics felt themselves to be mediators between human perception and eternal truths. Conscious of a world of injustice, suffering, and loss, they reached beyond surface realities to assure men of their capacity to find within themselves what Coleridge regarded as "A New Earth and New Heaven" ("Dejection: An Ode"). Whether denouncing social oppression or lamenting the transience of beauty, whether exploring the supernatural or celebrating the commonplace, the Romantic poets were impelled by a common desire to probe into "the very heart of man," to discover the sources of imaginative power, and to assert the infinite potential of the human spirit.

Herbert J. Rosengarten

WILLIAM BLAKE (1757 – 1827)

Song

How sweet I roam'd from field to field,
    And tasted all the summer's pride,
'Till I the prince of love beheld,
    Who in the sunny beams did glide!

He shew'd me lilies for my hair,
    And blushing roses for my brow;
He led me through his gardens fair,
    Where all his golden pleasures grow.

With sweet May dews my wings were wet,
    And Phoebus fir'd my vocal rage;
He caught me in his silken net,
    And shut me in his golden cage.

He loves to sit and hear me sing,
    Then, laughing, sports and plays with me;
Then stretches out my golden wing,
    And mocks my loss of liberty.

From Songs of Innocence and of Experience
Shewing the Two Contrary States of the Human Soul

From Songs of Innocence

Introduction

Piping down the valleys wild
Piping songs of pleasant glee
On a cloud I saw a child.
And he laughing said to me.

Pipe a song about a Lamb;
So I piped with merry chear,
Piper pipe that song again—
So I piped, he wept to hear.

Drop thy pipe thy happy pipe
Sing thy songs of happy chear,
So I sung the same again
While he wept with joy to hear

Piper sit thee down and write
In a book that all may read—
So he vanish'd from my sight.
And I pluck'd a hollow reed.

And I made a rural pen,
And I stain'd the water clear,
And I wrote my happy songs
Every child may joy to hear.

The Lamb

    Little Lamb who made thee
    Dost thou know who made thee
Gave thee life & bid thee feed.
By the stream & o'er the mead;
Gave thee clothing of delight,
Softest clothing wooly bright;
Gave thee such a tender voice,
Making all the vales rejoice!
    Little Lamb who made thee
    Dost thou know who made thee

    Little Lamb I'll tell thee,
    Little Lamb I'll tell thee!
He is called by thy name,
For he calls himself a Lamb:
He is meek & he is mild,
He became a little child:
I a child & thou a lamb,
We are called by his name.
    Little Lamb God bless thee.
    Little Lamb God bless thee.

The Chimney Sweeper

When my mother died I was very young,
And my father sold me while yet my tongue,
Could scarcely cry weep weep weep weep.[1]
So your chimneys I sweep & in soot I sleep.

---

1. Abbreviation of the street-cry "sweep!"

5   Theres little Tom Dacre, who cried when his head
    That curl'd like a lambs back, was shav'd, so I said.
    Hush Tom never mind it, for when your head's bare,
    You know that the soot cannot spoil your white hair.

    And so he was quiet, & that very night,
10 As Tom was a sleeping he had such a sight,
    That thousands of sweepers Dick, Joe Ned & Jack
    Were all of them lock'd up in coffins of black

    And by came an Angel who had a bright key,
    And he open'd the coffins & set them all free.
15 Then down a green plain leaping laughing they run
    And wash in a river and shine in the Sun.

    Then naked & white, all their bags left behind,
    They rise upon clouds, and sport in the wind.
    And the Angel told Tom if he'd be a good boy,
20 He'd have God for his father & never want joy.

    And so Tom awoke and we rose in the dark
    And got with our bags & our brushes to work.
    Tho' the morning was cold, Tom was happy & warm,
    So if all do their duty, they need not fear harm.

The Divine Image

To Mercy Pity Peace and Love,
All pray in their distress:
And to these virtues of delight
Return their thankfulness.

For Mercy Pity Peace and Love,
Is God our father dear:
And Mercy Pity Peace and Love,
Is Man his child and care.

For Mercy has a human heart
Pity, a human face:
And Love, the human form divine,
And Peace, the human dress.

Then every man of every clime,
That prays in his distress,
Prays to the human form divine
Love Mercy Pity Peace.

And all must love the human form,
In heathen, turk or jew.
Where Mercy, Love & Pity dwell
There God is dwelling too.

Holy Thursday[1]

Twas on a Holy Thursday their innocent faces clean
The children walking two & two in red & blue & green
Grey headed beadles[2] walkd before with wands as white as snow
Till into the high dome of Pauls they like Thames waters flow

O what a multitude they seemd these flowers of London town
Seated in companies they sit with radiance all their own
The hum of multitudes was there but multitudes of lambs
Thousands of little boys & girls raising their innocent hands

Now like a mighty wind they raise to heaven the voice of song
Or like harmonious thunderings the seats of heaven among
Beneath them sit the aged men wise guardians of the poor
Then cherish pity, lest you drive an angel from your door

1. Each year on Ascension Day special services were held
at St. Paul's Cathedral for the children of the Charity
Schools.

2. Parish officers appointed to keep order in religious
processions and in church.

From Songs of Experience

Introduction

Hear the voice of the Bard!
Who Present, Past, & Future sees
Whose ears have heard,
The Holy Word,
That walk'd among the ancient trees.[1]

Calling the lapsed Soul
And weeping in the evening dew;
That might controll,
The starry pole;
And fallen fallen light renew!

O Earth O Earth return!
Arise from out the dewy grass;
Night is worn,
And the morn
Rises from the slumberous mass.

Turn away no more:
Why wilt thou turn away
The starry floor
The watry shore[2]
Is giv'n thee till the break of day.

Earth's Answer

Earth rais'd up her head,
From the darkness dread & drear.
Her light fled:
Stony dread!
5   And her locks cover'd with grey despair.

Prison'd on watry shore
Starry Jealousy does keep my den
Cold and hoar
Weeping o'er
10 I hear the Father[1] of the ancient men.

Selfish father of men
Cruel jealous selfish fear
Can delight
Chain'd in night
15 The virgins of youth and morning bear.

Does spring hide its joy
When buds and blossoms grow?
Does the sower?
Sow by night?
20 Or the plowman in darkness plow?

Break this heavy chain,
That does freeze my bones around
Selfish! vain,
Eternal bane!
25 That free Love with bondage bound.

The Clod & the Pebble

Love seeketh not Itself to please,
Nor for itself hath any care;
But for another gives its ease,
And builds a Heaven in Hells despair.

So sang a little Clod of Clay,
Trodden with the cattles feet:
But a Pebble of the brook,
Warbled out these metres meet.

Love seeketh only Self to please,
To bind another to its delight;
Joys in anothers loss of ease,
And builds a Hell in Heavens despite.

Holy Thursday

Is this a holy thing to see,
In a rich and fruitful land,
Babes reducd to misery,
Fed with cold and usurous hand?

Is that trembling cry a song?
Can it be a song of joy?
And so many children poor?
It is a land of poverty!

1. Like Adam and Eve in the garden of Eden (Gen. iii.8), the Bard (i.e., Blake) has heard the voice of God.
2. For Blake, the stars and the ocean are associated with the rationalists' universe of fixed laws and earth-bound materialism. The call to "Earth" is thus an appeal to turn from a rigidly ordered concept of the universe to a new dawn of spiritual light.

1. The tyrannical and jealous god who imprisons the human soul in a world governed by reason and fear.

And their sun does never shine.
And their fields are bleak & bare.
And their ways are fill'd with thorns.
It is eternal winter there.

For where-e'er the sun does shine,
And where-e'er the rain does fall:
Babe can never hunger there,
Nor poverty the mind appall.

The Chimney Sweeper

A little black thing among the snow:
Crying weep, weep, in notes of woe!
Where are thy father & mother? say?
They are both gone up to the church to pray.

Because I was happy upon the heath,
And smil'd among the winters snow:
They clothed me in the clothes of death,
And taught me to sing the notes of woe.

And because I am happy, & dance & sing,
They think they have done me no injury:
And are gone to praise God & his Priest & King
Who make up a heaven of our misery.

The Sick Rose

O Rose thou art sick.
The invisible worm,
That flies in the night
In the howling storm:

Has found out thy bed
Of crimson joy:
And his dark secret love
Does thy life destroy.

The Tyger

Tyger Tyger, burning bright,
In the forests of the night;
What immortal hand or eye,
Could frame thy fearful symmetry?

5 In what distant deeps or skies
Burnt the fire of thine eyes!
On what wings dare he aspire?
What the hand, dare sieze the fire?

And what shoulder, & what art,
10 Could twist the sinews of thy heart?
And when thy heart began to beat,
What dread hand? & what dread feet?

What the hammer? what the chain,
In what furnace was thy brain?
15 What the anvil? what dread grasp,
Dare its deadly terrors clasp?

When the stars threw down their spears
And water'd heaven with their tears:
Did he smile his work to see?
20 Did he who made the Lamb make thee?

Tyger, Tyger burning bright,
In the forests of the night:
What immortal hand or eye,
Dare frame thy fearful symmetry?

The Garden of Love

I went to the Garden of Love,
And saw what I never had seen:
A Chapel was built in the midst,
Where I used to play on the green.

And the gates of this Chapel were shut,
And Thou shalt not. writ over the door;
So I turn'd to the Garden of Love,
That so many sweet flowers bore,

And I saw it was filled with graves,
And tomb-stones where flowers should be:
And Priests in black gowns, were walking their rounds,
And binding with briars, my joys & desires.

London

I wander thro' each charter'd[1] street,
Near where the charter'd Thames does flow.
And mark in every face I meet
Marks of weakness, marks of woe.

In every cry of every Man,
In every Infants cry of fear,
In every voice: in every ban,
The mind-forg'd manacles I hear

How the Chimney-sweepers cry
Every blackning Church appalls,
And the hapless Soldiers sigh,
Runs in blood down Palace walls

But most thro' midnight streets I hear
How the youthful Harlots curse
Blasts[2] the new-born Infants tear
And blights with plagues the Marriage hearse

Infant Sorrow

My mother groand! my father wept.
Into the dangerous world I leapt:
Helpless, naked, piping loud;
Like a fiend hid in a cloud.

Struggling in my fathers hands:
Striving against my swadling bands:
Bound and weary I thought best
To sulk upon my mothers breast.

The Mental Traveller

I traveld thro' a Land of Men
A Land of Men & Women too
And heard & saw such dreadful things
As cold Earth wanderers never knew

5 For there the Babe is born in joy
That was begotten in dire woe
Just as we Reap in joy the fruit
Which we in bitter tears did sow[1]

And if the Babe is born a Boy
10 He's given to a Woman Old
Who nails him down upon a rock[2]
Catches his shrieks in cups of gold

She binds iron thorns around his head
She pierces both his hands & feet
15 She cuts his heart out at his side
To make it feel both cold & heat

Her fingers number every Nerve
Just as a Miser counts his gold
She lives upon his shrieks & cries
20 And she grows young as he grows old

Till he becomes a bleeding youth
And she becomes a Virgin bright
Then he rends up his Manacles
And binds her down for his delight

25 He plants himself in all her Nerves
Just as a Husbandman his mould
And she becomes his dwelling place
And Garden fruitful seventy fold

30 An aged Shadow soon he fades
Wandring round an Earthly Cot
Full filled all with gems & gold
Which he by industry had got

And these are the gems of the Human Soul
The rubies & pearls of a lovesick eye
35 The countless gold of the akeing heart
The martyrs groan & the lovers sigh

They are his meat they are his drink
He feeds the Beggar & the Poor
And the wayfaring Traveller
40 For ever open is his door

His grief is their eternal joy
They make the roofs & walls to ring
Till from the fire on the hearth
A little Female Babe does spring

45 And she is all of solid fire
And gems & gold that none his hand
Dares stretch to touch her Baby form
Or wrap her in his swaddling-band

But She comes to the Man she loves
50 If young or old or rich or poor
They soon drive out the aged Host
A Beggar at anothers door

He wanders weeping far away
Untill some other take him in
55 Oft blind & age-bent sore distrest
Untill he can a Maiden win

---

1. An ironic allusion to the ancient charters guaranteeing
certain liberties and privileges to the city of London.
2. Used here in the sense of "blight" or "ruin," as well as
with the meaning of "strike with a curse."

1. Cf. Ps. cxxvi.5: "They that sow in tears shall reap in
joy."
2. The boy suffers torments like those of Prometheus, or
(in the next stanza) of Christ.

And to allay his freezing Age
The Poor Man takes her in his arms
The Cottage fades before his sight
60   The Garden & its lovely Charms

The Guests are scatterd thro' the land
For the Eye altering alters all
The Senses roll themselves in fear
And the flat Earth becomes a Ball[3]

65   The Stars Sun Moon all shrink away
A desart vast without a bound
And nothing left to eat or drink
And a dark desart all around

The honey of her Infant lips
70   The bread & wine of her sweet smile
The wild game of her roving Eye
Does him to Infancy beguile

For as he eats & drinks he grows
Younger & younger every day
75   And on the desart wild they both
Wander in terror & dismay

Like the wild Stag she flees away
Her fear plants many a thicket wild
While he pursues her night & day
80   By various arts of Love beguild

By various arts of Love & Hate
Till the wide desart planted oer
With Labyrinths of wayward Love
Where roams the Lion Wolf & Boar

85   Till he becomes a wayward Babe
And she a weeping Woman Old
Then many a Lover wanders here
The Sun & Stars are nearer rolld

The trees bring forth sweet Extacy
90   To all who in the desart roam
Till many a City there is Built
And many a pleasant Shepherds home

But when they find the frowning Babe
Terror strikes thro the region wide
95   They cry the Babe the Babe is Born
And flee away on Every side

For who dare touch the frowning form
His arm is witherd to its root
Lions Boars Wolves all howling flee
100   And every Tree does shed its fruit

And none can touch that frowning form
Except it be a Woman Old
She nails him down upon the Rock
And all is done as I have told

Mock on Mock on Voltaire Rousseau

Mock on Mock on Voltaire Rousseau[1]
Mock on Mock on tis all in vain
You throw the sand against the wind
And the wind blows it back again

And every sand becomes a Gem
Reflected in the beams divine
Blown back they blind the mocking Eye
But still in Israel's paths they shine

The Atoms of Democritus[2]
And Newtons Particles of light[3]
Are sands upon the Red sea shore
Where Israel's tents do shine so bright

ROBERT BURNS (1759-96)

Holy Willie's Prayer
And send the Godly in a pet to pray.[1]—Pope

Argument.

Holy Willie was a rather oldish batchelor Elder in the parish of Mauchline, and much and justly famed for that polemical chattering which ends in tippling Orthodoxy, and for that Spiritualized Bawdry which refines to Liquorish Devotion.— In a Sessional process with a gentleman in Mauchline, a Mr.

3. In the first book of *Milton*, Blake declares that the notion of the earth as a "globe rolling through voidness" is a "false appearance" and "a delusion of Ulro," Ulro being Blake's term for the lowest state of rationality and materialism in the fallen world.

1. Voltaire (1694–1778) and Rousseau (1712–78), leading figures of the French Enlightenment, are attacked here as

representatives of free-thinking rationalism.
2. Greek philosopher of the fifth century B.C., who taught that the world was made up of indestructible atoms.
3. Newton (1642–1727) theorized that light consisted of tiny particles emitted from luminous bodies in space.

1. Pope, *The Rape of the Lock*, iv.64.

Gavin Hamilton, Holy Willie, and his priest, father Auld, after full hearing in the Presbytry of Ayr, came off but second best; owing partly to the oratorical powers of Mr. Robt. Aiken, Mr. Hamilton's Counsel; but chiefly to Mr. Hamilton's being one of the most irreproachable and truly respectable characters in the country.—On losing his Process, the Muse overheard him at his devotions as follows—

O thou that in the heavens does dwell![2]
Wha, as it pleases best thysel,
Sends ane to heaven and ten to h-ll,
  A' for thy glory!
5 And no for ony gude or ill
  They've done before thee.—[3]

I bless and praise thy matchless might,
When thousands thou has left in night,
That I am here before thy sight,
10 For gifts and grace,
A burning and a shining light[4]
  To a' this place.—

What was I, or my generation,[5]
That I should get such exaltation?
15 I, wha deserv'd most just damnation,
  For broken laws
Sax thousand years ere my creation,
  Thro' Adam's cause!

When from my mother's womb I fell,
20 Thou might hae plunged me deep in hell,
To gnash my gooms,[6] and weep, and wail,
  In burning lakes,
Where damned devils roar and yell
  Chain'd to their stakes.—

25 Yet I am here, a chosen sample,
To shew thy grace is great and ample:
I'm here, a pillar o' thy temple
  Strong as a rock,
A guide, a ruler and example
30 To a' thy flock.—

O L—d thou kens[7] what zeal I bear,
When drinkers drink, and swearers swear,
And singin' there, and dancin' here,
  Wi' great an' sma';
35 For I am keepet by thy fear,
  Free frae them a'.—]

But yet—O L—d—confess I must—
At times I'm fash'd[8] wi' fleshly lust;
And sometimes too, in warldly trust
40 Vile Self gets in;
But thou remembers we are dust,
  Defil'd wi' sin.—

O L—d—yestreen[9]—thou kens—wi' Meg—
Thy pardon I sincerely beg!
45 O may't ne'er be a living plague,
  To my dishonor!
And I'll ne'er lift a lawless leg
  Again upon her.—

Besides, I farther maun[10] avow,
50 Wi' Leezie's lass, three times—I trow—
But L—d, that friday I was fou[11]
  When I cam near her;
Or else, thou kens, thy servant true
  Wad never steer[12] her.—

55 Maybe thou lets this fleshly thorn
Buffet thy servant e'en and morn,
Lest he o'er proud and high should turn,
  That he's sae gifted;
If sae, thy hand maun e'en be borne
60 Untill thou lift it.—

L—d bless thy Chosen in this place,
For here thou has a chosen race:
But G-d, confound their stubborn face,
  And blast their name,
65 Wha bring thy rulers to disgrace
  And open shame.—

L—d mind Gaun Hamilton's deserts!
He drinks, and swears, and plays at cartes,
Yet has sae mony taking arts
70 Wi' Great and Sma',
Frae G-d's ain priest the people's hearts
  He steals awa.—

And when we chasten'd him therefore,
Thou kens how he bred sic a splore,[13]
75 And set the warld in a roar
  O' laughin at us:
Curse thou his basket and his store,
  Kail[14] and potatoes.—

L—d hear my earnest cry and prayer
80 Against that Presbytry of Ayr!
Thy strong right hand, L—d, make it bare
  Upon their heads!
L—d visit them, and dinna spare,
  For their misdeeds!

2. Cf. Ps. cxxiii.1.
3. Holy Willie is describing the Calvinist doctrine of predestination, which holds that God has foreordained who shall be saved and who damned, regardless of their actions in life.
4. Cf. John v.35.
5. Family.
6. Gums.

7. Knows.
8. Troubled.
9. Yesterday evening.
10. Must.
11. Drunk.
12. Agitate, rouse.
13. Such an uproar.
14. A kind of cabbage.

85   O L—d my G-d, that glib-tongu'd Aiken!
      My very heart and flesh are quaking
      To think how I sat, sweating, shaking,
                And p-ss'd wi' dread,
      While Auld wi' hingin[15] lip gaed[16] sneaking
90   And hid his head!

      L—d, in thy day o' vengeance try him!
      L—d visit him that did employ him!
      And pass not in thy mercy by them,
                Nor hear their prayer;
95   But for thy people's sake destroy them,
                And dinna spare!

      But L—d, remember me and mine
      Wi' mercies temporal and divine!
      That I for grace and gear[17] may shine,
100   Excell'd by nane!
      And a' the glory shall be thine!
                AMEN! AMEN!

Tam o' Shanter. A Tale

Of Brownyis and of Bogillis[1] full is this buke. — Gawin Douglas

When chapman billies[2] leave the street,
And drouthy[3] neebors, neebors meet,
As market-days are wearing late,
An' folk begin to tak the gate;[4]
5   While we sit bousing at the nappy,[5]
And getting fou[6] and unco[7] happy,
We think na on the lang Scots miles,[8]
The mosses, waters, slaps,[9] and styles,
That lie between us and our hame,
10   Whare sits our sulky sullen dame,
Gathering her brows like gathering storm,
Nursing her wrath to keep it warm.

      This truth fand[10] honest *Tam o' Shanter*,
As he frae Ayr ae night did canter,
15   (Auld Ayr, wham ne'er a town surpasses,
For honest men and bonny lasses.)

      O *Tam*! hadst thou but been sae wise,
As ta'en thy ain wife *Kate*'s advice!
She tauld thee weel thou was a skellum,[11]
20   A blethering, blustering, drunken blellum;[12]
That frae November till October,
Ae market-day thou was nae sober;
That ilka melder,[13] wi' the miller,
Thou sat as lang as thou had siller;[14]
25   That every naig was ca'd a shoe on,[15]
The smith and thee gat roaring fou on;

That at the L—d's house, even on Sunday,
Thou drank wi' Kirkton Jean till Monday.
She prophesied that late or soon,
30   Thou would be found deep drown'd in Doon;[16]
Or catch'd wi' warlocks[17] in the mirk,[18]
By *Alloway*'s auld haunted kirk.

      Ah, gentle dames! it gars me greet,[19]
To think how mony counsels sweet,
35   How mony lengthen'd sage advices,
The husband frae the wife despises!

      But to our tale: Ae market-night,
Tam had got planted unco right;
Fast by an ingle, bleezing[20] finely,
40   Wi' reaming swats,[21] that drank divinely;
And at his elbow, Souter[22] *Johnny*,
His ancient, trusty, drouthy crony;
Tam lo'ed him like a vera brither;[23]
They had been fou for weeks thegither.
45   The night drave on wi' sangs and clatter;
And ay the ale was growing better:
The landlady and *Tam* grew gracious,
Wi' favours, secret, sweet, and precious:
The Souter tauld his queerest stories;
50   The landlord's laugh was ready chorus:
The storm without might rair[24] and rustle,
Tam did na mind the storm a whistle.

15. Hanging.
16. Went.
17. Possessions, property.

1. Good spirits and goblins. The epigraph is from Gavin Douglas' *Eneados*, VI.
2. Pedlar fellows.
3. Thirsty.
4. Road.
5. Ale.
6. Drunk.
7. Very.
8. The Scots mile was longer than the statute mile.
9. Gaps in a dyke or fence.
10. Found.

11. Scoundrel.
12. Idle babbler.
13. Each time you took corn to be ground at the mill ("melder" is the quantity of meal ground at one time).
14. Silver.
15. For every nag ("naig") that had a shoe hammered in.
16. A river in Ayrshire.
17. Caught by wizards.
18. Darkness
19. Makes me weep.
20. "ingle": fire. "bleezing": blazing.
21. Foaming new small ale.
22. Cobbler.
23. Very brother.
24. Roar.

Care, mad to see a man sae happy,
E'en drown'd himsel amang the nappy:
55 As bees flee hame wi' lades[25] o' treasure,
The minutes wing'd their way wi' pleasure:
Kings may be blest, but *Tam* was glorious,
O'er a' the ills o' life victorious!

But pleasures are like poppies spread,
60 You seize the flower, its bloom is shed;
Or like the snow falls in the river,
A moment white—then melts for ever;
Or like the borealis race,[26]
That flit ere you can point their place;
65 Or like the rainbow's lovely form
Evanishing amid the storm.—
Nae man can tether time or tide;
The hour approaches *Tam* maun ride;
That hour, o' night's black arch the key-stane,
70 That dreary hour he mounts his beast in;
And sic a night he taks the road in,
As ne'er poor sinner was abroad in.

The wind blew as 'twad blawn its last;
The rattling showers rose on the blast;
75 The speedy gleams the darkness swallow'd;
Loud, deep, and lang, the thunder bellow'd:
That night, a child might understand,
The Deil had business on his hand.

Weel mounted on his gray mare, *Meg*,
80 A better never lifted leg,
Tam skelpit[27] on thro' dub[28] and mire,
Despising wind, and rain, and fire;
Whiles holding fast his gude blue bonnet;
Whiles crooning o'er some auld Scots sonnet;
85 Whiles glowring[29] round wi' prudent cares,
Lest bogles[30] catch him unawares:
Kirk-Alloway was drawing nigh,
Whare ghaists and houlets[31] nightly cry.—

By this time he was cross the ford,
90 Whare, in the snaw, the chapman smoor'd;[32]
And past the birks and meikle stane,[33]
Whare drunken *Charlie* brak's neck-bane;
And thro' the whins,[34] and by the cairn,
Whare hunters fand the murder'd bairn;
95 And near the thorn, aboon[35] the well,
Whare *Mungo*'s mither hang'd hersel.—

Before him *Doon* pours all his floods;
The doubling storm roars thro' the woods;
The lightnings flash from pole to pole;
100 Near and more near the thunders roll:
When, glimmering thro' the groaning trees,
Kirk-Alloway seem'd in a bleeze;
Thro' ilka bore[36] the beams were glancing;
And loud resounded mirth and dancing.—

105 Inspiring bold *John Barleycorn*!
What dangers thou canst make us scorn!
Wi' tippeny,[37] we fear nae evil;
Wi' usquabae,[38] we'll face the devil!—
The swats sae ream'd in *Tammie*'s noddle,
110 Fair play,[39] he car'd na deils a boddle.[40]
But *Maggie* stood right sair[41] astonish'd,
Till, by the heel and hand admonish'd,
She ventured forward on the light;
And, vow! *Tam* saw an unco[42] sight!
115 Warlocks and witches in a dance;
Nae cotillion brent[43] new frae *France*,
But hornpipes, jigs, strathspeys, and reels,
Put life and mettle in their heels.
A winnock-bunker[44] in the east,
120 There sat auld Nick, in shape o' beast;
A towzie tyke,[45] black, grim, and large,
To gie them music was his charge:
He screw'd the pipes[46] and gart them skirl,[47]
Till roof and rafters a' did dirl.—[48]
125 Coffins stood round, like open presses,[49]
That shaw'd the dead in their last dresses;
And by some devilish cantraip slight[50]
Each in its cauld hand held a light.—
By which heroic *Tam* was able
130 To note upon the haly table,
A murderer's banes in gibbet airns;[51]
Twa span-lang,[52] wee, unchristen'd bairns;
A thief, new-cutted frae a rape,
Wi' his last gasp his gab[53] did gape;
135 Five tomahawks, wi' blude red-rusted;
Five scymitars, wi' murder crusted;
A garter, which a babe had strangled;
A knife, a father's throat had mangled,
Whom his ain son o' life bereft,
140 The grey hairs yet stack to the heft;
Wi' mair o' horrible and awefu',
Which even to name wad be unlawfu'.

---

25. Loads.
26. I.e., the lights of the Aurora Borealis.
27. Thrashed, slapped.
28. Mud, puddle.
29. Staring.
30. Spectres, goblins.
31. "ghaists": ghosts. "houlets": owls.
32. Was smothered.
33. "birks": birches. "meikle stane": big stone.
34. Furze-bushes.
35. Above.
36. Every crevice.
37. Two-pence worth of ale.
38. Whisky.
39. In justice to him.
40. He didn't care a single farthing (a "boddle" was a coin

of little value).
41. "Maggie": i.e., Tom's mare, Meg. "sair": sore.
42. Strange.
43. "cotillion": eighteenth-century French dance. "brent":
brand (new).
44. Window seat.
45. Shaggy mongrel.
46. Turned the drones to set them in tune.
47. Made them screech.
48. Shake, rattle.
49. Large cupboards.
50. Magic trick.
51. Fetters.
52. Small (literally, the span of an extended hand).
53. Mouth.

As *Tammie* glowr'd, amaz'd, and curious,
The mirth and fun grew fast and furious:
145 The piper loud and louder blew;
The dancers quick and quicker flew;
They reel'd, they set,[54] they cross'd, they cleekit,[55]
Till ilka carlin swat and reekit,[56]
And coost her duddies[57] to the wark,
150 And linket at it in her sark![58]

Now, *Tam*, O *Tam*! had thae been queans,[59]
A' plump and strapping in their teens,
Their sarks, instead o' creeshie flannen,[60]
Been snaw-white seventeen hunder linnen![61]
155 Thir breeks[62] o' mine, my only pair,
That ance were plush, o' gude blue hair,
I wad hae gi'en them off my hurdies,[63]
For ae blink o' the bonie burdies![64]

But wither'd beldams, auld and droll,
160 Rigwoodie[65] hags wad spean[66] a foal,
Lowping[67] and flinging on a crummock,[68]
I wonder didna turn thy stomach.

But *Tam* kend[69] what was what fu' brawlie,[70]
There was ae winsome wench and wawlie,[71]
165 That night enlisted in the core,
(Lang after kend on *Carrick* shore;
For mony a beast to dead she shot,
And perish'd mony a bony boat,
And shook baith meikle corn and bear,[72]
170 And kept the country-side in fear:)
Her cutty sark, o' Paisley harn,[73]
That while a lassie she had worn,
In longitude tho' sorely scanty,
It was her best, and she was vauntie. — [74]
175 Ah! little kend thy reverend grannie,
That sark she coft[75] for her wee Nannie,
Wi' twa pund[76] Scots, ('twas a' her riches),
Wad ever grac'd a dance of witches!

But here my Muse her wing maun cour;[77]
180 Sic flights are far beyond her pow'r;
To sing how Nannie lap and flang,[78]

(A souple jade she was, and strang),
And how *Tam* stood, like ane bewitch'd,
And thought his very een[79] enrich'd;
185 Even Satan glowr'd, and fidg'd fu' fain,[80]
And hotch'd[81] and blew wi' might and main:
Till first ae caper, syne[82] anither,
Tam tint[83] his reason a' thegither,
And roars out, 'Weel done, Cutty-sark!'
190 And in an instant all was dark:
And scarcely had he Maggie rallied,
When out the hellish legion sallied.

As bees bizz out wi' angry fyke,[84]
When plundering herds assail their byke;[85]
195 As open[86] pussie's mortal foes,
When, pop! she starts before their nose;
As eager runs the market-crowd,
When 'Catch the thief!' resounds aloud;
So Maggie runs, the witches follow,
200 Wi' mony an eldritch[87] skreech and hollow.

Ah, *Tam*! Ah, *Tam*! thou'll get thy fairin![88]
In hell they'll roast thee like a herrin!
In vain thy *Kate* awaits thy comin!
Kate soon will be a woefu' woman!
205 Now, do thy speedy utmost, Meg,
And win the key-stane[89] of the brig;
There at them thou thy tail may toss,
A running stream they dare na cross.
But ere the key-stane she could make,
210 The fient a tail[90] she had to shake!
For Nannie, far before the rest,
Hard upon noble Maggie prest,
And flew at *Tam* wi' furious ettle;[91]
But little wist she Maggie's mettle—
215 Ae spring brought off her master hale,[92]
But left behind her ain gray tail:
The carlin claught[93] her by the rump,
And left poor Maggie scarce a stump.

Now, wha this tale o' truth shall read,
220 Ilk man and mother's son, take heed:

54. Faced their partners.
55. Linked arms in the dance.
56. "carlin": witch. "reekit": smoked, steamed.
57. Cast off her clothes.
58. "linket": tripped, went briskly. "sark": shift.
59. Young girls.
60. Greasy flannel.
61. Finely woven linen, with 1,700 threads to the warp.
62. Breeches.
63. Buttocks.
64. Lasses.
65. Withered, coarse.
66. Wean (i.e., the hags would drive a foal off the teat with fright).
67. Leaping.
68. Staff with crooked head.
69. Knew.
70. Very well.
71. Fine, handsome.
72. "meikle corn": oats. "bear": barley.
73. "cutty": short. "harn": coarse linen.
74. Proud.

75. Bought.
76. Two pounds.
77. Lower, fold.
78. Leaped and flung.
79. Eyes.
80. Twitched with excitement.
81. Jerked about.
82. Then.
83. Lost.
84. Fuss, commotion.
85. "herds": herd-boys. "byke": hive.
86. Bark when following a scent.
87. Hideous.
88. Deserts, reward.
89. "It is a well known fact that witches, or any evil spirits, have no power to follow a poor wight any farther than the middle of the next running stream" (Burns's note).
90. The devil a tail (i.e., no tail at all).
91. Purpose.
92. Whole.
93. Clutched.

Whene'er to drink you are inclin'd,
Or cutty-sarks run in your mind,
Think, ye may buy the joys o'er dear,
Remember Tam o' Shanter's mare.

Ye Flowery Banks o' Bonie Doon

Ye flowery banks o' bonie Doon,[1]
  How can ye blume sae fair;
How can ye chant, ye little birds,
  And I sae fu' o' care!

5 Thou'll break my heart, thou bonie bird
  That sings upon the bough;
Thou minds me o' the happy days
  When my fause[2] luve was true.

Thou'll break my heart, thou bonie bird
10   That sings beside thy mate;
For sae I sat, and sae I sang,
  And wist[3] na o' my fate.

Aft hae I rov'd by bonie Doon,
  To see the wood-bine twine,
15 And ilka[4] bird sang o' its love,
  And sae did I o' mine.

Wi' lightsome heart I pu'd[5] a rose
  Frae aff its thorny tree,
And my fause luver staw[6] the rose,
20   But left the thorn wi' me.

Wi' lightsome heart I pu'd a rose,
  Upon a morn in June:
And sae I flourish'd on the morn,
  And sae was pu'd or[7] noon!

Song— For a' That and a' That—

Is there, for honest Poverty
  That hings[1] his head, and a' that;
The coward-slave, we pass him by,
  We dare be poor for a' that!
5 For a' that, and a' that,
  Our toils obscure, and a' that,
The rank is but the guinea's stamp,
  The Man's the gowd[2] for a' that.—

What though on hamely fare we dine,
10   Wear hoddin[3] grey, and a' that.
Gie fools their silks, and knaves their wine,
  A Man's a Man for a' that.
For a' that, and a' that,
  Their tinsel show, and a' that;
15 The honest man, though e'er sae poor,
  Is king o' men for a' that.—

Ye see yon birkie[4] ca'd, a lord,
  Wha struts, and stares, and a' that,
Though hundreds worship at his word,
20   He's but a coof[5] for a' that.
For a' that, and a' that,
  His ribband, star and a' that,
The man of independant mind,
  He looks and laughs at a' that.—

25 A prince can mak a belted knight,[6]
  A marquis, duke, and a' that;
But an honest man's aboon[7] his might,
  Gude faith he mauna fa'[8] that!
For a' that, and a' that,
30   Their dignities, and a' that,
The pith o' Sense, and pride o' Worth,
  Are higher rank than a' that.—

Then let us pray that come it may,
  As come it will for a' that,
35 That Sense and Worth, o'er a' the earth
  Shall bear the gree,[9] and a' that.
For a' that, and a' that,
  Its comin yet for a' that,
That Man to Man the warld o'er,
40   Shall brothers be for a' that.—

1. A river in Ayrshire.
2. False.
3. Knew.
4. Every.
5. Pulled.
6. Stole.
7. Ere.

1. Hangs.

2. Gold.
3. Coarse grey homespun cloth.
4. Lively fellow.
5. Fool.
6. Referring to the belt and spurs bestowed on knights,
etc., when they are raised to the dignity.
7. Above.
8. Must not lay claim to.
9. Come off best.

WILLIAM WORDSWORTH (1770–1850)

Lines Written in Early Spring

I heard a thousand blended notes,
While in a grove I sate reclined,
In that sweet mood when pleasant thoughts
Bring sad thoughts to the mind.

5 To her fair works did Nature link
The human soul that through me ran;
And much it grieved my heart to think
What man has made of man.

Through primrose tufts, in that green bower,
10 The periwinkle trailed its wreaths;
And 'tis my faith that every flower
Enjoys the air it breathes.

15 The birds around me hopped and played,
Their thoughts I cannot measure: -
But the least motion which they made,
It seemed a thrill of pleasure.

The budding twigs spread out their fan,
To catch the breezy air;
And I must think, do all I can,
20 That there was pleasure there.

If this belief from heaven be sent,
If such be Nature's holy plan,
Have I not reason to lament
What man has made of man?

Lines Composed a Few Miles above Tintern Abbey, on Revisiting the Banks of the Wye during a Tour. July 13, 1798

Five years have past;[1] five summers, with the length
Of five long winters! and again I hear
These waters, rolling from their mountain-springs
With a soft inland murmur. - Once again
5 Do I behold these steep and lofty cliffs,
That on a wild secluded scene impress
Thoughts of more deep seclusion; and connect
The landscape with the quiet of the sky.
The day is come when I again repose
10 Here, under this dark sycamore, and view
These plots of cottage-ground, these orchard-tufts,
Which at this season, with their unripe fruits,
Are clad in one green hue, and lose themselves
'Mid groves and copses. Once again I see
15 These hedge-rows, hardly hedge-rows, little lines
Of sportive wood run wild: these pastoral farms,
Green to the very door; and wreaths of smoke
Sent up, in silence, from among the trees!
With some uncertain notice, as might seem
20 Of vagrant dwellers in the houseless woods,
Or of some Hermit's cave, where by his fire
The Hermit sits alone.
                                These beauteous forms,
Through a long absence, have not been to me
As is a landscape to a blind man's eye:
25 But oft, in lonely rooms, and 'mid the din
Of towns and cities, I have owed to them
In hours of weariness, sensations sweet,
Felt in the blood, and felt along the heart;
And passing even into my purer mind,
30 With tranquil restoration: - feelings too
Of unremembered pleasure: such, perhaps,
As have no slight or trivial influence
On that best portion of a good man's life,
His little, nameless, unremembered, acts
35 Of kindness and of love. Nor less, I trust,

1. Wordsworth had paid his first visit to the ruins of
Tintern Abbey, near Monmouth, in August 1793.

To them I may have owed another gift,
Of aspect more sublime; that blessed mood,
In which the burden of the mystery,
In which the heavy and the weary weight
40   Of all this unintelligible world,
Is lightened: - that serene and blessed mood,
In which the affections² gently lead us on, -
Until, the breath of this corporeal frame
And even the motion of our human blood
45   Almost suspended, we are laid asleep
In body, and become a living soul:
While with an eye made quiet by the power
Of harmony, and the deep power of joy,
We see into the life of things.
                                      If this
50   Be but a vain belief, yet, oh! how oft -
In darkness and amid the many shapes
Of joyless daylight; when the fretful stir
Unprofitable, and the fever of the world,
Have hung upon the beatings of my heart -
55   How oft, in spirit, have I turned to thee,
O sylvan Wye! thou wanderer through the woods,
How often has my spirit turned to thee!

    And now, with gleams of half-extinguished thought,
With many recognitions dim and faint,
60   And somewhat of a sad perplexity,
The picture of the mind revives again:
While here I stand, not only with the sense
Of present pleasure, but with pleasing thoughts
That in this moment there is life and food
65   For future years. And so I dare to hope,
Though changed, no doubt, from what I was when first
I came among these hills; when like a roe
I bounded o'er the mountains, by the sides
Of the deep rivers, and the lonely streams,
70   Wherever nature led: more like a man
Flying from something that he dreads, than one
Who sought the thing he loved. For nature then
(The coarser pleasures of my boyish days,
And their glad animal movements all gone by)
75   To me was all in all. - I cannot paint
What then I was. The sounding cataract
Haunted me like a passion: the tall rock,
The mountain, and the deep and gloomy wood,
Their colours and their forms, were then to me
80   An appetite; a feeling and a love,
That had no need of a remoter charm,
By thought supplied, nor any interest
Unborrowed from the eye. - That time is past,
And all its aching joys are now no more,
85   And all its dizzy raptures. Not for this
Faint I, nor mourn nor murmur; other gifts
Have followed; for such loss, I would believe,
Abundant recompense. For I have learned
To look on nature, not as in the hour
90   Of thoughtless youth; but hearing oftentimes
The still, sad music of humanity,
Nor harsh nor grating, though of ample power
To chasten and subdue. And I have felt
A presence that disturbs me with the joy
95   Of elevated thoughts; a sense sublime

2. Feelings.

Of something far more deeply interfused,
Whose dwelling is the light of setting suns,
And the round ocean and the living air,
And the blue sky, and in the mind of man:
100   A motion and a spirit, that impels
All thinking things, all objects of all thought,
And rolls through all things. Therefore am I still
A lover of the meadows and the woods,
And mountains; and of all that we behold
105   From this green earth; of all the mighty world
Of eye, and ear, - both what they half create,
And what perceive; well pleased to recognize
In nature and the language of the sense,
The anchor of my purest thoughts, the nurse,
110   The guide, the guardian of my heart, and soul
Of all my moral being.
                            Nor perchance,
If I were not thus taught, should I the more
Suffer my genial spirits³ to decay:
For thou art with me here upon the banks
115   Of this fair river; thou my dearest Friend,⁴
My dear, dear Friend; and in thy voice I catch
The language of my former heart, and read
My former pleasures in the shooting lights
Of thy wild eyes. Oh! yet a little while
120   May I behold in thee what I was once,
My dear, dear Sister! and this prayer I make,
Knowing that Nature never did betray
The heart that loved her; 'tis her privilege,
Through all the years of this our life, to lead
125   From joy to joy: for she can so inform
The mind that is within us, so impress
With quietness and beauty, and so feed
With lofty thoughts, that neither evil tongues,
Rash judgements, nor the sneers of selfish men,
130   Nor greetings where no kindness is, nor all
The dreary intercourse of daily life,
Shall e'er prevail against us, or disturb
Our cheerful faith, that all which we behold
Is full of blessings. Therefore let the moon
135   Shine on thee in thy solitary walk;
And let the misty mountain-winds be free
To blow against thee: and, in after years,
When these wild ecstasies shall be matured
Into a sober pleasure; when thy mind
140   Shall be a mansion for all lovely forms,
Thy memory be as a dwelling-place
For all sweet sounds and harmonies; oh! then,
If solitude, or fear, or pain, or grief,
Should be thy portion, with what healing thoughts
145   Of tender joy wilt thou remember me,
And these my exhortations! Nor, perchance -
If I should be where I no more can hear
Thy voice, nor catch from thy wild eyes these gleams
Of past existence - wilt thou then forget
150   That on the banks of this delightful stream
We stood together; and that I, so long
A worshipper of Nature, hither came
Unwearied in that service: rather say
With warmer love - oh! with far deeper zeal
155   Of holier love. Nor wilt thou then forget,

---

3. Intellectual and creative powers.   4. Wordsworth's sister Dorothy.

That after many wanderings, many years
Of absence, these steep woods and lofty cliffs,
And this green pastoral landscape, were to me
More dear, both for themselves and for thy sake!

Strange Fits of Passion Have I Known

Strange fits of passion have I known:
And I will dare to tell,
But in the Lover's ear alone,
What once to me befell.

5 When she I loved looked every day
Fresh as a rose in June,
I to her cottage bent my way,
Beneath an evening moon.

Upon the moon I fixed my eye,
10 All over the wide lea;
With quickening pace my horse drew nigh
Those paths so dear to me.

And now we reached the orchard-plot;
And, as we climbed the hill,
15 The sinking moon to Lucy's cot
Came near, and nearer still.

In one of those sweet dreams I slept,
Kind Nature's gentlest boon!
And all the while my eyes I kept
20 On the descending moon.

My horse moved on; hoof after hoof
He raised, and never stopped:
When down behind the cottage roof,
At once, the bright moon dropped.

25 What fond and wayward thoughts will slide
Into a Lover's head!
'O mercy!' to myself I cried,
'If Lucy should be dead!'

She Dwelt among the Untrodden Ways

She dwelt among the untrodden ways
  Beside the springs of Dove,[1]
A Maid whom there were none to praise
  And very few to love:

A violet by a mossy stone
  Half hidden from the eye!
- Fair as a star, when only one
  Is shining in the sky.

She lived unknown, and few could know
  When Lucy ceased to be;
But she is in her grave, and, oh,
  The difference to me!

Three Years She Grew in Sun and Shower

Three years she grew in sun and shower,
Then Nature said, 'A lovelier flower
On earth was never sown;
This Child I to myself will take;
5 She shall be mine, and I will make
A Lady of my own.

'Myself will to my darling be
Both law and impulse: and with me
The Girl, in rock and plain,
10 In earth and heaven, in glade and bower,
Shall feel an overseeing power
To kindle or restrain.

'She shall be sportive as the fawn
That wild with glee across the lawn
15 Or up the mountain springs;
And hers shall be the breathing balm,
And hers the silence and the calm
Of mute insensate things.

'The floating clouds their state shall lend
20 To her; for her the willow bend;
Nor shall she fail to see
Even in the motions of the Storm
Grace that shall mould the Maiden's form
By silent sympathy.

1. Three English rivers bear this name, any one of which
Wordsworth may have had in mind.

25 'The stars of midnight shall be dear
To her; and she shall lean her ear
In many a secret place
Where rivulets dance their wayward round,
And beauty born of murmuring sound
30 Shall pass into her face.

'And vital feelings of delight
Shall rear her form to stately height,
Her virgin bosom swell;
Such thoughts to Lucy I will give
35 While she and I together live
Here in this happy dell.'

40 Thus Nature spake—The work was done—
How soon my Lucy's race was run!
She died, and left to me
This heath, this calm, and quiet scene;
The memory of what has been,
And never more will be.

A Slumber Did My Spirit Seal

A slumber did my spirit seal;
  I had no human fears:
She seemed a thing that could not feel
  The touch of earthly years.

No motion has she now, no force;
  She neither hears nor sees;
Rolled round in earth's diurnal course,
  With rocks, and stones, and trees.

I Travelled among Unknown Men

I travelled among unknown men,
  In lands beyond the sea;
Nor, England! did I know till then
  What love I bore to thee.

'Tis past, that melancholy dream!
  Nor will I quit thy shore
A second time; for still I seem
  To love thee more and more.

Among thy mountains did I feel
  The joy of my desire;
And she I cherished turned her wheel
  Beside an English fire.

Thy mornings showed, thy nights concealed,
  The bowers where Lucy played;
And thine too is the last green field
  That Lucy's eyes surveyed.

My Heart Leaps Up When I Behold

My heart leaps up when I behold
  A rainbow in the sky:
So was it when my life began;
So is it now I am a man;
So be it when I shall grow old,

  Or let me die!
The Child is father of the Man;
And I could wish my days to be
Bound each to each by natural piety.

Resolution and Independence

I
There was a roaring in the wind all night;
The rain came heavily and fell in floods;
But now the sun is rising calm and bright;
The birds are singing in the distant woods;
5 Over his own sweet voice the Stock-dove broods;
The Jay makes answer as the Magpie chatters;
And all the air is filled with pleasant noise of waters.

II
All things that love the sun are out of doors;
The sky rejoices in the morning's birth;
10 The grass is bright with rain-drops; - on the moors
The hare is running races in her mirth;
And with her feet she from the plashy earth

Raises a mist; that, glittering in the sun,
Runs with her all the way, wherever she doth run.

III

15 I was a Traveller then upon the moor;
I saw the hare that raced about with joy;
I heard the woods and distant waters roar;
Or heard them not, as happy as a boy:
The pleasant season did my heart employ:
20 My old remembrances went from me wholly;
And all the ways of men, so vain and melancholy.

IV

But, as it sometimes chanceth, from the might
Of joy in minds that can no further go,
As high as we have mounted in delight
25 In our dejection do we sink as low;
To me that morning did it happen so;
And fears and fancies thick upon me came;
Dim sadness - and blind thoughts, I knew not, nor could name.

V

I heard the sky-lark warbling in the sky;
30 And I bethought me of the playful hare:
Even such a happy Child of earth am I;
Even as these blissful creatures do I fare;
Far from the world I walk, and from all care;
But there may come another day to me -
35 Solitude, pain of heart, distress, and poverty.

VI

My whole life I have lived in pleasant thought,
As if life's business were a summer mood;
As if all needful things would come unsought
To genial[1] faith, still rich in genial good;
40 But how can He expect that others should
Build for him, sow for him, and at his call
Love him, who for himself will take no need at all?

VII

I thought of Chatterton,[2] the marvellous Boy,
The sleepless Soul that perished in his pride;
45 Of Him who walked in glory and in joy
Following his plough,[3] along the mountain-side:
By our own spirits are we deified:
We Poets in our youth begin in gladness;
But thereof come in the end despondency and madness.

VIII

50 Now, whether it were by peculiar grace,
A leading from above, a something given,
Yet it befell, that, in this lonely place,
When I with these untoward thoughts had striven,
Beside a pool bare to the eye of heaven
55 I saw a Man before me unawares:
The oldest man he seemed that ever wore grey hairs.

1. Cheering, inspiriting.
2. Thomas Chatterton (1752–70), a promising poet who committed suicide at seventeen.
3. The reference is to Robert Burns, who spent much of his life as an indigent farmer. Though Burns was lionized in his own lifetime, Wordsworth presents him here as a type of the neglected genius.

IX

As a huge stone is sometimes seen to lie
Couched on the bald top of an eminence;
Wonder to all who do the same espy,
60   By what means it could thither come, and whence;
So that it seems a thing endued with sense:
Like a sea-beast crawled forth, that on a shelf
Of rock or sand reposeth, there to sun itself;

X

Such seemed this Man, not all alive nor dead,
65   Nor all asleep - in his extreme old age:
His body was bent double, feet and head
Coming together in life's pilgrimage;
As if some dire constraint of pain, or rage
Of sickness felt by him in times long past,
70   A more than human weight upon his frame had cast.

XI

Himself he propped, limbs, body, and pale face,
Upon a long grey staff of shaven wood:
And, still as I drew near with gentle pace,
Upon the margin of that moorish flood
75   Motionless as a cloud the old Man stood,
That heareth not the loud winds when they call;
And moveth all together, if it move at all.

XII

At length, himself unsettling, he the pond
Stirred with his staff, and fixedly did look
80   Upon the muddy water, which he conned,[4]
As if he had been reading in a book:
And now a stranger's privilege I took;
And, drawing to his side, to him did say,
'This morning gives us promise of a glorious day.'

XIII

85   A gentle answer did the old Man make,
In courteous speech which forth he slowly drew:
And him with further words I thus bespake,
'What occupation do you there pursue?
This is a lonesome place for one like you.'
90   Ere he replied, a flash of mild surprise
Broke from the sable orbs of his yet-vivid eyes.

XIV

His words came feebly, from a feeble chest,
But each in solemn order followed each,
With something of a lofty utterance drest -
95   Choice word and measured phrase, above the reach
Of ordinary men; a stately speech;
Such as grave Livers do in Scotland use,
Religious men, who give to God and man their dues.

XV

He told, that to these waters he had come
100   To gather leeches, being old and poor:
Employment hazardous and wearisome!
And he had many hardships to endure:
From pond to pond he roamed, from moor to moor;
Housing, with God's good help, by choice or chance;
105   And in this way he gained an honest maintenance.

4. Studied.

XVI

The old Man still stood talking by my side;
But now his voice to me was like a stream
Scarce heard; nor word from word could I divide;
And the whole body of the Man did seem
110 Like one whom I had met with in a dream;
Or like a man from some far region sent,
To give me human strength, by apt admonishment.

XVII

My former thoughts returned: the fear that kills;
And hope that is unwilling to be fed;
115 Cold, pain, and labour, and all fleshly ills;
And mighty Poets in their misery dead.
- Perplexed, and longing to be comforted,
My question eagerly did I renew,
'How is it that you live, and what is it you do?'

XVIII

120 He with a smile did then his words repeat;
And said that, gathering leeches, far and wide
He travelled; stirring thus about his feet
The waters of the pools where they abide.
'Once I could meet with them on every side;
125 But they have dwindled long by slow decay;
Yet still I persevere, and find them where I may.'

XIX

While he was talking thus, the lonely place,
The old Man's shape, and speech - all troubled me:
In my mind's eye I seemed to see him pace
130 About the weary moors continually,
Wandering about alone and silently.
While I these thoughts within myself pursued,
He, having made a pause, the same discourse renewed.

XX

And soon with this he other matter blended,
135 Cheerfully uttered, with demeanour kind,
But stately in the main; and when he ended,
I could have laughed myself to scorn to find
In that decrepit Man so firm a mind.
'God,' said I, 'be my help and stay[5] secure;
140 I'll think of the Leech-gatherer on the lonely moor!'

Nuns Fret Not at Their Convent's Narrow Room

Nuns fret not at their convent's narrow room;
And hermits are contented with their cells;
And students with their pensive citadels;
Maids at the wheel, the weaver at his loom,
Sit blithe and happy; bees that soar for bloom,
High as the highest Peak of Furness-fells,[1]
Will murmur by the hour in foxglove bells:
In truth the prison, unto which we doom
Ourselves, no prison is: and hence for me,
In sundry moods, 'twas pastime to be bound
Within the Sonnet's scanty plot of ground;
Pleased if some Souls (for such there needs must be)
Who have felt the weight of too much liberty,
Should find brief solace there, as I have found.

---

5. Prop, support.   1. The hills west of Lake Windermere.

Composed upon Westminster Bridge, September 3, 1802[1]

Earth has not anything to show more fair:
Dull would he be of soul who could pass by
A sight so touching in its majesty:
This City now doth, like a garment, wear
The beauty of the morning; silent, bare,
Ships, towers, domes, theatres, and temples lie
Open unto the fields, and to the sky;

All bright and glittering in the smokeless air.
Never did sun more beautifully steep
In his first splendour, valley, rock, or hill;
Ne'er saw I, never felt, a calm so deep!
The river glideth at his own sweet will:
Dear God! the very houses seem asleep;
And all that mighty heart is lying still!

London, 1802[1]

Milton! thou shouldst be living at this hour:
England hath need of thee: she is a fen
Of stagnant waters: altar, sword, and pen,
Fireside, the heroic wealth of hall and bower,
Have forfeited their ancient English dower
Of inward happiness. We are selfish men;
Oh! raise us up, return to us again;

And give us manners, virtue, freedom, power.
Thy soul was like a Star, and dwelt apart:
Thou hadst a voice whose sound was like the sea
Pure as the naked heavens, majestic, free,
So didst thou travel on life's common way,
In cheerful godliness; and yet thy heart
The lowliest duties on herself did lay.

It Is a Beauteous Evening, Calm and Free

It is a beauteous evening, calm and free,
The holy time is quiet as a Nun
Breathless with adoration; the broad sun
Is sinking down in its tranquillity;
The gentleness of heaven broods o'er the Sea:
Listen! the mighty Being is awake,
And doth with his eternal motion make
A sound like thunder - everlastingly.
Dear Child![1] dear Girl! that walkest with me here,
If thou appear untouched by solemn thought,
Thy nature is not therefore less divine:
Thou liest in Abraham's bosom[2] all the year;
And worshipp'st at the Temple's inner shrine,
God being with thee when we know it not.

The World Is Too Much with Us; Late and Soon

The world is too much with us; late and soon,
Getting and spending, we lay waste our powers:
Little we see in Nature that is ours;
We have given our hearts away, a sordid boon!
This Sea that bares her bosom to the moon;
The winds that will be howling at all hours,
And are up-gathered now like sleeping flowers;

For this, for everything, we are out of tune;
It moves us not. - Great God! I'd rather be
A Pagan suckled in a creed outworn;
So might I, standing on this pleasant lea,
Have glimpses that would make me less forlorn;
Have sight of Proteus[1] rising from the sea;
Or hear old Triton[2] blow his wreathèd horn.

1. Dorothy Wordsworth's journals show that the date should probably be July 31, 1802, when she and her brother left London for Dover on their way to France.

1. "This was written immediately after my return from France to London, where I could not but be struck, as here described, with the vanity and parade of our own country, especially in great towns and cities, as contrasted with the quiet, and I may say the desolation, that the

revolution had produced in France" (Wordsworth's note).

1. Caroline, Wordsworth's daughter by Annette Vallon, born in 1792.
2. I.e., Heaven. See Luke xvi.22.

1. In Greek mythology, a sea god who could assume many different forms.
2. A son of Poseidon, half man, half fish.

Ode: Intimations of Immortality from Recollections of Early Childhood

The Child is Father of the Man;
And I could wish my days to be
Bound each to each by natural piety[1]

I

There was a time when meadow, grove, and stream,
The earth, and every common sight,
            To me did seem
            Apparelled in celestial light,
5   The glory and the freshness of a dream.
It is not now as it hath been of yore; -
            Turn wheresoe'er I may,
                By night or day,
The things which I have seen I now can see no more.

II

10   The Rainbow comes and goes,
                And lovely is the Rose;
                The Moon doth with delight
Look round her when the heavens are bare;
                Waters on a starry night
15   Are beautiful and fair;
    The sunshine is a glorious birth;
    But yet I know, where'er I go,
That there hath past away a glory from the earth.

III

Now, while the birds thus sing a joyous song,
20   And while the young lambs bound
            As to the tabor's sound,[2]
To me alone there came a thought of grief:
A timely utterance gave that thought relief,
            And I again am strong:
25 The cataracts blow their trumpets from the steep;
No more shall grief of mine the season wrong;
I hear the Echoes through the mountains throng,
The Winds come to me from the fields of sleep,
            And all the earth is gay;
30   Land and sea
        Give themselves up to jollity,
            And with the heart of May
        Doth every Beast keep holiday; -
            Thou Child of Joy,
35 Shout round me, let me hear thy shouts, thou happy
                Shepherd-boy!

IV

Ye blessèd Creatures, I have heard the call
    Ye to each other make; I see
The heavens laugh with you in your jubilee;
    My heart is at your festival,

---

1. These lines are from Wordsworth's poem "My Heart
Leaps Up."
2. The tabor is a small drum.

40   My head hath its coronal,[3]
The fulness of your bliss, I feel - I feel it all.
     Oh evil day! if I were sullen
     While Earth herself is adorning,
          This sweet May-morning,
45   And the Children are culling
          On every side,
     In a thousand valleys far and wide,
     Fresh flowers; while the sun shines warm,
And the Babe leaps up on his Mother's arm: -
50   I hear, I hear, with joy I hear!
     - But there's a Tree, of many, one,
A single Field which I have looked upon,
Both of them speak of something that is gone:
          The Pansy at my feet
55   Doth the same tale repeat:
Whither is fled the visionary gleam?
Where is it now, the glory and the dream?

V
Our birth is but a sleep and a forgetting:[4]
The Soul that rises with us, our life's Star,
60   Hath had elsewhere its setting,
               And cometh from afar:
          Not in entire forgetfulness,
          And not in utter nakedness,
But trailing clouds of glory do we come
65   From God, who is our home:
Heaven lies about us in our infancy!
Shades of the prison-house begin to close
          Upon the growing Boy,
               But He
70 Beholds the light, and whence it flows,
          He sees it in his joy;
The Youth, who daily farther from the east
          Must travel, still is Nature's Priest,
          And by the vision splendid
75   Is on his way attended;
At length the Man perceives it die away,
And fade into the light of common day.

VI
Earth fills her lap with pleasures of her own;
Yearnings she hath in her own natural kind,
80 And, even with something of a Mother's mind,
          And no unworthy aim,
          The homely Nurse doth all she can
To make her Foster-child, her Inmate Man,
          Forget the glories he hath known,
85 And that imperial palace whence he came.

VII
Behold the Child among his new-born blisses,
A six years' Darling of a pigmy size!
See, where 'mid work of his own hand he lies,
Fretted[5] by sallies of his mother's kisses,
90 With light upon him from his father's eyes!
See, at his feet, some little plan or chart,
Some fragment from his dream of human life,

---

3. A garland or circlet worn on the head.
4. Wordsworth's ideas about the pre-existence of the soul were derived in part from memories of his own childhood, in part from Platonic philosophy. However, he insisted that he did not intend to present these notions as systematic doctrine, only to make the best use of them he could "as a Poet," to explore man's consciousness of immortality.
5. Chequered over.

Shaped by himself with newly-learnèd art;
    A wedding or a festival,
95   A mourning or a funeral;
      And this hath now his heart,
    And unto this he frames his song:
      Then will he fit his tongue
To dialogues of business, love, or strife;
100   But it will not be long
      Ere this be thrown aside,
    And with new joy and pride
The little Actor cons another part;
Filling from time to time his 'humorous stage'[6]
105 With all the Persons, down to palsied Age,
That Life brings with her in her equipage;
    As if his whole vocation
    Were endless imitation.

VIII

Thou, whose exterior semblance doth belie
110   Thy Soul's immensity;
Thou best Philosopher, who yet dost keep
Thy heritage, thou Eye among the blind,
That, deaf and silent, read'st the eternal deep,
Haunted for ever by the eternal mind, -
115   Mighty Prophet! Seer blest!
    On whom those truths do rest,
Which we are toiling all our lives to find,
In darkness lost, the darkness of the grave;
Thou, over whom thy Immortality
120 Broods like the Day, a Master o'er a Slave,
A Presence which is not to be put by;
Thou little Child, yet glorious in the might
Of heaven-born freedom on thy being's height,
Why with such earnest pains dost thou provoke
125 The years to bring the inevitable yoke,
Thus blindly with thy blessedness at strife?
Full soon thy Soul shall have her earthly freight,
And custom lie upon thee with a weight,
Heavy as frost, and deep almost as life!

IX

130   O joy! that in our embers
    Is something that doth live,
    That nature yet remembers
    What was so fugitive!
The thought of our past years in me doth breed
135 Perpetual benediction: not indeed
For that which is most worthy to be blest;
Delight and liberty, the simple creed
Of Childhood, whether busy or at rest,
With new-fledged hope still fluttering in his breast: -
140   Not for these I raise
    The song of thanks and praise;
    But for those obstinate questionings
    Of sense and outward things,
    Fallings from us, vanishings;
145   Blank misgivings of a Creature
Moving about in worlds not realized,
High instincts before which our mortal Nature
Did tremble like a guilty Thing surprised:

---

6. Quoted from the dedicatory sonnet to Samuel Daniel's *Musophilus* (1599). "Humorous" here alludes to the tradition of dramatic characters representing different "humours" or aspects of temperament.

But for those first affections,[7]
150   Those shadowy recollections,
  Which, be they what they may,
Are yet the fountain light of all our day,
Are yet a master light of all our seeing;
  Uphold us, cherish, and have power to make
155 Our noisy years seem moments in the being
Of the eternal Silence: truths that wake,
   To perish never;
Which neither listlessness, nor mad endeavour,
   Nor Man nor Boy,
160 Nor all that is at enmity with joy,
Can utterly abolish or destroy!
   Hence in a season of calm weather
   Though inland far we be,
Our Souls have sight of that immortal sea
165   Which brought us hither,
  Can in a moment travel thither,
And see the Children sport upon the shore,
And hear the mighty waters rolling evermore.

X

Then sing, ye Birds, sing, sing a joyous song!
170   And let the young Lambs bound
   As to the tabor's sound!
We in thought will join your throng,
   Ye that pipe and ye that play,
   Ye that through your hearts today
175   Feel the gladness of the May!
What though the radiance which was once so bright
Be now for ever taken from my sight,
   Though nothing can bring back the hour
Of splendour in the grass, of glory in the flower;
180   We will grieve not, rather find
   Strength in what remains behind;
   In the primal sympathy
   Which having been must ever be;
   In the soothing thoughts that spring
185   Out of human suffering;
   In the faith that looks through death,
In years that bring the philosophic mind.

XI

And O, ye Fountains, Meadows, Hills, and Groves,
Forebode not any severing of our loves!
190 Yet in my heart of hearts I feel your might;
I only have relinquished one delight
To live beneath your more habitual sway.
I love the Brooks which down their channels fret,
Even more than when I tripped lightly as they;
195 The innocent brightness of a new-born Day
    Is lovely yet;
The Clouds that gather round the setting sun
Do take a sober colouring from an eye
That hath kept watch o'er man's mortality;
200 Another race hath been, and other palms are won.
Thanks to the human heart by which we live,
Thanks to its tenderness, its joys, and fears,
To me the meanest flower that blows can give
Thoughts that do often lie too deep for tears.

7. Feelings.

I Wandered Lonely as a Cloud

I wandered lonely as a cloud
That floats on high o'er vales and hills,
When all at once I saw a crowd,
A host, of golden daffodils;
5   Beside the lake, beneath the trees,
Fluttering and dancing in the breeze.

Continuous as the stars that shine
And twinkle on the milky way,
They stretched in never-ending line
10   Along the margin of a bay:
Ten thousand saw I at a glance,
Tossing their heads in sprightly dance.

The waves beside them danced; but they
Out-did the sparkling waves in glee:
15   A poet could not but be gay,
In such a jocund company:
I gazed - and gazed - but little thought
What wealth the show to me had brought:

For oft, when on my couch I lie
20   In vacant or in pensive mood,
They flash upon that inward eye
Which is the bliss of solitude;
And then my heart with pleasure fills,
And dances with the daffodils.

She Was a Phantom of Delight

She was a Phantom of delight
When first she gleamed upon my sight;
A lovely Apparition, sent
To be a moment's ornament;
5   Her eyes as stars of Twilight fair;
Like Twilight's, too, her dusky hair;
But all things else about her drawn
From May-time and the cheerful Dawn;
A dancing Shape, an Image gay,
10   To haunt, to startle, and way-lay.

I saw her upon nearer view,
A Spirit, yet a Woman too!
Her household motions light and free,
And steps of virgin-liberty;
15   A countenance in which did meet

Sweet records, promises as sweet;
A Creature not too bright or good
For human nature's daily food;
For transient sorrows, simple wiles,
20   Praise, blame, love, kisses, tears, and smiles.

And now I see with eye serene
The very pulse of the machine;
A Being breathing thoughtful breath,
A Traveller between life and death;
25   The reason firm, the temperate will,
Endurance, foresight, strength, and skill;
A perfect Woman, nobly planned,
To warn, to comfort, and command;
And yet a Spirit still, and bright
30   With something of angelic light.

The Solitary Reaper[1]

Behold her, single in the field,
Yon solitary Highland Lass!
Reaping and singing by herself;
Stop here, or gently pass!
5   Alone she cuts and binds the grain,
And sings a melancholy strain;
O listen! for the Vale profound
Is overflowing with the sound.

No Nightingale did ever chaunt
10   More welcome notes to weary bands
Of travellers in some shady haunt,
Among Arabian sands:
A voice so thrilling ne'er was heard
In spring-time from the Cuckoo-bird,
15   Breaking the silence of the seas
Among the farthest Hebrides.

Will no one tell me what she sings? -
Perhaps the plaintive numbers flow
For old, unhappy, far-off things,
20   And battles long ago:
Or is it some more humble lay,
Familiar matter of today?
Some natural sorrow, loss, or pain,
That has been, and may be again?

25   Whate'er the theme, the Maiden sang
As if her song could have no ending;
I saw her singing at her work,
And o'er the sickle bending; -
I listened, motionless and still;
30   And, as I mounted up the hill,
The music in my heart I bore,
Long after it was heard no more.

1. "This poem was suggested by a beautiful sentence in an MS. Tour in Scotland written by a friend, the last line being taken from it *verbatim*" (Wordsworth's note). The friend was Thomas Wilkinson, whose *Tours to the British Mountains* was published in 1824.

From The Prelude *or* Growth of a Poet's Mind
An Autobiographical Poem

From Book I. Introduction— Childhood and School-Time

  Fair seed-time had my soul, and I grew up
Fostered alike by beauty and by fear:
Much favoured in my birth-place, and no less
In that beloved Vale to which erelong
305 We were transplanted—there were we let loose
For sports of wider range. Ere I had told
Ten birth-days, when among the mountain slopes
Frost, and the breath of frosty wind, had snapped
The last autumnal crocus, 'twas my joy
310 With store of springes[1] o'er my shoulder hung
To range the open heights where woodcocks ran
Along the smooth green turf. Through half the night,
Scudding away from snare to snare, I plied
That anxious visitation;—moon and stars
315 Were shining o'er my head. I was alone,
And seemed to be a trouble to the peace
That dwelt among them. Sometimes it befel
In these night wanderings, that a strong desire
O'erpowered my better reason, and the bird
320 Which was the captive of another's toil[2]
Became my prey; and when the deed was done
I heard among the solitary hills
Low breathings coming after me, and sounds
Of undistinguishable motion, steps
325 Almost as silent as the turf they trod.

  Nor less when spring had warmed the cultured[3] Vale,
Roved we as plunderers where the mother-bird
Had in high places built her lodge; though mean
Our object and inglorious, yet the end
330 Was not ignoble. Oh! when I have hung
Above the raven's nest, by knots of grass
And half-inch fissures in the slippery rock
But ill-sustained, and almost (so it seemed)
Suspended by the blast that blew amain,
335 Shouldering the naked crag, oh, at that time
While on the perilous ridge I hung alone,
With what strange utterance did the loud dry wind
Blow through my ear! the sky seemed not a sky
Of earth—and with what motion moved the clouds!

340 Dust as we are, the immortal spirit grows
Like harmony in music; there is a dark
Inscrutable workmanship that reconciles
Discordant elements, makes them cling together
In one society. How strange that all
345 The terrors, pains, and early miseries,
Regrets, vexations, lassitudes interfused
Within my mind, should e'er have borne a part,
And that a needful part, in making up
The calm existence that is mine when I
350 Am worthy of myself! Praise to the end!
Thanks to the means which Nature deigned to employ;
Whether her fearless visitings, or those
That came with soft alarm, like hurtless light

1. Snares.
2. Trap, snare.   3. Cultivated.

Opening the peaceful clouds; or she may use
355   Severer interventions, ministry
More palpable, as best might suit her aim.

    One summer evening (led by her) I found
A little boat tied to a willow tree
Within a rocky cave, its usual home.
360   Straight I unloosed her chain, and stepping in
Pushed from the shore. It was an act of stealth
And troubled pleasure, nor without the voice
Of mountain-echoes did my boat move on;
Leaving behind her still, on either side,
365   Small circles glittering idly in the moon,
Until they melted all into one track
Of sparkling light. But now, like one who rows,
Proud of his skill, to reach a chosen point
With an unswerving line, I fixed my view
370   Upon the summit of a craggy ridge,
The horizon's utmost boundary; for above
Was nothing but the stars and the grey sky.
She was an elfin pinnace; lustily
I dipped my oars into the silent lake,
375   And, as I rose upon the stroke, my boat
Went heaving through the water like a swan;
When, from behind that craggy steep till then
The horizon's bound, a huge peak, black and huge,
As if with voluntary power instinct[4]
380   Upreared its head. I struck and struck again,
And growing still in stature the grim shape
Towered up between me and the stars, and still,
For so it seemed, with purpose of its own
And measured motion like a living thing,
385   Strode after me. With trembling oars I turned,
And through the silent water stole my way
Back to the covert of the willow tree;
There in her mooring-place I left my bark,—
And through the meadows homeward went, in grave
390   And serious mood; but after I had seen
That spectacle, for many days, my brain
Worked with a dim and undetermined sense
Of unknown modes of being; o'er my thoughts
There hung a darkness, call it solitude
395   Or blank desertion. No familiar shapes
Remained, no pleasant images of trees,
Of sea or sky, no colours of green fields;
But huge and mighty forms, that do not live
Like living men, moved slowly through the mind
400   By day, and were a trouble to my dreams.

    Wisdom and Spirit of the universe!
Thou Soul that art the eternity of thought,
That givest to forms and images a breath
And everlasting motion, not in vain
405   By day or star-light thus from my first dawn
Of childhood didst thou intwine for me
The passions that build up our human soul;
Not with the mean and vulgar works of man,
But with high objects, with enduring things—
410   With life and nature, purifying thus
The elements of feeling and of thought,
And sanctifying, by such discipline,

4. Imbued.

Both pain and fear, until we recognise
A grandeur in the beatings of the heart.
415   Nor was this fellowship vouchsafed to me
With stinted kindness. In November days,
When vapours rolling down the valley made
A lonely scene more lonesome, among woods
At noon, and 'mid the calm of summer nights,
420   When, by the margin of the trembling lake,
Beneath the gloomy hills homeward I went
In solitude, such intercourse was mine;
Mine was it in the fields both day and night,
And by the waters, all the summer long.

425   And in the frosty season, when the sun
Was set, and visible for many a mile
The cottage windows blazed through twilight gloom,
I heeded not their summons: happy time
It was indeed for all of us—for me
430   It was a time of rapture! Clear and loud
The village clock tolled six,—I wheeled about,
Proud and exulting like an untired horse
That cares not for his home. All shod with steel,
We hissed along the polished ice in games
435   Confederate, imitative of the chase
And woodland pleasures,—the resounding horn,
The pack loud chiming, and the hunted hare.
So through the darkness and the cold we flew,
And not a voice was idle; with the din
440   Smitten, the precipices rang aloud;
The leafless trees and every icy crag
Tinkled like iron; while far distant hills
Into the tumult sent an alien sound
Of melancholy not unnoticed, while the stars
445   Eastward were sparkling clear, and in the west
The orange sky of evening died away.
Not seldom from the uproar I retired
Into a silent bay, or sportively
Glanced sideway, leaving the tumultuous throng,
450   To cut across the reflex⁵ of a star
That fled, and, flying still before me, gleamed
Upon the grassy plain; and oftentimes,
When we had given our bodies to the wind,
And all the shadowy banks on either side
455   Came sweeping through the darkness, spinning still
The rapid line of motion, then at once
Have I, reclining back upon my heels,
Stopped short; yet still the solitary cliffs
Wheeled by me—even as if the earth had rolled
460   With visible motion her diurnal⁶ round!
Behind me did they stretch in solemn train,
Feebler and feebler, and I stood and watched
Till all was tranquil as a dreamless sleep.

Ye Presences of Nature in the sky
465   And on the earth! Ye Visions of the hills!
And Souls of lonely places! can I think
A vulgar hope was yours when ye employed
Such ministry, when ye through many a year
Haunting me thus among my boyish sports,
470   On caves and trees, upon the woods and hills,
Impressed upon all forms the characters⁷

5. Reflection.
6. Daily.   7. Marks, signs.

Of danger or desire; and thus did make
The surface of the universal earth
With triumph and delight, with hope and fear,
475 Work like a sea?
                     *   *   *
     Nor, sedulous as I have been to trace
545 How Nature by extrinsic passion first
Peopled the mind with forms sublime or fair,
And made me love them, may I here omit
How other pleasures have been mine, and joys
Of subtler origin; how I have felt,
550 Not seldom even in that tempestuous time,
Those hallowed and pure motions of the sense
Which seem, in their simplicity, to own
An intellectual charm; that calm delight
Which, if I err not, surely must belong
555 To those first-born affinities[8] that fit
Our new existence to existing things,
And, in our dawn of being, constitute
The bond of union between life and joy.

     Yes, I remember when the changeful earth,
560 And twice five summers on my mind had stamped
The faces of the moving year, even then
I held unconscious intercourse with beauty
Old as creation, drinking in a pure
Organic pleasure from the silver wreaths
565 Of curling mist, or from the level plain
Of waters coloured by impending[9] clouds.

     The sands of Westmoreland, the creeks and bays
Of Cumbria's[10] rocky limits, they can tell
How, when the Sea threw off his evening shade,
570 And to the shepherd's hut on distant hills
Sent welcome notice of the rising moon,
How I have stood, to fancies such as these
A stranger, linking with the spectacle
No conscious memory of a kindred sight,
575 And bringing with me no peculiar sense
Of quietness or peace; yet have I stood,
Even while mine eye hath moved o'er many a league
Of shining water, gathering as it seemed
Through every hair-breadth in that field of light
580 New pleasure like a bee among the flowers.

     Thus oft amid those fits of vulgar[11] joy
Which, through all seasons, on a child's pursuits
Are prompt attendants, 'mid that giddy bliss
Which, like a tempest, works along the blood
585 And is forgotten; even then I felt
Gleams like the flashing of a shield;—the earth
And common face of Nature spake to me
Rememberable things; sometimes, 'tis true,
By chance collisions and quaint accidents
590 (Like those ill-sorted unions,[12] work supposed
Of evil-minded fairies), yet not vain
Nor profitless, if haply they impressed
Collateral[13] objects and appearances,
Albeit lifeless then, and doomed to sleep
595 Until maturer seasons called them forth

8. Affinities possessed by the new-born infant.
9. Overhanging.
10. Cumberland's.
11. Commonplace.
12. I.e., incompatible couples.
13. Indirectly connected.

To impregnate and to elevate the mind.
—And if the vulgar joy by its own weight
Wearied itself out of the memory,
The scenes which were a witness of that joy
600   Remained in their substantial lineaments
Depicted on the brain, and to the eye
Were visible, a daily sight; and thus
By the impressive discipline of fear,
By pleasure and repeated happiness,
605   So frequently repeated, and by force
Of obscure feelings representative
Of things forgotten, these same scenes so bright,
So beautiful, so majestic in themselves,
Though yet the day was distant, did become
610   Habitually dear, and all their forms
And changeful colours by invisible links
Were fastened to the affections.[14]

From Book II. School-Time

         'Twere long to tell
What spring and autumn, what the winter snows,
And what the summer shade, what day and night,
355   Evening and morning, sleep and waking thought,
From sources inexhaustible, poured forth
To feed the spirit of religious love
In which I walked with Nature. But let this
Be not forgotten, that I still retained
360   My first creative sensibility;
That by the regular action of the world
My soul was unsubdued. A plastic[15] power
Abode with me; a forming hand, at times
Rebellious, acting in a devious mood;
365   A local spirit of his own, at war
With general tendency, but, for the most,
Subservient strictly to external things
With which it communed. An auxiliar light
Came from my mind, which on the setting sun
370   Bestowed new splendour; the melodious birds,
The fluttering breezes, fountains that ran on
Murmuring so sweetly in themselves, obeyed
A like dominion, and the midnight storm
Grew darker in the presence of my eye:
375   Hence my obeisance, my devotion hence,
And hence my transport.

                  Nor should this, perchance,
Pass unrecorded, that I still[16] had loved
The exercise and produce of a toil,
Than analytic industry to me
380   More pleasing, and whose character I deem
Is more poetic as resembling more
Creative agency. The song would speak
Of that interminable building reared
By observation of affinities
385   In objects where no brotherhood exists
To passive minds. My seventeeth year was come;
And, whether from this habit rooted now
So deeply in my mind, or from excess

14. Feelings.
15. Formative, creative.   16. Constantly, habitually.

In the great social principle of life
390 Coercing all things into sympathy,
To unorganic natures were transferred
My own enjoyments; or the power of truth
Coming in revelation, did converse
With things that really are; I, at this time,
395 Saw blessings spread around me like a sea.
Thus while the days flew by, and years passed on,
From Nature overflowing on my soul,
I had received so much, that every thought
Was steeped in feeling; I was only then
400 Contented, when with bliss ineffable
I felt the sentiment of Being spread
O'er all that moves and all that seemeth still;
O'er all that, lost beyond the reach of thought
And human knowledge, to the human eye
405 Invisible, yet liveth to the heart;
O'er all that leaps and runs, and shouts and sings,
Or beats the gladsome air; o'er all that glides
Beneath the wave, yea, in the wave itself,
And mighty depth of waters. Wonder not
410 If high the transport, great the joy I felt,
Communing in this sort through earth and heaven
With every form of creature, as it looked
Towards the Uncreated with a countenance
Of adoration, with an eye of love.
415 One song they sang, and it was audible,
Most audible, then, when the fleshly ear,
O'ercome by humblest prelude of that strain,
Forgot her functions, and slept undisturbed.

If this be error, and another faith
420 Find easier access to the pious mind,
Yet were I grossly destitute of all
Those human sentiments that make this earth
So dear, if I should fail with grateful voice
To speak of you, ye mountains, and ye lakes
425 And sounding cataracts, ye mists and winds
That dwell among the hills where I was born.
If in my youth I have been pure in heart,
If, mingling with the world, I am content
With my own modest pleasures, and have lived
430 With God and Nature communing, removed
From little enmities and low desires,
The gift is yours; if in these times of fear,
This melancholy waste of hopes o'erthrown,[17]
If, 'mid indifference and apathy
435 And wicked exultation, when good men
On every side fall off we know not how,
To selfishness, disguised in gentle names
Of peace and quiet and domestic love,
Yet mingled not unwillingly with sneers
440 On visionary minds; if, in this time
Of dereliction and dismay, I yet
Despair not of our nature, but retain
A more than Roman confidence, a faith
That fails not, in all sorrow my support,
445 The blessing of my life; the gift is yours,
Ye winds and sounding cataracts! 'tis yours,

17. These lines, written in 1799, refer to the general disillusion among ardent liberals consequent upon the excesses of the French Revolution and the military conquests of Napoleon.

Ye mountains! thine, O Nature! Thou hast fed
My lofty speculations; and in thee,
For this uneasy heart of ours, I find
450   A never-failing principle of joy
And purest passion.

SAMUEL TAYLOR COLERIDGE (1772–1834)

The Eolian Harp[1]
Composed at Clevedon, Somersetshire

My pensive Sara![2] thy soft cheek reclined
Thus on mine arm, most soothing sweet it is
To sit beside our Cot, our Cot o'ergrown
With white-flower'd Jasmin, and the broad-leav'd Myrtle,
5   (Meet emblems they of Innocence and Love!)
And watch the clouds, that late were rich with light,
Slow saddening round, and mark the star of eve
Serenely brilliant (such should Wisdom be)
Shine opposite! How exquisite the scents
10   Snatch'd from yon bean-field! and the world *so* hush'd!
The stilly murmur of the distant Sea
Tells us of silence.
                              And that simplest Lute,
Placed length-ways in the clasping casement, hark!
How by the desultory breeze caress'd,
15   Like some coy maid half yielding to her lover,
It pours such sweet upbraiding, as must needs
Tempt to repeat the wrong! And now, its strings
Boldlier swept, the long sequacious[3] notes
Over delicious surges sink and rise,
20   Such a soft floating witchery of sound
As twilight Elfins make, when they at eve
Voyage on gentle gales from Fairy-Land,
Where Melodies round[4] honey-dropping flowers,
Footless and wild, like birds of Paradise,[5]
25   Nor pause, nor perch, hovering on untam'd wing!
O! the one Life within us and abroad,
Which meets all motion and becomes its soul,
A light in sound, a sound-like power in light,
Rhythm in all thought, and joyance every where—
30   Methinks, it should have been impossible
Not to love all things in a world so fill'd;
Where the breeze warbles, and the mute still air
Is Music slumbering on her instrument.

And thus, my Love! as on the midway slope
35   Of yonder hill I stretch my limbs at noon,
Whilst through my half-clos'd eye-lids I behold
The sunbeams dance, like diamonds, on the main,
And tranquil muse upon tranquillity;
Full many a thought uncall'd and undetain'd,
40   And many idle flitting phantasies,
Traverse my indolent and passive brain,
As wild and various as the random gales
That swell and flutter on this subject Lute!

1. A stringed instrument so tuned as to produce chords
when placed in a current of air. It is named after Aeolus,
god of the winds.
2. Sara Fricker, whom Coleridge married in October 1795
and took to live in Clevedon on the Bristol Channel.

3. Successive.
4. Surround (verb).
5. Birds of New Guinea, once thought to spend their
entire lives on the wing.

And what if all of animated nature
45 Be but organic Harps diversely fram'd,
That tremble into thought, as o'er them sweeps
Plastic and vast, one intellectual breeze,
At once the Soul of each, and God of all?

But thy more serious eye a mild reproof
50 Darts, O belovéd Woman! nor such thoughts
Dim and unhallow'd dost thou not reject,
And biddest me walk humbly with my God.
Meek Daughter in the family of Christ!
Well hast thou said and holily disprais'd
55 These shapings of the unregenerate mind;
Bubbles that glitter as they rise and break
On vain Philosophy's aye-babbling spring.
For never guiltless may I speak of him,
The Incomprehensible! save when with awe
60 I praise him, and with Faith that inly *feels*;
Who with his saving mercies healéd me,
A sinful and most miserable man,
Wilder'd and dark, and gave me to possess
Peace, and this Cot, and thee, heart-honour'd Maid!

The Rime of the Ancient Mariner
In Seven Parts

Argument

How a Ship, having first sailed to the Equator, was driven by Storms to the cold Country towards the South Pole; how the Ancient Mariner cruelly and in contempt of the laws of hospitality killed a Seabird and how he was followed by many and strange Judgements: and in what manner he came back to his own Country.

Part I

An ancient Mariner meeteth three Gallants bidden to a wedding-feast, and detaineth one.

It is an ancient Mariner,
And he stoppeth one of three.
'By thy long grey beard and glittering eye,
Now wherefore stopp'st thou me?

The Bridegroom's doors are opened wide, 5
And I am next of kin;
The guests are met, the feast is set:
May'st hear the merry din.'

He holds him with his skinny hand,
'There was a ship,' quoth he. 10
'Hold off! unhand me, grey-beard loon!'[1]
Eftsoons[2] his hand dropt he.

The Wedding-Guest is spell-bound by the eye of the old seafaring man, and constrained to hear his tale.

He holds him with his glittering eye—
The Wedding-Guest stood still,
And listens like a three years' child: 15
The Mariner hath his will.

The Wedding-Guest sat on a stone:
He cannot choose but hear;
And thus spake on that ancient man,
The bright-eyed Mariner. 20

1. Ill-bred fellow. 2. At once.

The Mariner
tells how the
ship sailed
southward
with a good
wind and fair
weather, till it
reached the
line.

'The ship was cheered, the harbour cleared,
Merrily did we drop
Below the kirk, below the hill,
Below the lighthouse top.

The Sun came up upon the left,   25
Out of the sea came he!
And he shone bright, and on the right
Went down into the sea.

Higher and higher every day,
Till over the mast at noon—'[3]   30
The Wedding-Guest here beat his breast,
For he heard the loud bassoon.

*The Wedding-
Guest heareth
the bridal
music; but
the Mariner
continueth
his tale.*

The bride hath paced into the hall,
Red as a rose is she;
Nodding their heads before her goes   35
The merry minstrelsy.[4]

The Wedding-Guest he beat his breast,
Yet he cannot choose but hear;
And thus spake on that ancient man,
The bright-eyed Mariner.   40

*The ship
driven by a
storm toward
the south pole.*

'And now the STORM-BLAST came, and he
Was tyrannous and strong:
He struck with his o'ertaking wings,
And chased us south along.

With sloping masts and dipping prow,   45
As who[5] pursued with yell and blow
Still treads the shadow of his foe,
And forward bends his head,
The ship drove fast, loud roared the blast,
And southward aye[6] we fled.   50

And now there came both mist and snow,
And it grew wondrous cold:
And ice, mast-high, came floating by,
As green as emerald.

*The land of
ice, and of
fearful sounds
where no
living thing
was to be seen.*

And through the drifts the snowy clifts   55
Did send a dismal sheen:
Nor shapes of men nor beasts we ken—[7]
The ice was all between.

The ice was here, the ice was there,
The ice was all around: 60
It cracked and growled, and roared and howled,
Like noises in a swound![8]

*Till a great
sea-bird,
called the
Albatross,
came through
the snow-fog,
and was
received with
great joy and
hospitality.*

At length did cross an Albatross,
Thorough the fog it came;
As if it had been a Christian soul,   65
We hailed it in God's name.

It ate the food it ne'er had eat,
And round and round it flew.
The ice did split with a thunder-fit;
The helmsman steered us through!   70

3. The ship, southward bound, has reached the equator.   6. Ever, always.
4. Musicians.   7. Saw.
5. As one who.   8. Swoon.

And lo! the Albatross proveth a bird of good omen, and followeth the ship as it returned northward through fog and floating ice.

And a good south wind sprung up behind;
The Albatross did follow,
And every day, for food or play,
Came to the mariners' hollo!

In mist or cloud, on mast or shroud,   75
It perched for vespers nine;
Whiles all the night, through fog-smoke white,
Glimmered the white Moon-shine.'

The ancient Mariner inhospitably killeth the pious bird of good omen.

'God save thee, ancient Mariner!
From the fiends, that plague thee thus!—   80
Why look'st thou so?'— With my cross-bow
I shot the ALBATROSS.

Part II

The Sun now rose upon the right:[9]
Out of the sea came he,
Still hid in mist, and on the left   85
Went down into the sea.

And the good south wind still blew behind,
But no sweet bird did follow,
Nor any day for food or play
Came to the mariners' hollo!   90

His shipmates cry out against the ancient Mariner, for killing the bird of good luck.

And I had done a hellish thing,
And it would work 'em woe:
For all averred, I had killed the bird
That made the breeze to blow.
Ah wretch! said they, the bird to slay,   95
That made the breeze to blow!

But when the fog cleared off, they justify the same, and thus make themselves accomplices in the crime.

Nor dim nor red, like God's own head,
The glorious Sun uprist:
Then all averred, I had killed the bird
That brought the fog and mist.   100
'Twas right, said they, such birds to slay,
That bring the fog and mist.

The fair breeze continues; the ship enters the Pacific Ocean, and sails northward, even till it reaches the Line.

The fair breeze blew, the white foam flew,
The furrow followed free;
We were the first that ever burst   105
Into that silent sea.[10]

The ship hath been suddenly becalmed.

Down dropt the breeze, the sails dropt down,
'Twas sad as sad could be;
And we did speak only to break
The silence of the sea!   110

All in a hot and copper sky,
The bloody Sun, at noon,
Right up above the mast did stand,
No bigger than the Moon.

Day after day, day after day,   115
We stuck, nor breath nor motion;
As idle as a painted ship
Upon a painted ocean.

9. After rounding Cape Horn, the ship enters the Pacific and sails northward.
10. This is possibly a hint as to the period in which the Mariner's adventure takes place; the first European navigator to sail into the Pacific was Magellan in 1520.

Water, water, every where,
And all the boards did shrink;   120
Water, water, every where,
Nor any drop to drink.

The very deep did rot: O Christ!
That ever this should be!
Yea, slimy things did crawl with legs   125
Upon the slimy sea.

About, about, in reel and rout[11]
The death-fires[12] danced at night;
The water, like a witch's oils,
Burnt green, and blue and white.   130

*A Spirit had
followed them;
one of the in-
visible inhabi-
tants of this
planet, neither*

And some in dreams assuréd were
Of the Spirit that plagued us so;
Nine fathom deep he had followed us
From the land of mist and snow.

*departed souls nor angels; concerning whom the learned Jew, Josephus, and
the Platonic Constantinopolitan, Michael Psellus, may be consulted. They are
very numerous, and there is no climate or element without one or more.*

And every tongue, through utter drought,   135
Was withered at the root;
We could not speak, no more than if
We had been choked with soot.

*The shipmates,
in their sore
distress, would
fain throw the
whole guilt on
the ancient*

Ah! well a-day! what evil looks
Had I from old and young!   140
Instead of the cross, the Albatross
About my neck was hung.

Mariner: in sign whereof they hang the dead sea-bird round his neck.

Part III

There passed a weary time. Each throat
Was parched, and glazed each eye.
A weary time! a weary time!   145
How glazed each weary eye,
When looking westward, I beheld
A something in the sky.

*The ancient
Mariner be-
holdeth a sign
in the element
afar off.*

At first it seemed a little speck,
And then it seemed a mist;   150
It moved and moved, and took at last
A certain shape, I wist.[13]

A speck, a mist, a shape, I wist!
And still it neared and neared:
As if it dodged a water-sprite,   155
It plunged and tacked and veered.

*At its nearer
approach, it
seemeth him
to be a ship;
and at a dear
ransom he
freeth his
speech from
the bonds of
thirst.*

With throats unslaked, with black lips baked,
We could nor laugh nor wail;
Through utter drought all dumb we stood!
I bit my arm, I sucked the blood,   160
And cried, A sail! a sail!

11. "About, about": cf. *Macbeth* I.iii.32–34. "rout": disor-
derly crowd.
12. St. Elmo's fire, a luminescent glow sometimes seen on
a ship's mast or rigging during an electrical storm.
13. Knew.

With throats unslaked, with black lips baked,
Agape they heard me call:
A flash of joy;   Gramercy![14] they for joy did grin,
And all at once their breath drew in,   165
As they were drinking all.

And horror follows. For can it be a ship that comes onward without wind or tide?
See! see! (I cried) she tacks no more!
Hither to work us weal;[15]
Without a breeze, without a tide,
She steadies with upright keel!   170

The western wave was all a-flame.
The day was well nigh done!
Almost upon the western wave
Rested the broad bright Sun;
When that strange shape drove suddenly   175
Betwixt us and the Sun.

It seemeth him but the skeleton of a ship.
And straight the Sun was flecked with bars,
(Heaven's Mother send us grace!)
As if through a dungeon-grate he peered
With broad and burning face.   180

And its ribs are seen as bars on the face of the setting Sun.
Alas! (thought I, and my heart beat loud)
How fast she nears and nears!
Are those *her* sails that glance in the Sun,
Like restless gossameres?

The Spectre-Woman and her Death-mate, and no other on board the skeleton ship.
Are those *her* ribs through which the Sun   185
Did peer, as through a grate?
And is that Woman all her crew?
Is that a DEATH? and are there two?
Is DEATH that woman's mate?

Like vessel, like crew!
Her lips were red, *her* looks were free,   190
Her locks were yellow as gold:
Her skin was as white as leprosy,

Death and Life-in-Death have diced for the ship's crew, and she (the latter) winneth the ancient Mariner.
The Night-mare LIFE-IN-DEATH was she,
Who thicks man's blood with cold.

The naked hulk alongside came,   195
And the twain were casting dice;
'The game is done! I've won! I've won!'
Quoth she, and whistles thrice.

No twilight within the courts of the Sun.
The Sun's rim dips; the stars rush out:
At one stride comes the dark;   200
With far-heard whisper, o'er the sea,
Off shot the spectre-bark.

At the rising of the Moon,
We listened and looked sideways up!
Fear at my heart, as at a cup,
My life-blood seemed to sip!   205
The stars were dim, and thick the night,
The steersman's face by his lamp gleamed white;
From the sails the dew did drip—
Till clomb above the eastern bar[16]
The hornéd Moon, with one bright star   210
Within the nether tip.[17]

14. An exclamation of thanks.
15. Happiness, benefit.
16. "clomb": climbed. "bar": horizon.

17. Coleridge noted that a star-dogged moon was regarded by sailors as an evil omen.

<table>
<tr><td>*One after
another,*</td><td>One after one, by the star-dogged Moon,
Too quick for groan or sigh,
Each turned his face with a ghastly pang,
And cursed me with his eye.</td><td>215</td></tr>
</table>

*One after
another,*

One after one, by the star-dogged Moon,
Too quick for groan or sigh,
Each turned his face with a ghastly pang,
And cursed me with his eye.   215

*His shipmates
drop down
dead.*

Four times fifty living men,
(And I heard nor sigh nor groan)
With heavy thump, a lifeless lump,
They dropped down one by one.

*But Life-in-
Death begins
her work on
the ancient
Mariner.*

The souls did from their bodies fly,—   220
They fled to bliss or woe!
And every soul, it passed me by,
Like the whizz of my cross-bow!

Part IV

*The Wedding-
Guest feareth
that a Spirit
is talking to
him;*

'I fear thee, ancient Mariner!
I fear thy skinny hand!   225
And thou art long, and lank, and brown,
As is the ribbed sea-sand.

I fear thee and thy glittering eye,
And thy skinny hand, so brown.'—

*But the
ancient Ma-
riner assureth
him of his
bodily life, and
proceedeth to
relate his hor-
rible penance.*

Fear not, fear not, thou Wedding-Guest!   230
This body dropt not down.

Alone, alone, all, all alone,
Alone on a wide wide sea!
And never a saint took pity on
My soul in agony.   235

*He despiseth
the creatures
of the calm,*

The many men, so beautiful!
And they all dead did lie:
And a thousand thousand slimy things
Lived on; and so did I.

*And envieth
that they
should live,
and so many
lie dead.*

I looked upon the rotting sea,   240
And drew my eyes away;
I looked upon the rotting deck,
And there the dead men lay.

I looked to heaven, and tried to pray;
But or ever[18] a prayer had gusht,   245
A wicked whisper came, and made
My heart as dry as dust.

I closed my lids, and kept them close,
And the balls like pulses beat;
For the sky and the sea, and the sea and the sky   250
Lay like a load on my weary eye,
And the dead were at my feet.

*But the curse
liveth for him
in the eye of
the dead men.*

The cold sweat melted from their limbs,
Nor rot nor reek did they:
The look with which they looked on me   255
Had never passed away.

An orphan's curse would drag to hell
A spirit from on high;
But oh! more horrible than that
Is the curse in a dead man's eye!   260
Seven days, seven nights, I saw that curse,
And yet I could not die.

18. Ere ever.

In his lone-
liness and
fixedness he
yearneth to-
wards the
journeying
Moon, and the
stars that still
sojourn, yet
still move
onward; and
every where
the blue sky
belongs to

The moving Moon went up the sky,
And no where did abide:
Softly she was going up,   265
And a star or two beside—

Her beams bemocked the sultry main,
Like April hoar-frost spread;
But where the ship's huge shadow lay,
The charméd water burnt alway   270
A still and awful red.

them, and is their appointed rest, and their native country and their own
natural homes, which they enter unannounced, as lords that are certainly ex-
pected and yet there is a silent joy at their arrival.

By the light
of the Moon he
beholdeth
God's crea-
tures of the
great calm.

Beyond the shadow of the ship,
I watched the water-snakes:
They moved in tracks of shining white,
And when they reared, the elfish light   275
Fell off in hoary flakes.

Within the shadow of the ship
I watched their rich attire:
Blue, glossy green, and velvet black,
They coiled and swam; and every track   280
Was a flash of golden fire.

Their beauty
and their
happiness.

He blesseth
them in his
heart.

O happy living things! no tongue
Their beauty might declare:
A spring of love gushed from my heart,
And I blessed them unaware: 285
Sure my kind saint took pity on me,
And I blessed them unaware.

The spell
begins to
break.

The self-same moment I could pray;
And from my neck so free
The Albatross fell off, and sank   290
Like lead into the sea.

Part V
Oh sleep! it is a gentle thing,
Beloved from pole to pole!
To Mary Queen the praise be given!
She sent the gentle sleep from Heaven,   295
That slid into my soul.

By grace of
the holy
Mother, the
ancient
Mariner is
refreshed with
rain.

The silly[19] buckets on the deck,
That had so long remained,
I dreamt that they were filled with dew;
And when I awoke, it rained.   300

My lips were wet, my throat was cold,
My garments all were dank;
Sure I had drunken in my dreams,
And still my body drank.

I moved, and could not feel my limbs: 305
I was so light—almost
I thought that I had died in sleep,
And was a blesséd ghost.

19. Blessed (ME "sely").

*He heareth
sounds and
seeth strange
sights and
commotions in
the sky and
the element.*

And soon I heard a roaring wind:
It did not come anear;
But with its sound it shook the sails,
That were so thin and sere.[20]   310

The upper air burst into life!
And a hundred fire-flags sheen,[21]
To and fro they were hurried about!   315
And to and fro, and in and out,
The wan stars danced between.

And the coming wind did roar more loud,
And the sails did sigh like sedge;
And the rain poured down from one black cloud;   320
The Moon was at its edge.

The thick black cloud was cleft, and still
The Moon was at its side:
Like waters shot from some high crag,
The lightning fell with never a jag,   325
A river steep and wide.

*The bodies of
the ship's crew
are inspirited
and the
ship moves
on;*

The loud wind never reached the ship,
Yet now the ship moved on!
Beneath the lightning and the Moon
The dead men gave a groan.   330

They groaned, they stirred, they all uprose,
Nor spake, nor moved their eyes;
It had been strange, even in a dream,
To have seen those dead men rise.

The helmsman steered, the ship moved on;   335
Yet never a breeze up-blew;
The mariners all 'gan work the ropes,
Where they were wont to do;
They raised their limbs like lifeless tools—
We were a ghastly crew.   340

The body of my brother's son
Stood by me, knee to knee:
The body and I pulled at one rope,
But he said nought to me.

*But not by the
souls of the
men, nor by
dæmons of
earth or
middle air, but
by a blessed
troop of
angelic spirits,
sent down by
the invocation
of the guar-
dian saint.*

'I fear thee, ancient Mariner!'   345
Be calm, thou Wedding-Guest!
'Twas not those souls that fled in pain,
Which to their corses[22] came again,
But a troop of spirits blest:

For when it dawned—they dropped their arms,   350
And clustered round the mast;
Sweet sounds rose slowly through their mouths,
And from their bodies passed.

Around, around, flew each sweet sound,
Then darted to the Sun;   355
Slowly the sounds came back again,
Now mixed, now one by one.

---

20. Withered, worn.
21. Shone. Coleridge is describing the lights of the

Aurora Australis.
22. Corpses.

Sometimes a-dropping from the sky
I heard the sky-lark sing;
Sometimes all little birds that are,   360
How they seemed to fill the sea and air
With their sweet jargoning![23]

And now 'twas like all instruments,
Now like a lonely flute;
And now it is an angel's song,   365
That makes the heavens be mute.

It ceased; yet still the sails made on
A pleasant noise till noon,
A noise like of a hidden brook
In the leafy month of June,   370
That to the sleeping woods all night
Singeth a quiet tune.

Till noon we quietly sailed on,
Yet never a breeze did breathe:
Slowly and smoothly went the ship,   375
Moved onward from beneath.

The lonesome   Under the keel nine fathom deep,
Spirit from   From the land of mist and snow,
the south-pole   The spirit slid: and it was he
carries on the   That made the ship to go.   380
ship as far as   The sails at noon left off their tune,
the Line, in   And the ship stood still also.
obedience to
the angelic
troop, but still   The Sun, right up above the mast,
requireth   Had fixed her to the ocean.
vengeance.   But in a minute she 'gan stir,   385
                        With a short uneasy motion—
                        Backwards and forwards half her length
                        With a short uneasy motion.

Then like a pawing horse let go,
She made a sudden bound: 390
It flung the blood into my head,
And I fell down in a swound.

The Polar   How long in that same fit I lay,
Spirit's fellow-   I have not[24] to declare;
dæmons, the   But ere my living life returned,   395
invisible in-   I heard and in my soul discerned
habitants of   Two voices in the air.
the element,
take part in
his wrong;   'Is it he?' quoth one, 'Is this the man?
and two of   By him who died on cross,
them relate,   With his cruel bow he laid full low   400
one to the   The harmless Albatross.
other, that
penance long
and heavy for   The spirit who bideth by himself
the ancient   In the land of mist and snow,
Mariner hath   He loved the bird that loved the man
been accorded   Who shot him with his bow.'   405
to the Polar
Spirit, who
returneth   The other was a softer voice,
southward.   As soft as honey-dew:
                        Quoth he, 'The man hath penance done,
                        And penance more will do.'

23. Warbling.   24. Am unable.

Part VI
FIRST VOICE
'But tell me, tell me! speak again,   410
Thy soft response renewing—
What makes that ship drive on so fast?
What is the ocean doing?'

SECOND VOICE
'Still as a slave before his lord,
The ocean hath no blast;   415
His great bright eye most silently
Up to the Moon is cast—

If he may know which way to go;
For she guides him smooth or grim.
See, brother, see! how graciously   420
She looketh down on him.'

FIRST VOICE
'But why drives on that ship so fast,
Without or wave or wind?'

SECOND VOICE
'The air is cut away before,
And closes from behind.   425

Fly, brother, fly! more high, more high!
Or we shall be belated:
For slow and slow that ship will go,
When the Mariner's trance is abated.'

I woke, and we were sailing on   430
As in a gentle weather:
'Twas night, calm night, the moon was high;
The dead men stood together.

All stood together on the deck,
For a charnel-dungeon fitter: 435
All fixed on me their stony eyes,
That in the Moon did glitter.

The pang, the curse, with which they died,
Had never passed away:
I could not draw my eyes from theirs,   440
Nor turn them up to pray.

And now this spell was snapt: once more
I viewed the ocean green,
And looked far forth, yet little saw
Of what had else been seen—   445

Like one, that on a lonesome road
Doth walk in fear and dread,
And having once turned round walks on,
And turns no more his head;
Because he knows, a frightful fiend   450
Doth close behind him tread.

But soon there breathed a wind on me,
Nor sound nor motion made:
Its path was not upon the sea,
In ripple or in shade.   455

The Mariner hath been cast into a trance; for the angelic power causeth the vessel to drive northward faster than human life could endure.

The super-natural motion is retarded; the Mariner awakes, and his penance begins anew.

The curse is finally ex-piated.

It raised my hair, it fanned my cheek
Like a meadow-gale of spring—
It mingled strangely with my fears,
Yet it felt like a welcoming.

Swiftly, swiftly flew the ship,   460
Yet she sailed softly too:
Sweetly, sweetly blew the breeze—
On me alone it blew.

And the
ancient
Mariner be-
holdeth his
native
country.

Oh! dream of joy! is this indeed
The light-house top I see?   465
Is this the hill? is this the kirk?
Is this mine own countree?

We drifted o'er the harbour-bar,
And I with sobs did pray—
O let me be awake, my God!   470
Or let me sleep alway.

The harbour-bay was clear as glass,
So smoothly it was strewn!²⁵
And on the bay the moonlight lay,
And the shadow of the Moon.   475

The rock shone bright, the kirk no less,
That stands above the rock:
The moonlight steeped in silentness
The steady weathercock.

And the bay was white with silent light,   480
Till rising from the same,

The angelic
spirits leave
the dead
bodies,

Full many shapes, that shadows were,
In crimson colours came.

And appear in
their own
forms of light.

A little distance from the prow
Those crimson shadows were: 485
I turned my eyes upon the deck—
Oh, Christ! what saw I there!

Each corse lay flat, lifeless and flat,
And, by the holy rood!²⁶
A man all light, a seraph-man,²⁷   490
On every corse there stood.

This seraph-band, each waved his hand:
It was a heavenly sight!
They stood as signals to the land,
Each one a lovely light;   495

This seraph-band, each waved his hand,
No voice did they impart—
No voice; but oh! the silence sank
Like music on my heart.

But soon I heard the dash of oars,   500
I heard the Pilot's cheer;
My head was turned perforce away
And I saw a boat appear.

25. Calmed.
26. Cross.
27. The seraphim are the highest order of angels.

The Pilot and the Pilot's boy,
I heard them coming fast: 505
Dear Lord in Heaven! it was a joy
The dead men could not blast.

I saw a third— I heard his voice:
It is the Hermit good!
He singeth loud his godly hymns   510
That he makes in the wood.
He'll shrieve[28] my soul, he'll wash away
The Albatross's blood.

Part VII

*The Hermit of
the Wood,*

This Hermit good lives in that wood
Which slopes down to the sea.   515
How loudly his sweet voice he rears!
He loves to talk with marineres
That come from a far countree.

He kneels at morn, at noon, and eve—
He hath a cushion plump: 520
It is the moss that wholly hides
The rotted old oak-stump.

The skiff-boat neared: I heard them talk,
'Why, this is strange, I trow![29]
Where are those lights so many and fair,   525
That signal made but now?'

*Approacheth
the ship with
wonder.*

'Strange, by my faith!' the Hermit said—
'And they answered not our cheer!
The planks looked warped! and see those sails,
How thin they are and sere!   530
I never saw aught like to them,
Unless perchance it were

Brown skeletons of leaves that lag
My forest-brook along;
When the ivy-tod[30] is heavy with snow,   535
And the owlet whoops to the wolf below,
That eats the she-wolf's young.'

'Dear Lord! it hath a fiendish look—
(The Pilot made reply)
I am a-feared'— 'Push on, push on!'   540
Said the Hermit cheerily.

The boat came closer to the ship,
But I nor spake nor stirred;
The boat came close beneath the ship,
And straight a sound was heard.   545

*The ship
suddenly
sinketh.*

Under the water it rumbled on,
Still louder and more dread:
It reached the ship, it split the bay;
The ship went down like lead.

*The ancient
Mariner is
saved in the
Pilot's boat.*

Stunned by that loud and dreadful sound,   550
Which sky and ocean smote,
Like one that hath been seven days drowned

---

28. Shrive, to hear confession and give absolution to a
penitent.

29. Think.
30. Clump of ivy.

My body lay afloat;
But swift as dreams, myself I found
Within the Pilot's boat.   555

Upon the whirl, where sank the ship,
The boat spun round and round;
And all was still, save that the hill
Was telling of the sound.

I moved my lips—the Pilot shrieked   560
And fell down in a fit;
The holy Hermit raised his eyes,
And prayed where he did sit.

I took the oars: the Pilot's boy,
Who now doth crazy go,   565
Laughed loud and long, and all the while
His eyes went to and fro.
'Ha! ha!' quoth he, 'full plain I see,
The Devil knows how to row.'

And now, all in my own countree,   570
I stood on the firm land!
The Hermit stepped forth from the boat,
And scarcely he could stand.

'O shrieve me, shrieve me, holy man!'
The Hermit crossed his brow.[31]   575
'Say quick,' quoth he, 'I bid thee say—
What manner of man art thou?'

Forthwith this frame of mine was wrenched
With a woful agony,
Which forced me to begin my tale;   580
And then it left me free.

Since then, at an uncertain hour,
That agony returns:
And till my ghastly tale is told,
This heart within me burns.   585

I pass, like night, from land to land;
I have strange power of speech;
That moment that his face I see,
I know the man that must hear me:
To him my tale I teach.   590

What loud uproar bursts from that door!
The wedding-guests are there:
But in the garden-bower the bride
And bride-maids singing are:
And hark the little vesper bell,   595
Which biddeth me to prayer!

O Wedding-Guest! this soul hath been
Alone on a wide wide sea:
So lonely 'twas, that God himself
Scarce seeméd there to be.   600

---

31. Made the sign of the cross on his forehead.

O sweeter than the marriage-feast,
'Tis sweeter far to me,
To walk together to the kirk
With a goodly company!—

To walk together to the kirk,   605
And all together pray,
While each to his great Father bends,
Old men, and babes, and loving friends
And youths and maidens gay!

And to teach,
by his own
example, love
and reverence
to all things
that God made
and loveth.

Farewell, farewell! but this I tell   610
To thee, thou Wedding-Guest!
He prayeth well, who loveth well
Both man and bird and beast.

He prayeth best, who loveth best
All things both great and small;   615
For the dear God who loveth us,
He made and loveth all.

The Mariner, whose eye is bright,
Whose beard with age is hoar,
Is gone: and now the Wedding-Guest   620
Turned from the bridegroom's door.

He went like one that hath been stunned,
And is of sense forlorn:[32]
A sadder and a wiser man,
He rose the morrow morn.   625

Frost at Midnight

The Frost performs its secret ministry,
Unhelped by any wind. The owlet's cry
Came loud—and hark, again! loud as before.
The inmates of my cottage, all at rest,
5   Have left me to that solitude, which suits
Abstruser musings: save that at my side
My cradled infant[1] slumbers peacefully.
'Tis calm indeed! so calm, that it disturbs
And vexes meditation with its strange
10 And extreme silentness. Sea, hill, and wood,
This populous village! Sea, and hill, and wood,
With all the numberless goings-on of life,
Inaudible as dreams! the thin blue flame
Lies on my low-burnt fire, and quivers not;
15 Only that film,[2] which fluttered on the grate,
Still flutters there, the sole unquiet thing.
Methinks, its motion in this hush of nature
Gives it dim sympathies with me who live,
Making it a companionable form,
20 Whose puny flaps and freaks the idling Spirit
By its own moods interprets, every where
Echo or mirror seeking of itself,
And makes a toy of Thought.

32. Deprived.

1. Coleridge's son, Hartley.
2. Ash or soot fluttering on the grate. "In all parts of the kingdom these films are called *strangers* and supposed to portend the arrival of some absent friend" (Coleridge's note).

But O! how oft,
How oft, at school,[3] with most believing mind,
25 Presageful, have I gazed upon the bars,
To watch that fluttering *stranger*! and as oft
With unclosed lids, already had I dreamt
Of my sweet birth-place,[4] and the old church-tower,
Whose bells, the poor man's only music, rang
30 From morn to evening, all the hot Fair-day,
So sweetly, that they stirred and haunted me
With a wild pleasure, falling on mine ear
Most like articulate sounds of things to come!
So gazed I, till the soothing things, I dreamt,
35 Lulled me to sleep, and sleep prolonged my dreams!
And so I brooded all the following morn,
Awed by the stern preceptor's face, mine eye
Fixed with mock study on my swimming book:
Save if the door half opened, and I snatched
40 A hasty glance, and still my heart leaped up,
For still I hoped to see the *stranger's* face,
Townsman, or aunt, or sister more beloved,
My play-mate when we both were clothed alike!

Dear Babe, that sleepest cradled by my side,
45 Whose gentle breathings, heard in this deep calm,
Fill up the intersperséd vacancies
And momentary pauses of the thought!
My babe so beautiful! it thrills my heart
With tender gladness, thus to look at thee,
50 And think that thou shalt learn far other lore,
And in far other scenes! For I was reared
In the great city, pent 'mid cloisters dim,
And saw nought lovely but the sky and stars.
But *thou*, my babe! shalt wander like a breeze
55 By lakes and sandy shores, beneath the crags
Of ancient mountain, and beneath the clouds,
Which image in their bulk both lakes and shores
And mountain crags: so shalt thou see and hear
The lovely shapes and sounds intelligible
60 Of that eternal language, which thy God
Utters, who from eternity doth teach
Himself in all, and all things in himself.
Great universal Teacher! he shall mould
Thy spirit, and by giving make it ask.

65 Therefore all seasons shall be sweet to thee,
Whether the summer clothe the general earth
With greenness, or the redbreast sit and sing
Betwixt the tufts of snow on the bare branch
Of mossy apple-tree, while the nigh thatch
70 Smokes in the sun-thaw; whether the eave-drops fall
Heard only in the trances of the blast,
Or if the secret ministry of frost
Shall hang them up in silent icicles,
Quietly shining to the quiet Moon.

3. Christ's Hospital, London.
4. Ottery St. Mary, Devonshire.

Kubla Khan;
or, A Vision in a Dream. A Fragment[1]

In Xanadu did Kubla Khan[2]
A stately pleasure-dome decree:
Where Alph,[3] the sacred river, ran
Through caverns measureless to man
5   Down to a sunless sea.
So twice five miles of fertile ground
With walls and towers were girdled round:
And there were gardens bright sinuous rills,
Where blossomed many an incense-bearing tree;
10 And here were forests ancient as the hills,
Enfolding sunny spots of greenery.

But oh! that deep romantic chasm which slanted
Down the green hill athwart a cedarn cover!
A savage place! as holy and enchanted
15 As e'er beneath a waning moon was haunted
By woman wailing for her demon-lover!
And from this chasm, with ceaseless turmoil seething,
As if this earth in fast thick pants were breathing,
A mighty fountain momently[4] was forced:
20 Amid whose swift half-intermitted burst
Huge fragments vaulted like rebounding hail,
Or chaffy grain beneath the thresher's flail:
And 'mid these dancing rocks at once and ever
It flung up momently the sacred river.
25 Five miles meandering with a mazy motion
Through wood and dale the sacred river ran,
Then reached the caverns measureless to man,
And sank in tumult to a lifeless ocean:
And 'mid this tumult Kubla heard from far
30 Ancestral voices prophesying war!
    The shadow of the dome of pleasure
    Floated midway on the waves;
    Where was heard the mingled measure
    From the fountain and the caves.
35 It was a miracle of rare device,
A sunny pleasure-dome with caves of ice!

    A damsel with a dulcimer
    In a vision once I saw:

---

1. In a prefatory note, Coleridge described the genesis of his poem: "In the summer of the year 1797, the Author, then in ill health, had retired to a lonely farm-house between Porlock and Linton, on the Exmoor confines of Somerset and Devonshire. In consequence of a slight indisposition, an anodyne had been prescribed, from the effects of which he fell asleep in his chair at the moment that he was reading the following sentence, or words of the same substance, in 'Purchas's Pilgrimage': 'Here the Khan Kubla commanded a palace to be built, and a stately garden there-unto. And thus ten miles of fertile ground were inclosed with a wall.' The Author continued for about three hours in a profound sleep, at least of the external senses, during which time he has the most vivid confidence, that he could not have composed less than from two to three hundred lines; if that indeed can be called composition in which all the images rose up before him as *things*, with a parallel production of the correspondent expressions, without any sensation or consciousness of effort. On awaking he appeared to himself to have a distinct recollection of the whole, and taking his pen, ink, and paper, instantly and eagerly wrote down the lines that are here preserved. At this moment he was unfortunately called out by a person on business from Porlock, and detained by him above an hour, and on his return to his room, found, to his no small surprise and mortification, that though he still retained some vague and dim recollection of the general purport of the vision, yet, with the exception of some eight or ten scattered lines and images, all the rest had passed away like the images on the surface of a stream into which a stone has been cast, but, alas! without the after restoration of the latter!"

2. Kublai Khan (1215?–94), a descendant of Genghis Khan, founded the Mongol dynasty in China.

3. Suggested by the Greek river Alpheus. In Greek mythology, the river-god Alpheus pursued the nymph Arethusa by flowing under land and sea, and rose to join his beloved as a fountain in Sicily.

4. At every moment.

It was an Abyssinian maid,
40   And on her dulcimer she played,
Singing of Mount Abora.[5]
Could I revive within me
Her symphony and song,
To such a deep delight 'twould win me,
45   That with music loud and long,
I would build that dome in air,
That sunny dome! those caves of ice!
And all who heard should see them there,
And all should cry, Beware! Beware!
50   His flashing eyes, his floating hair!
Weave a circle round him thrice,
And close your eyes with holy dread,
For he on honey-dew hath fed,
And drunk the milk of Paradise.

Dejection: An Ode

Late, late yestreen[1] *I saw the new Moon,*
With the old Moon in her arms;
And I fear, I fear, my Master dear!
We shall have a deadly storm.
—**Ballad of Sir Patrick Spence**

I

Well! If the Bard was weather-wise, who made
    The grand old ballad of Sir Patrick Spence,
    This night, so tranquil now, will not go hence
Unroused by winds, that ply a busier trade
5   Than those which mould yon cloud in lazy flakes,
Or the dull sobbing draft, that moans and rakes
Upon the strings of this Æolian lute,[2]
        Which better far were mute.
    For lo! the New-moon winter-bright!
10   And overspread with phantom light,
        (With swimming phantom light o'erspread
        But rimmed and circled by a silver thread)
I see the old Moon in her lap, foretelling
    The coming-on of rain and squally blast.
15   And oh! that even now the gust were swelling,
    And the slant night-shower driving loud and fast!
Those sounds which oft have raised me, whilst they awed,
        And sent my soul abroad,
Might now perhaps their wonted impulse give,
20   Might startle this dull pain, and make it move and live!

II

A grief without a pang, void, dark, and drear,
    A stifled, drowsy, unimpassioned grief,
    Which finds no natural outlet, no relief,
        In word, or sigh, or tear—
25   O Lady! in this wan and heartless mood,
To other thoughts by yonder throstle[3] woo'd,
    All this long eve, so balmy and serene,
Have I been gazing on the western sky,
    And its peculiar tint of yellow green:

5. A fictitious name probably suggested by several of
Coleridge's sources, which are fully described in John
Livingston Lowes' *The Road to Xanadu* (1927).

1. Yesterday evening.
2. Stringed instrument that sounds notes
or chords when exposed to the wind.
3. Song-thrush.

30   And still I gaze—and with how blank an eye!
        And those thin clouds above, in flakes and bars,
        That give away their motion to the stars;
        Those stars, that glide behind them or between,
        Now sparkling, now bedimmed, but always seen:
35   Yon crescent Moon, as fixed as if it grew
        In its own cloudless, starless lake of blue;
        I see them all so excellently fair,
        I see, not feel, how beautiful they are!

III

            My genial spirits[4] fail;
40   And what can these avail
        To lift the smothering weight from off my breast?
            It were a vain endeavour,
            Though I should gaze for ever
        On that green light that lingers in the west:
45   I may not hope from outward forms to win
        The passion and the life, whose fountains are within.

IV

        O Lady! we receive but what we give,
        And in our life alone does Nature live:
        Ours is her wedding garment, ours her shroud!
50   And would we aught behold, of higher worth,
        Than that inanimate cold world allowed
        To the poor loveless ever-anxious crowd,
            Ah! from the soul itself must issue forth
        A light, a glory, a fair luminous cloud
55   Enveloping the Earth—
        And from the soul itself must there be sent
            A sweet and potent voice, of its own birth,
        Of all sweet sounds the life and element!

V

        O pure of heart! thou need'st not ask of me
60   What this strong music in the soul may be!
        What, and wherein it doth exist,
        This light, this glory, this fair luminous mist,
        This beautiful and beauty-making power.
            Joy, virtuous Lady! Joy that ne'er was given,
65   Save to the pure, and in their purest hour,
        Life, and Life's effluence, cloud at once and shower,
        Joy, Lady! is the spirit and the power,
        Which wedding Nature to us gives in dower
            A new Earth and new Heaven,
70   Undreamt of by the sensual and the proud—
        Joy is the sweet voice, Joy the luminous cloud—
                We in ourselves rejoice!
        And thence flows all that charms or ear or sight,
            All melodies the echoes of that voice,
75   All colours a suffusion from that light.

VI

        There was a time when, though my path was rough,
            This joy within me dallied with distress,
        And all misfortunes were but as the stuff
            Whence Fancy made me dreams of happiness:
80   For hope grew round me, like the twining vine,
        And fruits, and foliage, not my own, seemed mine.
        But now afflictions bow me down to earth:

---

4. Native powers.

Nor care I that they rob me of my mirth;
          But oh! each visitation
85 Suspends what nature gave me at my birth,
          My shaping spirit of Imagination.
For not to think of what I needs must feel,
          But to be still and patient, all I can;
And haply by abstruse research to steal
90   From my own nature all the natural man—
This was my sole resource, my only plan:
Till that which suits a part infects the whole,
And now is almost grown the habit of my soul.

VII

Hence, viper thoughts, that coil around my mind,
95   Reality's dark dream!
I turn from you, and listen to the wind,
          Which long has raved unnoticed. What a scream
Of agony by torture lengthened out
That lute sent forth! Thou Wind, that rav'st without,
100   Bare crag, or mountain-tairn,[5] or blasted tree,
Or pine-grove whither woodman never clomb,[6]
Or lonely house, long held the witches' home,
          Methinks were fitter instruments for thee,
Mad Lutanist! who in this month of showers,
105 Of dark-brown gardens, and of peeping flowers,
Mak'st Devils' yule, with worse than wintry song,
The blossoms, buds, and timorous leaves among.
          Thou Actor, perfect in all tragic sounds!
Thou mighty Poet, e'en to frenzy bold!
110   What tell'st thou now about?
          'Tis of the rushing of an host in rout,
With groans, of trampled men, with smarting wounds—
At once they groan with pain, and shudder with the cold!
But hush! there is a pause of deepest silence!
115 And all that noise, as of a rushing crowd,
With groans, and tremulous shudderings—all is over—
          It tells another tale, with sounds less deep and loud!
                A tale of less affright,
                And tempered with delight,
120 As Otway's self[7] had framed the tender lay,—
                'Tis of a little child
                Upon a lonesome wild,
Not far from home, but she hath lost her way:
And now moans low in bitter grief and fear,
125 And now screams loud, and hopes to make her mother hear.

VIII

'Tis midnight, but small thoughts have I of sleep:
Full seldom may my friend such vigils keep!
Visit her, gentle Sleep! with wings of healing,
          And may this storm be but a mountain-birth,
130 May all the stars hang bright above her dwelling,
          Silent as though they watched the sleeping Earth!
                With light heart may she rise,
                Gay fancy, cheerful eyes,
          Joy lift her spirit, joy attune her voice;
135 To her may all things live, from pole to pole,
Their life the eddying of her living soul!
          O simple spirit, guided from above,
Dear Lady! friend devoutest of my choice,
Thus mayest thou ever, evermore rejoice.

---

5. Small mountain lake.
6. Climbed.

7. Thomas Otway, seventeenth-century dramatist. Coleridge originally wrote "William's," and the "tender lay" alluded to is probably Wordsworth's "Lucy Gray."

GEORGE GORDON, LORD BYRON (1788–1824)

She Walks in Beauty

I

She walks in beauty, like the night
  Of cloudless climes and starry skies;
And all that's best of dark and bright
  Meet in her aspect and her eyes:
Thus mellow'd to that tender light
  Which heaven to gaudy day denies.

II

One shade the more, one ray the less,
  Had half impair'd the nameless grace
Which waves in every raven tress,
  Or softly lightens o'er her face;
Where thoughts serenely sweet express
  How pure, how dear their dwelling-place.

III

And on that cheek, and o'er that brow,
  So soft, so calm, yet eloquent,
The smiles that win, the tints that glow,
  But tell of days in goodness spent,
A mind at peace with all below,
  A heart whose love is innocent!

When Coldness Wraps This Suffering Clay

I

When coldness wraps this suffering clay,
  Ah! whither strays the immortal mind?
It cannot die, it cannot stay,
  But leaves its darken'd dust behind.
5 Then, unembodied, doth it trace
  By steps each planet's heavenly way?
Or fill at once the realms of space,
  A thing of eyes, that all survey?

II

Eternal, boundless undecay'd,
10 A thought unseen, but seeing all,
All, all in earth or skies display'd,
  Shall it survey, shall it recall:
Each fainter trace that memory holds
  So darkly of departed years,
15 In one broad glance the soul beholds,
  And all, that was, at once appears.

III

Before Creation peopled earth,
  Its eye shall roll through chaos back;
And where the farthest heaven had birth,
20 The spirit trace its rising track.
And where the future mars or makes,
  Its glance dilate o'er all to be,
While sun is quench'd or system breaks,
  Fix'd in its own eternity.

IV

25 Above or Love, Hope, Hate, or Fear,
  It lives all passionless and pure:
An age shall fleet like earthly year;
  Its years as moments shall endure.
Away, away, without a wing,
30 O'er all, through all, its thought shall fly,
A nameless and eternal thing,
  Forgetting what it was to die.

The Destruction of Sennacherib[1]

I

The Assyrian came down like the wolf on the fold,
And his cohorts were gleaming in purple and gold;
And the sheen of their spears was like stars on the sea,
When the blue wave rolls nightly on deep Galilee.

II

5 Like the leaves of the forest when Summer is green,
That host with their banners at sunset were seen:
Like the leaves of the forest when Autumn hath blown,
That host on the morrow lay wither'd and strown.

1. King of Assyria (702–681 B.C.). The story of his attack
on Judah, and of God's intervention, is told in 2 Kings xviii
and xix.

III

For the Angel of Death spread his wings on the blast,
10   And breathed in the face of the foe as he pass'd;
And the eyes of the sleepers wax'd deadly and chill,
And their hearts but once heaved, and for ever grew still!

IV

And there lay the steed with his nostril all wide,
But through it there roll'd not the breath of his pride;
15   And the foam of his gasping lay white on the turf,
And cold as the spray of the rock-beating surf.

V

And there lay the rider distorted and pale,
With the dew on his brow, and the rust on his mail:
And the tents were all silent, the banners alone,
20   The lances unlifted, the trumpet unblown.

VI

And the widows of Ashur[2] are loud in their wail,
And the idols are broke in the temple of Baal;[3]
And the might of the Gentile, unsmote by the sword,
Hath melted like snow in the glance of the Lord!

Prometheus[1]

I

Titan! to whose immortal eyes
   The sufferings of mortality,
      Seen in their sad reality,
Were not as things that gods despise;
5   What was thy pity's recompense?
A silent suffering, and intense;
The rock, the vulture, and the chain,
All that the proud can feel of pain,
The agony they do not show,
10   The suffocating sense of woe,
      Which speaks but in its loneliness,
And then is jealous lest the sky
Should have a listener, nor will sigh
      Until its voice is echoless.

II

15   Titan! to thee the strife was given
      Between the suffering and the will,
      Which torture where they cannot kill;
And the inexorable Heaven,
And the deaf tyranny of Fate,
20   The ruling principle of Hate,
Which for its pleasure doth create
The things it may annihilate,
Refused thee even the boon to die:
The wretched gift eternity
25   Was thine—and thou hast borne it well.

All that the Thunderer[2] wrung from thee
Was but the menace which flung back
On him the torments of thy rack;
The fate thou didst so well foresee,[3]
30   But would not to appease him tell;
And in thy Silence was his Sentence,
And in his Soul a vain repentance,
And evil dread so ill dissembled,
That in his hand the lightnings trembled.

III

35   Thy Godlike crime was to be kind,
      To render with thy precepts less
      The sum of human wretchedness,
And strengthen Man with his own mind;
But baffled as thou wert from high,
40   Still in thy patient energy,
In the endurance, and repulse
      Of thine impenetrable Spirit,
Which Earth and Heaven could not convulse,
      A mighty lesson we inherit:
45   Thou art a symbol and a sign
      To Mortals of their fate and force;
Like thee, Man is in part divine,
      A troubled stream from a pure source;
And Man in portions can foresee
50   His own funereal destiny;

---

2. The earliest capital of Assyria.
3. An Assyrian deity.

1. In defiance of Zeus, the Titan Prometheus stole fire from Olympus and gave it to mankind. For this he was

chained to a rock, and each day a vulture came to devour his liver, which Zeus caused to grow anew each night.
2. Zeus was the god of thunder and lightning.
3. Prometheus holds the secret of Zeus's fate, which he refuses to divulge.

His wretchedness, and his resistance,
And his sad unallied existence:
To which his Spirit may oppose
Itself— and equal to all woes,
55   And a firm will, and a deep sense,

Which even in torture can descry
    Its own concenter'd recompense,[4]
Triumphant where it dares defy,
And making Death a Victory.

From Childe Harold's Pilgrimage
A Romaunt

From Canto III

LXVIII
Lake Leman[1] woos me with its crystal face,
645   The mirror where the stars and mountains view
The stillness of their aspect in each trace
Its clear depth yields of their far height and hue:
There is too much of man here, to look through
With a fit mind the might which I behold;
650   But soon in me shall Loneliness renew
Thoughts hid, but not less cherish'd than of old,
Ere mingling with the herd had penn'd me in their fold.

LXIX
To fly from, need not be to hate, mankind:
All are not fit with them to stir and toil,
655   Nor is it discontent to keep the mind
Deep in its fountain, lest it overboil
In the hot throng, where we become the spoil
Of our infection, till too late and long
We may deplore and struggle with the coil,[2]
660   In wretched interchange of wrong for wrong
Midst a contentious world, striving where none are strong.

LXX
There, in a moment we may plunge our years
In fatal penitence, and in the blight
Of our own soul turn all our blood to tears,
665   And colour things to come with hues of Night;
The race of life becomes a hopeless flight
To those that walk in darkness: on the sea
The boldest steer but where their ports invite;
But there are wanderers o'er Eternity
670   Whose bark drives on and on, and anchor'd ne'er shall be.

LXXI
Is it not better, then, to be alone,
And love Earth only for its earthly sake?
By the blue rushing of the arrowy Rhone,[3]
Or the pure bosom of its nursing lake,
675   Which feeds it as a mother who doth make
A fair but froward infant her own care,
Kissing its cries away as these awake;—
Is it not better thus our lives to wear,
Than join the crushing crowd, doom'd to inflict or bear?

4. I.e., the reward lying at the very centre of suffering
itself.

1. The Lake of Geneva.

2. The turmoil of life.
3. The river which passes through the Lake of Geneva on
its way into France.

LXXII

680   I live not in myself, but I become
    Portion of that around me; and to me
    High mountains are a feeling, but the hum
    Of human cities torture: I can see
    Nothing to loathe in nature, save to be
685   A link reluctant in a fleshly chain,
    Class'd among creatures, when the soul can flee,
    And with the sky, the peak, the heaving plain
Of ocean, or the stars, mingle, and not in vain.

LXXIII

    And thus I am absorb'd, and this is life:
690   I look upon the peopled desert past,
    As on a place of agony and strife,
    Where, for some sin, to sorrow I was cast,
    To act and suffer, but remount at last
    With a fresh pinion;[4] which I feel to spring,
695   Though young, yet waxing vigorous as the blast
    Which it would cope with, on delighted wing,
Spurning the clay-cold bonds which round our being cling.

LXXIV

    And when, at length, the mind shall be all free
    From what it hates in this degraded form,
700   Reft of its carnal life, save what shall be
    Existent happier in the fly and worm,—-
    When elements to elements conform,
    And dust is as it should be, shall I not
    Feel all I see, less dazzling, but more warm?
705   The bodiless thought? the Spirit of each spot?
Of which, even now, I share at times the immortal lot?

LXXV

    Are not the mountains, waves, and skies, a part
    Of me and of my soul, as I of them?
    Is not the love of these deep in my heart
710   With a pure passion? should I not contemn
    All objects, if compared with these? and stem
    A tide of suffering, rather than forego
    Such feelings for the hard and worldly phlegm
    Of those whose eyes are only turn'd below,
715 Gazing upon the ground, with thoughts which dare not glow?

* * *

LXXXV

    Clear, placid Leman! thy contrasted lake,
    With the wild world I dwelt in, is a thing
    Which warns me, with its stillness, to forsake
800   Earth's troubled waters for a purer spring.
    This quiet sail is as a noiseless wing
    To waft me from distraction; once I loved
    Torn ocean's roar, but thy soft murmuring
    Sounds sweet as if a Sister's voice reproved,
805 That I with stern delights should e'er have been so moved.

LXXXVI

    It is the hush of night, and all between
    Thy margin and the mountains, dusk, yet clear,
    Mellow'd and mingling, yet distinctly seen,
    Save darken'd Jura,[5] whose capt heights appear
810   Precipitously steep; and drawing near,

4. Wing.   5. The mountain range between France and Switzerland.

There breathes a living fragrance from the shore,
Of flowers yet fresh with childhood; on the ear
Drops the light drip of the suspended oar,
Or chirps the grasshopper one good-night carol more.

LXXXVII

815 He is an evening reveller, who makes
His life an infancy, and sings his fill;
At intervals, some bird from out the brakes[6]
Starts into voice a moment, then is still.
There seems a floating whisper on the hill,
820 But that is fancy, for the starlight dews
All silently their tears of love instil,
Weeping themselves away, till they infuse
Deep into nature's breast the spirit of her hues.

LXXXVIII

Ye stars! which are the poetry of heaven!
825 If in your bright leaves we would read the fate
Of men and empires,—'tis to be forgiven,
That in our aspirations to be great,
Our destinies o'erleap their mortal state,
And claim a kindred with you; for ye are
830 A beauty and a mystery, and create
In us such love and reverence from afar,
That fortune, fame, power, life, have named themselves a star.

LXXXIX

All heaven and earth are still—though not in sleep,
But breathless, as we grow when feeling most;
835 And silent, as we stand in thoughts too deep:—
All heaven and earth are still: From the high host
Of stars, to the lull'd lake and mountain-coast,
All is concenter'd in a life intense,
Where not a beam, nor air, nor leaf is lost,
840 But hath a part of being, and a sense
Of that which is of all Creator and defence.

XC

Then stirs the feeling infinite, so felt
In solitude, where we are *least* alone;
A truth, which through our being then doth melt,
845 And purifies from self: it is a tone,
The soul and source of music, which makes known
Eternal harmony, and sheds a charm
Like to the fabled Cytherea's zone,[7]
Binding all things with beauty;—'twould disarm
850 The spectre Death, had he substantial power to harm.

XCI

Not vainly did the early Persian make
His altar the high places, and the peak
Of earth-o'ergazing mountains, and thus take
A fit and unwall'd temple, there to seek
855 The Spirit, in whose honour shrines are weak,
Uprear'd of human hands. Come, and compare
Columns and idol-dwellings, Goth or Greek,
With Nature's realms of worship, earth and air,
Nor fix on fond[8] abodes to circumscribe thy pray'r!

---

6. Thickets.
7. The girdle of Venus, which had the power to inspire
ardent love.
8. Foolish.

XCII

860 The sky is changed!—and such a change! Oh night,
And storm, and darkness, ye are wondrous strong,
Yet lovely in your strength, as is the light
Of a dark eye in woman! Far along,
From peak to peak, the rattling crags among
865 Leaps the live thunder! Not from one lone cloud,
But every mountain now hath found a tongue,
And Jura answers, through her misty shroud,
Back to the joyous Alps, who call to her aloud!

XCIII

And this is in the night:— Most glorious night!
870 Thou wert not sent for slumber! let me be
A sharer in thy fierce and far delight,—
A portion of the tempest and of thee!
How the lit lake shines, a phosphoric sea,
And the big rain comes dancing to the earth!
875 And now again 'tis black,— and now, the glee
Of the loud hills shakes with its mountain-mirth,
As if they did rejoice o'er a young earthquake's birth.

XCIV

Now, where the swift Rhone cleaves his way between
Heights which appear as lovers who have parted
880 In hate, whose mining depths so intervene,
That they can meet no more, though broken-hearted;
Though in their souls, which thus each other thwarted,
Love was the very root of the fond rage
Which blighted their life's bloom, and then departed:
885 Itself expired, but leaving them an age
Of years all winters,— war within themselves to wage.

XCV

Now, where the quick Rhone thus hath cleft his way,
The mightiest of the storms hath ta'en his stand:
For here, not one, but many, make their play,
890 And fling their thunder-bolts from hand to hand,
Flashing and cast around; of all the band,
The brightest through these parted hills hath fork'd
His lightnings,— as if he did understand,
That in such gaps as desolation work'd,
895 There the hot shaft should blast whatever therein lurk'd.

XCVI

Sky, mountains, river, winds, lake, lightnings! ye!
With night, and clouds, and thunder, and a soul
To make these felt and feeling, well may be
Things that have made me watchful; the far roll
900 Of your departing voices, is the knoll[9]
Of what in me is sleepless,— if I rest.
But where of ye, O tempests! is the goal?
Are ye like those within the human breast?
Or do ye find, at length, like eagles, some high nest?

XCVII

905 Could I embody and unbosom now
That which is most within me,— could I wreak
My thoughts upon expression, and thus throw
Soul, heart, mind, passions, feelings, strong or weak,
All that I would have sought, and all I seek,

9. Knell.

910 Bear, know, feel, and yet breathe—into *one* word,
And that one word were Lightning, I would speak;
But as it is, I live and die unheard,
With a most voiceless thought, sheathing it as a sword.

XCVIII

The morn is up again, the dewy morn,
915 With breath all incense, and with cheek all bloom,
Laughing the clouds away with playful scorn,
And living as if earth contain'd no tomb,—
And glowing into day: we may resume
The march of our existence: and thus I,
920 Still on thy shores, fair Leman! may find room
And food for meditation, nor pass by
Much, that may give us pause, if ponder'd fittingly.

From Don Juan

From Canto I

CC

My poem's epic,[1] and is meant to be
Divided in twelve books; each book containing,
1595 With love, and war, a heavy gale at sea,
A list of ships, and captains, and kings reigning,
New characters; the episodes are three:
A panoramic view of hell's in training,
After the style of Virgil and of Homer,
1600 So that my name of Epic's no misnomer.

CCI

All these things will be specified in time,
With strict regard to Aristotle's rules,[2]
The *Vade Mecum*[3] of the true sublime,
Which makes so many poets, and some fools:
1605 Prose poets like blank-verse, I'm fond of rhyme,
Good workmen never quarrel with their tools;
I've got new mythological machinery,
And very handsome supernatural scenery.

CCII

There's only one slight difference between
1610 Me and my epic brethren gone before,
And here the advantage is my own, I ween[4]
(Not that I have not several merits more,
But this will more peculiarly be seen);
They so embellish, that 'tis quite a bore
1615 Their labyrinth of fables to thread through,
Whereas this story's actually true.

CCIII

If any person doubt it, I appeal
To history, tradition, and to facts,
To newspapers, whose truth all know and feel,
1620 To plays in five, and operas in three acts;

1. At the time of his death, Byron had completed sixteen cantos of *Don Juan* and was at work on the seventeenth. The excerpt given here forms the conclusion to Canto I, which recounts the first of Juan's amorous adventures; later cantos take him from Spain to a Greek island, Turkey, Russia, and England.
2. Aristotle describes the principal characteristics of epic, tragedy, and comedy in his *Poetics*, which greatly influenced Renaissance and neo-classical ideas about literary form.
3. Latin, "go with me"—a generic name for a guide or handbook.
4. Believe.

All these confirm my statement a good deal,
　　But that which more completely faith exacts
Is, that myself, and several now in Seville,
　　Saw Juan's last elopement with the devil.[5]

CCIV

1625　If ever I should condescend to prose,
　　　I'll write poetical commandments, which
　　Shall supersede beyond all doubt all those
　　　That went before; in these I shall enrich
　　My text with many things that no one knows,
1630　　And carry precept to the highest pitch:
　　I'll call the work 'Longinus[6] o'er a Bottle,
　　Or, Every Poet his *own* Aristotle.'

CCV

　　Thou shalt believe in Milton, Dryden, Pope;
　　　Thou shalt not set up Wordsworth, Coleridge, Southey;[7]
1635　Because the first is crazed beyond all hope,
　　　The second drunk, the third so quaint and mouthy:
　　With Crabbe[8] it may be difficult to cope,
　　　And Campbell's Hippocrene[9] is somewhat drouthy:
　　Thou shalt not steal from Samuel Rogers, nor
1640　Commit—flirtation with the muse of Moore,

CCVI

　　Thou shalt not covet Mr. Sotheby's[10] Muse,
　　　His Pegasus,[11] nor anything that's his;
　　Thou shalt not bear false witness like 'the Blues'—[12]
　　　(There's *one*, at least, is very fond of this);
1645　Thou shalt not write, in short, but what I choose;
　　　This is true criticism, and you may kiss—
　　Exactly as you please, or not,—the rod;
　　But if you don't, I'll lay it on, by G—d!

CCVII

　　If any person should presume to assert
1650　　This story is not moral, first, I pray,
　　That they will not cry out before they're hurt,
　　　Then that they'll read it o'er again, and say
　　(But, doubtless, nobody will be so pert),
　　　That this is not a moral tale, though gay;
1655　Besides, in Canto Twelfth, I mean to show
　　The very place where wicked people go.

CCVIII

　　If, after all, there should be some so blind
　　　To their own good this warning to despise,
　　Let by some tortuosity of mind,
1660　　Not to believe my verse and their own eyes,

5. In popular legend, and in such dramatizations as Mozart's opera *Don Giovanni* (1787), the Spanish libertine Don Juan is carried off to Hell.
6. Greek rhetorician of the third century A.D., author of the treatise *On the Sublime*.
7. Robert Southey (1774–1843), made Poet-Laureate in 1813, and associated with Wordsworth and Coleridge as one of the Lake Poets whom Byron despised.
8. George Crabbe (1754–1832), Thomas Campbell (1777–1814), Samuel Rogers (1763–1855), and Thomas Moore (1779–1852) were poets whose work Byron generally admired, despite his comments here.

9. The fountain on Mount Helicon sacred to the Muses; its being "drouthy" (dry) indicates Campbell's lack of inspiration.
10. William Sotheby (1757–1833), minor poet and translator.
11. The winged horse, a conventional symbol for poetic inspiration.
12. Bluestockings, a term first given in the eighteenth century to intellectual women. The "one" in the next line refers to Byron's earnest and priggish wife Annabella, from whom he had separated with great bitterness in 1816.

And cry that they 'the moral cannot find,'
   I tell him, if a clergyman, he lies;
Should captains the remark, or critics, make,
They also lie too—under a mistake.

CCIX

1665 The public approbation I expect,
   And beg they'll take my word about the moral,
Which I with their amusement will connect
   (So children cutting teeth receive a coral);
Meantime they'll doubtless please to recollect
1670   My epical pretensions to the laurel:[13]
For fear some prudish readers should grow skittish,
I've bribed my Grandmother's Review—the British.[14]

CCX

I sent it in a letter to the Editor,
   Who thank'd me duly by return of post—
1675 I'm for a handsome article his creditor;
   Yet, if my gentle Muse he please to roast,
And break a promise after having made it her,
   Denying the receipt of what it cost,
And smear his page with gall instead of honey,
1680 All I can say is—that he had the money.

CCXI

I think that with this holy new alliance
   I may ensure the public, and defy
All other magazines of art or science,
   Daily, or monthly, or three monthly; I
1685 Have not essay'd to multiply their clients,
   Because they tell me 'twere in vain to try,
And that the Edinburgh Review and Quarterly
Treat a dissenting author very martyrly.

CCXII

'Non ego hoc ferrem calida juventa
1690   *Consule Planco,'*[15] Horace said, and so
Say I; by which quotation there is meant a
   Hint that some six or seven good years ago
(Long ere I dreamt of dating from the Brenta)[16]
   I was most ready to return a blow,
1695 And would not brook at all this sort of thing
In my hot youth—when George the Third was King.[17]

CCXIII

But now at thirty years my hair is gray—
   (I wonder what it will be like at forty?
I thought of a peruke[18] the other day—)
1700   My heart is not much greener; and, in short, I
Have squander'd my whole summer while 'twas May,
   And feel no more the spirit to retort; I
Have spent my life, both interest and principal,
And deem not, what I deem'd, my soul invincible.

---

13. The laurel wreath, symbol of poetic achievement.
14. Byron's playful claim to have bribed the *British Review* was solemnly denied by the journal in its issue for August 1819.
15. "I would not have borne this when I was a hot youth, during the consulship of Plancus" (Horace, *Odes* III.xiv).
16. A river near Venice, where Byron had taken up residence in 1817.
17. George III did not die till 1820; but in 1811 he was declared mad, and his son ruled for nine years as Prince Regent.
18. Wig.

CCXIV

1705 No more—no more—Oh! never more on me
　　The freshness of the heart can fall like dew,
　Which out of all the lovely things we see
　　Extracts emotions beautiful and new;
　Hived in our bosoms like the bag o' the bee.
1710 　Think'st thou the honey with those objects grew?
　Alas! 'twas not in them, but in thy power
　To double even the sweetness of a flower.

CCXV

　No more—no more—Oh! never more, my heart,
　　Canst thou be my sole world, my universe!
1715 Once all in all, but now a thing apart,
　　Thou canst not be my blessing or my curse:
　The illusion's gone for ever, and thou art
　　Insensible, I trust, but none the worse,
　And in thy stead I've got a deal of judgment,
1720 Though heaven knows how it ever found a lodgment.

CCXVI

　My days of love are over;[19] me no more
　　The charms of maid, wife, and still less of widow,
　Can make the fool of which they made before,—
　　In short, I must not lead the life I did do;
1725 The credulous hope of mutual minds is o'er,
　　The copious use of claret is forbid too,
　So for a good old-gentlemanly vice,
　I think I must take up with avarice.

CCXVII

　Ambition was my idol, which was broken
1730 　Before the shrines of Sorrow, and of Pleasure;
　And the two last have left me many a token
　　O'er which reflection may be made at leisure;
　Now, like Friar Bacon's brazen head, I've spoken,
　　'Time is, Time was, Time's past':[20]—a chymic[21] treasure
1735 Is glittering youth, which I have spent betimes—
　My heart in passion, and my head on rhymes.

CCXVIII

　What is the end of fame? 'tis but to fill
　　A certain portion of uncertain paper:
　Some liken it to climbing up a hill,
1740 　Whose summit, like all hills, is lost in vapour;
　For this men write, speak, preach, and heroes kill,
　　And bards burn what they call their 'midnight taper,'
　To have, when the original is dust,
　A name, a wretched picture, and worse bust.

CCXIX

1745 What are the hopes of man? Old Egypt's King
　　Cheops[22] erected the first pyramid
　And largest, thinking it was just the thing
　　To keep his memory whole, and mummy hid:
　But somebody or other rummaging,
1750 　Burglariously broke his coffin's lid:
　Let not a monument give you or me hopes,
　Since not a pinch of dust remains of Cheops.

---

19. An echo of Horace (*Odes* IV.i).
20. Words spoken by the Brazen Head in Robert Greene's play *Friar Bacon and Friar Bungay* (ca. 1589), IV.i.
21. Pertaining to alchemy.
22. The pharoah who built the Great Pyramid at Gizeh, near Cairo.

CCXX

But I, being fond of true philosophy,
   Say very often to myself, 'Alas!
1755 All things that have been born were born to die,
   And flesh (which Death mows down to hay) is grass;[23]
You've pass'd your youth not so unpleasantly,
   And if you had it o'er again—'twould pass—
So thank your stars that matters are no worse,
1760 And read your Bible, sir, and mind your purse.'

CCXXI

But for the present, gentle reader! and
   Still gentler purchaser! the bard—that's I—
Must, with permission, shake you by the hand,
   And so your humble servant, and good-bye!
1765 We meet again, if we should understand
   Each other; and if not, I shall not try
Your patience further than by this short sample—
'Twere well if others follow'd my example.

CCXXII

'Go, little book, from this my solitude!
1770   I cast thee on the waters—go thy ways!
And if, as I believe, thy vein be good,
   The world will find thee after many days.'
When Southey's read, and Wordsworth understood,
   I can't help putting in my claim to praise—
1775 The four first rhymes are Southey's, every line:[24]
For God's sake, reader! take them not for mine!

Stanzas Written on the Road between Florence and Pisa

Oh, talk not to me of a name great in story;
The days of our youth are the days of our glory;
And the myrtle and ivy[1] of sweet two-and-twenty
Are worth all your laurels,[2] though ever so plenty.

What are garlands and crowns to the brow that is wrinkled?
'Tis but as a dead flower with May-dew besprinkled.
Then away with all such from the head that is hoary!
What care I for the wreaths that can *only* give glory!

Oh FAME!—if I e'er took delight in thy praises,
'Twas less for the sake of thy high-sounding phrases,
Than to see the bright eyes of the dear one discover,
She thought that I was not unworthy to love her.

There chiefly I sought thee, *there* only I found thee;
Her glance was the best of the rays that surround thee;
When it sparkled o'er aught that was bright in my story,
I knew it was love, and I felt it was glory.

23. An echo of Isa. x1.6 and 1 Peter i.24.
24. Byron is indeed quoting from Southey: the lines cited
are from the "Epilogue" to Southey's *The Lay of the
Laureate.*

1. Symbols of love and youthful revelry.
2. The laurel wreath is an emblem of distinction.

On This Day I Complete My Thirty-Sixth Year[1]

'Tis time this heart should be unmoved,
   Since others it hath ceased to move:
Yet, though I cannot be beloved,
    Still let me love!

5 My days are in the yellow leaf;[2]
   The flowers and fruits of love are gone;
The worm, the canker, and the grief
    Are mine alone!

The fire that on my bosom preys
10 Is lone as some volcanic isle;
No torch is kindled at its blaze—
    A funeral pile.

The hope, the fear, the jealous care,
   The exalted portion of the pain
15 And power of love, I cannot share,
    But wear the chain.

But 'tis not *thus*—and 'tis not *here*—
   Such thoughts should shake my soul, nor *now*,
Where glory decks the hero's bier,
20   Or binds his brow.

The sword, the banner, and the field,
   Glory and Greece, around me see!
The Spartan, borne upon his shield,
    Was not more free.

25 Awake! (not Greece—she *is* awake!)
   Awake, my spirit! Think through *whom*
Thy life-blood tracks its parent lake,
    And then strike home!

Tread those reviving passions down,
30 Unworthy manhood!—unto thee
Indifferent should the smile or frown
    Of beauty be.

If thou regrett'st thy youth, *why live?*
   The land of honourable death
35 Is here:—up to the field, and give
    Away thy breath!

Seek out—less often sought than found—
   A soldier's grave, for thee the best;
Then look around, and choose thy ground,
40   And take thy rest.

PERCY BYSSHE SHELLEY (1792-1822)

Hymn to Intellectual[1] Beauty

1

The awful shadow of some unseen Power
   Floats though unseen amongst us,—visiting
   This various world with as inconstant wing
As summer winds that creep from flower to flower.—
5 Like moonbeams that behind some piny mountain shower,
     It visits with inconstant glance
     Each human heart and countenance;
Like hues and harmonies of evening,—
     Like clouds in starlight widely spread,—
10   Like memory of music fled,—
     Like aught that for its grace may be
Dear, and yet dearer for its mystery.

2

Spirit of BEAUTY, that dost consecrate
   With thine own hues all thou dost shine upon
15 Of human thought or form,—where art thou gone?
Why dost thou pass away and leave our state,
This dim vast vale of tears, vacant and desolate?
     Ask why the sunlight not forever
     Weaves rainbows o'er yon mountain river,
20 Why aught should fail and fade that once is shewn,

---

1. This poem was written on 22 January 1824, shortly after Byron's arrival at Missolonghi to help the Greeks in their struggle for liberation from the Turks. On 19 April he died there of a fever.

2. From *Macbeth* V.iii.22: "I have lived long enough: my way of life / Is fall'n into the sere, the yellow leaf."

1. Non-material, spiritual.

Why fear and dream and death and birth
Cast on the daylight of this earth
Such gloom,—why man has such a scope
For love and hate, despondency and hope?

3

25 No voice from some sublimer world hath ever
To sage or poet these responses given—
Therefore the name of God and ghosts and Heaven,
Remain the records of their vain endeavour,[2]
Frail spells—whose uttered charm might not avail to sever,
30 From all we hear and all we see,
Doubt, chance, and mutability.
Thy light alone—like mist o'er mountains driven,
Or music by the night wind sent
Through strings of some still instrument,[3]
35 Or moonlight on a midnight stream,
Gives grace and truth to life's unquiet dream.

4

Love, Hope, and Self-esteem, like clouds depart
And come, for some uncertain moments lent.
Man were immortal, and omnipotent,
40 Didst thou, unknown and awful as thou art,
Keep with thy glorious train firm state within his heart.
Thou messenger of sympathies,
That wax and wane in lovers' eyes—
Thou—that to human thought art nourishment,
45 Like darkness to a dying flame!
Depart not as thy shadow came,
Depart not—lest the grave should be,
Like life and fear, a dark reality.

5

While yet a boy I sought for ghosts, and sped
50 Through many a listening chamber, cave and ruin,
And starlight wood, with fearful steps pursuing
Hopes of high talk with the departed dead.
I called on poisonous names with which our youth is fed;
I was not heard—I saw them not—
55 When musing deeply on the lot
Of life, at that sweet time when winds are wooing
All vital things that wake to bring
News of buds and blossoming,—
Sudden, thy shadow fell on me;
60 I shrieked, and clasped my hands in extacy!

6

I vowed that I would dedicate my powers
To thee and thine—have I not kept the vow?
With beating heart and streaming eyes, even now
I call the phantoms of a thousand hours
65 Each from his voiceless grave: they have in visioned bowers
Of studious zeal or love's delight
Outwatched with me the envious night—
They know that never joy illumed my brow
Unlinked with hope that thou wouldst free
70 This world from its dark slavery,
That thou—O awful LOVELINESS,
Wouldst give whate'er these words cannot express.

2. I.e., not having been able to obtain divine truths, the
sages and poets have merely used such labels as "God and
ghosts and Heaven" to explain the mysteries of life.

3. An Aeolian harp, whose strings would sound as the
wind passed through them.

7

The day becomes more solemn and serene
   When noon is past—there is a harmony
75   In autumn, and a lustre in its sky,
Which through the summer is not heard or seen,
As if it could not be, as if it had not been!
      Thus let thy power, which like the truth
      Of nature on my passive youth
80 Descended, to my onward life supply
      Its calm—to one who worships thee,
      And every form containing thee,
      Whom, SPIRIT fair, thy spells did bind
To fear himself, and love all human kind.

Ozymandias[1]

I met a traveller from an antique land,
Who said—"Two vast and trunkless legs of stone
Stand in the desert. . . . Near them, on the sand,
Half sunk a shattered visage lies, whose frown,
And wrinkled lip, and sneer of cold command,
Tell that its sculptor well those passions read
Which yet survive, stamped on these lifeless things,
The hand that mocked them, and the heart that fed;
And on the pedestal, these words appear:
My name is Ozymandias, King of Kings,
Look on my Works, ye Mighty, and despair!
Nothing beside remains. Round the decay
Of that colossal Wreck, boundless and bare
The lone and level sands stretch far away."

Ode to the West Wind

I

O wild West Wind, thou breath of Autumn's being,
Thou, from whose unseen presence the leaves dead
Are driven, like ghosts from an enchanter fleeing,

Yellow, and black, and pale, and hectic red,[1]
5 Pestilence-stricken multitudes: O Thou,
Who chariotest to their dark wintry bed

The winged seeds, where they lie cold and low,
Each like a corpse within its grave, until
Thine azure sister of the Spring shall blow

10 Her clarion[2] o'er the dreaming earth, and fill
(Driving sweet buds like flocks to feed in air)
With living hues and odours plain and hill:

Wild Spirit, which art moving everywhere;
Destroyer and Preserver; hear, O hear!

II

15 Thou on whose stream, 'mid the steep sky's commotion,
Loose clouds like Earth's decaying leaves are shed,
Shook from the tangled boughs of Heaven and Ocean,

---

1. The Greek name for Rameses II, pharoah of Egypt in
the thirteenth century B.C.

1. The flushed, feverish colour often associated with
consumptive diseases.
2. A shrill-sounding trumpet.

Angels of rain and lightning: there are spread
On the blue surface of thine aery surge,
20   Like the bright hair uplifted from the head

Of some fierce Mænad,[3] even from the dim verge
Of the horizon to the zenith's height,
The locks of the approaching storm. Thou Dirge

Of the dying year, to which this closing night
25   Will be the dome of a vast sepulchre,
Vaulted with all thy congregated might

Of vapours, from whose solid atmosphere
Black rain and fire and hail will burst: O hear!

III

Thou who didst waken from his summer dreams
30   The blue Mediterranean, where he lay,
Lulled by the coil of his chrystalline streams,

Beside a pumice isle in Baiæ's bay,[4]
And saw in sleep old palaces and towers
Quivering within the wave's intenser day,

35   All overgrown with azure moss and flowers
So sweet, the sense faints picturing them! Thou
For whose path the Atlantic's level powers

Cleave themselves into chasms, while far below
The sea-blooms and the oozy woods which wear
40   The sapless foliage of the ocean,[5] know

Thy voice, and suddenly grow grey with fear,
And tremble and despoil themselves: O hear!

IV

If I were a dead leaf thou mightest bear;
If I were a swift cloud to fly with thee;
45   A wave to pant beneath thy power, and share

The impulse of thy strength, only less free
Than thou, O Uncontrollable! If even
I were as in my boyhood, and could be

The comrade of thy wanderings over Heaven
50   As then, when to outstrip thy skiey speed
Scarce seemed a vision; I would ne'er have striven

As thus with thee in prayer in my sore need.
Oh! lift me as a wave, a leaf, a cloud!
I fall upon the thorns of life! I bleed!

55   A heavy weight of hours has chained and bowed
One too like thee: tameless, and swift, and proud.

3. One of the frenzied female votaries of Dionysus, the Greek god of wine.
4. An island formed of porous lava, in the Bay of Baiae near Naples. Baiae was a favourite resort of the ancient Romans, who built large villas there.

5. "The vegetation at the bottom of the sea, of rivers, and of lakes, sympathizes with that of the land in the change of seasons, and is consequently influenced by the winds which announce it" (Shelley's note).

V

Make me thy lyre, even as the forest is:
What if my leaves are falling like its own!
The tumult of thy mighty harmonies

60 Will take from both a deep, autumnal tone,
Sweet though in sadness. Be thou, Spirit fierce,
My spirit! Be thou me, impetuous one!

Drive my dead thoughts over the universe
Like withered leaves to quicken a new birth!
65 And, by the incantation of this verse,

Scatter, as from an unextinguished hearth
Ashes and sparks, my words among mankind!
Be through my lips to unawakened Earth

The trumpet of a prophecy! O Wind,
70 If Winter comes, can Spring be far behind?

England in 1819

An old, mad, blind, despised, and dying King;[1]
Princes, the dregs of their dull race, who flow
Through public scorn,—mud from a muddy spring;
Rulers who neither see nor feel nor know,
But leechlike to their fainting country cling
Till they drop, blind in blood, without a blow.
A people starved and stabbed in th'untilled field;[2]
An army, whom liberticide and prey
Makes as a two-edged sword to all who wield;
Golden and sanguine laws which tempt and slay;
Religion Christless, Godless—a book sealed;
A senate, Time's worst statute,[3] unrepealed—
Are graves from which a glorious Phantom may
Burst, to illumine our tempestuous day.

To a Sky-Lark

Hail to thee, blithe Spirit!
    Bird thou never wert—
That from Heaven, or near it,
    Pourest thy full heart
5 In profuse strains of unpremeditated art.

Higher still and higher
    From the earth thou springest
Like a cloud of fire;
    The blue deep thou wingest,
10 And singing still dost soar, and soaring ever singest.

In the golden lightning
    Of the sunken Sun—
O'er which clouds are brightning,
    Thou dost float and run;
15 Like an unbodied joy whose race is just begun.

1. George III, king from 1760 to 1820, periodically suffered bouts of insanity, and in 1811 was replaced by his son who ruled as Prince Regent.
2. In August 1819, a peaceful rally held by reformers in St. Peter's Field in Manchester was violently attacked by militiamen, who killed at least six people. The incident came to be known as the Peterloo Massacre.
3. Probably an allusion to the legal disabilities under which Roman Catholics had suffered in England for several centuries.

The pale purple even
   Melts around thy flight,
Like a star of Heaven
   In the broad day-light
20   Thou art unseen,—but yet I hear thy shrill delight,

Keen as are the arrows
   Of that silver sphere,[1]
Whose intense lamp narrows
   In the white dawn clear
25   Until we hardly see—we feel that it is there.

All the earth and air
   With thy voice is loud,
As when Night is bare
   From one lonely cloud
30   The moon rains out her beams—and Heaven is overflowed.

What thou art we know not;
   What is most like thee?
From rainbow clouds there flow not
   Drops so bright to see
35   As from thy presence showers a rain of melody.

Like a Poet hidden
   In the light of thought,
Singing hymns unbidden,
   Till the world is wrought
40   To sympathy with hopes and fears it heeded not:

Like a high-born maiden
   In a palace-tower,
Soothing her love-laden
   Soul in secret hour,
45   With music sweet as love—which overflows her bower:

Like a glow-worm golden
   In a dell of dew,
Scattering unbeholden
   Its aerial hue
50   Among the flowers and grass which screen it from the view:

Like a rose embowered
   In its own green leaves—
By warm winds deflowered—
   Till the scent it gives
55   Makes faint with too much sweet heavy-winged thieves:

Sound of vernal showers
   On the twinkling grass,
Rain-awakened flowers,
   All that ever was
60   Joyous, and clear and fresh, thy music doth surpass.

1. The morning star.

Teach us, Sprite or Bird,
  What sweet thoughts are thine;
I have never heard
  Praise of love or wine
65 That panted forth a flood of rapture so divine:

Chorus Hymeneal[2]
  Or triumphal chaunt
Matched with thine would be all
  But an empty vaunt,
70 A thing wherein we feel there is some hidden want.

What objects are the fountains
  Of thy happy strain?
What fields or waves or mountains?
  What shapes of sky or plain?
75 What love of thine own kind? what ignorance of pain?

With thy clear keen joyance
  Languor cannot be—
Shadow of annoyance
  Never came near thee;
80 Thou lovest—but ne'er knew love's sad satiety.

Waking or asleep,
  Thou of death must deem
Things more true and deep
  Than we mortals dream,
85 Or how could thy notes flow in such a chrystal stream?

We look before and after,
  And pine for what is not—
Our sincerest laughter
  With some pain is fraught—
90 Our sweetest songs are those that tell of saddest thought.

Yet if we could scorn
  Hate and pride and fear;
If we were things born
  Not to shed a tear,
95 I know not how thy joy we ever should come near.

Better than all measures
  Of delightful sound—
Better than all treasures
  That in books are found—
100 Thy skill to poet were, thou Scorner of the ground!

Teach me half the gladness
  That thy brain must know,
Such harmonious madness
  From my lips would flow
105 The world should listen then—as I am listening now.

2. Pertaining to marriage (from Hymen, god of marriage).

Adonais

An Elegy on the Death of John Keats, Author of Endymion, Hyperion, Etc.

'Αστὴρ πρὶν μὲν ἔλαμπες ἐνὶ ζωοῖσιν ʿΕῶος'
νῦν δὲ θανὼν λάμπεις ʿΕσπερος ἐν φθιμένοις. —Plato[1]

1

I weep for Adonais[2]—he is dead!
O, weep for Adonais! though our tears
Thaw not the frost which binds so dear a head!
And thou, sad Hour, selected from all years
To mourn our loss, rouse thy obscure compeers,
And teach them thine own sorrow, say: with me
Died Adonais; till the Future dares
Forget the Past, his fate and fame shall be
An echo and a light unto eternity!

2

Where wert thou mighty Mother,[3] when he lay,
When thy Son lay, pierced by the shaft which flies
In darkness?[4] where was lorn Urania
When Adonais died? With veiled eyes,
'Mid listening Echoes, in her Paradise
She sate, while one, with soft enamoured breath,
Rekindled all the fading melodies,
With which, like flowers that mock the corse beneath,
He had adorned and hid the coming bulk of death.

3

O, weep for Adonais—he is dead!
Wake, melancholy Mother, wake and weep!
Yet wherefore? Quench within their burning bed
Thy fiery tears, and let thy loud heart keep
Like his, a mute and uncomplaining sleep;
For he is gone, where all things wise and fair
Descend;—oh, dream not that the amorous Deep
Will yet restore him to the vital air;
Death feeds on his mute voice, and laughs at our despair.

4

Most musical of mourners, weep again!
Lament anew, Urania!— He died,[5]
Who was the Sire of an immortal strain,
Blind, old, and lonely, when his country's pride,
The priest, the slave, and the liberticide,
Trampled and mocked with many a loathed rite
Of lust and blood; he went, unterrified,
Into the gulph of death; but his clear Sprite
Yet reigns o'er earth; the third among the sons of light.[6]

1. Thou wert the morning star among the living,   Ere thy fair light had fled— Now, having died, thou art as Hesperus, giving   New splendour to the dead.(Shelley's translation)
2. The name is derived from Adonis, the beautiful youth in Greek myth beloved by the goddess Aphrodite. He was killed by a wild boar, and from his blood sprang the anemone. Shelley's poem was in part suggested by the Greek poet Bion's "Lament for Adonis."
3. Urania (l. 12), in Greek mythology the muse of

astronomy. The name was also given to Aphrodite, goddess of love.
4. An allusion to the anonymous review of Keats's *Endymion* in the *Quarterly Review*, April 1818, which was popularly supposed to have hastened Keats's death The reviewer was John Wilson Croker.
5. I.e., John Milton.
6. In *A Defence of Poetry*, written in 1821, Shelley lists Homer, Dante, and Milton as the three great epic poets.

5

    Most musical of mourners, weep anew!
    Not all to that bright station dared to climb;
    And happier they their happiness who knew,
40   Whose tapers yet burn through that night of time
    In which suns perished; others more sublime,
    Struck by the envious wrath of man or God,
    Have sunk, extinct in their refulgent prime;
    And some yet live, treading the thorny road,
45 Which leads, through toil and hate, to Fame's serene abode.

6

    But now, thy youngest, dearest one, has perished
    The nursling of thy widowhood, who grew,
    Like a pale flower by some sad maiden cherished,[7]
    And fed with true love tears, instead of dew;
50   Most musical of mourners, weep anew!
    Thy extreme hope, the loveliest and the last,
    The bloom, whose petals nipt before they blew
    Died on the promise of the fruit, is waste;
The broken lily lies—the storm is overpast.

7

55   To that high Capital,[8] where kingly Death
    Keeps his pale court in beauty and decay,
    He came; and bought, with price of purest breath,
    A grave among the eternal.— Come away!
    Haste, while the vault of blue Italian day
60   Is yet his fitting charnel-roof! while still
    He lies, as if in dewy sleep he lay;
    Awake him not! surely he takes his fill
Of deep and liquid rest, forgetful of all ill.

8

    He will awake no more, oh, never more!—
65   Within the twilight chamber spreads apace,
    The shadow of white Death, and at the door
    Invisible Corruption waits to trace
    His extreme way[9] to her dim dwelling-place;
    The eternal Hunger sits, but pity and awe
70   Soothe her pale rage, nor dares she to deface
    So fair a prey, till darkness, and the law
Of change, shall o'er his sleep the mortal curtain draw.

9

    O, weep for Adonais!—The quick[10] Dreams,
    The passion-winged Ministers of thought,
75   Who were his flocks, whom near the living streams
    Of his young spirit he fed, and whom he taught
    The love which was its music, wander not,—
    Wander no more, from kindling brain to brain,
    But droop there, whence they sprung; and mourn their lot
80   Round the cold heart, where, after their sweet pain,
They ne'er will gather strength, or find a home again.

---

7. An allusion to Keats's poem *Isabella, or the Pot of Basil*, in which the heroine hides the head of her murdered lover in a pot of basil which she waters with her tears.

8. Rome, where Keats died on 23 February 1821.
9. His last journey.
10. Living.

10

And one with trembling hands clasps his cold head,
And fans him with her moonlight wings, and cries;
"Our love, our hope, our sorrow, is not dead;
85   See, on the silken fringe of his faint eyes,
Like dew upon a sleeping flower, there lies
A tear some Dream has loosened from his brain."
Lost Angel of a ruined Paradise!
She knew not 'twas her own; as with no stain
90   She faded, like a cloud which had outwept its rain.

11

One from a lucid[11] urn of starry dew
Washed his light limbs as if embalming them;
Another clipt her profuse locks, and threw
The wreath upon him, like an anadem,[12]
95   Which frozen tears instead of pearls begem;
Another in her wilful grief would break
Her bow and winged reeds, as if to stem
A greater loss with one which was more weak;
And dull the barbed fire against his frozen cheek.

12

100   Another Splendour on his mouth alit,
That mouth, whence it was wont to draw the breath
Which gave it strength to pierce the guarded wit,
And pass into the panting heart beneath
With lightning and with music: the damp death
105   Quenched its caress upon his icy lips;
And, as a dying meteor stains a wreath
Of moonlight vapour, which the cold night clips,[13]
It flushed through his pale limbs, and past to its eclipse.

13

And others came. . . Desires and Adorations,
110   Winged Persuasions and veiled Destinies,
Splendours, and Glooms, and glimmering Incarnations
Of hopes and fears, and twilight Phantasies;
And Sorrow, with her family of Sighs,
And Pleasure, blind with tears, led by the gleam
115   Of her own dying smile instead of eyes,
Came in slow pomp;— the moving pomp might seem
Like pageantry of mist on an autumnal stream.

14

All he had loved, and moulded into thought,
From shape, and hue, and odour, and sweet sound,
120   Lamented Adonais. Morning sought
Her eastern watchtower, and her hair unbound,
Wet with the tears which should adorn the ground,
Dimmed the aerial eyes that kindle day;
Afar the melancholy thunder moaned,
125   Pale Ocean in unquiet slumber lay,
And the wild winds flew round, sobbing in their dismay.

15

Lost Echo sits amid the voiceless mountains,
And feeds her grief with his remembered lay,
And will no more reply to winds or fountains,
130   Or amorous birds perched on the young green spray,

---

11. Shining, luminous.
12. Garland.   13. Embraces.

Or herdsman's horn, or bell at closing day;
Since she can mimic not his lips, more dear
Than those for whose disdain she pined away
Into a shadow of all sounds:[14]— a drear
135 Murmur, between their songs, is all the woodmen hear.

16

Grief made the young Spring wild, and she threw down
Her kindling buds, as if she Autumn were,
Or they dead leaves; since her delight is flown
For whom should she have waked the sullen year?
140 To Phœbus was not Hyacinth[15] so dear
Nor to himself Narcissus,[16] as to both
Thou Adonais: wan they stand and sere[17]
Amid the faint companions of their youth,
With dew all turned to tears; odour, to sighing ruth.

17

145 Thy spirit's sister, the lorn nightingale
Mourns not her mate with such melodious pain;
Not so the eagle, who like thee could scale
Heaven, and could nourish in the sun's domain
Her mighty youth[18] with morning, doth complain,
150 Soaring and screaming round her empty nest,
As Albion[19] wails for thee: the curse of Cain[20]
Light on his head who pierced thy innocent breast,
And scared the angel soul that was its earthly guest!

18

Ah woe is me! Winter is come and gone,
155 But grief returns with the revolving year;
The airs and streams renew their joyous tone;
The ants, the bees, the swallows reappear;
Fresh leaves and flowers deck the dead Seasons' bier;
The amorous birds now pair in every brake,[21]
160 And build their mossy homes in field and brere;[22]
And the green lizard, and the golden snake,
Like unimprisoned flames, out of their trance awake.

19

Through wood and stream and field and hill and Ocean
A quickening life from the Earth's heart has burst
165 As it has ever done, with change and motion,
From the great morning of the world when first
God dawned on Chaos; in its steam immersed
The lamps of Heaven flash with a softer light;
All baser things pant with life's sacred thirst;
170 Diffuse themselves; and spend in love's delight,
The beauty and the joy of their renewed might.

20

The leprous corpse touched by this spirit tender
Exhales itself in flowers of gentle breath;
Like incarnations of the stars, when splendour
175 Is changed to fragrance, they illumine death
And mock the merry worm that wakes beneath;

---

14. When Narcissus rejected her love, the nymph Echo
faded into a disembodied voice.
15. The youth Hyacinthus, beloved by Phoebus Apollo.
16. Narcissus fell in love with his own image in a fountain.
17. Withered, dried up.
18. According to ancient superstition, the eagle might
periodically gain renewed life by soaring towards the sun
and then plunging into the sea, thus shedding its old
feathers.
19. England.
20. See Gen. iv.11–12. The "head" of l. 152 is that of the
reviewer of *Endymion*.
21. Thicket.
22. Briar, thorny bush.

Nought we know, dies. Shall that alone which knows
Be as a sword consumed before the sheath
By sightless lightning?—th'intense atom glows
180   A moment, then is quenched in a most cold repose.

21

Alas! that all we loved of him should be,
But for our grief, as if it had not been,
And grief itself be mortal! Woe is me!
Whence are we, and why are we? of what scene
185   The actors or spectators? Great and mean
Meet massed in death, who lends what life must borrow.
As long as skies are blue, and fields are green,
Evening must usher night, night urge the morrow,
Month follow month with woe, and year wake year to sorrow.

22

190   *He* will awake no more, oh, never more!
"Wake thou," cried Misery, "childless Mother, rise
Out of thy sleep, and slake, in thy heart's core,
A wound more fierce than his with tears and sighs."
And all the Dreams that watched Urania's eyes,
195   And all the Echoes whom their sister's song
Had held in holy silence, cried: "Arise!"
Swift as a Thought by the snake Memory stung,
From her ambrosial rest the fading Splendour sprung.

23

She rose like an autumnal Night, that springs
200   Out of the East, and follows wild and drear
The golden Day, which, on eternal wings,
Even as a ghost abandoning a bier,
Had left the Earth a corpse. Sorrow and fear
So struck, so roused, so rapt Urania;
205   So saddened round her like an atmosphere
Of stormy mist; so swept her on her way
Even to the mournful place where Adonais lay.

24

Out of her secret Paradise she sped,
Through camps and cities rough with stone, and steel,
210   And human hearts, which to her aery tread
Yielding not, wounded the invisible
Palms of her tender feet where'er they fell:
And barbed tongues, and thoughts more sharp than they
Rent the soft Form they never could repel,
215   Whose sacred blood, like the young tears of May,
Paved with eternal flowers that undeserving way.

25

In the death chamber for a moment Death
Shamed by the presence of that living Might
Blushed to annihilation, and the breath
220   Revisited those lips, and life's pale light
Flashed through those limbs, so late her dear delight.
"Leave me not wild and drear and comfortless,
As silent lightning leaves the starless night!
Leave me not!" cried Urania: her distress
225   Roused Death: Death rose and smiled, and met her vain caress.

26

"Stay yet awhile! speak to me once again;
Kiss me, so long but as a kiss may live;

And in my heartless breast and burning brain
That word, that kiss shall all thoughts else survive
230   With food of saddest memory kept alive,
Now thou art dead, as if it were a part
Of thee, my Adonais! I would give
All that I am to be as thou now art!
But I am chained to Time, and cannot thence depart!

27
235   "O gentle child, beautiful as thou wert,
Why didst thou leave the trodden paths of men
Too soon, and with weak hands though mighty heart
Dare the unpastured dragon in his den?
Defenceless as thou wert, oh where was then
240   Wisdom the mirrored shield,[23] or scorn the spear?
Or hadst thou waited the full cycle, when
Thy spirit should have filled its crescent sphere,
The monsters of life's waste had fled from thee like deer.

28
"The herded wolves, bold only to pursue;
245   The obscene ravens, clamorous o'er the dead;
The vultures to the conqueror's banner true
Who feed where Desolation first has fed,
And whose wings rain contagion;— how they fled,
When like Apollo, from his golden bow,
250   The Pythian of the age[24] one arrow sped
And smiled!— The spoilers tempt no second blow,
They fawn on the proud feet that spurn them lying low.

29
"The sun comes forth, and many reptiles spawn;
He sets, and each ephemeral insect then
255   Is gathered into death without a dawn,
And the immortal stars awake again;
So is it in the world of living men:
A godlike mind soars forth, in its delight
Making earth bare and veiling heaven, and when
260   It sinks, the swarms that dimmed or shared its light
Leave to its kindred lamps the spirit's awful night."

30
Thus ceased she: and the mountain shepherds came
Their garlands sere, their magic mantles rent;
The Pilgrim of Eternity,[25] whose fame
265   Over his living head like Heaven is bent,
An early but enduring monument,
Came, veiling all the lightnings of his song
In sorrow; from her wilds Ierne[26] sent
The sweetest lyrist of her saddest wrong,
270   And love taught grief to fall like music from his tongue.

31
Midst others of less note, came one frail Form,[27]
A phantom among men; companionless
As the last cloud of an expiring storm
Whose thunder is its knell; he, as I guess,
275   Had gazed on Nature's naked loveliness,

---

23. Perseus slew Medusa, whose gaze could turn an onlooker into stone, by using his shield as a mirror and thus looking at her indirectly.
24. Like Pythian Apollo, who slew the serpent Python, Byron defeated his enemies with his "one arrow," the

satire *English Bards and Scotch Reviewers*.
25. Byron. See *Childe Harold*, Canto III, stanza LXX.
26. Ireland. The "sweetest lyrist" of l. 269 is Thomas Moore (1779–1852), author of *Irish Melodies*.
27. Shelley himself.

Actæon-like,[28] and now he fled astray
With feeble steps o'er the world's wilderness,
And his own thoughts, along that rugged way,
Pursued, like raging hounds, their father and their prey.

32

280
A pardlike[29] Spirit beautiful and swift—
A Love in desolation masked;—a Power
Girt round with weakness;—it can scarce uplift
The weight of the superincumbent hour;
It is a dying lamp, a falling shower,
285
A breaking billow;—even whilst we speak
Is it not broken? On the withering flower
The killing sun smiles brightly: on a cheek
The life can burn in blood, even while the heart may break.

33

His head was bound with pansies[30] overblown,
290
And faded violets, white, and pied, and blue;
And a light spear[31] topped with a cypress cone,
Round whose rude shaft dark ivy tresses grew
Yet dripping with the forest's noonday dew,
Vibrated, as the ever-beating heart
295
Shook the weak hand that grasped it; of that crew
He came the last, neglected and apart;
A herd-abandoned deer struck by the hunter's dart.

34

All stood aloof, and at his partial moan
Smiled through their tears; well knew that gentle band
300
Who in another's fate now wept his own;
As in the accents of an unknown land,
He sung new sorrow; sad Urania scanned
The Stranger's mien, and murmured: "who art thou?"
He answered not, but with a sudden hand
305
Made bare his branded and ensanguined brow,
Which was like Cain's or Christ's— Oh! that it should be so!

35

What softer voice is hushed over the dead?
Athwart what brow is that dark mantle thrown?
What form leans sadly o'er the white death-bed,
310
In mockery of monumental stone,
The heavy heart heaving without a moan?
If it be He,[32] who, gentlest of the wise,
Taught, soothed, loved, honoured the departed one;
Let me not vex, with inharmonious sighs
315
The silence of that heart's accepted sacrifice.

36

Our Adonais has drunk poison— oh!
What deaf and viperous murderer could crown
Life's early cup with such a draught of woe?
The nameless worm[33] would now itself disown:
320
It felt, yet could escape the magic tone
Whose prelude held all envy, hate, and wrong,

28. The hunter Actæon saw the goddess Diana bathing;
when the irate goddess turned him into a stag, he was torn
to pieces by his own hounds.
29. Leopard-like.
30. In the traditional symbolism of flowers, the pansy
represents thought and the violet is the type of modesty.
31. The thyrsus, a staff tipped with a pine cone and
wrapped with ivy or vine-leaves. Shelley pictures himself
as a follower of Dionysus, in whose rites the thyrsus was
borne.
32. Leigh Hunt (1784–1859), close friend of Keats.
33. Serpent. Another reference to the anonymous
reviewer of *Endymion*.

But what was howling in one breast alone,
  Silent with expectation of the song,
Whose master's hand is cold, whose silver lyre unstrung.

37

325 Live thou, whose infamy is not thy fame!
  Live! fear no heavier chastisement from me,
  Thou noteless blot on a remembered name!
  But be thyself, and know thyself to be!
  And ever at thy season be thou free
330 To spill the venom when thy fangs o'erflow:
  Remorse and Self-contempt shall cling to thee;
  Hot Shame shall burn upon thy secret brow,
And like a beaten hound tremble thou shalt—as now.

38

Nor let us weep that our delight is fled
335 Far from these carrion kites that scream below;
  He wakes or sleeps with the enduring dead;
  Thou canst not soar where he is sitting now.—
  Dust to the dust! but the pure spirit shall flow
  Back to the burning fountain whence it came,
340 A portion of the Eternal, which must glow
  Through time and change, unquenchably the same,
Whilst thy cold embers choke the sordid hearth of shame.

39

Peace, peace! he is not dead, he doth not sleep—
  He hath awakened from the dream of life—
345 'Tis we, who lost in stormy visions, keep
  With phantoms an unprofitable strife,
  And in mad trance, strike with our spirit's knife
  Invulnerable nothings.— *We* decay
  Like corpses in a charnel; fear and grief
350 Convulse us and consume us day by day,
And cold hopes swarm like worms within our living clay.

40

He has outsoared the shadow of our night;
  Envy and calumny and hate and pain,
  And that unrest which men miscall delight,
355 Can touch him not and torture not again;
  From the contagion of the world's slow stain
  He is secure, and now can never mourn
  A heart grown cold, a head grown grey in vain;
  Nor, when the spirit's self has ceased to burn,
360 With sparkless ashes load an unlamented urn.

41

He lives, he wakes—'tis Death is dead, not he;
  Mourn not for Adonais.—Thou young Dawn
  Turn all thy dew to splendour, for from thee
  The spirit thou lamentest is not gone;
365 Ye caverns and ye forests, cease to moan!
  Cease ye faint flowers and fountains, and thou Air
  Which like a mourning veil thy scarf hadst thrown
  O'er the abandoned Earth, now leave it bare
Even to the joyous stars which smile on its despair!

42

370 He is made one with Nature: there is heard
  His voice in all her music, from the moan
  Of thunder, to the song of night's sweet bird;

He is a presence to be felt and known
In darkness and in light, from herb and stone,
375   Spreading itself where'er that Power may move
Which has withdrawn his being to its own;
Which wields the world with never wearied love,
Sustains it from beneath, and kindles it above.

43

He is a portion of the loveliness
380   Which once he made more lovely: he doth bear
His part, while the one Spirit's plastic stress[34]
Sweeps through the dull dense world, compelling there,
All new successions to the forms they wear;
Torturing th'unwilling dross that checks its flight
385   To its own likeness, as each mass may bear;[35]
And bursting in its beauty and its might
From trees and beasts and men into the Heaven's light.

44

The splendours of the firmament of time
May be eclipsed, but are extinguished not;
390   Like stars to their appointed height they climb
And death is a low mist which cannot blot
The brightness it may veil. When lofty thought
Lifts a young heart above its mortal lair,
And love and life contend in it, for what
395   Shall be its earthly doom, the dead live there
And move like winds of light on dark and stormy air.

45

The inheritors of unfulfilled renown
Rose from their thrones, built beyond mortal thought,
Far in the Unapparent. Chatterton[36]
400   Rose pale, his solemn agony had not
Yet faded from him; Sidney, as he fought
And as he fell and as he lived and loved
Sublimely mild, a Spirit without spot,
Arose; and Lucan, by his death approved:[37]
405   Oblivion as they rose shrank like a thing reproved.

46

And many more, whose names on Earth are dark
But whose transmitted effluence cannot die
So long as fire outlives the parent spark,
Rose, robed in dazzling immortality.
410   "Thou art become as one of us," they cry,
"It was for thee yon kingless sphere has long
Swung blind in unascended majesty,
Silent alone amid an Heaven of song.
Assume thy winged throne, thou Vesper of our throng!"

47

415   Who mourns for Adonais? oh come forth
Fond[38] wretch! and know thyself and him aright.
Clasp with thy panting soul the pendulous[39] Earth;
As from a centre, dart thy spirit's light
Beyond all worlds, until its spacious might

34. Shaping force.
35. I.e., as far as the nature of the "unwilling dross," the resistant material substance shaped by the creative spirit, is capable of being refined into spiritual form.
36. Thomas Chatterton was a promising young poet who committed suicide in 1770 at the age of seventeen; Sir Philip Sidney, Elizabethan courtier and poet, died at thirty-two from wounds received in the battle of Zutphen (1586); the Roman writer Lucan killed himself in A.D. 65, when twenty-six years old, after his part in a plot against Nero had been discovered.
37. Vindicated.
38. Foolish.
39. Hanging, suspended.

420 Satiate the void circumference: then shrink
Even to a point within our day and night;
And keep thy heart light lest it make thee sink
When hope has kindled hope, and lured thee to the brink.

48
Or go to Rome, which is the sepulchre
425 O, not of him, but of our joy: 'tis nought
That ages, empires, and religions there
Lie buried in the ravage they have wrought;
For such as he can lend,—they borrow not
Glory from those who made the world their prey;
430 And he is gathered to the kings of thought
Who waged contention with their time's decay,
And of the past are all that cannot pass away.

49
Go thou to Rome,—at once the Paradise,
The grave, the city, and the wilderness;
435 And where its wrecks like shattered mountains rise,
And flowering weeds, and fragrant copses dress
The bones of Desolation's nakedness
Pass, till the Spirit of the spot shall lead
Thy footsteps to a slope of green access
440 Where, like an infant's smile, over the dead,
A light of laughing flowers along the grass is spread.[40]

50
And grey walls moulder round, on which dull Time
Feeds, like slow fire upon a hoary brand;
And one keen pyramid[41] with wedge sublime,
445 Pavilioning the dust of him who planned
This refuge for his memory, doth stand
Like flame transformed to marble; and beneath,
A field is spread, on which a newer band
Have pitched in Heaven's smile their camp of death
450 Welcoming him we lose with scarce extinguished breath.

51
Here pause: these graves are all too young as yet
To have outgrown the sorrow which consigned
Its charge to each; and if the seal is set,
Here, on one fountain of a mourning mind,
455 Break it not thou! too surely shalt thou find
Thine own well full, if thou returnest home,
Of tears and gall. From the world's bitter wind
Seek shelter in the shadow of the tomb.
What Adonais is, why fear we to become?

52
460 The One remains, the many change and pass;
Heaven's light forever shines, Earth's shadows fly;
Life, like a dome of many-coloured glass,
Stains the white radiance of Eternity,
Until Death tramples it to fragments.—Die,
465 If thou wouldst be with that which thou dost seek!
Follow where all is fled!—Rome's azure sky,
Flowers, ruins, statues, music, words, are weak
The glory they transfuse with fitting truth to speak.

40. Keats was buried in the Protestant Cemetery in
Rome, where Shelley's infant son William had been buried
in 1819.
41. The tomb of Gaius Cestus, a Roman tribune.

53

470
Why linger, why turn back, why shrink, my Heart?
Thy hopes are gone before; from all things here
They have departed; thou shouldst now depart!
A light is past from the revolving year,
And man, and woman; and what still is dear

475
Attracts to crush, repels to make thee wither.
The soft sky smiles,—the low wind whispers near:
'Tis Adonais calls! oh, hasten thither,
No more let Life divide what Death can join together.

54

That Light whose smile kindles the Universe,
That Beauty in which all things work and move,

480
That Benediction which the eclipsing Curse
Of birth can quench not, that sustaining Love
Which through the web of being blindly wove
By man and beast and earth and air and sea,
Burns bright or dim, as each are mirrors of

485
The fire for which all thirst;[42] now beams on me,
Consuming the last clouds of cold mortality.

55

The breath whose might I have invoked in song
Descends on me; my spirit's bark is driven,
Far from the shore, far from the trembling throng

490
Whose sails were never to the tempest given;
The massy earth and sphered skies are riven!
I am borne darkly, fearfully, afar:
Whilst burning through the inmost veil of Heaven,
The soul of Adonais, like a star,

495
Beacons from the abode where the Eternal are.

JOHN KEATS (1795–1821)

On First Looking into Chapman's Homer

Much have I travell'd in the realms of gold,
    And many goodly states and kingdoms seen;
    Round many western islands have I been
Which bards in fealty to Apollo hold.
Oft of one wide expanse had I been told
    That deep-brow'd Homer ruled as his demesne;
    Yet did I never breathe its pure serene[1]
Till I heard Chapman[2] speak out loud and bold:
Then felt I like some watcher of the skies
    When a new planet swims into his ken;
Or like stout Cortez when with eagle eyes
    He star'd at the Pacific—and all his men
Look'd at each other with a wild surmise—
    Silent, upon a peak in Darien.[3]

---

42. The "burning fountain" of l. 339.

1. A calm, clear expanse of air.
2. George Chapman (1559?–1634), whose translations of Homer's *Iliad* and *Odyssey* appeared 1611–16.

3. Keats makes a minor error here, in that it was the Spanish explorer Balboa, not Cortez, who crossed the Isthmus of Panama ("Darien") in 1513 and discovered the Pacific Ocean.

On Seeing the Elgin Marbles[1]

My spirit is too weak—mortality
  Weighs heavily on me like unwilling sleep,
  And each imagined pinnacle and steep
Of godlike hardship tells me I must die
Like a sick eagle looking at the sky.
  Yet 'tis a gentle luxury to weep
  That I have not the cloudy winds to keep
Fresh for the opening of the morning's eye.
Such dim-conceived glories of the brain
  Bring round the heart an undescribable feud;
So do these wonders a most dizzy pain,
  That mingles Grecian grandeur with the rude
Wasting of old time—with a billowy main—
A sun—a shadow of a magnitude.

On Sitting Down to Read *King Lear* Once Again

O golden-tongued Romance, with serene lute!
  Fair plumed syren, queen of far-away!
  Leave melodizing on this wintry day,
Shut up thine olden pages, and be mute.
Adieu! for, once again, the fierce dispute
  Betwixt damnation and impassion'd clay
  Must I burn through; once more humbly assay
The bitter-sweet of this Shaksperean fruit.
Chief Poet! and ye clouds of Albion,[1]
  Begetters of our deep eternal theme!
When through the old oak forest I am gone,
  Let me not wander in a barren dream:
But, when I am consumed in the fire,
Give me new phœnix[2] wings to fly at my desire.

When I Have Fears That I May Cease to Be

When I have fears that I may cease to be
  Before my pen has glean'd my teeming brain,
Before high piled books, in charactry,[1]
  Hold like rich garners the full ripen'd grain;
When I behold, upon the night's starr'd face,
  Huge cloudy symbols of a high romance,
And think that I may never live to trace
  Their shadows, with the magic hand of chance;
And when I feel, fair creature of an hour,
  That I shall never look upon thee more,
Never have relish in the fairy power
  Of unreflecting love;—then on the shore
Of the wide world I stand alone, and think
Till love and fame to nothingness do sink.

1. The sculptures from the Parthenon, brought to England by Lord Elgin and purchased from him by the government in 1816 to be housed in the British Museum.

1. England.

2. The mythical bird which, every five hundred years, would be born anew from the ashes of its funeral pyre.

1. Characters, i.e., the letters forming words.

The Eve of St. Agnes[1]

1

St. Agnes' Eve— Ah, bitter chill it was!
The owl, for all his feathers, was a-cold;
The hare limp'd trembling through the frozen grass,
And silent was the flock in woolly fold:
5   Numb were the Beadsman's fingers,[2] while he told
His rosary, and while his frosted breath,
Like pious incense from a censor old,
Seem'd taking flight for heaven, without a death,
Past the sweet Virgin's picture, while his prayer he saith.

2

10   His prayer he saith, this patient, holy man;
Then takes his lamp, and riseth from his knees,
And back returneth, meagre, barefoot, wan,
Along the chapel aisle by slow degrees:
The sculptur'd dead, on each side, seem to freeze,
15   Emprison'd in black, purgatorial rails:
Knights, ladies, praying in dumb orat'ries,[3]
He passeth by; and his weak spirit fails
To think how they may ache in icy hoods and mails.

3

Northward he turneth through a little door,
20   And scarce three steps, ere Music's golden tongue
Flatter'd to tears this aged man and poor;
But no— already had his deathbell rung;
The joys of all his life were said and sung:
His was harsh penance on St. Agnes' Eve:
25   Another way he went, and soon among
Rough ashes sat he for his soul's reprieve,
And all night kept awake, for sinners' sake to grieve.

4

That ancient Beadsman heard the prelude soft;
And so it chanc'd, for many a door was wide,
30   From hurry to and fro. Soon, up aloft,
The silver, snarling trumpets 'gan to chide:
The level chambers, ready with their pride,
Were glowing to receive a thousand guests:
The carved angels, ever eager-eyed,
35   Star'd, where upon their heads the cornice rests,
With hair blown back, and wings put cross-wise on their breasts.

5

At length burst in the argent revelry,[4]
With plume, tiara, and all rich array,
Numerous as shadows haunting fairily
40   The brain, new stuff'd, in youth, with triumphs gay
Of old romance. These let us wish away,
And turn, sole-thoughted, to one Lady there,
Whose heart had brooded, all that wintry day,
On love, and wing'd St. Agnes' saintly care,
45   As she had heard old dames full many times declare.

---

1. Patron saint of virgins, martyred in the fourth century. Keats used a popular superstition that if, on St. Agnes' Eve (20 January), a maiden observed certain rituals such as keeping a fast and maintaining silence before retiring, she would have a vision of her future husband.

2. A beadsman was paid to pray for the soul of others; as he prayed, he counted off ("told") each prayer on the beads of his rosary.

3. Small chapels for private worship.

4. Revelers clad in silvery garments.

6

They told her how, upon St. Agnes' Eve,
Young virgins might have visions of delight,
And soft adorings from their loves receive
Upon the honey'd middle of the night,
50　If ceremonies due they did aright;
As, supperless to bed they must retire,
And couch supine their beauties, lily white;
Nor look behind, nor sideways, but require
Of heaven with upward eyes for all that they desire.

7

55　Full of this whim was thoughtful Madeline:
The music, yearning like a god in pain,
She scarcely heard: her maiden eyes divine,
Fix'd on the floor, saw many a sweeping train
Pass by—she heeded not at all: in vain
60　Came many a tiptoe, amorous cavalier,
And back retir'd, not cool'd by high disdain;
But she saw not: her heart was otherwhere:
She sigh'd for Agnes' dreams, the sweetest of the year.

8

She danc'd along with vague, regardless eyes,
65　Anxious her lips, her breathing quick and short:
The hallow'd hour was near at hand: she sighs
Amid the timbrels,[5] and the throng'd resort
Of whisperers in anger, or in sport;
'Mid looks of love, defiance, hate, and scorn,
70　Hoodwink'd[6] with faery fancy; all amort,[7]
Save to St. Agnes and her lambs unshorn,[8]
And all the bliss to be before to-morrow morn.

9

So, purposing each moment to retire,
She linger'd still. Meantime, across the moors,
75　Had come young Porphyro, with heart on fire
For Madeline. Beside the portal doors,
Buttress'd from moonlight, stands he, and implores
All saints to give him sight of Madeline,
But for one moment in the tedious hours,
80　That he might gaze and worship all unseen;
Perchance speak, kneel, touch, kiss—in sooth such things have been.

10

He ventures in: let no buzz'd whisper tell:
All eyes be muffled, or a hundred swords
Will storm his heart, Love's fev'rous citadel:
85　For him, those chambers held barbarian hordes,
Hyena foemen, and hot-blooded lords,
Whose very dogs would execrations howl
Against his lineage: not one breast affords
Him any mercy, in that mansion foul,
90　Save one old beldame,[9] weak in body and in soul.

11

Ah, happy chance! the aged creature came,
Shuffling along with ivory-headed wand,[10]
To where he stood, hid from the torch's flame,

---

5. Tambourines.
6. Blinded.
7. Lifeless, as if dead.
8. On St. Agnes' Day two lambs were offered at the altar,

and their wool was spun and woven by nuns (see ll. 115–17).
9. Old woman.
10. Walking-stick.

Behind a broad hall-pillar, far beyond
95   The sound of merriment and chorus bland:
He startled her; but soon she knew his face,
And grasp'd his fingers in her palsied hand,
Saying, "Mercy, Porphyro! hie thee from this place;
They are all here to-night, the whole blood-thirsty race!

12
100   "Get hence! get hence! there's dwarfish Hildebrand;
He had a fever late, and in the fit
He cursed thee and thine, both house and land:
Then there's that old Lord Maurice, not a whit
More tame for his gray hairs— Alas me! flit!
105   Flit like a ghost away."— "Ah, Gossip¹¹ dear,
We're safe enough; here in this arm-chair sit,
And tell me how"— "Good Saints! not here, not here;
Follow me, child, or else these stones will be thy bier."

13
He follow'd through a lowly arched way,
110   Brushing the cobwebs with his lofty plume,
And as she mutter'd "Well-a— well-a-day!"
He found him in a little moonlight room,
Pale, lattic'd, chill, and silent as a tomb.
"Now tell me where is Madeline," said he,
115   "O tell me, Angela, by the holy loom
Which none but secret sisterhood may see,
When they St. Agnes' wool are weaving piously."

14
"St. Agnes! Ah! it is St. Agnes' Eve—
Yet men will murder upon holy days:
120   Thou must hold water in a witch's sieve,
And be liege-lord of all the Elves and Fays,
To venture so: it fills me with amaze
To see thee, Porphyro!— St. Agnes' Eve!
God's help! my lady fair the conjuror plays
125   This very night: good angels her deceive!
But let me laugh awhile, I've mickle¹² time to grieve."

15
Feebly she laugheth in the languid moon,
While Porphyro upon her face doth look,
Like puzzled urchin on an aged crone
130   Who keepeth clos'd a wond'rous riddle-book,
As spectacled she sits in chimney nook.
But soon his eyes grew brilliant, when she told
His lady's purpose; and he scarce could brook
Tears, at the thought of those enchantments cold,
135   And Madeline asleep in lap of legends old.

16
Sudden a thought came like a full-blown rose,
Flushing his brow, and in his pained heart
Made purple riot: then doth he propose
A stratagem, that makes the beldame start:
140   "A cruel man and impious thou art:
Sweet lady, let her pray, and sleep, and dream
Alone with her good angels, far apart
From wicked men like thee. Go, go!— I deem
Thou canst not surely be the same that thou didst seem."

11. Familiar acquaintance, friend.   12. Much.

17

145   "I will not harm her, by all saints I swear,"
      Quoth Porphyro: "O may I ne'er find grace
      When my weak voice shall whisper its last prayer,
      If one of her soft ringlets I displace,
      Or look with ruffian passion in her face:
150   Good Angela, believe me by these tears;
      Or I will, even in a moment's space,
      Awake, with horrid shout, my foemen's ears,
And beard them, though they be more fang'd than wolves and bears."

18

      "Ah! why wilt thou affright a feeble soul?
155   A poor, weak, palsy-stricken, churchyard thing,
      Whose passing-bell may ere the midnight toll;
      Whose prayers for thee, each morn and evening,
      Were never miss'd."—Thus plaining,[13] doth she bring
      A gentler speech from burning Porphyro;
160   So woful, and of such deep sorrowing,
      That Angela gives promise she will do
Whatever he shall wish, betide her weal or woe.

19

      Which was, to lead him, in close secrecy,
      Even to Madeline's chamber, and there hide
165   Him in a closet, of such privacy
      That he might see her beauty unespied,
      And win perhaps that night a peerless bride,
      While legion'd fairies pac'd the coverlet,
      And pale enchantment held her sleepy-eyed.
170   Never on such a night have lovers met,
Since Merlin paid his Demon all the monstrous debt.[14]

20

      "It shall be as thou wishest," said the Dame:
      "All cates[15] and dainties shall be stored there
      Quickly on this feast-night: by the tambour frame[16]
175   Her own lute thou wilt see: no time to spare,
      For I am slow and feeble, and scarce dare
      On such a catering trust my dizzy head.
      Wait here, my child, with patience; kneel in prayer
      The while: Ah! thou must needs the lady wed,
180   Or may I never leave my grave among the dead."

21

      So saying, she hobbled off with busy fear.
      The lover's endless minutes slowly pass'd;
      The dame return'd, and whisper'd in his ear
      To follow her; with aged eyes aghast
185   From fright of dim espial. Safe at last,
      Through many a dusky gallery, they gain
      The maiden's chamber, silken, hush'd, and chaste;
      Where Porphyro took covert, pleas'd amain.[17]
His poor guide hurried back with agues in her brain.

22

190   Her falt'ring hand upon the balustrade,
      Old Angela was feeling for the stair,
      When Madeline, St. Agnes' charmed maid,

13. Lamenting.
14. In Arthurian legend, the wizard Merlin, the son of a
devil, is beguiled and imprisoned forever by the Lady of
the Lake.

15. Choice foods.
16. A drum-like embroidery frame.
17. Greatly.

Rose, like a mission'd spirit,[18] unaware:
With silver taper's light, and pious care,
195   She turn'd, and down the aged gossip led
To a safe level matting. Now prepare,
Young Porphyro, for gazing on that bed;
She comes, she comes again, like ring-dove fray'd[19] and fled.

23

Out went the taper as she hurried in;
200   Its little smoke, in pallid moonshine, died:
She clos'd the door, she panted, all akin
To spirits of the air, and visions wide:
No uttered syllable, or, woe betide!
But to her heart, her heart was voluble,
205   Paining with eloquence her balmy side;
As though a tongueless nightingale should swell
Her throat in vain, and die, heart-stifled, in her dell.

24

A casement high and triple-arch'd there was,
All garlanded with carven imag'ries
210   Of fruits, and flowers, and bunches of knot-grass,[20]
And diamonded with panes of quaint device,
Innumerable of stains and splendid dyes,
As are the tiger-moth's deep-damask'd wings;
And in the midst, 'mong thousand heraldries,
215   And twilight saints, and dim emblazonings,[21]
A shielded scutcheon[22] blush'd with blood of queens and kings.

25

Full on this casement shone the wintry moon,
And threw warm gules[23] on Madeline's fair breast,
As down she knelt for heaven's grace and boon;
220   Rose-bloom fell on her hands, together prest,
And on her silver cross soft amethyst,
And on her hair a glory, like a saint:
She seem'd a splendid angel, newly drest,
Save wings, for heaven:— Porphyro grew faint:
225   She knelt, so pure a thing, so free from mortal taint.

26

Anon his heart revives: her vespers done,
Of all its wreathed pearls her hair she frees;
Unclasps her warmed jewels one by one;
Loosens her fragrant boddice; by degrees
230   Her rich attire creeps rustling to her knees:
Half-hidden, like a mermaid in sea-weed,
Pensive awhile she dreams awake, and sees,
In fancy, fair St. Agnes in her bed,
But dares not look behind, or all the charm is fled.

27

235   Soon, trembling in her soft and chilly nest,
In sort of wakeful swoon, perplex'd she lay,
Until the poppied warmth of sleep oppress'd
Her soothed limbs, and soul fatigued away;
Flown, like a thought, until the morrow-day;
240   Blissfully haven'd both from joy and pain;
Clasp'd like a missal where swart Paynims[24] pray;

18. An angel having a mission.
19. Frightened.
20. A common weed with pink flowers and intricate creeping stems.

21. Heraldic decorations.
22. The representation of a shield bearing a coat of arms.
23. An heraldic term for red.
24. Dark-hued pagans.

Blinded alike from sunshine and from rain,
As though a rose should shut, and be a bud again.

28

Stol'n to this paradise, and so entranced,
245 Porphyro gazed upon her empty dress,
And listen'd to her breathing, if it chanced
To wake into a slumberous tenderness;
Which when he heard, that minute did he bless,
And breath'd himself: then from the closet crept,
250 Noiseless as fear in a wide wilderness,
And over the hush'd carpet, silent, stept,
And 'tween the curtains peep'd, where, lo!— how fast she slept.

29

Then by the bed-side, where the faded moon
Made a dim, silver twilight, soft he set
255 A table, and, half anguish'd, threw thereon
A cloth of woven crimson, gold, and jet:—
O for some drowsy Morphean[25] amulet!
The boisterous, midnight, festive clarion,
The kettle-drum, and far-heard clarionet,
260 Affray his ears, though but in dying tone:—
The hall door shuts again, and all the noise is gone.

30

And still she slept an azure-lidded sleep,
In blanched linen, smooth, and lavender'd,
While he from forth the closet brought a heap
265 Of candied apple, quince, and plum, and gourd;[26]
With jellies soother[27] than the creamy curd,
And lucent syrops, tinct[28] with cinnamon;
Manna and dates, in argosy[29] transferr'd
From Fez; and spiced dainties, every one,
270 From silken Samarcand to cedar'd Lebanon.[30]

31

These delicates he heap'd with glowing hand
On golden dishes and in baskets bright
Of wreathed silver: sumptuous they stand
In the retired quiet of the night,
275 Filling the chilly room with perfume light.—
"And now, my love, my seraph fair, awake!
Thou art my heaven, and I thine eremite:[31]
Open thine eyes, for meek St. Agnes' sake,
Or I shall drowse beside thee, so my soul doth ache."

32

280 Thus whispering, his warm, unnerved arm
Sank in her pillow. Shaded was her dream
By the dusk curtains:— 'twas a midnight charm
Impossible to melt as iced stream:
The lustrous salvers in the moonlight gleam;
285 Broad golden fringe upon the carpet lies:
It seem'd he never, never could redeem
From such a stedfast spell his lady's eyes;
So mus'd awhile, entoil'd in woofed phantasies.[32]

---

25. Morpheus was the son of Sleep, and himself the god of
dreams.
26. Large fleshy fruit, such as watermelon.
27. Smoother.
28. Tinged.

29. Large merchant ship.
30. Fez and Samarcand were ancient commercial centres
in North Africa and Asia respectively.
31. Religious solitary.
32. Ensnared in intricate fantasies.

33

Awakening up, he took her hollow lute,—
290   Tumultuous,[33]— and, in chords that tenderest be,
He play'd an ancient ditty, long since mute,
In Provence call'd, "La belle dame sans mercy":[34]
Close to her ear touching the melody;—
Wherewith disturb'd, she utter'd a soft moan:
295   He ceased—she panted quick—and suddenly
Her blue affrayed eyes wide open shone:
Upon his knees he sank, pale as smooth-sculptured stone.

34

Her eyes were open, but she still beheld,
Now wide awake, the vision of her sleep:
300   There was a painful change, that nigh expell'd
The blisses of her dream so pure and deep:
At which fair Madeline began to weep,
And moan forth witless words with many a sigh;
While still her gaze on Porphyro would keep;
305   Who knelt, with joined hands and piteous eye,
Fearing to move or speak, she look'd so dreamingly.

35

"Ah, Porphyro!" said she, "but even now
Thy voice was at sweet tremble in mine ear,
Made tuneable with every sweetest vow;
310   And those sad eyes were spiritual and clear:
How chang'd thou art! how pallid, chill, and drear!
Give me that voice again, my Porphyro,
Those looks immortal, those complainings dear!
Oh leave me not in this eternal woe,
315   For if thou diest, my love, I know not where to go."

36

Beyond a mortal man impassion'd far
At these voluptuous accents, he arose,
Ethereal, flush'd, and like a throbbing star
Seen mid the sapphire heaven's deep repose;
320   Into her dream he melted, as the rose
Blendeth its odour with the violet,—
Solution sweet: meantime the frost-wind blows
Like Love's alarum pattering the sharp sleet
Against the window-panes; St. Agnes' moon hath set.

37

325   'Tis dark: quick pattereth the flaw-blown[35] sleet:
"This is no dream, my bride, my Madeline!"
'Tis dark: the iced gusts still rave and beat:
"No dream, alas! alas! and woe is mine!
Porphyro will leave me here to fade and pine.—
330   Cruel! what traitor could thee hither bring?
I curse not, for my heart is lost in thine,
Though thou forsakest a deceived thing;—
A dove forlorn and lost with sick unpruned[36] wing."

33. Here used in an archaic sense of disturbing or dis-
quieting.
34. "The beautiful lady without pity," title of a poem by
the fifteenth-century French writer Alain Chartier.

Provence, a region of southern France, is particularly
associated with the songs of medieval troubadors.
35. Blown by sudden gusts of wind.
36. Untrimmed—thus, disordered.

38

"My Madeline! sweet dreamer! lovely bride!
335   Say, may I be for aye thy vassal blest?
Thy beauty's shield, heart-shap'd and vermeil[37] dyed?
Ah, silver shrine, here will I take my rest
After so many hours of toil and quest,
A famish'd pilgrim,—saved by miracle.
340   Though I have found, I will not rob thy nest
Saving of thy sweet self; if thou think'st well
To trust, fair Madeline, to no rude infidel.

39

"Hark! 'tis an elfin-storm from faery land,
Of haggard seeming, but a boon indeed:
345   Arise—arise! the morning is at hand;—
The bloated wassaillers[38] will never heed:—
Let us away, my love, with happy speed;
There are no ears to hear, or eyes to see,—
Drown'd all in Rhenish[39] and the sleepy mead:
350   Awake! arise! my love, and fearless be,
For o'er the southern moors I have a home for thee."

40

She hurried at his words, beset with fears,
For there were sleeping dragons all around,
At glaring watch, perhaps, with ready spears—
355   Down the wide stairs a darkling way they found.—
In all the house was heard no human sound.
A chain-droop'd lamp was flickering by each door;
The arras,[40] rich with horseman, hawk, and hound,
Flutter'd in the besieging wind's uproar,
360   And the long carpets rose along the gusty floor.

41

They glide, like phantoms, into the wide hall;
Like phantoms, to the iron porch, they glide;
Where lay the Porter, in uneasy sprawl,
With a huge empty flaggon by his side:
365   The wakeful bloodhound rose, and shook his hide,
But his sagacious eye an inmate owns:[41]
By one, and one, the bolts full easy slide:—
The chains lie silent on the footworn stones;—
The key turns, and the door upon its hinges groans.

42

370   And they are gone: ay, ages long ago
These lovers fled away into the storm.
That night the Baron dreamt of many a woe,
And all his warrior-guests, with shade and form
Of witch, and demon, and large coffin-worm,
375   Were long be-nightmar'd. Angela the old
Died palsy-twitch'd, with meagre face deform;
The Beadsman, after thousand aves[42] told,
For aye unsought for slept among his ashes cold.

37. Vermilion red.
38. Revellers.
39. Rhine wine.

40. Rich tapestry.
41. Acknowledges.
42. The prayers beginning "Ave Maria."

La Belle Dame sans Merci[1]
A Ballad

1
O what can ail thee, knight at arms,
   Alone and palely loitering?
The sedge has wither'd from the lake,
   And no birds sing.

2
O what can ail thee, knight at arms,
   So haggard and so woe-begone?
The squirrel's granary is full,
   And the harvest's done.

3
I see a lily on thy brow
   With anguish moist and fever dew,
And on thy cheeks a fading rose
   Fast withereth too.

4
I met a lady in the meads,
   Full beautiful, a fairy's child;
Her hair was long, her foot was light,
   And her eyes were wild.

5
I made a garland for her head,
   And bracelets too, and fragrant zone;[2]
She look'd at me as she did love,
   And made sweet moan.

6
I set her on my pacing steed,
   And nothing else saw all day long,
For sidelong would she bend, and sing
   A fairy's song.

7
She found me roots of relish sweet,
   And honey wild, and manna dew,
And sure in language strange she said—
   I love thee true.

8
She took me to her elfin grot,[3]
   And there she wept, and sigh'd full sore,
And there I shut her wild wild eyes
   With kisses four.

9
And there she lulled me asleep,
   And there I dream'd—Ah! woe betide!
The latest[4] dream I ever dream'd
   On the cold hill's side.

10
I saw pale kings, and princes too,
   Pale warriors, death pale were they all;
They cried—"La belle dame sans merci
   Hath thee in thrall!"

11
I saw their starv'd lips in the gloam[5]
   With horrid warning gaped wide,
And I awoke and found me here
   On the cold hill's side.

12
And this is why I sojourn here,
   Alone and palely loitering,
Though the sedge is wither'd from the lake,
   And no birds sing.

If by Dull Rhymes Our English Must Be Chain'd

If by dull rhymes our English must be chain'd,
   And, like Andromeda,[1] the sonnet sweet
     Fetter'd, in spite of pained loveliness;
Let us find out, if we must be constrain'd,
   Sandals more interwoven and complete
To fit the naked foot of Poesy;
     Let us inspect the lyre, and weigh the stress
Of every chord, and see what may be gain'd
   By ear industrious, and attention meet;
     Misers of sound and syllable, no less
Than Midas[2] of his coinage, let us be
   Jealous of dead leaves in the bay wreath[3] crown;
So, if we may not let the muse be free,
   She will be bound with garlands of her own.

---

1. "The beautiful lady without pity." Keats took the title
from a poem by the French poet Alain Chartier.
2. Girdle.
3. Grotto.
4. Last.
5. Gloaming, twilight.

1. The beautiful daughter of Cassiopeia who was chained
to a rock as a sacrifice to a sea-monster, but rescued by
Perseus.
2. The legendary king of Phrygia whose touch turned
everything to gold.
3. Traditional symbol for literary achievement.

Ode to Psyche[1]

O Goddess! hear these tuneless numbers, wrung
    By sweet enforcement and remembrance dear,
And pardon that thy secrets should be sung
    Even into thine own soft-conched[2] ear:
5 Surely I dreamt to-day, or did I see
    The winged Psyche with awaken'd eyes?
I wander'd in a forest thoughtlessly,
    And, on the sudden, fainting with surprise,
Saw two fair creatures, couched side by side
10   In deepest grass, beneath the whisp'ring roof
    Of leaves and trembled blossoms, where there ran
        A brooklet, scarce espied:
'Mid hush'd, cool-rooted flowers, fragrant-eyed,
    Blue, silver-white, and budded Tyrian,[3]
15 They lay calm-breathing on the bedded grass;
    Their arms embraced, and their pinions[4] too;
    Their lips touch'd not, but had not bade adieu,
As if disjoined by soft-handed slumber,
And ready still past kisses to outnumber
20   At tender eye-dawn of aurorean[5] love:
        The winged boy I knew;
    But who wast thou, O happy, happy dove?
        His Psyche true!

O latest born[6] and loveliest vision far
25   Of all Olympus' faded hierarchy!
Fairer than Phœbe's sapphire-region'd star,[7]
    Or Vesper,[8] amorous glow-worm of the sky;
Fairer than these, though temple thou hast none,
    Nor altar heap'd with flowers;
30 Nor virgin-choir to make delicious moan
    Upon the midnight hours;
No voice, no lute, no pipe, no incense sweet
    From chain-swung censer teeming;
No shrine, no grove, no oracle, no heat
35   Of pale-mouth'd prophet dreaming.

O brightest! though too late for antique vows,
    Too, too late for the fond believing lyre,
When holy were the haunted forest boughs,
    Holy the air, the water, and the fire;
40 Yet even in these days so far retir'd
    From happy pieties, thy lucent fans,[9]
    Fluttering among the faint Olympians,
I see, and sing, by my own eyes inspired.
So let me be thy choir, and make a moan
45   Upon the midnight hours;
Thy voice, thy lute, thy pipe, thy incense sweet
    From swinged censer teeming;
Thy shrine, thy grove, thy oracle, thy heat
    Of pale-mouth'd prophet dreaming.

---

1. Psyche (Greek "soul," "mind") was a young maiden whose beauty aroused the jealousy of Venus. The goddess directed her son Cupid to make Psyche fall in love with an ugly creature, but instead Cupid fell in love with her himself. The lovers were parted, and Psyche underwent many trials imposed by Venus, until Jupiter reunited them in heaven.
2. A conch is a sea-shell.
3. Purple (from the purple dye made in ancient Tyre).
4. Wings.
5. Of the dawn (from Aurora, goddess of dawn).
6. Psyche's story was first told by the second-century Roman author Apuleius; consequently, as Keats told his brother and sister, "the Goddess was never worshipped or sacrificed to with any of the ancient fervour—and perhaps never thought of in the old religion."
7. The moon (of which Phoebe, or Diana, was goddess), floating in the blue spaces of the heavens.
8. Venus as the evening star.
9. Shining wings.

50   Yes, I will be thy priest, and build a fane[10]
     In some untrodden region of my mind,
Where branched thoughts, new grown with pleasant pain,
     Instead of pines shall murmur in the wind:
Far, far around shall those dark-cluster'd trees
55   Fledge[11] the wild-ridged mountains steep by steep;
And there by zephyrs, streams, and birds, and bees,
     The moss-lain Dryads[12] shall be lull'd to sleep;
And in the midst of this wide quietness
A rosy sanctuary will I dress
60   With the wreath'd trellis of a working brain,
     With buds, and bells, and stars without a name,
With all the gardener Fancy e'er could feign,
     Who breeding flowers, will never breed the same:
And there shall be for thee all soft delight
65   That shadowy thought can win,
A bright torch, and a casement ope at night,
     To let the warm Love in!

Ode to a Nightingale

confusion of whether awake or asleep.

1

My heart aches, and a drowsy numbness pains
     My sense, as though of hemlock[1] I had drunk,
Or emptied some dull opiate to the drains
     One minute past, and Lethe-wards[2] had sunk:
5   'Tis not through envy of thy happy lot,
     But being too happy in thine happiness,—
          That thou, light-winged Dryad[3] of the trees,
               In some melodious plot
     Of beechen green, and shadows numberless,
10   Singest of summer in full-throated ease.

2

O, for a draught of vintage! that hath been
     Cool'd a long age in the deep-delved earth,
Tasting of Flora[4] and the country green,
     Dance, and Provençal[5] song, and sunburnt mirth!
15   O for a beaker full of the warm South,
     Full of the true, the blushful Hippocrene,[6]
          With beaded bubbles winking at the brim,
               And purple-stained mouth;
     That I might drink, and leave the world unseen,   *wants to enter the*
20   And with thee fade away into the forest dim: *distilled world of summer.*

3

Fade far away, dissolve, and quite forget
     What thou among the leaves hast never known,
The weariness, the fever, and the fret
     Here, where men sit and hear each other groan;
25   Where palsy shakes a few, sad, last gray hairs,
     Where youth grows pale, and spectre-thin, and dies;
          Where but to think is to be full of sorrow
               And leaden-eyed despairs,
     Where Beauty cannot keep her lustrous eyes,
30   Or new Love pine at them beyond to-morrow.

10. Temple.
11. Cover as with feathers.
12. Wood-nymphs.

1. Poison derived from the hemlock plant.
2. Lethe was the river in Hades whose waters brought

forgetfulness.
3. Wood-nymph.
4. Goddess of flowers.
5. Of Provence, the region in France associated with the troubadors.
6. A fountain sacred to the muses, on Mt. Helicon.

4

Away! away! for I will fly to thee,   *— I will leave here and reach your world.*
  Not charioted by Bacchus[7] and his pards,[8]
But on the viewless wings of Poesy,
  Though the dull brain perplexes and retards:
35 Already with thee! tender is the night,   *— but now he is with the Nightengale*
    And haply[9] the Queen-Moon is on her throne,
      Cluster'd around by all her starry Fays;[10]
        But here there is no light,
    Save what from heaven is with the breezes blown
40   Through verdurous glooms and winding mossy ways.

5

I cannot see what flowers are at my feet,   *— if I don't think, I can't*
  Nor what soft incense hangs upon the boughs, *see the beauty in this world either.*
But, in embalmed[11] darkness, guess each sweet
  Wherewith the seasonable month endows   *mutability, movement of time.*
45 The grass, the thicket, and the fruit-tree wild;
    White hawthorn, and the pastoral eglantine;
      Fast fading violets cover'd up in leaves;
        And mid-May's eldest child,   *— transcendental state of ecstasy.*
    The coming musk-rose, full of dewy wine,
50   The murmurous haunt of flies on summer eves.

6

Darkling I listen; and, for many a time
  I have been half in love with easeful Death,
Call'd him soft names in many a mused rhyme,   *that is beautiful.*
  To take into the air my quiet breath;
55 Now more than ever seems it rich to die,   *instinctively singing.*
    To cease upon the midnight with no pain,
      While thou art pouring forth thy soul abroad
        In such an ecstasy!
    Still wouldst thou sing, and I have ears in vain—
60   To thy high requiem become a sod.

7

Thou wast not born for death, immortal Bird!
  No hungry generations tread thee down;
The voice I hear this passing night was heard
  In ancient days by emperor and clown:
65 Perhaps the self-same song that found a path
    Through the sad heart of Ruth,[12] when, sick for home,
      She stood in tears amid the alien corn;
        The same that oft-times hath
    Charm'd magic casements, opening on the foam
70   Of perilous seas, in faery lands forlorn.

8

   — language that makes us aware of our mutability
Forlorn! the very word is like a bell
  To toll me back from thee to my sole self!
Adieu! the fancy cannot cheat so well
  As she is fam'd to do, deceiving elf.
75 Adieu! adieu! thy plaintive anthem fades
    Past the near meadows, over the still stream,
      Up the hill-side; and now 'tis buried deep   *alienation*
        In the next valley-glades:
    Was it a vision, or a waking dream?
80   Fled is that music:— Do I wake or sleep?

---

7. Roman god of wine.
8. Leopards.
9. Perhaps.

10. Fairies.
11. Fragrant, perfumed.
12. An allusion to the biblical story in the book of Ruth

Ode on a Grecian Urn

1

Thou still unravish'd bride of quietness,
    Thou foster-child of silence and slow time,
Sylvan historian, who canst thus express
    A flowery tale more sweetly than our rhyme:
5   What leaf-fring'd legend haunts about thy shape
        Of deities or mortals, or of both,
            In Tempe[1] or the dales of Arcady?
        What men or gods are these? What maidens loth?
What mad pursuit? What struggle to escape?
10   What pipes and timbrels? What wild ecstasy?[2]

2

Heard melodies are sweet, but those unheard
    Are sweeter; therefore, ye soft pipes, play on;
Not to the sensual ear, but, more endear'd,
    Pipe to the spirit ditties of no tone:
15 Fair youth, beneath the trees, thou canst not leave
        Thy song, nor ever can those trees be bare;
            Bold lover, never, never canst thou kiss,
Though winning near the goal—yet, do not grieve;
        She cannot fade, though thou hast not thy bliss,
20   For ever wilt thou love, and she be fair!

3

Ah, happy, happy boughs! that cannot shed
    Your leaves, nor ever bid the spring adieu;
And, happy melodist, unwearied,
    For ever piping songs for ever new;
25 More happy love! more happy, happy love!
        For ever warm and still to be enjoy'd,
            For ever panting, and for ever young;
All breathing human passion far above,
        That leaves a heart high-sorrowful and cloy'd,
30   A burning forehead, and a parching tongue.

4

Who are these coming to the sacrifice?
    To what green altar, O mysterious priest,
Lead'st thou that heifer lowing at the skies,
    And all her silken flanks with garlands drest?
35 What little town by river or sea shore,
        Or mountain-built with peaceful citadel,
            Is emptied of this folk, this pious morn?
And, little town, thy streets for evermore
        Will silent be; and not a soul to tell
40   Why thou art desolate, can e'er return.

5

O Attic[3] shape! Fair attitude! with brede[4]
    Of marble men and maidens overwrought,[5]
With forest branches and the trodden weed;
    Thou, silent form, dost tease us out of thought
45 As doth eternity: Cold Pastoral!

---

1. A valley in Thessaly, here presented with Arcadia ("Arcady") as emblematic of the pastoral ideal.
2. The vase appears to depict a ritual in honour of the Greek god Dionysus, whose worshippers would often attain a state of frenzy.
3. From Attica, the region around ancient Athens.
4. Interwoven pattern.
5. Decorated over its surface.

When old age shall this generation waste,
    Thou shalt remain, in midst of other woe
Than ours, a friend to man, to whom thou say'st,
    "Beauty is truth, truth beauty,"—that is all
50   Ye know on earth, and all ye need to know.

Ode on Melancholy

1

No, no, go not to Lethe,[1] neither twist
    Wolf's-bane,[2] tight-rooted, for its poisonous wine;
Nor suffer thy pale forehead to be kiss'd
    By nightshade, ruby grape of Proserpine;[3]
5 Make not your rosary of yew-berries,[4]
    Nor let the beetle,[5] nor the death-moth[6] be
      Your mournful Psyche, nor the downy owl
A partner in your sorrow's mysteries;[7]
    For shade to shade will come too drowsily,
10   And drown the wakeful anguish of the soul.

2

But when the melancholy fit shall fall
    Sudden from heaven like a weeping cloud,
That fosters the droop-headed flowers all,
    And hides the green hill in an April shroud;
15 Then glut thy sorrow on a morning rose,
    Or on the rainbow of the salt sand-wave,
      Or on the wealth of globed peonies;
Or if thy mistress some rich anger shows,
    Emprison her soft hand, and let her rave,
20   And feed deep, deep upon her peerless eyes.

3

She dwells with Beauty—Beauty that must die;
    And Joy, whose hand is ever at his lips
Bidding adieu; and aching Pleasure nigh,
    Turning to poison while the bee-mouth sips:
25 Ay, in the very temple of Delight
    Veil'd Melancholy has her sovran shrine,
      Though seen of none save him whose strenuous tongue
    Can burst Joy's grape against his palate fine;
His soul shall taste the sadness of her might,
30   And be among her cloudy trophies hung.

To Autumn

1

Season of mists and mellow fruitfulness,
    Close bosom-friend of the maturing sun;
Conspiring with him how to load and bless
    With fruit the vines that round the thatch-eves run;
5 To bend with apples the moss'd cottage-trees,
    And fill all fruit with ripeness to the core;
      To swell the gourd, and plump the hazel shells

1. The river in Hades whose waters induced forgetfulness.
2. A poisonous plant, like nightshade (l. 4).
3. Queen of the infernal regions, and wife of Pluto.
4. The yew-tree, often planted in cemeteries, is traditionally associated with death.
5. The death-watch beetle; or possibly the Egyptian scarab.
6. The death's-head moth, whose markings resemble a skull. The reference to Psyche ("soul") in l. 7 suggests that Keats may also have in mind ancient representations of the soul as a butterfly, depicted as fluttering out of the mouth of the deceased.
7. Religious rites.

With a sweet kernel; to set budding more,
And still more, later flowers for the bees,
10   Until they think warm days will never cease,
        For summer has o'er-brimm'd their clammy cells.

2

Who hath not seen thee oft amid thy store?
    Sometimes whoever seeks abroad may find
Thee sitting careless on a granary floor,
15   Thy hair soft-lifted by the winnowing wind;
Or on a half-reap'd furrow sound asleep,
    Drows'd with the fume of poppies, while thy hook
        Spares the next swath and all its twined flowers:
And sometimes like a gleaner thou dost keep
20   Steady thy laden head across a brook;
    Or by a cyder-press, with patient look,
        Thou watchest the last oozings hours by hours.

3

Where are the songs of spring? Ay, where are they?
    Think not of them, thou hast thy music too,—
25   While barred clouds bloom the soft-dying day,
    And touch the stubble-plains with rosy hue;
Then in a wailful choir the small gnats mourn
    Among the river sallows,[1] borne aloft
        Or sinking as the light wind lives or dies;
30   And full-grown lambs loud bleat from hilly bourn;[2]
    Hedge-crickets sing; and now with treble soft
    The red-breast whistles from a garden-croft;
        And gathering swallows twitter in the skies.

WILLIAM CULLEN BRYANT (1794–1878)

Thanatopsis[1]

To him who in the love of Nature holds
Communion with her visible forms, she speaks
A various language; for his gayer hours
She has a voice of gladness, and a smile
5   And eloquence of beauty, and she glides
Into his darker musings, with a mild
And healing sympathy, that steals away
Their sharpness ere he is aware. When thoughts
Of the last bitter hour come like a blight
10   Over thy spirit, and sad images
Of the stern agony, and shroud, and pall,
And breathless darkness, and the narrow house,[2]
Make thee to shudder, and grow sick at heart;—
Go forth, under the open sky, and list
15   To Nature's teachings, while from all around—
Earth and her waters, and the depths of air,—
Comes a still voice— Yet a few days, and thee
The all-beholding sun shall see no more
In all his course; nor yet in the cold ground,
20   Where thy pale form was laid, with many tears,
Nor in the embrace of ocean, shall exist
Thy image. Earth, that nourished thee, shall claim
Thy growth, to be resolved to earth again,

1. Willow-trees.
2. Small stream.

1. A meditation upon death.
2. I.e., the grave.

And, lost each human trace, surrendering up
25 Thine individual being, shalt thou go
To mix for ever with the elements,
To be a brother to the insensible rock
And to the sluggish clod, which the rude swain
Turns with his share,[3] and treads upon. The oak
30 Shall send his roots abroad, and pierce thy mould.

　Yet not to thine eternal resting-place
Shalt thou retire alone,—nor couldst thou wish
Couch more magnificent. Thou shalt lie down
With patriarchs of the infant world—with kings,
35 The powerful of the earth—the wise, the good,
Fair forms, and hoary seers of ages past,
All in one mighty sepulchre. The hills
Rock-ribbed and ancient as the sun; the vales
Stretching in pensive quietness between;
40 The venerable woods; rivers that move
In majesty, and the complaining brooks
That make the meadows green; and, poured round all,
Old ocean's grey and melancholy waste—
Are but the solemn decorations all
45 Of the great tomb of man. The golden sun,
The planets, all the infinite host of heaven,
Are shining on the sad abodes of death,
Through the still lapse of ages. All that tread
The globe are but a handful to the tribes
50 That slumber in its bosom.—Take the wings
Of morning, traverse Barca's desert sands,[4]
Or lose thyself in the continuous woods
Where rolls the Oregon,[5] and hears no sound,
Save his own dashings—yet—the dead are there:
55 And millions in those solitudes, since first
The flight of years began, have laid them down
In their last sleep—the dead reign there alone.
So shalt thou rest, and what if thou withdraw
In silence from the living, and no friend
60 Take note of thy departure? All that breathe
Will share thy destiny. The gay will laugh
When thou art gone, the solemn brood of care
Plod on, and each one as before will chase
His favourite phantom; yet all these shall leave
65 Their mirth and their employments, and shall come,
And make their bed with thee. As the long train
Of ages glide away, the sons of men,
The youth in life's green spring, and he who goes
In the full strength of years, matron, and maid,
70 And the sweet babe, and the grey-headed man—
Shall one by one be gathered to thy side,
By those, who in their turn shall follow them.

　So live, that when thy summons comes to join
The innumerable caravan, which moves
75 To that mysterious realm, where each shall take
His chamber in the silent halls of death,
Thou go not, like the quarry-slave at night,
Scourged to his dungeon, but, sustained and soothed
By an unfaltering trust, approach thy grave
80 Like one who wraps the drapery of his couch
About him, and lies down to pleasant dreams.

3. Ploughshare.
4. The desert region of Barca in northern Africa (modern
Libya).
5. An early name given to the Columbia River.

To a Waterfowl

Whither, 'midst falling dew,
While glow the heavens with the last steps of day,
Far, through their rosy depths, dost thou pursue
    Thy solitary way?

5   Vainly the fowler's eye
Might mark thy distant flight to do thee wrong,
As, darkly seen against the crimson sky,
    Thy figure floats along.

      Seek'st thou the plashy brink
10 Of weedy lake, or marge of river wide,
Or where the rocking billows rise and sink
    On the chafed ocean side?

      There is a Power whose care
Teaches thy way along that pathless coast,—
15 The desert and illimitable air,—
    Lone wandering, but not lost.

      All day thy wings have fanned,
At that far height, the cold thin atmosphere,
Yet stoop not, weary, to the welcome land,
20   Though the dark night is near.

      And soon that toil shall end;
Soon shalt thou find a summer home and rest,
And scream among thy fellows; reeds shall bend,
    Soon, o'er thy sheltered nest.

25   Thou'rt gone, the abyss of heaven
Hath swallowed up thy form; yet, on my heart
Deeply hath sunk the lesson thou hast given,
    And shall not soon depart.

      He who, from zone to zone,
30 Guides through the boundless sky thy certain flight,
In the long way that I must tread alone,
    Will lead my steps aright.

To the Fringed Gentian

Thou blossom bright with autumn dew,
And coloured with the heaven's own blue,
That openest when the quiet light
Succeeds the keen and frosty night.

Thou comest not when violets lean
O'er wandering brooks and springs unseen,
Or columbines, in purple dressed,
Nod o'er the ground-bird's hidden nest;

Thou waitest late and com'st alone,
When woods are bare and birds are flown,
And frosts and shortening days portend
The aged year is near his end.

Then doth thy sweet and quiet eye
Look through its fringes to the sky,
Blue—blue—as if that sky let fall
A flower from its cerulean[1] wall.

I would that thus, when I shall see
The hour of death draw near to me,
Hope, blossoming within my heart,
May look to heaven as I depart.

1. Deep blue.

The Prairies

These are the gardens of the Desert, these
The unshorn fields, boundless and beautiful,
For which the speech of England has no name—[1]
The Prairies. I behold them for the first,
5   And my heart swells, while the dilated sight
Takes in the encircling vastness. Lo! they stretch
In airy undulations, far away,
As if the Ocean, in his gentlest swell,
Stood still, with all his rounded billows fixed,
10   And motionless for ever.—Motionless?—
No—they are all unchained again. The clouds
Sweep over with their shadows, and, beneath,
The surface rolls and fluctuates to the eye;
Dark hollows seem to glide along and chase
15   The sunny ridges. Breezes of the South!
Who toss the golden and the flame-like flowers,
And pass the prairie-hawk that, poised on high,
Flaps his broad wings, yet moves not—ye have played
Among the palms of Mexico and vines
20   Of Texas, and have crisped the limpid brooks
That from the fountains of Sonora[2] glide
Into the calm Pacific—have ye fanned
A nobler or a lovelier scene than this?
Man hath no part in all this glorious work:
25   The hand that built the firmament hath heaved
And smoothed these verdant swells, and sown their slopes
With herbage, planted them with island groves,
And hedged them round with forests. Fitting floor
For this magnificent temple of the sky—
30   With flowers whose glory and whose multitude
Rival the constellations! The great heavens
Seem to stoop down upon the scene in love,—
A nearer vault, and of a tenderer blue,
Than that which bends above our eastern hills.

35   As o'er the verdant waste I guide my steed,
Among the high rank grass that sweeps his sides
The hollow beating of his footstep seems
A sacrilegious sound. I think of those
Upon whose rest he tramples. Are they here—
40   The dead of other days?—and did the dust
Of these fair solitudes once stir with life
And burn with passion? Let the mighty mounds[3]
That overlook the rivers, or that rise
In the dim forest crowded with old oaks,
45   Answer. A race, that long has passed away,
Built them;—a disciplined and populous race
Heaped, with long toil, the earth, while yet the Greek
Was hewing the Pentelicus[4] to forms
Of symmetry, and rearing on its rock
50   The glittering Parthenon.[5] These ample fields
Nourished their harvests, here their herds were fed,
When haply by their stalls the bison lowed,
And bowed his maned shoulder to the yoke.
All day this desert murmured with their toils,
55   Till twilight blushed, and lovers walked, and wooed

1. I.e., the word "prairie" was introduced by the early
French explorers.
2. A state in northwest Mexico.
3. Burial mounds found in the Ohio and Mississippi valleys, thought to have been built by ancestors of the
American Indian tribes.
4. A mountain near Athens, renowned for its marble
quarries.
5. The temple of Athena in Athens.

In a forgotten language, and old tunes,
From instruments of unremembered form,
Gave the soft winds a voice. The red man came—
The roaming hunter tribes, warlike and fierce,
60   And the mound-builders vanished from the earth.
The solitude of centuries untold
Has settled where they dwelt. The prairie-wolf
Hunts in their meadows, and his fresh-dug den
Yawns by my path. The gopher mines the ground
65   Where stood their swarming cities. All is gone;
All—save the piles of earth that hold their bones,
The platforms where they worshipped unknown gods,
The barriers which they builded from the soil
To keep the foe at bay—till o'er the walls
70   The wild beleaguerers broke, and one by one
The strongholds of the plain were forced, and heaped
With corpses. The brown vultures of the wood
Flocked to those vast uncovered sepulchres,
And sat, unscared and silent, at their feast.
75   Haply some solitary fugitive,
Lurking in marsh and forest, till the sense
Of desolation and of fear became
Bitterer than death, yielded himself to die.
Man's better nature triumphed then. Kind words
80   Welcomed and soothed him; the rude conquerors
Seated the captive with their chiefs; he chose
A bride among their maidens, and at length
Seemed to forget—yet ne'er forgot—the wife
Of his first love, and her sweet little ones,
85   Butchered, amid their shrieks, with all his race.

Thus change the forms of being. Thus arise
Races of living things, glorious in strength,
And perish, as the quickening breath of God
Fills them, or is withdrawn. The red man, too,
90   Has left the blooming wilds he ranged so long,
And, nearer to the Rocky Mountains, sought
A wider hunting-ground. The beaver builds
No longer by these streams, but far away,
On waters whose blue surface ne'er gave back
95   The white man's face—among Missouri's springs,
And pools whose issues swell the Oregan,[6]
He rears his little Venice. In these plains
The bison feeds no more. Twice twenty leagues
Beyond remotest smoke of hunter's camp,
100   Roams the majestic brute, in herds that shake
The earth with thundering steps—yet here I meet
His ancient footprints stamped beside the pool.

Still this great solitude is quick with life.
Myriads of insects, gaudy as the flowers
105   They flutter over, gentle quadrupeds,
And birds, that scarce have learned the fear of man,
Are here, and sliding reptiles of the ground,
Startlingly beautiful. The graceful deer
Bounds to the wood at my approach. The bee,
110   A more adventurous colonist than man,
With whom he came across the eastern deep,
Fills the savannas with his murmurings,
And hides his sweets, as in the golden age,
Within the hollow oak. I listen long

6. The Columbia River.

115 To his domestic hum, and think I hear
The sound of that advancing multitude
Which soon shall fill these deserts. From the ground
Comes up the laugh of children, the soft voice
Of maidens, and the sweet and solemn hymn
120 Of Sabbath worshippers. The low of herds
Blends with the rustling of the heavy grain
Over the dark-brown furrows. All at once
A fresher wind sweeps by, and breaks my dream,
And I am in the wilderness alone.

EDGAR ALLAN POE (1809–49)

To Helen

Helen, thy beauty is to me
    Like those Nicéan[1] barks of yore,
That gently, o'er a perfumed sea,
    The weary, way-worn wanderer bore
    To his own native shore.

On desperate seas long wont to roam,
    Thy hyacinth hair,[2] thy classic face,
Thy Naiad[3] airs have brought me home
    To the glory that was Greece,
And the grandeur that was Rome.

Lo! in yon brilliant window-niche
    How statue-like I see thee stand,
    The agate lamp within thy hand!
Ah, Psyche,[4] from the regions which
    Are Holy-Land!

The City in the Sea

Lo! Death has reared himself a throne
In a strange city[1] lying alone
Far down within the dim West,
Where the good and the bad and the worst and the best
5 Have gone to their eternal rest.
There shrines and palaces and towers
(Time-eaten towers that tremble not!)
Resemble nothing that is ours.
Around, by lifting winds forgot,
10 Resignedly beneath the sky
The melancholy waters lie.

No rays from the holy heaven come down
On the long night-time of that town;
But light from out the lurid sea
15 Streams up the turrets silently—
Gleams up the pinnacles far and free
Up domes—up spires—up kingly halls—
Up fanes—up Babylon-like[2] walls—
Up shadowy long-forgotten bowers

1. Perhaps an allusion to the Greek colony of Nicaea, founded in the fourth century B.C., and an important trading centre under the Romans. "barks": vessels.
2. Hair clustered in curls, like the flower named after Hyacinthus, the youth loved by Apollo.
3. Water-nymph.
4. Psyche ("soul") was beloved by Cupid, who would visit her only in darkness; in defiance of his command, Psyche lit a lamp to see him while he slept, and woke him by spilling a drop of oil on him.

1. Though the reference to "the dim West" suggests the mythical city of Atlantis, Poe is probably recalling legends about the ruined cities of the plain whose destruction is described in Genesis xix, and which were thought to lie under the Dead Sea.
2. Babylon, capital of ancient Babylonia, stands in the Bible as a symbol of decadent wealth and sinfulness, doomed to suffer divine retribution. See Isaiah xiii, xiv. "fanes": temples.

20   Of sculptured ivy and stone flowers—
       Up many and many a marvellous shrine
       Whose wreathéd friezes intertwine
       The viol, the violet, and the vine.

       Resignedly beneath the sky
25   The melancholy waters lie.
       So blend the turrets and shadows there
       That all seem pendulous in air,
       While from a proud tower in the town
       Death looks gigantically down.

30   There open fanes and gaping graves
       Yawn level with the luminous waves;
       But not the riches there that lie
       In each idol's diamond eye—
       Not the gaily-jewelled dead
35   Tempt the waters from their bed;
       For no ripples curl, alas!

       Along that wilderness of glass—
       No swellings tell that winds may be
       Upon some far-off happier sea—
40   No heavings hint that winds have been
       On seas less hideously serene.

       But lo, a stir is in the air!
       The wave—there is a movement there!
       As if the towers had thrust aside,
45   In slightly sinking, the dull tide—
       As if their tops had feebly given
       A void within the filmy Heaven.
       The waves have now a redder glow—
       The hours are breathing faint and low—
50   And when, amid no earthly moans,
       Down, down that town shall settle hence,
       Hell, rising from a thousand thrones,[3]
       Shall do it reverence.

Dream-Land

       By a route obscure and lonely,
       Haunted by ill angels only,
       Where an Eidolon,[1] named Night,
       On a black throne reigns upright,
5   I have reached these lands but newly
       From an ultimate dim Thule[2]—
       From a wild weird clime that lieth, sublime,
            Out of Space— out of Time.

       Bottomless vales and boundless floods,
10   And chasms, and caves, and Titan[3] woods,
       With forms that no man can discover
       For the dews that drip all over;
       Mountains toppling evermore
       Into seas without a shore;
15   Seas that restlessly aspire,
       Surging, unto skies of fire;
       Lakes that endlessly outspread
       Their lone waters— lone and dead,—
       Their still waters— still and chilly
20   With the snows of the lolling lily.

       By the lakes that thus outspread
       Their lone waters, lone and dead,—
       Their sad waters, sad and chilly
       With the snows of the lolling lily,—
25   By the mountains— near the river
       Murmuring lowly, murmuring ever,—
       By the grey woods,— by the swamp
       Where the toad and the newt encamp,—

30   By the dismal tarns[4] and pools
            Where dwell the Ghouls,—
       By each spot the most unholy—
       In each nook most melancholy,—
       There the traveller meets aghast
35   Sheeted Memories of the Past—
       Shrouded forms that start and sigh
       As they pass the wanderer by—
       White-robed forms of friends long given,
       In agony, to the Earth— and Heaven.

       For the heart whose woes are legion
       'Tis a peaceful, soothing region—
       For the spirit that walks in shadow
       O! it is an Eldorado![5]
       But the traveller, travelling through it,
       May not— dare not openly view it;
45   Never its mysteries are exposed
       To the weak human eye unclosed;
       So wills its King, who hath forbid
       The uplifting of the fringed lid;
       And thus the sad Soul that here passes
50   Beholds it but through darkened glasses.

       By a route obscure and lonely,
       Haunted by ill angels only,
       Where an Eidolon, name NIGHT,
       On a black throne reigns upright,
55   I have wandered home but newly
       From this ultimate dim Thule.

3. "Hell from beneath is moved for thee to meet *thee* at thycoming: it stirreth up the dead for thee, *even* all the chief ones of the earth; it hath raised up from their thrones all the kings of the nations" (Isa. xiv.9).

1. Phantom.
2. The name given by the ancients to an island at the northern tip of the known world, variously identified by later writers as Iceland or the Shetland Isles. Here Poe echoes Virgil's phrase "*ultima Thule*" (farthest Thule), from the *Georgics*, I.30.
3. The Titans were the giant offspring of Uranus, god of Heaven, and Gaea, goddess of Earth.
4. Mountain lakes.
5. The legendary South American city of fabulous wealth, sought in vain by European explorers.

The Raven

Once upon a midnight dreary, while I pondered, weak and weary,
Over many a quaint and curious volume of forgotten lore—
While I nodded, nearly napping, suddenly there came a tapping,
As of some one gently rapping, rapping at my chamber door—
5 "'Tis some visiter," I muttered, "tapping at my chamber door—
        Only this and nothing more."

Ah, distinctly I remember it was in the bleak December;
And each separate dying ember wrought its ghost upon the floor.
Eagerly I wished the morrow;—vainly I had sought to borrow
10 From my books surcease of sorrow—sorrow for the lost Lenore[1]—
For the rare and radiant maiden whom the angels name Lenore—
        Nameless *here* for evermore.

And the silken, sad, uncertain rustling of each purple curtain
Thrilled me—filled me with fantastic terrors never felt before;
15 So that now, to still the beating of my heart, I stood repeating
"'Tis some visiter entreating entrance at my chamber door—
Some late visiter entreating entrance at my chamber door;—
        This it is and nothing more."

Presently my soul grew stronger; hesitating then no longer,
20 "Sir," said I, "or Madam, truly your forgiveness I implore;
But the fact is I was napping, and so gently you came rapping,
And so faintly you came tapping, tapping at my chamber door,
That I scarce was sure I heard you"—here I opened wide the door;—
        Darkness there and nothing more.

25 Deep into that darkness peering, long I stood there wondering, fearing,
Doubting, dreaming dreams no mortal ever dared to dream before;
But the silence was unbroken, and the stillness gave no token,
And the only word there spoken was the whispered word, "Lenore?"
This I whispered, and an echo murmured back the word, "Lenore!"
30   Merely this and nothing more.

Back into the chamber turning, all my soul within me burning,
Soon again I heard a tapping somewhat louder than before.
"Surely," said I, "surely that is something at my window lattice;
Let me see, then, what thereat is, and this mystery explore—
35 Let my heart be still a moment and this mystery explore;—
        'Tis the wind and nothing more!"

Open here I flung the shutter, when, with many a flirt and flutter,
In there stepped a stately Raven of the saintly days of yore;
Not the least obeisance made he; not a minute stopped or stayed he;
40 But, with mien of lord or lady, perched above my chamber door—
Perched upon a bust of Pallas[2] just above my chamber door—
        Perched, and sat, and nothing more.

Then this ebony bird beguiling my sad fancy into smiling,
By the grave and stern decorum of the countenance it wore,
45 "Though thy crest be shorn and shaven, thou," I said, "art sure no craven,
Ghastly grim and ancient Raven wandering from the Nightly shore—
Tell me what thy lordly name is on the Night's Plutonian[3] shore!"
        Quoth the Raven "Nevermore."

1. Poe may have chosen this name because of its association with the German ballad by Bürger (1747–94), in
which the heroine Lenore is carried off by the ghost of her
lover after his death, and wedded to him at the grave-side.
2. Athena, goddess of wisdom.
3. From Pluto, king of the underworld.

50 Much I marvelled this ungainly fowl to hear discourse so plainly,
Though its answer little meaning— little relevancy bore;
For we cannot help agreeing that no living human being
Ever yet was blessed with seeing bird above his chamber door—
Bird or beast upon the sculptured bust above his chamber door,
         With such name as "Nevermore."

55 But the Raven, sitting lonely on the placid bust, spoke only
That one word, as if his soul in that one word he did outpour.
Nothing farther then he uttered—not a feather then he fluttered—
Till I scarcely more than muttered "Other friends have flown before—
On the morrow *he* will leave me, as my Hopes have flown before."
60   Then the bird said "Nevermore."

Startled at the stillness broken by reply so aptly spoken,
"Doubtless," said I, "what it utters is its only stock and store
Caught from some unhappy master whom unmerciful Disaster
Followed fast and followed faster till his songs one burden[4] bore —
65 Till the dirges of his Hope that melancholy burden bore
         Of 'Never — nevermore.'"

But the Raven still beguiling my sad fancy into smiling,
Straight I wheeled a cushioned seat in front of bird, and bust and door;
Then, upon the velvet sinking, I betook myself to linking
70 Fancy unto fancy, thinking what this ominous bird of yore —
What this grim, ungainly, ghastly, gaunt, and ominous bird of yore
         Meant in croaking "Nevermore."

This I sat engaged in guessing, but no syllable expressing
To the fowl whose fiery eyes now burned into my bosom's core;
75 This and more I sat divining, with my head at ease reclining
On the cushion's velvet lining that the lamp-light gloated o'er,
But whose velvet-violet lining with the lamp-light gloating o'er,
         She shall press, ah, nevermore!

Then, methought, the air grew denser, perfumed from an unseen censer
80 Swung by seraphim whose foot-falls tinkled on the tufted floor.
"Wretch," I cried, "thy God hath lent thee — by these angels he hath sent thee
Respite — respite and nepenthe[5] from thy memories of Lenore;
Quaff, oh quaff this kind nepenthe and forget this lost Lenore!"
         Quoth the Raven "Nevermore."

85 "Prophet!" said I, "thing of evil! — prophet still, if bird or devil! —
Whether Tempter sent, or whether tempest tossed thee here ashore,
Desolate yet all undaunted, on this desert land enchanted —
On this home by Horror haunted — tell me truly, I implore —
Is there — *is* there balm in Gilead?[6] — tell me — tell me, I implore!"
90   Quoth the Raven "Nevermore."

"Prophet!" said I, "thing of evil! — prophet still, if bird or devil!
By that Heaven that bends above us — by that God we both adore —
Tell this soul with sorrow laden if, within the distant Aidenn,[7]
It shall clasp a sainted maiden whom the angels name Lenore —
95 Clasp a rare and radiant maiden whom the angels name Lenore."
         Quoth the Raven "Nevermore."

---

4. Refrain, chorus.
5. In classical myth, a drug that dispelled sorrow.

6. "*Is* there no balm in Gilead . . . ?" (Jer. viii.22). Gilead was famous for its herbs and spices.
7. Eden.

"Be that word our sign of parting, bird or fiend!" I shrieked, upstarting —
"Get thee back into the tempest and the Night's Plutonian shore!
Leave no black plume as a token of that lie thy soul hath spoken!
100   Leave my loneliness unbroken! — quit the bust above my door!
Take thy beak from out my heart, and take thy form from off my door!"
       Quoth the Raven "Nevermore."

And the Raven, never flitting, still is sitting, *still* is sitting
On the pallid bust of Pallas just above my chamber door;
105   And his eyes have all the seeming of a demon's that is dreaming,
And the lamp-light o'er him streaming throws his shadow on the floor;
And my soul from out that shadow that lies floating on the floor
       Shall be lifted — nevermore!

Introduction: 1832–1900

"Close thy *Byron*; open thy *Goethe*." This terse instruction, delivered by Thomas Carlyle in 1834, points to the movement which poets were asked to make in the late nineteenth century away from the socially disengaged, flippant, sensual, and dark side of Romanticism towards an earnest, idealistic, self-renouncing, and highly serious concern with moral, spiritual, and social matters. Of course, the influence of the major Romantic poets was all-pervasive in the second half of the nineteenth century: behind Tennyson and D. G. Rossetti stands Keats, behind Browning and Swinburne stands Shelley, behind Arnold and Longfellow stands Wordsworth, and behind the Canadian "Confederation" poets stand these same Romantics (as well as their successors in England and America). But the age demanded that its poets be selective in their choice of literary ancestors and selective, too, in their poetic stance and subject matter. It demanded, and its most popular poets— Tennyson in England, Longfellow in America, and Roberts in Canada—acceded to the demand, that its poetry be didactic and sentimental and that its poets be sages and seers, authors of good works to elevate their readers and of prophetic visions of their society's bright future. "Most of what now passes with us for religion and philosophy will be replaced by poetry" was the extravagant claim made by Matthew Arnold, whose lecture tours of America and Canada in 1883 and 1886, like those of Charles Dickens, met with an enthusiasm symbolic of the esteem in which literary figures were held on both sides of the Atlantic.

Such expectations and such esteem came with a price. Many poets allowed that their art might be the handmaiden of, if not the replacement for, religion but feared that the demands of their materialistic society would result in the death of the individual imagination. The dilemma of the late-nineteenth-century poet became increasingly one of whether to serve art for its own sake and to follow the imagination down whatever dark passages it afforded, or to place his or her art at the service of society and to become involved with the problems of an industrial, conceited, complacent, and urbanized civilization which many sensitive people perceived to be sliding towards destruction and, in the process, exacting an unconscionable toll in human misery and spiritual perversion. Was not the amputation of mind and body implied by the description of a worker as a "hand" simply too much to pay for a materialistic progress and technological advancement founded on a viciously unrestrained capitalism and a grinding work ethic? For many the answer to such a question was clear, though the solution (utilitarianism? socialism? transcendentalism? unitrinianism? escape?) was more difficult to find—though not for want of seeking. It was an age, after all, of great energy and creativity, of asking, testing, questing, exploring, inventing, and refusing, as Tennyson said, "to yield."

The age that produced *The Communist Manifesto* and Queen Victoria's palace-full of children, Billy the Kid and the C.P.R., Louis Riel and anaesthetics, the American Civil War and Emily Carr, *Dr. Jekyll and Mr. Hyde* and Sigmund Freud was a complex one in which nations and people were divided against themselves and each other. England, as Benjamin Disraeli perceived, consisted of "two nations," the "rich and the poor"; America, as a slave-owning society whose constitution guaranteed "liberty" for all, contained a cruel paradox at its heart; and Canada, Roberts' "Child of Nations, giant-limbed," was then as now a pair of Siamese twins, with a Native ancestor, joined at the head rather than the heart. Such dichotomies resulted in conflicts at every level of human activity and interaction in the three nations and were joined by others of consequence for the poetry of the period. The controversy between religion and science, fuelled by the Higher Criticism of the Bible, which raised questions regarding the accuracy of the Scriptures, and by Charles Darwin's theory of evolution, which raised questions concerning the relation among various theories of nature and progress, drew many people into a conflict with each other and between their own faith and knowledge. The sexual repressiveness and orthodoxy of the mainly Protestant middle classes put women in an intolerable position, demanding that they mother large families but denying them the pleasures that can accompany the process, and led to distorted images of woman as much as to such unconventional and anti-conventional phenomena as Oscar Wilde, the Pre-Raphaelite "stunner," the joyous affirmations of Whitman, and the sensual (and pagan) lucubrations of Swinburne. Little wonder that, in an age of such variety and conflict, where social philosophies, religious beliefs, and scientific theories flourished and fought, and where the public life of the individual was rigorously separated from the private, Arnold could experience a sense of "wandering between two worlds, one dead / The other powerless to be born." Freud needed merely to invent the terminology for such problems.

Confronted with a society whose values and direction they questioned, many poets, including Tennyson and Browning, Longfellow and Whittier, Roberts and Scott, turned (naturally, because of the period's strong sense of history) to the past, to classical Greece, to the Middle Ages, to the Renaissance, or to their own childhood or the past of other cultures (such as that of the Indians). They did so sometimes merely to escape the unattractive present, but more often to comment in a distant and indirect manner on the psychological and sexual, spiritual and moral, artistic and aesthetic problems and choices of their own age and place. Often these poets chose the longer, narrative poem in an attempt to create sustained effects, to explore complexities of character, and to dramatize conflict in an engaging story. (In so doing they pushed poetry in the direction of the novel, which was, of course, the most outstanding and popular form of the period.) Often, in a lyrical vein, the poets turned their backs on the city and all that it stood for to seek in the minute particulars, the transcendant vistas, and "the kinship of earth" the answers to the materialistic individualism and religious uncertainty of the age. Some poets saw in the outsider's life of the gypsy, the vagabond, the hermit, or the bohemian an attractive means of avoiding confrontation with a sick society and, in turn, of confronting that society with a healing, or at least expanding, image of a better way of life. It must not be thought, however, that the poets of the late nineteenth century did not directly confront their society with its own malaise; on the contrary, poems such as Clough's "The Latest Decalogue" and Lampman's "To a Millionaire" depict frontally what these poets saw as the evil causes and effects of their time; and Lampman's "The City of the End of Things" is one of several poems of the age of steam and progress which diagnoses the metropolis as a necropolis, as a realm of death-in-life and, in so doing, points not only towards the dreadful consequences of materialism but also towards modern works such as *The Waste Land* of T. S. Eliot.

Poems diagnosing the diseases of a sick society provide one link between the late nineteenth century and the modern age. Poetic techniques provide another. For, although writers of our own century rejected and disparaged their nineteenth-century parents (often using terms tellingly reminiscent of Wordsworth's similarly motivated reference to the poetic diction of the weaker verse of the eighteenth century as "gaudy and inane"), they also learned from certain of them, particularly those who, like Whitman, moved beyond fixed structures such as the sonnet to explore the possibilities of freer forms or who, like Browning, wrote lines whose rough colloquialism and discordant, even grotesque, noises contrast markedly with the mellifluous harmonies and glamorous syntax of a Tennyson, a Longfellow, or a Carman. Ezra Pound battled but absorbed the influence of Whitman's "barbaric yawp" and oceanic free verse, and he owes debts to Browning and the Pre-Raphaelites. Yeats's early work (like that of Wallace Stevens) has roots in the Pre-Raphaelites as well as in the decadent nineties of Wilde and Dowson; Eliot's entire canon has continuities with the Tennyson whom Auden describes as a poet "whose talents were / For an articulate despair"; and, last and least of this catalogue, John Masefield, the poet laureate from 1930 to 1967, was inspired to become a poet by Duncan Campbell Scott's "The Piper of Arll." Mention must also be made of two late-nineteenth-century poets, Hopkins and Dickinson, whose posthumously published work has been peculiarly appealing and inspirational to readers and poets of our own century for its reaching alike towards psychological realism and a revitalized language of poetry.

If it is true that literary movements, like individuals, rebel against their fathers but retain an affection for their grandfathers, then it should follow that at the present time, with the reaction against modernism gathering momentum, a love for the poetry of the late nineteenth century is as inevitable as it is warranted.

D. M. R. Bentley

ALFRED, LORD TENNYSON (1809–92)

Mariana

Mariana in the moated grange[1]*—Measure for Measure*

With blackest moss the flower-plots
  Were thickly crusted, one and all:
The rusted nails fell from the knots
  That held the pear to the gable-wall.
5 The broken sheds looked sad and strange:
  Unlifted was the clinking latch;
  Weeded and worn the ancient thatch
Upon the lonely moated grange.
    She only said, 'My life is dreary,
10   He cometh not,' she said;
    She said, 'I am aweary, aweary,
      I would that I were dead!'

Her tears fell with the dews at even;
  Her tears fell ere the dews were dried;
15 She could not look on the sweet heaven,
  Either at morn or eventide.
After the flitting of the bats,
  When thickest dark did trance the sky,
  She drew her casement-curtain by,
20 And glanced athwart the glooming flats.
    She only said, 'The night is dreary,
      He cometh not,' she said;
    She said, 'I am aweary, aweary,
      I would that I were dead!'

25 Upon the middle of the night,
  Waking she heard the night-fowl crow:
The cock sung out an hour ere light:
  From the dark fen the oxen's low
Came to her: without hope of change,
30 In sleep she seemed to walk forlorn,
  Till cold winds woke the gray-eyed morn
About the lonely moated grange.
    She only said, 'The day is dreary,
      He cometh not,' she said;
35   She said, 'I am aweary, aweary,
      I would that I were dead!'

About a stone-cast from the wall
  A sluice with blackened waters slept,
And o'er it many, round and small,
40 The clustered marish-mosses crept.[2]
Hard by a poplar shook alway,
  All silver-green with gnarlèd bark:
  For leagues no other tree did mark
The level waste, the rounding gray.
45   She only said, 'My life is dreary,
      He cometh not,' she said;
    She said, 'I am aweary, aweary,
      I would that I were dead!'

And ever when the moon was low,
50 And the shrill winds were up and away,
In the white curtain, to and fro,
  She saw the gusty shadow sway.
But when the moon was very low,
  And wild winds bound within their cell,[3]
55 The shadow of the poplar fell
Upon her bed, across her brow.
    She only said, 'The night is dreary,
      He cometh not,' she said;
    She said, 'I am aweary, aweary,
60   I would that I were dead!'

All day within the dreamy house,
  The doors upon their hinges creaked;
The blue fly sung in the pane; the mouse
  Behind the mouldering wainscot shrieked,
65 Or from the crevice peered about.
  Old faces glimmered through the doors,
  Old footsteps trod the upper floors,
Old voices called her from without.
    She only said, 'My life is dreary,
70   He cometh not,' she said;
    She said, 'I am aweary, aweary,
      I would that I were dead!'

The sparrow's chirrup on the roof,
  The slow clock ticking, and the sound
75 Which to the wooing wind aloof
  The poplar made, did all confound
Her sense; but most she loathed the hour
  When the thick-moted sunbeam lay
  Athwart the chambers, and the day
80 Was sloping toward his western bower.
    Then, said she, 'I am very dreary,
      He will not come,' she said;
    She wept, 'I am aweary, aweary,
      Oh God, that I were dead!'

---

1. In Shakespeare's *Measure for Measure* III.i, a "dejected Mariana" resides at a farmhouse (grange), weeping for the lover who has deserted her.

2. Lumps of marsh-moss floating on the surface of the water.

3. The cave of Aeolus, god of the winds, in which the winds are imprisoned.

The Kraken[1]

Below the thunders of the upper deep;
Far, far beneath in the abysmal sea,
His ancient, dreamless, uninvaded sleep
The Kraken sleepeth: faintest sunlights flee
About his shadowy sides: above him swell
Huge sponges of millennial growth and height;
And far away into the sickly light,
From many a wondrous grot and secret cell

Unnumbered and enormous polypi[2]
Winnow with giant arms the slumbering green.
There hath he lain for ages and will lie
Battening upon huge seaworms in his sleep,
Until the latter fire[3] shall heat the deep;
Then once by man and angels to be seen,
In roaring he shall rise and on the surface die.

The Lady of Shalott

Part I

On either side the river lie
Long fields of barley and of rye,
That clothe the wold[1] and meet the sky;
And through the field the road runs by   40
5   To many-towered Camelot;[2]
And up and down the people go,
Gazing where the lilies blow[3]
Round an island there below,
          The island of Shalott.   45

10   Willows whiten, aspens quiver,
Little breezes dusk and shiver
Through the wave that runs for ever
By the island in the river
          Flowing down to Camelot.   50
15   Four gray walls, and four gray towers,
Overlook a space of flowers,
And the silent isle imbowers
          The Lady of Shalott.

By the margin, willow-veiled,   55
20   Slide the heavy barges trailed
By slow horses; and unhailed
The shallop[4] flitteth silken-sailed
          Skimming down to Camelot:
But who hath seen her wave her hand?   60
25   Or at the casement seen her stand?
Or is she known in all the land,
          The Lady of Shalott?

Only reapers, reaping early
In among the bearded barley,   65
30   Hear a song that echoes cheerly
From the river winding clearly,
          Down to towered Camelot:
And by the moon the reaper weary,
Piling sheaves in uplands airy,   70
35   Listening, whispers ''Tis the fairy
          Lady of Shalott.'

Part II

There she weaves by night and day
A magic web with colours gay.
She has heard a whisper say,
A curse is on her if she stay
          To look down to Camelot.
She knows not what the curse may be,
And so she weaveth steadily,
And little other care hath she,
          The Lady of Shalott.

And moving through a mirror[5] clear
That hangs before her all the year,
Shadows of the world appear.
There she sees the highway near
          Winding down to Camelot:
There the river eddy whirls,
And there the surly village-churls,[6]
And the red cloaks of market girls,
          Pass onward from Shalott.

Sometimes a troop of damsels glad,
An abbot on an ambling pad,[7]
Sometimes a curly shepherd-lad,
Or long-haired page in crimson clad,
          Goes by to towered Camelot;
And sometimes through the mirror blue
The knights come riding two and two:
She hath no loyal knight and true,
          The Lady of Shalott.

But in her web she still delights
To weave the mirror's magic sights,
For often through the silent nights
A funeral, with plumes and lights
          And music, went to Camelot:
Or when the moon was overhead,
Came two young lovers lately wed;
'I am half sick of shadows,' said
          The Lady of Shalott.

1. A mythical sea-serpent of enormous size.
2. Octopuses.
3. The fire of the apocalypse. See Rev. viii.8–9, xvi.3–9, and xiii.1.

1. Hilly or rolling countryside.
2. Legendary city and location of King Arthur's court.

3. Bloom.
4. A small, open boat used mainly in shallow waters.
5. Weavers placed mirrors behind their tapestries in order to see their work from the proper side.
6. Peasants.
7. A horse that moves at a gentle pace.

Part III

A bow-shot from her bower-eaves,
He rode between the barley-sheaves,
75 The sun came dazzling through the leaves,
And flamed upon the brazen greaves[8]
    Of bold Sir Lancelot.
A red-cross knight[9] for ever kneeled
To a lady in his shield,
80 That sparkled on the yellow field,
    Beside remote Shalott.

The gemmy bridle glittered free,
Like to some branch of stars we see
Hung in the golden Galaxy.
85 The bridle bells rang merrily
    As he rode down to Camelot:
And from his blazoned baldric[10] slung
A mighty silver bugle hung,
And as he rode his armour rung,
90   Beside remote Shalott.

All in the blue unclouded weather
Thick-jewelled shone the saddle-leather,
The helmet and the helmet-feather
Burned like one burning flame together,
95   As he rode down to Camelot.
As often through the purple night,
Below the starry clusters bright,
Some bearded meteor, trailing light,
    Moves over still Shalott.

100 His broad clear brow in sunlight glowed;
On burnished hooves his war-horse trode;
From underneath his helmet flowed
His coal-black curls as on he rode,
    As he rode down to Camelot.
105 From the bank and from the river
He flashed into the crystal mirror,
'Tirra lirra,' by the river
    Sang Sir Lancelot.

She left the web, she left the loom,
110 She made three paces through the room,
She saw the water-lily bloom,
She saw the helmet and the plume,
    She looked down to Camelot.
Out flew the web and floated wide;
115 The mirror cracked from side to side;
'The curse is come upon me,' cried
    The Lady of Shalott.

Part IV

In the stormy east-wind straining,
The pale yellow woods were waning,
120 The broad stream in his banks complaining,
Heavily the low sky raining
    Over towered Camelot;

Down she came and found a boat
Beneath a willow left afloat,
125 And round about the prow she wrote
    The Lady of Shalott.

And down the river's dim expanse
Like some bold seër in a trance,
Seeing all his own mischance—
130 With a glassy countenance
    Did she look to Camelot.
And at the closing of the day
She loosed the chain, and down she lay;
The broad stream bore her far away,
135   The Lady of Shalott.

Lying, robed in snowy white
That loosely flew to left and right—
The leaves upon her falling light—
Through the noises of the night
140   She floated down to Camelot:
And as the boat-head wound along
The willowy hills and fields among,
They heard her singing her last song,
    The Lady of Shalott.

145 Heard a carol, mournful, holy,
Chanted loudly, chanted lowly,
Till her blood was frozen slowly,
And her eyes were darkened wholly,
    Turned to towered Camelot.
150 For ere she reached upon the tide
The first house by the water-side,
Singing in her song she died,
    The Lady of Shalott.

Under tower and balcony,
155 By garden-wall and gallery,
A gleaming shape she floated by,
Dead-pale between the houses high,
    Silent into Camelot.
Out upon the wharfs they came,
160 Knight and burgher, lord and dame,
And round the prow they read her name,
    The Lady of Shalott.

Who is this? and what is here?
And in the lighted palace near
165 Died the sound of royal cheer;
And they crossed themselves for fear,
    All the knights at Camelot:
But Lancelot mused a little space;
He said, 'She has a lovely face;
170 God in his mercy lend her grace,
    The Lady of Shalott.'

---

8. Armour for the leg below the knee.
9. A knight, as in Spenser's *Faerie Queene*, whose emblem is the red cross of St. George.

10. Ornamental belt worn over one shoulder to support a bugle or sword.

The Lotos-Eaters[1]

'Courage!' he[2] said, and pointed toward the land,
'This mounting wave will roll us shoreward soon.'
In the afternoon they came unto a land
In which it seemèd always afternoon.
5   All round the coast the languid air did swoon,
Breathing like one that hath a weary dream.
Full-faced above the valley stood the moon;
And like a downward smoke, the slender stream
Along the cliff to fall and pause and fall did seem.

10   A land of streams! some, like a downward smoke,
Slow-dropping veils of thinnest lawn,[3] did go;
And some through wavering lights and shadows broke,
Rolling a slumbrous sheet of foam below.
They saw the gleaming river seaward flow
15   From the inner land: far off, three mountain-tops,
Three silent pinnacles of agèd snow,
Stood sunset-flushed: and, dewed with showery drops,
Up-clomb the shadowy pine above the woven copse.

The charmèd sunset lingered low adown
20   In the red West: through mountain clefts the dale
Was seen far inland, and the yellow down[4]
Bordered with palm, and many a winding vale
And meadow, set with slender galingale;[5]
A land where all things always seemed the same!
25   And round about the keel with faces pale,
Dark faces pale against that rosy flame,
The mild-eyed melancholy Lotos-eaters came.

Branches they bore of that enchanted stem,
Laden with flower and fruit, whereof they gave
30   To each, but whoso did receive them,
And taste, to him the gushing of the wave
Far far away did seem to mourn and rave
On alien shores; and if his fellow spake,
His voice was thin, as voices from the grave;
35   And deep-asleep he seemed, yet all awake,
And music in his ears his beating heart did make.

They sat them down upon the yellow sand,
Between the sun and moon upon the shore;
And sweet it was to dream of Fatherland,
40   Of child, and wife, and slave; but evermore
Most weary seemed the sea, weary the oar,
Weary the wandering fields of barren foam.
Then some one said, 'We will return no more;'
And all at once they sang, 'Our island home[6]
45   Is far beyond the wave; we will no longer roam.'

---

1. The principal source of Tennyson's poem is the *Odyssey* IX.82–104 where, as Ulysses tells it, he and his men, while returning from the Trojan War, "set foot on the land of the lotos-eaters, who eat a flowery food . . . and the lotos-eaters . . . gave [my comrades] of the lotos to taste. And whosoever of them ate of the honey-sweet fruit of the lotos, had no longer any wish to bring back word or to return, but they were fain to abide among the lotos-eaters, feeding on the lotos, and forgetful of their homeward way."
2. Odysseus (Ulysses).
3. A fine, sheer cotton fabric.
4. Gently sloping, high ground.
5. A species of sedge with an aromatic root of ancient medicinal repute.
6. Ithaca.

Choric Song

I

There is sweet music here that softer falls
Than petals from blown roses on the grass,
Or night-dews on still waters between walls
Of shadowy granite, in a gleaming pass;
50 Music that gentlier on the spirit lies,
Than tired eyelids upon tired eyes;
Music that brings sweet sleep down from the blissful skies.
Here are cool mosses deep,
And through the moss the ivies creep,
55 And in the stream the long-leaved flowers weep,
And from the craggy ledge the poppy hangs in sleep.

II

Why are we weighed upon with heaviness,
And utterly consumed with sharp distress,
While all things else have rest from weariness?
60 All things have rest: why should we toil alone,
We only toil, who are the first of things,
And make perpetual moan,
Still from one sorrow to another thrown:
Nor ever fold our wings,
65 And cease from wanderings,
Nor steep our brows in slumber's holy balm;
Nor harken what the inner spirit sings,
'There is no joy but calm!'
Why should we only toil, the roof and crown of things?

III

70 Lo! in the middle of the wood,
The folded leaf is wooed from out the bud
With winds upon the branch, and there
Grows green and broad, and takes no care,
Sun-steeped at noon, and in the moon
75 Nightly dew-fed; and turning yellow
Falls, and floats adown the air.
Lo! sweetened with the summer light,
The full-juiced apple, waxing over-mellow,
Drops in a silent autumn night.
80 All its allotted length of days,
The flower ripens in its place,
Ripens and fades, and falls, and hath no toil,
Fast-rooted in the fruitful soil.

IV

Hateful is the dark-blue sky,
85 Vaulted o'er the dark-blue sea.
Death is the end of life; ah, why
Should life all labour be?
Let us alone. Time driveth onward fast,
And in a little while our lips are dumb.
90 Let us alone. What is it that will last?
All things are taken from us, and become
Portions and parcels of the dreadful Past.
Let us alone. What pleasure can we have
To war with evil? Is there any peace
95 In ever climbing upon the climbing wave?
All things have rest, and ripen toward the grave
In silence; ripen, fall and cease:
Give us long rest or death, dark death, or dreamful ease.

V

How sweet it were, hearing the downward stream,
100   With half-shut eyes ever to seem
Falling asleep in a half-dream!
To dream and dream, like yonder amber light,
Which will not leave the myrrh-bush on the height;
To hear each other's whispered speech;
105   Eating the Lotos day by day,
To watch the crisping[7] ripples on the beach,
And tender curving lines of creamy spray;
To lend our hearts and spirits wholly
To the influence of mild-minded melancholy;
110   To muse and brood and live again in memory,
With those old faces of our infancy
Heaped over with a mound of grass,
Two handfuls of white dust, shut in an urn of brass!

VI

Dear is the memory of our wedded lives,
115   And dear the last embraces of our wives
And their warm tears: but all hath suffered change:
For surely now our household hearths are cold:
Our sons inherit us: our looks are strange:
And we should come like ghosts to trouble joy.
120   Or else the island princes[8] over-bold
Have eat our substance, and the minstrel sings
Before them of the ten years' war in Troy,   ʼ
And our great deeds, as half-forgotten things.
Is there confusion in the little isle?[9]
125   Let what is broken so remain.
The Gods are hard to reconcile:
'Tis hard to settle order once again.
There *is* confusion worse than death,
Trouble on trouble, pain on pain,
130   Long labour unto agèd breath,
Sore task to hearts worn out by many wars
And eyes grown dim with gazing on the pilot-stars.

VII

But, propt on beds of amaranth and moly,[10]
How sweet (while warm airs lull us, blowing lowly)
135   With half-dropt eyelid still,
Beneath a heaven dark and holy,
To watch the long bright river drawing slowly
His waters from the purple hill—
To hear the dewy echoes calling
140   From cave to cave through the thick-twinèd vine—
To watch the emerald-coloured water falling
Through many a woven acanthus[11]-wreath divine!
Only to hear and see the far-off sparkling brine,
Only to hear were sweet, stretched out beneath the pine.

7. Closely curling.
8. Those who had remained behind on Odysseus' island home of Ithaca during the Trojan War and were suitors for the hand of his wife Penelope.
9. Ithaca.
10. "Amaranth": a fabled never-fading flower, an emblem of immortality. "Moly": a mythical herb given by Hermes to Odysseus as a counter-charm against the spells of Circe; it is sometimes reputed to induce forgetfulness.
11. A prickly plant whose leaves served as models for decorations such as those on Corinthian columns.

VIII

145 The Lotos blooms below the barren peak:
The Lotos blows by every winding creek:
All day the wind breathes low with mellower tone:
Through every hollow cave and alley lone
Round and round the spicy downs the yellow Lotos-dust is blown.
150 We have had enough of action, and of motion we,
Rolled to starboard, rolled to larboard, when the surge was seething free,
Where the wallowing monster spouted his foam-fountains in the sea.
Let us swear an oath, and keep it with an equal mind,
In the hollow Lotos-land to live and lie reclined
155 On the hills like Gods[12] together, careless of mankind.
For they lie beside their nectar, and the bolts[13] are hurled
Far below them in the valleys, and the clouds are lightly curled
Round their golden houses, girdled with the gleaming world:
Where they smile in secret, looking over wasted lands,
160 Blight and famine, plague and earthquake, roaring deeps and fiery sands,
Clanging fights, and flaming towns, and sinking ships, and praying hands.
But they smile, they find a music centred in a doleful song
Steaming up, a lamentation and an ancient tale of wrong,
Like a tale of little meaning though the words are strong;
165 Chanted from an ill-used race of men that cleave the soil,
Sow the seed, and reap the harvest with enduring toil,
Storing yearly little dues of wheat, and wine and oil;
Till they perish and they suffer—some, 'tis whispered—down in hell
Suffer endless anguish, others in Elysian[14] valleys dwell,
170 Resting weary limbs at last on beds of asphodel.[15]
Surely, surely, slumber is more sweet than toil, the shore
Than labour in the deep mid-ocean, wind and wave and oar;
Oh rest ye, brother mariners, we will not wander more.

The Eagle

Fragment

He clasps the crag with crookèd hands;
Close to the sun in lonely lands,
Ringed with the azure world, he stands.

The wrinkled sea beneath him crawls;
He watches from his mountain walls,
And like a thunderbolt he falls.

Ulysses[1]

It little profits that an idle king,
By this still hearth, among these barren crags,
Matched with an agèd wife,[2] I mete and dole
Unequal laws[3] unto a savage race,
5 That hoard, and sleep, and feed, and know not me.

I cannot rest from travel: I will drink
Life to the lees: all times I have enjoyed
Greatly, have suffered greatly, both with those
That loved me, and alone; on shore, and when
10 Through scudding drifts[4] the rainy Hyades[5]

---

12. Tennyson's description of the gods is based, in part, on Lucretius' account of Epicureanism in *De rerum natura.*
13. Thunderbolts.
14. Referring to Elysium, the Islands of the Blest, where, in Greek mythology, those favoured by the gods enjoy a pleasant life after death.
15. Perennial herbs of the lily family. In Greek mythology, plants associated particularly with the dead.

1. Tennyson's principal source for this poem is Dante's *Inferno* XXVI.90–120, where Ulysses (Odysseus), the veteran of the Trojan War and of the adventures described in the *Odyssey*, tells how he became restless on Ithaca and, with a small, faithful crew, set out on a final voyage to explore the world to the west.
2. Penelope.
3. Administer primitive laws.
4. Wind-driven rain.
5. Stars whose appearance was thought to bring rain.

Vext the dim sea: I am become a name;
For always roaming with a hungry heart
Much have I seen and known; cities of men
And manners, climates, councils, governments,
15 Myself not least, but honoured of them all;
And drunk delight of battle with my peers,
Far on the ringing plains of windy Troy.
I am a part of all that I have met;
Yet all experience is an arch wherethrough
20 Gleams that untravelled world, whose margin fades
For ever and for ever when I move.
How dull it is to pause, to make an end,
To rust unburnished, not to shine in use!
As though to breathe were life. Life piled on life
25 Were all too little, and of one to me
Little remains: but every hour is saved
From that eternal silence, something more,
A bringer of new things; and vile it were
For some three suns to store and hoard myself,
30 And this gray spirit yearning in desire
To follow knowledge like a sinking star,
Beyond the utmost bound of human thought.

 This is my son, mine own Telemachus,
To whom I leave the sceptre and the isle—
35 Well-loved of me, discerning to fulfil
This labour, by slow prudence to make mild
A rugged people, and through soft degrees
Subdue them to the useful and the good.
Most blameless is he, centred in the sphere
40 Of common duties, decent not to fail
In offices of tenderness, and pay
Meet adoration to my household gods,
When I am gone. He works his work, I mine.

 There lies the port; the vessel puffs her sail:
45 There gloom the dark broad seas. My mariners,
Souls that have toiled, and wrought, and thought with me—
That ever with a frolic welcome took
The thunder and the sunshine, and opposed
Free hearts, free foreheads—you and I are old;
50 Old age hath yet his honour and his toil;
Death closes all: but something ere the end,
Some work of noble note, may yet be done,
Not unbecoming men that strove with Gods.
The lights begin to twinkle from the rocks:
55 The long day wanes: the slow moon climbs: the deep
Moans round with many voices. Come, my friends,
'Tis not too late to seek a newer world.
Push off, and sitting well in order smite
The sounding furrows; for my purpose holds
60 To sail beyond the sunset, and the baths
Of all the western stars,[6] until I die.
It may be that the gulfs will wash us down:
It may be we shall touch the Happy Isles,[7]
And see the great Achilles, whom we knew.
65 Though much is taken, much abides; and though
We are not now that strength which in old days

---

6. In Greek cosmology the stars of the western sky descended into the body of water which, it was believed, encircled the plain of earth.

7. Elysium, the place where, in Greek mythology, the favourites of the gods (such as Achilles) enjoy a pleasant afterlife, was believed to lie in the ocean to the far west.

Moved earth and heaven; that which we are, we are;
One equal temper of heroic hearts,
Made weak by time and fate, but strong in will
70   To strive, to seek, to find, and not to yield.

Morte d'Arthur[1]

So all day long the noise of battle rolled
Among the mountains by the winter sea;
Until King Arthur's table, man by man,
Had fallen in Lyonnesse[2] about their Lord,
5   King Arthur: then, because his wound was deep,
The bold Sir Bedivere uplifted him,
Sir Bedivere, the last of all his knights,
And bore him to a chapel nigh the field,
A broken chancel with a broken cross,
10   That stood on a dark strait of barren land.
On one side lay the Ocean, and on one
Lay a great water, and the moon was full.

   Then spake King Arthur to Sir Bedivere:
'The sequel of today unsolders all
15   The goodliest fellowship of famous knights
Whereof this world holds record. Such a sleep
They sleep—the men I loved. I think that we
Shall never more, at any future time,
Delight our souls with talk of knightly deeds,
20   Walking about the gardens and the halls
Of Camelot,[3] as in the days that were.
I perish by this people which I made,—
Though Merlin[4] sware that I should come again
To rule once more—but let what will be, be,
25   I am so deeply smitten through the helm
That without help I cannot last till morn.
Thou therefore take my brand[5] Excalibur,
Which was my pride: for thou rememberest how
In those old days, one summer noon, an arm
30   Rose up from out the bosom of the lake,
Clothed in white samite,[6] mystic, wonderful,
Holding the sword—and how I rowed across
And took it, and have worn it, like a king:
And, wheresoever I am sung or told
35   In aftertime, this also shall be known:
But now delay not: take Excalibur,
And fling him far into the middle mere:[7]
Watch what thou seëst, and lightly[8] bring me word.'

   To him replied the bold Sir Bedivere:
40   'It is not meet, Sir King, to leave thee thus,
Aidless, alone, and smitten through the helm.
A little thing may harm a wounded man.
Yet I thy hest will all perform at full,
Watch what I see, and lightly bring thee word.'

1. This poem was first published within a framework
entitled "The Epic" which hints at the poet's ambition to
write an "epic" in "some twelve books" on King Arthur
and addresses the issue of whether such an epic should be
written in modern idiom ("the fashion of the day") or
should "take the style of those heroic times." In 1869
"Morte d'Arthur" was incorporated into Tennyson's
Idylls of the King as "The Passing of Arthur." Its
principal source is Malory's *Morte d'Arthur* XXI.4–5.

2. In Arthurian legend, a country lying off the coast of
England between Cornwall and the Scilly Islands.
3. See note 2 to "The Lady of Shalott."
4. Magician and prophet in the court of Arthur.
5. Sword.
6. A rich, silk cloth.
7. Lake.
8. Speedily.

45   So saying, from the ruined shrine he stept
And in the moon athwart the place of tombs,
Where lay the mighty bones of ancient men,
Old knights, and over them the sea-wind sang
Shrill, chill, with flakes of foam. He, stepping down
50 By zig-zag paths, and juts of pointed rock,
Came on the shining levels of the lake.

    There drew he forth the brand Excalibur,
And o'er him, drawing it, the winter moon,
Brightening the skirts of a long cloud, ran forth
55 And sparkled keen with frost against the hilt:
For all the haft twinkled with diamond sparks,
Myriads of topaz-lights, and jacinth-work
Of subtlest jewellery. He gazed so long
That both his eyes were dazzled, as he stood,
60 This way and that dividing the swift mind,
In act to throw: but at the last it seemed
Better to leave Excalibur concealed
There in the many-knotted waterflags,
That whistled stiff and dry about the marge.
65 So strode he back slow to the wounded King.

    Then spake King Arthur to Sir Bedivere:
'Hast thou performed my mission which I gave?
What is it thou hast seen? or what hast heard?'

    And answer made the bold Sir Bedivere:
70 'I heard the ripple washing in the reeds,
And the wild water lapping on the crag.'

    To whom replied King Arthur, faint and pale:
'Thou hast betrayed thy nature and thy name,
Not rendering true answer, as beseemed
75 Thy fëalty, nor like a noble knight:
For surer sign had followed, either hand,
Or voice, or else a motion of the mere.
This is a shameful thing for men to lie.
Yet now, I charge thee, quickly go again
80 As thou art lief[9] and dear, and do the thing
I bad thee, watch, and lightly bring me word.'

    Then went Sir Bedivere the second time
Across the ridge, and paced beside the mere,
Counting the dewy pebbles, fixed in thought;
85 But when he saw the wonder of the hilt,
How curiously and strangely chased, he smote
His palms together, and he cried aloud,

    'And if indeed I cast the brand away,
Surely a precious thing, one worthy note,
90 Should thus be lost for ever from the earth,
Which might have pleased the eyes of many men.
What good should follow this, if this were done?
What harm, undone? deep harm to disobey,
Seeing obedience is the bond of rule.
95 Were it well to obey then, if a king demand
An act unprofitable, against himself?
The King is sick, and knows not what he does.
What record, or what relic of my lord
Should be to aftertime, but empty breath

9. Beloved.

100   And rumours of a doubt? but were this kept,
    Stored in some treasure-house of mighty kings,
    Some one might show it at a joust of arms,
    Saying, "King Arthur's sword, Excalibur,
    Wrought by the lonely maiden of the Lake.
105   Nine years she wrought it, sitting in the deeps
    Upon the hidden bases of the hills."
    So might some old man speak in the aftertime
    To all the people, winning reverence.
    But now much honour and much fame were lost.'

110   So spake he, clouded with his own conceit,[10]
    And hid Excalibur the second time,
    And so strode back slow to the wounded King.

      Then spoke King Arthur, breathing heavily:
    'What is it thou hast seen? or what hast heard?'

115   And answer made the bold Sir Bedivere:
    'I heard the water lapping on the crag,
    And the long ripple washing in the reeds.'

      To whom replied King Arthur, much in wrath:
    'Ah, miserable and unkind, untrue,
120   Unknightly, traitor-hearted! Woe is me!
    Authority forgets a dying king,
    Laid widowed of the power in his eye
    That bowed the will. I see thee what thou art,
    For thou, the latest-left of all my knights,
125   In whom should meet the offices of all,
    Thou wouldst betray me for the precious hilt;
    Either from lust of gold, or like a girl
    Valuing the giddy pleasure of the eyes.
    Yet, for a man may fail in duty twice,
130   And the third time may prosper, get thee hence:
    But, if thou spare to fling Excalibur,
    I will arise and slay thee with my hands.'

      Then quickly rose Sir Bedivere, and ran,
    And, leaping down the ridges lightly, plunged
135   Among the bulrush-beds, and clutched the sword,
    And strongly wheeled and threw it. The great brand
    Made lightnings in the splendour of the moon,
    And flashing round and round, and whirled in an arch,
    Shot like a streamer of the northern morn,[11]
140   Seen where the moving isles[12] of winter shock
    By night, with noises of the northern sea.
    So flashed and fell the brand Excalibur:
    But ere he dipt the surface, rose an arm
    Clothed in white samite, mystic, wonderful,
145   And caught him by the hilt, and brandished him
    Three times, and drew him under in the mere.
    And lightly went the other to the King.

      Then spoke King Arthur, drawing thicker breath:
    'Now see I by thine eyes that this is done.
150   Speak out: what is it thou hast heard, or seen?'

      And answer made the bold Sir Bedivere:
    'Sir King, I closed mine eyelids, lest the gems

10. His own fanciful imaginings.
11. Of the aurora borealis or northern lights.   12. Icebergs.

Should blind my purpose, for I never saw,
Nor shall see, here or elsewhere, till I die,
155 Not though I live three lives of mortal men,
So great a miracle as yonder hilt.
Then with both hands I flung him, wheeling him;
But when I looked again, behold an arm,
Clothed in white samite, mystic, wonderful,
160 That caught him by the hilt, and brandished him
Three times, and drew him under in the mere.'

And answer made King Arthur, breathing hard:
'My end draws nigh; 'tis time that I were gone.
Make broad thy shoulders to receive my weight,
165 And bear me to the margin; yet I fear
My wound hath taken cold, and I shall die.'

So saying, from the pavement he half rose,
Slowly, with pain, reclining on his arm,
And looking wistfully with wide blue eyes
170 As in a picture. Him Sir Bedivere
Remorsefully regarded through his tears,
And would have spoken, but he found not words,
Then took with care, and kneeling on one knee,
O'er both his shoulders drew the languid hands,
175 And rising bore him through the place of tombs.

But, as he walked, King Arthur panted hard,
Like one that feels a nightmare on his bed
When all the house is mute. So sighed the King,
Muttering and murmuring at his ear, 'Quick, quick!
180 I fear it is too late, and I shall die.'
But the other swiftly strode from ridge to ridge,
Clothed with his breath, and looking, as he walked,
Larger than human on the frozen hills.
He heard the deep behind him, and a cry
185 Before. His own thought drove him, like a goad.
Dry[13] clashed his harness in the icy caves
And barren chasms, and all to left and right
The bare black cliff clanged round him, as he based
His feet on juts of slippery crag that rang
190 Sharp-smitten with the dint of armèd heels—
And on a sudden, lo! the level lake,
And the long glories of the winter moon.

Then saw they how there hove a dusky barge,
Dark as a funeral scarf from stem to stern,
195 Beneath them; and descending they were ware
That all the decks were dense with stately forms
Black-stoled, black-hooded, like a dream—by these
Three Queens with crowns of gold—and from them rose
A cry that shivered to the tingling stars,
200 And, as it were one voice, an agony
Of lamentation, like a wind, that shrills
All night in a waste land, where no one comes,
Or hath come, since the making of the world.

Then murmured Arthur, 'Place me in the barge,'
205 And to the barge they came. There those three Queens
Put forth their hands, and took the King, and wept.
But she, that rose the tallest of them all
And fairest, laid his head upon her lap,

13. Harsh.

And loosed the shattered casque,[14] and chafed his hands,
210 And called him by his name, complaining loud,
And dropping bitter tears against his brow
Striped with dark blood: for all his face was white
And colourless, and like the withered moon
Smote by the fresh beam of the springing east;
215 And all his greaves and cuisses[15] dashed with drops
Of onset; and the light and lustrous curls—
That made his forehead like a rising sun
High from the daïs-throne—were parched with dust;
Or, clotted into points and hanging loose,
220 Mixed with the knightly growth that fringed his lips.
So like a shattered column lay the King;
Not like that Arthur who, with lance in rest,
From spur to plume a star of tournament,
Shot through the lists at Camelot, and charged
225 Before the eyes of ladies and of kings.

   Then loudly cried the bold Sir Bedivere,
'Ah! my Lord Arthur, whither shall I go?
Where shall I hide my forehead and my eyes?
For now I see the true old times are dead,
230 When every morning brought a noble chance,
And every chance brought out a noble knight.
Such times have been not since the light that led
The holy Elders with the gift of myrrh.[16]
But now the whole ROUND TABLE is dissolved
235 Which was an image of the mighty world;
And I, the last, go forth companionless,
And the days darken round me, and the years,
Among new men, strange faces, other minds.'

   And slowly answered Arthur from the barge:
240 'The old order changeth, yielding place to new,
And God fulfils Himself in many ways,
Lest one good custom should corrupt the world.
Comfort thyself: what comfort is in me?
I have lived my life, and that which I have done
245 May He within Himself make pure! but thou,
If thou shouldst never see my face again,
Pray for my soul. More things are wrought by prayer
Than this world dreams of. Wherefore, let thy voice
Rise like a fountain for me night and day.
250 For what are men better than sheep or goats
That nourish a blind life within the brain,
If, knowing God, they lift not hands of prayer
Both for themselves and those who call them friend?
For so the whole round earth is every way
255 Bound by gold chains about the feet of God.
But now farewell. I am going a long way
With these thou seëst—if indeed I go—
(For all my mind is clouded with a doubt)
To the island-valley of Avilion;[17]
260 Where falls not hail, or rain, or any snow,
Nor ever wind blows loudly; but it lies
Deep-meadowed, happy, fair with orchard-lawns
And bowery hollows crowned with summer sea,
Where I will heal me of my grievous wound.'

14. Helmet.
15. Armour for the legs ("greaves") and thighs
("cuisses"), here covered with blood from battle ("onset").
16. The star of Bethlehem which led the three wise men
to the infant Christ.
17. Avalon, the Earthly Paradise to which heroes are
taken after death and from which Arthur will one day
return.

265   So said he, and the barge with oar and sail
       Moved from the brink, like some full-breasted swan
       That, fluting a wild carol ere her death,
       Ruffles her pure cold plume, and takes the flood
       With swarthy webs. Long stood Sir Bedivere
270   Revolving many memories, till the hull
       Looked one black dot against the verge of dawn,
       And on the mere the wailing died away.

Break, Break, Break

Break, break, break,
   On thy cold gray stones, O Sea!
And I would that my tongue could utter
   The thoughts that arise in me.

O well for the fisherman's boy,
   That he shouts with his sister at play!
O well for the sailor lad,
   That he sings in his boat on the bay!

And the stately ships go on
   To their haven under the hill;
But O for the touch of a vanished hand,
   And the sound of a voice that is still!

Break, break, break,
   At the foot of thy crags, O Sea!
But the tender grace of a day that is dead
   Will never come back to me.

Song from The Princess

Tears, Idle Tears[1]

   'Tears, idle tears, I know not what they mean,
Tears from the depth of some divine despair
Rise in the heart, and gather to the eyes,
In looking on the happy Autumn-fields,
And thinking of the days that are no more.

   'Fresh as the first beam glittering on a sail,
That brings our friends up from the underworld,
Sad as the last which reddens over one
That sinks with all we love below the verge;
So sad, so fresh, the days that are no more.

   'Ah, sad and strange as in dark summer dawns
The earliest pipe of half-awakened birds
To dying ears, when unto dying eyes
The casement slowly grows a glimmering square;
So sad, so strange, the days that are no more.

   'Dear as remembered kisses after death,
And sweet as those by hopeless fancy feigned
On lips that are for others; deep as love,
Deep as first love, and wild with all regret;
O Death in Life, the days that are no more.'

1. Tennyson said of this poem: "This song came to me on
the yellowing autumn-tide at Tintern Abbey, full for me of
its bygone memories. It is the sense of the abiding in the
transient." Tintern Abbey would have associations for
Tennyson not only with Wordsworth's "Tintern Abbey"
but also perhaps with Arthur Hallam (see note to "In the
Valley of Cauteretz") who was buried nearby.

In the Valley of Cauteretz

All along the valley, stream that flashest white,
Deepening thy voice with the deepening of the night,
All along the valley, where thy waters flow,
I walked with one[1] I loved two and thirty years ago.
All along the valley, while I walked today,
The two and thirty years were a mist that rolls away;
For all along the valley, down thy rocky bed,
Thy living voice to me was as the voice of the dead,
And all along the valley, by rock and cave and tree,
The voice of the dead was a living voice to me.

Flower in the Crannied Wall

Flower in the crannied wall,
I pluck you out of the crannies,
I hold you here, root and all, in my hand,
Little flower—but *if* I could understand
What you are, root and all, and all in all,
I should know what God and man is.

Crossing the Bar

Sunset and evening star,
    And one clear call for me!
And may there be no moaning of the bar,
    When I put out to sea,

But such a tide as moving seems asleep,
    Too full for sound and foam,
When that which drew from out the boundless deep
    Turns again home.

Twilight and evening bell,
    And after that the dark!
And may there be no sadness of farewell,
    When I embark;

For though from out our bourne of Time and Place
    The flood may bear me far,
I hope to see my Pilot[1] face to face
    When I have crost the bar.

ROBERT BROWNING (1812-89)

Porphyria's Lover[1]

The rain set early in tonight,
    The sullen wind was soon awake,
It tore the elm-tops down for spite,
    And did its worst to vex the lake:
5   I listened with heart fit to break.

When glided in Porphyria; straight
    She shut the cold out and the storm,
And kneeled and made the cheerless grate
    Blaze up, and all the cottage warm;
10   Which done, she rose, and from her form

1. Guide, particularly one employed to conduct a ship in and out of port.

1. The general title of "Madhouse Cells" which Browning once assigned to this poem and a companion piece is indicative of its psychologically complex presentation of an abnormal mind.

1. Arthur Hallam, the young Tennyson's closest friend, whose untimely death at the age of twenty-two in 1833 had a profound and lasting effect on the poet. Cauteretz is in the Pyrenees Mountains on the border between France and Spain.

Withdrew the dripping cloak and shawl,
   And laid her soiled gloves by, untied
Her hat and let the damp hair fall,
   And, last, she sat down by my side
15   And called me. When no voice replied,
She put my arm about her waist,
   And made her smooth white shoulder bare,
And all her yellow hair displaced,
   And, stooping, made my cheek lie there,
20   And spread, o'er all, her yellow hair,
Murmuring how she loved me—she
   Too weak, for all her heart's endeavour,
To set its struggling passion free
   From pride, and vainer ties dissever,
25   And give herself to me for ever.
But passion sometimes would prevail,
   Nor could tonight's gay feast restrain
A sudden thought of one so pale
   For love of her, and all in vain:
30   So, she was come through wind and rain.
Be sure I looked up at her eyes
   Happy and proud; at last I knew
Porphyria worshipped me; surprise
   Made my heart swell, and still it grew
35   While I debated what to do.

That moment she was mine, mine, fair,
   Perfectly pure and good: I found
A thing to do, and all her hair
   In one long yellow string I wound
40   Three times her little throat around,
And strangled her. No pain felt she;
   I am quite sure she felt no pain.
As a shut bud that holds a bee,
   I warily oped her lids: again
45   Laughed the blue eyes without a stain.
And I untightened next the tress
   About her neck; her cheek once more
Blushed bright beneath my burning kiss:
   I propped her head up as before,
50   Only, this time my shoulder bore
Her head, which droops upon it still:
   The smiling rosy little head,
So glad it has its utmost will,
   That all it scorned at once is fled,
55   And I, its love, am gained instead!
Porphyria's love: she guessed not how
   Her darling one wish would be heard.
And thus we sit together now,
   And all night long we have not stirred,
60   And yet God has not said a word!

Soliloquy of the Spanish Cloister

I
Gr-r-r—there go, my heart's abhorrence!
   Water your damned flower-pots, do!
If hate killed men, Brother Lawrence,
   God's blood, would not mine kill you!
5   What? your myrtle-bush wants trimming?
   Oh, that rose has prior claims—
Needs its leaden vase filled brimming?
   Hell dry you up with its flames!

II
At the meal we sit together:
10   *Salve tibi!*[1] I must hear
Wise talk of the kind of weather,
   Sort of season, time of year:
Not a plenteous cork-crop: scarcely
   Dare we hope oak-galls,[2] *I doubt:*
15   *What's the Latin name for 'parsley'?*
   What's the Greek name for Swine's Snout?[3]

III
Whew! We'll have our platter burnished,
   Laid with care on our own shelf!
With a fire-new spoon we're furnished,
20   And a goblet for ourself,
Rinsed like something sacrificial
   Ere 'tis fit to touch our chaps[4]—
Marked with L. for our initial!
   (He-he! There his lily snaps!)

IV
25   *Saint,* forsooth! While brown Dolores
   Squats outside the Convent bank
With Sanchicha, telling stories,
   Steeping tresses in the tank,
Blue-black, lustrous, thick like horsehairs,
30   —Can't I see his dead eye glow,
Bright as 'twere a Barbary corsair's?[5]
   (That is, if he'd let it show!)

V
When he finishes refection,[6]
   Knife and fork he never lays
35   Cross-wise, to my recollection,
   As do I, in Jesu's praise.
I the Trinity illustrate,
   Drinking watered orange-pulp—
In three sips the Arian[7] frustrate;
40   While he drains his at one gulp.

VI
Oh, those melons? If he's able
   We're to have a feast! so nice!
One goes to the Abbot's table,
   All of us get each a slice.
45   How go on your flowers? None double?
   Not one fruit-sort can you spy?
Strange!—And I, too, at such trouble,
   Keep them close-nipped on the sly!

1. (Latin) "Hail to thee!"
2. Abnormal growth on the bark or leaves of the oak tree. Used in dyeing and in making ink.
3. Dandelion (in Latin *rostrum porcinum*).
4. Cheeks.

5. A pirate ("corsair") from the Barbary coast of North Africa.
6. A meal. Refreshment after hunger or fatigue.
7. An heretical follower of Arius (256–336) who denied that Christ is of the same substance as God and questioned the doctrine of the Holy Trinity.

VII

There's a great text in Galatians,[8]
50   Once you trip on it, entails
Twenty-nine distinct damnations,
    One sure, if another fails:
If I trip him just a-dying,
    Sure of heaven as sure can be,
55 Spin him round and send him flying
    Off to hell, a Manichee?[9]

VIII

Or, my scrofulous[10] French novel
    On grey paper with blunt type!
Simply glance at it, you grovel
60   Hand and foot in Belial's gripe:[11]
If I double down its pages
    At the woeful sixteenth print,
When he gathers his greengages,[12]
    Ope a sieve and slip it in't?

IX

65 Or, there's Satan!—one might venture
    Pledge one's soul to him, yet leave
Such a flaw in the indenture[13]
    As he'd miss till, past retrieve,
Blasted lay that rose-acacia
70   We're so proud of! *Hy, Zy, Hine*[14]...
'St, there's Vespers![15] *Plena gratiâ*
    Ave, Virgo![16] Gr-r-r—you swine!

My Last Duchess[1]
Ferrara

That's my last Duchess painted on the wall,
Looking as if she were alive. I call
That piece a wonder, now: Frà Pandolf's[2] hands
Worked busily a day, and there she stands.
5 Will't please you sit and look at her? I said
'Frà Pandolf' by design, for never read
Strangers like you that pictured countenance,
The depth and passion of its earnest glance,
But to myself they turned (since none puts by
10 The curtain I have drawn for you, but I)
And seemed as they would ask me, if they durst,
How such a glance came there; so, not the first
Are you to turn and ask thus. Sir, 'twas not
Her husband's presence only, called that spot
15 Of joy into the Duchess' cheek: perhaps
Frà Pandolf chanced to say 'Her mantle laps
Over my lady's wrist too much,' or 'Paint
Must never hope to reproduce the faint
Half-flush that dies along her throat:' such stuff
20 Was courtesy, she thought, and cause enough
For calling up that spot of joy. She had
A heart—how shall I say?—too soon made glad,
Too easily impressed; she liked whate'er
She looked on, and her looks went everywhere.

8. There is no such text—a mistake Browning himself acknowledged; however, see Gal. v.15–23 and Deut. xviii.15–45 for various sins and curses.
9. One who adheres to the heretical belief that everything springs from two supreme principles, the one good and the other evil, that are at war in the Universe.
10. Diseased.
11. The grip of the Devil.
12. Exquisitely flavoured plums.
13. A legal agreement with mutual covenants entered into by two or more people.
14. These are probably the most discussed words in Browning. Are they an onomatopoeic rendering (or distortion) of the bell sounds? An invocation to Satan as part of a pact to blast the "rose-acacia"? A slurred version of a Mass refrain? Nonsense words to conjure demons? A malicious snarl? A conjuration of Mars derived from a medieval

manual of magic formulae which the monk is rehearsing to use later for the destruction of the "rose-acacia"?
15. Evening service announced by the ringing of a summoning bell.
16. "Full of grace, / Hail, Virgin"; the speaker is inverting the normal order of the words ("Hail Mary, full of grace") in the Latin prayer to the Blessed Virgin.

1. This poem is based on events in the life of Alfonso II, the first Duke of Ferrara in Italy. In 1558 he married the fourteen-year-old Lucrezia de Medici who died three years later, in 1561, with poisoning suspected. After the death of Lucrezia, the Duke negotiated, through an intermediary named Nikolaus Madruz, with Count Ferdinand I of Tyrol, whose capital was Innsbruck, for the hand of his daughter, whom he eventually married in 1565.
2. Probably a fictive painter.

25   Sir, 'twas all one! My favour at her breast,
The dropping of the daylight in the West,
The bough of cherries some officious fool
Broke in the orchard for her, the white mule
She rode with round the terrace—all and each
30   Would draw from her alike the approving speech,
Or blush, at least. She thanked men,—good! but thanked
Somehow—I know not how—as if she ranked
My gift of a nine-hundred-years-old name
With anybody's gift. Who'd stoop to blame
35   This sort of trifling? Even had you skill
In speech—(which I have not)—to make your will
Quite clear to such an one, and say, 'Just this
Or that in you digusts me; here you miss,
Or there exceed the mark'—and if she let
40   Herself be lessoned so, nor plainly set
Her wits to yours, forsooth, and made excuse,
—E'en then would be some stooping; and I choose
Never to stoop. Oh sir, she smiled, no doubt,
Whene'er I passed her; but who passed without
45   Much the same smile? This grew; I gave commands;[3]
Then all smiles stopped together. There she stands
As if alive. Will't please you rise? We'll meet
The company below, then. I repeat,
The Count your master's known munificence
50   Is ample warrant that no just pretence
Of mine for dowry will be disallowed;
Though his fair daughter's self, as I avowed
At starting, is my object. Nay, we'll go
Together down, sir. Notice Neptune, though,
55   Taming a sea-horse, thought a rarity,
Which Claus of Innsbruck[4] cast in bronze for me!

Home-Thoughts, from Abroad[1]

I

Oh, to be in England
Now that April's there,
And whoever wakes in England
Sees, some morning, unaware,
That the lowest boughs and the brushwood sheaf
Round the elm-tree bole are in tiny leaf,
While the chaffinch sings on the orchard bough
In England—now!

II

And after April, when May follows,
And the whitethroat builds, and all the swallows!
Hark, where my blossomed pear-tree in the hedge
Leans to the field and scatters on the clover
Blossoms and dewdrops—at the bent spray's edge—
That's the wise thrush; he sings each song twice over,
Lest you should think he never could recapture
The first fine careless rapture!
And though the fields look rough with hoary dew,
All will be gay when noontide wakes anew
The buttercups, the little children's dower[2]
—Far brighter than this gaudy melon-flower!

---

4. Probably a fictive sculptor.

3. According to H. Corson in his *Introduction to the Study of Browning's Poetry* (1903), Browning said: "I meant that the commands were that she should be put to death. . . . Or he might have had her shut up in a convent."

1. Browning was in Italy in 1838 and in 1844, but on neither occasion in the spring.
2. Gift.

The Bishop Orders His Tomb at Saint Praxed's Church[1]
Rome, 15—

Vanity, saith the preacher, vanity![2]
Draw round my bed: is Anselm keeping back?
Nephews—sons mine...ah God, I know not! Well—
She, men would have to be your mother once,
5   Old Gandolf envied me, so fair she was!
What's done is done, and she is dead beside,
Dead long ago, and I am Bishop since,
And as she died so must we die ourselves,
And thence ye may perceive the world's a dream.
10   Life, how and what is it? As here I lie
In this state-chamber, dying by degrees,
Hours and long hours in the dead night, I ask
'Do I live, am I dead?' Peace, peace seems all.
Saint Praxed's ever was the church for peace;
15   And so, about this tomb of mine. I fought
With tooth and nail to save my niche, ye know:
—Old Gandolf cozened[3] me, despite my care;
Shrewd was that snatch from out the corner South
He graced his carrion with, God curse the same!
20   Yet still my niche is not so cramped but thence
One sees the pulpit o' the epistle-side,[4]
And somewhat of the choir, those silent seats,
And up into the airy dome where live
The angels, and a sunbeam's sure to lurk:
25   And I shall fill my slab of basalt[5] there,
And 'neath my tabernacle[6] take my rest,
With those nine columns round me, two and two,
The odd one at my feet where Anselm stands:
Peach-blossom marble all, the rare, the ripe
30   As fresh-poured red wine of a mighty pulse.
—Old Gandolf with his paltry onion-stone,[7]
Put me where I may look at him! True peach,
Rosy and flawless: how I earned the prize!
Draw close: that conflagration of my church
35   —What then? So much was saved if aught were missed!
My sons, ye would not be my death? Go dig
The white-grape vineyard where the oil-press stood,
Drop water gently till the surface sink,
And if ye find...Ah God, I know not, I!...
40   Bedded in store of rotten fig-leaves soft,
And corded up in a tight olive-frail,[8]
Some lump, ah God, of *lapis lazuli*,[9]
Big as a Jew's head cut off at the nape,[10]
Blue as a vein o'er the Madonna's breast...
45   Sons, all have I bequeathed you, villas, all,
That brave Frascati[11] villa with its bath,
So, let the blue lump poise between my knees,

1. In *Modern Painters* IV.xx.34, John Ruskin says of this poem: "I know no other piece of modern English...in which there is so much told, as in these lines, of the Renaissance spirit,—its worldliness, inconsistency, pride, hypocrisy, ignorance of itself, love of art, of luxury, and of good Latin." Santa Prassede's Basilica, which is named for the second-century virgin saint who gave her riches to the Church and to the poor, is in Rome. Although Browning's Bishop, and his predecessor, Gandolf, are fictive, various historical personages, including Cardinal Ippolito d'Este the Younger and the uncle of the Duke in "My Last Duchess," have been proposed as models for the Bishop.
2. See Eccl. i.2: "Vanity of vanities, saith the Preacher, vanity of vanities; all is vanity."

3. Tricked.
4. The Epistle is read from the right side of the altar (as one faces it) during Mass.
5. Dark gray or black stone.
6. See Exod. xxv–xxviii regarding the tabernacle which Moses is orderd by the Lord to construct.
7. An inferior quality of marble.
8. Basket.
9. Rich blue stone used for ornamental purposes.
10. The Bishop is perhaps thinking of John the Baptist's head.
11. Picturesque town near Rome, famous as a resort and for its wine.

Like God the Father's globe on both his hands
Ye worship in the Jesu Church[12] so gay,
50 For Gandolf shall not choose but see and burst!
Swift as a weaver's shuttle fleet our years:[13]
Man goeth to the grave, and where is he?[14]
Did I say basalt for my slab, sons? Black[15]—
'Twas ever antique-black I meant! How else
55 Shall ye contrast my frieze[16] to come beneath?
The bas-relief in bronze ye promised me,
Those Pans and Nymphs ye wot[17] of, and perchance
Some tripod, thyrsus, with a vase or so,
The Saviour at his sermon on the mount,
60 Saint Praxed in a glory, and one Pan
Ready to twitch the Nymph's last garment off,
And Moses with the tables[18] . . . but I know
Ye mark me not! What do they whisper thee,
Child of my bowels, Anselm? Ah, ye hope
65 To revel down my villas while I gasp
Bricked o'er with beggar's mouldy travertine[19]
Which Gandolf from his tomb-top chuckles at!
Nay, boys, ye love me—all of jasper,[20] then!
'Tis jasper ye stand pledged to, lest I grieve
70 My bath[21] must needs be left behind, alas!
One block, pure green as a pistachio-nut,
There's plenty jasper somewhere in the world—
And have I not Saint Praxed's ear to pray
Horses for ye, and brown Greek manuscripts,
75 And mistresses with great smooth marbly limbs?
—That's if ye carve my epitaph aright,
Choice Latin, picked phrase, Tully's[22] every word,
No gaudy ware like Gandolf's second line—
Tully, my masters? Ulpian[23] serves his need!
80 And then how I shall lie through centuries,
And hear the blessed mutter of the mass,
And see God made and eaten all day long,[24]
And feel the steady candle-flame, and taste
Good strong thick stupefying incense-smoke!
85 For as I lie here, hours of the dead night,
Dying in state and by such slow degrees,
I fold my arms as if they clasped a crook,[25]
And stretch my feet forth straight as stone can point,
And let the bedclothes, for a mortcloth,[26] drop
90 Into great laps and folds of sculptor's-work:
And as yon tapers dwindle, and strange thoughts
Grow, with a certain humming in my ears,
About the life before I lived this life,
And this life too, popes, cardinals and priests,

12. The Chiesa del Gesu in Rome has an altar with a representation of the Holy Trinity in which an angel holds a large globe of lapis lazuli.
13. See Job vii.6: "My days are swifter than a weaver's shuttle, and are spent without hope."
14. See Job vii.9: "Man giveth up the ghost, and where is he?"
15. A valuable black stone.
16. A sculptured or ornamented band.
17. Know.
18. The Bishop wants a bas-relief (i.e., a sculpture consisting of a flat surface with slightly raised figures) combining, in the Renaissance manner, Christian with Pagan motifs—Christ, Moses, and St. Praxed in a halo ("a glory") with Pan, known in Greek mythology for his lustful pursuit of various Nymphs, and such emblems of the good life as a "tripod," a three-legged stool associated with priestesses, and a "thyrsus," a processional staff associated with Bacchus, the god of wine, revelry, and fertility.
19. Limestone.
20. Coloured quartz used for decorative purposes.
21. Building in which people bathe.
22. Marcus Tullius Cicero (106–43 B.C.), Roman writer renowned for his elegant and ornate style.
23. Domitius Ulpianus (A.D. 170–228), a voluminous and inferior Roman writer.
24. A reference to the Roman Catholic doctrine of transubstantiation.
25. The staff of a bishop.
26. Pall.

95 Saint Praxed at his sermon on the mount,[27]
  Your tall pale mother with her talking eyes,
  And new-found agate urns as fresh as day,
  And marble's language, Latin pure, discreet,
  —Aha, ELUCESCEBAT[28] quoth our friend?
100 No Tully, said I, Ulpian at the best!
  Evil and brief hath been my pilgrimage.[29]
  All *lapis*, all, sons! Else I give the Pope
  My villas! Will ye ever eat my heart?
  Ever your eyes were as a lizard's quick,
105 They glitter like your mother's for my soul,
  Or ye would heighten my impoverished frieze,
  Piece out its starved design, and fill my vase
  With grapes, and add a vizor and a Term,[30]
  And to the tripod ye would tie a lynx
110 That in his struggle throws the thyrsus down,
  To comfort me on my entablature[31]
  Whereon I am to lie till I must ask
  'Do I live, am I dead?' There, leave me, there!
  For ye have stabbed me with ingratitude
115 To death—ye wish it—God, ye wish it! Stone—
  Gritstone,[32] a-crumble! Clammy squares which sweat
  As if the corpse they keep were oozing through—
  And no more *lapis* to delight the world!
  Well go! I bless ye. Fewer tapers there,
120 But in a row: and, going, turn your backs
  —Ay, like departing altar-ministrants,
  And leave me in my church, the church for peace,
  That I may watch at leisure if he leers—
  Old Gandolf, at me, from his onion-stone,
125 As still he envied me, so fair she was!

Childe Roland to the Dark Tower Came
(See Edgar's song in *Lear*)[1]

I

My first thought was, he lied in every word,
 That hoary cripple, with malicious eye
 Askance[2] to watch the working of his lie
On mine, and mouth scarce able to afford
5 Suppression of the glee, that pursed and scored
 Its edge, at one more victim gained thereby.

27. The fact that the Bishop mixes up St. Praxed and Christ indicates that his mind is confused. There is also the possibility that the Bishop, who seems to think St. Praxed was a man ("*his* sermon"), is confused regarding the gender of his church's saint. Browning wrote that "the blunder as to the sermon is the result of the dying man's haziness. He would not reveal himself as he does but for that."
28. "He was illustrious." In the "pure, discreet" Latin of Cicero the word would be *elucebat*.
29. See Gen. xlvii.9: "The days of the years of my pilgrimage are anhundred and thirty years: few and evil have the days of the years of my life been."
30. "Visor": the moveable face guard of a helmet, a mask. "Term": a statuary bust in continuity with its pedestal.
31. This word is misused; Browning may have been thinking of an entablement—a platform supporting a statue or effigy.
32. Coarse, cheap sandstone.

1. The title of this poem comes from Shakespeare's *King Lear* III.iv.187–90, where it is spoken by Edgar disguised as a madman. (Browning originally thought that the words were spoken by the Fool.) A "Childe" is a youth of high birth before he has advanced to the status of a Knight. Browning maintained that the poem came to him "as a kind of dream" and that it was written in one day. He also stated that it was "only a fantasy" with "no allegorical intention," though when asked if it meant "he that endureth to the end shall be saved" he replied "Just about that." The poem has been the subject of much interest and controversy among the critics, who have suggested numerous debts in the poem (e.g., to the stories of *Jack the Giant-Killer* and *Jack and the Beanstalk*, to medieval quest literature, to Dante's *Inferno*, XXXI, and to Bunyan's *Pilgrim's Progress*) and have attempted, despite Browning's statement of intention, to read it allegorically in terms, for example, of the industrialization of England, of Browning's creative career, of a coming to maturity, and so on.
2. Sideways, obliquely out of the corner of the eye.

II

What else should he be set for, with his staff?
    What, save to waylay with his lies, ensnare
    All travellers who might find him posted there,
10 And ask the road? I guessed what skull-like laugh
Would break, what crutch 'gin write my epitaph
    For pastime in the dusty thoroughfare,

III

If at his counsel I should turn aside
    Into that ominous tract which, all agree,
15   Hides the Dark Tower. Yet acquiescingly
I did turn as he pointed: neither pride
Nor hope rekindling at the end descried,
    So much as gladness that some end might be.

IV

For, what with my whole world-wide wandering,
20   What with my search drawn out through years, my hope
    Dwindled into a ghost not fit to cope
With that obstreperous joy success would bring,—
I hardly tried now to rebuke the spring
    My heart made, finding failure in its scope.

V

25 As when a sick man very near to death[3]
    Seems dead indeed, and feels begin and end
    The tears and takes the farewell of each friend,
And hears one bid the other go, draw breath
Freelier outside, ('since all is o'er,' he saith,
30   'And the blow fallen no grieving can amend;')

VI

While some discuss if near the other graves
    Be room enough for this, and when a day
    Suits best for carrying the corpse away,
With care about the banners, scarves and staves:
35 And still the man hears all, and only craves
    He may not shame such tender love and stay.

VII

Thus, I had so long suffered in this quest,
    Heard failure prophesied so oft, been writ
    So many times among 'The Band'—to wit,
40 The knights who to the Dark Tower's search addressed
Their steps—that just to fail as they, seemed best,
    And all the doubt was now—should I be fit?

VIII

So, quiet as despair, I turned from him,
    That hateful cripple, out of his highway
45   Into the path he pointed. All the day
Had been a dreary one at best, and dim
Was settling to its close, yet shot one grim
    Red leer to see the plain catch its estray.[4]

IX

For mark! no sooner was I fairly found
50   Pledged to the plain, after a pace or two,
    Than, pausing to throw backward a last view

---

3. See John Donne, "A Valediction: Forbidding Mourning," ll. 1–4 and Tennyson, *The Princess* VII.136–39.

4. Stray animal.

O'er the safe road, 'twas gone; grey plain all round:
Nothing but plain to the horizon's bound.
    I might go on; naught else remained to do.

X

55 So, on I went. I think I never saw
    Such starved ignoble nature; nothing throve:
    For flowers—as well expect a cedar grove!
But cockle, spurge,[5] according to their law
Might propagate their kind, with none to awe,
60   You'd think; a burr had been a treasure-trove.

XI

No! penury, inertness and grimace,
    In some strange sort, were the land's portion, 'See
    Or shut your eyes,' said Nature peevishly,
'It nothing skills:[6] I cannot help my case:
65 'Tis the Last Judgement's fire must cure this place,
    Calcine[7] its clods and set my prisoners free.'

XII

If there pushed any ragged thistle-stalk
    Above its mates, the head was chopped; the bents[8]
    Were jealous else. What made those holes and rents
70 In the dock's[9] harsh swarth leaves, bruised as to balk
All hope of greenness? 'tis a brute must walk
    Pashing[10] their life out, with a brute's intents.

XIII

As for the grass, it grew as scant as hair
    In leprosy; thin dry blades pricked the mud
75   Which underneath looked kneaded up with blood.
One stiff blind horse,[11] his every bone a-stare,
Stood stupefied, however he came there:
    Thrust out past service from the devil's stud!

XIV

Alive? he might be dead for aught I know,
80   With that red gaunt and colloped[12] neck a-strain,
    And shut eyes underneath the rusty mane;
Seldom went such grotesqueness with such woe;
I never saw a brute I hated so;
    He must be wicked to deserve such pain.

XV

85 I shut my eyes and turned them on my heart.
    As a man calls for wine before he fights,
    I asked one draught of earlier, happier sights,
Ere fitly I could hope to play my part.
Think first, fight afterwards—the soldier's art:
90   One taste of the old time sets all to rights.

XVI

Not it! I fancied Cuthbert's reddening face
    Beneath its garniture of curly gold,
    Dear fellow, till I almost felt him fold

---

5. Types of weed.
6. It is no use.
7. To reduce to powder through the action of heat.
8. Coarse grass such as that found on neglected ground.
9. Coarse plants, troublesome weeds.
10. Crushing, trampling.

11. Browning maintained that the portrait of the horse derived from a tapestry which he owned, but Edgar Allan Poe's "Metzengerstein" has been suggested as another source of inspiration.
12. Beaten, ridged.

An arm in mine to fix me to the place,
95   That way he used. Alas, one night's disgrace!
  Out went my heart's new fire and left it cold.

XVII

Giles then, the soul of honour—there he stands
  Frank as ten years ago when knighted first.
  What honest man should dare (he said) he durst.
100 Good—but the scene shifts—faugh! what hangman-hands
Pin to his breast a parchment? His own bands
  Read it. Poor traitor, spit upon and curst!

XVIII

Better this present than a past like that;
  Back therefore to my darkening path again!
105 No sound, no sight as far as eye could strain.
Will the night send a howlet[13] or a bat?
I asked: when something on the dismal flat
  Came to arrest my thoughts and change their train.

XIX

A sudden little river crossed my path
110 As unexpected as a serpent comes.
  No sluggish tide congenial to the glooms;
This, as it frothed by, might have been a bath
For the fiend's glowing hoof—to see the wrath
  Of its black eddy bespate[14] with flakes and spumes.

XX

115 So petty yet so spiteful! All along,
  Low scrubby alders kneeled down over it;
  Drenched willows flung them headlong in a fit
Of mute despair, a suicidal throng:
The river which had done them all the wrong,
120 Whate'er that was, rolled by, deterred no whit.

XXI

Which, while I forded,—good saints, how I feared
  To set my foot upon a dead man's cheek,
  Each step, or feel the spear I thrust to seek
For hollows, tangled in his hair or beard!
125 —It may have been a water-rat I speared,
  But, ugh! it sounded like a baby's shriek.

XXII

Glad was I when I reached the other bank.
  Now for a better country. Vain presage!
  Who were the strugglers, what war did they wage,
130 Whose savage trample thus could pad[15] the dank
Soil to a plash?[16] Toads in a poisoned tank,
  Or wild cats in a red-hot iron cage—

XXIII

The fight must so have seemed in that fell cirque.[17]
  What penned them there, with all the plain to choose?
135 No foot-print leading to that horrid mews,[18]
None out of it. Mad brewage set to work
Their brains, no doubt, like galley-slaves the Turk
  Pits for his pastime, Christians against Jews.

13. Owl.
14. Bespattered.
15. Tread.
16. Shallow pool, puddle.

17. A kind of circular valley among mountains. An amphitheatre.
18. See note 11 to "Fra Lippo Lippi."

XXIV

And more than that—a furlong on—why, there!
140   What bad use was that engine for, that wheel,
        Or brake,[19] not wheel—that harrow to fit reel
Men's bodies out like silk? with all the air
Of Tophet's[20] tool, on earth left unaware,
        Or brought to sharpen its rusty teeth of steel.

XXV

145 Then came a bit of stubbed[21] ground, once a wood,
        Next a marsh, it would seem, and now mere earth
        Desperate and done with; (so a fool finds mirth,
Makes a thing and then mars it, till his mood
Changes and off he goes!) within a rood[22]—
150   Bog, clay and rubble, sand and stark black dearth.

XXVI

Now blotches rankling, coloured gay and grim,
        Now patches where some leanness of the soil's
        Broke into moss or substances like boils;
Then came some palsied oak, a cleft in him
155 Like a distorted mouth that splits its rim
        Gaping at death, and dies while it recoils.

XXVII

And just as far as ever from the end!
        Naught in the distance but the evening, naught
        To point my footstep further! At the thought,
160 A great black bird, Apollyon's[23] bosom-friend,
Sailed past, nor beat his wide wing dragon-penned[24]
        That brushed my cap—perchance the guide I sought.

XXVIII

For, looking up, aware I somehow grew,
        'Spite of the dusk, the plain had given place
165   All round to mountains—with such name to grace
Mere ugly heights and heaps now stolen in view.
How thus they had surprised me,—solve it, you!
        How to get from them was no clearer case.

XXIX

Yet half I seemed to recognize some trick
170   Of mischief happened to me, God knows when—
        In a bad dream perhaps. Here ended, then,
Progress this way. When, in the very nick
Of giving up, one time more, came a click
        As when a trap shuts—you're inside the den!

XXX

175 Burningly it came on me all at once,
        This was the place! those two hills on the right,
        Crouched like two bulls locked horn in horn in fight;
While to the left, a tall scalped mountain . . . Dunce,
Dotard,[25] a-dozing at the very nonce,
180   After a life spent training for the sight!

---

19. A large, heavy harrow used for breaking clods, here
seen as an instrument of torture, like a rack.
20. In the Bible, an accursed, hell-like place.
21. Abounding in stumps (stubs).
22. A quarter of an acre.

23. A creature from "the bottomless pit" in Rev. ix.11 and
a monster with "wings like a dragon" in *Pilgrim's Progress*.
24. Winged.
25. Stupid ("Dunce"), senile ("Dotard") person.

XXXI

What in the midst lay but the Tower itself?
   The round squat turret, blind as the fool's heart,[26]
   Built of brown stone, without a counterpart
In the whole world. The tempest's mocking elf
185   Points to the shipman thus the unseen shelf
   He strikes on, only when the timbers start.

XXXII

Not see? because of night perhaps?—why, day
   Came back again for that! before it left,
   The dying sunset kindled through a cleft:
190   The hills, like giants at a hunting, lay,
Chin upon hand, to see the game at bay,—
   'Now stab and end the creature—to the heft!'[27]

XXXIII

Not hear? when noise was everywhere? it tolled
   Increasing like a bell. Names in my ears
195   Of all the lost adventurers my peers,—
How such a one was strong, and such was bold,
And such was fortunate, yet each of old
   Lost, lost! one moment knelled the woe of years.

XXXIV

There they stood, ranged along the hill-sides, met
200   To view the last of me, a living frame
   For one more picture! in a sheet of flame
I saw them and I knew them all. And yet
Dauntless the slug-horn[28] to my lips I set,
   And blew. *'Childe Roland to the Dark Tower came.'*

Fra Lippo Lippi[1]

I am poor brother Lippo, by your leave!
You need not clap your torches to my face.
Zooks,[2] what's to blame? you think you see a monk!
What, 'tis past midnight, and you go the rounds,
5   And here you catch me at an alley's end
Where sportive ladies leave their doors ajar?
The Carmine's[3] my cloister: hunt it up,
Do,—harry out, if you must show your zeal,
Whatever rat, there, haps on his wrong hole,
10   And nip each softling of a wee white mouse,
Weke, weke, that's crept to keep him company!
Aha, you know your betters! Then, you'll take
Your hand away that's fiddling on my throat,
And please to know me likewise. Who am I?
15   Why, one, sir, who is lodging with a friend
Three streets off—he's a certain . . . how d'ye call?
Master—a . . . Cosimo of the Medici,[4]
I' the house that caps the corner. Boh! you were best!

26. See Ps. xiv.1: "The fool hath said in his heart, there is no God. They are corrupt, they have done abominable works, there is none that doeth good."
27. Handle of sword or dagger.
28. "Slughorn" means war-cry or slogan. Apparently Browning was mislead by the poet Chatterton's use of the word to mean trumpet or horn. Both meanings are pertinent to the conclusion of the poem.

1. Information on Fra Lippo Lippi (1406–69) gleaned by Browning from Georgio Vasari's *Lives of the Artists* (1550) was probably augmented by opinions and judgements concerning the Florentine friar and painter's life and work in François Rio's *The Poetry of Christian Art* (1836, trans. 1851) and Anna Jameson's *Early Italian Painters* (1845).
2. An abbreviated form of "Gad-zooks," a minced oath apparently from "God's hooks."
3. The Carmelite monestary in Florence.
4. A powerful Florentine ruler and patron of the arts whose "house" was the Medici Riccardi Palace.

Remember and tell me, the day you're hanged,
20　How you affected such a gullet's-gripe![5]
But you, sir, it concerns you that your knaves
Pick up a manner nor discredit you:
Zooks, are we pilchards,[6] that they sweep the streets
And count fair prize what comes into their net?
25　He's Judas to a tittle, that man is![7]
Just such a face! Why, sir, you make amends.
Lord, I'm not angry! Bid your hangdogs go
Drink out this quarter-florin[8] to the health
Of the munificent House that harbours me
30　(And many more beside, lads! more beside!)
And all's come square again. I'd like his face—
His, elbowing on his comrade in the door
With the pike and lantern,—for the slave that holds
John Baptist's head a-dangle by the hair
35　With one hand ('Look you, now,' as who should say)
And his weapon in the other, yet unwiped!
It's not your chance to have bit of chalk,
A wood-coal or the like? or you should see!
Yes, I'm the painter, since you style me so.
40　What, brother Lippo's doings, up and down,
You know them and they take[9] you? like enough!
I saw the proper twinkle in your eye—
'Tell you, I liked your looks at very first.
Let's sit and set things straight now, hip to haunch.
45　Here's spring come, and the nights one makes up bands
To roam the town and sing out carnival,[10]
And I've been three weeks shut within my mew,[11]
A-painting for the great man, saints and saints
And saints again. I could not paint all night—
50　Ouf! I leaned out of window for fresh air.
There came a hurry of feet and little feet,
A sweep of lute-strings, laughs, and whifts of song,—
Flower o' the broom,
Take away love, and our earth is a tomb!
55　*Flower o' the quince,*
I let Lisa go, and what good in life since?
Flower o' the thyme[12]—and so on. Round they went.
Scarce had they turned the corner when a titter
Like the skipping of rabbits by moonlight,—three slim shapes,
60　And a face that looked up...zooks, sir, flesh and blood,
That's all I'm made of! Into shreds it went,
Curtain and counterpane and coverlet,
All the bed-furniture—a dozen knots,
There was a ladder! Down I let myself,
65　Hands and feet, scrambling somehow, and so dropped,
And after them. I came up with the fun
Hard by Saint Lawrence,[13] hail fellow, well met,—
Flower o' the rose,
If I've been merry, what matter who knows?
70　And so as I was stealing back again
To get to bed and have a bit of sleep
Ere I rise up tomorrow and go work
On Jerome[14] knocking at his poor old breast
With his great round stone to subdue the flesh,

5. How you dared to grasp the throat of such a well-connected person.
6. Small, sardine-like fish.
7. He is the image of Judas.
8. Name given to different coins of different values but first applied to a Florentine coin because it was stamped with a lily flower.
9. Appeal to you.
10. The feast or season of rejoicing that precedes Lent.
11. Cage, cell.
12. An Italian folksong beginning with a reference to a flower is called a *stornello*.
13. The church of San Lorenzo in Florence.
14. Saint Jerome (340–420), famous for his extreme asceticism.

75 You snap[15] me of the sudden. Ah, I see!
Though your eye twinkles still, you shake your head—
Mine's shaved—a monk, you say—the sting's in that!
If Master Cosimo announced himself,
Mum's the word naturally; but a monk!
80 Come, what am I a beast for? tell us, now!
I was a baby when my mother died
And father died and left me in the street.
I starved there, God knows how, a year or two
On fig-skins, melon-parings, rinds and shucks,
85 Refuse and rubbish. One fine frosty day,
My stomach being empty as your hat,
The wind doubled me up and down I went.
Old Aunt Lapaccia[16] trussed me with one hand,
(Its fellow was a stinger as I knew)
90 And so along the wall, over the bridge,
By the straight cut to the convent. Six words there,
While I stood munching my first bread that month:
'So, boy, you're minded,' quoth the good fat father
Wiping his own mouth, 'twas refection-time,[17]—
95 'To quit this very miserable world?
Will you renounce'...'the mouthful of bread?' thought I;
By no means! Brief, they made a monk of me;
I did renounce the world, its pride and greed,
Palace, farm, villa, shop and banking-house,
100 Trash, such as these poor devils of Medici
Have given their hearts to—all at eight years old.
Well, sir, I found in time, you may be sure,
'Twas not for nothing—the good bellyful,
The warm serge and the rope that goes all round,
105 And day-long blessed idleness beside!
'Let's see what the urchin's fit for'—that came next.
Not overmuch their way, I must confess.
Such a to-do! They tried me with their books:
Lord, they'd have taught me Latin in pure waste!
110 *Flower o' the clove,*
All the Latin I construe is, 'amo' I love!
But, mind you, when a boy starves in the streets
Eight years together, as my fortune was,
Watching folk's faces to know who will fling
115 The bit of half-stripped grape-bunch he desires,
And who will curse or kick him for his pains,—
Which gentleman processional and fine,
Holding a candle to the Sacrament,
Will wink and let him lift a plate and catch
120 The droppings of the wax to sell again,
Or holla for the Eight[18] and have him whipped,—
How say I?—nay, which dog bites, which lets drop
His bone from the heap of offal in the street,—
Why, soul and sense of him grow sharp alike,
125 He learns the look of things, and none the less
For admonition from the hunger-pinch.
I had a store of such remarks, be sure,
Which, after I found leisure, turned to use.
I drew men's faces on my copy-books,
130 Scrawled them within the antiphonary's marge,[19]
Joined legs and arms to the long music-notes,
Found eyes and nose and chin for A's and B's,

15. Grasp.
16. The aunt who, according to Vasari, looked after Lippo for six years after he was orphaned.
17. See note 6 to "Soliloquy of the Spanish Cloister."

18. The eight magistrates of Florence.
19. Lippi drew faces in the book containing passages for learners to imitate and in the margins of his choral music book.

And made a string of pictures of the world
Betwixt the ins and outs of verb and noun,
135   On the wall, the bench, the door. The monks looked black.
'Nay,' quoth the Prior, 'turn him out, d'ye say?
In no wise. Lose a crow and catch a lark.
What if at last we get our man of parts,
We Carmelites, like those Camaldolese
140   And Preaching Friars,[20] to do our church up fine
And put the front on it that ought to be!'
And hereupon he bade me daub away.
Thank you! my head being crammed, the walls a blank,
Never was such prompt disemburdening.
145   First, every sort of monk, the black and white,
I drew them, fat and lean: then, folk at church,
From good old gossips waiting to confess
Their cribs[21] of barrel-droppings, candle-ends,—
To the breathless fellow at the altar-foot,
150   Fresh from his murder, safe and sitting there
With the little children round him in a row
Of admiration, half for his beard and half
For that white anger of his victim's son
Shaking a fist at him with one fierce arm,
155   Signing himself with the other because of Christ
(Whose sad face on the cross sees only this
After the passion of a thousand years)
Till some poor girl, her apron o'er her head,
(Which the intense eyes looked through) came at eve
160   On tiptoe, said a word, dropped in a loaf,
Her pair of earrings and a bunch of flowers
(The brute took growling), prayed, and so was gone.
I painted all, then cried. "Tis ask and have;
Choose, for more's ready!'—laid the ladder flat,
165   And showed my covered bit of cloister-wall.
The monks closed in a circle and praised loud
Till checked, taught what to see and not to see,
Being simple bodies,—'That's the very man!
Look at the boy who stoops to pat the dog!
170   That woman's like the Prior's niece[22] who comes
To care about his asthma: it's the life!'
But there my triumph's straw-fire flared and funked;[23]
Their betters took their turn to see and say:
The Prior and the learned pulled a face
175   And stopped all that in no time. 'How? what's here?
Quite from the mark of painting, bless us all!
Faces, arms, legs and bodies like the true
As much as pea and pea! it's devil's-game!
Your business is not to catch men with show,
180   With homage to the perishable clay,
But lift them over it, ignore it all,
Make them forget there's such a thing as flesh.
Your business is to paint the souls of men—
Man's soul, and it's a fire, smoke . . . no, it's not . . .
185   It's vapour done up like a new-born babe—
(In that shape when you die it leaves your mouth)
It's . . . well, what matters talking, it's the soul!
Give us no more of body than shows soul!
Here's Giotto,[24] with his Saint a-praising God,
190   That sets us praising,—why not stop with him?

20. Different religious orders.
21. Petty thefts, filchings.
22. Here, as above (l. 136), a Prior is the superior of a
priory or a monastery; his niece is almost certainly not a
relation, but one with whom he has relations.
23. Gone up in smoke.
24. The Florentine painter (ca. 1267–1337).

Why put all thoughts of praise out of our head
With wonder at lines, colours, and what not?
Paint the soul, never mind the legs and arms!
Rub all out, try at it a second time.
195   Oh, that white smallish female with the breasts,
She's just my niece... Herodias,[25] I would say,—
Who went and danced and got men's heads cut off!
Have it all out!' Now, is this sense, I ask?
A fine way to paint soul, by painting body
200   So ill, the eye can't stop there, must go further
And can't fare worse! Thus, yellow does for white
When what you put for yellow's simply black,
And any sort of meaning looks intense
When all beside itself means and looks naught.
205   Why can't a painter lift each foot in turn,
Left foot and right foot, go a double step,
Make his flesh liker and his soul more like,
Both in their order? Take the prettiest face,
The Prior's niece... patron-saint—is it so pretty
210   You can't discover if it means hope, fear,
Sorrow or joy? won't beauty go with these?
Suppose I've made her eyes all right and blue,
Can't I take breath and try to add life's flash,
And then add soul and heighten them threefold?
215   Or say there's beauty with no soul at all—
(I never saw it—put the case the same—)
If you get simple beauty and naught else,
You get about the best thing God invents:
That's somewhat: and you'll find the soul you have missed,
220   Within yourself, when you return him thanks.
'Rub all out!' Well, well, there's my life, in short,
And so the thing has gone on ever since.
I'm grown a man no doubt, I've broken bounds:
You should not take a fellow eight years old
225   And make him swear to never kiss the girls.
I'm my own master, paint now as I please—
Having a friend, you see, in the Corner-house!
Lord, it's fast holding by the rings in front—
Those great rings serve more purposes than just
230   To plant a flag in, or tie up a horse!
And yet the old schooling sticks, the old grave eyes
Are peeping o'er my shoulder as I work,
The heads shake still—'It's art's decline, my son!
You're not of the true painters, great and old;
235   Brother Angelico's the man, you'll find;
Brother Lorenzo[26] stands his single peer:
Fag[27] on at flesh, you'll never make the third!'
Flower o' the pine,
You keep your mistr... manners, and I'll stick to mine!
240   I'm not the third, then: bless us, they must know!
Don't you think they're the likeliest to know,
They with their Latin? So, I swallow my rage,
Clench my teeth, suck my lips in tight, and paint
To please them—sometimes do and sometimes don't;
245   For, doing most, there's pretty sure to come
A turn, some warm eve finds me at my saints—
A laugh, a cry, the business of the world—
(Flower o' the peach,
Death for us all, and his own life for each!)

---

25. The mother of Salome whose dancing (not that of Herodias herself) secured for Herodias the head of John the Baptist (see Matt. xiv.1-12).

26. Fra Angelico (1387-1455) and his teacher Lorenzo Monaco (ca. 1370-ca. 1425).
27. Labour hard until exhausted.

250 And my whole soul revolves, the cup runs over,[28]
    The world and life's too big to pass for a dream,
    And I do these wild things in sheer despite,
    And play the fooleries you catch me at,
    In pure rage! The old mill-horse, out at grass
255 After hard years, throws up his stiff heels so,
    Although the miller does not preach to him
    The only good of grass is to make chaff.[29]
    What would men have? Do they like grass or no—
    May they or mayn't they? all I want's the thing
260 Settled for ever one way. As it is,
    You tell too many lies and hurt yourself:
    You don't like what you only like too much,
    You do like what, if given you at your word,
    You find abundantly detestable.
265 For me, I think I speak as I was taught;
    I always see the garden and God there
    A-making man's wife:[30] and, my lesson learned,
    The value and significance of flesh,
    I can't unlearn ten minutes afterwards.

270   You understand me: I'm a beast, I know.
    But see, now—why, I see as certainly
    As that the morning star's about to shine,
    What will hap some day. We've a youngster here
    Comes to our convent, studies what I do,
275 Slouches and stares and lets no atom drop:
    His name is Guidi[31]—he'll not mind the monks—
    They call him Hulking Tom, he lets them talk—
    He picks my practice up—he'll paint apace,
    I hope so—though I never live so long,
280 I know what's sure to follow. You be judge!
    You speak no Latin more than I, belike,
    However, you're my man, you've seen the world
    —The beauty and the wonder and the power,
    The shapes of things, their colours, lights and shades,
285 Changes, surprises,—and God made it all!
    —For what? Do you feel thankful, ay or no,
    For this fair town's face, yonder river's line,
    The mountain round it and the sky above,
    Much more the figures of man, woman, child,
290 These are the frame to? What's it all about?
    To be passed over, despised? or dwelt upon,
    Wondered at? oh, this last of course!—you say.
    But why not do as well as say,—paint these
    Just as they are, careless what comes of it?
295 God's works—paint any one, and count it crime
    To let a truth slip. Don't object, 'His works
    Are here already; nature is complete:
    Suppose you reproduce her'—(which you can't)
    'There's no advantage! you must beat her, then.'
300 For, don't you mark? we're made so that we love
    First when we see them painted, things we have passed
    Perhaps a hundred times nor cared to see;
    And so they are better, painted—better to us,
    Which is the same thing. Art was given for that;
305 God uses us to help each other so,
    Lending our minds out. Have you noticed, now,
    Your cullion's[32] hanging face? A bit of chalk,
    And trust me but you should, though! How much more,

---

28. See Ps. xxiii.5: "my cup runneth over."
29. Straw.
30. Eve in the garden of Eden.

31. Tomasso Guidi (1401–ca. 1428), nicknamed Masaccio ("Hulking Tom") was Lippi's teacher, not his pupil.
32. A low wretch.

If I drew higher things with the same truth!
310   That were to take the Prior's pulpit-place,
Interpret God to all of you! Oh, oh,
It makes me mad to see what men shall do
And we in our graves! This world's no blot for us,
Nor blank; it means intensely, and means good:
315   To find its meaning is my meat and drink.
'Ay, but you don't so instigate to prayer!'
Strikes in the Prior: 'when your meaning's plain
It does not say to folk—remember matins,[33]
Or, mind you fast next Friday!' Why, for this
320   What need of art at all? A skull and bones,
Two bits of stick nailed crosswise, or, what's best,
A bell to chime the hour with, does as well.
I painted a Saint Laurence six months since
At Prato, splashed with the fresco[34] in fine style:
325   'How looks my painting, now the scaffold's down?'
I ask a brother: 'Hugely,' he returns—
'Already not one phiz[35] of your three slaves
Who turn the Deacon off his toasted side,
But's scratched and prodded to our heart's content,
330   The pious people have so eased their own
With coming to say prayers there in a rage:
We get on fast to see the bricks beneath.
Expect another job this time next year,
For pity and religion grow i' the crowd—
335   Your painting serves its purpose!' Hang the fools!

     —That is—you'll not mistake an idle word
Spoke in a huff by a poor monk, Got wot,
Tasting the air this spicy night which turns
The unaccustomed head like Chianti[36] wine!
340   Oh, the church knows! don't misreport me, now!
It's natural a poor monk out of bounds
Should have his apt word to excuse himself:
And hearken how I plot to make amends.
I have bethought me: I shall paint a piece
345   . . . There's for you! Give me six months, then go, see,
Something in Sant' Ambrogio's![37] Bless the nuns!
They want a cast o' my office.[38] I shall paint
God in the midst, Madonna and her babe,
Ringed by a bowery flowery angel-brood,
350   Lilies and vestments and white faces, sweet
As puff on puff of grated orris-root[39]
When ladies crowd to Church at midsummer.
And then i' the front, of course a saint or two—
Saint John,[40] because he saves the Florentines,
355   Saint Ambrose,[41] who puts down in black and white
The convent's friends and gives them a long day,
And Job, I must have him there past mistake,
The man of Uz[42] (and Us without the z,
Painters who need his patience). Well, all these
360   Secured at their devotion, up shall come
Out of a corner when you least expect,
As one by a dark stair into a great light,

33. Morning prayer.
34. Lippo has depicted the martyrdom of St. Laurence, who was roasted to death in 258, in a large wall-painting ("fresco") in Prato, a town near Florence.
35. Face.
36. Strong red wine from the Chianti district of Italy.
37. A convent in Florence for which Lippi painted his *Coronation of the Virgin*, described in the succeeding lines.

38. Sample of my work.
39. Powder from the roots of certain varieties of iris was used for medicinal and cosmetic purposes.
40. The patron-saint of Florence.
41. A seeming confusion of the St. Ambrose who was the fourth-century Archbishop of Milan and Ambrose the Camaldulian (1386–1439), who was a translator of Greek theologians and a friend of Cosimo de Medici.
42. See Job. i.1.

Music and talking, who but Lippo! I!—
Mazed, motionless and moonstruck[43]—I'm the man!
365 Back I shrink—what is this I see and hear?
I, caught up with my monk's-things by mistake,
My old serge gown and rope that goes all round,
I, in this presence, this pure company!
Where's a hole, where's a corner for escape?
370 Then steps a sweet angelic slip of a thing[44]
Forward, puts out a soft palm—"Not so fast!"
—Addresses the celestial presence, 'nay—
He made you and devised you, after all,
Though he's none of you! Could Saint John there draw—
375 His camel-hair[45] make up a painting-brush?
We come to brother Lippo for all that,
Iste perfecit opus![46] So, all smile—
I shuffle sideways with my blushing face
Under the cover of a hundred wings
380 Thrown like a spread of kirtles[47] when you're gay
And play hot cockles,[48] all the doors being shut,
Till, wholly unexpected, in there pops
The hothead husband! Thus I scuttle off
To some safe bench behind, not letting go
385 The palm of her, the little lily thing
That spoke the good word for me in the nick,
Like the Prior's niece... Saint Lucy, I would say.
And so all's saved for me, and for the church
A pretty picture gained. Go, six months hence!
390 Your hand, sir, and good-bye: no lights, no lights!
The street's hushed, and I know my own way back,
Don't fear me! There's the grey beginning. Zooks!

Prospice[1]

Fear death? —to feel the fog in my throat,
    The mist in my face,
When the snows begin, and the blasts denote
    I am nearing the place,
5 The power of the night, the press of the storm,
    The post of the foe;
Where he stands, the Arch Fear in a visible form,
    Yet the strong man must go:
For the journey is done and the summit attained,
10   And the barriers fall,
Though a battle's to fight ere the guerdon[2] be gained,
    The reward of it all.
I was ever a fighter, so — one fight more,
    The best and the last!
15 I would hate that death bandaged my eyes, and forbore,
    And bade me creep past.
No! let me taste the whole of it, fare like my peers
    The heroes of old,
Bear the brunt, in a minute pay glad life's arrears

43. Confused ("Mazed") and slightly mad ("moonstruck").
44. St. Lucy (whose name means "light"), a figure in the *Coronation of the Virgin.*
45. See Mark i.6: "And John was clothed with camel's hair."
46. Latin meaning: "This man arranged the work," The words, which occur on a scroll in the *Coronation*, were thought in Browning's day to mean "This man did the work." Hence, it was thought that the figure in the painting was Lippi himself, though in fact it is Canon Maringhi, who commissioned the painting in 1441.
47. A short gown, petticoat.

48. Literally a game, but metaphorically a reference to spirited sexual activity.

1. The Latin title translates as "Look forward." This uncharacteristically personal poem probably has its origins in the poet's feelings following his wife's death in 1861, at about which time he transcribed the following translation from Dante's *Convivio* II.9: "Thus I believe, thus I affirm, thus I am certain it is, that from this life I shall pass to another, there, where the lady lives of whom my soul was enamoured."
2. Reward, requital.

20 Of pain, darkness and cold.
For sudden the worst turns the best to the brave,
   The black minute's at end,
And the elements' rage, the fiend-voices that rave,
   Shall dwindle, shall blend,
25 Shall change, shall become first a peace out of pain,
   Then a light, then thy breast,
O thou soul of my soul! I shall clasp thee again,
   And with God be the rest!

ARTHUR HUGH CLOUGH (1819–61)

The Latest Decalogue[1]

Thou shalt have one God only; who
Would be at the expense of two?
No graven images may be
Worshipped, except the currency:
5 Swear not at all; for for thy curse
Thine enemy is none the worse:
At church on Sunday to attend
Will serve to keep the world thy friend:
Honor thy parents; that is, all
10 From whom advancement may befall:
Thou shalt not kill; but needst not strive
Officiously to keep alive:
Do not adultery commit;

15 Advantage rarely comes of it:
Thou shalt not steal; an empty feat,
When it's so lucrative to cheat:
Bear not false witness; let the lie
Have time on its own wings to fly:
Thou shalt not covet; but tradition
20 Approves all forms of competition.

The sum of all is, thou shalt love,
If anybody, God above:
At any rate shall never labor
More than thyself to love thy neighbour.[2]

MATTHEW ARNOLD (1822–88)

In Harmony with Nature[1]
To a Preacher

'In harmony with Nature?' Restless fool,
Who with such heat dost preach what were to thee,
When true, the last impossibility—
To be like Nature strong, like Nature cool!

Know, man hath all which Nature hath, but more,
And in that *more* lie all his hopes of good.
Nature is cruel, man is sick of blood;
Nature is stubborn, man would fain adore;

Nature is fickle, man hath need for rest;
Nature forgives no debt, and fears no grave;
Man would be mild, and with safe conscience blest.

Man must begin, know this, where Nature ends;
Nature and man can never be fast friends.
Fool, if thou canst not pass her, rest her slave!

1. The original decalogue was the ten commandments
given to Moses by God on Mount Sinai.
2. These last four lines were not originally published with
the poem. Discovered in one of the poet's manuscripts,
they were appended to the poem in 1951.

1. Originally published under the title "To an Independent Preacher, who preached that we should be 'In
Harmony with Nature.'"

Isolation. To Marguerite[1]

We were apart; yet, day by day,
I bade my heart more constant be.
I bade it keep the world away,
And grow a home for only thee;
5 Nor feared but thy love likewise grew,
Like mine, each day, more tried, more true.

The fault was grave! I might have known,
What far too soon, alas! I learned—
The heart can bind itself alone,
10 And faith may oft be unreturned.
Self-swayed our feelings ebb and swell—
Thou lov'st no more;— Farewell! Farewell!

Farewell!— and thou, thou lonely heart,
Which never yet without remorse
15 Even for a moment didst depart
From thy remote and spheréd course
To haunt the place where passions reign—
Back to thy solitude again!

Back! with the conscious thrill of shame
20 Which Luna felt, that summer-night,
Flash through her pure immortal frame,
When she forsook the starry height
To hang over Endymion's sleep
Upon the pine-grown Latmian steep.[2]

25 Yet she, chaste queen, had never proved
How vain a thing is mortal love,
Wandering in Heaven, far removed.
But thou hast long had place to prove
This truth—to prove, and make thine own:
30 'Thou hast been, shalt be, art, alone.'

Or, if not quite alone, yet they
Which touch thee are unmating things—
Ocean and clouds and night and day;
Lorn autumns and triumphant springs;
35 And life, and others' joy and pain,
And love, if love, of happier men.

Of happier men—for they, at least,
Have *dreamed* two human hearts might blend
In one, and were through faith released
40 From isolation without end
Prolonged; nor knew, although not less
Alone than thou, their loneliness.

To Marguerite— Continued

Yes! in the sea of life enisled,
With echoing straits[1] between us thrown,
Dotting the shoreless watery wild,
We mortal millions live *alone*.
5 The islands feel the enclasping flow,
And then their endless bounds they know.

But when the moon their hollows lights,
And they are swept by balms of spring,
And in their glens, on starry nights,
10 The nightingales divinely sing;
And lovely notes, from shore to shore,
Across the sounds and channels pour —

Oh! then a longing like despair
Is to their farthest caverns sent;
15 For surely once, they feel, we were
Parts of a single continent!
Now round us spreads the watery plain —
Oh might our marges meet again!

Who ordered, that their longing's fire
20 Should be, as soon as kindled, cooled?
Who renders vain their deep desire? —
A God, a God their severance ruled!
And bade betwixt their shores to be
The unplumbed, salt, estranging sea.

Dover Beach[1]

The sea is calm to-night.
The tide is full, the moon lies fair
Upon the straits; on the French coast the light
Gleams and is gone; the cliffs of England stand,

1. This and the following poem, "To Marguerite—Continued," are amongst those inspired by a girl (whether French or English there is some dispute) whom Arnold apparently met in Switzerland in the late 1840s.
2. According to the Greek myth, it was on the slopes of Mount Latmos that the handsome shepherd Endymion was seen and beloved by Luna, the goddess of chastity and of the moon. (Note the subtle references to the moon, its effects and course, in lines 11 and 16.) Luna put

Endymion into a perpetual sleep and descended every night from the sky to embrace him.

1. Perhaps the English Channel, dividing the British Isles from the continent of Europe, but not to the exclusion of the metaphorical meanings.

1. On the English Channel roughly opposite Calais in France.

5   Glimmering and vast, out in the tranquil bay.
    Come to the window, sweet is the night-air!
    Only, from the long line of spray
    Where the sea meets the moon-blanched land,
    Listen! you hear the grating roar
10 Of pebbles which the waves draw back, and fling,
    At their return, up the high strand,
    Begin, and cease, and then again begin,
    With tremulous cadence slow, and bring
    The eternal note of sadness in.

15 Sophocles[2] long ago
    Heard it on the Ægæan, and it brought
    Into his mind the turbid[3] ebb and flow
    Of human misery; we
    Find also in the sound a thought,
20 Hearing it by this distant northern sea.

    The Sea of Faith
    Was once, too, at the full, and round earth's shore
    Lay like the folds of a bright girdle furled.[4]
    But now I only hear
25 Its melancholy, long, withdrawing roar,
    Retreating, to the breath
    Of the night-wind, down the vast edges drear
    And naked shingles[5] of the world.

    Ah, love, let us be true
30 To one another! for the world, which seems
    To lie before us like a land of dreams,
    So various, so beautiful, so new,
    Hath really neither joy, nor love, nor light,
    Nor certitude, nor peace, nor help for pain;
35 And we are here as on a darkling plain
    Swept with confused alarms of struggle and flight,
    Where ignorant armies clash by night.[6]

Lines Written in Kensington Gardens[1]

    In this lone, open glade I lie,
    Screened by deep boughs on either hand;
    And at its end, to stay the eye,
    Those black-crowned, red-boled pine-trees stand!

5   Birds here make song, each bird has his,
    Across the girdling city's hum.
    How green under the boughs it is!
    How thick the tremulous sheep-cries come!

    Sometimes a child will cross the glade
10 To take his nurse his broken toy;
    Sometimes a thrush flit overhead
    Deep in her unknown day's employ.

2. Sophocles (496–06 B.C.) was Arnold's favourite Greek dramatist; Arnold may have been thinking here of Sophocles' *Antigone*, 583 ff. or his *Trachiniae*, 112 ff.
3. Troubled, muddy.
4. The precise meaning of this line is not clear; a girdle is an item of clothing, an ornamental sash worn around the waist, but it is difficult to visualize a girdle "furled"—i.e., wrapped up—in "folds," particularly as an image applied to the sea.
5. Large pebbles and beaches covered with such pebbles.

6. Arnold's source for the final lines of the poem is Thucydides' description of the Battle of Epipolae (413 B.C.) in his *History of the Peloponnesian War* which translates in part: "The Athenians were getting into a state of . . . great confusion and perplexity . . . in a battle by night . . . how could anyone know anything clearly?" He may also have had in mind the European conflicts of 1848–49.

1. A park in the fashionable heart of London.

Here at my feet what wonders pass,
What endless, active life is here!
15   What blowing daisies, fragrant grass!
An air-stirred forest, fresh and clear.

Scarce fresher is the mountain-sod
Where the tired angler lies, stretched out,
And, eased of basket and of rod,
20   Counts his day's spoil, the spotted trout.

In the huge world, which roars hard by,
Be others happy if they can!
But in my helpless cradle I
Was breathed on by the rural Pan.²

25   I, on men's impious uproar hurled,
Think often, as I hear them rave,
That peace has left the upper world
And now keeps only in the grave.

30   Yet here is peace for ever new!
When I who watch them am away,
Still all things in this glade go through
The changes of their quiet day.

Then to their happy rest they pass!
The flowers upclose, the birds are fed,
35   The night comes down upon the grass,
The child sleeps warmly in his bed.

Calm soul of all things! make it mine
To feel, amid the city's jar,
That there abides a peace of thine,
40   Man did not make, and cannot mar.

The will to neither strive nor cry,
The power to feel with others give!
Calm, calm me more! nor let me die
Before I have begun to live.

The Scholar-Gipsy¹

Go, for they call you, shepherd,² from the hill;
    Go, shepherd, and untie the wattled cotes!³
        No longer leave thy wistful flock unfed,
    Nor let thy bawling fellows rack their throats,
5   Nor the cropped herbage shoot another head.
            But when the fields are still,
    And the tired men and dogs all gone to rest,
        And only the white sheep are sometimes seen
        Cross and recross the strips of moon-blanched green,
10   Come, shepherd, and again begin the quest!

Here, where the reaper was at work of late—
    In this high field's dark corner, where he leaves
        His coat, his basket, and his earthen cruse,⁴
    And in the sun all morning binds the sheaves,
15   Then here, at noon, comes back his stores to use—
            Here will I sit and wait,
    While to my ear from uplands far away
        The bleating of the folded flocks is borne,
        With distant cries of reapers in the corn⁵—
20   All the live murmur of a summer's day.

2. The Greek god, part man and part goat, of shepherds and flocks.

1. The following, a pastiche of sentences from Joseph Glanville's *The Vanity of Dogmatizing* (1661) which inspired "The Scholar-Gipsy," was given by Arnold as an explanatory note to the poem: "There was very lately a lad in the University at Oxford, who was by his poverty forced to leave his studies there; and at last to join himself to a company of vagabound gipsies. Among these extravagant people, by the insinuating subtility of his carriage, he quickly got so much of their love and esteem as that they discovered to him their mystery. After he had been a pretty while well ['well' dropped inadvertently *1869* and the error left uncorrected in later editions] exercised in the trade, there chanced to ride by a couple of scholars, who had formerly been of his acquaintance. They quickly spied out their old friend among the gipsies; and he gave them an account of the necessity which drove him to that kind of life, and told them that the people he went with were not such imposters as they were taken for, but that they had a traditional kind of learning among them, and could do wonders by the power of imagination, their fancy binding that of others: that himself had learned much of their art, and when he had compassed the whole secret, he intended, he said, to leave their company, and give the world an account of what he had learned." In a letter to his brother, Arnold explains that "The Scholar-Gipsy" was "meant to fix the remembrance of [the] delightful wanderings" which the pair had enjoyed with the poet's friend and fellow-poet Arthur Hugh Clough in the Cumner Hills near the university town of Oxford.
2. The shepherd who has been helping the poet in his search for traces of the "scholar-gipsy" is sometimes identified with Clough.
3. Sheepfolds constructed of woven sticks.
4. Pottery mug or bottle.
5. Wheat.

Screened is this nook o'er the high, half-reaped field,
    And here till sun-down, shepherd! will I be.
      Through the thick corn the scarlet poppies peep,
    And round green roots and yellowing stalks I see
25   Pale pink convolvulus in tendrils creep;
        And air-swept lindens yield
    Their scent, and rustle down their perfumed showers
    Of bloom on the bent grass where I am laid,
    And bower me from the August sun with shade;
30 And the eye travels down to Oxford's towers.

And near me on the grass lies Glanvil's book—
    Come, let me read the oft-read tale again!
      The story of the Oxford scholar poor,
    Of pregnant parts[6] and quick inventive brain,
35   Who, tired of knocking at preferment's door,
        One summer-morn forsook
    His friends, and went to learn the gipsy-lore,
    And roamed the world with that wild brotherhood,
    And came, as most men deemed, to little good,
40 But came to Oxford and his friends no more.

But once, years after, in the country-lanes,
    Two scholars, whom at college erst he knew,
      Met him, and of his way of life enquired;
    Whereat he answered, that the gipsy-crew,
45   His mates, had arts to rule as they desired
        The workings of men's brains,
    And they can bind them to what thoughts they will.
    'And I,' he said, 'the secret of their art,
    When fully learned, will to the world impart;
50 But it needs heaven-sent moments for this skill.'

This said, he left them, and returned no more.
    But rumours hung about the country-side,
      That the lost Scholar long was seen to stray,
    Seen by rare glimpses, pensive and tongue-tied,
55   In hat of antique shape, and cloak of grey,
        The same the gipsies wore.
    Shepherds had met him on the Hurst[7] in spring;
    At some lone alehouse in the Berkshire moors,
    On the warm ingle-bench,[8] the smock-frocked boors[9]
60 Had found him seated at their entering,

But, 'mid their drink and clatter, he would fly.
    And I myself seem half to know thy[10] looks,
      And put the shepherds, wanderer! on thy trace;
    And boys who in lone wheatfields scare the rooks
65   I ask if thou hast passed their quiet place;
        Or in my boat I lie
    Moored to the cool bank in the summer-heats,
    'Mid wide grass meadows which the sunshine fills,
    And watch the warm, green-muffled Cumner hills,
70 And wonder if thou haunt'st their shy retreats.

---

6. Full of ideas.
7. Cumner Hurst, a hill near Oxford. Until the final two
stanzas, the place-names mentioned refer to features of
the country-side surrounding Oxford.

8. Fire-side seat.
9. Countryfolk.
10. The "scholar-gipsy" is now being addressed.

For most, I know, thou lov'st retiréd ground!
  Thee at the ferry Oxford riders blithe,
    Returning home on summer-nights, have met
  Crossing the stripling Thames[11] at Bab-lock-hithe,
75   Trailing in the cool stream thy fingers wet,
      As the punt's rope chops round;[12]
  And leaning backward in a pensive dream,
    And fostering in thy lap a heap of flowers
    Plucked in shy fields and distant Wychwood bowers,
80 And thine eyes resting on the moonlit stream.

And then they land, and thou art seen no more!
  Maidens, who from the distant hamlets come
    To dance around the Fyfield elm in May,
  Oft through the darkening fields have seen thee roam,
85   Or cross a stile into the public way.
      Oft thou hast given them store
Of flowers—the frail-leafed, white anemone,[13]
    Dark bluebells drenched with dews of summer eves,
    And purple orchises[14] with spotted leaves—
90 But none hath words she can report of thee.

And, above Godstow Bridge, when hay-time's here
  In June, and many a scythe in sunshine flames,
    Men who through those wide fields of breezy grass
  Where black-winged swallows haunt the glittering Thames,
95   To bathe in the abandoned lasher pass,[15]
      Have often passed thee near
Sitting upon the river bank o'ergrown;
    Marked thine outlandish garb, thy figure spare,
    Thy dark vague eyes, and soft abstracted air—
100 But, when they came from bathing, thou wast gone!

At some lone homestead in the Cumner hills,
  Where at her open door the housewife darns,
    Thou hast been seen, or hanging on a gate
  To watch the threshers in the mossy barns.
105   Children, who early range these slopes and late
      For cresses from the rills,
Have known thee eying, all an April-day,
    The springing pastures and the feeding kine;
    And marked thee, when the stars come out and shine,
110 Through the long dewy grass move slow away.

In autumn, on the skirts of Bagley Wood—
  Where most the gipsies by the turf-edged way
    Pitch their smoked tents, and every bush you see
  With scarlet patches tagged and shreds of grey,
115   Above the forest-ground called Thessaly—
      The blackbird, picking food,
Sees thee, nor stops his meal, nor fears at all;
    So often has he known thee past him stray,
    Rapt, twirling in thy hand a withered spray,
120 And waiting for the spark from heaven to fall.

And once, in winter, on the causeway chill
  Where home through flooded fields foot-travellers go,
    Have I not passed thee on the wooden bridge,

---

11. The relatively narrow, upper reaches of the river.
12. The rope securing the flat-bottomed pleasure boat to the shore shifts and splashes around as the boat responds to changes in the river's current.
13. Flower of the buttercup family, noted for the ease with which it drops its petals.
14. Orchids.
15. Pool which once carried rushing water over a weir or small dam.

Wrapped in thy cloak and battling with the snow,
125   Thy face tow'rd Hinksey and its wintry ridge?
      And thou hast climbed the hill,
And gained the white brow of the Cumner range;
    Turned once to watch, while thick the snowflakes fall,
    The line of festal light in Christ-Church hall[16]—
130   Then sought thy straw in some sequestered grange.[17]

But what—I dream! Two hundred years are flown
    Since first thy story ran through Oxford halls,
      And the grave Glanvil did the tale inscribe
That thou wert wandered from the studious walls
135   To learn strange arts, and join a gipsy-tribe;
      And thou from earth art gone
Long since, and in some quiet churchyard laid—
    Some country-nook, where o'er thy unknown grave
    Tall grasses and white flowering nettles wave,
140   Under a dark, red-fruited yew-tree's shade.

— No, no, thou hast not felt the lapse of hours!
    For what wears out the life of mortal men?
      'Tis that from change to change their being rolls;
    'Tis that repeated shocks, again, again,
145   Exhaust the energy of strongest souls
      And numb the elastic powers.
Till having used our nerves with bliss and teen,[18]
    And tired upon a thousand schemes our wit,
    To the just-pausing Genius[19] we remit
150   Our worn-out life, and are— what we have been.

Thou hast not lived, why should'st thou perish, so?
    Thou hadst one aim, one business, one desire;
      Else wert thou long since numbered with the dead!
Else hadst thou spent, like other men, thy fire!
155   The generations of thy peers are fled,
      And we ourselves shall go;
But thou possessest an immortal lot,
    And we imagine thee exempt from age
    And living as thou liv'st on Glanvil's page,
160   Because thou hadst— what we, alas! have not.

For early didst thou leave the world, with powers
    Fresh, undiverted to the world without,
      Firm to their mark, not spent on other things;
Free from the sick fatigue, the languid doubt,
165   Which much to have tried, in much been baffled, brings.
      O life unlike to ours!
Who fluctuate idly without term or scope,
    Of whom each strives, nor knows for what he strives,
    And each half-lives a hundred different lives;
170   Who wait like thee, but not, like thee, in hope.

Thou waitest for the spark from heaven! and we,
    Light half-believers of our casual creeds,
      Who never deeply felt, nor clearly willed,
Whose insight never has borne fruit in deeds,
175   Whose vague resolves never have been fulfilled;
      For whom each year we see

16. A hall is a communal dining room at a college.
17. See note 1 to Tennyson's "Mariana."
18. Unhappiness.
19. In Roman religion, the spirit of a man which gives him the power to create. Here it seems to be the spirit of the universe which pauses briefly to receive the individual man's soul at death.

Breeds new beginnings, disappointments new;
　　Who hesitate and falter life away,
　　And lose to-morrow the ground won to-day—
180　Ah! do not we, wanderer! await it too?

Yes, we await it!— but it still delays,
　　And then we suffer! and amongst us one,[20]
　　Who most has suffered, takes dejectedly
His seat upon the intellectual throne;
185　　And all his store of sad experience he
　　　Lays bare of wretched days;
　　Tells us his misery's birth and growth and signs,
　　And how the dying spark of hope was fed,
　　And how the breast was soothed, and how the head,
190　And all his hourly varied anodynes.[21]

This for our wisest! and we others pine,
　　And wish the long unhappy dream would end,
　　And waive all claim to bliss, and try to bear;
With close-lipped patience for our only friend,
195　　Sad patience, too near neighbour to despair—
　　　But none has hope like thine!
　　Thou through the fields and through the woods dost stray,
　　Roaming the country-side, a truant boy,
　　Nursing thy project in unclouded joy,
200　And every doubt long blown by time away.

O born in days when wits were fresh and clear,
　　And life ran gaily as the sparkling Thames;
　　Before this strange disease of modern life,
　　With its sick hurry, its divided aims,
205　　Its heads o'ertaxed, its palsied hearts, was rife—
　　　Fly hence, our contact fear!
　　Still fly, plunge deeper in the bowering wood!
　　Averse, as Dido[22] did with gesture stern
　　From her false friend's approach in Hades turn,
210　Wave us away, and keep thy solitude!

Still nursing the unconquerable hope,
　　Still clutching the inviolable shade,
　　With a free, onward impulse brushing through,
　　By night, the silvered branches of the glade—
215　　Far on the forest-skirts, where none pursue,
　　　On some mild pastoral slope
　　Emerge, and resting on the moonlit pales
　　Freshen thy flowers as in former years
　　With dew, or listen with enchanted ears,
220　From the dark dingles,[23] to the nightingales!

But fly our paths, our feverish contact fly!
　　For strong the infection of our mental strife,
　　Which, though it gives no bliss, yet spoils for rest;
　　And we should win thee from thy own fair life,
225　　Like us distracted, and like us unblest.
　　　Soon, soon thy cheer would die,
　　Thy hopes grow timorous, and unfixed thy powers,
　　And thy clear aims be cross and shifting made;
　　And then thy glad perennial youth would fade,
230　Fade, and grow old at last, and die like ours.

20. Goethe and Tennyson (the more likely candidate) have been suggested as the unnamed "one" here.
21. Drugs or pastimes that allay pain or soothe the mind.
22. In Greek mythology, the founder and Queen of Carthage who committed suicide after being deserted by her lover Aeneas and who, when she subsequently encountered Aeneas in hell (Hades), turned sternly away from him.
23. Small wooded ravines.

Then fly our greetings, fly our speech and smiles!
　　—As some grave Tyrian trader,²⁴ from the sea,
　　　　Descried at sunrise an emerging prow
　　　　Lifting the cool-haired creepers stealthily,
235　　　　　The fringes of a southward-facing brow
　　　　　　Among the Ægean isles;²⁵
　　And saw the merry Grecian coaster come,
　　　　Freighted with amber grapes, and Chian²⁶ wine,
　　　　Green, bursting figs, and tunnies²⁷ steeped in brine—
240　　And knew the intruders on his ancient home,

　　The young light-hearted masters of the waves—
　　　　And snatched his rudder, and shook out more sail;
　　　　　And day and night held on indignantly
　　　　O'er the blue Midland waters with the gale,
245　　　　　Betwixt the Syrtes and soft Sicily,²⁸
　　　　　　To where the Atlantic raves
　　Outside the western straight;²⁹ and unbent sails
　　　　There, where down cloudy cliffs, through sheets of foam,
　　　　Shy traffickers, the dark Iberians³⁰ come;
250　　And on the beach undid his corded bales.³¹

Philomela¹

Hark! ah, the nightingale—
The tawny-throated!
Hark, from that moonlit cedar what a burst!
What triumph! hark!—what pain!

5　O wanderer from a Grecian shore,
　Still, after many years, in distant lands,
　Still nourishing in thy bewildered brain
　That wild, unquenched, deep-sunken, old-world pain—
　Say, will it never heal?
10　And can this fragrant lawn
　With its cool trees, and night,
　And the sweet, tranquil Thames,
　And moonshine, and the dew,
　To thy racked heart and brain
15　Afford no balm?

24. Trader from Tyre, a maritime city in ancient Phoenicia. Carthage was once a colony of Tyre.
25. Islands off the coast of Greece.
26. Chios, a large island off the coast of Asia Minor was famous for its wine and figs.
27. Fish of the mackerel family found in the Mediterranean.
28. Between the north coast of Africa (where the two gulfs, the Syrtes, were considered perilous to ships) and the island of Sicily.
29. The straits of Gibraltar between the Mediterranean Sea and the Atlantic Ocean.
30. Perhaps descendants of the Arabs on the Spanish (Iberian) peninsula.
31. Arnold may have had in mind the following passage from Herodotus' *History* IV.196: "The Carthaginians . . . relate [that] . . . there is . . . a nation, beyond the Pillars of Hercules (i.e., the straits of Gibraltar), which they are wont to visit, where they no sooner arrive but forthwith they unlade their wares . . . along the beach, leave them, and [return] aboard their ships . . . . The natives . . . come down to the shore, and laying out to view so much gold as they think the worth of the wares, withdraw to a distance. The Carthaginians upon this come ashore and look. If they think the gold enough, they take it and go their way . . . ." The behaviour of the Tyrian trader both in avoiding the

boistrous intruders to his "ancient home" (penultimate stanza) and in using a method of trade which avoids direct "contact" (l. 221) with his buyers (ultimate stanza) is analogous to the shy and solitary behaviour of the "scholar-gipsy" earlier in the poem.

1. In Greek mythology, Philomela was the sister of Procne. The latter's husband, Tereus the King of Thrace, fell in love with Philomela, and, after seducing or raping her at his palace, cut out her tongue and hid her away so that she would not reveal his actions. Philomela, however, was able to depict her misfortunes on a piece of needlework which she sent to Procne who, to avenge her sister, killed her own son Itys and served his flesh to Tereus. Before Tereus could kill the two sisters, all three were changed into birds, Tereus into a hoopoe, Philomela into a swallow, and Procne into a nightingale. Apparently Arnold initially wrote his poem with this version of the story in mind, and should have entitled the poem "Procne"; he realized, however, that tradition (traceable to Latin versions of the myth) associates Philomela with the nightingale whose mournful song is his poem's subject. This seems to explain why the poem is entitled "Philomela" yet, at l. 21, still links the nightingale with Procne.

Dost thou to-night behold,
Here, through the moonlight on this English grass,
The unfriendly palace in the Thracian wild?
Dost thou again peruse
20   With hot cheeks and seared eyes
The too clear web,[2] and thy dumb sister's shame?
Dost thou once more assay
Thy flight, and feel come over thee,
Poor fugitive, the feathery change
25   Once more, and once more seem to make resound
With love and hate, triumph and agony,
Lone Daulis,[3] and the high Cephissian vale?
Listen, Eugenia[4]—
How thick the bursts come crowding through the leaves!
30   Again—thou hearest?
Eternal passion!
Eternal pain!

DANTE GABRIEL ROSSETTI (1828–82)

My Sister's Sleep[1]

She fell asleep on Christmas Eve:
  At length the long-ungranted shade
  Of weary eyelids overweigh'd
The pain nought else might yet relieve.

5   Our mother, who had leaned all day
  Over the bed from chime to chime,
  Then raised herself for the first time,
And as she sat her down, did pray.

Her little work-table was spread
10   With work to finish. For the glare
  Made by her candle, she had care
To work some distance from the bed.

Without, there was a cold moon up,
  Of winter radiance sheer and thin;
15   The hollow halo it was in
Was like an icy crystal cup.[2]

Through the small room, with subtle sound
  Of flame, by vents the fireshine drove[3]
  And reddened. In its dim alcove
20   The mirror shed a clearness round.

I had been sitting up some nights,
  And my tired mind felt weak and blank;
  Like a sharp strengthening wine it drank
The stillness and the broken lights.

25   Twelve struck. That sound, by dwindling years
  Heard in each hour, crept off; and then
  The ruffled silence spread again,
Like water that a pebble stirs.

Our mother rose from where she sat:
30   Her needles, as she laid them down,
  Met lightly, and her silken gown
Settled: no other noise than that.

"Glory unto the Newly Born!"[4]
  So, as said angels, she did say;
35   Because we were in Christmas Day,
Though it would still be long till morn.

Just then in the room over us
  There was a pushing back of chairs,
  As some who had sat unawares
40   So late, now heard the hour, and rose.

With anxious softly-stepping haste
  Our mother went where Margaret lay,
  Fearing the sounds o'erhead—should they
Have broken her long watched-for rest!

45   She stopped an instant, calm, and turned;
  But suddenly turned back again;
  And all her features seemed in pain
With woe, and her eyes gazed and yearned.

---

2. Philomela's needlework.
3. Daulis is a city which was occupied by the Tracians and ruled over by Tereus; it is in Phocis, a region through which runs the Cephisus river.
4. Fictional listener.

1. The Margaret of the poem is fictive; neither of Rossetti's two sisters had died when the poem was written and published in 1847–48.

2. In early versions of the poem, the moon is "hollow, like an altar cup." This and other revisions were made to the poem in 1869 in an attempt, as Rossetti said in a letter, to "eliminate the religious element altogether" from "My Sister's Sleep."
3. Was fanned.
4. A reference perhaps to the Christmas hymn "Hark, the Herald Angels Sing."

For my part, I but hid my face,
50   And held my breath, and spoke no word:
There was none spoken; but I heard
The silence for a little space.

Our mother bowed herself and wept:
And both my arms fell, and I said,
55   "God knows I knew that she was dead."
And there, all white, my sister slept.

Then kneeling, upon Christmas morn
A little after twelve o'clock,
We said, ere the first quarter struck,
60   "Christ's blessing on the newly born!"

The Blessed Damozel[1]

The blessed damozel leaned out
From the gold bar of Heaven;
Her eyes were deeper than the depth
Of waters stilled at even;
5   She had three lilies in her hand,
And the stars in her hair were seven.

Her robe, ungirt from clasp to hem,
No wrought[2] flowers did adorn,
But a white rose of Mary's gift,
10   For service meetly worn;
Her hair that lay along her back
Was yellow like ripe corn.[3]

Herseemed she scarce had been a day
One of God's choristers;
15   The wonder was not yet quite gone
From that still look of hers;
Albeit, to them she left, her day
Had counted as ten years.

(To one, it is ten years of years.
20   . . . Yet now, and in this place,
Surely she leaned o'er me—her hair
Fell all about my face . . .
Nothing: the autumn-fall of leaves.
The whole year sets apace.)

25   It was the rampart of God's house
That she was standing on;
By God built over the sheer depth
The which is Space begun;
So high, that looking downward thence
30   She scarce could see the sun.

It lies in Heaven, across the flood
Of ether,[4] as a bridge.
Beneath, the tides of day and night
With flame and darkness ridge
35   The void, as low as where this earth
Spins like a fretful midge.[5]

Around her, lovers, newly met
'Mid deathless love's acclaims,
Spoke evermore among themselves
40   Their heart-remembered names;
And the souls mounting up to God
Went by her like thin flames.

And still she bowed herself and stooped
Out of the circling charm;
45   Until her bosom must have made
The bar she leaned on warm,
And the lilies lay as if asleep
Along her bended arm.

From the fixed place of Heaven she saw
50   Time like a pulse shake fierce
Through all the worlds. Her gaze still strove
Within the gulf to pierce
Its path; and now she spoke as when
The stars sang in their spheres.

55   The sun was gone now; the curled moon
Was like a little feather
Fluttering far down the gulf; and now
She spoke through the still weather.
Her voice was like the voice the stars
60   Had when they sang together.[6]

(Ah sweet! Even now, in that bird's song,
Strove not her accents there,
Fain to be hearkened? When those bells
Possessed the mid-day air,
65   Strove not her steps to reach my side
Down all the echoing stair?)

"I wish that he were come to me,
For he will come," she said.
"Have I not prayed in Heaven?—on earth,
70   Lord, Lord, has he not pray'd?
Are not two prayers a perfect strength?
And shall I feel afraid?

1. The Anglo-Norman form of damsel—a young unmarried woman, a maiden, a virgin.
2. Worked, embroidered.
3. Wheat.
4. Hypothetical substance which was supposed to be

diffused in space beyond the earth's atmosphere.
5. Common name for a variety of small flies and insects.
6. See Job xxxviii.7: "When the morning stars sang together, and all the sons of God shouted for joy."

"When round his head the aureole clings,
   And he is clothed in white,
75 I'll take his hand and go with him
   To the deep wells of light;[7]
As unto a stream we will step down,
   And bathe there in God's sight.

"We two will stand beside that shrine,
80   Occult,[8] withheld, untrod,
Whose lamps are stirred continually
   With prayer sent up to God;
And see our old prayers, granted, melt
   Each like a little cloud.

85 "We two will lie i' the shadow of
   That living mystic tree[9]
Within whose secret growth the Dove[10]
   Is sometimes felt to be,
While every leaf that His plumes touch
90   Saith His Name audibly.

"And I myself will teach to him,
   I myself, lying so,
The songs I sing here; which his voice
   Shall pause in, hushed and slow,
95 And find some knowledge at each pause,
   Or some new thing to know."

(Alas! we two, we two, thou say'st!
   Yea, one wast thou with me
That once of old. But shall God lift
100   To endless unity
The soul whose likeness with thy soul
   Was but its love for thee?)

"We two," she said, "will seek the groves
   Where the lady Mary is,
105 With her five handmaidens, whose names
   Are five sweet symphonies,
Cecily, Gertrude, Magdalen,
   Margaret and Rosalys.

110 "Circlewise sit they, with bound locks
   And foreheads garlanded;
Into the fine cloth white like flame
   Weaving the golden thread,
To fashion the birth-robes for them
   Who are just born, being dead.

115 "He shall fear, haply, and be dumb:
   Then will I lay my cheek
To his, and tell about our love,
   Not once abashed or weak:
And the dear Mother will approve
120   My pride, and let me speak.

"Herself shall bring us, hand in hand,
   To Him round whom all souls
Kneel, the clear-ranged unnumbered heads
   Bowed with their aureoles:
125 And angels meeting us shall sing
   To their citherns and citoles.[11]

"There will I ask of Christ the Lord
   Thus much for him and me:—
Only to live as once on earth
130   With Love,—only to be,
As then awhile, for ever now
   Together, I and he."

She gazed and listened and then said,
   Less sad of speech than mild,—
135 "All this is when he comes." She ceased.
   The light thrilled towards her, fill'd
With angels in strong level flight.
   Her eyes prayed, and she smil'd.

(I saw her smile.) But soon their path
140   Was vague in distant spheres:
And then she cast her arms along
   The golden barriers,
And laid her face between her hands,
   And wept. (I heard her tears.)

The Card-Dealer[1]

Could you not drink her gaze like wine?
   Yet though its splendour swoon
Into the silence languidly
   As a tune into a tune,
5 Those eyes unravel the coiled night
   And know the stars at noon.

The gold that's heaped beside her hand,
   In truth rich prize it were;
And rich the dreams that wreathe her brows
10   With magic stillness there;
And he were rich who should unwind
   That woven golden hair.

---

7. See Rev. xxii.1 regarding the "pure river of water of life" in Heaven.
8. Hidden, mysterious, invisible.
9. See Rev. xxii.2 regarding "the tree of life" in Heaven.
10. The Holy Ghost.
11. Antique stringed instruments.

1. When this poem was first published in 1852 it was subtitled "Vingt-et-un. From a picture." Rossetti himself, in a letter of 1848, explained the card-dealer as a personification of "intellectual enjoyment" and the card-game, Twenty-one, as a reference to "the age at which the mind is most likely to be beguiled for a time from its proper purpose," though critics have been more inclined to see the dealer and her game as metaphoric of the inscrutable processes of Fate. According to a note appended to the poem in 1852 the picture that inspired "The Card-Dealer" is "one painted by . . . Theodore Von Holst; and represents a beautiful woman, richly dressed, who is sitting at a lamp-lit table, dealing out cards with a peculiar fixedness of expression." Never appended to the poem was a fraudulent motto written in French by Rossetti and purporting to be from the *Calendrier de la Vie* (1630); translated, it reads "Ambition, Cupidity, / And delicious Voluptuousness, / Are the sisters of Destiny / After the twenty-first year."

Around her, where she sits, the dance[2]
   Now breathes its eager heat;
15 And not more lightly or more true
   Fall there the dancers' feet
Than fall her cards on the bright board
   As 'twere a heart that beat.

Her fingers let them softly through,
20   Smooth polished silent things;
And each one as it falls reflects
   In swift light-shadowings,
Blood-red and purple, green and blue,
   The great eyes of her rings.

25 Whom plays she with? With thee, who lov'st
   Those gems upon her hand;
With me, who search her secret brows;
   With all men, bless'd or bann'd.
We play together, she and we,
30   Within a vain strange land:

A land without any order,—
   Day even as night, (one saith,)—
Where who lieth down ariseth not
   Nor the sleeper awakeneth;
35 A land of darkness as darkness itself
   And of the shadow of death.[3]

What be her cards, you ask? Even these:—
   The heart, that doth but crave
More, having fed; the diamond,
40   Skilled to make base seem brave;
The club, for smiting in the dark;
   The spade, to dig a grave.

And do you ask what game she plays?
   With me 'tis lost or won;
45 With thee it is playing still; with him
   It is not well begun;
But 'tis a game she plays with all
   Beneath the sway o' the sun.

Thou seest the card that falls,—she knows
50   The card that followeth:
Her game in thy tongue is called Life,
   As ebbs thy daily breath:
When she shall speak, thou'lt learn her tongue
   And know she calls it Death.

The Woodspurge[1]

The wind flapped loose, the wind was still,
Shaken out dead from tree and hill:
I had walked on at the wind's will,—
I sat now, for the wind was still.

Between my knees my forehead was,—
My lips, drawn in, said not Alas!
My hair was over in the grass,
My naked ears heard the day pass.

My eyes, wide open, had the run
Of some ten weeds to fix upon;
Among those few, out of the sun,
The woodspurge flowered, three cups in one.

From perfect grief there need not be
Wisdom or even memory:
One thing then learnt remains to me,—
The woodspurge has a cup of three.

From The House of Life
A Sonnet-Sequence

[Introductory Sonnet]

A Sonnet is a moment's monument,—
   Memorial from the Soul's eternity
   To one dead deathless hour. Look that it be,
Whether for lustral[1] rite or dire portent,
Of its own arduous fulness reverent:
   Carve it in ivory or in ebony,
   As Day or Night may rule; and let Time see
Its flowering crest impearled and orient.[2]

---

2. The dance of life.
3. See Job x.22: "A land of darkness, as darkness itself;
and of the shadow of death, without any order, and where
the light is as darkness."

1. There is some question as to whether this poem was
inspired by an event in Rossetti's life or by an illustration

in a botany book such as Gerard's *Herbal* (1626), a copy of
which was owned by the poet. In *Tales about Plants*
(1839) by "Peter Parley" (S. G. Goodrich) spurges are
described as "weed-like" plants in which "the seed vessel,
or fruit . . . is always divided into three distinct cells. . . ."

1. Cleansing, purificatory.
2. Precious, shining.

> A Sonnet is a coin: its face reveals
>   The soul,—its converse, to what Power 'tis due:—
> Whether for tribute to the august appeals
>   Of Life, or dower in Love's high retinue,
> It serve; or, 'mid the dark wharf's cavernous breath,
> In Charon's palm it pay the toll to Death.³

Silent Noon

[XIX]

Your hands lie open in the long fresh grass,—
    The finger-points look through like rosy blooms:
    Your eyes smile peace. The pasture gleams and glooms
'Neath billowing skies that scatter and amass.
All round our nest, far as the eye can pass,
    Are golden kingcup-fields¹ with silver edge
    Where the cow-parsley² skirts the hawthorn-hedge.
'Tis visible silence, still as the hour-glass.

Deep in the sun-searched growths the dragon-fly
Hangs like a blue thread loosened from the sky:—
    So this wing'd hour is dropt to us from above.
Oh! clasp we to our hearts, for deathless dower,
This close-companioned inarticulate hour
    When twofold silence was the song of love.

Willowwood

XLIX

I sat with Love upon a woodside well,
    Leaning across the water, I and he;
    Nor ever did he speak nor looked at me,
But touched his lute wherein was audible
5 The certain secret thing he had to tell:
    Only our mirrored eyes met silently
    In the low wave; and that sound came to be
The passionate voice I knew; and my tears fell.

And at their fall, his eyes beneath grew hers;
10 And with his foot and with his wing-feathers
    He swept the spring that watered my heart's drouth.¹
Then the dark ripples spread to waving hair,
And as I stooped, her own lips rising there
    Bubbled with brimming kisses at my mouth.

L

15 And now Love sang: but his was such a song,
    So meshed with half-remembrance hard to free,
    As souls disused in death's sterility
May sing when the new birthday tarries long.
And I was made aware of a dumb throng
20   That stood aloof, one form by every tree,
    All mournful forms, for each was I or she,
The shades of those our days that had no tongue.

3. In Greek mythology, Charon was the ferryman who conveyed the dead in his boat across the river Styx to Hades, a task for which each passenger paid him a coin. The dead were buried with a coin in their mouths to pay Charon's fee.

1. Fields containing buttercups.
2. Popular name for several herbs of the carrot family which are supposed to be eaten by cattle.

1. Drought, thirst.

They looked on us, and knew us and were known;
   While fast together, alive from the abyss,
25   Clung the soul-wrung implacable close kiss;
And pity of self through all made broken moan
Which said "For once, for once, for once alone!"
   And still Love sang, and what he sang was this:—

LI

"O ye, all ye that walk in Willowwood,
30   That walk with hollow faces burning white;
What fathom-depth of soul-struck widowhood,
   What long, what longer hours, one lifelong night,
Ere ye again, who so in vain have wooed
   Your last hope lost, who so in vain invite
35   Your lips to that their unforgotten food,
   Ere ye, ere ye again shall see the light!

Alas! the bitter banks in Willowwood,
   With tear-spurge wan, with blood-wort[2] burning red:
Alas! if ever such a pillow could
40   Steep deep the soul in sleep till she were dead,—
Better all life forget her than this thing,
That Willowwood should hold her wandering!"

LII

So sang he: and as meeting rose and rose
   Together cling through the wind's wellaway[3]
45   Nor change at once, yet near the end of day
The leaves drop loosened where the heart-stain glows,—
So when the song died did the kiss unclose;
   And her face fell back drowned, and was as grey
   As its grey eyes; and if it ever may
50 Meet mine again I know not if Love knows.

Only I know that I leaned low and drank
A long draught from the water where she sank,
   Her breath and all her tears and all her soul:
And as I leaned, I know I felt Love's face
55 Pressed on my neck with moan of pity and grace,
   Till both our heads were in his aureole.

The One Hope

[CI]
When vain desire at last and vain regret
   Go hand in hand to death, and all is vain,
   What shall assuage the unforgotten pain
And teach the unforgetful to forget?
Shall Peace be still a sunk stream long unmet,—
   Or may the soul at once in a green plain
   Stoop through the spray of some sweet life-fountain
And cull the dew-drenched flowering amulet?[1]

---

2. Perennial herb with deep red dye in its roots. For
"spurge" see note to Rossetti's "The Woodspurge."
3. Lamentation.

1. Something worn or carried to act as a charm or
preservative against evil or death. Perhaps Rossetti had
in mind the talismans granted by the Cumaean Sibyl to
give her devotees free passage over the river Acheron to
the fields of Paradise or the "coronet of flowers" which the
heroine of the *Hypnerotomachia Poliphili* (1499) receives
when she has passed through death to join her beloved.

Ah! when the wan soul in that golden air
    Between the scriptured petals[2] softly blown
    Peers breathless for the gift of grace unknown,—
Ah! let none other alien spell soe'er
But only the one Hope's one name be there,—
    Not less nor more, but even that word alone.

CHRISTINA ROSSETTI (1830–94)

Song

When I am dead, my dearest,
    Sing no sad songs for me;
Plant thou no roses at my head,
    Nor shady cypress tree:
Be the green grass above me
    With showers and dewdrops wet:
And if thou wilt, remember,
    And if thou wilt, forget.

I shall not see the shadows,
    I shall not feel the rain;
I shall not hear the nightingale
    Sing on as if in pain:[1]
And dreaming through the twilight
    That doth not rise nor set,
Haply I may remember,
    And haply may forget.

After Death

The curtains were half drawn, the floor was swept
    And strewn with rushes, rosemary and may[1]
    Lay thick upon the bed on which I lay,
Where through the lattice ivy-shadows crept.
He leaned above me, thinking that I slept
    And could not hear him; but I heard him say,
    "Poor child, poor child": and as he turned away
Came a deep silence, and I knew he wept.
He did not touch the shroud, or raise the fold
    That hid my face, or take my hand in his,
        Or ruffle the smooth pillows for my head:
        He did not love me living; but once dead
    He pitied me; and very sweet it is
To know he still is warm though I am cold.

A Birthday

My heart is like a singing bird
    Whose nest is in a watered shoot:
My heart is like an apple-tree
    Whose boughs are bent with thickest fruit;
My heart is like a rainbow shell
    That paddles in a halcyon sea;
My heart is gladder than all these
    Because my love is come to me.

Raise me a dais of silk and down;
    Hang it with vair[1] and purple dyes;
Carve it in doves and pomegranates,
    And peacocks with a hundred eyes;
Work it in gold and silver grapes,
    In leaves and silver fleurs-de-lys;
Because the birthday of my life
    Is come, my love is come to me.

---

2. Probably the petals of the "flowering amulet"; the Greeks believed that the petals of the hyacinth were inscribed ("scriptured") with letters indicating what was to be the lot of the soul in eternity.

1. See note 1 to Arnold's "Procne."

1. Hawthorn flowers.

1. A kind of squirrel fur, bluish-grey and white, represented heraldically by rows of blue and white shields or bells.

An Apple Gathering

I plucked pink blossoms from mine apple-tree
 And wore them all that evening in my hair:
Then in due season when I went to see
 I found no apples there.

5 With dangling basket all along the grass
 As I had come I went the selfsame track:
My neighbours mocked me while they saw me pass
 So empty-handed back.

Lilian and Lilias smiled in trudging by,
10 Their heaped-up basket teazed me like a jeer;
Sweet-voiced they sang beneath the sunset sky,
 Their mother's home was near.

Plump Gertrude passed me with her basket full,
 A stronger hand than hers helped it along;
15 A voice talked with her through the shadows cool
 More sweet to me than song.

Ah Willie, Willie, was my love less worth
 Than apples with their green leaves piled above?
I counted rosiest apples on the earth
20 Of far less worth than love.

So once it was with me you stooped to talk
 Laughing and listening in this very lane;
To think that by this way we used to walk
 We shall not walk again!

25 I let my neighbours pass me, ones and twos
 And groups; the latest said the night grew chill,
And hastened: but I loitered; while the dews
 Fell fast I loitered still.

Uphill

Does the road wind up-hill all the way?
 Yes, to the very end.
Will the day's journey take the whole long day?
 From morn to night, my friend.

But is there for the night a resting-place?
 A roof for when the slow dark hours begin.
May not the darkness hide it from my face?
 You cannot miss that inn.

Shall I meet other wayfarers at night?
 Those who have gone before.
Then must I knock, or call when just in sight?
 They will not keep you standing at that door.

Shall I find comfort, travel-sore and weak?
 Of labor you shall find the sum.
Will there be beds for me and all who seek?
 Yea, beds for all who come.

WILLIAM MORRIS (1834–96)

The Haystack in the Floods[1]

Had she come all the way for this,
To part at last without a kiss?
Yea, had she borne the dirt and rain
That her own eyes might see him slain
5 Beside the haystack in the floods?

Along the dripping leafless woods,
The stirrup touching either shoe,
She rode astride as troopers do;
With kirtle kilted[2] to her knee,
10 To which the mud splash'd wretchedly;
And the wet dripp'd from every tree
Upon her head and heavy hair,
And on her eyelids broad and fair;
The tears and rain ran down her face.
15 By fits and starts they rode apace,
And very often was his place
Far off from her; he had to ride
Ahead, to see what might betide
When the roads cross'd; and sometimes, when
20 There rose a murmuring from his men,
Had to turn back with promises;
Ah me! she had but little ease;
And often for pure doubt and dread
She sobb'd, made giddy in the head
25 By the swift riding; while, for cold,
Her slender fingers scarce could hold
The wet reins; yea, and scarcely, too,
She felt the foot within her shoe
Against the stirrup: all for this,
30 To part at last without a kiss
Beside the haystack in the floods.

For when they near'd that old soak'd hay,
They saw across the only way
That Judas, Godmar, and the three
35 Red running lions dismally
Grinn'd from his pennon, under which
In one straight line along the ditch,
They counted thirty heads.

So then,
40 While Robert turn'd round to his men,
She saw at once the wretched end,
And, stooping down, tried hard to rend
Her coif[3] the wrong way from her head,
And hid her eyes; while Robert said:
45 "Nay, love, 'tis scarcely two to one,

At Poictiers where we made them run
So fast—why, sweet my love, good cheer,
The Gascon frontier is so near,
Nought after this."

50 But, "O!" she said,
"My God! my God! I have to tread
The long way back without you; then
The court at Paris; those six men;
The gratings of the Chatelet;
55 The swift Seine on some rainy day
Like this, and people standing by
And laughing, while my weak hands try
To recollect how strong men swim.
All this, or else a life with him,[4]
60 For which I should be damned at last.
Would God that this next hour were past!"

He answer'd not, but cried his cry,
"St. George for Marny!" cheerily;
And laid his hand upon her rein.
65 Alas! no man of all his train
Gave back that cheery cry again;
And, while for rage his thumb beat fast
Upon his sword-hilts, some one cast
About his neck a kerchief long,
70 And bound him.

Then they went along
To Godmar; who said: "Now, Jehane,
Your lover's life is on the wane
So fast, that, if this very hour
75 You yield not as my paramour,
He will not see the rain leave off—
Nay, keep your tongue from gibe and scoff,
Sir Robert, or I slay you now."

She laid her hand upon her brow,
80 Then gazed upon the palm, as though
She thought her forehead bled, and—"No!"
She said, and turn'd her head away,
As there were nothing else to say,
And everything were settled: red
85 Grew Godmar's face from chin to head:
"Jehane, on yonder hill there stands
My castle, guarding well my lands:
What hinders me from taking you,
And doing that I list to do

---

1. This poem, which takes its inspiration from the
Chronicle of Jean Froissart (1338–1410), is set against
the backdrop of the Hundred Years' War and takes place
after the defeat of the French by the English at Poitiers
(1356). Sir Robert of Marny, an English Knight, and
Jehane, his French mistress, are attempting to cross the
"Gascon frontier" to safety when they are apprehended by
Godmar, a knight on the French side.

2. With skirt or outer petticoat tucked up.
3. A covering for the head worn by women.
4. The suggestion is that, if captured, Jehane will either
be taken back to the Chatelet prison in Paris to face a
court of six judges, trial by water (as a suspected witch),
and almost inevitable death or have to consent to become
Godmar's mistress.

90   To your fair wilful body, while
      Your knight lies dead?"

                    A wicked smile
      Wrinkled her face, her lips grew thin,
      A long way out she thrust her chin:
95   "You know that I should strangle you
      While you were sleeping; or bite through
      Your throat, by God's help—ah!" she said,
      "Lord Jesus, pity your poor maid!
      For in such wise they hem me in,
100   I cannot choose but sin and sin,
      Whatever happens: yet I think
      They could not make me eat or drink,
      And so should I just reach my rest."
      "Nay, if you do not my behest,
105   O Jehane! though I love you well,"
      Said Godmar, "would I fail to tell
      All that I know?" "Foul lies," she said.
      "Eh? lies, my Jehane? by God's head,
      At Paris folks would deem them true!
110   Do you know, Jehane, they cry for you:
      'Jehane the brown! Jehane the brown!
      Give us Jehane to burn or drown!'—
      Eh—gag me Robert!—sweet my friend,
      This were indeed a piteous end
115   For those long fingers, and long feet,
      And long neck, and smooth shoulders sweet;
      An end that few men would forget
      That saw it—So, an hour yet:
      Consider, Jehane, which to take
120   Of life or death!"
                    So, scarce awake,
      Dismounting, did she leave that place,
      And totter some yards: with her face
      Turn'd upward to the sky she lay,
125   Her head on a wet heap of hay,
      And fell asleep: and while she slept,
      And did not dream, the minutes crept
      Round to the twelve again; but she,
      Being waked at last, sigh'd quietly,

130   And strangely childlike came, and said:
      "I will not." Straightway Godmar's head,
      As though it hung on strong wires, turn'd
      Most sharply round, and his face burn'd.

      For Robert—both his eyes were dry,
135   He could not weep, but gloomily
      He seem'd to watch the rain; yea, too,
      His lips were firm; he tried once more
      To touch her lips; she reach'd out, sore
      And vain desire so tortured them,
140   The poor grey lips, and now the hem
      Of his sleeve brush'd them.

                    With a start
      Up Godmar rose, thrust them apart;
      From Robert's throat he loosed the bands
145   Of silk and mail; with empty hands
      Held out, she stood and gazed, and saw
      The long bright blade without a flaw
      Glide out from Godmar's sheath, his hand
      In Robert's hair; she saw him bend
150   Back Robert's head; she saw him send
      The thin steel down; the blow told well,
      Right backward the knight Robert fell,
      And moaned as dogs do, being half dead,
      Unwitting, as I deem: so then
155   Godmar turn'd grinning to his men,
      Who ran, some five or six, and beat
      His head to pieces at their feet.

      Then Godmar turn'd again and said:
      "So, Jehane, the first fitte[5] is read!
160   Take note, my lady, that your way
      Lies backward to the Chatelet!"
      She shook her head and gazed awhile
      At her cold hands with a rueful smile,
      As though this thing had made her mad.

165   This was the parting that they had
      Beside the haystack in the floods.

---

5. Part of a literary work, like a chapter.

ALGERNON CHARLES SWINBURNE (1837–1909)

The Leper[1]

Nothing is better, I well think,
　　Than love; the hidden well-water
Is not so delicate to drink:
　　This was well seen of me and her.

5　I served her in a royal house;
　　I served her wine and curious meat.
For will to kiss between her brows,
　　I had no heart to sleep or eat.

Mere scorn God knows she had of me,
10　A poor scribe, nowise great or fair,
Who plucked his clerk's hood back to see
　　Her curled-up lips and amorous hair.

I vex my head with thinking this.
　　Yea, though God always hated me,
15　And hates me now that I can kiss
　　Her eyes, plait up her hair to see

How she then wore it on the brows,
　　Yet am I glad to have her dead
Here in this wretched wattled house
20　Where I can kiss her eyes and head.

Nothing is better, I well know,
　　Than love; no amber in cold sea
Or gathered berries under snow:
　　That is well seen of her and me.

25　Three thoughts I make my pleasure of:
　　First I take heart and think of this:
That knight's gold hair she chose to love,
　　His mouth she had such will to kiss.

Then I remember that sundawn
30　I brought him by a privy way
Out at her lattice, and thereon
　　What gracious words she found to say.

(Cold rushes for such little feet—
　　Both feet could lie into my hand.
35　A marvel was it of my sweet
　　Her upright body could so stand.)

40　'Sweet friend, God give you thank and grace;
　　Now am I clean and whole of shame,
Nor shall men burn me in the face
　　For my sweet fault that scandals them.'

I tell you over word by word.
　　She, sitting edgewise on her bed,
Holding her feet, said thus. The third,
　　A sweeter thing than these, I said.

45　God, that makes time and ruins it
　　And alters not, abiding God,
Changed with disease her body sweet,
　　The body of love wherein she abode.

Love is more sweet and comelier
50　Than a dove's throat strained out to sing.
All they spat out and cursed at her
　　And cast her forth for a base thing.

They cursed her, seeing how God had wrought
　　This curse to plague her, a curse of his.
55　Fools were they surely, seeing not
　　How sweeter than all sweet she is.

He that had held her by the hair,
　　With kissing lips blinding her eyes,
Felt her bright bosom, strained and bare,
60　Sigh under him, with short mad cries

Out of her throat and sobbing mouth
　　And body broken up with love,
With sweet hot tears his lips were loth
　　Her own should taste the savour of.

65　Yea, he inside whose grasp all night
　　Her fervent body leapt or lay,
Stained with sharp kisses red and white,
　　Found her a plague to spurn away.

I hid her in this wattled house,
70　I served her water and poor bread.
For joy to kiss between her brows
　　Time upon time I was nigh dead.

1. Swinburne appended a fraudulent note to this poem. It purported to be from the *Grandes Chroniques de France* (1505) but was actually in his own approximation of sixteenth-century French. It translates as follows: "In those days the country was full of unclean persons and lepers. This caused the King great dismay, seeing that God must be greatly offended. Now it came to pass that a noble woman, Yolande de Sallières by name, was afflicted and sorely wasted by this ugly disease; all her friends and relations having before their very eyes the anger of God thrust her forth from their homes, resolving never to shelter or succour a body cursed by God and an abomination to all men. In former days, this lady had been a beauty most pleasing to behold, generous with her body and of easy virtue. However, none of those lovers who had frequently embraced and tenderly kissed her wanted now to shelter so hideous a woman and so detestable a sinner. A clerk who had once served her in the office of lackey and go-between in matters venerial took her in and hid her in a little hut. There the poor woman died a cruel and wretched death; and after her died the said clerk who had cared for her out of true love for six months, washing her, clothing her, and unclothing her every day with his own hands. They even say that the naughty man, the cursed clerk, remembering the great former loveliness of this ruined beauty pleasured himself aplenty in kissing her on her dreadful, leprous lips and pressing her gently to him with lover's hands. Wherefore, he died of the same awful disease. This took place in Gastinois near Fontainebellant. And when King Phillipe heard of this happening he was greatly amazed by it" (trans. Robin F. Jones).

Bread failed; we got but well-water
   And gathered grass with dropping seed;
75 I had such joy of kissing her,
   I had small care to sleep or feed.

Sometimes when service made me glad
   The sharp tears leapt between my lids,
Falling on her, such joy I had
80   To do the service God forbids.

'I pray you let me be at peace,
   Get hence, make room for me to die.'
She said that: her poor lip would cease,
   Put up to mine, and turn to cry.

85 I said, 'Bethink yourself how love
   Fared in us twain, what either did;
Shall I unclothe my soul thereof?
   That I should do this, God forbid.'

Yea, though God hateth us, he knows
90   That hardly in a little thing
Love faileth of the work it does
   Till it grow ripe for gathering.

Six months, and now my sweet is dead
   A trouble takes me; I know not
95 If all were done well, all well said,
   No word or tender deed forgot.

Too sweet, for the least part in her,
   To have shed life out by fragments; yet,
Could the close mouth catch breath and stir,
100   I might see something I forget.

Six months, and I sit still and hold
   In two cold palms her cold two feet.
Her hair, half grey half ruined gold,
   Thrills me and burns me in kissing it.

105 Love bites and stings me through, to see
   Her keen face made of sunken bones.
Her worn-off eyelids madden me,
   That were shot through with purple once.

110 She said, 'Be good with me; I grow
   So tired for shame's sake, I shall die
If you say nothing': even so.
   And she is dead now, and shame put by.

Yea, and the scorn she had of me
   In the old time, doubtless vexed her then.
115 I never should have kissed her. See
   What fools God's anger makes of men!

She might have loved me a little too,
   Had I been humbler for her sake.
But that new shame could make love new
120   She saw not—yet her shame did make.

I took too much upon my love,
   Having for such mean service done
Her beauty and all the ways thereof,
   Her face and all the sweet thereon.

125 Yea, all this while I tended her,
   I know the old love held fast his part,
I know the old scorn waxed heavier,
   Mixed with sad wonder, in her heart.

It may be all my love went wrong—
130   A scribe's work writ awry and blurred,
Scrawled after the blind evensong—
   Spoilt music with no perfect word.

But surely I would fain have done
   All things the best I could. Perchance
135 Because I failed, came short of one,
   She kept at heart that other man's.

I am grown blind with all these things:
   It may be now she hath in sight
Some better knowledge; still there clings
140   The old question. Will not God do right?

Stage Love

When the game began between them for a jest,
He played king and she played queen to match the best;
Laughter soft as tears, and tears that turned to laughter,
These were things she sought for years and sorrowed after.

Pleasure with dry lips, and pain that walks by night;
All the sting and all the stain of long delight;
These were things she knew not of, that knew not of her,
When she played at half a love with half a lover.

Time was chorus, gave them cues to laugh or cry;
They would kill, befool, amuse him, let him die;
Set him webs to weave to-day and break to-morrow,
Till he died for good in play, and rose in sorrow.

What the years mean; how time dies and is not slain;
How love grows and laughs and cries and wanes again;
These were things she came to know, and take their measure,
When the play was played out so for one man's pleasure.

The Garden of Proserpine

Here, where the world is quiet;
  Here, where all trouble seems
Dead winds' and spent waves' riot
  In doubtful dreams of dreams;
5 I watch the green field growing
For reaping folk and sowing,
For harvest-time and mowing,
  A sleepy world of streams.

I am tired of tears and laughter,
10 And men that laugh and weep;
Of what may come hereafter
  For men that sow to reap:
I am weary of days and hours,
Blown buds of barren flowers,
15 Desires and dreams and powers
  And everything but sleep.

Here life has death for neighbour,
  And far from eye or ear
Wan waves and wet winds labour,
20 Weak ships and spirits steer;
They drive adrift, and whither
They wot not who make thither;
But no such winds blow hither,
  And no such things grow here.

25 No growth of moor or coppice,
  No heather-flower or vine,
But bloomless buds of poppies,
  Green grapes of Proserpine,
Pale beds of blowing rushes
30 Where no leaf blooms or blushes
Save this whereout she crushes
  For dead men deadly wine.

Pale, without name or number,
  In fruitless fields of corn,
35 They bow themselves and slumber
  All night till light is born;
And like a soul belated,
In hell and heaven unmated,
By cloud and mist abated
40 Comes out of darkness morn.

Though one were strong as seven,
  He too with death shall dwell,
Nor wake with wings in heaven,
  Nor weep for pains in hell;
45 Though one were fair as roses,
His beauty clouds and closes;
And well though love reposes,
  In the end it is not well.

50 Pale, beyond porch and portal,
  Crowned with calm leaves, she stands
Who gathers all things mortal
  With cold immortal hands;
Her languid lips are sweeter
Than love's who fears to greet her
55 To men that mix and meet her
  From many times and lands.

She waits for each and other,
  She waits for all men born;
Forgets the earth her mother,
60 The life of fruits and corn;
And spring and seed and swallow
Take wing for her and follow
Where summer song rings hollow
  And flowers are put to scorn.

65 There go the loves that wither,
  The old loves with wearier wings;
And all dead years draw thither,
  And all disastrous things;
Dead dreams of days forsaken,
70 Blind buds that snows have shaken,
Wild leaves that winds have taken,
  Red strays of ruined springs.

We are not sure of sorrow,
  And joy was never sure;
75 Today will die tomorrow;
  Time stoops to no man's lure;
And love, grown faint and fretful,
With lips but half regretful
Sighs, and with eyes forgetful
80 Weeps that no love endure.

From too much love of living,
  From hope and fear set free,
We thank with brief thanksgiving
  Whatever gods may be
85 That no life lives for ever;
That dead men rise up never;
That even the weariest river
  Winds somewhere safe to sea.

Then star nor sun shall waken,
90 Nor any change of light:
Nor sound of waters shaken,
  Nor any sound or sight:
Nor wintry leaves nor vernal,
Nor days nor things diurnal;
95 Only the sleep eternal
  In an eternal night.

RALPH WALDO EMERSON (1803–82)

Each and All

Little thinks, in the field, yon red-cloaked clown
Of thee from the hill-top looking down;
The heifer that lows in the upland farm,
Far-heard, lows not thine ear to charm;
5 The sexton,[1] tolling his bell at noon,
Deems not that great Napoleon
Stops his horse, and lists with delght,
Whilst his files sweep round yon Alpine height;
Nor knowest thou what argument
10 Thy life to thy neighbor's creed has lent.
All are needed by each one;
Nothing is fair or good alone.
I thought the sparrow's note from heaven,
Singing at dawn on the alder bough;
15 I brought him home, in his nest, at even;
He sings the song, but it cheers not now,
For I did not bring home the river and sky;—
He sang to my ear,— they sang to my eye.
The delicate shells lay on the shore;
20 The bubbles of the latest wave
Fresh pearls to their enamel gave,
And the bellowing of the savage sea
Greeted their safe escape to me.
I wiped away the weeds and foam,
25 I fetched my sea-born treasures home;
But the poor, unsightly, noisome[2] things

30 Had left their beauty on the shore
With the sun and the sand and the wild uproar.
The lover watched his graceful maid,
As 'mid the virgin train she strayed,
Nor knew her beauty's best attire
Was woven still by the snow-white choir.
At last she came to his hermitage,[3]
35 Like the bird from the woodlands to the cage:—
The gay enchantment was undone,
A gentle wife, but fairy none.
Then I said, "I covet truth;
Beauty is unripe childhood's cheat;
I leave it behind with the games of youth:"—
40 As I spoke, beneath my feet
The ground-pine curled its pretty wreath,
Running over the club-moss burrs;
I inhaled the violet's breath;
Around me stood the oaks and firs;
45 Pine-cones and acorns lay on the ground;
Over me soared the eternal sky,
Full of light and of deity;
Again I saw, again I heard,
The rolling river, the morning bird;—
50 Beauty through my senses stole;
I yielded myself to the perfect whole.

The Rhodora[1]
On Being Asked, Whence Is the Flower?

In May, when sea-winds pierced our solitudes,
I found the fresh Rhodora in the woods,
Spreading its leafless blooms in a damp nook,
To please the desert and the sluggish brook.
The purple petals, fallen in the pool,
Made the black water with their beauty gay;
Here might the red-bird come his plumes to cool,
And court the flower that cheapens his array.
Rhodora! if the sages ask thee why
This charm is wasted on the earth and sky,
Tell them, dear, that if eyes were made for seeing,
Then Beauty is its own excuse for being:
Why thou wert there, O rival of the rose!
I never thought to ask, I never knew:
But, in my simple ignorance, suppose
The self-same Power that brought me there brought you.

---

1. The caretaker of a church.
2. Offensive to the smell or other senses.
3. The home of a hermit or solitary.

1. Shrub found in New England and Canada which produces delicate pink flowers before or with its leaves in the spring.

The Snow-Storm

Announced by all the trumpets of the sky,
Arrives the snow, and, driving o'er the fields,
Seems nowhere to alight: the whited air
Hides hills and woods, the river, and the heaven,
5   And veils the farm-house at the garden's end.
The sled and traveler stopped, the courier's feet
Delayed, all friends shut out, the housemates sit
Around the radiant fireplace, enclosed
In a tumultuous privacy of storm.

10   Come see the north wind's masonry.
Out of an unseen quarry evermore
Furnished with tile, the fierce artificer
Curves his white bastions with projected roof
Round every windward stake, or tree, or door.
15   Speeding, the myriad-handed, his wild work
So fanciful, so savage, nought cares he
For number or proportion. Mockingly,
On coop or kennel he hangs Parian[1] wreaths;
A swan-like form invests the hidden thorn;
20   Fills up the farmer's lane from wall to wall,
Maugre[2] the farmer's sighs; and at the gate
A tapering turret overtops the work.
And when his hours are numbered, and the world
Is all his own, retiring, as he were not,
25   Leaves, when the sun appears, astonished Art
To mimic in slow structures, stone by stone,
Built in an age, the mad wind's night-work,
The frolic architecture of the snow.

Ode to Beauty

Who gave thee, O Beauty,
The keys of this breast,—
Too credulous lover
Of blest and unblest?
5   Say, when in lapsed ages
Thee knew I of old?
Or what was the service
For which I was sold?
When first my eyes saw thee,
10   I found me thy thrall,
By magical drawings,
Sweet tyrant of all!
I drank at thy fountain
False waters of thirst;
15   Thou intimate stranger,
Thou latest and first!
Thy dangerous glances
Make women of men;
New-born, we are melting
20   Into nature again.

Lavish, lavish promiser,
Nigh persuading gods to err!
Guest of million painted forms,
Which in turn thy glory warms!

25   The frailest leaf, the mossy bark,
The acorn's cup, the raindrop's arc,
The swinging spider's silver line,
The ruby of the drop of wine,
The shining pebble of the pond,
30   Thou inscribest with a bond,
In thy momentary play,
Would bankrupt nature to repay.

Ah, what avails it
To hide or to shun
35   Whom the Infinite One
Hath granted his throne?
The heaven high over
Is the deep's lover;
The sun and sea,
40   Informed by thee,
Before me run
And draw me on,
Yet fly me still,
As Fate refuses
45   To me the heart Fate for me chooses.
Is it that my opulent soul
Was mingled from the generous whole;
Sea-valleys and the deep of skies

1. The island of Paros in the Aegean Sea was noted for its
fine, white marble which was used by ancient Greek
sculptors for their best works.
2. Notwithstanding, in spite of.

Furnished several supplies;
50 And the sands whereof I'm made
Draw me to them, self-betrayed?
I turn the proud portfolio
Which holds the grand designs
Of Salvator, of Guercino,
55 And Piranesi's lines.[1]
I hear the lofty paeans[2]
Of the masters of the shell,
Who heard the starry music
And recount the numbers well;
60 Olympian[3] bards who sung
Divine Ideas below,
Which always find us young
And always keep us so.
Oft, in streets or humblest places,
65 I detect far-wandered graces,
Which, from Eden wide astray,
In lowly homes have lost their way.

Thee gliding through the sea of form,
Like the lightning through the storm,
70 Somewhat not to be possessed,
Somewhat not to be caressed,
No feet so fleet could ever find,
No perfect form could ever bind.
Thou eternal fugitive,

75 Hovering over all that live,
Quick and skilful to inspire
Sweet, extravagant desire,
Starry space and lily-bell
Filling with thy roseate smell,
80 Wilt not give the lips to taste
Of the nectar which thou hast.

All that's good and great with thee
Works in close conspiracy;
Thou hast bribed the dark and lonely
85 To report thy features only,
And the cold and purple morning
Itself with thoughts of thee adorning;
The leafy dell, the city mart,
Equal trophies of thine art;
90 E'en the flowing azure air
Thou hast touched for my despair;
And, if I languish into dreams,
Again I meet the ardent beams.
Queen of things! I dare not die
95 In Being's deeps past ear and eye;
Lest there I find the same deceiver
And be the sport of Fate forever.
Dread Power, but dear! if God thou be,
Unmake me quite, or give thyself to me!

Brahma[1]

If the red slayer think he slays,
    Or if the slain think he is slain,
They know not well the subtle ways
    I keep, and pass, and turn again.

Far or forgot to me is near;
    Shadow and sunlight are the same;
The vanished gods to me appear;
    And one to me are shame and fame.

They reckon ill who leave me out;
    When me they fly, I am the wings;
I am the doubter and the doubt,
    And I the hymn the Brahmin[2] sings.

The strong gods pine for my abode,
    And pine in vain the sacred Seven;[3]
But thou, meek lover of the good!
    Find me, and turn thy back on heaven.

Days

Daughters of Time, the hypocritic Days,
Muffled and dumb like barefoot dervishes,[1]
And marching single in an endless file,
Bring diadems and fagots[2] in their hands.
To each they offer gifts after his will,
Bread, kingdoms, stars, and sky that holds them all.

1. The portable case for holding large drawings ("portfolio") contains the work of the painters Salvator Rosa (1615–73), Giovanni Francesco Barbieri ("Guercino") (1591–1666), and Giambattista Piranesi (1720–78).
2. Songs of praise—specifically, ancient Greek hymns in honour of Apollo, the god of music and poetry, who is reputed to have constructed the lyre from a turtle shell.
3. In Greek mythology the summit of Mount Olympus was regarded as the residence of the gods; here Emerson pictures divinely inspired poets singing on the lower reaches of the mountain.

1. The title of this poem is the designation generally applied to the Supreme Soul of the universe in orthodox Hindu belief; Brahma is the impersonal, all-embracing divine essence, the original source and ultimate goal of all that exists. In addition, the word brahma means a devotional rite, prayer or hymn (see l. 12).
2. Priest and worshipper of Brahma.
3. Saints of the Brahman faith.

1. Mohammedan holy man who leads an ascetic life.
2. Crowns ("diadems"), the emblems of royalty, and bundles of sticks ("fagots"), emblems of military power.

I, in my pleached[3] garden, watched the pomp,
Forgot my morning wishes, hastily
Took a few herbs and apples, and the Day
Turned and departed silent. I, too late,
Under her solemn fillet[4] saw the scorn.

Terminus[1]

It is time to be old,
To take in sail:—
The god of bounds,
Who sets to seas a shore,
5　Came to me in his fatal rounds,
And said, 'No more!
No farther shoot
Thy broad ambitious branches, and thy root.
Fancy departs: no more invent,
10　Contract they firmament
To compass of a tent.
There's not enough for this and that,
Make thy option which of two;
Economize the failing river,
15　Not the less revere the Giver,
Leave the many and hold the few.
Timely wise accept the terms,
Soften the fall with wary foot;
A little while
20　Still plan and smile,
And—fault of novel germs—

Mature the unfallen fruit.
Curse, if thou wilt, thy sires,
Bad husbands of their fires,
25　Who, when they gave thee breath,
Failed to bequeath
The needful sinew stark as once,
The Baresark[2] marrow to thy bones,
But left a legacy of ebbing veins,
30　Inconstant heat and nerveless reins,—
Amid the Muses, left thee deaf and dumb,
Amid the gladiators, halt and numb.'

As the bird trims her to the gale,
I trim myself to the storm of time,
35　I man the rudder, reef the sail,
Obey the voice at eve obeyed at prime:
'Lowly faithful, banish fear,
Right onward drive unharmed;
The port, well worth the cruise, is near,
40　And every wave is charmed.'

JOHN GREENLEAF WHITTIER (1807–92)

Abraham Davenport[1]

In the old days (a custom laid aside
With breeches and cocked hats) the people sent
Their wisest men to make the public laws.
And so, from a brown homestead, where the Sound
5　Drinks the small tribute of the Mianas,
Waved over by the woods of Rippowams,[2]
And hallowed by pure lives and tranquil deaths,
Stamford sent up to the councils of the State
Wisdom and grace in Abraham Davenport.

---

3. Interwoven.
4. Headband.

1. The Roman god of boundaries and limits.
2. Berserk—literally, "bare-shirt," in reference to ancient Scandinavian warriors of extreme fierceness who fought without armour.

1. Abraham Davenport (1715–89), who was a lawyer in Stamford, Connecticut, and a staunch patriot during the American Revolution, was for twenty-five years a member of the state legislature of Connecticut before being advanced to the Council of Assistants (i.e., becoming a state senator), a position which he held from 1766 to 1784. President Dwight said of him and of the incident related in Whittier's poem: "Colonel Davenport was possessed of a vigorous understanding, and invincible firmness of mind; of integrity, and justice, unquestioned even by his enemies; of veracity, exact in a degree nearly singular; and of . . . weight of character. . . . He was early a professor of the Christian religion; and adorned its doctrines by an exemplary conformity to its precepts. . . . The 19th of May, 1780, was a remarkable day. Candles were lighted in many houses; the birds were silent, and disappeared; and the fowls retired to roost. The Legislature of Connecticut was then in session at Hartford. A very general opinion prevailed, that the day of Judgement was at hand. The House of Representatives, being unable to transact their business, adjourned. A proposal to adjourn the Council was under consideration. When the opinion of Colonel Davenport was asked, he answered, 'I am against an adjournment. The day of Judgement is either approaching, or it is not. If it is not, there is no cause for adjournment; if it is, I choose to be found doing my duty. I wish, therefore, that candles may be brought.' "
2. Topographical features of western Connecticut.

10   'Twas on a May-day of the far old year
Seventeen hundred eighty, that there fell
Over the bloom and sweet life of the Spring,
Over the fresh earth and the heaven of noon,
A horror of great darkness, like the night
15 In day of which the Norland sagas tell,—
The Twilight of the Gods.[3] The low-hung sky
Was black with ominous clouds, save where its rim
Was fringed with a dull glow, like that which climbs
The crater's sides from the red hell below.
20 Birds ceased to sing, and all the barn-yard fowls
Roosted; the cattle at the pasture bars
Lowed, and looked homeward; bats on leathern wings
Flitted abroad; the sounds of labor died;
Men prayed, and women wept; all ears grew sharp
25 To hear the doom-blast of the trumpet[4] shatter
The black sky, that the dreadful face of Christ
Might look from the rent clouds, not as He looked
A loving guest at Bethany,[5] but stern
As Justice and inexorable Law.

30   Meanwhile in the old State House, dim as ghosts,
Sat the lawgivers of Connecticut,
Trembling beneath their legislative robes.
"It is the Lord's Great Day! Let us adjourn,"
Some said; and then, as if with one accord,
35 All eyes were turned to Abraham Davenport.
He rose, slow cleaving with his steady voice
The intolerable hush. "This well may be
The Day of Judgment which the world awaits;
But be it so or not, I only know
40 My present duty, and my Lord's command
To occupy till He come. So at the post
Where He hath set me in His providence,
I choose, for one, to meet Him face to face,—
No faithless servant frightened from my task,
45 But ready when the Lord of the harvest[6] calls;
And therefore, with all reverence, I would say,
Let God do His work, we will see to ours.
Bring in the candles." And they brought them in.

    Then by the flaring lights the Speaker read,
50 Albeit with husky voice and shaking hands,
An act to amend an act to regulate
The shad and alewive[7] fisheries. Whereupon
Wisely and well spake Abraham Davenport,
Straight to the question, with no figures of speech
55 Save the ten Arab signs,[8] yet not without
The shrewd dry humor natural to the man:
His awe-struck colleagues listening all the while,
Between the pauses of his argument,
To hear the thunder of the wrath of God
60 Break from the hollow trumpet of the cloud.

    And there he stands in memory to this day,
Erect, self-poised, a rugged face, half seen
Against the background of unnatural dark,
A witness to the ages as they pass,
65 That simple duty hath no place for fear.

---

3. The *Götterdämmerung*, the day of final reckoning and destruction, in Norse and Germanic mythology.
4. Announcing the Day of Judgement.
5. See Matt. xxvi.6–13 for the incident where Christ was attended in the house of Simon the leper by the woman who anointed him with precious ointment.
6. See Luke x.2.
7. Fish of the herring family.
8. Numerals.

HENRY WADSWORTH LONGFELLOW (1807–82)

The Jewish Cemetery at Newport[1]

How strange it seems! These Hebrews in their graves,
   Close by the street of this fair seaport town,
Silent beside the never-silent waves,
   At rest in all this moving up and down!

5   The trees are white with dust, that o'er their sleep
   Wave their broad curtains in the southwind's breath,
While underneath these leafy tents they keep
   The long, mysterious Exodus[2] of Death.

And these sepulchral stones, so old and brown,
10   That pave with level flags their burial-place,
Seem like the tablets of the Law, thrown down
   And broken by Moses at the mountain's base.[3]

The very names recorded here are strange,
   Of foreign accent, and of different climes;
15 Alvares and Rivera interchange
   With Abraham and Jacob of old times.

"Blessed be God, for he created Death!"
   The mourners said, "and Death is rest and peace;"
Then added, in the certainty of faith,
20   "And giveth Life that nevermore shall cease."

Closed are the portals of their Synagogue,
   No Psalms of David now the silence break,
No Rabbi reads the ancient Decalogue
   In the grand dialect the Prophets spake.

25 Gone are the living, but the dead remain,
   And not neglected; for a hand unseen,
Scattering its bounty, like a summer rain,
   Still keeps their graves and their remembrance green.

How came they here? What burst of Christian hate,
30   What persecution, merciless and blind,
Drove o'er the sea—that desert desolate—
   These Ishmaels and Hagars of mankind?[4]

They lived in narrow streets and lanes obscure,
   Ghetto and Judenstrass,[5] in mirk and mire;
35 Taught in the school of patience to endure
   The life of anguish and the death of fire.

All their lives long, with the unleavened bread
   And bitter herbs of exile and its fears,
The wasting famine of the heart they fed,
40   And slaked its thirst with marah[6] of their tears.

1. Longfellow visited the Jewish Cemetery in Newport, Rhode Island, on 9 July 1852.
2. The migration of the Israelites from Egypt to the Promised Land is recorded in the book of Exodus.
3. See Exod. xxxii.19: "Moses' anger waxed hot [at the sight of the golden calf], and he cast the tables out of his hand, and brake them beneath the mount."
4. See Gen. xvi and xxi for the exile and wanderings of Abraham's concubine Hagar and her son Ishmael.
5. (German) "Street of Jews."
6. (Hebrew) "bitterness," in reference to the bitter stream found by the Israelites in the wilderness (see Exod. xv.23–26). "Unleavened bread" and "bitter herbs" are associated with the Jewish celebration of the Passover.

Anathema maranatha![7] was the cry
   That rang from town to town, from street to street:
At every gate the accursed Mordecai[8]
   Was mocked and jeered, and spurned by Christian feet.

45 Pride and humiliation hand in hand
   Walked with them through the world where'er they went;
Trampled and beaten were they as the sand,
   And yet unshaken as the continent.

For in the background figures vague and vast
50   Of patriarchs and of prophets rose sublime,
And all the great traditions of the Past
   They saw reflected in the coming time.

And thus forever with reverted look
   The mystic volume of the world they read,
55 Spelling it backward, like a Hebrew book,
   Till life became a Legend of the Dead.

But ah! what once has been shall be no more!
   The groaning earth in travail and in pain
Brings forth its races, but does not restore,
60   And the dead nations never rise again.

Nature

As a fond mother, when the day is o'er,
   Leads by the hand her little child to bed,
   Half willing, half reluctant to be led,
And leave his broken playthings on the floor,
Still gazing at them through the open door,
   Nor wholly reassured and comforted
   By promises of others in their stead,
Which, though more splendid, may not please him more;
So Nature deals with us, and takes away
   Our playthings one by one, and by the hand
Leads us to rest so gently, that we go
Scarce knowing if we wish to go or stay,
   Being too full of sleep to understand
   How far the unknown transcends the what we know.

The Tide Rises, the Tide Falls

The tide rises, the tide falls,
The twilight darkens, the curlew[1] calls;
Along the sea-sands damp and brown
The traveller hastens toward the town,
   And the tide rises, the tide falls.

Darkness settles on roofs and walls,
But the sea, the sea in the darkness calls;
The little waves, with their soft, white hands,
Efface the footprints in the sands,
   And the tide rises, the tide falls.

The morning breaks; the steeds in their stalls
Stamp and neigh, as the hostler[2] calls;
The day returns, but nevermore
Returns the traveller to the shore,
   And the tide rises, the tide falls.

7. See 1 Cor. xvi.22: "If any man love not the Lord Jesus
Christ let him be Anathema Maran-atha ('destroyed when
the Lord comes')." These words came to be applied
specifically to the Jews.
8. See Esther iii for the story of how Haman's jealousy
over the Jew Mordecai prompted him to attempt to effect
the destruction of all Jews in the kingdom.

1. Bird allied to the snipe found and heard frequently at
the sea-side.
2. Stable-boy.

Ultima Thule[1]
Dedication: To G. W. G.[2]

With favoring winds, o'er sunlit seas,
We sailed for the Hesperides,[3]
The land where golden apples grow;
But that, ah! that was long ago.

How far since then the ocean streams
Have swept us from that land of dreams,
That land of fiction and of truth,
The lost Atlantis[4] of our youth!

Whither, ah, whither? Are not these
The tempest-haunted Orcades,[5]
Where sea-gulls scream, and breakers roar,
And wreck and sea-weed line the shore?

Ultima Thule! Utmost Isle!
Here in thy harbors for a while
We lower our sails; a while we rest
From the unending, endless quest.

WALT WHITMAN (1819–92)

Out of the Cradle Endlessly Rocking

Out of the cradle endlessly rocking,
Out of the mocking-bird's throat, the musical shuttle,
Out of the Ninth-month[1] midnight,
Over the sterile sands and the fields beyond, where the child leaving his bed wander'd alone,
        bareheaded, barefoot,
5   Down from the shower'd halo,
Up from the mystic play of shadows twining and twisting as if they were alive,
Out from the patches of briers and blackberries,
From the memories of the bird that chanted to me,
From your memories sad brother, from the fitful risings and fallings I heard,
10   From under that yellow half-moon late-risen and swollen as if with tears,
From those beginning notes of yearning and love there in the mist,
From the thousand responses of my heart never to cease,
From the myriad thence-arous'd words,
From the word stronger and more delicious than any,
15   From such as now they start the scene revisiting,
As a flock, twittering, rising, or overhead passing,
Borne hither, ere all eludes me, hurriedly,
A man, yet by these tears a little boy again,
Throwing myself on the sand, confronting the waves,
20   I, chanter of pains and joys, uniter of here and hereafter,
Taking all hints to use them, but swiftly leaping beyond them,
A reminiscence sing.

Once Paumanok,[2]
When the lilac-scent was in the air and Fifth-month[3] grass was growing,
25   Up this seashore in some briers,
Two feather'd guests from Alabama, two together,
And their nest, and four light-green eggs spotted with brown,
And every day the he-bird to and fro near at hand,
And every day the she-bird crouch'd on her nest, silent, with bright eyes,
30   And every day I, a curious boy, never too close, never disturbing them,
Cautiously peering, absorbing, translating.

1. The name given by the Romans to the most northern country known—hence, the goal of the final journey.
2. George Washington Greene, friend with whom the poet had discussed his life's goals as a young man.
3. The "Daughters of the Evening" who, in Greek mythology, were supposed to live in the remote West guarding a tree that bore golden apples.
4. A continent believed by the Greeks to have existed in the far West and to have sunk below the Atlantic ocean.
5. The Orkney Islands off the coast of Scotland.

1. September, with suggestions also of the human period of gestation and, hence, of fertility and birth.
2. The Indian name for Long Island, where Whitman was born on 31 May 1819.
3. May.

Shine! shine! shine!
Pour down your warmth, great sun!
While we bask, we two together.

35 *Two together!*
Winds blow south or winds blow north,
Day come white, or night come black,
Home, or rivers and mountains from home,
Singing all time, minding no time,
40 *While we two keep together.*

Till of a sudden,
May-be kill'd, unknown to her mate,
One forenoon the she-bird crouch'd not on the nest,
Nor return'd that afternoon, nor the next,
45 Nor ever appear'd again.

And thenceforward all summer in the sound of the sea,
And at night under the full of the moon in calmer weather,
Over the hoarse surging of the sea,
Or flitting from brier to brier by day,
50 I saw, I heard at intervals the remaining one, the he-bird,
The solitary guest from Alabama.

Blow! blow! blow!
Blow up sea-winds along Paumanok's shore;
I wait and I wait till you blow my mate to me.

55 Yes, when the stars glisten'd,
All night long on the prong of a moss-scallop'd stake,
Down almost amid the slapping waves,
Sat the lone singer wonderful causing tears.

He call'd on his mate,
60 He pour'd forth the meanings which I of all men know.

Yes my brother I know,
The rest might not, but I have treasur'd every note,
For more than once dimly down to the beach gliding,
Silent, avoiding the moonbeams, blending myself with the shadows,
65 Recalling now the obscure shapes, the echoes, the sounds and sights after their sorts,
The white arms out in the breakers tirelessly tossing,
I, with bare feet, a child, the wind wafting my hair,
Listen'd long and long.

Listen'd to keep, to sing, now translating the notes,
70 Following you my brother.

Soothe! soothe! soothe!
Close on its wave soothes the wave behind,
And again another behind embracing and lapping, every one close,
But my love soothes not me, not me.

75 *Low hangs the moon, it rose late,*
It is lagging—O I think it is heavy with love, with love.

O madly the sea pushes upon the land,
With love, with love.

O night! do I not see my love fluttering out among the breakers?
80 *What is that little black thing I see there in the white?*

Loud! loud! loud!
Loud I call to you, my love!

     High and clear I shoot my voice over the waves,
     Surely you must know who is here, is here,
85   *You must know who I am, my love.*

     Low-hanging moon!
     What is that dusky spot in your brown yellow?
     O it is the shape, the shape of my mate!
     O moon do not keep her from me any longer.

90   *Land! land! O land!*
     Whichever way I turn, O I think you could give me my mate back again if you only would,
     For I am almost sure I see her dimly whichever way I look.

     O rising stars!
     Perhaps the one I want so much will rise, will rise with some of you.

95   *O throat! O trembling throat!*
     Sound clearer through the atmosphere!
     Pierce the woods, the earth,
     Somewhere listening to catch you must be the one I want.

     Shake out carols!
100   *Solitary here, the night's carols!*
     Carols of lonesome love! death's carols!
     Carols under that lagging, yellow, waning moon!
     O under that moon where she droops almost down into the sea!
     O reckless despairing carols.

105   *But soft! sink low!*
     Soft! let me just murmur,
     And do you wait a moment you husky-nois'd sea,
     For somewhere I believe I heard my mate responding to me,
     So faint, I must be still, be still to listen,
110   *But not altogether still, for then she might not come immediately to me.*

     Hither my love!
     Here I am! here!
     With this just-sustain'd note I announce myself to you,
     This gentle call is for you my love, for you.

115   *Do not be decoy'd elsewhere,*
     That is the whistle of the wind, it is not my voice,
     That is the fluttering, the fluttering of the spray,
     Those are the shadows of leaves.

     O darkness! O in vain!
120   *O I am very sick and sorrowful.*

     O brown halo in the sky near the moon, drooping upon the sea!
     O troubled reflection in the sea!
     O throat! O throbbing heart!
     And I singing uselessly, uselessly all the night.

125   *O past! O happy life! O songs of joy!*
     In the air, in the woods, over fields,
     Loved! loved! loved! loved! loved!
     But my mate no more, no more with me!
     We two together no more.

130   The aria[4] sinking,
       All else continuing, the stars shining,
       The winds blowing, the notes of the bird continuous echoing,
       With angry moans the fierce old mother incessantly moaning,
       On the sands of Paumanok's shore gray and rustling,
135   The yellow half-moon enlarged, sagging down, drooping, the face of the sea almost touching,
       The boy ecstatic, with his bare feet the waves, with his hair the atmosphere dallying,
       The love in the heart long pent, now loose, now at last tumultuously bursting,
       The aria's meaning, the ears, the soul, swiftly depositing,
       The strange tears down the cheeks coursing,
140   The colloquy there, the trio, each uttering,
       The undertone, the savage old mother incessantly crying,
       To the boy's soul's questions sullenly timing, some drown'd secret hissing,
       To the outsetting bard.

       Demon or bird! (said the boy's soul,)
145   Is it indeed toward your mate you sing? or is it really to me?
       For I, that was a child, my tongue's use sleeping, now I have heard you,
       Now in a moment I know what I am for, I awake,
       And already a thousand singers, a thousand songs, clearer, louder and more sorrowful than yours,
       A thousand warbling echoes have started to life within me, never to die.

150   O you singer solitary, singing by yourself, projecting me,
       O solitary me listening, never more shall I cease perpetuating you,
       Never more shall I escape, never more the reverberations,
       Never more the cries of unsatisifed love be absent from me,
       Never again leave me to be the peaceful child I was before what there in the night,
155   By the sea under the yellow and sagging moon,
       The messenger there arous'd, the fire, the sweet hell within,
       The unknown want, the destiny of me.

       O give me the clew! (it lurks in the night here somewhere,)
       O if I am to have so much, let me have more!

160   A word then, (for I will conquer it,)
       The word final, superior to all,
       Subtle, sent up—what is it?—I listen;
       Are you whispering it, and have been all the time, you sea-waves?
       Is that it from your liquid rims and wet sands?

165   Whereto answering, the sea,
       Delaying not, hurrying not,
       Whisper'd me through the night, and very plainly before daybreak,
       Lisp'd to me the low and delicious word death,
       And again death, death, death, death,
170   Hissing melodious, neither like the bird nor like my arous'd child's heart,
       But edging near as privately for me rustling at my feet,
       Creeping thence steadily up to my ears and laving me softly all over,
       Death, death, death, death, death.

       Which I do not forget,
175   But fuse the song of my dusky demon and brother,
       That he sang to me in the moonlight on Paumanok's gray beach,
       With the thousand responsive songs at random,
       My own songs awaked from that hour,
       And with them the key, the word up from the waves,
180   The word of the sweetest song and all songs,
       That strong and delicious word which, creeping to my feet,
       (Or like some old crone rocking the cradle, swathed in sweet garments, bending aside,)
       The sea whisper'd me.

4. Melody sung by a single voice, as in an opera.

When I Heard the Learn'd Astronomer

When I heard the learn'd astronomer,
When the proofs, the figures, were ranged in columns before me,
When I was shown the charts and diagrams, to add, divide, and measure them,
When I sitting heard the astronomer where he lectured with much applause in the lecture-room,
How soon unaccountable I became tired and sick,
Till rising and gliding out I wander'd off by myself,
In the mystical moist night-air, and from time to time,
Look'd up in perfect silence at the stars.

The Dalliance of the Eagles

Skirting the river road, (my forenoon walk, my rest,)
Skyward in air a sudden muffled sound, the dalliance of the eagles,
The rushing amorous contact high in space together,
The clinching interlocking claws, a living, fierce, gyrating wheel,
Four beating wings, two beaks, a swirling mass tight grappling,
In tumbling turning clustering loops, straight downward falling,
Till o'er the river pois'd, the twain yet one, a moment's lull,
A motionless still balance in the air, then parting, talons loosing,
Upward again on slow, firm pinions slanting, their separate diverse flight,
She hers, he his, pursuing.

When Lilacs Last in the Dooryard Bloom'd[1]

1
When lilacs last in the dooryard bloom'd,
And the great star early droop'd in the western sky in the night,
I mourn'd, and yet shall mourn with ever-returning spring.

Ever-returning spring, trinity sure to me you bring,
5   Lilac blooming perennial and drooping star in the west,
And thought of him I love.

2
O powerful western fallen star!
O shades of night—O moody, tearful night!
O great star disappear'd—O the black murk that hides the star!
10   O cruel hands that hold me powerless—O helpless soul of me!
O harsh surrounding cloud that will not free my soul.

3
In the dooryard fronting an old farm-house near the white-wash'd palings,
Stands the lilac-bush tall-growing with heart-shaped leaves of rich green,
With many a pointed blossom rising delicate, with the perfume strong I love,
15   With every leaf a miracle—and from this bush in the dooryard,
With delicate-color'd blossoms and heart-shaped leaves of rich green,
A sprig with its flower I break.

4
In the swamp in secluded recesses,
A shy and hidden bird is warbling a song.

20   Solitary the thrush,
The hermit withdrawn to himself, avoiding the settlements,
Sings by himself a song.

---

1. This poem is one of Whitman's elegiac "Memories of
President Lincoln," who became president of the United
States in 1861 and was assassinated in 1865.

Song of the bleeding throat,
Death's outlet song of life, (for well dear brother I know,
25 If thou wast not granted to sing thou would'st surely die.)

5
Over the breast of the spring, the land, amid cities,
Amid lanes and through old woods, where lately the violets peep'd from the ground, spotting
the gray debris,
Amid the grass in the fields each side of the lanes, passing the endless grass,
Passing the yellow-spear'd wheat, every grain from its shroud in the dark-brown fields uprisen,
30 Passing the apple-tree blows of white and pink in the orchards,
Carrying a corpse to where it shall rest in the grave,
Night and day journeys a coffin.

6
Coffin that passes through lanes and streets,[2]
Through day and night with the great cloud darkening the land,
35 With the pomp of the inloop'd flags with the cities draped in black,
With the show of the States themselves as of crape-veil'd women standing,
With processions long and winding and the flambeaus of the night,
With the countless torches lit, with the silent sea of faces and the unbared heads,
With the waiting depot, the arriving coffin, and the sombre faces,
40 With dirges through the night, with the thousand voices rising strong and solemn,
With all the mournful voices of the dirges pour'd around the coffin,
The dim-lit churches and the shuddering organs—where amid these you journey,
With the tolling tolling bells' perpetual clang,
Here, coffin that slowly passes,
45 I give you my sprig of lilac.

7
(Nor for you, for one alone,
Blossoms and branches green to coffins all I bring,
For fresh as the morning, thus would I chant a song for you O sane and sacred death.

All over bouquets of roses,
50 O death, I cover you over with roses and early lilies,
But mostly and now the lilac that blooms the first,
Copious I break, I break the sprigs from the bushes,
With loaded arms I come, pouring for you,
For you and the coffins all of you O death.)

8
55 O western orb sailing the heaven,
Now I know what you must have meant as a month since I walk'd,
As I walk'd in silence the transparent shadowy night,
As I saw you had something to tell as you bent to me night after night,
As you droop'd from the sky low down as if to my side, (while the other stars all look'd on,)
60 As we wander'd together the solemn night, (for something I know not what kept me from sleep,)
As the night advanced, and I saw on the rim of the west how full you were of woe,
As I stood on the rising ground in the breeze in the cool transparent night,
As I watch'd where you pass'd and was lost in the netherward black of the night,
As my soul in its trouble dissatisfied sank, as where you sad orb,
65 Concluded, dropt in the night, and was gone.

9
Sing on there in the swamp,
O singer bashful and tender, I hear your notes, I hear your call,
I hear, I come presently, I understand you,
But a moment I linger, for the lustrous star has detain'd me,
70 The star my departing comrade holds and detains me.

2. On its way from Washington, D.C., to burial in Springfield, Illinois, Lincoln's coffin passed through several states. At many cities and towns mourners paid their last respects to the murdered president.

10

O how shall I warble myself for the dead one there I loved?
And how shall I deck my song for the large sweet soul that has gone?
And what shall my perfume be for the grave of him I love?

Sea-winds blown from east and west,
75   Blown from the Eastern sea and blown from the Western sea, till there on the prairies meeting,
These and with these and the breath of my chant,
I'll perfume the grave of him I love.

11

O what shall I hang on the chamber walls?
And what shall the pictures be that I hang on the walls,
80   To adorn the burial-house of him I love?

Pictures of growing spring and farms and homes,
With the Fourth-month eve at sundown, and the gray smoke lucid and bright,
With floods of the yellow gold of the gorgeous, indolent, sinking sun, burning, expanding the air,
With the fresh sweet herbage under foot, and the pale green leaves of the trees prolific,
85   In the distance the flowing glaze, the breast of the river, with a wind-dapple here and there,
With ranging hills on the banks, with many a line against the sky, and shadows,
And the city at hand with dwellings so dense, and stacks of chimneys,
And all the scenes of life and the workshops, and the workmen homeward returning.

12

Lo, body and soul— this land,
90   My own Manhattan with spires, and the sparkling and hurrying tides, and the ships,
The varied and ample land, the South and the North in the light, Ohio's shores and flashing
                  Missouri,
And ever the far-spreading prairies cover'd with grass and corn.

Lo, the most excellent sun so calm and haughty,
The violet and purple morn with just-felt breezes,
95   The gentle soft-born measureless light,
The miracle spreading bathing all, the fulfill'd noon,
The coming eve delicious, the welcome night and the stars,
Over my cities shining all, enveloping man and land.

13

Sing on, sing on you gray-brown bird,
100   Sing from the swamps, the recesses, pour your chant from the bushes,
Limitless out of the dusk, out of the cedars and pines.

Sing on dearest brother, warble your reedy song,
Loud human song, with voice of uttermost woe.

O liquid and free and tender!
105   O wild and loose to my soul—O wondrous singer!
You only I hear—yet the star holds me, (but will soon depart,)
Yet the lilac with mastering odor holds me.

14

Now while I sat in the day and look'd forth,
In the close of the day with its light and the fields of spring, and the farmers preparing their crops,
110   In the large unconscious scenery of my land with its lakes and forests,
In the heavenly aerial beauty, (after the perturb'd winds and the storms,)
Under the arching heavens of the afternoon swift passing, and the voices of children and women,
The many-moving sea-tides, and I saw the ships how they sail'd,
And the summer approaching with richness, and the fields all busy with labor,
115   And the infinite separate houses, how they all went on, each with its meals and minutia of daily
                  usages,

And the streets how their throbbings throbb'd, and the cities pent—lo, then and there,
Falling upon them all and among them all, enveloping me with the rest,
Appear'd the cloud, appear'd the long black trail,
And I knew death, its thought, and the sacred knowledge of death.

120 Then with the knowledge of death as walking one side of me,
And the thought of death close-walking the other side of me,
And I in the middle as with companions, and as holding the hands of companions,
I fled forth to the hiding receiving night that talks not,
Down to the shores of the water, the path by the swamp in the dimness,
125 To the solemn shadowy cedars and ghostly pines so still.

And the singer so shy to the rest receiv'd me,
The gray-brown bird I know receiv'd us comrades three,
And he sang the carol of death, and a verse for him I love.

From deep secluded recesses,
130 From the fragrant cedars and the ghostly pines so still,
Came the carol of the bird.

And the charm of the carol rapt me,
As I held as if by their hands my comrades in the night,
And the voice of my spirit tallied the song of the bird.

135 *Come lovely and soothing death,*
Undulate round the world, serenely arriving, arriving,
In the day, in the night, to all, to each,
Sooner or later delicate death.

Prais'd be the fathomless universe,
140 *For life and joy, and for objects and knowledge curious,*
And for love, sweet love—but praise! praise! praise!
For the sure-enwinding arms of cool-enfolding death.

Dark mother always gliding near with soft feet,
Have none chanted for thee a chant of fullest welcome?
145 *Then I chant it for thee, I glorify thee above all,*
I bring thee a song that when thou must indeed come, come unfalteringly.

Approach strong deliveress,
When it is so, when thou hast taken them I joyously sing the dead,
Lost in the loving floating ocean of thee,
150 *Laved in the flood of thy bliss O death.*

From me to thee glad serenades,
Dances for thee I propose saluting thee, adornments and feastings for thee,
And the sights of the open landscape and the high-spread sky are fitting,
And life and the fields, and the huge and thoughtful night.

155 *The night in silence under many a star,*
The ocean shore and the husky whispering wave whose voice I know,
And the soul turning to thee O vast and well-veil'd death,
And the body gratefully nestling close to thee.

Over the tree-tops I float thee a song,
160 *Over the rising and sinking waves, over the myriad fields and the prairies wide,*
Over the dense-pack'd cities all and the teeming wharves and ways,
I float this carol with joy, with joy to thee O death.

15

To the tally of my soul,
Loud and strong kept up the gray-brown bird,
165   With pure deliberate notes spreading filling the night.

Loud in the pines and cedars dim,
Clear in the freshness moist and the swamp-perfume,
And I with my comrades there in the night.

While my sight that was bound in my eyes unclosed,
170   As to long panoramas of visions.

And I saw askant the armies,
I saw as in noiseless dreams hundreds of battle-flags,
Borne through the smoke of the battles and pierc'd with missiles I saw them,
And carried hither and yon through the smoke, and torn and bloody,
175   And at last but a few shreds left on the staffs, (and all in silence,)
And the staffs all splinter'd and broken.

I saw battle-corpses, myriads of them,
And the white skeletons of young men, I saw them,
I saw the debris and debris of all the slain soldiers of the war,
180   But I saw they were not as was thought,
They themselves were fully at rest, they suffer'd not,
The living remain'd and suffer'd, the mother suffer'd,
And the wife and the child and the musing comrade suffer'd,
And the armies that remain'd suffer'd.

16

185   Passing the visions, passing the night,
Passing, unloosing the hold of my comrades' hands,
Passing the song of the hermit bird and the tallying song of my soul,
Victorious song, death's outlet song, yet varying ever-altering song,
As low and wailing, yet clear the notes, rising and falling, flooding the night,
190   Sadly sinking and fainting, as warning and warning, and yet again bursting with joy,
Covering the earth and filling the spread of the heaven,
As that powerful psalm in the night I heard from recesses,
Passing, I leave thee lilac with heart-shaped leaves,
I leave thee there in the dooryard, blooming, returning with spring.

195   I cease from my song for thee,
From my gaze on thee in the west, fronting the west, communing with thee,
O comrade lustrous with silver face in the night.

Yet each to keep and all, retrievements out of the night,
The song, the wondrous chant of the gray-brown bird,
200   And the tallying chant, the echo arous'd in my soul,
With the lustrous and drooping star with the countenance full of woe,
With the holders holding my hand nearing the call of the bird,
Comrades mine and I in the midst, and their memory ever to keep, for the dead I loved so well,
For the sweetest, wisest soul of all my days and lands—and this for his dear sake,
205   Lilac and star and bird twined with the chant of my soul,
There in the fragrant pines and the cedars dusk and dim.

A Noiseless Patient Spider

A noiseless patient spider,
I mark'd where on a little promontory it stood isolated,
Mark'd how to explore the vacant vast surrounding,
It launch'd forth filament, filament, filament, out of itself,
Ever unreeling them, ever tirelessly speeding them.

And you O my soul where you stand,
Surrounded, detached, in measureless oceans of space,
Ceaselessly musing, venturing, throwing, seeking the spheres to connect them,
Till the bridge you will need be form'd, till the ductile anchor hold,
Till the gossamer thread you fling catch somewhere, O my soul.

To a Locomotive in Winter

Thee for my recitative,
Thee in the driving storm even as now, the snow, the winter-day declining,
Thee in thy panoply, thy measur'd dual throbbing and thy beat convulsive,
Thy black cylindric body, golden brass and silvery steel,
Thy ponderous side-bars, parallel and connecting rods, gyrating, shuttling at thy sides,
Thy metrical, now swelling pant and roar, now tapering in the distance,
Thy great protruding head-light fix'd in front,
Thy long, pale, floating vapor-pennants, tinged with delicate purple,
The dense and murky clouds out-belching from thy smoke-stack,
Thy knitted frame, thy springs and valves, the tremulous twinkle of thy wheels,
Thy train of cars behind, obedient, merrily following,
Through gale or calm, now swift, now slack, yet steadily careering;
Type of the modern— emblem of motion and power— pulse of the continent,
For once come serve the Muse and merge in verse, even as here I see thee,
With storm and buffeting gusts of wind and falling snow,
By day thy warning ringing bell to sound its notes,
By night thy silent signal lamps to swing.

Fierce-throated beauty!
Roll through my chant with all thy lawless music, thy swinging lamps at night,
Thy madly-whistled laughter, echoing, rumbling like an earthquake, rousing all,
Law of thyself complete, thine own track firmly holding,
(No sweetness debonair of tearful harp or glib piano thine,)
Thy trills of shrieks by rocks and hills return'd,
Launch'd o'er the prairies wide, across the lakes,
To the free skies unpent and glad and strong.

Joy, Shipmate, Joy![1]

Joy, shipmate, joy!
(Pleas'd to my soul at death I cry,)
Our life is closed, our life begins,
The long, long anchorage we leave,

The ship is clear at last, she leaps!
She swiftly courses from the shore,
Joy, shipmate, joy!

EMILY DICKINSON (1830–86)

67

Success is counted sweetest
By those who ne'er succeed.
To comprehend a nectar
Requires sorest need.

Not one of all the purple Host
Who took the Flag today
Can tell the definition
So clear of Victory

As he defeated— dying—
On whose forbidden ear
The distant strains of triumph
Burst agonized and clear!

1. This is one of the "Songs of Parting" which conclude the
1871 edition of *Leaves of Grass*.

76

Exultation is the going
Of an inland soul to sea,
Past the houses—past the headlands—
Into deep Eternity—

Bred as we, among the mountains,
Can the sailor understand
The divine intoxication
Of the first league out from land?

214

I taste a liquor never brewed—
From Tankards scooped in Pearl—
Not all the Vats upon the Rhine
Yield such an Alcohol!

When "Landlords" turn the drunken Bee
Out of the Foxglove's door—
When Butterflies—renounce their "drams"—
I shall but drink the more!

Inebriate of Air—am I—
And Debauchee of Dew—
Reeling—thro endless summer days—
From inns of Molten Blue—

Till Seraphs swing their snowy Hats—
And Saints—to windows run—
To see the little Tippler
Leaning against the—Sun—

241

I like a look of Agony,
Because I know it's true—
Men do not sham Convulsion,
Nor simulate, a Throe—

The Eyes glaze once—and that is Death—
Impossible to feign
The Beads upon the Forehead
By homely Anguish strung.

258

There's a certain Slant of light,
Winter Afternoons—
That oppresses, like the Heft
Of Cathedral Tunes—

None may teach it—Any—
'Tis the Seal Despair—
An imperial affliction
Sent us of the Air—

Heavenly Hurt, it gives us—
We can find no scar,
But internal difference,
Where the Meanings, are—

When it comes, the Landscape listens—
Shadows—hold their breath—
When it goes, 'tis like the Distance
On the look of Death—

290

Of Bronze— and Blaze—
The North—Tonight—
So adequate—it forms—
So preconcerted with itself—
So distant—to alarms—
An Unconcern so sovereign
To Universe, or me—
Infects my simple spirit
With Taints of Majesty—
Till I take vaster attitudes—
And strut upon my stem—
Disdaining Men, and Oxygen,
For Arrogance of them—

My Splendors, are Menagerie—
But their Competeless Show
Will entertain the Centuries
When I, am long ago,
An Island in dishonored Grass—
Whom none but Beetles—know.

303

The Soul selects her own Society—
Then—shuts the Door—
To her divine Majority—
Present no more—

Unmoved—she notes the Chariots—pausing—
At her low Gate—
Unmoved— an Emperor be kneeling
Upon her Mat—

I've known her—from an ample nation—
Choose One—
Then—close the Valves of her attention—
Like Stone—

324

Some keep the Sabbath going to Church—
I keep it, staying at Home—
With a Bobolink for a Chorister—
And an Orchard, for a Dome—

Some keep the Sabbath in Surplice—
I just wear my Wings—
And instead of tolling the Bell, for Church,
Our little Sexton—sings.

God preaches, a noted Clergyman—
And the sermon is never long,
So instead of getting to Heaven, at last—
I'm going, all along.

328

A Bird came down the Walk—
He did not know I saw—
He bit an Angleworm in halves
And ate the fellow, raw,

And then he drank a Dew
From a convenient Grass—
And then hopped sidewise to the Wall
To let a Beetle pass—

He glanced with rapid eyes
That hurried all around—
They looked like frightened Beads, I thought—
He stirred his Velvet Head

Like one in danger, Cautious,
I offered him a Crumb
And he unrolled his feathers
And rowed him softer home—

Than Oars divide the Ocean,
Too silver for a seam—
Or Butterflies, off Banks of Noon
Leap, plashless as they swim.

341

After great pain, a formal feeling comes—
The Nerves sit ceremonious, like Tombs—
The stiff Heart questions was it He, that bore,
And Yesterday, or Centuries before?

The Feet, mechanical, go round—
Of Ground, or Air, or Ought—
A Wooden way
Regardless grown,
A Quartz contentment, like a stone—

This is the Hour of Lead—
Remembered, if outlived,
As Freezing persons, recollect the Snow—
First—Chill— then Stupor—then the letting go—

401

What Soft—Cherubic Creatures—
These Gentlewomen are—
One would as soon assault a Plush—
Or violate a Star—

Such Dimity Convictions—
A Horror so refined
Of freckled Human Nature—
Of Deity—ashamed—

It's such a common—Glory—
A Fisherman's—Degree—
Redemption—Brittle Lady—
Be so—ashamed of Thee—

435

Much Madness is divinest Sense—
To a discerning Eye—
Much Sense—the starkest Madness—
'Tis the Majority

In this, as All, prevail—
Assent—and you are sane—
Demur—you're straightway dangerous—
And handled with a Chain—

449

I died for Beauty—but was scarce
Adjusted in the Tomb
When One who died for Truth, was lain
In an adjoining Room—

He questioned softly "Why I failed"?
"For Beauty", I replied—
"And I—for Truth—Themself Are One—
We Brethren, are", He said—

And so, as Kinsmen, met a Night—
We talked between the Rooms—
Until the Moss had reached our lips—
And covered up—our names—

465

I heard a Fly buzz—when I died—
The Stillness in the Room
Was like the Stillness in the Air—
Between the Heaves of Storm—

The Eyes around—had wrung them dry—
And Breaths were gathering firm
For that last Onset—when the King
Be witnessed—in the Room—

I willed my Keepsakes—Signed away
What portion of me be
Assignable—and then it was
There interposed a Fly—

With Blue—uncertain stumbling Buzz—
Between the light—and me—
And then the Windows failed—and then
I could not see to see—

526

To hear an Oriole sing
May be a common thing—
Or only a divine.

It is not of the Bird
Who sings the same, unheard,
As unto Crowd—

The Fashion of the Ear
Attireth that it hear
In Dun, or fair—

So whether it be Rune,
Or whether it be none
Is of within.

The "Tune is in the Tree—"
The Skeptic—showeth me—
"No Sir! In Thee!"

585

I like to see it lap the Miles—
And lick the Valleys up—
And stop to feed itself at Tanks—
And then—prodigious step

Around a Pile of Mountains—
And supercilious peer
In Shanties—by the sides of Roads—
And then a Quarry pare

To fit its Ribs
And crawl between
Complaining all the while
In horrid—hooting stanza—
Then chase itself down Hill—

And neigh like Boanerges[1]—
Then—punctual as a Star
Stop—docile and omnipotent
At its own stable door—

---

1. Name meaning "sons of thunder" given by Christ to
James and John (see Mark iii.17)—hence, a loud preacher.

712

Because I could not stop for Death—
He kindly stopped for me—
The Carriage held but just Ourselves—
And Immortality.

5 We slowly drove— He knew no haste
And I had put away
My labor and my leisure too,
For His Civility—

We passed the School, where Children strove
10 At Recess— in the Ring—
We passed the Fields of Gazing Grain—
We passed the Setting Sun—

Or rather—He passed Us—
The Dews drew quivering and chill—
15 For only Gossamer, my Gown—
My Tippet—only Tulle—

We paused before a House that seemed
A Swelling of the Ground—
The Roof was scarcely visible—
20 The Cornice—in the Ground—

Since then—'tis Centuries—and yet
Feels shorter than the Day
I first surmised the Horses' Heads
Were toward Eternity—

986

A narrow Fellow in the Grass
Occasionally rides—
You may have met Him—did you not
His notice sudden is—

5 The Grass divides as with a Comb—
A spotted shaft is seen—
And then it closes at your feet
And opens further on—

He likes a Boggy Acre
10 A Floor too cool for Corn—
Yet when a Boy, and Barefoot—
I more than once at Noon

Have passed, I thought, a Whip lash
Unbraiding in the Sun
15 When stooping to secure it
It wrinkled, and was gone—

Several of Nature's People
I know, and they know me—
I feel for them a transport
20 Of cordiality—

But never met this Fellow
Attended, or alone
Without a tighter breathing
And Zero at the Bone—

1052

I never saw a Moor—
I never saw the Sea—
Yet know I how the Heather looks
And what a Billow be.

I never spoke with God
Nor visited in Heaven—
Yet certain am I of the spot
As if the Checks were given—

1100

The last Night that She lived
It was a Common Night
Except the Dying— this to Us
Made Nature different

5 We noticed smallest things—
Things overlooked before
By this great light upon our Minds
Italicized— as 'twere.

As We went out and in
10 Between Her final Room
And Rooms where Those to be alive
Tomorrow were, a Blame

That Others could exist
While She must finish quite
15 A Jealousy for Her arose
So nearly infinite—

We waited while She passed—
It was a narrow time—
Too jostled were Our Souls to speak
20 At length the notice came.

She mentioned, and forgot—
Then lightly as a Reed
Bent to the Water, struggled scarce—
Consented, and was dead—

25 And We—We placed the Hair—
And drew the Head erect—
And then an awful leisure was
Belief to regulate—

1263

There is no Frigate like a Book
To take us Lands away
Nor any Coursers like a Page
Of prancing Poetry—

This Traverse may the poorest take
Without oppress of Toll—
How frugal is the Chariot
That bears the Human soul.

1463

A Route of Evanescence
With a revolving Wheel—
A Resonance of Emerald—
A Rush of Cochineal[1]—

And every Blossom on the Bush
Adjusts its tumbled Head—
The mail from Tunis, probably,
An easy Morning's Ride—

1732

My life closed twice before its close—
It yet remains to see
If Immortality unveil
A third event to me

So huge, so hopeless to conceive
As these that twice befell.
Parting is all we know of heaven,
And all we need of hell.

1760

Elysium[1] is as far as to
The very nearest Room
If in that Room a Friend await
Felicity or Doom—

What fortitude the Soul contains,
That it can so endure
The accent of a coming Foot—
The opening of a Door—

ISABELLA VALANCY CRAWFORD (1850–87)

Said the Canoe

My masters twain made me a bed
Of pine-boughs resinous, and cedar;
Of moss, a soft and gentle breeder
Of dreams of rest; and me they spread
5   With furry skins and, laughing, said:
"Now she shall lay her polished sides
As queens do rest, or dainty brides,
Our slender lady of the tides!"

My masters twain their camp-soul lit;
10   Streamed incense from the hissing cones;
Large crimson flashes grew and whirled;
Thin golden nerves of sly light curled
Round the dun camp; and rose faint zones,
Half way about each grim bole knit,
15   Like a shy child that would bedeck
With its soft clasp a Brave's red neck,
Yet sees the rough shield on his breast,
The awful plumes shake on his crest,
And, fearful, drops his timid face,
20   Nor dares complete the sweet embrace.

Into the hollow hearts of brakes[1]—
Yet warm from sides of does and stags
Passed to the crisp, dark river-flags[2]—
Sinuous, red as copper-snakes,
25   Sharp-headed serpents, made of light,
Glided and hid themselves in night.

My masters twain the slaughtered deer
Hung on forked boughs with thongs of leather:
Bound were his stiff, slim feet together,
30   His eyes like dead stars cold and drear.
The wandering firelight drew near
And laid its wide palm, red and anxious,
On the sharp splendour of his branches,
On the white foam grown hard and sere
35   On flank and shoulder.
Death—hard as breast of granite boulder—
        Under his lashes
Peered thro' his eyes at his life's grey ashes.

1. Red dye.

1. Paradise in Greek mythology. Also known as the
Islands of the Blest, and thought to be located in the far
west.

1. Thickets.
2. Popular name for plants with sword-shaped leaves
which grow mostly in moist situations.

My masters twain sang songs that wove—
40 As they burnished hunting-blade and rifle—
A golden thread with a cobweb trifle,
Loud of the chase and low of love:

"O Love! art thou a silver fish,
Shy of the line and shy of gaffing,
45 Which we do follow, fierce, yet laughing,
Casting at thee the light-winged wish?
And at the last shall we bring thee up
From the crystal darkness, under the cup
    Of lily folden
50   On broad leaves golden?

"O Love! art thou a silver deer
With feet as swift as wing of swallow,
While we with rushing arrows follow?
And at the last shall we draw near
55 And o'er thy velvet neck cast thongs
Woven of roses, stars and songs—
    New chains all moulden
    Of rare gems olden?"

60 They hung the slaughtered fish like swords
    On saplings slender; like scimitars,
    Bright, and ruddied from new-dead wars,
Blazed in the light the scaly hordes.

They piled up boughs beneath the trees,
    Of cedar web and green fir tassel.
65   Low did the pointed pine tops rustle,
The camp-fire blushed to the tender breeze.

The hounds laid dewlaps on the ground
    With needles of pine, sweet, soft and rusty,
    Dreamed of the dead stag stout and lusty;
70 A bat by the red flames wove its round.

The darkness built its wigwam walls
    Close round the camp, and at its curtain
    Pressed shapes, thin, woven and uncertain
As white locks of tall waterfalls.

WILLIAM WILFRED CAMPBELL (1858–1918)

Indian Summer

Along the line of smoky hills
    The crimson forest stands,
And all the day the blue-jay calls
    Throughout the autumn lands.

Now by the brook the maple leans
    With all his glory spread,
And all the sumachs[1] on the hills
    Have turned their green to red.

Now by great marshes wrapt in mist,
    Or past some river's mouth,
Throughout the long, still autumn day
    Wild birds are flying south.

How One Winter Came in the Lake Region[1]

For weeks and weeks the autumn world stood still,
    Clothed in the shadow of a smoky haze;
The fields were dead, the wind had lost its will,
And all the lands were hushed by wood and hill,
5   In those grey, withered days.

Behind a mist the blear sun rose and set,
    At night the moon would nestle in a cloud;
The fisherman, a ghost, did cast his net;
The lake its shores forgot to chafe and fret,
10   And hushed its caverns loud.

Far in the smoky woods the birds were mute,
    Save that from blackened tree a jay would scream,
Or far in swamps the lizard's lonesome lute
Would pipe in thirst, or by some gnarlèd root
15   The tree-toad trilled his dream.

1. Trees, shrubs, or vines whose leaves turn to brilliant
colours in the autumn.

1. Campbell spent part of his youth in Meaford and
Wiarton, Ontario, where the waters of Georgian Bay, and
with them the characteristic scenery of the Great Lakes
region, particularly that of the northern or "upper" lakes,
provided the inspiration for the Lake lyrics which he very
probably wrote later while residing in New England and
New Brunswick.

From day to day still hushed the season's mood,
   The streams stayed in their runnels shrunk and dry;
Suns rose aghast by wave and shore and wood,
And all the world, with ominous silence, stood
20   In weird expectancy.

When one strange night the sun like blood went down,
   Flooding the heavens in a ruddy hue;
Red grew the lake, the sere² fields parched and brown,
Red grew the marshes where the creeks stole down,
25   But never a wind-breath blew.

That night I felt the winter in my veins,
   A joyous tremor of the icy glow;
And woke to hear the North's wild vibrant strains,
While far and wide, by withered woods and plains,
30   Fast fell the driving snow.

CHARLES G. D. ROBERTS (1860–1943)

Tantramar Revisited¹

Summers and summers have come, and gone with the flight of the swallow;
Sunshine and thunder have been, storm, and winter, and frost;
Many and many a sorrow has all but died from remembrance,
Many a dream of joy fall'n in the shadow of pain.
5   Hands of chance and change have marred, or moulded, or broken,
Busy with spirit or flesh, all I most have adored;
Even the bosom of Earth is strewn with heavier shadows,—
Only in these green hills, aslant to the sea, no change!
Here where the road that has climbed from the inland valleys and woodlands,
10 Dips from the hill-tops down, straight to the base of the hills,—
Here, from my vantage-ground, I can see the scattering houses,
Stained with time, set warm in orchards, meadows, and wheat,
Dotting the broad bright slopes outspread to southward and eastward,
Wind-swept all day long, blown by the south-east wind.

15 Skirting the sunbright uplands stretches a riband of meadow,
Shorn of the labouring grass, bulwarked well from the sea,
Fenced on its seaward border with long clay dykes from the turbid
Surge and flow of the tides vexing the Westmoreland shores.
Yonder, toward the left, lie broad the Westmoreland marshes,—
20 Miles on miles they extend, level, and grassy, and dim,
Clear from the long red sweep of flats to the sky in the distance,
Save for the outlying heights, green-rampired² Cumberland Point;
Miles on miles outrolled, and the river-channels divide them,—
Miles on miles of green, barred by the hurtling gusts.
25 Miles on miles beyond the tawny bay is Minudie.
There are the low blue hills; villages gleam at their feet.
Nearer a white sail shines across the water, and nearer
Still are the slim, grey masts of fishing boats dry on the flats.
Ah, how well I remember those wide red flats, above tide-mark
30 Pale with scurf of the salt, seamed and baked in the sun!

---

2. Dry, withered.

1. In *The Week* [Toronto], the periodical which Roberts
left his native New Brunswick to edit in 1883, the poem is
entitled "Westmoreland Revisited." The Tantramar River
and Marsh, Westmoreland and Cumberland Point are
topographical features of the area near Westcock in eastern New Brunswick where the poet grew up. Minudie is a
village in Nova Scotia, across the Bay of Fundy from
Westcock.
2. Bulwarked.

Well I remember the piles of blocks and ropes, and the net-reels
Wound with the beaded nets, dripping and dark from the sea!
Now at this season the nets are unwound; they hang from the rafters
Over the fresh-stowed hay in upland barns, and the wind
35   Blows all day through the chinks, with the streaks of sunlight, and sways them
Softly at will; or they lie heaped in the gloom of a loft.

Now at this season the reels are empty and idle; I see them
Over the lines of the dykes, over the gossiping grass.
Now at this season they swing in the long strong wind, thro' the lonesome
40   Golden afternoon, shunned by the foraging gulls.
Near about sunset the crane will journey homeward above them;
Round them, under the moon, all the calm night long,
Winnowing soft grey wings of marsh-owls wander and wander,
Now to the broad, lit marsh, now to the dusk of the dike.
45   Soon, thro' their dew-wet frames, in the live keen freshness of morning,
Out of the teeth of the dawn blows back the awakening wind.
Then, as the blue day mounts, and the low-shot shafts of the sunlight
Glance from the tide to the shore, gossamers jewelled with dew
Sparkle and wave, where late sea-spoiling fathoms of drift-net
50   Myriad-meshed, uploomed sombrely over the land.

Well I remember it all. The salt, raw scent of the margin;
While, with men at the windlass, groaned each reel, and the net,
Surging in ponderous lengths, uprose and coiled in its station;
Then each man to his home,— well I remember it all!

55   Yet, as I sit and watch, this present peace of the landscape,—
Stranded boats, these reels empty and idle, the hush,
One grey hawk slow-wheeling above yon cluster of haystacks,—
More than the old time stir this stillness welcomes me home.
Ah, the old-time stir, how once it stung me with rapture,—
60   Old-time sweetness, the winds freighted with honey and salt!
Yet will I stay my steps and not go down to the marshland,—
Muse and recall far off, rather remember than see,—
Lest on too close sight I miss the darling illusion,
Spy at their task even here the hands of chance and change.

The Sower[1]

A brown, sad-coloured hillside, where the soil
    Fresh from the frequent harrow, deep and fine,
    Lies bare; no break in the remote sky-line,
Save where a flock of pigeons streams aloft,
Startled from feed in some low-lying croft,
    Or far-off spires with yellow of sunset shine;
    And here the Sower, unwittingly divine,
Exerts the silent forethought of his toil.

Alone he treads the glebe,[2] his measured stride
    Dumb in the yielding soil; and though small joy
    Dwell in his heavy face, as spreads the blind
Pale grain from his dispensing palm aside,
    This plodding churl grows great in his employ;—
    God-like, he makes provision for mankind.

1. The poem was inspired by a copy of the painting of the
same name by Jean François Millet (1814–75).   2. A cultivated field. Land belonging to the Church.

The Potato Harvest

A high bare field, brown from the plough, and borne
   Aslant from sunset; amber wastes of sky
   Washing the ridge; a clamour of crows that fly
In from the wide flats where the spent tides mourn
To yon their rocking roosts in pines wind-torn;
   A line of grey snake-fence, that zigzags by
   A pond and cattle; from the homestead nigh
The long deep summonings of the supper horn.

Black on the ridge, against that lonely flush,
   A cart, and stoop-necked oxen; ranged beside
     Some barrels; and the day-worn harvest-folk,
Here emptying their baskets, jar the hush
   With hollow thunders. Down the dusk hillside
     Lumbers the wain;[1] and day fades out like smoke.

The Winter Fields

Winds here, and sleet, and frost that bites like steel.
   The low bleak hill rounds under the low sky.
   Naked of flock and fold the fallows lie,
Thin streaked with meagre drift. The gusts reveal
By fits the dim grey snakes of fence, that steal
   Through the white dusk. The hill-foot poplars sigh,
   While storm and death with winter trample by,
And the iron fields ring sharp, and blind lights reel.

Yet in the lonely ridges, wrenched with pain,
   Harsh solitary hillocks, bound and dumb,
Grave glebes[1] close-lipped beneath the scourge and chain,
   Lurks hid the germ of ecstasy—the sum
Of life that waits on summer, till the rain
   Whisper in April and the crocus come.

The Salt Flats

Here clove the keels of centuries ago
   Where now unvisited the flats lie bare.
   Here seethed the sweep of journeying waters, where
No more the tumbling floods of Fundy[1] flow,
And only in the samphire[2] pipes creep slow
   The salty currents of the sap. The air
   Hums desolately with wings that seaward fare,
Over the lonely reaches beating low.

The wastes of hard and meagre weeds are thronged
With murmurs of a past that time has wronged;
   And ghosts of many an ancient memory
Dwell by the brackish pools and ditches blind,
In these low-lying pastures of the wind,
   These marshes pale and meadows by the sea.

1. A large farm wagon.

1. See "The Sower," note 2.

1. The Bay of Fundy.
2. A seacoast plant that is sometimes pickled and eaten.

In the Wide Awe and Wisdom of the Night

In the wide awe and wisdom of the night
   I saw the round world rolling on its way,
Beyond significance of depth or height,
   Beyond the interchange of dark and day.
I marked the march to which is set no pause,
   And that stupendous orbit round whose rim
The great sphere sweeps, obedient unto laws
   That utter the eternal thought of Him.
I compassed time, outstripped the starry speed,
   And in my still Soul apprehended space,
Till, weighing laws which these but blindly heed,
   At last I came before Him face to face,—
And knew the universe of no such span
As the august infinitude of man.

Philander's Song
(From "The Sprightly Pilgrim")[1]

I sat and read Anacreon.[2]
   Moved by the gay, delicious measure
I mused that lips were made for love,
   And love to charm a poet's leisure.

And as I mused a maid came by
   With something in her look that caught me.
Forgotten was Anacreon's line,
   But not the lesson he had taught me.

BLISS CARMAN (1861 – 1929)

Low Tide on Grand Pré[1]

The sun goes down, and over all
   These barren reaches by the tide
Such unelusive glories fall,
   I almost dream they yet will bide
5   Until the coming of the tide.

And yet I know that not for us,
   By any ecstasy of dream,
He lingers to keep luminous
   A little while the grievous stream,
10   Which frets, uncomforted of dream—

A grievous stream, that to and fro
   Athrough the fields of Acadie
Goes wandering, as if to know
   Why one beloved face[2] should be
15   So long from home and Acadie.

Was it a year or lives ago
   We took the grasses in our hands,
And caught the summer flying low
   Over the waving meadow lands,
20   And held it there between our hands?

The while the river at our feet—
   A drowsy inland meadow stream—
At set of sun the after-heat
   Made running gold, and in the gleam
25   We freed our birch upon the stream.

There down along the elms at dusk
   We lifted dripping blade to drift,
Through twilight scented fine like musk,[3]
   Where night and gloom awhile uplift,
30   Nor sunder soul and soul adrift.

1. Merely the subtitle of the poem.
2. The sixth-century B.C. Greek poet whose poems, only fragments of which survive, are chiefly celebrations of wine and love.

1. The Grand Pré ("great meadow") area of New Brunswick, the province in whose capital city, Fredericton, Carman was born and raised, lies near Minas Basin on the Bay of Fundy. Not only does it have historical resonances with the expulsion of the Acadians (see ll. 12 and 15), but it also would have had personal associations for the poet who as a boy spent several summers vacationing there with his family.
2. The "one beloved" has been identified with various women, including Julie Plante, a Frederiction girl with whom Carman went on several canoe trips but who married a Boston man, and the poet's mother whose death in 1886 was a severe blow to him.
3. A heavy, sweet odour.

And that we took into our hands
   Spirit of life or subtler thing—
Breathed on us there, and loosed the bands
   Of death, and taught us, whispering,
35   The secret of some wonder-thing.

Then all your face grew light, and seemed
   To hold the shadow of the sun;
The evening faltered, and I deemed
   That time was ripe, and years had done
40   Their wheeling underneath the sun.

So all desire and all regret,
   And fear and memory, were naught;
One to remember or forget
   The keen delight our hands had caught;
45   Morrow and yesterday were naught.

The night has fallen, and the tide . . .
   Now and again comes drifting home,
Across these aching barrens wide,
   A sigh like driven wind or foam:
50   In grief the flood is bursting home.

A Windflower[1]

Between the roadside and the wood,
   Between the dawning and the dew,
A tiny flower before the sun,
   Ephemeral in time, I grew.

And there upon the trail of spring,
   Not death nor love nor any name
Known among men in all their lands
   Could blur the wild desire with shame.

But down my dayspan of the year
   The feet of straying winds came by;
And all my trembling soul was thrilled
   To follow one lost mountain cry.

And then my heart beat once and broke
   To hear the sweeping rain forebode
Some ruin in the April world,
   Between the woodside and the road.

To-night can bring no healing now;
   The calm of yesternight is gone;
Surely the wind is but the wind,
   And I a broken waif thereon.

A Sea Child

The lover of child Marjory
   Had one white hour of life brim full;
Now the old nurse, the rocking sea,
   Hath him to lull.

The daughter of child Marjory
   Hath in her veins, to beat and run,
The glad indomitable sea,
   The strong white sun.

The Grave-Tree

Let me have a scarlet maple
For the grave-tree at my head,[1]
With the quiet sun behind it,
In the years when I am dead.

5 Let me have it for a signal,
Where the long winds stream and stream,
Clear across the dim blue distance,
Like a horn blown in a dream;

Scarlet when the April vanguard
10 Bugles up the laggard Spring,
Scarlet when the bannered Autumn,
Marches by unwavering.

It will comfort me with honey
When the shining rifts and showers
15 Sweep across the purple valley
And bring back the forest flowers.

It will be my leafy cabin,
Large enough when June returns
And I hear the golden thrushes
20 Flute and hesitate by turns.

And in fall, some yellow morning,
When the stealthy frost has come,
Leaf by leaf it will befriend me
As with comrades going home.

25 Let me have the Silent Valley
And the hill that fronts the east,
So that I can watch the morning
Redden and the stars released.

Leave me in the Great Lone Country,
30 For I shall not be afraid
With the shy moose and the beaver
There within my scarlet shade.

1. The anemone, see note 1 to Lampman's "The Frogs."

1. Carman is buried in Fredericton, New Brunswick. His wish that a scarlet maple tree be planted over his grave was fulfilled by the University of New Brunswick in 1954.

I would sleep, but not too soundly,
Where the sunning partridge drums,
35 Till the crickets hush before him
When the Scarlet Hunter comes.

That will be in warm September,
In the stillness of the year,
When the river-blue is deepest
40 And the other world is near.

When the apples burn their reddest
And the corn is in the sheaves,
I shall stir and waken lightly
At a footfall in the leaves.

45 It will be the Scarlet Hunter
Come to tell me time is done;
On the idle hills forever
There will stand the idle sun.

There the wind will stay to whisper
50 Many wonders to the reeds;
But I shall not fear to follow
Where my Scarlet Hunter leads.

I shall know him in the darkling
Murmur of the river bars,
55 While his feet are on the mountains
Treading out the smoldering stars.

I shall know him, in the sunshine
Sleeping in my scarlet tree,
Long before he halts beside it
60 Stooping down to summon me.

Then fear not, my friends, to leave me
In the boding autumn vast;
There are many things to think of
When the roving days are past.

65 Leave me by the scarlet maple,
When the journeying shadows fail,
Waiting till the Scarlet Hunter
Pass upon the endless trail.

From Songs of the Sea Children

Song VI

Love,[1] by that loosened hair,
Well now I know
Where the lost Lilith[2] went
So long ago.

Love, by those starry eyes
I understand
How the sea maidens lure
Mortals from land.

Love, by that welling laugh
Joy claims its own
Sea-born and wind-wayward
Child of the sun.

A Vagabond Song

There is something in the autumn that is native to my blood—
Touch of manner, hint of mood;
And my heart is like a rhyme,
With the yellow and the purple and the crimson keeping time.

The scarlet of the maples can shake me like a cry
Of bugles going by.
And my lonely spirit thrills
To see the frosty asters like a smoke upon the hills.

There is something in October sets the gypsy blood astir;
We must rise and follow her,
When from every hill of flame
She calls and calls each vagabond by name.

1. Jessie Kappeler, with whom Carman had a love affair in the mid-1890s.
2. In Assyrian and Hebrew myth, Lilith was the wife of Adam before Eve. Carman would certainly have known

Dante Gabriel Rossetti's depection of Lilith, the "fabled snaked-woman" whose long hair was the world's "first gold," in his sonnet "Body's Beauty" and in his ballad "Eden Bower."

From Sappho[1]

Song XXIII

I loved thee, Atthis, in the long ago,
When the great oleanders[2] were in flower
In the broad herded meadows full of sun.
And we would often at the fall of dusk
Wander together by the silver stream,
When the soft grass-heads were all wet with dew
And purple-misted in the fading light.
And joy I knew and sorrow at thy voice,
And the superb magnificence of love,—
The loneliness that saddens solitude,
And the sweet speech that makes it durable,—
The bitter longing and the keen desire,
The sweet companionship through quiet days
In the slow ample beauty of the world,
And the unutterable glad release
Within the temple of the holy night.
O Atthis, how I loved thee long ago
In that fair perished summer by the sea!

Vestigia

I took a day to search for God,
And found Him not. But as I trod
By rocky ledge, through woods untamed,
Just where one scarlet lily flamed,
5 I saw His footprint in the sod.

Then suddenly, all unaware,
Far off in the deep shadows, where
A solitary hermit thrush
Sang through the holy twilight hush—
10 I heard His voice upon the air.

And even as I marvelled how
God gives us Heaven here and now,
In a stir of wind that hardly shook
The poplar leaves beside the brook—
15 His hand was light upon my brow.

At last with evening as I turned
Homeward, and thought what I had learned
And all that there was still to probe—
I caught the glory of His robe
20 Where the last fires of sunset burned.

Back to the world with quickening start
I looked and longed for any part
In making saving Beauty be...
And from that kindling ecstasy
25 I knew God dwelt within my heart.

ARCHIBALD LAMPMAN (1861 – 99)

The Frogs

I

Breathers of wisdom won without a quest,
   Quaint uncouth dreamers, voices high and strange;
   Flutists of lands where beauty hath no change,
And wintry grief is a forgotten guest,
5 Sweet murmurers of everlasting rest,

---

1. Born on the island of Lesbos in the seventh century B.C., Sappho wrote several books of poetry of which only fragments have survived. Her expressions of love, often for other women, are characterized by their naturalness, tenderness, and, on occasion, strong passion. Carman's poem was inspired by Fragment 49. In the translation made by J. A. Symonds for Wharton the first line reads: "I loved thee once, Atthis, long ago."
2. Evergreen shrubs with beautiful red or white flowers which are common in the Mediterranean area.

For whom glad days have ever yet to run,
And moments are as aeons, and the sun
But ever sunken half-way toward the west.

Often to me who heard you in your day,
10   With close rapt ears, it could not choose but seem
That earth, our mother, searching in what way
      Men's hearts might know her spirit's inmost dream;
         Ever at rest beneath life's change and stir,
         Made you her soul, and bade you pipe for her.

II

15   In those mute days when spring was in her glee,
      And hope was strong, we knew not why or how,
      And earth, the mother, dreamed with brooding brow,
Musing on life, and what the hours might be,
When love should ripen to maternity,
20   Then like high flutes in silvery interchange
      Ye piped with voices still and sweet and strange,
And ever as ye piped, on every tree

The great buds swelled; among the pensive woods
      The spirits of first flowers awoke and flung
25   From buried faces the close-fitting hoods,
      And listened to your piping till they fell,
      The frail spring-beauty with her perfumed bell,
The wind-flower, and the spotted adder-tongue.[1]

III

All the day long, wherever pools might be
30   Among the golden meadows, where the air
      Stood in a dream, as it were moorèd there
For ever in a noon-tide reverie,
Or where the birds made riot of their glee
      In the still woods, and the hot sun shone down,
35   Crossed with warm lucent shadows on the brown
Leaf-paven pools, that bubbled dreamily,

Or far away in whispering river meads[2]
      And watery marshes where the brooding noon,
Full with the wonder of its own sweet boon,
40   Nestled and slept among the noisless reeds,
      Ye sat and murmured, motionless as they,
      With eyes that dreamed beyond the night and day.

IV

And when day passed and over heaven's height,
      Thin with the many stars and cool with dew,
45   The fingers of the deep hours slowly drew
The wonder of the ever-healing night,
No grief or loneliness or rapt delight
      Or weight of silence ever brought to you
      Slumber or rest; only your voices grew
50   More high and solemn; slowly with hushed flight

Ye saw the echoing hours go by, long-drawn,
      Nor ever stirred, watching with fathomless eyes,
      And with your countless clear antiphonies

---

1. Colloquial names for wild plants which appear in the early spring; "spring-beauty": plant of the purslane family with delicate pink flowers; "wind-flower": the anemone, a flower of the buttercup family, noted for the ease with which it drops its petals; "adder-tongue": a bulbous herb of the lily family.
2. Moist, low-lying grasslands. Poetical word for meadow.

Filling the earth and heaven, even till dawn,
55   Last-risen, found you with its first pale gleam,
       Still with soft throats unaltered in your dream.

V

And slowly as we heard you, day by day,
       The stillness of enchanted reveries
       Bound brain and spirit and half-closèd eyes,
60 In some divine sweet wonder-dream astray;
To us no sorrow or upreared dismay
       Nor any discord came, but evermore
       The voices of mankind, the outer roar,
Grew strange and murmurous, faint and far away.

65 Morning and noon and midnight exquisitely,
       Rapt with your voices, this alone we knew,
Cities might change and fall, and men might die,
       Secure were we, content to dream with you
              That change and pain are shadows faint and fleet,
70   And dreams are real, and life is only sweet.

Heat

From plains that reel to southward, dim,
       The road runs by me white and bare;
Up the steep hill it seems to swim
       Beyond, and melt into the glare.
5   Upward half-way, or it may be
       Nearer the summit, slowly steals
A hay-cart, moving dustily
       With idly clacking wheels.

By his cart's side the wagoner
10   Is slouching slowly at his ease,
Half-hidden in the windless blur
       Of white dust puffing to his knees.
This wagon on the height above,
       From sky to sky on either hand,
15 Is the sole thing that seems to move
       In all the heat-held land.

Beyond me in the fields the sun
       Soaks in the grass and hath his will;
I count the marguerites[1] one by one;
20   Even the buttercups are still.
On the brook yonder not a breath
       Disturbs the spider or the midge.
The water-bugs draw close beneath
       The cool gloom of the bridge.

25 Where the far elm-tree shadows flood
       Dark patches in the burning grass,
The cows, each with her peaceful cud,
       Lie waiting for the heat to pass.
From somewhere on the slope near by
30   Into the pale depth of the noon
A wandering thrush slides leisurely
       His thin revolving tune.

In intervals of dreams I hear
       The cricket from the droughty ground;
35 The grasshoppers spin into mine ear
       A small innumerable sound.
I lift mine eyes sometimes to gaze:
       The burning sky-line blinds my sight:
The woods far off are blue with haze:
40   The hills are drenched in light.

And yet to me not this or that
       Is always sharp or always sweet;
In the sloped shadow of my hat
       I lean at rest, and drain the heat;
45 Nay more, I think some blessèd power
       Hath brought me wandering idly here:
In the full furnace of this hour
       My thoughts grow keen and clear.

1. Daisy-like flowers.

Among the Timothy[1]

Long hours ago, while yet the morn was blithe,
　Nor sharp athirst had drunk the beaded dew,
A mower came, and swung his gleaming scythe
　Around this stump, and, shearing slowly, drew
5　Far round among the clover, ripe for hay,
　　A circle clean and gray;
And here among the scented swathes that gleam,
　Mixed with dead daisies, it is sweet to lie
And watch the grass and the few-clouded sky,
10　Nor think but only dream.

For when the noon was turning, and the heat
　Fell down most heavily on field and wood,
I too came hither, borne on restless feet,
　Seeking some comfort for an aching mood.
15　Ah! I was weary of the drifting hours,
　　The echoing city towers,
The blind gray streets, the jingle of the throng,
　Weary of hope that like a shape of stone
Sat near at hand without a smile or moan,
20　And weary most of song.

And those high moods of mine that sometime made
　My heart a heaven, opening like a flower
A sweeter world where I in wonder strayed,
　Begirt with shapes of beauty and the power
25　Of dreams that moved through that enchanted clime
　　With changing breaths of rhyme,
Were all gone lifeless now, like those white leaves
　That hang all winter, shivering dead and blind
Among the sinewy beeches in the wind,
30　That vainly calls and grieves.

Ah! I will set no more mine overtaskèd brain
　To barren search and toil that beareth nought,
For ever following with sore-footed pain
　The crossing pathways of unbournèd thought;
35　But let it go, as one that hath no skill,
　　To take what shape it will,
An ant slow-burrowing in the earthy gloom,
　A spider bathing in the dew at morn,
Or a brown bee in wayward fancy borne
40　From hidden bloom to bloom.

Hither and thither o'er the rocking grass
　The little breezes, blithe as they are blind,
Teasing the slender blossoms pass and pass,
　Soft-footed children of the gipsy wind,
45　To taste of every purple-fringèd head
　　Before the bloom is dead;
And scarcely heed the daisies that, endowed
　With stems so short they cannot see, up-bear
Their innocent sweet eyes distressed, and stare
50　Like children in a crowd.

---

1. Originally entitled "Among the Millet," this poem may have been renamed in order to give it a more local colouring. Millet, a cereal native to India, is cultivated in Europe as well as in North America (though not in Lampman's Ottawa Valley) while timothy, a coarse, pasture grass first cultivated in America, was in Lampman's day a common agricultural plant in the Ottawa and St. Lawrence Valleys.

In his *At the Mermaid Inn* column in *The Globe and Mail* [Toronto] for 6 February 1892, Duncan Campbell Scott writes: "the critics across the water may look perplexed and ask our poets what they mean by 'timothy,' or some other colloquial term, but in the main we must depend for local colour on whatever there is of real difference in our manner of looking at the old world with its changeful beauty."

Not far to fieldward in the central heat,
   Shadowing the clover, a pale poplar stands
With glimmering leaves that, when the wind comes, beat
   Together like innumerable small hands,
55   And with the calm, as in vague dreams astray,
      Hang wan and silver-gray;
Like sleepy maenads, who in pale surprise,
   Half-wakened by a prowling beast, have crept
   Out of the hidden covert, where they slept,
60   At noon with languid eyes.

The crickets creak, and through the noonday glow,
   That crazy fiddler of the hot mid-year.
The dry cicada plies his wiry bow
   In long-spun cadence, thin and dusty sere;
65   From the green grass the small grasshoppers' din
      Spreads soft and silvery thin;
And ever and anon a murmur steals
   Into mine ears of toil that moves alway,
   The crackling rustle of the pitch-forked hay
70   And lazy jerk of wheels.

As so I lie and feel the soft hours wane,
   To wind and sun and peaceful sound laid bare,
That aching dim discomfort of the brain
   Fades off unseen, and shadowy-footed care
75   Into some hidden corner creeps at last
      To slumber deep and fast;
And gliding on, quite fashioned to forget,
   From dream to dream I bid my spirit pass
   Out into the pale green ever-swaying grass
80   To brood, but no more fret.

And hour by hour among all shapes that grow
   Of purple mints and daisies gemmed with gold
In sweet unrest my visions come and go;
   I feel and hear and with quiet eyes behold;
85   And hour by hour, the ever-journeying sun,
      In gold and shadow spun,
Into mine eyes and blood, and through the dim
   Green glimmering forest of the grass shines down,
   Till flower and blade, and every cranny brown,
90   And I are soaked with him.

The Railway Station

The darkness brings no quiet here, the light
   No waking: ever on my blinded brain
   The flare of lights, the rush, and cry, and strain,
The engines' scream, the hiss and thunder smite:
I see the hurrying crowds, the clasp, the flight,
   Faces that touch, eyes that are dim with pain:
   I see the hoarse wheels turn, and the great train
Move labouring out into the bourneless night.
So many souls within its dim recesses,
   So many bright, so many mournful eyes:
Mine eyes that watch grow fixed with dreams and guesses;
   What threads of life, what hidden histories,
What sweet or passionate dreams and dark distresses,
   What unknown thoughts, what various agonies!

In November

The hills and leafless forests slowly yield
  To the thick-driving snow. A little while
  And night shall darken down. In shouting file
The woodmen's carts go by me homeward-wheeled,
Past the thin fading stubbles, half concealed,
  Now golden-gray, sowed softly through with snow,
  Where the last ploughman follows still his row,
Turning black furrows through the whitening field.
Far off the village lamps begin to gleam,
  Fast drives the snow, and no man comes this way;
    The hills grow wintry white, and bleak winds moan
    About the naked uplands. I alone
  Am neither sad, nor shelterless, nor gray,
Wrapped round with thought, content to watch and dream.

Distance

To the distance! ah, the distance!
  Blue and broad and dim!
Peace is not in burgh[1] or meadow
  But beyond the rim.

Aye, beyond it, far beyond it;
  Follow still my soul,
Till this earth is lost in heaven,
  And thou feel'st the whole.

The City of the End of Things

Beside the pounding cataracts
Of midnight streams unknown to us
'Tis builded in the leafless tracts
And valleys huge of Tartarus.[1]
5 Lurid and lofty and vast it seems;
It hath no rounded name that rings,
But I have heard it called in dreams
The City of the End of Things.

Its roofs and iron towers have grown
10 None knoweth how high within the night,
But in its murky streets far down
A flaming terrible and bright
Shakes all the stalking shadows there,
Across the walls, across the floors,
15 And shifts upon the upper air
From out a thousand furnace doors;
And all the while an awful sound
Keeps roaring on continually,
And crashes in the ceaseless round
20 Of a gigantic harmony.
Through its grim depths re-echoing
And all its weary height of walls,
With measured roar and iron ring,
The inhuman music lifts and falls.
25 Where no thing rests and no man is,
And only fire and night hold sway;
The beat, the thunder and the hiss
Cease not, and change not, night nor day.
And moving at unheard commands,
30 The abysses and vast fires between,

35 Flit figures that with clanking hands
Obey a hideous routine;
They are not flesh, they are not bone,
They see not with the human eye,
And from their iron lips is blown
A dreadful and monotonous cry;
And whoso of our mortal race
Should find that city unaware,
Lean Death would smite him face to face,
40 And blanch him with its venomed air:
Or caught by the terrific spell,
Each thread of memory snapt and cut,
His soul would shrivel and its shell
Go rattling like an empty nut.

45 It was not always so, but once,
In days that no man thinks upon,
Fair voices echoed from its stones,
The light above it leaped and shone:
Once there were multitudes of men,
50 That built that city in their pride,
Until its might was made, and then
They withered age by age and died.
But now of that prodigious race,
Three only in an iron tower,
55 Set like carved idols face to face,
Remain the masters of its power;
And at the city gate a fourth,
Gigantic and with dreadful eyes,
Sits looking toward the lightless north,
60 Beyond the reach of memories;

1. Town.

1. In Greek mythology, a region of the underworld where the wicked—particularly those who have committed an outrage against the gods—suffer punishment for their misdeeds on earth.

Fast rooted to the lurid floor,
A bulk that never moves a jot,
In his pale body dwells no more,
Or mind or soul,—an idiot!
65 But sometime in the end those three
Shall perish and their hands be still,
And with the master's touch shall flee
Their incommunicable skill.
A stillness absolute as death
70 Along the slacking wheels shall lie,
And, flagging at a single breath,
The fires that moulder out and die.
The roar shall vanish at its height,
And over that tremendous town
75 The silence of eternal night
Shall gather close and settle down.
All its grim grandeur, tower and hall,
Shall be abandoned utterly,
And into rust and dust shall fall
80 From century to century;
Nor ever living thing shall grow,
Nor trunk of tree, nor blade of grass;
No drop shall fall, no wind shall blow,
Nor sound of any foot shall pass:
85 Alone of its accursèd state,
One thing the hand of Time shall spare,
For the grim Idiot at the gate
Is deathless and eternal there.

On the Companionship with Nature

Let us be much with Nature; not as they
That labour without seeing, that employ
Her unloved forces, blindly without joy;
Nor those whose hands and crude delights obey
The old brute passion to hunt down and slay;
But rather as children of one common birth,
Discerning in each natural fruit of earth
Kinship and bond with this diviner clay.
Let us be with her wholly at all hours,
With the fond lover's zest, who is content
If his ear hears, and if his eye but sees;
So shall we grow like her in mould and bent,
Our bodies stately as her blessèd trees,
Our thoughts as sweet and sumptuous as her flowers.

To a Millionaire

The world in gloom and splendour passes by,
And thou in the midst of it with brows that gleam,
A creature of that old distorted dream
That makes the sound of life an evil cry.
Good men perform just deeds, and brave men die,
And win not honour such as gold can give,
While the vain multitudes plod on, and live,
And serve the curse that pins them down: But I
Think only of the unnumbered broken hearts,
The hunger and the mortal strife for bread,
Old age and youth alike mistaught, misfed,
By want and rags and homelessness made vile,
The griefs and hates, and all the meaner parts
That balance thy one grim misgotten pile.

From The Largest Life

Sonnet III

There is a beauty at the goal of life,
A beauty growing since the world began,
Through every age and race, through lapse and strife
Till the great human soul complete her span.
Beneath the waves of storm that lash and burn,
The currents of blind passion that appall,
To listen and keep watch till we discern
The tide of sovereign truth that guides it all;
So to address our spirits to the height,
And so attune them to the valiant whole,
That the great light be clearer for our light,
And the great soul the stronger for our soul:
To have done this is to have lived, though fame
Remember us with no familiar name.

At the Long Sault: May, 1660[1]

Under the day-long sun there is life and mirth
   In the working earth,
And the wonderful moon shines bright
   Through the soft spring night,
The innocent flowers in the limitless woods are springing
   Far and away
   With the sound and the perfume of May,
And ever up from the south the happy birds are winging,
   The waters glitter and leap and play
   While the grey hawk soars.

But far in an open glade of the forest set
   Where the rapid plunges and roars,
Is a ruined fort with a name that men forget,—
   A shelterless pen
   With its broken palisade,
   Behind it, musket in hand,
   Beyond message or aid
   In this savage heart of the wild,
   Mere youngsters, grown in a moment to men,
   Grim and alert and arrayed,
   The comrades of Daulac stand.
   Ever before them, night and day,
   The rush and skulk and cry
   Of foes, not men but devils, panting for prey;
   Behind them the sleepless dream
Of the little frail-walled town,[2] far away by the plunging stream,
   Of maiden and matron and child,
With ruin and murder impending, and none but they
To beat back the gathering horror
Deal death while they may,
   And then die.

Day and night they have watched while the little plain
Grew dark with the rush of the foe, but their host
Broke ever and melted away, with no boast

1. Several accounts of the defence by Dollard des Ormeaux (Daulac) and a small band of French Canadians and Indians of the dilapidated fort on the Long Sault in the spring of 1660 may have been known to Lampman. Perhaps the chief source of the poem was the American historian Francis Parkman's *The Old Régime in Canada* (1874) which contains a lengthy and spirited account of the incident which in Lampman's day was called "the Canadian Thermopylae."
2. Quebec City.

35   But to number their slain;
       And now as the days renew
       Hunger and thirst and care
       Were they never so stout, so true,
       Press at their hearts; but none
40   Falters or shrinks or utters a coward word,
       Though each setting sun
       Brings from the pitiless wild new hands to the Iroquois[3] horde,
       And only to them despair.

       Silent, white-faced, again and again
45   Charged and hemmed round by furious hands,
       Each for a moment faces them all and stands
       In his little desperate ring; like a tired bull moose
       Whom scores of sleepless wolves, a ravening pack,
       Have chased all night, all day
50   Through the snow-laden woods, like famine let loose;
       And he turns at last in his track
       Against a wall of rock and stands at bay;
       Round him with terrible sinews and teeth of steel
       They charge and recharge; but with many a furious plunge and wheel,
55   Hither and thither over the trampled snow,
       He tosses them bleeding and torn;
       Till, driven, and ever to and fro
       Harried, wounded and weary grown,
       His mighty strength gives way
60   And all together they fasten upon him and drag him down.

       So Daulac turned him anew[4]
       With a ringing cry to his men
       In the little raging forest glen,
       And his terrible sword in the twilight whistled and slew.
65   And all his comrades stood
       With their backs to the pales, and fought
       Till their strength was done;
       The thews that were only mortal flagged and broke
       Each struck his last wild stroke,
70   And they fell one by one,
       And the world that had seemed so good
       Passed like a dream and was naught.

       And then the great night came
       With the triumph-songs of the foe and the flame
75   Of the camp-fires.
       Out of the dark the soft wind woke,
       The song of the rapid rose alway
       And came to the spot where the comrades lay,
       Beyond help or care,
80   With none but the red men round them
       To gnash their teeth and stare.

       All night by the foot of the mountain
          The little town lieth at rest,
       The sentries are peacefully pacing;
85   And neither from East nor from West

       Is there rumour of death or of danger;
          None dreameth tonight in his bed
       That ruin was near and the heroes
          That met it and stemmed it are dead.

---

3. See note 2 to Duncan Campbell Scott's "Watkwenies."
4. When Duncan Campbell Scott edited this poem for publication in 1943 (it was unfinished when Lampman died in 1899), not only did he make what he calls a "very few cuts" to it, but he also effected a "rearrangement of the lines from 'so Daulac turned him anew' " and, moreover, "used town instead of burg in the 26th line of the lyric" because he "didn't like burg."

90 But afar in the ring of the forest,
    Where the air is so tender with May
And the waters are wild in the moonlight,
    They lie in their silence of clay.

The numberless stars out of heaven
95   Look down with a pitiful glance;
And the lilies asleep in the forest
    Are closed like the lilies of France.

DUNCAN CAMPBELL SCOTT (1862–1947)

The Piper of Arll[1]

There was in Arll a little cove
Where the salt wind came cool and free:
A foamy beach that one would love,
If he were longing for the sea.

5 A brook hung sparkling on the hill,
The hill swept far to ring the bay;
The bay was faithful, wild or still,
To the heart of the ocean far away.

There were three pines above the comb[2]
10 That, when the sun flared and went down,
Grew like three warriors reaving[3] home
The plunder of a burning town.

A piper lived within the grove,
Tending the pasture of his sheep;
15 His heart was swayed with faithful love,
From the springs of God's ocean clear and deep.

And there a ship one evening stood,
Where ship had never stood before;
A pennon bickered red as blood,
20 An angel glimmered at the prore.[4]

About the coming on of dew,
The sails burned rosy, and the spars
Were gold, and all the tackle grew
Alive with ruby-hearted stars.

25 The piper heard an outland tongue,[5]
With music in the cadenced fall;
And when the fairy lights[6] were hung,
The sailors gathered one and all,

And leaning on the gunwales dark,
30 Crusted with shells and dashed with foam,
With all the dreaming hills to hark,
They sang their longing songs of home.

When the sweet airs had fled away,
The piper, with a gentle breath,
35 Moulded a tranquil melody
Of lonely love and longed-for death.

When the fair sound began to lull,
From out the fireflies and the dew,
A silence held the shadowy hull,
40 Until the eerie tune was through.

Then from the dark and dreamy deck
An alien song began to thrill;
It mingled with the drumming beck,
And stirred the braird[7] upon the hill.

45 Beneath the stars each sent to each
A message tender, till at last
The piper slept upon the beach,
The sailors slumbered round the mast.

Still as a dream till nearly dawn,
50 The ship was bosomed on the tide;
The streamlet, murmuring on and on,
Bore the sweet water to her side.

Then shaking out her lawny[8] sails,
Forth on the misty sea she crept;
55 She left the dawning of the dales,[9]
Yet in his cloak the piper slept.

And when he woke he saw the ship,
Limned black against the crimson sun;
Then from the disc he saw her slip,
60 A wraith of shadow—she was gone.

He threw his mantle on the beach,
He went apart like one distraught,
His lips were moved—his desperate speech
Stormed his inviolable thought.

---

1. An imaginary place. This poem, which clearly owes a debt to Coleridge's "Rime of the Ancient Mariner," was particularly admired by John Masefield.
2. A narrow valley on the side of a hill.
3. Carrying.
4. Ship's prow.

5. Foreign language.
6. Small lights.
7. First shoots of corn or other crops.
8. Sails of a fine cotton fabric.
9. Valleys.

65   He broke his human-throated reed,
And threw it in the idle rill;
But when his passion had its mead,[10]
He found it in the eddy still.

He mended well the patient flue,
70   Again he tried its varied stops;
The closures answered right and true,
And starting out in piercing drops,

A melody began to drip
That mingled with a ghostly thrill
75   The vision-spirit of the ship,
The secret of his broken will.

Beneath the pines he piped and swayed,
Master of passion and of power;
He was his soul and what he played,
80   Immortal for a happy hour.

He, singing into nature's heart,
Guiding his will by the world's will,
With deep, unconscious, childlike art
Had sung his soul out and was still.

85   And then at evening came the bark
That stirred his dreaming heart's desire;
It burned slow lights along the dark
That died in glooms of crimson fire.

The sailors launched a sombre boat,
90   And bent with music at the oars;
The rhythm throbbing every throat,
And lapsing round the liquid shores,

Was that true tune the piper sent,
Unto the wave-worn mariners,
95   When with the beck and ripple blent
He heard that outland song of theirs.

Silent they rowed him, dip and drip,
The oars beat out an exequy,[11]
They laid him down within the ship,
100   They loosed a rocket to the sky.

It broke in many a crimson sphere
That grew to gold and floated far,
And left the sudden shore-line clear,
With one slow-changing, drifting star.

105   Then out they shook the magic sails,
That charmed the wind in other seas,
From where the west line pearls and pales,
They waited for a ruffling breeze.

But in the world there was no stir,
110   The cordage[12] slacked with never a creak,
They heard the flame begin to purr
Within the lantern at the peak.

They could not cry, they could not move,
They felt the lure from the charmed sea;
115   They could not think of home or love
Or any pleasant land to be.

They felt the vessel dip and trim,
And settle down from list to list;
They saw the sea-plain heave and swim
120   As gently as a rising mist.

And down so slowly, down and down,
Rivet by rivet, plank by plank;
A little flood of ocean flown
Across the deck, she sank and sank.

125   From knee to breast the water wore,
It crept and crept; ere they were ware
Gone was the angel at the prore,
They felt the water float their hair.

They saw the salt plain spark and shine,
130   They threw their faces to the sky;
Beneath a deepening film of brine
They saw the star-flash blur and die.

She sank and sank by yard and mast,
Sank down the shimmering gradual dark;
135   A little drooping pennon last
Showed like the black fin of a shark.

And down she sank till, keeled in sand,
She rested safely balanced true,
With all her upward gazing band,
140   The piper and the dreaming crew.

And there, unmarked of any chart,
In unrecorded deeps they lie,
Empearled within the purple heart
Of the great sea for aye and aye.

145   Their eyes are ruby in the green
Long shaft of sun that spreads and rays,
And upward with a wizard sheen
A fan of sea-light leaps and plays.

Tendrils of or and azure[13] creep,
150   And globes of amber light are rolled,
And in the gloaming[14] of the deep
Their eyes are starry pits of gold.

And sometimes in the liquid night
The hull is changed, a solid gem,
155   That glows with a soft stony light,
The lost prince of a diadem.

And at the keel a vine is quick,[15]
That spreads its bines and works and weaves
O'er all the timbers veining thick
160   A plenitude of silver leaves.

---

10. Had worked itself out.
11. Funeral rite.
12. Ropes in the rigging of a ship.

13. The heraldic colours gold ("or") and blue ("azure").
14. Twilight.
15. Alive.

Watkwenies[1]

Vengeance was once her nation's lore and law:
When the tired sentry stooped above the rill,
Her long knife flashed, and hissed, and drank its fill;
Dimly below her dripping wrist she saw,
One wild hand, pale as death and weak as straw,
Clutch at the ripple in the pool; while shrill
Sprang through the dreaming hamlet on the hill,
The war-cry of the triumphant Iroquois.[2]

Now clothed with many an ancient flap and fold,
And wrinkled like an apple kept till May,
She weighs the interest-money[3] in her palm,
And, when the Agent calls her valiant name,
Hears, like the war-whoops of her perished day,
The lads playing snow-snake[4] in the stinging cold.

The Onondaga Madonna[1]

She stands full-throated and with careless pose,
This woman of a weird and waning race,
The tragic savage lurking in her face,
Where all her pagan passion burns and glows;
Her blood is mingled with her ancient foes,
And thrills with war and wildness in her veins;
Her rebel lips are dabbled with the stains
Of feuds and forays and her father's woes.

And closer in the shawl about her breast,
The latest promise of her nation's doom,
Paler[2] than she her baby clings and lies,
The primal warrior gleaming from his eyes;
He sulks, and burdened with his infant gloom,
He draws his heavy brows and will not rest.

On the Way to the Mission[1]

They dogged him all one afternoon,
Through the bright snow,
Two whitemen servants of greed;
He knew that they were there,
5   But he turned not his head;
He was an Indian trapper;
He planted his snow-shoes firmly,
He dragged the long toboggan
Without rest.

10 The three figures drifted
Like shadows in the mind of a seer;
The snow-shoes were whisperers
On the threshold of awe;
The toboggan made the sound of wings,
15 A wood-pigeon sloping to her nest.

The Indian's face was calm.
He strode with the sorrow of fore-knowledge,
But his eyes were jewels of content
Set in circles of peace.

20 They would have shot him;
But momently in the deep forest,
They saw something flit by his side:
Their hearts stopped with fear.
Then the moon rose.
25 They would have left him to the spirit,
But they saw the long toboggan
Rounded well with furs,
With many a silver fox-skin,[2]
With the pelts of mink and of otter.
30 They were the servants of greed;

1. The Woman Who Conquers.
2. A member of the confederacy of Indian peoples that included the Cayuga, Mohawk, Oneida, Onondaga, and Seneca tribes.
3. Probably treaty money, the annual cash payment of about five dollars paid to registered Indians, though why the woman has the money in her hand *before* her name is called by the agent (who represents the federal government when treaty payments are made) seems unclear.
4. A game in which a spear is thrown as far as possible along a shallow trench in the snow.

1. See note 2 to "Watkwenies."
2. Therefore with less Indian blood.

1. This poem has affinities with an incident in Major Robert Rogers' play *Ponteach: or the Savages of America* (1766). In I.ii two Europeans shoot a "couple" of Indians and then steal their furs. "Mission": headquarters of a church engaged in bringing Christianity to the Indians.
2. An extremely rare and valuable fur, obtained from the ordinary red fox in the colour phase characterized by black fur overlaid by silvery guard hair.

When the moon grew brighter
And the spruces were dark with sleep,
They shot him.
When he fell on a shield of moonlight 50
35 One of his arms clung to his burden;
The snow was not melted:
The spirit passed away.

Then the servants of greed
Tore off the cover to count their gains;
40 They shuddered away into the shadows, 55
Hearing each the loud heart of the other.
Silence was born.

There in the tender moonlight,
As sweet as they were in life,
45 Glimmered the ivory features,
Of the Indian's wife.

In the manner of Montagnais[3] women
Her hair was rolled with braid;
Under her waxen fingers
A crucifix was laid.

He was drawing her down to the Mission,
To bury her there in spring,
When the bloodroot comes and the windflower[4]
To silver everything.

But as a gift of plunder
Side by side were they laid,
The moon went on to her setting
And covered them with shade.

The Forsaken[1]

I

Once in the winter
Out on a lake
In the heart of the north-land,
Far from the Fort
5 And far from the hunters,
A Chippewa[2] woman
With her sick baby,
Crouched in the last hours
Of a great storm.
10 Frozen and hungry,
She fished through the ice
With a line of the twisted
Bark of the cedar,
And a rabbit-bone hook
15 Polished and barbed;
Fished with the bare hook
All through the wild day,
Fished and caught nothing;
While the young chieftain
20 Tugged at her breasts,
Or slept in the lacings
Of the warm *tikanagan*.[3]
All the lake-surface
Streamed with the hissing
25 Of millions of iceflakes
Hurled by the wind;
Behind her the round

Of a lonely island
Roared like a fire
30 With the voice of the storm
In the deeps of the cedars.
Valiant, unshaken,
She took of her own flesh,
Baited the fish-hook,
35 Drew in a gray-trout,[4]
Drew in his fellows,
Heaped them beside her,
Dead in the snow.
Valiant, unshaken,
40 She faced the long distance,
Wolf-haunted and lonely,
Sure of her goal
And the life of her dear one:
Tramped for two days,
45 On the third in the morning,
Saw the strong bulk
Of the Fort by the river,
Saw the wood-smoke
Hang soft in the spruces,
50 Heard the keen yelp
Of the ravenous huskies
Fighting for whitefish:[5]
Then she had rest.

3. Indians inhabiting the northern part of Quebec and Labrador.
4. Plants whose white flowers appear in the early spring.

1. While apparently based on a factual incident recounted to Scott on one of his trips to the North, this poem may owe part of its inspiration to Wordsworth's "The Complaint of a Forsaken Indian Woman" and to the following passage, itself the source of Wordsworth's poem, from Samuel Hearne's *A Journey from Prince of Wales's Fort in Hudson's Bay to the Northern Ocean* . . . (1795): "One of the Indian's wives . . . had for a few days past become so weak as to be incapable of travelling. . . . Without much ceremony, she was left unassisted, to perish above-ground. . . . [The Indians] say it is better to leave one who

is past recovery, than for the whole family to sit down by them and starve to death. . . . After covering them well up with deer skins, etc. they take their leave, and walk away crying. . . . A custom apparently so unnatural is perhaps not to be found among any other of the human race: if properly considered, however, it may with justice be ascribed to necessity and self-preservation, rather than to the want of humanity and social feeling. . . ."
2. An Indian tribe of the region north of Lakes Superior and Huron.
3. A cradle-board used to carry a baby safely. It is constructed of a rectangular board onto which is attached a moss bag—i.e., a bag which is laced at the front and which contains dry moss.
4. Lake trout. North American char.
5. Commonly found North American food fish.

II

Years and years after,
55 When she was old and withered,
When her son was an old man
And his children filled with vigour,
They came in their northern tour on the verge of winter,
To an island in a lonely lake.
60 There one night they camped, and on the morrow
Gathered their kettles and birch-bark[6]
Their rabbit-skin robes[7] and their mink-traps,
Launched their canoes and slunk away through the islands,
Left her alone forever,
65 Without a word of farewell,
Because she was old and useless,
Like a paddle broken and warped,
Or a pole[8] that was splintered.
Then, without a sigh,
70 Valiant, unshaken,
She smoothed her dark locks under her kerchief,
Composed her shawl in state,
Then folded her hands ridged with sinews and corded with veins,
Folded them across her breasts spent with the nourishing of children,
75 Gazed at the sky past the tops of the cedars,
Saw two spangled nights arise out of the twilight,
Saw two days go by filled with the tranquil sunshine,
Saw, without pain, or dread, or even a moment of longing:
Then on the third great night there came thronging and thronging
80 Millions of snowflakes out of a windless cloud;
They covered her close with a beautiful crystal shroud,
Covered her deep and silent.
But in the frost of the dawn,
Up from the life below,
85 Rose a column of breath
Through a tiny cleft in the snow,
Fragile, delicately drawn,
Wavering with its own weakness,
In the wilderness a sign of the spirit,
90 Persisting still in the sight of the sun
Till day was done.
Then all light was gathered up by the hand of God and hid in His breast,
Then there was born a silence deeper than silence,
Then she had rest.

6. Birchbark rogans—i.e., small bowls or buckets constructed of birchbark which is sewn together with spruce roots and made watertight with spruce gum.
7. A warm robe consisting of long strips of rabbit-skin woven together.

8. A setting-pole, usually about ten feet in length and tipped with an iron ferrule at each end, was used for guiding a canoe in shallow water or for ascending swiftly running streams.

At Gull Lake: August, 1810[1]

Gull Lake set in the rolling prairie[2]—
Still there are reeds on the shore,
As of old the poplars shimmer
As summer passes;
5 Winter freezes the shallow lake to the core;
Storm passes,
Heat parches the sedges and grasses,
Night comes with moon-glimmer,
Dawn with the morning-star;
10 All proceeds in the flow of Time
As a hundred years ago.

Then two camps were pitched on the shore,
The clustered teepees
Of Tabashaw Chief of the Saulteaux.
15 And on a knoll tufted with poplars
Two gray tents of a trader—
Nairne of the Orkneys.[3]
Before his tents under the shade of the poplars
Sat Keejigo,[4] third of the wives
20 Of Tabashaw Chief of the Saulteaux;
Clad in the skins of antelopes
Broidered with porcupine quills
Coloured with vivid dyes,
Vermilion here and there
25 In the roots of her hair,
A half-moon of powder-blue
On her brow, her cheeks
Scored with light ochre streaks.
Keejigo daughter of Launay
30 The Normandy[5] hunter
And Oshawan of the Saulteaux,
Troubled by fugitive visions
In the smoke of the camp-fires,
In the close dark of the teepee,
35 Flutterings of colour
Along the flow of the prairies,
Spangles of flower tints
Caught in the wonder of dawn,
Dreams of sounds unheard—
40 The echoes of echo,
Star she was named for
Keejigo, star of the morning,
Voices of storm—
Wind-rush and lightning,—
45 The beauty of terror;
The twilight moon
Coloured like a prairie lily,
The round moon of pure snow,

The beauty of peace;
50 Premonitions of love and of beauty
Vague as shadows cast by a shadow.
Now she had found her hero,
And offered her body and spirit
With abject unreasoning passion,
55 As Earth abandons herself
To the sun and the thrust of the lightning.
Quiet were all the leaves of the poplars,
Breathless the air under their shadow,
As Keejigo spoke of these things to her heart
60 In the beautiful speech of the Saulteaux.

The flower lives on the prairie,
The wind in the sky,
I am here my beloved;
The wind and the flower.

65 *The crane hides in the sand-hills,*
Where does the wolverine hide?
I am here my beloved,
Heart's-blood on the feathers
The foot caught in the trap.

70 *Take the flower in your hand,*
The wind in your nostrils;
I am here my beloved;
Release the captive
Heal the wound under the feathers.

75 A storm-cloud was marching
Vast on the prairie,
Scored with livid ropes of hail,
Quick with nervous vines of lightning—
Twice had Nairne turned her away
80 Afraid of the venom of Tabashaw,
Twice had the Chief fired at his tents
And now when two bullets
Whistled above the encampment
He yelled "Drive this bitch to her master."

85 Keejigo went down a path by the lake;
Thick at the tangled edges,
The reeds and the sedges
Were gray as ashes
Against the death-black water;
90 The lightning scored with double flashes
The dark lake-mirror and loud
Came the instant thunder.

1. The probable source of this poem is the entry for August 29, 1800, in the *Journal* of Alexander Henry, Jr. (d. 1814) which reads in part: "At night I [Henry] was troubled by the visit of a young woman from the other side [of the Red River (in Manitoba)]. . . . She told me . . . that she had left her husband [Tabashaw (a Saulteaux chief)] and come to live with me. . . . Just then we heard a great bustle across the river . . . the husband, . . . knowing of his wife's intention, had determined to shoot at my tent; but his gun only flashed. . . . On his wife's return . . . the Indian . . . caught up a large fire-brand, . . . and rubbed it in her face with all his might, until the fire was extinguished.

Then letting her up, 'Now,' says he, 'go and see your beloved, and ask him if he likes you as well as he did before.' Her face was in a horrid condition. . . . Thus ended a very unpleasant affair. . . ."
2. Gull Lake is north of Red Deer, Alberta.
3. The Orkney Islands lie off the north coast of Scotland.
4. The woman is unnamed in Henry's journal. Henry lists "Kejikong," the Ojibway word for "sky," in a glossary in his Journal, however, and the poem associates Keejigo with the "morning-star" (itself the offspring of the sun and moon in the mythology of the Prairie Indians).
5. Region in France.

Her lips still moved to the words of her music,
"Release the captive,
95   Heal the wound under the feathers."

At the top of the bank
The old wives caught her and cast her down
Where Tabashaw crouched by his camp-fire.
He snatched a live brand from the embers,
100   Seared her cheeks,
Blinded her eyes,
Destroyed her beauty with fire,
Screaming, "Take that face to your lover."
Keejigo held her face to the fury
105   And made no sound.
The old wives dragged her away
And threw her over the bank
Like a dead dog.

Then burst the storm—
110   The Indians' screams and the howls of the dogs
Lost in the crash of hail
That smashed the sedges and reeds,
Stripped the poplars of leaves,
Tore and blazed onwards,
115   Wasting itself with riot and tumult—
Supreme in the beauty of terror.

The setting sun struck the retreating cloud
With a rainbow, not an arc but a column
Built with the glory of seven metals;
120   Beyond in the purple deeps of the vortex
Fell the quivering vines of the lightning.
The wind withdrew the veil from the shrine of the moon,
She rose changing her dusky shade for the glow
Of the prairie lily, till free of all blemish of colour
125   She came to her zenith without a cloud or a star,
A lovely perfection, snow-pure in the heaven of midnight.
After the beauty of terror the beauty of peace.

But Keejigo came no more to the camps of her people;
Only the midnight moon knew where she felt her way,
130   Only the leaves of autumn, the snows of winter
Knew where she lay.

Introduction: 1900 – 45

What we call for convenience the "Modern" period originated, as the name itself suggests, in a sense of radical discontinuity with the immediate past. The classic Victorian assumptions about religion, sex, society, human nature, and human progress had been under vigorous examination by the Victorians themselves, and by 1900 the assumptions were clearly breaking down. The Boer War began the discrediting of British imperialism, a development which had long-term implications for both England and Canada. Irish nationalism, the spread of mass literacy, the suffragette movement, the growing wealth and power of the United States, Laurier's sanguine boast that the twentieth century would belong to Canada—all these suggested that the new century would be different from the nineteenth. More dramatic than these events, however, was World War I's senseless destruction and suffering, which were seen as exposing the final bankruptcy of the old order. The Russian Revolution of 1917 was also seen as a portent, either alarming or beneficent, of mankind's future. In the 1930s the economic depression, the rise of Fascism, and the approach of another war deepened the sense of crisis.

The disciplines of economics, anthropology, and psychology altered the perceptions of the age in ways which had important effects upon the literature which it produced. Marxism, with its ostensibly scientific analysis of the economic basis of human behaviour, offered a way of dealing with the miseries of industrial society. J. G. Frazer's *The Golden Bough* (1890) suggested that religion had its origins in ancient fertility rituals whose meaning was embodied in myth and symbol; myth could therefore be a way of re-connecting people with their own deepest impulses. The psycho-analytic writings of Sigmund Freud and Carl Gustav Jung directed attention to the unconscious and subconscious minds. Common to all these ideas was a perception that modern industrial life had alienated people from the roots of their being—from the possibility of doing meaningful work, from their spiritual and mythic origins, from the most vital elements in their cultural tradition, from their own bodies and sexuality. These theories are manifest in various ways in the poetry which was written in the early twentieth century.

Modern poetry is distinguished not only by new intellectual attitudes towards the world, but also by new poetic techniques and new attitudes towards the nature of poetry itself. Modern poetry began with Imagism, and Imagism may very well have begun with a working visit which the English thinker T. E. Hulme made to Canada in 1906 – 07. Haunted by the stark vastness of the prairies and the sense of human limitation which that vastness conveyed, he saw the inadequacy of current poetic conventions to render this kind of experience. On his return to London he discussed with Ezra Pound and others the possibilities for a new poetic language. Central to these discussions was a rejection of a worn-out, self-indulgent romanticism in favour of a renewed "classicism," and a replacing of decorative verbal ornament by precision and clarity of image. Pound argued for "direct treatment of the 'thing'" and asserted that poets should use "absolutely no word that does not contribute to the presentation" and should "compose in the sequence of the musical phrase, not in sequence of a metronome." The "Imagist" poems which grew out of these principles were short, finely crafted descriptive lyrics in free verse such as Pound's "In a Station of the Metro," Livesay's "Signpost," Smith's "The Lonely Land," and Williams' "The Red Wheelbarrow."

Imagism's insistence on economy, clarity, and freshness was an important contribution to the new poetry which began just before World War I. Its possibilities were limited, but other influences combined with it to make possible a complex and diversified poetic idiom. The poems of Gerard Manley Hopkins, published posthumously in 1918, provided a model for a rhythmical pattern which was neither free verse nor conventionally syllabic, and their difficult, densely worked imagery was also a significant influence. The intellectual values of wit and irony were encouraged by a renewed interest in John Donne and other "metaphysical" poets of the seventeenth century, and in such hitherto unfashionable poets as John Skelton and John Dryden. The oblique allusiveness of French *symboliste* poetry, the compression of the Japanese *haiku,* and the rhythms and vocabulary of contemporary speech and songs were other elements which helped to form modern poetry.

From its very beginnings, that poetry was characterized by a sense of experimentation, a deliberate and self-conscious effort to renew poetic language by using words and images in unfamiliar and unexpected ways, so that readers are constantly required to adjust their expectations. As a result, much of the poetry of the Moderns is distinguished by the heavy demands which it makes on its readers. Obvious examples are Eliot's *The Waste Land* and Pound's *Hugh Selwyn Mauberley,* which pay the reader a compliment by assuming enormous erudition. Both poems are by American expatriates who are eager to show that they have mastered European culture and who deliberately limit their audience so that the poems have something of the appeal of gnostic texts. This is not a universal tendency; cummings' irreverence towards his "busted statues" contrasts with Eliot's lament for "a heap of broken images." But certainly esoteric learning informs the poems of Yeats, Klein, and Stevens, for example. The typographical experiments of cummings, the technical language of Pratt, Smith's "difficult, lonely music," and Frost's regional accent all work to similar ends, which are to separate serious from frivolous readers and to require the reader to participate actively in making the poem.

The theoretical basis of Modernism in English-language poetry was largely an Anglo-American creation, but Canadian poets, though they learned much from Yeats, Eliot, Auden, Pound, and Williams, were not merely pale imitators of their seniors. They took what they needed and applied it to their own circumstances. In particular their quest is to locate themselves not in myth and tradition, but in the unpeopled spaces which had first surprised T. E. Hulme, and in geologic and paleontologic time. The alienation of the artist in Klein's "Portrait of the Poet as Landscape" is not primarily a function of a decadent, materialistic environment, but of the lingering frontier conditions and colonialist lack of self-confidence which gave Canadian poetry, like the rest of its culture, a shape and set of images somewhat different from those of American or English poetry. Like all the Moderns, however, the Canadian poets shared the problem of creating a poetic language which could render their experience of life in the early twentieth century.

Paul Denham

GERARD MANLEY HOPKINS (1844–99)

God's Grandeur

The world is charged with the grandeur of God.
   It will flame out, like shining from shook foil;[1]
   It gathers to a greatness, like the ooze of oil[2]
Crushed. Why do men then now not reck his rod?
Generations have trod, have trod, have trod;
   And all is seared with trade; bleared, smeared with toil;
   And wears man's smudge and shares man's smell: the soil
Is bare now, nor can foot feel, being shod.

And for all this, nature is never spent;
   There lives the dearest freshness deep down things;
And though the last lights off the black West went
   Oh, morning, at the brown brink eastward, springs—
Because the Holy Ghost over the bent
   World broods with warm breast and with ah! bright wings.

The Windhover[1]
To Christ our Lord

I caught this morning morning's minion, king-
   dom of daylight's dauphin,[2] dapple-dawn-drawn Falcon, in his riding
   Of the rolling level underneath him steady air, and striding
High there, how he rung upon the rein of a wimpling wing
In his ecstasy! then off, off forth on swing,
   As a skate's heel sweeps smooth on a bow-bend: the hurl and gliding
   Rebuffed the big wind. My heart in hiding
Stirred for a bird,—the achieve of, the mastery of the thing!

Brute beauty and valour and act, oh, air, pride, plume, here
   Buckle! AND the fire that breaks from thee then, a billion
Times told lovelier, more dangerous, O my chevalier![3]

   No wonder of it: shéer plód makes plough down sillion[4]
Shine, and blue-bleak embers, ah my dear,
   Fall, gall themselves, and gash gold-vermilion.

Pied Beauty

Glory be to God for dappled things—
   For skies of couple-colour as brinded[1] cow;
     For rose-moles all in stipple upon trout that swim;
Fresh-firecoal chestnut-falls;[2] finches' wings;
   Landscape plotted and pieced—fold, fallow, and plough;
     And áll trádes, their gear and tackle and trim.
All things counter, original, spare, strange;
    Whatever is fickle, freckled (who knows how?)
      With swift, slow; sweet, sour; adazzle, dim;
   He fathers-forth whose beauty is past change:
                Praise him.

---

1. Leaf or tinsel.
2. Olive oil.

1. Kestrel or falcon, which hovers in the air with its head to the wind.
2. Heir to the throne of France.

3. Knight, horseman, nobleman.
4. A ridge between two furrows.

1. Brindled, streaked.
2. Fallen chestnuts.

Spring and Fall
to a young child

Márgarét, áre you gríeving
Over Goldengrove[1] unleaving?
Leáves, líke the things of man, you
With your fresh thoughts care for, can you?
Áh! ás the heart grows older
It will come to such sights colder
By and by, nor spare a sigh
Though worlds of wanwood[2] leafmeal[3] lie;

And yet you *will* weep and know why.
Now no matter, child, the name:
Sórrow's spríngs áre the same.
Nor mouth had, no nor mind, expressed
What heart heard of, ghost guessed:
It ís the blight man was born for,
It is Margaret you mourn for.

I wake and feel the fell of dark, not day.
What hours, O what black hoürs we have spent
This night! what sights you, heart, saw; ways you went!
And more must, in yet longer light's delay.

With witness I speak this. But where I say
Hours I mean years, mean life. And my lament
Is cries countless, cries like dead letters sent
To dearest him that lives alas! away.

I am gall, I am heartburn. God's most deep decree
Bitter would have me taste: my taste was me;
Bones built in me, flesh filled, blood brimmed the curse.

Selfyeast of spirit a dull dough sours. I see
The lost are like this, and their scourge to be
As I am mine, their sweating selves; but worse.

No worst, there is none. Pitched past pitch of grief,
More pangs will, schooled at forepangs, wilder wring.
Comforter, where, where is your comforting?
Mary, mother of us, where is your relief?
My cries heave, herds-long; huddle in a main, a chief-
woe, world-sorrow; on an age-old anvil wince and sing—
Then lull, then leave off. Fury had shrieked 'No ling-
ering! Let me be fell:[1] force[2] I must be brief'.
O the mind, mind has mountains; cliffs of fall
Frightful, sheer, no-man-fathomed. Hold them cheap
May who ne'er hung there. Nor does long our small
Durance[3] deal with that steep or deep. Here! creep,
Wretch, under a comfort serves in a whirlwind: all
Life death does end and each day dies with sleep.

1. Rural district in North Wales near St. Beuno's College where Hopkins studied theology, 1874–77.
2. In Old English "wan" meant dark or discoloured.
3. According to W. H. Gardner, Hopkins' editor, the word functions as an adverb on the analogy of "piecemeal."

1. Fierce, cruel, ruthless.
2. Perforce.
3. Endurance.

WILLIAM BUTLER YEATS (1865–1939)

Down by the Salley Gardens

Down by the salley[1] gardens my love and I did meet;
She passed the salley gardens with little snow-white feet.
She bid me take love easy, as the leaves grow on the tree;
But I, being young and foolish, with her would not agree.

In a field by the river my love and I did stand,
And on my leaning shoulder she laid her snow-white hand.
She bid me take life easy, as the grass grows on the weirs;
But I was young and foolish, and now am full of tears.

When You Are Old

When you are old and grey and full of sleep,
And nodding by the fire, take down this book,
And slowly read, and dream of the soft look
Your eyes had once, and of their shadows deep;

How many loved your moments of glad grace,
And loved your beauty with love false or true,
But one man loved the pilgrim soul in you,
And loved the sorrows of your changing face;

And bending down beside the glowing bars,
Murmur, a little sadly, how Love fled
And paced upon the mountains overhead
And hid his face amid a crowd of stars.

The Magi[1]

Now as at all times I can see in the mind's eye,
In their stiff, painted clothes, the pale unsatisfied ones
Appear and disappear in the blue depth of the sky
With all their ancient faces like rain-beaten stones,
And all their helms of silver hovering side by side,
And all their eyes still fixed, hoping to find once more,
Being by Calvary's turbulence unsatisfied,
The uncontrollable mystery on the bestial floor.

Easter 1916[1]

I have met them at close of day
Coming with vivid faces
From counter or desk among grey
Eighteenth-century houses.
5 I have passed with a nod of the head
Or polite meaningless words,
Or have lingered awhile and said
Polite meaningless words,
And thought before I had done
10 Of a mocking tale or a gibe
To please a companion
Around the fire at the club,
Being certain that they and I
But lived where motley is worn:
15 All changed, changed utterly:
A terrible beauty is born.

1. Sallow, a species of willow.

1. The Wise Men from the East. See Matt. ii.

1. The Easter Rebellion of 1916 was an unsuccessful uprising by Irish nationalists against the British government. Some of its leaders, mentioned in the poem, were hanged or shot.

That woman's days were spent
In ignorant good-will,
Her nights in argument
20 Until her voice grew shrill.[2]
What voice more sweet than hers
When, young and beautiful,
She rode to harriers?
This man had kept a school
25 And rode our wingèd horse;[3]
This other his helper and friend
Was coming into his force;
He might have won fame in the end,
So sensitive his nature seemed,
30 So daring and sweet his thought.
This other man I had dreamed
A drunken, vainglorious lout.[4]
He had done most bitter wrong
To some who are near my heart,
35 Yet I number him in the song;
He, too, has resigned his part
In the casual comedy;
He, too, has been changed in his turn,
Transformed utterly:
40 A terrible beauty is born.

Hearts with one purpose alone
Through summer and winter seem
Enchanted to a stone
To trouble the living stream.
45 The horse that comes from the road,
The rider, the birds that range
From cloud to tumbling cloud,
Minute by minute they change;
A shadow of cloud on the stream

50 Changes minute by minute;
A horse-hoof slides on the brim,
And a horse plashes within it;
The long-legged moor-hens dive,
And hens to moor-cocks call;
55 Minute by minute they live:
The stone's in the midst of all.

Too long a sacrifice
Can make a stone of the heart.
O when may it suffice?
60 That is Heaven's part, our part
To murmur name upon name,
As a mother names her child
When sleep at last has come
On limbs that had run wild.
65 What is it but nightfall?
No, no, not night but death;
Was it needless death after all?
For England may keep faith
For all that is done and said.
70 We know their dream; enough
To know they dreamed and are dead;
And what if excess of love
Bewildered them till they died?
I write it out in a verse—
75 MacDonagh[5] and MacBride
And Connolly[6] and Pearse
Now and in time to be,
Wherever green is worn,
Are changed, changed utterly:
80 A terrible beauty is born.

September 25, 1916

The Second Coming[1]

Turning and turning in the widening gyre[2]
The falcon cannot hear the falconer;
Things fall apart; the centre cannot hold;
Mere anarchy is loosed upon the world,
5 The blood-dimmed tide is loosed, and everywhere
The ceremony of innocence is drowned;
The best lack all conviction, while the worst
Are full of passionate intensity.

Surely some revelation is at hand;
10 Surely the Second Coming is at hand.
The Second Coming! Hardly are those words out
When a vast image out of *Spiritus Mundi*[3]
Troubles my sight: somewhere in sands of the desert

2. Constance Gore-Booth Markievicz, who became a strident nationalist. Her death sentence was commuted.
3. Patrick Pearse (1879–1916), schoolteacher, poet, and leader of the movement to re-establish Gaelic in Ireland. He led the fighting in the Dublin Post Office.
4. Major John MacBride, who had married Maud Gonne, Yeats's early love.
5. Thomas MacDonagh (1878–1916), poet.
6. James Connolly (1870–1916), one of the leaders of the uprising.

1. See Matt. xxiv. and 1 John ii.18.
2. A cone- or spiral-shaped movement. Yeats saw history as cyclical, and his own age (the Christian era) as reaching the end of its cycle or gyre, whereupon a new age would begin.
3. Spirit of the world, a kind of collective unconscious in which the memories of the human race are stored and with which the poet must put himself in touch.

15 A shape with lion body and the head of a man,
A gaze blank and pitiless as the sun,
Is moving its slow thighs, while all about it
Reel shadows of the indignant desert birds.
The darkness drops again; but now I know
That twenty centuries of stony sleep
20 Were vexed to nightmare by a rocking cradle,[4]
And what rough beast, its hour come round at last,
Slouches towards Bethlehem to be born?

Sailing to Byzantium[1]

[handwritten: teach my soul that I may sing when I get old.]

I

[handwritten: as soon as you are born you are destined to die]
[handwritten: yeates wants to become a work of art]

That is no country for old men. The young
In one another's arms, birds in the trees
—Those dying generations—at their song,
The salmon-falls, the mackerel-crowded seas,
5 Fish, flesh, or fowl, commend all summer long
[handwritten: life force embodied]
Whatever is begotten, born, and dies.
Caught in that sensual music all neglect
Monuments of unageing intellect. *[handwritten: - they have none so now can't age.]*

II

An aged man is but a paltry thing,
10 A tattered coat upon a stick, unless
[handwritten: have nothing of their body left so must find it inside]
Soul clap its hands and sing, and louder sing
For every tatter in its mortal dress,
Nor is there singing school but studying
Monuments of its own magnificence;
15 And therefore I have sailed the seas and come
To the holy city of Byzantium.

III

O sages standing in God's holy fire
As in the gold mosaic of a wall,
Come from the holy fire, perne[2] in a gyre,
20 And be the singing-masters of my soul.
Consume my heart away; sick with desire
And fastened to a dying animal *[handwritten: his aging body.]*
It knows not what it is; and gather me
Into the artifice of eternity.

IV

[handwritten: earthly mortal.]

25 Once out of nature I shall never take
My bodily form from any natural thing,
But such a form as Grecian goldsmiths make
Of hammered gold and gold enamelling
To keep a drowsy Emperor awake; *[handwritten: immortal]*
30 Or set upon a golden bough to sing *[handwritten: everlasti]*
To lords and ladies of Byzantium
Of what is past, or passing, or to come.[3]

1927

[handwritten: image of timeless eternity.]

Leda and the Swan[1]

A sudden blow: the great wings beating still
Above the staggering girl, her thighs caressed
By the dark webs, her nape caught in his bill,
He holds her helpless breast upon his breast.

How can those terrified vague fingers push
The feathered glory from her loosening thighs?
And how can body, laid in that white rush,
But feel the strange heart beating where it lies?

A shudder in the loins engenders there
The broken wall, the burning roof and tower
And Agamemnon dead.
                    Being so caught up,
So mastered by the brute blood of the air,
Did she put on his knowledge with his power
Before the indifferent beak could let her drop?

1923

---

4. The present era began with Christ's birth.

1. Later Constantinople, now Istanbul. Byzantium in the fifth century A.D. represented an ideal for Yeats: "I think that in early Byzantium, maybe never before or since in recorded history, religious, aesthetic, and practical life were one, that architects and artificers . . . spoke to the multitude and the few alike" (Yeats, *A Vision* [London: Macmillan, 1962], p. 279).
2. A pirn is a spool or bobbin; Yeats makes it a verb, meaning to spin round.
3. "I have read somewhere that in the Emperor's palace at Byzantium was a tree made of gold and silver, and artificial birds that sang" (Yeats, *Collected Poems* [London: Macmillan, 1963], p. 532).

1. Zeus took the form of a swan to approach the mortal Leda; as a result of their sexual union Leda gave birth to Helen and Clytemnestra. Helen married Menelaus and then eloped to Troy with Paris, thus initiating the Trojan War. Clytemnestra murdered her husband Agamemnon, who had sacrificed their daughter Iphegenia in order to secure a fair wind from the gods so that his ships could sail to assist Menelaus, Agamemnon's brother, in attacking Troy. Thus began the Greek era of civilization.

Among School Children

I

I walk through the long schoolroom questioning;
A kind old nun in a white hood replies;
The children learn to cipher and to sing,   35
To study reading-books and histories,
5 To cut and sew, be neat in everything
In the best modern way—the children's eyes
In momentary wonder stare upon
A sixty-year-old smiling public man.   40

II

I dream of a Ledaean body, bent
10 Above a sinking fire, a tale that she
Told of a harsh reproof, or trivial event
That changed some childish day to tragedy—
Told, and it seemed that our two natures blent   45
Into a sphere from youthful sympathy,
15 Or else, to alter Plato's parable,[1]
Into the yolk and white of the one shell.

III

And thinking of that fit of grief or rage
I look upon one child or t'other there   50
And wonder if she stood so at that age—
20 For even daughters of the swan can share
Something of every paddler's heritage—
And had that colour upon cheek or hair,
And thereupon my heart is driven wild: 55
She stands before me as a living child.

IV

25 Her present image floats into the mind—
Did Quattrocento[2] finger fashion it
Hollow of cheek as though it drank the wind
And took a mess of shadows for its meat?   60
And I though never of Ledaean kind
30 Had pretty plumage once—enough of that,
Better to smile on all that smile, and show
There is a comfortable kind of old scarecrow.

V

What youthful mother, a shape upon her lap
Honey of generation[3] had betrayed,
And that must sleep, shriek, struggle to escape
As recollection or the drug decide,
Would think her son, did she but see that shape
With sixty or more winters on its head,
A compensation for the pang of his birth,
Or the uncertainty of his setting forth?

VI

Plato thought nature but a spume that plays
Upon a ghostly paradigm of things;[4]
Solider Aristotle played the taws
Upon the bottom of a king of kings;[5]
World-famous golden-thighed Pythagoras[6]
Fingered upon a fiddle-stick or strings
What a star sang and careless Muses heard:
Old clothes upon old sticks to scare a bird.

VII

Both nuns and mothers worship images,
But those the candles light are not as those
That animate a mother's reveries,
But keep a marble or a bronze repose.
And yet they too break hearts—O Presences
That passion, piety or affection knows,
And that all heavenly glory symbolise—
O self born mockers of man's enterprise;

VIII

Labour is blossoming or dancing where
The body is not bruised to pleasure soul,
Nor beauty born out of its own despair,
Nor blear-eyed wisdom out of midnight oil.
O chestnut-tree, great-rooted blossomer,
Are you the leaf, the blossom or the bole?
O body swayed to music, O brightening glance,
How can we know the dancer from the dance?

Byzantium

The unpurged images of day recede;
The Emperor's drunken soldiery are abed;   10
Night resonance recedes, night-walkers' song
After great cathedral gong;
5 A starlit or a moonlit dome disdains
All that man is,
All mere complexities,   15
The fury and the mire of human veins.

Before me floats an image, man or shade,
Shade more than man, more image than a shade;
For Hades' bobbin[1] bound in mummy-cloth
May unwind the winding path;
A mouth that has no moisture and no breath
Breathless mouths may summon;
I hail the superhuman;
I call it death-in-life and life-in-death.

1. In *The Symposium*, Plato explained love by suggesting that originally man was one and later divided in two; love is a seeking to be re-united.
2. Fifteenth century in Italy.
3. A drug which blots out the memory of pre-natal happiness.
4. Plato saw nature as mere appearance, veiling the ultimate reality of forms.

5. Aristotle believed that reality inhered in the matter of nature. He was tutor to Alexander the Great, whom he disciplined with the "taws" or strap.
6. Early Greek philosopher with an interest in the mathematical properties of music and the music of the spheres.

1. Spool on which man's fate is wound and unwound.

Miracle, bird or golden handiwork,
More miracle than bird or handiwork,
Planted on the star-lit golden bough,
20   Can like the cocks of Hades crow,
Or, by the moon embittered, scorn aloud
In glory of changeless metal
Common bird or petal
And all complexities of mire or blood.

25   At midnight on the Emperor's pavement flit
Flames that no faggot feeds, nor steel has lit,
Nor storm disturbs, flames begotten of flame,
Where blood-begotten spirits come
And all complexities of fury leave,
30   Dying into a dance,
An agony of trance,
An agony of flame that cannot singe a sleeve.

35   Astraddle on the dolphin's[2] mire and blood,
Spirit after spirit! The smithies break the flood,
The golden smithies of the Emperor!
Marbles of the dancing floor
Break bitter furies of complexity,
Those images that yet
Fresh images beget,
40   That dolphin-torn, that gong-tormented sea.

1930

Crazy Jane Talks with the Bishop

I met the Bishop on the road
And much said he and I.
'Those breasts are flat and fallen now,
Those veins must soon be dry;
Live in a heavenly mansion,
Not in some foul sty.'

'Fair and foul are near of kin,
And fair needs foul,' I cried.
'My friends are gone, but that's a truth
Nor grave nor bed denied,
Learned in bodily lowliness
And in the heart's pride.

'A woman can be proud and stiff
When on love intent;
But Love has pitched his mansion in
The place of excrement;
For nothing can be sole or whole
That has not been rent.'

The Circus Animals' Desertion

I
I sought a theme and sought for it in vain,
I sought it daily for six weeks or so.
Maybe at last, being but a broken man,
I must be satisifed with my heart, although
5   Winter and summer till old age began
My circus animals were all on show,
Those stilted boys, that burnished chariot,
Lion and woman[1] and the Lord knows what.

II
What can I but enumerate old themes?
10   First that sea-rider Oisin[2] led by the nose
Through three enchanted islands, allegorical dreams,
Vain gaiety, vain battle, vain repose,
Themes of the embittered heart, or so it seems,
That might adorn old songs or courtly shows;
15   But what cared I that set him on to ride,
I, starved for the bosom of his faery bride?

2. Symbol of the soul's journey from one state to another.

1. The Sphinx.

2. Legendary Irish hero, subject of an early poem by
Yeats, "The Wandering of Oisin."

And then a counter-truth filled out its play,
The Countess Cathleen[3] was the name I gave it;
She, pity-crazed, had given her soul away,
20 But masterful Heaven had intervened to save it.
I thought my dear[4] must her own soul destroy,
So did fanaticism and hate enslave it,
And this brought forth a dream and soon enough
This dream itself had all my thought and love.

25 And when the Fool and Blind Man stole the bread
Cuchulain[5] fought the ungovernable sea;
Heart-mysteries there, and yet when all is said
It was the dream itself enchanted me:
Character isolated by a deed
30 To engross the present and dominate memory.
Players and painted stage took all my love,
And not those things that they were emblems of.

III
Those masterful images because complete
Grew in pure mind, but out of what began?
35 A mound of refuse or the sweepings of a street,
Old kettles, old bottles, and a broken can,
Old iron, old bones, old rags, that raving slut
Who keeps the till. Now that my ladder's gone,
I must lie down where all the ladders start,
40 In the foul rag-and-bone shop of the heart.

D. H. LAWRENCE (1885–1930)

Piano

Softly, in the dusk, a woman is singing to me;
Taking me back down the vista of years, till I see
A child sitting under the piano, in the boom of the tingling strings
And pressing the small, poised feet of a mother who smiles as she sings.

In spite of myself, the insidious mastery of song
Betrays me back, till the heart of me weeps to belong
To the old Sunday evenings at home, with winter outside
And hymns in the cosy parlour, the tinkling piano our guide.

So now it is vain for the singer to burst into clamour
With the great black piano appassionato. The glamour
Of childish days is upon me, my manhood is cast
Down in the flood of remembrance, I weep like a child for the past.

Snake

A snake came to my water-trough
On a hot, hot day, and I in pyjamas for the heat,
To drink there.

In the deep, strange-scented shade of the great dark carob-tree
5 I came down the steps with my pitcher
And must wait, must stand and wait, for there he was at the trough before me.

---

3. Title of an early play by Yeats. The Countess sold her soul to the devil to get food for the starving, but went to heaven anyway because of her mercy.

4. Maud Gonne, Yeats's early love.
5. Another Irish hero of legend, treated in Yeats's play *On Baile's Strand*.

He reached down from a fissure in the earth-wall in the gloom
And trailed his yellow-brown slackness soft-bellied down, over the edge of the stone trough
And rested his throat upon the stone bottom,
10   And where the water had dripped from the tap, in a small clearness,
He sipped with his straight mouth,
Softly drank through his straight gums, into his slack long body,
Silently.

Someone was before me at my water-trough,
15   And I, like a second comer, waiting.

He lifted his head from his drinking, as cattle do,
And looked at me vaguely, as drinking cattle do,
And flickered his two-forked tongue from his lips, and mused a moment,
And stooped and drank a little more,
20   Being earth-brown, earth-golden from the burning bowels of the earth
On the day of Sicilian July, with Etna smoking.

The voice of my education said to me
He must be killed,
For in Sicily the black, black snakes are innocent, the gold are venomous.

25   And voices in me said, If you were a man
You would take a stick and break him now, and finish him off.

But must I confess how I liked him,
How glad I was he had come like a guest in quiet, to drink at my water-trough
And depart peaceful, pacified, and thankless,
30   Into the burning bowels of this earth?

Was it cowardice, that I dared not kill him?
Was it perversity, that I longed to talk to him?
Was it humility, to feel so honoured?
I felt so honoured.

35   And yet those voices:
If you were not afraid, you would kill him!

And truly I was afraid, I was most afraid,
But even so, honoured still more
That he should seek my hospitality
40   From out the dark door of the secret earth.

He drank enough
And lifted his head, dreamily, as one who has drunken,
And flickered his tongue like a forked night on the air, so black;
Seeming to lick his lips,
45   And looked around like a god, unseeing, into the air,
And slowly turned his head,
And slowly, very slowly, as if thrice adream,
Proceeded to draw his slow length curving round
And climb again the broken bank of my wall-face.

50   And as he put his head into that dreadful hole,
And as he slowly drew up, snake-easing his shoulders, and entered farther,
A sort of horror, a sort of protest against his withdrawing into that horrid black hole,
Deliberately going into the blackness, and slowly drawing himself after,
Overcame me now his back was turned.

55   I looked round, I put down my pitcher,
I picked up a clumsy log
And threw it at the water-trough with a clatter.

I think it did not hit him,
But suddenly that part of him that was left behind convulsed in undignified haste,
60 Writhed like lightning, and was gone
Into the black hole, the earth-lipped fissure in the wall-front,
At which, in the intense still noon, I stared with fascination.

And immediately I regretted it.
I thought how paltry, how vulgar, what a mean act!
65 I despised myself and the voices of my accursed human education.

And I thought of the albatross,[1]
And I wished he would come back, my snake.

For he seemed to me again like a king,
Like a king in exile, uncrowned in the underworld,
70 Now due to be crowned again.

And so, I missed my chance with one of the lords
Of life.
And I have something to expiate;
A pettiness.

Taormina.[2]

Bavarian Gentians

Not every man has gentians[1] in his house
in Soft September, at slow, sad Michaelmas.[2]

Bavarian[3] gentians, big and dark, only dark
darkening the day-time, torch-like with the smoking blueness of Pluto's[4] gloom,
ribbed and torch-like, with their blaze of darkness spread blue
down flattening into points, flattened under the sweep of white day
torch-flower of the blue-smoking darkness, Pluto's dark-blue daze,
black lamps from the halls of Dis, burning dark blue,
giving off darkness, blue darkness, as Demeter's pale lamps give off light,
lead me then, lead the way.

Reach me a gentian, give me a torch!
let me guide myself with the blue, forked torch of this flower
down the darker and darker stairs, where blue is darkened on blueness
even where Persephone goes, just now, from the frosted September
to the sightless realm where darkness is awake upon the dark
and Persephone herself is but a voice
or a darkness invisible enfolded in the deeper dark
of the arms Plutonic, and pierced with the passion of dense gloom,
among the splendour of torches of darkness, shedding darkness on the lost bride and her groom.

---

1. Killed pointlessly in Coleridge's "The Ancient Mariner."
2. Sicilian town where Lawrence lived from March 1920 to February 1922.

1. Plants with funnel-shaped flowers in a variety of colours and bitter, medicinal juice.
2. 29 September.

3. Bavaria is a district in southern Germany.
4. Pluto (also Dis) is the classical god of the underworld. He abducted Persephone, daughter of Demeter (the corn-goddess), and carried her off to Hades. Persephone was eventually allowed to return to earth each spring, thus comforting her mother and restoring the earth's fertility. In the autumn she descended to Hades again as Pluto's wife.

The Ship of Death

I

Now it is autumn and the falling fruit
and the long journey towards oblivion.

The apples falling like great drops of dew
to bruise themselves an exit from themselves.

5   And it is time to go, to bid farewell
to one's own self, and find an exit
from the fallen self.

II

Have you built your ship of death, O have you?
O build your ship of death, for you will need it.

10   The grim frost is at hand, when the apples will fall
thick, almost thundrous, on the hardened earth.

And death is on the air like a smell of ashes!
Ah! can't you smell it?

And in the bruised body, the frightened soul
15   finds itself shrinking, wincing from the cold
that blows upon it through the orifices.

III

And can a man his own quietus make
with a bare bodkin?[1]

With daggers, bodkins, bullets, man can make
20   a bruise or break of exit for his life;
but is that a quietus, O tell me, is it quietus?

Surely not so! for how could murder, even self-murder
ever a quietus make?

IV

O let us talk of quiet that we know,
25   that we can know, the deep and lovely quiet
of a strong heart at peace!

How can we this, our own quietus, make?

V

Build then the ship of death, for you must take
the longest journey, to oblivion.

30   And die the death, the long and painful death
that lies between the old self and the new.

Already our bodies are fallen, bruised, badly bruised,
already our souls are oozing through the exit
of the cruel bruise.

35   Already the dark and endless ocean of the end
is washing in through the breaches of our wounds,
already the flood is upon us.

---

1. A dagger or poniard. See *Hamlet* III.i.75–76.

Oh build your ship of death, your little ark[2]
and furnish it with food, with little cakes, and wine
40 for the dark flight down oblivion.

VI

Piecemeal the body dies, and the timid soul
has her footing washed away, as the dark flood rises.

We are dying, we are dying, we are all of us dying
and nothing will stay the death-flood rising within us
45 and soon it will rise on the world, on the outside world.

We are dying, we are dying, piecemeal our bodies are dying
and our strength leaves us,
and our soul cowers naked in the dark rain over the flood,
cowering in the last branches of the tree of our life.

VII

50 We are dying, we are dying, so all we can do
is now to be willing to die, and to build the ship
of death to carry the soul on the longest journey.

A little ship, with oars and food
and little dishes, and all accoutrements
55 fitting and ready for the departing soul.

Now launch the small ship, now as the body dies
and life departs, launch out, the fragile soul
in the fragile ship of courage, the ark of faith
with its store of food and little cooking pans
60 and change of clothes,
upon the flood's black waste
upon the waters of the end
upon the sea of death, where still we sail
darkly, for we cannot steer, and have no port.

65 There is no port, there is nowhere to go
only the deepening blackness darkening still
blacker upon the soundless, ungurgling flood
darkness at one with darkness, up and down
and sideways utterly dark, so there is no direction any more.
70 And the little ship is there; yet she is gone.
She is not seen, for there is nothing to see her by.
She is gone! gone! and yet
somewhere she is there.
Nowhere!

VIII

75 And everything is gone, the body is gone
completely under, gone, entirely gone.
The upper darkness is heavy as the lower,
between them the little ship
is gone
80 she is gone.

It is the end, it is oblivion.

2. An image suggestive of Noah's ark, of Egyptian and
Etruscan funeral ships, and of the boatman Charon, who
ferried dead souls across the river Styx.

IX

And yet out of eternity, a thread
separates itself on the blackness,
a horizontal thread
85   that fumes a little with pallor upon the dark.

Is it illusion? or does the pallor fume
A little higher?
Ah wait, wait, for there's the dawn,
the cruel dawn of coming back to life
90   out of oblivion.

Wait, wait, the little ship
drifting, beneath the deathly ashy grey
of a flood-dawn.

Wait, wait! even so, a flush of yellow
95   and strangely, O chilled wan soul, a flush of rose.

A flush of rose, and the whole thing starts again.

X

The flood subsides, and the body, like a worn sea-shell
emerges strange and lovely.
And the little ship wings home, faltering and lapsing
100   on the pink flood,
and the frail soul steps out, into her house again
filling the heart with peace.

Swings the heart renewed with peace
even of oblivion.

105   Oh build your ship of death, oh build it!
for you will need it.
For the voyage of oblivion awaits you.

T. S. ELIOT (1888–1965)

The Love Song of J. Alfred Prufrock

S'io credessi che mia risposta fosse
a persona che mai tornasse al mondo,
questa fiamma staria senza più scosse.
Ma per ciò che giammai di questo fondonon
tornò vivo alcun, s'i'odo il vero,
senza tema d'infamia ti rispondo.[1]

Let us go then, you and I,   — we are all trapped in hell.
When the evening is spread out against the sky   damned eternal.
Like a patient etherised upon a table;
Let us go, through certain half-deserted streets,
5   The muttering retreats
Of restless nights in one-night cheap hotels
And sawdust restaurants with oyster-shells:
Streets that follow like a tedious argument
Of insidious intent
10   To lead you to an overwhelming question . . .
Oh, do not ask, 'What is it?'
Let us go and make our visit.

1. In Dante's *Inferno*, Guido da Montefeltro tells the narrator of his shame in Hell: "If I thought my answer were to one who would ever return to the world, this flame would shake no more [i.e., I would be silent], but since none ever returned alive from this depth, if what I hear be true, I answer you without fear of infamy."

In the room the women come and go
Talking of Michelangelo.[2]

15   The yellow fog that rubs its back upon the window-panes,
The yellow smoke that rubs its muzzle on the window-panes,
Licked its tongue into the corners of the evening,
Lingered upon the pools that stand in drains,
Let fall upon its back the soot that falls from chimneys,
20   Slipped by the terrace, made a sudden leap,
And seeing that it was a soft October night,
Curled once about the house, and fell asleep.

And indeed there will be time
For the yellow smoke that slides along the street
25   Rubbing its back upon the window-panes;
There will be time, there will be time
To prepare a face to meet the faces that you meet;
There will be time to murder and create,
And time for all the works and days[3] of hands
30   That lift and drop a question on your plate;
Time for you and time for me,
And time yet for a hundred indecisions,
And for a hundred visions and revisions,
Before the taking of a toast and tea.

35   In the room the women come and go
Talking of Michelangelo.

And indeed there will be time
To wonder, 'Do I dare?' and, 'Do I dare?'
Time to turn back and descend the stair,
40   With a bald spot in the middle of my hair—
(They will say: 'How his hair is growing thin!')
My morning coat, my collar mounting firmly to the chin,
My necktie rich and modest, but asserted by a simple pin—
(They will say: 'But how his arms and legs are thin!')
45   Do I dare
Disturb the universe?
In a minute there is time
For decisions and revisions which a minute will reverse.

For I have known them all already, known them all—
50   Have known the evenings, mornings, afternoons,
I have measured out my life with coffee spoons;
I know the voices dying with a dying fall[4]
Beneath the music from a farther room.
   So how should I presume?

55   And I have known the eyes already, known them all—
The eyes that fix you in a formulated phrase,
And when I am formulated, sprawling on a pin,
When I am pinned and wriggling on the wall,
Then how should I begin
60   To spit out all the butt-ends of my days and ways?
   And how should I presume?

And I have known the arms already, known them all—
Arms that are braceleted and white and bare
(But in the lamplight, downed with light brown hair!)
65   Is it perfume from a dress
That makes me so digress?

2. (1475–1564), Italian painter, sculptor, and architect, one of the greatest artists of the Renaissance.

3. Allusion to the early Greek poet Hesiod's poem about farming, *Works and Days* (eighth century B.C.).
4. See Shakespeare, *Twelfth Night* I.i.

Arms that lie along a table, or wrap about a shawl.
>And should I then presume?
>And how should I begin?

       .   .   .   .   .

70   Shall I say, I have gone at dusk through narrow streets
And watched the smoke that rises from the pipes
Of lonely men in shirt-sleeves, leaning out of windows? . . .

I should have been a pair of ragged claws
Scuttling across the floors of silent seas.

       .   .   .   .   .

75   And the afternoon, the evening, sleeps so peacefully!
Smoothed by long fingers,
Asleep . . . tired . . . or it malingers,
Stretched on the floor, here beside you and me.
Should I, after tea and cakes and ices,
80   Have the strength to force the moment to its crisis?
But though I have wept and fasted, wept and prayed,
Though I have seen my head (grown slightly bald) brought in upon a platter,[5]
I am no prophet—and here's no great matter;
I have seen the moment of my greatness flicker,
85   And I have seen the eternal Footman hold my coat, and snicker,
And in short, I was afraid.

And would it have been worth it, after all,
After the cups, the marmalade, the tea,
Among the porcelain, among some talk of you and me,
90   Would it have been worth while,
To have bitten off the matter with a smile,
To have squeezed the universe into a ball
To roll it towards some overwhelming question,
To say: 'I am Lazarus, come from the dead,[6]
95   Come back to tell you all, I shall tell you all'—
If one, settling a pillow by her head,
>Should say: 'That is not what I meant at all.
>That is not it, at all.'

And would it have been worth it, after all,
100   Would it have been worth while,
After the sunsets and the dooryards and the sprinkled streets,
After the novels, after the teacups, after the skirts that trail along the floor—
And this, and so much more?—
It is impossible to say just what I mean!
105   But as if a magic lantern threw the nerves in patterns on a screen:
Would it have been worth while
If one, settling a pillow or throwing off a shawl,
And turning toward the window, should say:
>'That is not it at all,
110   That is not what I meant, at all.'

       .   .   .   .   .

No! I am not Prince Hamlet, nor was meant to be;
Am an attendant lord, one that will do
To swell a progress, start a scene or two,
Advise the prince; no doubt, an easy tool,
115   Deferential, glad to be of use,
Politic, cautious, and meticulous;
Full of high sentence, but a bit obtuse;
At times, indeed, almost ridiculous—
Almost, at times, the Fool.

[handwritten note: Prufrock does not act in the end as Hamlet did. He's buffeted by winds of fortune, indulging in self pity. not going to take fate into own hands.]

5. See Matt. xiv.3–11 and Mark vi.17–28.   6. See John xi.1–44.

120   I grow old ...I grow old ...
      I shall wear the bottoms of my trousers rolled.   *clinging to youth.*

      Shall I part my hair behind? Do I dare to eat a peach?   *laxative (hypochondriac).*
      I shall wear white flannel trousers, and walk upon the beach.
      I have heard the mermaids singing, each to each.

125   I do not think that they will sing to me.

      I have seen them riding seaward on the waves
      Combing the white hair of the waves blown back
      When the wind blows the water white and black.

      We have lingered in the chambers of the sea
130   By sea-girls wreathed with seaweed red and brown
      Till human voices wake us, and we drown.   *Lose ability to communicate. he drowns.*

Gerontion[1]

Thou hast nor youth nor age
But as it were an after dinner sleep
Dreaming of both.[2]

      Here I am, an old man in a dry month,
      Being read to by a boy, waiting for rain.
      I was neither at the hot gates[3]
      Nor fought in the warm rain
5   Nor knee deep in the salt marsh, heaving a cutlass,
      Bitten by flies, fought.
      My house is a decayed house,
      And the Jew squats on the window sill, the owner,
      Spawned in some estaminet[4] of Antwerp,
10   Blistered in Brussels, patched and peeled in London.
      The goat coughs at night in the field overhead;
      Rocks, moss, stonecrop, iron, merds.[5]
      The woman keeps the kitchen, makes tea,
      Sneezes at evening, poking the peevish gutter.
15   I an old man,
      A dull head among windy spaces.

      Signs are taken for wonders. 'We would see a sign!'[6]
      The word within a word, unable to speak a word,
      Swaddled with darkness.[7] In the juvescence of the year
20   Came Christ the tiger[8]

      In depraved May, dogwood and chestnut, flowering judas,
      To be eaten, to be divided, to be drunk[9]
      Among whispers; by Mr. Silvero
      With caressing hands, at Limoges
25   Who walked all night in the next room;
      By Hakagawa, bowing among the Titians;
      By Madame de Tornquist, in the dark room
      Shifting the candles; Fräulein von Kulp
      Who turned in the hall, one hand on the door.
30   Vacant shuttles
      Weave the wind. I have no ghosts,
      An old man in a draughty house
      Under a windy knob.

---

1. A coinage from Greek meaning "little old man."
2. Shakespeare, *Measure for Measure* III.i.32–34.
3. Of Thermopylae, the mountain pass where the Greeks defeated the Persians in 480 B.C.
4. Cafe.

5. Dung.
6. See Matt. xii.38–39.
7. See John i.1–5.
8. See Rev. v.5 and William Blake's poem "The Tyger."
9. See Luke xxii.15–20.

After such knowledge, what forgiveness? Think now
35 History has many cunning passages, contrived corridors
And issues, deceives with whispering ambitions,
Guides us by vanities. Think now
She gives when our attention is distracted
And what she gives, gives with such supple confusions
40 That the giving famishes the craving. Gives too late
What's not believed in, or is still believed,
In memory only, reconsidered passion. Gives too soon
Into weak hands, what's thought can be dispensed with
Till the refusal propagates a fear. Think
45 Neither fear nor courage saves us. Unnatural vices
Are fathered by our heroism. Virtues
Are forced upon us by our impudent crimes.
These tears are shaken from the wrath-bearing tree.

The tiger springs in the new year. Us he devours. Think at last
50 We have not reached conclusion, when I
Stiffen in a rented house. Think at last
I have not made this show purposelessly
And it is not by any concitation[10]
Of the backward devils.
55 I would meet you upon this honestly.
I that was near your heart was removed therefrom
To lose beauty in terror, terror in inquisition.
I have lost my passion: why should I need to keep it
Since what is kept must be adulterated?
60 I have lost my sight, smell, hearing, taste and touch:
How should I use them for your closer contact?

These with a thousand small deliberations
Protract the profit of their chilled delirium,
Excite the membrane, when the sense has cooled,
65 With pungent sauces, multiply variety
In a wilderness of mirrors. What will the spider do,
Suspend its operations, will the weevil
Delay? De Bailhache, Fresca, Mrs. Cammel, whirled
Beyond the circuit of the shuddering Bear
70 In fractured atoms. Gull against the wind, in the windy straits
Of Belle Isle, or running on the Horn.
White feathers in the snow, the Gulf claims,
And an old man driven by the Trades[11]
To a sleepy corner.

75   Tenants of the house,
Thoughts of a dry brain in a dry season.

10. Stirring up.
11. Trade-winds.

The Waste Land
1922

'Nam Sibyllam quidem Cumis ego ipse oculis meisvidi
in ampulla pendere, et cum illi pueri dicerent:
Σίβυλλα τί θέλεις; respondebat illa: ἀποθανεῖν θέλω.' [1]

For Ezra Pound
il miglior fabbro. [2]

I. The Burial of the Dead[3]

April is the cruellest month, breeding
Lilacs out of the dead land, mixing
Memory and desire, stirring
Dull roots with spring rain.
5   Winter kept us warm, covering
Earth in forgetful snow, feeding
A little life with dried tubers.
Summer surprised us, coming over the Starnbergersee[4]
With a shower of rain; we stopped in the colonnade,
10   And went on in sunlight, into the Hofgarten,[5]
And drank coffee, and talked for an hour.
Bin gar keine Russin, stamm' aus Litauen, echt deutsch.[6]
And when we were children, staying at the arch-duke's,
My cousin's, he took me out on a sled,
15   And I was frightened. He said, Marie,
Marie, hold on tight. And down we went.
In the mountains, there you feel free.
I read, much of the night, and go south in the winter.

What are the roots that clutch, what branches grow
20   Out of this stony rubbish? Son of man,[7]
You cannot say, or guess, for you know only
A heap of broken images, where the sun beats,
And the dead tree gives no shelter, the cricket no relief,[8]
And the dry stone no sound of water. Only
25   There is shadow under this red rock,[9]
(Come in under the shadow of this red rock),
And I will show you something different from either
Your shadow at morning striding behind you
Or your shadow at evening rising to meet you;
30   I will show you fear in a handful of dust.
        Frisch weht der Wind
        Der Heimat zu
        Mein Irisch Kind,
        Wo weilest du? [10]

---

1. (Latin and Greek) From Petronius, *The Satyricon* (first century A.D.): "For I myself saw with my own eyes the Sybil of Cumae hanging in a cage, and when the boys said to her, 'Sybil, what do you want?' she replied, 'I want to die.'" Granted immortality by Apollo, the Sybil, a prophet, forgot to ask for perpetual youth, so she kept on getting older and more wretched.
2. (Italian) "The better craftsman." Pound suggested drastic revisions to Eliot's original version of the poem, which was much longer than the present one. In his own notes to the poem, Eliot also acknowledges his debt to James Frazer's *The Golden Bough* (1890), which explores the meanings of ancient fertility myths and rituals, and to Jessie Weston's *From Ritual to Romance* (1920), which related those myths to the medieval legend of the Holy Grail. "Indeed, so deeply am I indebted, Miss Weston's book will elucidate the difficulties of the poem much better than my notes can do..." (Eliot's note).
3. Title of the Anglican burial service.
4. A resort lake near Munich, Germany.
5. A public park in Munich.
6. (German) "I am not Russian at all, I come from Lithuania, a true German."
7. "Cf. Ezekiel 2:1" (Eliot's note).
8. "Cf. Ecclesiastes 12:5" (Eliot's note).
9. See Isa. xxxii.2.
10. "V. *Tristan un Isolde*, I, verses 5–8" (Eliot's note). In Wagner's opera, a sailor sings of his absent love: "Fresh blows the wind to the homeland; my Irish child, where are you waiting?"

35   'You gave me hyacinths first a year ago;
        'They called me the hyacinth girl.'
        — Yet when we came back, late, from the hyacinth garden,
        Your arms full, and your hair wet, I could not
        Speak, and my eyes failed, I was neither
40   Living nor dead, and I knew nothing,
        Looking into the heart of light, the silence.
        Oed' und leer das Meer.[11]

        Madame Sosostris,[12] famous clairvoyante,
        Had a bad cold, nevertheless
45   Is known to be the wisest woman in Europe,
        With a wicked pack of cards.[13] Here, said she,
        Is your card, the drowned Phoenician Sailor,
        (Those are pearls that were his eyes.[14] Look!)
        Here is Belladonna,[15] the Lady of the Rocks,
50   The lady of situations.
        Here is the man with three staves, and here the Wheel,
        And here is the one-eyed merchant, and this card,
        Which is blank, is something he carries on his back,
        Which I am forbidden to see. I do not find
55   The Hanged Man. Fear death by water.
        I see crowds of people, walking round in a ring.
        Thank you. If you see dear Mrs. Equitone,
        Tell her I bring the horoscope myself:
        One must be so careful these days.

60   Unreal City,[16]
        Under the brown fog of a winter dawn,
        A crowd flowed over London Bridge, so many,
        I had not thought death had undone so many.[17]
        Sighs, short and infrequent, were exhaled,[18]
65   And each man fixed his eyes before his feet.
        Flowed up the hill and down King William Street,
        To where Saint Mary Woolnoth[19] kept the hours
        With a dead sound on the final stroke of nine.[20]
        There I saw one I knew, and stopped him, crying: 'Stetson!
70   'You who were with me in the ships at Mylae![21]
        'That corpse you planted last year in your garden,
        'Has it begun to sprout? Will it bloom this year?
        'Or has the sudden frost disturbed its bed?
        'O keep the Dog far hence, that's friend to men,
75   'Or with his nails he'll dig it up again![22]
        'You! hypocrite lecteur! — mon semblable, — mon frère!'[23]

---

11. "Id. III, verse 24" (Eliot's note). "Empty and desolate the sea."
12. A mock Egyptian-sounding name.
13. The Tarot pack, described by Jessie Weston. "I am not familiar with the exact constitution of the Tarot pack of cards, from which I have obviously departed to suit my own convenience. The Hanged Man, a member of the traditional pack, fits my purpose in two ways: because he is associated in my mind with the Hanged God of Frazer, and because I associate him with the hooded figure in the passage of the disciples to Emmaus in Part V. The Phoenician Sailor and the Merchant appear later; also the 'crowds of people', and Death by Water is executed in Part IV. The Man with Three Staves (an authentic member of the Tarot pack) associates, quite arbitrarily, with the Fisher King himself" (Eliot's note).
14. See Shakespeare, *The Tempest* I.ii.399.
15. Beautiful lady, the Virgin Mary; also a poison, deadly nightshade.
16. "Cf. Baudelaire: Fourmillante cité, cité pleine de rêves, / Où le spectre en plein jour raccroche le passant"
(Eliot's note). The lines from Baudelaire's poem "Les Sept Vieillards" may be translated as: "Swarming city, city full of dreams, where the spectre accosts the passerby in broad daylight."
17. "Cf. *Inferno* III, 55–57" (Eliot's note). The Italian may be translated as: "So long a train of people, I should never have believed that death had undone so many."
18. "Cf. *Inferno* IV, 25–27" (Eliot's note). "Here was no plaint that could be heard, except of sighs, which caused the eternal air to tremble."
19. A church in the financial district ("City") of London.
20. "A phenomenon which I have often noticed" (Eliot's note).
21. Site of a naval battle between Rome and Carthage in 260 B.C.
22. "Cf. the Dirge in Webster's *White Devil*" (Eliot's note). In Webster's play (ca. 1608) the dirge runs, in part: "But keep the wolf hence, that's foe to men, / For with his nails he'll dig them up again."
23. "V. Baudelaire, Preface to *Fleurs du Mal*" (Eliot's note). The French translates as: "Hypocritical reader! My likeness! My brother!"

II. A Game of Chess[24]

The Chair she sat in, like a burnished throne,
Glowed on the marble,[25] where the glass
Held up by standards wrought with fruited vines
80 From which a golden Cupidon peeped out
(Another hid his eyes behind his wing)
Doubled the flames of sevenbranched candelabra
Reflecting light upon the table as
The glitter of her jewels rose to meet it,
85 From satin cases poured in rich profusion.
In vials of ivory and coloured glass
Unstoppered, lurked her strange synthetic perfumes,
Unguent, powdered, or liquid—troubled, confused
And drowned the sense in odours; stirred by the air
90 That freshened from the window, these ascended
In fattening the prolonged candle-flames,
Flung their smoke into the laquearia,[26]
Stirring the pattern on the coffered ceiling.
Huge sea-wood fed with copper
95 Burned green and orange, framed by the coloured stone,
In which sad light a carvèd dolphin swam.
Above the antique mantel was displayed
As though a window gave upon the sylvan scene[27]
The change of Philomel, by the barbarous king
100 So rudely forced;[28] yet there the nightingale[29]
Filled all the desert with inviolable voice
And still she cried, and still the world pursues,
'Jug Jug' to dirty ears.
And other withered stumps of time
105 Were told upon the walls; staring forms
Leaned out, leaning, hushing the room enclosed.
Footsteps shuffled on the stair.
Under the firelight, under the brush, her hair
Spread out in fiery points
110 Glowed into words, then would be savagely still.

'My nerves are bad to-night. Yes, bad. Stay with me.
'Speak to me. Why do you never speak. Speak.
'What are you thinking of? What thinking? What?
'I never know what you are thinking. Think.'

115 I think we are in rats' alley[30]
Where the dead men lost their bones.

'What is that noise?'
          The wind under the door.[31]
'What is that noise now? What is the wind doing?'
120   Nothing again nothing.
                                      'Do
'You know nothing? Do you see nothing? Do you remember
'Nothing?'

24. The title evokes two plays by Thomas Middleton (1580–1627), *A Game at Chess* and *Women Beware Women*. In the latter, a woman is distracted by a chess game while her daughter-in-law is seduced.
25. "Cf. *Antony and Cleopatra*, II. ii, l. 190" (Eliot's note).
26. A panelled ceiling. "V. *Aeneid*, I, 726..." (Eliot's note). Eliot goes on to quote the Latin line, which is from a description of a banquet given by Dido, Queen of Carthage, for her lover Aeneas. Dido and Aeneas, along with Antony and Cleopatra, were perhaps the most famous mortal lovers of antiquity.
27. "V. Milton, *Paradise Lost*, IV, 140" (Eliot's note). Milton's passage is a description of Eden.
28. "V. Ovid, *Metamorphoses*, VI, Philomela" (Eliot's note). Tereus raped Philomela, sister of his wife Procne, and then cut out her tongue to silence her. Philomela was later changed into a nightingale, Procne into a swallow.
29. "Cf. Part III, l. 204" (Eliot's note).
30. "Cf. Part III, l. 195" (Eliot's note).
31. "Cf. Webster: 'Is the wind in that door still?'" (Eliot's note). See Webster, *The Devil's Law Case* III.ii.162.

I remember
125   Those are pearls that were his eyes.
'Are you alive, or not? Is there nothing in your head?'
                                                    But

O O O O that Shakespeherian Rag—
It's so elegant
130   So intelligent[32]
'What shall I do now? What shall I do?'
'I shall rush out as I am, and walk the street
'With my hair down, so. What shall we do tomorrow?
'What shall we ever do?'
135   The hot water at ten.
And if it rains, a closed car at four.
And we shall play a game of chess,[33]
Pressing lidless eyes and waiting for a knock upon the door.

When Lil's husband got demobbed,[34] I said—
140   I didn't mince my words, I said to her myself,
HURRY UP PLEASE ITS TIME[35]
Now Albert's coming back, make yourself a bit smart.
He'll want to know what you done with that money he gave you
To get yourself some teeth. He did, I was there.
145   You have them all out, Lil, and get a nice set,
He said, I swear, I can't bear to look at you.
And no more can't I, I said, and think of poor Albert,
He's been in the army four years, he wants a good time,
And if you don't give it him, there's others will, I said.
150   Oh is there, she said. Something o' that, I said.
Then I'll know who to thank, she said, and give me a straight look.
HURRY UP PLEASE ITS TIME
If you don't like it you can get on with it, I said.
Others can pick and choose if you can't.
155   But if Albert makes off, it won't be for lack of telling.
You ought to be ashamed, I said, to look so antique.
(And her only thirty-one.)
I can't help it, she said, pulling a long face,
It's them pills I took, to bring it off, she said.
160   (She's had five already, and nearly died of young George.)
The chemist said it would be all right, but I've never been the same.
You *are* a proper fool, I said.
Well, if Albert won't leave you alone, there it is, I said,
What you get married for if you don't want children?
165   HURRY UP PLEASE ITS TIME
Well, that Sunday Albert was home, they had a hot gammon,
And they asked me in to dinner, to get the beauty of it hot—
HURRY UP PLEASE ITS TIME
HURRY UP PLEASE ITS TIME
170   Goonight Bill. Goonight Lou. Goonight May. Goonight.
Ta ta. Goonight. Goonight.
Good night, ladies, good night, sweet ladies, good night, good night.[36]

III. The Fire Sermon

The river's tent is broken; the last fingers of leaf
Clutch and sink into the wet bank. The wind

---

32. Adapted from a ragtime piece popular around 1912.
33. "Cf. the game of chess in Middleton's *Women Beware Women*" (Eliot's note).

34. Demobilized, discharged from the army.
35. Call of the English pub-keeper at closing time.
36. See Ophelia's final words in *Hamlet* IV.v.72.

175 Crosses the brown land, unheard. The nymphs are departed.
Sweet Thames, run softly, till I end my song.[37]
The river bears no empty bottles, sandwich papers,
Silk handkerchiefs, cardboard boxes, cigarette ends
Or other testimony of summer nights. The nymphs are departed.
180 And their friends, the loitering heirs of City directors;
Departed, have left no addresses.
By the waters of Leman I sat down and wept...[38]
Sweet Thames, run softly till I end my song,
Sweet Thames, run softly, for I speak not loud or long.
185 But at my back in a cold blast I hear
The rattle of the bones, and chuckle spread from ear to ear.

A rat crept softly through the vegetation
Dragging its slimy belly on the bank
While I was fishing in the dull canal
190 On a winter evening round behind the gashouse
Musing upon the king my brother's wreck[39]
And on the king my father's death before him.
White bodies naked on the low damp ground
And bones cast in a little low dry garret,
195 Rattled by the rat's foot only, year to year.
But at my back from time to time I hear[40]
The sound of horns and motors, which shall bring
Sweeney to Mrs. Porter in the spring.[41]
O the moon shone bright on Mrs. Porter
200 And on her daughter
They wash their feet in soda water[42]
Et O ces voix d'enfants, chantant dans la coupole![43]

Twit twit twit
Jug jug jug jug jug jug
205 So rudely forc'd.
Tereu[44]

Unreal City
Under the brown fog of a winter noon
Mr. Eugenides, the Smyrna merchant
210 Unshaven, with a pocket full of currants
C.i.f. London: documents at sight,[45]
Asked me in demotic French
To luncheon at the Cannon Street Hotel
Followed by a weekend at the Metropole.

215 At the violet hour, when the eyes and back
Turn upward from the desk, when the human engine waits
Like a taxi throbbing waiting,

---

37. "V. Spenser, *Prothalamion*" (Eliot's note). Edmund Spenser's poem is a marriage song.
38. See the mourning of the exiled Jews in Babylon, Ps. cxxxvii. Lake Leman is Lake Geneva, near Lausanne, where Eliot worked on the poem. "Leman" is also an archaic word meaning an illicit lover.
39. "Cf. *The Tempest*, I, ii" (Eliot's note).
40. "Cf. Marvell, *To His Coy Mistress*" (Eliot's note).
41. "Cf. Day, *Parliament of Bees:*
    When of the sudden, listening, you shall hear,
    A noise of horns and hunting, which shall bring
    Actaeon to Diana in the spring,
    Where all shall see her naked skin...."
        (Eliot's note)

Actaeon saw the goddess Diana bathing and was changed into a stag and hunted to death.
42. From an Australian troop song in World War I.
43. (French) "And O those children's voices, singing in the cupola!" "V. Verlaine, *Parsifal*" (Eliot's note). Parsifal was a knight questing for the Holy Grail; Wagner wrote an opera about him.
44. Conventional representations of the nightingale's song by the Elizabethans.
45. "The currants were quoted at a price 'carriage and insurance free to London'; and the Bill of Lading, etc., were to be handed to the buyer upon payment of the sight draft" (Eliot's note).

I Tiresias,[46] though blind, throbbing between two lives,
Old man with wrinkled female breasts, can see
220   At the violet hour, the evening hour that strives
Homeward, and brings the sailor home from sea,[47]
The typist home at teatime, clears her breakfast, lights
Her stove, and lays out food in tins.
Out of the window perilously spread
225   Her drying combinations touched by the sun's last rays,
On the divan are piled (at night her bed)
Stockings, slippers, camisoles, and stays.

I Tiresias, old man with wrinkled dugs
Perceived the scene, and foretold the rest—
230   I too awaited the expected guest.
He, the young man carbuncular, arrives,
A small house agent's clerk, with one bold stare,
One of the low on whom assurance sits
As a silk hat on a Bradford[48] millionaire.
235   The time is now propitious, as he guesses,
The meal is ended, she is bored and tired,
Endeavours to engage her in caresses
Which still are unreproved, if undesired.
Flushed and decided, he assaults at once;
240   Exploring hands encounter no defence;
His vanity requires no response,
And makes a welcome of indifference.
(And I Tiresias have foresuffered all
Enacted on this same divan or bed;
245   I who have sat by Thebes below the wall
And walked among the lowest of the dead.)[49]
Bestows one final patronising kiss,
And gropes his way, finding the stairs unlit . . .

She turns and looks a moment in the glass,
250   Hardly aware of her departed lover;
Her brain allows one half-formed thought to pass:
'Well now that's done: and I'm glad it's over.'
When lovely woman stoops to folly and[50]
Paces about her room again, alone,
255   She smoothes her hair with automatic hand,
And puts a record on the gramophone.

'This music crept by me upon the waters'[51]
And along the Strand, up Queen Victoria Street.
O City city, I can sometimes hear
260   Beside a public bar in Lower Thames Street,
The pleasant whining of a mandoline

---

46. "Tiresias, although a mere spectator and not indeed a 'character', is yet the most important personage in the poem, uniting all the rest. Just as the one-eyed merchant, seller of currants, melts into the Phoenician Sailor, and the latter is not wholly distinct from Ferdinand Prince of Naples, so all the women are one woman, and the two sexes meet in Tiresias. What Tiresias *sees*, in fact, is the substance of the poem . . ." (Eliot's note). Eliot goes on to quote nineteen lines in Latin from Ovid's *Metamorphoses* III, which is an account of how Tiresias was changed from a man into a woman, and years later back into a man. Jupiter and Juno, disputing whether men or women took greater pleasure from love, asked Tiresias to decide, since he had been both man and woman; when he said that women did, Juno, offended, blinded him, but Jupiter mollified this punishment by granting him the gift of prophecy.
47. "This may not appear as exact as Sappho's lines, but I had in mind the 'longshore' or 'dory' fisherman, who returns at nightfall" (Eliot's note). Sappho's lines are an address to Hesperus, the Evening Star. See also Robert Louis Stevenson's "Requiem": "Home is the sailor, home from the sea, / And the hunter home from the hill."
48. An industrial city in Yorkshire.
49. Tiresias lived and prophesied in Thebes for several generations. After his death he continued to prophesy in Hades, where Odysseus questioned him; see Pound's Canto I.
50. "V. Goldsmith, the song in *The Vicar of Wakefield*" (Eliot's note). In Oliver Goldsmith's novel (1766) the seduced Olivia sings: "When lovely woman stoops to folly, / And finds too late that men betray, / What charm can soothe her melancholy? / What art can wash her guilt away? / The only art her guilt to cover, / To hide her shame from every eye, / To give repentance to her lover, / And wring his bosom, is— to die."
51. "V. *The Tempest*, as above" (Eliot's note).

And a clatter and a chatter from within
Where fishmen lounge at noon: where the walls
Of Magnus Martyr hold
265 Inexplicable splendour of Ionian white and gold.[52]

The river sweats[53]
Oil and tar
The barges drift
With the turning tide
270 Red sails
Wide
To leeward, swing on the heavy spar.
The barges wash
Drifting logs
275 Down Greenwich reach[54]
Past the Isle of Dogs.
   Weialala leia
   Wallala leialala

Elizabeth and Leicester[55]
280 Beating oars
The stern was formed
A gilded shell
Red and gold
The brisk swell
285 Rippled both shores
Southwest wind
Carried down stream
The peal of bells
White towers
290   Weialala leia
   Wallala leialala

'Trams and dusty trees.
Highbury bore me. Richmond and Kew
Undid me.[56] By Richmond I raised by knees
295 Supine on the floor of a narrow canoe.'

'My feet are at Moorgate, and my heart
Under my feet. After the event
He wept. He promised "a new start."
I made no comment. What should I resent?'

300 'On Margate Sands.
I can connect
Nothing with nothing.
The broken fingernails of dirty hands.
My people humble people who expect
305 Nothing.'
  la la

52. "The interior of St. Magnus Martyr is to my mind one of the finest among Wren's interiors..." (Eliot's note).
53. "The Song of the (three) Thames-daughters begins here. From line 292 to 306 inclusive they speak in turn. V. *Götterdämmerung* III, i: the Rhine-daughters" (Eliot's note). In Wagner's opera, *Die Götterdämmerung* (The Twilight of the Gods), the last of the four operas in his *Ring* cycle, the Rhine-maidens lament that, since the gold of the Nibelungs over which they watched has been stolen, their river is no longer beautiful. The refrain "Weialala leia" is taken directly from the opera. The river scene also owes something to the opening of Conrad's *Heart of Darkness*.
54. A section of the Thames downstream from London, bordered by Greenwich and the Isle of Dogs.

55. "V. Froude, *Elizabeth*, Vol I, ch. iv, letter of De Quadra to Philip of Spain: 'In the afternoon we were in a barge, watching the games on the river. (The queen) was alone with Lord Robert [Earl of Leicester] and myself on the poop, when they began to talk nonsense, and went so far that Lord Robert at last said, as I was on the spot there was no reason why they should not be married if the queen pleased'" (Eliot's note).
56. "Cf. *Purgatorio*, V. 133..." (Eliot's note). Eliot then quotes two lines from Dante, which may be translated: "Remember me, who am La Pia; Siena made me, Maremma unmade me." They are spoken by a Sienese woman condemned to die for infidelity in the Maremma marshes; Pound uses the same passage in *Hugh Selwyn Mauberley*. The places named are all in or near London; Margate is a resort town on the Thames estuary.

To Carthage then I came[57]

Burning burning burning burning[58]
O Lord Thou pluckest me out
310   O Lord Thou pluckest[59]

burning

IV. Death by Water[60]

Phlebas the Phoenician, a fortnight dead,
Forgot the cry of gulls, and the deep sea swell
And the profit and loss.
315   A current under sea
Picked his bones in whispers. As he rose and fell
He passed the stages of his age and youth
Entering the whirlpool.
                     Gentile or Jew
320   O you who turn the wheel and look to windward,
Consider Phlebas, who was once handsome and tall as you.

V. What the Thunder Said[61]

      After the torchlight red on sweaty faces
After the frosty silence in the gardens
After the agony in stony places
325   The shouting and the crying
Prison and palace and reverberation
Of thunder of spring over distant mountains
He who was living is now dead
We who were living are now dying
330   With a little patience

      Here is no water but only rock
Rock and no water and the sandy road
The road winding above among the mountains
Which are mountains of rock without water
335   If there were water we should stop and drink
Amongst the rock one cannot stop or think
Sweat is dry and feet are in the sand
If there were only water amongst the rock
Dead mountain mouth of carious teeth that cannot spit
340   Here one can neither stand nor lie nor sit
There is not even silence in the mountains
But dry sterile thunder without rain
There is not even solitude in the mountains
But red sullen faces sneer and snarl
345   From doors of mudcracked houses
                     If there were water

And no rock
If there were rock
And also water
350   And water

57. "V. St. Augustine's *Confessions:* 'to Carthage then I came, where a cauldron of unholy loves sang all about mine ears'" (Eliot's note).
58. "The complete text of the Buddha's Fire Sermon (which corresponds in importance to the Sermon on the Mount) from which these words are taken, will be found translated in the late Henry Clarke Warren's *Buddhism in Translation* (Harvard Oriental Series)..." (Eliot's note).
59. "From St. Augustine's *Confessions* again. The collocation of these two representatives of eastern and western asceticism, as the culmination of this part of the poem, is not an accident" (Eliot's note).
60. The title recalls not only the allusions to *The Tempest*, but also the accounts in Frazer and Weston of the rites of Adonis or Tammuz. An effigy of the god was thrown into the sea or river and later taken out; the rising of the drowned god was necessary to renew the earth's fertility.
61. "In the first part of Part V three themes are employed: the journey to Emmaus, the approach to the Chapel Perilous (see Miss Weston's book) and the present decay of eastern Europe" (Eliot's note).

A spring
A pool among the rock
If there were the sound of water only
Not the cicada
355   And dry grass singing
But sound of water over a rock
Where the hermit-thrush sings in the pine trees
Drip drop drip drop drop drop drop[62]
But there is no water

360   Who is the third who walks always beside you?[63]
When I count, there are only you and I together
But when I look ahead up the white road
There is always another one walking beside you
Gliding wrapt in a brown mantle, hooded
365   I do not know whether a man or a woman
— But who is that on the other side of you?

       What is that sound high in the air[64]
Murmur of maternal lamentation
Who are those hooded hordes swarming
370   Over endless plains, stumbling in cracked earth
Ringed by the flat horizon only
What is the city over the mountains
Cracks and reforms and bursts in the violet air
Falling towers
375   Jerusalem Athens Alexandria
Vienna London
Unreal

       A woman drew her long black hair out tight
And fiddled whisper music on those strings
380   And bats with baby faces in the violet light
Whistled, and beat their wings
And crawled head downward down a blackened wall
And upside down in air were towers
Tolling reminiscent bells, that kept the hours
385   And voices singing out of empty cisterns and exhausted wells.

       In this decayed hole among the mountains
In the faint moonlight, the grass is singing
Over the tumbled graves, about the chapel[65]
There is the empty chapel, only the wind's home.
390   It has no windows, and the door swings,
Dry bones can harm no one.
Only a cock stood on the rooftree
Co co rico co co rico
In a flash of lightning. Then a damp gust
395   Bringing rain

---

62. "This is *Turdus aonalaschkae pallasii*, the hermit-thrush which I have heard in Quebec Province. Chapman says *(Handbook of Birds of Eastern North America)* 'it is most at home in secluded woodland and thickety retreats. . . . Its notes are not remarkable for variety or volume, but in purity and sweetness of tone and exquisite modulation they are unequalled.' Its 'water-dripping song' is justly celebrated" (Eliot's note).
63. "The following lines were stimulated by the account of one of the Antarctic expeditions (I forget which, but I think one of Shackleton's): it was related that the party of explorers, at the extremity of their strength, had the constant delusion that there was *one more member* than could actually be counted" (Eliot's note). See also Luke xxiv.13–34.
64. "Cf. Hermann Hesse, *Blick ins Chaos* . . ." (Eliot's note). Eliot quotes in German a passage from Hesse's text. A translation is: "Already half of Europe, already at least half of eastern Europe, on the way to Chaos, travels drunken in sacred madness along the edge of the abyss, and sings the while, sings drunkenly and hymn-like as Dmitri Karamazov [in Dostoievski's *Brothers Karamazov*] sang. Shocked by these songs the bourgeois laughs; the saint and the prophet hear them with tears."
65. The Chapel Perilous of the Grail legend, where the questing knight meets his final test.

Ganga[66] was sunken, and the limp leaves
Waited for rain, while the black clouds
Gathered far distant, over Himavant.[67]
The jungle crouched, humped in silence.
400   Then spoke the thunder
DA[68]
Datta: what have we given?
My friend, blood shaking my heart
The awful daring of a moment's surrender
405   Which an age of prudence can never retract
By this, and this only, we have existed
Which is not to be found in our obituaries
Or in memories draped by the beneficent spider[69]
Or under seals broken by the lean solicitor
410   In our empty rooms
DA
Dayadhvam: I have heard the key
Turn in the door once and turn once only[70]
We think of the key, each in his prison
415   Thinking of the key, each confirms a prison
Only at nightfall, aethereal rumours
Revive for a moment a broken Coriolanus[71]
DA
Damyata: The boat responded
420   Gaily, to the hand expert with sail and oar
The sea was calm, your heart would have responded
Gaily, when invited, beating obedient
To controlling hands

I sat upon the shore
Fishing, with the arid plain behind me[72]
425   Shall I at least set my lands in order?[73]
London Bridge is falling down falling down falling down
Poi s'ascose nel foco che gli affina[74]
Quando fiam uti chelidon[75] — O swallow swallow
Le Prince d'Aquitaine à la tour abolie[76]
430   These fragments I have shored against my ruins
Why then Ile fit you. Hieronymo's mad againe.[77]
Datta. Dayadhvam. Damyata.
Shantih shantih shantih[78]

---

66. The sacred Ganges river.
67. A mountain in the Himalayas.
68. "'Datta, dayadhvam, damyata' (Give, sympathise, control). The fable of the meaning of the Thunder is found in the *Brihadaranyaka—Upanishad*, 5, 1..." (Eliot's note). In the Hindu story, gods, men, and demons asked their father Prajapati, "Speak to us, Lord." To each he replied in the thunder with the one word "Da," and each group interpreted it in a different way: "Datta" to give alms, "Dayadhvam" to have compassion, "Damyata" to practise self-control.
69. "Cf. Webster, *The White Devil*, V, vi: '...they'll remarry / Ere the worm pierce your winding-sheet, ere the spider / Make a thin curtain for your epitaphs'" (Eliot's note).
70. "Cf. *Inferno*, XXXIII, 46..." (Eliot's note). Eliot quotes the Italian passage, which may be translated: "And I heard below the door of the horrible tower being locked up." The traitor Ugolino is describing his punishment. Eliot continues: "Also F.H. Bradley, *Appearance and Reality*, p. 346, 'My external sensations are no less private to myself than are my thoughts or my feelings. In either case my experience falls within my own circle, a circle closed on the outside; and, with all its elements alike, every sphere is opaque to the others which surround it.... In brief, regarded as an existence which appears in a soul, the whole world for each is peculiar and private to

that soul.'"
71. Roman general, subject of Shakespeare's play.
72. "V. Weston, *From Ritual to Romance;* chapter on the Fisher King" (Eliot's note).
73. See Isa. xxxviii.l.
74. "V. *Purgatorio*, XXVI, 148..." (Eliot's note). Eliot quotes four lines in Italian, the last of which is the line he uses in the poem. They read: "'Now I pray you, by the goodness that guides you to the summit of this stairway, be mindful in due season of my pain.' Then he hid himself in the fire which refines them."
75. (Latin) "When shall I be as the swallow?" Eliot's note reads: "V. *Pervigilium Veneris*. Cf. Philomela in Parts II and III." In this version Philomela is identified with the swallow.
76. "V. Gerard de Nerval, Sonnet *El Desdichado*" (Eliot's note). The line translates "The prince of Aquitaine at the ruined tower." The Tower struck by Lightning is a card in the Tarot pack suggesting pride humbled.
77. "V. Kyd's *Spanish Tragedy*" (Eliot's note). Thomas Kyd's play (1594) is subtitled *Hieronymo's Mad Againe*. It is an early revenge tragedy; "Why then Ile fit you" is Hieronymo's reply when requested to write a play. Acting a part in it, he kills his son's murderer.
78. "Repeated as here, a formal ending to an Upanishad. 'The Peace which passeth understanding' is our equivalent to this word" (Eliot's note).

The Hollow Men
1925

Mistah Kurtz—he dead.[1]

A penny for the Old Guy[2]

I

We are the hollow men
We are the stuffed men
Leaning together
Headpiece filled with straw. Alas!
5 Our dried voices, when
We whisper together
Are quiet and meaningless
As wind in dry grass
Or rats' feet over broken glass
10 In our dry cellar

Shape without form, shade without colour,
Paralysed force, gesture without motion;

Those who have crossed
With direct eyes, to death's other Kingdom
15 Remember us—if at all—not as lost
Violent souls, but only
As the hollow men
The stuffed men.

II

Eyes I dare not meet in dreams
20 In death's dream kingdom
These do not appear:
There, the eyes are
Sunlight on a broken column
There, is a tree swinging
25 And voices are
In the wind's singing
More distant and more solemn
Than a fading star.

Let me be no nearer
30 In death's dream kingdom
Let me also wear
Such deliberate disguises
Rat's coat, crowskin, crossed staves
In a field
35 Behaving as the wind behaves
No nearer—

Not that final meeting
In the twilight kingdom

III

40 This is the dead land
This is cactus land
Here the stone images
Are raised, here they receive
The supplication of a dead man's hand
Under the twinkle of a fading star.

45 Is it like this
In death's other kingdom
Waking alone
At the hour when we are
Trembling with tenderness
50 Lips that would kiss
Form prayers to broken stone.

IV

The eyes are not here
There are no eyes here
In this valley of dying stars
55 In this hollow valley
This broken jaw of our lost kingdoms

In this last of meeting places
We grope together
And avoid speech
60 Gathered on this beach of the tumid river[3]

Sightless, unless
The eyes reappear
As the perpetual star
Multifoliate rose[4]
65 Of death's twilight kingdom
The hope only
Of empty men.

1. This is the announcement of the death of Kurtz in Joseph Conrad's *Heart of Darkness*. Marlow, the narrator, says of Kurtz, a highly gifted man whose moral vacuity has been exposed by the conditions of the jungle: "Whether he knew of this deficiency himself I can't say. I think the knowledge came to him at last—only at the very last. But the wilderness had found him out early, and had taken on him a terrible vengeance for the fantastic invasion. I think it had whispered to him things about himself which he did not know, things of which he had no conception till he took counsel with this great solitude—and the whisper had proved irresistibly fascinating. It echoed loudly within him because he was hollow at the core...."

2. On 5 November 1605, the Gunpowder Plot was discovered; Guy Fawkes and other conspirators had secreted gunpowder in the cellars under the English Parliament with a view to blowing it up. On Guy Fawkes Day, children exhibit straw effigies of Guy Fawkes and use the quoted phrase to solicit coins to buy fireworks.

3. See Dante, *Inferno* III, where the damned souls assemble to cross the river Acheron into Hell. The most repulsive are those who have been neither faithful nor unfaithful, good nor evil, but uncommitted.

4. See Dante, *Paradiso* XXXI–XXXII, where Paradise is imaged as a celestial rose.

V

Here we go round the prickly pear
Prickly pear prickly pear
70   *Here we go round the prickly pear*
At five o'clock in the morning.

Between the idea
And the reality
Between the motion
75   And the act
Falls the Shadow

For Thine is the Kingdom

Between the conception
And the creation
80   Between the emotion
And the response
Falls the Shadow

Life is very long

Between the desire
85   And the spasm
Between the potency
And the existence
Between the essence
And the descent
90   Falls the Shadow

For Thine is the Kingdom

For Thine is
Life is
For Thine is the

95   *This is the way the world ends*
This is the way the world ends
This is the way the world ends
Not with a bang but a whimper.

Journey of the Magi[1]

'A cold coming we had of it,
Just the worst time of the year
For a journey, and such a long journey:
The ways deep and the weather sharp,
5   The very dead of winter.'[2]
And the camels galled, sore-footed, refractory,
Lying down in the melting snow.
There were times we regretted
The summer palaces on slopes, the terraces,
10   And the silken girls bringing sherbet.
Then the camel men cursing and grumbling
And running away, and wanting their liquor and women,
And the night-fires going out, and the lack of shelters,
And the cities hostile and the towns unfriendly

1. See Matt. ii.1–12.
2. The lines in quotation marks are adapted from a

Nativity sermon by the seventeenth-century Bishop of
Winchester, Lancelot Andrewes.

15 And the villages dirty and charging high prices:
A hard time we had of it.
At the end we preferred to travel all night,
Sleeping in snatches,
With the voices singing in our ears, saying
20 That this was all folly.

   Then at dawn we came down to a temperate valley,
Wet, below the snow line, smelling of vegetation,
With a running stream and a water-mill beating the darkness,
And three trees on the low sky,
25 And an old white horse galloped away in the meadow.
Then we came to a tavern with vine-leaves over the lintel,
Six hands at an open door dicing for pieces of silver,
But there was no information, and so we continued
And arrived at evening, not a moment too soon
30 Find the place; it was (you may say) satisfactory.

All this was a long time ago, I remember,
And I would do it again, but set down
This set down
This: were we led all that way for
35 Birth or Death? There was a Birth, certainly,
We had evidence and no doubt. I had seen birth and death,
But had thought they were different; this Birth was
Hard and bitter agony for us, like Death, our death.
We returned to our places, these Kingdoms,
40 But no longer at ease here, in the old dispensation,
With an alien people clutching their gods.
I should be glad of another death.

W. H. AUDEN (1907 – 73)

Sir,[1] no man's enemy, forgiving all
But will his negative inversion, be prodigal:
Send to us power and light, a sovereign touch[2]
Curing the intolerable neural itch,
The exhaustion of weaning, the liar's quinsy,[3]
And the distortions of ingrown virginity.
Prohibit sharply the rehearsed response
And gradually correct the coward's stance;
Cover in time with beams those in retreat
That, spotted, they turn though the reverse were great;
Publish each healer that in city lives
Or country houses at the end of drives;
Harrow the house of the dead; look shining at
New styles of architecture, a change of heart.

O What Is That Sound

O what is that sound which so thrills the ear
   Down in the valley drumming, drumming?
Only the scarlet soldiers, dear,
   The soldiers coming.

1. This poem and "Spain 1937" were eventually repudiated by Auden because he no longer agreed with the sentiments expressed in them.
2. The "king's touch" was reputed to have curative powers.
3. Tonsillitis.

5　O what is that light I see flashing so clear
　　Over the distance brightly, brightly?
　O nly the sun on their weapons, dear,
　　As they step lightly.

　O what are they doing with all that gear,
10　　What are they doing this morning, this morning?
　Only their usual manoeuvres, dear,
　　Or perhaps a warning.

　O why have they left the road down there,
　　Why are they suddenly wheeling, wheeling?
15　Perhaps a change in their orders, dear.
　　Why are you kneeling?

　O haven't they stopped for the doctor's care,
　　Haven't they reined their horses, their horses?
　Why, they are none of them wounded, dear,
20　　None of these forces.

　O is it the parson they want, with white hair,
　　Is it the parson, is it, is it?
　No, they are passing his gateway, dear,
　　Without a visit.

25　O it must be the farmer who lives so near.
　　It must be the farmer so cunning, so cunning?
　They have passed the farmyard already, dear,
　　And now they are running.

　O where are you going? Stay with me here!
30　　Were the vows you swore deceiving, deceiving?
　No, I promised to love you, dear,
　　But I must be leaving.

　O it's broken the lock and splintered the door,
　　O it's the gate where they're turning, turning;
35　Their boots are heavy on the floor
　　And their eyes are burning.

On This Island

　Look, stranger, on this island now
　The leaping light for your delight discovers,
　Stand stable here
　And silent be,
5　That through the channels of the ear
　May wander like a river
　The swaying sound of the sea.

　Here at the small field's ending pause
　When the chalk wall falls to the foam and its tall ledges
10　Oppose the pluck
　And knock of the tide,
　And the shingle scrambles after the sucking surf,
　And the gull lodges
　A moment on its sheer side.

15　Far off like floating seeds the ships
　Diverge on urgent voluntary errands,
　And the full view

Indeed may enter
And move in memory as now these clouds do,
20   That pass the harbour mirror
And all the summer through the water saunter.

Lullaby

Lay your sleeping head, my love,
Human on my faithless arm;
Time and fevers burn away
Individual beauty from
5   Thoughtful children, and the grave
Proves the child ephemeral:
But in my arms till break of day
Let the living creature lie,
Mortal, guilty, but to me
10   The entirely beautiful.

Soul and body have no bounds:
To lovers as they lie upon
Her tolerant enchanted slope
In their ordinary swoon,
15   Grave the vision Venus sends
Of supernatural sympathy,
Universal love and hope;
While an abstract insight wakes
Among the glaciers and the rocks
20   The hermit's carnal ecstasy.

Certainty, fidelity
On the stroke of midnight pass
Like vibrations of a bell
And fashionable madmen raise
25   Their pedantic boring cry:
Every farthing of the cost,
All the dreaded cards foretell,
Shall be paid, but from this night
Not a whisper, not a thought,
30   Not a kiss nor look be lost.

Beauty, midnight, vision dies:
Let the winds of dawn that blow
Softly round your dreaming head
Such a day of welcome show
35   Eye and knocking heart may bless,
Find out mortal world enough;
Noons of dryness find you fed
By the involuntary powers,
Nights of insult let you pass
40   Watched by every human love.

Spain 1937[1]

Yesterday all the past. The language of size
Spreading to China along the trade-routes; the diffusion
        Of the counting-frame and the cromlech;[2]
Yesterday the shadow-reckoning in the sunny climates.

5   Yesterday the assessment of insurance by cards,
The divination of water; yesterday the invention
        Of cart-wheels and clocks, the taming of
Horses; yesterday the bustling world of the navigators.

Yesterday the abolition of fairies and giants;
10   The fortress like a motionless eagle eyeing the valley,
        The chapel built in the forest;
Yesterday the carving of angels and of frightening gargoyles;

The trial of heretics among the columns of stone;
Yesterday the theological feuds in the taverns
15   And the miraculous cure at the fountain;
Yesterday the Sabbath of Witches. But to-day the struggle.

Yesterday the installation of dynamos and turbines;
The construction of railways in the colonial desert;
        Yesterday the classic lecture
20   On the origin of Mankind. But to-day the struggle.

1. The Spanish Civil War (1936–39) began when General
Franco's Fascists took up arms against the duly elected
left-wing Spanish republican government. The Fascists
were supported by Hitler and Mussolini, the Republicans
by the U.S.S.R. and by various left-wing intellectuals and
workers from North America and western Europe, but
not by the governments of the western democracies.
Auden and others saw the war as a test of democracy's
will to resist fascist aggression.
2. A prehistoric circle of upright stones.

Yesterday the belief in the absolute value of Greek;
The fall of the curtain upon the death of a hero;
       Yesterday the prayer to the sunset,
And the adoration of madmen. But to-day the struggle.

25   As the poet whispers, startled among the pines
Or, where the loose waterfall sings, compact, or upright
       On the crag by the leaning tower:
'O my vision. O send me the luck of the sailor.'

And the investigator peers through his instruments
30   At the inhuman provinces, the virile bacillus
       Or enormous Jupiter finished:
'But the lives of my friends. I inquire, I inquire.'

And the poor in their fireless lodgings dropping the sheets
Of the evening paper: 'Our day is our loss. O show us
35   History the operator, the
Organiser, Time the refreshing river.'

And the nations combine each cry, invoking the life
That shapes the individual belly and orders
       The private noctural terror:
40   'Did you not found once the city state of the sponge,

'Raise the vast military empires of the shark
And the tiger, establish the robin's plucky canton?
       Intervene. O descend as a dove or
A furious papa or a mild engineer: but descend.'

45   And the life, if it answers at all, replies from the heart
And the eyes and the lungs, from the shops and squares of the city:
       'O no, I am not the Mover,
Not to-day, not to you. To you I'm the

'Yes-man, the bar-companion, the easily-duped:
50   I am whatever you do; I am your vow to be
       Good, your humorous story;
I am your business voice; I am your marriage.

'What's your proposal? To build the Just City? I will.
I agree. Or is it the suicide pact, the romantic
55   Death? Very well, I accept, for
I am your choice, your decision: yes, I am Spain.'

Many have heard it on remote peninsulas,
On sleepy plains, in the aberrant fishermen's islands,
       In the corrupt heart of the city;
60   Have heard and migrated like gulls or the seeds of a flower.

They clung like burrs to the long expresses that lurch
Through the unjust lands, through the night, through the alpine tunnel;
       They floated over the oceans;
They walked the passes: they came to present their lives.

65   On that arid square, that fragment nipped off from hot
Africa, soldered so crudely to inventive Europe,
       On that tableland scored by rivers,
Our fever's menacing shapes are precise and alive.

To-morrow, perhaps, the future: the research on fatigue
70   And the movements of packers; the gradual exploring of all the

                    Octaves of radiation;
          To-morrow the enlarging of consciousness by diet and breathing.

          To-morrow the rediscovery of romantic love;
          The photographing of ravens; all the fun under
75   Liberty's masterful shadow;
          To-morrow the hour of the pageant-master and the musician.

          To-morrow for the young the poets exploding like bombs,
          The walks by the lake, the winter of perfect communion;
                    To-morrow the bicycle races
80   Through the suburbs on summer evenings: but to-day the struggle.

          To-day the inevitable increase in the chances of death;
          The conscious acceptance of guilt in the fact of murder;
                    To-day the expending of powers
          On the flat ephemeral pamphlet and the boring meeting.

85   To-day the makeshift consolations; the shared cigarette;
          The cards in the candle-lit barn and the scraping concert,
                    The masculine jokes; to-day the
          Fumbled and unsatisfactory embrace before hurting.

          The stars are dead; the animals will not look:
90   We are left alone with our day, and the time is short and
                    History to the defeated
          May say Alas but cannot help or pardon.

As I Walked Out One Evening

As I walked out one evening,
  Walking down Bristol Street,
The crowds upon the pavement
  Were fields of harvest wheat.
	25 'In the burrows of the Nightmare
	  Where Justice naked is,
	Time watches from the shadow
	  And coughs when you would kiss.

5 And down by the brimming river
  I heard a lover sing
Under an arch of the railway:
  'Love has no ending.
	'In headaches and in worry
	30 Vaguely life leaks away,
	And Time will have his fancy
	  To-morrow or to-day.

'I'll love you, dear, I'll love you
10 Till China and Africa meet,
And the river jumps over the mountain
  And the salmon sing in the street,
	'Into many a green valley
	  Drifts the appalling snow;
	35 Time breaks the threaded dances
	  And the diver's brilliant bow.

'I'll love you till the ocean
  Is folded and hung up to dry
15 And the seven stars[1] go squawking
  Like geese about the sky.
	'O plunge your hands in water,
	  Plunge them in up to the wrist;
	Stare, stare in the basin
	40 And wonder what you've missed.

'The years shall run like rabbits,
  For in my arms I hold
The Flower of the Ages,
20 And the first love of the world.'
	'The glacier knocks in the cupboard,
	  The desert sighs in the bed,
	And the crack in the tea-cup opens
	  A lane to the land of the dead.

But all the clocks in the city
  Began to whirr and chime:
'O let not Time deceive you,
  You cannot conquer Time.
	45 'Where the beggars raffle the banknotes
	  And the Giant is enchanting to Jack,
	And the Lily-white Boy is a Roarer,
	  And Jill goes down on her back.

1. The Pleiades in the constellation Taurus.

50   'O look, look in the mirror,
       O look in your distress;
     Life remains a blessing
       Although you cannot bless.

55   'O stand, stand at the window
       As the tears scald and start;
     You shall love your crooked neighbour
       With your crooked heart.'

     It was late, late in the evening,
       The lovers they were gone;
     The clocks had ceased their chiming,
60   And the deep river ran on.

Musée des Beaux Arts[1]

[handwritten: society ignores death only the intellects and master understand.]

[handwritten left margin: sense of mundane]

     About suffering they were never wrong,
     The Old Masters: how well they understood
     Its human position; how it takes place
     While someone else is eating or opening a window or just walking dully along;
5   How, when the aged are reverently, passionately waiting
     For the miraculous birth, there always must be
     Children who did not specially want it to happen, skating
     On a pond at the edge of the wood:
     They never forgot
10   That even the dreadful martyrdom must run its course
     Anyhow in a corner, some untidy spot
     Where the dogs go on with their doggy life and the torturer's horse
     Scratches its innocent behind on a tree.

     In Breughel's *Icarus*, for instance: how everything turns away
15   Quite leisurely from the disaster; the ploughman may
     Have heard the splash, the forsaken cry,
     But for him it was not an important failure; the sun shone
     As it had to on the white legs disappearing into the green
     Water; and the expensive delicate ship that must have seen
20   Something amazing, a boy falling out of the sky,
     Had somewhere to get to and sailed calmly on.

[handwritten left margin: none at all cares rich nor poor conscious nor unconscious]

[handwritten: — we must go on despite our suffering.]

In Memory of W. B. Yeats
(d. Jan. 1939)

I

     He disappeared in the dead of winter:
     The brooks were frozen, the airports almost deserted,
     And snow disfigured the public statues;
     The mercury sank in the mouth of the dying day.
5   What instruments we have agree
     The day of his death was a dark cold day.

     Far from his illness
     The wolves ran on through the evergreen forests,
     The peasant river was untempted by the fashionable quays:
10   By mourning tongues
     The death of the poet was kept from his poems.

     But for him it was his last afternoon as himself,
     An afternoon of nurses and rumours;
     The provinces of his body revolted,

1. (French) Museum of Fine Arts. The painting *The Fall of Icarus* by Pieter Breughel (or Brueghel) (1520–69) hangs in the Palace of the Royal Museums of Painting and Sculpture in Brussels. Icarus flew too close to the sun on artificial wings which his father Daedalus had made of feathers and wax; the sun melted the wax and he fell into the sea. In the picture, Icarus' splash in the water is a small and seemingly insignificant part of the whole composition.

15 The squares of his mind were empty,
Silence invaded the suburbs,
The current of his feeling failed; he became his admirers.

Now he is scattered among a hundred cities
And wholly given over to unfamiliar affections,
20 To find his happiness in another kind of wood
And be punished under a foreign code of conscience.
The words of a dead man
Are modified in the guts of the living.

But in the importance of noise of to-morrow
25 When the brokers are roaring like beasts on the floor of the Bourse,[1]
And the poor have the sufferings to which they are fairly accustomed,
And each in the cell of himself is almost convinced of his freedom,
A few thousand will think of this day
As one thinks of a day when one did something slightly unusual.
30 What instruments we have agree
The day of his death was a dark cold day.

II

You were silly like us; your gift survived it all:
The parish of rich women,[2] physical decay,
Yourself. Mad Ireland hurt you into poetry.
35 Now Ireland has her madness and her weather still,
For poetry makes nothing happen: it survives
In the valley of its making where executives
Would never want to tamper, flows on south
From ranches of isolation and the busy griefs,
40 Raw towns that we believe and die in; it survives,
A way of happening, a mouth.

III

Earth, receive an honoured guest:
William Yeats is laid to rest.
Let the Irish vessel lie
45 Emptied of its poetry.[3]

55 Follow, poet, follow right
To the bottom of the night,
With your unconstraining voice
Still persuade us to rejoice;

In the nightmare of the dark
All the dogs of Europe bark,
And the living nations wait,
Each sequestered in its hate;

With the farming of a verse
Make a vineyard of the curse,
60 Sing of human unsuccess
In a rapture of distress;

50 Intellectual disgrace
Stares from every human face,
And the seas of pity lie
Locked and frozen in each eye.

In the deserts of the heart
Let the healing fountain start,
In the prison of his days
65 Teach the free man how to praise.

1. Stock exchange.
2. Yeats's confidantes included Mrs. Olivia Shakespeare,
Lady Augusta Gregory, and Dorothy Wellesley.
3. The first version of this poem included three additional
stanzas at this point. They read:
  Time that is intolerant
  Of the brave and innocent,
  And indifferent in a week
  To a beautiful physique,

  Worships language and forgives
  Everyone by whom it lives;
  Pardons cowardice, conceit,
  Lays its honours at their feet.

  Time that with this strange excuse
  Pardoned Kipling and his views,
  And will pardon Paul Claudel,
  Pardons him for writing well.

    Rudyard Kipling (1865–1936) was an apologist for British imperialism; Paul Claudel (1868–1955), French poet and dramatist, was an extreme conservative. Yeats's own political views, unlike Auden's at the time, were also conservative and anti-democratic.

The Unknown Citizen

(To JS/07/M/378
This Marble Monument
Is Erected by the State)

He was found by the Bureau of Statistics to be
One against whom there was no official complaint,
And all the reports on his conduct agree
That, in the modern sense of an old-fashioned word, he was a saint,
5   For in everything he did he served the Greater Community.
Except for the War till the day he retired
He worked in a factory and never got fired,
But satisfied his employers, Fudge Motors Inc.
Yet he wasn't a scab or odd in his views,
10   For his Union reports that he paid his dues,
(Our report on his Union shows it was sound)
And our Social Psychology workers found
That he was popular with his mates and liked a drink.
The Press are convinced that he bought a paper every day
15   And that his reactions to advertisements were normal in every way.
Policies taken out in his name prove he was fully insured,
And his Health-card shows he was once in hospital but left it cured.
Both Producers Research and High-Grade Living declare
He was fully sensible to the advantages of the Instalment Plan
20   And had everything necessary to the Modern Man,
A phonograph, a radio, a car and a frigidaire.
Our researchers into Public Opinion are content
That he held the proper opinions for the time of year;
When there was peace, he was for peace; when there was war, he went.
25   He was married and added five children to the population,
Which our Eugenist[1] says was the right number for a parent of his generation,
And our teachers report that he never interfered with their education.
Was he free? Was he happy? The question is absurd:
Had anything been wrong, we should certainly have heard.

DYLAN THOMAS (1914–53)

And Death Shall Have No Dominion

And death shall have no dominion.[1]
Dead men naked they shall be one
With the man in the wind and the west moon;
When their bones are picked clean and the clean bones gone,
5   They shall have stars at elbow and foot;
Though they go mad they shall be sane,
Though they sink through the sea they shall rise again;
Though lovers be lost love shall not;
And death shall have no dominion.

10   And death shall have no dominion.
Under the windings of the sea
They lying long shall not die windily;
Twisting on racks when sinews give way,
Strapped to a wheel, yet they shall not break;
15   Faith in their hands shall snap in two,
And the unicorn evils run them through;
Split all ends up they shan't crack;
And death shall have no dominion.

1. Someone concerned with improving humanity through
selective breeding.   1. See Rom. vi.9.

And death shall have no dominion.
20 No more may gulls cry at their ears
Or waves break loud on the seashores;
Where blew a flower may a flower no more
Lift its head to the blows of the rain;
Though they be mad and dead as nails,
25 Heads of the characters hammer through daisies;
Break in the sun till the sun breaks down,
And death shall have no dominion.

The Force That through the Green Fuse Drives the Flower

The force that through the green fuse drives the flower
Drives my green age; that blasts the roots of trees
Is my destroyer.
And I am dumb to tell the crooked rose
5 My youth is bent by the same wintry fever.

The force that drives the water through the rocks
Drives my red blood; that dries the mouthing streams
Turns mine to wax.
And I am dumb to mouth unto my veins
10 How at the mountain spring the same mouth sucks.

The hand that whirls the water in the pool
Stirs the quicksand; that ropes the blowing wind
Hauls my shroud sail.
And I am dumb to tell the hanging man
15 How of my clay is made the hangman's lime.

The lips of time leech to the fountain head;
Love drips and gathers, but the fallen blood
Shall calm her sores.
And I am dumb to tell a weather's wind
20 How time has ticked a heaven round the stars.

And I am dumb to tell the lover's tomb
How at my sheet goes the same crooked worm.

After the Funeral
(In memory of Ann Jones)[1]

After the funeral, mule praises, brays,
Windshake of sailshaped cars, muffle-toed tap
Tap happily of one peg in the thick
Grave's foot, blinds down the lids, the teeth in black,
5 The spittled eyes, the salt ponds in the sleeves,
Morning smack of the spade that wakes up sleep,
Shakes a desolate boy who slits his throat
In the dark of the coffin and sheds dry leaves,
That breaks one bone to light with a judgment clout,
10 After the feast of tear-stuffed time and thistles
In a room with a stuffed fox and a stale fern,
I stand, for this memorial's sake, alone
In the snivelling hours with dead, humped Ann
Whose hooded, fountain heart once fell in puddles
15 Round the parched worlds of Wales and drowned each sun
(Though this for her is a monstrous image blindly
Magnified out of praise; her death was a still drop;

1. Thomas' aunt, who died of cancer in February 1933.

She would not have me sinking in the holy
Flood of her heart's fame; she would lie dumb and deep
20   And need no druid[2] of her broken body).
But I, Ann's bard on a raised hearth, call all
The seas to service that her wood-tongued virtue
Babble like a bellbuoy over the hymning heads,
Bow down the walls of the ferned and foxy woods
25   That her love sing and swing through a brown chapel,
Bless her bent spirit with four, crossing birds.
Her flesh was meek as milk, but this skyward statue
With the wild breast and blessed and giant skull
Is carved from her in a room with a wet window
30   In a fiercely mourning house in a crooked year.
I know her scrubbed and sour humble hands
Lie with religion in their cramp, her threadbare
Whisper in a damp word, her wits drilled hollow,
Her fist of a face died clenched on a round pain;
35   And sculptured Ann is seventy years of stone.
These cloud-sopped, marble hands, this monumental
Argument of the hewn voice, gesture and psalm,
Storm me forever over her grave until
The stuffed lung of the fox twitch and cry Love
40   And the strutting fern lay seeds on the black sill.

Fern Hill[1]

Now as I was young and easy under the apple boughs
About the lilting house and happy as the grass was green,
    The night above the dingle starry,
        Time let me hail and climb
5   Golden in the heydays of his eyes,
And honoured among wagons I was prince of the apple towns
And once below a time I lordly had the trees and leaves
        Trail with daisies and barley
    Down the rivers of the windfall light.

10   And as I was green and carefree, famous among the barns
About the happy yard and singing as the farm was home,
    In the sun that is young once only,
        Time let me play and be
        Golden in the mercy of his means,
15   And green and golden I was huntsman and herdsman, the calves
Sang to my horn, the foxes on the hills barked clear and cold,
        And the sabbath rang slowly
    In the pebbles of the holy streams.

All the sun long it was running, it was lovely, the hay
20   Fields high as the house, the tunes from the chimneys, it was air
        And playing, lovely and watery
            And fire green as grass.
        And nightly under the simple stars
As I rode to sleep the owls were bearing the farm away,
25   All the moon long I heard, blessed among stables, the nightjars
        Flying with the ricks, and the horses
            Flashing into the dark.

---

2. Priest of the ancient Celtic religion.

1. Fernhill was a farm owned by Ann and Jim Jones, Thomas' aunt and uncle, in Carmarthenshire in southwest Wales. Thomas spent summer holidays there as a boy.

And then to awake, and the farm, like a wanderer white
With the dew, come back, the cock on his shoulder: it was all
30   Shining, it was Adam and maiden,
            The sky gathered again
      And the sun grew round that very day.
So it must have been after the birth of the simple light
In the first, spinning place, the spellbound horses walking warm
35   Out of the whinnying green stable
            On to the fields of praise.

And honoured among foxes and pheasants by the gay house
Under the new made clouds and happy as the heart was long,
      In the sun born over and over,
40   I ran my heedless ways,
      My wishes raced through the house high hay
And nothing I cared, at my sky blue trades, that time allows
In all his tuneful turning so few and such morning songs
            Before the children green and golden
45   Follow him out of grace,

Nothing I cared, in the lamb white days, that time would take me
Up to the swallow thronged loft by the shadow of my hand,
      In the moon that is always rising,
            Nor that riding to sleep
50   I should hear him fly with the high fields
And wake to the farm forever fled from the childless land.
Oh as I was young and easy in the mercy of his means,
            Time held me green and dying
      Though I sang in my chains like the sea.

Do Not Go Gentle into That Good Night

Do not go gentle into that good night,   *— Do not fight death.*
Old age should burn and rave at close of day; *— fight against death.*
Rage, rage against the dying of the light.

Though wise men at their end know dark is right,   *— wise men believe in god*
Because their words had forked no lightning they   *they will die yet not*
Do not go gentle into that good night.   *peacefully.*
                                                   preach to people.

Good men, the last wave by, crying how bright
Their frail deeds might have danced in a green bay, *← deeds that they have done.*
Rage, rage against the dying of the light.

Wild men who caught and sang the sun in flight,
And learn, too late, they grieved it on its way,
Do not go gentle into that good night.

Grave men, near death, who see with blinding sight
Blind eyes could blaze like meteors and be gay,
Rage, rage against the dying of the light.

And you, my father, there on the sad height,   *— son talking to his father*
Curse, bless, me now with your fierce tears, I pray. *telling him not to die*
Do not go gentle into that good night.   *easily.*
Rage, rage against the dying of the light.

ROBERT FROST (1874–1963)

Mending Wall

Something there is that doesn't love a wall,
That sends the frozen-ground-swell under it
And spills the upper boulders in the sun,
And makes gaps even two can pass abreast.
5   The work of hunters is another thing:
I have come after them and made repair
Where they have left not one stone on a stone,
But they would have the rabbit out of hiding,
To please the yelping dogs. The gaps I mean,
10   No one has seen them made or heard them made,
But at spring mending-time we find them there.
I let my neighbor know beyond the hill;
And on a day we meet to walk the line
And set the wall between us once again.
15   We keep the wall between us as we go.
To each the boulders that have fallen to each.
And some are loaves and some so nearly balls
We have to use a spell to make them balance:
"Stay where you are until our backs are turned!"
20   We wear our fingers rough with handling them.
Oh, just another kind of outdoor game,
One on a side. It comes to little more:
There where it is we do not need the wall:
He is all pine and I am apple orchard.
25   My apple trees will never get across
And eat the cones under his pines, I tell him.
He only says, "Good fences make good neighbors."
Spring is the mischief in me, and I wonder
If I could put a notion in his head:
30   "*Why* do they make good neighbors? Isn't it
Where there are cows? But here there are no cows.
Before I built a wall I'd ask to know
What I was walling in or walling out,
And to whom I was like to give offense.
35   Something there is that doesn't love a wall,
That wants it down." I could say "Elves" to him,
But it's not elves exactly, and I'd rather
He said it for himself. I see him there,
Bringing a stone grasped firmly by the top
40   In each hand, like an old-stone savage armed.
He moves in darkness as it seems to me,
Not of woods only and the shade of trees.
He will not go behind his father's saying,
And he likes having thought of it so well
45   He says again, "Good fences make good neighbors."

The Wood-Pile

Out walking in the frozen swamp one gray day,
I paused and said, "I will turn back from here.
No, I will go no farther—and we shall see."
The hard snow held me, save where now and then
5   One foot went through. The view was all in lines
Straight up and down of tall slim trees
Too much alike to mark or name a place by
So as to say for certain I was here

Or somewhere else: I was just far from home.
10 A small bird flew before me. He was careful
To put a tree between us when he lighted,
And say no word to tell me who he was
Who was so foolish as to think what *he* thought.
He thought that I was after him for a feather—
15 The white one in his tail; like one who takes
Everything said as personal to himself.
One flight out sideways would have undeceived him.
And then there was a pile of wood for which
I forgot him and let his little fear
20 Carry him off the way I might have gone,
Without so much as wishing him good-night.
He went behind it to make his last stand.
It was a cord of maple, cut and split
And piled—and measured, four by four by eight.
25 And not another like it could I see.
No runner tracks in this year's snow looped near it.
And it was older sure than this year's cutting,
Or even last year's or the year's before.
The wood was gray and the bark warping off it
30 And the pile somewhat sunken. Clematis
Had wound strings round and round it like a bundle.
What held it, though, on one side was a tree
Still growing, and on one a stake and prop,
These latter about to fall. I thought that only
35 Someone who lived in turning to fresh tasks
Could so forget his handiwork on which
He spent himself, the labor of his ax,
And leave it there far from a useful fireplace
To warm the frozen swamp as best it could
40 With the slow smokeless burning of decay.

The Road Not Taken

Two roads diverged in a yellow wood,
And sorry I could not travel both
And be one traveler, long I stood
And looked down one as far as I could
To where it bent in the undergrowth;

Then took the other, as just as fair,
And having perhaps the better claim,
Because it was grassy and wanted wear;
Though as for that, the passing there
Had worn them really about the same,

And both that morning equally lay
In leaves no step had trodden black.
Oh, I kept the first for another day!
Yet knowing how way leads on to way,
I doubted if I should ever come back.

I shall be telling this with a sigh
Somewhere ages and ages hence:
Two roads diverged in a wood, and I—
I took the one less traveled by,
And that has made all the difference.

Birches

When I see birches bend to left and right
Across the lines of straighter darker trees,
I like to think some boy's been swinging them.
But swinging doesn't bend them down to stay
5 As ice storms do. Often you must have seen them
Loaded with ice a sunny winter morning
After a rain. They click upon themselves
As the breeze rises, and turn many-colored
As the stir cracks and crazes their enamel.
10 Soon the sun's warmth makes them shed crystal shells
Shattering and avalanching on the snow crust—
Such heaps of broken glass to sweep away

You'd think the inner dome of heaven had fallen.
They are dragged to the withered bracken by the load,
15   And they seem not to break; though once they are bowed
So low for long, they never right themselves:
You may see their trunks arching in the woods
Years afterwards, trailing their leaves on the ground
Like girls on hands and knees that throw their hair
20   Before them over their heads to dry in the sun.
But I was going to say when Truth broke in
With all her matter of fact about the ice storm,
I should prefer to have some boy bend them
As he went out and in to fetch the cows—
25   Some boy too far from town to learn baseball,
Whose only play was what he found himself,
Summer or winter, and could play alone.
One by one he subdued his father's trees
By riding them down over and over again
30   Until he took the stiffness out of them,
And not one but hung limp, not one was left
For him to conquer. He learned all there was
To learn about not launching out too soon
And so not carrying the tree away
35   Clear to the ground. He always kept his poise
To the top branches, climbing carefully
With the same pains you use to fill a cup
Up to the brim, and even above the brim.
Then he flung outward, feet first, with a swish,
40   Kicking his way down through the air to the ground.
So was I once myself a swinger of birches.
And so I dream of going back to be.
It's when I'm weary of considerations,
And life is too much like a pathless wood
45   Where your face burns and tickles with the cobwebs
Broken across it, and one eye is weeping
From a twig's having lashed across it open.
I'd like to get away from earth awhile
And then come back to it and begin over.
50   May no fate willfully misunderstand me
And half grant what I wish and snatch me away
Not to return. Earth's the right place for love:
I don't know where it's likely to go better.
I'd like to go by climbing a birch tree,
55   And climb black branches up a snow-white trunk
Toward heaven, till the tree could bear no more,
But dipped its top and set me down again.
That would be good both going and coming back.
One could do worse than be a swinger of birches.

"Out, Out— "[1]

The buzz saw snarled and rattled in the yard
And made dust and dropped stove-length sticks of wood,
Sweet-scented stuff when the breeze drew across it.
And from there those that lifted eyes could count
5   Five mountain ranges one behind the other
Under the sunset far into Vermont.
And the saw snarled and rattled, snarled and rattled,
As it ran light, or had to bear a load.
And nothing happened: day was all but done.

1. The title is from Shakespeare's *Macbeth* V.v.23–26: "Out, out, brief candle! / Life's but a walking shadow, a poor player / That struts and frets his hour upon the stage / And then is heard no more."

10　Call it a day, I wish they might have said
　　To please the boy by giving him the half hour
　　That a boy counts so much when saved from work.
　　His sister stood beside them in her apron
　　To tell them "Supper." At the word, the saw,
15　As if to prove saws knew what supper meant,
　　Leaped out at the boy's hand, or seemed to leap—
　　He must have given the hand. However it was,
　　Neither refused the meeting. But the hand!
　　The boy's first outcry was a rueful laugh,
20　As he swung toward them holding up the hand,
　　Half in appeal, but half as if to keep
　　The life from spilling. Then the boy saw all—
　　Since he was old enough to know, big boy
　　Doing a man's work, though a child at heart—
25　He saw all spoiled. "Don't let him cut my hand off—
　　The doctor, when he comes. Don't let him, sister!"
　　So. But the hand was gone already.
　　The doctor put him in the dark of ether.
　　He lay and puffed his lips out with his breath.
30　And then—the watcher at his pulse took fright.
　　No one believed. They listened at his heart.
　　Little—less—nothing!—and that ended it.
　　No more to build on there. And they, since they
　　Were not the one dead, turned to their affairs.

Nothing Gold Can Stay

Nature's first green is gold,
Her hardest hue to hold,
Her early leaf's a flower;
But only so an hour.
Then leaf subsides to leaf.
So Eden sank to grief,
So dawn goes down to day.
Nothing gold can stay.

Acquainted with the Night

I have been one acquainted with the night.
I have walked out in rain—and back in rain.
I have outwalked the furthest city light.

I have looked down the saddest city lane.
I have passed by the watchman on his beat
And dropped my eyes, unwilling to explain.

I have stood still and stopped the sound of feet
When far away an interrupted cry
Came over houses from another street,

But not to call me back or say good-by;
And further still at an unearthly height
One luminary clock against the sky

Proclaimed the time was neither wrong nor right.
I have been one acquainted with the night.

The Most of It

He thought he kept the universe alone;
For all the voice in answer he could wake
Was but the mocking echo of his own
From some tree-hidden cliff across the lake.
Some morning from the boulder-broken beach
He would cry out on life, that what it wants
Is not its own love back in copy speech,
But counter-love, original response.

And nothing ever came of what he cried
Unless it was the embodiment that crashed
In the cliff's talus on the other side,
And then in the far-distant water splashed,
But after a time allowed for it to swim,
Instead of proving human when it neared

And someone else additional to him,
As a great buck it powerfully appeared,
Pushing the crumpled water up ahead,
And landed pouring like a waterfall,
And stumbled through the rocks with horny tre
And forced the underbrush—and that was all.

The Gift Outright

The land was ours before we were the land's.
She was our land more than a hundred years
Before we were her people. She was ours
In Massachusetts, in Virginia,
But we were England's, still colonials,
Possessing what we still were unpossessed by,
Possessed by what we now no more possessed.
Something we were withholding made us weak

Until we found out that it was ourselves
We were withholding from our land of living,
And forthwith found salvation in surrender.
Such as we were we gave ourselves outright
(The deed of gift was many deeds of war)
To the land vaguely realizing westward,
But still unstoried, artless, unenhanced,
Such as she was, such as she would become.

WALLACE STEVENS (1879–1955)

The Snow Man

One must have a mind of winter
To regard the frost and the boughs
Of the pine-trees crusted with snow;

And have been cold a long time
To behold the junipers shagged with ice,
The spruces rough in the distant glitter

Of the January sun; and not to think
Of any misery in the sound of the wind,
In the sound of a few leaves,

Which is the sound of the land
Full of the same wind
That is blowing in the same bare place

For the listener, who listens in the snow,
And, nothing himself, beholds
Nothing that is not there and the nothing that is

The Emperor of Ice-Cream

Call the roller of big cigars,
The muscular one, and bid him whip
In kitchen cups concupiscent curds.
Let the wenches dawdle in such dress
As they are used to wear, and let the boys
Bring flowers in last month's newspapers.
Let be be finale of seem.
The only emperor is the emperor of ice-cream.

Take from the dresser of deal,
Lacking the three glass knobs, that sheet
On which she embroidered fantails[1] once
And spread it so as to cover her face.
If her horny feet protrude, they come
To show how cold she is, and dumb.
Let the lamp affix its beam.
The only emperor is the emperor of ice-cream.

Sunday Morning

I
Complacencies of the peignoir, and late
Coffee and oranges in a sunny chair,
And the green freedom of a cockatoo
Upon a rug mingle to dissipate
5   The holy hush of ancient sacrifice.
She dreams a little, and she feels the dark
Encroachment of that old catastrophe,

1. Pigeons.

As a calm darkens among water-lights.
The pungent oranges and bright, green wings
10   Seem things in some procession of the dead,
Winding across wide water, without sound.
The day is like wide water, without sound,
Stilled for the passing of her dreaming feet
Over the seas, to silent Palestine,
15   Dominion of the blood and sepulchre.

II

Why should she give her bounty to the dead?
What is divinity if it can come
Only in silent shadows and in dreams?
Shall she not find in comforts of the sun,
20   In pungent fruit and bright, green wings, or else
In any balm or beauty of the earth,
Things to be cherished like the thought of heaven?
Divinity must live within herself:
Passions of rain, or moods in falling snow;
25   Grievings in loneliness, or unsubdued
Elations when the forest blooms; gusty
Emotions on wet roads on autumn nights;
All pleasures and all pains, remembering
The bough of summer and the winter branch.
30   These are the measures destined for her soul.

III

Jove[1] in the clouds had his inhuman birth.
No mother suckled him, no sweet land gave
Large-mannered motions to his mythy mind.
He moved among us, as a muttering king,
35   Magnificent, would move among his hinds,[2]
Until our blood, commingling, virginal,
With heaven, brought such requital to desire
The very hinds discerned it, in a star.
Shall our blood fail? Or shall it come to be
40   The blood of paradise? And shall the earth
Seem all of paradise that we shall know?
The sky will be much friendlier then than now,
A part of labor and a part of pain,
And next in glory to enduring love,
45   Not this dividing and indifferent blue.

IV

She says, "I am content when wakened birds,
Before they fly, test the reality
Of misty fields, by their sweet questionings;
But when the birds are gone, and their warm fields
50   Return no more, where, then, is paradise?"
There is not any haunt of prophecy,
Nor any old chimera[3] of the grave,
Neither the golden underground, nor isle
Melodious, where spirits gat them home,
55   Nor visionary south, nor cloudy palm
Remote on heaven's hill, that has endured
As April's green endures; or will endure
Like her remembrance of awakened birds,
Or her desire for June and evening, tipped
60   By the consummation of the swallow's wings.

1. Jupiter or Zeus, supreme god in Greek and Roman myth.
2. Farm labourers, shepherds.
3. A fanciful monster.

V

She says, "But in contentment I still feel
The need of some imperishable bliss."
Death is the mother of beauty; hence from her,
Alone, shall come fulfilment to our dreams

65   And our desires. Although she strews the leaves
Of sure obliteration on our paths,
The path sick sorrow took, the many paths
Where triumph rang its brassy phrase, or love
Whispered a little out of tenderness,

70   She makes the willow shiver in the sun
For maidens who were wont to sit and gaze
Upon the grass, relinquished to their feet.
She causes boys to pile new plums and pears
On disregarded plate. The maidens taste

75   And stray impassioned in the littering leaves.

VI

Is there no change of death in paradise?
Does ripe fruit never fall? Or do the boughs
Hang always heavy in that perfect sky,
Unchanging, yet so like our perishing earth,

80   With rivers like our own that seek for seas
They never find, the same receding shores
That never touch with inarticulate pang?
Why set the pear upon those river-banks
Or spice the shores with odors of the plum?

85   Alas, that they should wear our colors there,
The silken weavings of our afternoons,
And pick the strings of our insipid lutes!
Death is the mother of beauty, mystical,
Within whose burning bosom we devise

90   Our earthly mothers waiting, sleeplessly.

VII

Supple and turbulent, a ring of men
Shall chant in orgy on a summer morn
Their boisterous devotion to the sun,
Not as a god, but as a god might be,

95   Naked among them, like a savage source.
Their chant shall be a chant of paradise,
Out of their blood, returning to the sky;
And in their chant shall enter, voice by voice,
The windy lake wherein their lord delights,

100   The trees, like serafin,[4] and echoing hills,
That choir among themselves long afterward.
They shall know well the heavenly fellowship
Of men that perish and of summer morn.
And whence they came and whither they shall go

105   The dew upon their feet shall manifest.

VIII

She hears, upon that water without sound,
A voice that cries, "The tomb in Palestine
Is not the porch of spirits lingering.
It is the grave of Jesus, where he lay."

110   We live in an old chaos of the sun,
Or old dependency of day and night,
Or island solitude, unsponsored, free,
Of that wide water, inescapable.

___

4. Seraphim. See Isa. vi.2–7.

115 Deer walk upon our mountains, and the quail
Whistle about us their spontaneous cries;
Sweet berries ripen in the wilderness;
And, in the isolation of the sky,
At evening, casual flocks of pigeons make
120 Ambiguous undulations as they sink,
Downward to darkness, on extended wings.

Anecdote of the Jar

I placed a jar in Tennessee,
And round it was, upon a hill.
It made the slovenly wilderness
Surround that hill.

The wilderness rose up to it,
And sprawled around, no longer wild.
The jar was round upon the ground
And tall and of a port in air.

It took dominion everywhere.
The jar was gray and bare.
It did not give of bird or bush,
Like nothing else in Tennessee.

Peter Quince[1] at the Clavier

I

Just as my fingers on these keys
Make music, so the selfsame sounds
On my spirit make a music, too.

5 Music is feeling, then, not sound;
And thus it is that what I feel,
Here in this room, desiring you,

Thinking of your blue-shadowed silk,
Is music. It is like the strain
Waked in the elders by Susanna.[2]

10 Of a green evening, clear and warm,
She bathed in her still garden, while
The red-eyed elders watching, felt

The basses of their beings throb
In witching chords, and their thin blood
15 Pulse pizzicati of Hosanna.

25 Upon the bank, she stood
In the cool
Of spent emotions.
She felt, among the leaves,
The dew
Of old devotions.

30 She walked upon the grass,
Still quavering.
The winds were like her maids,
On timid feet,
Fetching her woven scarves,
35 Yet wavering.

A breath upon her hand
Muted the night.
She turned—
A cymbal crashed,
40 And roaring horns.

II

In the green water, clear and warm,
Susanna lay.
She searched
The touch of springs,
20 And found
Concealed imaginings.
She sighed,
For so much melody.

III

Soon, with a noise like tambourines,
Came her attendant Byzantines.[3]

They wondered why Susanna cried
Against the elders by her side;

45 And as they whispered, the refrain
Was like a willow swept by rain.

1. A comic character in Shakespeare's *Midsummer Night's Dream* who directs a play about Pyramus and Thisbe.
2. The story of Susanna is one of the Apocryphal books of the Old Testament. Two Hebrew elders spied on the beautiful Susanna at her bath and then attempted to seduce her. She brought charges against them; they successfully defended themselves and she was about to be executed when proved innocent by the prophet Daniel. The elders were then executed instead.
3. Susanna's attendants.

Anon, their lamps' uplifted flame
Revealed Susanna and her shame.

And then, the simpering Byzantines
50 Fled, with a noise like tambourines.

IV
Beauty is momentary in the mind—
The fitful tracing of a portal;
But in the flesh it is immortal.

The body dies; the body's beauty lives.
55 So evenings die, in their green going,

A wave, interminably flowing.
So gardens die, their meek breath scenting
The cowl of winter, done repenting.
So maidens die, to the auroral
60 Celebration of a maiden's choral.
Susanna's music touched the bawdy strings
Of those white elders; but, escaping,
Left only Death's ironic scraping.
Now, in its immortality, it plays
65 On the clear viol of her memory,
And makes a constant sacrament of praise.

Thirteen Ways of Looking at a Blackbird

I
Among twenty snowy mountains,
The only moving thing
Was the eye of the blackbird.

II
I was of three minds,
5 Like a tree
In which there are three blackbirds.

III
The blackbird whirled in the autumn winds.
It was a small part of the pantomime.

IV
A man and a woman
10 Are one.
A man and a woman and a blackbird
Are one.

V
I do not know which to prefer,
The beauty of inflections
15 Or the beauty of innuendoes,
The blackbird whistling
Or just after.

VI
Icicles filled the long window
With barbaric glass.
20 The shadow of the blackbird
Crossed it, to and fro.
The mood
Traced in the shadow
An indecipherable cause.

VII
25 O thin men of Haddam,[1]
Why do you imagine golden birds?
Do you not see how the blackbird
Walks around the feet
Of the women about you?

VIII
30 I know noble accents
And lucid, inescapable rhythms;
But I know, too,
That the blackbird is involved
In what I know.

IX
35 When the blackbird flew out of sight,
It marked the edge
Of one of many circles.

X
At the sight of blackbirds
Flying in a green light,
40 Even the bawds of euphony
Would cry out sharply.

XI
He rode over Connecticut
In a glass coach.
Once, a fear pierced him,
45 In that he mistook
The shadow of his equipage
For blackbirds.

XII
The river is moving.
The blackbird must be flying.

XIII
50 It was evening all afternoon.
It was snowing
And it was going to snow.
The blackbird sat
In the cedar-limbs.

1. A town in Connecticut, near Hartford.

The Idea of Order at Key West[1]

She sang beyond the genius of the sea.
The water never formed to mind or voice,
Like a body wholly body, fluttering
Its empty sleeves; and yet its mimic motion
5   Made constant cry, caused constantly a cry,
That was not ours although we understood,
Inhuman, of the veritable ocean.

The sea was not a mask. No more was she.
The song and water were not medleyed sound
10   Even if what she sang was what she heard,
Since what she sang was uttered word by word.
It may be that in all her phrases stirred
The grinding water and the gasping wind;
But it was she and not the sea we heard.

15   For she was the maker of the song she sang.
The ever-hooded, tragic-gestured sea
Was merely a place by which she walked to sing.
Whose spirit is this? we said, because we knew
It was the spirit that we sought and knew
20   That we should ask this often as she sang.

If it was only the dark voice of the sea
That rose, or even colored by many waves;
If it was only the outer voice of sky
And cloud, of the sunken coral water-walled,
25   However clear, it would have been deep air,
The heaving speech of air, a summer sound
Repeated in a summer without end
And sound alone. But it was more than that,
More even than her voice, and ours, among
30   The meaningless plungings of water and the wind,
Theatrical distances, bronze shadows heaped
On high horizons, mountainous atmospheres
Of sky and sea.
               It was her voice that made
35   The sky acutest at its vanishing.
She measured to the hour its solitude.
She was the single artificer of the world
In which she sang. And when she sang, the sea,
Whatever self it had, became the self
40   That was her song, for she was the maker. Then we,
As we beheld her striding there alone,
Knew that there never was a world for her
Except the one she sang and, singing, made.

Ramon Fernandez,[2] tell me, if you know,
45   Why, when the singing ended and we turned
Toward the town, tell why the glassy lights,
The lights in the fishing boats at anchor there,
As the night descended, tilting in the air,
Mastered the night and portioned out the sea,
50   Fixing emblazoned zones and fiery poles,
Arranging, deepening, enchanting night.

1. One of a chain of islands off the south coast of Florida.
2. French literary critic (1894–1944), but Stevens says he
did not intend a specific allusion.

Oh! Blessed rage for order, pale Ramon,
The maker's rage to order words of the sea,
Words of the fragrant portals, dimly-starred,
55   And of ourselves and of our origins,
In ghostlier demarcations, keener sounds.

The Sense of the Sleight-of-Hand Man

One's grand flights, one's Sunday baths,
One's tootings at the weddings of the soul
Occur as they occur. So bluish clouds
Occurred above the empty house and the leaves
Of the rhododendrons rattled their gold,
As if someone lived there. Such floods of white
Came bursting from the clouds. So the wind
Threw its contorted strength around the sky.

Could you have said the bluejay suddenly
Would swoop to earth? It is a wheel, the rays
Around the sun. The wheel survives the myths.
The fire eye in the clouds survives the gods.
To think of a dove with an eye of grenadine
And pines that are cornets, so it occurs,
And a little island full of geese and stars:
It may be that the ignorant man, alone,
Has any chance to mate his life with life
That is the sensual, pearly spouse, the life
That is fluent in even the wintriest bronze.

Of Modern Poetry

The poem of the mind in the act of finding
What will suffice. It has not always had
To find: the scene was set; it repeated what
Was in the script.
5   Then the theatre was changed
To something else. Its past was a souvenir.
It has to be living, to learn the speech of the place.
It has to face the men of the time and to meet
The women of the time. It has to think about war
10   And it has to find what will suffice. It has
To construct a new stage. It has to be on that stage
And, like an insatiable actor, slowly and
With meditation, speak words that in the ear,
In the delicatest ear of the mind, repeat,
15   Exactly, that which it wants to hear, at the sound
Of which, an invisible audience listens,
Not to the play, but to itself, expressed
In an emotion as of two people, as of two
Emotions becoming one. The actor is
20   A metaphysician in the dark, twanging
An instrument, twanging a wiry string that gives
Sounds passing through sudden rightnesses, wholly
Containing the mind, below which it cannot descend,
Beyond which it has no will to rise.
25   It must
Be the finding of a satisfaction, and may
Be of a man skating, a woman dancing, a woman
Combing. The poem of the act of the mind.

[handwritten annotations:]
changing of the times or what poetrys goal is.

not talking about religion, religious beliefs life.

only musicians or skillful readers of poetry can here with the delicatest ear.

comprehension of poetry. two minds reader of poet

abstruse, conceal, difficult metaphysician - intellecual. poet trying to find something on his own.

WILLIAM CARLOS WILLIAMS (1883–1963)

Tract

I will teach you my townspeople
how to perform a funeral
for you have it over a troop
of artists—
5 unless one should scour the world—
you have the ground sense necessary.

See! the hearse leads.
I begin with a design for a hearse.
For Christ's sake not black—
10 nor white either—and not polished!
Let it be weathered—like a farm wagon—
with gilt wheels (this could be
applied fresh at small expense)
or no wheels at all:
15 a rough dray to drag over the ground.

Knock the glass out!
My God—glass, my townspeople!
For what purpose! Is it for the dead
to look out or for us to see
20 how well he is housed or to see
the flowers or the lack of them—
or what?
To keep the rain and snow from him?
He will have a heavier rain soon:
25 pebbles and dirt and what not.
Let there be no glass—
and no upholstery, phew!
and no little brass rollers
and small easy wheels on the bottom—
30 my townspeople what are you thinking of?

A rough plain hearse then
with gilt wheels and no top at all.
On this the coffin lies
by its own weight.

35   No wreaths please—
especially no hot house flowers.
Some common memento is better,
something he prized and is known by:
his old clothes—a few books perhaps—
40 God knows what! You realize
how we are about these things
my townspeople—
something will be found—anything
even flowers if he had come to that.
45 So much for the hearse.

For heaven's sake though see to the driver!
Take off the silk hat! In fact
that's no place at all for him—
up there unceremoniously
50 dragging our friend out to his own dignity!
Bring him down—bring him down!
Low and inconspicuous! I'd not have him ride
on the wagon at all—damn him—
the undertaker's understrapper!
55 Let him hold the reins
and walk at the side
and inconspicuously too!

Then briefly as to yourselves:
Walk behind—as they do in France,
60 seventh class, or if you ride
Hell take curtains! Go with some show
of inconvenience; sit openly—
to the weather as to grief.

Or do you think you can shut grief in?
65 What—from us? We who have perhaps
nothing to lose? Share with us
share with us—it will be money
in your pockets.
                    Go now
70 I think you are ready.

Spring and All

By the road to the contagious hospital[1]
under the surge of the blue
mottled clouds driven from the
northeast—a cold wind. Beyond, the
5 waste of broad, muddy fields
brown with dried weeds, standing and fallen

patches of standing water
the scattering of tall trees

All along the road the reddish
10 purplish, forked, upstanding, twiggy
stuff of bushes and small trees
with dead, brown leaves under them
leafless vines—

Lifeless in appearance, sluggish
15 dazed spring approaches—

---

1. Hospital for contagious diseases.

They enter the new world naked,
cold, uncertain of all
save that they enter. All about them
the cold, familiar wind—

20 Now the grass, tomorrow
the stiff curl of wildcarrot leaf
One by one objects are defined—
It quickens: clarity, outline of leaf

25 But now the stark dignity of
entrance—Still, the profound change
has come upon them: rooted, they
grip down and begin to awaken

The Red Wheelbarrow

so much depends
upon

a red wheel
barrow

glazed with rain
water

beside the white
chickens.

This Is Just to Say

I have eaten
the plums
that were in
the icebox

and which
you were probably
saving
for breakfast

Forgive me
they were delicious
so sweet
and so cold

The Yachts

contend in a sea which the land partly encloses
shielding them from the too-heavy blows
of an ungoverned ocean which when it chooses

tortures the biggest hulls, the best man knows
5   to pit against its beatings, and sinks them pitilessly.
Mothlike in mists, scintillant in the minute

brilliance of cloudless days, with broad bellying sails
they glide to the wind tossing green water
from their sharp prows while over them the crew crawls

10 ant-like, solicitously grooming them, releasing,
making fast as they turn, lean far over and having
caught the wind again, side by side, head for the mark.

In a well guarded arena of open water surrounded by
lesser and greater craft which, sycophant, lumbering
15 and flittering follow them, they appear youthful, rare

as the light of a happy eye, live with the grace
of all that in the mind is fleckless, free and
naturally to be desired. Now the sea which holds them

is moody, lapping their glossy sides, as if feeling
20 for some slightest flaw but fails completely.
Today no race. Then the wind comes again. The yachts

move, jockeying for a start, the signal is set and they
are off. Now the waves strike at them but they are too
well made, they slip through, though they take in canvas.

25 Arms with hands grasping seek to clutch at the prows.
Bodies thrown recklessly in the way are cut aside.
It is a sea of faces about them in agony, in despair

until the horror of the race dawns staggering the mind,
the whole sea become an entanglement of watery bodies
30 lost to the world bearing what they cannot hold. Broken,

beaten, desolate, reaching from the dead to be taken up
they cry out, failing, failing! their cries rising
in waves still as the skillful yachts pass over.

The Poor

It's the anarchy of poverty
delights me, the old
yellow wooden house indented
among the new brick tenements

Or a cast-iron balcony
with panels showing oak branches
in full leaf. It fits
the dress of the children

reflecting every stage and
custom of necessity—
Chimneys, roofs, fences of
wood and metal in an unfenced

age and enclosing next to
nothing at all: the old man
in a sweater and soft black
hat who sweeps the sidewalk—

his own ten feet of it
in a wind that fitfully
turning his corner has
overwhelmed the entire city

The Dance

In Brueghel's great picture, The Kermess,[1]
the dancers go round, they go round and
around, the squeal and the blare and the
tweedle of bagpipes, a bugle and fiddles
tipping their bellies (round as the thick-
sided glasses whose wash they impound)

their hips and their bellies off balance
to turn them. Kicking and rolling about
the Fair Grounds, swinging their butts, those
shanks must be sound to bear up under such
rollicking measures, prance as they dance
in Breughel's great picture, The Kermess.

The Dish of Fruit

The table describes
nothing: four legs, by which
it becomes a table. Four lines
by which it becomes a quatrain,

the poem that lifts the dish
of fruit, if we say it is like
a table— how will it describe
the contents of the poem?

1. Pieter Brueghel (or Breughel) (ca. 1520–69) was a
Flemish painter of peasant life. A kermess is an outdoor
festival held on a town's patron saint's day. The picture,
which is in the Vienna Kunsthistorisches Museum, is
usually identified as *The Peasant Dance*, and the standard
interpretation of it is as a depiction of gluttony, lust, and
the neglect of God.

The Sparrow
(To My Father)

This sparrow
    who comes to sit at my window
        is a poetic truth
more than a natural one.
5   His voice,
        his movements,
his habits—
    how he loves to
        flutter his wings
10 in the dust—
    all attest it;
        granted, he does it
to rid himself of lice
    but the relief he feels
15   makes him
cry out lustily—
    which is a trait
        more related to music
than otherwise.
20   Wherever he finds himself
        in early spring,
on back streets
    or beside palaces,
        he carries on
25 unaffectedly
    his amours.
        It begins in the egg,
his sex genders it:
    What is more pretentiously
30   useless
or about which
    we more pride ourselves?
        It leads as often as not
to our undoing.
35   The cockerel, the crow
        with their challenging voices
cannot surpass
    the insistence
        of his cheep!
40 Once
    at El Paso[1]
        toward evening,
I saw—and heard!—
    ten thousand sparrows
45   who had come in from
the desert
    to roost. They filled the trees
        of a small park. Men fled
(with ears ringing!)
50   from their droppings,
        leaving the premises
to the alligators
    who inhabit
        the fountain. His image
55 is familiar
    as that of the aristocratic
        unicorn, a pity

there are not more oats eaten
    nowadays
60   to make living easier
for him.[2]
    At that,
        his small size,
keen eyes,
65   serviceable beak
        and general truculence
assure his survival—
    to say nothing
        of his innumerable
70 brood.
        Even the Japanese
        know him
and have painted him
    sympathetically,
75   with profound insight
into his minor
    characteristics.
        Nothing even remotely
subtle
80   about his lovemaking.
        He crouches
before the female,
    drags his wings,
        waltzing,
85 throws back his head
    and simply—
        yells! The din
is terrific.
    The way he swipes his bill
90   across a plank
to clean it,
    is decisive.
        So with everything
he does. His coppery
95   eyebrows
        give him the air
of being always
    a winner—and yet
        I saw once,
100 the female of his species
    clinging determinedly
        to the edge of
a water pipe,
    catch him
105   by his crown-feathers
to hold him
    silent,
        subdued,
hanging above the city streets
110 until
        she was through with him.
What was the use
    of that?

1. A town in west Texas.
2. Sparrows eat the partly digested oats in horse droppings; the automobile thus deprived them of a source of
food.

115 *She* hung there
herself,
        puzzled at her success.
           I laughed heartily.
Practical to the end,
    it is the poem
120   of his existence
that triumphed
        finally;
           a wisp of feathers
flattened to the pavement,
125   wings spread symmetrically
           as if in flight,

the head gone,
        the black escutcheon of the breast
           undecipherable,
130 an effigy of a sparrow,
        a dried wafer only,
           left to say
and it says it
        without offense,
135   beautifully;
This was I,
    a sparrow.
           I did my best;
farewell.

EZRA POUND (1885-1972)

The Return

See, they return; ah, see the tentative
    Movements, and the slow feet,
      The trouble in the pace and the uncertain
Wavering!

See, they return, one, and by one,
With fear, as half-awakened;
As if the snow should hesitate
And murmur in the wind,
        and half turn back;
These were the "Wing'd-with-Awe,"
    Inviolable.

Gods of the wingèd shoe!
With them the silver hounds,
      sniffing the trace of air!

Haie! Haie!
      These were the swift to harry;
These the keen-scented;
These were the souls of blood. [1]

Slow on the leash,
      pallid the leash-men!

In a Station of the Métro[1]

The apparition of these faces in the crowd;
Petals on a wet, black bough.

Lament of the Frontier Guard

By the North Gate, the wind blows full of sand,
Lonely from the beginning of time until now!
Trees fall, the grass goes yellow with autumn.
I climb the towers and towers
      to watch out the barbarous land:
5 Desolate castle, the sky, the wide desert.
There is no wall left to this village.
Bones white with a thousand frosts,
High heaps, covered with trees and grass;
Who brought this to pass?
10 Who has brought the flaming imperial anger?
Who has brought the army with drums and with kettle-drums?
Barbarous kings.
A gracious spring, turned to blood-ravenous autumn,
A turmoil of wars-men, spread over the middle kingdom,
15 Three hundred and sixty thousand,

1. Odysseus in Book XI of the *Odyssey* offered the dead a
bowl of blood so that he might speak with them. See
Pound's Canto I.

1. The Paris subway or underground train system.

And sorrow, sorrow like rain.
Sorrow to go, and sorrow, sorrow returning.
Desolate, desolate fields,
And no children of warfare upon them,
   No longer the men for offence and defence.
20 Ah, how shall you know the dreary sorrow at the North Gate,
With Rihoku's[1] name forgotten,
And we guardsmen fed to the tigers.

By Rihaku (Li T'ai Po)

Hugh Selwyn Mauberley
(Life and Contacts)
"Vocat œstus in umbram."— Nemesianus, Ec. IV[1]
E. P. Ode pour l'election de son sepulchre[2]

I

For three years, out of key with his time,
He strove to resuscitate the dead art
Of poetry; to maintain "the sublime"
In the old sense. Wrong from the start—

5 No, hardly, but seeing he had been born
In a half savage country, out of date;
Bent resolutely on wringing lilies from the acorn;
Capaneus;[3] trout for factitious bait;

 Ἴδμεν γάρ τοι πάνθ᾽, ὅσ᾽ ἐνὶ Τροίῃ[4]
10 Caught in the unstopped ear;
Giving the rocks small lee-way
The chopped seas held him, therefore, that year.

His true Penelope[5] was Flaubert,[6]
He fished by obstinate isles;
15 Observed the elegance of Circe's[7] hair
Rather than the mottoes on sun-dials.

Unaffected by "the march of events,"
He passed from men's memory in *l'an trentuniesme*
De son eage;[8] the case presents
20 No adjunct to the Muses' diadem.

II

The age demanded an image
Of its accelerated grimace,
Something for the modern stage,
Not, at any rate, an Attic grace;

---

1. Variant of Rihaku, Japanese form of the name Li T'ai Po (A.D. 701–62), a great Chinese poet. The poem is a translation of one of Li Po's poems.

1. (Latin) "The heat calls us into the shade," a line from the *Eclogues* of Nemesianus, a third-century poet of Carthage.
2. The title means "E.P. Ode for the selection of his tomb," adapted from the title of an ode of Pierre de Ronsard (1524–85).
3. One of the Seven against Thebes, killed by Zeus with a thunderbolt.

4. (Greek) "For we know all the toils of wide Troy," part of the song of the sirens in the *Odyssey*, Book XII. Odysseus stopped his crewmen's ears with wax to prevent their succumbing to the sirens' lure, but he himself listened while bound to a mast.
5. Wife of Odysseus who waited faithfully at home for him.
6. Gustav Flaubert (1821–80), French novelist.
7. Enchantress who detained Odysseus for a year.
8. (French) "the thirty-first year of his age," a line adapted from the fifteenth-century French poet Francois Villon.

25 Not, not certainly, the obscure reveries
    Of the inward gaze;
    Better mendacities
    Than the classics in paraphrase!

    The "age demanded" chiefly a mound in plaster,
30   Made with no loss of time,
    A prose kinema,[9] not, not assuredly, alabaster
    Or the "sculpture" of rhyme.

III

    The tea-rose tea-gown, etc.
    Supplants the mousseline of Cos,[10]
35   The pianola "replaces"
    Sappho's barbitos.[11]

    Christ follows Dionysus,[12]
    Phallic and ambrosial
    Made way for macerations;
40   Caliban casts out Ariel.[13]

    All things are a flowing,
    Sage Heracleitus[14] says;
    But a tawdry cheapness
    Shall outlast our days.

45   Even the Christian beauty
    Defects—after Samothrace;[15]
    We see τὸ καλόν [16]
    Decreed in the market place.

    Faun's flesh is not to us,
50   Nor the saint's vision.
    We have the press for wafer;
    Franchise for circumcision.

    All men, in law, are equals.
    Free of Pisistratus,[17]
55   We choose a knave or an eunuch
    To rule over us.

    O bright Apollo,[18]
    τίν' ἄνδρα, τίν' ἥρωα, τινα θεόν, [19]
    What god, man, or hero
60   Shall I place a tin wreath upon!

IV

    These fought in any case,
    and some believing,
                 pro domo,[20] in any case . . .

9. (Greek) motion: also cinema.
10. Muslin from the Aegean island of Cos.
11. A lyre used by the Greek poetess Sappho (seventh century B.C.).
12. Greek god of fertility and poetic inspiration. His worship was frenzied and ecstatic.
13. In Shakespeare's *The Tempest*, Caliban was an earth-bound slave of Prospero, Ariel an imaginative spirit of the air.

14. Greek philosopher, ca. 500 B.C.
15. Greek island, source of the statue *Winged Victory*.
16. (Greek) the Beautiful.
17. Athenian tyrant, patron of the arts.
18. God of the sun and of poetry.
19. (Greek) "What man, what hero, what god," adapted from Pindar's second *Olympian Ode*.
20. (Latin) "for home."

Some quick to arm,
65 some for adventure,
some from fear of weakness,
some from fear of censure,
some for love of slaughter, in imagination,
learning later...
70 some in fear, learning love of slaughter;

Died some, pro patria,
                non "dulce" non "et decor"[21]...
walked eye-deep in hell
believing in old men's lies, then unbelieving
75 came home, home to a lie,
home to many deceits,
home to old lies and new infamy;
usury age-old and age-thick
and liars in public places.

80 Daring as never before, wastage as never before.
Young blood and high blood,
fair cheeks, and fine bodies;

fortitude as never before

frankness as never before,
85 disillusions as never told in the old days,
hysterias, trench confessions,
laughter out of dead bellies.

V

There died a myriad,
And of the best, among them,
90 For an old bitch gone in the teeth,
For a botched civilization,

Charm, smiling at the good mouth,
Quick eyes gone under earth's lid,

For two gross of broken statues,
95 For a few thousand battered books.

Yeux glauques[22]

Gladstone[23] was still respected,
When John Ruskin produced
"Kings' Treasuries";[24] Swinburne
And Rossetti still abused.

100 Fœtid Buchanan[25] lifted up his voice
When that faun's head of hers
Became a pastime for
Painters and adulterers.

The Burne-Jones cartons
105 Have preserved her eyes;

---

21. Adapted from Horace's *Odes* III.ii: *Dulce et decorum
est pro patria mori*: "It is sweet and fitting to die for one's
country."
22. The title is French for glaucous or yellow-green eyes,
an allusion to Elizabeth Siddal, model for several pre-
Raphaelite paintings, including "King Cophetua and the
Beggar-Maid" by Edward Burne-Jones (1833–98), now in
the Tate Gallery in London. Swinburne and Rossetti were
pre-Raphaelite poets.

23. William Ewart Gladstone (1809–98), Liberal Prime
Minister of England.
24. The title of a lecture in John Ruskin's *Sesame and
Lilies* (1865).
25. Robert W. Buchanan (1841–1901) attacked the pre-
Raphaelites as "the Fleshly School of Poetry"; one of the
poems he criticized was Rossetti's "Jenny," about a London prostitute.

Still, at the Tate, they teach
Cophetua to rhapsodize;

Thin like brook-water,
With a vacant gaze.
110 The English Rubaiyat[26] was still-born
In those days.

The thin, clear gaze, the same
Still darts out faun-like from the half-ruin'd face,
Questing and passive....
115 "Ah, poor Jenny's case"...

Bewildered that a world
Shows no surprise
At her last maquero's[27]
Adulteries.

"Siena Mi Fe'; Disfecemi Maremma"[28]

120 Among the pickled fœtuses and bottled bones,
Engaged in perfecting the catalogue,
I found the last scion of the
Senatorial families of Strasbourg, Monsieur Verog.[29]

For two hours he talked of Galliffet;[30]
125 Of Dowson; of the Rhymer's Club;
Told me how Johnson (Lionel) died
By falling from a high stool in a pub...

But showed no trace of alcohol
At the autopsy, privately performed—
130 Tissue preserved—the pure mind
Arose toward Newman[31] as the whiskey warmed.

Dowson found harlots cheaper than hotels;
Headlam[32] for uplift; Image[33] impartially imbued
With raptures for Bacchus, Terpsichore[34] and the Church.
135 So spoke the author of "The Dorian Mood,"
M. Verog, out of step with the decade,
Detached from his contemporaries,
Neglected by the young,
Because of these reveries.

Brennbaum[35]

140 The sky-like limpid eyes,
The circular infant's face,
The stiffness from spats to collar
Never relaxing into grace;

26. Edward Fitzgerald (1809–83) translated *The Rubaiyat of Omar Khayyam* in 1859, but it was at first ignored.
27. "maquereau": pimp.
28. The title is Italian, from Dante's *Purgatorio*: "Siena made me, Maremma unmade me," spoken by a Sienese woman condemned to die in the Maremma marshes for her infidelity.
29. Victor Plarr (1863–1929), French poet from Strasbourg, librarian of the Royal College of Surgeons, member (along with poets Ernest Dowson and Lionel Johnson) of the Rhymers Club and author of *In the Dorian Mood* (1896).
30. French General in the Franco-Prussian War.

31. John Henry Newman (1801–90), founder of the Oxford Movement in the Anglican Church. He converted to Roman Catholicism (as did Lionel Johnson) and became a Cardinal.
32. The Rev. Stuart Headlam, friend of the Decadent poets, lecturer on the dance and theatre.
33. Selwyn Image, publisher of the Decadent poets and friend of Headlam, with whom he founded the Church and Stage Guild.
34. Greek Muse of the Dance.
35. (German) "burnt tree" or burning bush. Probably Max Beerbohm (1872–1956), English essayist and humorist known as "the Incomparable Max." He was not Jewish.

The heavy memories of Horeb, Sinai and the forty years,[36]
145 Showed only when the daylight fell
Level across the face
Of Brennbaum "The Impeccable."

Mr. Nixon[37]

In the cream gilded cabin of his steam yacht
Mr. Nixon advised me kindly, to advance with fewer
150 Dangers of delay. "Consider
          "Carefully the reviewer.

"I was as poor as you are;
"When I began I got, of course,
"Advance on royalties, fifty at first," said Mr. Nixon,
155 "Follow me, and take a column,
"Even if you have to work free.

"Butter reviewers. From fifty to three hundred
"I rose in eighteen months;
"The hardest nut I had to crack
160 "Was Dr. Dundas.

"I never mentioned a man but with the view
"Of selling my own works.
"The tip's a good one, as for literature
"It gives no man a sinecure.

165 "And no one knows, at sight, a masterpiece.
"And give up verse, my boy,
"There's nothing in it."

      .   .   .   .

Likewise a friend of Blougram's[38] once advised me:
Don't kick against the pricks,[39]
170 Accept opinion. The "Nineties" tried your game
And died, there's nothing in it.

X
Beneath the sagging roof
The stylist has taken shelter,
175 Unpaid, uncelebrated,
At last from the world's welter

Nature receives him;
With a placid and uneducated mistress
He exercises his talents
And the soil meets his distress.

180 The haven from sophistications and contentions
Leaks through its thatch;
He offers succulent cooking;
The door has a creaking latch.

XI
"Conservatrix of Milésien"[40]
185 Habits of mind and feeling,
Possibly. But in Ealing[41]
With the most bank-clerkly of Englishmen?

36. See Exod. iii and xix; also Deut. ii.
37. Possibly Arnold Bennett (1867–1931), English novelist.
38. From Robert Browning's poem, *Bishop Blougram's Apology*.
39. See Acts ix.5.

40. Refers to *Milesian Tales*, erotic stories by Aristides of Miletus, first century B.C., and to a phrase by Remy de Gourmont (1858–1915) to the effect that women are "conservatrices des traditions milésiennes," conservors of Milesian traditions.
41. Suburb of London.

No, "Milésian" is an exaggeration.
No instinct has survived in her
190   Older than those her grandmother
Told her would fit her station.

XII

"Daphne[42] with her thighs in bark
Stretches toward me her leafy hands,"—
Subjectively. In the stuffed-satin drawing-room
195   I await The Lady Valentine's commands,

Knowing my coat has never been
Of precisely the fashion
To stimulate, in her,
A durable passion;

200   Doubtful, somewhat, of the value
Of well-gowned approbation
Of literary effort,
But never of The Lady Valentine's vocation:

Poetry, her border of ideas,
205   The edge, uncertain, but a means of blending
With other strata
Where the lower and higher have ending;

A hook to catch the Lady Jane's attention,
A modulation toward the theatre,
210   Also, in the case of revolution,
A possible friend and comforter.

.   .   .   .

Conduct, on the other hand, the soul
"Which the highest cultures have nourished"[43]
To Fleet St. where
215   Dr. Johnson[44] flourished;

Beside this thoroughfare
The sale of half-hose has
Long since superseded the cultivation
Of Pierian[45] roses.

Envoi (1919)[46]

220   *Go, dumb-born book,*
Tell her that sang me once that song of Lawes:
Hadst thou but song
As thou hast subjects known,
Then were there cause in thee that should condone
225   *Even my faults that heavy upon me lie,*
And build her glories their longevity.

Tell her that sheds
Such treasure in the air,
Recking naught else but that her graces give
230   *Life to the moment,*

42. A nymph transformed into a laurel tree to escape the pursuit of Apollo.
43. Translation of a phrase from *Complainte des Pianos* by French poet Jules Laforgue.
44. Samuel Johnson (1709–84), poet, critic, essayist, and man of letters in eighteenth-century London. Literary life in his time centred on Fleet Street.
45. Of Pieria, near Olympus, seat of the Muses.
46. This poem is modelled on a lyric, "Go, lovely rose," by Edmund Waller (1606–87); the poem was set to music by Henry Lawes (1598–1662).

> *I would bid them live*
> *As roses might, in magic amber laid,*
> *Red overwrought with orange and all made*
> *One substance and one colour*
235 *Braving time.*
>
> *Tell her that goes.*
> *With song upon her lips*
> *But sings not out the song, nor knows*
> *The maker of it, some other mouth,*
240 *May be as fair as hers,*
> *Might, in new ages, gain her worshippers,*
> *When our two dusts with Waller's shall be laid,*
> *Siftings on siftings in oblivion,*
> *Till change hath broken down*
245 *All things save Beauty alone.*

Mauberley
1920

"Vacuos exercet in aera morsus."[47]

I

Turned from the "eau-forte
Par Jacquemart"[48]
To the strait head
Of Messalina:[49]

250 "His true Penelope
Was Flaubert,"
And his tool
The engraver's.

Firmness,
255 Not the full smile,
His art, but an art
In profile;

Colourless
Pier Francesca,[50]
260 Pisanello[51] lacking the skill
To forge Achaia.[52]

II

*"Qu'est ce qu'ils savent de l'amour, et
qu'est ce qu'ils peuvent en comprendre?
    S'ils ne comprennent pas la poésie,
s'ils ne sentent pas la musique, qu'est ce
qu'ils peuvent comprendre de cette passion en comparaison avec laquelle la rose
est grossière et le parfum des violettes un
tonnerre?"* — Caid Ali[53]

47. (Latin) "He bites emptily at the air," said of a dog attacking a monster in Ovid's *Metamorphoses* VII. Dog and monster are both later turned to stone.
48. "Etching by Jaquemart," a French graphic artist (1837–80).
49. Dissolute wife of the Roman emperor Claudius.
50. Piero della Francesca (ca. 1420–92), Italian painter.
51. Vittore Pisano (ca. 1397–1455), Italian medallist and painter.
52. Ancient Greece.
53. (French) "What do they know of love, and what can they understand? If they do not understand poetry, if they do not feel music, what can they understand of this passion in comparison with which the rose is gross and the perfume of violets a clap of thunder?" Caid Ali is an invented name.

For three years, diabolus in the scale,[54]
He drank ambrosia,
All passes, ANANGKE[55] prevails,
265   Came end, at last, to that Arcadia.[56]

He had moved amid her phantasmagoria,
Amid her galaxies,
NUKTOS 'AGALMA[57]

  • • • • • • • • • •

Drifted . . . drifted precipitate,
270   Asking time to be rid of . . .
Of his bewilderment; to designate
His new found orchid . . .

To be certain . . . certain . . .
(Amid ærial flowers) . . . time for arrangements—
275   Drifted on
To the final estrangement;

Unable in the supervening blankness
To sift TO AGATHON[58] from the chaff
Until he found his sieve . . .
280   Ultimately, his seismograph:

—Given that is his "fundamental passion,"
This urge to convey the relation
Of the eye-lid and cheek-bone
By verbal manifestation;

285   To present the series
Of curious heads in medallion—

He had passed, inconscient, full gaze,
The wide-banded irides[59]
And botticellian sprays[60] implied
290   In their diastasis;[61]

Which anæthesis,[62] noted a year late,
And weighed, revealed his great affect,
(Orchid), mandate
Of Eros,[63] a retrospect.

295   Mouths biting empty air,
The still stone dogs,
Caught in metamorphosis, were
Left him as epilogues.

"The Age Demanded"
Vide[64] *Poem II. Page 544*

For this agility chance found
300   Him of all men, unfit
As the red-beaked steeds of
The Cytheræan[65] for a chain bit.

---

54. The devil in the musical scale, the interval of the augmented fourth, which causes discord.
55. (Greek) necessity, fate.
56. Rustic paradise.
57. (Greek) night's jewel, the evening star.
58. (Greek) the good.
59. Plural of iris, flower and part of eye.
60. Sandro Botticelli (ca. 1444–1510), Italian painter.

Sprays may allude to the flowers in his painting *Primavera* (Spring), or to the waves in *The Birth of Venus*.
61. Separation.
62. Loss of feeling.
63. Cupid, god of love.
64. (Latin) see.
65. Aphrodite, whose chariot was drawn by doves.

The glow of porcelain
Brought no reforming sense
305 To his perception
Of the social inconsequence

Thus, if her colour
Came against his gaze,
Tempered as if
310 It were through a perfect glaze

He made no immediate application
Of this to relation of the state
To the individual, the month was more temperate
Because this beauty had been.

315   The coral isle, the lion-coloured sand
       Burst in upon the porcelain revery:
       Impetuous troubling
       Of his imagery.

Mildness, amid the neo-Nietzschean[66] clatter,
320 His sense of graduations,
Quite out of place amid
Resistance to current exacerbations,

Invitation, mere invitation to perceptivity
Gradually led him to the isolation
325 Which these presents place
Under a more tolerant, perhaps, examination.

By constant elimination
The manifest universe
Yielded an armour
330 Against utter consternation,

A Minoan[67] undulation,
Seen, we admit, amid ambrosial circumstances
Strengthened him against
The discouraging doctrine of chances,

335 And his desire for survival,
Faint in the most strenuous moods,
Became an Olympian *apathein*[68]
In the presence of selected perceptions.

A pale gold, in the aforesaid pattern,
340 The unexpected palms
Destroying, certainly, the artist's urge,
Left him delighted with the imaginary
Audition of the phantasmal sea-surge,

Incapable of the least utterance or composition,
345 Emendation, conservation of the "better tradition,"
Refinement of medium, elimination of superfluities,
August attraction or concentration.

Nothing, in brief, but maudlin confession,
Irresponse to human aggression.
350 Amid the precipitation, down-float

---

66. Friedrich Nietzsche (1844–1900), controversial German philosopher.

67. Ancient Cretan civilization.
68. Apathy.

Of insubstantial manna,
Lifting the faint susurrus[69]
Of his subjective hosannah.

Ultimate affronts to
355   Human redundancies;

Non-esteem of self-styled "his betters"
Leading, as he well knew,
To his final
Exclusion from the world of letters.

IV
360   Scattered Moluccas[70]
Not knowing, day to day,
The first day's end, in the next noon;
The placid water
Unbroken by the Simoon;[71]

365   Thick foliage
Placid beneath warm suns,
Tawn fore-shores
Washed in the cobalt of oblivions;

Or through dawn-mist
370   The grey and rose
Of the juridical
Flamingoes;

A consciousness disjunct,
Being but this overblotted
375   Series
Of intermittences;

Coracle[72] of Pacific voyages,
The unforecasted beach;
Then on an oar
380   Read this:

"I was
And I no more exist;
Here drifted
An hedonist."

Medallion

385   Luini[73] in porcelain!
The grand piano
Utters a profane
Protest with her clear soprano.

The sleek head emerges
390   From the gold-yellow frock
As Anadyomene[74] in the opening
Pages of Reinach.[75]

---

69. Whisper or rustling sound.
70. The Spice Islands.
71. Violent windstorm in the desert.
72. Small boat made by covering a light wooden frame with hide.
73. Bernardo Luini (ca. 1475–1532), Italian painter.
74. "Foam-born," applied to Aphrodite (Venus), who rose from the sea.
75. Salomon Reinach (1858–1932), French archaeologist, author of *Apollo* (1904).

Honey-red, closing the face-oval,
A basket-work of braids which seem as if they were
395   Spun in King Minos'[76] hall
From metal, or intractable amber;

The face-oval beneath the glaze,
Bright in its suave bounding-line, as,
Beneath half-watt rays,
400   The eyes turn topaz.

Canto I

And then went down to the ship,[1]
Set keel to breakers, forth on the godly sea, and
We set up mast and sail on that swart ship,
Bore sheep aboard her, and our bodies also
5   Heavy with weeping, and winds from sternward
Bore us out onward with bellying canvas,
Circe's[2] this craft, the trim-coifed goddess.
Then sat we amidships, wind jamming the tiller,
Thus with stretched sail, we went over sea till day's end.
10   Sun to his slumber, shadows o'er all the ocean,
Came we then to the bounds of deepest water,
To the Kimmerian lands,[3] and peopled cities
Covered with close-webbed mist, unpierced ever
With glitter of sun-rays
15   Nor with stars stretched, nor looking back from heaven
Swartest night stretched over wretched men there.
The ocean flowing backward, came we then to the place
Aforesaid by Circe.
Here did they rites, Perimedes and Eurylochus,[4]
20   And drawing sword from my hip
I dug the ell-square pitkin;[5]
Poured we libations unto each the dead,
First mead and then sweet wine, water mixed with white flour.
Then prayed I many a prayer to the sickly death's-heads;
25   As set in Ithaca, sterile bulls of the best
For sacrifice, heaping the pyre with goods,
A sheep to Tiresias only, black and a bell-sheep.
Dark blood flowed in the fosse,
Souls out of Erebus,[6] cadaverous dead, of brides
30   Of youths and of old who had borne much;
Souls stained with recent tears, girls tender,
Men many, mauled with bronze lance heads,
Battle spoil, bearing yet dreory[7] arms,
These many crowded about me; with shouting,
35   Pallor upon me, cried to my men for more beasts;
Slaughtered the herds, sheep slain of bronze;
Poured ointment, cried to the gods,
To Pluto the strong, and praised Proserpine;[8]
Unsheathed the narrow sword,
40   I sat to keep off the impetuous impotent dead,
Till I should hear Tiresias.
But first Elpenor came, our friend Elpenor,[9]

76. Legendary king of Crete.

1. The Canto, one of 116, is a free adaptation of the opening lines of the *Odyssey*, Book XI, which describe Odysseus' visit to the underworld. Pound is working not from Homer's Greek, but from a Renaissance Latin version by Andreas Divus (1538).
2. Enchantress, who had told Odysseus that he must visit Hades in order to inquire of Tiresias how he could return to his home in Ithaca.
3. The Crimea.
4. Two of Odysseus' men.
5. A small pit. An ell is an old measure, about 45 inches.
6. A dark, gloomy place through which the dead pass on their way to Hades.
7. (Old English) bloody.
8. King and Queen of Hades.
9. One of Odysseus's late companions.

Unburied, cast on the wide earth,
Limbs that we left in the house of Circe,
45   Unwept, unwrapped in sepulchre, since toils urged other.
Pitiful spirit. And I cried in hurried speech:
"Elpenor, how art thou come to this dark coast?
"Cam'st thou afoot, outstripping seamen?"
      And he in heavy speech:
50   "Ill fate and abundant wine. I slept in Circe's ingle.
"Going down the long ladder unguarded,
"I fell against the buttress,
"Shattered the nape-nerve, the soul sought Avernus.
"But thou, O King, I bid remember me, unwept, unburied,
55   "Heap up mine arms, be tomb by sea-bord, and inscribed:
"*A man of no fortune, and with a name to come.*
"And set my oar up, that I swung mid fellows."

And Anticlea came,[10] whom I beat off, and then Tiresias Theban,
Holding his golden wand, knew me, and spoke first:
60   "A second time? why? man of ill star,
"Facing the sunless dead and this joyless region?
"Stand from the fosse, leave me my bloody bever
"For soothsay."
      And I stepped back,
65   And he strong with the blood, said then: "Odysseus
"Shalt return through spiteful Neptune, over dark seas,
"Lose all companions." And then Anticlea came.
Lie quite Divus. I mean, that is Andreas Divus,
In officina Wecheli, 1538, out of Homer.
70   And he sailed, by Sirens and thence outward and away
And unto Circe.
      Venerandam,"[11]
In the Cretan's phrase, with the golden crown, Aphrodite,
Cypri munimenta sortita est,[12] mirthful, orichalchi,[13] with golden
75   Girdles and breast bands, thou with dark eyelids
Bearing the golden bough[14] of Argicida.[15] So that:

e. e. cummings (1894 – 1962)

when god lets my body be

From each brave eye shall sprout a tree
fruit that dangles therefrom

the purpled world will dance upon
Between my lips which did sing

a rose shall beget the spring
that maidens whom passion wastes

will lay between their little breasts
My strong fingers beneath the snow

Into strenuous birds shall go
my love walking in the grass

their wings will touch with her face
and all the while shall my heart be

With the bulge and nuzzle of the sea

10. Mother of Odysseus.
11. (Latin) "worthy of admiration," a phrase applied to Aphrodite in the translations of the Homeric hymns by Georgius Dartona "the Cretan," included in the Divus volume.
12. (Latin) The citadels of Cyprus were her realm.
13. Copper (orichalci).

14. In Vergil's *Aeneid*, Book VI, a golden bough is Aeneas' passport to the underworld. Aeneas was one of the unsuccessful defenders of Troy against the Greeks.
15. "slayer of Argus" (i.e., Hermes) or "slayer of Greeks" (i.e., Aphrodite, who supported the Trojans in the Trojan war).

in Just-
spring   when the world is mud-
luscious the little
lame balloonman

.

whistles   far   and wee

and eddieandbill come
running from marbles and
piracies and it's
spring

when the world is puddle-wonderful

the queer
old balloonman whistles
far   and   wee
and bettyandisbel come dancing

from hop-scotch and jump-rope and

it's
spring
and
    the

        goat-footed[1]

balloonMan   whistles
far
and
wee

O sweet spontaneous
earth how often have
the
doting

    fingers of
prurient philosophers pinched
and
poked

thee
, has the naughty thumb
of science prodded
thy

    beauty   . how
often have religions taken
thee upon their scraggy knees
squeezing and

buffeting thee that thou mightest conceive
gods
        (but
true

to the incomparable
couch of death thy
rhythmic
lover

            thou answerest

them only with

                spring)

---

the Cambridge[1] ladies who live in furnished souls
are unbeautiful and have comfortable minds
(also, with the church's protestant blessings
daughters, unscented shapeless spirited)
they believe in Christ and Longfellow,[2] both dead,
are invariably interested in so many things—
at the present writing one still finds
delighted fingers knitting for the is it Poles?
perhaps. While permanent faces coyly bandy
scandal of Mrs. N and Professor D
.... the Cambridge ladies do not care, above
Cambridge if sometimes in its box of
sky lavender and cornerless, the
moon rattles like a fragment of angry candy

---

1. Pan, god of shepherds and huntsmen, also has goats'
feet. He played on a reed pipe.

1. A suburb of Boston, Massachusetts, and site of Harvard University, where Cummings was educated.
2. Henry Wadsworth Longfellow (1807–82), poet, Harvard professor, and member of Cambridge society.

Spring is like a perhaps hand
(which comes carefully
out of Nowhere)arranging
a window,into which people look(while
people stare
arranging and changing placing
carefully there a strange
thing and a known thing here)and

changing everything carefully

spring is like a perhaps
Hand in a window
(carefully to
and fro moving New and
Old things,while
people stare carefully
moving a perhaps
fraction of flower here placing
an inch of air there)and

without breaking anything.

(ponder,darling,these busted statues
of yon motheaten forum be aware
notice what hath remained
—the stone cringes
5 clinging to the stone,how obsolete

lips utter their extant smile . . . .
remark

a few deleted of texture
or meaning monuments and dolls

10 resist Them Greediest Paws of careful
time all of which is extremely
unimportant)whereas Life

matters if or

15 when the your- and my-
idle vertical worthless
self unite in a peculiarly
momentary

partnership(to instigate
constructive
20   Horizontal
business . . . . even so,let us make haste
—consider well this ruined aqueduct

lady,
which used to lead something into somewhere)

"next to of course god america i
love you land of the pilgrims' and so forth oh
say can you see by the dawn's early my
country 'tis of centuries come and go
and are no more what of it we should worry
in every language even deafanddumb
thy sons acclaim your glorious name by gorry
by jingo by gee by gosh by gum

why talk of beauty what could be more beautiful than these heroic happy dead
who rushed like lions to the roaring slaughter
they did not stop to think they died instead
then shall the voice of liberty be mute?"

He spoke. And drank rapidly a glass of water

---

since feeling is first
who pays any attention
to the syntax of things
will never wholly kiss you;

wholly to be a fool
while Spring is in the world

my blood approves,
and kisses are a better fate
than wisdom

lady i swear by all flowers. Don't cry
—the best gesture of my brain is less than
your eyelids' flutter which says

we are for each other: then
laugh, leaning back in my arms
for life's not a paragraph

And death i think is no parenthesis

anyone lived in a pretty how town
(with up so floating many bells down)
spring summer autumn winter
he sang his didn't he danced his did.

5   Women and men(both little and small)
cared for anyone not at all
they sowed their isn't they reaped their same
sun moon stars rain

children guessed(but only a few
10   and down they forgot as up they grew
autumn winter spring summer)
that noone loved him more by more

when by now and tree by leaf
she laughed his joy she cried his grief
15   bird by snow and stir by still
anyone's any was all to her

someones married their everyones
laughed their cryings and did their dance
(sleep wake hope and then)they
20   said their nevers they slept their dream

stars rain sun moon
(and only the snow can begin to explain
how children are apt to forget to remember
with up so floating many bells down)

25   one day anyone died i guess
(and noone stooped to kiss his face)
busy folk buried them side by side
little by little and was by was

all by all and deep by deep
30   and more by more they dream their sleep
noone and anyone earth by april
wish by spirit and if by yes.

Women and men(both dong and ding)
summer autumn winter spring
35   reaped their sowing and went their came
sun moon stars rain

---

pity this busy monster,manunkind,

not. Progress is a comfortable disease:
your victim(death and life safely beyond)

plays with the bigness of his littleness
—electrons deify one razorblade
into a mountainrange;lenses extend

unwish through curving wherewhen till unwish
returns on its unself.

A world of made
is not a world of born— pity poor flesh

and trees,poor stars and stones,but never this
fine specimen of hypermagical

ultraomnipotence. We doctors know

a hopeless case if— listen:there's a hell
of a good universe next door;let's go

---

when your honest redskin toma
hawked and scaled his victim ,

not to save a world for stalin
was he aiming ;

spare the child and spoil the rod
quoth the palmist .

---

honour corruption villainy holiness
riding in fragrance of sunlight(side by side
all in a singing wonder of blossoming yes
riding)to him who died that death should be dead

humblest and proudest eagerly wandering
(equally all alive in miraculous day)
merrily moving through sweet forgiveness of spring
(over the under the gift of the earth of the sky

knight and ploughman pardoner wife and nun
merchant frere clerk somnour miller and reve
and geoffrey and all)come up from the never of when
come into the now of forever come riding alive

down while crylessly drifting through vast most
nothing's own nothing children go of dust

E. J. PRATT (1883–1964)

The Flood-Tide

He paused a moment by the sea,
   Then stooped, and with a leisured hand
He wrote in casual tracery
   Her name upon the flux of sand.

The waves beat up and swiftly spun
   A silver web at every stride;
He watched their long, thin fingers run
   The letters back into the tide.

But she had written where the tide
   Could never its grey waters fling;
She watched the longest wave subside
   Ere it could touch the lettering.

Sea-Gulls

For one carved instant as they flew,
The language had no simile—
Silver, crystal, ivory
Were tarnished. Etched upon the horizon blue.
The frieze must go unchallenged, for the lift
And carriage of the wings would stain the drift
Of stars against a tropic indigo
Or dull the parable of snow.

Now settling one by one
Within green hollows or where curled
Crests caught the spectrum from the sun,
A thousand wings are furled.
No clay-born lilies of the world
Could blow as free
As those wild orchids of the sea.

Erosion

It took the sea a thousand years,
A thousand years to trace
The granite features of this cliff,
In crag and scarp and base.

It took the sea an hour one night,
An hour of storm to place
The sculpture of these granite seams
Upon a woman's face.

The Sea-Cathedral

Vast and immaculate! No pilgrim bands,
In ecstasy before the Parian[1] shrines,
Knew such a temple built by human hands,
With this transcendent rhythm in its lines;
5 Like an epic on the North Atlantic stream
It moved, and fairer than a Phidian[2] dream.

1. White marble from the island of Paros, used for
sculpture.

2. Phidias (ca. 490–448 B.C.), Athenian sculptor.

Rich gifts unknown to kings were duly brought
At dawn and sunset and at cloudless noons,
Gifts from the sea-gods and the sun who wrought
10   Cascades and rainbows; flung them in festoons
Over the spires, with emerald, amethyst,
Sapphire and pearl out of their fiery mist.

And music followed when a litany,
Begun with the ring of foam bells and the purl
15   Of linguals as the edges cut the sea,
Crashed upon a rising storm with whirl
Of floes from far-off spaces where Death rides
The darkened belfries of his evening tides.

Within the sunlight, vast, immaculate!
20   Beyond all reach of earth in majesty,
It passed on southwards slowly to its fate—
To be drawn down by the inveterate sea
Without one chastening fire made to start
From altars built around its polar heart.

From Stone to Steel

From stone to bronze, from bronze to steel
Along the road-dust of the sun,
Two revolutions of the wheel
From Java[1] to Geneva[2] run.

The snarl Neanderthal is worn
Close to the smiling Aryan[3] lips,
The civil polish of the horn
Gleams from our praying finger tips.

The evolution of desire
Has but matured a toxic wine,
Drunk long before its heady fire
Reddened Euphrates[4] or the Rhine.[5]

Between the temple and the cave
The boundary lies tissue-thin:
The yearlings still the alters crave
As satisfaction for a sin.

The road goes up, the road goes down—
Let Java or Geneva be—
But whether to the cross or crown,
The path lies through Gethsemane.[6]

The Prize Cat

Pure blood domestic, guaranteed,
Soft-mannered, musical in purr,
The ribbon had declared the breed,
Gentility was in the fur.

Such feline culture in the gads[1]
No anger ever arched her back—
What distance since those velvet pads
Departed from the leopard's track!

And when I mused how Time had thinned
The jungle strains within the cells,
How human hands had disciplined
Those prowling optic parallels;

I saw the generations pass
Along the reflex of a spring,
A bird had rustled in the grass,
The tab had caught it on the wing:

1. Part of modern Indonesia, site of fossil excavations in
1890 and again in 1931–32. Bones of an early type of
pre-historic (Neanderthal) man were discovered there;
the type was nicknamed Java Man.
2. In Switzerland, headquarters of the League of Nations
from 1919 to the Second World War.
3. Hitler, who came to power in Germany in 1933,
regarded the Aryan "race" as the only source of civilization.

4. River in modern Iraq and one of the great river valleys
of ancient Mesopotamian civilization.
5. River in western Germany and the Netherlands.
6. See Matt. xxvi. 36–56.

1. Spikes or pointed tools. Here it refers to the cat's
claws.

Behind the leap so furtive-wild
Was such ignition in the gleam,
I thought an Abyssinian[2] child
Had cried out in the whitethroat's[3] scream.

The Truant

"What have you there?" the great Panjandrum[1] said
To the Master of the Revels[2] who had led
A bucking truant with a stiff backbone
Close to the foot of the Almighty's throne.

5   "Right Reverend, most adored,
And forcibly acknowledged Lord
By the keen logic of your two-edged sword!
This creature has presumed to classify
Himself—a biped, rational, six feet high
10   And two feet wide; weighs fourteen stone;
Is guilty of a multitude of sins.
He has abjured his choric origins,
And like an undomesticated slattern,
Walks with tangential step unknown
15   Within the weave of the atomic pattern.
He has developed concepts, grins
Obscenely at your Royal bulletins,
Possesses what he calls a will
Which challenges your power to kill."

20   "What is his pedigree?"

"The base is guaranteed, your Majesty—
Calcium, carbon, phosphorus, vapour
And other fundamentals spun
From the umbilicus of the sun,
25   And yet he says he will not caper
Around your throne, nor toe the rules
For the ballet of the fiery molecules."
"His concepts and denials—scrap them, burn them—
To the chemists with them promptly."

                          "Sire,
30   The stuff is not amenable to fire.
Nothing but their own kind can overturn them.
The chemists have sent back the same old story—
'With our extreme gelatinous apology,
We beg to inform your Imperial Majesty,
35   Unto whom be dominion and power and glory,
There still remains that strange precipitate
Which has the quality to resist
Our oldest and most trusted catalyst.
It is a substance we cannot cremate
40   By temperatures known to our Laboratory.'"

2. Abyssinia, or Ethiopia, was invaded by Italy under Mussolini in 1935.
3. White-throated sparrow.

1. Originally part of a nonsense phrase, "the grand Panjandrum," invented by Samuel Foote (1720–77), English dramatist. A mock title for a self-important official. Elizabeth Brewster has suggested in conversation that Pratt's use of the adjective "great" rather than "grand" may indicate that he knew the term through a Victorian children's verse, "The Great Panjandrum himself," which was published as a picture-book in 1885 with illustrations by Randolph Caldecott.
2. Originally an official appointed to lead entertainments at the English court.

And the great Panjandrum's face grew dark—
"I'll put those chemists to their annual purge,
And I myself shall be the thaumaturge
To find the nature of this fellow's spark.
45   Come, bring him nearer by yon halter rope:
I'll analyse him with the cosmoscope."

Pulled forward with his neck awry,
The little fellow six feet short,
Aware he was about to die,
50   Committed grave contempt of court
By answering with a flinchless stare
The Awful Presence seated there.

The ALL HIGH swore until his face was black.
He called him a coprophagite,
55   A genus *homo*, egomaniac,
Third cousin to the family of worms,
A sporozoan from the ooze of night,
Spawn of a spavined troglodyte:
He swore by all the catalogue of terms
60   Known since the slang of carboniferous Time.
He said that he could trace him back
To pollywogs and earwigs in the slime.
And in his shrillest tenor he began
Reciting his indictment of the man,
65   Until he closed upon this capital crime—
"You are accused of singing out of key,
(A foul unmitigated dissonance)
Of shuffling in the measures of the dance,
Then walking out with that defiant, free
70   Toss of your head, banging the doors,
Leaving a stench upon the jacinth floors.
You have fallen like a curse
On the mechanics of my Universe.

"Herewith I measure out your penalty—
75   Hearken while you hear, look while you see:
I send you now upon your homeward route
Where you shall find
Humiliation for your pride of mind.
I shall make deaf the ear, and dim the eye,
80   Put palsy in your touch, make mute
Your speech, intoxicate your cells and dry
Your blood and marrow, shoot
Arthritic needles through your cartilage,
And having parched you with old age,
85   I'll pass you wormwise through the mire;
And when your rebel will
Is mouldered, all desire
Shrivelled, all your concepts broken,
Backward in dust I'll blow you till
90   You join my spiral festival of fire.
Go, Master of the Revels— I have spoken."

And the little genus *homo*, six feet high,
Standing erect, countered with this reply—
"You dumb insouciant invertebrate,
95   You rule a lower than a feudal state—
A realm of flunkey decimals that run,
Return; return and run; again return,
Each group around its little sun,
And every sun a satellite.

100 There they go by day and night,
Nothing to do but run and burn,
Taking turn and turn about,
Light-year in and light-year out,
Dancing, dancing in quadrillions,
105 Never leaving their pavilions.

"Your astronomical conceit
Of bulk and power is anserine.[3]
Your ignorance so thick,
You did not know your own arithmetic.
110 We flung the graphs about your flying feet;
We measured your diameter—
Merely a line
Of zeros prefaced by an integer.
Before we came
115 You had no name.
You did not know direction or your pace;
We taught you all you ever knew
Of motion, time and space.
We healed you of your vertigo
120 And put you in our kindergarten show,
Perambulated you through prisms, drew
Your mileage through the Milky Way,
Lassoed your comets when they ran astray,
Yoked Leo, Taurus, and your team of Bears
125 To pull our kiddy cars of inverse squares.

"Boast not about your harmony,
Your perfect curves, your rings
Of *pure and endless light*[4]—'Twas we
Who pinned upon your Seraphim their wings,
130 And when your brassy heavens rang
With joy that morning while the planets sang
Their choruses of archangelic lore,[5]
'Twas we who ordered the notes upon their score
Out of our winds and strings.
135 Yes! all your shapely forms
Are ours—parabolas of silver light,
Those blueprints of your spiral stairs
From nadir depth to zenith height,
Coronas, rainbows after storms,
140 Auroras on your eastern tapestries
And constellations over western seas.

"And when, one day, grown conscious of your age,
While pondering an eolith,
We turned a human page
145 And blotted out a cosmic myth
With all its baby symbols to explain
The sunlight in Apollo's eyes,
Our rising pulses and the birth of pain,
Fear, and that fern-and-fungus breath
150 Stalking our nostrils to our caves of death—
That day we learned how to anatomize
Your body, calibrate your size
And set a mirror up before your face
To show you what you really were—a rain

3. Goose-like.
4. From "The World," a poem by Henry Vaughan (1622–95), in which eternity is likened to "a great ring of pure and endless light."
5. See Job xxxviii.7.

155   Of dull Lucretian[6] atoms crowding space,
       A series of concentric waves which any fool
       Might make by dropping stones within a pool,
       Or an exploding bomb forever in flight
       Bursting like hell through Chaos and Old Night.

160   "You oldest of the hierarchs
       Composed of electronic sparks,
       We grant you speed,
       We grant you power, and fire
       That ends in ash, but we concede
165   To you no pain nor joy nor love nor hate,
       No final tableau of desire,
       No causes won or lost, no free
       Adventure at the outposts— only
       The degradation of your energy
170   When at some late
       Slow number of your dance your sergeant-major Fate
       Will catch you blind and groping and will send
       You reeling on that long and lonely
       Lockstep of your wave-lengths towards your end.

175   "We who have met
       With stubborn calm the dawn's hot fusillades;
       Who have seen the forehead sweat
       Under the tug of pulleys on the joints,
       Under the liquidating tally
180   Of the cat-and-truncheon bastinades;
       Who have taught our souls to rally
       To mountain horns and the sea's rockets
       When the needle ran demented through the points;
       We who have learned to clench
185   Our fists and raise our lightless sockets
       To morning skies after the midnight raids,
       Yet cocked our ears to bugles on the barricades,
       And in cathedral rubble found a way to quench
       A dying thirst within a Galilean valley—
190   No! by the Rood,[7] we will not join your ballet."

Cycles

There was a time we knew our foes,
Could recognize their features well,
Name them before we bartered blows;
So in our challenges could tell
5   What the damned quarrel was about,
As with our fists we slugged it out.

When distance intervened, the call
Of trumpets sped the spear and arrow;
From stone and sling to musket ball
10 The path was blasted to the marrow;
But still we kept our foes in sight,
Dusk waiting for the morning light.

We need no more that light of day,
No need of faces to be seen;
15 The squadrons in the skies we slay
Through moving shadows on a screen:
By nailing echoes under sea
We kill with like geometry.

Now since the Lord of Love is late
20 In being summoned to the ring
To keep in bounds the range of hate,
The Lord of Hosts to whom we sing
As Marshal of both man and brute
May be invoked as substitute.

---

6. Lucretius (ca. 99–55 B.C.), Roman author of a philosophical poem, *De Rerum Natura*, asserted that the basis
of all things was atoms falling through space.
7. The Cross.

25 Whether from heaven or from hell,
    May he return as referee,
    And, keen-eared to an honest bell,
    Splitting the foul from fair, feel free
    To send us forth into the lists,
30 Armed only with our naked fists.

    And then before our voice is dumb,
    Before our blood-shot eyes go blind,
    The Lord of Love and Life may come
    To lead our ebbing veins to find
35 Enough for their recovery
    Of plasma from Gethsemane.[1]

F. R. SCOTT (1889–   )

Lakeshore

    The lake is sharp along the shore
    Trimming the bevelled edge of land
    To level curves; the fretted sand
    Goes slanting down through liquid air
5   Till stones below shift here and there
    Floating upon their broken sky
    All netted by the prism wave
    And rippled where the currents are.

    I stare through windows at this cave
10 Where fish, like planes, slow-motioned, fly.
    Poised in a still of gravity
    The narrow minnow, flicking fin,
    Hangs in a paler, ochre sun,
    His doorways open everywhere.

15 And I am a tall frond that waves
    Its head below its rooted feet
    Seeking the light that leads it down
    To forest floors beyond its reach
    Vivid with gloom and Beebe[1] dreams.

20 The water's deepest colonnades
    Contract the blood, and to this home
    That stirs the dark amphibian
    With me the naked swimmers come
    Drawn to their prehistoric womb.

25 They too are liquid as they fall
    Like tumbled water loosed above
    Until they lie, diagonal,

    Within the cool and sheltered grove
    Stroked by the fingertips of love.

30 Silent, our sport is drowned in fact
    Too virginal for speech or sound
    And each is personal and laned
    Along his private aqueduct.

    Too soon the tether of the lungs
35 Is taut and straining, and we rise
    Upon our undeveloped wings
    Toward the prison of our ground
    A secret anguish in our thighs
    And mermaids in our memories.

40 This is our talent, to have grown
    Upright in posture, false-erect,
    A landed gentry, circumspect,
    Tied to a horizontal soil
    The floor and ceiling of the soul;
45 Striving, with cold and fishy care
    To make an ocean of the air.

    Sometimes, upon a crowded street,
    I feel the sudden rain come down
    And in the old, magnetic sound
50 I hear the opening of a gate
    That loosens all the seven seas.
    Watching the whole creation drown
    I muse, alone, on Ararat.

Old Song

    far voices
    and fretting leaves
    this music the
    hillside gives

    but in the deep
    Laurentian river
    an elemental song
    for ever

    a quiet calling
    of no mind
    out of long æons
    when dust was blind
    and ice hid sound

    only a moving
    with no note
    granite lips
    a stone throat

1. See Matt. xxvi.36–56.

1. Charles William Beebe (1877–1962), American author, biologist, and explorer. In 1934 he descended in a bath-ysphere to a depth of 3,028 feet to explore the life of the ocean depths. In another version of the poem the phrase was "eerie dreams."

Eden

Adam stood by a sleeping lion
Feeling its fur with his toes.
He did not hear Eve approaching,
Like a shy fawn she crept close.

5   The stillness deepened. He turned.
She stood there, too solemn for speech.
He knew that something had happened
Or she never would stay out of reach.

"What is it? What have you found?"
10 He stared as she held out her hand.
The innocent fruit was shining.
The truth burned like a brand.

"It is good to eat," she said,
"And pleasant to the eyes,
15 And—this is the reason I took it—
It is going to make us wise!"

She was like that, the beauty,
Always simple and strong.
She was leading him into trouble
20 But he could not say she was wrong.

Anyway, what could he do?
She'd already eaten it first.
She could not have all the wisdom.
He'd have to eat and be cursed.

25 So he ate, and their eyes were opened.
In a flash they knew they were nude.
Their ignorant innocence vanished.
Taste began shaping the crude.

This was no Fall, but Creation,
30 For although the Terrible Voice
Condemned them to sweat and to labour,
They had conquered the power of choice.

Even God was astonished.
"This man is become one of Us.
35 If he eat of the Tree of Life . . . !"
Out they went in a rush.

As the Flaming Sword receded
Eve walked a little ahead.
"If we keep on using this knowledge
40 I think we'll be back," she said.

The Canadian Authors Meet

Expansive puppets percolate self-unction
Beneath a portrait of the Prince of Wales.
Miss Crotchet's muse has somehow failed to function,
Yet she's a poetess. Beaming, she sails

5   From group to chattering group, with such a dear
Victorian saintliness; as is her fashion,
Greeting the other unknowns with a cheer—
Virgins of sixty who still write of passion.

The air is heavy with Canadian topics,
10 And Carman, Lampman, Roberts, Campbell, Scott,
Are measured for their faith and philanthropics,
Their zeal for God and King, their earnest thought.

The cakes are sweet, but sweeter is the feeling
That one is mixing with the *literati*;
15 It warms the old, and melts the most congealing.
Really, it is a most delightful party.

Shall we go round the mulberry bush, or shall
We gather at the river,¹ or shall we
Appoint a poet Laureate² this Fall,
20 Or shall we have another cup of tea?

O Canada, O Canada, Oh can
A day go by without new authors springing
To paint the native maple, and to plan
More ways to set the selfsame welkin ringing?

1. From the refrain of an evangelical hymn.
2. In England, the official court poet. In 1921, at its
founding meeting, the Canadian Authors' Association, the
body satirized in this poem, acclaimed Bliss Carman as an
unofficial Canadian poet Laureate.

Bonne Entente

The advantages of living with two cultures
Strike one at every turn,
Especially when one finds a notice in an office building:
"This elevator will not run on Ascension Day";
Or reads in the *Montreal Star*:
"Tomorrow being the Feast of the Immaculate Conception,
There will be no collection of garbage in the city";
Or sees on the restaurant menu the bilingual dish:

        DEEP APPLE PIE

    TARTE AUX POMMES PROFONDES

Advice

Beware the casual need
By which the heart is bound;
Pluck out the quickening seed
That falls on stony ground.

Forgo the shallow gain,
The favour of an hour.
Escape, by early pain,
The death before the flower.

Dancing

Long ago
when I first danced
I danced
holding her
5 back and arm
making her move
as I moved

she was best
when she was
10 least herself
lost herself

Now I dance
seeing her
dance away from
15 me   she
looks at me
dancing   we
are closer
held in the movement of the dance
20 I no longer dance
with myself
we are two
not one
the dance
25 is one

A. J. M. SMITH (1902–80)

Like an Old Proud King in a Parable

A bitter king in anger to be gone
From fawning courtier and doting queen
Flung hollow sceptre and gilt crown away,
And breaking bound of all his counties green
He made a meadow in the northern stone
And breathed a palace of inviolable air
To cage a heart that carolled like a swan,
And slept alone, immaculate and gay,
With only his pride for a paramour.

O who is that bitter king? It is not I.

Let me, I beseech thee, Father, die
From this fat royal life, and lie

As naked as a bridegroom by his bride,
And let that girl be the cold goddess Pride:

And I will sing to the barren rock
Your difficult, lonely music, heart,
Like an old proud king in a parable.

Ode: On the Death of William Butler Yeats

An old thorn tree in a stony place
Where the mountain stream has run dry,
Torn in the black wind under the race
Of the icicle-sharp kaleidoscopic white sky,
5   Bursts into sudden flower.

Under the central dome of winter and night
A wild swan spreads his fanatic wing.
Ancestralled energy of blood and power
Beats in his sinewy breast. And now the ravening
10   Soul, fulfilled, his first-last hour
      Upon him, chooses to exult.

Over the edge of shivering Europe,
Over the chalk front of Kent, over Eire,
Dwarfing the crawling waves' amoral savagery,
15   Daring the hiding clouds' rhetorical tumult,
      The white swan plummets the mountain top.

The stream has suddenly pushed the papery leaves!
It digs a rustling channel of clear water
On the scarred flank of Ben Bulben.[1]
20   The twisted tree is incandescent with flowers.
The swam leaps singing into the cold air:
      This is a glory not for an hour:

      Over the Galway shore
      The white bird is flying
25   Forever, and crying
      To the tumultuous throng
Of the sky his cold and passionate song.

The Lonely Land

Cedar and jagged fir
uplift sharp barbs
against the gray
and cloud-piled sky;
5   and in the bay
blown spume and windrift
and thin, bitter spray
snap
at the whirling sky;
10   and the pine trees
lean one way.

A wild duck calls
to her mate,
and the ragged
15   and passionate tones
stagger and fall,
and recover,
and stagger and fall,
on these stones—
20   are lost
in the lapping of water
on smooth, flat stones.

1. Mountain in County Sligo, Ireland, near where Yeats is
buried.

This is a beauty
of dissonance,
25 this resonance
of stony strand,
this smoky cry
curled over a black pine
like a broken
30 and wind-battered branch
when the wind

bends the tops of the pines
and curdles the sky
from the north.

35 This is the beauty
of strength
broken by strength
and still strong.

The Fountain

This fountain sheds her flowery spray
Like some enchanted tree of May
Immortalized in feathery frost
With nothing but its fragrance lost.
Yet nothing has been done amiss
In this white metamorphosis,
For fragrance here has grown to form,
And Time is fooled, although he storm.

Through Autumn's sodden disarray
These blossoms fall, but not away;
They build a tower of silver light
Where Spring holds court in Winter's night;
And while chaotic darkness broods
The golden groves to solitudes,
Here shines, in this transfigured spray,
The cold, immortal ghost of day.

The Adolescence of Leda[1]

Observe this youthful, rather sexy swan
    Rolling his downy neck among the reeds,
        Framed in a crystalline flat space of water.

Here in the tedium of the afternoon
    The Princess comes, and sews, or dreams, or reads,
        Fleeing her girl-friends' innocent chatter.

Look how he paddles his brick-red feet,
    Silently gliding into the dubious shade
        Of an old low twisted overhanging alder,

Where water midges, many a shining fleet,
    (U.S. destroyers at Villefranche[2] displayed)
        Anchor until declining day grows colder.

Now watch! To please the girl his snowy plume
    Like a pure flower in the shaggy green
        Rises and rustles—Stifle your clownish laughter!

See, she lies panting in the mossy gloom
    Of tunnelled boughs—but no, the willows screen
    All that portends, now and hereafter.

News of the Phoenix

They say the Phoenix[1] is dying, some say dead.
Dead without issue is what one message said,
But that has been suppressed, officially denied.

I think myself the man who sent it lied.
In any case, I'm told, he has been shot,
As a precautionary measure, whether he did or not.

1. In Greek myth, Zeus took the form of a swan in order
to approach Leda; see Yeats's "Leda and the Swan."
2. French town on the Mediterranean near Nice.

1. A fabulous bird which lived in the desert for five
hundred years, then burnt itself to ashes on a pyre and
emerged renewed to go through the same cycle repeated-
ly—hence a symbol of regeneration and the life cycle.

A. M. KLEIN (1909–72)

Out of the Pulver[1] and the Polished Lens

i.
The paunchy sons of Abraham[2]
Spit on the maculate streets of Amsterdam,
Showing Spinoza, Baruch *alias* Benedict,[3]
He and his God are under interdict.

5   Ah, what theology there is in spatted spittle,
And in anathema what sacred prose
Winnowing the fact from the suppose!
Indeed, what better than these two things can whittle
The scabrous heresies of Yahweh's[4] foes,
10   Informing the breast where Satan gloats and crows
That saving it leave false doctrine, jot and tittle,
No vigilant thumb will leave its orthodox nose?
What better than ram's horn blown,
And candles blown out by maledictory breath,
15   Can bring the wanderer back to his very own,
The infidel back to his faith?

Nothing, unless it be that from the ghetto
A soldier of God advance to teach the creed,
Using as rod the irrefutable stiletto.

ii.
20   Uriel da Costa[5]
Flightily ranted
Heresies one day,
Next day recanted.

Rabbi and bishop,
25   Each vies to smuggle
Soul of da Costa
Out of its struggle.

Confessional hears his
Glib paternoster;
30   Synagogue sees his
Penitent posture.

What is the end of
This catechism?
Bullet brings dogma
35   That suffers no schism.

iii.
Malevolent scorpions befoul thy chambers,
O my heart; they scurry across its floor,
Leaving the slimy vestiges of doubt.

1. Powder, dust (obsolete). Cf. pulverize.
2. Jews.
3. Baruch (Benedict) de Spinoza (1632–77), born to a family of exiled Portuguese Jews living in Amsterdam, made his living as a lens-grinder. He developed a philosophic system based on a kind of pantheism: God is revealed not in the Scriptures but in the world; hence everything is an aspect of God. Morality is based on the "intellectual love" of God because love of God necessitates love of our fellow creatures. He was excommunicated from his synagogue because his views implied that the Scriptures were unimportant. He died of consumption in The Hague.
4. Hebrew name of God (Jehovah).
5. Uriel da Costa (1590–1647) was born in Portugal to a Jewish family who had converted to Roman Catholicism under pressure from the Inquisition; he reconverted to Judaism and moved to more tolerant Amsterdam. Becoming impatient with the rigidity of the Jewish community there, he wrote several rationalist attacks on it and was twice excommunicated and twice recanted. Eventually the humiliation of recantation led him to shoot himself.

Banish memento of the vermin; let
40 No scripture on the wall affright you; no
Ghost of da Costa; no, nor any threat.
Ignore, O heart, even as didst ignore
The bribe of florins jingling in the purse.

iv.

Jehovah is factotum of the rabbis;
45 And Christ endures diurnal Calvary;
Polyglot God is exiled to the churches;
Synods tell God to be or not to be.

The Lord within his vacuum of heaven
Discourses his domestic policies,
50 With angels who break off their loud hosannas
To help him phrase infallible decrees.

Soul of Spinoza, Baruch Spinoza bids you,
Forsake the god suspended in mid-air,
Seek you that other Law, and let Jehovah
55 Play his game of celestial solitaire.

v.

   Reducing providence to theorems, the horrible
atheist compiled such lore that proved, like proving
two and two make four, that in the crown of God we
all are gems. From glass and dust of glass he brought
60 to light, out of the pulver and the polished lens, the
prism and the flying mote; and hence the infinitesimal
and infinite.
   Is it a marvel, then, that he forsook the abracadabra
of the synagogue, and holding with timelessness a duo-
65 logue, deciphered a new scripture in the book? Is it
a marvel that he left old fraud for passion intellectual
of God?

vi.

Unto the crown of bone cry *Suzerain!*[6]
Do genuflect before the jewelled brain!
70 Lavish the homage of the vassal; let
The blood grow heady with strong epithet;
Or cirque of the Cabbalist![7] O proud skull!
Of alchemy. O crucible!
Sanctum sanctorum;[8] grottoed hermitage
75 Where sits the bearded sage!
O golden bowl of Koheleth![9] and of fate
O hourglass within the pate!
Circling, O planet in the occiput![10]
O Macrocosm, sinew-shut!
80 Yea, and having uttered this loud *Te Deum*[11]
Ye have been singularly dumb.

vii.

I am weak before the wind; before the sun
    I faint; I lose my strength;
I am utterly vanquished by a star;
85   I go to my knees, at length

6. Feudal overlord.
7. Student of the Cabbala or Kabbalah, esoteric and mystical teachings of Judaism.
8. (Latin) Holy of holies— the inner sanctuary of the temple. See Exod. xxvi.34.
9. Hebrew name for the Book of Ecclesiastes. For the golden bowl, see Eccl. xii.6.
10. The head, specifically the back of the head.
11. Latin hymn of praise, beginning *Te Deum laudamus*, "we praise Thee our God."

Before the song of a bird; before
  The breath of spring or fall
I am lost; before these miracles
  I am nothing at all.

viii.

90   Lord, accept my hallelujahs; look not askance at
these my petty words; unto perfection a fragment
makes its prayer.
    For thou art the world, and I am part thereof; thou
art the blossom and I its fluttering petal.
95   I behold thee in all things, and in all things: lo, it
is myself; I look into the pupil of thine eye, it is my
very countenance I see.

    Thy glory fills the earth; it is the earth; the noise
of the deep, the moving of many waters, is it not thy
100   voice aloud, O Lord, aloud that all may hear?
    The wind through the almond-trees spreads the fra-
grance of thy robes; the turtle-dove twittering utters
diminutives of thy love; at the rising of the sun I behold thy countenance.

105   Yea, and in the crescent moon, thy little finger's
finger-nail.
    If I ascend up into heaven, thou art there; If I make
my bed in hell, behold thou art there.
    Thou art everywhere; a pillar to thy sanctuary is
110   every blade of grass.
    Wherefore I said to the wicked, Go to the ant, thou
sluggard, seek thou an audience with God.
    On the swift wings of a star, even on the numb legs
of a snail, thou dost move, O Lord.
115   A babe in swaddling clothes laughs at the sunbeams
on the door's lintel; the sucklings play with thee; with
thee Kopernik[12] holds communion through a lens.
    I am thy son, O Lord, and brother to all that lives
am I.
120   The flowers of the field, they are kith and kin to
me; the lily my sister, the rose is my blood and flesh.
    Even as the stars in the firmament move, so does my
inward heart, and even as the moon draws the tides
in the bay, so does it the blood in my veins.
125   For thou art the world, and I am part thereof;
    Howbeit, even in dust I am resurrected; and even
in decay I live again.

ix.

Think of Spinoza, then, not as you think
Of Shabbathai Zvi[13] who for a time of life
130   Took to himself the Torah for a wife,
And underneath the silken canopy
Made public: Thou art hallowed unto me.

12. Nicholas Copernicus (or Koppernik) (1473–1543),
Polish astronomer who put forth the theory that the
planets, including the earth, revolve around the sun.
13. Or Shabbetai Zevi (1628–76), cabbalist of Smyrna,
who proclaimed himself Messiah and did other bizarre
things, such as celebrating his own marriage with the
Torah (the Pentateuch, the Law) under a canopy as is
customary at Jewish weddings.

Think of Spinoza, rather, plucking tulips
Within the garden of Mynheer,[14] forgetting
135   Dutchmen and Rabbins, and consumptive fretting,
Plucking his tulips in the Holland sun,
Remembering the thought of the Adored,
Spinoza, gathering flowers for the One,
The ever-unwedded lover of the Lord.

The Still Small Voice[1]

The candles splutter; and the kettle hums;
The heirloomed clock enumerates the tribes,
Upon the wine-stained table-cloth lie crumbs
Of matzoh[2] whose wide scattering describes
Jews driven in far lands upon this earth.
The kettle hums; the candles splutter; and
Winds whispering from shutters tell re-birth
Of beauty rising in an eastern land,

Of paschal sheep driven in cloudy droves;
Of almond-blossoms colouring the breeze;
Of vineyards upon verdant terraces;
Of golden globes in orient orange-groves.
And those assembled at the table dream
Of small schemes that an April wind doth scheme,
And cry from out the sleep assailing them:
Jerusalem, next year! Next year, Jerusalem![3]

Reb[1] Levi Yitschok Talks to God

Reb Levi Yitschok, crony of the Lord,
Familiar of heaven, broods these days.
His heart erupts in sighs. He will have a word
At last, with Him of the mysterious ways.

5   He will go to the synagogue of Berditchev,[2]
And there sieve out his plaints in a dolorous sieve.

Rebono shel Olam[3]—he begins—
Who helps you count our little sins?
Whosoever it be, saving Your grace,
10   I would declare before his face,
He knows no ethics,
No, nor arithmetics.

For if from punishments we judge the sins,
Thy midget Hebrews, even when they snore,
15   Are most malefic djinns,[4]
And wicked to the core of their heart's core;
Not so didst thou consider them,
Thy favourite sons of yore.
How long wilt thou ordain it, Lord, how long
20   Will Satan fill his mickle-mouth with mirth,
Beholding him free, the knave who earned the thong,
And Israel made the buttocks of the earth?

The moon grinned from the window-pane; a cat
Standing upon a gable, humped and spat;
25   *Somewhere a loud mouse nibbled at a board,*
A spider wove a niche in the House of the Lord.

---

14. (Dutch) Sir, Mr.

1. See 1 Kings xix.22.
2. Unleavened bread eaten at Passover. See Exod.
xii.15–20.
3. The phrase "Next year in Jerusalem," spoken at the

Passover meal, expressed the desire of the Jews of the
Diaspora to return to Israel.

1. Rabbi, Teacher.
2. A town in Volhynia in the Ukraine.
3. (Hebrew) Master of the Universe.
4. Spirits productive of evil. "Djinns" is Arabic.

Reb Levi Yitschok talking to himself,
Addressed his infant arguments to God:
Why hast thou scattered him like biblic dust,
30   To make a union with unhallowed sod,
Building him temples underneath a mound,
Compatriot of the worm in rain-soaked ground?

The lion of Judah!⁵ no such parable
Is on my lips; no lion, nor lion's whelp,
35   But a poor bag'o'bones goat which seeks thy help,
A scrawny goat, its rebel horns both broken,
Its beard uncouthly plucked, its tongue so dumbly lolling
Even its melancholy ma-a- remains unspoken.

The candles flicker,
40   *And peeping through the windows, the winds snicker.*
The mice digest some holy rune,
And gossip of the cheeses of the moon . . .

Where is the trumpeted Messiah? Where
The wine long-soured into vinegar?
45   Have cobwebs stifled his mighty shofar?⁶ Have
Chilblains weakened his ass's one good hoof?

So all night long Reb Levi Yitschok talked,
Preparing words on which the Lord might brood.
How long did even angels guard a feud?
50   When would malign Satanas be unfrocked?
Why were the tortured by their echoes mocked?
Who put Death in his ever-ravenous mood?
Good men groaned; Hunger; bad men belched of food;
Wherefore? And why? Reb Levi Yitschok talked . . .
55   Vociferous was he in his monologue.
He raged, he wept. He suddenly went mild
Begging the Lord to lead him through the fog;
Reb Levi Yitschok, an ever-querulous child,
Sitting on God's knees in the synagogue,
60   Unanswered even when the sunrise smiled.

Psalm IV: A Psalm of Abraham, Touching His Green Pastures

From pastures green, whereon I lie,
Beside still waters, far from crowds,
I lift hosannahs to the sky
And hallelujahs to the clouds,

Only to see where clouds should sit,
And in that space the sky should fill,
The fierce carnivorous Messerschmidt,
The Heinkel¹ on the kill.

They'll not be green for very long,
Those pastures of my peace, nor will
The heavens be a place for song,
Nor the still waters still.

---

5. See Gen. xlix.9 and Hos. v.14.
6. Ceremonial horn sounded on holy days and solemn
occasions.

1. Fighter planes of the German Luftwaffe in World War
II.

Pastoral of the City Streets

I

Between distorted forests, clapped into geometry,
in meadows of macadam,
heat-fluff-a-host-of-dandelions dances on the air.
Everywhere glares the sun's glare,
5   the asphalt shows hooves.

           In meadows of macadam
grazes the dray horse, nozzles his bag of pasture,
is peaceful. Now and then flicks through farmer straw
his ears, like pulpit-flowers; quivers
10   his hide; swishes his tempest tail
a black and sudden nightmare for the fly.
The sun shines, sun shines down
new harness on his withers, saddle, and rump.

On curbrock and on stairstump the clustered kids
15   resting let slide some afternoon: then restless
hop to the game of the sprung haunches; skid
to the safe place; jump up: stir a wind in the heats:
laugh, puffed and sweat-streaked.

O for the crystal stream!

20   Comes a friend's father
with his pet of a hose,
and plays the sidewalk black
cavelike and cool.

O crisscross beneath the spray, those pelting petals and peas
25   those white soft whisks
brushing off heat!
O underneath these acrobatic fountains
among the crystal,
like raindrops a sunshower of youngsters dance:
30   small-nippled self-hugged boys
and girls with water sheer, going *Ah* and *Ah*.

II

And at twilight,
the sun like a strayed neighbourhood creature
having been chased
35   back to its cover
the children count a last game, or talk, or rest,
beneath the bole of the tree of the single fruit of glass
now ripening,
a last game, talk, or rest,
40   until mothers like evening birds call from the stoops.

Monsieur Gaston

You remember the big Gaston, for whom everyone predicted
a bad end?—
Gaston, the neighbour's gossip and his mother's cross?
You remember him *vaurien*,[1] always out of a job,
5   with just enough clinking coinage
for pool, bright neckties, and blondes,—

---

1. (French) Good-for-nothing.

the scented Gaston in the poolroom lolling
in meadows of green baize?
In clover now. Through politics. *Monsieur* Gaston.

10   They say the Minister of a certain department does not move
without him; and they say, to make it innocent,—
chauffeur.
But everyone understands. Why, wherever our Gaston smiles
a nightclub rises and the neons flash.
15   To his slightest whisper
the bottled rye, like a fawning pet-dog, gurgles.
The burlesque queen will not undress
unless Monsieur Gaston says yes.
And the Madame will shake her head behind the curtain-rods
20   unless he nods.

A changed man, Gaston; almost a civil servant,
keeps records, appointments, women; speaks tough English;
is very much respected.
You should hear with what greetings his distinguished approach is greeted;
25   you should see the gifts he gets,
with compliments for his season.

Portrait of the Poet as Landscape[1]

I

Not an editorial-writer, bereaved with bartlett,[2]
mourns him, the shelved Lycidas.[3]
No actress squeezes a glycerine tear for him.
The radio broadcast lets his passing pass.
5   And with the police, no record. Nobody, it appears,
either under his real name or his alias,
missed him enough to report.

It is possible that he is dead, and not discovered.
It is possible that he can be found some place
10   in a narrow closet, like the corpse in a detective story,
standing, his eyes staring, and ready to fall on his face.
It is also possible that he is alive
and amnesiac, or mad, or in retired disgrace,
or beyond recognition lost in love.

15   We are sure only that from our real society
he has disappeared; he simply does not count,
except in the pullulation of vital statistics—
somebody's vote, perhaps, an anonymous taunt
of the Gallup poll, a dot in a government table—
20   but not felt, and certainly far from eminent—
in a shouting mob, somebody's sigh.

O, he who unrolled our culture from his scroll[4]—
the prince's quote, the rostrum-rounding roar—
who under one name made articulate
25   heaven, and under another the seven-circled air,[5]

1. Klein's original title was "Portrait of the Poet as
Nobody."
2. John Bartlett's *Familiar Quotations*, originally pub
lished in 1855, was a standard source of proverbial wisdom.
3. Title and subject of a pastoral elegy by John Milton.
Lycidas is the conventional pastoral name Milton gave to
Edward King, a young poet who drowned in the Irish Sea
in 1637.
4. The first scroll is the Torah, the record of God's
creative and culture-defining words. The poet's activity is
thus an imitation of God's.
5. The Spheres of the sun, moon, and five visible planets
which, according to the old Ptolemaic system, moved
around the earth.

is, if he is at all, a number, an x,
a Mr. Smith in a hotel register,—
incognito, lost, lacunal.

II

The truth is he's not dead, but only ignored—
30   like the mirroring lenses forgotten on a brow
that shine with the guilt of their unnoticed world.
The truth is he lives among neighbours, who, though they will allow
him a passable fellow, think him eccentric, not solid,
a type that one can forgive, and for that matter, forego.

35   Himself he has his moods, just like a poet.
Sometimes, depressed to nadir, he will think all lost,
will see himself as throwback, relict, freak,
his mother's miscarriage, his great-grandfather's ghost,
and he will curse his quintuplet senses, and their tutors
40   in whom he put, as he should not have put, his trust.

Then he will remember his travels over that body—
the torso verb, the beautiful face of the noun,
and all those shaped and warm auxiliaries!
A first love it was, the recognition of his own.
45   Dear limbs adverbial, complexion of adjective,
dimple and dip of conjugation!

And then remember how this made a change in him
affecting for always the glow and growth of his being;
how suddenly was aware of the air, like shaken tinfoil,
50   of the patents of nature, the shock of belated seeing,
the lonelinesses peering from the eyes of crowds;
the integers of thought; the cube-roots of feeling.

Thus, zoomed to zenith, sometimes he hopes again,
and sees himself as a character, with a rehearsed role:
55   the Count of Monte Cristo,[6] come for his revenges;
the unsuspected heir, with papers; the risen soul;
or the chloroformed prince awaking from his flowers;
or—deflated again—the convict on parole.

III

He is alone; yet not completely alone.
60   Pins on a map of a colour similar to his,
each city has one, sometimes more than one;
here, caretakers of art, in colleges;
in offices, there, with arm-bands, and green-shaded;
and there, pounding their catalogued beats in libraries,—

65   everywhere menial, a shadow's shadow.
And always for their egos—their outmoded art.
Thus, having lost the bevel in the ear,
they know neither up nor down, mistake the part
for the whole, curl themselves in a comma,
70   talk technics, make a colon their eyes. They distort—

such is the pain of their frustration—truth
to something convolute and cerebral.
How they do fear the slap of the flat of the platitude!

---

6. Title character of a novel by Alexandre Dumas, published in 1844–5. Unjustly imprisoned by his enemies, the character escapes and seeks revenge under various names.

Now Pavlov's[7] victims, their mouths water at bell,
75 the platter empty.
                    See they set twenty-one jewels
into their watches; the time they do not tell!

Some, patagonian[8] in their own esteem,
and longing for the multiplying word,
80 join party and wear pins, now have a message,
an ear, and the convention-hall's regard.
Upon the knees of ventriloquists, they own,
of their dandled brightness, only the paint and board.

And some go mystical, and some go mad.
85 One stares at a mirror all day long, as if
to recognize himself; another courts
angels,—for here he does not fear rebuff;
and a third, alone, and sick with sex, and rapt,
doodles him symbols convex and concave.

90 O schizoid solitudes! O purities
curdling upon themselves! Who live for themselves,
or for each other, but for nobody else;
desire affection, private and public loves;
are friendly, and then quarrel and surmise
95 the secret perversions of each other's lives.

IV
He suspects that something has happened, a law
been passed, a nightmare ordered. Set apart,
he finds himself, with special haircut and dress,
as on a reservation. Introvert.
100 He does not understand this; sad conjecture
muscles and palls thrombotic on his heart.

He thinks an impostor, having studied his personal biography,
his gestures, his moods, now has come forward to pose
in the shivering vacuums his absence leaves.
105 Wigged with his laurel, that other, and faked with his face,
he pats the heads of his children, pecks his wife,
and is at home, and slippered, in his house.

So he guesses at the impertinent silhouette
that talks to his phone-piece and slits open his mail.
110 Is it the local tycoon who for a hobby
plays poet, he so epical in steel?
The orator, making a pause? Or is that man
he who blows his flash of brass in the jittering hall?

Or is he cuckolded by the troubadour
115 rich and successful out of celluloid?
Or by the don who unrhymes atoms? Or
the chemist death built up? Pride, lost impostor'd pride,
it is another, another, whoever he is,
who rides where he should ride.

7. Ivan Petrovich Pavlov (1849–1936), Russian psychol-
ogist who developed the concept of the conditioned reflex
by showing that, if an animal salivates at the sight of food
while a bell is simultaneously rung, he can be conditioned
to salivate at the sound alone.
8. Gigantic. The Indians of Patagonia, in the extreme
south of South America, were reputed to be the tallest
human beings.

V

120   *Fame*, the adrenalin:[9] to be talked about;
to be a verb; to be introduced as *The:*
to smile with endorsement from slick paper; make
caprices anecdotal; to nod to the world; to see
ones name like a song upon the marquees played;
125   to be forgotten with embarrassment; to be—
to be.

It has its attractions, but is not the thing;
nor is it the ape mimesis who speaks from the tree
ancestral; nor the merkin joy...
130   Rather it is stark infelicity
which stirs him from his sleep, undressed, asleep
to walk upon roofs and window-sills and defy
the gape of gravity.

VI

Therefore he seeds illusions. Look, he is
135   the nth Adam taking a green inventory
in world but scarcely uttered, naming, praising,
the flowering fiats[10] in the meadow, the
syllabled fur, stars aspirate, the pollen
whose sweet collision sounds eternally.
140   For to praise

the world—he, solitary man—is breath
to him. Until it has been praised, that part
has not been. Item by exciting item—
air to his lungs, and pressured blood to his heart—
145   they are pulsated, and breathed, until they map,
not the world's, but his own body's chart!

And now in imagination he has climbed
another planet, the better to look
with single camera view upon this earth—
150   its total scope, and each afflated tick,
its talk, its trick, its tracklessness—and this,
this he would like to write down in a book!

To find a new function for the declassé craft
archaic like the fletcher's; to make a new thing;
155   to say the word that will become sixth sense;
perhaps by necessity and indirection bring
new forms to life, anonymously, new creeds—
O, somehow pay back the daily larcenies of the lung!

These are not mean ambitions. It is already something
160   merely to entertain them. Meanwhile, he
makes of his status as zero a rich garland,[11]
a halo of his anonymity,
and lives alone, and in his secret shines
like phosphorus.[12] At the bottom of the sea.

---

9. See *Lycidas*, ll. 70–73.
10. Words of creation (e.g., *Fiat lux*, let there be light).
11. Wreath of laurel conferred on poets by Apollo.
12. White phosphorus in its pure form glows in the dark and must be stored under water because it ignites on exposure to air. Phosphorus is essential to plant and animal life.

DOROTHY LIVESAY (1909 –   )

Signpost

Spring is forever a question
And no one really knows
Whether to dig in his garden
Or follow the flight of the crows
Led by a veering signpost—
The old wind's nose!

The Difference

Your way of loving is too slow for me.
For you, I think, must know a tree by heart
Four seasons through, and note each single leaf
With microscopic glance before it falls—
And after watching soberly the turn
Of autumn into winter and the slow
Awakening again, the rise of sap—
Then only will you cry: "I love this tree!"

As if the beauty of the thing could be
Made lovelier or marred by any mood
Of wind, or by the sun's caprice; as if
All beauty had not sprung up with the seed—
With such slow ways you find no time to love
A falling flame, a flower's brevity.

Wilderness Stone

I dreamed that I dwelt in a house
On the edge of a field
With a fire for warmth
And a roof for shield.

But when I awoke I saw
There was nothing at all
But rain for my roof
And wind for my wall.

Dark ways we led each other, though we sought
Only to catch the sun—
A happiness quick shared before the night:
Once to possess, and then divide the joy
Was all our thought. But somewhere evil crept
A twisted thing, between us, broke the blades
Of grass, the flowers grown round us close,

Shattered the laughter that was clean
As morning air, that we had tossed between us.
And so we lost the way—you mine, I yours,
And quarrelled in the darkness— we who still
Were longing to be kind, to do no hurt.
Two innocents expelled, outside the gate.

Day and Night

1

Dawn, red and angry, whistles loud and sends
A geysered shaft of steam searching the air.
Scream after scream announces that the churn
Of life must move, the giant arm command.
5   Men in a stream, a moving human belt
Move into sockets, every one a bolt.
The fun begins, a humming, whirring drum—
Men do a dance in time to the machines.

2

One step forward
Two steps back[1]
Shove the lever,
Push it back

While Arnot whirls
A roundabout
And Geoghan[2] shuffles
Bolts about.

One step forward
Hear it crack
Smashing rhythm—
Two steps back

Your heart-beat pounds
Against your throat
The roaring voices
Drown your shout

Across the way
A writhing whack
Sets you spinning
Two steps back—

One step forward
Two steps back.

3

Day and night are rising and falling
Night and day shift gears and slip rattling
Down the runway, shot into storerooms
Where only arms and a note-book remember
The record of evil, the sum of commitments.
We move as through sleep's revolving memories
Piling up hatred, stealing the remnants,
Doors forever folding before us—
And where is the recompense, on what agenda
Will you set love down? Who knows of peace?

Day and night
Night and day
Light rips into ribbons
What we say.

I called to love
Deep in dream:
Be with me in the daylight
As in gloom.

1. Dorothy Livesay comments on the origin of this poem:
"This documentary is dominated by themes of struggle:
class against class, race against race. The sound of Negro
spirituals mingled in my mind with Cole Porter's "Night
and Day" and with Lenin's words (I quote from memory):
'To go two steps forward we may have to take one step
back.' That phrase captured my imagination for it seemed
to me that the capitalist system was putting that concept
into reverse" (*The Documentaries* [Toronto: Ryerson,
1968], p. 17).

Vladimir Ilyich Lenin's book about the 1903 London
Congress of the Russian Social Democratic Party was
called *One Step Forward, Two Steps Back* (1904). At this
time the party split into Bolsheviks and Mensheviks;
Lenin's book was intended to discredit the Mensheviks.
In1921, his New Economic Policy amounted to a partial
retreat from the pure Marxist principles to a re-
introduction of some capitalist methods.
2. "fictitious names . . . mechanical Robot figures"
(Dorothy Livesay in correspondence with the editor).

Be with me in the pounding
50 In the knives against my back
Set your voice resounding
Above the steel's whip crack.

High and sweet
Sweet and high
55 Hold, hold up the sunlight
In the sky!

Day and night
Night and day
Tear up all the silence
60 Find the words I could not say...

4

We were stoking coal in the furnaces; red hot
They gleamed, burning our skins away, his and mine.
We were working together, night and day, and knew
Each other's stroke; and without words, exchanged
65 An understanding about kids at home,
The landlord's jaw, wage-cuts and overtime.
We were like buddies, see? Until they said
That nigger is too smart the way he smiles
And sauces back the foreman; he might say
70 Too much one day, to others changing shifts.
Therefore they cut him down, who flowered at night
And raised me up, day hanging over night—
So furnaces could still consume our withered skin.

Shadrach, Meshach and Abednego
75 Turn in the furnace, whirling slow.[3]
        Lord, I'm burnin' in the fire
        Lord, I'm steppin' on the coals
        Lord, I'm blacker than my brother
        Blow your breath down here.

80   Boss, I'm smothered in the darkness
        Boss, I'm shrivellin' in the flames
        Boss, I'm blacker than my brother
        Blow your breath down here.
Shadrach, Meshach and Abednego
85 Burn in the furnace, whirling slow.

5

Up in the roller room, men swing steel
Swing it, zoom; and cut it, crash.
Up in the dark the welder's torch
Makes sparks fly like lightning reel.

90 Now I remember storm on a field
The trees bow tense before the blow
Even the jittering sparrows' talk
Ripples into the still tree shield.

We are in storm that has no cease
95 No lull before, no after time
When green with rain the grasses grow
And air is sweet with fresh increase.

3. See Dan. iii.8–30.

We bear the burden home to bed
The furnace glows within our hearts:
100 Our bodies hammered through the night
Are welded into bitter bread.

Bitter, yes:
But listen, friend:
We are mightier
105 In the end.

We have ears
Alert to seize
A weakness
In the foreman's ease

110 We have eyes
To look across
The bosses' profit
At our loss.

Are you waiting?
115 Wait with us
After evening
There's a hush—

Use it not
For love's slow count:
120 Add up hate
And let it mount

Until the lifeline
Of your hand
Is calloused with
125 A fiery brand!

Add up hunger,
Labour's ache
These are figures
That will make

130 The page grow crazy
Wheels go still,
Silence sprawling
On the till—

Add your hunger,
135 Brawn and bones,
Take your earnings:
Bread, not stones!

6
Into thy maw I commend my body[4]
But the soul shines without
140 A child's hands as a leaf are tender
And draw the poison out.

Green of new leaf shall deck my spirit
Laughter's roots will spread:
Though I am overalled and silent
145 Boss, I'm far from dead!

4. See Luke xxiii.46.

One step forward
Two steps back
Will soon be over:
Hear it crack!

150   The wheels may whirr
A roundabout
And neighbour's shuffle
Drown your shout

The wheel must limp
155   Till it hangs still
And crumpled men
Pour down the hill.

Day and night
Night and day
160   Till life is turned
The other way!

Page One

1
Reared on snow she was
Manacled in ice
Ten frostbound winters of her life
In bondage to this Lear
5   This blue lipped, fondling father
Whose hard chains
Clanked on her feet
Pinched the poor fingers stiff with pain.
Play, an ordeal to be endured
10   As feathery snow
Festooned the faces
Ridiculed the shapes
A rigid fence
Lay bundled on the hill
15   And snow made ladies out of trees
Those bare and gangling boys.

Feasted on snow
And cold's glass palaces she knew
The ice yard where huge blocks were river flung
20   To fortress out a field
And in the corridors of crisp
And rainbow shafted crystal
She traced the pattern of a princess' day
And was her godmother
25   And listened to her pray.

O might there always be
Those wishes three

That dazzling evanescent dress
Those pearls, those tears
30   That slipper made of glass—

But not for me.

But not for me
Whistled the winter wisdom of the wind:

35 The ice that bound her could not be her home
Native this land, but not
The boundary of her home.

2
When spring sneaked sucking at the snow
Its tongue devouring humps and hills
Sipping at icicles until they dripped
40 In ignominious patter on
The rude brown water barrel's yawn—
Then rivulets began to run
The sound of shovels rasped the air
Grinding on chunks embedded firm
45 Demanding still a further term;
And in the slush, all sparkle gone
Water began to make its home
To sigh and sing, to crack and swing
Its column in the underground.

50 At such a moment, such a day
Her head was lifted suddenly
Her ears believed, her heart heard
The sky's hallooing honking word.
Here, in this wasting winter, geese
55 Briefly for feeding came to rest
Here they were transients, who knew
Some other home lay farther on
Some grass upshaken
A forest to be taken;
60 And following their arrowed alphabet
Straining to see their jet-
Propulsion through the unstained sky
She felt her feet untried
Her winter thongs unpried.
65 She was a moving miracle of wing and sound
No one home hers, but all homes to be found.

On Looking into Henry Moore[1]

1
Sun, stun me, sustain me
Turn me to stone:
Stone, goad me and gall me
Urge me to run.

5 When I have found
Passivity in fire
And fire in stone
Female and male
I'll rise alone
10 Self-extending and self-known.

2
The message of the tree is this:
Aloneness is the only bliss

Self-adoration is not in it
(Narcissus tried, but could not win it)

15 Rather, to extend the root
Tombwards, be at home with death

But in the upper branches know
A green eternity of fire and snow.

3
The fire in the farthest hills
20 Is where I'd burn myself to bone:
Clad in the armour of the sun
I'd stand anew, alone

Take off this flesh, this hasty dress
Prepare my half-self for myself:
25 One unit, as a tree or stone
Woman in man, and man in womb.

1. English sculptor (1898–), of whom Livesay has said: "I think he was androgynous. He saw the humanity of man and woman, the complete thing, which I've been striving to express." (Interview with Alan Twigg, *NeWest Review*, 5 February 1980, p. 4.)

The Unquiet Bed

The woman I am
is not what you see
I'm not just bones
and crockery

the woman I am
knew love and hate
hating the chains
that parents make

longing that love
might set men free
yet hold them fast
in loyalty

the woman I am
is not what you see
move over love
make room for me

Introduction: 1945-80

Perhaps we should call our era "The Age of X." It is part of the nature of our second half of the twentieth century that we expect to be faced with an unnamed quantity every week. Afghanistan and Chile come to us not through history but as quick daily events on colour video tapes. The arts, too, resemble child prodigies who have left home early. Dante knew that he could give years to fashioning his premeditated *Divine Comedy* because one could assume that, well after he was finished, his civilization would hold the vision of heaven, earth, and hell that fed his imagination before he began. In our time a poet is likely to present a destroyed work because, while resting between efforts, he read in the paper that life on earth has been here a billion years longer than formerly imagined.

Meanwhile three thousand poems have been published, and their authors are going back to their desks. It is no wonder that there is no canon for contemporary verse. It is only now that the Modernist period of before and after World War I is settling into the standard anthologies and organizing itself around the great figures of W. B. Yeats, T. S. Eliot, Ezra Pound, and William Carlos Williams. So any collection of poets since World War II will necessarily be a package of samples.

The Modernist poets often saw the new century as an age that was overturning ideas of order long composed by political thought and religious belief. The survival of order was to be sought in art itself. Some Modernists looked to the tradition for bearings; others wanted to up-end the museums and build something new from the debris.

But the poets of our time in Britain, Canada, and the United States were born in the twentieth century. To them it has been the normal thing to buy a new map of Africa every year, or to open a new book of verse and see a concrete poem spring into the air. "What does not change / is the will to change," wrote Charles Olson shortly after World War II. Olson is probably speaking not only of our time, but also from a New World stance. In every country there are those poets who try to maintain an orderly voice in the middle of a riot, and those who speak loudly into a tape recorder while they are being whirled through the air toward Oz. (And there are many poets in the centre who look askance at both extremes.) In our time the British poets, though they include some rock and roll crazies, tend toward a nostalgic humanism, the meticulous decent calm of Philip Larkin or the confident craftsmanship of Basil Bunting, whose lines are informed by Northumberland Quaker stonemasons and the chamber music of Vivaldi.

There are genteel poets in the United States, too: the reasonable New England brahmin Robert Lowell, or pastoral empiricist W. S. Merwin, who hears a stream playing its flute and not roiling with industrial waste. But the Americans are more likely to open their ears to extreme forms; whereas the British poets seem to be writing meditatively, composing in more-or-less regular metres *about* the world they have seen this year, the American poets consider the act of writing to be the task of the scribe at the edge, to get down in whatever way possible the voice or voices that are coming unannounced from God-knows-where. Thus there is Frank O'Hara, curator at New York's Museum of Modern Art, making poems that could be hung with the works of the Action painters, or Robert Duncan on the other side of the continent, proposing that his lines are mysteriously dictated to highly educated fingers that partake of mind rather than serve it.

Canadian poetry in English has, since the end of World War II, come to disresemble British poetry and has taken on New World configurations. Whereas Canadian verse in the thirties often derived from Stephen Spender and W. H. Auden, in the seventies it could be the language of a planet fantasized by Jorge Luis Borges. Much of Canada's recent poetry articulates an uncovering of experiential citizenship. John Newlove's "The Pride" announces that the bones on the prairie are more clearly his ancestors than are the names in Old World churchyards. Margaret Atwood and Al Purdy both direct our senses to the remains of human marks made on their portion of the continent.

Yet we live as beings aware of their mortality have always lived, in the geography of language. Poet bpNichol builds, or rather makes visible, an environment of words and their elements. Margaret Avison's English does not describe the experience of the human spirit, but probes it with necessary and beautiful respect, a syllable at a time. James Reaney's "First Letter: To the Avon River above Stratford, Canada" is one of Canada's most important poems, focusing as it does upon the revealed body of language in order to realize the baptism of a renewed mind in a post-colonial world.

One of the most noteworthy changes brought about in our century has been the land-rush made by the muse of English-language poetry. A hundred years ago English poetry was one of the great possessions of Imperial Britain, and superior verse in the language around the globe was rare. Even in the Modernist period, when half the best English poetry was written by non-Britons, many of those foreigners were living in England or nearby. But in our half of the century Britain is only one of the custodians of the language and its art. Poets in New Zealand, Singapore, or Trinidad no longer feel as if they are feeding into the hopper at Oxford when they practise their occupation. In the past few decades the British poets have come in great numbers to live and write among the people of the New World, much as Eliot and Pound and H. D. migrated to London half a hundred years earlier.

But in "The Age of X" it is no more than one interesting strategy for the poet to set up in a cottage where Coleridge once mused. Allen Ginsberg's vision in the Wales of Tintern Abbey flashes in a present also graved by his vision on a railroad dock at San Francisco Bay. But neither manifestation will define the late-twentieth century design. One can wager that there is a poet recently emigrated from Morawhanna to Glace Bay, and she is being visited by the muse of lyric poetry at this very moment.

George Bowering

BASIL BUNTING (1900 –   )

From Briggflatts[1]

I

Brag, sweet tenor bull,
descant on Rawthey's madrigal,[2]
each pebble its part
for the fells'[3] late spring.
5 Dance tiptoe, bull,
black against may.
Ridiculous and lovely
chase hurdling shadows
morning into noon.
10 May[4] on the bull's hide
and through the dale
furrows fill with may,
paving the slowworm's way.[5]

A mason times his mallet
15 to a lark's twitter,
listening while the marble rests,
lays his rule
at a letter's edge,
fingertips checking,
20 till the stone spells a name
naming none,
a man abolished.
Painful lark, labouring to rise!
The solemn mallet says:
25 In the grave's slot
he lies. We rot.

Decay thrusts the blade,
wheat stands in excrement
trembling. Rawthey trembles.
30 Tongue stumbles, ears err
for fear of spring.
Rub the stone with sand,
wet sandstone rending
roughness away. Fingers
35 ache on the rubbing stone.
The mason says: Rocks
happen by chance.
No one here bolts the door,
love is so sore.

40 Stone smooth as skin,
cold as the dead they load
on a low lorry[6] by night.
The moon sits on the fell
but it will rain.
45 Under sacks on the stone
two children lie,
hear the horse stale,[7]
the mason whistle,
harness mutter to shaft,
50 felloe[8] to axle squeak,
rut thud the rim,
crushed grit.

Stocking to stocking, jersey to jersey,
head to a hard arm,
55 they kiss under the rain,
bruised by their marble bed.
In Garsdale,[9] dawn;
at Hawes,[10] tea from the can.
Rain stops, sacks
60 steam in the sun, they sit up.
Copper-wire moustache,
sea-reflecting eyes
and Baltic plainsong speech
declare: By such rocks
65 men killed Bloodaxe.[11]

Fierce blood throbs in his tongue,
lean words.
Skulls cropped for steel caps
huddle round Stainmore.[12]
70 Their becks[13] ring on limestone,
whisper to peat.
The clogged cart pushes the horse downhill.
In such soft air
they trudge and sing,
75 laying the tune frankly on the air.
All sounds fall still,
fellside bleat,
hide-and-seek peewit.[14]

---

1. This is the first of four sections of *Briggflatts*, subtitled
"An Autobiography." Named after a Quaker community
in Northumberland, in northeast England. The poem is
often read to Vivaldi's *The Seasons*.
2. A madrigal is a lyric poem on a pastoral subject. A
descant is an ornamental counterpoint. Here they are
performed by the natural elements at Briggflatts, including the Rawthey River.
3. Northern English moorlands.
4. The flower of the hawthorn.
5. A legless lizard.

6. An English truck.
7. Urinate.
8. Outer circle of wheel.
9. Small town in region.
10. Small town in region.
11. Eric Bloodaxe: "Piece his story together from the
Anglo-Saxon Chronicle, the Orkneyinga Saga, and
Heimskringla, as you fancy." (Bunting's note.)
12. Stainmore Pass, North Durham: local place name.
13. Brooks.
14. Lapwing, a bird.

Her pulse their pace,
80 palm countering palm,
till a trench is filled,
stone white as cheese
jeers at the dale.
Knotty wood, hard to rive,
85 smoulders to ash;
smell of October apples.
The road again,
at a trot.
Wetter, warmed, they watch
90 the mason meditate
on name and date.

Rain rinses the road,
the bull streams and laments.
Sour rye porridge from the hob
95 with cream and black tea,
meat, crust and crumb.
Her parents in bed
the children dry their clothes.
He has untied the tape
100 of her striped flannel drawers
before the range. Naked
on the pricked rag mat
his fingers comb
thatch of his manhood's home.

105 Gentle generous voices weave
over bare night
words to confirm and delight
till bird dawn.
Rainwater from the butt[15]
110 she fetches and flannel
to wash him inch by inch,
kissing the pebbles.
Shining slowworm part of the marvel.
The mason stirs:
115 Words!
Pens are too light.
Take a chisel to write.

Every birth a crime,
every sentence life.
120 Wiped of mould and mites
would the ball run true?
No hope of going back.
Hounds falter and stray,
shame deflects the pen.
125 Love murdered neither bleeds nor stifles
but jogs the draftsman's elbow.
What can he, changed, tell
her, changed, perhaps dead?
Delight dwindles. Blame
130 stays the same.

Brief words are hard to find,
shapes to carve and discard:
Bloodaxe, king of York,
king of Dublin, king of Orkney.[16]
135 Take no notice of tears;
letter the stone to stand
over love laid aside lest
insufferable happiness impede
flight to Stainmore,
140 to trace
lark, mallet,
becks, flocks
and axe knocks.

Dung will not soil the slowworm's
145 mosaic. Breathless lark
drops to nest in sodden trash;
Rawthey truculent, dingy.
Drudge at the mallet, the may is down,
fog on fells. Guilty of spring
150 and spring's ending
amputated years ache after
the bull is beef, love a convenience.
It is easier to die than to remember.
Name and date
155 split in soft slate
a few months obliterate.

What the Chairman Told Tom[1]

Poetry? It's a hobby.
I run model trains.
Mr Shaw there breeds pigeons.

It's not work. You dont sweat.
5 Nobody pays for it.
You *could* advertise soap.

Art, that's opera; or repertory—
The Desert Song.[2]
Nancy was in the chorus.

10 But to ask for twelve pounds a week—
married, aren't you?—
you've got a nerve.

How could I look a bus conductor
in the face
15 if I paid you twelve pounds?

Who says it's poetry, anyhow?
My ten year old
can do it *and* rhyme.

I get three thousand and expenses,
20 a car, vouchers,
but I'm an accountant.

They do what I tell them,
my company.
What do *you* do?

15. Barrel.
16. Scottish island, conquered by Norway in 1093.

1. Tom Pickard, poet from Newcastle-on-Tyne.
2. Exotic operetta by Sigmund Romberg.

25 Nasty little words, nasty long words,
it's unhealthy.
I want to wash when I meet a poet.

They're Reds, addicts,
all delinquents.
30 What you write is rot.

Mr Hines says so, and he's a schoolteacher,
he ought to know.
Go and find *work*.

STEVIE SMITH (1902–71)

A Father for a Fool

Little Master Home-from-School
This is the Parkland you must rule,
What does it feel like to have a father for a fool?
Your father mortgaged the estate
5 Lost his money and blamed fate,
And shot himself through the head too late.
There's a father for a fool,
My little Master Home-from-School.

Why does Auntie wear such funny hats
10 And invert her sentences, now that's
Positive proof she must be bats.
Why has Parker got all the horses out for me?
Why doesn't Ma meet the train as usually?
Here's hoping they give us shrimps for tea.

15 Little Master Home-from-School
Your Ma lies dead, she lies too cool,
She's stone-cold dead of a broken heart, the fool.
Jingle-jog the horse go,
And Parker's thinking what I know:
20 Here comes Master Home-from-School
That had a father for a fool.

Louise

Why is the child so pale,
Sitting alone in that sawny[1] way
On an upturned valise
In a suburban sitting-room?
5 Louise,
Can't you give moma a smile?
Come and say How-do-you-do
To Mr Tease.

Why is the child so pale?
10 They have come overnight by rail
From Budapest;
Oh the poor child.

And the money has given out,
And they've telegraphed home for more,
15 And meanwhile they are having to stay
In a small-beerish way

1. Simpleton.

With Mr and Mrs Tease, as I have said,
Of Harringay Park, instead
Of having a comfortable bed
20   At the Ritz.

The child is pale and precocious,
She knows all the capitals of Europe,
She knows all there is to know about Wagons-Lits[2]
And First Class accommodation,
25   But she has never been long enough in any nation
Completely to unpack:
Always her thoughts are centred
On the nearest railway station.

Moma and nurse and Louise,
30   A hatbox, a trunk, a valise,
And one was lost at Marseille,

    'Oh if I only could stay
    Just for two weeks in one place'
    Thinks the child of the doleful face.

35   Moma has had a cup of tea,
She is feeling better
'Cheer up, girlie' she says
'I've a letter here from your poppa,
It will take him some time to raise the bucks . . .
40   Shucks, child,
Go and help Nursie unpack,
We're here for two weeks at least
Then we leave for Athens and the Near East.'

In the suburban sitting-room
45   The poor child sits in a mazy fit:
Such a quick answer to a prayer
Shakes one a bit.

My Cats
(a Witch speaks)

I like to toss him up and down
A heavy cat weighs half a Crown
With a hey do diddle my cat Brown.

I like to pinch him on the sly
When nobody is passing by
With a hey do diddle my cat Fry.

I like to ruffle up his pride
And watch him skip and turn aside
With a hey do diddle my cat Hyde.

Hey Brown and Fry and Hyde my cats
That sit on tombstones for your mats.

The Blue from Heaven
A Legend of King Arthur of Britain

King Arthur rode in another world
And his twelve knights rode behind him
And Guinevere[1] was there
Crying: Arthur, where are you, dear?

5   Why is the King so blue?
Why is he this blue colour?
It is because the sun is shining
And he rides under the blue cornflowers.

---

2. European railroad sleeping-car.

1. Wife of King Arthur.

High wave the cornflowers
10 That shed the pale blue light
And under the tall cornflowers
Rides King Arthur and his twelve knights.

And Guinevere is there
Crying: Arthur, where are you, dear?

15 First there were twelve knights riding
And then there was only one
And King Arthur said to the one knight,
Be gone.

All I ask for now, said Arthur,
20 Is the beautiful colour blue
And to ride in the blue sunshine
And Guinevere I do not wish for you.

Oh lord, said Guinevere,
I do not see the colour blue
25 And I wish to ride where our knights rode,
After you.

Go back, go back, Guinevere,
Go back to the palace, said the King,
So she went back to the palace
30 And her grief did not seem to her a small thing.

The Queen has returned to the palace
Crying: Arthur, where are you, dear?
And every day she speaks of Arthur's grandeur
To the knights who are there.

35 That the King has fallen from the power
Of his grandeur all agree
And the falling off of Arthur
Becomes their theme presently.

And if it were only temporarily
40 And it was not for ever
They speak, but the Queen knows
He will come back never.

Yes, Arthur has passed away,
Gladly he has laid down his reigning power,
45 He has gone to ride in the blue light
Of the peculiar towering cornflowers.

PHILIP LARKIN (1922–   )

Poetry of Departures

Sometimes you hear, fifth-hand,
As epitaph:
He chucked up everything
And just cleared off,
5 And always the voice will sound
Certain you approve
This audacious, purifying,
Elemental move.

And they are right, I think.
10 We all hate home
And having to be there:
I detest my room,
Its specially-chosen junk,
The good books, the good bed,
15 And my life, in perfect order:
So to hear it said

He walked out on the whole crowd
Leaves me flushed and stirred,
Like *Then she undid her dress*
20 Or *Take that you bastard*;
Surely I can, if he did?
And that helps me stay
Sober and industrious.
But I'd go today,

25 Yes, swagger the nut-strewn roads,
Crouch in the fo'c'sle[1]
Stubbly with goodness, if
It weren't so artificial,
Such a deliberate step backwards
30 To create an object:
Books; china; a life
Reprehensibly perfect.

1. Forecastle, superstructure at bow of ship.

Church Going

Once I am sure there's nothing going on
I step inside, letting the door thud shut.
Another church: matting, seats, and stone,
And little books; sprawlings of flowers, cut
For Sunday, brownish now; some brass and stuff
Up at the holy end; the small neat organ;
And a tense, musty, unignorable silence,
Brewed God knows how long. Hatless, I take off
My cycle-clips in awkward reverence,

5

Move forward, run my hand around the font
From where I stand, the roof looks almost new
Cleaned, or restored? Someone would know: I don't.
Mounting the lectern, I peruse a few
Hectoring large-scale verses, and pronounce
'Here endeth' much more loudly than I'd meant.
The echoes snigger briefly. Back at the door
I sign the book, donate an Irish sixpence,
Reflect the place was not worth stopping for.

10

15

Yet stop I did: in fact I often do,
And always end much at a loss like this,
Wondering what to look for; wondering, too,
When churches fall completely out of use
What we shall turn them into, if we shall keep
A few cathedrals chronically on show,
Their parchment, plate and pyx[1] in locked cases,
And let the rest rent-free to rain and sheep.
Shall we avoid them as unlucky places?

20

25

Or, after dark, will dubious women come
To make their children touch a particular stone;
Pick simples[2] for a cancer; or on some
Advised night see walking a dead one?
Power of some sort or other will go on
In games, in riddles, seemingly at random;
But superstition, like belief, must die,
And what remains when disbelief has gone?
Grass, weedy pavement, brambles, buttress, sky,

30

35

A shape less recognisable each week,
A purpose more obscure. I wonder who
Will be the last, the very last, to seek
This place for what it was; one of the crew
That tap and jot and know what rood-lofts were?
Some ruin-bibber, randy for antique,
Or Christmas-addict, counting on a whiff
Of gowns-and-bands and organ-pipes and myrrh?
Or will he be my representative,

40

45

Bored, uninformed, knowing the ghostly silt
Dispersed, yet tending to this cross of ground
Through suburb scrub because it held unsplit
So long and equably what since is found
Only in separation—marriage, and birth,
And death, and thoughts of these—for which was built
This special shell? For, though I've no idea
What this accoutred frowsty[3] barn is worth,
It pleases me to stand in silence here;

50

1. Container for Eucharist wafers.

2. Medicinal plants.
3. Musty.

55   A serious house on serious earth it is,
     In whose blent air all our compulsions meet,
     Are recognised, and robed as destinies.
     And that much never can be obsolete,
     Since someone will forever be surprising
60   A hunger in himself to be more serious,
     And gravitating with it to this ground,
     Which, he once heard, was proper to grow wise in,
     If only that so many dead lie round.

The Whitsun Weddings

  That Whitsun,[1] I was late getting away:
     Not till about
  One-twenty on the sunlit Saturday
  Did my three-quarters-empty train pull out,
5   All windows down, all cushions hot, all sense
     Of being in a hurry gone. We ran
  Behind the backs of houses, crossed a street
  Of blinding windscreens, smelt the fish-dock; thence
  The river's level drifting breadth began,
10   Where sky and Lincolnshire[2] and water meet.

  All afternoon, through the tall heat that slept
     For miles inland,
  A slow and stopping curve southwards we kept.
  Wide farms went by, short-shadowed cattle, and
15   Canals with floatings of industrial froth;
  A hothouse flashed uniquely: hedges dipped
  And rose: and now and then a smell of grass
  Displaced the reek of buttoned carriage-cloth
  Until the next town, new and nondescript,
20   Approached with acres of dismantled cars.

  At first, I didn't notice what a noise
     The weddings made
  Each station that we stopped at: sun destroys
  The interest of what's happening in the shade,
25   And down the long cool platforms whoops and skirls[3]
  I took for porters larking with the mails,
  And went on reading. Once we started, though,
  We passed them, grinning and pomaded, girls
  In parodies of fashion, heels and veils,
30   All posed irresolutely, watching us go,

  As if out on the end of an event
     Waving goodbye
  To something that survived it. Struck, I leant
  More promptly out next time, more curiously,
35   And saw it all again in different terms:
  The fathers with broad belts under their suits
  And seamy foreheads; mothers loud and fat;
  An uncle shouting smut; and then the perms,
  The nylon gloves and jewellery-substitutes,
40   The lemons, mauves, and olive-ochres that

1. White Sunday or Pentecost, seventh Sunday after Easter.

2. County in east-central England.
3. Shrill piercing sound, as made by a pipe.

Marked off the girls unreally from the rest.
    Yes, from cafés
And banquet-halls up yards, and bunting-dressed
Coach-party annexes, the wedding-days
45 Were coming to an end. All down the line
Fresh couples climbed aboard: the rest stood round;
The last confetti and advice were thrown,
And, as we moved, each face seemed to define
Just what it saw departing: children frowned
50 At something dull; fathers had never known

Success so huge and wholly farcical;
    The women shared
The secret like a happy funeral;
While girls, gripping their handbags tighter, stared
55 At a religious wounding. Free at last,
And loaded with the sum of all they saw,
We hurried towards London, shuffling gouts of steam.
Now fields were building-plots, and poplars cast
Long shadows over major roads, and for
60 Some fifty minutes, that in time would seem

Just long enough to settle hats and say
    I nearly died,
A dozen marriages got under way.
They watched the landscape, sitting side by side
65 — An Odeon[4] went past, a cooling tower,
And someone running up to bowl[5] — and none
Thought of the others they would never meet
Or how their lives would all contain this hour.
I thought of London spread out in the sun,
70 Its postal districts packed like squares of wheat:

There we were aimed. And as we raced across
    Bright knots of rail
Past standing Pullmans,[6] walls of blackened moss
Came close, and it was nearly done, this frail
75 Travelling coincidence; and what it held
Stood ready to be loosed with all the power
That being changed can give. We slowed again,
And as the tightened brakes took hold, there swelled
A sense of falling, like an arrow-shower
80 Sent out of sight, somewhere becoming rain.

MICHAEL HAMBURGER (1924 –   )

Tides

To wake without fail when milk bottles shake in their racks,
Scrape one's face in the morning, every morning,
Take the same route to work and say 'good morning'
To the same row of scraped or powdered faces—
5 I cursed the roundness of this earth, I raged
At every self-perpetuating motion,
Hated the sea, that basher of dumb rock,
For all her factory of weeds and fishes,
The thumps, the thuds, the great reverberations—
10 Too much in rhythm; jarring, but by rote.

4. A movie theatre.
5. In the game of cricket, equivalent to pitching.   6. Railway sleeping-cars.

The metronome it was in my own head
That ticked and ticked; caged cricket in my head
That chirped and chirped until I had no ear
For syncopation, counterpoint of stillness
15 Beating against all music—of the sea,
Of birds and men, of season and machine,
Even of cricket and of metronome.
In silence I learned to listen; in the dark to look.

And unrepeatable now each morning's light
20 Modulates, shuffles, probes the daily faces
Often too suddenly different, like the street,
This weathered wall re-pointed, that new one cracked,
Apple trees that I prune while I forget
The shape of last year's boughs, cankered or grown,
25 And where that stump is, one that died in blossom;
Forget the hill's curve under the aerial masts.

No, wheels, grind on; seasons, repeat yourselves;
Milk bottles, rattle; familiars, gabble 'good morning';
Breed, hatch, digest your weeds and fishes, sea,
30 Omit no beat, nor rise to tidal waves.
Various enough the silences cut in
Between the rock cave's boom and the small wader's cry.

For a Family Album

Four heads in one lamp's light
And each head bowed into peculiar darkness,
Reading, drawing, alone.
A camera would have caught them, held them there
Half-lit in the room's warm halflight,
Left them, refused to tell
How long till that lamp was broken,
Your hair pinned up or cut or tinted or waved.

I cannot even describe them, caught no more
Than a flash of light that ripped open
The walls of our half-lit room;
Or the negative— a black wedge
Rammed into light so white that it hurt to look.

Leave this page blank.
You'd neither like nor believe
The picture no lens could have taken:

Tied to my rooted bones
In your chairs you were flying, flying.

Babes in the Wood[1]
in memoriam E. and W. M.

No, they didn't get out,
Nor did they die, then.
They grew up, learning
To live on what they could find,
5 To build shelters, fend off
Wild boars that rooted around them,
Inquisitive bears.

They grew old, never knowing it,
Holding hands, lisping
10 Love's baby talk
Against buzzard and owl,
The half-light of day
And darker night—
Till the dawn when he lay dumb.

1. See the fairy tale in which abandoned children perish
and are buried by sympathetic birds. Hence the sense of
the title: innocents in unfamiliar setting.

15 Come down, birdy, she said,
It's a cold hand I hold,
And hold it I must while he
Lies here for me to see.
I am weak, I am old,
20 The damp has warped my bones,
I cannot bury him.

It was ants that obliged.
But birdy said the woman
Who found her way out.

Memory

My wives do not write.
Sweetly young, hair flowing,
They walk where they belong,
Riverside, lakeside,
5 Mountainside, hillside,
Woodland or grassy plain.

One I consoled—
Black-haired, sad
In her forest clearing—
10 Another I followed
From a wellspring up in the scree[1]
To a pool's golden rushes.

Did I leave them, forsake them?
I travelled,
15 Remember no parting.
Ways, I recall, transitions,
The shadows, the colours turning,
Herbs acrid or heady,
Sweet wives the world over,
20 Sweet virgins walking where they belong—

Unchanged, unchanging regions,
And they unchanged.

But by the knee a stranger
Clawed me, held on;
25 I fought: my grappling hand
Slid deep into rotten flesh,
A hole behind his ear.
I knocked him down and ran,
Clegs[2] covering me,
30 A grey crust;
Ran to the church, thinking
They could not enter there,
But still they clung, stinging,

And up I climbed, climbed
35 To the belfry, pursued
By a man half-decayed.

Sweet wives, sweet virgins
Walk still unchanged,
Do not write, do not miss me,
40 Never forget.
It was the sunshine, the shadows,
It was the herbs and the haze.

ELIZABETH JENNINGS (1926–   )

The Resurrection

I was the one who waited in the garden
Doubting the morning and the early light.
I watched the mist lift off its own soft burden,
Permitting not believing my own sight.

If there were sudden noises I dismissed
Them as a trick of sound, a sleight of hand.
Not by a natural joy could I be blessed
Or trust a thing I could not understand.

Maybe I was a shadow thrown by one
Who, weeping, came to lift away the stone,
Or was I but the path on which the sun,
Too heavy for itself, was loosed and thrown?

1. Stone rubble that has fallen down a hillside.   2. Horseflies.

I heard the voices and the recognition
And love like kisses heard behind thin walls.
Were they my tears which fell, a real contrition?
Or simply April with its waterfalls?

It was by negatives I learnt my place.
The garden went on growing and I sensed
A sudden breeze that blew across my face.
Despair returned but now it danced, it danced.

Attempted Suicides

We have come back.
Do not be surprised if we blink our eyes
If we stare oddly
If we hide in corners.
5   It is we, not you, who should show surprise.

For everything looks strange.
Roofs are made of paper
Hands are muslin
Babies look eatable.
10   There has been too much change.

And where do we come from?
Where did the pills take us,
The gas,
The water left pouring?
15   Limbo? Hell? Mere forgetfulness?

20   It was a lost moment,
There were no dreams,
There was simply the beyond-endurance
And then the coming-to
To you and you and you and you.

Do not ask us,
As if we were Lazarus,[1]
What it was like.
We never got far enough.
25   Now we touch ourselves and feel strange.
We have a whole world to arrange.

Caravaggio's[1] "Narcissus"[2] in Rome

Look at yourself, the shine, the sheer
Embodiment thrown back in some
Medium like wood or glass. You stare,
And many to this gallery come
5   Simply to see this picture. Clear
As glass it is. It holds the eye
By subject and by symmetry.

Yes, something of yourself is said
In this great shining figure. You
10   Must have come to self-knowledge, read
Yourself within that image who
Draws every visitor. You made
From gleaming paint that tempting thing—
Man staring at his suffering.

15   And at his joy. But you stopped where
We cannot pause, merely make sure
The picture took you from the stare,
Fatal within: Chagall[3] or Blake[4]
Have exorcized your gazing for
20   A meaning that you could not find
In the cold searchings of your mind.

1. Brother of Mary and Martha, brought back from the grave by Jesus. See John ii.

1. Italian painter (1565–1609).
2. In Greek mythology, youth who spurned Echo, and pined away for love of his own image in a pond.
3. Marc Chagall (1887–   ), Russo-French painter.
4. William Blake (1757–1827), great English poet and artist.

The Minotaur[1]

Daedalus[2] designed this. Famous for buildings he did Minos'[3] will.
          Minos, full of revenge, yet could not
Kill this creature begotten by his wife and a bull coupling.
          Poseidon[4] punished him in this way,
5   Making for us a pattern as perfect and intricate as that labyrinth.[5]
          We want the danger, the escape, above all
We want a happy love story to cancel a passion which was prodigal
              only of
A half-bull. Ariadne[6] waited on this, patient as Penelope.[7] She had seen
10   the handsome Athenians one by one
Go into Daedalus' design and die there. But she possessed joyfully the
          power of a thread and a secret.

At first sight, as even classical writers will show and allow us, she
          fell in love with Theseus[8] who arrived
15   Apparently just a victim. But she, and we want this too, always this
          necessity and ceremony,
Gave him the thread, the clue, the condition to be his wife. Theseus,
          quick with courage and passion,
Took the twine from her, smiled and walked into the darkness
20   watchfully but fearlessly and found
The Minotaur sleeping. Beautiful indeed but now to be beaten to
          death by young fists, exalted
In no bull-ring with panoply[9] but providing us with the desired peril
          before love succeeds,
25   Leading us gently into labyrinths within us where half-bulls
          sometimes wake in our own darkness
And where we must always all be both Theseus and Ariadne.

CHARLES TOMLINSON (1927 –   )

Paring the Apple

There are portraits and still-lives.

And there is paring the apple.

And then? Paring it slowly,
From under cool-yellow
Cold-white emerging. And ...?

The spring of concentric peel
Unwinding off white,
The blade hidden, dividing.

There are portraits and still-lives
And the first, because 'human'
Does not excel the second, and
Neither is less weighted
With a human gesture, then paring the apple
With a human stillness.

The cool blade
Severs between coolness, apple-rind
Compelling a recognition.

---

1. In Greek mythology, the Cretan monster, half-bull, half-human, offspring of King Minos' wife Pasiphae and a beautiful bull.
2. Architect hired by King Minos to build the labyrinth for containment of the Minotaur.
3. King of Crete.
4. Greek god of the sea and other bodies of water.
5. The maze built to hold the Minotaur.
6. Minos' daughter who supplied thread so that Theseus might find his way out of the labyrinth.
7. Wife of Odysseus. She worked at her loom as she awaited his return from his long voyage.
8. Prince of Athens. He was placed into the labyrinth together with other Athenian youths whose lives paid tribute to Minos' rule.
9. Shining suit of armour.

Crow

The inspecting eye
shows cold
amid the head's
disquieted iridescence.
5 The whole bird sits
rocking at a vantage
clumsily. The glance
alone is steady
and a will behind it
10 rights the stance,
corrects all disposition
to ungainly action.
Acting, it will be
as faultless as its eye
15 in a concerted drop
on carrion; or watch

20 it fly—the insolence
transfers to wing-tip
and the action wears
an ease that's merciless,
all black assumption,
mounting litheness.
The blown bird,
inaccessible its intimations
25 of the wind, 'Stay
where you are' is
what it says and we
poor swimmers
in that element
30 stay, to bear
with clumsy eye
affronted witness at its ways in air.

Composition

for John Berger[1]

Courbet[2] might have painted this
gigantic head: heavy, yellow
petal-packed bloom of the chrysanthemum.

He would have caught the way
5 the weight of it looms from the cheap-green
vase this side the window it lolls in.

But he would have missed the space
triangled between stalk and curtain
along a window-frame base.

10 The opulence of the flower
would have compelled him to ignore
the ship-shape slotted verticals

of the door in the house beyond
dwarfed by the wand of the stem;
15 and the gate before it would not

have echoed those parallels to his eye
with its slatted wood, its two
neat side-posts of concrete.

The triangle compacts the lot: there
20 is even room in it for the black
tyre and blazing wheel-hub of a car

parked by the entrance. But the eye
of Courbet is glutted with petals
as solid as meat that press back the sky.

Ariadne[1] and the Minotaur[2]

When Theseus[3] went down
she stood alone surrounded
by the sense of what finality it was
she entered now: the hot rocks offered her
5 neither resistance nor escape, but ran
viscous with the image of betrayal:
the pitted and unimaginable face
the minotaur haunted her with
kept forming there
10 along the seams and discolorations
and in the diamond sweat
of mica: the sword and thread
had been hers to give, and she
had given them, to this easer of destinies:

---

1. English novelist and art critic (b. 1926).
2. Gustave Courbet (1819–77), French realist painter.

1. Daughter of King Minos of Crete. She gave Theseus

the thread he used to find his way out of the labyrinth.
2. Half-bull, half-human monster, offspring of Minos' wife Pasiphae. It was kept in the labyrinth, to which Athenian boys were sentenced.
3. Prince of Athens, bare-handed killer of the Minotaur.

15 if she had gone
    alone out of the sun and down where he
    had threaded the way for her,
    if she had gone
    winding the ammonite[4] of space
20 to where at the cold heart
    from the dark stone the bestial warmth
    would rise to meet her
    unarmed in acquiescence, unprepared
    her spindle of packthread . . . her fingers felt now
25 for the image in the sunlit rock, and her ears
    at the shock of touch took up a cry
    out of the labyrinth[5]
    into their own, a groaning
    that filled the stone mouth
30 hollowly: between the lips of stone
    appeared he whom she had sent
    to go where her unspeakable
    intent unspoken had been to go
    herself, and heaved unlabyrinthed at her feet
35 their mutual completed crime—

40 a put-by destiny, a dying
    look that sought her
    out of eyes the light extinguished,
    eyes she should have led
    herself to light: and the rays
    that turned to emptiness in them
    filling the whole of space with loss,
    a waste of irrefutable sunlight spread
    from Crete[6] to Naxos.[7]

GAEL TURNBULL (1928–   )

A Fragment of Truth.

While working in the garden recently, I dug up a
    small fragment of truth.

It was stuck all over with clay and must have been
    buried for many years but I recognized what it
    was almost at once.

At first we kept it on the mantlepiece in the
    livingroom, but it was often embarrassing because
    of visitors and I eventually put it on my desk
    in the study, for a paper-weight.

I asked several close friends what they thought I
    ought to do with it, but no one was sure. "Keep
    it for your children," some said. "It's a great
    curiosity." Others suggested the local museum.

While we were away on holiday, someone broke into
    the house and stole it. The police said that
    they would make inquiries and asked me, "Could
    you identify it again as yours, if you saw it?"

Perhaps. But now I'm not sure if I do want it back.
    After all, if whoever it was should have found
    some use for it . . .

---

4. Cephalopod chambered shell.
5. The maze within which Minos kept the Minotaur and to
which he sent the condemned Athenian youths.

6. Island home of Minos, ruler of the Mediterranean.
7. Island upon which Theseus left Ariadne after escaping
Crete.

The Priests of Paris

The priests in Paris are the Priests of Paris.
The black ones, striding along the pavements, always
    striding somewhere, always purposefully going,
some with hats like platters, some in skull caps,
5   some with shaven pates,
some carrying valises full of important documents
    concerning the distribution of souls,
some smoking wrinkled stubs of cigarettes which put
    them in communion with other souls,
10 some with their hands folded under their black capes,
    making invocations with their fingers to conjure
    new souls into being;
black flapping drapes of the priests of Paris as they
    go past on their urgent errands.
15 Beneath their charcoal robes they guard the secret
    purposes of the city, they guard the delicate
    pollen of happiness,
that Paris may flourish and its leaves wave gently
    in the slow air, that its white roots of flesh
20   may be moist,
under the dark earth of the priestly garments they
    conserve the deep juices, withholding them,
    intently feeding them,
on their errands as they go past, and no one talks
25   to them, no one looks at them,
as if to pretend that they were not necessary, as if
    to pretend that Paris could flourish without them,
    as if to pretend that their purpose was towards
    some far-off non-Parisian heaven.

A Case

They call me that we have a case at the hospital.
It is a fine night, not late, only a little after eleven.
When I arrive, they tell me, "Mr. H - is going to
operate. The patient is in the first bed on the left
5 in the men's ward." I go in.

It is dark but some light comes from a wall fixture
above the bed. He is a man in early life. I begin to
ask the usual questions. I explain that I will give
the anaesthetic for the operation. He says, "My name
10 is Pisgah." I nod and go on with my questions and
examination. He appears tired and in some distress.
The exact nature of his condition is still in doubt.

It is true, when he tells me his name, I have a
momentary surprise, which I suppress. The name is that
15 of the mountain mentioned in the Bible from which Moses
is said to have viewed the Promised Land. As a child,
the name had intrigued me. It also occurs in a hymn,
as if it were a man's name: Pisgah's Mount. I had often
thought, singing the verse: who was Pisgah? I had used
20 the name later, rather at random, for a person who
existed in a story I was writing.

It was a story upon which I had exerted myself and
then, in one sense, abandoned. Pisgah, in fact, was the
person in that story with whom I was most concerned. I
25 had written two extended versions, and others more
fragmentary, without being able to bring them to any
satisfaction.

That I had not finished those pieces did not mean
that I had abandoned the work. To abandon a piece of
30 writing is one thing. To abandon a work, is another. A
particular piece of writing is a means, for a writer,
which may not always finally serve the work. Thus, I
write this, which also serves, for the moment.

I give the anaesthetic while my friend Mr. H - does
35 the surgery. The details of the case are of no consequence.
It goes well. Towards the end, when my attention is not
too pressed with technical details, I have the chance to
look more closely at Pisgah's face.

It is the face of a man asleep. As he sleeps, he is
40 remote, both from himself and from us. Yet he sleeps
by my will. I check his pulse, his blood pressure, his
colour, his muscle tone, and gently assist each breath.

In the story I had often had the experience that Pisgah
was difficult to lay hold upon. His character seemed to
45 change. Even the details of what he did or said. I had
wanted to discover who exactly he was. So that I could,
in some way, come to terms with him, to finish the story.
Now, suddenly, I felt him alive against my hand. And that
life dependent upon my attention. If my attention should
50 fail, I might lose him for ever.

I speak occasionally with Mr. H -. Sometimes about
the details of what he is doing. Sometimes about other
things entirely. Neither of us speaks of the man with
whom, in our several ways, we are involved.

55 Later, before leaving the hospital, I make a last
routine visit to Pisgah's bed. He is now partly awake
and responds to a touch on the face or a simple question.
I look again into that face, somewhat firmer now, and
occasionally tightened by the first twinges of pain from
60 the incision.

"Who are you?" I ask. He smiles faintly, out of his
half sleep, as if amused that after all this time I
should not know.

ROY FISHER (1930 -   )

For Realism

For 'realism':
the sight of Lucas's
lamp factory on a summer night;
a shift coming off about nine,
5 pale light, dispersing,
runnels of people chased,

by pavements drying off
quickly after them,
away among the wrinkled brown houses
10   where there are cracks for them to go;

sometimes, at the corner of Farm and Wheeler Streets,
standing in that stained, half-deserted place

—pale light for staring up
four floors high
15   through the blind window walls
of a hall of engines,
shady humps left alone,
no lights on in there
except the sky—

20   there presses in
—and not as conscience—
what concentrates down in the warm hollow:

plenty of life there still,
the foodshops open late, and people
25   going about constantly, but not far;

there's a man in a blue suit
facing into a corner,
straddling to keep his shoes dry;
women step, talking, over the stream,
30   and when the men going by call out, he answers.

Above, dignity A new precinct
comes over the scraped hill,
flats on the ridge get the last light.

Down Wheeler Street, the lamps
35   already gone, the windows have
lake stretches of silver
gashed out of tea green shadows,
the after-images of brickwork.

A conscience
40   builds, late, on the ridge. A realism
tries to record, before they're gone,
what silver filth these drains have run.

Discovering the Form

Discovering the form of vibrancy
in one of the minor hilltops,

the whorl of an ear
twisting somewhere under the turf,
a curve you have to guess at.

In a house out of sight round the shoulder,
out of ordinary earshot,
a desperate mother, shut in with her child,
raves back at it when it cries,
on and on and on, in misery and fear.

Round on the quiet side of the hill
their shrieks fill an empty meadow.

Emblem
for Basil Bunting[1]

Wing
    torn out of stone
like a paper fan

Hung in a sky
    so hard
the stone seems paper

Bare stems of ivy
    silver themselves
into the stones

And hold up the wall
    like an armature[2]
till they force it apart

Corner

Dark projecting corner
of shiny mahogany
standing out
among shadowy walls.

5   Beside it the face
gleams. Somebody standing

or halted in walking out.
A teacher—
    there are no
teachers here, no lessons.
10 It's not a teacher.
    Somebody—

the settings are made
to show faces off.
People have to expect to be seen.
They can clear themselves of enigma
15 if the settings allow,
if the enigma—

Keats's[1] death-mask
a face built out from a corner.

If you're living
20 any decor
can make a wraith of you.

Epitaph: Lorine Niedecker[1]

Certain trees
came separately from the wood

and with no special
thought of returning

TED HUGHES (1930 –   )

View of a Pig

The pig lay on a barrow dead.
It weighed, they said, as much as three men.
Its eyes closed, pink-white eyelashes.
Its trotters stuck straight out.

5   Such weight and thick pink bulk
Set in death seemed not just dead.
It was less than lifeless, further off.
It was like a sack of wheat.

1. Major British poet (b. 1900).
2. Protective covering of a plant.

1. John Keats (1795–1821), great English Romantic poet.
His death mask, reproduced in casts by Gherardi, is
peculiarly realistic.

1. American poet (1903–70). Her adjective for her poetry
was "condensary."

I thumped it without feeling remorse.
One feels guilty insulting the dead,
Walking on graves. But this pig
Did not seem able to accuse.

It was too dead. Just so much
A poundage of lard and pork.
Its last dignity had entirely gone.
It was not a figure of fun.

Too dead now to pity.
To remember its life, din, stronghold
Of earthly pleasure as it had been,
Seemed a false effort, and off the point.

Too deadly factual. Its weight
Oppressed me—how could it be moved?
And the trouble of cutting it up!
The gash in its throat was shocking, but not pathetic.

Once I ran at a fair in the noise
To catch a greased piglet
That was faster and nimbler than a cat;
Its squeal was the rending of metal.

Pigs must have hot blood, they feel like ovens.
Their bite is worse than a horse's—
They chop a half-moon clean out.
They eat cinders, dead cats.

Distinctions and admirations such
As this one was long finished with.
I stared at it a long time. They were going to scald it,
Scald it and scour it like a doorstep.

Cadenza[1]

The violinist's shadow vanishes.

The husk of a grasshopper
Sucks a remote cyclone and rises.

The full, bared throat of a woman walking water,
The loaded estuary of the dead.

And I am the cargo
Of a coffin attended by swallows.

And I am the water
Bearing the coffin that will not be silent.

The clouds are full of surgery and collisions
But the coffin escapes—as a black diamond,

A ruby brimming blood,
An emerald beating its shores,

The sea lifts swallow wings and flings
A summer lake open,

1. Virtuoso passage near the end of a solo.

Sips and bewilders its reflection,
Till the whole sky dives shut like a burned land back to its spark—

A bat with a ghost in its mouth
Struck at by lightnings of silence—

20   Blue with sweat, the violinist
Crashes into the orchestra, which explodes.

Crow's Theology

Crow[1] realized God loved him—
Otherwise, he would have dropped dead.
So that was proved.
Crow reclined, marvelling, on his heart-beat.

And he realized that God spoke Crow—
Just existing was His revelation.

But what
Loved the stones and spoke stone?
They seemed to exist too.
And what spoke that strange silence
After his clamour of caws faded?

And what loved the shot-pellets
That dribbled from those strung-up mummifying crows?
What spoke the silence of lead?

Crow realized there were two Gods—

One of them much bigger than the other
Loving his enemies
And having all the weapons.

The Bear

In the huge, wide-open, sleeping eye of the mountain
The bear is the gleam in the pupil
Ready to awake
And instantly focus.

5   The bear is gluing
Beginning to end
With glue from people's bones
In his sleep.

The bear is digging
10   In his sleep
Through the wall of the Universe
With a man's femur.

The bear is a well
Too deep to glitter
15   Where your shout
Is being digested.

The bear is a river
Where people bending to drink
See their dead selves.

---

1. Mythical hero of Hughes's booklength suite, *Crow*.

20   The bear sleeps
     In a kingdom of walls
     In a web of rivers.

     He is the ferryman
     To dead land.

25   His price is everything.

The Ancient Briton Lay under His Rock

Under the oaks, the polished leaves of Sunday.

     He was happy no longer existing
     Happy being nursery school history
     A few vague words
5   A stump of local folk-lore.

     A whorl in our ignorance.

     That valley needed him, dead in his cave-mouth,
     Bedded on bones of cave-bear, sabre-tooth.
     We needed him. The Mighty Hunter.

10   We dug for him. We dug to be sure.

     Stinging brows, Sunday after Sunday.
     Iron levers.

     We needed that waft from the cave
     The dawn dew-chilling of emergence,
15   The hunting grounds untouched all around us.

     Meanwhile his pig-headed rock existed.
     A slab of time, it surely did exist.
     Loyal to the day, it did not cease to exist.

     As we dug it waddled and squirmed deeper.
20   As we dug, slowly, a good half ton,
     It escaped us, taking its treasure down.

     And lay beyond us, looking up at us

     Labouring in the prison
     Of our eyes, our sun, our Sunday bells.

ADRIAN MITCHELL (1932–   )

I Tried, I Really Tried

     Mesh-faced loudspeakers outshouted Fleet Street,[1]
     Their echoes overlapping down Shoe Lane
     And Bouverie Street, pronouncing
     WASH YOURSELF POET.
5   Blurred black police cars from the BBC[2]
     Circled me blaring: WASH YOURSELF POET
     AND DON'T FORGET YOUR NAVEL.

1. Street next to stream of same name, a sewer that runs into the Thames. Name given to newspaper business located there.

2. The British Broadcasting Corporation, English public radio.

My ears were clogged with savoury gold wax
And so I failed WASH to hear at first WASH
10   WASH WASH YOURSELF
Since I was naked and they wore
Chrome-armoured cars and under the cars man-made fibre suits and under the suits Y-front pants
        and under the pants official groin protectors and under the groin protectors automatics,
I obediently ran to the city's pride,
The Thames, that Lord Mayor's Procession of mercury,
15   And jumped from Westminster Bridge.
Among half-human mud I bathed
Using a dead cat for a loofah,[3]
Detergent foam for gargle.
I dived, heard the power station's rumble and the moan of sewers.
20   The bubbles of my breath exploded along the waterskin.
Helmeted in dead newspapers, I sprang
Into the petrol-flavoured air
And Big Ben, like a speak-your-weight machine
Intoned WATCH YOURSELF POET.
25   Clothed in the muck of London, I yelled back:
I HAVE BEEN WASHED IN THE BLOOD OF THE THAMES, BIG BROTHER,
AND FROM NOW ON I SHALL USE NO OTHER.

Leaflets

(for Brian Patten[1] and my twelve students at Bradford)

Outside the plasma supermarket
I stretch out my arm to the shoppers and say:
"Can I give you one of these?"

I give each of them a leaf from a tree.

The first shopper thanks me.
The second puts the leaf in his mack[2] pocket where his wife won't see.
The third says she is not interested in leaves. She looks like a mutilated willow.
The fourth says: "Is it art?" I say that it is a leaf.
The fifth looks through his leaf and smiles at the light beyond.
The sixth hurls down his leaf and stamps it till dark purple mud oozes through.
The seventh says she will press it in her album.
The eighth complains that it is an oak leaf and says he would be on my side if I were also handing
        out birch leaves, apple leaves, privet leaves and larch leaves. I say that it is a leaf.
The ninth takes the leaf carefully and then, with a backhand fling, gives it its freedom.
It glides, following surprise curving alleys through the air.
It lands. I pick it up.
The tenth reads both sides of the leaf twice and then says: "Yes, but it doesn't say who we should
                        kill."

But you took your leaf like a kiss.

They tell me that, on Saturdays,
You can be seen in your own city centre
Giving away forests, orchards, jungles.

Ten Ways to Avoid Lending Your Wheelbarrow to Anybody

1 Patriotic

May I borrow your wheelbarrow?
I didn't lay down my life in World War II
so that you could borrow my wheelbarrow.

---

3. Egyptian plant pod, used as bathing brush.

1. English poet and song-writer (b. 1939).
2. Mackintosh: an English raincoat.

2   Snobbish

May I borrow your wheelbarrow?
5   Unfortunately Lord Goodman is using it.

3   Overweening

May I borrow your wheelbarrow?
It is too mighty a conveyance to be wielded
by any mortal save myself.

4   Pious

May I borrow your wheelbarrow?
10   My wheelbarrow is reserved for religious ceremonies.

5   Melodramatic

May I borrow your wheelbarrow?
I would sooner be broken on its wheel
and buried in its barrow.

6   Pathetic

May I borrow your wheelbarrow?
15   I am dying of schizophrenia
and all you can talk about is wheelbarrows.

7   Defensive

May I borrow your wheelbarrow?
Do you think I'm made of wheelbarrows?

8   Sinister

May I borrow your wheelbarrow?
20   It is full of blood.

9   Lecherous

May I borrow your wheelbarrow?
Only if I can fuck your wife in it.

10   Philosophical

May I borrow your wheelbarrow?
What is a wheelbarrow?

D. M. THOMAS (1935 –   )

Cecie

The evening that you died was the first I could not
Overhear you bed-down with your 'dear Nellie':
No farting and whispering. The house lay cursed
Not with one death only: with its own.
5   Who, you asked in my head, will lace my brother's
Shoes up in the morning, empty the chamberpots
And dress my sister? There was no reply.
I heard you struggle to sit up in the coffin.
You'd have worked all night and worked off that deep hurt.

10   Dear aunt, if Christ had come, as well he might, to you,
You'd have scrubbed his feet with good soapy water
Left from Monday's wash, pocketed a few
Fresh loaves and fishes for your poor sister;

Burnt your hand on the boiler, muttered, 'That's nothin',
15   Run out, lisle stocking flapping, to dig the garden.

You demand—clucking at the grave in such a state,
From our habit of taking you for granted—shears,
Scrubbing-brush, water, not for your sake but hers
You lie beside again. An image of you: triangle:
20   Lawn, mower and you (no taller than it)
Leaning a force three times your fleshless weight.
70, your death shocked us like a child's.

In all but stoicism you *were* a child.
Rampaging through the village you never left,
25   Blackberry-faced, hot pasties[1] in your apron,
Scuttling, chuckling. No breasts to hold or suck at.

You had no life. No lovers that I know of.
Yet we all loved you. You were filled with love
No-one repaid. Death can't be a still
30   Nor a cobwebbed house any longer, full of your labour,
Farting, scurrying. You have no death.
So much living is living still.

Rubble

I sit in my mother's cramped bedsit,[1]
on edge in body and spirit.
The light too bright for her eyes.
The radio too loud for her ears.
5   The low fire too hot for her
seized limbs appalling me.

Yet she wants to live.
Yet to rejoin her husband.
To win, lose, tie, go on running.

10   Almost it is a quarter to nine
when I can jump up, heat
her milk and water, kettle
for her bottle, pull out the commode,
compel myself to kiss her, and go.

15   She is a fledgling
broken on the road
I want to be out of sight of.
But alive, or the world will fold.

It is as though the black hole
20   drawing her into itself
is conditioning my love
to require absence. She knows

it. She is content. There is
a queer radiance in the space
25   between us which my eyes
avoid occupying: the radium
Madame Curie[2] found, when desolate
she returned at night to the empty table.

---

1. Meat pies cooked in a paste without a cooking dish.

1. Bed-sitting room: cheap English lodging.
2. Marie Curie (1867–1934), Polish-French chemist.

Blue Lake

Picture a man, or a woman,
In a deck-chair, by a blue lake,
Reading a poetry-book.

Suddenly a knee jerks
5 In surprise at finding
A poem called 'Blue Lake',

About a man, or a woman,
In a deck-chair, by a blue lake,
Reading a poetry-book.

10 Whose knee jerks
In surprise at finding
A poem entitled 'Blue Lake',

Concerning a man, or a woman,
On a white wall, by a blue lake,
15 Reading a poetry-book.

Whose knee jerks
In amazement, discovering
A poem entitled 'Blue Lake',

Concerning a man, or a woman, or a child,
20 On a white wall, by a blue lake,
Reading a poetry-book.

Whose knee jerks
In amazement, discovering
A poem entitled 'Grey Lake'.

25 It concerns a child,
On a white wall, by a grey lake,
Reading a poetry-book.

Whose knee jerks
In recognition, discovering
30 A poem entitled 'Grey Lake',

Concerning a child,
On a white wall, by a grey lake,
Reading a fishing magazine.

Who sits up straight
35 In recognition, discovering
A poem entitled 'White Shark'.

It concerns a child,
On a white wall, by a grey sea,
Reading a fishing magazine.

40 Who sits up straight
In illumination, discovering
A poem entitled 'White Shark',

Which concerns a child,
On a white wall, by a grey sea,
45 Dreaming of a white shark,

Which never sleeps, would slash
Its own gut if it could turn
Sharp enough, which dreams

Continuously it is a man, or a woman,
50 In a deck-chair, by a blue lake,
Reading a poetry-book.

The Dream Game

There was a black girl
who was so beautiful all the white men slept with her.
She had a hunter, an analyst, a manufacturer, and a poet.
And so clever
5 she picked up their language from their conversations.

She grew unhappy as
she couldn't dream, and not to dream was a kind of
constipation to the black girl, a growing burden
she grew fat with,
10 so that they had to buy her a pantigirdle.

We'll make you a dream,
said the analyst, and you must guess what it is.
When she had gone he explained to the others, smiling,
they wouldn't make up a dream
15 for the black girl, she would make up her own.

If her questions, if her guesses,
he said, contain in the last word the letter e, say yes,
if not, say no. The hunter, the manufacturer,

and the poet smiled,
20   and they called the black girl back into the room.

They instructed her
to ask them each in turn a question about the dream
they had made up for her. She could go on questioning
for as long as
25   she liked. It was important she find her dream.

How their laughter
exploded at her frequent marvellous guesses.
Black girl, they said, this is black magic! and their
beer spluttered out
30   of their mouths in uncontrollable mirth as she

unwound her dream, her dream
that all four of them had murdered her with knives,
cut her up in the kitchen and re-cycled her
into trees, into paper
35   on which beautiful elegies were written about her.

CHARLES OLSON (1910–70)

The Ring Of

it was the west wind caught her up, as
she rose
from the genital
wave, and bore her from the delicate
5   foam, home
to her isle

and those lovers
of the difficult, the hours
of the goldèn day welcomed her, clad her, were
10   as though they had made her, were wild
to bring this new thing born
of the ring of the sea pink
& naked, this girl, brought her
to the face of the gods, violets
15   in her hair

Beauty, and she
said no to zeus[1] & them all, all were not or
was it she chose the ugliest
to bed with, or was it straight
20   and to expiate the nature of beauty, was it?

knowing hours, anyway,
she did not stay long, or the lame
was only one part, & the handsome
mars[2] had her And the child
25   had that name, the arrow of
as the flight of, the move of
his mother who adorneth

1. Ruler of the heavens and the presiding god of the
Greek Pantheon.

2. Roman name of Ares, with whom Aphrodite mated to
have Eros, god of love.

with myrtle³ the dolphin and words
they rise, they do who
30   are born of like
elements

I, Maximus of Gloucester, to You

Off-shore, by islands hidden in the blood
jewels & miracles, I, Maximus¹
a metal hot from boiling water, tell you
what is a lance, who obeys the figures of
5   the present dance

1
the thing you're after
may lie around the bend
of the nest (second, time slain, the bird! the bird!

And there! (strong) thrust, the mast! flight
10   (of the bird
o kylix,² o
Antony of Padua³
sweep low, o bless

the roofs, the old ones, the gentle steep ones
15   on whose ridge-poles the gulls sit, from which they depart,

                        And the flake-racks
of my city!

2
love is form, and cannot be without
important substance (the weight
20   say, 58 carats each one of us, perforce
our goldsmith's scale

                  feather to feather added
                  (and what is mineral, what
                  is curling hair, the string
25   you carry in your nervous beak, these

                  make bulk, these, in the end, are
                  the sum

                  (o my lady of good voyage⁴
                  in whose arm, whose left arm rests
30   no boy but a carefully carved wood, a painted face, a schooner!
a delicate mast, as bow-sprit for

                        forwarding

3
the underpart is, though stemmed, uncertain
is, as sex is, as moneys are, facts!

3. Mediterranean flowering shrub, sacred to Aphrodite.

1. The archetypal figure, Jung's "homo maximus." Also
see Maximus of Tyre, second century A.D. Greek philosopher concerned with community.

2. Stone anchor.
3. Franciscan saint (1195–1231), patron saint of Portuguese fishermen in Gloucester, Mass.
4. Church in Gloucester, bearing statue herein described.

35   facts, to be dealt with, as the sea is, the demand
     that they be played by, that they only can be, that they must
     be played by, said he, coldly, the
     ear!

     By ear, he sd.
40   But that which matters, that which insists, that which will last,
     that! o my people, where shall you find it, how, where, where shall you listen
     when all is become billboards, when, all, even silence, is spray-gunned?

     when even our bird, my roofs,
     cannot be heard

45   when even you, when sound itself is neoned in?

     when, on the hill, over the water
     where she who used to sing,
     when the water glowed,
     black, gold, the tide
50   outward, at evening

     when bells came like boats
     over the oil-slicks, milkweed[5]
     hulls

     And a man slumped,
55   attentionless,
     against pink shingles

     o sea city)

4
     one loves only form,
     and form only comes
60   into existence when
     the thing is born

           born of yourself, born
           of hay and cotton struts,
           of street-pickings, wharves, weeds
65   you carry in, my bird

                     of a bone of a fish
                     of a straw, or will
                     of a color, of a bell
                     of yourself, torn

5
70   love is not easy
     but how shall you know,
     New England, now
     that pejoracracy is here, how
     that street-cars, o Oregon, twitter
75   in the afternoon, offend
     a black-gold loin?

           how shall you strike,
           o swordsman, the blue-red back
           when, last night, your aim
80   was mu-sick, mu-sick, mu-sick[6]
           And not the cribbage game?

5. Phoenician boats that crossed the Atlantic.   6. Popular jukebox song of 1949–50.

(o Gloucester-man,[7]
weave
your birds and fingers
85   new, your roof-tops,
clean shit upon racks
sunned on
American

braid
90   with others like you, such
extricable surface
as faun and oral,
satyr lesbos vase[8]

o kill kill kill kill kill[9]
95   those
who advertise you
out)

6
in! in! the bow-sprit, bird, the beak
in, the bend is, in, goes in, the form
100   that which you make, what holds, which is
the law of object, strut after strut, what you are, what you must be, what
the force can throw up, can, right now hereinafter erect,
the mast, the mast, the tender
mast!

105   The nest, I say, to you, I Maximus, say
under the hand, as I see it, over the waters
from this place where I am, where I hear,
can still hear

from where I carry you a feather
110   as though, sharp, I picked up,
in the afternoon delivered you
a jewel,
                    it flashing more than a wing,
than any old romantic thing,
115   than memory, than place,
than anything other than that which you carry

than that which is,
call it a nest, around the head of, call it
the next second

120   than that which you
can do!

Maximus to Gloucester, Letter 27 [withheld][1]

I come back to the geography of it,
the land falling off to the left
where my father shot his scabby golf
and the rest of us played baseball
5   into the summer darkness until no flies
could be seen and we came home
to our various piazzas where the women
buzzed

7. Citizen or sailing ship pertaining to Gloucester, Mass.,
location of many of Olson's poems.
8. Reference to ancient Greek transition from oral poetry
(pre-Homeric) to Sappho's verse, known to us in fragments.

9. See *King Lear* IV.vi.191.

1. Though written in 1954, the poem was not included in
the *Maximus* sequence until 1960.

To the left the land fell to the city,
to the right, it fell to the sea

I was so young my first memory
is of a tent spread to feed lobsters
to Rexall[2] conventioneers, and my father,
a man for kicks, came out of the tent roaring
with a bread-knife in his teeth to take care of
a druggist they'd told him had made a pass at
my mother, she laughing, so sure, as round
as her face, Hines[3] pink and apple,
under one of those frame hats women then

This, is no bare incoming
of novel abstract form, this

is no welter or the forms
of those events, this,

Greeks,[4] is the stopping
of the battle[5]

It is the imposing
of all those antecedent predecessions, the precessions[6]

of me, the generation of those facts
which are my words, it is coming

from all that I no longer am, yet am,
the slow westward motion of

more than I am

There is no strict personal order[7]

for my inheritance.

No Greek will be able

to discriminate my body.[8]

An American

is a complex of occasions,

themselves a geometry

of spatial nature.

I have this sense,

that I am one

with my skin

Plus this—plus this:

---

2. A North American drugstore chain.
3. The family name of Olson's mother.
4. "It was the defect of the Greek analysis of generation that it conceived it in terms of the bare incoming of novel abstract form" (Alfred North Whitehead, *Adventures of Ideas* [New York, 1933], p. 242).
5. The Celtic bards of Wales were said to have the power and influence to bring battles to an end, and to decide victors and losers.
6. Slow westward motion of equinoctal points along the ecliptic.
7. Whitehead, p. 242.
8. Whitehead, p. 242.

45   that forever the geography

which leans in

on me I compell

backwards I compell Gloucester[9]

to yield, to

50   change

      Polis[10]

is this

ROBERT LOWELL (1917–77)

To Delmore Schwartz[1]
(Cambridge 1946)

We couldn't even keep the furnace lit!
Even when we had disconnected it,
the antiquated
refrigerator gurgled mustard gas
5   through your mustard-yellow house,
and spoiled our long maneuvered visit
from T.S. Eliot's brother, Henry Ware. . . .

Your stuffed duck craned toward Harvard from my trunk:
its bill was a black whistle, and its brow
10   was high and thinner than a baby's thumb;
its webs were tough as toenails on its bough.
It was your first kill; you had rushed it home,
pickled in a tin wastebasket of rum—
it looked through us, as if it'd died dead drunk.
15   You must have propped its eyelids with a nail,
and yet it lived with us and met our stare,
Rabelaisian,[2] lubricious, drugged. And there,
perched on my trunk and typing-table,
it cooled our universal
20   *Angst*[3] a moment, Delmore. We drank and eyed
the chicken-hearted shadows of the world.
Underseas fellows, nobly mad,
we talked away our friends. "Let Joyce and Freud,
the Masters of Joy,
25   be our guests here," you said. The room was filled
with cigarette smoke circling the paranoid,
inert gaze of Coleridge, back
from Malta[4]—his eyes lost in flesh, lips baked and black.
Your tiger kitten, *Oranges*,
30   cartwheeled for joy in a ball of snarls.

9. Massachusetts coastal city, *locus* of Olson's poems.
10. A community of citizens.

1. American poet (1913–66).

2. Francois Rabelais (1494–1553), bawdy French satirist.
3. Philosophical term designating social anxiety.
4. Possibly the portrait done in 1805 in Italy by American painter Washington Allston.

You said:
"*We poets in our youth begin in sadness;*
thereof in the end come despondency and madness;[5]
Stalin has had two cerebral hemorrhages!"
35   The Charles
River[6] was turning silver. In the ebb-
light of morning, we stuck
the duck
-'s web-
40   foot, like a candle, in a quart of gin we'd killed.

For the Union Dead[1]

"Relinquunt Omnia Servare Rem Publicam."[2]

The old South Boston Aquarium stands
in a Sahara of snow now. Its broken windows are boarded.
The bronze weathervane cod has lost half its scales.
The airy tanks are dry.

5   Once my nose crawled like a snail on the glass;
my hand tingled
to burst the bubbles
drifting from the noses of the cowed, compliant fish.

My hand draws back. I often sigh still
10   for the dark downward and vegetating kingdom
of the fish and reptile. One morning last March,
I pressed against the new barbed and galvanized

fence on the Boston Common. Behind their cage,
yellow dinosaur steamshovels were grunting
15   as they cropped up tons of mush and grass
to gouge their underworld garage.

Parking spaces luxuriate like civic
sandpiles in the heart of Boston.
A girdle of orange, Puritan-pumpkin colored girders
20   braces the tingling Statehouse,

shaking over the excavations, as it faces Colonel Shaw[3]
and his bell-cheeked Negro infantry
on St. Gaudens'[4] shaking Civil War relief,
propped by a plank splint against the garage's earthquake.

25   Two months after marching through Boston,
half the regiment was dead;
at the dedication,
William James[5] could almost hear the bronze Negroes breathe.

Their monument sticks like a fishbone
30   in the city's throat.
Its Colonel is as lean
as a compass-needle.

---

5. Lowell's lines are a rewriting of Schwartz's rewriting
of Wordsworth's lines from "Resolution and Independence." Schwartz's lines actually read: "We poets in our
youth begin in sadness / But thereof come, for some,
exaltation, ascendancy & gladness."
6. Harvard University sits on its banks.

1. Soldiers killed while fighting for the North in the U.S.
Civil War.
2. "They give up everything to save the republic."
3. Massachusetts officer in the Civil War.
4. A sculptor (1848–1907).
5. Harvard philosopher and teacher (1842–1910).

He has an angry wrenlike vigilance,
a greyhound's gentle tautness;
35   he seems to wince at pleasure,
and suffocate for privacy.

He is out of bounds now. He rejoices in man's lovely,
peculiar power to choose life and die—
when he leads his black soldiers to death,
40   he cannot bend his back.

On a thousand small town New England greens,
the old white churches hold their air
of sparse, sincere rebellion; frayed flags
quilt the graveyards of the Grand Army of the Republic.

45   The stone statues of the abstract Union Soldier
grow slimmer and younger each year—
wasp-wasted, they doze over muskets
and muse through their sideburns . . .

Shaw's father wanted no monument
50   except the ditch,
where his son's body was thrown
and lost with his "niggers."

The ditch is nearer.
There are no statues for the last war here;
55   on Boyleston Street, a commercial photograph
shows Hiroshima[6] boiling

over a Mosler Safe, the "Rock of Ages"
that survived the blast. Space is nearer.
When I crouch to my television set,
60   the drained faces of Negro school-children rise like balloons.

Colonel Shaw
is riding on his bubble,
he waits
for the blessèd break.

65   The Aquarium is gone. Everywhere,
giant finned cars nose forward like fish;
a savage servility
slides by on grease.

Fall 1961

Back and forth, back and forth
goes the tock, tock, tock
of the orange, bland, ambassadorial
face of the moon
5   on the grandfather clock.

All autumn, the chafe and jar
of nuclear war;
we have talked our extinction to death.
I swim like a minnow
10   behind my studio window.

Our end drifts nearer,
the moon lifts,
radiant with terror.
The state
15   is a diver under a glass bell.

A father's no shield
for his child.
We are like a lot of wild
spiders crying together,
20   but without tears.

6. First Japanese city destroyed by American atomic
bomb (1945).

Nature holds up a mirror.
One swallow makes a summer.
It's easy to tick
off the minutes,
25   but the clockhands stick.

Back and forth!
Back and forth, back and forth—
my one point of rest
is the orange and black
30   oriole's swinging nest!

ROBERT DUNCAN (1919–   )

The Law I Love Is Major Mover

from which flow destructions of the Constitution.[1]
No nation stands unstirrd
in whose courts. *I, John, testify:*[2]
I saw. But he who judges must
5   know mercy
as a man knows a woman
        in marriage,

for She is fair, whom we, masters, serve.

The Which, says John Adams,[3]
10   "requires the continual exercise of virtue
        "beyond the reach
        "of human infirmity, even in its best estate."

Responsibility is to keep
        the ability to respond.
15   The myriad of spiders' eyes that Rexroth[4] saw
        reflecting light
are glamorless, are testimony
        clear and true.

The shaman[5] sends himself
20   The universe is filld with eyes then, intensities,
        with intent,
        outflowings of good or evil,
        benemaledictions of the dead,

        but
25   the witness brings self up before the Law.
It is the Law before the witness that
        makes Justice.

There is no touch that is not each
        to each   reciprocal.

30   The scale of five, eight, or twelve tones
        performs a judgment
previous to music. The music restores
        health to the land.

The land? The Boyg
35   in Peer Gynt[6] speaks.
On the stage it was shown: a moving obscurity.

---

1. E.g., the American Constitution, the final test in
American legal matters.
2. See Rev. xxii.20.
3. Second president of the United States (1797–1801).

4. Kenneth Rexroth, American poet who lives, as does
Duncan, in San Francisco.
5. Diviner of spirit world in American Indian culture.
6. Play by Henrik Ibsen (1826–1906).

I try to read you, lad, who offer no text.
Not terror now, dumb grief it is,
diabolus—but little devils
40   are garbled men that speak garble.
Your chosen place is less than hell,
nor hate nor love breeds. There,
disorder is not, order is not, not no
even simpleton need demands my ear.

45   Hear!

Hear! Beautiful damnd man that lays down his law lays down himself creates hell
a sentence unfolding healthy heaven.

Thou wilt not allow the suns to move
nor man to mean desire move,
50   nor rage for war and wine,
here where the mind nibbles,
nor embrace the law under which you lie,
that will not fall upon your face
or upon knees, all
55   but twisted out of shape, crippled
by angelic Syntax.

Look!   the Angel that made a man of Jacob[7]
made Israël in His embrace

60   was the Law,   was Syntax.

Him I love is major mover.

A New Poem (for Jack Spicer)[1]

You are right. What we call Poetry is the boat.
The first boat, the body—but it was a bed.
The bed, but it was a car.
And the driver or sandman, the boatman,
5   the familiar stranger, first lover,
is not with me.

You are wrong.
What we call Poetry is the lake itself,
the bewildering circling water way—
10   having our power in what we know nothing of,
in this having neither father nor son,

our never having come into it,
our never having left it,
our misnaming it, our
15   giving it the lie so that it lies.

I would not be easy
calling the shadowy figure who refuses to guide the boat
but crosses and recrosses the heart . . .

—He breaks a way among the lily pads.
20   He breaks away from the directions
we cannot give—

7. Gen. xxxii.

1. Major American poet, contemporary and friend of
Duncan.

I would not be easy calling him
        the Master of Truth,
but Master he is of turning right and wrong.

25   I cannot make light of it.
    The boat has its own light.

    The weight of the boat
    is not in the boat. He will not
    give me images but I must
30   give him images.
    He will not give me his name
    but I must give him . . .

    name after name I give him.
    But I will not name the grave easily,
35   the boat of bone
    so light it turns as if earth
    were wind and water.

    Ka,² I call him. The shadow
    wavers and wears my own face.

40   Kaka,³ I call him. The
    whole grey cerement replaces itself and shows
    a hooded hole.

    From what we call Poetry a cock crows
    away off there at the break of something.

45   Lake of no shores I can name,
    Body of no day or night I can account for,
    snoring in the throws of sleep I came
    sleepless to the joint of this poem,
    as if there were a hinge in the ways.

50   Door opend or closed,
    knuckled down where faces of a boat join,
    Awake Asleep
    from the hooded hold of the boat
    join in. The farthest shore is so near
55   crows fly up and we know it is America.

    No crow flies. It is not America.
    From what we call Poetry
    a bird I cannot name crows.

From Passages¹

5: The Moon

    so pleasing   a light

        round,   haloed,   partially

---

2. Shadowy double (and son) of Osiris on his becoming Ra, most important of Egyptian gods.
3. Son of Ra. Also a parrot of the Antipodes, thus one of the speaking birds of the poem?

1. A continuing sequence of poems by Duncan.

disclosed,   a ring,

      night's wedding signet   •

5   may be

a great lady drawing

     her tide-skirts up   •

          in whirls

        and loosening to the gilt

10   shore-margins   of her sea-robes

•   or he,   his consent

      releasing dreams,

  the dazzling path remaining

          over the waves,

15   a lord too,   lunar moth king

          Oberon[2]   •   gleaming amidst clouds.

     From what source

  the light of their faces,   the

        light of their eyes,   the dark

20   glance that illumines,   the kindling look

     as if over the shimmer of the lake

       his flesh radiant   •

  My Lord-and-Lady Moon

        upon whom

25   as if with love

     the sun at the source of light

           reflects   •

      Lifted   •

Mount Shasta[3] in snowy reverie

30   •   floats

---

2. In medieval folklore, king of the fairies.
3. Snowy volcanic mountain in northern California.

DENISE LEVERTOV (1923–   )

With Eyes at the Back of Our Heads

With eyes at the back of our heads
we see a mountain
not obstructed with woods but laced
here and there with feathery groves.

5   The doors before us in a facade
that perhaps has no house in back of it
are too narrow, and one is set high
with no doorsill. The architect sees

the imperfect proposition and
10   turns eagerly to the knitter.
Set it to rights!
The knitter begins to knit.

For we want
to enter the house, if there is a house,
15   to pass through the doors at least
into whatever lies beyond them,

we want to enter the arms
of the knitted garment. As one
is re-formed, so the other,
20   in proportion.

When the doors widen
when the sleeves admit us
the way to the mountain will clear,

the mountain we see with
25   eyes at the back of our heads, mountain
green, mountain
cut of limestone, echoing
with hidden rivers, mountain
of short grass and subtle shadows.

To the Muse[1]

I have heard it said,
and by a wise man,
that you are not one who comes and goes

but having chosen
5   you remain in your human house,
and walk

in its garden for air and the delights
of weather and seasons.

Who builds
10   a good fire in his hearth
shall find you at it
with shining eyes and a ready tongue.

Who shares
even water and dry bread with you
15   will not eat without joy

and wife or husband
who does not lock the door of the marriage
against you, finds you

not as unwelcome third in the room, but as
20   the light of the moon on flesh and hair.

He told me, that wise man,
that when it seemed the house was
empty of you,

---

1. In Greek mythology, one of the nine daughters of Zeus
and Mnemosyne, who watched over poets and sometimes
extended inspiration to them.

the fire crackling for no one,
25   the bread hard to swallow in solitude,
the gardens a tedious maze,

you were not gone away
but hiding yourself in secret rooms.
The house is no cottage, it seems,

30   it has stairways, corridors, cellars,
a tower perhaps,
unknown to the host.

The host, the housekeeper, it is
who fails you. He had forgotten
35   to make room for you at the hearth
or set a place for you at the table
or leave the doors unlocked for you.

Noticing you are not there
(when did he last see you?)
40   he cries out you are faithless,

have failed him,
writes you stormy letters demanding you return
it is intolerable

to maintain this great barracks without your presence,
45   it is too big, it is too small, the walls
menace him, the fire smokes

and gives off no heat. But to what address
can he mail the letters?
                    And all the while

you are indwelling,
50   a gold ring lost in the house.
A gold ring lost in the house.
You are in the house!

Then what to do to find the room where you are?
Deep cave of obsidian² glowing with red, with green,
55   with black light,
high room in the lost tower where you sit spinning,

crack in the floor where the gold ring
waits to be found?

                    No more rage but a calm face,
60   trim the fire, lay the table, find some
flowers for it: is that the way?
Be ready with quick sight to catch
a gleam between the floorboards,

there, where he had looked
65   a thousand times and seen nothing?
                    Light of the house,

the wise man spoke
words of comfort. You are near,
perhaps you are sleeping and don't hear.

2. A black volcanic glass, prized for its beauty, hardness,
and mysterious shift in colour.

70   Not even a wise man
      can say, do thus and thus, that presence
      will be restored.
                         Perhaps

      a becoming aware a door is swinging, as if
75   someone had passed through the room a moment ago— perhaps
      looking down, the sight
      of the ring back on its finger?

The Garden Wall

      Bricks of the wall,
      so much older than the house—
      taken I think from a farm pulled down
                  when the street was built—
5   narrow bricks of another century.

      Modestly, though laid with panels and parapets,
      a wall behind the flowers—
      roses and hollyhocks, the silver
      pods of lupine, sweet-tasting
10   phlox, gray
      lavender—
                  unnoticed—
                               but I discovered
      the colors in the wall that woke
15   when spray from the hose
      played on its pocks and warts—

      a hazy red, a
      grain gold, a mauve
      of small shadows, sprung
20   from the quiet dry brown—

                  archetype
      of the world always a step
      beyond the world, that can't
      be looked for, only
25   as the eye wanders,
      found.

ROBERT CREELEY (1926 –   )

The Innocence

Looking to the sea, it is a line
of unbroken mountains.

It is the sky.
It is the ground. There
we live, on it.

It is a mist
now tangent to another
quiet. Here the leaves
come, there
is the rock in evidence

or evidence.
What I come to do
is partial, partially kept.

I Know a Man

As I sd to my
friend, because I am
always talking,—John, I

sd, which was not his
name, the darkness sur-
rounds us, what

can we do against
it, or else, shall we &
why not, buy a goddamn big car,

drive, he sd, for
christ's sake, look
out where yr going.

Speech

Simple things
one wants to say
like, what's the day
like, out there—
who am I
and where.

Prayer to Hermes[1]
for Rafael Lopez-Pedraza[2]

Hermes, god
of crossed sticks,
crossed existence,
protect these feet

5   I offer. Imagination
is the wonder
of the real, and I am
sore afflicted with

the devil's doubles,
10   the twos, of this
half-life,
this twilight.

Neither one nor two
but a mixture
15   walks here
in me—

feels forward,
finds behind
the track, yet
20   cannot stand

still or be here
elemental, be more
or less a man,
a woman.

25   What I understand
of this life,
what was right
in it, what was wrong,

30   I have forgotten
in these days
of physical change.
I see the ways

of knowing, of
securing, life grow
35   ridiculous. A weakness,
a tormenting, relieving weakness

comes to me. My hand
I see at arm's end—
five fingers, fist—
40   is not mine?

Then must I forever
walk on, *walk on*—
as I have and
as I can?

45   Neither truth, nor love,
nor body itself—
nor anyone of any—
become me?

Yet questions
50   are tricks,
for me—
and always will be.

This moment the grey,
suffusing fog
55   floats in the quiet courtyard
beyond the window—

1. In Greek mythology, the son of Zeus, and the god of
roads, of crossroads, and of roadmarkers.

2. Spanish poet.

this morning grows now
to noon, and somewhere above
the sun warms the air
60   and wetness drips as ever

under the grey, diffusing
clouds. This weather,
this winter, comes closer.
This— *physical* sentence.

65   I give all
to you, hold
nothing back,
have no strength to.

My luck
70   is your gift,
my melodious
breath, my stumbling,

75   my twisted commitment,
my vagrant
drunkenness, my confused
flesh and blood.

All who know me
say, *why* this man's
persistent pain, the scarifying
80   openness he makes do with?

Agh! brother spirit,
what do they know
of whatever *is* the instant
cannot wait a minute—

85   *will* find heaven in hell,
will be there again even now,
and *will* tell of itself
all, *all* the world.

La Noche

In the court-
yard at midnight, at

midnight. The moon is
locked in itself, to

a man a
familiar thing.

For W.C.W.[1]

The rhyme is after
all the repeated
insistence.

There, you say, and
there, and there,
and *and* becomes

just so. And
what one wants is
what one wants,

yet complexly
as you
say.

Let's
let it go.
I want—

Then there is—
and,
I want.

ALLEN GINSBERG (1926–   )

Sunflower Sutra[1]

I walked on the banks of the tincan banana dock and sat down under the huge shade of a Southern
                    Pacific locomotive to look at the sunset over the box house hills and cry.
Jack Kerouac[2] sat beside me on a busted rusty iron pole, companion, we thought the same thoughts
            of the soul, bleak and blue and sad-eyed, surrounded by the gnarled steel roots of trees
                                                                            of machinery.

---

1. William Carlos Williams (1883–1963), great American
poet and a powerful influence on Creeley's work.

1. Narrative lecture as taught by the Buddha.
2. American novelist and poet (1922–69), great friend of
Ginsberg.

The oily water on the river mirrored the red sky, sun sank on top of final Frisco[3] peaks, no fish in
    that stream, no hermit in those mounts, just ourselves rheumy-eyed and hungover like old
        bums on the riverbank, tired and wily.
Look at the Sunflower, he said, there was a dead gray shadow against the sky, big as a man, sitting
    dry on top of a pile of ancient sawdust—

5   —I rushed up enchanted—it was my first sunflower, memories of Blake[4]—my visions—Harlem[5]
    and Hells of the Eastern rivers, bridges clanking Joes Greasy Sandwiches, dead baby carriages,
      black treadless tires forgotten and unretreaded, the poem of the riverbank, condoms & pots,
      steel knives, nothing stainless, only the dank muck and the razor sharp artifacts passing
        into the past—
and the gray Sunflower poised against the sunset, crackly bleak and dusty with the smut and smog
    and smoke of olden locomotives in its eye—
corolla of bleary spikes pushed down and broken like a battered crown, seeds fallen out of its face,
    soon-to-be-toothless mouth of sunny air, sunrays obliterated on its hairy head like a dried
      wire spiderweb,
leaves stuck out like arms out of the stem, gestures from the sawdust root, broke pieces of plaster
    fallen out of the black twigs, a dead fly in its ear,

10 Unholy battered old thing you were, my sunflower O my soul, I loved you then!
The grime was no man's grime but death and human locomotives,
all that dress of dust, that veil of darkened railroad skin, that smog of cheek, that eyelid of black
    mis'ry, that sooty hand or phallus or protuberance of artificial worse-than-dirt—
      industrial—modern—all that civilization spotting your crazy golden crown—
and those blear thoughts of death and dusty loveless eyes and ends and withered roots below, in the
    home-pile of sand and sawdust, rubber dollar bills, skin of machinery, the guts and innards of
    the weeping coughing car, the empty lonely tincans with their rusty tongues alack, what more
    could I name, the smoked ashes of some cock cigar, the cunts of wheelbarrows and the milky
    breasts of cars, wornout asses out of chairs & sphincters of dynamos—all these
entangled in your mummied roots—and you there standing before me in the sunset, all your glory in
    your form!

15 A perfect beauty of a sunflower! a perfect excellent lovely sunflower existence! a sweet natural eye
    to the new hip moon, woke up alive and excited grasping in the sunset shadow sunrise
      golden monthly breeze!
How many flies buzzed round you innocent of your grime, while you cursed the heavens of the
    railroad and your flower soul?
Poor dead flower? when did you forget you were a flower? when did you look at your skin and decide
    you were an impotent dirty old locomotive? the ghost of a locomotive? the specter and shade
    of a once powerful mad American locomotive?
You were never no locomotive, Sunflower, you were a sunflower!
And you Locomotive, you are a locomotive, forget me not!
20 So I grabbed up the skeleton thick sunflower and stuck it at my side like a scepter,
and deliver my sermon to my soul, and Jack's soul too, and anyone who'll listen,
    —We're not our skin of grime, we're not our dread bleak dusty imageless locomotive, we're all
    beautiful golden sunflowers inside, we're blessed by our own seed & golden hairy naked
    accomplishment-bodies growing into mad black formal sunflowers in the sunset, spied on by
our eyes under the shadow of the mad locomotive riverbank sunset Frisco hilly tincan evening
    sitdown vision.

—*Berkeley 1955*

---

3. Nickname given by Eastern Americans to San Francisco.
4. See his poem, "Ah Sun-Flower."

5. In uptown Manhattan where Ginsberg had an halluci-
nation of Blake's voice.

Wales Visitation

White fog lifting & falling on mountain-brow
      Trees moving in rivers of wind
              The clouds arise
  as on a wave, gigantic eddy lifting mist
5   above teeming ferns exquisitely swayed
                along a green crag
      glimpsed thru mullioned glass in valley raine—

Bardic,[1] O Self, Visitacione, tell naught
  but what seen by one man in a vale in Albion,[2]
10   of the folk, whose physical sciences end in Ecology,
        the wisdom of earthly relations,
  of mouths & eyes interknit ten centuries visible
      orchards of mind language manifest human,
  of the satanic thistle that raises its horned symmetry
15   flowering above sister grass-daisies' pink tiny
          bloomlets angelic as lightbulbs—

Remember 160 miles from London's symmetrical thorned tower
      & network of TV pictures flashing bearded your Self
  the lambs on the tree-nooked hillside this day bleating
20   heard in Blake's old ear, & the silent thought of Wordsworth in
               eld Stillness
  clouds passing through skeleton arches of Tintern Abbey[3]—
      Bard Nameless as the Vast, babble to Vastness!

All the Valley quivered, one extended motion, wind
25   undulating on mossy hills
    a giant wash that sank white fog delicately down red runnels
         on the mountainside
    whose leaf-branch tendrils moved asway
        in granitic undertow down—
30 and lifted the floating Nebulous upward, and lifted the arms of the trees
       and lifted the grasses an instant in balance
       and lifted the lambs to hold still
  and lifted the green of the hill, in one solemn wave

35 A solid mass of Heaven, mist-infused, ebbs thru the vale,
    a wavelet of Immensity, lapping gigantic through Llanthony Valley,[4]
  the length of all England, valley upon valley under Heaven's ocean
               tonned with cloud-hang,
40   Heaven balanced on a grassblade—
  Roar of the mountain wind slow, sigh of the body,
        One Being on the mountainside stirring gently
          Exquisite scales trembling everywhere in balance,
  one motion thru the cloudy sky-floor shifting on the million
45   feet of daisies,
  one Majesty the motion that stirred wet grass quivering
      to the farthest tendril of white fog poured down
         through shivering flowers on the mountain's head—

50 No imperfection in the budded mountain,
      Valleys breathe, heaven and earth move together,
    daisies push inches of yellow air, vegetables tremble,
      green atoms shimmer in grassy mandalas,[5]
  sheep speckle the mountainside, revolving their jaws with empty eyes,
55   horses dance in the warm rain,

---

1. Pertaining to ancient order of Welsh singing poets.
2. Old Celtic name for Britain, favoured by poets.
3. Locale of celebrated pastoral poem by William

Wordsworth.
4. Southeastern Wales.
5. Circles symbolic of the universe, especially in India.

tree-lined canals network through live farmland,
　　　　　blueberries fringe stone walls
　　　　on hill breasts nippled with hawthorn,
60　　pheasants croak up meadow-bellies haired with fern—

Out, out on the hillside, into the ocean sound, into delicate
　　　　　　　　gusts of wet air,
Fall on the ground, O great Wetness, O Mother, No harm on thy body!
65　Stare close, no imperfection in the grass,
　　　　　each flower Buddha-eye, repeating the story,
　　　　　　　the myriad-formed soul
Kneel before the foxglove raising green buds, mauve bells drooped
　　　　doubled down the stem trembling antennae,
70　　& look in the eyes of the branded lambs that stare
　　　　breathing stockstill under dripping hawthorn—
I lay down mixing my beard with the wet hair of the mountainside,
　　　　smelling the brown vagina-moist ground, harmless,
　　　　　tasting the violet thistle-hair, sweetness—
75　One being so balanced, so vast, that its softest breath
　　　　moves every floweret in the stillness on the valley floor,
　　　trembles lamb-hair hung gossamer rain-beaded in the grass,
lifts trees on their roots, birds in the great draught
　　　　hiding their strength in the rain, bearing same weight,

80　Groan thru breast and neck, a great Oh! to earth heart
　　　　　Calling our Presence together
　　　The great secret is no secret
　　　　Senses fit the winds,
　　　　　Visible is visible,
85　　rain mist curtains wave through the bearded vale,
　　　　grey atoms wet the wind's Kaballah[6]

Crosslegged on a rock in dusk rain,
　　　　rubber booted in soft grass, mind moveless,
　　breath trembles in white daisies by the roadside,
90　　　　Heaven breath and my own symmetric
　　Airs wavering thru antlered green fern
drawn in my navel, same breath as breathes thru Capel-Y-Ffn,[7]
　　　Sounds of Aleph[8] and Aum[9]
　　　　through forests of gristle,
95　　my skull and Lord Hereford's Knob equal,
　　　　All Albion one.

What did I notice? Particulars! The
　　　　vision of the great One is myriad—
　　smoke curls upward from ash tray,
100　　　　house fire burned low,
The night, still wet & moody black heaven
　　　　starless
　　upward in motion with wet wind.

July 29, 1967 (LSD) – August 3, 1967 (London)

6. Secret mystical Jewish theosophy which originated
during the Middle Ages.
7. Holy place, southeast Wales.

8. First letter of Hebrew alphabet.
9. Sound uttered during Indian meditational discipline.

FRANK O'HARA (1926–66)

In Memory of My Feelings
To Grace Hartigan[1]

1

My quietness has a man in it, he is transparent
and he carries me quietly, like a gondola, through the streets.
He has several likenesses, like stars and years, like numerals.

My quietness has a number of naked selves,
5   so many pistols I have borrowed to protect myselves
from creatures who too readily recognize my weapons
and have murder in their heart!
                    though in winter
they are warm as roses, in the desert
10   taste of chilled anisette.
                   At times, withdrawn,
I rise into the cool skies
and gaze on at the imponderable world with the simple identification
of my colleagues, the mountains. Manfred[2] climbs to my nape,
15   speaks, but I do not hear him,
                     I'm too blue.
An elephant takes up his trumpet,
money flutters from the windows of cries, silk stretching its mirror
across shoulder blades. A gun is "fired."
20   One of me rushes
to window #13 and one of me raises his whip and one of me
flutters up from the center of the track amidst the pink flamingoes,
and underneath their hooves as they round the last turn my lips
are scarred and brown, brushed by tails, masked in dirt's lust,
25   definition, open mouths gasping for the cries of the bettors for the lungs
of earth.
          So many of my transparencies could not resist the race!
Terror in earth, dried mushrooms, pink feathers, tickets,
a flaking moon drifting across the muddied teeth,
30   the imperceptible moan of covered breathing,
                         love of the serpent!
I am underneath its leaves as the hunter crackles and pants
and bursts, as the barrage balloon drifts behind a cloud
and animal death whips out its flashlight,
35   whistling
and slipping the glove off the trigger hand. The serpent's eyes
redden at sight of those thorny fingernails, he is so smooth!
                     My transparent selves
flail about like vipers in a pail, writhing and hissing
40   without panic, with a certain justice of response
and presently the aquiline serpent comes to resemble the Medusa.[3]

2

The dead hunting
and the alive, ahunted.
                  My father, my uncle,
45   my grand-uncle and the several aunts. My
grand-aunt dying for me, like a talisman, in the war,
before I had even gone to Borneo
her blood vessels rushed to the surface

---

1. American artist (1922–). O'Hara was a curator at the
Museum of Modern Art in New York.
2. Lord Byron's romantic hero, references to whom occur
throughout the poem.
3. In Greek mythology, a gorgon with snakes for hair; the
sight of her turned men to stone.

and burst like rockets over the wrinkled
50 invasion of the Australians, her eyes aslant
like the invaded, but blue like mine.
An atmosphere of supreme lucidity,
                                humanism,
the mere existence of emphasis,
55   a rusted barge
painted orange against the sea
full of Marines reciting the Arabian ideas
which are a proof in themselves of seasickness
which is a proof in itself of being hunted.
60 A hit? *ergo* swim.
                        My 10   my 19,
my 9,   and the several years. My
12 years since they all died, philosophically speaking.
And now the coolness of a mind
65 like a shuttered suite in the Grand Hotel[4]
where mail arrives for my incognito,
                             whose façade
has been slipping into the Grand Canal[5] for centuries;
rockets splay over a *sposalizio*,[6]
70   fleeing into the night
from their Chinese memories, and it is a celebration,
the trying desperately to count them as they die.
But who will stay to be these numbers
when all the lights are dead?

3
75 The most arid stretch is often richest,
the hand lifting towards a fig tree from hunger
                               digging
and there is water, clear, supple, or there
deep in the sand where death sleeps, a murmurous bubbling
80 proclaims the blackness that will ease and burn.
You preferred the Arabs? but they didn't stay to count
their inventions, racing into sands, converting themselves into
so many,
                  embracing, at Ramadan,[7] the tenderest effigies of
85 themselves with penises shorn by the hundreds, like a camel
ravishing a goat.
                    And the mountainous-minded Greeks could speak
of time as a river and step across it into Persia, leaving the pain
at home to be converted into statuary. I adore the Roman copies.
90 And the stench of the camel's spit I swallow,
and the stench of the whole goat. For we have advanced, France,
together into a new land, like the Greeks, where one feels nostalgic
for mere ideas, where truth lies on its deathbed like an uncle
and one of me has a sentimental longing for number,
95 as has another for the ball gowns of the Directoire[8] and yet
another for "Destiny, Paris, destiny!"
                    or "Only a king may kill a king."

How many selves are there in a war hero asleep in names? under
a blanket of platoon and fleet, orderly. For every seaman
100 with one eye closed in fear and twitching arm at a sigh for Lord Nelson,
he is all dead; and now a meek subaltern writhes in his bedclothes
with the fury of a thousand, violating an insane mistress
who has only herself to offer his multitudes.

4. Title of great 1932 motion picture, grand allegory of
post-WWI life.
5. Main thoroughfare of Venice.

6. A wedding ceremony.
7. Month of fasting in Moslem year.
8. Period of 1795-99 in revolutionary France.

                                                    Rising,
105   he wraps himself in the burnoose of memories against the heat of life
       and over the sands he goes to take an algebraic postion *in re*
       a sun of fear shining not too bravely. He will ask himselves to
       vote on fear before he feels a tremor,
                              as runners arrive from the mountains
110   bearing snow, proof that the mind's obsolescence is still capable
       of intimacy. His mistress will follow him across the desert
       like a goat, towards a mirage which is something familiar about
       one of his innumerable wrists,
                              and lying in an oasis one day,
115   playing catch with coconuts, they suddenly smell oil.

       4
       Beneath these lives
       the ardent lover of history hides,
                                    tongue out
       leaving a globe of spit on a taut spear of grass
120   and leaves off rattling his tail a moment
       to admire this flag.
                       I'm looking for my Shanghai Lil.[9]
       Five years ago, enamored of fire-escapes, I went to Chicago,
       an eventful trip: the fountains! the Art Institute, the Y
125   for both sexes, absent Christianity.
                              At 7, before Jane
       was up, the copper lake stirred against the sides
       of a Norwegian freighter; on the deck a few dirty men,
       tired of night, watched themselves in the water
130   as years before the German prisoners on the *Prinz Eugen*
       dappled the Pacific with their sores, painted purple
       by a Naval doctor.
                       Beards growing, and the constant anxiety
       over looks. I'll shave before she wakes up. Sam Goldwyn[10]
135   spent $2,000,000 on Anna Sten,[11] but Grushenka[12] left America.
       One of me is standing in the waves, an ocean bather,
       or I am naked with a plate of devils at my hip.
                                    Grace
       to be born and live as variously as possible. The conception
140   of the masque barely suggests the sordid identifications.
       I am a Hittite[13] in love with a horse. I don't know what blood's
       in me I feel like an African prince I am a girl walking downstairs
       in a red pleated dress with heels I am a champion taking a fall
       I am a jockey with a sprained ass-hole I am the light mist
145   in which a face appears
       and it is another face of blonde I am a baboon eating a banana
       I am a dictator looking at his wife I am a doctor eating a child
       and the child's mother smiling I am a Chinaman climbing a mountain
       I am a child smelling his father's underwear I am an Indian
150   sleeping on a scalp
                       and my pony is stamping in the birches,
       and I've just caught sight of the *Niña*, the *Pinta* and the *Santa Maria*.
                       What land is this, so free?
                                    I watch
155   the sea at the back of my eyes, near the spot where I think
       in solitude as pine trees groan and support the enormous winds,
       they are humming *L'Oiseau de feu!* [14]
                              They look like gods, these whitemen,
       and they are bringing me the horse I fell in love with on the frieze.

9. Marlene Dietrich, in *Shanghai Express* (1932).
10. American producer of extravagant movies (1882–1974).
11. Actress who appeared with Gary Cooper in the 1935 movie *The Wedding Night*.
12. The heroine of *Grand Hotel* (1932), played by Greta Garbo.
13. Ancient people of Asia Minor, 1500 B.C.
14. Ballet by Igor Stravinsky (1910).

5

160 And now it is the serpent's turn.
I am not quite you, but almost, the opposite of visionary.
You are coiled around the central figure,
                                   the heart
that bubbles with red ghosts, since to move is to love
165 and the scrutiny of all things is syllogistic,
the startled eyes of the dikdik, the bush full of white flags
fleeing a hunter,
                    which is our democracy
                                    but the prey
170 is always fragile and like something, as a seashell can be
a great Courbet,[15] if it wishes. To bend the ear of the outer world.

                                When you turn your head
can you feel your heels, undulating? that's what it is
to be a serpent. I haven't told you of the most beautiful things
175 in my lives, and watching the ripple of their loss disappear
along the shore, underneath ferns,
                             face downward in the ferns
my body, the naked host to my many selves, shot
by a guerrilla warrior or dumped from a car into ferns
180 which are themselves *journalières*.[16]
                    The hero, trying to unhitch his parachute,
stumbles over me. It is our last embrace.
                             And yet
I have forgotten my loves, and chiefly that one, the cancerous
185 statue which my body could no longer contain,
                                    against my will
                                    against my love
becomes art,
                 I could not change it into history
190 and so remember it,
                    and I have lost what is always and everywhere
present, the scene of my selves, the occasion of these ruses,
which I myself and singly must now kill
                    and save the serpent in their midst.

JOHN ASHBERY (1927–   )

Hotel Dauphin[1]

It was not something identical with my carnation-world
But its smallest possession—a hair or a sneeze—
I wanted. I remember
Dreaming on tan plush the wrong dreams

5 Of asking fortunes, now lost
In what snows? Is there anything
We dare credit? And we get along.
The soul resumes its teachings. Winter boats

Are visible in the harbor. A child writes
10 "La pluie."[2] All noise is engendered
As we sit listening. I lose myself
In others' dreams.

---

15. Gustave Courbet (1819–87), French realist painter.
16. Journeymen.

1. A hotel found on the French Riveria.
2. The rain.

Why no vacation from these fortunes, from the white hair
Of the old? These dreams of tennis?
15   Fortunately, the snow, cutting like a knife,
Protects too itself from us.

Not so with this rouge I send to you
At old Christmas. Here the mysteries
And the color of holly are embezzled—
20   Poor form, poor watchman for my holidays,

My days of name-calling and blood-letting.
Do not fear the exasperation of death
(Whichever way I go is solitary)
Or the candles blown out by your passing.

25   It breathes a proper farewell, the panic
Under sleep like grave under stone,
Warning of sad renewals of the spirit.
In cheap gardens, fortunes. Or we might never depart.

Faust[1]

If only the phantom[2] would stop reappearing!
Business, if you wanted to know, was punk at the opera.
The heroine no longer appeared in *Faust*.
The crowds strolled sadly away. The phantom
5   Watched them from the roof, not guessing the hungers
That must be stirred before disappointment can begin.

One day as morning was about to begin
A man in brown with a white shirt reappearing
At the bottom of his yellow vest, was talking hungers
10   With the silver-haired director of the opera.
On the green-carpeted floor no phantom
Appeared, except yellow squares of sunlight, like those in *Faust*.

That night as the musicians for *Faust*
Were about to go on strike, lest darkness begin
15   In the corridors, and through them the phantom
Glide unobstructed, the vision reappearing
Of blonde Marguerite[3] practicing a new opera
At her window awoke terrible new hungers

In the already starving tenor. But hungers
20   Are just another topic, like the new Faust
Drifting through the tunnels of the opera
(In search of lost old age? For they begin
To notice a twinkle in his eye. It is cold daylight reappearing
At the window behind him, itself a phantom

25   Window, painted by the phantom
Scene painters, sick of not getting paid, of hungers
For a scene below of tiny, reappearing
Dancers, with a sandbag falling like a note in *Faust*
Through purple air. And the spectators begin
30   To understand the bleeding tenor star of the opera.)

1. Alchemist who sold his soul to the Devil: hero of
dramatic works by Marlowe and Goethe and later of opera
by Charles Francois Gounoud (1857).

2. Pathetic hero of renowned 1925 movie, *The Phantom
of the Opera*.
3. Character in *Faust*.

That night the opera
Was crowded to the rafters. The phantom
Took twenty-nine curtain calls. "Begin!
Begin!" In the wings the tenor hungers
35   For the heroine's convulsive kiss, and Faust
Moves forward, no longer young, reappearing

And reappearing for the last time. The opera
Faust would no longer need its phantom
On the bare, sunlit stage the hungers could begin.

Voyage in the Blue

As on a festal day in early spring
The tidelands maneuver and the air is quick with imitations:
Ships, hats appear. And those,
The mind-readers, who are never far off. But
5   To get to know them we must avoid them.

And so, into our darkness life seeps,
Keeping its part of the bargain. But what of
Houses, standing ruined, desolate just now:
Is this not also beautiful and wonderful?
10   For where a mirage has once been, life must be.

The pageant, growing ever more curious, reaches
An ultimate turning point. Now everything is going to be
Not dark, but on the contrary, charged with so much light
It looks dark, because things are now packed so closely together.
15   We see it with our teeth. And once this

Distant corner is rounded, everything
Is not to be made new again. We shall be inhabited
In the old way, as ideal things came to us,
Yet in the having we shall be growing, rising above it
20   Into an admixture of deep blue enameled sky and bristly gold stars.

The way the date came in
Made no sense, it never had any.
It should have been a caution to you
To listen more carefully to the words
25   Under the wind as it moved toward us.

Perhaps, sinking into the pearl stain of that passionate eye
The minutes came to seem the excrement of all they were passing through,
A time when colors no longer mattered.
They are to us as qualities we were not meant to catch
30   As being too far removed from our closed-in state.

And ideally the chime of this
Will come to have the fascination of a remembered thing
Without avatars,[1] or so remote, like a catastrophe
In some unheard-of country, that our concern
35   Will be only another fact in a long list of important facts.

You and I and the dog
Are here, this is what matters for now.
In other times things will happen that cannot possibly involve us now
And this is good, a true thing, perpendicular to the ground
40   Like the freshest, least complicated and earliest of memories.

1. Manifestations of ideals from the past.

We have them all, those people, and now they have us.
Their decision was limited, waiting for us to make the first move.
But now that we have done so the results are unfathomable, as though
A single implication could sway the whole universe on its stem.
45   We are fashionably troubled by this new edge of what had seemed finite

Before and now seems infinite though encircled by gradual doubts
Of whatever came over us. Perhaps the old chic was less barren,
More something to be looked forward to, than this
Morning in the orchards under an unclouded sky,
50   This painful freshness of each thing being exactly itself.

Perhaps all that is wanted is time.
People cover us, they are older
And have lived before. They want no part of us,
Only to be dying, and over with it.
55   Out of step with all that is passing along with them

But living with it deep into the midst of things.
It is civilization that counts, after all, they seem
To be saying, and we are as much a part of it as anybody else
Only we think less about it, even not at all, until some
60   Fool comes shouting into the forest at nightfall

News of some thing we know and care little of,
As the distant castle rejoices to the joyous
Sound of hooves, releasing rooks straight up into the faultless air
And meanwhile weighs its shadow ever heavier on the mirroring
65   Surface of the river, surrounding the little boat with three figures in it.

What Is Poetry

The medieval town, with frieze
Of boy scouts from Nagoya?[1] The snow

That came when we wanted it to snow?
Beautiful images? Trying to avoid

Ideas, as in this poem? But we
Go back to them as to a wife, leaving

The mistress we desire? Now they
Will have to believe it

As we believe it. In school
All the thought got combed out:

What was left was like a field.
Shut your eyes, and you can feel it for miles around.

Now open them on a thin vertical path.
It might give us— what?— some flowers soon?

[handwritten: Real poets create and express ideas; they cannott escape it.

Poets are above society]

1. Large city in Japan.

W. S. MERWIN (1927 –   )

Caesar

My shoes are almost dead
And as I wait at the doors of ice
I hear the cry go up for him Caesar Caesar

But when I look out the window I see only the flatlands
And the slow vanishing of the windmills
The centuries draining the deep fields

Yet this is still my country
The thug on duty says What would you change
He looks at his watch he lifts
Emptiness out of the vases
And holds it up to examine

So it is evening
With the rain starting to fall forever

One by one he calls night out of the teeth
And at last I take up
My duty

Wheeling the president past banks of flowers
Past the feet of empty stairs
Hoping he's dead

Come Back

You came back to us in a dream and we were not here
In a light dress laughing you ran down the slope
To the door
And knocked for a long time thinking it strange

Oh come back we were watching all the time
With the delight choking us and the piled
Grief scrambling like guilt to leave us
At the sight of you
Looking well
And besides our questions our news
All of it paralyzed until you were gone

Is it the same way there

The Indigestion of the Vampire

Look at this red pear
Hanging from a good family

Where the butcher hung the rag on the tree.

The bat's bloated again
Hooked on his dark nimbus
Getting over it.
Here is the cure of pity
Upside down.

10 Elsewhere the laundry
Is buried,
The deer tracks left by his teeth
Look for the cross-roads,
The veins that are still good
Hold out their hands.

Here's his story.

15 His bridges are not burned only folded.
In a while the swollen life
He calls his own
Will shrink back till it fits the mirrors,
20 No worse for no wear;
The eyes will come
To conceal movement again;
He will find his voice to fly by.

25 That's how he does it: rock-a-bye,
Hanging there with his silence all wool
And others at heart,
Two pounds in his pound bag,

Shaped like a tear but
Not falling for anyone.

Dusk in Winter

The sun sets in the cold without friends
Without reproaches after all it has done for us
It goes down believing in nothing
When it has gone I hear the stream running after it
It has brought its flute it is a long way

Whenever I Go There

Whenever I go there everything is changed

The stamps on the bandages the titles
Of the professors of water

The portrait of Glare the reasons for
The white mourning

In new rocks new insects are sitting
With the lights off
And once more I remember that the beginning

Is broken

No wonder the addresses are torn

To which I make my way eating the silence of animals
Offering snow to the darkness

Today belongs to few and tomorrow to no one

SYLVIA PLATH (1932–63)

Lady Lazarus[1]

I have done it again.
One year in every ten
I manage it——

A sort of walking miracle, my skin
5 Bright as a Nazi lampshade,
My right foot

A paperweight,
My face a featureless, fine
Jew linen.

1. Brother of Mary and Martha, raised from the dead by
Jesus (John xi.12).

10   Peel off the napkin
      O my enemy.
      Do I terrify?——

      The nose, the eye pits, the full set of teeth?
      The sour breath
15   Will vanish in a day.

      Soon, soon the flesh
      The grave cave ate will be
      At home on me

      And I a smiling woman.
20   I am only thirty.
      And like the cat I have nine times to die.

      This is Number Three.
      What a trash
      To annihilate each decade.

25   What a million filaments.
      The peanut-crunching crowd
      Shoves in to see

      Them unwrap me hand and foot——
      The big strip tease.
30   Gentlemen, ladies

      These are my hands
      My knees.
      I may be skin and bone,

      Nevertheless, I am the same, identical woman.
35   The first time it happened I was ten.
      It was an accident.

      The second time I meant
      To last it out and not come back at all.
      I rocked shut

40   As a seashell.
      They had to call and call
      And pick the worms off me like sticky pearls.

      Dying
      Is an art, like everything else.
45   I do it exceptionally well.

      I do it so it feels like hell.
      I do it so it feels real.
      I guess you could say I've a call.

      It's easy enough to do it in a cell.
50   It's easy enough to do it and stay put.
      It's the theatrical

      Comeback in broad day
      To the same place, the same face, the same brute
      Amused shout:

55   'A miracle!'
      That knocks me out.
      There is a charge

For the eyeing of my scars, there is a charge
For the hearing of my heart——
60   It really goes.

And there is a charge, a very large charge
For a word or touch
Or a bit of blood

Or a piece of my hair or my clothes.
65   So, so, Herr Doktor.[2]
So, Herr Enemy.

I am your opus,
I am your valuable,
The pure gold baby

70   That melts to a shriek.
I turn and burn.
Do not think I underestimate your great concern.

Ash, ash——
You poke and stir.
75   Flesh, bone, there is nothing there——

A cake of soap,
A wedding ring,
A gold filling.

Herr God, Herr Lucifer[3]
80   Beware
Beware.

Out of the ash
I rise with my red hair
And I eat men like air.

EARLE BIRNEY (1904 –   )

Bushed

He invented a rainbow but lightning struck it
shattered it into the lake-lap of a mountain
so big his mind slowed when he looked at it

Yet he built a shack on the shore
5   learned to roast porcupine belly and
wore the quills on his hatband

At first he was out with the dawn
whether it yellowed bright as wood-columbine
or was only a fuzzed moth in a flannel of storm
10   But he found the mountain was clearly alive
sent messages whizzing down every hot morning
boomed proclamations at noon and spread out
a white guard of goat
before falling asleep on its feet at sundown

2. Reference to Nazi death-camp doctor. See l. 5.
3. Satan: the brightest of the angels who fell from Heaven
after their revolt.

15   When he tried his eyes on the lake   ospreys
    would fall like valkyries
    choosing the cut-throat
    He took then to waiting
    till the night smoke rose from the boil of the sunset

20   But the moon carved unknown totems
    out of the lakeshore
    owls in the beardusky woods derided him
    moosehorned cedars circled his swamps and tossed
    their antlers up to the stars
25   Then he knew   though the mountain slept   the winds
    were shaping its peak to an arrowhead
    poised

    And now he could only
    bar himself in and wait
30   for the great flint to come singing into his heart

(1952)

Ellesmereland[1] I

Explorers say that harebells[2] rise
from the cracks of Ellesmereland
and cod swim fat beneath the ice
that grinds its meagre sands
No man is settled on that coast
The harebells are alone
Nor is there talk of making man
from ice cod bell or stone

1952

Ellesmereland II

And now in Ellesmereland there sits
a town of twenty men
They guard the floes that reach to the Pole
a hundred leagues and ten
The warders watch the sky watch them
the stricken hills eye both
A Mountie visits twice a year
And there is talk of growth

1965

> ARRIVALS   Wolfville
> *Locals*
> From Halifax   30 Mins L

It was the hand that caught in me

Sudden as a beast the blizzard
had whirled on us   was gone
as quick over the hill and howling
5   through the next village   whose spire

---

1. Ellesmere Island. The northernmost point of Canada.

2. Sometimes called bluebells, a wildflower.

could be glimpsed blotting out now
in a grey fury

And we are wading   a straggle of passengers
in town shoes   through a snowscape
10   clean and cosy as any Christmas card
the small firs like spunwhite candy
spaced on the ice-cream hillocks

Already the sunlight smoulders down
burning on the narrow tracks at the crossing
15   and fires the sleet that sheathes one flank
and the bland diesel-face of our train
so small and innocent now it has stopped

You wouldnt think from that little jolt we got!
. . . Speedin . . . Naw, in that storm he jes couldn see

20   Green as a great bruise
where the smooth flesh of the drifts
has been savaged   the auto lies
crumpled and akimbo
like a beetle battered by catspaw

25   Flung it fifty feet . . . Yeah an him further . . .
This year's chevvy . . . Well we stopped fast enough

We stand   the unsilent   stamping
staring   to reduce to livable size
what is casually spreadeagled here in the snow

30   Should be a law about level cross—
Sure but we oughta wistled wen— Hell we did!
. . . Anybody know who he is?

We too anonymous   one to the other
but our breaths write on the air
35   the kinship of being alive
surrounding the perfect stranger

Christ it's too cold I'm gittin back . . .
Yep ain't nothin we kin do . . . Hey look
he's only gone three hunderd . . .

40   A thin man unprompted is gathering papers
slewed from a briefcase over the raddled banks
He slaps them free of flakes
and packs them carefully back in the case
Now he teeters   not knowing what to do with it
45   The brakeman plods up with a plaid blanket

Train gonna be held up till police come?
. . . No I'm stayin
Conductor was up to that farm phonin em

The man with the case silently lays it
50   next to the open palm
the blanket has failed to cover
He offers his only remark

Assizes is on up to Wolfville
Them's law papers

55　The halfburied engine continues to tick
　　with cooling　　something live under the snow
　　Each time we are startled

　　Lawyer eh?...Musta stalled on the track
　　grabbed his case　got half out his door...
60　Yep　nearly made it...Young feller too

　　　The sun has given way again to a black sky
　　　Most have tramped back to the train
　　　The rest of us circle about
　　　as if for somewhere to put down the guilt

65　Yer all lucky we dint go offa the tracks
　　...He's right　Can't blame the crew none

　　　Diesel shrieks and we jump
　　　The brakeman gestures　　Turning at once
　　　We leave him beating his arms for warmth
70　turn in a pleasure of hurry　to hop
　　　like schoolboys back in the steps we made
　　　eager for heat and motion　arrivals
　　　and shaping already what happened

　　　The train moves to its goal
75　and scatters us from the scene forever
　　　The manner of hills　words　faces
　　　slides from the gloss protecting each mind
　　　We will forget even that scotched face perhaps
　　　waiting till the gay rug came down
80　in a Christmas world

　　　But not surely the longfingered hand
　　　stretched in some arresting habit of eloquence
　　　to the last irrational judgement
　　　roaring in from the storm

85　Or is it only in me that the hand hooked
　　　and I who must manage it now like a third?

Sinalóa[1]

　　Si, seōr, is halligators here, your guidebook say it,
　　si, jaguar in the montaās, maybe helephants, quién sabe?[2]
　　You like, those palm trees in the sunset? Certamente[3] very nice,
　　it happen each night in the guía tourista.[4]
5　But who the hell eat jaguar, halligator, you heat them?
　　Mira[5] my fren, wat this town need is muy[6] big breakwater—
　　　I like take hax to them jeezly palmas.

---

1. State on west coast of Mexico.　　　4. Tourist guide.
2. Who knows?　　　　　　　　　　　5. Look.
3. Certainly.　　　　　　　　　　　　6. Very.

So you want buy machete? Por favor,[7] I give you
sousand machetes you give me one grand bulldozer, hey?
10   Wat this country is lack, seõr, is real good goosin,
is need pinehapple shove hup her bottom
(sure, sure, is bella[8] all those water-ayacints)
is need drains for sugarcane in them pitorescos[9] swamps—
        and shoot all them anarquista[10] egrets.

15   Hokay, you like bugambilla, ow you say, flower-hung cliffs?
Is how old, the Fort? Is Colhuan,[11] muy viejo,[12] before Moses, no?
Is for you, seõr, take em away, send us helevator for w'eat.
It like me[13] to see all them fine boxcar stuff full rice,
sugar, flax, all rollin down to those palmstudded ports
20   were Cortez[14] and all that crap (you heat history?)—
        and bugger the pink flamingos.

Amigo, we make you present all them two-weel hoxcart,
you send em Québec, were my brudder was learn to be padre—
we take ditchdiggers, tractors, Massey-Arris yes?
25   Sinalóa want ten sousand mile irrigation canals,
absolutamente. Is fun all that organ-cactus fence?
Is for the birds, seõr; is more better barbwire, verdad?[15]—
        and chingar[16] those cute little burros.

Sin argumento, my fren, is a beautiful music,
30   all them birds. Pero,[17] wy you no like to hear combos,
refrigerator trucks? Is wonderful on straight new ighway.
jampack with melons, peppers, bananas, tomatoes, si, si. . . .
Chirrimoyas?[18] Mangos? You like! Is for Indios, solamente,
is bruise, no can ship, is no bueno, believe me, seõr—
35   and defecar[19] on those goddam guidebook.

father grouse

some mornings trying to write
i get like an old ruffed partridge
flopping off & on the nest
scared somebody'll steal
5   those handsome brown eggs
i havent quite laid yet

flinching from cloud shadows
hearing a fox behind every bush
snakes in the grass
10   shots on the hill —
limping & trembling around
from what looked like a man
but was only a dumb moose
till i crumple down beat
15   with nothing done
& then the phone rings

but listen!
it isnt another mag salesman
or the Poets' League about dues
20   out of that lovely earpiece
comes a voice spreading sunshine
all through the woods
& i sit back drumming softly
to the loveliest partridge of all
25   (whose eggs they really are)
& feeling energy-control
right down to my wingtips

after we hang up quietly
i am warming up the eggs again
30   if i cant lay i can hatch
maybe something of me
will show in the chicks

July 1974

7. Please.
8. Beautiful.
9. Picturesque.
10. Anarchist.
11. Properly *Culhuan*, designating the coalition government of Mexican peoples immediately prior to the Spanish invasion of 1519.
12. Very old.
13. Translation of Spanish form.
14. Spanish conqueror of Mexico (1485–1547).
15. True?
16. A Mexican obscenity.
17. But.
18. Properly *chirimayos*, a fruit peculiar to Mexico.
19. Excrete.

IRVING LAYTON (1912–   )

A Tall Man Executes a Jig

I

So the man spread his blanket on the field
And watched the shafts of light between the tufts
And felt the sun push the grass towards him;
The noise he heard was that of whizzing flies,
5 The whistlings of some small imprudent birds,
And the ambiguous rumbles of cars
That made him look up at the sky, aware
Of the gnats that tilted against the wind
And in the sunlight turned to jigging motes.
10 Fruitflies he'd call them except there was no fruit
About, spoiling to hatch these glitterings,
These nervous dots for which the mind supplied
The closing sentences from Thucydides,[1]
Or from Euclid[2] having a savage nightmare.

II

15 Jig, jig, jig, jig. Like minuscule black links
Of a chain played with by some playful
Unapparent hand or the palpitant
Summer haze bored with the hour's stillness.
He felt the sting and tingle afterwards
20 Of those leaving their unorthodox unrest,
Leaving their undulant excitation
To drop upon his sleeveless arm. The grass,
Even the wildflowers became black hairs
And himself a maddened speck among them.
25 Still the assaults of the small flies made him
Glad at last, until he saw purest joy
In their frantic jiggings under a hair,
So changed from those in the unrestraining air.

III

He stood up and felt himself enormous.
30 Felt as might Donatello[3] over stone,
Or Plato,[4] or as a man who has held
A loved and lovely woman in his arms
And feels his forehead touch the emptied sky
Where all antinomies flood into light.
35 Yet jig jig jig, the haloing black jots
Meshed with the wheeling fire of the sun:
Motion without meaning, disquietude
Without sense or purpose, ephemerides[5]
That mottled the resting summer air till
40 Gusts swept them from his sight like wisps of smoke.
Yet they returned, bringing a bee who, seeing
But a tall man, left him for a marigold.

IV

He doffed his aureole of gnats and moved
Out of the field as the sun sank down,
45 A dying god upon the blood-red hills.

1. Greek historian, fifth century B.C.
2. Greek mathematician, third century B.C. Father of geometry.
3. Italian sculptor, fifteenth century.
4. Greek philosopher, fourth century B.C.
5. Tiny insects.

Ambition, pride, the ecstasy of sex,
And all circumstance of delight and grief,
That blood upon the mountain's side, that flood
Washed into a clear incredible pool
50   Below the ruddied peaks that pierced the sun.
He stood still and waited. If ever
The hour of revelation was come
It was now, here on the transfigured steep.
The sky darkened. Some birds chirped. Nothing else.
55   He thought the dying god had gone to sleep:
An Indian fakir on his mat of nails.

V

And on the summit of the asphalt road
Which stretched towards the fiery town, the man
Saw one hill raised like a hairy arm, dark
60   With pines and cedars against the stricken sun
— The arm of Moses or of Joshua.[6]
He dropped his head and let fall the halo
Of mountains, purpling and silent as time,
To see temptation coiled before his feet:
65   A violated grass snake that lugged
Its intestine like a small red valise.
A cold-eyed skinflint it now was, and not
The manifest of that joyful wisdom,
The mirth and arrogant green flame of life;
70   Or earth's vivid tongue that flicked in praise of earth.

VI

And the man wept because pity was useless.
"Your jig's up; the flies come like kites," he said
And watched the grass snake crawl towards the hedge,
Convulsing and dragging into the dark
75   The satchel filled with curses for the earth,
For the odours of warm sedge, and the sun,
A blood-red organ in the dying sky.
Backwards it fell into a grassy ditch
Exposing its underside, white as milk,
80   And mocked by wisps of hay between its jaws;
And then it stiffened to its final length.
But though it opened its thin mouth to scream
A last silent scream that shook the black sky,
Adamant and fierce, the tall man did not curse.

VII

85   Beside the rigid snake the man stretched out
In fellowship of death; he lay silent
And stiff in the heavy grass with eyes shut,
Inhaling the moist odours of the night
Through which his mind tunnelled with flicking tongue
90   Backwards to caves, mounds, and sunken ledges
And desolate cliffs where come only kites,
And where of perished badgers and racoons
The claws alone remain, gripping the earth.
Meanwhile the green snake crept upon the sky,
95   Huge, his mailed coat glittering with stars that made
The night bright, and blowing thin wreaths of cloud
Athwart the moon; and as the weary man
Stood up, coiled above his head, transforming all.

6. Leaders of Israelite nation out of Egypt.

The Cold Green Element

At the end of the garden walk
the wind and its satellite wait for me;
their meaning I will not know
      until I go there,
5   but the black-hatted undertaker

who, passing, saw my heart beating in the grass,
is also going there. Hi, I tell him,
a great squall in the Pacific blew a dead poet
      out of the water,
10   who now hangs from the city's gates.

Crowds depart daily to see it, and return
with grimaces and incomprehension;
if its limbs twitched in the air
      they would sit at its feet
15   peeling their oranges.

And turning over I embrace like a lover
the trunk of a tree, one of those
for whom the lightning was too much
      and grew a brilliant
20   hunchback with a crown of leaves.

The ailments escaped from the labels
of medicine bottles are all fled to the wind;
I've seen myself lately in the eyes
      of old women,
25   spent streams mourning my manhood,

in whose old pupils the sun became
a bloodsmear on broad catalpa[1] leaves
and hanging from ancient twigs,
      my murdered selves
30   sparked the air like the muted collisions

of fruit. A black dog howls down my blood,
a black dog with yellow eyes;
he too by someone's inadvertence
      saw the bloodsmear
35   on the broad catalpa leaves.

But the furies[2] clear a path for me to the worm
who sang for an hour in the throat of a robin,
and misled by the cries of young boys
      I am again
40   a breathless swimmer in that cold green element.

Keine Lazarovitch 1870–1959

When I saw my mother's head on the cold pillow,
Her white waterfalling hair in the cheeks' hollows,
I thought, quietly circling my grief, of how
She had loved God but cursed extravagantly his creatures.

1. North American tree with heart-shaped leaves.
2. Vengeful goddesses in Greek and Roman mythologies.

For her final mouth was not water but a curse,
A smal black hole, a black rent in the universe,
Which damned the green earth, stars and trees in its stillness
And the inescapable lousiness of growing old.

And I record she was comfortless, vituperative,
Ignorant, glad, and much else besides; I believe
She endlessly praised her black eyebrows, their thick weave,
Till plagiarizing Death leaned down and took them for his mould.

And spoiled a dignity I shall not again find,
And the fury of her stubborn limited mind;
Now none will shake her amber beads and call God blind,
Or wear them upon a breast so radiantly.

O fierce she was, mean and unaccommodating;
But I think now of the toss of her gold earrings,
Their proud carnal assertion, and her youngest sings
While all the rivers of her red veins move into the sea.

Berry Picking

Silently my wife walks on the still wet furze
Now darkgreen the leaves are full of metaphors
Now lit up is each tiny lamp of blueberry.
The white nails of rain have dropped and the sun is free.

And whether she bends or straightens to each bush
To find the children's laughter among the leaves
Her quiet hands seem to make the quiet summer hush—
Berries or children, patient she is with these.

I only vex and perplex her; madness, rage
Are endearing perhaps put down upon the page;
Even silence daylong and sullen can then
Enamour as restraint or classic discipline.

So I envy the berries she puts in her mouth,
The red and succulent juice that stains her lips;
I shall never taste that good to her, nor will they
displease her with a thousand barbarous jests.

How they lie easily for her hand to take,
Part of the unoffending world that is hers;
Here beyond complexity she stands and stares
And leans her marvellous head as if for answers.

No more the easy soul my childish craft deceives
Nor the simpler one for whom yes is always yes;
No, now her voice comes to me from a far way off
Though her lips are redder than the raspberries.

Divine Image

Swiftly darting in the setting light,
The doomed sparrow feels the falcon's wings.
How beautiful are they both in flight.

MARGARET AVISON (1918 –   )

Searching and Sounding

In July this early sky is
a slope-field, a tangled
shining—blue-green, moist, in
heaped up pea-vines, in milk-hidden
5   tendrils, in light so strong
it seems a shadow of
further light, were the heart
large enough to find its succulence
and feed and not be glutted there.

10   I look for you
who only know the
melding and the forming of such heart,

and find you here
in the sour air
15   of a morning-after rooming-house hall-bedroom;
not in Gethsemane's[1] grass, perfumed with prayer,
but here,
seeking to cool the gray-stubbled cheek
    and the filth-choked throat
    and the scalding self-loathing heart, and
20   failing, for he is
sick,
for I . . .

I run from you to
the blinding blue of the
25   loveliness of this wasting
morning, and know
it is only with you
I can find the fields of brilliance
to burn out the sockets of the eyes that want no
30   weeping
though I am he
        or I am
a babbling boy
aged twenty, mentally distracted, blunted
35   by sedatives and too-long innocence
without your hand, teaching his the ax-heft or
    throttle-bar or
      grease-monkey's[2] gun or
        any craft or art.

40   And as I run I cry
"But I need something human
somebody now, here, with me."
Running from you.
The sunlight is sundered by cloud-mass.

45   My heart is sore, as its
bricked-in ovens smoulder,
for I know whose hand at my elbow
I fling from me as I run.

1. Garden near Jerusalem where Christ was arrested.
2. An automotive mechanic.

But you have come and sounded
50   a music around me, newly,

as though you can clear
all tears from our eyes only
if we sound the wells of weeping with
another's heart, and hear
55   another's music only.

Lord, the light deepens as the
summer day goes down
in lakes of stillness.
Dwarf that I am, and spent,
60   touch my wet face with
the little light I can bear now, to mirror,
and keep me
close, into sleeping.
— — —
From the pearl and gray of daybreak
65   you have brought me to
sandstone, baldness, the place
of jackals, the sparrow's skull,
tumbled skeletons of what were
hills clothed in forest
70   and spongy meadows, the place of
baked stone, dryness, famine,
of howling among the tombs.

From the first dews, the
grasses at their budding,
75   fragrance of mountain snow
and sunfat cedars
to the farthest reaches
where your Descent began, on the beach gravel
ground by sea-slimed teeth...
80   those bloodless horses....

To what strange fruits in
the ocean's orchards?

Reaching
with Light that is perfect, needed no
85   kernels to swell nor juices to syrop nor
no further making— *all* newness—
all being
that the remotest fishrib,
the hairiest pink-thing there
90   might as one fragment
make towards the fullness you
put off, there, on the
ravening shore I view, from
my gull-blanched cliffs,
95   and shiver.
GATHER my fragments towards
the radium, the
all-swallowing moment
once more.

The Dumbfounding

When you walked here,
took skin, muscle, hair,
eyes, larynx, we
withheld all honor: "His house is clay,
5   how can he tell us of his far country?"

Your not familiar pace
in flesh, across the waves,
woke only our distrust.
Twice-torn we cried "A ghost"
10   and only on our planks counted you fast.

Dust wet with your spittle
cleared mortal trouble.
We called you a blasphemer,
a devil-tamer.

15   The evening you spoke of going away
we could not stay.
All legions massed. You had to wash, and rise,
alone, and face
out of the light, for us.

20   You died.
We said,
"The worst is true, our bliss
has come to this."

When you were seen by men
25   in holy flesh again
we hoped so despairingly for such report
we closed their windpipes for it.

Now you have sought
and seek, in all our ways, all thoughts,
30   streets, musics—and we make of these a din
trying to lock you out, or in,
to be intent. And dying.

Yet you are
constant and sure,
35   the all-lovely, all-men's-way
to that far country.

Winning one, you again
all ways would begin
life: to make new
40   flesh, to empower
the weak in nature
to restore
or stay the sufferer;

lead through the garden to
45   trash, rubble, hill,
where, the outcast's outcast, you
sound dark's uttermost, strangely light-brimming, until
time be full.

The Swimmer's Moment

For everyone
The swimmer's moment at the whirlpool comes,
But many at that moment will not say,
"This is the whirlpool, then."
5   By their refusal they are saved
From the black pit, and also from contesting
The deadly rapids, and emerging in
The mysterious, and more ample, further waters.
And so their bland-blank faces turn and turn
10   Pale and forever on the rim of suction
They will not recognize.
Of those who dare the knowledge
Many are whirled into the ominous center
That, gaping vertical, seals up
15   For them an eternal boon of privacy,
So that we turn away from their defeat
With a despair, not for their deaths, but for
Ourselves, who cannot penetrate their secret
Nor even guess at the anonymous breadth
20   Where one or two have won:
(The silver reaches of the estuary).

AL PURDY (1918-   )

The Cariboo Horses

At 100 Mile House[1] the cowboys ride in rolling
stagey cigarettes with one hand reining
half-tame brorco rebels on a morning grey as stone
— so much like riding dangerous women
5   with whiskey coloured eyes—
such women as once fell dead with their lovers
with fire in their heads and slippery froth on thighs
—Beaver and Carrier[2] women maybe or
        Blackfoot squaws far past the edge of this valley
10   on the other side of those two toy mountain ranges
        from the sunfierce plains beyond—

But only horses
                waiting in stables
hitched at taverns
15   standing at dawn
pastured outside the town with
jeeps and fords and chevvys and
busy muttering stake trucks rushing
importantly over roads of man's devising
20   over the safe known roads of the ranchers
families and merchants of the town—
                On the high prairie
are only horse and rider
                wind in dry grass
25   clopping in silence under the toy mountains
dropping sometimes and
                lost in the dry grass
                golden oranges of dung—

1. A town on Highway 97, in the Cariboo region of central British Columbia.

2. Beaver and Carrier are ethnic divisions of British Columbian interior native peoples. The Blackfeet are a prairie tribe.

Only horses
30   no stopwatch memories or palace ancestors
not Kiangs³ hauling undressed stone in the Nile Valley
and having stubborn Egyptian tantrums or
Onagers⁴ racing thru Hither Asia and
the last Quagga⁵ screaming in African highlands
35   lost relatives of these
        whose hooves were thunder
the ghosts of horses battering thru the wind
whose names were the wind's common usage
whose life was the sun's
40   arriving here at chilly noon
        in the gasoline smell of the
        dust and waiting 15 minutes
        at the grocer's—

Winter at Roblin Lake

Seeing the sky darken & the fields
turn brown & the lake lead-grey
as some enormous scrap of sheet metal
& wind grabs the world around the equator
I am most thankful then for knowing about
        the little gold hairs on your belly

Old Alex

"85 years old, that miserable alcoholic
old bastard is never gonna die," the man said
where he got bed and board. But he did.
I'll say this for Alex' immortality tho:
5   if they dig him up in a thousand years,
and push a spigot into his belly why
his fierce cackle'll drive a nail in silence,
his laugh split cordwood and trees kow-tow
like green butlers, the staggering world
10   get drunk and sober men run scared.
So you say: was I fond of him?
No—not exactly anyhow. Once
he told his sons and daughters to bugger off,
and then vomited on their memory. It'd be
15   like liking toadstools or a gun pointing at you—
He sat home three weeks drinking whiskey,
singing harsh songs and quoting verse and chapter
from the Bible: his mean and privileged piety
dying slowly: they rolled him onto a stretcher
20   like an old pig and prettied him with cosmetics,
sucked his blood out with a machine and
dumped him into the ground like garbage.

I don't mourn. Nobody does. Like mourning an ulcer.
Why commemorate disease in a poem then?
25   I don't know. But his hate was lovely,
given freely and without stint. His smallness
had the quality of making everyone else feel noble,
and thus fools. I search desperately
for good qualities, and end up crawling

3. Wild asses of eastern Asia.
4. Wild asses of central Asia.   5. Zebra-like animal of southern Africa. Now extinct.

30   inside that decaying head and wattled throat
    to scream obscenities like papal blessings,
    knowing now and again I'm at least God.
    Well, who remembers a small purple and yellow bruise long?
    But when he was here he was a sunset!

The Horseman of Agawa[1]
(Indian rock-painting under the cliffs of Lake Superior)

It's spring and the steel platforms tourists usually stand on
are not installed yet so we take our chances
but I have to abandon my beer and use both hands for safety
We clamber down rocks unsteady as children
5   reach slanting stone ledges under the hundred-foot walls
my wife skipping ahead so nimbly I'm jealous of her
and say "Wait for me, dammit" but she won't
then take my shoes off and go barefoot

She sees the painting first and calls "Here!"
10   her face flattens and dissolves into no expression
I balance myself beside her on the tilted ledge
that slides off into deep water and the rock hurts my feet
but I feel the same way she does as the rock horseman canters
by two feet from my nose forever or nearly
15   We stand there and hold onto each other for balance above the big lake
that holds a million or so rainbows
stillborn under the luminous water and water
dripping down from above in the almost silence my feet hurt

The painted horseman rides over four moons (or suns) on his trail
20   whose meaning must be a four-day journey somewhere
the red iron oxide faded from Lake Superior storms
and maybe two hundred years since the Ojibway artist stood there
balanced above water like us
and drew with his fingers on the stone canvas
25   with fish eggs or bear grease to make the painting permanent
pitting fish eggs and bear grease against eternity
which is kind of ludicrous or kind of beautiful I guess

I have too many thoughts about the horseman
I might select one and say this is a signpost this painting
30   (in fact I've just done that)
a human-as-having-babies signpost
but also dammit part of the spirit
a thought taken out from inside the head and carefully left here
like saying I love you to stone
35   I think that after the Ojibway are all dead
and all the bombs in the white world have fizzed into harmlessness
the ghost of one inept hunter who always got lost
and separated from his friends because he had a lousy sense of direction
that man can come here to get his bearings calling out
40   to his horse his dog or himself because he's alone
in the fog in the night in the rain in his mind and say
'My friends where are you?'
and the rock walls will seize his voice
and break it into a million amplified pieces of echoes
45   that will find the ghosts of his friends in the tombs of their dust

But I mistrust the mind-quality that tempts me
to embroider and exaggerate things

---

1. Name of a town, a river, and a region in Lake Superior   Provincial Park, north of Sault Ste. Marie, Ontario.

I just watch my wife's face
she is quiet as she generally is because I do most of the talking
50 it is forty years old and has felt the pain of children
the pettiness of day-to-day living and getting thousands of meals
but standing on the rock face of Lake Superior
it is not lessened in any way
with a stillness of depth that reaches where I can't follow
55 all other thoughts laid aside in her brain
on her face I see the Ojibway horseman painting the rock with red fingers
and he speaks to her as I could not
in pictures without handles of words
into feeling into being here by direct transmission
60 from the stranded Ojibway horseman
And I change it all back into words again for that's the best I can do
but they only point the way we came from for who knows where we are
under the tall stone cliffs with water dripping down on us
or returned from a long journey and calling out to our friends
65 But the rock blazes into light when we leave the place
or else the sun shines somewhere else and I didn't notice it
and my secret knowing is knowing what she knows
and can't say and I can only indicate
reclaim my half-empty beer and drink it and tie my shoes
70 follow her up the tangled rocks past the warning sign for strangers
and wait till she turns around

JAMES REANEY (1926–   )

First Letter[1]
To the Avon River[2] above Stratford, Canada

What did the Indians call you?
For you do not flow
With English accents.
I hardly know
5 What I should call you
  Because before
I drank coffee or tea
  I drank you
  With my cupped hands
10 And you did not taste English to me
  And you do not sound
  Like Avon
  Or swans & bards[3]
But rather like the sad wild fowl
15   In prints drawn
  By Audubon[4]
And like dear bad poets
  Who wrote
  Early in Canada
20 And never were of note.
You are the first river
  I crossed
And like the first whirlwind
  The first rainbow
25   First snow, first
  Falling star I saw,

You, for other rivers are my law.
  These other rivers:
  The Red & the Thames[5]
30   Are never so sweet
To skate upon, swim in
  Or for baptism of sin.
  Silver and light
The sentence of your voice,
35   With a soprano
Continuous cry you shall
  Always flow
  Through my heart.
The rain and the snow of my mind
40 Shall supply the spring of that river
  Forever.
Though not your name
Your coat of arms I know
  And motto:
45 A shield of reeds and cresses
  Sedges, crayfishes
The hermaphroditic leech
Minnows, muskrats and farmers' geese
And printed above this shield
50 One of my earliest wishes
"To flow like you."

1. This is the opening poem of a book entitled *Twelve Letters to a Small Town*.
2. The place names in Southwest Ontario are usually taken from British geography.
3. Swans and William Shakespeare are associated with both Stratfords.
4. French artist of early nineteenth century, famous for prints of North American birds.
5. They flow through Winnipeg, Manitoba, and London, Ontario, two places where Reaney has lived.

The Tall Black Hat

As a child, I dreamt of tomorrow
Of the word "tomorrow" itself.
The word was a man in a tall black hat
Who walked in black clothes through
5　Green fields of quiet rain that
Beneath gray cloudfields grew.

Tall as trees or Abraham Lincoln[1]
Were that man's brothers
Who when they become To-day
10　Die and dissolve one by one
Like licorice morning shadows
When held in the mouth of the sun.

Yesterday is an old greataunt
Rocked off in her rocking chair
15　To cellars where old light and snow
And all yesterdays go;
To-day was a small girl bringing
China cupfuls of water and air
And cages of robins singing,
20　"It is positively no crime

To have pleasure in Present Time."
But Tomorrow is most impressive
Like the hired man back from the fair
He comes to the child still sleeping
25　With pockets of longer hair,
A handful of longer fingers
And the Indian I remember
At dusk, crossing Market Square.

The man in the tall black hat
30　Brought the gipsy who was drunk
And the white faced cat
Who stepped before my stepmother
The very first time she came.

He gave the child a yellow leaf,
35　He holds the arrow for my heart,
He dropped the playing card in the lane,
He brought the dancing weasel,
And the old man playing the jewsharp.

He brings the wind and the sun
40　And the stalks of dead teazle[2]
Seen on a windless winter walk,
He fetches a journey's direction
From his garden of weathervanes
And mines, like diamonds, the tears
45　For the glittering windowpanes
Of rain and sorrow.

All the days of all the years
The dark provider hunts me
Whom I named Sir Thomas Tomorrow
50　After my dream of him,
And in the grave fields of mystery
This black man has brothers
Who have followed him and come
Ever since with all I must see,
55　With Earth, Heaven and the tenor drum
I played in the C.O.T.C.,[3]
The sound of bells and stars in a tree
Are stuck to their thumb
And lie in their tall black hats and pockets
60　Like pictures in locked and closed lockets.

At midnight he knocked and arrived
As the old woman really rocked away
And he took off his tall hat which
Changed into a small white cup,
65　White as the new light of day.
To the girl as small as a switch,
The girl who wakes me up,
His tallness and blackness shrank
To leave behind on the floor
70　From his pockets of come to pass
Puzzles and lonely birds to see
Diamonded names upon window glass,
A whistle, a straw and a tree.

But see out where small in the dawn
75　Through the hanging wingflash dance
Of the little flies, the wrens and the doves
Who are the seconds and minutes and hours
Floating over the acres of distance,
See his brother with feet of slate
80　Begin to walk through the wet flowers
Towards me with his speck of Future
And a tall black hatful of Fate.

The Katzenjammer Kids[1]

With porcupine locks
And faces which, when
More closely examined,
Are composed of measle-pink specks,
5　These two dwarf imps,
The Katzenjammer Kids,

1. American president (1861–65), famous for his stove-pipe hat.
2. A European thistle.
3. Canadian Officers' Training Corps, a university organization.

1. An American comic strip, especially popular in the 1940s. The details of the poem describe typical events in the strip.

Flitter through their Desert Island world.
Sometimes they get so out of hand
That a blue Captain
10   With stiff whiskers of black wicker
And an orange Inspector
With a black telescope
Pursue them to spank them
All through that land
15   Where cannibals cut out of brown paper
In cardboard jungles feast and caper,
Where the sea's sharp waves continually
Waver against the shore faithfully
And the yellow sun above is thin and flat
20   With a collar of black spikes and spines
To tell the innocent childish heart that
It shines
And warms (see where she stands and stammers)
The dear fat mother of the Katzenjammers.
25   Oh, for years and years she has stood
At the window and kept fairly good
Guard over the fat pies that she bakes
For her two children, those dancing heartaches.
Oh, the blue skies of that funny paper weather!
30   The distant birds like two eyebrows close together!
And the rustling paper roar
Of the waves
Against the paper sands of the paper shore!

D. G. JONES (1929 –   )

For Françoise Adnet

It is that time of day, time
To chop the beans, to peel
Potatoes for the evening meal.

The fullness of time
5   Grows, at this hour,
Like the shadows on the crockery.

Mademoiselle's mauve gloves,
Alone, tell of the afternoon, the dried
Flowers, the delicate hands among the stalks.

10   For once things are what they are,
Until my little girl
Comes in from outdoors, the melting snow

15   Cool in her nostrils,
Sky, blue without clouds,
Behind her eyes.

But even these dissolve.
Fingering an orange
She lets her bare legs dangle.

Time is space, it glows
20   Like the white tablecloth,
The breadboard where I slice the onions.

The kitchen floats in my tears—
And the sun
In its brazier of urban trees.

The Stream Exposed with All Its Stones

The stream exposed with all its stones
Flung on a raw field
Is covered, once again,

With snow.

It is not hidden. It
Still flows.

The houses in the valley, standing
Motionless below,
Seem wrapped in sunlight like a snow

And are deceptive. Even stones
Deceive us.

The creator goes
Rampaging through our lives: winter
Is a masquerade.

I tell you
Nakedness is a disguise: the white
Is dark below.

This silence is the water's cry.

I tell you in those silent houses girls
Are dancing like the stones.

Dance for One Leg
(for Avrum Malus)[1]

Not to be driven, above all
by oneself

to improvise

as fields
5   forget the glacier and the driven plough
and move like milk.

The tall man with a cast becomes
a whitewashed wall
where flowers grow: *Pour ton amour*

10   *Pour te consoler.*

The one leg learns to dance.

His house has many windows.

His house is blank, a white
among the drifts of white.

15   How did they come here, the children
playing age (the one who rocks
in the rocking chair, the girl
in the diminutive long dress), the friend

each separate

20   the mother of the girl (her beauty
the exhausted grass)

except that deaths
like winters are occasion for a fire
a break is an occasion

25   to discover love.

They dance

the tall man with a cast
dances

thus, together

30   as estranged bones knit, as fields
invested in the driven snow
forget themselves

become one flesh.

1. A writer and teacher in the Eastern Townships,
Quebec.

A Garland of Milne[1]

He lived in the bush, the wilderness
but he made light of it

He was at home, sitting
with the small birds around him
5   gathering seeds, the bare

earth showing through the snow
the sun falling
scenting the air

For him it was a garden

10   Wildflowers picked in the woods
he placed in a pickle jar
perhaps to sketch

A tent made a pleasance

He let the trees stand where they were

15   and he went quietly
where islands curled up for the winter

A wife could not abide
that god-forsaken country

but a woman came
20   as silently as trees
and stayed

being cut in the grain, like Eve

He wanted nothing

He lay in wait for ponds, the still
25   moments when the snow
fell from the branches

Flowers he knew most naked in a bowl

He left it to Monet[2] to paint
the waterlilies in their wild
30   and dangerous state

The titans he contained in a cartouche[3]

A battlefield or a deserted house
had a life of its own

No violence

35   Who flies with the whirlwind is at rest

No one in France
could make such galaxies
of glass and water

intricate with flowers

40   All space came out in flowers
miraculous, erupting from a void or mouth

And every breath
a wind or sun, a season or delight
drew colour from the earth

45   as if a brush
stroked virgin canvas

The hills flew little flags beyond
the painting place

The darkest night drew fires
50   like jack-o'-lanterns from the street

The children danced like flames

And gaily, gaily glowed the islands
under the storm's spout

The light was never spent

55   A solemn gaiety awoke
in the white poppy

amid the sanguine and magenta reds

LEONARD COHEN (1934 –   )

For Anne

With Annie gone,
Whose eyes to compare
With the morning sun?

Not that I did compare,
But I do compare
Now that she's gone.

1. David Milne, Canadian painter (1882–1953).
2. French Impressionist painter (1840–1926).

3. Oval frame used to enclose important figures in Egyptian hieroglyphics. But see other meanings.

I Have Not Lingered in European Monasteries

I have not lingered in European monasteries
and discovered among the tall grasses tombs of knights
who fell as beautifully as their ballads tell;
I have not parted the grasses
5   or purposefully left them thatched.

I have not released my mind to wander and wait
in those great distances
between the snowy mountains and the fishermen,
like a moon,
10   or a shell beneath the moving water.

I have not held my breath
so that I might hear the breathing of God,
or tamed my heartbeat with an exercise,
or starved for visions.
15   Although I have watched him often
I have not become the heron,
leaving my body on the shore,
and I have not become the luminous trout,
leaving my body in the air.

20   I have not worshipped wounds and relics,
or combs of iron,
or bodies wrapped and burnt in scrolls.

I have not been unhappy for ten thousand years.
During the day I laugh and during the night I sleep.
25   My favourite cooks prepare my meals,
my body cleans and repairs itself,
and all my work goes well.

As the Mist Leaves No Scar

As the mist leaves no scar
On the dark green hill,
So my body leaves no scar
On you, nor ever will.

When wind and hawk encounter,
What remains to keep?
So you and I encounter,
Then turn, then fall to sleep.

As many nights endure
Without a moon or star,
So will we endure
When one is gone and far.

Hitler the Brain-Mole

Hitler the brain-mole looks out of my eyes
Goering boils ingots of gold in my bowels
My Adam's Apple bulges with the whole head of Goebbels
No use to tell a man he's a Jew
I'm making a lampshade out of your kiss
Confess! confess!
    is what you demand
although you believe you're giving me everything

The Bus

I was the last passenger of the day,
I was alone on the bus,
I was glad they were spending all that money
just getting me up Eighth Avenue.
Driver! I shouted, it's you and me tonight,
let's run away from this big city
to a smaller city more suitable to the heart,
let's drive past the swimming pools of Miami Beach,
you in the driver's seat, me several seats back,
but in the racial cities we'll change places
so as to show how well you've done up North,
and let us find ourselves some tiny American fishing village
in unknown Florida
and park right at the edge of the sand,
a huge bus pointing out,
metallic, painted, solitary,
with New York plates.

Two Went to Sleep

Two went to sleep
almost every night
one dreamed of mud
one dreamed of Asia
5 visiting a zeppelin
visiting Nijinsky[1]
Two went to sleep
one dreamed of ribs
one dreamed of senators
10 Two went to sleep
two travellers
The long marriage
in the dark
The sleep was old
15 the travellers were old
one dreamed of oranges
one dreamed of Carthage[2]
Two friends asleep
years locked in travel
20 Good night my darling
as the dreams waved goodbye
one travelled lightly
one walked through water
visiting a chess game
25 visiting a booth
always returning
to wait out the day
One carried matches
one climbed a beehive
30 one sold an earphone
one shot a German

Two went to sleep
every sleep went together
wandering away
35 from an operating table
one dreamed of grass
one dreamed of spokes
one bargained nicely
one was a snowman
40 one counted medicine
one tasted pencils
one was a child
one was a traitor
visiting heavy industry
45 visiting the family
Two went to sleep
none could foretell
one went with baskets
one took a ledger
50 one night happy
one night in terror
Love could not bind them
Fear could not either
they went unconnected
55 they never knew where
always returning
to wait out the day
parting with kissing
parting with yawns
60 visiting Death till
they wore out their welcome
visiting Death till
the right disguise worked

---

1. Vaslav Nijinsky (1890–1950), famous Russian ballet dancer and choreographer. He spent the later part of his life in an insane asylum.

2. Ancient city of Northern Africa, predominant sea power in western Mediterranean until defeated by Rome in second century B.C.

JOHN NEWLOVE (1938–)

The Pride

1.
The image/   the pawnees[1]
in their earth-lodge villages,
the clear image
of teton sioux, wild
5   fickle people the chronicler says,

the crazy dogs, men
tethered with leather dog-thongs
to a stake, fighting until dead,

image: arikaras
10   with traded spanish sabre blades
mounted on the long
heavy buffalo lances,
riding the sioux
down, the centaurs,[2] the horsemen
15   scouring the level plains
in war or hunt
until smallpox got them,
the warriors,

image— of a desolate country,
20   a long way between fires,
unfound lakes, mirages, cold rocks,
and lone men going through it,
cree with good guns
causing terror in athabaska[3]
25   among the inhabitants, frightened
stone-age people, "so that
they fled at the mere sight
of a strange smoke miles away."

2.
This western country crammed
30   with the ghosts of indians,
haunting the coastal stones and shores,
the forested pacific islands,
mountains, hills and plains:

beside the ocean ethlinga,
35   man in the moon, empties
his bucket, on
a sign from spirit
of the wind ethlinga
empties his bucket, refreshing
40   the earth, and it rains
on the white cities;

that black joker, broken-
jawed raven, most prominent
among haida and tsimshian tribes
45   is in the kwakiutl

1. Pawnees, Sioux, Arikaras, Cree, Shoshonis, Snakes, and Peigans are plains tribes. Nootka, Kwakiutl, Haida, and Tsimshian are coastal tribes.
2. In Greek mythology, monsters born of Ixion; they have the heads, trunks, and arms of human beings, and the bodies of horses.
3. Territory now embraced by northern Alberta and Saskatchewan.

dance masks too—
it was he who brought fire,
food and water to man,
the trickster;

50 and thunderbird hilunga,
little thought of
by haida for lack of thunderstorms
in their district, goes
by many names, exquisite disguises
55 carved in the painted wood,

he is nootka tootooch, the wings
causing thunder and the tongue
or flashing eyes engendering
rabid white lightning,
60 whose food was whales,

called kwunusela by the kwakiutl,
it was he who laid down the house-logs
for the people at the place
where kwunusela alighted;

65 in full force and virtue
and terror of the law, eagle—
he is authority, the sun
assumed his form once,
the sun which used to be
70 a flicker's egg, success-
fully transformed;

and malevolence comes to the land,
the wild woman of the woods—
grinning, she wears
75 a hummingbird in her hair,
d'sonoqua, the furious one—

they are all ready
to be found, the legends
and the people, or
80 all their ghosts and memories,
whatever is strong enough
to be remembered.

3.
But what image, bewildered
son of all men
85 under the hot sun,
do you worship,
what completeness
do you hope to have
from these tales,
90 a half-understood massiveness, mirage,
in men's minds—what
is your purpose;

with what force
will you proceed
95 along a line
neither straight nor short,
whose future
you cannot know
or result foretell,

100   whose meaning is still
       obscured as the incidents
       occur and accumulate?

4.
       The country moves on;
       there are orchards in the interior,
105   the mountain passes
       are broken, the foothills
       covered with cattle and fences,
       and the fading hills covered;

       but the plains are bare,
110   not barren, easy
       for me to love their people,
       for me to love their people
       without selection.

5.
       In 1787, the old cree saukamappee, aged 75 or thereabout, speaking then of
115   things that had happened when he was 16, just a man, told david thompson
       about the raids the shoshonis, the snakes, had made on the westward-
       reaching peigan, of their war-parties sometimes sent 10 days' journey to
       enemy camps, the man all afoot in battle array for the encounter, crouching
       behind their giant shields. The peigan armed with guns drove these snakes
120   out of the plains, the plains where their strength had been, where they had
       been settled since living memory (though nothing is remembered beyond a
       grandfather's time), to the west of the rockies:

       these people moved without rest,
       backward and forward with the wind,
125   the seasons, the game, great herds,
       in hunger and abundance—

       in summer and in the bloody fall
       they gathered on the killing grounds,
       fat and shining with fat, amused
130   with the luxuries of war and death,

       relieved from the steam of knowledge,
       consoled by the stream of blood
       and steam rising from the fresh hides
       and tired horses, wheeling in their pride
135   on the sweating horses, their pride.

6.
       Those are all stories;
       the pride, the grand poem
       of our land, of the earth itself,
       will come, welcome, and
140   sought for, and found,
       in a line of running verse,
       sweating, our pride;

       we seize on
       what has happened before,
145   one line only
       will be enough,
       a single line
       and then the sunlit brilliant image suddenly floods us
       with understanding, shocks our
150   attentions, and all desire
       stops, stands alone;

we stand alone,
we are no longer lonely
but have roots,
155 and the rooted words
recur in the mind, mirror, so that
we dwell on nothing else, in nothing else,
touched, repeating them,
at home freely
160 at last, in amazement;

"the unyielding phrase
in tune with the epoch,"
the thing made up
of our desires,
165 not of its words, not only
of them, but of something else
as well, that which we desire
so ardently, that which
will not come when
170 it is summoned alone,
but grows in us
and idles about and hides
until the moment is due—

the knowledge of
175 our origins, and where
we are in truth,
whose land this is
and is to be.

7.
The unyielding phrase:
180 when the moment is due, then
it springs upon us
out of our own mouths,
unconsidered, overwhelming
in its knowledge, complete—

185 not this handful
of fragments, as the indians
are not composed of
the romantic stories
about them, or of the stories
190 they tell only, but
still ride the soil
in us, dry bones a part
of the dust in our eyes,
needed and troubling
195 in the glare, in
our breath, in our
ears, in our mouths,
in our bodies entire, in our minds, until
at last
200 we become them

in our desires, our desires,
mirages, mirrors, that are theirs, hard-
riding desires, and they
become our true forbears, moulded
205 by the same wind or rain,
and in this land we
are their people, come
back to life again.

No Song

said the bird
in its attitude

caw

declining
the privilege
of music
or melody

caw

standing
on its tree

caw

fingering
the absolute
wood
beneath

The Flower

I am too tense,
decline to dance
verbally. The flower
is not in its colour,
but in the seed.

MARGARET ATWOOD (1939 –   )

Some Objects of Wood and Stone

i   Totems[1]

We went to the park
where they kept the wooden people:
static, multiple
uprooted and trans-
5 planted.

Their faces were restored,
freshly-painted.
In front of them
the other wooden people
10 posed for each others' cameras
and nearby a new booth
sold replicas and souvenirs.

One of the people was real.
It lay on its back, smashed
15 by a toppling fall or just
the enduring of minor winters.

20 Only one of the heads had
survived intact, and it was
also beginning to decay
but there was a
life in the progressing
of old wood back to
the earth, obliteration

25 that the clear-hewn
standing figures lacked.

As for us, perennial watchers,
tourists of another kind
there is nothing for us to worship;
30 no pictures of ourselves, no blue-
sky summer fetishes, no postcards
we can either buy, or
smiling
be.

1. Popular name for house frontal poles, mortuary and
memorial poles, carved and painted by the native peoples   of the British Columbia coast.

There are few totems that remain
35 living for us.
Though in passing,
through glass we notice

dead trees in the seared meadows
dead roots bleaching in the swamps.

ii   Pebbles

40 Talking was difficult. Instead
we gathered coloured pebbles
from the places on the beach
where they occurred.

They were sea-smoothed, sea-completed.
45 They enclosed what they intended
to mean in shapes
as random and necessary
as the shapes of words

and when finally
50 we spoke
the sounds of our voices fell
into the air   single and
solid and rounded and really
there
55 and then dulled, and then like sounds
gone,   a fistful of gathered
pebbles there was no point
in taking home, dropped on a beachful
of other coloured pebbles

60 and when we turned to go
a flock of small
birds flew scattered by the
fright of our sudden moving
and disappeared: hard

65 sea pebbles
thrown solid for an instant
against the sky

flight of words

iii   Carved Animals

The small carved
70 animal is passed from
hand to hand
around the circle
until the stone grows warm

touching, the hands do not know
75 the form of animal
which was made or
the true form of stone
uncovered

and the hands, the fingers the
80 hidden small bones
of the hands bend to hold the shape,
shape themselves, grow
cold with the stone's cold, grow
also animal, exchange
85 until the skin wonders
if stone is human

In the darkness later
and even when the animal
has gone, they keep
90 the image of that
inner shape

hands holding warm
hands holding
the half-formed air

Progressive Insanities of a Pioneer

i

He stood, a point
on a sheet of green paper
proclaiming himself the centre,

with no walls, no borders
5 anywhere; the sky no height
above him, totally un-
enclosed
and shouted:

Let me out!

ii

10 He dug the soil in rows,
imposed himself with shovels
He asserted
into the furrows, I
am not random.

15   The ground
      replied with aphorisms:

      a tree-sprout, a nameless
      weed, words
      he couldn't understand.

      iii

20   The house pitched
      the plot staked
      in the middle of nowhere.

      At night the mind
      inside, in the middle
25   of nowhere.

      The idea of an animal
      patters across the roof.

      In the darkness the fields
      defend themselves with fences
30   in vain:
                  everything
                  is getting in.

      iv

      By daylight he resisted.
      He said, disgusted
35   with the swamp's clamourings and the outbursts
      of rocks,
                  This is not order
                  but the absence
                  of order.

40   He was wrong, the unanswering
      forest implied:

                  It was
                  an ordered absence

      v

      For many years
45   he fished for a great vision,
      dangling the hooks of sown
      roots under the surface
      of the shallow earth.

      It was like
50   enticing whales with a bent
      pin. Besides he thought

      in that country
      only the worms were biting.

      vi

      If he had known unstructured
55   space is a deluge
      and stocked his log house-
      boat with all the animals

      even the wolves,

he might have floated.

60 But obstinate he
stated, The land is solid
and stamped,

watching his foot sink
down through stone
65 up to the knee.

vii

Things
refused to name themselves; refused
to let him name them.

The wolves hunted
70 outside.

On his beaches, his clearings,
by the surf of under-
growth breaking
at his feet, he foresaw
75 disintegration
                        and in the end
through eyes
made ragged by his
effort, the tension
80 between subject and object,

the green
vision, the unnamed
whale invaded.

———————————

you fit into me
like a hook into an eye

a fish hook
an open eye

You Are Happy

The water turns
a long way down over the raw stone,
ice crusts around it

We walk separately
along the hill to the open
beach, unused
picnic tables, wind
shoving the brown waves, erosion, gravel
rasping on gravel.

In the ditch a deer
carcass, no head. Bird
running across the glaring
road against the low pink sun.

When you are this
cold you can think about
nothing but the cold, the images

hitting into your eyes
like needles, crystals, you are happy.

DAPHNE MARLATT (1942 –   )

Imperial Cannery,[1] 1913

Standing inside the door (the river . . .) how shadow lies
just inside the cannery floor, sun, pouring down outside
the river streaming slow, slow, by. Now she feels old enough,
now she is wearing her long print dress & leaning into the
5   threshold, waiting for work, the wheel that time is, Whose hands
are standing still, hers, empty, Whose friends also surround her,
waiting, waiting all morning for the fish to come. Nothing moves
but occasional strands of long hair the subtle wind is lifting,
up off the river, the Fraser, mouth of the Fraser here where it
10   debouches, into marsh, delta, swirling around & past those
pilings of the cannery wharf they are standing on, muddy &
pale grey teeming, invisible fish . . .

                          Now she is old enough to be her
mother inside, working, with the smallest one standing by her skirt
15   in grubby dress, & the blood streams down the wooden cutting board
as the 'iron chink' (that's what they call it) beheads each fish . . .

Now she is old enough for the wheel's turn, she is feeling her
body in its light dress wind blows thru, as past the faces of
her friends, likewise silent, impassive. Wind blows thru
20   those open doors (two) because, in the dark where machines are,
& the cans, & the steam, & a cavern of men with rolled up
sleeves & straw hats, & men in oilcloth slickers spattered with
fish gut, beyond & across the corner of that dark stands
another door, & the sail of a boat crossing the river, wind,
25   wind . . . An open door, where men unload their hauls of fish, the
collector's boat, float, sliding one, a hundred, on top of another,
their own scale grease that keeps them alive in sea they're
taken from to dry, in open sun on an open dock.

                          But she is in her
30   element, dreaming of sails, her father's, or a friend's son, at the
Imperial which owns their boat, their net, their debt. But the
Fraser gives of itself, incessantly, rich (so the dream goes),
& wooden houses jammed on pilings close together, leaning, with
wooden walks & muddy alleys, laundry, & the dry marsh grass that
35   stutters out of silt the dykes retain, from a flowing
ever eroding & running river . . .

dreaming, of fabric she saw at Walker's Emporium, & the ribbon. A
woman of means she dreams, barefoot on the dock in the wind, leaning
into her threshold of work, machines, the wheel that keeps turning
40   turning out of its wooden sleeve, the blade with teeth marked:
for marriage, for birth, for death.

A by-channel; a small backwater:

                 slough, Finn Slough[1] (or Gilmour,
by Gilmour Island), slough for sale as 'deep sea frontage,'
has been always, simply, backwater clutch of shacks, floats,
sheds: a swamp & dusty marsh grass sheltering mosquito boats,
5   small gillnetters & other vessels in this amphibious place,

---

1. Salmon-processing cannery at Steveston, B.C., a small
town south of Vancouver. The population was largely of
Japanese origin.

1. Local name for waterway near Steveston, a fishing
town south of Vancouver, B.C.

half earth half water, half river half sea, tide fills, swiftly,
pushing muddy fingers into timbers of the float, crawling round
pilings & rushes, glinting up a web of net stranding float where
a man & a woman bend, knotting holes deadheads & other refuse a murky
10　river roils, have torn, ripped, & otherwise scorned, sometimes from
leadline to cork . . .
　　　　　　　　　　　　　　　　The slow effort of
this people's morning: rise with predawn birdsong & coffee
stretching stiffer & stiffer bones, pack lunch, pad past the
15　cloistered silence of tv, crunch of gravel, drive (green Pinto)[2]
down to where their boats lie, light filtering immense
vegetation.

　　　　　Check fuel, untie & start the engine ('a 7 Easthope
& a 15, wasn't it a 15 Easthope they had too? They thought they really
20　had something on the go - now when they look back they think it's a
joke, you know, why, have we actually been fishing with those?'

'That was the onetime king engine' on this coast, days when
nobody had any money, they bought a used car engine for two bucks,
had it delivered down to the slough, the poor

25　　　　　　　　　　　　　　　　shelter of swamp
houses, float ('when I look at it now it looks like a summer cabin')
under the lee of a dyke Finnish squatters & other folk whose lives
are inextricably tied with the tide that inundates their day, their
time measured only by: this sucking at vegetal silence swallows shred,
30　from the boom of idle boats, from the ridgepole of shadowy netshed
jets drone: this land up for deep sea frontage ('oh yes, it'll be
freighters & cement scow, barges & containerized shipping all the
way up to New Westminister,[3]
　　　　　　　　　　　you can't stop progress, can you?'

35　　　　　　　　　　　How *accept* its creeping up?
like a disease, like time, the tide they still know how to run,
with it, up under ('remember how your net got wrapped & rolled?')
that barge, danger at dark or fog, still after the fish which still
run shadowy lines thru all that murk against the shifting bars of
40　shipping channel, slipping that traffic, that bottom:

　　　　　　　　　　　　　　　'You sure find out
when you get all the rubbish from down there - lot of bark, papers,
bathroom papers - it's real messy sometimes. Trees & twigs &
branches, branches of trees even floating down there. & then there's,
45　I dunno what kind of plant it is, it's like a crabapple limb & it's
just full of little twigs, & that's a wicked one when it gets caught in
to a thin net. & ends of logs that have been cut, you know, stump
ends & round blocks drifting. The sawmills open their gates, you know
& let all their loose stuff out - when that comes dashing there's even
50　sawdust in the river.'

　　　　　At bottom of this slippery time, it's her boat,
her feet on, managing the freshet, swollen, flooding (highest tides
of the year last week) water on water swell, with a wind running
norwesterly 'it gets pretty choppy here,' 'I've been here with a blow
55　that's bin blowing 47 miles an hour - just big big waves washing
way up above the rocks.' 'See it's narrow & when the wind blows
those waves break & cross, it gets *real* rough.'

2.　Small American automobile, named after an irregularly
coloured horse.

3.　A small city up the Fraser River from Steveston.

She runs in the

throat of time, voicing the very swifts & shallows of that river,
60 urging, in the dash of it, enough to keep up, to live on. When nets
are up 50%, fuel's up, & the packers taking chum salmon, undressed,
at 20 cents a pound, 'the same they sell in the stores dressed at $1.20,
while they're selling the roe they don't even pay us for at $2.20
a pound, clear profit' . . .

65 Somehow they survive the oily waters swirling

under packers piling, bargeloads of herring sucked up, truckloads
left to rot, salmon on ice in the packerboats collecting twenty hours
a day,

Somehow they survive, this people, these fish,
70 survive the refuse bottom, filthy water, their choked lives,
in a singular dance of survival, each from each. At the
narrows, in the pressure of waves so checked & held by
'deep-sea frontage' it's the river's push against her, play of
elements her life comes rolling on, hair flying. In gumboots,
75 on deck with rubber apron ('it's no dance dress'), she'll take
all that river gives, willing only to stand her ground (rolling,
with it, right under her feet, her life, rolling, out from under,
right on out to sea . . .

MICHAEL ONDAATJE (1943 –   )

Birth of Sound

At night the most private of a dog's long body groan.
It comes with his last stretch
in the dark corridor outside our room.
The children turn.
A window tries to split with cold
the other dog hoofing the carpet for lice.
We're all alone.

King Kong Meets Wallace Stevens

Take two photographs—
Wallace Stevens and King Kong
(Is it significant that I eat bananas as I write this?)

Stevens is portly, benign, a white brush cut
striped tie. Businessman but
for the dark thick hands, the naked brain
the thought in him.

Kong is staggering
lost in New York streets again
a spawn of annoyed cars at his toes.
The mind is nowhere.
Fingers are plastic, electric under the skin.
He's at the call of Metro-Goldwyn-Mayer.

Meanwhile W. S. in his suit
is thinking chaos is thinking fences.
In his head the seeds of fresh pain
his exorcising,
the bellow of locked blood.

The hands drain from his jacket,
pose in the murderer's shadow.

Letters & Other Worlds

"for there was no more darkness for him and, no doubt
like Adam before the fall, he could see in the dark"

My father's body was a globe of fear
His body was a town we never knew
He hid that he had been where we were going
His letters were a room he seldom lived in
5   In them the logic of his love could grow

My father's body was a town of fear
He was the only witness to its fear dance
He hid where he had been that we might lose him
His letters were a room his body scared

10   He came to death with his mind drowning.
On the last day he enclosed himself
in a room with two bottles of gin, later
fell the length of his body
so that brain blood moved
15   to new compartments
that never knew the wash of fluid
and he died in minutes of a new equilibrium.

His early life was a terrifying comedy
and my mother divorced him again and again.
20   He would rush into tunnels magnetized
by the white eye of trains
and once, gaining instant fame,
managed to stop a Perahara in Ceylon[1]
—the whole procession of elephants dancers
25   local dignitaries—by falling
dead drunk onto the street.

As a semi-official, and semi-white at that,
the act was seen as a crucial
turning point in the Home Rule Movement
30   and led to Ceylon's independence in 1948.

(My mother had done her share too—
her driving so bad
she was stoned by villagers
whenever her car was recognized)

35   For 14 years of marriage
each of them claimed he or she
was the injured party.
Once on the Colombo docks
saying goodbye to a recently married couple

1. Spectacular spring pageant in celebration of the Holy
Tooth, an important Buddhist relic.

40   my father, jealous
at my mother's articulate emotion,
dove into the waters of the harbour
and swam after the ship waving farewell.
My mother pretending no affiliation
45   mingled with the crowd back to the hotel.

Once again he made the papers
though this time my mother
with a note to the editor
corrected the report—saying he was drunk
50   rather than broken hearted at the parting of friends.
The married couple received both editions
of *The Ceylon Times* when their ship reached Aden.[2]

And then in his last years
he was the silent drinker,
55   the man who once a week
disappeared into his room with bottles
and stayed there until he was drunk
and until he was sober.

There speeches, head dreams, apologies,
60   the gentle letters, were composed.
With the clarity of architects
he would write of the row of blue flowers
his new wife had planted,
the plans for electricity in the house,
65   how my half-sister fell near a snake
and it had awakened and not touched her.
Letters in a clear hand of the most complete empathy
his heart widening and widening and widening
to all manner of change in his children and friends
70   while he himself edged
into the terrible acute hatred
of his own privacy
till he balanced and fell
the length of his body
75   the blood screaming in
the empty reservoir of bones
the blood searching in his head without metaphor

'The Gate in His Head'
for Victor Coleman[1]

Victor, the shy mind
revealing the faint scars
coloured strata of the brain,
not clarity but the sense of shift

5   a few lines, the tracks of thought

Landscape of busted trees
the melted tires in the sun
Stan's[2] fishbowl
with a book inside
10   turning its pages

2. Until 1968, a British Colony. Now part of South
Yemen.

1. A Toronto poet who periodically resides on the Sechelt
Peninsula.

2. Stan Bevington, Toronto publisher of both Ondaatje
and Coleman. Founder of Coach House Press.

like some sea animal
camouflaging itself
the typeface clarity
going slow blonde in the sun full water

15 My mind is pouring chaos
in nets onto the page.
A blind lover, dont know
what I love till I write it out.
And then from Gibson's[3] your letter
20 with a blurred photograph of a gull.
Caught vision. The stunning white bird
an unclear stir.

And that is all this writing should be then.
The beautiful formed things caught at the wrong moment
25 so they are shapeless, awkward
moving to the clear.

bpNichol (1944 –   )

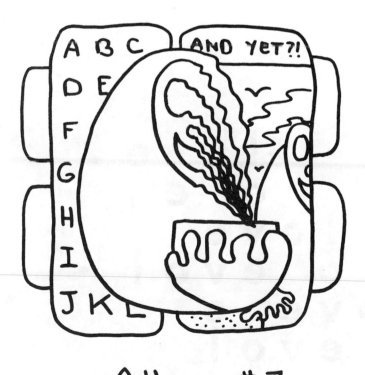

Allegory #7

3. A community on the Sechelt Peninsula, north of Vancouver.

Turnips Are

turnips are
inturps are
urnspit are
tinspur are
5   rustpin are
stunrip are
piturns are
ritpuns are
punstir are
10 nutrips are
suntrip are
untrips are
spinrut are
runspit are
15 pitnurs are
runtsip are
puntsir are
turnsip are
tipruns are
20 turpsin are
spurtin

blues

Postcard Between
for Margaret Avison[1]

looked up & saw
the winter sun

                clouds
half covering it

5   somewhere near
washington street
it came

into my ear
this morning

10   again

a woman or
the sea
moved over me

like the clouds
15   till

          no focus

grown used to
by degrees

and I thot

20   "i have done with it"

vague
       like the clouds
         my language was

sun
25   disappearing from view

this poem for you

---

1. Major Canadian poet, author of *Winter Sun*.

Acknowledgements

Michael Alexander   Ed. *The Earliest English Poems: A Bilingual Edition* (University of California Press, 1970). Selections from The Exeter Book ("The Wanderer" and "The Wife's Complaint") and from *Beowulf* ("The Lay of the Last Survivor").

John Ashbery   "Hotel Dauphin" from *Some Trees*. Copyright © 1956 John Ashbery. Reprinted by permission of the author. "Voyage in Blue" from *Self Portrait in a Convex Mirror* and "What Is Poetry" from *Houseboat Days*. Reprinted by permission of Viking Penguin Ltd.

Margaret Atwood   "Some Objects of Wood and Stone" from *The Circle Game* and "you fit into me" from *Power Politics*, both published by House of Anansi. Reprinted with permission of Margaret Atwood. "Progressive Insanities of a Pioneer" from *The Animals in That Country* and "You Are Happy" from *You Are Happy* by Margaret Atwood. © Oxford University Press Canada. Reprinted by permission of the publisher.

W. H. Auden   "Sir, no man's enemy" and "Spain" reprinted by permission of Faber and Faber Ltd. from *The English Auden*. Other selections reprinted by permission of Faber and Faber Ltd. from *Collected Poems* by W. H. Auden.

Margaret Avison   "The Swimmer's Moment" from *Winter Sun* and "Searching and Sounding" and "The Dumbfounding" from *The Dumbfounding* by Margaret Avison. Reprinted with the permission of the author.

Beowulf   Excerpts from the poem ("The Fight with Grendel's Dam" and "Hrothgar's Advice") are from Kevin Crossley-Holland, trans. *"Beowulf": A New Translation* (New York: Farrar, Straus and Giroux, 1968).

Earle Birney   "Bushed," "Ellesmereland I and II," "Arrivals Wolfville," "Sinalóa," and "father grouse" from *Collected Poems of Earle Birney* and *Fall by Fury* by Earle Birney. Reprinted by permission of The Canadian Publishers, McClelland and Stewart, Limited, Toronto.

Basil Bunting   Selections from *Collected Poems*, © Basil Bunting 1978. Reprinted by permission of Oxford University Press.

J. J. Campbell   Ed. *The Advent Lyrics of the Exeter Book* (Princeton University Press). Selections I, III, VI, and X are from this text.

James Carney   Ed. *Medieval Irish Lyrics* (University of California Press, 1967). Selections by Columbanus and Sedulius Scottus are from this text.

Geffrey Chaucer   Selections are from John H. Fisher, ed., *The Complete Poetry and Prose of Geoffrey Chaucer* (New York: Holt, Rinehart and Winston, 1977).

Leonard Cohen   Selections from *Selected Poems* by Leonard Cohen. Reprinted with the permission of the author.

Robert Creeley   "The Innocence" and "I Know a Man" from *Selected Poems* by Robert Creeley. Copyright © 1976 by Robert Creeley. "La Noche" from *For Love* by Robert Creeley. Copyright © 1962 by Robert Creeley. Reprinted by permission of Charles Scribner's Sons. "Speech" and "Prayer to Hermes" from Robert Creeley, *Later*. Copyright © 1979 by Robert Creeley. Reprinted by permission of New Directions. "A Piece" and "For W.C.W." from *Words* by Robert Creeley. Reprinted by permission of the author.

e. e. cummings   "o sweet spontaneous," copyright 1923, 1951 by e.e. cummings. Reprinted from his volume *Complete Poems 1913–1962* by permission of Harcourt Brace Jovanovich, Inc. "pity this busy monster, manunkind" and "anyone lived in a pretty how town," copyright 1944 by e. e. cummings; renewed 1972 by Nancy T. Andrews. Reprinted by permission of Harcourt Brace Jovanovich, Inc., from *Complete Poems 1913–1962*. "When your honest redskin toma" and "honour corruption villainy holiness," copyright 1950 by e. e. cummings. Reprinted from his volume *Complete Poems 1913–1962* by permission of Harcourt Brace Jovanovich, Inc. "in Just–," "when god lets my body be," "the Cambridge ladies who live in furnished souls," and "Spring is like a perhaps hand" from *Tulips & Chimneys* by e. e. cummings, with the permission of Liveright Publishing Corporation. Copyright 1923, 1925 and renewed 1951, 1953 by e. e. cummings. Copyright © 1973, 1976 by Nancy I. Andrews. Copyright © 1973, 1976 by George James Firmage. "(ponder, darling, these busted statues," "next to of course god america i," and "since feeling is first" from *IS 5* by e. e. cummings, with the permission of Liveright Publishing Corporation. Copyright 1926 by Horace Liveright. Copyright renewed 1954 by e. e. cummings.

Robert Duncan   "A New Poem (for Jack Spicer)" from *Root and Branches*, copyright © 1964 by Robert Duncan. "The Moon, Passages 5" from *Bending the Bow*, copyright © 1968 by Robert Duncan. "The Law I Love Is Major Mover" from Robert Duncan, *The Opening of the Field*. Copyright © 1960 by Robert Duncan. All selections reprinted by permission of New Directions Publishing Corporation, New York.

T.S. Eliot   Selections reprinted by permission of Faber and Faber Ltd. from *Collected Poems 1909-1962* by T.S. Eliot.

Roy Fisher   Selections from *Poems 1955-80* by Roy Fisher, © Roy Fisher 1980. Reprinted by permission of Oxford University Press.

Robert Frost   All selections from *The Poetry of Robert Frost*, edited by Edward Connery Lathem. Copyright 1916, 1923, 1928, 1930, 1939, © 1969 by Holt, Rinehart and Winston. Copyright 1942, 1944, 1951, © 1956, 1958 by Robert Frost.   Copyright © 1967, 1970 by Lesly Frost Ballantine. Reprinted by permission of Holt, Rinehart and Winston, Publishers.

Allen Ginsberg   "Sunflower Sutra" from *Howl and Other Poems* by Allen Ginsberg. Copyright © 1956, 1959 by Allen Ginsberg. Reprinted by permission of City Lights Books. "Wales Visitation" from *Planet News* by Allen Ginsberg. Copyright © 1968 by Allen Ginsberg. Reprinted by permission of City Lights Books.

Michael Hamburger   "Tides" from *Weather & Season 1958-1962*; "Babes in the Wood" from *Real Estate*; and "For a Family Album" and "Memory" from *Travelling*. Selections reprinted with the permission of the author.

Robert Henryson   "The Complaint of Orpheus" is from Charles Elliot, ed., *Robert Henryson's Poems* (Oxford: Clarendon Press, 1963).

Gerard Manley Hopkins   Selections from *The Poems of Gerard Manley Hopkins*, 4th Edition (1967), edited by W. H. Gardner and N. H. MacKenzie and published by Oxford University Press for the Society of Jesus.

Ted Hughes   "View of a Pig" from *Lupercal*; "Cadenza" and "The Bear" from *Crow*; and "The Ancient Briton Lay under his Rock" from *Remains of Elmet* by Ted Hughes. Reprinted by permission of Faber and Faber Ltd.

Elizabeth Jennings   "The Minotaur" from *Growing Points* by Elizabeth Jennings. Reprinted by permission of Carcanet New Press. Other selections from *Collected Poems* by Elizabeth Jennings. Reprinted by permission of Macmillan Company.

D. G. Jones   "For François Adnet" from *Sun Is Axeman*; "A Garland of Milne" and "Dance For One Leg" from *Under the Thunder the Flowers Light up the Earth*; and "The Stream Exposed with All Its Stones" from *Phrases from Orpheus*. Selections reprinted with the permission of the author.

C. W. Kennedy   Ed. Early *English Christian Poetry* (New York: Oxford University Press, 1963). *The Dream of the Cross* and selections from pseudo-Caedmon ("The Fall of Lucifer") and Physiologus ("The Panther" and "The Whale") are from this text.

A. M. Klein   Selections are from *The Collected Poems of A. M. Klein*, compiled by Miriam Waddington. Copyright © McGraw-Hill Ryerson Limited, 1974. Reprinted by permission of the publisher.

Philip Larkin   "Church Going" and "Poetry of Departures" from *The Less Deceived* by permission of The Marvell Press, England. "The Whitsun Weddings" reprinted by permission of Faber and Faber Ltd. from *The Whitsun Weddings* by Philip Larkin.

D. H. Lawrence   From *The Complete Poems of D. H. Lawrence*, published by William Heinemann Ltd. Selections reprinted with the permission of Lawrence Pollinger Ltd. and the Estate of the late Frieda Lawrence Ravagli.

Irving Layton   "A Tall Man Executes a Jig," "The Cold Green Element," "Keine Lazarovitch 1870-1959," "Berry Picking," and "Divine Image" from *The Collected Poems of Irving Layton* by Irving Layton. Reprinted by permission of The Canadian Publishers, McClelland and Stewart, Limited, Toronto.

Denise Levertov   "With Eyes at the Back of Our Heads" from Denise Levertov, *Collected Earlier Poems 1940-1960*. Copyright © 1958 by Denise Levertov. "To the Muse" and "The Garden Wall" from Denise Levertov, *O Taste and See*. Copyright © 1964 by Denise Levertov Goodman. Selections reprinted by permission of New Directions Publishing Corporation, New York.

Dorothy Livesay   Selections are from *Collected Poems: The Two Seasons* by Dorothy Livesay. Copyright © Dorothy Livesay, 1972. Reprinted by permission of McGraw-Hill Ryerson Limited.

Robert Lowell   Reprinted by permission of Farrar, Straus & Giroux, Inc. "To Delmore Schwartz" from *Life Studies* by Robert Lowell. Copyright © 1956, 1959 by Robert Lowell. "For the Union Dead" and "Fall 1961" from *For the Union Dead* by Robert Lowell. Copyright © 1960, 1962 by Robert Lowell.

Daphne Marlatt   "Imperial Cannery, 1913" and "A by-channel..." from *Steveston*, published by Coach House Press. Reprinted with the permission of Daphne Marlatt.

W.S. Merwin   "The Indigestion of the Vampire" from *The Moving Target* by W.S. Merwin. Copyright © 1963 by W.S. Merwin. Reprinted by permission of Atheneum Publishers. Other selections from *The Lice* by W.S. Merwin. Copyright © 1966, 1967 by W.S. Merwin. "Come Back" appeared originally in the *New Yorker*. Reprinted by permission of Atheneum Publishers.

Adrian Mitchell "I Tried, I Really Tried" and "Leaflets" from *Out Loud* by Adrian Mitchell. Reprinted by permission of Cape Goliard Press. "Ten Ways to Avoid Lending Your Wheelbarrow to Anybody" from *The Apeman Cometh* by Adrian Mitchell. Reprinted by permission of Jonathan Cape Ltd.

John Newlove "The Pride" from *The Fat Man*, "No Song" from *Black Night Window*, and "The Flower" from *The Cave* by John Newlove. Reprinted by permission of The Canadian Publishers, McClelland and Stewart, Limited, Toronto.

bpNichol Selections by bpNichol are reprinted with the permission of the author.

Frank O'Hara "In Memory of My Feelings" from *The Collected Poems of Frank O'Hara* by Frank O'Hara, edited by Donald Allen. Copyright © 1971 by Alfred A. Knopf, Inc. Reprinted by permission of Alfred A. Knopf, Inc.

Charles Olson "Letter 27 [withheld]" and "The Ring of" reprinted by permission of George F. Butterick, executor, Estate of Charles Olson. "I, Maximus of Gloucester, to You" reprinted by permission of Corinth Books.

Michael Ondaatje "Birth of Sound" and "Gate in his head" from *Rat Jelly*, published by Coach House Press, and "King Kong Meets Wallace Stevens" and "Letters and other worlds" from *There's a Trick with a Knife I'm Learning to Do*, published by McClelland and Stewart. Copyright © Michael Ondaatje. Reprinted with permission of the author.

Sylvia Plath "Lady Lazarus" from *Ariel* by Sylvia Plath. Published by Faber & Faber (London). Copyright Ted Hughes, 1965. Reprinted by permission.

Ezra Pound "Canto I" from *The Cantos of Ezra Pound*. Copyright 1934 by Ezra Pound. Other selections from Ezra Pound, *Personae*. Copyright 1926 by Ezra Pound. Reprinted by permission of New Directions Publishing Corporation.

E. J. Pratt From *Collected Poems of E. J. Pratt*, edited by N. Frye and published by Macmillan Company Ltd. Selections reprinted with the permission of Claire Pratt.

Al Purdy Selections from *Being Alive: Poems 1958-1978* by Al Purdy. Reprinted by permission of The Canadian Publishers, McClelland and Stewart, Limited, Toronto.

James Reaney "The Tall Black Hat," "The Katzenjammer Kids," and "First Letter: To the Avon River above Stratford, Canada" from *Poems* by James Reaney. Reprinted by permission of Press Porcépic Ltd.

F. R. Scott "The Canadian Authors Meet," "Advice," and "Old Song" from *Overture*; "Lakeshore," "Bonne Entente," and "Eden" from *Events and Signals*, and "Dancing" from *The Dance Is One*. Selections are reprinted with the permission of F. R. Scott.

John Skelton Selections from *The Complete Poems of John Skelton*, edited by Philip Henderson. Reprinted by permission of J. M. Dent & Sons Ltd.

A. J. M. Smith From *Poems, New and Collected* by A. J. M. Smith. Selections reprinted by permission of The Canadian Publishers, McClelland and Stewart, Limited, Toronto.

Stevie Smith From *The Collected Poems of Stevie Smith*, published by Allen Lane. Selections reprinted by permission of James MacGibbon, executor for Stevie Smith.

Wallace Stevens "Anecdote of the Jar," copyright 1923 and renewed 1951 by Wallace Stevens. "The Sense of the Sleight-of-Hand Man," copyright 1942 by Wallace Stevens and renewed 1970 by Holly Stevens. "The Idea of Order at Key West," copyright 1936 by Wallace Stevens and renewed 1964 by Holly Stevens. These poems, together with the other selections, are reprinted from *The Collected Poems of Wallace Stevens*, by Wallace Stevens, by permission of Alfred A. Knopf, Inc.

D. M. Thomas "The Dream Game" from *The Honeymoon Voyage* by D. M. Thomas. Reprinted by permission of Martin Secker & Warburg Limited. Other selections from *Love and Other Deaths* by D. M. Thomas. Reprinted by permission of Granada Publishing Ltd.

Dylan Thomas From Dylan Thomas, *The Poems*, published by J. M. Dent. Selections reprinted by permission of the publisher and of the Trustees for the Copyright of the late Dylan Thomas.

J. R. R. Tolkien "Sir Orfeo" from '*Sir Gawain & The Green Knight*,' '*Pearl*,' and '*Sir Orfeo*,' trans. by J. R. R. Tolkien. Reprinted by permission of George Allen & Unwin.

Charles Tomlinson Selections from *Selected Poems 1951-1974*, © Charles Tomlinson 1978, by permission of Oxford University Press.

Gael Turnbull Selections from *A Trampoline* by Gael Turnbull. Reprinted by permission of Jonathan Cape Ltd.

Helen Waddell Selections from Boethius, Alcuin, and Colman are from Helen Waddell, ed. *Medieval Latin Lyrics* (New York: Norton, 1977).

William Carlos Williams "Tract," "The Red Wheelbarrow," "Spring and All," "This Is Just to Say," "The Yachts," and "The Poor" from *The Collected Earlier Poems* of William Carlos Williams, copyright 1938 by New Directions. "The Dance" and "The Dish of Fruit" from *The Collected Later Poems* of William Carlos Williams, copyright 1944, 1948 by William Carlos Williams. "The Sparrow" from William Carlos Williams, *Pictures from Brueghel and Other Poems*, copyright

1955 by William Carlos Williams. Reprinted by permission of New Directions Publishing Corporation.

W. B. Yeats   From *Collected Poems* published by The Macmillan Company. Selections reprinted with the permission of Michael and Anne Yeats and Macmillan London Limited.

The editors also wish to acknowledge their indebtedness to the following standard editions in the preparation of this anthology's first section: C. F. Brown, ed., *Religious Lyrics of the Fifteenth Century* (Oxford, 1939); R. H. Robbins, ed., *Secular Lyrics of the XIVth and XVth Centuries*, 2nd ed. (Oxford: Clarendon Press, 1955); and R. D. Stevick, ed., *One Hundred Middle English Lyrics* (Bobbs-Merrill).

Author Index

Title Index